D0148888

The Heath Anthology of American Literature

Volume E

Contemporary Period: 1945 to the Present

The Heath Anthology of American Literature

SIXTH EDITION

Volume E
Contemporary Period: 1945 to the Present

Paul Lauter
Trinity College
General Editor

John Alberti
North Kentucky University
Editor, Instructor's Guide

Mary Pat Brady
Cornell University

Jackson R. Bryer
University of Maryland

King-Kok Cheung
University of California, Los Angeles

Kirk Curnutt
Troy University

Anne Goodwyn Jones
Allegheny College

Richard Yarborough
University of California, Los Angeles
Associate General Editor

James Kyung-Jin Lee
University of California,
Santa Barbara

Wendy Martin
Claremont Graduate University

Quentin Miller
Suffolk University

Bethany Schneider
Bryn Mawr College

Ivy T. Schweitzer
Dartmouth College

Sandra A. Zagarell
Oberlin College

WADSWORTH
CENGAGE Learning

Australia • Brazil • Japan • Korea • Mexico • Singapore • Spain • United Kingdom • United States

WADSWORTH
CENGAGE Learning™

**The Heath Anthology of American Literature, Sixth Edition
Volume E, *Contemporary Period: 1945 to the Present***
Edited by Paul Lauter, Richard Yarborough, John Alberti, Mary Pat Brady, Jackson R. Bryer, King-Kok Cheung, Kirk Curnutt, Anne Goodwyn Jones, James Kyung-Jin Lee, Wendy Martin, Quentin Miller, Bethany Schneider, Ivy T. Schweitzer, and Sandra A. Zagarell

Senior Publisher: Lyn Uhl

Publisher: Michael Rosenberg

Senior Development Editor: Kathy
    Sands-Boehmer

Assistant Editor: Megan Garvey

Editorial Assistant: Erin Pass

Media Editor: Amy Gibbons

Marketing Manager: Christina Shea

Marketing Coordinator: Ryan Ahern

Marketing Communications Manager:
    Beth Rodio

Senior Content Project Manager:
    Rosemary Winfield

Art and Design Manager: Jill Haber

Composition Buyer: Chuck Dutton

Manufacturing Manager: Marcia Locke

Permissions Editor: Katie Huha

Photo Manager: Jennifer Meyer Dare

Photo Researcher: Stacey Dong

Senior Art Director: Cate Rickard Barr

Cover Image: © Shutterstock

Compositor: NK Graphics

© 2010, 2006 Wadsworth, Cengage Learning

ALL RIGHTS RESERVED. No part of this work covered by the copyright herein may be reproduced, transmitted, stored, or used in any form or by any means graphic, electronic, or mechanical, including but not limited to photocopying, recording, scanning, digitizing, taping, Web distribution, information networks, or information storage and retrieval systems, except as permitted under Section 107 or 108 of the 1976 United States Copyright Act, without the prior written permission of the publisher.

For product information and technology assistance, contact us at
Cengage Learning Academic Resource Center, 1-800-423-0563.
For permission to use material from this text or product, submit all requests online at
www.cengage.com/permissions.
Further permissions questions can be e-mailed to
permissionrequest@cengage.com.

Library of Congress Control Number: 2008927720

ISBN-10: 0-5472-0180-X

ISBN-13: 978-0-5472-0180-1

Wadsworth
20 Channel Center Street
Boston, MA 02210
USA

Cengage Learning products are represented in Canada by Nelson Education, Ltd.

For your course and learning solutions, visit
www.cengage.com.

Purchase any of our products at your local college store or at our preferred online store at **www.ichapters.com**.

Printed in the United States of America
2 3 4 5 6 7 13 12 11 10

CONTENTS

CONTEMPORARY PERIOD: 1945 TO THE PRESENT

2241

2687 Cluster: E Pluribus Unum—Landmark Legislation

2725 A Sheaf of Vietnam Conflict Poetry and Prose

2781 New World Disorder: Recent Literature

3073 A Sheaf of Prison Literature

PREFACE

In this sixth edition of *The Heath Anthology of American Literature,* we have extended the innovative tradition established by the very first edition of the anthology. That first edition implemented the slogan of the Reconstructing American Literature project that led to the publication of the *Heath Anthology:* "So that the work of Frederick Douglass, Mary Wilkins Freeman, Agnes Smedley, Zora Neale Hurston, and others is read with the work of Nathaniel Hawthorne, Henry James, William Faulkner, Ernest Hemingway, and others." Consequently, that first edition, while providing very rich selections of traditionally canonical authors, also contained the widest selection of writing by women and authors of diverse racial, ethnic, and regional origins ever assembled in an academic textbook. That is still the case in the sixth edition of the *Heath Anthology*—still innovating, still leading.

The *Heath Anthology*'s breadth and depth of coverage is extended in this sixth edition. Volume A includes entries from Northeast woodlands tribes as well as a section on New Netherland literature. Volume B contains significant newly anthologized texts like Phoebe Cary's hilarious poetic parodies, Hawthorne's striking early story "Alice Doane's Appeal," and a substantial selection from Julia Ward Howe's strange and long-unavailable *The Hermaphrodite.* Volume C now offers an independent entry by accomplished nineteenth-century poet Sarah Piatt and one of the English-language fiction and poetry by the versatile Japanese writer Yone Noguchi. Volume D now includes poems and stories by Américo Paredes, relevant commentaries on culture by period thinkers such as Walter Lippmann, Gilbert Seldes, and Margaret Sanger, as well as new selections from Gertrude Stein, Katherine Anne Porter, and John Steinbeck. Two of the most prominent living fiction writers—Philip Roth and Don DeLillo—are represented for the first time in Volume E.

One major objective of the *Heath Anthology* has always been to enable students to understand literary texts in relation to the cultural and historical contexts out of which they developed and to which they initially spoke. One innovation for this edition has been to provide four clusters in each volume on similar cultural and historical issues—Nature and Religion; Aesthetics; America in the World, the World in America; and E Pluribus Unum. These clusters consist of shorter selections that are relevant to each topic. They can be used as the basis for self-contained assignments or studied in relation to the primary texts in each volume. With the *Heath Anthology*'s unusually wide selection, they provide instructors with broadened opportunities to help students perceive continuity and change in the literary and cultural history of what is now the United States.

Another major goal of the *Heath Anthology* has been to broaden our understanding of what constitutes the "literary." On the one hand, we want to provide students with a large selection of well-known texts whose literary power and cultural relevance had been established by generations of critics and teachers—

William Bradford's "Of Plymouth Plantation," Benjamin Franklin's *Autobiography,* "Young Goodman Brown," "Self-Reliance," "Civil Disobedience," "Annabel Lee," "Daisy Miller," "The Open Boat," *The Waste Land,* "Hills Like White Elephants," "Sonny's Blues," "Howl." At the same time, we wish to provide exemplary texts that, because of their forms or subjects, have seldom been taught and often little read. Thus, we include, for example, "sorrow songs" or spirituals, nineteenth-century folk songs and stories, *corridos* and blues lyrics, and poems written on the walls of Angel Island prison by Chinese detainees. Likewise, we include nonfictional forms such as the spiritual autobiographies of Thomas Shepard and Elizabeth Ashbridge, sketches by Fanny Fern, polemical letters by Angelina and Sarah Grimké, columns by Finley Peter Dunne, José Martí's important "Our America," Randolph Bourne's "Trans-National America," Martin Luther King's "I Have a Dream," and chapters from Gloria Anzaldúa's *Borderlands / La Frontera.* The sixth edition extends this goal by including journal entries from several members of the Lewis and Clark expedition, letters protesting Cherokee removal, "proletarian" folk songs, a number of graphic narratives by Art Spiegelman, Lynda Barry, and others. In addition, each volume includes a glossy insert of paintings, photographs, book jackets, and documents that illuminate the culture of each historical period. These reproductions are, we think, not only attractive in themselves but useful as objects of study parallel to the volume's literary texts.

The *Heath Anthology* has also from its beginning balanced longer complete works with shorter texts by the wide variety of authors included in our anthology. Thus, for example, the sixth edition includes the full texts of Royall Tyler's "The Contrast," Mercy Otis Warren's "The Group," Melville's "Benito Cereno" and "Billy Budd," Frederick Douglass's *Narrative,* Abraham Cahan's "The Imported Bridegroom," Kate Chopin's *The Awakening,* Nella Larsen's *Passing,* Arthur Miller's *The Crucible,* among many other longer works. At the same time, student preferences and instructor suggestions have led us to make available, packaged with the anthology, a choice of a number of important longer works in separate volumes of the New Riverside Reader series. These include *The Scarlet Letter, Typee, The Portrait of a Lady, Huckleberry Finn, The Red Badge of Courage,* and *The Damnation of Theron Ware.* The availability of these independent volumes not only satisfies student preferences for such separate texts but provides instructors with increased variety in terms of easily accessible novels that they can teach along with the anthology's basic selections.

The particular character of the *Heath Anthology* has always depended on the participation in the project of a wide community of scholars and teachers. Unlike other anthologies, the *Heath* includes introductory notes that have been written by scholars who specialize in a particular author. In their diverse yet consistent approaches, these notes illustrate for students how writing about literature is not limited to any single standard. More important, perhaps, these contributing editors, together with readers, consultants, and users of the anthology, have provided guidance to our unusually large and diverse editorial board as we determine the changes that will make the anthology most useful. The *Heath* community has also remained active in constructing the complementary materials that have made the *Heath Anthology,* despite the unique diversity of its content, particularly user friendly. These include the twice-yearly *Heath Newsletter,* which is designed in particular to support teaching innovation; the *Instructor's Guide* (online and in paper), edited by John Alberti, which offers suggestions for approaching texts and authors, model assignments, and useful exam and discussion questions; and the innovative *Heath Anthology* website. The *Heath* website, available at www.cengage.com/english/ heath6e, contains the *Instructor's Guide,* a detailed time line, bibliographical materials, and links to a large number of visual and auditory resources that are very useful in the classroom.

Changes in individual volumes reflect the *Heath Anthology*'s continuing commitment to bringing contemporary scholarship into classroom practice:

- In Volume A, we have reorganized the Native American entries to better reflect current scholarship and to include a broader representation of native cultures. In addition to drawing on recent scholarship on New Netherland life, we have extended the literature of exploration forward to the nineteenth century with the expedition of Lewis and Clark to the northwest.

- In Volume B, in addition to the changes mentioned above, the four new clusters will help to focus classroom discussion of critical early nineteenth-century phenomena like the Second Great Awakening, the rise of the abolitionist movement, the conflict over expansionism and Indian "removal," and the debates over reform in the rapidly industrializing and urbanizing United States. These clusters help make clear how deeply involved the writers of the early nineteenth century were with the world that they helped shape and to which they spoke.

- Volume C has added or restored a broad range of works, including Charles Chesnutt's "Po' Sandy," Kate Chopin's "The Storm" and "The Story of an Hour," Henry James's "The Beast in the Jungle," Sarah Orne Jewett's "The Foreigner," Alice Dunbar-Nelson's "Mr. Baptiste" and "The Praline Woman," Sui-Sin Far's "The Wisdom of the New," and an additional story by Jack London, "Koolau the Leper." We have added two new sheafs—"A Latino Chorus for Social Change" and "Filipino and Filipina Writing"—and restored the "Sheaf of Poetry by Late Nineteenth-Century American Women" to its original size. We have grouped the literature by writers from New Orleans in a subsection on "New Orleans and America" that features the life and culture of that city. Finally, our four clusters adapt the themes common to all five volumes to the rich, variegated, and often contentious circumstances of the United States between 1865 and 1910.

- Volume D continues to demonstrate the diversity of the literary period known as modernism by introducing readers to the array of modernisms that constitute it—the hermetic experiments of Ezra Pound and T. S. Eliot, the more commercial expression of loss and uncertainty in popular efforts by F. Scott Fitzgerald and Edna St. Vincent Millay, the ethnically complex fusion of African American and dominant-culture aesthetics that typify the Harlem Renaissance, and the political activism of the proletarian movement of the 1930s and its internal debates over the social functions of art. Volume D now includes the full text of Nella Larsen's *Passing,* as well as revised selections from

Katherine Anne Porter, Richard Wright, John Steinbeck, and other writers. These changes have been undertaken in an effort to reconceptualize reputations, confront pedagogical complacencies, and reignite interest in overlooked works. The major change from previous editions of this volume is the inclusion of four clusters that are designed to dramatize the upheavals that characterized the first half of the American twentieth century. Despite the avowals of some of its leading figures, these excerpts demonstrate that the literature of modernism did not exist outside of history—the explosion of consumerism, the rise of popular-culture appropriations of modernist ideals in advertising, and such hot-button topics as immigration, racial discrimination, and the regulation of political freedom. In keeping with the mission of reiterating this fact, another significant change to this edition is the addition of a folk music cluster that demonstrates the narrative continuities between popular music and the written word.

•Volume E has been revised to reflect changes in the notion of what can be called contemporary. The new structure of the volume advances the idea that the years including and surrounding the Vietnam War mark a turning point in literary tastes, styles, and subjects. Two distinct periods of literary history are beginning to emerge—from the end of World War II to the early 1970s and from the mid-1970s to the present. The latter period, more than any other in history, reflects American literature's consciousness of its diversity, a consciousness that *Heath Anthology* editors have labored to uncover in earlier periods.

Acknowledgments

We want to extend our thanks to all of the contributing editors who devoted their time and scholarship to introductory notes, choices of texts, and teaching materials. For the current edition, they include Paula Bernat Bennett (Emerita), Southern Illinois University; Renée Bergland, Simmons College; Mary Pat Brady, Cornell University; Hillary Chute, Harvard University; Denise Cruz, Indiana University; Gene Jarrett, Boston University; Daniel Heath Justice, University of Toronto; Ann Keniston, University of Nevada, Reno; James Kyung-Jin Lee, University of California, Santa Barbara; Katherine E. Ledford, Appalachian State University; Viet Nguyen, University of Southern California; Robert Dale Parker, University of Illinois at Urbana-Champaign; Elizabeth Petrino, Fairfield University; Ramón Saldívar, Stanford University; Lavina Shankar, Bates College; Scott Slovic, University of Nevada, Reno; Mayumi Takada, Bryn Mawr College; Darlene Unrue, University of Nevada, Las Vegas; and Joanne van der Woude, Columbia University.

Thanks to Oberlin College for funding student researchers and to Amanda Shubert and Hillary Smith for the incomparable work they have done in that capacity. We also want to thank student researchers Carson Thomas and Kyle Lewis from Dartmouth College for excellent editorial help.

We especially want to thank those who reviewed this edition: Jennifer Adkison, Idaho State University; John Battenburg, California Polytechnic State University; Michael Berndt, Normandale Community College; Patricia Bostian,

Central Piedmont Community College; Steve Brahlek, Palm Beach Community College; Amy Braziller, Red Rocks Community College; Francis Broussard, Southeastern Louisiana University; Mark Cantrell, University of Miami; Adrienne Cassel, Sinclair Community College; Susan Castillo, Kings College, London; Linda Coblentz, University of Houston–Downtown; Linda Daigle, Houston Community College; Cynthia Denham, Snead State Community College; Robert Dunne, Central Connecticut State University; Philip Egan, Western Michigan; Gregory Eislien, Kansas State; Michael Elliott, Emory University; Brad Evans, Rutgers University; Paul Ferlazzo, Northern Arizona University; Tom Fick, Southeastern Louisiana University; Africa R. Fine, Palm Beach Community College; Joe Fulton, Baylor University; Eric Gardner, Saginaw Valley State University; Susan Gilmore, Central Connecticut State University; Yoshinobu Hakutani, Kent State University; Emily Hegarty, Nassau Community College; Kathleen Hicks, Arizona State University; Rebecca Hite, Southeastern Louisiana University; Barbara Hodne, University of Minnesota–Minneapolis; Martha Holder, Wytheville Community College; Daniel Heath Justice, University of Toronto; Homer Kemp, Tennessee Technical University; Kristie Knott, Westfield State College; Camille Langston, St. Mary's University; Katherine Ledford, Appalachian State University; Max Loges, Lamar University; Christopher Lukasik, Purdue University; Stephen Mathis, North Haverhill Community College; Brian Norman, Idaho State University; John Parks, Miami University; Cyrus Patell, New York University; Joan Reeves, Northeast Alabama Community College; Carla Rineer, Millersville University; Jane Rosecrans, J. Sargeant Reynolds Community College; Michael Sirmons, Austin Community College; Scott Slawinski, Western Michigan University; Emily Todd, Westfield State College; Gregory Tomso, University of West Florida; Bill Toth, Western New Mexico University; Joanne Van der Woude, Columbia University; Mark Van Wienen, Northern Illinois; Bryan Waterman, New York University; Megan Wesling, University of California, Santa Cruz; and Susan Wolstenholme, Cayuga Community College.

We also want to thank those who contributed to this as well as to earlier editions of this work: Susan Abbotson, Rhode Island College; Thomas P. Adler, Purdue University; Jesse Alemán, University of New Mexico; Elizabeth Ammons, Tufts University; William L. Andrews, University of Kansas; Frances R. Aparicio, University of Michigan; Elaine Sargent Apthorp, San Jose State University; Evelyn Avery, Towson State University; Liahna Babener, Montana State University; Barbara A. Bardes, Loyola University of Chicago; Helen Barolini; Marleen Barr, Virginia Polytechnic Institute and State University; Sam S. Baskett, Michigan State University; Rosalie Murphy Baum, University of South Florida; Herman Beavers, University of Pennsylvania; Eileen T. Bender, Indiana University at Bloomington; Renée L. Bergland, Simmons College; Juda Bennett, The College of New Jersey; Carol Marie Bensick, University of California, Riverside; David Bergman, Towson State University; Susan L. Blake, Lafayette College; Michael Boccia, Tufts University; Robert H. Brinkmeyer, Jr., University of Mississippi; Joanna Brooks, San Diego State University; Carol A. Burns, Southern Illinois University Press; Cynthia Butos, Trinity College; John F. Callahan, Lewis and Clark College; Jane Campbell, Purdue University, Calumet; Christine Cao, University of California, Los Angeles; Jean Ferguson Carr, University of Pittsburgh; Juliana Chang, Santa

Clara University; Allan Chavkin, Southwest Texas State University; Bell Gale Chevigny (Emeritus), Purchase College, State University of New York; Randolph Chilton, University of St. Francis; Beverly Lyon Clark, Wheaton College; C. B. Clark, Oklahoma City University; Amanda J. Cobb, New Mexico State University; Arthur B. Coffin, Montana State University; the late Constance Coiner, Binghamton University, State University of New York; James W. Coleman, University of North Carolina at Chapel Hill; Martha E. Cook, Longwood College; Angelo Costanzo, Shippensburg University; Patti Cowell, Colorado State University; John W. Crowley, Syracuse University; Sister Martha Curry, Wayne State University; Walter C. Daniel, University of Missouri–Columbia; Cathy N. Davidson, Duke University; Sharon L. Dean, Rivier College; Jane Krause DeMouy; Dorothy L. Denniston, Brown University; Kathryn Zabelle Derounian-Stodola, University of Arkansas at Little Rock; Joseph Dewey, University of Pittsburgh at Johnstown; the late Margaret Dickie, University of Georgia; Elizabeth Maddock Dillon, Northeastern University; Joanne Dobson, Fordham University; Raymond F. Dolle, Indiana State University; Sheila Hurst Donnelly, Orange County Community College; Carole K. Doreski, Daniel Webster College; Michael J. Drexler, Brown University; Sally Ann Drucker, North Carolina State University; Arlene A. Elder, University of Cincinnati; the late Everett Emerson (Emeritus), University of North Carolina at Chapel Hill; Bernard F. Engel, Michigan State University; Hugh English, City University of New York; Betsy Erkkila, Northwestern University; Lillian Faderman, California State University, Fresno; Charles Fanning, Southern Illinois University; Robert M. Farnsworth, University of Missouri–Kansas City; Dominika Ferens, Wroclaw University; Laraine Fergenson, City University of New York, Bronx Community College; Judith Fetterley, University at Albany, State University of New York; Joseph Fichtelberg, Hofstra University; Cheryl J. Fish, Manhattan Community College, City University of New York; Lucy M. Freibert, University of Louisville; George S. Friedman, Towson State University; Susan Stanford Friedman, University of Wisconsin–Madison; Albert Furtwangler, Mount Allison University; Diana Hume George, Pennsylvania State University at Erie, The Behrend College; Allison Giffen, New Mexico State University; Leah Blatt Glasser, Mount Holyoke College; Wendell P. Glick, University of Minnesota; William Goldhurst, University of Florida; Rita K. Gollin, State University of New York, Geneseo; Suzanne Gossett, Loyola University of Chicago; Philip Gould, Brown University; Maryemma Graham, University of Kansas; Theodora Rapp Graham, Pennsylvania State University, Harrisburg; Robert M. Greenberg, Temple University; Barry Gross, Michigan State University; James Guimond, Rider College; Minrose C. Gwin, University of New Mexico; Alfred Habegger; Joan F. Hallisey, Regis College; Jeffrey A. Hammond, St. Mary's College of Maryland; Earl N. Harbert, Northeastern University; Sharon M. Harris, University of Connecticut; Susan K. Harris, University of Kansas; Trudier Harris, University of North Carolina–Chapel Hill; Ellen Louise Hart, University of California, Santa Cruz; the late William L. Hedges, Goucher College; Joan D. Hedrick, Trinity College; Allison Heisch, San Jose State University; Robert Hemenway, University of Kentucky; Desirée Henderson, University of Texas at Arlington; Kristin Herzog, University of Massachusetts, Lowell; Donald R. Hettinga, Calvin College; Danielle Hinrichs, University of Southern California; Hilary W. Holladay, Independent

Scholars Association of the North Carolina Triangle at Chapel Hill; Elvin Holt, Southwest Texas State University; Kenneth Alan Hovey, University of Texas at San Antonio; Akasha (Gloria) Hull, University of California, Santa Cruz; James M. Hutchisson, The Citadel; Susan Clair Imbarrato, Minnesota State University, Moorhead; Gregory S. Jackson, Rutgers University; Ronna C. Johnson, Tufts University; Paul Jones, University of North Carolina–Chapel Hill; Joyce Ann Joyce, Temple University; Nancy Carol Joyner, Western Carolina University; Rose Yalow Kamel, University of Sciences in Philadelphia; Carolyn L. Karcher, Temple University; Janet Kaufman, University of Iowa; Richard S. Kennedy, Temple University; Carol Farley Kessler, Pennsylvania State University; Elizabeth L. Keyser, Hollins University; Karen L. Kilcup, University of North Carolina–Greensboro; Daniel Y. Kim, Brown University; Elaine H. Kim, University of California, Berkeley; Marcy Jane Knopf-Newman, Boise State University; Maureen Konkle, University of Missouri–Columbia; Michael Kreyling, Vanderbilt University; Lawrence La Fountain-Stokes, University of Michigan, Ann Arbor; Him Mark Lai; David M. Larson, Cleveland State University; Estella Lauter, University of Wisconsin–Green Bay; Barry Leeds, Central Connecticut State University; George S. Lensing, University of North Carolina–Chapel Hill; James A. Levernier, University of Arkansas at Little Rock; Walter K. Lew, University of California, Los Angeles; Cliff Lewis, University of Massachusetts at Lowell; Patricia Liggins-Hill, University of San Francisco; Genny Lim, New College of California; Shirley Geok-lin Lim, University of California, Santa Barbara; John Lowe, Louisiana State University; Juanita Luna-Lawhn, San Antonio College; Etta Madden, Southwest Missouri State University; Joseph Mancini, Jr., George Washington University; Daniel Marder, University of Tulsa; Robert A. Martin; Derek C. Maus, University of North Carolina–Chapel Hill; Kate McCullough, Cornell University; Deborah E. McDowell, University of Virginia; Joseph R. McElrath, Florida State University; Peggy McIntosh, Wellesley College Center for Research on Women; the late Nellie Y. McKay, University of Wisconsin–Madison; D. H. Melhem, Union for Experimenting Colleges and Universities; Michael J. Mendelsohn, University of Tampa; Gabriel Miller, Rutgers University; James A. Miller, George Washington University; Jeanne-Marie A. Miller, Howard University; Keith D. Miller, Arizona State University; Arthenia J. Bates Millican; Daniel Moos, Rhode Island College; James S. Moy, University of Wisconsin–Madison; Joel Myerson, University of South Carolina; Cary Nelson, University of Illinois at Urbana–Champaign; Margaret F. Nelson, Oklahoma State University; Charles H. Nichols (Emeritus), Brown University; Vera Norwood, University of New Mexico; Michael O'Brien, Miami University; Margaret Anne O'Connor, University of North Carolina–Chapel Hill; Genaro M. Padilla, University of California, Berkeley; Linda Pannill, Transylvania University; James W. Parins, University of Arkansas at Little Rock; Grace H. Park, University of California, Los Angeles; Vivian M. Patraka, Bowling Green State University; John J. Patton, Atlantic Cape Community College; James Robert Payne, New Mexico State University; Richard Pearce, Wheaton College; Michael W. Peplow, Western International University; Ronald Primeau, Central Michigan University; John Purdy, Western Washington University; Jennifer L. Randisi, University of California, Berkeley; Geoffrey Rans, University of Western Ontario; Julius Rowan Raper, University of North

Carolina–Chapel Hill; Kelly Reames; John M. Reilly, Howard University; Thelma Shinn Richard, Arizona State University; Phillip M. Richards, Colgate University; Marilyn Richardson; John-Michael Rivera, University of Colorado; Evelyn Hoard Roberts, Saint Louis Community College at Meramec; James A. Robinson, University of Maryland; William H. Robinson, Rhode Island College; Kenneth M. Roemer, University of Texas at Arlington; Judith Roman-Royer, Indiana University East; Nicholas D. Rombes, Jr., Pennsylvania State University; the late Lora Romero, Stanford University; Robert C. Rosen, William Paterson University; Deborah S. Rosenfelt, University of Maryland; Karen E. Rowe, University of California, Los Angeles; A. LaVonne Brown Ruoff (Emerita), University of Illinois at Chicago; Roshni Rustomji-Kerns, Stanford University; Doreen Alvarez Saar, Drexel University; Enrique Sacerio-Garí, Bryn Mawr College; Douglas C. Sackman, University of Puget Sound; Ramón Saldívar, Stanford University; Sonia Saldívar-Hull, University of California, Los Angeles; Thomas Scanlan, Ohio University; Gary Scharnhorst, University of New Mexico; Judith Scheffler, West Chester University; Bethany Ridgway Schneider, Bryn Mawr College; George J. Searles, Mohawk Valley Community College; Cynthia Secor, Higher Education Resource Services, Mid-America, at the University of Denver; David S. Shields, University of South Carolina; Thelma J. Shinn, Arizona State University; Frank C. Shuffelton, University of Rochester; Peggy Skaggs, Angelo State University; Katharine Capshaw Smith, University of Connecticut; Beth Helen Stickney, City University of New York; Catharine R. Stimpson, New York University; Janis P. Stout, Texas A & M University; Jim Sullivan, Mira Costa College; the late Claudia Tate, Princeton University; Ronnie Theisz, Black Hills State University; John Edgar Tidwell, University of Kansas; Eleanor Q. Tignor, City University of New York, La Guardia Community College; Jane Tompkins, University of Illinois at Chicago; Steven C. Tracy; Eleanor W. Traylor, Howard University; Richard Tuerk, Texas A&M University–Commerce; Bonnie TuSmith, Northeastern University; George Uba, California State University, Northridge; Paula Uruburu, Hofstra University; Donald Vanouse, State University of New York College at Oswego; Daniel Walden, Pennsylvania State University; Arthur E. Waterman, Georgia State University; Sybil Weir, San Jose State University; Judith Wellman, State University of New York College at Oswego; James L. W. West III, Pennsylvania State University; Thomas R. Whitaker, Yale University; Barbara A. White, University of New Hampshire; Margaret B. Wilkerson, University of California, Berkeley; the late Kenny J. Williams, Duke University; Marcellette G. Williams, Michigan State University; James C. Wilson, University of Cincinnati; Norma Clark Wilson, University of South Dakota; Amy E. Winans, Susquehanna University; Kate H. Winter, State University of New York at Albany; Frederick Woodard, University of Iowa; Jean Fagan Yellin (Emeritus), Pace University; Amy Marie Yerkes, Johns Hopkins University; Judith Yung, University of California, Santa Cruz.

The Heath Anthology of American Literature

Volume E

Contemporary Period: 1945 to the Present

CONTEMPORARY PERIOD:
1945 TO THE PRESENT

WHEN the United States emerged from World War II, it was unquestionably the most powerful nation the world had yet known. Its factories and farms had been crucial to the Allies' military victory. Its technology had produced the atomic bomb, a weapon of unsurpassed terror. Unlike many other industrial powers, its cities were untouched by the war's devastation, and its industries quickly converted their enormous productive capacities from making guns and tanks to producing cars and refrigerators. American engineers talked of producing virtually free power through atomic fission. And as Johnny came marching home, Rosie was told to leave riveting to raise babies in the newly built suburbs.

A quarter of a century later, the United States had essentially been defeated by a small Asian nation on the distant battlefield of Vietnam. Its factories, like some of its large cities, were in decay. Its monopoly on weapons of mass destruction had long disappeared into a balance of terror. Indeed, the fabric of American society was being shredded in harsh and sometimes violent conflicts over war, human rights, and continuing and deepening poverty. Johnny and Rosie had probably gone separate ways; the house in the suburbs had begun to disintegrate. Far from creating a harmonious chorus singing "one for all, all for one," Americans had issued a cacophony of competing voices, all demanding a large piece of the action.

The literature chosen to represent the last half of the twentieth century attempts to show the differences of outlook and attitude as well as the rich spectrum of cultural and aesthetic perspectives. The dissolution of cultural and even national boundaries has helped shape such writers as Sherman Alexie and Helena María Viramontes. Most of the writers of this period have lived with the fear of the Bomb, the agony of the Vietnam War, the exhilaration of the March on Washington; their works sometimes chronicle, sometimes protest, and sometimes ignore these events. Yet like everyone else, writers are in some measure creatures of their time, and since they are often—in Henry James's words—people on whom "nothing is lost," we will find their world and ours inscribed in their books.

"What validates us as human beings validates us as writers," Gloria Anzaldúa affirms as she urges people to express their beliefs and their individuality through the act of writing. The validation of all human experience through a printed text is more nearly possible now than ever before in American history. Publishers have become more interested in work by minorities and women, homosexuals and political radicals, and the appearance in print of some of the most important writing of the twentieth century foretells even greater opportunities to come. In fact, as large-scale commercial publishing has become more concentrated, with big publishers swallowed by bigger conglomerates, many groups have established smaller independent houses to create more specialized lists. Today, Arte Publico, Thunder's Mouth Press, Kitchen Table/Women of Color Press, Crossing Press, West End Press, and other publishers offer alternatives to the commercial concentration on "soon-to-be-major-movie" titles. The Internet has also transformed the nature of publishing, popularizing on-line journals and web logs that turn spontaneous observations into objects of scrutiny.

New kinds of publishing opportunities have met with criticism, however. Some readers claim that too much recent writing deals with odysseys of sexual freedom, descriptions of economic inequity, seemingly personal treatments of troubled families, and individual characters who experience madness or other shattering life happenings. They decry what they see as "inappropriate" subject matter conveyed through techniques so experimental as to be unreadable or, conversely, so simple as to be unliterary. This kind of negative response is also a United States literary tradition: such complaints have met new writing in almost every period because many readers feel more comfortable reading fiction, drama, and poetry that is distant, even remote, from their own life experience.

Yet contemporary American literature is remarkable because it does portray a variety of experiences, not only the sensational or the confessional. Today's writers often use unpleasant subject matter warningly, presenting it with enough chill that reading the text becomes admonitory. Contemporary literature does not wear blinders, and it is not intended for readers who live in an unreal world. Except for some science fiction and science fantasy, much contemporary literature is not escapist. It rather follows the direction of modernist writer William Carlos Williams, who demanded that the immediate objects and situations of the twentieth century become the subject of its art. Like Charles Sheeler's paintings of Ford Motor Company's River Rouge plant in Michigan, contemporary writers too use what surrounds them. Their artistry consists in shaping literature from that daily milieu, often crowded and chaotic, and often seemingly inartistic.

There is a difference, however, between the modern and the contemporary. Whereas the modern writer or artist focused on the objects of his or her culture, contemporary writers and artists are more intent on describing people's emotional states. The emotions that much writing chooses as its subject are more difficult to mirror than was Williams's red wheelbarrow. Late in the twentieth century, when Carolyn Forché writes about the brutal dismembering of war (and the military man's delight in the torture that has become a daily event), or Etheridge Knight laments the marginality of the lives of prison inmates, or James Welch shows the loss of hope in the lives of young Native Americans, our attention is drawn to the emotional meaning of that telling. Style supports meaning, as it did during modernism, but with somewhat different effects. Much contemporary writing has stopped pretending that there is an order, a hierarchy, to experience, or that education can bring shape out of the chaos of twentieth-century life. While the modernists believed that knowledge meant control, many postmodernists have accepted an utter lack of order as today's cultural norm. What chaos theory means to the contemporary psyche is that randomness, surprise, and dysfunction are as valuable as more orderly patterns of experience—and the literature about it—that dominated letters earlier, in the twentieth century. To insist that the word is valuable as word, that the form of writing is not necessarily an extension of its meaning but perhaps works against its perceived meaning, and that the writer's thought is no more valuable than that of any other living person is as viable in today's culture as the modernist code. Thomas Pynchon, Donald Barthelme, John Ashbery, Jessica Hagedorn, Raymond Carver, Kimiko Hahn, Joy Harjo, Leslie Marmon Silko, and David Foster Wallace are among the postmodernist writers included here.

A second critical difference between modern and postmodern literature involves difference itself. The 1950s are often said to have offered a unified vision of American culture. We then knew, or so the myth has it, what constituted American, indeed "Western," history and culture, and therefore we knew what students should study and critics should criticize. And it is certainly true that curricula and literary texts of the period offer a degree of uniformity unimaginable today. But in fact the seeds of today's diversity had already been sown and were rapidly sprouting, as the Civil Rights movement began to change American society and therefore American culture as well. In many respects, the question for ethnic and minority writers, as for ethnic and minority people, had been how they might fit themselves into mainstream culture. This question oversimplifies a complex process, but what constituted the center and the margins had remained relatively clear. The very manner in which writers like Ann Petry and Ralph Ellison were received illustrates something of the power of normative definitions, since they could be accounted for as a "naturalistic" and a "symbolist" writer, respectively, whose plots in *The Street* and *Invisible Man* simply happened to focus more than others on race.

But in the 1950s older definitions of cultural norms based upon race and ethnicity were, after years of attack, falling. In 1954 the Supreme Court agreed that separate education for black and white students produced inherently unequal opportunities for minorities, thus setting aside the legal basis for segregated schools. In 1955, Rosa Parks refused to accept the concept that black people belonged at the back of the bus; her arrest for refusing to give up her seat to a white and move to the rear set the stage for the Montgomery bus boycott and the prominence of the young black minister Martin Luther King, Jr. These and hundreds of other instances of resistance ultimately pluralized American culture. That is, the question shifted from how an ethnic minority writer might fit *into* mainstream culture to how alternative centers of culture, alternative understandings of its nature and functions, might be established *by* minority writers and *for* minority communities.

The developing movements for change spread ideas about, for example, black pride, and thus generated a new consciousness about culture and history among those who had been marginalized. Writers of color and white women responded to the imperative to speak for themselves and for others like themselves who had been silenced in history. But more: to do so, they had to define their own distinctive voices, create their own artistic forms and critical discourses, develop their own institu-

---

If I am right, the problem that has no name stirring in the minds of so many American women today is not a matter of loss of femininity or too much education, or the demands of domesticity. It is far more important than anyone recognizes. It is the key to these other new and old problems which have been torturing women and their husbands and children, and puzzling their doctors and educators for years. It may well be the key to our future as a nation and a culture. We can no longer ignore that voice within women that says: "I want something more than my husband and my children and my home."

Betty Friedan
"The Problem That Has No Name"

tions—especially publishing houses—their own foci for cultural work. The Black Arts movement, El Teatro Campesino, anthologies like *Black Fire, Time to Greeze!,* and *That's What She Said,* the dozens of new magazines and festivals—these all represent significant moments in the development of alternative cultural centers. To some degree, these "centers" have been geographically differentiated. Detroit, San Francisco, Houston, Albuquerque, and Atlanta have, in their different ways, become central to certain significant cultural movements. But the issue is less that of place than of power: the power to define literary form and value. No longer can "ethnic literature" be defined as being *about* ethnics so much as *by* ethnics.

There is another, perhaps more far-reaching consequence of this radical pluralization of American literary traditions. As contemporary United States literature has lost its dominantly Anglo-American and largely male definition, it has become more accessible and perhaps more interesting to many from outside the United States, those readers who view the new American literature focused on ethnicity, race, and the "subaltern" as a vital part of a global dialogue about the relationship of colonized peoples to their (mainly European) colonizers. Paradoxically, it may be that the very decentering of American literature has made it more integral to international culture.

New themes and subjects call for new techniques, and the contemporary period includes literature as technically varied as that in any time before it. Earlier modernism—with its difficult but unforgettable texts such as Faulkner's *The Sound and the Fury,* Toomer's *Cane,* and Eliot's *The Waste Land*—strongly influences some contemporary writers who see formal innovation as a means not only for extending the domain of what is termed "literature" but also for shaking readers free from their conventional assumptions about their world. For other contemporary writers, however, formal innovation is of less consequence than expressing the experiences of communities that had previously been marginalized, and challenging readers with issues like AIDS and ambiguous sexual definition, which are painful and, to some, unwelcome. Much recent literature makes use of oral elements, which remain particularly strong in many minority cultures, as well as echoing traditional rituals and tales, like "La Llorona" and "Yellow Woman." Contemporary authors often blend realistic elements with elliptical or surreal details, rejecting the notion that writing must "represent" a knowable reality lying "behind" the surface of language, suggesting instead that any narrative—whether called history or a novel—is a fictional construction subject to deconstruction and reassembly by changing communities of readers.

"Postmodernism," the name often given to recent cultural developments, has no single agreed-upon definition, but it surely involves the decentering of literary and cultural authority, as well as the dissolution of traditional boundaries like those between "high" and "popular" cultures or between "American" and "other" literatures. Whatever else it may imply, the postmodern era presents little that is stable, unitary, and comforting for readers, offering instead the pleasures of uncertainty, diversity, and change.

This anthology aims to give today's readers a *representative* selection of contemporary writing. Space prohibits any attempt at comprehensiveness, but the works that follow show the sheer excellence of the writing of our time, the late twentieth century as well as the nascent twenty-first.

The "American Century": From Victory to Vietnam

World War II ushered in a widespread spirit of optimism that most Americans had not felt for two decades. In 1941, just before the war began, Henry Luce, the publisher of *Life* magazine, wrote, "Throughout the 17th century and the 18th century and the 19th century, this continent teemed with manifold projects and magnificent purposes. Above them all and weaving them all together into the most exciting flag of all the world and of all history was the triumphal purpose of freedom. It is in this spirit that all of us are called, each to his own measure of capacity, and each in the widest horizon of his vision, to create the first great American Century."

Indeed, the twentieth century came to be known as the American Century, largely because of the economic prosperity of the United States and its military might. The United States imagined itself as a hardworking, resourceful nation that would sacrifice in times of need and enjoy its prosperity in times of plenty. Part of this cultural optimism came from the transition from the Great Depression, which had blighted the nation in the 1930s, to the spirit of victory following World War II, which ended in 1945. All of America seemed to be involved in fighting the war—the American soldiers who landed on the French coast to help end the spread of Nazism and fascism, the scientists who developed the atomic bomb that would give the United States its enduring title of superpower, the women who filled the factory jobs while men were fighting overseas, the children who gathered tin cans to be recycled into bullets and other materials necessary for war.

This version of the story is not without its contradictions or its long-term implications. A culture that appears ebullient and victorious on the surface is invariably masking misery. In 1945, when soldiers were disembarking from ships to reunite with their sweethearts, returning to housing shortages that soon led to the creation of affordable suburban housing developments and to make the babies that would produce the largest native-born population explosion in U.S. history, the story of the American Century was continuing, but a number of other stories were beginning as well.

At home, the United States was certainly enjoying the start of a long period of prosperity, but the jubilant nation was not without its troubles. The atomic bombs that had concluded the war marked the beginning of the atomic age, when competition between nuclear powers produced widespread anxiety and advanced the terrifying notion that the world could be destroyed instantly. Everyone was at risk. And although the United States was the most powerful nation on earth, within its borders were powerless groups of people.

In 1942, the first year of the war, President Franklin Roosevelt had signed Executive Order 9066, which had resulted in the relocation of more than 100,000 people of Japanese descent—more than half of whom were U.S. citizens—to "war relocation," or "internment," camps. Discrimination against Asian Americans was thus backed by the power of the executive branch of government, just as discrimination against African Americans in the South was backed by the power of state legislatures, state judges, and the police.

Although African American soldiers who returned home after World War II did not face the lynch mobs that attacked some black soldiers after World War I, segregation was still the law in the American South in 1945. The civil rights movement turned violent over the next two decades, culminating in the race riots in the Watts section of Los Angeles in August 1965 and in over a hundred cities (Detroit and Newark were the most prominent) in July 1967.

The tide of immigration from Europe that rose the 1920s had abated, but new immigration from Puerto Rico and Spanish-speaking countries in the western hemisphere radically changed the demographics of the forty-eight states. Like many immigrant groups before them, Spanish speakers were subjected to discrimination as they struggled to preserve their heritage in a nation that had once again forgotten its multicultural promise.

Although the hope was that global politics would be more stable in the aftermath of World War II, the United States and the Soviet Union, wartime allies, were soon squaring off. In 1946, the year after World War II ended, British Prime Minister Winston Churchill warned that an "iron curtain" was descending over eastern Europe. The United States now had a formidable adversary in its former ally, the Soviet Union. Within the next few years, this adversary launched the first satellite into space with the intention of gathering intelligence and had developed its own atomic bomb.

Also in 1946, Ho Chi Minh became president of North Vietnam. While the United States set up a new agency known as the Central Intelligence Agency (the descendant of the wartime Office of Strategic Services) to gather information about what was going on behind the iron curtain, a new enemy was quietly materializing in Southeast Asia. Over the next two decades, America gradually became deeply involved in the conflict in Vietnam. By the late 1960s, America found itself at war, and young American men were being drafted to fight it. Americans who were born in 1946 and after found themselves debating,

arguing about, and protesting the mandatory draft for the war in Vietnam in the late 1960s. More than 60,000 Americans died in that war, and in 1970 on the campus of Kent State University in Ohio, four protesters were shot and killed by National Guard members who were struggling to control members of a young generation vociferously exercising their right to free speech.

In addition to the wars that have traditionally helped to define history, a number of cultural changes, many of them wrought by opposition to the war in Vietnam, undeniably affected the literature of the second half of the twentieth century. One especially visible change was the modern American suburb, and one of its best-known developers was a man named William Levitt. In building Levittown, an instant community halfway between New York City and the defense industry plants on Long Island, he was responding to the need for affordable housing in the aftermath of World War II. As Levittown was being built from 1947 to 1951, the demand for its modest houses on curved streets and cul-de-sacs off a main thoroughfare was overwhelming: reunited couples needed a place to raise their families. The houses were essentially identical, but this homogeneity did not seem to bother these middle-class families, and Levittown became the model for the countless similar communities that have sprouted throughout the United States since the end of World War II.

As a result of these suburban developments, U.S. cities languished from the 1950s through the 1980s, and rural regions steadily became smaller as suburbs began to sprawl outward and encroach into farmland. American culture and the U.S. landscape would never be the same. The American dream in the 1950s (and even to this day) was a married couple, a comfortable yet modest home, a picket fence, a couple of kids, and a dog—and it all began in Levittown.

These suburban homes were likely to contain two culturally significant items—a car and a television. Detroit churned out automobiles in the 1950s to help the economy make a switch from wartime to civilian production and to answer a pent-up demand for cars, and a host of other industries (fast-food chains and drive-in theaters, followed by malls and strip malls) were initially associated with the baby boomers, who started driving in the early 1960s. The automobile and the interstate highway system, a development initiated by President Dwight D. Eisenhower in the 1950s as a key component of a national defense system, allowed American families to travel easily throughout their nation, increasing a trend toward isolationism while allowing Americans to enjoy their vaunted sense of freedom. The interstate highway system also replaced the national railway system as the primary means of transporting goods.

The economic benefits of the interstate system are manifold (trucks can go more places than trains can), but the environmental costs have proved to be great. This has been made clearer as scientists have become aware of the perils, social costs, and health risks of global warming, poor air quality, and the depletion of nonrenewable natural resources.

The impact of television on American culture cannot be underestimated. Television quickly replaced the radio as the main form of family entertainment. Because of its visual and audio content, television was even more appealing than its predecessor—more like life, more like the movies and easily packaged to fit into a living room. As a way to sell products, television was also unparalleled, and its ubiquity contributed to a consumerist mentality that has dominated U.S. culture ever since. Nightly news broadcasts gradually overtook newspapers as America's primary source of information. In fact, the television news broadcasts from the Vietnam War in the late 1960s were one reason that opinion about the war was so divided: war isn't pretty. Indeed, Vietnam came to be known as the living room war, and a device that was designed for en-

tertainment became the vehicle for delivering national traumas. Nonetheless, in the 1950s and early 1960s television was still primarily a form of entertainment that showed American families idealized versions of themselves on *The Donna Reed Show, The Dick Van Dyke Show,* and *Leave It to Beaver.*

The rise of television and the development of the modern suburb had profound implications for American literary culture during this period. If families were watching more television, they must have been reading fewer books, which meant that literature began to have less influence on middle-class culture than in the previous half century. Writers responded to this cultural change with innovation—and sometimes despair. Also, the depiction of American culture on television reflected the rise of the suburbs and therefore was homogeneous in many ways. Not until the 1970s were members of ethnic or racial minorities represented consistently on television. Literature began to feel the burden of correcting for television-produced misperceptions about American society.

In preceding decades, authors who chronicled the experiences of members of minority groups or who sought to record the experiences of citizens living at the margins of society were likely to hunt for small, alternative publishing houses, which proliferated after the war. Rather than cater to mainstream American tastes, which appeared to be growing flat and bland from a steady diet of television, innovative American authors of every ethnic and racial background pursued publishing or performance venues that did not demand that their works be scrubbed clean. During the 1950s and early 1960s, avant-garde publishing houses cropped up, poets could be found performing their poetry in nightclubs and coffeehouses, and the off-Broadway play began to gain legitimacy in the American theater. The spirit of individualism and rebellion that has always characterized American culture remained alive throughout the 1950s: it was just less apparent.

Arguably the best and most enduring literature of this period is some of the most experimental and iconoclastic. This is not to say that some mainstream or popular works are not worthy of our attention. Grace Metalious's scandalous novel *Peyton Place* (1956) exposed the sexual affairs of a fictional small town in New England. Sloan Wilson's *The Man in the Gray Flannel Suit* (1955), also a popular 1956 film, revealed the simmering discontent of a typical suburban commuter, a veteran of World War II. These novels were hugely popular in their day but have not withstood serious critical literary analysis over time.

However, Ralph Ellison's *Invisible Man* (1952) achieved critical acclaim as well as popular success, and Ellison became the first African American to win the National Book Award. (See his acceptance speech, published as "Brave Words for a Startling Occasion," in this volume.) Many critics count Ellison's novel among the greatest works of American fiction. The nameless narrator (usually referred to as "Invisible Man"), an African American who considers himself invisible, endures a series of humiliations that stem from his racial identity. Unconsciously following the Great Migration from the South (the region of his birth) to New York City, Invisible Man gradually becomes aware of his marginality in American society, though he continues to believe in the validity of American ideals at the book's conclusion.

Awareness of marginality was a hallmark of the literary 1950s. Two other works of fiction that achieved popular and critical success were James Baldwin's *Giovanni's Room* (1956) and Jack Kerouac's *On the Road* (1957). Baldwin, an African American living in exile in Paris in the 1950s, gained attention for his bildungsroman *Go Tell It on the Mountain* (1953) and his manifesto, a collection of essays entitled *Notes of a Native Son* (1955). Both reflected his experiences as a poor black youth, but both largely ignored another facet of his identity, his bisexuality. *Giovanni's Room* tackled this subject in a way that had not been broached before this time. Baldwin's publisher was scared of the explicit homoerotic content of the book, which is ironic, considering that the novel scrutinizes the forces that would lead a young man to suppress his homosexual desires in order to conform to the heterosexual lifestyle considered normal by his culture.

Kerouac's *On the Road* also dabbles in bisexuality, but that is only one of many experiences chronicled in a novel that might be considered deviant by conservatives. Kerouac's novel, written in a fluid, spontaneous style, describes characters who experiment with illegal drugs, drink excessive amounts of alcohol, hitchhike, travel like hoboes on boxcars, and drive at more than 100 miles per hour—all in pursuit of some elusive "IT," some quasi-spiritual experience that will give meaning to their lives because they have rejected the values and lifestyles of mainstream Americans. As a central figure of the so-called beat generation, Kerouac's writings influenced a vast number of young people who were discontented with the suburban lifestyle into which they were born. Kerouac's friend Allen Ginsberg, the other leading figure of the beat movement, published the long poem "Howl" in 1956. The explicit homosexual content of this poem caused an even greater uproar than Baldwin's novel did. Following a performance of the poem at the now-famous City Lights bookstore in San Francisco, U.S. customs agents tried to ban the published version of Ginsberg's poem by seizing copies of the book as they arrived in the port. This case of censorship did not hold up in a local court, and "Howl" became a sensation as well as a classic. Baldwin's story "Sonny's Blues," Kerouac's piece "The Vanishing American Hobo," and Ginsberg's "Howl" (as well as other poems of his) can all be found in this volume.

Poor, marginalized men like Ellison, Baldwin, Kerouac, and Ginsberg struggled to get their experiences and visions into print, but women writers of the 1950s and 1960s were also revealing a widespread resistance to the cultural expectations, especially those that would keep them barefoot, pregnant, and in the kitchen. In 1963, Betty Friedan published *The Feminine Mystique,* a nonfiction work that explored the discontentment that so many middle-class women were experiencing. In the suburbs, convenience items like dishwashers, vacuum cleaners, and washing machines made domestic work less arduous, but many women were questioning whether their role as homemaker was fulfilling. This questioning became a full-fledged social and political movement in the 1960s and 1970s— what is now called second-wave feminism (the first wave was the feminism of the late nineteenth and early twentieth centuries). We can see the origins of second-wave feminism in women's writings of the 1950s. Poetry by Adrienne Rich and Anne Sexton, for example, often focuses on women who want to reject a gender-stereotyped, preordained lifestyle. Rich eventually became a leading figure in the feminist movement, and Sexton committed suicide.

Sexton was part of a school of poetry that developed in the late 1950s and early 1960s known as confessional poetry. Its leading figure was Robert Lowell, an influential poet who had written in a more traditional modernist style through the early 1950s. In 1960, with the publication of his volume *Life Studies,* Lowell paved the way for a generation of poets to follow. Confessional poetry focuses on subjective experience, often as it connects to a perceived broader social ill. The "I" of the poem is central, not a mask or persona, as it had been in modern poetry, but a subject for deep scrutiny. In this sense, confessional poetry parallels beat poetry, which flourished at the same time and also rendered personal experience in writing. However, the confessional style is more influenced by classical poetic forms than by the jazz rhythms or spontaneity that dictates the form of beat poetry. Confessional poetry tends to privilege extreme emotional states. Its speakers tend toward neurosis. Like Sexton, Sylvia Plath was a student of Lowell's, wrote in the confessional mode, and committed suicide. All three poets are represented in this volume, and their influence on more recent poets is profound.

It could be argued that American drama reached its golden age in the third quarter of the twentieth century. Some of the most enduring and well-respected figures in American drama—Arthur Miller, Tennessee Williams, and Edward Albee— were active then. Following in the footsteps of their predecessor, Eugene O'Neill, these three writers continued to experiment with the form and content of plays. Like the confessional school of poetry, the theater of the 1950s tended to focus on the problems of people who were, at least in Miller's conception, ordinary individuals with tragic flaws. Miller's influential essay "Tragedy and the Common Man" argued that the strains of classical tragedy could still be heard on the contemporary stage but that the theater now concerned itself with types that audience members could immediately recognize as their neighbors or themselves rather than the "great men" of classical drama. Miller's most famous plays, *Death of a Salesman* (1949) and *The Crucible* (1953, included here), embody the ideas that he sets forth in this essay. Williams's plays, like Miller's, reveal the despair of ordinary characters trapped by the expectations of their culture. Albee tended to turn midcentury despair into a kind of insanity on the stage. Magnified only slightly, the discontent of the contemporary world became grotesque in his hands, and he paved the way for the next generation of playwrights, like Sam Shepard, who indulged even more in the absurd. Williams's short play "Portrait of a Madonna" and Albee's "The Sand Box" can be found in this volume.

For the first time, African American playwrights were also gaining notoriety in the American theater. Lorraine Hansberry's play *A Raisin in the Sun* (1959) became the first play by an African American to be produced on Broadway. Had it not been for her premature death, Hansberry likely would have joined the next generation of experimental black playwrights, including George C. Wolfe and Ntozake Shange, as they made even more space on the American stage for the black experience in the 1970s and 1980s. James Baldwin's 1964 play *Blues for Mister Charlie,* though not uniformly well received, cleared a path for a number of plays by angry, even radical, black activists, notably Amiri Baraka (who was born LeRoi Jones), whose 1964 play *Dutchman* is included in this volume. The intent or effect of Baldwin's and Baraka's plays was to examine the tragedies of modern times and to see them in terms of race relations, which were reaching a boiling point in the mid-1960s. Baraka is a particularly influential figure in the black arts movement of the late 1960s that sought to express the political aims of radical black activism in art.

Arthur Miller's prominence in the theater in the 1950s and 1960s indicates another trend in American literature of this period—the rise to prominence of Jewish writers. Especially in the realm of fiction, Jewish voices and the Jewish experience had not been widely visible in the early twentieth century but began to emerge in the 1950s and 1960s. The most prominent, critically respected, award-winning writers of this period were, for the first time in American literary history, not from an Anglo/Christian background. Bernard Malamud, Philip Roth, Grace Paley, Norman Mailer, and the Nobel laureate Saul Bellow all became active in the years following the end of World War II, and they remain some of the most significant authors of the twentieth century. Roth continues to gain notoriety in the twenty-first.

As *The Heath Anthology of American Literature* shows, American literature has always been more diverse than it appeared to be, but only in the second half of the twentieth century was that diversity recognized or rewarded by the mainstream literary establishment. The trend continues and expands exponentially in the final quarter of the twentieth century and in the first decade of the twenty-first century, which are introduced in the second half of this volume— New World Disorder: Recent Literature.

Ann Petry 1908–1997

Born in 1908 in Old Saybrook, Connecticut, Ann Petry liked to characterize herself as a gambler and survivor: the former, because she was a black woman who decided to write for a living, and the latter, because she published eight books.

The younger daughter of middle-class, New England-born parents, Ann Lane grew up in Old Saybrook and spent much of her time in her family's drugstore. She joined the family business after graduating from the Connecticut College of Pharmacy in New Haven. But in 1938, after marrying George Petry, an aspiring writer from New Iberia, Louisiana, she left behind her sheltered life in the seaside town and moved to New York City. There she decided to concentrate on her writing, an interest she had pursued on the side for years. As a reporter for a Harlem weekly, she became familiar with the poverty and demoralization afflicting inner-city blacks. She also learned about the city through her involvement in an after-school program for Harlem children. It was during this period that she got the idea for *The Street* (1946), the tale of Lutie Johnson's desperate struggle to earn a living in Harlem and protect her young son from corruption. Petry's first novel became a national bestseller, the first for an American black woman. To date, it has sold more than a million and a half copies.

The Street showcases Petry's mastery of naturalism. Lutie's endless war with hostile forces begins with her braving a ferociously cold wind and culminates in her struggle with a would-be rapist. Set during World War II, *The Street* illustrates the myriad degradations faced by black men and children as well as black women. In addition to telling Lutie's story, the novel takes up the perspectives of Bub, her lonely eight-year-old son; Jones, the depraved building superintendent; Mrs. Hedges, a malevolent madam; and even Boots Smith, the bitterly resentful band leader.

After *The Street*'s success, the Petrys returned to the reclusive quiet of Old Saybrook, where they settled permanently and had a daughter, Elisabeth Ann. In 1947 Petry published *Country Place,* a novel as unflinching in its portrayal of a white New England town as *The Street* is in its portrayal of a Harlem ghetto. Set in the years just after World War II and narrated by the white druggist 'Doc' Fraser, *Country Place* concerns marital infidelities and a litany of other betrayals. Although it lacks *The Street*'s depth of characterization, *Country Place* reveals Petry's continuing fascination with troubled communities.

In Petry's third novel, *The Narrows* (1953), blacks and whites coexist uneasily in the small city of Monmouth, Connecticut. The novel, which takes place in the fifties, revolves around a doomed relationship between Link Williams, an educated young black man, and Camilla Treadway, a wealthy young white woman. What begins as their private love affair ends in murder and public polarization of the races.

Miss Muriel and Other Stories (1971) includes 13 stories, several of which are set in Wheeling, New York, a fictional town similar to Old Saybrook. Like her novels, Petry's short fiction deals with devastating fissures in insular communities. The tension in these stories often results from distrust among people who cannot conquer their own or anyone else's prejudices of race and gender.

Petry's books for younger readers include a historical biography, *Harriet Tubman: Conductor on the Underground Railroad* (1955), and *Tituba of Salem Village* (1964), the story, based on real events, of a slave woman convicted of witchcraft. More didactic than her works for adults, these books are eloquent studies in African American heritage and individual fortitude.

Hilary Holladay
University of Massachusetts–Lowell

PRIMARY WORKS

The Street, 1946; *Country Place,* 1947; *The Narrows,* 1953; *Harriet Tubman: Conductor on the Underground Railroad,* 1955; *Tituba of Salem Village,* 1964; *Miss Muriel and Other Stories,* 1971.

The Witness

It had been snowing for twenty-four hours, and as soon as it stopped, the town plows began clearing the roads and sprinkling them with a mixture of sand and salt. By nightfall the main roads were what the roadmaster called clean as a whistle. But the little winding side roads and the store parking lots and the private walkways lay under a thick blanket of snow.

Because of the deep snow, Charles Woodruff parked his station wagon, brand-new, expensive, in the road in front of the Congregational church rather than risk getting stuck in the lot behind the church. He was early for the minister's class so he sat still, deliberately savoring the new-car smell of the station wagon. He found himself sniffing audibly and thought the sound rather a greedy one and so got out of the car and stood on the snow-covered walk, studying the church. A full moon lay low on the horizon. It gave a wonderful luminous quality to the snow, to the church, and to the branches of the great elms dark against the winter sky.

He ducked his head down because the wind was coming in gusts straight from the north, blowing the snow so it swirled around him, stinging his face. It was so cold that his toes felt as though they were freezing and he began to stamp his feet. Fortunately his coat insulated his body against the cold. He hadn't really planned to buy a new coat but during the Christmas vacation he had been in New York City and he had gone into one of those thickly carpeted, faintly perfumed, crystal-chandeliered stores that sell men's clothing and he had seen the coat hanging on a rack—a dark gray cashmere coat, lined with nutria and adorned by a collar of black Persian lamb. A tall, thin salesman who smelled of heather saw him looking at the coat and said: "Try it on, sir—it's toast-warm, cloud-light, guaranteed to make you feel like a prince—do try it on, here let me hold your coat, sir." The man's voice sounded as though he were purring and he kept brushing against Woodruff like a cat, and managed to sell him the coat, a narrow-brimmed felt hat, and a pair of fur-lined gloves.

If Addie had been alive and learned he had paid five hundred dollars for an overcoat, she would have argued with him fiercely, nostrils flaring, thin arched eyebrows lifted. Standing there alone in the snow, in front of the church, he permitted himself a small indulgence. He pretended Addie was standing beside him. He spoke to her, aloud: "You always said I had to dress more elegantly than my students so they would respect my clothes even if they didn't respect my learning. You said—"

He stopped abruptly, thinking he must look like a lunatic, standing in the snow, stamping his feet and talking to himself. If he kept it up long enough, someone would call the state police and a bulletin about him would go clattering out over the teletype: "Attention all cruisers, attention all cruisers, a black man, repeat, a black man is standing in front of the Congregational church in Wheeling, New York; description follows, description follows, thinnish, tallish black man, clipped moustache, expensive (extravagantly expensive, outrageously expensive, unjustifiably expensive) overcoat, felt hat like a Homburg, eyeglasses glittering in the moonlight, feet stamping in the moonlight, mouth muttering in the moonlight. Light of the moon we danced. Glimpses of the moon revisited . . ."

There was no one in sight, no cars passing. It was so still it would be easy to believe that the entire population of the town had died and lay buried under the snow and that he was the sole survivor, and that would be ironic because he did not really belong in this all-white community.

The thought of his alien presence here evoked an image of Addie—dark-skinned, intense, beautiful. He was sixty-five when she died. He had just retired as professor of English at Virginia College for Negroes. He had spent all of his working life there. He had planned to write a grammar to be used in first-year English classes, to perfect his herb garden, catalogue his library, tidy up his files, and organize his clippings—a wealth of material in those clippings. But without Addie these projects seemed inconsequential—like the busy work that grade school teachers devise to keep children out of mischief. When he was offered a job teaching in a high school in a small town in New York, he accepted it quickly.

Everybody was integrating and so this little frozen Northern town was integrating, too. Someone probably asked why there were no black teachers in the school system and the school board and the Superintendent of Schools said they were searching for 'one'—and the search yielded that brand-new black widower, Charles Woodruff (nigger in the woodpile, he thought, and then, why that word, a word he despised and never used so why did it pop up like that, does a full moon really affect the human mind) and he was eager to escape from his old environment and so for the past year he had taught English to academic seniors in Wheeling High School.

No problems. No hoodlums. All of his students were being herded toward college like so many cattle. He referred to them (mentally) as the Willing Workers of America. He thought that what was being done to them was a crime against nature. They were hard-working, courteous, pathetic. He introduced a new textbook, discarded a huge anthology that was filled with mutilated poetry, mutilated essays, mutilated short stories. His students liked him and told him so. Other members of the faculty said he was lucky but just wait until another year—the freshmen and the sophomores were "a bunch of hoodlums"—"a whole new ball game"—

Because of his success with his English classes, Dr. Shipley, the Congregational minister, had asked him if he would assist (Shipley used words like "assist" instead of "help") him with a class of delinquent boys—the class met on Sunday nights. Woodruff felt he should make some kind of contribution to the life of this small town which had treated him with genuine friendliness so he had said yes.

But when he first saw those seven boys assembled in the minister's study, he knew that he could neither help nor assist the minister with them—they were beyond his reach, beyond the minister's reach. They sat silent, motionless, their shoulders hunched as though against some chill they found in the air of that small book-lined room. Their eyelids were like shutters drawn over their eyes. Their long hair covered their foreheads, obscuring their eyebrows, reaching to the collars of their jackets. Their legs, stretched out straight in front of them, were encased in pants that fit as tightly as the leotards of a ballet dancer.

He kept looking at them, studying them. Suddenly, as though at a signal, they all looked at him. This collective stare was so hostile that he felt himself stiffen and sweat broke out on his forehead. He assumed that the same thing had happened to Dr. Shipley because Shipley's eyeglasses kept fogging up, though the room was not overly warm.

Shipley had talked for an hour. He began to get hoarse. Though he paused now and then to ask a question and waited hopefully for a reply, there was none. The boys sat mute and motionless.

After they left, filing out, one behind the other, Woodruff had asked Shipley about them—who they were and why they attended this class in religion.

Shipley said, "They come here under duress. The Juvenile Court requires their attendance at this class."

"How old are they?"

"About sixteen. Very bright. Still in high school. They're all sophomores—that's why you don't know them. Rambler, the tall thin boy, the ringleader, has an IQ in the genius bracket. As a matter of fact, if they weren't so bright, they'd be in reform school. This class is part of an effort to—well—to turn them into God-fearing responsible young citizens."

"Are their families poor?"

"No, indeed. The parents of these boys are—well, they're the backbone of the great middle class in this town."

After the third meeting of the class where the same hostile silence prevailed, Woodruff said, "Dr. Shipley, do you think we are accomplishing anything?" He had said "we" though he was well aware that these new young outlaws spawned by the white middle class were, praise God, Shipley's problem—the white man's problem. This cripplingly tight shoe was usually on the black man's foot. He found it rather pleasant to have the position reversed.

Shipley ran his fingers through his hair. It was very short hair, stiff-looking, crew-cut.

"I don't know," he said frowning. "I really don't know. They don't even respond to a greeting or a direct question. It is a terribly frustrating business, an exhausting business. When the class is over, I feel as though I had spent the entire evening lying prone under the unrelieved weight of all their bodies."

Woodruff, standing outside the church, stamping his feet, jumped and then winced because he heard a sound like a gunshot. It was born on the wind so that it seemed close at hand. He stood still, listening. Then he started moving quickly toward the religious education building which housed the minister's study.

He recognized the sound—it was made by the car the boys drove. It had no muffler and the snorting, back-firing sounds made by the spent motor were like a series of gunshots. He wanted to be out of sight when the boys drove up in their rusted car. Their lithe young bodies were a shocking contrast to the abused and ancient vehicle in which they traveled. The age of the car, its dreadful condition, was like a snarled message aimed at the adult world: All we've got is the crumbs, the leftovers, whatever the fat cats don't want and can't use; the turnpikes and the throughways and the seventy-mile-an-hour speedways are filled with long, low, shiny cars built for speed, driven by bald-headed, big-bellied rat finks and we're left with the junk, the worn-out beat-up chassis, the thin tires, the brakes that don't hold, the transmission that's shot to hell. He had seen them push the car out of the parking lot behind the church. It wouldn't go in reverse.

Bent over, peering down, picking his way through the deep snow lest he stumble and fall, Woodruff tried to hurry and the explosive sound of that terrible engine kept getting closer and closer. He envisioned himself as a black beetle in a fur-collared coat silhouetted against the snow trying to scuttle out of danger. Danger: Why should he think he was in danger? Perhaps some sixth sense was trying to warn him and his beetle's antenna (did beetles have antennae, did they have five senses and some of them an additional sense, extrasensory—) picked it up—by the pricking of my thumbs, something wicked this way comes.

Once inside the building he drew a deep breath. He greeted Dr. Shipley, hung his hat and coat on the brass hat rack, and then sat down beside Shipley behind the old fumed oak desk. He braced himself for the entrance of the boys.

There was the sound of the front door opening followed by the click-clack sound of their heavy boots, in the hall. Suddenly they were all there in the minister's study. They brought cold air in with them. They sat down with their jackets on—great quilted dark jackets that had been designed for European ski slopes. At the first meeting of the class, Dr. Shipley had suggested they remove their jackets and they simply sat and stared at him until he fidgeted and looked away obviously embarrassed. He never again made a suggestion that was direct and personal.

Woodruff glanced at the boys and then directed his gaze away from them, thinking, if a bit of gilt braid and a touch of velvet were added to their clothing, they could pass for the seven dark bastard sons of some old and evil twelfth-century king. Of course they weren't all dark. Three of them were blond, two had brown hair, one had red hair, only one had black hair. All of them were white. But there was about them an aura of something so evil, so dark, so suggestive of the far reaches of the night, of the black horror of nightmares, that he shivered deep inside himself whenever he saw them. Though he thought of them as being black, this was not the blackness of human flesh, warm, soft to the touch, it was the blackness and the coldness of the hole from which D.H. Lawrence's snake emerged.

The hour was almost up when to Woodruff's surprise, Rambler, the tall boy, the one who drove the ramshackle car, the one Shipley said was the leader of the group, began asking questions about cannibalism. His voice was husky, low in pitch, and he almost whispered when he spoke. Woodruff found himself leaning forward in an effort to hear what the boy was saying. Dr. Shipley leaned forward, too.

Rambler said, "Is it a crime to eat human flesh?"

Dr. Shipley said, surprised, "Yes. It's cannibalism. It is a sin and it is also a crime." He spoke slowly, gently, as though he were wooing a timid, wild animal that had ventured out of the woods and would turn tail and scamper back if he spoke in his normal voice.

"Well, if the cats who go for this human flesh bit don't think it's a sin and if they eat it because they haven't any other food, it isn't a sin for them, is it?" The boy spoke quickly, not pausing for breath, running his words together.

"There are many practices and acts that are acceptable to non-Christians which are sinful. Christians condemn such acts no matter what the circumstances."

Woodruff thought uncomfortably, why does Shipley have to sound so pompous, so righteous, so from-off-the-top-of-Olympus? The boys were all staring at him, bright-eyed, mouths slightly open, long hair obscuring their foreheads. Then Rambler said, in his husky whispering voice, "What about you, Doc?"

Dr. Shipley said, "Me?" and repeated it, his voice losing its coaxing tone, rising in pitch, increasing in volume. "Me? What do you mean?"

"Well, man, you're eatin' human flesh, ain't you?"

Woodruff had no idea what the boy was talking about. But Dr. Shipley was looking down at his own hands with a curious self-conscious expression and Woodruff saw that Shipley's nails were bitten all the way down to the quick.

The boy said, "It's self-cannibalism, ain't it, Doc?"

Shipley put his hands on the desk, braced himself, preparatory to standing up. His thin, bony face had reddened. Before he could move, or speak, the boys stood up and began to file out of the room. Rambler leaned over and ran his hand through the minister's short-cut, bristly hair and said, "Don't sweat it, Doc."

Woodruff usually stayed a half-hour or more after the class ended. Dr. Shipley liked to talk and Woodruff listened to him patiently, though he thought Shipley had a second-rate mind and rambled when he talked. But Shipley sat with his head bowed, a pose not conducive to conversation and Woodruff left almost immediately after the boys, carrying in his mind's eye a picture of all those straight, narrow backs with the pants so tight they were like elastic bandages on their thighs, and the oversized bulky jackets and the long, frowsy hair. He thought they looked like paper dolls, cut all at once, exactly alike with a few swift slashes of scissors wielded by a skilled hand. Addie could do that—take paper and fold it and go snip, snip, snip with the scissors and she'd have a string of paper dolls, all fat, or all thin, or all bent over, or all wearing top hats, or all bearded Santas or all Cheshire cats. She had taught arts and crafts in the teacher-training courses for elementary-school teachers at Virginia College and so was skilled in the use of crayon and scissors.

He walked toward his car, head down, picking his way through the snow and then he stopped, surprised. The boys were standing in the road. They had surrounded a girl. He didn't think she was a high school girl though she was young. She had long blond hair that spilled over the quilted black jacket she was wearing. At first he couldn't tell what the boys were doing but as he got closer to them, he saw that they were moving toward their ancient car and forcing the girl to move with them though she was resisting. They were talking to each other and to her, their voices companionable, half-playful.

"So we all got one in the oven."

"So it's all right if it's all of us."

The girl said, "No."

"Aw, come on, Nellie, hurry up."

"It's colder'n hell, Nellie. Move!"

They kept pushing her toward the car and she turned on them and said, "Quit it."

"Aw, get in."

One of them gave her a hard shove, sent her closer to the car and she screamed and Rambler clapped his hand over her mouth and she must have bitten his hand because he snatched it away and then she screamed again because he slapped her and then two of them picked her up and threw her on the front seat and one of them stayed there, holding her.

Woodruff thought, There are seven of them, young, strong, satanic. He ought to go home where it was quiet and safe, mind his own business—black man's business; leave this white man's problem for a white man, leave it alone, not his, don't interfere, go home to the bungalow he rented—ridiculous type of architecture in this cold climate, developed for India, a hot climate, and that open porch business—

He said, "What are you doing?" He spoke with the voice of authority, the male schoolteacher's voice and thought, Wait, slow down, cool it, you're a black man speaking with a white man's voice.

They turned and stared at him; as they turned, they all assumed what he called the stance of the new young outlaw: the shoulders hunched, the hands in the pockets. In the moonlight he thought they looked as though they belonged in a frieze around a building—the hunched-shoulder posture repeated again and again, made permanent in stone. Classic.

"What are you doing?" he said again, voice louder, deeper.

"We're standin' here."

"You can see us, can't you?"

"Why did you force that girl into your car?"

"You're dreamin'."

"I saw what happened. And that boy is holding her in there."

"You been readin' too much."

They kept moving in, closing in on him. Even on this cold, windy night he could smell them and he loathed the smell—cigarettes, clothes washed in detergents and not rinsed enough and dried in automatic driers. They all smelled like that these days, even those pathetic college-bound drudges, the Willing Workers of America, stank so that he was always airing out his classroom. He rarely ever encountered the fresh clean smell of clothes that had been washed in soap and water, rinsed in boiling water, dried in the sun—a smell that he associated with new-mown hay and flower gardens and—Addie.

There was a subtle change in the tone of the voice of the next speaker. It was more contemptuous and louder.

"What girl, ho-daddy, what girl?"

One of them suddenly reached out and knocked his hat off his head, another one snatched his glasses off and threw them in the road and there was the tinkling sound of glass shattering. It made him shudder. He was half-blind without his glasses, peering about, uncertain of the shape of objects—like the woman in the Thurber cartoon, oh, yes, of course, three balloons and an H or three cats and a dog—only it was one of those scrambled alphabet charts.

They unbuttoned his overcoat, went through the pockets of his pants, of his jacket. One of them took his wallet, another took his car keys, picked up his hat, and then was actually behind the wheel of his station wagon and was moving off in it.

He shouted, "My car. Damn you, you're stealing my car—" his brand-new station wagon; he kept it immaculate, swept it out every morning, washed the windows. He tried to break out of that confining circle of boys and they simply pushed him back toward their car.

"Don't sweat it, man. You goin' ride with us and this little chick-chick."

"You goin' be our pro-tec-shun, ho-daddy. You goin' be our protec-shun."

They took his coat off and put it around him backward without putting his arms in the sleeves and then buttoned it up. The expensive coat was just like a strait jacket—it pinioned his arms to his sides. He tried to work his way out of it by flexing his muscles, hoping that the buttons would pop off or a seam would give, and thought, enraged, They must have stitched the goddamn coat to last for a thousand years and put the goddamn buttons on the same way. The fur collar pressed against his throat, choking him.

Woodruff was forced into the back seat, two boys on each side of him. They were sitting half on him and half on each other. The one holding his wallet examined its contents. He whistled. "Hey!" he said, "Ho-daddy's got one hundred and forty-four bucks. We got us a rich ho-daddy—"

Rambler held out his hand and the boy handed the money over without a protest, not even a sigh. Then Rambler got into the front seat behind the wheel. The girl was quiet only because the boy beside her had his hand around her throat and from the way he was holding his arm, Woodruff knew he was exerting a certain amount of pressure.

"Give the man a hat," Rambler said.

One of the boys felt around until he found a cap. They were so close to each other that each of his movements slightly disrupted their seating arrangement. When the boy shifted his weight, the rest of them were forced to shift theirs.

"Here you go," the boy said. He pulled a black wool cap down on Woodruff's head, over his eyes, over his nose.

He couldn't see anything. He couldn't breathe through his nose. He had to breathe through his mouth or suffocate. The freezing cold air actually hurt the inside of his mouth. The overcoat immobilized him and the steady pressure of the fur collar against his windpipe was beginning to interfere with his normal rate of breathing. He knew that his whole circulatory system would gradually begin to slow down. He frowned, thinking what a simple and easily executed method of rendering a person helpless—just an overcoat and a knit cap. Then he thought, alarmed, If they should leave me out in the woods like this, I would be dead by morning. What do they want of me anyway?

He cleared his throat preparatory to questioning them but Rambler started the car and he could not make himself heard above the sound of the engine. He thought the noise would shatter his eardrums and he wondered how these boys could bear it—the terrible cannon fire sound of the engine and the rattling of the doors and the windows. Then they were off and it was like riding in a jeep—only worse because the seat was broken and they were jounced up out of the seat and then back down into a hollowed-out place, all of them on top of each other. He tried to keep track of the turns the car made but he couldn't, there were too many of them. He assumed that whenever they stopped it was because of a traffic light or a stop sign.

It seemed to him they had ridden for miles and miles when the car began to jounce up and down more violently than ever and he decided they had turned onto a rough, rutted road. Suddenly they stopped. The car doors were opened and the boys pushed him out of the car. He couldn't keep his balance and he stumbled and fell flat on his face in the snow and they all laughed. They had to haul him to his feet for his movements were so constricted by the overcoat that he couldn't get up without help.

The cap had worked up a little so that he could breathe more freely and he could see anything that was in his immediate vicinity. Either they did not notice that the cap had been pushed out of place or they didn't care. As they guided him along he saw that they were in a cemetery that was filled with very old tombstones. They were approaching a small building and his station wagon was parked to one side. The boy who had driven it opened the door of the building and Woodruff saw that it was lighted inside by a big bulb that dangled from the ceiling. There were shovels and rakes inside and a grease-encrusted riding mower, bags of grass seed, and a bundle of material that looked like the artificial grass used around new graves.

Rambler said, "Put the witness here."

They stood him against the back wall, facing the wall.

"He's here and yet he ain't here."

"Ho-daddy's here—and yet—he ain't here."

"He's our witness."

And then Rambler's voice again, "If he moves, ice him with a shovel."

The girl screamed and then the sound was muffled, only a kind of far-off moaning sound coming through something. They must have gagged her. All the sounds were muffled—it was like trying to see something in a fog or hear something when other sounds overlay the one thing you're listening for. What had they brought him here for? They would go away and leave him with the girl but the girl would know that he hadn't—

How would she know? They had probably blindfolded her, too. What were they doing? He could see shadows on the wall. Sometimes they moved, sometimes they were still, and then the shadows moved again and then there would be laughter. Silence after that and then thuds, thumps, silence again. Terrible sounds behind him. He started to turn around and someone poked him in the back, sharply, with the handle of a shovel or a rake. He began to sweat despite the terrible cold.

He tried to relax by breathing deeply and he began to feel as though he were going to faint. His hands and feet were numb. His head ached. He had strained so to hear what was going on behind him that he was afraid he had impaired his own hearing.

When Rambler said, "Come on, ho-daddy, it's your turn," he was beginning to lose all feeling in his arms and legs.

Someone unbuttoned his coat, plucked the cap off his head. He let his breath out in a long drawn-out sigh. He doubted that he could have survived much longer with that pressure on his throat. The boys looked at him curiously. They threw his coat on the hard-packed dirt floor and tossed the cap on top of it. He thought that the black knit cap they'd used, like a sailor's watch cap, was as effective a blindfold as could be found—providing, of course, the person couldn't use his hands to remove it.

The girl was lying on the floor, half-naked. They had put some burlap bags under her. She looked as though she were dead.

They pushed him toward her saying, "It's your turn."

He balked, refusing to move.

"You don't want none?"

They laughed. "Ho-daddy don't want none."

They pushed him closer to the girl and someone grabbed one of his hands and placed it on the girl's thigh, on her breasts, and then they laughed again. They handed him his coat, pulled the cap down on his head.

"Let's go, ho-daddy. Let's go."

Before he could put his coat back on they hustled him outdoors. One of them threw his empty wallet at him and another aimed his car keys straight at his head. The metal stung as it hit his cheek. Before he could catch them the keys disappeared in the snow. The boys went back inside the building and emerged carrying the girl, half-naked, head hanging down limply the way the head of a corpse would dangle.

"The girl—" Woodruff said.

"You're our witness, ho-daddy. You're our big fat witness."

They propped the girl up in the back seat of their car. "You're the only witness we got," they repeated it, laughing. "Take good care of yourself."

"She'll freeze to death like that," he protested.

"Not Nellie."

"She likes it."

"Come on, man, let's go, let's go, let's go," Rambler said impatiently.

Woodruff's arms and hands were so numb that he had trouble getting his coat on. He had to take his gloves off and poke around in the snow with his bare hands before he could retrieve his wallet and the car keys. The pain in his hands was as sharp and intense as if they had been burned.

Getting into his car he began to shake with fury. Once he got out of this wretched cemetery he would call the state police. Young animals. He had called them outlaws; they weren't outlaws, they were animals. In his haste he dropped the keys and had to feel around on the floor of the car for them.

When he finally got the car started he was shivering and shaking and his stomach was quivering so that he didn't dare try to drive. He turned on the heater and watched the tiny taillight on Rambler's car disappear—an old car and the taillight was like the end of a pencil glowing red in the dark. The loud explosive sound of the engine gradually receded. When he could no longer hear it, he flicked on the light in his car and looked at his watch. It was quarter past three. Wouldn't the parents of those godforsaken boys wonder where they were at that hour? Perhaps they didn't care—perhaps they were afraid of them—just as he was.

Though he wanted to get home as quickly as possible, so he could get warm, so he could think, he had to drive slowly, peering out at the narrow rutted road because he was half blind without his glasses. When he reached the cemetery gates he stopped, not knowing whether to turn right or left for he had no idea where he was. He took a chance and turned right and followed the macadam road, still going slowly, saw a church on a hill and recognized it as the Congregational church in Brooksville, the next town, and knew he was about five miles from home.

By the time he reached his own driveway, sweat was pouring from his body just like water coming out of a showerhead—even his eyelashes were wet; it ran down his ears, dripped off his nose, his lips, even the palms of his hands.

In the house he turned on the lights, in the living room, in the hall, in his bedroom. He went to his desk, opened a drawer and fished out an old pair of glasses. He had had them for years. They looked rather like Peter Cooper's glasses—he'd seen them once in the Cooper Union Museum in New York—small-lensed, with narrow, silvery-looking frames. They evoked an image of a careful scholarly man. When he had started wearing glasses, he had selected frames like Peter Cooper's. Addie had made him stop wearing them. She said they gave him the look of another era, made it easy for his students to caricature him—the tall, slender figure, slightly stooped, the steel-rimmed glasses. She said that his dark, gentle eyes looked as though they were trapped behind those little glasses.

Having put on the glasses, he went to the telephone and stood with one hand resting on it, sweating again, trembling again. He turned away, took off his overcoat and hung it on a hanger and placed it in the hall closet.

He began to pace up and down the living room—a pleasant spacious room, simply furnished. It had a southern exposure and there were big windows on that side of the room. The windows faced a meadow. The thought crossed his mind, lightly, like the silken delicate strand of a cobweb, that he would have to leave here and he brushed it away—not quite away, a trace remained.

He wasn't going to call the police. Chicken. That was the word his students used. Fink was another one. He was going to chicken out. He was going to fink out.

Why wasn't he going to call the police? Well, what would he tell them? That he'd been robbed? Well, that was true. That he'd been kidnapped? Well, that was true, too, but it seemed like a harsh way of putting it. He'd have to think about that one. That he'd been witness to a rape? He wasn't even certain that they had raped the girl. No? Who was he trying to kid? Himself? Himself.

So why wasn't he going to the police? He hadn't touched the girl. But those horrible little hoods, toads rather, why toads, toe of frog ingredient of witches' brew, poisonous substance in the skin—bufotenine, a hallucinogen found in the skin of the frog, of the toad. Those horrible toadlike hoods would say he had touched her. Well, he had. Hadn't he? They had made sure of that. Would the police believe him? The school board? The PTA? "Where there's smoke there must be fire." "I'm not going to let my daughter stay in his class."

He started shivering again and made himself a cup of tea and sat down on the window seat in the living room to drink it and then got up and turned off the lights and looked out at the snow. The moonlight was so bright that he could see wisps of tall grass in the meadow—yellow against the snow. Immediately he thought of the long blond hair of that starvation-thin young girl. Bleached hair? Perhaps. It didn't lessen the outrage. She was dressed just like the boys—big quilted jacket, skin-tight pants, even her hair worn like theirs, obscuring the forehead, the sides of the face.

There was a sudden movement outside the window and he frowned and leaned forward, wondering what was moving about at this hour. He saw a pair of rabbits, leaping, running, literally playing games with each other. He had never before seen such free joyous movement, not even children at play exhibited it. There was always something unrelaxed about the eyes of children, about the way they held their mouths, wrinkled their foreheads—they looked as though they had been cornered and were impelled to defend themselves or that they were impelled to pursue some object that forever eluded them.

Watching this joyous heel-kicking play of the rabbits, he found himself thinking,

I cannot continue to live in the same small town with that girl and those seven boys. The boys knew, before he did, that he wasn't going to report this—this incident—these crimes. They were bright enough to know that he would quickly realize how neatly they had boxed him in and thus would keep quiet. If he dared enter a complaint against them they would accuse him of raping the girl, would say they found him in the cemetery with her. Whose story would be believed? "Where there's smoke there's fire."

Right after that he started packing. He put his clothes into a foot locker. He stacked his books on the floor of the station wagon. He was surprised to find among the books a medical textbook that had belonged to John—Addie's brother.

He sat down and read all the material on angina pectoris. At eight o'clock he called the school and said he wasn't feeling well (which was true) and that he would not be in. Then he called the office of the local doctor and made an appointment for that afternoon.

When he talked to the doctor he described the violent pain in his chest that went from the shoulder down to his finger tips on the left side, causing a squeezing, crushing sensation that left him feeling faint, dizzy.

The doctor, a fat man in an old tweed jacket and a limp white shirt, said after he examined him, "Angina. You'll have to take three or four months off until we can get this thing under control."

"I will resign immediately."

"Oh, no. That isn't necessary. Besides I've been told you're the best English teacher we've ever had. It would be a great pity to lose you."

"No," Woodruff said, "it is better to resign." Come back here and look at that violated little girl? Come back here? Ever?

He scarcely listened to the detailed instructions he was to follow, did not even glance at the three prescriptions he was handed, for he was eager to be on his way. He composed a letter of resignation in his mind. When he went back to the bungalow he wrote it quickly and then put it on the front seat of the station wagon to be mailed en route.

Then he went back into the house and stayed there just long enough to call his landlord. He said he'd had a heart attack and was going back to Virginia to convalesce, that he had turned the thermostat down to sixty-five and he would return the house keys by mail. The landlord said, My goodness, you just paid a month in advance, I'll mail you a refund, what's your new address, so sorry, ideal tenant.

Woodruff hung up the receiver and said, "Peace be with you, brother—" There was already an echo in the room though it wasn't empty—all he'd removed were his books and his clothes.

He put on his elegant overcoat. When he got back to Virginia, he would give the coat away, his pleasure in it destroyed now for he would always remember the horrid feel of the collar tight across his throat, even the feel of the fabric under his finger tips would evoke an image of the cemetery, the tool shed, and the girl.

He drove down the road rather slowly. There were curves in the road and he couldn't go fast, besides he liked to look at this landscape. It was high rolling land. Snow lay over it—blue-white where there were shadows cast by the birch trees and the hemlocks, yellow-white and sparkling in the great meadow where he had watched the heel-kicking freedom of the rabbits at play.

At the entrance to the highway he brought the car to a halt. As he sat there waiting for an opportunity to get into the stream of traffic, he heard close at hand the loud explosive sound of an engine—a familiar sound. He was so alarmed that he momentarily experienced all the symptoms of a heart attack, the sudden terrible inability to breathe and the feeling that something was squeezing his chest, kneading it so that pain ran through him as though it were following the course of his circulatory system.

He knew from the sound that the car turning off the highway, entering the same road that he was now leaving, was Rambler's car. In the sunlight, silhouetted against the snow, it looked like a junkyard on wheels, fenders dented, sides dented, chassis rusted. All the boys were in the car. Rambler was driving. The thin blond girl was in the front seat—a terrible bruise under one eye. For a fraction of a second Woodruff looked straight into Rambler's eyes, just visible under the long, untidy hair. The expression was cold, impersonal, analytical.

After he got on the highway, he kept looking in the rearview mirror. There was no sign of pursuit. Evidently Rambler had not noticed that the car was loaded for flight—books and cartons on the seats, foot locker on the floor, all this was out of his range of vision. He wondered what they were doing. Wrecking the interior of the bungalow? No. They were probably waiting for him to return so they could blackmail him. Blackmail a black male.

On the turnpike he kept going faster and faster—eighty-five miles an hour, ninety, ninety-five, one hundred. He felt exhilarated by this tremendous speed. It was clearing his mind, heartening him, taking him out of himself.

He began to rationalize about what had happened. He decided that Rambler and his friends didn't give a damn that he Woodruff, was a black man. They couldn't care less. They were very bright boys, bright enough to recognize him for what he was: a black man in his sixties, conditioned all his life by the knowledge that "White woman taboo for you" (as one of his African students used to say). The moment he attempted to intervene there in front of the church, they decided to take him with them. They knew he wasn't going to the police about any matter which involved sex and a white girl, especially where there was the certainty that all seven of them would accuse him of having relations with the girl. They had used his presence in that tool shed to give an extra exquisite fillip to their dreadful game.

He turned on the radio and waited impatiently for music, any kind of music, thinking it would distract him. He got one of those stations that play what he called thump-and-blare music. A husky-voiced woman was shouting a song—not singing, shouting:

> I'm gonna turn on the big beat
> I'm gonna turn up the high heat
> For my ho-daddy, ho-daddy,
> For my ho-daddy, ho-daddy.

He flipped the switch, cutting off the sound and he gradually diminished the speed of the car, slowing, slowing, slowing. "We got us a rich ho-daddy." That's what one of the boys had said there in front of the church when he plucked the money out of Woodruff's wallet. A rich ho-daddy? A black ho-daddy. A witness. Another poor scared black bastard who was a witness.

1971

Theodore Roethke 1908–1963

Theodore Roethke was born in Saginaw, Michigan, and spent his childhood in and around his father's large commercial greenhouses, with their luxuriance of protected natural growth. It was there, among the acres of roses and carnations, and in cellars rank with rotten manure and rooting slips, that he developed his participatory awareness of the small things of nature. These two, the greenhouses and the almost godlike father directing a crew of skilled florists and helpers, would become the most pervasive shaping presences in his poetry—the greenhouses a humanly created Eden surrounded by open fields of eternity, and the father a center of powerful conflicting emotions of love and hate.

Roethke apparently began to write poems during his undergraduate years at the University of Michigan, where he received a B.A. in 1929, but if so, he wrote in secret. His doing so is only one early instance of his habitual wearing of masks to hide an inner vulnerability and seriousness. It was not until his graduate school years, first at Michigan and then at Harvard, that he either discussed or wrote poetry openly. His first publications came in 1930 and 1931. His teaching career, which would prove to be lifelong, began in the fall of 1931 at Lafayette College in Easton, Pennsylvania. Toward the end of his four-year term there, he served also as tennis coach, a game he played with intense and even rude aggressiveness. Later he would teach at several other colleges and universities before settling, from 1947 until his death, at the University of Washington.

Another pattern that would also prove to be lifelong emerged by 1931, or even before. By the time he went to Easton to teach, Roethke was already a heavy drinker, having frequent bouts of drunkenness during which he sometimes became rowdy and even destructive. Friends would later recall his drinking as a kind of search for oblivion. Certainly the drinking was both evidence and a contributing cause of the complex and severe emotional problems that led to his being hospitalized several times for what was usually diagnosed as manic-depression. Throughout his life he swung between extremes—of mood, of bravado or torturing self-doubt, of self-righteousness or guilt, of certainty that he was America's preeminent poet or despair over his supposed lack of achievement. He seems to have felt that nothing he did would have earned his father's approval.

In 1953, Roethke married Beatrice O'Connell, a former student of his and also a former fashion model. At the time of their marriage, Beatrice was totally unaware of his history of mental illness; he told her nothing. Before a year was out, she had seen him through one of his typical crises, though a fairly mild one involving only two weeks of hospitalization. She rose to the need and proved remarkably supportive over the years, a real companion as well as caretaker. It must not have been easy. He was extraordinarily demanding, as well as dependent, and was an inveterate casual pawer of women. His difficulties relating to women apparently sprang from very complex feelings toward his mother which, if less disturbing than those toward his father, were at any rate troubled. However, several of his late poems record Roethke's great care and concern for his wife, and one of his most significant works, "Meditations of an Old Woman," draws partly on his regard for his mother.

Besides its disciplined exploration of rhythmic variation and symbolist style, Roethke's poetry is characterized by a deep, even mystical, animism, a close attention to minute living things and natural processes, and a continuing use of childhood anxieties and his own ambivalent feelings toward his father in developing a motif of the soul journey. For Roethke, this journey went toward reconciliation and oneness. In his late poem "The Rose" (from "North American Sequence") his father would be joined with an evocation of the greenhouse world as images of perfect beatitude: "What need for heaven, then, / With that man and those roses?" Among his many honors and awards were the Pulitzer Prize, the Bollingen Prize, a Fulbright Award, and two Guggenheim Fellowships.

Janis Stout
Texas A & M University

PRIMARY WORKS

Open House, 1941; *The Lost Son and Other Poems*, 1948; *Praise to the End!*, 1951; *The Waking: Poems 1933–53*, 1953; *Words for the Wind: The Collected Verse of Theodore Roethke*, 1957; *I Am! Says the Lamb*, 1961; *Party at the Zoo*, 1963; *The Far Field*, 1964; *Sequence, Sometimes Metaphysical*, 1964; *The Collected Poems of Theodore Roethke*, 1968.

Frau Bauman, Frau Schmidt, and Frau Schwartze[1]

Gone the three ancient ladies
Who creaked on the greenhouse ladders,
Reaching up white strings
To wind, to wind
5   The sweet-pea tendrils,[2] the smilax,[3]
Nasturtiums, the climbing
Roses, to straighten
Carnations, red
Chrysanthemums; the stiff
10 Stems, jointed like corn,
They tied and tucked,—
These nurses of nobody else.
Quicker than birds, they dipped
Up and sifted the dirt;
15 They sprinkled and shook;
They stood astride pipes,
Their skirts billowing out wide into tents,
Their hands twinkling with wet;
Like witches they flew along rows
20 Keeping creation at ease;
With a tendril for needle
They sewed up the air with a stem;
They teased out the seed that the cold kept asleep,—

[1]Common German names; Roethke's family was German.

[2]Small twigs of vining plants.
[3]A climbing plant with prickly stems.

All the coils, loops, and whorls.
25 They trellised[4] the sun; they plotted for more than themselves.

I remember how they picked me up, a spindly[5] kid,
Pinching and poking my thin ribs
Till I lay in their laps, laughing,
Weak as a whiffet;[6]
30 Now, when I'm alone and cold in my bed,
They still hover over me,
These ancient leathery crones,
With their bandannas stiffened with sweat,
And their thorn-bitten wrists,
35 And their snuff-laden breath blowing lightly over me in my first
    sleep.

1948

Root Cellar

Nothing would sleep in that cellar,[1] dank as a ditch,
Bulbs broke out of boxes hunting for chinks in the dark,
Shoots dangled and drooped,
Lolling obscenely from mildewed crates,
5 Hung down long yellow evil necks, like tropical snakes.
And what a congress[2] of stinks!—
Roots ripe as old bait,
Pulpy stems, rank, silo-rich,[3]
Leaf-mold, manure, lime, piled against slippery planks.
10 Nothing would give up life:
Even the dirt kept breathing a small breath.

1948

---

[4]Trained up on a frame, usually made of laths, as a plant is trained into a chosen shape. Roethke's tribute to the three greenhouse workers/nature goddesses has reached mythic proportions.
[5]Skinny.
[6]A small, young, or unimportant person; probably a corruption of *whippet,* a small dog.

[1]The cellar of the poet's father's commercial greenhouse in Saginaw, Michigan. "Root Cellar" is one of the famous "greenhouse poems."
[2]Literally, a coming together; thus a collection or assortment.
[3]Rank from long storage; a silo is a storage building for grain.

Big Wind

Where were the greenhouses going,
Lunging into the lashing
Wind driving water
So far down the river
5   All the faucets stopped?—
So we drained the manure-machine
For the steam plant,
Pumping the stale mixture
Into the rusty boilers,
10   Watching the pressure gauge
Waver over to red,
As the seams hissed
And the live steam
Drove to the far
15   End of the rose-house,
Where the worst wind was,
Creaking the cypress window-frames,
Cracking so much thin glass
We stayed all night,
20   Stuffing the holes with burlap;
But she rode it out,
That old rose-house,
She hove[1] into the teeth of it,
The core and pith of that ugly storm,
25   Ploughing with her stiff prow,
Bucking into the wind-waves
That broke over the whole of her,
Flailing her sides with spray,
Flinging long strings of wet across the roof-top,
30   Finally veering, wearing themselves out, merely
Whistling thinly under the wind-vents;
She sailed until the calm morning,
Carrying her full cargo of roses.

1948

---

[1]Past tense of heave; in nautical usage, to heave to is to keep the ship heading into the wind. Here, the term is part of an extended conceit of greenhouse as boat or ship.

from The Lost Son

1.   *The Flight*

At Woodlawn[1] I heard the dead cry:
I was lulled by the slamming of iron,
A slow drip over stones,
Toads brooding wells.[2]
5   All the leaves stuck out their tongues;
I shook the softening chalk of my bones,
Saying,
Snail, snail, glister[3] me forward,
Bird, soft-sigh me home,
10   Worm, be with me.
This is my hard time.

Fished in an old wound,[4]
The soft pond of repose;
Nothing nibbled my line,
15   Not even the minnows came.

Sat in an empty house
Watching shadows crawl,
Scratching.
There was one fly.
20   Voice, come out of the silence.
Say something.
Appear in the form of a spider
Or a moth beating the curtain.

Tell me:
25   Which is the way I take;
Out of what door do I go,
Where and to whom?

Dark hollows said, lee to the wind,
The moon said, back of an eel,
30   The salt said, look by the sea,
Your tears are not enough praise,

---

[1]A cemetery.
[2]Read "brooding in wells."
[3]A variant of *glisten* or *glitter,* referring to the shining track as they move along.

[4]Casting about for meaning or reassurance, he figuratively casts his line into the subconscious, wounded as it was; simultaneously, he casts his line into memories of childhood.

You will find no comfort here,
In the kingdom of bang and blab.[5]
Running lightly over spongy ground,

35   Past the pasture of flat stones,
The three elms,
The sheep strewn on a field,
Over a rickety bridge
Toward the quick-water, wrinkling and rippling.

40   Hunting along the river,
Down among the rubbish, the bug-riddled foliage,
By the muddy pond-edge, by the bog-holes,
By the shrunken lake, hunting, in the heat of summer.

The shape of a rat?
45   It's bigger than that.
It's less than a leg
And more than a nose,
Just under the water
It usually goes.
50   Is it soft like a mouse?
Can it wrinkle its nose?
Could it come in the house
On the tips of its toes?

           Take the skin of a cat
55   And the back of an eel,
Then roll them in grease,—
That's the way it would feel.

It's sleek as an otter
With wide webby toes
60   Just under the water
It usually goes.

4.   *The Return*

The way to the boiler was dark,
Dark all the way,
Over slippery cinders
Through the long greenhouse.

[5]Empty verbiage; perhaps a view of everyday
society.

5   The roses kept breathing in the dark.
       They had many mouths to breathe with.
       My knees made little winds underneath
       Where the weeds slept.

       There was always a single light
10   Swinging by the fire-pit,[1]
       Where the fireman pulled out roses,
       The big roses, the big bloody clinkers.[2]

       Once I stayed all night.
       The light in the morning came slowly over the white
15   Snow.
       There were many kinds of cool
       Air.
       Then came steam.

       Pipe-knock.

20 Scurry of warm over small plants.
    Ordnung! ordnung![3]
    Papa is coming!

       A fine haze moved off the leaves;
       Frost melted on far panes;
25   The rose, the chrysanthemum turned toward the light.
       Even the hushed forms, the bent yellowy weeds
       Moved in a slow up-sway.

5.   *It was beginning winter*

       It was beginning winter,
       An in-between time,
       The landscape still partly brown:
       The bones of weeds kept swinging in the wind,
5   Above the blue snow.

       It was beginning winter,
       The light moved slowly over the frozen field,
       Over the dry seed-crowns,

---

[1]Where the boiler was heated, to provide steam   [3]German, "order"; here, given as a military-like
  for keeping the greenhouse warm.   command.
[2]Red coals.

The beautiful surviving bones
10 Swinging in the wind.

Light traveled over the wide field;
Stayed.
The weeds stopped swinging.
The mind moved, not alone,
15 Through the clear air, in the silence.

Was it light?
Was it light within?
Was it light within light?
Stillness becoming alive,
20 Yet still?

A lively understandable spirit
Once entertained you.
It will come again.
Be still.
25 Wait.

1948

from Meditations of an Old Woman

First Meditation

1

On love's worst ugly day,
The weeds hiss at the edge of the field,
The small winds make their chilly indictments.
Elsewhere, in houses, even pails can be sad;
5 While stones loosen on the obscure hillside,
And a tree tilts from its roots,
Toppling down an embankment.

The spirit moves, but not always upward,
While animals eat to the north,
10 And the shale slides an inch in the talus,
The bleak wind eats at the weak plateau,
And the sun brings joy to some.
But the rind, often, hates the life within.

How can I rest in the days of my slowness?
15 I've become a strange piece of flesh,
Nervous and cold, bird-furtive,[1] whiskery,
With a cheek soft as a hound's ear.
What's left is light as a seed;
I need an old crone's knowing.

2

20 Often I think of myself as riding—
Alone, on a bus through western country.
I sit above the back wheels, where the jolts are hardest,
And we bounce and sway along toward the midnight,
The lights tilting up, skyward, as we come over a little rise,
25 Then down, as we roll like a boat from a wave-crest.

All journeys, I think, are the same:
The movement is forward, after a few wavers,
And for a while we are all alone,
Busy, obvious with ourselves,
30 The drunken soldier, the old lady with her peppermints;
And we ride, we ride, taking the curves
Somewhat closer, the trucks coming
Down from behind the last ranges,
Their black shapes breaking past;
35 And the air claps between us,
Blasting the frosted windows,
And I seem to go backward,
Backward in time:

Two song sparrows, one within a greenhouse,
40 Shuttling[2] its throat while perched on a wind-vent,
And another, outside, in the bright day,
With a wind from the west and the trees all in motion.
One sang, then the other,
The songs tumbling over and under the glass,
45 And the men beneath them wheeling in dirt to the cement
benches,
The laden wheelbarrows creaking and swaying,
And the up-spring of the plank when a foot left the
runway.

---

[1]As furtive as a bird.
[2]With a back-and-forth motion like the shuttle
of a loom; referring to the vibration of a singing
bird's throat.

50 Journey within a journey:[3]
The ticket mislaid or lost, the gate
Inaccessible, the boat always pulling out
From the rickety wooden dock,
The children waving;
55 Or two horses plunging in snow, their lines tangled,
A great wooden sleigh careening behind them,
Swerving up a steep embankment.
For a moment they stand above me,
Their black skins shuddering:
60 Then they lurch forward,
Lunging down a hillside.

3

As when silt drifts and sifts down through muddy pond-water,
Settling in small beads around weeds and sunken branches,
And one crab, tentative, hunches himself before moving along the
65   bottom,
Grotesque, awkward, his extended eyes looking at nothing in
        particular,
Only a few bubbles loosening from the ill-matched tentacles,
The tail and smaller legs slipping and sliding slowly backward—
70 So the spirit tries for another life,
Another way and place in which to continue;
Or a salmon, tired, moving up a shallow stream,
Nudges into a back-eddy, a sandy inlet,
Bumping against sticks and bottom-stones, then swinging
75 Around, back into the tiny maincurrent, the rush of brownish-
        white water,
Still swimming forward—
So, I suppose, the spirit journeys.

4

I have gone into the waste lonely places
80 Behind the eye;[4] the lost acres at the edge of smoky cities.
What's beyond never crumbles like an embankment,

---

[3]Throughout, cf. "The spirit moves but not al-ways upward": the spiritual journey includes periods of frustration which, traditionally, the mystic accepts as integral parts of the whole. Cf. T. S. Eliot's "the way up is the way down," *Four Quartets.*

[4]The mystic journey entails a journey inward, the journey of introspection.

Explodes like a rose, or thrusts wings over the Caribbean.
There are no pursuing forms, faces on walls:
Only the motes of dust in the immaculate hallways,
85 The darkness of falling hair, the warnings from lint and spiders,
The vines graying to a fine powder.
There is no riven tree, or lamb dropped by an eagle.[5]

There are still times, morning and evening:
The cerulean,[6] high in the elm,
90 Thin and insistent as a cicada,[7]
And the far phoebe,[8] singing,
The long plaintive notes floating down,
Drifting through leaves, oak and maple,
Or the whippoorwill, along the smoky ridges,
95 A single bird calling and calling;
A fume reminds me, drifting across wet gravel;
A cold wind comes over stones;
A flame, intense, visible,
Plays over the dry pods,[9]
100 Runs fitfully along the stubble,
Moves over the field,
Without burning.
        In such times, lacking a god,
        I am still happy.

from *Fourth Meditation*

2

What is it to be a woman?
To be contained, to be a vessel?
To prefer a window to a door?
A pool to a river?
5 To become lost in a love,
Yet remain only half aware of the intransient glory?
To be a mouth, a meal of meat?
To gaze at a face with the fixed eyes of a spaniel?

I think of the self-involved:
10 The ritualists of the mirror, the lonely drinkers,

---

[5]The old woman's spiritual journey is not characterized by high drama but by full attention to the everyday.
[6]Blue; the sky.
[7]A variety of locust having an insistent harsh sound.

[8]A bird.
[9]Empty seed pods; the time is late autumn or winter, when all that is left in the grain fields is stubble.

The minions[1] of benzedrine and paraldehyde,[2]
And those who submerge themselves deliberately in trivia,
Women who become their possessions,
Shapes stiffening into metal,
15 Match-makers, arrangers of picnics—
What do their lives mean,
And the lives of their children?—
The young, brow-beaten early into a baleful[3] silence,
Frozen by a father's lip, a mother's failure to answer.
20 Have they seen, ever, the sharp bones of the poor?
Or known, once, the soul's authentic hunger,
Those cat-like immaculate creatures
For whom the world works?

What do they need?
25 O more than a roaring boy,
For the sleek captains of intuition cannot reach them;
They feel neither the tearing iron
Nor the sound of another footstep—
How I wish them awake!
30 May the high flower of the hay climb into their hearts;
May they lean into light and live;
May they sleep in robes of green, among the ancient ferns;
May their eyes gleam with the first dawn;
May the sun gild them a worm;
35 May they be taken by the true burning;
May they flame into being!—
I see them as figures walking in a greeny garden,
Their gait formal and elaborate, their hair a glory,
The gentle and beautiful still-to-be-born;
40 The descendants of the playful tree-shrew that survived the archaic
        killers,
The fang and the claw, the club and the knout,[4] the irrational
        edict,
The fury of the hate-driven zealot, the meanness of the human
45   weasel;
Who turned a corner in time, when at last he grew a thumb;
A prince of small beginnings, enduring the slow stretches of
        change,
Who spoke first in the coarse short-hand of the subliminal[5] depths,
50 Made from his terror and dismay a grave philosophical language;
A lion of flame, pressed to the point of love,
Yet moves gently among the birds.

1958

---

[1]Slaves.
[2]Drugs; benzedrine is a stimulant, paraldehyde a sedative.
[3]Sorrowful.
[4]A leather whip for flogging.
[5]Beneath the threshold (*limen*) of consciousness.

Elegy

Her face like a rain-beaten stone on the day she rolled off
With the dark hearse, and enough flowers for an alderman,[1]—
And so she was, in her way, Aunt Tilly.

Sighs, sighs, who says they have sequence?
5 Between the spirit and the flesh,—what war?
She never knew;
For she asked no quarter[2] and gave none,
Who sat with the dead when the relatives left,
Who fed and tended the infirm, the mad, the epileptic,
10 And, with a harsh rasp of a laugh at herself,
Faced up to the worst.

I recall how she harried the children away all the late summer
From the one beautiful thing in her yard, the peachtree;
How she kept the wizened,[3] the fallen, the misshapen for herself,
15 And picked and pickled the best, to be left on rickety doorsteps.

And yet she died in agony,
Her tongue, at the last, thick, black as an ox's.

Terror of cops, bill collectors, betrayers of the poor,—
I see you[4] in some celestial[5] supermarket,
20 Moving serenely among the leeks and cabbages,
Probing the squash,
Bearing down, with two steady eyes,
On the quaking butcher.

1958

My Papa's Waltz

The whiskey on your breath
Could make a small boy dizzy;
But I hung on like death:
Such waltzing was not easy.

---

[1] A public official, like a city councilman.
[2] Mercy granted to a surrendering foe.
[3] Shriveled.
[4] The poet addresses his dead Aunt Tilly, whom he characterizes as a terror to three representa-tive groups of oppressors—policemen, bill collectors, and betrayers of the poor.
[5] Heavenly; he envisions Aunt Tilly in an after-life very much like her accustomed life on earth.

5 We romped until the pans
Slid from the kitchen shelf;
My mother's countenance
Could not unfrown itself.

The hand that held my wrist
10 Was battered on one knuckle;
At every step you missed
My right ear scraped a buckle.

You beat time on my head
With a palm caked hard by dirt,
15 Then waltzed me off to bed
Still clinging to your shirt.

                                        1948

Eudora Welty 1909–2002

Like that of Jane Austen, the canvas of Eudora Welty is small. She had, as she wrote in *One Writer's Beginnings* (1983), a "sheltered life" but one full of emotional daring. For nearly a century, Welty lived in the small town of Jackson, Mississippi, where she was born in 1909. Her artistic sensibility is the product of a childhood framed by family and rooted in story. And this sensibility accounts for one of her great strengths as a writer: her ability to infuse the tradition of southern manners with the complex emotional truths of the twentieth-century South out of which she wrote.

Welty's formal education included attendance at Mississippi State College for Women, the University of Wisconsin, and the Columbia University School of Business; her first job, publicity assistant for the Works Progress Administration (WPA), helped to sharpen her eye and ear for the tasks of a fiction writer. Welty's first short story appeared in 1936 and, with the help of Robert Penn Warren and Cleanth Brooks, she published six other stories over the next three years. *A Curtain of Green,* Welty's first collection of stories, was published in 1941 with an excellent preface by Katherine Anne Porter. The forties also saw publication of Welty's first short novel (*The Robber Bridegroom,* 1942), a second collection of stories (*The Wide Net,* 1943), a second novel (*Delta Wedding,* 1946), and a collection of interrelated stories (*The Golden Apples,* 1949). *The Ponder Heart,* a short novel, appeared in 1954, and a collection entitled *The Bride of the Innesfallen* was published the following year. In 1970, Welty's longest novel, *Losing Battles,* was published, and her WPA-inspired photographs, *One Time, One Place,* appeared in 1971. *The Optimist's Daughter,* a novel awarded the Pulitzer Prize in 1972, was followed by a collection of essays, *The Eye of the Story* (1978), *The Collected Stories of Eudora Welty* (1980), and *One Writer's Beginnings* (1983). More recently, Welty co-edited *The Norton Book of Friendship* (1991). A collection of her book reviews (*A Writer's Eye*) appeared in 1994. Four years later, Library of America published two collections of Welty's work (*Eudora Welty: Complete Novels* and *Eudora Welty: Stories, Essays and Memoir*), edited by Richard Ford and Michael Kreyling. She was awarded the Medal of Arts in 1987.

Although critics disagree about how

Welty's fiction should be read, they have consistently recognized its importance. New Critics Robert Penn Warren and Cleanth Brooks included a sampling of Welty's short stories in their classic text *Understanding Fiction* (1943). Since then, Welty has been claimed not only by critics of southern gothic literature, folklore, and mythology but also by modern and feminist critics. Her stories are a staple of American literature anthologies, and she continues to find an audience in colleges and universities across the country.

Welty said that she wrote out of an impulse "to praise," and her fiction is often a celebration of life in all its mystery and complexity. Her characters are imbued with a sense of place (an emotional and associational texture described by Welty in her essay "Place in Fiction") and are easily recognizable by their distinctive narrative voices. An admirer of William Faulkner's work, Welty had a similar interest in "the problems of the human heart in conflict with itself." In her work these problems are most often centered on a conflict between the desire to belong (whether to family or lover) and to preserve a separate identity. The root of this conflict is love, and Welty's stories, however grotesque or comic, transcend regionalism in their universal themes.

Inasmuch as she grew up listening to and reading fairy tale, legend, and myth, Welty's narrative technique owes as much to an oral as to a written tradition. Welty's ability to hear the rhythms and patterns of speech is apparent in her narrative voices, which range from the hill country to the Mississippi Delta and the city. Her images are often grounded in the natural world, and her style is lyric and evocative.

Jennifer L. Randisi
Independent Scholar

PRIMARY WORKS

A Curtain of Green, 1941; *The Robber Bridegroom*, 1942; *The Wide Net*, 1943; *Delta Wedding*, 1946; *The Golden Apples*, 1949; *The Ponder Heart*, 1954; *The Bride of Innesfallen*, 1955; *Losing Battles*, 1970; *One Time, One Place*, 1971; *The Optimist's Daughter*, 1972; *The Eye of the Story*, 1978; *The Collected Stories of Eudora Welty*, 1980; *One Writer's Beginnings*, 1983; *A Writer's Eye: Collected Book Reviews*, 1994; *The Collected Stories*, 1998; *Country Churchyards*, 2000.

The Wide Net

This story is for John Fraiser Robinson

William Wallace Jamieson's wife Hazel was going to have a baby. But this was October, and it was six months away, and she acted exactly as though it would be tomorrow. When he came in the room she would not speak to him, but would look as straight at nothing as she could, with her eyes glowing. If he only touched her she stuck out her tongue or ran around the table. So one night he went out with two of the boys down the road and stayed out all night. But that was the worst thing yet, because when he came home in the early morning Hazel had vanished. He went through the house not believing his eyes, balancing with both hands out, his yellow cowlick rising on end, and then he turned the kitchen inside out looking for her, but it did no good. Then when he got back to the front room he saw she had left him a little letter, in an envelope. That was doing something behind someone's back. He took out the letter, pushed it open, held it out at a distance from his eyes. . . . After one look he was scared to read the exact words, and he crushed the whole thing in his hand instantly, but what it had said was that she would not put up with him after that and was going to the river to drown herself.

"Drown herself . . . But she's in mortal fear of the water!"

He ran out front, his face red like the red plums hanging on the bushes there, and down in the road he gave a loud shout for Virgil Thomas, who was just going in his own house, to come out again. He could just see the edge of Virgil, he had almost got in, he had one foot inside the door.

They met half-way between the farms, under the shade tree.

"Haven't you had enough of the night?" asked Virgil. There they were, their pants all covered with dust and dew, and they had had to carry the third man home flat between them.

"I've lost Hazel, she's vanished, she went to drown herself."

"Why, that ain't like Hazel," said Virgil.

William Wallace reached out and shook him. "You heard me. Don't you know we have to drag the river?"

"Right this minute?"

"You ain't got nothing to do till spring."

"Let me go set foot inside the house and speak to my mother and tell her a story, and I'll come back."

"This will take the wide net," said William Wallace. His eyebrows gathered, and he was talking to himself.

"How come Hazel to go and do that way?" asked Virgil as they started out.

William Wallace said, "I reckon she got lonesome."

"That don't argue—drown herself for getting lonesome. My mother gets lonesome."

"Well," said William Wallace. "It argues for Hazel."

"How long is it now since you and her was married?"

"Why, it's been a year."

"It don't seem that long to me. A year!"

"It was this time last year. It seems longer," said William Wallace, breaking a stick off a tree in surprise. They walked along, kicking at the flowers on the road's edge. "I remember the day I seen her first, and that seems a long time ago. She was coming along the road holding a little frying-size chicken from her grandma, under her arm, and she had it real quiet. I spoke to her with nice manners. We knowed each other's names, being bound to, just didn't know each other to speak to. I says, 'Where are you taking the fryer?' and she says, 'Mind your manners,' and I kept on till after while she says, 'If you want to walk me home, take littler steps.' So I didn't lose time. It was just four miles across the field and full of blackberries, and from the top of the hill there was Dover below, looking sizeable-like and clean, spread out between the two churches like that. When we got down, I says to her, 'What kind of water's in this well?' and she says, 'The best water in the world.' So I drew a bucket and took out a dipper and she drank and I drank. I didn't think it was that remarkable, but I didn't tell her."

"What happened that night?" asked Virgil.

"We ate the chicken," said William Wallace, "and it was tender. Of course that wasn't all they had. The night I was trying their table out, it sure had good things to eat from one end to the other. Her mama and papa sat at the head and foot and we was face to face with each other across it, with I remember a pat of butter between. They had real sweet butter, with a tree drawed down it, elegant-like. Her mama eats like a man. I had brought her a whole hatful of berries and she didn't even pass them to her husband. Hazel, she would leap up and take a pitcher of new milk and fill up the glasses. I had heard how they couldn't have a singing at the church without a fight over her."

"Oh, she's a pretty girl, all right," said Virgil. "It's a pity for the ones like her to grow old, and get like their mothers."

"Another thing will be that her mother will get wind of this and come after me," said William Wallace.

"Her mother will eat you alive," said Virgil.

"She's just been watching her chance," said William Wallace. "Why did I think I could stay out all night."

"Just something come over you."

"First it was just a carnival at Carthage, and I had to let them guess my weight . . . and after that . . ."

"It was nice to be sitting on your neck in a ditch singing," prompted Virgil, "in the moonlight. And playing on the harmonica like you can play."

"Even if Hazel did sit home knowing I was drunk, that wouldn't kill her," said William Wallace. "What she knows ain't ever killed her yet. . . . She's smart, too, for a girl," he said.

"She's a lot smarter than her cousins in Beulah," said Virgil, "and especially Edna Earle, that never did get to be what you'd call a heavy thinker. Edna Earle could sit and ponder all day on how the little tail of the 'C' got through the 'L' in a Coca-Cola sign."

"Hazel *is* smart," said William Wallace. They walked on. "You ought to see her pantry shelf, it looks like a hundred jars when you open the door. I don't see how she could turn around and jump in the river."

"It's a woman's trick."

"I always behaved before. Till the one night—last night."

"Yes, but the one night," said Virgil. "And she was waiting to take advantage."

"She jumped in the river because she was scared to death of the water and that was to make it worse," he said. "She remembered how I used to have to pick her up and carry her over the oak-log bridge, how she'd shut her eyes and make a dead-weight and hold me round the neck, just for a little creek. I don't see how she brought herself to jump."

"Jumped backwards," said Virgil. "Didn't look."

When they turned off, it was still early in the pink and green fields. The fumes of morning, sweet and bitter, sprang up where they walked. The insects ticked softly, their strength in reserve; butterflies chopped the air, going to the east, and the birds flew carelessly and sang by fits and starts, not the way they did in the evening in sustained and drowsy songs.

"It's a pretty *day* for sure," said William Wallace. "It's a pretty *day* for it."

"I don't see a sign of her ever going along here," said Virgil.

"Well," said William Wallace. "She wouldn't have dropped anything. I never saw a girl to leave less signs of where she's been."

"Not even a plum seed," said Virgil, kicking the grass.

In the grove it was so quiet that once William Wallace gave a jump, as if he could almost hear a sound of himself wondering where she had gone. A descent of energy came down on him in the thick of the woods and he ran at a rabbit and caught it in his hands.

"Rabbit . . . Rabbit . . ." He acted as if he wanted to take it off to himself and hold it up and talk to it. He laid a palm against its pushing heart. "Now . . . There now . . ."

"Let her go, William Wallace, let her go." Virgil, chewing on an elderberry whistle he had just made, stood at his shoulder: "What do you want with a live rabbit?"

William Wallace squatted down and set the rabbit on the ground but held it under his hand. It was a little old, brown rabbit. It did not try to move. "See there?"

"Let her go."

"She can go if she wants to, but she don't want to."

Gently he lifted his hand. The round eye was shining at him sideways in the green gloom.

"Anybody can freeze a *rabbit,* that wants to," said Virgil, Suddenly he gave a far-reaching blast on the whistle, and the rabbit went in a streak. "Was you out catching cotton-tails, or was you out catching your wife?" he said, taking the turn to the open fields. "I come along to keep you on the track."

"Who'll we get now?" They stood on top of a hill and William Wallace looked critically over the countryside. "Any of the Malones?"

"I was always scared of the Malones," said Virgil. "Too many *of* them."

"This is my day with the net, and they would have to watch out," said William Wallace. "I reckon some Malones, and the Doyles, will be enough. The six Doyles and their dogs, and you and me, and two little nigger boys is enough, with just a few Malones."

"That ought to be enough," said Virgil, "no matter what."

"I'll bring the Malones, and you bring the Doyles," said William Wallace, and they separated at the spring.

When William Wallace came back, with a string of Malones just showing behind him on the hilltop, he found Virgil with the two little Rippen boys waiting behind him, solemn little towheads. As soon as he walked up, Grady, the one in front, lifted his hand to signal silence and caution to his brother Brucie, who began panting merrily and untrustworthily behind him.

Brucie bent readily under William Wallace's hand-pat, and gave him a dreamy look out of the tops of his round eyes, which were pure green-and-white like clover tops. William Wallace gave him a nickel. Grady hung his head; his white hair lay in a little tail in the nape of his neck.

"Let's let them come," said Virgil.

"Well, they can come then, but if we keep letting everybody come it is going to be too many," said William Wallace.

"They'll appreciate it, those little old boys," said Virgil. Brucie held up at arm's length a long red thread with a bent pin tied on the end; and a look of helpless and intense interest gathered Grady's face like a drawstring—his eyes, one bright with a sty, shone pleadingly under his white bangs, and he snapped his jaw and tried to speak. . . . "Their papa was drowned in the Pearl River," said Virgil.

There was a shout from the gully.

"Here come all the Malones," cried William Wallace. "I asked four of them would they come, but the rest of the family invited themselves."

"Did you ever see a time when they didn't," said Virgil. "And yonder from the other direction comes the Doyles, still with biscuit crumbs on their cheeks, I bet, now it's nothing to do but eat as their mother said."

"If two little niggers would come along now, or one big nigger," said William Wallace. And the words were hardly out of his mouth when two little Negro boys came along, going somewhere, one behind the other, stepping high and gay in their overalls, as though they waded in honeydew to the waist.

"Come here, boys. What's your names?"

"Sam and Robbie Bell."

"Come along with us, we're going to drag the river."

"You hear that, Robbie Bell?" said Sam.

They smiled.

The Doyles came noiselessly, their dogs made all the fuss. The Malones, eight giants with great long black eyelashes, were already stamping the ground and pawing each other, ready to go. Everybody went up together to see Doc.

Old Doc owned the wide net. He had a house on top of the hill and he sat and looked out from a rocker on the front porch.

"Climb the hill and come in!" he began to intone across the valley. "Harvest's over . . . slipped up on everybody . . . corn's all in, hogs gettin' ripe . . . hay cut . . . molasses made around here. . . . Big explosion's over, supervisors elected, some pleased, some not. . . . We're hearing talk of war!"

When they got closer, he was saying, "Many's been saved at revival, twenty-two last Sunday including a Doyle, ought to counted two. Hope they'll be a blessing to Dover community besides a shining star in Heaven. Now what?" he asked, for they had arrived and stood gathered in front of the steps.

"If nobody is using your wide net, could we use it?" asked William Wallace.

"You just used it a month ago," said Doc. "It ain't your turn."

Virgil jogged William Wallace's arm and cleared his throat. "This time is kind of special," he said. "We got reason to think William Wallace's wife Hazel is in the river, drowned."

"What reason have you got to think she's in the river drowned?" asked Doc. He took out his old pipe. "I'm asking the husband."

"Because she's not in the house," said William Wallace.

"Vanished?" and he knocked out the pipe.

"Plum vanished."

"Of course a thousand things could have happened to her," said Doc, and he lighted the pipe.

"Hand him up the letter, William Wallace," said Virgil. "We can't wait around till Doomsday for the net while Doc sits back thinkin'."

"I tore it up, right at the first," said William Wallace. "But I know it by heart. It said she was going to jump straight in the Pearl River and that I'd be sorry."

"Where do you come in, Virgil?" asked Doc.

"I was in the same place William Wallace sat on his neck in, all night, and done as much as he done, and come home the same time."

"You-all were out cuttin' up, so Lady Hazel has to jump in the river, is that it? Cause and effect? Anybody want to argue with me? Where do these others come in, Doyles, Malones, and what not?"

"Doc is the smartest man around," said William Wallace, turning to the solidly waiting Doyles, "but it sure takes time."

"These are the ones that's collected to drag the river for her," said Virgil.

"Of course I am not going on record to say so soon that *I* think she's drowned," Doc said, blowing out blue smoke.

"Do you think . . ." William Wallace mounted a step, and his hands both went into fists. "Do you think she was *carried off?*"

"Now that's the way to argue, see it from all sides," said Doc promptly. "But who by?"

Some Malone whistled, but not so you could tell which one.

"There's no booger around the Dover section that goes around carrying off young girls that's married," stated Doc.

"She was always scared of the Gypsies." William Wallace turned scarlet. "She'd sure turn her ring around on her finger if she passed one, and look in the other direction so they couldn't see she was pretty and carry her off. They come in the end of summer."

"Yes, there are the Gypsies, kidnappers since the world began. But was it to be you that would pay the grand ransom?" asked Doc. He pointed his finger. They all laughed then at how clever old Doc was and clapped William Wallace on the back. But that turned into a scuffle and they fell to the ground.

"Stop it, or you can't have the net," said Doc. "You're scaring my wife's chickens."

"It's time we was gone," said William Wallace.

The big barking dogs jumped to lean their front paws on the men's chests.

"My advice remains, Let well enough alone," said Doc. "Whatever this mysterious event will turn out to be, it has kept one woman from talking a while. However, Lady Hazel is the prettiest girl in Mississippi, you've never seen a prettier one and you never will. A golden-haired girl." He got to his feet with the nimbleness that was always his surprise, and said, "I'll come along with you."

The path they always followed was the Old Natchez Trace. It took them through the deep woods and led them out down below on the Pearl River, where they could begin dragging it upstream to a point near Dover. They walked in silence around William Wallace, not letting him carry anything, but the net dragged heavily and the buckets were full of clatter in a place so dim and still.

Once they went through a forest of cucumber trees and came up on a high ridge. Grady and Brucie, who were running ahead all the way, stopped in their tracks; a whistle had blown and far down and far away a long freight train was passing. It seemed like a little festival procession, moving with the slowness of ignorance or a dream, from distance to distance, the tiny pink and gray cars like secret boxes. Grady was counting the cars to himself, as if he could certainly see each one clearly, and Brucie watched his lips, hushed and cautious, the way he would watch a bird drinking. Tears suddenly came to Grady's eyes, but it could only be because a tiny man walked along the top of the train, walking and moving on top of the moving train.

They went down again and soon the smell of the river spread over the woods, cool and secret. Every step they took among the great walls of vines and among the passion-flowers started up a little life, a little flight.

"We're walking along in the changing-time," said Doc. "Any day now the change will come. It's going to turn from hot to cold, and we can kill the hog that's ripe and have fresh meat to eat. Come one of these nights and we can wander down here and tree a nice possum. Old Jack Frost will be pinching things up. Old Mr. Winter will be standing in the door. Hickory tree there will be yellow. Sweet-gum red, hickory yellow, dogwood red, sycamore yellow." He went along rapping the tree trunks with his knuckle. "Magnolia and live-oak never die. Remember that. Persimmons will all get fit to eat, and the nuts will be dropping like rain all through the woods here. And run, little quail, run, for we'll be after you too."

They went on and suddenly the woods opened upon light, and they had reached the river. Everyone stopped, but Doc talked on ahead as though nothing had happened. "Only today," he said, "today, in October sun, it's all gold—sky and tree and water. Everything just before it changes looks to be made of gold."

William Wallace looked down, as though he thought of Hazel with the shining eyes, sitting at home and looking straight before her, like a piece of pure gold, too precious to touch.

Below them the river was glimmering, narrow, soft, and skin-colored, and slowed nearly to stillness. The shining willow trees hung round them. The net that was being drawn out, so old and so long-used, it too looked golden, strung and tied with golden threads.

Standing still on the bank, all of a sudden William Wallace, on whose word they were waiting, spoke up in a voice of surprise. "What is the name of this river?"

They looked at him as if he were crazy not to know the name of the river he had fished in all his life. But a deep frown was on his forehead, as if he were compelled to wonder what people had come to call this river, or to think there was a mystery in the name of the river they all knew so well, the same as if it were some great far torrent of waves that dashed through the mountains somewhere, and almost as if it were a river in some dream, for they could not give him the name of that.

"Everybody knows Pearl River is named the Pearl River," said Doc.

A bird note suddenly bold was like a stone thrown into the water to sound it.

"It's deep here," said Virgil, and jogged William Wallace. "Remember?"

William Wallace stood looking down at the river as if it were still a mystery to him. There under his feet, which hung over the bank, it was transparent and yellow like an old bottle lying in the sun, filling with light.

Doc clattered all his paraphernalia.

Then all of a sudden all the Malones scattered jumping and tumbling down the bank. They gave their loud shout. Little Brucie started after them, and looked back.

"Do you think she jumped?" Virgil asked William Wallace.

II

Since the net was so wide, when it was all stretched it reached from bank to bank of the Pearl River, and the weights would hold it all the way to the bottom. Jug-like sounds filled the air, splashes lifted in the sun, and the party began to move upstream. The Malones with great groans swam and pulled near the shore, the Doyles swam and pushed from behind with Virgil to tell them how to do it best; Grady and Brucie with his thread and pin trotted along the sandbars hauling buckets and lines. Sam and Robbie Bell, naked and bright, guided the old oarless rowboat that always drifted at the shore, and in it, sitting up tall with his hat on, was Doc—he went along without ever touching water and without ever taking his eyes off the net. William Wallace himself did everything but most of the time he was out of sight, swimming about under water or diving, and he had nothing to say any more.

The dogs chased up and down, in and out of the water, and in and out of the woods.

"Don't let her get too heavy, boys," Doc intoned regularly, every few minutes, "and she won't let nothing through."

"She won't let nothing through, she won't let nothing through," chanted Sam and Robbie Bell, one at his front and one at his back.

The sandbars were pink or violet drifts ahead. Where the light fell on the river, in a wandering from shore to shore, it was leaf-shaped spangles that trembled softly, while the dark of the river was calm. The willow trees leaned overhead under muscadine vines, and their trailing leaves hung like waterfalls in the morning air. The thing that seemed like silence must have been the endless cry of all the crickets and locusts in the world, rising and falling.

Every time William Wallace took hold of a big eel that slipped the net, the Malones all yelled, "Rassle with him, son!"

"Don't let her get too heavy, boys," said Doc.

"This is hard on catfish," William Wallace said once.

There were big and little fishes, dark and bright, that they caught, good ones and bad ones, the same old fish.

"This is more shoes than I ever saw got together in any store," said Virgil when they emptied the net to the bottom. "Get going!" he shouted in the next breath.

The little Rippens who had stayed ahead in the woods stayed ahead on the river. Brucie, leading them all, made small jumps and hops as he went, sometimes on one foot, sometimes on the other.

The winding river looked old sometimes, when it ran wrinkled and deep under high banks where the roots of trees hung down, and sometimes it seemed to be only a young creek, shining with the colors of wildflowers. Sometimes sandbars in the shapes of fishes lay nose to nose across, without the track of even a bird.

"Here comes some alligators," said Virgil. "Let's let them by."

They drew out on the shady side of the water, and three big alligators and four middle-sized ones went by, taking their own time.

"Look at their great big old teeth!" called a shrill voice. It was Grady making his only outcry, and the alligators were not showing their teeth at all.

"The better to eat folks with," said Doc from his boat, looking at him severely.

"Doc, you are bound to declare all you know," said Virgil. "Get going!"

When they started off again the first thing they caught in the net was the baby alligator.

"That's just what we wanted!" cried the Malones.

They set the little alligator down on a sandbar and he squatted perfectly still; they could hardly tell when it was he started to move. They watched with set faces his incredible mechanics, while the dogs after one bark stood off in inquisitive humility, until he winked.

"He's ours!" shouted all the Malones. "We're taking him home with us!"

"He ain't nothing but a little-old baby," said William Wallace.

The Malones only scoffed, as if he might be only a baby but he looked like the oldest and worst lizard.

"What are you going to do with him?" asked Virgil.

"Keep him."

"I'd be more careful what I took out of this net," said Doc.

"Tie him up and throw him in the bucket," the Malones were saying to each other, while Doc was saying, "Don't come running to me and ask me what to do when he gets big."

They kept catching more and more fish, as if there was no end in sight.

"Look, a string of lady's beads," said Virgil. "Here, Sam and Robbie Bell."

Sam wore them around his head, with a knot over his forehead and loops around his ears, and Robbie Bell walked behind and stared at them.

In a shadowy place something white flew up. It was a heron, and it went away over the dark treetops. William Wallace followed it with his eyes and Brucie clapped his hands, but Virgil gave a sigh, as if he knew that when you go looking for what is lost, everything is a sign.

An eel slid out of the net.

"Rassle with him, son!" yelled the Malones. They swam like fiends.

"The Malones are in it for the fish," said Virgil.

It was about noon that there was a little rustle on the bank.

"Who is that yonder?" asked Virgil, and he pointed to a little undersized man with short legs and a little straw hat with a band around it, who was following along on the other side of the river.

"Never saw him and don't know his brother," said Doc.

Nobody had ever seen him before.

"Who invited you?" cried Virgil hotly. "Hi . . . !" and he made signs for the little undersized man to look at him, but he would not.

"Looks like a crazy man, from here," said the Malones.

"Just don't pay any attention to him and maybe he'll go away," advised Doc.

But Virgil had already swum across and was up on the other bank. He and the stranger could be seen exchanging a word apiece and then Virgil put out his hand the way he would pat a child and patted the stranger to the ground. The little man got up again just as quickly, lifted his shoulders, turned around, and walked away with his hat tilted over his eyes.

When Virgil came back he said, "Little-old man claimed he was harmless as a baby. I told him to just try horning in on this river and anything in it."

"What did he look like up close?" asked Doc.

"I wasn't studying how he looked," said Virgil. "But I don't like anybody to come looking at me that I am not familiar with." And he shouted, "Get going!"

"Things are moving in too great a rush," said Doc.

Brucie darted ahead and ran looking into all the bushes, lifting up their branches and looking underneath.

"Not one of the Doyles has spoke a word," said Virgil.

"That's because they're not talkers," said Doc.

All day William Wallace kept diving to the bottom. Once he dived down and down into the dark water, where it was so still that nothing stirred, not even a fish, and so dark that it was no longer the muddy world of the upper river but the dark clear world of deepness, and he must have believed this was the deepest place in the whole Pearl River, and if she was not here she would not be anywhere. He was gone such a long time that the others stared hard at the surface of the water, through which the bubbles came from below. So far down and all alone, had he found Hazel? Had he suspected down there, like some secret, the real, the true trouble that Hazel had fallen into, about which words in a letter could not speak . . . how (who knew?) she had been filled to the brim with that elation that they all remembered, like their own secret, the elation that comes of great hopes and changes, sometimes simply of the harvest time, that comes with a little course of its own like a tune to run in the head, and there was nothing she could do about it—they knew—and so it had turned into this. It could be nothing but the old trouble that William Wallace was finding out, reaching and turning in the gloom of such depths.

"Look down yonder," said Grady softly to Brucie.

He pointed to the surface, where their reflections lay colorless and still side by side. He touched his brother gently as though to impress him.

"That's you and me," he said.

Brucie swayed precariously over the edge, and Grady caught him by the seat of his overalls. Brucie looked, but showed no recognition. Instead, he backed away, and seemed all at once unconcerned and spiritless, and pressed the nickel William Wallace had given him into his palm, rubbing it into his skin. Grady's inflamed eyes rested on the brown water. Without warning he saw something . . . perhaps the image in the river seemed to be his father, the drowned man—with arms open, eyes open, mouth open. . . . Grady stared and blinked, again something wrinkled up his face.

And when William Wallace came up it was in an agony from submersion, which seemed an agony of the blood and of the very heart, so woeful he looked. He was staring and glaring around in astonishment, as if a long time had gone by, away from the pale world where the brown light of the sun and the river and the little party watching him trembled before his eyes.

"What did you bring up?" somebody called—was it Virgil?

One of his hands was holding fast to a little green ribbon of plant, root and all. He was surprised, and let it go.

It was afternoon. The trees spread softly, the clouds hung wet and tinted. A buzzard turned a few slow wheels in the sky, and drifted upwards. The dogs promenaded the banks.

"It's time we ate fish," said Virgil.

On a wide sandbar on which seashells lay they dragged up the haul and built a fire.

Then for a long time among clouds of odors and smoke, all half-naked except Doc, they cooked and ate catfish. They ate until the Malones groaned and all the Doyles stretched out on their faces, though for long after, Sam and Robbie Bell sat up to their own little table on a cypress stump and ate on and on. Then they all were silent and still, and one by one fell asleep.

"There ain't a thing better than fish," muttered William Wallace. He lay stretched on his back in the glimmer and shade of trampled sand. His sunburned forehead and cheeks seemed to glow with fire. His eyelids fell. The shadow of a willow branch dipped and moved over him. "There is nothing in the world as good as . . . fish. The fish of Pearl River." Then slowly he smiled. He was asleep.

But it seemed almost at once that he was leaping up, and one by one up sat the others in their ring and looked at him, for it was impossible to stop and sleep by the river.

"You're feeling as good as you felt last night," said Virgil, setting his head on one side.

"The excursion is the same when you go looking for your sorrow as when you go looking for your joy," said Doc.

But William Wallace answered none of them anything, for he was leaping all over the place and all, over them and the feast and the bones of the feast, trampling the sand, up and down, and doing a dance so crazy that he would die next. He took a big catfish and hooked it to his belt buckle and went up and down so that they all hollered, and the tears of laughter streaming down his cheeks made him put his hand up, and the two days' growth of beard began to jump out, bright red.

But all of a sudden there was an even louder cry, something almost like a cheer, from everybody at once, and all pointed fingers moved from William Wallace to the river. In the center of three light-gold rings across the water was lifted first an old hoary head ("It has whiskers!" a voice cried) and then in an undulation loop after loop and hump after hump of a long dark body, until there were a dozen rings of ripples, one behind the other, stretching all across the river, like a necklace.

"The King of the Snakes!" cried all the Malones at once, in high tenor voices and leaning together.

"The King of the Snakes," intoned old Doc in his profound bass.

"He looked you in the eye."

William Wallace stared back at the King of the Snakes with all his might.

It was Brucie that darted forward, dangling his little thread with the pin tied to it, going toward the water.

"That's the King of the Snakes!" cried Grady, who always looked after him.

Then the snake went down.

The little boy stopped with one leg in the air, spun around on the other, and sank to the ground.

"Git up," Grady whispered. "It was just the King of the Snakes. He went off whistling. Git up. It wasn't a thing but the King of the Snakes."

Brucie's green eyes opened, his tongue darted out, and he sprang up; his feet were heavy, his head light, and he rose like a bubble coming to the surface.

Then thunder like a stone loosened and rolled down the bank.

They all stood unwilling on the sandbar, holding to the net. In the eastern sky were the familiar castles and the round towers to which they were used, gray, pink, and blue, growing darker and filling with thunder. Lightning flickered in the sun along their thick walls. But in the west the sun shone with such a violence that in an illumination like a long-prolonged glare of lightning the heavens looked black and white; all color left the world, the goldenness of everything was like a memory, and only heat, a kind of glamor and oppression, lay on their heads. The thick heavy trees on the other side of the river were brushed with mile-long streaks of silver, and a wind touched each man on the forehead. At the same time there was a long roll of thunder that began behind them, came up and down mountains and valleys of air, passed over their heads, and left them listening still. With a small, near noise a mockingbird followed it, the little white bars of its body flashing over the willow trees.

"We are here for a storm now," Virgil said. "We will have to stay till it's over."

They retreated a little, and hard drops fell in the leathery leaves at their shoulders and about their heads.

"Magnolia's the loudest tree there is in a storm," said Doc.

Then the light changed the water, until all about them the woods in the rising wind seemed to grow taller and blow inward together and suddenly turn dark. The rain struck heavily. A huge tail seemed to lash through the air and the river broke in a wound of silver. In silence the party crouched and stooped beside the trunk of the great tree, which in the push of the storm rose full of a fragrance and unyielding weight. Where they all stared, past their tree, was another tree, and beyond that another and another, all the way down the bank of the river, all towering and darkened in the storm.

"The outside world is full of endurance," said Doc. "Full of endurance."

Robbie Bell and Sam squatted down low and embraced each other from the start.

"Runs in our family to get struck by lightnin'," said Robbie Bell. "Lightnin' drawed a pitchfork right on our grandpappy's cheek, stayed till he died. Pappy got struck by some bolts of lightnin' and was dead three days, dead as that-there axe."

There was a succession of glares and crashes.

"This'n's goin' to be either me or you," said Sam. "Here come a little bug. If he go to the left, be me, and to the right, be you."

But at the next flare a big tree on the hill seemed to turn into fire before their eyes, every branch, twig, and leaf, and a purple cloud hung over it.

"Did you hear that crack?" asked Robbie Bell. "That were its bones."

"Why do you little niggers talk so much!" said Doc. "Nobody's profiting by this information."

"We always talks this much," said Sam, "but now everybody so quiet, they hears us."

The great tree, split and on fire, fell roaring to earth. Just at its moment of falling, a tree like it on the opposite bank split wide open and fell in two parts.

"Hope they ain't goin' to be no balls of fire come rollin' over the water and fry all the fishes with they scales on," said Robbie Bell.

The water in the river had turned purple and was filled with sudden currents and whirlpools. The little willow trees bent almost to its surface, bowing one after another down the bank and almost breaking under the storm. A great curtain of wet leaves was borne along before a blast of wind, and every human being was covered.

"Now us got scales," wailed Sam. "Us is the fishes."

"Hush up, little-old colored children," said Virgil. "This isn't the way to act when somebody takes you out to drag a river."

"Poor lady's-ghost, I bet it is scareder than us," said Sam.

"All I hoping is, us don't find her!" screamed Robbie Bell.

William Wallace bent down and knocked their heads together. After that they clung silently in each other's arms, the two black heads resting, with wind-filled cheeks and tight-closed eyes, one upon the other until the storm was over.

"Right over yonder is Dover," said Virgil. "We've come all the way. William Wallace, you have walked on a sharp rock and cut your foot open."

III

In Dover it had rained, and the town looked somehow like new. The wavy heat of late afternoon came down from the watertank and fell over everything like shiny mosquito-netting. At the wide place where the road was paved and patched with tar, it seemed newly embedded with Coca-Cola tops. The old circus posters on the store were nearly gone, only bits, the snowflakes of white horses, clinging to its side. Morning-glory vines started almost visibly to grow over the roofs and cling round the ties of the railroad track, where bluejays lighted on the rails, and umbrella chinaberry trees hung heavily over the whole town, dripping intermittently upon the tin roofs.

Each with his counted fish on a string, the members of the river-dragging party walked through the town. They went toward the town well, and there was Hazel's mother's house, but no sign of her yet coming out. They all drank a dipper of the water, and still there was not a soul on the street. Even the bench in front of the store was empty, except for a little corn-shuck doll.

But something told them somebody had come, for after one moment people began to look out of the store and out of the post office. All the bird dogs woke up to see the Doyle dogs and such a large number of men and boys materialize suddenly with such a big catch of fish, and they ran out barking. The Doyle dogs joyously barked back. The bluejays flashed up and screeched above the town, whipping through their tunnels in the chinaberry trees. In the café a nickel clattered inside a music box and a love song began to play. The whole town of Dover began to throb in its wood and tin, like an old tired heart, when the men walked through once more, coming around again and going down the street carrying the fish, so drenched, exhausted, and muddy that no one could help but admire them.

William Wallace walked through the town as though he did not see anybody or hear anything. Yet he carried his great string of fish held high where it could be seen by all. Virgil came next, imitating William Wallace exactly, then the modest Doyles crowded by the Malones, who were holding up their alligator, tossing it in the air, even, like a father tossing his child. Following behind and pointing authoritatively at the ones in front strolled Doc, with Sam and Robbie Bell still chanting in his wake. In and out of the whole little line Grady and Brucie jerked about. Grady, with his head ducked, and stiff as a rod, walked with a springy limp; it made him look forever angry and unapproachable. Under his breath he was whispering, "Sty, sty, git out of my eye, and git on somebody passin' by." He traveled on with narrowed shoulders, and kept his eye unerringly upon his little brother, wary and at the same time proud, as though he held a flying June-bug on a string. Brucie, making a twanging noise with his lips, had shot forth again, and he was darting rapidly everywhere at once, delighted and tantalized, running in circles around William Wallace, pointing to his fish. A frown of pleasure like the print of a bird's foot was stamped between his faint brows, and he trotted in some unknown realm of delight.

"Did you ever see so many fish?" said the people in Dover.

"How much are your fish, mister?"

"Would you sell your fish?"

"Is that all the fish in Pearl River?"

"How much you sell them all for? Everybody's?"

"Take 'em free," said William Wallace suddenly and loud. The Malones were upon him and shouting, but it was too late. "I don't want no more of 'em. I want my wife!" he yelled, just at the moment when Hazel's mother walked out of her front door.

"You can't head her mother off," said Virgil. "Here she comes in full bloom."

"What have you done with my child?" Hazel's mother shouted.

But William Wallace turned his back on her, that was all, and on everybody, for that matter, and that was the breaking-up of the party.

Just as the sun went down, Doc climbed his back steps, sat in his chair on the back porch where he sat in the evenings, and lighted his pipe. William Wallace hung out the net and came back and Virgil was waiting for him, so they could say good evening to Doc.

"All in all," said Doc, when they came up, "I've never been on a better river-dragging, or seen better behavior. If it took catching catfish to move the Rock of Gibraltar, I believe this outfit could move it."

"Well, we didn't catch Hazel," said Virgil.

"What did you say?" asked Doc.

"He don't really pay attention," said Virgil. "I said, 'We didn't catch Hazel.'"

"Who says Hazel was to be caught?" asked Doc. "She wasn't in there. Girls don't like the water—remember that. Girls don't just haul off and go jumping in the river to get back at their husbands. They got other ways."

"Didn't you ever think she was in there?" asked William Wallace. "The whole time?"

"Nary once," said Doc.

"He's just smart," said Virgil, putting his hand on William Wallace's arm. "It's only because we didn't find her that he wasn't looking for her."

"I'm beholden to you for the net, anyway," said William Wallace.

"You're welcome to borry it again," said Doc.

On the way home Virgil kept saying, "Calm down, calm down, William Wallace."

"If he wasn't such an old skinny man I'd have wrung his neck for him," said William Wallace. "He had no business coming."

"He's too big for his britches," said Virgil. "Don't nobody know everything. And just because it's his net. Why does it have to be his net?"

"If it wasn't for being polite to old men, I'd have skinned him alive," said William Wallace.

"I guess he don't really know nothing about wives at all, his wife's so deaf," said Virgil.

"He don't know Hazel," said William Wallace. "I'm the only man alive knows Hazel: would she jump in the river or not, and I say she would. She jumped in because I was sitting on the back of my neck in a ditch singing, and that's just what she ought to done. Doc ain't got no right to say one word about it."

"Calm down, calm down, William Wallace," said Virgil.

"If it had been you that talked like that, I'd have broke every bone in your body," said William Wallace. "Just let you talk like that. You're my age and size."

"But I ain't going to talk like that," said Virgil. "What have I done the whole time but keep this river-dragging going straight and running even, without no hitches? You couldn't have drug the river a foot without me."

"What are you talking about! Without who!" cried William Wallace. "This wasn't your river-dragging! It wasn't your wife!" He jumped on Virgil and they began to fight.

"Let me up." Virgil was breathing heavily.

"Say it was my wife. Say it was my river-dragging."

"Yours!" Virgil was on the ground with William Wallace's hand putting dirt in his mouth.

"Say it was my net."

"Your net!"

"Get up then."

They walked along getting their breath, and smelling the honeysuckle in the evening. On a hill William Wallace looked down, and at the same time there went drifting by the sweet sounds of music outdoors. They were having the Sacred Harp Sing on the grounds of an old white church glimmering there at the crossroads, far below. He stared away as if he saw it minutely, as if he could see a lady in white take a flowered cover off the organ, which was set on a little slant in the shade, dust the keys, and start to pump and play. . . . He smiled faintly, as he would at his mother, and at Hazel, and at the singing women in his life, now all one young girl standing up to sing under the trees the oldest and longest ballads there were.

Virgil told him good night and went into his own house and the door shut on him.

When he got to his own house, William Wallace saw to his surprise that it had not rained at all. But there, curved over the roof, was something he had never seen before as long as he could remember, a rainbow at night. In the light of the moon, which had risen again, it looked small and of gauzy material, like a lady's summer dress, a faint veil through which the stars showed.

He went up on the porch and in at the door, and all exhausted he had walked through the front room and through the kitchen when he heard his name called. After a moment, he smiled, as if no matter what he might have hoped for in his wildest heart, it was better than that to hear his name called out in the house. The voice came out of the bedroom.

"What do you want?" he yelled, standing stock-still.

Then she opened the bedroom door with the old complaining creak, and there she stood. She was not changed a bit.

"How do you feel?" he said.

"I feel pretty good. Not too good," Hazel said, looking mysterious.

"I cut my foot," said William Wallace, taking his shoe off so she could see the blood.

"How in the world did you do that?" she cried, with a step back.

"Dragging the river. But it don't hurt any longer."

"You ought to have been more careful," she said. "Supper's ready and I wondered if you would ever come home, or if it would be last night all over again. Go and make yourself fit to be seen," she said, and ran away from him.

After supper they sat on the front steps a while.

"Where were you this morning when I came in?" asked William Wallace when they were ready to go in the house.

"I was hiding," she said. "I was still writing on the letter. And then you tore it up."

"Did you watch me when I was reading it?"

"Yes, and you could have put out your hand and touched me. I was so close."

But he bit his lip, and gave her a little tap and slap, and then turned her up and spanked her.

"Do you think you will do it again?" he asked.

"I'll tell my mother on you for this!"

"Will you do it again?"

"No!" she cried.

"Then pick yourself up off my knee."

It was just as if he had chased her and captured her again. She lay smiling in the crook of his arm. It was the same as any other chase in the end.

"I will do it again if I get ready," she said. "Next time will be different, too."

Then she was ready to go in, and rose up and looked out from the top step, out across their yard where the China tree was and beyond, into the dark fields where the lightning-bugs flickered away. He climbed to his feet too and stood beside her, with the frown on his face, trying to look where she looked. And after a few minutes she took him by the hand and led him into the house, smiling as if she were smiling down on him.

1943

Charles Olson 1910–1970

As poet, essayist, letter writer, and teacher, Charles Olson was a seminal figure in the generation after Ezra Pound and William Carlos Williams. His first book, *Call Me Ishmael,* is an interpretation of Melville's *Moby-Dick* that deserves a place beside D. H. Lawrence's *Studies in Classic American Literature,* Williams's *In the American Grain,* and Edward Dahlberg's *Can These Bones Live.* His long sequence, *The Maximus Poems,* is the major attempt at a "personal epic" after Pound's *Cantos* and Williams's *Paterson.* He increasingly thought of himself as a "mythographer" or "archaeologist of morning" who aimed to reconnect us with the natural process from which we have been alienated by the rationalist thought of the last 2,500 years.

Born in Worcester, Massachusetts, Olson grew up there while spending summers in Gloucester, the city he later celebrated in *The Maximus Poems.* He attended Wesleyan University, from which he received a B.A. and an M.A. with a thesis on Melville. He then embarked on a search for Melville's library and tracked down many of his books, including his personally annotated Hawthorne and Shakespeare. Olson taught English for two years at Clark University, took a summer job on the schooner *Doris W. Hawkes,* and entered Harvard's American Civilization program, where he studied with the historian Frederick Merk and the literary scholar F. O. Matthiessen. After completing the coursework for the Ph.D., he returned to Gloucester to take up a Guggenheim Fellowship for studies in Melville. In 1940 he met Constance Wilcock, who became his common-law wife, and began working in New York for the American Civil Liberties Union and then for the Common Council for American Unity. From 1942 to 1944, he worked for the Office of War Information in Washington and then became director of the Foreign Nationalities Division, Democratic National Committee. In 1945, disenchanted with politics, he decided to commit himself to writing. During that year he wrote *Call Me Ishmael* (based on his earlier Melville research), several poems, and an essay in qualified defense of Ezra Pound, the boldly mimetic "This Is Yeats Speaking."

Over the next three years, Olson met Pound and also the geographer Carl Sauer (an important influence on his thought), worked on a book about the American West, wrote a dance-play based on *Moby-Dick,* and began to lecture at Black Mountain College as a replacement for his friend and mentor, Edward Dahlberg. In 1949 he wrote his important postmodernist poem "The Kingfishers." In 1950 he began corresponding with Robert Creeley, wrote the first Maximus poem, and published "Projective Verse," in which he reasserted Creeley's principle, "FORM IS NEVER MORE THAN AN EXTENSION OF CONTENT," and Dahlberg's clue to poetic process, "ONE PERCEPTION MUST IMMEDIATELY AND DIRECTLY LEAD TO A FURTHER PERCEPTION." In 1951 he began his association with Cid Corman and the magazine *Origin,* traveled to the Yucatán to study Mayan culture, and wrote "Human Universe," in which he argued that art "is the only twin life has" because it "does not seek to describe but to enact."

That year he also joined Black Mountain full time, where he remained (except for a leave in 1952 for further research on Mayan glyphs) as faculty member and then rector until the college closed in 1956. While there he separated from Constance and took as common-law wife Elizabeth Kaiser. Olson effectively turned Black Mountain into an arts center. Among his associates were the painters Franz Kline and Robert Rauschenberg, the dancer Merce Cunningham, and the musician John Cage. In 1957 Olson returned to Gloucester, from which he traveled to various colleges for lectures and readings. In 1963 he began to teach at the State University of New York at Buffalo. In 1964 his wife, Elizabeth, was killed in an automobile accident—a tragedy from which Olson never recovered. He returned to Gloucester in 1965 and then accepted in 1969 a position at the University of Connecticut, where he taught for a few weeks before his death. During these years, he had continued to work on *The Maximus Poems,* which he never completed. The third book of that sequence was posthumously arranged from his notes by his former students Charles Boer and George F. Butterick.

Olson's poetry is often elliptical and allusive, with a range that can include Sumerian myth, Heraclitus, Hesiod, the linguist B. L. Whorf, the cyberneticist Norbert Wiener, the philosopher Alfred North Whitehead, the psychologist C. G. Jung, and the details of both ancient and modern history. His style tends to be meditative and didactic, but with frequent lyricism. It is often made difficult by incomplete syntax, heavy reliance upon abstract terms, brief notations, and a disjunctive or paratactic forward motion that piles up incremental meanings and produces an effect of continual self-revision. These traits are in accord with Olson's understanding of art as "enactment." His constantly twisting utterance seeks not to describe but to enact the movements of a speaker who is himself in "process" as he grapples with the matter in hand. As Olson said once at Goddard College, "I myself would wish that all who spoke and wrote, spoke always from a place that is *new* at that moment that they do speak. . . ."

Thomas R. Whitaker
Yale University

PRIMARY WORKS

Poetry: *Y & X,* 1949; *In Cold Hell, In Thicket,* 1953; *The Maximus Poems / 1–10,* 1953; *The Maximus Poems / 11–22,* 1956; *The Maximus Poems,* 1960; *The Distances,* 1960; *The Maximus Poems IV, V, VI,* 1968; *Archaeologist of Morning,* 1973; *The Maximus Poems,* 1983; *The Collected Poems,* 1987; *A Nation of Nothing but Poetry: Supplementary Poems,* 1989; *Selected Poems,* 1993. Prose: *Call Me Ishmael,* 1947; *A Bibliography on America for Ed Dorn,* 1964; *Human Universe and Other Essays,* 1965; *Proprioception,* 1965; *Stocking Cap,* 1966; *Causal Mythology,* 1969; *The Special View of History,* 1970; *Poetry and Truth: The Beloit Lectures and Poems,* 1971; *Additional Prose,* 1974; *The Post Office,* 1975.

The Kingfishers[1]

I

What does not change / is the will to change[2]

He[3] woke, fully clothed, in his bed. He
remembered only one thing, the birds, how
when he came in, he had gone around the rooms
5 and got them back in their cage, the green one first,
she with the bad leg, and then the blue,
the one they had hoped was a male

Otherwise? Yes, Fernand, who had talked lispingly of Albers[4] &
Angkor Vat.[5]
10 He had left the party without a word. How he got up, got into his
coat,
I do not know. When I saw him, he was at the door, but it did not
matter,
he was already sliding along the wall of the night, losing himself
15 in some crack of the ruins. That it should have been he who said,
"The kingfishers!
who cares
for their feathers[6]
now?"
20 His last words had been, "The pool is slime."[7] Suddenly everyone,
ceasing their talk, sat in a row around him, watched
they did not so much hear, or pay attention, they
wondered, looked at each other, smirked, but listened,
he repeated and repeated, could not go beyond his thought

---

[1]This poem about personal, poetic, and cultural crisis answers Pound and Eliot in many ways, beginning with the title. The "kingfishers," as literal and complex subjects of meditation, imply a reversal of Eliot's kind of symbolism (the "Fisher King" of *The Waste Land* and the "kingfisher's wing" in "Burnt Norton").

[2]A revision of Heraclitus's Fragment 83, "Change alone is unchanging," to emphasize the human will and history. Eliot's "Burnt Norton" begins with Heraclitus's Fragments 2 and 60.

[3]Third-person reference to the poet: concerned with parakeets that friends hope to mate, he then remembers "Fernand," a character based on an art curator in Washington.

[4]Josef Albers, noted painter and teacher, who was rector of Black Mountain College when Olson was first hired.

[5]Early twelfth-century temple in Cambodia.

[6]The feathers of the kingfisher had ceremonial use and were a valuable article of trade in the Mayan-Aztec culture that Olson had begun to study at the time of this poem.

[7]The sacrificial pool at Chichén Itzá in which messengers to the gods, wearing feathered headdresses, were drowned.

25   "The pool the kingfishers' feathers were wealth why
did the export stop?"

It was then he left

2

I thought of the E on the stone,[8] and of what Mao[9] said
30 la lumiere"
               but the kingfisher
de l'aurore"
               but the kingfisher flew west
est devant nous!
               he got the color of his breast
35   from the heat of the setting sun![10]

The features are, the feebleness of the feet (syndactylism of the 3rd &
    4th digit)
the bill, serrated, sometimes a pronounced beak, the wings
where the color is, short and round, the tail
40 inconspicuous.

But not these things were the factors. Not the birds.
The legends are
legends. Dead, hung up indoors, the kingfisher
will not indicate a favoring wind,
45 or avert the thunderbolt. Nor, by its nesting,
still the waters, with the new year, for seven days.
It is true, it does nest with the opening year, but not on the waters.
It nests at the end of a tunnel bored by itself in a bank. There,
six or eight white and translucent eggs are laid, on fishbones
50 not on bare clay, on bones thrown up in pellets by the birds.

                        On these rejectamenta
(as they accumulate they form a cup-shaped structure) the young are
    born.

[8]The symbol, perhaps an epsilon, carved on the omphalos, or navel stone, at the oracle of Delphi. Plutarch's essay, "The E at Delphi," offers several conjectures as to the lost meaning of this symbol.

[9]Mao Tse-tung, whose revolutionary army was winning the civil war in China during the spring of 1949. A passage from Mao's call to action in a 1948 report to the Communist Party was sent to Olson by a French friend, Jean Riboud. The passage concludes: *"La lumière de l'aurore est devant nous. Nous devons nous lever et agir"* ("The light of dawn is before us. We must rise and act").

[10]This legend, those given below, and the items of biological information are drawn from the article on the kingfisher in *The Encyclopaedia Britannica* (11th ed.).

And, as they are fed and grow, this nest of excrement and decayed
55   fish becomes

                    a dripping, fetid mass

Mao concluded:
           nous devons
                nous lever
60   et agir!

3

When the attentions change / the jungle
leaps in
        even the stones are split
                they rive[11]
65 Or,
    enter
that other conqueror[12] we more naturally recognize
he so resembles ourselves

But the E
70 cut so rudely on that oldest stone
sounded otherwise,
was differently heard

as, in another time, were treasures used:

(and, later, much later, a fine ear thought
75 a scarlet coat)

        "of green feathers feet, beaks and eyes
        of gold

        "animals likewise,
        resembling snails

80   "a large wheel, gold, with figures of unknown four-foots,
        and worked with tufts of leaves, weight
        3800 ounces

---

[11]These lines synthesize Pound and Williams on renewal: *Canto XX:* "jungle,/Basis of renewal, renewals"; *Paterson,* Book II: "unless the mind change . . . without invention nothing lies under the witch-hazel bush . . . "; "A Sort of a Song": "Invent!/Saxifrage is my flower that splits/the rocks."

[12]I.e., a destroyer of civilization like Hernando Cortés, the conqueror of Mexico, to whom the poem alludes below.

"last, two birds, of thread and featherwork, the quills
gold, the feet
85   gold, the two birds perched on two reeds
gold, the reeds arising from two embroidered mounds,
one yellow, the other
white.

"And from each reed hung
90   seven feathered tassels.[13]

In this instance, the priests
(in dark cotton robes, and dirty,
their dishevelled hair matted with blood, and flowing wildly
over their shoulders)
95 rush in among the people, calling on them
to protect their gods

And all now is war
where so lately there was peace,
and the sweet brotherhood, the use
100 of tilled fields.

4

Not one death but many,[14]
not accumulation but change, the feed-back proves, the feed-back is
the law[15]

Into the same river no man steps twice[16]
105   When fire dies air dies
No one remains, nor is, one

Around an appearance, one common model, we grow up
many. Else how is it,
if we remain the same,
110 we take pleasure now

[13]Montezuma's gifts to Cortés, as described in William H. Prescott, *History of the Conquest of Mexico.* See also Williams's "The Destruction of Tenochtitlán," in *In the American Grain.*

[14]A phrase drawn, perhaps, from Pablo Neruda, *The Heights of Macchu Picchu.*

[15]The first of several allusions to Norbert Wiener, *Cybernetics: or Control and Communication in the Animal and the Machine.* Wiener describes the circular and self-corrective processes of "feedback" as enabling the precise steering or control of any process, mechanical, biological, or social.

[16]Heraclitus, Fragment 91, quoted by the moderator Ammonius in Plutarch's "The E at Delphi." Part 4 of section II puts in modern terms Ammonius's vision of Heraclitian change, ending with a rephrasing of the admonition "Know thyself," which was the climax of Ammonius's argument.

in what we did not take pleasure before? love
contrary objects? admire and/or find fault? use
other words, feel other passions, have
nor figure, appearance, disposition, tissue
115 the same?
   To be in different states without a change
   is not a possibility

We can be precise. The factors are
in the animal and/or the machine the factors are
120 communication and/or control, both involve
the message. And what is the message? The message is
a discrete or continuous sequence of measurable events distributed in
   time[17]

is the birth of air, is
125 the birth of water,[18] is
a state between
the origin and
the end, between
birth and the beginning of
130 another fetid nest

is change, presents
no more than itself

And the too strong grasping of it,
when it is pressed together and condensed,
135 loses it

This very thing you are

II

   They buried their dead in a sitting posture
   serpent cane razor ray of the sun

   And she sprinkled water on the head of the child, crying
140   "Cioa-coatl! Cioa-coatl!"
     with her face to the west[19]

---

[17]Quoted from Wiener, *Cybernetics,* p. 8.
[18]Ammonius cites Heraclitus's dictum (Fragment 76) in Plutarch's "The E at Delphi": "the death of heat is birth for steam, and the death of steam is birth for water, but the case is even more clearly to be seen in our own selves. . . ."

Olson's emphasis on "birth" reverses that of Eliot when echoing the same dictum in "Little Gidding": "This is the death of air" and "the death of water."
[19]Factual details of Mayan burial and baptismal ceremonies.

> Where the bones are found, in each personal heap
> with what each enjoyed, there is always
> the Mongolian louse[20]

145 The light is in the east. Yes. And we must rise, act. Yet
in the west, despite the apparent darkness (the whiteness
which covers all), if you look, if you can bear, if you can, long enough

> as long as it was necessary for him, my guide
> to look into the yellow of that longest-lasting rose[21]

150 so you must, and, in that whiteness, into that face, with what candor,[22]
> look

and, considering the dryness of the place
> the long absence of an adequate race

> (of the two who first came, each a conquistador, one
155 > healed, the other[23]
> tore the eastern idols down, toppled
> the temple walls, which, says the excuser
> were black from human gore)

> hear
160 hear, where the dry blood talks
> where the old appetite walks

> la piu saporita et migliore
> che si possa truovar al mondo[24]

> where it hides, look
165 in the eye how it runs
> in the flesh / chalk[25]

---

[20]Evidence sometimes offered to support the theory that Amerindian culture is of Asian origin.

[21]In Dante's *Divine Comedy,* the Latin poet Virgil guides Dante through Hell and Purgatory, but it is St. Bernard who finally directs his vision to the white rose (*candida rosa*) of Paradise, likened to the sun at dawn (*Paradiso, XXXI,* 118-129). In Olson's poem, where the paradisal appears "in" or "under" the infernal, Virgil and Bernard are implicitly combined. The model for that combination is provided by Pound's *Cantos,* a journey through the hell of the modern world toward a vision of the paradisal.

[22]Echoing Pound, *Canto LXXIV* ("what whiteness will you add to this whiteness,/what candor?"), which paraphrases the *Analects* of Confucius. Pound's lines point to the natural "process" and also to the "city of Dioce whose terraces are the colour of stars," understood as paradisal antitheses to the tragedy of war.

[23]Cabeza de Vaca, who "healed," and Cortés, who so destroyed the idols in Tenochtitlán, and was so justified by Prescott.

[24]From Marco Polo's account of cannibalism in Asia: "the most savory and best that can be found in the world."

[25]The "eye" and "flesh" of the living Mayans and the "chalk" of the Mayan glyphs.

but under these petals
in the emptiness
regard the light, contemplate
the flower
170   whence it arose

with what violence benevolence is bought
what cost in gesture justice brings
what wrongs domestic rights involve
175   what stalks
this silence

what pudor pejorocracy[26] affronts
how awe, night-rest and neighborhood can rot[27]
what breeds where dirtiness is law
180   what crawls
below

III[28]

I am no Greek, hath not th'advantage.[29]
And of course, no Roman:
he can take no risk that matters,
185   the risk of beauty least of all.

But I have my kin,[30] if for no other reason than
(as he said, next of kin)[31] I commit myself, and,
given my freedom, I'd be a cad
if I didn't. Which is most true.

190   It works out this way, despite the disadvantage.
I offer, in explanation, a quote:

---

[26]"Rule by the worst," an antonym of "aristocracy" coined by Pound in *Canto LXXIX*.

[27]Recalling Shakespeare, *Timon of Athens*, 4. 1. 17–20: "Domestic awe, night-rest, and neighborhood,/Instruction, manners, mysteries and trades,/Degrees, observances, customs and laws,/Decline to your confounding contraries."

[28]After two sections in the juxtapositional mode of *The Waste Land* and *The Cantos*, and deriving partly from the montage technique of the film-artist Sergei Eisenstein, Section III presents a first-person statement in response to Eliot and Pound, using quatrains that glance at those in Pound's "Hugh Selwyn Mauberley."

[29]Parodying Eliot's "The Love Song of J. Alfred Prufrock: "I am not Prince Hamlet, nor was meant to be." Williams had already answered Eliot and Pound in the epigraph to *Paterson:* "a reply to Greek and Latin with the bare hands."

[30]Answering Pound's talk about "my kin of the spirit" in "In Durance."

[31]The "next of kin" is here acknowledged to be Pound, who said in his Preface to *Guide to Kulchur:* "It is my intention . . . to COMMIT myself on as many points as possible. . . . Given my freedom, I may be a fool to use it, but I wd. be a cad not to."

si j'ai du goût, ce n'est guères
que pour la terre et les pierres.[32]

Despite the discrepancy (an ocean   courage   age)
195   this is also true: if I have any taste
it is only because I have interested myself
in what was slain in the sun

I pose you your question:[33]

shall you uncover honey / where maggots are?

200   I hunt among stones

1950

For Sappho, Back[1]

I

With a dry eye, she
saw things out of the corner of,
with a bold
she looked on any man,
5 with a shy eye

---

[32]Arthur Rimbaud, "Faim" ("Hunger"), lines 1-2, in *Delires* (*Deliriums*), a section of *Une Saison en enfer* (*A Season in Hell*): "If I have any taste, it is only for earth and stones." For Olson, Rimbaud enacts the return to the "familiar" after the intellectual estrangement of Western culture. See *The Special View of History:* "It is this which Heraclitus meant when he laid down the law which was vitiated by Socrates and only restored by Rimbaud: that man is estranged from that [with] which he is most familiar." See "Maximus, to himself," page 1952, note 2.

[33]A revision of Samson's riddle in Judges 14:14: "Out of the eater came forth meat, and out of the strong came forth sweetness." The carcass of the lion slain by Samson contained a swarm of bees and honey.

[1]Sappho was a Greek lyric poet, born c. 630 B.C, who lived and wrote on the island of Lesbos off the coast of Asia Minor, and who has been much admired by modern American poets. Except for three poems, her work is now known only in fragments, many of which were discovered in the twentieth century on papyrus that had been re-used to make mummy shrouds. Her verse, both passionate and detached, celebrates a love of women and of all delicate things. Olson read the translations by J. M. Edmonds in the Loeb Classical Library *Lyra Graeca* (Volume 1). Olson's tribute, which begins in the past tense but moves to a continuing present, makes of Sappho a trope for woman, poetry, dance, and creative nature beyond all rational analysis.

With a cold eye, with her eye she looked on, she looked out, she
who was not so different as you might imagine from,
who had, as nature hath, an eye to look upon her makings, to,
in her womb, know
10 how red, and because it is red, how
handsome blood is, how, because it is unseen, how
because it goes about its business as she does,
as nature's things have that way of doing, as
in the delight of her eye she
15 creates constants

    And, in the thickness of her blood, some

variants

II

As blood is, as flesh can be
is she, self-housed, and moving
20 moving in impeccability to be
clear, clear! to be
as, what is rhythm but
her limpidity?
    She
25 who is as certain as the morning is
when it arises, when it is spring, when, from wetness comes its
  brightness
as fresh as this beloved's fingers, lips
each new time she new turns herself to
30 tendernesses, she
turns her most objective, scrupulous attention, her own
self-causing
   each time it is,
   as is the morning, is
35   the morning night and revelation of her
   nakedness, new
   forever new, as fresh as is the scruple of her eye, the accurate
   kiss

III

If you would know what woman is, what
40 strength the reed of man unknows, forever
cannot know, look, look! in these eyes, look
as she passes, on this moving thing, which moves

as grass blade by grass blade moves, as
syllable does throw light on fellow syllable, as,
45 in this rare creature, each hidden, each moving thing
is light to its known, unknown brother,
as objects stand one by one by another, so
is this universe, this flow, this woman, these eyes
are sign

IV

50 The intimate, the intricate, what shall perplex, forever
is a matter, is it not, not of confusions to be studied and made literal,
but of a dry dance by which, as shoots one day make leaves, as
the earth's crust, when ice draws back, wrings mountains
from itself, makes valleys in whose palms
55 root-eating fisher folk spring up—
by such a dance, in which the dancer contradicts
the waste and easy gesture, contains
the heave within,
within, because the human is so light a structure, within
60 a finger, say, or there
within the gentlest swaying of
                              (of your true hips)

In such containment
                    And in search for that which is the shoot, the thrust
65 of what you are
            (of what you were so delicately born)
                              of what fruits
of your own making you are
                    the hidden constance of which all the rest
70 is awkward variation

                this! this
                is what gives beauty to her eye, inhabitation
                to her tender-taken bones, is what illumines
                all her skin with satin glow
75   when love blows over, turning
                as the leaf turns in the wind
                and, with that shock of recognition,[2] shows
                its other side, the joy, the sort of terror of

                a dancer going off

                                              1951

[2]A phrase made famous by Edmund Wilson's *The Shock of Recognition,* 1943, which treats a self-consciousness among American writers that has manifested itself in "moments when genius becomes aware of its kin" (p. viii).

I, Maximus of Gloucester, to You[1]

Off-shore, by islands hidden in the
    blood[2]
jewels & miracles, I, Maximus
a metal hot from boiling water, tell you
5   what is a lance, who obeys the figures of
the present dance

1

the thing you're after
may lie around the bend
of the nest (second, time slain, the bird! the bird!

10 And there! (strong) thrust, the mast! flight

                                    (of the bird
                                    o kylix,[3] o
                                    Antony of Padua[4]
                                    sweep low, o bless

15 the roofs, the old ones, the gentle steep ones
on whose ridge-poles the gulls sit, from which they depart,

                                    And the flake-racks
of my city!

---

[1]The first "letter" of *The Maximus Poems.* Like "Paterson" in Williams's *Paterson,* Maximus is a complex figure. Most often, in this exploratory and self-corrective sequence, he is an aspect of the six-foot-eight-inch poet himself, probing the geography, history, and present needs of Gloucester, on Cape Ann in Massachusetts, which is for him "the last *polis* or city" in the northwestward migration of European culture from the eastern Mediterranean. But his name also suggests both Maximus of Tyre, a second-century A.D. Greek eclectic philosopher whom Olson encountered while reading about Sappho, and C. G. Jung's "homo maximus" or Self, which includes the ego-consciousness and the unconscious collective archetypes, and is the final goal of psychological "individuation." The title of this poem recalls the form of address used by St. Paul in his letters to the church-communities (e.g., *Colossians* 1: 1–3); but Maximus's initial oracular stance will be undercut by the opening lines of "Letter 2": ". . . . tell you? ha! who/can tell another how/to manage the swimming?"

[2]Suggesting an inner voice that projects itself to the east of Gloucester. *The Maximus Poems* later stress the fact that Maximus of Tyre lived on an island (off-shore from Asia Minor) which was made into a peninsula by a mole built by Alexander the Great, even as Cape Ann is an island made into a peninsula by the highway bridge of Route 128.

[3]An ancient Greek shallow cup with tall stem, evoked by the bird's flight and the shape of Gloucester harbor. These invocational lines recall and revise the seagull imagery that opens Hart Crane's modern "epic," *The Bridge* (see "To Brooklyn Bridge" in this volume).

[4]Franciscan friar and saint (1195–1231), patron of the Portuguese fishing community of Gloucester.

2

love is form, and cannot be without
20 important substance (the weight
say, 58 carats each one of us, perforce
our goldsmith's scale

                   feather to feather added
                   (and what is mineral, what
25   is curling hair, the string
                you carry in your nervous beak, these

                make bulk, these, in the end, are
                the sum[5]
                (o my lady of good voyage[6]
30   in whose arm, whose left arm rests
no boy but a carefully carved wood, a painted face, a schooner!
a delicate mast, as bow-sprit for

                       forwarding

3

the underpart is, though stemmed, uncertain
35 is, as sex is, as moneys are, facts!
facts, to be dealt with, as the sea is, the demand
that they be played by, that they only can be, that they must
be played by, said he, coldly, the
ear!

40 By ear, he sd.
But that which matters, that which insists, that which will last,
that! o my people, where shall you find it, how, where, where shall
    you listen
when all is become billboards, when, all, even silence, is spray-gunned?

45 when even our bird, my roofs,
cannot be heard

when even you, when sound itself is neoned in?

---

[5]An allusion to the preface of Williams's *Paterson:* "To make a start,/out of particulars/and make them general, rolling/up the sum, by defective means—."

[6]At the top of the Church of Our Lady of Good Voyage, in the Portuguese community of Gloucester, is a statue of Our Lady holding a schooner. She is the invoked muse of the poem, the guide on its voyage.

when, on the hill, over the water
where she who used to sing,
50 when the water glowed,
black, gold, the tide
outward, at evening

when bells came like boats
over the oil-slicks, milkweed
55 hulls

And a man slumped,
attentionless,
against pink shingles

o sea city)

4

60 one loves only form,
and form only comes
into existence when
the thing is born

born of yourself, born
65 of hay and cotton struts,
of street-pickings, wharves, weeds
you carry in, my bird

of a bone of a fish
of a straw, or will
70 of a color, of a bell
of yourself, torn

5

love is not easy
but how shall you know,
New England, now
75 that pejorocracy[7] is here, how
that street-cars, o Oregon, twitter[8]

---

[7]See note 26 to "The Kingfishers," above.
[8]At the time of the poem, streetcars in the East (though presumably not in Oregon) were piping in recorded music for the passengers.

in the afternoon, offend
a black-gold loin?

how shall you strike,[9]
80   o swordsman, the blue-red back
when, last night, your aim
was mu-sick, mu-sick, mu-sick[10]
And not the cribbage game?

(o Gloucester-man,
85   weave
your birds and fingers
new, your roof-tops,
clean shit upon racks
sunned on
90   American
braid
with others like you, such
extricable surface
as faun and oral,
95   satyr lesbos vase[11]

o kill kill kill kill kill[12]
those
who advertise you
out)

6

100 in! in! the bow-sprit, bird, the beak
in, the bend is, in, goes in, the form
that which you make, what holds, which is
the law of object, strut after strut, what you are, what you must be, what
the force can throw up, can, right now hereinafter erect,
105 the mast, the mast, the tender
mast!

The nest, I say, to you, I Maximus, say
under the hand, as I see it, over the waters

---

[9]A "striker" is a swordfish harpooner.
[10]Recalling a popular song, "Music, Music, Music."
[11]The lines suggest the classical Greek ("oral culture" and the island of Lesbos) and also modes of sexuality.
[12]Echoing Shakespeare, *King Lear*, 4. 6. 191.

from this place where I am, where I hear,
110   can still hear

from where I carry you a feather
as though, sharp, I picked up,
in the afternoon delivered you
a jewel,
115   it flashing more than a wing,
than any old romantic thing,
than memory, than place,
than anything other than that which you carry

than that which is,
120   call it a nest, around the head of, call it
the next second

than that which you
can do!

1953

Maximus, to himself[1]

I have had to learn the simplest things
last. Which made for difficulties.
Even at sea I was slow, to get the hand out, or to cross
a wet deck.
5   The sea was not, finally, my trade.
But even my trade, at it, I stood estranged
from that which was most familiar.[2] Was delayed,
and not content with the man's argument
that such postponement
10 is now the nature of
obedience,
           that we are all late
           in a slow time,
           that we grow up many

---

[1]The twelfth poem in *The Maximus Poems.*
[2]Olson often quoted, and later chose as epi-graph for *The Special View of History,* a dictum he attributed to Heraclitus: "Man is estranged from that [with] which he is most familiar."

That seems to be Olson's own condensation of Heraclitus's Fragments 1 and 2, which he here ("the man's argument") paraphrases at greater length.

15   And the single
            is not easily
            known

It could be, though the sharpness (the *achiote*)[3]
I note in others,
20 makes more sense
than my own distances. The agilities

        they show daily
        who do the world's
        businesses
25   And who do nature's
        as I have no sense
        I have done either

I have made dialogues,
have discussed ancient texts,
30 have thrown what light I could, offered
what pleasures
doceat[4] allows

        But the known?
This, I have had to be given,
35 a life, love, and from one man[5]
the world.

        Tokens.
        But sitting here
        I look out as a wind
40   and water man, testing
        And missing
        some proof

I know the quarters
of the weather, where it comes from,
45 where it goes. But the stem of me,

---

[3]Spanish: The seeds of the annatto tree, which are surrounded by a dark red pulp. When crushed to a paste, *achiote* can impart to food a deep, golden-yellow color. Delicate in flavor but often combined with further seasoning, *achiote* is widely used in Yucatán cooking, where Olson would have encountered it.
[4]Teaching, or to teach (from Latin *docere*).

Pound, in *Make It New*, p. 8, quotes Rudolf Agricola's statement of the three proper functions of literature: "*Ut doceat, ut moveat, ut delectet*" ("to teach, to move, or to delight").
[5]Robert Creeley, Olson's friend and colleague, to whom (as "the Figure of Outward") he dedicated *The Maximus Poems*.

this I took from their welcome,
or their rejection, of me

And my arrogance
was neither diminished
50   nor increased,
by the communication

2

It is undone business
I speak of, this morning,
with the sea
55 stretching out
from my feet

1956

Elizabeth Bishop 1911–1979

Elizabeth Bishop was the only child of William Thomas Bishop and Gertrude (Bulmer) Bishop. William, the oldest son of John W. Bishop of Prince Edward Island, was a contractor responsible for many public buildings in Boston (including the Museum of Fine Arts and the Boston Public Library). He married Gertrude Bulmer of Great Village, Nova Scotia, and died when Elizabeth was but eight months old. When the poet was four years old, her mother, after years of nervous breakdowns, was permanently placed in a mental institution. Elizabeth spent summers with her maternal grandparents in Nova Scotia and was intermittently cared for by her paternal grandparents in Worcester and later by a married but childless aunt in and around Boston. Bishop's childhood was spent in the company of adults; in her early years, she had little opportunity for contact with members of her own generation.

Chronically ill with asthma, Bishop was unable to attend school until 1927, when she enrolled at Walnut Hill School in Nat-

ick, Massachusetts. Sailing (two months at "The Nautical Camp for Girls" on Cape Cod), reading, and music were her early and enduring enthusiasms. When she entered Vassar College in 1930 she was undecided as to whether she would major in music, literature, or medicine. Though that Vassar class would come to be known as a particularly literary group (Muriel Rukeyser and Mary McCarthy were co-editors with Bishop of the student literary magazine, *Con Spirito*), Bishop did not meet her literary mentor, Marianne Moore, at Vassar but in the entry way of the New York Public Library. The Vassar College librarian had arranged a meeting after Bishop expressed an interest in Marianne Moore's poetry; the meeting led to a lifelong friendship.

Marianne Moore was Bishop's first life example, editor, confidante, and typist. In an age when women lacked women as role models, Moore emerged as one of the earliest as well as most significant reference points in the younger poet's world. As Bishop would later recall, Moore offered a rare confluence of manners and morals, a life as distinctly styled as her poetry. Correspondence between the poets reveals a protégée influenced by, yet resistant to, the poetic style of her mentor. While comparisons are inevitable, Bishop repeatedly distinguished her aesthetic as quite traditional in comparison with Moore's unique brand of modernism. Curiously, poets as diverse as George Herbert and Gerard Manley Hopkins, Emerson, Thoreau, and Neruda greatly influenced Bishop's early work.

Robert Lowell's intuitive and precise review of *North & South* (*Sewanee Review*, 1947) brought the poets together for a lifetime of correspondence. Though Lowell repeatedly confessed his debt to Bishop's poetry, her debt to his is less well known. For Bishop, Lowell represented the quintessential American: male and historically significant. Indeed, he became her "other." Even as *Questions of Travel* seems a reply to Lowell's earlier *Life Studies, Geography III* seems unimaginable without Lowell's struggle to place life at the center of the lyric.

Although Moore and Lowell served as her sponsors, Bishop returned that favor in correspondence, friendship, and support of May Swenson. The voluminous collection of letters between these poets (Washington University Library Special Collections) describes a mutual female bonding and support. Swenson is as tough-minded as the young Bishop was but she refuses to see the role of mentor as exclusively Bishop's. Swenson enters into a lively critical discussion with Bishop, often assuming the role of teacher herself. The reserve that marks the Moore-Bishop letters fades into an eloquent democracy in the Bishop-Swenson letters.

Bishop's literary development is best known through letters because she spent most of her adult life in Brazil, away from the stresses and competitiveness of the New York literary world. Though Moore, Lowell, Randall Jarrell, and Swenson kept her informed about the American poetry world, she was able to live a life of tropical remove with her Brazilian friend, Lota Costellat de Macedo Soares. Witness to overwhelming poverty, political instabilities, and a mixture of foreign cultures, Bishop, armed with a small trust fund, could afford to keep these distractions at bay while she traveled, observed, and wrote.

Keenly observed description and a dependence upon the things of this world characterize Bishop's work. In language, she is a direct descendant of what Perry Miller called the American plain stylists. Like Robert Frost, she effects a wide tonal range within a remarkably narrow range of words, often accomplished through formal means. In "Filling Station," Bishop uses the restrictions of form to impose limitations upon the tone and atmosphere of the poem. Solitary figures in the landscape abound in her poems and suggest the familiar Romantic lyric of the isolated hero, the Wordsworthian self-discoverer; yet she systematically rejects epiphany, preferring the familiarity of the phenomenal world. Bishop's early interest in surrealism surfaces throughout her work in dreamscapes of different sorts. "The Man-Moth" explores the nightmarish uncertainties of the night world, while invoking the poet's interest in the perceptions of exiles. Like many American writers, she prizes the isolated moral force. Like Emerson's poetry, Bishop sees, names, and gives the landscape a moral form and purpose.

Much has been made of Bishop's reticence. Octavio Paz proclaimed it a power, a womanly strength; Sylvia Plath and Adrienne Rich, searching for appropriate woman poets as models, rejected it as a kind of repression. Bishop's refusal to appear in women's anthologies did not stem from an avoidance of women's issues (she had lived her life as an independent artist), but rather from a lifelong commitment to the transcendent potential of art, a belief that literature should address that world beyond life's limitations.

C. K. Doreski
Boston University

PRIMARY WORKS

North & South, 1946; *Poems: North & South—A Cold Spring* (Pulitzer Prize, 1956); *Questions of Travel*, 1965; *The Complete Poems*, 1969; *Geography III*, 1976; *The Complete Poems, 1927–1979*, 1983; *The Collected Prose*, 1984.

The Fish

I caught a tremendous fish
and held him beside the boat
half out of water, with my hook
fast in a corner of his mouth.
5 He didn't fight.
He hadn't fought at all.
He hung a grunting weight,
battered and venerable
and homely. Here and there
10 his brown skin hung in strips
like ancient wallpaper,
and its pattern of darker brown
was like wallpaper:
shapes like full-blown roses
15 stained and lost through age.
He was speckled with barnacles,
fine rosettes of lime,
and infested
with tiny white sea-lice,
20 and underneath two or three
rags of green weed hung down.
While his gills were breathing in
the terrible oxygen
—the frightening gills,
25 fresh and crisp with blood,
that can cut so badly—
I thought of the coarse white flesh
packed in like feathers,
the big bones and the little bones,
30 the dramatic reds and blacks
of his shiny entrails,
and the pink swim-bladder
like a big peony.
I looked into his eyes
35 which were far larger than mine
but shallower, and yellowed,

the irises backed and packed
with tarnished tinfoil
seen through the lenses
40 of old scratched isinglass.
They shifted a little, but not
to return my stare.
—It was more like the tipping
of an object toward the light.
45 I admired his sullen face,
the mechanism of his jaw,
and then I saw
that from his lower lip
—if you could call it a lip—
50 grim, wet, and weaponlike,
hung five old pieces of fish-line,
or four and a wire leader
with the swivel still attached,
with all their five big hooks
55 grown firmly in his mouth.
A green line, frayed at the end
where he broke it, two heavier lines,
and a fine black thread
still crimped from the strain and snap
60 when it broke and he got away.
Like medals with their ribbons
frayed and wavering,
a five-haired beard of wisdom
trailing from his aching jaw.
65 I stared and stared
and victory filled up
the little rented boat,
from the pool of bilge
where oil had spread a rainbow
70 around the rusted engine
to the bailer rusted orange,
the sun-cracked thwarts,
the oarlocks on their strings,
the gunnels—until everything
75 was rainbow, rainbow, rainbow!
And I let the fish go.

1946

The Man-Moth[1]

Here, above,
cracks in the buildings are filled with battered moonlight.
The whole shadow of Man is only as big as his hat.
It lies at his feet like a circle for a doll to stand on,
5 and he makes an inverted pin, the point magnetized to the moon.
He does not see the moon; he observes only her vast properties,
feeling the queer light on his hands, neither warm nor cold,
of a temperature impossible to record in thermometers.

But when the Man-Moth
10 pays his rare, although occasional, visits to the surface,
the moon looks rather different to him. He emerges
from an opening under the edge of one of the sidewalks
and nervously begins to scale the faces of the buildings.
He thinks the moon is a small hole at the top of the sky,
15 proving the sky quite useless for protection.
He trembles, but must investigate as high as he can climb.

Up the façades,
his shadow dragging like a photographer's cloth behind him,
he climbs fearfully, thinking that this time he will manage
20 to push his small head through that round clean opening
and be forced through, as from a tube, in black scrolls on the
     light.
(Man, standing below him, has no such illusions.)
But what the Man-Moth fears most he must do, although
25 he fails, of course, and falls back scared but quite unhurt.

Then he returns
to the pale subways of cement he calls his home. He flits,
he flutters, and cannot get aboard the silent trains
fast enough to suit him. The doors close swiftly.
30 The Man-Moth always seats himself facing the wrong way
and the train starts at once at its full, terrible speed,
without a shift in gears or a gradation of any sort.
He cannot tell the rate at which he travels backwards.

Each night he must
35 be carried through artificial tunnels and dream recurrent dreams.
Just as the ties recur beneath his train, these underlie
his rushing brain. He does not dare look out the window,

---

[1]Newspaper misprint for "mammoth."

for the third rail, the unbroken draught of poison,
runs there beside him. He regards it as a disease
40 he has inherited the susceptibility to. He has to keep
his hands in his pockets, as others must wear mufflers.

    If you catch him,
hold up a flashlight to his eye. It's all dark pupil,
an entire night itself, whose haired horizon tightens
45 as he stares back, and closes up the eye. Then from the lids
one tear, his only possession, like the bee's sting, slips.
Slyly he palms it, and if you're not paying attention
he'll swallow it. However, if you watch, he'll hand it over,
cool as from underground springs and pure enough to drink.

                                                    1946

At the Fishhouses

Although it is a cold evening,
down by one of the fishhouses
an old man sits netting,
his net, in the gloaming almost invisible,
5   a dark purple-brown,
and his shuttle worn and polished.
The air smells so strong of codfish
it makes one's nose run and one's eyes water.
The five fishhouses have steeply peaked roofs
10 and narrow, cleated gangplanks slant up
to storerooms in the gables
for the wheelbarrows to be pushed up and down on.
All is silver: the heavy surface of the sea,
swelling slowly as if considering spilling over,
15 is opaque, but the silver of the benches,
the lobster pots, and masts, scattered
among the wild jagged rocks,
is of an apparent translucence
like the small old buildings with an emerald moss
20 growing on their shoreward walls.
The big fish tubs are completely lined
with layers of beautiful herring scales
and the wheelbarrows are similarly plastered
with creamy iridescent coats of mail,
25 with small iridescent flies crawling on them.
Up on the little slope behind the houses,

set in the sparse bright sprinkle of grass,
is an ancient wooden capstan,
cracked, with two long bleached handles
30 and some melancholy stains, like dried blood,
where the ironwork has rusted.
The old man accepts a Lucky Strike.
He was a friend of my grandfather.
We talk of the decline in the population
35 and of codfish and herring
while he waits for a herring boat to come in.
There are sequins on his vest and on his thumb.
He has scraped the scales, the principal beauty,
from unnumbered fish with that black old knife,
40 the blade of which is almost worn away.

Down at the water's edge, at the place
where they haul up the boats, up the long ramp
descending into the water, thin silver
tree trunks are laid horizontally
45 across the gray stones, down and down
at intervals of four or five feet.

Cold dark deep and absolutely clear,
element bearable to no mortal,
to fish and to seals . . . One seal particularly
50 I have seen here evening after evening.
He was curious about me. He was interested in music;
like me a believer in total immersion,
so I used to sing him Baptist hymns.
I also sang "A Mighty Fortress Is Our God."
55 He stood up in the water and regarded me
steadily, moving his head a little.
Then he would disappear, then suddenly emerge
almost in the same spot, with a sort of shrug
as if it were against his better judgment.
60 Cold dark deep and absolutely clear,
the clear gray icy water . . . Back, behind us,
the dignified tall firs begin.
Bluish, associating with their shadows,
a million Christmas trees stand
65 waiting for Christmas. The water seems suspended
above the rounded gray and blue-gray stones.
I have seen it over and over, the same sea, the same,
slightly, indifferently swinging above the stones,
icily free above the stones,
70 above the stones and then the world.
If you should dip your hand in,

your wrist would ache immediately,
your bones would begin to ache and your hand would burn
as if the water were a transmutation of fire
75 that feeds on stones and burns with a dark gray flame.
If you tasted it, it would first taste bitter,
then briny, then surely burn your tongue.
It is like what we imagine knowledge to be:
dark, salt, clear, moving, utterly free,
80 drawn from the cold hard mouth
of the world, derived from the rocky breasts
forever, flowing and drawn, and since
our knowledge is historical, flowing, and flown.

1955

Filling Station

Oh, but it is dirty!
—this little filling station,
oil-soaked, oil-permeated
to a disturbing, over-all
5 black translucency.
Be careful with that match!

Father wears a dirty,
oil-soaked monkey suit
that cuts him under the arms,
10 and several quick and saucy
and greasy sons assist him
(it's a family filling station),
all quite thoroughly dirty.

Do they live in the station?
15 It has a cement porch
behind the pumps, and on it
a set of crushed and grease-
impregnated wickerwork;
on the wicker sofa
20 a dirty dog, quite comfy.

Some comic books provide
the only note of color—
of certain color. They lie

upon a big dim doily
25 draping a taboret[1]
(part of the set), beside
a big hirsute begonia.

Why the extraneous plant?
Why the taboret?
30 Why, oh why, the doily?
(Embroidered in daisy stitch
with marguerites, I think,
and heavy with gray crochet.)

Somebody embroidered the doily.
35 Somebody waters the plant,
or oils it, maybe. Somebody
arranges the rows of cans
so that they softly say:
ESSO—SO—SO—SO
40 to high-strung automobiles.
Somebody loves us all.

1965

Bienvenido N. Santos 1911–1996

Throughout his career, Bienvenido N. Santos meditated again and again on a condition that is perhaps best diagnosed by the narrator of his story "Scent of Apples": "certain ideals, certain beliefs, even illusions peculiar to the exile." For Santos, exile was much more than a literary trope. He often described himself and his work as indelibly marked by the alienation, loneliness, and longing that were produced by a lifetime of transnational experiences.

As a writer, Santos came to think of himself as "belong[ing] to the literature of two great countries: the Philippines, land of my birth; and the United States, sanctuary, a second home." Santos was one of the first Filipino writers to publish literature in English in both countries, and he had a prolific, noteworthy career. In 1941, after he completed his undergraduate education at the University of the Philippines, Santos was awarded a scholarship for study abroad and attended the University of Illinois at Urbana-Champaign, where he received a master of arts in English. But when the United States became involved World War II, many Filipinas and Filipinos were unable to return home. In 1942, the U.S. government summoned Santos to work for the war effort in Washington, D.C. Santos wrote speeches and articles as part of a public relations venture to educate Americans about the war in the Pacific, and he toured the country giving lectures about the Philippines. This experience became the autobiographical basis for stories like "Scent of Apples."

Although Santos eventually became a U.S. citizen, he lived, taught, and wrote in both countries until he died. He participated in creative writing workshops at

[1]Small stand.

Columbia, Harvard, and the University of Iowa, and he taught at a wide range of institutions, such as Ohio State University, University of Iowa, Wichita State University, University of the Philippines, Ateneo de Manila University, and De La Salle University in Manila. He held honorary doctorates from institutions in both countries, and he received multiple awards, including the Manila Critics Circle National Book Award and fellowships from the Rockefeller Foundation, Guggenheim Foundation, and National Endowment for the Arts.

In the United States, "Scent of Apples" is Santos's best-known work. He originally published the story in the Philippines as part of the collection *You Lovely People,* and he later included it in the warmly praised, U.S-published collection *Scent of Apples* (1979). "Scent of Apples" highlights recurring formal and thematic features in Santos's short stories. In the story, an unnamed "first class Filipino" narrator encounters Celestino Fabia, who describes himself as "just a Filipino farmer" in Michigan. Ultimately, the narrator sympathizes with Fabia's need to believe in an idealized memory of "our Filipino women" as a link to his lost home in the Philippines. Through the developing relationship between these men and a contrast in their narrative perspectives, the story reflects on Filipino immigration and exile; the tensions between an older group of Filipinos who migrated to the United States as laborers and a younger, mobile, and elite generation of Filipinos; and the place of women in the imaginations of Filipinos abroad.

Denise Cruz
Indiana University, Bloomington

WORKS

You Lovely People, 1955; *The Wounded Stag: Fifty-Four Poems,* 1956; *Brother My Brother,* 1960; *Villa Magdalena,* 1965; *The Volcano,* 1965; *The Day the Dancers Came,* 1967; *Scent of Apples,* 1979; *The Praying Man,* 1982; *The Man Who (Thought He) Looked Like Robert Taylor,* 1983; *Distances in Time,* 1983; *Dwell in the Wilderness,* 1985; *What the Hell for You Left Your Heart in San Francisco,* 1987; *Memory's Fictions: A Personal History,* 1993; *Postscript to a Saintly Life,* 1994; *Letters,* 1995.

Scent of Apples

When I arrived in Kalamazoo it was October and the war was still on. Gold and silver stars hung on pennants above silent windows of white and brick-red cottages. In a backyard an old man burned leaves and twigs while a grey-haired woman sat on the porch, her red hands quiet on her lap, watching the smoke rising above the elms, both of them thinking of the same thought perhaps, about a tall, grinning boy with blue eyes and flying hair, who went out to war: where could he be now this month when leaves were turning into gold and the fragrance of gathered apples was in the wind?

It was a cold night when I left my room at the hotel for a usual speaking arrangement. I walked but a little way. A heavy wind coming up from Lake Michigan was icy on the face. It felt like winter straying early in the northern woodlands. Under the lampposts the leaves shone like bronze. And they rolled on the pavements like the ghost feet of a thousand autumns long dead, long before the boys left for faraway lands without great icy winds and promise of winter early in the air, lands without apple trees, *the singing and the gold!*

It was the same night I met Celestino Fabia, "just like a Filipino farmer" as he called himself, who had a farm about thirty miles east of Kalamazoo.

"You came all that way on a night like this just to hear me talk?" I asked.

"I've seen no Filipino for so many years now," he answered quickly. "So when I saw your name in the papers where it says you come from the Islands and that you're going to talk, I come right away."

Earlier that night I had addressed a college crowd, mostly women. It appeared that they wanted me to talk about my country; they wanted me to tell them things about it because my country had become a lost country. Everywhere in the land the enemy stalked. Over it a great silence hung; and their boys were there, unheard from, or they were on their way to some little known island on the Pacific, young boys all, hardly men, thinking of harvest moons and smell of forest fire.

It was not hard talking about our own people. I knew them well and I loved them. And they seemed so far away during those terrible years that I must have spoken of them with a little fervor, a little nostalgia.

In the open forum that followed, the audience wanted to know whether there was much difference between our women and the American women. I tried to answer the question as best as I could, saying, among other things, that I did not know much about American women, except that they looked friendly, but differences or similarities in inner qualities such as naturally belonged to the heart or to the mind, I could only speak about with vagueness.

While I was trying to explain away the fact that it was not easy to make comparisons, a man rose from the rear of the hall, wanting to say something. In the distance, he looked slight and old and very brown. Even before he spoke, I knew that he was, like me, a Filipino.

"I'm a Filipino," he began, loud and clear, in a voice that seemed used to wide open spaces, "I'm just a Filipino farmer out in the country." He waved his hand towards the door. "I left the Philippines more than twenty years ago and have never been back. Never will perhaps. I want to find out, sir, are our Filipino women the same like they were twenty years ago?"

As he sat down, the hall filled with voices, hushed and intrigued. I weighed my answer carefully. I did not want to tell a lie yet I did not want to say anything that would seem platitudinous, insincere. But more important than these considerations, it seemed to me that moment as I looked towards my countryman, I must give him an answer that would not make him so unhappy. Surely, all these years, he must have held on to certain ideals, certain beliefs, even illusions peculiar to the exile.

"First," I said as the voices gradually died down and every eye seemed upon me, "First, tell me what our women were like twenty years ago."

The man stood to answer. "Yes," he said, "you're too young . . . Twenty years ago our women were nice, they were modest, they wore their hair long, they dressed proper and went for no monkey business. They were natural, they went to church regular, and they were faithful." He had spoken slowly, and now in what seemed like an afterthought, added, "It's the men who ain't."

Now I knew what I was going to say.

"Well," I began, "it will interest you to know that our women have changed— but definitely! The change, however, has been on the outside only. Inside, here," pointing to the heart, "they are the same as they were twenty years ago. God-fearing, faithful, modest, and *nice*."

The man was visibly moved. "I'm very happy, sir," he said, in the manner of one who, having stakes on the land, had found no cause to regret one's sentimental investment.

After this, everything that was said and done in that hall that night seemed like an anti-climax; and later, as we walked outside, he gave me his name and told me of his farm thirty miles east of the city.

We had stopped at the main entrance to the hotel lobby. We had not talked very much on the way. As a matter of fact, we were never alone. Kindly American friends talked to us, asked us questions, said goodnight. So now I asked him whether he cared to step into the lobby with me and talk.

"No, thank you," he said, "you are tired. And I don't want to stay out too late."

"Yes, you live very far."

"I got a car," he said, "besides . . ."

Now he smiled, he truly smiled. All night I had been watching his face and I wondered when he was going to smile.

"Will you do me a favor, please," he continued smiling almost sweetly. "I want you to have dinner with my family out in the country. I'd call for you tomorrow afternoon, then drive you back. Will that be all right?"

"Of course," I said. "I'd love to meet your family." I was leaving Kalamazoo for Muncie, Indiana, in two days. There was plenty of time.

"You will make my wife very happy," he said.

"You flatter me."

"Honest. She'll be very happy. Ruth is a country girl and hasn't met many Filipinos. I mean Filipinos younger than I, cleaner looking. We're just poor farmer folk, you know, and we don't get to town very often. Roger, that's my boy, he goes to school in town. A bus takes him early in the morning and he's back in the afternoon. He's nice boy."

I bet he is," I agreed. "I've seen the children of some of the boys by their American wives and the boys are tall, taller than the father, and very good looking."

"Roger, he'd be tall. You'll like him."

Then he said goodbye and I waved to him as he disappeared in the darkness.

The next day he came, at about three in the afternoon. There was a mild, ineffectual sun shining; and it was not too cold. He was wearing an old brown tweed jacket and worsted trousers to match. His shoes were polished, and although the green of his tie seemed faded, a colored shirt hardly accentuated it. He looked younger than he appeared the night before now that he was clean shaven and seemed ready to go to a party. He was grinning as we met.

"Oh, Ruth can't believe it. She can't believe it," he kept repeating as he led me to his car—a nondescript thing in faded black that had known better days and many hands. "I says to her, I'm bringing you a first class Filipino, and she says, aw, go away, quit kidding, there's no such thing as first class Filipino. But Roger, that's my boy, he believed me immediately. What's he like, daddy, he asks. Oh, you will see, I says, he's first class. Like you daddy? No, no, I laugh at him, your daddy ain't first class. Aw, but you are, daddy, he says. So you can see what a nice boy he is, so innocent. Then Ruth starts griping about the house, but the house is a mess, she says. True it's a mess, it's always a mess, but you don't mind, do you? We're poor folks, you know."

The trip seemed interminable. We passed through narrow lanes and disappeared into thickets, and came out on barren land overgrown with weeds in places. All around were dead leaves and dry earth. In the distance were apple trees.

"Aren't those apple trees?" I asked wanting to be sure.

"Yes, those are apple trees," he replied. "Do you like apples? I got lots of 'em. I got an apple orchard, I'll show you."

All the beauty of the afternoon seemed in the distance, on the hills, in the dull soft sky.

"Those trees are beautiful on the hills," I said.

"Autumn's a lovely season. The trees are getting ready to die, and they show their colors, proud-like."

"No such thing in our own country," I said.

That remark seemed unkind, I realized later. It touched him off on a long deserted tangent, but ever there perhaps. How many times did the lonely mind take unpleasant detours away from the familiar winding lanes towards home for fear of this, the remembered hurt, the long lost youth, the grim shadows of the years; how many times indeed, only the exile knows.

It was a rugged road we were travelling and the car made so much noise that I could not hear everything he said, but I understood him. He was telling his story for the first time in many years. He was remembering his own youth. He was thinking of home. In these odd moments there seemed no cause for fear no cause at all, no pain. That would come later. In the night perhaps. Or lonely on the farm under the apple trees.

In this old Visyan town, the streets are narrow and dirty and strewn with corral shells. You have been there? You could not have missed our house, it was the biggest in town, one of the oldest, ours was a big family. The house stood right on the edge of the street. A door opened heavily and you enter a dark hall leading to the stairs. There is the smell of chickens roosting on the low topped walls, there is the familiar sound they make and you grope your way up a massive staircase, the bannisters smooth upon the trembling hand. Such nights, they are no better than days, windows are closed against the sun; they close heavily.

Mother sits in her corner looking very white and sick. This was her world, her domain. In all these years I cannot remember the sound of her voice. Father was different. He moved about. He shouted. He ranted. He lived in the past and talked of honor as though it were the only thing.

I was born in that house. I grew up there into a pampered brat. I was mean. One day I broke their hearts. I saw mother cry wordlessly as father heaped his curses upon me and drove me out of the house, the gate closing heavily after me. And my brothers and sisters took up my father's hate for me and multiplied it numberless times in their own broken hearts. I was no good.

But sometimes, you know, I miss that house, the roosting chickens on the low-topped walls. I miss my brothers and sisters. Mother sitting in her chair, looking like a pale ghost in a corner of the room. I would remember the great live posts, massive tree trunks from the forests. Leafy plants grew on the sides, buds pointing downwards, wilted and died before they could become flowers. As they fell on the floor, father bent to pick them and throw them out into the corral streets. His hands were strong. I have kissed those hands . . . many times, many times.

Finally we rounded a deep curve and suddenly came upon a shanty, all but ready to crumble in a heap on the ground, its plastered walls were rotting away, the floor was hardly a foot from the ground. I thought of the cottages of the poor colored folk in the south, the hovels of the poor everywhere in the land. This one stood all by itself as though by common consent all the folk that used to live here had decided to stay away, despising it, ashamed of it. Even the lovely season could not color it with beauty.

A dog barked loudly as we approached. A fat blonde woman stood at the door with a little boy by her side. Roger seemed newly scrubbed. He hardly took his eyes off me. Ruth had a clean apron around her shapeless waist. Now as she shook my hands in sincere delight I noticed shamefacedly (that I should notice) how rough her hands, how coarse and red with labor, how ugly! She was no longer young and her smile was pathetic.

As we stepped inside and the door closed behind us, immediately I was aware of the familiar scent of apples. The room was bare except for a few ancient pieces of second-hand furniture. In the middle of the room stood a stove to keep the family warm in winter. The walls were bare. Over the dining table hung a lamp yet unlighted.

Ruth got busy with the drinks. She kept coming in and out of a rear room that must have been the kitchen and soon the table was heavy with food, fried chicken legs and rice, and green peas and corn on the ear. Even as we ate, Ruth kept standing, and going to the kitchen for more food. Roger ate like a little gentleman.

"Isn't he nice looking?" his father asked.

"You are a handsome boy, Roger," I said.

The boy smiled at me. "You look like Daddy," he said.

Afterwards I noticed an old picture leaning on the top of a dresser and stood to pick it up. It was yellow and soiled with many fingerings. The faded figure of a woman in Philippine dress could yet be distinguished although the face had become a blur.

"Your . . ." I began.

"I don't know who she is," Fabia hastened to say. "I picked that picture many years ago in a room on La Salle Street in Chicago. I have often wondered who she is."

"The face wasn't a blur in the beginning?"

"Oh, no. It was a young face and good."

Ruth came with a plate full of apples.

"Ah," I cried, picking out a ripe one, "I've been thinking where all the scent of apples come from. The room is full of it."

"I'll show you," said Fabia.

He showed me a backroom, not very big. It was half-full of apples.

"Every day," he explained, "I take some of them to town to sell to the groceries. Prices have been low. I've been losing on the trips."

"These apples will spoil," I said.

"We'll feed them to the pigs."

Then he showed me around the farm. It was twilight now and the apple trees stood bare against a glowing western sky. In apple blossom time it must be lovely here, I thought. But what about wintertime?

One day, according to Fabia, a few years ago, before Roger was born, he had an attack of acute appendicitis. It was deep winter. The snow lay heavy everywhere. Ruth was pregnant and none too well herself. At first she did not know what to do. She bundled him in warm clothing and put him on a cot near the stove. She shoveled the snow from their front door and practically carried the suffering man on her shoulders, dragging him through the newly made path towards the road where they waited for the U.S. Mail car to pass. Meanwhile snowflakes poured all over them and she kept rubbing the man's arms and legs as she herself nearly froze to death.

"Go back to the house, Ruth!" her husband cried, "you'll freeze to death."

But she clung to him wordlessly. Even as she massaged his arms and legs, her tears rolled down her cheeks. "I won't leave you, I won't leave you," she repeated.

Finally the U.S. Mail car arrived. The mailman, who knew them well, helped them board the car, and, without stopping on his usual route, took the sick man and his wife direct to the nearest hospital.

Ruth stayed in the hospital with Fabia. She slept in a corridor outside the patients' ward and in the day time helped in scrubbing the floor and washing the dishes and cleaning the men's things. They didn't have enough money and Ruth was willing to work like a slave.

"Ruth's a nice girl," said Fabia, "like our own Filipino women."

Before nightfall, he took me back to the hotel. Ruth and Roger stood at the door holding hands and smiling at me. From inside the room of the shanty, a low light flickered. I had a last glimpse of the apple trees in the orchard under the darkened sky as Fabia backed up the car. And soon we were on our way back to town. The dog had started barking. We could hear it for some time, until finally, we could not hear it anymore, and all was darkness around us, except where the head lamps revealed a stretch of road leading somewhere.

Fabia did not talk this time. I didn't seem to have anything to say myself. But when finally we came to the hotel and I got down, Fabia said, "Well, I guess I won't be seeing you again."

It was dimly lighted in front of the hotel and I could hardly see Fabia's face. Without getting off the car, he moved to where I had sat, and I saw him extend his hand. I gripped it.

"Tell Ruth and Roger," I said, "I love them."

He dropped my hand quickly. "They'll be waiting for me now," he said.

"Look," I said, not knowing why I said it, "one of these days, very soon, I hope, I'll be going home. I could go to your town."

"No," he said softly, sounding very much defeated but brave, "Thanks a lot. But, you see, nobody would remember me now."

Then he started the car, and as it moved away, he waved his hand.

"Goodbye," I said, waving back into the darkness. And suddenly the night was cold like winter straying early in these northern woodlands.

I hurried inside. There was a train the next morning that left for Muncie, Indiana, at a quarter after eight.

1979

Tennessee Williams 1911–1983

Although invariably ranked second (just behind Eugene O'Neill) among American dramatists, Tennessee Williams is indisputably the most important southern playwright yet to emerge. Born Thomas Lanier Williams, in Columbus, Mississippi, where his much loved maternal grandfather was an Episcopalian minister, by 1919 he had been transplanted with his family to St. Louis, Missouri. The contrast between these two cultures—an agrarian South that looked back nostalgically to a partly mythical past of refinement and gentility, and a forward-looking urban North that valued pragmatism and practicality over civility and beauty—would haunt Williams throughout his life, providing one of the enduring tensions in his plays.

After attending the University of Missouri and Washington University in St. Louis, Williams followed his graduation from the University of Iowa in 1938 with a period of wandering around the country and a succession of odd jobs, including an unsuccessful stint as a scriptwriter in Hollywood. One of his filmscripts, however, became the genesis for his first great theatrical success during the 1944–45 season, *The Glass Menagerie.* In that "memory play," the autobiographical narrator, Tom Wingfield, hopes that by reliving his desertion of his domineering mother and physically and psychically fragile sister, Laura, he will find release from the guilt of the past, thereby allowing his full maturation as a poet. Williams's biographers Donald Spoto and Lyle Leverich remark (as have others before them) on the playwright's lasting and decisive love for his schizophrenic sister Rose, clearly the model for Laura, and at least partially for Blanche in the classic *A Streetcar Named Desire* (1947), Catherine in *Suddenly Last Summer* (1958), the sister Clare in *Out Cry* (1973), and even for the largely factual Zelda Fitzgerald in Williams's final Broadway play, *Clothes for a Summer Hotel* (1980). No other American dramatist has created women characters of such complexity, portrayed with deep understanding and sensitivity.

In his opening narration in *Menagerie,* Tom speaks of "an emissary from a world of reality that we were somehow set apart from" who threatens to upset the fragile escape into illusion that serves repeatedly in Williams's dramas as a refuge for those who are physically, emotionally, or spiritually misbegotten and vulnerable, and yet because of this somehow special. One of Williams's chief characteristics as a dramatist is his compassion for misfits and outsiders, perhaps fed early on by his own sexual orientation (he frankly discusses his homosexuality in the confessional *Memoirs*) and later, in the two decades before his death, by the increasingly negative critical reception of works that become excessively private. If there is a central ethical norm by which his characters must live, it is surely that espoused by the nonjudgmental artist Hannah in *Night of the Iguana* (1961): "Nothing human disgusts me unless it's unkind, violent."

Williams was a prolific author, a two-time winner of the Pulitzer Prize for Drama (for *Streetcar* and *Cat on a Hot Tin Roof* [1955]) and a four-time recipient of the New York Drama Critics Circle Award (for the above two plays as well as for *Menagerie* and *Iguana*). Along with two dozen full-length plays and two collections of one-acts, he wrote two novels, four collections of short fiction—among his finest stories, influenced by Hawthorne and Poe, are "Desire and the Black Masseur" and "One Arm"—two volumes of poetry, and several screenplays. Most are charged with a highly expressive symbolism and imbued with his recurrent attitudes and motifs: a somewhat sentimental valuation of the lost and lonely; a worship of sexuality as a means of transcending aloneness; a castigation of repression and excessive guilt; an abhorrence of the underdeveloped heart that refuses to reach out to others; a fear of time, the enemy that robs one of physical beauty and artistic vitality; and an insistence on the need for the courage to endure, to always continue onward—as Williams himself did as a writer.

Thomas P. Adler
Purdue University

PRIMARY WORKS

Battle of Angels, 1945; *The Glass Menagerie*, 1945; *Twenty-Seven Wagons Full of Cotton & Other One-Act Plays*, 1946; *You Touched Me!*, 1947; *A Streetcar Named Desire*, 1947; *One Arm and Other Short Stories*, 1948; *Summer and Smoke*, 1948; *American Blues: Five Short Stories*, 1948; *The Roman Spring of Mrs. Stone*, 1950; *The Rose Tattoo*, 1951; *I Rise in Flame, Cried the Phoenix*, 1951; *Camino Real*, 1953; *Hard Candy*, 1954; *Cat on a Hot Tin Roof*, 1955; *In the Winter Of Cities*, 1956; *Baby Doll*, 1956; *Orpheus Descending*, 1958; *The Fugitive Kind*, 1958; *Suddenly Last Summer*, 1958; *Sweet Bird of Youth*, 1959; *Period of Adjustment*, 1960; *The Milk Train Doesn't Stop Here Any More*, 1964; *The Knightly Quest: A Novella & Four Short Stories*, 1966; *Kingdom of Earth*, 1967; *Two-Character Play*, 1969; *Dragon Country*, 1970; *Small Craft Warnings*, 1972; *Out Cry*, 1973; *Eight Mortal Ladies Possessed*, 1974; *Moise And The World Of Reason*, 1975; *Memoirs*, 1975; *Eccentricities of a Nightingale*, 1976; *Where I Live: Selected Essays*, 1978; *Something Cloudy, Something Clear*, 1981; *Clothes for a Summer Hotel*, 1981; *A House not Meant to Stand*, 1982; *In Masks Outrageous and Austere*, 1983; *Collected Stories*, 1986.

Portrait of a Madonna

Respectfully dedicated to the talent and charm of Miss Lillian Gish.[1]

CHARACTERS

Miss Lucretia Collins
The Porter
The Elevator Boy
The Doctor
The Nurse
Mr. Abrams

SCENE: *The living room of a moderate-priced city apartment. The furnishings are old-fashioned and everything is in a state of neglect and disorder. There is a door in the back wall to a bedroom, and on the right to the outside hall.*

MISS COLLINS: Richard! (*The door bursts open and Miss Collins rushes out, distract-edly. She is a middle-aged spinster, very slight and hunched of figure with a desiccated face that is flushed with excitement. Her hair is arranged in curls that would become a young girl and she wears a frilly negligee which might have come from an old hope chest of a period considerably earlier.*) No, no, no, no! I don't care if the whole church hears about it! (*She frenziedly snatches up the phone.*) Manager, I've got to speak to the manager! Hurry, oh, please hurry, there's a *man*—! (*wildly aside as if to an invisible figure*) Lost all respect, absolutely no respect! . . . Mr. Abrams? (*in a tense hushed voice*) I don't want any reporters to hear about this but something awful has been going on upstairs. Yes, this is Miss Collins' apartment on the top floor. I've refrained from making any complaint because of my connections with

---

[1]Lillian Gish (1896–1993): A demure actress of almost angelic appearance, often the heroine in distress, whose long career spanned virtually the entire history of silent and sound film.

the church. I used to be assistant to the Sunday School superintendent and I once had the primary class. I helped them put on the Christmas pageant. I made the dress for the Virgin and Mother, made robes for the Wise Men. Yes, and now this has happened, I'm not responsible for it, but night after night after night this man has been coming into my apartment and—indulging his senses! Do you understand? Not once but repeatedly, Mr. Abrams! I don't know whether he comes in the door or the window or up the fire-escape or whether there's some secret entrance they know about at the church, but he's here now, in my bedroom, and I can't force him to leave, I'll have to have some assistance! No, he isn't a thief, Mr. Abrams, he comes of a very fine family in Webb, Mississippi, but this woman has ruined his character, she's destroyed his respect for ladies! Mr. Abrams? Mr. Abrams! Oh, goodness! *(She slams up the receiver and looks distractedly about for a moment; then rushes back into the bedroom.)* Richard! *(The door slams shut. After a few moments an old porter enters in drab gray cover-alls. He looks about with a sorrowfully humorous curiosity, then timidly calls.)*

PORTER: Miss Collins? *(The elevator door slams open in hall and the Elevator Boy, wearing a uniform, comes in.)*

ELEVATOR BOY: Where is she?

PORTER: Gone in 'er bedroom.

ELEVATOR BOY: *(grinning)* She got him in there with her?

PORTER: Sounds like it. *(Miss Collins' voice can be heard faintly protesting with the mysterious intruder.)*

ELEVATOR BOY: What'd Abrams tell yuh to do?

PORTER: Stay here an' keep a watch on 'er till they git here.

ELEVATOR BOY: Jesus.

PORTER: Close 'at door.

ELEVATOR BOY: I gotta leave it open a little so I can hear the buzzer. Ain't this place a holy sight though?

PORTER: Don't look like it's had a good cleaning in fifteen or twenty years. I bet it ain't either. Abrams'll bust a bloodvessel when he takes a lookit them walls.

ELEVATOR BOY: How comes it's in this condition?

PORTER: She wouldn't let no one in.

ELEVATOR BOY: Not even the paper-hangers?

PORTER: Naw. Not even the plumbers. The plaster washed down in the bathroom underneath hers an' she admitted her plumbin' had been stopped up. Mr. Abrams had to let the plumber in with this here pass-key when she went out for a while.

ELEVATOR BOY: Holy Jeez. I wunner if she's got money stashed around here. A lotta freaks do stick away big sums of money in ole mattresses an' things.

PORTER: She ain't. She got a monthly pension check or something she always turned over to Mr. Abrams to dole it out to 'er. She tole him that Southern ladies was never brought up to manage finanshul affairs. Lately the checks quit comin'.

ELEVATOR BOY: Yeah?

PORTER: The pension give out or somethin'. Abrams says he got a contribution from the church to keep 'er on here without 'er knowin' about it. She's proud as a peacock's tail in spite of 'er awful appearance.

ELEVATOR BOY: Lissen to 'er in there!

PORTER: What's she sayin'?

ELEVATOR BOY: Apologizin' to him! For callin' the *police!*

PORTER: She thinks police 're comin'?

MISS COLLINS: *(from bedroom)* Stop it, it's got to stop!

ELEVATOR BOY: Fightin' to protect her honor again! What a commotion, no wunner folks are complainin'!

PORTER: *(lighting his pipe)* This here'll be the last time.

ELEVATOR BOY: She's goin' out, huh?

PORTER: *(blowing out the match)* Tonight.

ELEVATOR BOY: Where'll she go?

PORTER: *(slowly moving to the old gramophone)* She'll go to the state asylum.

ELEVATOR BOY: Holy G!

PORTER: Remember this ole number? *(He puts on a record of "I'm Forever Blowing Bubbles.")*

ELEVATOR BOY: Naw. When did that come out?

PORTER: Before your time, sonny boy. Machine needs oilin'. *(He takes out small oil-can and applies oil about the crank and other parts of gramophone.)*

ELEVATOR BOY: How long is the old girl been here?

PORTER: Abrams says she's been livin' here twenty-five, thirty years, since before he got to be manager even.

ELEVATOR BOY: Livin' alone all that time?

PORTER: She had an old mother died of an operation about fifteen years ago. Since then she ain't gone out of the place excep' on Sundays to church or Friday nights to some kind of religious meeting.

ELEVATOR BOY: Got an awful lot of ol' magazines piled aroun' here.

PORTER: She used to collect 'em. She'd go out in back and fish 'em out of the incinerator.

ELEVATOR BOY: What'n hell for?

PORTER: Mr. Abrams says she used to cut out the Campbell soup kids. Them red-tomato-headed kewpie dolls that go with the soup advertisements. You seen 'em, ain'tcha?

ELEVATOR BOY: Uh-huh.

PORTER: She made a collection of 'em. Filled a big lot of scrapbooks with them paper kiddies an' took 'em down to the Children's Hospitals on Xmas Eve an' Easter Sunday, exactly twicet a year. Sounds better, don't it? *(referring to gramophone, which resumes its faint, wheedling music)* Eliminated some a that crankin' noise . . .

ELEVATOR BOY: I didn't know that she'd been nuts *that* long.

PORTER: Who's nuts an' who ain't? If you ask me the world is populated with people that's just as peculiar as she is.

ELEVATOR BOY: Hell. She don't have brain *one.*

PORTER: There's important people in Europe got less'n she's got. Tonight they're takin' her off'n' lockin' her up. They'd do a lot better to leave 'er go an' lock up some a them maniacs over there. She's harmless; they ain't. They kill millions of people an' go scot free!

ELEVATOR BOY: An ole woman like her is disgusting, though, imaginin' somebody's raped her.

PORTER: Pitiful, not disgusting. Watch out for them cigarette ashes.

ELEVATOR BOY: What's uh diff'rence? So much dust you can't see it. All a this here goes out in the morning, don't it?

PORTER: Uh-huh.

ELEVATOR BOY: I think I'll take a couple a those ole records as curiosities for my girl friend. She's got a portable in 'er bedroom, she says it's better with music!

PORTER: Leave 'em alone. She's still got 'er property rights.

ELEVATOR BOY: Aw, she's got all she wants with them dreamlovers of hers!

PORTER: Hush up! (*He makes a warning gesture as Miss Collins enters from bedroom. Her appearance is that of a ravaged woman. She leans exhaustedly in the doorway, hands clasped over her flat, virginal bosom.*)

MISS COLLINS: (*breathlessly*) Oh, Richard—Richard . . .

PORTER: (*coughing*) Miss—Collins.

ELEVATOR BOY: Hello, Miss Collins.

MISS COLLINS: (*just noticing the men*) Goodness! You've arrived already! Mother didn't tell me you were here! (*Self-consciously she touches her ridiculous corkscrew curls with the faded pink ribbon tied through them. Her manner becomes that of a slightly coquettish but prim little Southern belle.*) I must ask you gentlemen to excuse the terrible disorder.

PORTER: That's all right, Miss Collins.

MISS COLLINS: It's the maid's day off. Your No'thern girls receive such excellent domestic training, but in the South it was never considered essential for a girl to have anything but prettiness and charm! (*She laughs girlishly.*) Please do sit down. Is it too close? Would you like a window open?

PORTER: No, Miss Collins.

MISS COLLINS: (*advancing with delicate grace to the sofa*) Mother will bring in something cool after while. . . . Oh, my! (*She touches her forehead.*)

PORTER: (*kindly*) Is anything wrong, Miss Collins?

MISS COLLINS: Oh, no, no, thank you, nothing! My head is a little bit heavy. I'm always a little bit—malarial—this time of year! (*She sways dizzily as she starts to sink down on the sofa.*)

PORTER: (*helping her*) Careful there, Miss Collins.

MISS COLLINS: (*vaguely*) Yes, it is, I hadn't noticed before. (*She peers at them nearsightedly with a hesitant smile.*) You gentlemen have come from the church?

PORTER: No, ma'am. I'm Nick, the porter, Miss Collins, and this boy here is Frank that runs the elevator.

MISS COLLINS: (*stiffening a little*) Oh? . . . I don't understand.

PORTER: (*gently*) Mr. Abrams just asked me to drop in here an' see if you was getting along all right.

MISS COLLINS: Oh! Then he must have informed you of what's been going on in here!

PORTER: He mentioned some kind of—disturbance.

MISS COLLINS: Yes! Isn't it outrageous? But it mustn't go any further, you understand. I mean you mustn't repeat it to other people.

PORTER: No, I wouldn't say nothing.

MISS COLLINS: Not a word of it, please!

ELEVATOR BOY: Is the man still here, Miss Collins?

MISS COLLINS: Oh, no. No, he's gone now.

ELEVATOR BOY: How did he go, out the bedroom window, Miss Collins?

MISS COLLINS: (*vaguely*) Yes. . . .

ELEVATOR BOY: I seen a guy that could do that once. He crawled straight up the side of the building. They called him The Human Fly! Gosh, that's a wonderful publicity angle, Miss Collins—"Beautiful Young Society Lady Raped by The Human Fly!"

PORTER: (*nudging him sharply*) Git back in your cracker box!

MISS COLLINS: Publicity? No! It would be so humiliating! Mr. Abrams surely hasn't reported it to the papers!

PORTER: No, ma'am. Don't listen to this smarty pants.

MISS COLLINS: (*touching her curls*) Will pictures be taken, you think? There's one of him on the mantel.

ELEVATOR BOY: (*going to be mantel*) This one here, Miss Collins?

MISS COLLINS: Yes. Of the Sunday School faculty picnic. I had the little kindergardeners that year and he had the older boys. We rode in the cab of a railroad locomotive from Webb to Crystal Springs. (*She covers her ears with a girlish grimace and toss of her curls.*) Oh, how the steam-whistle blew! Blew! (*giggling*) Blewwwww! It frightened me so, he put his arm round my shoulders! But she was there, too, though she had no business being. She grabbed his hat and stuck it on the back of her head and they—they *rassled* for it, they actually *rassled* together! Everyone said it was *shameless!* Don't you think that it was?

PORTER: Yes, Miss Collins.

MISS COLLINS: That's the picture, the one in the silver frame up there on the mantel. We cooled the watermelon in the springs and afterwards played games. She hid somewhere and he took ages to find her. It got to be dark and he hadn't found her yet and everyone whispered and giggled about it and finally they came back together—her hangin' on to his arm like a common little strumpet—and Daisy Belle Huston shrieked out, "Look, everybody, the seat of Evelyn's skirt!" It was—covered with—grass-stains! Did you ever hear of anything as outrageous? It didn't faze her, though, she laughed like it was something very, very amusing! Rather *triumphant* she was!

ELEVATOR BOY: Which one is him, Miss Collins?

MISS COLLINS: The tall one in the blue shirt holding onto one of my curls. He loved to play with them.

ELEVATOR BOY: Quite a Romeo—1910 model, huh?

MISS COLLINS: (*vaguely*) Do you? It's nothing, really, but I like the lace on the collar. I said to Mother, "Even if I don't wear it, Mother, it will be *so* nice for my hope-chest!"

ELEVATOR BOY: How was he dressed tonight when he climbed into your balcony, Miss Collins?

MISS COLLINS: Pardon?

ELEVATOR BOY: Did he still wear that nifty little stick-candy-striped blue shirt with the celluloid collar?

MISS COLLINS: He hasn't changed.

ELEVATOR BOY: Oughta be easy to pick him up in that. What color pants did he wear?

MISS COLLINS: (*vaguely*) I don't remember.

ELEVATOR BOY: Maybe he didn't wear any. Shimmied out of 'em on the way up the wall! You could get him on grounds of indecent exposure, Miss Collins!

PORTER: (*grasping his arm*) Cut that or git back in your cage! Understand?

ELEVATOR BOY: (*snickering*) Take it easy. She don't hear a thing.

PORTER: Well, you keep a decent tongue or get to hell out. Miss Collins here is a lady. You understand that?

ELEVATOR BOY: Okay. She's Shoiley Temple.

PORTER: She's a *lady!*

ELEVATOR BOY: Yeah! (*He returns to the gramophone and looks through the records.*)

MISS COLLINS: I really shouldn't have created this disturbance. When the officers come I'll have to explain that to them. But you can understand my feelings, can't you?

PORTER: Sure, Miss Collins.

MISS COLLINS: When men take advantage of common white-trash women who smoke in public there is probably some excuse for it, but when it occurs to a lady who is single and always com-*pletely* above reproach in her moral behavior, there's really nothing to do but call for police protection! Unless of course the girl is fortunate enough to have a father and brothers who can take care of the matter privately without any scandal.

PORTER: Sure. That's right, Miss Collins.

MISS COLLINS: Of course it's bound to cause a great deal of very disagreeable talk. Especially 'round the *church!* Are you gentlemen Episcopalian?

PORTER: No, ma'am. Catholic, Miss Collins.

MISS COLLINS: Oh. Well, I suppose you know in England we're known as the English Catholic church. We have direct Apostolic succession through St. Paul who christened the Early Angles—which is what the original English people were called—and established the English branch of the Catholic church over there. So when you hear ignorant people claim that our church was founded by—by Henry the *Eighth*—that horrible, *lech*erous old man who had so many wives—as many as *Blue*-beard they say!—you can see how ridiculous it *is* and how thoroughly ob-*nox*ious to anybody who really *knows* and under*stands* Church *His*tory!

PORTER: *(comfortingly)* Sure, Miss Collins. Everybody knows that.

MISS COLLINS: I wish they *did,* but they need to be in*struc*ted! Before he died, my father was Rector at the Church of St. Michael and St. George at Glorious Hill, Mississippi.[2]... I've literally grown up right in the very *shad*ow of the Episcopal church. At Pass Christian and Natchez, Biloxi, Gulfport, Port Gibson, Columbus and Glorious Hill! *(with gentle, bewildered sadness)* But you know I sometimes suspect that there has been some kind of spiritual schism in the modern church. These northern dioceses have completely departed from the good old church traditions. For instance our Rector at the Church of the Holy Communion has never darkened my door. It's a fashionable church and he's terribly busy, but even so you'd think he might have time to make a stranger in the congregation feel at home. But he doesn't though! Nobody seems to have the time any more.... *(She grows more excited as her mind sinks back into illusion.)* I ought not to mention this, but do you know they actually take a malicious de-*light* over there at the Holy Communion—where I've recently transferred my letter[3]—in what's been going on here at night in this apartment? *Yes!! (She laughs wildly and throws up her hands.)* They take a malicious de*LIGHT* in it!! *(She catches her breath and gropes vaguely about her wrapper.)*

PORTER: You lookin' for somethin', Miss Collins?

MISS COLLINS: My—handkerchief ... *(She is blinking her eyes against tears.)*

PORTER: *(removing a rag from his pocket)* Here. Use this, Miss Collins. It's just a rag but it's clean, except along that edge where I wiped off the phonograph handle.

MISS COLLINS: Thanks. You gentlemen are very kind. Mother will bring in something cool after while....

---

[2]A mythical town, also the site of Williams's *Summer and Smoke* (1947). There is an Episcopal Church of St. Michael and St. George near the campus of Washington University in St. Louis where Williams was enrolled from 1936–1937. A Church of the Holy Communion is also found in St. Louis.

[3]Letter from the Rector of one's former church necessary for formal acceptance into full membership in a new parish community.

ELEVATOR BOY: *(placing a record on machine)* This one is got some kind of foreign title. *(The record begins to play Tschaikowsky's "None But the Lonely Heart.")*

MISS COLLINS: *(stuffing the rag daintily in her bosom)* Excuse me, please. Is the weather nice outside?

PORTER: *(huskily)* Yes, it's nice, Miss Collins.

MISS COLLINS: *(dreamily)* So wa'm for this time of year. I wore my little astrakhan cape to service but had to *carry* it *home,* as the weight of it actually seemed *oppres*sive to me. *(Her eyes fall shut.)* The sidewalks seem so dreadfully long in summer. . . .

ELEVATOR BOY: This ain't summer, Miss Collins.

MISS COLLINS: *(dreamily)* I used to think I'd never get to the end of that last block. And that's the block where all the trees went down in the big tornado. The walk is simply *glit*-tering with sunlight. *(pressing her eyelids)* Impossible to shade your face and I *do* perspire so freely! *(She touches her forehead daintily with the rag.)* Not a branch, not a leaf to give you a little protection! You simply *have* to en-*dure* it. Turn your hideous red face away from all the front-porches and walk as fast as you decently *can* till you get *by* them! Oh, dear, dear Savior, sometimes you're not so lucky and you *meet* people and have to *smile!* You can't *avoid* them unless you cut *across* and that's so *ob*-vious, you know. . . . People would say you're pe*cul*iar. . . . His house is right in the middle of that awful leafless block, *their* house, his and *hers,* and they have an automobile and always get home early and sit on the porch and *watch* me walking by—Oh, Father in Heaven—with a ma*lic*ious de*light! (She averts her face in remembered torture.)* She has such *penetrating* eyes, they look straight through me. She sees that terrible choking thing in my throat and the pain I have in *here*—*(touching her chest)*—and she points it out and laughs and whispers to him, "There she goes with her shiny big red nose, the poor old maid—that *loves* you!" *(She chokes and hides her face in the rag.)*

PORTER: Maybe you better forget all that, Miss Collins.

MISS COLLINS: Never, never forget it! Never, never! I left my parasol once—the one with long white fringe that belonged to Mother—I left it behind in the cloakroom at the church so I didn't have anything to cover my face with when I walked by, and I couldn't turn back either, with all those people behind me—giggling back of me, poking fun at my clothes! Oh, dear, dear! I had to walk straight forward—past the last elm tree and into that *merciless* sunlight. Oh! It beat down on me, *scorching* me! *Whips! . . .* Oh, Jesus! . . . Over my face and my body! . . . I tried to walk on fast but was dizzy and they kept closer behind me—! I stumbled, I nearly fell, and all of them burst out laughing! My face turned so *horribly* red, it got so red and wet, I knew how ugly it was in all that merciless glare—not a single shadow to hide in! And then—*(Her face contorts with fear.)*—their automobile drove up in front of their house, right where I had to pass by it, and *she* stepped out, in white, so fresh and easy, her stomach round with a baby, the first of the *six.* Oh, God! . . . And he stood smiling behind her, white and easy and cool, and they stood there waiting for me. *Waiting!* I had to keep on. What else could I do? I couldn't turn *back,* could I? *No!* I said dear *God,* strike me *dead!* He didn't, though. I put my head way down like I couldn't see them! You know what she did? She stretched out her hand to *stop* me! And *he*—he stepped up straight in front of me, *smiling,* blocking the walk with his terrible big white body! *"Lucretia,"* he said, "Lucretia *Collins!"* I—I tried to speak but I couldn't, the breath went out of my body! I covered my face and—ran! . . . Ran! . . . *Ran! (beating the arm of the sofa)* Till I reached the end of the block—and the elm trees—*started* again. . . . Oh, Merciful Christ in Heaven, how *kind* they were! *(She leans back exhaustedly, her hand relaxed on sofa. She pauses and the music ends.)* I said to Mother, "Mother, we've got to leave town!" We *did* after that. And now after all these years he's finally remembered and come *back!* Moved away from that house and the woman and come *here*—I saw him in the back of the church one day. I wasn't sure—but it *was.* The night after that was the night that he first broke in—and indulged his senses with me. . . . He doesn't realize that I've changed, that I can't feel again the way that I used to feel, now that he's got six children by that Cincinnati girl—three in high-school already! Six! Think of that? Six children! I don't know what he'll say when he knows another one's coming! He'll probably blame *me* for it because a man always *does!* In spite of the fact that he *forced* me!

ELEVATOR BOY: *(grinning)* Did you say—a *baby,* Miss Collins?

MISS COLLINS: *(lowering her eyes but speaking with tenderness and pride)* Yes—I'm expecting a *child.*

ELEVATOR BOY: Jeez! *(He claps his hand over his mouth and turns away quickly.)*

MISS COLLINS: Even if it's not legitimate, I think it has a perfect right to its father's name—don't you?

PORTER: Yes. Sure, Miss Collins.

MISS COLLINS: A child is innocent and pure. No matter how it's conceived. And it must *not* be made to suffer! So I intend to dispose of the little property Cousin Ethel left me and give the child a private education where it won't come under the evil influence of the Christian church! I want to make sure that it doesn't grow up in the shadow of the cross and then have to walk along blocks that scorch you with terrible sunlight! *(The elevator buzzer sounds from the hall.)*

PORTER: Frank! Somebody wants to come up. *(The Elevator Boy goes out. The elevator door bangs shut. The Porter clears his throat.)* Yes, it'd be better—to go off some place else.

MISS COLLINS: If only I had the courage—but I don't. I've grown so used to it here, and people outside—it's always so *hard* to *face* them!

PORTER: Maybe you won't—have to face nobody, Miss Collins. *(The elevator door clangs open.)*

MISS COLLINS: *(rising fearfully)* Is someone coming—here?

PORTER: You just take it easy, Miss Collins.

MISS COLLINS: If that's the officers coming for Richard, tell them to go away. I've decided not to prosecute Mr. Martin. *(Mr. Abrams enters with the Doctor and the Nurse. The Elevator Boy gawks from the doorway. The Doctor is the weary, professional type, the Nurse hard and efficient. Mr. Abrams is a small, kindly person, sincerely troubled by the situation.)*

MISS COLLINS: *(shrinking back, her voice faltering)* I've decided not to—prosecute Mr. Martin.

DOCTOR: Miss Collins?

MR. ABRAMS: *(with attempted heartiness)* Yes, this is the lady you wanted to meet, Dr. White.

DOCTOR: Hmmm. *(briskly to the Nurse)* Go in her bedroom and get a few things together.

NURSE: Yes, sir. *(She goes quickly across to the bedroom.)*

MISS COLLINS: *(fearfully shrinking)* Things?

DOCTOR: Yes, Miss Tyler will help you pack up an overnight bag. *(smiling mechani-*

cally) A strange place always seems more homelike the first few days when we have a few of our little personal articles around us.

MISS COLLINS: A strange—place?

DOCTOR: *(carelessly, making a memorandum)* Don't be disturbed, Miss Collins.

MISS COLLINS: I know! *(excitedly)* You've come from the Holy Communion to place me under arrest! On moral charges!

MR. ABRAMS: Oh, no, Miss Collins, you got the wrong idea. This is a doctor who—

DOCTOR: *(impatiently)* Now, now, you're just going away for a while till things get straightened out. *(He glances at his watch.)* Two-twenty-five! Miss Tyler?

NURSE: Coming!

MISS COLLINS: *(with slow and sad comprehension)* Oh. . . . I'm going away. . . .

MR. ABRAMS: She was always a lady, Doctor, such a perfect lady.

DOCTOR: Yes. No doubt.

MR. ABRAMS: It seems too bad!

MISS COLLINS: Let me—write him a note. A pencil? Please?

MR. ABRAMS: Here, Miss Collins. *(She takes the pencil and crouches over the table. The Nurse comes out with a hard, forced smile, carrying a suitcase.)*

DOCTOR: Ready, Miss Tyler?

NURSE: All ready, Dr. White. *(She goes up to Miss Collins.)* Come along, dear, we can tend to that later!

MR. ABRAMS: *(sharply)* Let her finish the note!

MISS COLLINS: *(straightening with a frightened smile)* It's—finished.

NURSE: All right, dear, come along. *(She propels her firmly toward the door.)*

MISS COLLINS: *(turning suddenly back)* Oh, Mr. Abrams!

MR. ABRAMS: Yes, Miss Collins?

MISS COLLINS: If he should come again—and find me gone—I'd rather you didn't tell him—about the baby. . . . I think its better for *me* to tell him *that. (gently smiling)* You know how men *are,* don't you?

MR. ABRAMS: Yes, Miss Collins.

PORTER: Goodbye, Miss Collins. *(The Nurse pulls firmly at her arm. She smiles over her shoulder with a slight apologetic gesture.)*

MISS COLLINS: Mother will bring in—something cool—after while . . . *(She disappears down the hall with the Nurse. The elevator door clangs shut with the metallic sound of a locked cage. The wires hum.)*

MR. ABRAMS: She wrote him a note.

PORTER: What did she write, Mr. Abrams?

MR. ABRAMS: "Dear—Richard. I'm going away for a while. But don't worry, I'll be back. I have a secret to tell you. Love—Lucretia." *(He coughs.)* We got to clear out this stuff an' pile it down in the basement till I find out where it goes.

PORTER: *(dully)* Tonight, Mr. Abrams?

MR. ABRAMS: *(roughly to hide his feeling)* No, no, not tonight, you old fool. Enough has happened tonight! *(then gently)* We can do it tomorrow. Turn out that bedroom light—and close the window. *(Music playing softly becomes audible as the men go out slowly, closing the door, and the light fades out.)*

Curtain

1945

Tillie Lerner Olsen 1913–2007

Tillie Olsen's parents, Samuel and Ida Lerner, took part in the 1905 revolution in Russia, fleeing to the United States when it failed. Her father worked at a variety of jobs, from farming to packinghouse work, eventually becoming state secretary of the Nebraska Socialist Party. The young Tillie Lerner read avidly in her public library, becoming conversant with American and world literature. Forced to leave school after the eleventh grade to go to work, she pressed ties, trimmed meat in the packing houses, and acted as a domestic and a waitress. She also became an activist in the Young Communist League, going to jail in Kansas City after attempting to organize packinghouse workers. At nineteen she began work on the novel that many years later would become *Yonnondio: From the Thirties;* in the same year, she bore her first child, a daughter. In the early thirties, she moved to northern California, continuing to write and to do political work. She combined the two in such reportage as "The Strike," an essay about the great general strike that spread up and down the Coast from San Francisco in 1934.

In 1936, Tillie Lerner became involved with her YCL companion Jack Olsen, whom she eventually married. In the years that followed, she bore three more children, struggling to combine mothering with work out of the home to help support her growing family. During the 1950s, she and her family, like so many progressives of the thirties and forties, were harassed destructively by the FBI. Yet in the fifties too Olsen began writing again: "I Stand Here Ironing," "Hey Sailor, What Ship?" and "O Yes," written in the mid-fifties, followed by "Tell Me a Riddle," which won the O. Henry Award in 1961 for best short story of the year. These stories, originally conceived as part of a novel about three generations of a Russian Jewish family, celebrate the stubborn endurance of human love and of the passion for justice, in spite of the injuries inflicted by poverty, racism, and the patriarchal order.

The same theme informs *Yonnondio: From the Thirties,* a novel revised and published forty years after its inception by the "older writer in arduous partnership with that long ago younger one." The story of the Holbrook family's efforts to survive on the farms and in the packing houses of the Midwest in the twenties, the novel creates in Mazie Holbrook and in her mother Anna a figure who reappears throughout Olsen's work, fiction and criticism alike: the potential female artist/activist silenced by poverty, by the willingly assumed burdens of caring for loved others, by the expectations associated with her sex. *Silences,* Olsen's collected critical essays, continues this theme. The book is a sustained prose poem about all the forms of silencing that befall writers—especially, though not exclusively, women; especially, though not exclusively, those who must struggle for sheer survival.

Concerned with the "circumstances" of class, race, and gender as the soil which nurtures or impedes human achievement, Olsen's work constitutes a vitally important link between the radical movements of the thirties and the culture, ideas, and literature of the women's liberation movement. Her fiction and essays, finely crafted and emotionally powerful, make an important contribution to American literature, an achievement acknowledged in Olsen's receipt of many prestigious awards and four honorary doctorates. She contributed to what she called "the larger tradition of social concern" not only as a writer but also as a scholar and teacher. Her efforts helped to reclaim many "lost" women writers and to initiate the democratization of the literary canon reflected in the contours of this anthology.

Deborah S. Rosenfelt
University of Maryland at College Park

PRIMARY WORKS

Tell Me a Riddle, 1961; *Yonnondio: From the Thirties*, 1974; *Silences*, 1978; *Mother to Daughter, Daughter to Mother: A Daybook and Reader*, 1984.

O Yes

1

They are the only white people there, sitting in the dimness of the Negro church that had once been a corner store, and all through the bubbling, swelling, seething of before the services, twelve-year-old Carol clenches tight her mother's hand, the other resting lightly on her friend, Parialee Phillips, for whose baptism she has come.

The white-gloved ushers hurry up and down the aisle, beckoning people to their seats. A jostle of people. To the chairs angled to the left for the youth choir, to the chairs angled to the right for the ladies' choir, even up to the platform, where behind the place for the dignitaries and the mixed choir, the new baptismal tank gleams— and as if pouring into it from the ceiling, the blue-painted River of Jordan, God standing in the waters, embracing a brown man in a leopard skin and pointing to the letters of gold:

REJOICE

D   L

O IS O

V

G   E

I AM THE WAY   THE TRUTH   THE LIFE

At the clear window, the crucified Christ embroidered on the starched white curtain leaps in the wind of the sudden singing. And the choirs march in. Robes of wine, of blue, of red.

"We stands and sings too," says Parialee's mother, Alva, to Helen; though already Parialee has pulled Carol up. Singing, little Lucinda Phillips fluffs out her many petticoats; singing, little Bubbie bounces up and down on his heels.

> *Any day now I'll reach that land of freedom,*
> *Yes, o yes*
> *Any day now, know that promised land*

The youth choir claps and taps to accent the swing of it. Beginning to tap, Carol stiffens. "Parry, look. Somebody from school."

"Once more once," says Parialee, in the new way she likes to talk now.

"Eddie Garlin's up there. He's in my math."

"Couple cats from Franklin Jr. chirps in the choir. No harm or alarm."

Anxiously Carol scans the faces to see who else she might know, who else might know her, but looks quickly down to Lucinda's wide skirts, for it seems Eddie looks back at her, sullen or troubled, though it is hard to tell, faced as she is into the window of curtained sunblaze.

I know my robe will fit me well
I tried it on at the gates of hell

If I were a record she would play it over and over, Carol thought, to untwine the intertwined voices, to search how the many rhythms rock apart and yet are one glad rhythm.

When I get to heaven gonna sing and shout
Nobody be able to turn me out

"That's Mr. Chairback Evans going to invocate," Lucinda leans across Parry to explain. "He don't invoke good like Momma."

"Shhhh."

"Momma's the only lady in the church that invocates. She made the prayer last week. (Last month, Lucy.) I made the children's 'nouncement last time. (That was way back Thanksgiving.) And Bubbie's 'nounced too. Lots of times."

"Lucy-inda. SIT!"

Bible study announcements and mixed-choir practice announcements and Teen Age Hearts meeting announcements.

If Eddie said something to her about being there, worried Carol, if he talked to her right in front of somebody at school.

Messengers of Faith announcements and Mamboettes announcement and Committee for the Musical Tea.

Parry's arm so warm. Not realizing, starting up the old game from grade school, drumming a rhythm on the other's arm to see if the song could be guessed. "Parry, guess."

But Parry is pondering the platform.

The baptismal tank? "Parry, are you scared . . . the baptizing?"

"This cat? No." Shaking her head so slow and scornful, the barrette in her hair, sun fired, strikes a long rail of light. And still ponders the platform.

New Strangers Baptist Church invites you and Canaan Fair Singers announcements and Battle of Song and Cosmpolites meet. "O Lord, I couldn't find no ease," a solo. The ladies' choir:

O what you say seekers, o what you say seekers,
Will you never turn back no more?

The mixed choir sings:

Ezekiel saw that wheel of time
Every spoke was of humankind . . .

And the slim worn man in the pin-stripe suit starts his sermon. On the Nature of God. How God is long-suffering. Oh, how long has he suffered. Calling the roll of the mighty nations, that rose and fell and now are dust for grinding the face of Man.

O voice of drowsiness and dream to which Carol does not need to listen. As long ago. Parry warm beside her too, as it used to be, there in the classroom at Mann

Elementary, and the feel of drenched in sun and dimness and dream. Smell and sound of the chalk wearing itself away to nothing, rustle of books, drumming tattoo of fingers on her arm: *Guess.*

And as the preacher's voice spins happy and free, it is the used-to-be play-yard. Tag. Thump of the volley ball. Ecstasy of the jump rope. Parry, do pepper. Carol, do pepper. Parry's bettern Carol, Carol's bettern Parry . . .

Did someone scream?

It seemed someone screamed—but all were sitting as before, though the sun no longer blared through the windows. She tried to see up where Eddie was, but the ushers were standing at the head of the aisle now, the ladies in white dresses like nurses or waitresses wear, the men holding their white-gloved hands up so one could see their palms.

"And God is Powerful," the preacher was chanting. "Nothing for him to scoop out the oceans and pat up the mountains. Nothing for him to scoop up the miry clay and create man. Man, I said, create Man."

The lady in front of her moaned, *"O yes"* and others were moaning *"O yes."*

"And when the earth mourned the Lord said, Weep not, for all will be returned to you, every dust, every atom. And the tired dust settles back, goes back. Until that Judgment Day. That great day."

"O yes."

The ushers were giving out fans. Carol reached for one and Parry said: "What *you* need one for?" but she took it anyway.

"You think Satchmo can blow; you think Muggsy can blow; you think Dizzy can blow?" He was straining to an imaginary trumpet now, his head far back and his voice coming out like a trumpet.

"Oh Parry, he's so good."

"Well. Jelly jelly."

"Nothing to Gabriel on that great getting-up morning. And the horn wakes up Adam and, Adam runs to wake up Eve, and Eve moans; Just one more minute, let me sleep, and Adam yells, Great Day, woman, don't you know it's the Great Day?"

"Great Day, Great Day," the mixed choir behind the preacher rejoices:

> *When our cares are past*
> *when we're home at last . . .*

"And Eve runs to wake up Cain." Running round the platform, stooping and shaking imaginary sleepers, "and Cain runs to wake up Abel." Looping, scalloping his voice—"Grea-aaa-aat Daaaay." All the choirs thundering:

> *Great Day*
> *When the battle's fought*
> *And the victory's won*

Exultant spirals of sound. And Carol caught into it (Eddie forgotten, the game forgotten) chanting with Lucy and Bubbie: *"Great Day."*

"Ohhhhhhhhhh," his voice like a trumpet again, "the re-unioning. Ohhhhhhhh, the rejoicing. After the ages immemorial of longing."

Someone *was* screaming. And an awful thrumming sound with it, like feet and hands thrashing around, like a giant jumping of a rope.

"*Great Day.*" And no one stirred or stared as the ushers brought a little woman out into the aisle, screaming and shaking, just a little shrunk-up woman, not much taller than Carol, the biggest thing about her her swollen hands and the cascades of tears wearing her face.

The shaking inside Carol too. Turning and trembling to ask: "What? . . . that lady?" But Parry still ponders the platform; little Lucy loops the chain of her bracelet round and round; and Bubbie sits placidly, dreamily. Alva Phillips is up fanning a lady in front of her; two lady ushers are fanning other people Carol cannot see. And her mother, her mother looks in a sleep.

Yes. He raised up the dead from the grave. He made old death behave.

Yes. Yes. From all over, hushed. *O Yes*

He was your mother's rock. Your father's mighty tower. And he gave us a little baby. A little baby to love.

I am so glad

Yes, your friend, when you're friendless. Your father when you're fatherless. Way maker. Door opener.

Yes

When it seems you can't go on any longer, he's there. You can, he says, you can.

Yes

And that burden you been carrying—ohhhhh that burden—not for always will it be. No, not for always.

Stay with me, Lord

I will put my Word in you and it is power. I will put my Truth in you and it is power.

O Yes

Out of your suffering I will make you to stand as a stone. A tried stone. Hewn out of the mountains of ages eternal. Ohhhhhhhhhhh. Out of the mire I will lift your feet. Your tired feet from so much wandering. From so much work and wear and hard times.

Yes

From so much journeying—and never the promised land. And I'll wash them in the well your tears made. And I'll shod them in the gospel of peace, and of feeling good. Ohhhhhhhh.

O Yes.

Behind Carol, a trembling wavering scream. Then the thrashing. Up above, the singing:

> *They taken my blessed Jesus and flogged him to the woods*
> *And they made him hew out his cross and they dragged him to Calvary*
>
> *Shout brother, Shout shout shout. He never cried a word.*

Powerful throbbing voices. Calling and answering to each other.

> *They taken my blessed Jesus and whipped him up the hill*
> *With a knotty whip and a raggedy thorn he never cried a word*
> *Shout, sister. Shout shout shout. He never cried a word.*
>
> *Go tell the people the Saviour has risen*
> *Has risen from the dead and will live forevermore*
> *And won't have to die no more.*

Halleloo.

> *Shout, brother, shout*
> *We won't have to die no more!*

A single exultant lunge of shriek. Then the thrashing. All around a clapping. Shouts with it. The piano whipping, whipping air to a froth. Singing now.

> *I once was lost who now am found*
> *Was blind who now can see*

On Carol's fan, a little Jesus walked on wondrously blue waters to where bearded disciples spread nets out of a fishing boat. If she studied the fan—became it—it might make a wall around her. If she could make what was happening (*what was happening?*) into a record small and round to listen to far and far as if into a seashell—the stamp and rills and spirals all tiny (but never any screaming).

> *wade wade in the water*
>
> *Jordan's water is chilly and wild*
> *I've got to get home to the other side*
> *God's going to trouble the waters*

The music leaps and prowls. Ladders of screamings. Drumming feet of ushers running. And still little Lucy fluffs her skirts, loops the chain on her bracelet; still Bubbie sits and rocks dreamily; and only eyes turn for an instant to the aisle as if nothing were happening. "Mother, let's go home," Carol begs, but her mother holds her so tight. Alva Phillips, strong Alva, rocking too and chanting, *O Yes*. No, do not look.

> *Wade,*
> *Sea of trouble all mingled with fire*
> *Come on my brethren it's time to go higher*
> *Wade wade*

The voices in great humming waves, slow, slow (when did it become the humming?), everyone swaying with it, too, moving like in slow waves and singing, and up where Eddie is, a new cry, wild and open, "O help me, Jesus," and when Carol opens her eyes she closes them again, quick, but still can see the new known face from school (not Eddie), the thrashing, writhing body, struggling against the ushers with the look of grave and loving support on their faces, and hear the torn, tearing cry: "Don't take me away, life everlasting, don't take me away."

And now the rhinestones in Parry's hair glitter wicked, the white hands of the ushers, fanning, foam in the air; the blue-painted waters of Jordan swell and thunder; Christ spirals on his cross in the window, and she is drowned under the sluice of the slow singing and the sway.

So high up and forgotten the waves and the world, so stirless the deep cool green and the wrecks of what had been. Here now Hostess Foods, where Alva Phillips works her nights—but different from that time Alva had taken them through before work, for it is all sunken under water, the creaking loading platform where they had left the night behind; the closet room where Alva's swaddles of sweaters, boots, and cap hung, the long hall lined with pickle barrels, the sharp freezer door swinging open.

Bubbles of breath that swell. A gulp of numbing air. She swims into the chill room where the huge wheels of cheese stand, and Alva swims too, deftly oiling each machine: slicers and wedgers and the convey, that at her touch start to roll and grind. The light of day blazes up and Alva is holding a cup, saying: Drink this, baby.

"DRINK IT." Her mother's voice and the numbing air demanding her to pay attention. Up through the waters and into the car.

"That's right, lambie, now lie back." Her mother's lap.

"Mother."

"Shhhhh. You almost fainted, lambie."

Alva's voice. "You gonna be all right, Carol . . . Lucy, I'm telling you for the last time, you and Buford get back into that church. Carol is *fine.*"

"Lucyinda, if I had all your petticoats I could float." Crying. "Why didn't you let me wear my full skirt with the petticoats, Mother."

"Shhhhh, lamb." Smoothing her cheek. "Just breathe, take long deep breaths."

". . . How you doing now, you little ol' consolation prize?" It is Parry, but she does not come in the car or reach to Carol through the open window: "No need to cuss and fuss. You going to be sharp as a tack, Jack."

Answering automatically: "And cool as a fool."

Quick, they look at each other.

"Parry, we have to go home now, don't we, Mother? I almost fainted, didn't I, Mother? . . . Parry, I'm sorry I got sick and have to miss your baptism."

"Don't feel sorry. I'll feel better you not there to watch. It was our mommas wanted you to be there, not me."

"Parry!" Three voices.

"Maybe I'll come over to play kickball after. If you feeling better. Maybe. Or bring the pogo." Old shared joys in her voice. "Or any little thing."

In just a whisper: "Or any little thing. Parry. Goodbye, Parry."

And why does Alva have to talk now?

"You all right? You breathin' deep like your momma said? Was it too close 'n hot in there? Did something scare you, Carrie?"

Shaking her head to lie, "No."

"I blame myself for not paying attention. You not used to people letting go that way. Lucy and Bubbie, Parialee, they used to it. They been coming since they lap babies."

"Alva, that's all right. Alva, Mrs. Phillips."

"You *was* scared. Carol, it's something to study about. You'll feel better if you understand."

Trying not to listen.

"You not used to hearing what people keeps inside, Carol. You know how music can make you feel things? Glad or sad or like you can't sit still? That was religion music, Carol."

"I have to breathe deep, Mother said."

"Not everybody feels religion the same way. Some it's in their mouth, but some it's like a hope in the blood, their bones. And they singing songs every word that's real to them, Carol, every word out of they own life. And the preaching finding lodgment in their hearts."

The screaming was tuning up in her ears again, high above Alva's patient voice and the waves lapping and fretting.

"Maybe somebody's had a hard week, Carol, and they locked up with it. Maybe a lot of hard weeks bearing down."

"Mother, my head hurts."

"And they're home, Carol, church is home. Maybe the only place they can feel how they feel and maybe let it come out. So they can go on. And it's all right."

"Please, Alva. Mother, tell Alva my head hurts."

"Get Happy, we call it, and most it's a good feeling, Carol. When you got all that locked up inside you."

"Tell her we have to go home. It's all right, Alva. Please, Mother. Say good-bye. Good-bye."

When I was carrying Parry and her father left me, and I fifteen years old, one thousand miles away from home, sin-sick and never really believing, as still I don't believe all, scorning, for what have it done to help, waiting there in the clinic and maybe sleeping, a voice called: Alva, Alva. So mournful and so sweet: Alva. Fear not, I have loved you from the foundation of the universe. And a little small child tugged on my dress. He was carrying a parade stick, on the end of it a star that outshined the sun. Follow me, he said. And the real sun went down and he hidden his stick. How dark it was, how dark. I could feel the darkness with my hands. And when I could see, I screamed. Dump trucks run, dumping bodies in hell, and a convey line run, never ceasing with souls, weary ones having to stamp and shove them along, and the air like fire. Oh I never want to hear such screaming. Then the little child jumped on a motorbike making a path no bigger than my little finger. But first he greased my feet with the hands of my momma when I was a knee baby. They shined like the sun was on them. Eyes he placed all around my head, and as I journeyed upward after him, it seemed I heard a mourning: "Mama Mama you must help carry the world." The rise and fall of nations I saw. And the voice called again Alva Alva, and I flew into a world of light, multitudes singing, Free, free, I am so glad.

2

Helen began to cry, telling her husband about it.

"You and Alva ought to have your heads examined, taking her there cold like that," Len said. "All right, wreck my best handkerchief. Anyway, now that she's had a bath, her Sunday dinner. . . ."

"And been fussed over," seventeen-year-old Jeannie put in.

"She seems good as new. Now *you* forget it, Helen."

"I can't. Something . . . deep happened. If only I or Alva had told her what it would be like. . . . But I didn't realize."

You don't realize a lot of things, Mother, Jeannie said, but not aloud.

"So Alva talked about it after instead of before. Maybe it meant more that way."

"Oh Len, she didn't listen."

"You don't know if she did or not. Or what there was in the experience for her. . . ."

Enough to pull that kid apart two ways even more, Jeannie said, but still not aloud.

"I was so glad she and Parry were going someplace together again. Now that'll be between them too. Len, they really need, miss each other. What happened in a few months? When I think of how close they were, the hours of makebelieve and dressup and playing ball and collecting. . . ."

"Grow up, Mother." Jeannie's voice was harsh. "Parialee's collecting something else now. Like her own crowd. Like jivetalk and rhythmandblues. Like teachers who treat her like a dummy and white kids who treat her like dirt; boys who think she's really something and chicks who. . . ."

"Jeannie, I know. It hurts."

"Well, maybe it hurts Parry too. Maybe. At least she's got a crowd. Just don't let it hurt Carol though, 'cause there's nothing she can do about it. That's all through, her and Parialee Phillips, put away with their paper dolls."

"No, Jeannie, no."

"It's like Ginger and me. Remember Ginger, my best friend in Horace Mann. But you hardly noticed when it happened to us, did you . . . because she was white? Yes, Ginger, who's got two kids now, who quit school year before last. Parry's never going to finish either. What's she got to do with Carrie any more? They're going different places. Different places, different crowds. And they're sorting. . . ."

"Now wait, Jeannie. Parry's just as bright, just as capable."

"They're in junior high, Mother. Don't you know about junior high? How they sort? And it's all where you're going. Yes and Parry's colored and Carrie's white. And you have to watch everything, what you wear and how you wear it and who you eat lunch with and how much homework you do and how you act to the teacher and what you laugh at. . . . And run with your crowd."

"It's that final?" asked Len. "Don't you think kids like Carol and Parry can show it doesn't *have* to be that way."

"They can't. They can't. They don't let you."

"No need to shout," he said mildly. "And who do you mean by 'they' and what do you mean by 'sorting'?"

How they sort. A foreboding of comprehension whirled within Helen. What was it Carol had told her of the Welcome Assembly the first day in junior high? The models showing How to Dress and How Not to Dress and half the girls in their loved new clothes watching their counterparts up on the stage—*their* straight skirt, their sweater, their earrings, lipstick, hairdo—"How Not to Dress," "a bad reputation for your school." It was nowhere in Carol's description, yet picturing it now, it seemed to Helen that a mute cry of violated dignity hung in the air. Later there had been a story of going to another Low 7 homeroom on an errand and seeing a teacher trying to wipe the forbidden lipstick off a girl who was fighting back and cursing. Helen could hear Carol's frightened, self-righteous tones: ". . . and I hope they expel her; she's the kind that gives Franklin Jr. a bad rep; she doesn't care about anything and always gets into fights." Yet there was nothing in these incidents to touch the heavy comprehension that waited. . . . Homework, the wonderings those times Jeannie and Carol needed help: "What if there's no one at home to give the help, and the teachers with their two hundred and forty kids a day can't or don't or the kids don't ask and they fall hopelessly behind, what then?"—but this too was unrelated. And what had it been that time about Parry? "Mother, Melanie and Sharon won't go if they know Parry's coming." Then of course you'll go with Parry, she's been your friend longer, she had answered, but where was it they were going and what had finally happened? Len, my head hurts, she felt like saying, in Carol's voice in the car, but Len's eyes were grave on Jeannie who was saying passionately:

"If you think it's so goddam important why do we have to live here where it's for real; why don't we move to Ivy like Betsy (yes, I know, money), where it's the deal to be buddies, in school anyway, three coloured kids and their father's a doctor or judge or something big wheel and one always gets elected President or head song girl or something to prove oh how we're democratic. . . . What do you want of that poor kid anyway? Make up your mind. Stay friends with Parry—but be one of the kids. Sure. Be a brain—but not a square. Rise on up, college prep, but don't get separated. Yes, stay one of the kids but. . . ."

"Jeannie. You're not talking about Carol at all, are you, Jeannie? Say it again. I wasn't listening. I was trying to think."

"She will not say it again," Len said firmly, "you look about ready to pull a Carol. One a day's our quota. And you, Jeannie, we'd better cool it. Too much to talk about for one session. . . . Here, come to the window and watch the Carol and Parry you're both all worked up about."

In the wind and the shimmering sunset light, half the children of the block are playing down the street. Leaping, bouncing, hallooing, tugging the kites of spring. In the old synchronized understanding, Carol and Parry kick, catch, kick, catch. And now Parry jumps on her pogo stick (the last time), Carol shadowing her, and Bubbie, arching his body in a semicircle of joy, bounding after them, high, higher, higher.

And the months go by and supposedly it is forgotten, except for the now and then when, self-important, Carol will say: I really truly did nearly faint, didn't I, Mother, that time I went to church with Parry?

And now seldom Parry and Carol walk the hill together. Melanie's mother drives by to pick up Carol, and the several times Helen has suggested Parry, too, Carol is quick to explain: "She's already left" or "She isn't ready; she'll make us late."

And after school? Carol is off to club or skating or library or someone's house, and Parry can stay for kickball only on the rare afternoons when she does not have to hurry home where Lucy, Bubbie, and the cousins wait to be cared for, now Alva works the four to twelve-thirty shift.

No more the bending together over the homework. All semester the teachers have been different, and rarely Parry brings her books home, for where is there space or time and what is the sense? And the phone never rings with: what you going to wear tomorrow, are you bringing your lunch, or come on over, let's design some clothes for Katy Keane comic-book contest. And Parry never drops by with Alva for Saturday snack to or from grocery shopping.

And the months go by and the sorting goes on and seemingly it is over until that morning when Helen must stay home from work, so swollen and feverish is Carol with mumps.

The afternoon before, Parry had come by, skimming up the stairs, spilling books and binders on the bed: Hey frail, lookahere and wail, your momma askin for homework, what she got against YOU? . . . looking quickly once then not looking again and talking fast. . . . Hey, you bloomed. You gonna be your own pumpkin, hallowe'en? Your momma know yet it's mu-umps? And lumps. Momma says: no distress, she'll be by tomorrow morning see do you need anything while your momma's to work. . . . (Singing: *whole lotta shakin going on.*) All your 'signments is inside; Miss Rockface says the teachers to write 'em cause I mightn't get it right all right.

But did not tell: Does your mother work for Carol's mother? Oh, you're neighbors! Very well, I'll send along a monitor to open Carol's locker but you're only to take these things I'm writing down, nothing else. Now say after me: Miss Campbell is trusting me to be a good responsible girl. And go right to Carol's house. After school. Not stop anywhere on the way. Not lose anything. And only take. What's written on the list.

You really gonna mess with that book stuff? Sign on *mine* says do-not-open-until-eX-mas. . . . That Mrs. Fernandez doll she didn't send nothin, she was the only, says feel better and read a book to report if you feel like and I'm the most for takin care for you; she's my most, wish I could get her but she only teaches 'celerated. . . . Flicking the old read books on the shelf but not opening to mock-declaim as once she used to . . . Vicky, Eddie's g.f. in Rockface office, she's on suspended for sure, yellin to Rockface: you bitchkitty don't you give me no more bad shit. That Vicky she can sure sling-ating-ring it. Staring out the window as if the tree not there in which they had hid out and rocked so often. . . . For sure. (*Keep mo-o-vin.*) Got me a new pink top and lilac skirt. Look sharp with this purple? Cinching in the wide belt as if delighted with what newly swelled above and swelled below. Wear it Saturday night to Sweet's, Modernaires Sounds of Joy, Leroy and Ginny and me goin if Momma'll stay home. IF. (*Shake my baby shake.*) How come old folks still likes to party? Huh? Asking of Rembrandt's weary old face looking from the wall. How come (softly) you long-gone you. Touching her face to his quickly, lightly. NEXT mumps is your buddybud Melanie's turn to tote your stuff. *I'm* gettin the hoovus goovus. Hey you so unneat, don't care what you bed with. Removing the books and binders, ranging them on the dresser one by one, marking lipstick faces—bemused or mocking or amazed—on each paper jacket. Better. Fluffing out smoothing the quilt with exaggerated energy. Any little thing I can get, cause I gotta blow. Tossing up and catching their year-ago, arm-in-arm graduation picture, replacing it deftly, upside down, into its mirror crevice. Joe. Bring your joy juice or fizz water or kickapoo? Adding a frown line to one bookface. Twanging the paper fishkite, the Japanese windbell overhead, setting the mobile they had once made of painted eggshells and decorated straws to twirling and rocking. And is gone.

She talked to the lipstick faces after, in her fever, tried to stand on her head to match the picture, twirled and twanged with the violent overhead.

Sleeping at last after the disordered night. Having surrounded herself with the furnishings of that world of childhood she no sooner learned to live in comfortably, then had to leave.

The dollhouse stands there to arrange and rearrange; the shell and picture card collections to re-sort and remember; the population of dolls given away to little sister, borrowed back, propped all around to dress and undress and caress.

She has thrown off her nightgown because of the fever, and her just budding breast is exposed where she reaches to hold the floppy plush dog that had been her childhood pillow.

Not anything would Helen have disturbed her. Except that in the unaccustomed-ness of a morning at home, in the bruised restlessness after the sleepless night, she clicks on the radio—and the storm of singing whirls into the room:

> *. . . of trouble all mingled with fire*
> *Come on my brethern we've got to go higher*
> *Wade, wade. . . .*

And Carol runs down the stairs, shrieking and shrieking. "Turn it off, Mother, turn it off." Hurling herself at the dial and wrenching it so it comes off in her hand.

"Ohhhhh," choked and convulsive, while Helen tries to hold her, to quiet.

"Mother, why did they sing and scream like that?"

"At Parry's church?"

"Yes." Rocking and strangling the cries. "I hear it all the time." Clinging and beseeching. ". . . What was it, Mother? Why?"

Emotion, Helen thought of explaining, *a characteristic of the religion of all oppressed peoples, yes your very own great-grandparents*—thought of saying. And discarded.

Aren't you now, haven't you had feelings in yourself so strong they had to come out some way? ("what howls restrained by decorum")—thought of saying. And discarded.

Repeat Alva: *hope . . . every word out of their own life. A place to let go. And church is home.* And discarded.

The special history of the Negro people—history?—just you try living what must be lived every day—thought of saying. And discarded.

And said nothing.

And said nothing.

And soothed and held.

"Mother, a lot of the teachers and kids don't like Parry when they don't even know what she's like. Just because. . . ." Rocking again, convulsive and shamed. "And I'm not really her friend any more."

No news. Betrayal and shame. Who betrayed? Whose shame? Brought herself to say aloud: "But may be friends again. As Alva and I are."

The sobbing a whisper. "That girl Vicky who got that way when I fainted, she's in school. She's the one keeps wearing lipstick and they wipe it off and she's always in trouble and now maybe she's expelled. Mother."

"Yes, lambie."

"She acts so awful outside but I remember how she was in church and whenever I see her now I have to wonder. And hear . . . like I'm her, Mother, like I'm her." Clinging and trembling. "Oh why do I have to feel it happens to me too?

"Mother, I want to forget about it all, and not care,—like Melanie. Why can't I forget? Oh why is it like it is and why do I have to care?"

Caressing, quieting.

Thinking: *caring asks doing. It is a long baptism into the seas of humankind, my daughter. Better immersion than to live untouched. . . . Yet how will you sustain?*
Why is it like it is?
Sheltering her daughter close, mourning the illusion of the embrace.
And why do I have to care?
While in her, her own need leapt and plunged for the place of strength that was not—where one could scream or sorrow while all knew and accepted, and gloved and loving hands waiting to support and understand.

1956

Muriel Rukeyser 1913–1980

From the outset, Muriel Rukeyser was at once a political poet and a visionary. At times, those qualities were intensified, and in those moments she was simultaneously a revolutionary and a mystic. But to grasp the forces that drive her work—throughout the nearly 600 packed pages of her *Collected Poems*—we have to come to terms with a visionary impulse rooted in time, embedded in a struggle with lived history. Consider as cases in point the rhapsodic images she crafts to voice the mother's anguish at the death of her sons in "Absalom," and Rukeyser's own shared sense of loss in "Martin Luther King, Malcolm X," two poems from the beginning and the end of a career that spanned five decades of American history. But that is not all. To understand her work, we must also embrace the larger, wiser notion of politics that underlies all her poetry. For she understood early on what so many of us could not: that politics encompasses all the ways that social life is hierarchically structured and made meaningful. Politics is not only the large-scale public life of nations. It is also the advantages, inequities and illusions that make daily life very different for different groups among us. Thus Rukeyser understood that race and gender are integral parts of our social and political life. Never officially a feminist, she nonetheless devoted herself to voicing women's distinctive experience throughout her career.

Although Rukeyser was quite capable of writing short, tightly controlled poems—"The Minotaur" below is a good example—it may well be that her most rich and suggestive accomplishments are her poem sequences. Two of the poems in this selection are thus taken from longer sequences; "Absalom" is from "The Book of the Dead" and "*Les Tendresses Bestiales*" (the bestial tendernesses) is from "Ajanta," a poem sequence that takes its title from the name of a famous group of painted caves in India. "The Book of the Dead," in particular, is one of the major poem sequences of American modernism. Based on Rukeyser's own research in West Virginia, it combines historical background, congressional testimony, and the voices of a number of victims in telling the story of a 1930s industrial scandal: a company building a tunnel for a dam decided to double its profit by rapidly mining silica at the same time (without any of the necessary precautions). A great many workers died of lung disease as a result. "The Book of the Dead" is thus also one of Rukeyser's many poems that reflect and contribute to her political activism. "How We Did It," also reprinted here, is another; it recalls a demonstration about the Vietnam War, a war that Rukeyser experienced still more directly during a peace mission to South Vietnam in 1972.

During the 1930s Rukeyser regularly wrote for Communist Party publications like *New Masses*. She was in Spain to cover the antifascist Olympics in Barcelona when the Spanish Civil War broke out. She described that experience in the long poem "Mediterranean" and returned to the subject throughout her life. Years later, in 1975, she went to South Korea to protest the poet Kim Chi-Ha's imprisonment and anticipated execution; the poem sequence "The Gates" grew out of that trip. Rukeyser meditates on her poetics in *The Life of Poetry* (1949). She also published a novel, *The Orgy* (1966), as well as two biographies, *Willard Gibbs* (1942) and *The Traces of Thomas Harriot* (1971).

Cary Nelson
University of Illinois

PRIMARY WORKS

Willard Gibbs, 1942; *One Life*, 1957; *Body of Waking*, 1958; *Waterlily Fire*, 1962; *The Orgy*, 1965; *Bubbles*, 1967; *The Speed of Darkness*, 1968; *Mazes*, 1970; *The Traces of Thomas Hariot*, 1971; *Theory of Flight*, 1971; *The Life of Poetry*, 1974; *The Gates*, 1976; *The Collected Poems*, 1979, *Out of Silence: Selected Poems*, 1992; *Selected Poems*, 2004.

Absalom

I first discovered what was killing these men.
I had three sons who worked with their father in the tunnel:
Cecil, aged 23, Owen, aged 21, Shirley, aged 17.
They used to work in a coal mine, not steady work
5 for the mines were not going much of the time.
A power Co. foreman learned that we made home brew,
he formed a habit of dropping in evenings to drink,
persuading the boys and my husband—
give up their jobs and take this other work.
10 It would pay them better.
Shirley was my youngest son; the boy.
He went into the tunnel.

      My heart   my mother   my heart   my mother
      My heart   my coming into being.

15 My husband is not able to work.
He has it, according to the doctor.
We have been having a very hard time making a living since
    this trouble came to us.
I saw the dust in the bottom of the tub.
20 The boy worked there about eighteen months,
came home one evening with a shortness of breath.
He said, "Mother, I cannot get my breath."
Shirley was sick about three months.
I would carry him from his bed to the table,
25 from his bed to the porch, in my arms.

My heart is mine in the place of hearts,
They gave me back my heart, it lies in me.

When they took sick, right at the start, I saw a doctor.
I tried to get Dr. Harless to X-ray the boys.
30 He was the only man I had any confidence in,
the company doctor in the Kopper's mine,
but he would not see Shirley.
He did not know where his money was coming from.
I promised him half if he'd work to get compensation,
35 but even then he would not do anything.
I went on the road and begged the X-ray money,
the Charleston hospital made the lung pictures,
he took the case after the pictures were made.
And two or three doctors said the same thing.
40 The youngest boy did not get to go down there with me,
he lay and said, "Mother, when I die,
"I want you to have them open me up and
"see if that dust killed me.
"Try to get compensation,
45 "you will not have any way of making your living
"when we are gone,
"and the rest are going too."

       I have gained mastery over my heart
       I have gained mastery over my two hands
50   *I have gained mastery over the waters*
       I have gained mastery over the river.

The case of my son was the first of the line of lawsuits.
They sent the lawyers down and the doctors down;
they closed the electric sockets in the camps.
55 There was Shirley, and Cecil, Jeffrey and Oren,
Raymond Johnson, Clev and Oscar Anders,
Frank Lynch, Henry Palf, Mr. Pitch, a foreman;
a slim fellow who carried steel with my boys,
his name was Darnell, I believe. There were many others,
60 the towns of Glen Ferris, Alloy, where the white rock lies,
six miles away; Vanetta, Gauley Bridge,
Gamoca, Lockwood, the gullies,
the whole valley is witness.
I hitchhike eighteen miles, they make checks out.
65 They asked me how I keep the cow on $2.
I said one week, feed for the cow, one week, the children's
    flour.
The oldest son was twenty-three.
The next son was twenty-one.
70 The youngest son was eighteen.

They called it pneumonia at first.
They would pronounce it fever.
Shirley asked that we try to find out.
That's how they learned what the trouble was.

75   *I open out a way, they have covered my sky with crystal*
      I come forth by day, I am born a second time,
      I force a way through, and I know the gate
      I shall journey over the earth among the living.

He shall not be diminished, never;
80 I shall give a mouth to my son.

                                                    1938

The Minotaur

Trapped, blinded, led; and in the end betrayed
Daily by new betrayals as he stays
Deep in his labyrinth, shaking and going mad.
Betrayed. Betrayed. Raving, the beaten head
5 Heavy with madness, he stands, half-dead and proud.
No one again will ever see his pride.
No one will find him by walking to him straight
But must be led circuitously about,
Calling to him and close and, losing the subtle thread,
10 Lose him again; while he waits, brutalized
By loneliness.   Later, afraid
Of his own suffering.   At last, savage and made
Ravenous, ready to prey upon the race
If it so much as learn the clews of blood
15 Into his pride his fear his glistening heart.
Now is the patient deserted in his fright
And love carrying salvage round the world
Lost in a crooked city; roundabout,
By the sea, the precipice, all the fantastic ways
20 Betrayal weaves its trap; loneliness knows the thread,
And the heart is lost, lost, trapped, blinded and led,
Deserted at the middle of the maze.

                                                    1944

Rite

My father groaned; my mother wept.
Among the mountains of the west
A deer lifted her golden throat.

They tore the pieces of the kill
5 While two dark sisters laughed and sang.—
The hidden lions blare until

The hunters charge and burn them all.
And in the black apartment halls
Of every city in the land

10 A father groans; a mother weeps;
A girl to puberty has come;
They shriek this, this is the crime

The gathering of the powers in.
At this first sign of her next life
15 America is stricken dumb.

The sharpening of your rocky knife!
The first blood of a woman shed!
The sacred word: Stand Up You Dead.

Mothers go weep; let fathers groan,
20 The flag of infinity is shown.
Now you will never be alone.

1958

The Poem as Mask

Orpheus

When I wrote of the women in their dances and wildness, it
    was a mask,
on their mountain, gold-hunting, singing, in orgy,
it was a mask; when I wrote of the god,
5 fragmented, exiled from himself, his life, the love gone down
    with song,
it was myself, split open, unable to speak, in exile from myself.

There is no mountain, there is no god, there is memory
of my torn life, myself split open in sleep, the rescued child
10 beside me among the doctors, and a word
of rescue from the great eyes.

No more masks! No more mythologies!

Now, for the first time, the god lifts his hand,
the fragments join in me with their own music.

1968

Martin Luther King, Malcolm X

Bleeding of the mountains
the noon bleeding
he is shot through the voice
all things being broken

5 The moon returning in her blood
looks down   grows white
loses color
and blazes

. . . and the near star gone—

10 voices of cities
drumming in the moon

bleeding of my right hand
my black voice bleeding

1973

How We Did It

We all traveled into that big room,
some from very far away
we smiled at some we knew
we did not as we talked agree
5 our hearts went fast thinking of morning

when we would walk along the path.
We spoke.   Late night.   We disagreed.
We knew we would climb the Senate steps.
We knew we would present our claim
10 we would demand : be strong now : end the war.
How would we do it?   What would we ask?
"We will be warned," one said. "They will warn us and
    take us."
"We can speak and walk away."
15 "We can lie down as if in mourning."
"We can lie down as a way of speech,
speaking of all the dead in Asia."
Then Eqbal said, "We are not at this moment
a revolutionary group, we are
20 a group of dissenters.   Let some, then,
walk away, let some stand until they want to leave,
let some lie down and let some be arrested.   Some of us.
Let each do what he feels at that moment
tomorrow."   Eqbal's dark face.
25 The doctor spoke, of friendships made in jail.
We looked into each other's eyes
and went all to our rooms, to sleep,
waiting for morning.

1976

Carlos Bulosan 1913–1956

The first Filipino writer to bring Filipino concerns to national attention, Carlos Bulosan came to Seattle in 1930, steerage class, inculcated with the ideals of brotherhood and equality he had learned in American schools in the Philippines. Arriving at the start of the Great Depression, he quickly learned the bitter truth that when jobs are scarce, minorities and immigrants become scapegoats, and the egalitarian rhetoric was far from reality for such as he. From the 1870s, the Chinese had been targets of such racial hatred; in the 1930s, the Filipinos were perceived as the latest influx of the "yellow horde" who worked for little pay, taking jobs away from whites. In his brief experience as a migrant laborer, Bulosan endured living conditions worse than those

he had left behind. Bulosan found "that in many ways it was a crime to be a Filipino in California. I came to know that the public streets were not free to my people: we were stopped each time these vigilant patrolmen saw us driving a car. We were suspect each time we were seen with a white woman."

In Los Angeles, Bulosan met labor organizer Chris Mensalves. Together they organized a union of fish cannery workers, and Bulosan, working as a dishwasher, wrote for the union paper. Writing became a means of defining his life, and his concern for just treatment for Filipino workers became one of his major themes. In 1936 the effects of poverty and constant moving led to tuberculosis. Bulosan entered the hospital, and in 1938 he was discharged, after three operations for lung lesions and an extended convalescence. His enforced confinement became his education. Bulosan read at least a book a day, from Whitman and Poe through Hemingway, Dreiser, and Steinbeck.

With some of the most important Pacific action of World War II occurring in the Philippine Islands, names such as Bataan and Corregidor became household words, and the climate was right for Bulosan to rise to national prominence. The *Saturday Evening Post* paid nearly a thousand dollars for Bulosan's essay "Freedom from Want" (an essay which was illustrated by Norman Rockwell and displayed in the Federal Building in San Francisco); his work appeared in *The New Yorker, Harper's Bazaar, Town and Country, Poetry* and other prestigious magazines, and he was featured on the cover of news magazines. His book of reminiscences, *Laughter of My Father,* was broadcast to American soldiers around the world, and *Look* declared his autobiographic novel, *America Is in the Heart,* one of the fifty most important American books ever published.

However, Bulosan died in 1956, in poverty and obscurity. The political climate had changed, and narratives of the underdog, the remorselessly common person, were no longer appealing. In Asian American literature, though, Carlos Bulosan's impassioned work has an enduring place.

The following selections from chapters 13 and 14 of *America Is in the Heart* describe Carlos's arrival in the United States at age seventeen, penniless, idealistic, and naive. Thrust into a violent, dog-eat-dog world, Carlos struggles to maintain his belief in himself and the faith in the American ideals of democracy and justice that he had been taught in the Philippines. *America Is in the Heart* is a reminder to Americans to live up to the ideals set forth by the founders and a searing record of the painful experience of Filipino immigrants in the United States in the 1930s.

Amy Ling
late of University of Wisconsin at Madison

King-Kok Cheung
University of California, Los Angeles

PRIMARY WORKS

The Voice of Bataan, 1943; *The Dark People,* 1944; *Laughter of My Father,* 1944; *America Is in the Heart,* 1946; *The Power of the People,* 1977.

from America Is in the Heart

from Chapter XIII

We arrived in Seattle on a June day. My first sight of the approaching land was an exhilarating experience. Everything seemed native and promising to me. It was like coming home after a long voyage, although as yet I had no home in this city. Everything seemed familiar and kind—the white faces of the buildings melting in the soft afternoon sun, the gray contours of the surrounding valleys that seemed to vanish in the last periphery of light. With a sudden surge of joy, I knew that I must find a home in this new land.

I had only twenty cents left, not even enough to take me to Chinatown where, I had been informed, a Filipino hotel and two restaurants were located. Fortunately two oldtimers put me in a car with four others, and took us to a hotel on King Street, the heart of Filipino life in Seattle. Marcelo, who was also in the car, had a cousin named Elias who came to our room with another oldtimer. Elias and his unknown friend persuaded my companions to play a strange kind of card game. In a little while Elias got up and touched his friend suggestively; then they disappeared and we never saw them again.

It was only when our two countrymen had left that my companions realized what happened. They had taken all their money. Marcelo asked me if I had any money. I gave him my twenty cents. After collecting a few more cents from the others, he went downstairs and when he came back he told us that he had telegraphed for money to his brother in California.

All night we waited for the money to come, hungry and afraid to go out in the street. Outside we could hear shouting and singing; then a woman screamed lustily in one of the rooms down the hall. Across from our hotel a jazz band was playing noisily; it went on until dawn. But in the morning a telegram came to Marcelo which said:

YOUR BROTHER DIED AUTOMOBILE ACCIDENT LAST WEEK

Marcelo looked at us and began to cry. His anguish stirred an aching fear in me. I knelt on the floor looking for my suitcase under the bed. I knew that I had to go out now—alone. I put the suitcase on my shoulder and walked toward the door, stopping for a moment to look back at my friends who were still standing silently around Marcelo. Suddenly a man came into the room and announced that he was the proprietor.

"Well, boys," he said, looking at our suitcases, "where is the rent?"

"We have no money, sir," I said, trying to impress him with my politeness.

"That is too bad," he said quickly, glancing furtively at our suitcases again. "That is just too bad." He walked outside and went down the hall. He came back with a short, fat Filipino, who looked at us stupidly with his dull, small eyes, and spat his cigar out of the window.

"There they are, Jake," said the proprietor.

Jake looked disappointed. "They are too young," he said.

"You can break them in, Jake," said the proprietor.

"They will be sending babies next," Jake said.

"You can break them in, can't you, Jake?" the proprietor pleaded. "This is not the first time you have broken babies in. You have done it in the sugar plantations in Hawaii, Jake!"

"Hell!" Jake said, striding across the room to the proprietor. He pulled a fat roll of bills from his pocket and gave twenty-five dollars to the proprietor. Then he turned to us and said, "All right, Pinoys, you are working for me now. Get your hats and follow me."

We were too frightened to hesitate. When we lifted our suitcases the proprietor ordered us not to touch them.

"I'll take care of them until you come back from Alaska," he said. "Good fishing, boys!"

In this way we were sold for five dollars each to work in the fish canneries in Alaska, by a Visayan from the island of Leyte to an Ilocano from the province of La Union. Both were oldtimers; both were tough. They exploited young immigrants until one of them, the hotel proprietor, was shot dead by an unknown assailant. We were forced to sign a paper which stated that each of us owed the contractor twenty dollars for bedding and another twenty for luxuries. What the luxuries were, I have never found out. The contractor turned out to be a tall, heavy-set, dark Filipino, who came to the small hold of the boat barking at us like a dog. He was drunk and saliva was running down his shirt.

"And get this, you devils!" he shouted at us. "You will never come back alive if you don't do what I say!"

It was the beginning of my life in America, the beginning of a long flight that carried me down the years, fighting desperately to find peace in some corner of life.

I had struck up a friendship with two oldtimers who were not much older than I. One was Conrado Torres, a journalism student at a university in Oregon, who was fired with a dream to unionize the cannery workers. I discovered that he had come from Binalonan, but could hardly remember the names of people there because he had been very young when he had come to America. Conrado was small and dark, with slant eyes and thick eyebrows; but his nose was thin above a wise, sensuous mouth. He introduced me to Paulo Lorca, a gay fellow, who had graduated from law school in Los Angeles. This surreptitious meeting at a cannery in Rose Inlet was the beginning of a friendship that grew simultaneously with the growth of the trade union movement and progressive ideas among the Filipinos in the United States.

In those days labor unions were still unheard of in the canneries, so the contractors rapaciously exploited their workers. They had henchmen in every cannery who saw to it that every attempt at unionization was frustrated and the instigators of the idea punished. The companies also had their share in the exploitation; our bunkhouses were unfit for human habitation. The lighting system was bad and dangerous to our eyes, and those of us who were working in the semi-darkness were severely affected by the strong ammonia from the machinery.

I was working in a section called "wash lye." Actually a certain amount of lye was diluted in the water where I washed the beheaded fish that came down on a small escalator. One afternoon a cutter above me, working in the poor light, slashed off his right arm with the cutting machine. It happened so swiftly, he did not cry out. I saw his arm floating down the water among the fish heads.

It was only at night that we felt free, although the sun seemed never to disappear from the sky. It stayed on in the western horizon and its magnificence inflamed the snows on the island, giving us a world of soft, continuous light, until the moon rose at about ten o'clock to take its place. Then trembling shadows began to form on the rise of the brilliant snow in our yard, and we would come out with baseball bats, gloves and balls, and the Indian girls who worked in the cannery would join us, shouting huskily like men.

We played far into the night. Sometimes a Filipino and an Indian girl would run off into the moonlight; we could hear them chasing each other in the snow. Then we would hear the girl giggling and laughing deliciously in the shadows. Paulo was always running off with a girl named LaBelle. How she acquired that name in Alaska,

I never found out. But hardly had we started our game when off they ran, chasing each other madly and suddenly disappearing out of sight.

Toward the end of the season La Belle gave birth to a baby. We were sure, however, that the father was not in our group. We were sure that she had got it from one of the Italian fishermen on the island. La Belle did not come to work for two days, but when she appeared on the third day with the baby slung on her back, she threw water into Conrado's face.

"Are you going to marry me or not?" she asked him.

Conrado was frightened. He was familiar with the ways of Indians, so he said: "Why should I marry you?"

"We'll see about that!" La Belle shouted, running to the door. She came back with an official of the company. "That's the one!" she said, pointing to Conrado.

"You'd better come to the office with us," said the official.

Conrado did not know what to do. He looked at me for help. Paulo left his washing machine and nodded to me to follow him. We went with them into the building which was the town hall.

"You are going to marry this Indian girl and stay on the island for seven years as prescribed by law," said the official to Conrado. "And as the father of the baby, you must support both mother and child, and, if you have four more children by the time your turn is up, you will be sent back to the mainland with a bonus."

"But, sir, the baby is not mine," said Conrado weakly.

Paulo stepped up quickly beside him and said: "The baby is mine, sir. I guess I'll have to stay."

La Belle looked at Paulo with surprise. After a moment, however, she began to smile with satisfaction. Paulo was well-educated and spoke good English. But I think what finally drove Conrado from La Belle's primitive mind were Paulo's curly hair, his even, white teeth. Meekly she signed the paper after Paulo.

"I'll stay here for seven years, all right," Paulo said to me. "I'm a mess in Los Angeles anyway—so I'll stay with this dirty Indian girl."

"Stop talking like that if you know what is good for you," La Belle said, giving him the baby.

"I guess you are right," Paulo said.

"You shouldn't have done it for me," Conrado said.

"It's all right," Paulo laughed. "I'll be in the United States before you know it."

I still do not understand why Paulo interceded for Conrado. When the season was over Paulo came to our bunks in the boat and asked Conrado to send him something to drink. I did not see him again.

from Chapter XIV

When I landed in Seattle for the second time, I expected a fair amount of money from the company. But the contractor, Max Feuga, came into the play room and handed us slips of paper. I looked at mine and was amazed at the neatly itemized expenditures that I was supposed to have incurred during the season. Twenty-five dollars for withdrawals, one hundred for board and room, twenty for bedding, and another twenty for something I do not now remember. At the bottom was the actual amount I was to receive after all the deductions: *thirteen dollars!*

I could do nothing. I did not even go to the hotel where I had left my suitcase. I went to a Japanese dry goods store on Jackson Street and bought a pair of corduroy pants and a blue shirt. It was already twilight and the cannery workers were in the crowded Chinese gambling houses, losing their season's earnings and drinking boot-leg whisky. They became quarrelsome and abusive to their own people when they lost, and subservient to the Chinese gambling lords and marijuana peddlers. They pawed at the semi-nude whores with their dirty hands and made suggestive gestures, running out into the night when they were rebuffed for lack of money.

I was already in America, and I felt good and safe. I did not understand why. The gamblers, prostitutes and Chinese opium smokers did not excite me, but they aroused in me a feeling of flight. I knew that I must run away from them, but it was not that I was afraid of contamination. I wanted to see other aspects of American life, for surely these destitute and vicious people were merely a small part of it. Where would I begin this pilgrimage, this search for a door into America?

I went outside and walked around looking into the faces of my countrymen, wondering if I would see someone I had known in the Philippines. I came to a build-ing which brightly dressed white women were entering, lifting their diaphanous gowns as they climbed the stairs. I looked up and saw the huge sign:

MANILA DANCE HALL

The orchestra upstairs was playing; Filipinos were entering. I put my hands in my pockets and followed them, beginning to feel lonely for the sound of home.

The dance hall was crowded with Filipino cannery workers and domestic ser-vants. But the girls were very few, and the Filipinos fought over them. When a boy liked a girl he bought a roll of tickets from the hawker on the floor and kept dancing with her. But the other boys who also liked the same girl shouted at him to stop, curs-ing him in dialects and sometimes throwing rolled wet papers at him. At the bar the glasses were tinkling, the bottles popping loudly, and the girls in the back room were smoking marijuana. It was almost impossible to breathe.

Then I saw Marcelo's familiar back. He was dancing with a tall blonde in a green dress, a girl so tall that Marcelo looked like a dwarf climbing a tree. But the girl was pretty and her body was nicely curved and graceful, and she had a way of swaying that aroused confused sensations in me. It was evident that many of the boys wanted to dance with her; they were shouting maliciously at Marcelo. The way the blonde waved to them made me think that she knew most of them. They were nearly all old-timers and strangers to Marcelo. They were probably gamblers and pimps, because they had fat rolls of money and expensive clothing.

But Marcelo was learning very fast. He requested one of his friends to buy an-other roll of tickets for him. The girl was supposed to tear off one ticket every three minutes, but I noticed that she tore off a ticket for every minute. That was ten cents a minute. Marcelo was unaware of what she was doing; he was spending his whole season's earnings on his first day in America. It was only when one of his friends shouted to him in the dialect that he became angry with the girl. Marcelo was not tough, but his friend was an oldtimer. Marcelo pushed the girl toward the gaping by-standers. His friend opened a knife and gave it to him.

Then something happened that made my heart leap. One of the blonde girl's admirers came from behind and struck Marcelo with a piece of lead pipe. Marcelo's friend whipped out a pistol and fired. Marcelo and the boy with the lead pipe fell on the floor simultaneously, one on top of the other, but the blonde girl ran into the crowd screaming frantically. Several guns banged at once, and the lights went out. I saw Marcelo's friend crumple in the fading light.

At once the crowd seemed to flow out of the windows. I went to a side window and saw three heavy electric wires strung from the top of the building to the ground. I reached for them and slid to the ground. My palms were burning when I came out of the alley. Then I heard the sirens of police cars screaming infernally toward the place. I put my cap in my pocket and ran as fast as I could in the direction of a neon sign two blocks down the street.

It was a small church where Filipino farm workers were packing their suitcases and bundles. I found out later that Filipino immigrants used their churches as rest houses while they were waiting for work. There were two large trucks outside. I went to one of them and sat on the running board, holding my hands over my heart for fear it would beat too fast. The lights in the church went out and the workers came into the street. The driver of the truck in which I was sitting pointed a strong flashlight at me.

"Hey, you, are you looking for a job?" he asked.

"Yes, sir," I said.

"Get in the truck," he said, jumping into the cab. "Let's go, Flo!" he shouted to the other driver.

I was still trembling with excitement. But I was glad to get out of Seattle—to anywhere else in America. I did not care where so long as it was in America. I found a corner and sat down heavily. The drivers shouted to each other. Then we were off to work.

It was already midnight and the lights in the city of Seattle were beginning to fade. I could see the reflections on the bright lake in Bremerton. I was reminded of Baguio. Then some of the men began singing. The driver and two men were arguing over money. A boy in the other truck was playing a violin. We were on the highway to Yakima Valley.

After a day and a night of driving we arrived in a little town called Moxee City. The apple trees were heavy with fruit and the branches drooped to the ground. It was late afternoon when we passed through the town; the hard light of the sun punctuated the ugliness of the buildings. I was struck dumb by its isolation and the dry air that hung oppressively over the place. The heart-shaped valley was walled by high treeless mountains, and the hot breeze that blew in from a distant sea was injurious to the apple trees.

The leader of our crew was called Cornelio Paez; but most of the oldtimers suspected that it was not his real name. There was something shifty about him, and his so-called bookkeeper, a pockmarked man we simply called Pinoy (which is a term generally applied to all Filipino immigrant workers), had a strange trick of squinting sideways when he looked at you. There seemed to be an old animosity between Paez and his bookkeeper.

But we were drawn together because the white people of the Yakima Valley were suspicious of us. Years before, in the town of Toppenish, two Filipino apple pickers had been found murdered on the road to Sunnyside. At that time, there was ruthless persecution of the Filipinos throughout the Pacific Coast, instigated by orchardists who feared the unity of white and Filipino workers. A small farmer in Wapato who had tried to protect his Filipino workers had had his house burned. So however much we distrusted each other under Paez, we knew that beyond the walls of our bunkhouse were our real enemies, waiting to drive us out of Yakima Valley.

I had become acquainted with an oldtimer who had had considerable experience in the United States. His name was Julio, and it seemed that he was hiding from some trouble in Chicago. At night, when the men gambled in the kitchen, I would stand silently behind him and watch him cheat the other players. He was very deft, and his eyes were sharp and trained. Sometimes when there was no game, Julio would teach me tricks.

Mr. Malraux, our employer, had three daughters who used to work with us after school hours. He was a Frenchman who had gone to Moxee City when it consisted of only a few houses. At that time the valley was still a haven for Indians, but they had been gradually driven out when farming had been started on a large scale. Malraux had married an American woman in Spokane and begun farming; the girls came one by one, helping him on the farm as they grew. When I arrived in Moxee City they were already in their teens.

The oldest girl was called Estelle; she had just finished high school. She had a delightful disposition and her industry was something that men talked about with approval. The other girls, Maria and Diane, were still too young to be going about so freely; but whenever Estelle came to our bunkhouse they were always with her.

It was now the end of summer and there was a bright moon in the sky. Not far from Moxee City was a wide grassland where cottontails and jack rabbits roamed at night. Estelle used to drive her father's old car and would pick up some of us at the bunkhouse; then we would go hunting with their dogs and a few antiquated shotguns.

When we came back from hunting we would go to the Malraux house with some of the men who had musical instruments. We would sit on the lawn for hours singing American songs. But when they started singing Philippine songs their voices were so sad, so full of yesterday and the haunting presence of familiar seas, as if they had reached the end of creation, that life seemed ended and no bright spark was left in the world.

But one afternoon toward the end of the season, Paez went to the bank to get our paychecks and did not come back. The pockmarked bookkeeper was furious.

"I'll get him this time!" he said, running up and down the house. "He did that last year in California and I didn't get a cent. I know where to find the bastard!"

Julio grabbed him by the neck. "You'd better tell me where to find him if you know what is good for you," he said angrily, pushing the frightened bookkeeper toward the stove.

"Let me alone!" he shouted.

Julio hit him between the eyes, and the bookkeeper struggled violently. Julio hit him again. The bookkeeper rolled on the floor like a baby. Julio picked him up and threw him outside the house. I thought he was dead, but his legs began to move. Then he opened his eyes and got up quickly, staggering like a drunken stevedore toward the highway. Julio came out of the house with brass knuckles, but the bookkeeper was already disappearing behind the apple orchard. Julio came back and began hitting the door of the kitchen with all his force, in futile anger.

I had not seen this sort of brutality in the Philippines, but my first contact with it in America made me brave. My bravery was still nameless, and waiting to express itself. I was not shocked when I saw that my countrymen had become ruthless toward one another, and this sudden impact of cruelty made me insensate to pain and kindness, so that it took me a long time to wholly trust other men. As time went by I became as ruthless as the worst of them, and I became afarid that I would never feel like a human being again. Yet no matter what bestiality encompassed my life, I felt sure that somewhere, sometime, I would break free. This faith kept me from completely succumbing to the degradation into which many of my countrymen had fallen. It finally paved my way out of our small, harsh life, painfully but cleanly, into a world of strange intellectual adventures and self-fulfillment.

1946

Robert Hayden 1913–1980

Born Asa Bundy Sheffey in Detroit, Michigan, Hayden grew up in a poor, racially mixed neighborhood. Because his parents were divorced when he was quite young, his mother left him with neighbors, William and Sue Ellen Hayden, who gave him their name and raised him. His mother's periodic reappearances coupled with the jealousy of his foster mother made him "a divided person," and his art includes images of warring forces within the self.

Nearsighted and introverted, Hayden spent many hours reading and writing, and published his first poem at eighteen. Between 1932 and 1936, he attended Detroit City College (now Wayne State University); between 1936 and 1938, he worked for the Federal Writers Project of the Works Progress Administration (WPA), and in 1944 completed an M.A. in English at the University of Michigan. (In 1940 he had married Erma Morris, a musician and teacher.) In 1946 he began teaching at Fisk University and in 1969 joined the English Department of the University of Michigan, where he taught until his death.

Much of his life Hayden wrote good poetry with little recognition. He was sustained by some awards and by friendships with other poets: a Rosenwald Fellowship in 1947, a Ford Foundation grant to write and travel in Mexico in 1954–1955, and

the Grand Prize for Poetry at the First World Festival of Negro Arts in 1966. During the 1970s he was published by Liveright (*Angle of Ascent,* 1975), elected a fellow of the American Academy of Poets, and in 1976 chosen as Consultant in Poetry to the Library of Congress, the first African American ever to hold that post.

Hayden's philosophy of art remained constant throughout his life. Opposed to ethnocentrism, he refused to allow race to define subject matter. He also refused to believe that black social and political frustrations demanded poetry aimed exclusively at a black readership. Two criteria pertained for all artists: expert craft and universal subject matter. Universality, moreover, did not mean denial of racial material; it meant building out of personal and ethnic experience to human insights that could reach across group lines. Hayden's Baha'i faith, which he adopted in the 1940s, helped him believe in the unity of people and in the spiritual importance of art.

Some of the major themes of Hayden's poetry are the tensions between the imagination and the tragic nature of life, the past in the present, art as a form of spiritual redemption, and the nurturing power of early life and history. Most of his work falls into categories of "spirit of place" poems, folk character poems, Detroit neighborhood poems, and historical poems. This latter group, best known by the long poem "Middle Passage," is aimed at "correcting the misconceptions and destroying some of the stereotypes and clichés which surround Negro history." In the context of the racial militance of the 1960s and 1970s,

Hayden's work has sometimes been found wanting by younger poets. His output for over forty years, however, suggests the deepest of commitments both to his own race and to humanity as a whole.

Robert M. Greenberg
Temple University

PRIMARY WORKS

Heart-Shape in the Dust, 1940; *The Lion and the Archer,* with Myron O'Higgins, 1948; *Figure of Time,* 1955; *A Ballad of Remembrance,* 1962; *Selected Poems,* 1966; *Words in the Mourning Time,* 1970; *The Night-Blooming Cereus,* 1972; *Angle of Ascent: New and Selected Poems,* 1975; *American Journal,* 1982; *Collected Prose,* 1984; *Collected Poems,* 1985.

Tour 5[1]

The road winds down through autumn hills
in blazonry of farewell scarlet
and recessional gold,
past cedar groves, through static villages
5 whose names are all that's left
of Choctaw, Chickasaw.

We stop a moment in a town
watched over by Confederate sentinels,
buy gas and ask directions of a rawboned man
10 whose eyes revile us as the enemy.

Shrill gorgon[2] silence breathes behind
his taut civility
and in the ever-tauntening air,
dark for us despite its Indian summer glow.
15 We drive on, following the route
of highwaymen and phantoms,

Of slaves and armies.
Children, wordless and remote,
wave at us from kindling porches.

---

[1] Alludes to an auto route in a guidebook that includes the old Natchez Trace, originally an Indian trail that later became "a dangerous and sinister road used by escaped criminals, highwaymen, murderers."

[2] Snaky-haired sisters in Greek mythology who turned those who looked at them to stone.

20 And now the land is flat for miles,
       the landscape lush, metallic, flayed,
       its brightness harsh as bloodstained swords.

                                             1962

Those Winter Sundays

       Sundays too my father got up early
       and put his clothes on in the blueblack cold,
       then with cracked hands that ached
       from labor in the weekday weather made
   5   banked fires blaze. No one ever thanked him.

       I'd wake and hear the cold splintering, breaking.
       When the rooms were warm, he'd call,
       and slowly I would rise and dress,
       fearing the chronic angers of that house,

10   Speaking indifferently to him,
       who had driven out the cold
       and polished my good shoes as well.
       What did I know, what did I know
       of love's austere and lonely offices?

                                             1962

Summertime and the Living . . .[1]

       Nobody planted roses, he recalls,
       but sunflowers gangled there sometimes,
       tough-stalked and bold
       and like the vivid children there unplanned.
   5   There circus-poster horses curveted
       in trees of heaven
       above the quarrels and shattered glass,
       and he was bareback rider of them all.

---

[1]Lyric ("Summertime and the living is easy")
from George and Ira Gershwin's *Porgie and
Bess.*

No roses there in summer—
10 oh, never roses except when people died—
and no vacations for his elders,
so harshened after each unrelenting day
that they were shouting-angry.
But summer was, they said, the poor folks' time
15 of year. And he remembers
how they would sit on broken steps amid

The fevered tossings of the dusk, the dark,
wafting hearsay with funeral-parlor fans
or making evening solemn by
20 their quietness. Feels their Mosaic eyes
upon him, though the florist roses
that only sorrow could afford
long since have bidden them Godspeed.
Oh, summer summer summertime—

25 Then grim street preachers shook
their tambourines and Bibles in the face
of tolerant wickedness;
then Elks parades and big splendiferous
Jack Johnson[2] in his diamond limousine
30 set the ghetto burgeoning
with fantasies
of Ethiopia spreading her gorgeous wings.[3]

1962

Mourning Poem for the Queen of Sunday

Lord's lost Him His mockingbird,
His fancy warbler;
Satan sweet-talked her,
four bullets hushed her.
5 Who would have thought
she'd end that way?

Four bullets hushed her. And the world a-clang with evil.
Who's going to make old hardened sinner men tremble now
and the righteous rock?

[2]A black folk-hero, Jack Johnson (1878–1946) won the world heavyweight boxing championship in 1908. He was the subject of the Broadway play and Hollywood movie *The Great White Hope.*

[3]Adapts an often-quoted biblical reference to Ethiopia.

10   Oh who and oh who will sing Jesus down
     to help with struggling and doing without and being colored
     all through blue Monday?
     Till way next Sunday?

         All those angels
15   in their cretonne clouds and finery
         the true believer saw
         when she rared back her head and sang,
         all those angels are surely weeping.
         Who would have thought
20   she'd end that way?

     Four holes in her heart. The gold works wrecked.
     But she looks so natural in her big bronze coffin
     among the Broken Hearts and Gates-Ajar,
     it's as if any moment she'd lift her head
25 from its pillow of chill gardenias
     and turn this quiet into shouting Sunday
     and make folks forget what she did on Monday.

         Oh, Satan sweet-talked her,
         and four bullets hushed her.
30   Lord's lost Him His diva,
         His fancy warbler's gone.
         Who would have thought,
         who would have thought she'd end that way?

                                        1962

Bernard Malamud 1914–1986

Author of eight novels and numerous short stories, Bernard Malamud preferred to view himself as a universal writer who "happened to be Jewish, also American." Malamud's diverse subjects, varied readers, and prestigious national awards underscore his status as a major twentieth century writer and a prominent American Jewish author.

Malamud consistently transformed the raw materials of his life into imaginative fiction. Born in 1914 to Max and Bertha Malamud, hard working Russian Jews who ran a Brooklyn grocery (the setting for *The Assistant*), the author attended Erasmus High School, received a B.A. from City College and an M.A. from Columbia University. After teaching evenings in New York City high schools for several years, Malamud moved to Oregon with his wife Ann and their young son Paul. For a decade he taught at Oregon State University in Corvallis, the subject of his academic satire, *A New Life*. During that period, he published some of his finest fiction: *The Natural,* an allegorical baseball story made into a film; *The Assistant,* and *The Magic Barrel,* a short story collection that won the National Book Award.

In 1961 Malamud accepted a teaching position at Bennington College that allowed him to spend the warm months in Vermont and the winters in New York City. The move was also conducive to his writing. *The Fixer,* somewhat based on Russian persecution of Mendel Beiliss, a Jew, won both a National Book Award and a Pulitzer Prize. Within the next decade, Malamud published *Pictures of Fidelman,* a series of stories connected by an Italian setting and Jewish American protagonist, *The Tenants,* a bleak encounter between an African American and Jewish American writer, and *Rembrandt's Hat,* a short story collection. *Dubin's Lives,* which appeared in 1979, includes a variety of familiar settings (Vermont, New York, and Italy) as well as characters and themes.

Although his last completed novel, *God's Grace* (1982), is his gloomiest, with its post–nuclear war setting and cast of island primates, it contains a reflective, tormented Jew who struggles to understand and to control his grim environment. In fact, though the settings and situations of Malamud's works vary, his bumbling, suffering, at times comic, heroes resemble each other. Whether a Jewish grocer, college professor, novelist, artist, fixer or even Italian assistant or black angel, all are students of life who learn the importance of being human. In Malamud's fiction, a good Jew is a good man. Malamud's world is peopled with Jews and non-Jews in frequently surprising ways. In *The Fixer,* a Jewish spy betrays an embattled prisoner, while a Russian guard attempts to save him. In *The Assistant,* a Jew transforms a gentile into a good person and therefore into a good Jew.

Though Malamud's fiction reflects his immigrant Jewish background and American experience, above all it reveals a unique imagination which can mingle history and fantasy, comedy and tragedy. A combination of such elements seems to characterize *The People,* the novel Malamud was composing when he died. In contrast to his later, more pessimistic works, *The People,* published posthumously in 1989, unites a lonely Jewish immigrant with a needy Indian tribe in what promises to be a mutually beneficial association.

Even without *The People,* Malamud's legacy is enormous. A leader of the post-World War II Jewish literary renaissance, Malamud changed the landscape of American literature, introducing mainstream America to marginal ethnic characters, to immigrant urban settings, to Jewish-American dialect and, most important, to a world with which Americans could empathize. Something of a magician, Malamud transformed the particular into the universal so that poor Jews symbolized all individuals struggling to survive with dignity and humanity.

Evelyn Avery
Towson University

PRIMARY WORKS

The Natural, 1952; *The Assistant,* 1957; *The Magic Barrel,* 1958; *A New Life,* 1961; *Idiots First,* 1963; *The Fixer,* 1966; *Pictures of Fidelman: An Exhibition,* 1969; *The Tenants,* 1971; *Rembrandt's Hat,* 1973; *Dubin's Lives,* 1979; *God's Grace,* 1982; *The Stories of Bernard Malamud,* 1984; *The People and Uncollected Stories,* 1989; *The Complete Stories of Bernard Malamud,* 1997.

The Magic Barrel

Not long ago there lived in uptown New York, in a small, almost meager room, though crowded with books, *Leo Finkle,* a rabbinical student at the Yeshiva University. Finkle, after six years of study, was to be ordained in June and had been advised by an acquaintance that he might find it easier to win himself a congregation if he were married. Since he had no present prospects of marriage, after two tormented days of turning it over in his mind, he called in Pinye Salzman, a marriage broker whose two-line advertisement he had read in the *Forward*.

The matchmaker appeared one night out of the dark fourth-floor hallway of the graystone rooming house where Finkle lived, grasping a black, strapped portfolio that had been worn thin with use. Salzman, who had been long in the business, was of slight but dignified build, wearing an old hat, and an overcoat too short and tight for him. He smelled frankly of fish, which he loved to eat, and although he was missing a few teeth, his presence was not displeasing, because of an amiable manner curiously contrasted with mournful eyes. His voice, his lips, his wisp of beard, his bony fingers were animated, but give him a moment of repose and his mild blue eyes revealed a depth of sadness, a characteristic that put Leo a little at ease although the situation, for him, was inherently tense.

He at once informed Salzman why he had asked him to come, explaining that but for his parents, who had married comparatively late in life, he was alone in the world. He had for six years devoted himself almost entirely to his studies, as a result of which, understandably, he had found himself without time for social life and the company of young women. Therefore he thought it the better part of trial and error—of embarrassing fumbling—to call in an experienced person to advise him on these matters. He remarked in passing that the function of the marriage broker was ancient and honorable, highly approved in the Jewish community, because it made practical the necessary without hindering joy. Moreover, his own parents had been brought together by a matchmaker. They had made, if not a financially profitable marriage—since neither had possessed any worldly goods to speak of—at least a successful one in the sense of their everlasting devotion to each other. Salzman listened in embarrassed surprise, sensing a sort of apology. Later, however, he experienced a glow of pride in his work, an emotion that had left him years ago, and he heartily approved of Finkle.

The two went to their business. Leo had led Salzman to the only clear place in the room, a table near a window that overlooked the lamp-lit city. He seated himself at the matchmaker's side but facing him, attempting by an act of will to suppress the unpleasant tickle in his throat. Salzman eagerly unstrapped his portfolio and removed a loose rubber band from a thin packet of much-handled cards. As he flipped through them, a gesture and sound that physically hurt Leo, the student pretended not to see and gazed steadfastly out the window. Although it was still February, winter was on its last legs, signs of which he had for the first time in years begun to notice. He now observed the round white moon, moving high in the sky through a cloud menagerie, and watched with half-open mouth as it penetrated a huge hen, and dropped out of her like an egg laying itself. Salzman, though pretending through eyeglasses he had just slipped on to be engaged in scanning the writing on the cards, stole occasional glances at the young man's distinguished face, noting with pleasure the long, severe scholar's nose, brown eyes heavy with learning, sensitive yet ascetic lips, and a certain almost hollow quality of the dark cheeks. He gazed around at shelves upon shelves of books and let out a soft, contented sigh.

When Leo's eyes fell upon the cards, he counted six spread out in Salzman's hand.

"So few?" he asked in disappointment.

"You wouldn't believe me how much cards I got in my office," Salzman replied. "The drawers are already filled to the top, so I keep them now in a barrel, but is every girl good for a new rabbi?"

Leo blushed at this, regretting all he had revealed of himself in a curriculum vitae he had sent to Salzman. He had thought it best to acquaint him with his strict standards and specifications, but in having done so, felt he had told the marriage broker more than was absolutely necessary.

He hesitantly inquired, "Do you keep photographs of your clients on file?"

"First comes family, amount of dowry, also what kind promises," Salzman replied, unbuttoning his tight coat and settling himself in the chair. "After comes pictures, rabbi."

"Call me Mr. Finkle. I'm not yet a rabbi."

Salzman said he would, but instead called him doctor, which he changed to rabbi when Leo was not listening too attentively.

Salzman adjusted his horn-rimmed spectacles, gently cleared his throat, and read in an eager voice the contents of the top card:

"Sophie P. Twenty-four years. Widow one year. No children. Educated high school and two years college. Father promises eight thousand dollars. Has wonderful wholesale business. Also real estate. On the mother's side comes teachers, also one actor. Well known on Second Avenue."

Leo gazed up in surprise. "Did you say a widow?"

"A widow don't mean spoiled, rabbi. She lived with her husband maybe four months. He was a sick boy she made a mistake to marry him."

"Marrying a widow has never entered my mind."

"This is because you have no experience. A widow, especially if she is young and healthy like this girl, is a wonderful person to marry. She will be thankful to you the rest of her life. Believe me, if I was looking now for a bride, I would marry a widow."

Leo reflected, then shook his head.

Salzman hunched his shoulders in an almost imperceptible gesture of disappointment. He placed the card down on the wooden table and began to read another:

"Lily H. High school teacher. Regular. Not a substitute. Has savings and new Dodge car. Lived in Paris one year. Father is successful dentist thirty-five years. Interested in professional man. Well-Americanized family. Wonderful opportunity.

"I know her personally," said Salzman. "I wish you could see this girl. She is a doll. Also very intelligent. All day you could talk to her about books and theyater and what not. She also knows current events."

"I don't believe you mentioned her age?"

"Her age?" Salzman said, raising his brows. "Her age is thirty-two years."

Leo said after a while, "I'm afraid that seems a little too old."

Salzman let out a laugh. "So how old are you, rabbi?"

"Twenty-seven."

"So what is the difference, tell me, between twenty-seven and thirty-two? My own wife is seven years older than me. So what did I suffer?— Nothing. If Rothschild's daughter wants to marry you, would you say on account her age, no?"

"Yes," Leo said dryly.

Salzman shook off the no in the yes. "Five years don't mean a thing. I give you my word that when you will live with her for one week you will forget her age. What does it mean five years—that she lived more and knows more than somebody who is younger? On this girl, God bless her, years are not wasted. Each one that it comes makes better the bargain."

"What subject does she teach in high school?"

"Languages. If you heard the way she speaks French, you will think it is music. I am in the business twenty-five years, and I recommend her with my whole heart. Believe me, I know what I'm talking, rabbi."

"What's on the next card?" Leo said abruptly.

Salzman reluctantly turned up the third card:

"Ruth K. Nineteen years. Honor student. Father offers thirteen thousand cash to the right bridegroom. He is a medical doctor. Stomach specialist with marvelous practice. Brother-in-law owns own garment business. Particular people."

Salzman looked as if he had read his trump card.

"Did you say nineteen?" Leo asked with interest.

"On the dot."

"Is she attractive?" He blushed. "Pretty?"

Salzman kissed his fingertips. "A little doll. On this I give you my word. Let me call the father tonight and you will see what means pretty."

But Leo was troubled. "You're sure she's that young?"

"This I am positive. The father will show you the birth certificate."

"Are you positive there isn't something wrong with her?" Leo insisted.

"Who says there is wrong?"

"I don't understand why an American girl her age should go to a marriage broker."

A smile spread over Salzman's face.

"So for the same reason you went, she comes."

Leo flushed. "I am pressed for time."

Salzman, realizing he had been tactless, quickly explained. "The father came, not her. He wants she should have the best, so he looks around himself. When we will locate the right boy he will introduce him and encourage. This makes a better marriage than if a young girl without experience takes for herself. I don't have to tell you this."

"But don't you think this young girl believes in love?" Leo spoke uneasily.

Salzman was about to guffaw but caught himself and said soberly, "Love comes with the right person, not before."

Leo parted dry lips but did not speak. Noticing that Salzman had snatched a glance at the next card, he cleverly asked, "How is her health?"

"Perfect," Salzman said, breathing with difficulty. "Of course, she is a little lame on her right foot from an auto accident that it happened to her when she was twelve years, but nobody notices on account she is so brilliant and also beautiful."

Leo got up heavily and went to the window. He felt curiously bitter and upbraided himself for having called in the marriage broker. Finally, he shook his head.

"Why not?" Salzman persisted, the pitch of his voice rising.

"Because I detest stomach specialists."

"So what do you care what is his business? After you marry her do you need him? Who says he must come every Friday night in your house?"

Ashamed of the way the talk was going, Leo dismissed Salzman, who went home with heavy, melancholy eyes.

Though he had felt only relief at the marriage broker's departure, Leo was in low spirits the next day. He explained it as arising from Salzman's failure to produce a suitable bride for him. He did not care for his type of clientele. But when Leo found himself hesitating whether to seek out another matchmaker, one more polished than Pinye, he wondered if it could be—his protestations to the contrary, and although he honored his father and mother—that he did not, in essence, care for the matchmaking institution? This thought he quickly put out of mind yet found himself still upset. All day he ran around in the woods—missed an important appointment, forgot to give out his laundry, walked out of a Broadway cafeteria without paying and had to run back with the ticket in his hand; had even not recognized his landlady in the street when she passed with a friend and courteously called out, "A good evening to you, Doctor Finkle." By nightfall, however, he had regained sufficient calm to sink his nose into a book and there found peace from his thoughts.

Almost at once there came a knock on the door. Before Leo could say enter, Salzman, commercial cupid, was standing in the room. His face was gray and meager, his expression hungry, and he looked as if he would expire on his feet. Yet the marriage broker managed, by some trick of the muscles, to display a broad smile.

"So good evening. I am invited?"

Leo nodded, disturbed to see him again, yet unwilling to ask the man to leave.

Beaming still, Salzman laid his portfolio on the table. "Rabbi, I got for you tonight good news."

"I've asked you not to call me rabbi. I'm still a student."

"Your worries are finished. I have for you a first-class bride."

"Leave me in peace concerning this subject." Leo pretended lack of interest.

"The world will dance at your wedding."

"Please, Mr. Salzman, no more."

"But first must come back my strength," Salzman said weakly. He fumbled with the portfolio straps and took out of the leather case an oily paper bag, from which he extracted a hard, seeded roll and a small smoked whitefish. With a quick motion of his hand he stripped the fish out of its skin and began ravenously to chew. "All day in a rush," he muttered.

Leo watched him eat.

"A sliced tomato you have maybe?" Salzman hesitantly inquired.

"No."

The marriage broker shut his eyes and ate. When he had finished he carefully cleaned up the crumbs and rolled up the remains of the fish, in the paper bag. His spectacled eyes roamed the room until he discovered, amid some piles of books, a one-burner gas stove. Lifting his hat he humbly asked, "A glass tea you got, rabbi?"

Conscience-stricken, Leo rose and brewed the tea. He served it with a chunk of lemon and two cubes of lump sugar, delighting Salzman.

After he had drunk his tea, Salzman's strength and good spirits were restored.

"So tell me, rabbi," he said amiably, "you considered some more the three clients I mentioned yesterday?"

"There was no need to consider."

"Why not?"

"None of them suits me."

"What then suits you?"

Leo let it pass because he could give only a confused answer.

Without waiting for a reply, Salzman asked, "You remember this girl I talked to you—the high school teacher?"

"Age thirty-two?"

But, surprisingly, Salzman's face lit in a smile. "Age twenty-nine."

Leo shot him a look. "Reduced from thirty-two?"

"A mistake," Salzman avowed. "I talked today with the dentist. He took me to his safety deposit box and showed me the birth certificate. She was twenty-nine years last August. They made her a party in the mountains where she went for her vacation. When her father spoke to me the first time I forgot to write the age and I told you thirty-two, but now I remember this was a different client, a widow."

"The same one you told me about, I thought she was twenty-four?"

"A different. Am I responsible that the world is filled with widows?"

"No, but I'm not interested in them, nor, for that matter, in schoolteachers."

Salzman pulled his clasped hands to his breast. Looking at the ceiling he devoutly exclaimed, "Yiddishe kinder, what can I say to somebody that he is not interested in high school teachers? So what then you are interested?"

Leo flushed but controlled himself.

"In what else will you be interested," Salzman went on, "if you not interested in this fine girl that she speaks four languages and has personally in the bank ten thousand dollars? Also her father guarantees further twelve thousand. Also she has a new car, wonderful clothes, talks on all subjects, and she will give you a first-class home and children. How near do we come in our life to paradise?"

"If she's so wonderful, why wasn't she married ten years ago?"

"Why?" said Salzman with a heavy laugh. "—Why? Because she is *partikiler*. This is why. She wants the *best*."

Leo was silent, amused at how he had entangled himself. But Salzman had aroused his interest in Lily H., and he began seriously to consider calling on her. When the marriage broker observed how intently Leo's mind was at work on the facts he had supplied, he felt certain they would soon come to an agreement.

Late Saturday afternoon, conscious of Salzman, Leo Finkle walked with Lily Hirschorn along Riverside Drive. He walked briskly and erectly, wearing with distinction the black fedora he had that morning taken with trepidation out of the dusty hat box on his closet shelf, and the heavy black Saturday coat he had thoroughly whisked clean. Leo also owned a walking stick, a present from a distant relative, but quickly put temptation aside and did not use it. Lily, petite and not unpretty, had on something signifying the approach of spring. She was au courant, animatedly, with all sorts of subjects, and he weighed her words and found her surprisingly sound—score another for Salzman, whom he uneasily sensed to be somewhere around, hiding perhaps high in a tree along the street, flashing the lady signals with a pocket mirror; or perhaps a cloven-hoofed Pan, piping nuptial ditties as he danced his invisible way before them, strewing wild buds on the walk and purple grapes in their path, symbolizing fruit of a union, though there was of course still none.

Lily startled Leo by remarking, "I was thinking of Mr. Salzman, a curious figure, wouldn't you say?"

Not certain what to answer, he nodded.

She bravely went on, blushing, "I for one am grateful for his introducing us. Aren't you?"

He courteously replied, "I am."

"I mean," she said with a little laugh—and it was all in good taste, or at least gave the effect of being not in bad—"do you mind that we came together so?"

He was not displeased with her honesty, recognizing that she meant to set the relationship aright, and understanding that it took a certain amount of experience in life, and courage, to want to do it quite that way. One had to have some sort of past to make that kind of beginning.

He said that he did not mind. Salzman's function was traditional and honorable—valuable for what it might achieve, which, he pointed out, was frequently nothing.

Lily agreed with a sigh. They walked on for a while and she said after a long silence, again with a nervous laugh, "Would you mind if I asked you something a little bit personal? Frankly, I find the subject fascinating." Although Leo shrugged, she went on half embarrassedly, "How was it that you came to your calling? I mean, was it a sudden passionate inspiration?"

Leo, after a time, slowly replied, "I was always interested in the Law."

"You saw revealed in it the presence of the Highest?"

He nodded and changed the subject. "I understand that you spent a little time in Paris, Miss Hirschorn?"

"Oh, did Mr. Salzman tell you, Rabbi Finkle?" Leo winced but she went on, "It was ages ago and almost forgotten. I remember I had to return for my sister's wedding."

And Lily would not be put off. "When," she asked in a slightly trembly voice, "did you become enamored of God?"

He stared at her. Then it came to him that she was talking not about Leo Finkle but a total stranger, some mystical figure, perhaps even passionate prophet that Salzman had dreamed up for her—no relation to the living or dead. Leo trembled with rage and weakness. The trickster had obviously sold her a bill of goods, just as he had him, who'd expected to become acquainted with a young lady of twenty-nine, only to behold, the moment he had laid eyes upon her strained and anxious face, a woman past thirty-five and aging rapidly. Only his self-control had kept him this long in her presence.

"I am not," he said gravely, "a talented religious person," and in seeking words to go on, found himself possessed by shame and fear. "I think," he said in a strained manner, "that I came to God not because I loved Him but because I did not."

This confession he spoke harshly because its unexpectedness shook him.

Lily wilted. Leo saw a profusion of loaves of bread go flying like ducks high over his head, not unlike the winged loaves by which he had counted himself to sleep last night. Mercifully, then, it snowed, which he would not put past Salzman's machinations.

He was infuriated with the marriage broker and swore he would throw him out of the room the moment he reappeared. But Salzman did not come that night, and when Leo's anger had subsided, an unaccountable despair grew in its place. At first he thought this was caused by his disappointment in Lily, but before long it became evident that he had involved himself with Salzman without a true knowledge of his own intent. He gradually realized—with an emptiness that seized him with six hands—that he had called in the broker to find him a bride because he was incapable of doing it himself. This terrifying insight he had derived as a result of his meeting and conversation with Lily Hirschorn. Her probing questions had somehow irritated him into revealing—to himself more than her—the true nature of his relationship to God, and from that it had come upon him, with shocking force, that apart from his parents, he had never loved anyone. Or perhaps it went the other way, that he did not love God so well as he might, because he had not loved man. It seemed to Leo that his whole life stood starkly revealed and he saw himself for the first time as he truly was—unloved and loveless. This bitter but somehow not fully unexpected revelation brought him to a point of panic, controlled only by extraordinary effort. He covered his face with his hands and cried.

The week that followed was the worst of his life. He did not eat and lost weight. His beard darkened and grew ragged. He stopped attending seminars and almost never opened a book. He seriously considered leaving the Yeshiva, although he was deeply troubled at the thought of the loss of all his years of study—saw them like pages torn from a book, strewn over the city—and at the devastating effect of this decision upon his parents. But he had lived without knowledge of himself, and never in the Five Books and all the Commentaries—mea culpa—had the truth been revealed to him. He did not know where to turn, and in all this desolating loneliness there was no *to whom,* although he often thought of Lily but not once could bring himself to go downstairs and make the call. He became touchy and irritable, especially with his landlady, who asked him all manner of personal questions; on the other hand, sensing his own disagreeableness, he waylaid her on the stairs and apologized abjectly, until, mortified, she ran from him. Out of this, however, he drew the consolation that he was a Jew and that a Jew suffered. But gradually, as the long and terrible week drew to a close, he regained his composure and some idea of purpose in life: to go on as planned. Although he was imperfect, the ideal was not. As for his quest of a bride, the thought of continuing afflicted him with anxiety and heartburn, yet perhaps with this new knowledge of himself he would be more successful than in the past. Perhaps love would now come to him and a bride to that love. And for this sanctified seeking who needed a Salzman?

The marriage broker, a skeleton with haunted eyes, returned that very night. He looked, withal, the picture of frustrated expectancy—as if he had steadfastly waited the week at Miss Lily Hirschorn's side for a telephone call that never came.

Casually coughing, Salzman came immediately to the point: "So how did you like her?"

Leo's anger rose and he could not refrain from chiding the matchmaker: "Why did you lie to me, Salzman?"

Salzman's pale face went dead white, the world had snowed on him.

"Did you not state that she was twenty-nine?" Leo insisted.

"I give you my word—"

"She was thirty-five, if a day. *At least* thirty-five."

"Of this don't be too sure. Her father told me—"

"Never mind. The worst of it is that you lied to her."

"How did I lie to her, tell me?"

"You told her things about me that weren't true. You made me out to be more, consequently less than I am. She had in mind a totally different person, a sort of semimystical Wonder Rabbi."

"All I said, you was a religious man."

"I can imagine."

Salzman sighed. "This is my weakness that I have," he confessed. "My wife says to me I shouldn't be a salesman, but when I have two fine people that they would be wonderful to be married, I am so happy that I talk too much." He smiled wanly. "This is why Salzman is a poor man."

Leo's anger left him. "Well, Salzman, I'm afraid that's all."

The marriage broker fastened hungry eyes on him.

"You don't want any more a bride?"

"I do," said Leo, "but I have decided to seek her in another way. I am no longer interested in an arranged marriage. To be frank, I now admit the necessity of premarital love. That is, I want to be in love with the one I marry."

"Love?" said Salzman, astounded. After a moment he remarked, "For us, our love is our life, not for the ladies. In the ghetto they—"

"I know, I know," said Leo. "I've thought of it often. Love, I have said to myself, should be a product of living and worship rather than its own end. Yet for myself I find it necessary to establish the level of my need and fulfill it."

Salzman shrugged but answered, "Listen, rabbi, if you want love, this I can find for you also. I have such beautiful clients that you will love them the minute your eyes will see them."

Leo smiled unhappily. "I'm afraid you don't understand."

But Salzman hastily unstrapped his portfolio and withdrew a manila packet from it.

"Pictures," he said, quickly laying the envelope on the table.

Leo called after him to take the pictures away, but as if on the wings of the wind, Salzman had disappeared.

March came. Leo had returned to his regular routine. Although he felt not quite himself yet—lacked energy—he was making plans for a more active social life. Of course it would cost something, but he was an expert in cutting corners; and when there were no corners left he would make circles rounder. All the while Salzman's pictures had lain on the table, gathering dust. Occasionally as Leo sat studying, or enjoying a cup of tea, his eyes fell on the manila envelope, but he never opened it.

The days went by and no social life to speak of developed with a member of the opposite sex—it was difficult, given the circumstances of his situation. One morning Leo toiled up the stairs to his room and stared out the window at the city. Although the day was bright his view of it was dark. For some time he watched the people in the street below hurrying along and then turned with a heavy heart to his little room. On the table was the packet. With a sudden relentless gesture he tore it open. For a half hour he stood by the table in a state of excitement, examining the photographs of the ladies Salzman had included. Finally, with a deep sigh he put them down. There were six, of varying degrees of attractiveness, but look at them long enough and they all became Lily Hirschorn: all past their prime, all starved behind bright smiles, not a true personality in the lot. Life, despite their frantic yoohooings, had passed them by; they were pictures in a briefcase that stank of fish. After a while, however, as Leo attempted to return the photographs into the envelope, he found in it another, a snapshot of the type taken by a machine for a quarter. He gazed at it a moment and let out a low cry.

Her face deeply moved him. Why, he could at first not say. It gave him the impression of youth—spring flowers, yet age—a sense of having been used to the bone, wasted; this came from the eyes, which were hauntingly familiar, yet absolutely strange. He had a vivid impression that he had met her before, but try as he might he could not place her although he could almost recall her name, as if he had read it in her own handwriting. No, this couldn't be; he would have remembered her. It was not, he affirmed, that she had an extraordinary beauty—no, though her face was attractive enough; it was that *something* about her moved him. Feature for feature, even some of the ladies of the photographs could do better; but she leaped forth to his heart—had *lived,* or wanted to—more than just wanted, perhaps regretted how she had lived—had somehow deeply suffered: it could be seen in the depths of those reluctant eyes, and from the way the light enclosed and shone from her, and within her, opening realms of possibility: this was her own. Her he desired. His head ached and eyes narrowed with the intensity of his gazing, then as if an obscure fog had blown up in the mind, he experienced fear of her and was aware that he had received an impression, somehow, of evil. He shuddered, saying softly, it is thus with us all. Leo brewed some tea in a small pot and sat sipping it without sugar, to calm himself. But before he had finished drinking, again with excitement he examined the face and found it good: good for Leo Finkle. Only such a one could understand him and help him seek whatever he was seeking. She might, perhaps, love him. How she had happened to be among the discards in Salzman's barrel he could never guess, but he knew he must urgently go find her.

Leo rushed downstairs, grabbed up the Bronx telephone book, and searched for Salzman's home address. He was not listed, nor was his office. Neither was he in the Manhattan book. But Leo remembered having written down the address on a slip of paper after he had read Salzman's advertisement in the "personals" column of the *Forward.* He ran up to his room and tore through his papers, without luck. It was exasperating. Just when he needed the matchmaker he was nowhere to be found. Fortunately Leo remembered to look in his wallet. There on a card he found his name written and a Bronx address. No phone number was listed, the reason— Leo now recalled—he had originally communicated with Salzman by letter. He got on his coat, put a hat on over his skullcap and hurried to the subway station. All the way to the far end of the Bronx he sat on the edge of his seat. He was more than once tempted to take out the picture and see if the girl's face was as he remembered, but he refrained, allowing the snapshot to remain in his inside coat pocket, content to have her so close. When the train pulled into the station he was waiting at the door and bolted out. He quickly located the street Salzman had advertised.

The building he sought was less than a block from the subway, but it was not an office building, nor even a loft, nor a store in which one could rent office space. It was a very old tenement house. Leo found Salzman's name in pencil on a soiled tag under the bell and climbed three dark flights to his apartment. When he knocked, the door was opened by a thin, asthmatic, gray-haired woman, in felt slippers.

"Yes?" she said, expecting nothing. She listened without listening. He could have sworn he had seen her, too, before but knew it was an illusion.

"Salzman—does he live here? Pinye Salzman," he said, "the matchmaker?"

She stared at him a long minute. "Of course."

He felt embarrassed. "Is he in?"

"No." Her mouth, though left open, offered nothing more.

"The matter is urgent. Can you tell me where his office is?"

"In the air." She pointed upward.

"You mean he has no office?" Leo asked.

"In his socks."

He peered into the apartment. It was sunless and dingy, one large room divided by a half-open curtain, beyond which he could see a sagging metal bed. The near side of the room was crowded with rickety chairs, old bureaus, a three-legged table, racks of cooking utensils, and all the apparatus of a kitchen. But there was no sign of Salzman or his magic barrel, probably also a figment of the imagination. An odor of frying fish made Leo weak to the knees.

"Where is he?" he insisted. "I've got to see your husband."

At length she answered, "So who knows where he is? Every time he thinks a new thought he runs to a different place. Go home, he will find you."

"Tell him Leo Finkle."

She gave no sign she had heard.

He walked downstairs, depressed.

But Salzman, breathless, stood waiting at his door.

Leo was astounded and overjoyed. "How did you get here before me?"

"I rushed."

"Come inside."

They entered. Leo fixed tea, and a sardine sandwich for Salzman. As they were drinking he reached behind him for the packet of pictures and handed them to the marriage broker.

Salzman put down his glass and said expectantly, "You found somebody you like?"

"Not among these."

The marriage broker turned away.

"Here is the one I want." Leo held forth the snapshot.

Salzman slipped on his glasses and took the picture into his trembling hand. He turned ghastly and let out a groan.

"What's the matter?" cried Leo.

"Excuse me. Was an accident this picture. She isn't for you."

Salzman frantically shoved the manila packet into his portfolio. He thrust the snapshot into his pocket and fled down the stairs.

Leo, after momentary paralysis, gave chase and cornered the marriage broker in the vestibule. The landlady made hysterical outcries but neither of them listened.

"Give me back the picture, Salzman."

"No." The pain in his eyes was terrible.

"Tell me who she is then."

"This I can't tell you. Excuse me."

He made to depart, but Leo, forgetting himself, seized the matchmaker by his tight coat and shook him frenziedly.

"Please," sighed Salzman. "*Please.*"

Leo ashamedly let him go. "Tell me who she is," he begged. "It's very important for me to know."

"She is not for you. She is a wild one—wild, without shame. This is not a bride for a rabbi."

"What do you mean wild?"

"Like an animal. Like a dog. For her to be poor was a sin. This is why to me she is dead now."

"In God's name, what do you mean?"

"Her I can't introduce to you," Salzman cried.

"Why are you so excited?"

"Why, he asks," Salzman said, bursting into tears. "This is my baby, my Stella, she should burn in hell."

Leo hurried up to bed and hid under the covers. Under the covers he thought his life through. Although he soon fell asleep he could not sleep her out of his mind. He woke, beating his breast. Though he prayed to be rid of her, his prayers went unanswered. Through days of torment he endlessly struggled not to love her; fearing success, he escaped it. He then concluded to convert her to goodness, himself to God. The idea alternately nauseated and exalted him.

He perhaps did not know that he had come to a final decision until he encountered Salzman in a Broadway cafeteria. He was sitting alone at a rear table, sucking the bony remains of a fish. The marriage broker appeared haggard, and transparent to the point of vanishing.

Salzman looked up at first without recognizing him. Leo had grown a pointed beard and his eyes were weighted with wisdom.

"Salzman," he said, "love has at last come to my heart."

"Who can love from a picture?" mocked the marriage broker.

"It is not impossible."

"If you can love her, then you can love anybody. Let me show you some new clients that they just sent me their photographs. One is a little doll."

"Just her I want," Leo murmured.

"Don't be a fool, doctor. Don't bother with her."

"Put me in touch with her, Salzman," Leo said humbly. "Perhaps I can be of service."

Salzman had stopped eating and Leo understood with emotion that it was now arranged.

Leaving the cafeteria, he was, however, afflicted by a tormenting suspicion that Salzman had planned it all to happen this way.

Leo was informed by letter that she would meet him on a certain corner, and she was there one spring night, waiting under a street lamp. He appeared, carrying a small bouquet of violets and rosebuds. Stella stood by the lamppost, smoking. She wore white with red shoes, which fitted his expectations, although in a troubled moment he had imagined the dress red, and only the shoes white. She waited uneasily and shyly. From afar he saw that her eyes—clearly her father's—were filled with desperate innocence. He pictured, in her, his own redemption. Violins and lit candles revolved in the sky. Leo ran forward with flowers outthrust.

Around the corner, Salzman, leaning against a wall, chanted prayers for the dead.

1958

Ralph Ellison 1914–1994

Ralph Waldo Ellison was born in Oklahoma City of parents who migrated from South Carolina and Georgia. His father, Lewis, a construction foreman and later the owner of a small ice and coal business, named his son after Emerson, hoping he would be a poet. After losing his father when he was three, Ellison and his younger brother, Herbert, were raised by their mother, Ida, who worked as a nursemaid, janitress, and domestic and was active in politics. Ellison used to enjoy telling how she had canvassed for Eugene V. Debs and other Socialist candidates and later been jailed for defying Oklahoma City's segregation ordinances.

Ellison was drawn to music, playing cornet and trumpet from an early age and, in 1933, going to study classical composition at Tuskegee Institute under William L. Dawson. Of his musical influences he later said, "The great emphasis in my school was upon classical music, but such great jazz musicians as Hot Lips Page, Jimmy Rushing, and Lester Young were living in Oklahoma City. . . . As it turned out, the perfection, the artistic dedication which helped

me as a writer, was not so much in the classical emphasis as in the jazz itself."

In July 1936, after his junior year at Tuskegee, Ellison went to New York to earn money for his senior year and to study music and sculpture, and he stayed. In June 1937 his friendship with Richard Wright began and led him toward becoming a writer. Ellison also made the acquaintance of Langston Hughes and the painter Romare Bearden. In Dayton, Ohio, where he went to visit his ailing mother, and remained for six months after her unexpected death in October 1937, he began to write seriously, mostly nights in the second-story law office of Attorney William O. Stokes, using Stokes's letterhead and typewriter.

Returning to New York, from 1938 until 1942 Ellison worked on the New York Federal Writers Project of the Works Progress Administration (WPA). Starting in the late 1930s, he contributed reviews, essays, and short fiction to *New Masses, Tomorrow, The Negro Quarterly* (of which he was for a time managing editor), *The New Republic, The Saturday Review, Antioch*

Review, The Reporter, and other periodicals. During World War II he served in the merchant marine as a cook and baker and afterward worked at a variety of jobs, including freelance photography and the building and installation of audio systems.

Over a period of seven years, Ellison wrote *Invisible Man,* which was recognized upon its publication in 1952 as one of the most important works of fiction of its time. It was on the best-seller list for sixteen weeks and won the National Book Award. Its critical reputation and popularity have only continued to grow in the more than four decades since its publication. Ellison has described his novel's structure as that of a symphonic jazz composition with a central theme (or bass line) and harmonic variations (or riffs) often expressed in virtuoso solo performances. *Invisible Man* speaks for all readers and reflects the contradictions and complexities of American life through the prism of African American experience.

Although an excerpt from a second novel was published in *Noble Savage* in 1960, and seven other selections in literary magazines between then and 1977, no other long work of fiction has yet appeared. *Shadow and Act* (1964) and *Going to the Territory* (1986) collect essays and interviews written over more than forty years. Since Ellison's death four posthumous works have appeared: *The Collected Essays of Ralph Ellison* (1995), *Conversations with Ralph Ellison* (1995), *Flying Home and Other Stories* (1996), and *Juneteenth* (1999).

"A Party down at the Square" (undated), unpublished in Ellison's lifetime, is a tour de force. By narrating a lynching in the voice of a Cincinnati white boy visiting his uncle in Alabama, Ellison, while still a young writer, crosses the narrative color line and defies the "segregation of the word" he found lingering in American literature when he wrote "Twentieth-Century Fiction and the Black Mask of Humanity" (1946). Ellison's technique in "A Party down at the Square" compels readers to experience the human condition in extremis, mediated by a stranger whose morality is a commitment to be noncommital. The white boy's most telling response comes from his insides when, to his shame, he throws up. His sensations signify a resistance to values he has been taught not to question. There is nothing like this story in the rest of Ellison's work.

"Flying Home" (1944) anticipates the theme of invisibility and the technique of solos and breaks with which Ellison took flight in *Invisible Man.* Just when Todd, Ellison's northern protagonist, believes that he has learned to use his wiles to escape the limitations of race, language, and geography, circumstances force him to confront the strange "old country" of the South. A literary descendant of Icarus, as well as Joyce's Stephen Dedalus, Todd, one of the black eagles from the Negro air school at Tuskegee, flies too close to the sun, collides with a buzzard (a "jimcrow"), and falls to earth in rural Alabama. There, he is saved by Jefferson, whose folktales and actions enable Todd to recognize where he is and who he is and to come back to life by following the old black peasant and his son out of a labyrinthine Alabama valley.

In "Brave Words for a Startling Occasion" (1953), Ellison's acceptance address for the National Book Award, he celebrates the richness and diversity of American speech and the American language. And he identifies the task of the American writer as "always to challenge the apparent forms of reality—that is, the fixed manners and values of the few—and to struggle with it until it reveals its mad, variimplicated chaos, its false faces, and on until it surrenders its insight, its truth."

John F. Callahan
Lewis and Clark College

PRIMARY WORKS

Invisible Man, 1952; *Shadow and Act,* 1964; *Going to the Territory,* 1986; *The Collected Essays of Ralph Ellison,* 1995; *Flying Home and Other Stories,* 1996; *Juneteenth,* 1999.

A Party Down at the Square

I don't know what started it. A bunch of men came by my Uncle Ed's place and said there was going to be a party down at the Square, and my uncle hollered for me to come on and I ran with them through the dark and rain and there we were at the Square. When we got there everybody was mad and quiet and standing around looking at the nigger. Some of the men had guns, and one man kept goosing the nigger in his pants with the barrel of a shotgun, saying he ought to pull the trigger, but he never did. It was right in front of the courthouse, and the old clock in the tower was striking twelve. The rain was falling cold and freezing as it fell. Everybody was cold, and the nigger kept wrapping his arms around himself trying to stop the shivers.

Then one of the boys pushed through the circle and snatched off the nigger's shirt, and there he stood, with his black skin all shivering in the light from the fire, and looking at us with a scaired look on his face and putting his hands in his pants pockets. Folks started yelling to hurry up and kill the nigger. Somebody yelled: "Take your hands out of your pockets, nigger; we gonna have plenty heat in a minnit." But the nigger didn't hear him and kept his hands where they were.

I tell you the rain was cold. I had to stick my hands in my pockets they got so cold. The fire was pretty small, and they put some logs around the platform they had the nigger on and then threw on some gasoline, and you could see the flames light up the whole Square. It was late and the streetlights had been off for a long time. It was so bright that the bronze statue of the general standing there in the Square was like something alive. The shadows playing on his moldy green face made him seem to be smiling down at the nigger.

They threw on more gas, and it made the Square bright like it gets when the lights are turned on or when the sun is setting red. All the wagons and cars were standing around the curbs. Not like Saturday though—the niggers weren't there. Not a single nigger was there except this Bacote nigger and they dragged him there tied to the back of Jed Wilson's truck. On Saturday there's as many niggers as white folks.

Everybody was yelling crazy 'cause they were about to set fire to the nigger, and I got to the rear of the circle and looked around the Square to try to count the cars. The shadows of the folks was flickering on the trees in the middle of the Square. I saw some birds that the noise had woke up flying through the trees. I guess maybe they thought it was morning. The ice had started the cobblestones in the street to shine where the rain was falling and freezing. I counted forty cars before I lost count. I knew folks must have been there from Phenix City by all the cars mixed in with the wagons.

God, it was a hell of a night. It was some night all right. When the noise died down I heard the nigger's voice from where I stood in the back, so I pushed my way up front. The nigger was bleeding from his nose and ears, and I could see him all red where the dark blood was running down his black skin. He kept lifting first one foot and then the other, like a chicken on a hot stove. I looked down at the platform they had him on, and they had pushed a ring of fire up close to his feet. It must have been hot to him with the flames almost touching his big black toes. Somebody yelled for the nigger to say his prayers, but the nigger wasn't saying anything now. He just kinda moaned with his eyes shut and kept moving up and down on his feet, first one foot and then the other.

I watched the flames burning the logs up closer and closer to the nigger's feet. They were burning good now, and the rain had stopped and the wind was rising, making the flames flare higher. I looked, and there must have been thirty-five women in the crowd, and I could hear their voices clear and shrill mixed in with those of the men. Then it happened. I heard the noise about the same time everyone else did. It was like the roar of a cyclone blowing up the gulf, and everyone was looking up into the air to see what it was. Some of the faces looked surprised and scaired, all but the nigger. He didn't even hear the noise. He didn't even look up. Then the roar came closer, right above our heads and the wind was blowing higher and higher and the sound seemed to be going in circles.

Then I saw her. Through the clouds and fog I could see a red and green light on her wings. I could see them just for a second; then she rose up into the low clouds. I looked out for the beacon over the tops of the buildings in the direction of the air-field that's forty miles away, and it wasn't circling around. You usually could see it sweeping around the sky at night, but it wasn't there. Then, there she was again, like a big bird lost in the fog. I looked for the red and green lights, and they weren't there anymore. She was flying even closer to the tops of the buildings than before. The wind was blowing harder, and leaves started flying about, making funny shadows on the ground, and tree limbs were cracking and falling.

It was a storm all right. The pilot must have thought he was over the landing field. Maybe he thought the fire in the Square was put there for him to land by. Gosh, but it scaired the folks. I was scaired too. They started yelling: "He's going to land. He's going to land." And: "He's going to fall." A few started for their cars and wagons. I could hear the wagons creaking and chains jangling and cars spitting and missing as they started the engines up. Off to my right, a horse started pitching and striking his hooves against a car.

I didn't know what to do. I wanted to run, and I wanted to stay and see what was going to happen. The plane was close as hell. The pilot must have been trying to see where he was at, and her motors were drowning out all the sounds. I could even feel the vibration, and my hair felt like it was standing up under my hat. I happened to look over at the statue of the general standing with one leg before the other and leaning back on a sword, and I was fixing to run over and climb between his legs and sit there and watch when the roar stopped some, and I looked up and she was gliding just over the top of the trees in the middle of the Square.

Her motors stopped altogether and I could hear the sound of branches cracking and snapping off below her landing gear. I could see her plain now, all silver and shining in the light of the fire with T.W.A. in black letters under her wings. She was sailing smoothly out of the Square when she hit the high power lines that follow the Birmingham highway through the town. It made a loud crash. It sounded like the wind blowing the door of a tin barn shut. She only hit with her landing gear, but I could see the sparks flying, and the wires knocked loose from the poles were spitting blue sparks and whipping around like a bunch of snakes and leaving circles of blue sparks in the darkness.

The plane had knocked five or six wires loose, and they were dangling and swinging, and every time they touched they threw off more sparks. The wind was making them swing, and when I got over there, there was a crackling and spitting screen of blue haze across the highway. I lost my hat running over, but I didn't stop to look for it. I was among the first and I could hear the others pounding behind me across the grass of the Square. They were yelling to beat all hell, and they came up fast, pushing and shoving, and someone got pushed against a swinging wire. It made a sound like when a blacksmith drops a red hot horseshoe into a barrel of water, and the steam comes up. I could smell the flesh burning. The first time I'd ever smelled it. I got up close and it was a woman. It must have killed her right off. She was lying in a puddle stiff as a board, with pieces of glass insulators that the plane had knocked off the poles lying all around her. Her white dress was torn, and I saw one of her tits hanging out in the water and her thighs. Some woman screamed and fainted and almost fell on a wire, but a man caught her. The sheriff and his men were yelling and driving folks back with guns shining in their hands, and everything was lit up blue by the sparks. The shock had turned the woman almost as black as the nigger. I was trying to see if she wasn't blue too, or if it was just the sparks, and the sheriff drove me away. As I backed off trying to see, I heard the motors of the plane start up again somewhere off to the right in the clouds.

The clouds were moving fast in the wind and the wind was blowing the smell of something burning over to me. I turned around, and the crowd was headed back to the nigger. I could see him standing there in the middle of the flames. The wind was making the flames brighter every minute. The crowd was running. I ran too. I ran back across the grass with the crowd. It wasn't so large now that so many had gone when the plane came. I tripped and fell over the limb of a tree lying in the grass and bit my lip. It ain't well yet I bit it so bad. I could taste the blood in my mouth as I ran over. I guess that's what made me sick. When I got there, the fire had caught the nigger's pants, and the folks were standing around watching, but not too close on account of the wind blowing the flames. Somebody hollered, "Well, nigger, it ain't so cold now, is it? You don't need to put your hands in your pockets now." And the nigger looked up with his great white eyes looking like they was 'bout to pop out of his head, and I had enough. I didn't want to see anymore. I wanted to run somewhere to puke, but I stayed. I stayed right there in the front of the crowd and looked.

The nigger tried to say something I couldn't hear for the roar of the wind in the fire, and I strained my ears. Jed Wilson hollered, "What you say there, nigger?" And it came back through the flames in his nigger voice: "Will one a you gentlemen please cut my throat?" he said. "Will somebody please cut my throat like a Christian?" And Jed hollered back, "Sorry, but ain't no Christians around tonight. Ain't no Jew-boys neither. We're just one hundred percent Americans."

Then the nigger was silent. Folks started laughing at Jed. Jed's right popular with the folks, and next year, my uncle says, they plan to run him for sheriff. The heat was too much for me, and the smoke was making my eyes to smart. I was trying to back away when Jed reached down and brought up a can of gasoline and threw it in the fire on the nigger. I could see the flames catching the gas in a puff as it went in in a silver sheet and some of it reached the nigger, making spurts of blue fire all over his chest.

Well, that nigger was tough. I have to give it to that nigger; he was really tough. He had started to burn like a house afire and was making the smoke smell like burning hides. The fire was up around his head, and the smoke was so thick and black we couldn't see him. And him not moving—we thought he was dead. Then he started out. The fire had burned the ropes they had tied him with, and he started jumping and kicking about like he was blind, and you could smell his skin burning. He kicked so hard that the platform, which was burning too, fell in, and he rolled out of the fire at my feet. I jumped back so he wouldn't get on me. I'll never forget it. Every time I eat barbeque I'll remember that nigger. His back was just like a barbecued hog. I could see the prints of his ribs where they start around from his backbone and curve down and around. It was a sight to see, that nigger's back. He was right at my feet, and somebody behind pushed me and almost made me step on him, and he was still burning.

I didn't step on him though, and Jed and somebody else pushed him back into the burning planks and logs and poured on more gas. I wanted to leave, but the folks were yelling and I couldn't move except to look around and see the statue. A branch the wind had broken was resting on his hat. I tried to push out and get away because my guts were gone, and all I got was spit and hot breath in my face from the woman and two men standing directly behind me. So I had to turn back around. The nigger rolled out of the fire again. He wouldn't stay put. It was on the other side this time. I couldn't see him very well through the flames and smoke. They got some tree limbs and held him there this time and he stayed there till he was ashes. I guess he stayed there. I know he burned to ashes because I saw Jed a week later, and he laughed and showed me some white finger bones still held together with little pieces of the nigger's skin. Anyway, I left when somebody moved around to see the nigger. I pushed my way through the crowd, and a woman in the rear scratched my face as she yelled and fought to get up close.

I ran across the Square to the other side, where the sheriff and his deputies were guarding the wires that were still spitting and making a blue fog. My heart was pounding like I had been running a long ways, and I bent over and let my insides go. Everything came up and spilled in a big gush over the ground. I was sick, and tired, and weak, and cold. The wind was still high, and large drops of rain were beginning to fall. I headed down the street to my uncle's place past a store where the wind had broken a window, and glass lay over the sidewalk. I kicked it as I went by. I remember somebody's fool rooster crowing like it was morning in all that wind.

The next day I was too weak to go out, and my uncle kidded me and called me "the gutless wonder from Cincinnati." I didn't mind. He said you get used to it in time. He couldn't go out hisself. There was too much wind and rain. I got up and looked out of the window, and the rain was pouring down and dead sparrows and limbs of trees were scattered all over the yard. There had been a cyclone all right. It swept a path right through the county, and we were lucky we didn't get the full force of it.

It blew for three days steady, and put the town in a hell of a shape. The wind blew sparks and set fire to the white-and-green-trimmed house on Jackson Avenue that had the big concrete lions in the yard and burned it down to the ground. They had to kill another nigger who tried to run out of the county after they burned this Bacote nigger. My Uncle Ed said they always have to kill niggers in pairs to keep the other niggers in place. I don't know though, the folks seem a little skittish of the niggers. They all came back, but they act pretty sullen. They look mean as hell when you pass them down at the store. The other day I was down to Brinkley's store, and a white cropper said it didn't do no good to kill the niggers 'cause things don't get no better. He looked hungry as hell. Most of the croppers look hungry. You'd be surprised how hungry white folks can look. Somebody said that he'd better shut his damn mouth, and he shut up. But from the look on his face he won't stay shut long. He went out of the store muttering to himself and spit a big chew of tobacco right down on Brinkley's floor. Brinkley said he was sore 'cause he wouldn't let him have credit. Anyway, it didn't seem to help things. First it was the nigger and the storm, then the plane, then the woman and the wires, and now I hear the airplane line is investigating to find who set the fire that almost wrecked their plane. All that in one night, and all of it but the storm over one nigger. It was some night all right. It was some party too. I was right there, see. I was right there watching it all. It was my first party and my last. God, but that nigger was tough. That Bacote nigger was some nigger!

Flying Home

When Todd came to, he saw two faces suspended above him in a sun so hot and blinding that he could not tell if they were black or white. He stirred, feeling a pain that burned as though his whole body had been laid open to the sun, which glared into his eyes. For a moment an old fear of being touched by white hands seized him. Then the very sharpness of the pain began slowly to clear his head. Sounds came to him dimly. *He done come to.* Who are they? he thought. *Naw he ain't, I coulda sworn he was white.* Then he heard clearly:

"You hurt bad?"

Something within him uncoiled. It was a Negro sound.

"He's still out," he heard.

"Give 'im time. . . . Say, son, you hurt bad?"

Was he? There was that awful pain. He lay rigid, hearing their breathing and trying to weave a meaning between them and his being stretched painfully upon the ground. He watched them warily, his mind traveling back over a painful distance. Jagged scenes, swiftly unfolding as in a movie trailer, reeled through his mind, and he saw himself piloting a tailspinning plane and landing and falling from the cockpit and trying to stand. Then, as in a great silence, he remembered the sound of crunching bone and, now, looking up into the anxious faces of an old Negro man and a boy from where he lay in the same field, the memory sickened him and he wanted to remember no more.

"How you feel, son?"

Todd hesitated, as though to answer would be to admit an unacceptable weakness. Then, "It's my ankle," he said.

"Which one?"

"The left."

With a sense of remoteness he watched the old man bend and remove his boot, feeling the pressure ease.

"That any better?"

"A lot. Thank you."

He had the sensation of discussing someone else, that his concern was with some far more important thing, which for some reason escaped him.

"You done broke it bad," the old man said. "We have to get you to a doctor."

He felt that he had been thrown into a tailspin. He looked at his watch; how long had he been here? He knew there was but one important thing in the world, to get the plane back to the field before his officers were displeased.

"Help me up," he said. "Into the ship."

"But it's broke too bad . . ."

"Give me your arm!"

"But, son . . ."

Clutching the old man's arm, he pulled himself up, keeping his left leg clear, thinking, I'd never make him understand, as the leather-smooth face came parallel with his own.

"Now, let's see."

He pushed the old man back, hearing a bird's insistent shrill. He swayed, giddily. Blackness washed over him, like infinity.

"You best sit down."

"No, I'm okay."

"But, son. You jus gonna make it worse . . ."

It was a fact that everything in him cried out to deny, even against the flaming pain in his ankle. He would have to try again.

"You mess with that ankle they have to cut your foot off," he heard.

Holding his breath, he started up again. It pained so badly that he had to bite his lips to keep from crying out and he allowed them to help him down with a pang of despair.

"It's best you take it easy. We gon git you a doctor."

Of all the luck, he thought. Of all the rotten luck, now I have done it. The fumes of high-octane gasoline clung in the heat, taunting him.

"We kin ride him into town on old Ned," the boy said.

Ned? He turned, seeing the boy point toward an ox team, browsing where the buried blade of a plow marked the end of a furrow. Thoughts of himself riding an ox through the town, past streets full of white faces, down the concrete runways of the airfield, made swift images of humiliation in his mind. With a pang he remembered his girl's last letter. "Todd," she had written, "I don't need the papers to tell me you had the intelligence to fly. And I have always known you to be as brave as anyone else. The papers annoy me. Don't you be contented to prove over and over again that you're brave or skillful just because you're black, Todd. I think they keep beating that dead horse because they don't want to say why you boys are not yet fighting. I'm really disappointed, Todd. Anyone with brains can learn to fly, but then what. What about using it, and who will you use it for? I wish, dear, you'd write about this. I sometimes think they're playing a trick on us. It's very humiliating. . . ." He whipped cold sweat from his face, thinking, What does she know of humiliation? She's never been down South. *Now* the humiliation would come. When you must have them judge you, knowing that they never accept your mistakes as your own but hold it against your whole race—that was humiliation. Yes, and humiliation was when you could never be simply yourself; when you were always a part of this old black ignorant man. Sure, he's all right. Nice and kind and helpful. But he's not you. Well, there's one humiliation I can spare myself.

"No," he said. "I have orders not to leave the ship. . . ."

"Aw," the old man said. Then turning to the boy, "Teddy, then you better hustle down to Mister Graves and get him to come. . . ."

"No, wait!" he protested before he was fully aware. Graves might be white. "Just have him get word to the field, please. They'll take care of the rest."

He saw the boy leave, running.

"How far does he have to go?"

"Might' nigh a mile."

He rested back, looking at the dusty face of his watch. By now they know something has happened, he thought. In the ship there was a perfectly good radio, but it was useless. The old fellow would never operate it. That buzzard knocked me back a hundred years, he thought. Irony danced within him like the gnats circling the old man's head. With all I've learned, I'm dependent upon this "peasant's" sense of time and space. His leg throbbed. In the plane, instead of time being measured by the rhythms of pain and a kid's legs, the instruments would have told him at a glance. Twisting upon his elbows, he saw where dust had powdered the plane's fuselage, feeling the lump form in his throat that was always there when he thought of flight. It's crouched there, he thought, like the abandoned shell of a locust. I'm naked without it. Not a machine, a suit of clothes you wear. And with a sudden embarrassment and wonder he whispered, "It's the only dignity I have. . . ."

He saw the old man watching, his torn overalls clinging limply to him in the heat. He felt a sharp need to tell the old man what he felt. But that would be meaningless. If I tried to explain why I need to fly back, he'd think I was simply afraid of white officers. But it's more than fear . . . a sense of anguish clung to him like the veil of sweat that hugged his face. He watched the old man, hearing him humming snatches of a tune as he admired the plane. He felt a furtive sense of resentment. Such old men often came to the field to watch the pilots with childish eyes. At first it had made him proud; they had been a meaningful part of a new experience. But soon he realized they did not understand his accomplishments and they came to shame and embarrass him, like the distasteful praise of an idiot. A part of the meaning of flying had gone, then, and he had not been able to regain it. If I were a prize-fighter I would be more human, he thought. Not a monkey doing tricks, but a man. They were pleased simply that he was a Negro who could fly, and that was not enough. He felt cut off from them by age, by understanding, by sensibility, by technology, and by his need to measure himself against the mirror of other men's appreciation. Somehow he felt betrayed, as he had when as a child he grew to discover that his father was dead. Now, for him, any real appreciation lay with his white officers; and with them he could never be sure. Between ignorant black men and condescending whites, his course of flight seemed mapped by the nature of things away from all needed and natural landmarks. Under some sealed orders, couched in ever more technical and mysterious terms, his path curved swiftly away from both the shame the old man symbolized and the cloudy terrain of white man's regard. Flying blind, he knew but one point of landing and there he would receive his wings. After that the enemy would appreciate his skill and he would assume his deepest meaning, he thought sadly, neither from those who condescended nor from those who praised without understanding, but from the enemy who would recognize his manhood and skill in terms of hate. . . .

He sighed, seeing the oxen making queer, prehistoric shadows against the dry brown earth.

"You just take it easy, son," the old man soothed. "That boy won't take long. Crazy as he is about airplanes."

"I can wait," he said.

"What kinda airplane you call this here'n?"

"An Advanced Trainer," he said, seeing the old man smile. His fingers were like gnarled dark wood against the metal as he touched the low-slung wing.

" 'Bout how fast can she fly?"

"Over two hundred an hour."

"Lawd! That's so fast I bet it don't seem like you moving!"

Holding himself rigid, Todd opened his flying suit. The shade had gone and he lay in a ball of fire.

"You mind if I take a look inside? I was always curious to see . . ."

"Help yourself. Just don't touch anything."

He heard him climb upon the metal wing, grunting. Now the questions would start. Well, so you don't have to think to answer. . . .

He saw the old man looking over into the cockpit, his eyes bright as a child's.

"You must have to know a lot to work all these here things."

Todd was silent, seeing him step down and kneel beside him.

"Son, how come you want to fly way up there in the air?"

Because it's the most meaningful act in the world . . . because it makes me less like you, he thought.

But he said: "Because I like it, I guess. It's as good a way to fight and die as I know."

"Yeah? I guess you right," the old man said. "But how long you think before they gonna let you all fight?"

He tensed. This was the question all Negroes asked, put with the same timid hopefulness and longing that always opened a greater void within him than that he had felt beneath the plane the first time he had flown. He felt lightheaded. It came to him suddenly that there was something sinister about the conversation, that he was flying unwillingly into unsafe and uncharted regions. If he could only be insulting and tell this old man who was trying to help him to shut up!

"I bet you one thing . . ."

"Yes?"

"That you was plenty scared coming down."

He did not answer. Like a dog on a trail the old man seemed to smell out his fears, and he felt anger bubble within him.

"You sho scared *me*. When I seen you coming down in that thing with it a-rollin' and a-jumpin' like a pitchin' hoss, I thought sho you was a goner. I almost had me a stroke!"

He saw the old man grinning. "Ever'thin's been happening round here this morning, come to think of it."

"Like what?" he asked.

"Well, first thing I know, here come two white fellers looking for Mister Rudolph, that's Mister Graves' cousin. That got me worked up right away. . . ."

"Why?"

"Why? 'Cause he done broke outa the crazy house, that's why. He liable to kill somebody," he said. "They oughta have him by now though. Then here *you* come. First I think it's one of them white boys. Then doggone if you don't fall outa there. Lawd, I'd done heard about you boys but I haven't never *seen* one o' you all. Caint tell you how it felt to see somebody what look like me in a airplane!"

The old man talked on, the sound streaming around Todd's thoughts like air flowing over the fuselage of a flying plane. You were a fool, he thought, remembering how before the spin the sun had blazed, bright against the billboard signs beyond the town, and how a boy's blue kite had bloomed beneath him, tugging gently in the wind like a strange, odd-shaped flower. He had once flown such kites himself and tried to find the boy at the end of the invisible cord. But he had been flying too high and too fast. He had climbed steeply away in exultation. Too steeply, he thought. And one of the first rules you learn is that if the angle of thrust is too steep the plane goes into a spin. And then, instead of pulling out of it and going into a dive you let a buzzard panic you. A lousy buzzard!

"Son, what made all that blood on the glass?"

"A buzzard," he said, remembering how the blood and feathers had sprayed back against the hatch. It had been as though he had flown into a storm of blood and blackness.

"Well, I declare! They's lots of 'em around here. They after dead things. Don't eat nothing what's alive."

"A little bit more and he would have made a meal out of me," Todd said grimly.

"They had luck all right. Teddy's got a name for 'em, calls 'em jimcrows," the old man laughed.

"It's a damned good name."

"They the damnedest birds. Once I seen a hoss all stretched out like he was sick, you know. So I hollers, 'Gid up from there, suh!' Just to make sho! An,' doggone, son, if I don't see two old jimcrows come flying right up outa that hoss's insides! Yessuh! The sun was shinin' on 'em and they couldn'ta been no greasier if they'd been eating barbecue!"

Todd thought he would vomit; his stomach quivered.

"You made that up," he said.

"Nawsuh! Saw him just like you."

"Well, I'm glad it was you."

"You see lots a funny things down here, son."

"No, I'll let you see them," he said.

"By the way, the white folks round here don't like to see you boys up there in the sky. They ever bother you?"

"No."

"Well, they'd like to."

"Someone always wants to bother someone else," Todd said. "How do you know?"

"I just know."

"Well," he said defensively, "no one has bothered us."

Blood pounded in his ears as he looked away into space. He tensed, seeing a black spot in the sky, and strained to confirm what he could not clearly see.

"What does that look like to you?" he asked excitedly.

"Just another bad luck, son."

Then he saw the movement of wings with disappointment. It was gliding smoothly down, wings outspread, tail feathers gripping the air, down swiftly—gone behind the green screen of trees. It was like a bird he had imagined there, only the sloping branches of the pines remained, sharp against the pale stretch of sky. He lay barely breathing and stared at the point where it had disappeared, caught in a spell of loathing and admiration. Why did they make them so disgusting and yet teach them to fly so well? *It's like when I was up in heaven,* he heard, starting.

The old man was chuckling, rubbing his stubbled chin.

"What did you say?"

"Sho, I died and went to heaven . . . maybe by time I tell you about it they be done come after you."

"I hope so," he said wearily.

"You boys ever sit around and swap lies?"

"Not often. Is this going to be one?"

"Well, I ain't so sho, on account of it took place when I was dead."

The old man paused. "That wasn't no lie 'bout the buzzards though."

"All right," he said.

"Sho you want to hear 'bout heaven?"

"Please," he answered, resting his head upon his arm.

"Well, I went to heaven and right away started to sproutin' me some wings. Six-foot ones, they was. Just like them the white angels had. I couldn't hardly believe it. I was so glad that I went off on some clouds by myself and tried 'em out. You know, 'cause I didn't want to make a fool outa myself the first thing . . ."

It's an old tale, Todd thought. Told me years ago. Had forgotten. But at least it will keep him from talking about buzzards.

He closed his eyes, listening.

". . . First thing I done was to git up on a low cloud and jump off. And doggone, boy, if them wings didn't work! First I tried the right; then I tried the left; then I tried 'em both together. Then, Lawd, I started to move on out among the folks. I let 'em see me . . ."

He saw the old man gesturing flight with his arms, his face full of mock pride as he indicated an imaginary crowd, thinking, *It'll be in the newspapers,* as he heard, ". . . so I went and found me some colored angels—somehow I didn't believe I was an angel till I seen a real black one, ha, yes! Then I was sho—but they tole me I better come down 'cause us colored folks had to wear a special kin'a harness when we flew. That was how come *they* wasn't flyin'. Oh yes, an' you had to be extra strong for a black man even, to fly with one of them harnesses . . ."

This is a new turn, Todd thought. What's he driving at?

"So I said to myself, I ain't gonna be bothered with no harness! Oh naw! 'Cause if God let you sprout wings you oughta have sense enough not to let nobody make you wear something what gits in the way of flyin'. So I starts to flyin'. Hecks, son," he chuckled, his eyes twinkling, "you know I had to let eve'body know that old Jefferson could fly good as anybody else. And I could too, fly smooth as a bird! I could even loop-the-loop—only I had to make sho to keep my long white robe down roun' my ankles . . ."

Todd felt uneasy. He wanted to laugh at the joke, but his body refused, as of an independent will. He felt as he had as a child when after he had chewed a sugar-coated pill which his mother had given him, she had laughed at his efforts to remove the terrible taste.

". . . Well," he heard. "I was doing all right till I got to speeding. Found out I could fan up a right strong breeze, I could fly so fast. I could do all kin'sa stunts too. I started flying up to the stars and divin' down and zooming roun' the moon. Man, I like to scare the devil outa some ole white angels. I was raisin' hell. Not that I meant any harm, son. But I was just feeling good. It was so good to know I was free at last. I accidentally knocked the tips offa some stars and they tell me I caused a storm and a coupla lynchings down here in Macon County—though I swear I believe them boys what said that was making up lies on me . . ."

He's mocking me, Todd thought angrily. He thinks it's a joke. Grinning down at me . . . His throat was dry. He looked at his watch; why the hell didn't they come? Since they had to, why? *One day I was flying down one of them heavenly streets.* You got yourself into it, Todd. Like Jonah in the whale.

"Justa throwin' feathers in eve'body's face. An' ole Saint Peter called me in. Said, 'Jefferson, tell me two things, what you doin' flyin' without a harness; an' how come you flyin' so fast?' So I tole him I was flyin' without a harness 'cause it got in my way, but I couldn'ta been flyin' so fast, 'cause I wasn't usin' but one wing. Saint Peter said, 'You wasn't flyin' with but *one* wing?' 'Yessuh,' I says, scared-like. So he says, 'Well, since you got sucha extra fine pair of wings you can leave off yo harness awhile. But from now on none of that there one-wing flyin', 'cause you gittin' up too damn much speed!' "

And with one mouth full of bad teeth you're making too damned much talk, thought Todd. Why don't I send him after the boy? His body ached from the hard ground, and seeking to shift his position he twisted his ankle and hated himself for crying out.

"It gittin' worse?"

"I . . . I twisted it," he groaned.

"Try not to think about it, son. That's what I do."

He bit his lip, fighting pain with counter-pain as the voice resumed its rhythmical droning. Jefferson seemed caught in his own creation.

". . . After all that trouble I just floated roun' heaven in slow motion. But I forgot like colored folks will do and got to flyin' with one wing agin. This time I was restin' my ole broken arm and got to flyin' fast enough to shame the devil. I was comin' so fast, Lawd, I got myself called befo ole Saint Peter agin. He said, 'Jeff, didn't I warn you 'bout that speedin'?' 'Yessuh,' I says, 'but it was an accident.' He looked at me sad-like and shook his head and I knowed I was gone. He said, 'Jeff, you and that speedin' is a danger to the heavenly community. If I was to let you keep on flyin', heaven wouldn't be nothin' but uproar. Jeff, you got to go!' Son, I argued and pleaded with that old white man, but it didn't do a bit of good. They rushed me straight to them pearly gates and gimme a parachute and a map of the state of Alabama . . ."

Todd heard him laughing so that he could hardly speak, making a screen between them upon which his humiliation glowed like fire.

"Maybe you'd better stop a while," he said, his voice unreal.

"Ain't much more," Jefferson laughed. "When they gimme the parachute ole Saint Peter ask me if I wanted to say a few words before I went. I felt so bad I couldn't hardly look at him, specially with all them white angels standin' around. Then somebody laughed and made me mad. So I tole him, 'Well, you done took my wings. And you puttin' me out. You got charge of things so's I can't do nothin' about it. But you got to admit just this: While I was up here I was the flyin'est son-of-a-bitch what ever hit heaven!'"

At the burst of laughter Todd felt such an intense humiliation that only great violence would wash it away. The laughter which shook the old man like a boiling purge set up vibrations of guilt within him which not even the intricate machinery of the plane would have been adequate to transform and he heard himself screaming, "Why do you laugh at me this way?"

He hated himself at that moment, but he had lost control. He saw Jefferson's mouth fall open. "What—?"

"Answer me!"

His blood pounded as though it would surely burst his temples, and he tried to reach the old man and fell, screaming, "Can I help it because they won't let us actually fly? Maybe we are a bunch of buzzards feeding on a dead horse, but we can hope to be eagles, can't we? *Can't we?*"

He fell back, exhausted, his ankle pounding. The saliva was like straw in his mouth. If he had the strength he would strangle this old man. This grinning gray-headed clown who made him feel as he felt when watched by the white officers at the field. And yet this old man had neither power, prestige, rank, nor technique. Nothing that could rid him of this terrible feeling. He watched him, seeing his face struggle to express a turmoil of feeling.

"What you mean, son? What you talking 'bout . . . ?"

"Go away. Go tell your tales to the white folks."

"But I didn't mean nothing like that . . . I . . . I wasn't tryin' to hurt your feelings . . ."

"Please. Get the hell away from me!"

"But I didn't, son. I didn't mean all them things a-tall."

Todd shook as with a chill, searching Jefferson's face for a trace of the mockery he had seen there. But now the face was somber and tired and old. He was confused. He could not be sure that there had ever been laughter there, that Jefferson had ever really laughed in his whole life. He saw Jefferson reach out to touch him and shrank away, wondering if anything except the pain, now causing his vision to waver, was real. Perhaps he had imagined it all.

"Don't let it get you down, son," the voice said pensively.

He heard Jefferson sigh wearily, as though he felt more than he could say. His anger ebbed, leaving only the pain.

"I'm sorry," he mumbled.

"You just wore out with pain, was all . . ."

He saw him through a blur, smiling. And for a second he felt the embarrassed silence of understanding flutter between them.

"What was you doin' flyin' over this section, son? Wasn't you scared they might shoot you for a crow?"

Todd tensed. Was he being laughed at again? But before he could decide, the pain shook him and a part of him was lying calmly behind the screen of pain that had fallen between them, recalling the first time he had ever seen a plane. It was as though an endless series of hangars had been shaken ajar in the airbase of his memory and from each, like a young wasp emerging from its cell, arose the memory of the plane.

The first time I ever saw a plane I was very small and planes were new in the world. I was four and a half and the only plane that I had ever seen was a model suspended from the ceiling of the automobile exhibit at the state fair. But I did not know that it was only a model. I did not know how large a real plane was, nor how expensive. To me it was a fascinating toy, complete in itself, which my mother said could only be owned by rich little white boys. I stood rigid with admiration, my head straining backward as I watched the gray little plane describing arcs above the gleaming tops of the automobiles. And I vowed that, rich or poor, some day I would own such a toy. My mother had to drag me out of the exhibit, and not even the merry-go-round, the Ferris wheel, or the racing horses could hold my attention for the rest of the fair. I was too busy imitating the tiny drone of the plane with my lips, and imitating with my hands the motion, swift and circling, that it made in flight.

After that I no longer used the pieces of lumber that lay about our backyard to construct wagons and autos . . . now it was used for airplanes. I built biplanes, using pieces of board for wings, a small box for the fuselage, another piece of wood for the rudder. The trip to the fair had brought something new into my small world. I asked my mother repeatedly when the fair would come back again. I'd lie in the grass and watch the sky and each flighting bird became a soaring plane. I would have been good a year just to have seen a plane again. I became a nuisance to everyone with my questions about airplanes. But planes were new to the old folks, too, and there was little that they could tell me. Only my uncle knew some of the answers. And better still, he could carve propellers from pieces of wood that would whirl rapidly in the wind, wobbling noisily upon oiled nails.

I wanted a plane more than I'd wanted anything; more than I wanted the red wagon with rubber tires, more than the train that ran on a track with its train of cars. I asked my mother over and over again:

"Mama?"

"What do you want, boy?" she'd say.

"Mama, will you get mad if I ask you?" I'd say.

"What do you want now, I ain't got time to be answering a lot of fool questions. What you want?"

"Mama, when you gonna get me one . . . ?" I'd ask.

"Get you one what?" she'd say.

"You know, Mama; what I been asking you . . ."

"Boy," she'd say, "if you don't want a spanking you better come on 'n tell me what you talking about so I can get on with my work."

"*Aw, Mama, you know . . .*"

"*What I just tell you?*" she'd say.

"*I mean when you gonna buy me a airplane.*"

"*AIRPLANE! Boy, is you crazy? How many times I have to tell you to stop that foolishness. I done told you them things cost too much. I bet I'm gon wham the living daylight out of you if you don't quit worrying me 'bout them things!*"

But this did not stop me, and a few days later I'd try all over again.

Then one day a strange thing happened. It was spring and for some reason I had been hot and irritable all morning. It was a beautiful spring. I could feel it as I played barefoot in the backyard. Blossoms hung from the thorny black locust trees like clusters of fragrant white grapes. Butterflies flickered in the sunlight above the short new dew-wet grass. I had gone in the house for bread and butter and coming out I heard a steady unfamiliar drone. It was unlike anything I had ever heard before. I tried to place the sound. It was no use. It was a sensation like that I had when searching for my father's watch, heard ticking unseen in a room. It made me feel as though I had forgotten to perform some task that my mother had ordered . . . then I located it, overhead. In the sky, flying quite low and about a hundred yards off, was a plane! It came so slowly that it seemed barely to move. My mouth hung wide; my bread and butter fell into the dirt. I wanted to jump up and down and cheer. And when the idea struck I trembled with excitement: *Some little white boy's plane's done flew away and all I got to do is stretch out my hands and it'll be mine!* It was a little plane like that at the fair, flying no higher than the eaves of our roof. Seeing it come steadily forward I felt the world grow warm with promise. I opened the screen and climbed over it and clung there, waiting. I would catch the plane as it came over and swing down fast and run into the house before anyone could see me. Then no one could come to claim the plane. It droned nearer. Then when it hung like a silver cross in the blue directly above me I stretched out my hand and grabbed. It was like sticking my finger through a soap bubble. The plane flew on, as though I had simply blown my breath after it. I grabbed again, frantically, trying to catch the tail. My fingers clutched the air and disappointment surged tight and hard in my throat. Giving one last desperate grasp, I strained forward. My fingers ripped from the screen. I was falling, the ground burst hard against me. I drummed the earth with my heels and when my breath returned, I lay there bawling.

My mother rushed through the door.

"*What's the matter, chile! What on earth is wrong with you?*"

"*It's gone! It's gone!*"

"*What gone?*"

"*The airplane . . .*"

"*Airplane?*"

"*Yessum, jus like the one at the fair . . . I . . . I tried to stop it an' it kep right on going . . .*"

"*When, boy?*"

"*Just now,*" I cried through my tears.

"*Where it go, boy, what way?*"

"*Yonder, there . . .*"

She scanned the sky, her arms akimbo and her checkered apron flapping in the wind, as I pointed to the fading plane. Finally she looked down at me, slowly shaking her head.

"It's gone! It's gone!" I cried.

"Boy, is you a fool?" she said. "Don't you see that there's a real airplane 'stead of one of them toy ones?"

"Real . . . ?" I forgot to cry. "Real?"

"Yass, real. Don't you know that thing you reaching for is bigger'n a auto? You here trying to reach for it and I bet it's flying 'bout two hundred miles higher'n this roof." She was disgusted with me. "You come on in this house before somebody else sees what a fool you done turned out to be. You must think these here li'l ole arms of your'n is mighty long . . ."

I was carried into the house and undressed for bed and the doctor was called. I cried bitterly; as much from the disappointment of finding the plane so far beyond my reach as from the pain.

When the doctor came I heard my mother telling him about the plane and asking if anything was wrong with my mind. He explained that I had had a fever for several hours. But I was kept in bed for a week and I constantly saw the plane in my sleep, flying just beyond my fingertips, sailing so slowly that it seemed barely to move. And each time I'd reach out to grab it I'd miss and through each dream I'd hear my grandma warning:

"Young man, young man
Yo arm's too short
To box with God. . . ."

"Hey, son!"

At first he did not know where he was and looked at the old man pointing, with blurred eyes.

"Ain't that one of you all's airplanes coming after you?"

As his vision cleared he saw a small black shape above a distant field, soaring through waves of heat. But he could not be sure and with the pain he feared that somehow a horrible recurring fantasy of being split in twain by the whirling blades of a propeller had come true.

"You think he sees us?" he heard.

"See? I hope so."

"He's coming like a bat outa hell!"

Straining, he heard the faint sound of a motor and hoped it would soon be over.

"How you feeling?"

"Like a nightmare," he said.

"Hey, he's done curved back the other way!"

"Maybe he saw us," he said. "Maybe he's gone to send out the ambulance and ground crew." And, he thought with despair, maybe he didn't even see us.

"Where did you send the boy?"

"Down to Mister Graves," Jefferson said. "Man what owns this land."

"Do you think he phoned?"

Jefferson looked at him quickly.

"Aw sho. Dabney Graves is got a bad name on accounta them killings, but he'll call though . . ."

"What killings?"

"Them five fellers . . . ain't you heard?" he asked with surprise.

"No."

"Eve'body knows 'bout Dabney Graves, especially the colored. He done killed enough of us."

Todd had the sensation of being caught in a white neighborhood after dark.

"What did they do?" he asked.

"Thought they was men," Jefferson said. "An' some he owed money, like he do me . . ."

"But why do you stay here?"

"You black, son."

"I know, but . . ."

"You have to come by the white folks, too."

He turned away from Jefferson's eyes, at once consoled and accused. And I'll have to come by them soon, he thought with despair. Closing his eyes, he heard Jefferson's voice as the sun burned blood-red upon his lids.

"I got nowhere to go," Jefferson said, "an' they'd come after me if I did. But Dabney Graves is a funny fellow. He's all the time making jokes. He can be mean as hell, then he's liable to turn right around and back the colored against the white folks. I seen him do it. But me, I hates him for that more'n anything else. 'Cause just as soon as he gits tired helping a man he don't care what happens to him. He just leaves him stone-cold. And then the other white folks is double hard on anybody he done helped. For him it's just a joke. He don't give a hilla beans for nobody—but hisself . . ."

Todd listened to the thread of detachment in the old man's voice. It was as though he held his words at arm's length before him to avoid their destructive meaning.

"He'd just as soon do you a favor and then turn right around and have you strung up. Me, I stays outa his way 'cause down here that's what you gotta do."

If my ankle would only ease for a while, he thought. The closer I spin toward the earth the blacker I become, flashed through his mind. Sweat ran into his eyes and he was sure that he would never see the plane if his head continued whirling. He tried to see Jefferson, what it was that Jefferson held in his hand. It was a little black man, another Jefferson! A little black Jefferson that shook with fits of belly laughter while the other Jefferson looked on with detachment. Then Jefferson looked up from the thing in his hand and turned to speak but Todd was far away, searching the sky for a plane in a hot dry land on a day and age he had long forgotten. He was going mysteriously with his mother through empty streets where black faces peered from behind drawn shades and someone was rapping at a window and he was looking back to see a hand and a frightened face frantically beckoning from a cracked door and his mother was looking down the empty perspective of the street and shaking her head and hurrying him along and at first it was only a flash he saw and a motor was droning as through the sun's glare he saw it gleaming silver as it circled and he was seeing a burst like a puff of white smoke and hearing his mother yell, "Come along, boy, I got no time for them fool airplanes, I got no time," and he saw it a second time, the plane flying high, and the burst appeared suddenly and fell slowly, billowing out and sparkling like fireworks and he was watching and being hurried along as the air filled with a flurry of white pinwheeling cards that caught in the wind and scattered over the rooftops and into the gutters and a woman was running and snatching a card and reading it and screaming and he darted into the shower, grabbing as in winter he grabbed for snowflakes and bounding away at his mother's, "Come on here, boy! Come on, I say!" And he was watching as she took the card away seeing her face grow puzzled and turning taut as her voice quavered, "Niggers Stay from the Polls," and died to a moan of terror as he saw the eyeless sockets of a white hood staring at him from the card and above he saw the plane spiraling gracefully, agleam in the sun like a fiery sword. And seeing it soar he was caught, transfixed between a terrible horror and a horrible fascination.

The sun was not so high now, and Jefferson was calling, and gradually he saw three figures moving across the curving roll of the field.

"Look like some doctors, all dressed in white," said Jefferson.

They're coming at last, Todd thought. And he felt such a release of tension within him that he thought he would faint. But no sooner did he close his eyes than he was seized and he was struggling with three white men who were forcing his arms into some kind of coat. It was too much for him, his arms were pinned to his sides and as the pain blazed in his eyes, he realized that it was a straitjacket. What filthy joke was this?

"That oughta hold him, Mister Graves," he heard.

His total energies seemed focused in his eyes as he searched for their faces. That was Graves, the other two wore hospital uniforms. He was poised between two poles of fear and hate as he heard the one called Graves saying,

"He looks kinda purty in that there suit, boys. I'm glad you dropped by."

"This boy ain't crazy, Mister Graves," one of the others said. "He needs a doctor, not us. Don't see how you led us way out here anyway. It might be a joke to you, but your cousin Rudolph liable to kill somebody. White folks or niggers don't make no difference . . ."

Todd saw the man turn red with anger. Graves looked down upon him, chuckling.

"This nigguh belongs in a straitjacket, too, boys. I knowed that the minnit Jeff's kid said something 'bout a nigguh flyer. You all know you caint let the nigguh git up that high without his going crazy. The nigguh brain ain't built right for high altitudes . . ."

Todd watched the drawling red face, feeling that all the unnamed horror and obscenities that he had ever imagined stood materialized before him.

"Let's git outa here," one of the attendants said.

Todd saw the other reach toward him, realizing for the first time that he lay upon a stretcher as he yelled:

"Don't put your hands on me!"

They drew back, surprised.

"What's that you say, nigguh?" asked Graves.

He did not answer and thought that Graves' foot was aimed at his head. It landed in his chest and he could hardly breathe. He coughed helplessly, seeing Graves' lips stretch taut over his yellow teeth, and tried to shift his head. It was as though a half-dead fly was dragging slowly across his face, and a bomb seemed to burst within him. Blasts of hot, hysterical laughter tore from his chest, causing his eyes to pop, and he felt that the veins in his neck would surely burst. And then a part of him stood behind it all, watching the surprise in Graves' red face and his own hysteria. He thought he would never stop, he would laugh himself to death. It rang in his ears like Jefferson's laughter and he looked for him, centering his eyes desperately upon his face, as though somehow he had become his sole salvation in an insane world of outrage and humiliation. It brought a certain relief. He was suddenly aware that although his body was still contorted, it was an echo that no longer rang in his ears. He heard Jefferson's voice with gratitude.

"Mister Graves, the army done tole him not to leave his airplane."

"Nigguh, army or no, you gittin' off my land! That airplane can stay 'cause it was paid for by taxpayers' money. But you gittin' off. An' dead or alive, it don't make no difference to me."

Todd was beyond it now, lost in a world of anguish.

"Jeff," Graves said. "You and Teddy come and grab holt. I want you to take this here black eagle over to that nigguh airfield and leave him."

Jefferson and the boy approached him silently. He looked away, realizing and doubting at once that only they could release him from his overpowering sense of isolation.

They bent for the stretcher. One of the attendants moved toward Teddy.

"Think you can manage it, boy?"

"I think I can, suh," Teddy said.

"Well, you better go behind then, and let yo pa go ahead so's to keep that leg elevated."

He saw the white men walking ahead as Jefferson and the boy carried him along in silence. Then they were pausing, and he felt a hand wiping his face, then he was moving again. And it was as though he had been lifted out of his isolation, back into the world of men. A new current of communication flowed between the man and boy and himself. They moved him gently. Far away he heard a mocking-bird liquidly calling. He raised his eyes, seeing a buzzard poised unmoving in space. For a moment the whole afternoon seemed suspended, and he waited for the horror to seize him again. Then like a song within his head he heard the boy's soft humming and saw the dark bird glide into the sun and glow like a bird of flaming gold.

1944

Brave Words for a Startling Occasion[1]

First, as I express my gratitude for this honor which you have bestowed on me, let me say that I take it that you are rewarding my efforts rather than my not quite fully achieved attempt at a major novel. Indeed, if I were asked in all seriousness just what I considered to be the chief significance of *Invisible Man* as a fiction, I would reply:

[1]Address for Presentation Ceremony, National Book Award, January 27, 1953.

its experimental attitude, and its attempt to return to the mood of personal moral responsibility for democracy which typified the best of our nineteenth-century fiction. That my first novel should win this most coveted prize must certainly indicate that there is a crisis in the American novel. You as critics have told us so, and current fiction sales would indicate that the reading public agrees. Certainly the younger novelists concur. The explosive nature of events mocks our brightest efforts. And the very "facts" which the naturalists assumed would make us free have lost the power to protect us from despair. Controversy now rages over just what aspects of American experience are suitable for novelistic treatment. The prestige of the theorists of the so-called novel of manners has been challenged. Thus, after a long period of stability we find our assumptions concerning the novel being called into question. And though I was only vaguely aware of it, it was this growing crisis which shaped the writing of *Invisible Man*.

After the usual apprenticeship of imitation and seeking with delight to examine my experience through the discipline of the novel, I became gradually aware that the forms of so many of the works which impressed me were too restricted to contain the experience which I knew. The diversity of American life with its extreme fluidity and openness seemed too vital and alive to be caught for more than the briefest instant in the tight, well-made Jamesian novel, which was, for all its artistic perfection, too concerned with "good taste" and stable areas. Nor could I safely use the forms of the "hard-boiled" novel, with its dedication to physical violence, social cynicism and understatement. Understatement depends, after all, upon commonly held assumptions, and my minority status rendered all such assumptions questionable. There was also a problem of language, and even dialogue, which, with its hard-boiled stance and its monosyllabic utterance, is one of the shining achievements of twentieth-century American writing. For despite the notion that its rhythms were those of everyday speech, I found that when compared with the rich babel of idiomatic expression around me, a language full of imagery and gesture and rhetorical canniness, it was embarrassingly austere. Our speech I found resounding with an alive language swirling with over three hundred years of American living, a mixture of the folk, the Biblical, the scientific and the political. Slangy in one stance, academic in another, loaded poetically with imagery at one moment, mathematically bare of imagery in the next. As for the rather rigid concepts of reality which informed a number of the works which impressed me and to which I owe a great deal, I was forced to conclude that reality was far more mysterious and uncertain, and more exciting, and still, despite its raw violence and capriciousness, more promising. To attempt to express that American experience which has carried one back and forth and up and down the land and across, and across again the great river, from freight train to Pullman car, from contact with slavery to contact with a world of advanced scholarship, art and science, is simply to burst such neatly understated forms of the novel asunder.

A novel whose range was both broader and deeper was needed. And in my search I found myself turning to our classical nineteenth-century novelists. I felt that except for the work of William Faulkner something vital had gone out of American prose after Mark Twain. I came to believe that the writers of that period took a much greater responsibility for the condition of democracy and, indeed, their works were imaginative projections of the conflicts within the human heart which arose when the sacred principles of the Constitution and the Bill of Rights clashed with the practical exigencies of human greed and fear, hate and love. Naturally I was attracted to these writers as a Negro. Whatever they thought of my people per se, in their imaginative economy the Negro symbolized both the man lowest down and the mysterious, underground aspect of human personality. In a sense the Negro was the gauge of the human condition as it waxed and waned in our democracy. These writers were willing to confront the broad complexities of American life, and we are the richer for their having done so.

Thus to see America with an awareness of its rich diversity and its almost magical fluidity and freedom, I was forced to conceive of a novel unburdened by the narrow naturalism which has led, after so many triumphs, to the final and unrelieved despair which marks so much of our current fiction. I was to dream of a prose which was flexible, and swift as American change is swift, confronting the inequalities and brutalities of our society forthrightly, yet thrusting forth its images of hope, human fraternity and individual self-realization. It would use the richness of our speech, the idiomatic expression and the rhetorical flourishes from past periods which are still alive among us. And despite my personal failures, there must be possible a fiction which, leaving sociology to the scientists, can arrive at the truth about the human condition, here and now, with all the bright magic of a fairy tale.

What has been missing from so much experimental writing has been the passionate will to dominate reality as well as the laws of art. This will is the true source of the experimental attitude. We who struggle with form and with America should remember Eidothea's advice to Menelaus when in the *Odyssey* he and his friends are seeking their way home. She tells him to seize her father, Proteus, and to hold him fast "however he may struggle and fight. He will turn into all sorts of shapes to try you," she says, "into all the creatures that live and move upon the earth, into water, into blazing fire; but you must hold him fast and press him all the harder. When he is himself, and questions you in the same shape that he was when you saw him in his bed, let the old man go; and then, sir, ask which god it is who is angry, and how you shall make your way homewards over the fish-giving sea."

For the novelist, Proteus stands for both America and the inheritance of illusion through which all men must fight to achieve reality; the offended god stands for our sins against those principles we all hold sacred. The way home we seek is that condition of man's being at home in the world, which is called love, and which we term democracy. Our task then is always to challenge the apparent forms of reality—that is, the fixed manners and values of the few—and to struggle with it until it reveals its mad, vari-implicated chaos, its false faces, and on until it surrenders its insight, its truth. We are fortunate as American writers in that with our variety of racial and national traditions, idioms and manners, we are yet one. On its profoundest level American experience is of a whole. Its truth lies in its diversity and swiftness of change. Through forging forms of the novel worthy of it, we achieve not only the promise of our lives, but we anticipate the resolution of those world problems of humanity which for a moment seem to those who are in awe of statistics completely insoluble.

Whenever we as Americans have faced serious crises we have returned to fundamentals; this, in brief, is what I have tried to do.

1953

Arthur Miller 1915–2005

Until the age of fourteen, Arthur Miller lived on East 112th Street in Harlem, New York, the son of a prosperous manufacturer of women's coats. With the Depression, his father lost his business and the family moved to Brooklyn into a small but comfortable house. Miller attended Abraham Lincoln High School, where he played football, sustaining a knee injury. Following graduation, he worked at various odd jobs ranging from singer on a local radio station to truck driver to clerk in an automobile parts warehouse. He saved his pay for two years to attend college but was unable to enroll because of poor grades in high school. On the long daily subway ride into Manhattan from Brooklyn, he began reading *The Brothers Karamazov* (which he thought was a detective story), the book that he later referred to as "the great book of wonder" and which presumably aroused his interest in serious literature.

After two attempts, in 1934 Miller finally was admitted to the University of Michigan in Ann Arbor, where he became a journalism major. During the spring of 1936, Miller wrote a play, *No Villain*, that won a Hopwood Award in Drama, an annual contest that carried an award of $250. During this same year, Miller was working his way through college by waiting tables, feeding mice in the university laboratories, and gaining experience as a reporter and night editor of the student newspaper. Transferring his degree program to English, Miller began to study plays eagerly and revised *No Villain* for the Theatre Guild's Bureau of New Plays

Contest with a new title, *They Too Arise*. In 1937 Miller enrolled in a playwriting class taught by Kenneth T. Rowe; that year *They Too Arise* received a major award of $1,250 from the Bureau of New Plays and was produced in Ann Arbor and Detroit. In June his second Hopwood entry received another $250, and Miller decided that playwriting was his future. After narrowly missing winning a third Hopwood Award for *The Great Disobedience*, Miller graduated in 1938 and returned to Brooklyn.

Over the next six years, Miller wrote radio plays and scripts while continuing to look for a play producer. In 1944 his first Broadway play, *The Man Who Had All the Luck*, opened—but closed after four performances. Two years later, Miller appeared on Broadway again with *All My Sons*, a play like most of his major dramas that explored relationships between family members, quite often between fathers, sons, and brothers. *All My Sons* won the New York Drama Critics Circle Award. In 1945 Miller published a novel, *Focus*, that dealt with anti-Semitism. In 1949 *Death of a Salesman* was produced at the Morosco Theater in New York and firmly established its author as a major American playwright. The play won the Pulitzer Prize, the New York Drama Critics' Circle Award, the Antoinette Perry Award, the Theater Club Award, and the Donaldson Award, among many others. It remains one of the most definitive stage works of all time as a study of the American character and culture.

In 1950 Miller adapted Ibsen's *An Enemy of the People*. By 1953 the specter of McCarthyism and its search for Communists in and out of the government and the entertainment business had nearly paralyzed the country. Along with other members of the intellectual community, Miller felt that he had to write in protest. In the introduction to volume one of his *Collected Plays*, Miller noted that he had "known of the Salem witch-hunt for many years before 'McCarthyism' had arrived, and it had always remained an inexplicable darkness to me. When I looked into it now, however, it was with the contemporary situation at my back, particularly the mystery of the handing over of conscience, which seemed to me the central and informing fact of the time." To inform himself of the facts and temper of the Salem events, Miller traveled to Massachusetts, the location of the trials at Danvers (originally Salem Village) and present-day Salem, where he read the original transcripts and documents. The parallel then fell into place between Salem in 1692 and McCarthyism in 1952—the play was almost ready at hand in the transcripts. "No character is in the play," Miller said in a *New York Times* article, "who did not take a similar role in Salem, 1692." The play so precisely reflected the political atmosphere of 1952 that many reviewers were forced to pretend there was no connection. In 1955 Miller was called to testify before the House Committee on Un-American Activities; like John Proctor, he refused to testify against others accused of being Communist sympathizers or party members and was convicted for contempt of Congress (the decision was reversed in 1957). *The Crucible* to date has been produced more often than any of Miller's other plays. As a historical, cultural, and political rendition of one of the most terrifying chapters in American history, and as a reminder of how conscience handed over to others can debase the social contract, *The Crucible* remains unique. It won the Antoinette Perry and Donaldson awards for 1953's best play.

Miller's dramatic themes and interests have always been closely related to what's "in the air," which has led him to being described as a "social dramatist." In the plays following *The Crucible*, Miller ranged far and experimentally in theme, form, and content. Such plays as *A View from the Bridge* (1956, two-act version); his film script for *The Misfits* (1960), now a classic film; *After the Fall* (1964), a dramatic representation of his family, political troubles, and marriage to Marilyn Monroe; *The Price* (1968); *The Archbishop's Ceiling* (1977); and *The American Clock* (1984), among others, deal directly or indirectly with the family, the 1930s Depression, politics, and the American dream. One of Miller's more recent plays, *The Ride Down Mount Morgan*, opened in London in October 1991 to enthusiastic acclaim by British critics.

Robert A. Martin
Michigan State University

PRIMARY WORKS

The Golden Years, 1939; *The Man Who Had All the Luck*, 1944; *Focus*, 1945; *All My Sons*, 1947; *Death of a Salesman*, 1949; *The Crucible*, 1953; *A View from the Bridge*, 1956; *Arthur Miller's Collected Plays*, 1957; *The Misfits*, 1961; *After the Fall*, 1964; *Incident at Vichy*, 1964; *I Don't Need You Any More*, 1967; *The Price*, 1968; *The Creation of the World and Other Business*, 1972; *The Theater Essays of Arthur Miller*, 1978; *Playing for Time*, 1980; *The American Clock*, 1983; *The Archbishop's Ceiling*, 1984; *The Two-Way Mirror* (*Elegy for a Lady* and *Some Kind of Love Story*), 1984; *Danger: Memory* (*I Can't Remember Anything* and *Clara*), 1986; *Timebends: A Life*, 1987; *The Ride Down Mt. Morgan*, 1991; *The Last Yankee*, 1993; *Broken Glass*, 1994; *Mr. Peters' Connections*, 1998; *Resurrection Blues*, 2002; *Finishing the Picture*, 2004.

The Crucible

A Play in Four Acts

Characters

REVEREND PARRIS

BETTY PARRIS

TITUBA

ABIGAIL WILLIAMS

SUSANNA WALCOTT

MRS. ANN PUTNAM

THOMAS PUTNAM

MERCY LEWIS

MARY WARREN

JOHN PROCTOR

REBECCA NURSE

GILES COREY

REVEREND JOHN HALE

ELIZABETH PROCTOR

FRANCIS NURSE

EZEKIEL CHEEVER

MARSHAL HERRICK

JUDGE HATHORNE

DEPUTY GOVERNOR DANFORTH

SARAH GOOD

HOPKINS

A Note on the Historical Accuracy of This Play

This play is not history in the sense in which the word is used by the academic historian. Dramatic purposes have sometimes required many characters to be fused into one; the number of girls involved in the "crying-out" has been reduced; Abigail's age has been raised; while there were several judges of almost equal authority, I have symbolized them all in Hathorne and Danforth. However, I believe that the reader will discover here the essential nature of one of the strangest and most awful chapters in human history. The fate of each character is exactly that of his historical model, and there is no one in the drama who did not play a similar—and in some cases exactly the same—role in history.

As for the characters of the persons, little is known about most of them excepting what may be surmised from a few letters, the trial record, certain broadsides written at the time, and references to their conduct in sources of varying reliability. They may therefore be taken as creations of my own, drawn to the best of my ability in conformity with their known behavior, except as indicated in the commentary I have written for this text.

Act One
(An Overture)

A small upper bedroom in the home of Reverend Samuel Parris, Salem, Massachusetts, in the spring of the year 1692.

There is a narrow window at the left. Through its leaded panes the morning sunlight streams. A candle still burns near the bed, which is at the right. A chest, a chair, and a small table are the other furnishings. At the back a door opens on the landing of the stairway to the ground floor. The room gives off an air of clean spareness. The roof rafters are exposed, and the wood colors are raw and unmellowed.

As the curtain rises, Reverend Parris is discovered kneeling beside the bed, evidently in prayer. His daughter, Betty Parris, aged ten, is lying on the bed, inert.

At the time of these events Parris was in his middle forties. In history he cut a villainous path, and there is very little good to be said for him. He believed he was being persecuted wherever he went, despite his best efforts to win people and God to his side. In meeting, he felt insulted if someone rose to shut the door without first asking his permission. He was a widower with no interest in children, or talent with them. He regarded them as young adults, and until this strange crisis he, like the rest of Salem, never conceived that the children were anything but thankful for being permitted to walk straight, eyes slightly lowered, arms at the sides, and mouths shut until bidden to speak.

His house stood in the "town"—but we today would hardly call it a village. The meeting house was nearby, and from this point outward—toward the bay or inland—there were a few small-windowed, dark houses snuggling against the raw Massachusetts winter. Salem had been established hardly forty years before. To the European world the whole province was a barbaric frontier inhabited by a sect of fanatics who, nevertheless, were shipping out products of slowly increasing quantity and value.

No one can really know what their lives were like. They had no novelists—and would not have permitted anyone to read a novel if one were handy. Their creed forbade anything resembling a theater or "vain enjoyment." They did not celebrate Christmas, and a holiday from work meant only that they must concentrate even more upon prayer.

Which is not to say that nothing broke into this strict and somber way of life. When a new farmhouse was built, friends assembled to "raise the roof," and there would be special foods cooked and probably some potent cider passed around. There was a good supply of ne'er-do-wells in Salem, who dallied at the shovelboard in Bridget Bishop's tavern. Probably more than the creed, hard work kept the morals of the place from spoiling, for the people were forced to fight the land like heroes for every grain of corn, and no man had very much time for fooling around.

That there were some jokers, however, is indicated by the practice of appointing a two-man patrol whose duty was to "walk forth in the time of God's worship to take notice of such as either lye about the meeting house, without attending to the word and ordinances, or that lye at home or in the fields without giving good account thereof, and to take the names of such persons, and to present them to the magistrates, whereby they may be accordingly proceeded against." This predilection for minding other people's business was time-honored among the people of Salem, and it undoubtedly created many of the suspicions which were to feed the coming madness. It was also, in my opinion, one of the things that a John Proctor would rebel against, for the time of the armed camp had almost passed, and since the country was reasonably—although not wholly—safe, the old disciplines were beginning to rankle. But, as in all such matters, the issue was not clear-cut, for danger was still a possibility, and in unity still lay the best promise of safety.

The edge of the wilderness was close by. The American continent stretched endlessly west, and it was full of mystery for them. It stood, dark and threatening, over their shoulders night and day, for out of it Indian tribes marauded from time to time, and Reverend Parris had parishioners who had lost relatives to these heathen.

The parochial snobbery of these people was partly responsible for their failure to convert the Indians. Probably they also preferred to take land from heathens rather than from fellow Christians. At any rate, very few Indians were converted, and the Salem folk believed that the virgin forest was the Devil's last preserve, his home base and the citadel of his final stand. To the best of their knowledge the American forest was the last place on earth that was not paying homage to God.

For these reasons, among others, they carried about an air of innate resistance, even of persecution. Their fathers had, of course, been persecuted in England. So now they and their church found it necessary to deny any other sect its freedom, lest their New Jerusalem be defiled and corrupted by wrong ways and deceitful ideas.

They believed, in short, that they held in their steady hands the candle that would light the world. We have inherited this belief, and it has helped and hurt us. It helped them with the discipline it gave them. They were a dedicated folk, by and large, and they had to be to survive the life they had chosen or been born into in this country.

The proof of their belief's value to them may be taken from the opposite character of the first Jamestown settlement, farther south, in Virginia. The Englishmen who landed there were motivated mainly by a hunt for profit. They had thought to pick off the wealth of the new country and then return rich to England. They were a band of individualists, and a much more ingratiating group than the Massachusetts men. But Virginia destroyed them. Massachusetts tried to kill off the Puritans, but they combined; they set up a communal society which, in the beginning, was little more than an armed camp with an autocratic and very devoted leadership. It was, however, an autocracy by consent, for they were united from top to bottom by a commonly held ideology whose perpetuation was the reason and justification for all their sufferings. So their self-denial, their purposefulness, their suspicion of all vain pursuits, their hard-handed justice, were altogether perfect instruments for the conquest of this space so antagonistic to man.

But the people of Salem in 1692 were not quite the dedicated folk that arrived on the *Mayflower*. A vast differentiation had taken place, and in their own time a revolution had unseated the royal government and substituted a junta which was at this moment in power. The times, to their eyes, must have been out of joint, and to the common folk must have seemed as insoluble and complicated as do ours today. It is not hard to see how easily many could have been led to believe that the time of confusion had been brought upon them by deep and darkling forces. No hint of such speculation appears on the court record, but social disorder in any age breeds such mystical suspicions, and when, as in Salem, wonders are brought forth from below the social surface, it is too much to expect people to hold back very long from laying on the victims with all the force of their frustrations.

The Salem tragedy, which is about to begin in these pages, developed from a paradox. It is a paradox in whose grip we still live, and there is no prospect yet that we will discover its resolution. Simply, it was this: for good purposes, even high purposes, the people of Salem developed a theocracy, a combine of state and religious power whose function was to keep the community together, and to prevent any kind of disunity that might open it to destruction by material or ideological enemies. It was forged for a necessary purpose and accomplished that purpose. But all organization is and must be grounded on the idea of exclusion and prohibition, just as two objects cannot occupy the same space. Evidently the time came in New England when the repressions of order were heavier than seemed warranted by the dangers against which the order was organized. The witch-hunt was a perverse manifestation of the panic which set in among all classes when the balance began to turn toward greater individual freedom.

When one rises above the individual villainy displayed, one can only pity them all, just as we shall be pitied someday. It is still impossible for man to organize his social life without repressions, and the balance has yet to be struck between order and freedom.

The witch-hunt was not, however, a mere repression. It was also, and as importantly, a long overdue opportunity for everyone so inclined to express publicly his guilt and sins, under the cover of accusations against the victims. It suddenly became possible—and patriotic and holy—for a man to say that Martha Corey had come into his bedroom at night, and that, while his wife was sleeping at his side, Martha laid herself down on his chest and "nearly suffocated him." Of course it was her spirit only, but his satisfaction at confessing himself was no lighter than if it had been Martha herself. One could not ordinarily speak such things in public.

Long-held hatreds of neighbors could now be openly expressed, and vengeance taken, despite the Bible's charitable injunctions. Land-lust which had been expressed before by constant bickering over boundaries and deeds, could now be elevated to the arena of morality; one could cry witch against one's neighbor and feel perfectly justified in the bargain. Old scores could be settled on a plane of heavenly combat between Lucifer and the Lord; suspicions and the envy of the miserable toward the happy could and did burst out in the general revenge.

Reverend Parris is praying now, and, though we cannot hear his words, a sense of his confusion hangs about him. He mumbles, then seems about to weep; then he weeps, then prays again; but his daughter does not stir on the bed.

The door opens, and his Negro slave enters. Tituba is in her forties. Parris brought her with him from Barbados, where he spent some years as a merchant before entering the ministry. She enters as one does who can no longer bear to be barred from the sight of her beloved, but she is also very frightened because her slave sense has warned her that, as always, trouble in this house eventually lands on her back.

TITUBA, *already taking a step backward:* My Betty be hearty soon?

PARRIS: Out of here!

TITUBA, *backing to the door:* My Betty not goin' die . . .

PARRIS, *scrambling to his feet in a fury:* Out of my sight! *She is gone.* Out of my—*He is overcome with sobs. He clamps his teeth against them and closes the door and leans against it, exhausted.* Oh, my God! God help me! *Quaking with fear, mumbling to himself through his sobs, he goes to the bed and gently takes Betty's hand.* Betty. Child. Dear child. Will you wake, will you open up your eyes! Betty, little one . . .

He is bending to kneel again when his niece, Abigail Williams, seventeen, enters—a strikingly beautiful girl, an orphan, with an endless capacity for dissembling. Now she is all worry and apprehension and propriety.

ABIGAIL: Uncle? *He looks to her.* Susanna Walcott's here from Doctor Griggs.

PARRIS: Oh? Let her come, let her come.

ABIGAIL, *leaning out the door to call to Susanna, who is down the hall a few steps:* Come in, Susanna.

Susanna Walcott, a little younger than Abigail, a nervous, hurried girl, enters.

PARRIS, *eagerly:* What does the doctor say, child?

SUSANNA, *craning around Parris to get a look at Betty:* He bid me come and tell you, reverend sir, that he cannot discover no medicine for it in his books.

PARRIS: Then he must search on.

SUSANNA: Aye, sir, he have been searchin' his books since he left you, sir. But he bid me tell you, that you might look to unnatural things for the cause of it.

PARRIS, *his eyes going wide:* No—no. There be no unnatural cause here. Tell him I have sent for Reverend Hale of Beverly, and Mr. Hale will surely confirm that. Let him look to medicine and put out all thought of unnatural causes here. There be none.

SUSANNA: Aye, sir. He bid me tell you. *She turns to go.*

ABIGAIL: Speak nothin' of it in the village, Susanna.

PARRIS: Go directly home and speak nothing of unnatural causes.

SUSANNA: Aye, sir. I pray for her. *She goes out.*

ABIGAIL: Uncle, the rumor of witchcraft is all about; I think you'd best go down and deny it yourself. The parlor's packed with people, sir. I'll sit with her.

PARRIS, *pressed, turns on her:* And what shall I say to them? That my daughter and my niece I discovered dancing like heathen in the forest?

ABIGAIL: Uncle, we did dance; let you tell them I confessed it—and I'll be whipped if I must be. But they're speakin' of witchcraft. Betty's not witched.

PARRIS: Abigail, I cannot go before the congregation when I know you have not opened with me. What did you do with her in the forest?

ABIGAIL: We did dance, uncle, and when you leaped out of the bush so suddenly, Betty was frightened and then she fainted. And there's the whole of it.

PARRIS: Child. Sit you down.

ABIGAIL, *quavering, as she sits:* I would never hurt Betty. I love her dearly.

PARRIS: Now look you, child, your punishment will come in its time. But if you trafficked with spirits in the forest I must know it now, for surely my enemies will, and they will ruin me with it.

ABIGAIL: But we never conjured spirits.

PARRIS: Then why can she not move herself since midnight? This child is desperate! *Abigail lowers her eyes.* It must come out—my enemies will bring it out. Let me know what you done there. Abigail, do you understand that I have many enemies?

ABIGAIL: I have heard of it, uncle.

PARRIS: There is a faction that is sworn to drive me from my pulpit. Do you understand that?

ABIGAIL: I think so, sir.

PARRIS: Now then, in the midst of such disruption, my own household is discovered to be the very center of some obscene practice. Abominations are done in the forest—

ABIGAIL: It were sport, uncle!

PARRIS, *pointing at Betty:* You call this sport? *She lowers her eyes. He pleads:* Abigail, if you know something that may help the doctor, for God's sake tell it to me. *She is silent.* I saw Tituba waving her arms over the fire when I came on you. Why was she doing that? And I heard a screeching and gibberish coming from her mouth. She were swaying like a dumb beast over that fire!

ABIGAIL: She always sings her Barbados songs, and we dance.

PARRIS: I cannot blink what I saw, Abigail, for my enemies will not blink it. I saw a dress lying on the grass.

ABIGAIL, *innocently:* A dress?

PARRIS—*it is very hard to say:* Aye, a dress. And I thought I saw—someone naked running through the trees!

ABIGAIL, *in terror:* No one was naked! You mistake yourself, uncle!

PARRIS, *with anger:* I saw it! *He moves from her. Then, resolved:* Now tell me true, Abigail. And I pray you feel the weight of truth upon you, for now my ministry's at stake, my ministry and perhaps your cousin's life. Whatever abomination you have done, give me all of it now, for I dare not be taken unaware when I go before them down there.

ABIGAIL: There is nothin' more. I swear it, uncle.

PARRIS, *studies her, then nods, half convinced:* Abigail, I have fought here three long years to bend these stiff-necked people to me, and now, just now when some good respect is rising for me in the parish, you compromise my very character. I have given you a home, child, I have put clothes upon your back—now give me upright answer. Your name in the town—it is entirely white, is it not?

ABIGAIL, *with an edge of resentment:* Why, I am sure it is, sir. There be no blush about my name.

PARRIS, *to the point:* Abigail, is there any other cause than you have told me, for your being discharged from Goody Proctor's service? I have heard it said, and I tell you as I heard it, that she comes so rarely to the church this year for she will not sit so close to something soiled. What signified that remark?

ABIGAIL: She hates me, uncle, she must, for I would not be her slave. It's a bitter woman, a lying, cold, sniveling woman, and I will not work for such a woman!

PARRIS: She may be. And yet it has troubled me that you are now seven month out of their house, and in all this time no other family has ever called for your service.

ABIGAIL: They want slaves, not such as I. Let them send to Barbados for that. I will not black my face for any of them! *With ill-concealed resentment at him:* Do you begrudge my bed, uncle?

PARRIS: No—no.

ABIGAIL, *in a temper:* My name is good in the village! I will not have it said my name is soiled! Goody Proctor is a gossiping liar!

Enter Mrs. Ann Putnam. She is a twisted soul of forty-five, a death-ridden woman, haunted by dreams.

PARRIS, *as soon as the door begins to open:* No—no, I cannot have anyone. *He sees her, and a certain deference springs into him, although his worry remains.* Why, Goody Putnam, come in.

MRS. PUTNAM, *full of breath, shiny-eyed:* It is a marvel. It is surely a stroke of hell upon you.

PARRIS: No, Goody Putnam, it is—

MRS. PUTNAM, *glancing at Betty:* How high did she fly, how high?

PARRIS: No, no, she never flew—

MRS. PUTNAM, *very pleased with it:* Why, it's sure she did. Mr. Collins saw her goin' over Ingersoll's barn, and come down light as bird, he says!

PARRIS: Now, look you, Goody Putnam, she never— *Enter Thomas Putnam, a well-to-do hard-handed landowner, near fifty.* Oh, good morning, Mr. Putnam.

PUTNAM: It is a providence the thing is out now! It is a providence. *He goes directly to the bed.*

PARRIS: What's out, sir, what's—

Mrs. Putnam goes to the bed.

PUTNAM, *looking down at Betty:* Why, *her* eyes is closed! Look you, Ann.

MRS. PUTNAM: Why, that's strange. *To Parris:* Ours is open.

PARRIS, *shocked:* Your Ruth is sick?

MRS. PUTNAM, *with vicious certainty:* I'd not call it sick; the Devil's touch is heavier than sick. It's death, y'know, it's death drivin' into them, forked and hoofed.

PARRIS: Oh, pray not! Why, how does Ruth ail?

MRS. PUTNAM: She ails as she must—she never waked this morning, but her eyes open and she walks, and hears naught, sees naught, and cannot eat. Her soul is taken, surely.

Parris is struck.

PUTNAM, *as though for further details:* They say you've sent for Reverend Hale of Beverly?

PARRIS, *with dwindling conviction now:* A precaution only. He has much experience in all demonic arts, and I—

MRS. PUTNAM: He has indeed; and found a witch in Beverly last year, and let you remember that.

PARRIS: Now, Goody Ann, they only thought that were a witch, and I am certain there be no element of witchcraft here.

PUTNAM: No witchcraft! Now look you, Mr. Parris—

PARRIS: Thomas, Thomas, I pray you, leap not to witchcraft. I know that you—you least of all, Thomas, would ever wish so disastrous a charge laid upon me. We cannot leap to witchcraft. They will howl me out of Salem for such corruption in my house.

A word about Thomas Putnam. He was a man with many grievances, at least one of which appears justified. Some time before, his wife's brother-in-law, James Bayley, had been turned down as minister of Salem. Bayley had all the qualifications, and a two-thirds vote into the bargain, but a faction stopped his acceptance, for reasons that are not clear.

Thomas Putnam was the eldest son of the richest man in the village. He had fought the Indians at Narragansett, and was deeply interested in parish affairs. He undoubtedly felt it poor payment that the village should so blatantly disregard his candidate for one of its more important offices, especially since he regarded himself as the intellectual superior of most of the people around him.

His vindictive nature was demonstrated long before the witchcraft began. Another former Salem minister, George Burroughs, had had to borrow money to pay for his wife's funeral, and, since the parish was remiss in his salary, he was soon bankrupt. Thomas and his brother John had Burroughs jailed for debts the man did not owe. The incident is important only in that Burroughs succeeded in becoming minister where Bayley, Thomas Putnam's brother-in-law, had been rejected; the motif of resentment is clear here. Thomas Putnam felt that his own name and the honor of his family had been smirched by the village, and he meant to right matters however he could.

Another reason to believe him a deeply embittered man was his attempt to break his father's will, which left a disproportionate amount to a stepbrother. As with every other public cause in which he tried to force his way, he failed in this.

So it is not surprising to find that so many accusations against people are in the handwriting of Thomas Putnam, or that his name is so often found as a witness corroborating the supernatural testimony, or that his daughter led the crying-out at the most opportune junctures of the trials, especially when—But we'll speak of that when we come to it.

PUTNAM—*at the moment he is intent upon getting Parris, for whom he has only contempt, to move toward the abyss:* Mr. Parris, I have taken your part in all contention here, and I would continue; but I cannot if you hold back in this. There are hurtful, vengeful spirits layin' hands on these children.

PARRIS: But, Thomas, you cannot—

PUTNAM: Ann! Tell Mr. Parris what you have done.

MRS. PUTNAM: Reverend Parris, I have laid seven babies unbaptized in the earth. Believe me, sir, you never saw more hearty babies born. And yet, each would wither in my arms the very night of their birth. I have spoke nothin', but my heart has clamored intimations. And now, this year, my Ruth, my only—I see her turning strange. A secret child she has become this year, and shrivels like a sucking mouth were pullin' on her life too. And so I thought to send her to your Tituba—

PARRIS: To Tituba! What may Tituba—?

MRS. PUTNAM: Tituba knows how to speak to the dead, Mr. Parris.

PARRIS: Goody Ann, it is a formidable sin to conjure up the dead!

MRS. PUTNAM: I take it on my soul, but who else may surely tell us what person murdered my babies?

PARRIS, *horrified:* Woman!

MRS. PUTNAM: They were murdered, Mr. Parris! And mark this proof! Mark it! Last night my Ruth were ever so close to their little spirits; I know it, sir. For how else is she struck dumb now except some power of darkness would stop her mouth? It is a marvelous sign, Mr. Parris!

PUTNAM: Don't you understand it, sir? There is a murdering witch among us, bound to keep herself in the dark. *Parris turns to Betty, a frantic terror rising in him.* Let your enemies make of it what they will, you cannot blink it more.

PARRIS, *to Abigail:* Then you were conjuring spirits last night.

ABIGAIL, *whispering:* Not I, sir—Tituba and Ruth.

PARRIS *turns now, with new fear, and goes to Betty, looks down at her, and then, gazing off:* Oh, Abigail, what proper payment for my charity! Now I am undone.

PUTNAM: You are not undone! Let you take hold here. Wait for no one to charge you—declare it yourself. You have discovered witchcraft—

PARRIS: In my house? In my house, Thomas? They will topple me with this! They will make of it a—

Enter Mercy Lewis, the Putnams' servant, a fat, sly, merciless girl of eighteen.

MERCY: Your pardons. I only thought to see how Betty is.

PUTNAM: Why aren't you home? Who's with Ruth?

MERCY: Her grandma come. She's improved a little, I think—she give a powerful sneeze before.

MRS. PUTNAM: Ah, there's a sign of life!

MERCY: I'd fear no more, Goody Putnam. It were a grand sneeze; another like it will shake her wits together, I'm sure. *She goes to the bed to look.*

PARRIS: Will you leave me now, Thomas? I would pray a while alone.

ABIGAIL: Uncle, you've prayed since midnight. Why do you not go down and—

PARRIS: No—no. *To Putnam:* I have no answer for that crowd. I'll wait till Mr. Hale arrives. *To get Mrs. Putnam to leave:* If you will, Goody Ann . . .

PUTNAM: Now look you, sir. Let you strike out against the Devil, and the village will bless you for it! Come down, speak to them—pray with them. They're thirsting for your word, Mister! Surely you'll pray with them.

PARRIS, *swayed:* I'll lead them in a psalm, but let you say nothing of witchcraft yet. I will not discuss it. The cause is yet unknown. I have had enough contention since I came; I want no more.

MRS. PUTNAM: Mercy, you go home to Ruth, dy'y'hear?

MERCY: Aye, mum.

Mrs. Putnam goes out.

PARRIS, *to Abigail:* If she starts for the window, cry for me at once.

ABIGAIL: I will, uncle.

PARRIS, *to Putnam:* There is a terrible power in her arms today. *He goes out with Putnam.*

ABIGAIL, *with hushed trepidation:* How is Ruth sick?

MERCY: It's weirdish, I know not—she seems to walk like a dead one since last night.

ABIGAIL, *turns at once and goes to Betty, and now, with fear in her voice:* Betty? *Betty doesn't move. She shakes her.* Now stop this! Betty! Sit up now!

Betty doesn't stir. Mercy comes over.

MERCY: Have you tried beatin' her? I gave Ruth a good one and it waked her for a minute. Here, let me have her.

ABIGAIL, *holding Mercy back:* No, he'll be comin' up. Listen, now; if they be questioning us, tell them we danced—I told him as much already.

MERCY: Aye. And what more?

ABIGAIL: He knows Tituba conjured Ruth's sisters to come out of the grave.

MERCY: And what more?

ABIGAIL: He saw you naked.

MERCY, *clapping her hands together with a frightened laugh:* Oh, Jesus!

Enter Mary Warren, breathless. She is seventeen, a subservient, naive, lonely girl.

MARY WARREN: What'll we do? The village is out! I just come from the farm; the whole country's talkin' witchcraft! They'll be callin' us witches, Abby!

MERCY, *pointing and looking at Mary Warren:* She means to tell, I know it.

MARY WARREN: Abby, we've got to tell. Witchery's a hangin' error, a hangin' like they done in Boston two year ago! We must tell the truth, Abby! You'll only be whipped for dancin', and the other things!

ABIGAIL: Oh, *we'll* be whipped!

MARY WARREN: I never done none of it, Abby. I only looked!

MERCY, *moving menacingly toward Mary:* Oh, you're a great one for lookin', aren't you, Mary Warren? What a grand peeping courage you have!

Betty, on the bed, whimpers. Abigail turns to her at once.

ABIGAIL: Betty? *She goes to Betty.* Now, Betty, dear, wake up now. It's Abigail. *She sits Betty up and furiously shakes her.* I'll beat you, Betty! *Betty whimpers.* My, you seem improving. I talked to your papa and I told him everything. So there's nothing to—

BETTY, *darts off the bed, frightened of Abigail, and flattens herself against the wall:* I want my mama!

ABIGAIL, *with alarm, as she cautiously approaches Betty:* What ails you, Betty? Your mama's dead and buried.

BETTY: I'll fly to Mama. Let me fly! *She raises her arms as though to fly, and streaks for the window, gets one leg out.*

ABIGAIL, *pulling her away from the window:* I told him everything; he knows now, he knows everything we—

BETTY: You drank blood, Abby! You didn't tell him that!

ABIGAIL: Betty, you never say that again! You will never—

BETTY: You did, you did! You drank a charm to kill John Proctor's wife! You drank a charm to kill Goody Proctor!

ABIGAIL, *smashes her across the face:* Shut it! Now shut it!

BETTY, *collapsing on the bed:* Mama, Mama! *She dissolves into sobs.*

ABIGAIL: Now look you. All of you. We danced. And Tituba conjured Ruth Putnam's dead sisters. And that is all. And mark this. Let either of you breathe a word, or the edge of a word, about the other things, and I will come to you in the black of some terrible night and I will bring a pointy reckoning that will shudder you. And you know I can do it; I saw Indians smash my dear parents' heads on the pillow next to mine, and I have seen some reddish work done at night, and I can make you wish you had never seen the sun go down! *She goes to Betty and roughly sits her up.* Now, you—sit up and stop this!

But Betty collapses in her hands and lies inert on the bed.

MARY WARREN, *with hysterical fright:* What's got her? *Abigail stares in fright at Betty.* Abby, she's going to die! It's a sin to conjure, and we—

ABIGAIL, *starting for Mary:* I say shut it, Mary Warren!

Enter John Proctor. On seeing him, Mary Warren leaps in fright.

Proctor was a farmer in his middle thirties. He need not have been a partisan of any faction in the town, but there is evidence to suggest that he had a sharp and bitting way with hypocrites. He was the kind of man—powerful of body, even-tempered, and not easily led—who cannot refuse support to partisans without drawing their deepest resentment. In Proctor's presence a fool felt his foolishness instantly—and a Proctor is always marked for calumny therefore.

But as we shall see, the steady manner he displays does not spring from an untroubled soul. He is a sinner, a sinner not only against the moral fashion of the time, but against his own vision of decent conduct. These people had no ritual for the washing away of sins. It is another trait we inherited from them, and it has helped to discipline us as well as to breed hypocrisy among us. Proctor, respected and even feared in Salem, has come to regard himself as a kind of fraud. But no hint of this has yet appeared on the surface, and as he enters from the crowded parlor below it is a man in his prime we see, with a quiet confidence and an unexpressed, hidden force. Mary Warren, his servant, can barely speak for embarrassment and fear.

MARY WARREN: Oh! I'm just going home, Mr. Proctor.

PROCTOR: Be you foolish, Mary Warren? Be you deaf? I forbid you leave the house, did I not? Why shall I pay you? I am looking for you more often than my cows!

MARY WARREN: I only come to see the great doings in the world.

PROCTOR: I'll show you a great doin' on your arse one of these days. Now get you home; my wife is waitin' with your work! *Trying to retain a shred of dignity, she goes slowly out.*

MERCY LEWIS, *both afraid of him and strangely titillated:* I'd best be off. I have my Ruth to watch. Good morning, Mr. Proctor.

Mercy sidles out. Since Proctor's entrance, Abigail has stood as though on tiptoe, absorbing his presence, wide-eyed. He glances at her, then goes to Betty on the bed.

ABIGAIL: Gah! I'd almost forgot how strong you are, John Proctor!

PROCTOR, *looking at Abigail now, the faintest suggestion of a knowing smile on his face:* What's this mischief here?

ABIGAIL, *with a nervous laugh:* Oh, she's only gone silly somehow.

PROCTOR: The road past my house is a pilgrimage to Salem all morning. The town's mumbling witchcraft.

ABIGAIL: Oh, posh! *Winningly she comes a little closer, with a confidential, wicked air.* We were dancin' in the woods last night, and my uncle leaped in on us. She took fright, is all.

PROCTOR, *his smile widening:* Ah, you're wicked yet, aren't y'! *A trill of expectant laughter escapes her, and she dares come closer, feverishly looking into his eyes.* You'll be clapped in the stocks before you're twenty.

He takes a step to go, and she springs into his path.

ABIGAIL: Give me a word, John. A soft word. *Her concentrated desire destroys his smile.*

PROCTOR: No, no, Abby. That's done with.

ABIGAIL, *tauntingly:* You come five mile to see a silly girl fly? I know you better.

PROCTOR, *setting her firmly out of his path:* I come to see what mischief your uncle's brewin' now. *With final emphasis:* Put it out of mind, Abby.

ABIGAIL, *grasping his hand before he can release her:* John—I am waitin' for you every night.

PROCTOR: Abby, I never give you hope to wait for me.

ABIGAIL, *now beginning to anger—she can't believe it:* I have something better than hope, I think!

PROCTOR: Abby, you'll put it out of mind. I'll not be comin' for you more.

ABIGAIL: You're surely sportin' with me.

PROCTOR: You know me better.

ABIGAIL: I know how you clutched my back behind your house and sweated like a stallion whenever I come near! Or did I dream that? It's she put me out, you cannot pretend it were you. I saw your face when she put me out, and you loved me then and you do now!

PROCTOR: Abby, that's a wild thing to say—

ABIGAIL: A wild thing may say wild things. But not so wild, I think. I have seen you since she put me out; I have seen you nights.

PROCTOR: I have hardly stepped off my farm this sevenmonth.

ABIGAIL: I have a sense for heat, John, and yours has drawn me to my window, and I have seen you looking up, burning in your loneliness. Do you tell me you've never looked up at my window?

PROCTOR: I may have looked up.

ABIGAIL, *now softening:* And you must. You are no wintry man. I know you, John. I *know* you. *She is weeping.* I cannot sleep for dreamin'; I cannot dream but I wake and walk about the house as though I'd find you comin' through some door. *She clutches him desperately.*

PROCTOR, *gently pressing her from him, with great sympathy but firmly:* Child—

ABIGAIL, *with a flash of anger:* How do you call me child!

PROCTOR: Abby, I may think of you softly from time to time. But I will cut off my hand before I'll ever reach for you again. Wipe it out of mind. We never touched, Abby.

ABIGAIL: Aye, but we did.

PROCTOR: Aye, but we did not.

ABIGAIL, *with a bitter anger:* Oh, I marvel how such a strong man may let such a sickly wife be—

PROCTOR, *angered—at himself as well:* You'll speak nothin' of Elizabeth!

ABIGAIL: She is blackening my name in the village! She is telling lies about me! She is a cold, sniveling woman, and you bend to her! Let her turn you like a—

PROCTOR, *shaking her:* Do you look for whippin'?

A psalm is heard being sung below.

ABIGAIL, *in tears:* I look for John Proctor that took me from my sleep and put knowledge in my heart! I never knew what pretense Salem was, I never knew the lying lessons I was taught by all these Christian women and their covenanted men! And now you bid me tear the light out of my eyes? I will not, I cannot! You loved me, John Proctor, and whatever sin it is, you love me yet! *He turns abruptly to go out. She rushes to him.* John, pity me, pity me!

The words "going up to Jesus" are heard in the psalm, and Betty claps her ears suddenly and whines loudly.

ABIGAIL: Betty? *She hurries to Betty, who is now sitting up and screaming. Proctor goes to Betty as Abigail is trying to pull her hands down, calling "Betty!"*

PROCTOR, *growing unnerved:* What's she doing? Girl, what ails you? Stop that wailing!

The singing has stopped in the midst of this, and now Parris rushes in.

PARRIS: What happened? What are you doing to her? Betty! *He rushes to the bed, crying, "Betty, Betty!" Mrs. Putnam enters, feverish with curiosity, and with her Thomas Putnam and Mercy Lewis. Parris, at the bed, keeps lightly slapping Betty's face, while she moans and tries to get up.*

ABIGAIL: She heard you singin' and suddenly she's up and screamin'.

MRS. PUTNAM: The psalm! The psalm! She cannot bear to hear the Lord's name!

PARRIS: No, God forbid. Mercy, run to the doctor! Tell him what's happened here! *Mercy Lewis rushes out.*

MRS. PUTNAM: Mark it for a sign, mark it!

Rebecca Nurse, seventy-two, enters. She is white-haired, leaning upon her walking-stick.

PUTNAM, *pointing at the whimpering Betty:* That is a notorious sign of witchcraft afoot, Goody Nurse, a prodigious sign!

MRS. PUTNAM: My mother told me that! When they cannot bear to hear the name of—

PARRIS, *trembling:* Rebecca, Rebecca, go to her, we're lost. She suddenly cannot bear to hear the Lord's—

Giles Corey, eighty-three, enters. He is knotted with muscle, canny, inquisitive, and still powerful.

REBECCA: There is hard sickness here, Giles Corey, so please to keep the quiet.

GILES: I've not said a word. No one here can testify I've said a word. Is she going to fly again? I hear she flies.

PUTNAM: Man, be quiet now!

Everything is quiet. Rebecca walks across the room to the bed. Gentleness exudes from her. Betty is quietly whimpering, eyes shut. Rebecca simply stands over the child, who gradually quiets.

And while they are so absorbed, we may put a word in for Rebecca. Rebecca was the wife of Francis Nurse, who, from all accounts, was one of those men for whom both sides of the argument had to have respect. He was called upon to arbitrate disputes as though he were an unofficial judge, and Rebecca also enjoyed the high opinion most people had for him. By the time of the delusion, they had three hundred acres, and their children were settled in separate homesteads within the same estate. However, Francis had originally rented the land, and one theory has it that, as he gradually paid for it and raised his social status, there were those who resented his rise.

Another suggestion to explain the systematic campaign against Rebecca, and inferentially against Francis, is the land war he fought with his neighbors, one of whom was a Putnam. This squabble grew to the proportions of a battle in the woods between partisans of both sides, and it is said to have lasted for two days. As for Rebecca herself, the general opinion of her character was so high that to explain how anyone dared cry her out for a witch—and more, how adults could bring themselves to lay hands on her—we must look to the fields and boundaries of that time.

As we have seen, Thomas Putnam's man for the Salem ministry was Bayley. The Nurse clan had been in the faction that prevented Bayley's taking office. In addition, certain families allied to the Nurses by blood or friendship, and whose farms were contiguous with the Nurse farm or close to it, combined to break away from the Salem town authority and set up Topsfield, a new and independent entity whose existence was resented by old Salemites.

That the guiding hand behind the outcry was Putnam's is indicated by the fact that, as soon as it began, this Topsfield-Nurse faction absented themselves from church in protest and disbelief. It was Edward and Jonathan Putnam who signed the first complaint against Rebecca; and Thomas Putnam's little daughter was the one who fell into a fit at the hearing and pointed to Rebecca as her attacker. To top it all, Mrs. Putnam—who is now staring at the bewitched child on the bed—soon accused Rebecca's spirit of "tempting her to iniquity," a charge that had more truth in it than Mrs. Putnam could know.

MRS. PUTNAM, *astonished:* What have you done?

Rebecca, in thought, now leaves the bedside and sits.

PARRIS, *wondrous and relieved:* What do you make of it, Rebecca?

PUTNAM, *eagerly:* Goody Nurse, will you go to my Ruth and see if you can wake her?

REBECCA, *sitting:* I think she'll wake in time. Pray calm yourselves. I have eleven children, and I am twenty-six times a grandma, and I have seen them all through their silly seasons, and when it come on them they will run the Devil bowlegged keeping up with their mischief. I think she'll wake when she tires of it. A child's spirit is like a child, you can never catch it by running after it; you must stand still, and, for love, it will soon itself come back.

PROCTOR: Aye, that's the truth of it, Rebecca.

MRS. PUTNAM: This is no silly season, Rebecca. My Ruth is bewildered, Rebecca; she cannot eat.

REBECCA: Perhaps she is not hungered yet. *To Parris:* I hope you are not decided to go in search of loose spirits, Mr. Parris. I've heard promise of that outside.

PARRIS: A wide opinion's running in the parish that the Devil may be among us, and I would satisfy them that they are wrong.

PROCTOR: Then let you come out and call them wrong. Did you consult the wardens before you called this minister to look for devils?

PARRIS: He is not coming to look for devils!

PROCTOR: Then what's he coming for?

PUTNAM: There be children dyin' in the village, Mister!

PROCTOR: I seen none dyin'. This society will not be a bag to swing around your head, Mr. Putnam. *To Parris:* Did you call a meeting before you—?

PUTNAM: I am sick of meetings; cannot the man turn his head without he have a meeting?

PROCTOR: He may turn his head, but not to Hell!

REBECCA: Pray, John, be calm. *Pause. He defers to her.* Mr. Parris, I think you'd best send Reverend Hale back as soon as he come. This will set us all to arguin' again in the society, and we thought to have peace this year. I think we ought rely on the doctor now, and good prayer.

MRS. PUTNAM: Rebecca, the doctor's baffled!

REBECCA: If so he is, then let us go to God for the cause of it. There is prodigious danger in the seeking of loose spirits. I fear it, I fear it. Let us rather blame ourselves and—

PUTNAM: How may we blame ourselves? I am one of nine sons; the Putnam seed have peopled this province. And yet I have but one child left of eight—and now she shrivels!

REBECCA: I cannot fathom that.

MRS. PUTNAM, *with a growing edge of sarcasm:* But I must! You think it God's work you should never lose a child, nor grandchild either, and I bury all but one? There are wheels within wheels in this village, and fires within fires!

PUTNAM, *to Parris:* When Reverend Hale comes, you will proceed to look for signs of witchcraft here.

PROCTOR, *to Putnam:* You cannot command Mr. Parris. We vote by name in this society, not by acreage.

PUTNAM: I never heard you worried so on this society, Mr. Proctor. I do not think I saw you at Sabbath meeting since snow flew.

PROCTOR: I have trouble enough without I come five mile to hear him preach only hellfire and bloody damnation. Take it to heart, Mr. Parris. There are many others who stay away from church these days because you hardly ever mention God any more.

PARRIS, *now aroused:* Why, that's a drastic charge!

REBECCA: It's somewhat true; there are many that quail to bring their children—

PARRIS: I do not preach for children, Rebecca. It is not the children who are unmindful of their obligations toward this ministry.

REBECCA: Are there really those unmindful?

PARRIS: I should say the better half of Salem village—

PUTNAM: And more than that!

PARRIS: Where is my wood? My contract provides I be supplied with all my firewood. I am waiting since November for a stick, and even in November I had to show my frostbitten hands like some London beggar!

GILES: You are allowed six pound a year to buy your wood, Mr. Parris.

PARRIS: I regard that six pound as part of my salary. I am paid little enough without I spend six pound on firewood.

PROCTOR: Sixty, plus six for firewood—

PARRIS: The salary is sixty-six pound, Mr. Proctor! I am not some preaching farmer with a book under my arm; I am a graduate of Harvard College.

GILES: Aye, and well instructed in arithmetic!

PARRIS: Mr. Corey, you will look far for a man of my kind at sixty pound a year! I am not used to this poverty; I left a thrifty business in the Barbados to serve the Lord. I do not fathom it, why am I persecuted here? I cannot offer one proposition but there be a howling riot of argument. I have often wondered if the Devil be in it somewhere; I cannot understand you people otherwise.

PROCTOR: Mr. Parris, you are the first minister ever did demand the deed to this house—

PARRIS: Man! Don't a minister deserve a house to live in?

PROCTOR: To live in, yes. But to ask ownership is like you shall own the meeting house itself; the last meeting I were at you spoke so long on deeds and mortgages I thought it were an auction.

PARRIS: I want a mark of confidence, is all! I am your third preacher in seven years. I do not wish to be put out like the cat whenever some majority feels the whim. You people seem not to comprehend that a minister is the Lord's man in the parish; a minister is not to be so lightly crossed and contradicted—

PUTNAM: Aye!

PARRIS: There is either obedience or the church will burn like Hell is burning!

PROCTOR: Can you speak one minute without we land in Hell again? I am sick of Hell!

PARRIS: It is not for you to say what is good for you to hear!

PROCTOR: I may speak my heart, I think!

PARRIS, *in a fury:* What, are we Quakers? We are not Quakers here yet, Mr. Proctor. And you may tell that to your followers!

PROCTOR: My followers!

PARRIS—*now he's out with it:* There is a party in this church. I am not blind; there is a faction and a party.

PROCTOR: Against you?

PUTNAM: Against him and all authority!

PROCTOR: Why, then I must find it and join it.

There is shock among the others.

REBECCA: He does not mean that.

PUTNAM: He confessed it now!

PROCTOR: I mean it solemnly, Rebecca; I like not the smell of this "authority."

REBECCA: No, you cannot break charity with your minister. You are another kind, John. Clasp his hand, make your peace.

PROCTOR: I have a crop to sow and lumber to drag home. *He goes angrily to the door and turns to Corey with a smile.* What say you, Giles, let's find the party. He says there's a party.

GILES: I've changed my opinion of this man, John. Mr. Parris, I beg your pardon. I never thought you had so much iron in you.

PARRIS, *surprised:* Why, thank you, Giles!

GILES: It suggests to the mind what the trouble be among us all these years. *To all:* Think on it. Wherefore is everybody suing everybody else? Think on it now, it's a deep thing, and dark as a pit. I have been six time in court this year—

PROCTOR, *familiarly, with warmth, although he knows he is approaching the edge of Giles' tolerance with this:* Is it the Devil's fault that a man cannot say you good morning without you clap him for defamation? You're old, Giles, and you're not hearin' so well as you did.

GILES—*he cannot be crossed:* John Proctor, I have only last month collected four pound damages for you publicly sayin' I burned the roof off your house, and I—

PROCTOR, *laughing:* I never said no such thing, but I've paid you for it, so I hope I can call you deaf without charge. Now come along, Giles, and help me drag my lumber home.

PUTNAM: A moment, Mr. Proctor. What lumber is that you're draggin', if I may ask you?

PROCTOR: My lumber. From out my forest by the riverside.

PUTNAM: Why, we are surely gone wild this year. What anarchy is this? That tract is in my bounds, it's in my bounds, Mr. Proctor.

PROCTOR: In your bounds! *Indicating Rebecca:* I bought that tract from Goody Nurse's husband five months ago.

PUTNAM: He had no right to sell it. It stands clear in my grandfather's will that all the land between the river and—

PROCTOR: Your grandfather had a habit of willing land that never belonged to him, if I may say it plain.

GILES: That's God's truth; he nearly willed away my north pasture but he knew I'd break his fingers before he'd set his name to it. Let's get your lumber home, John. I feel a sudden will to work coming on.

PUTNAM: You load one oak of mine and you'll fight to drag it home!

GILES: Aye, and we'll win too, Putnam—this fool and I. Come on! *He turns to Proctor and starts out.*

PUTNAM: I'll have my men on you, Corey! I'll clap a writ on you!

Enter Reverend John Hale of Beverly.

Mr. Hale is nearing forty, a tight-skinned, eager-eyed intellectual. This is a beloved errand for him; on being called here to ascertain witchcraft he felt the pride of the specialist whose unique knowledge has at last been publicly called for. Like almost all men of learning, he spent a good deal of his time pondering the invisible world, especially since he had himself encountered a witch in his parish not long before. That woman, however, turned into a mere pest under his searching scrutiny, and the child she had allegedly been afflicting recovered her normal behavior after Hale had given her his kindness and a few days of rest in his own house. However, that experience never raised a doubt in his mind as to the reality of the underworld or the existence of Lucifer's many-faced lieutenants. And his belief is not to his discredit. Better minds than Hale's were—and still are—convinced that there is a society of spirits beyond our ken. One cannot help noting that one of his lines has never yet raised a laugh in any audience that has seen this play; it is his assurance that "We cannot look to superstition in this. The Devil is precise." Evidently we are not quite certain even now whether diabolism is holy and not to be scoffed at. And it is no accident that we should be so bemused.

Like Reverend Hale and the others on this stage, we conceive the Devil as a necessary part of a respectable view of cosmology. Ours is a divided empire in which certain ideas and emotions and actions are of God, and their opposites are of Lucifer. It is as impossible for most men to conceive of a morality without sin as of an earth without "sky." Since 1692 a great but superficial change has wiped out God's beard and the Devil's horns, but the world is still gripped between two diametrically opposed absolutes. The concept of unity, in which positive and negative are attributes of the same force, in which good and evil are relative, ever changing, and always joined to the same phenomenon—such a concept is still reserved to the physical sciences and to the few who have grasped the history of ideas. When it is recalled that until the Christian era the underworld was never regarded as a hostile area, that all gods were useful and essentially friendly to man despite occasional lapses; when we see the steady and methodical inculcation into humanity of the idea of man's worthlessness—until redeemed—the necessity of the Devil may become evident as a weapon, a weapon designed and used time and time again in every age to whip men into a surrender to a particular church or church-state.

Our difficulty in believing the—for want of a better word—political inspiration of the Devil is due in great part to the fact that he is called up and damned not only by our social antagonists but by our own side, whatever it may be. The Catholic Church, through its Inquisition, is famous for cultivating Lucifer as the arch-fiend, but the Church's enemies relied no less upon the Old Boy to keep the human mind enthralled. Luther was himself accused of alliance with Hell, and he in turn accused his enemies. To complicate matters further, he believed that he had had contact with the Devil and had argued theology with him. I am not surprised at this, for at my own university a professor of history—a Lutheran, by the way—used to assemble his graduate students, draw the shades, and commune in the classroom with Erasmus. He was never, to my knowledge, officially scoffed at for this, the reason being that the university officials, like most of us, are the children of a history which still sucks at the Devil's teats. At this writing, only England has held back before the temptations of contemporary diabolism. In the countries of the Communist ideology, all resistance of any import is linked to the totally malign capitalist succubi, and in America any man who is not reactionary in his views is open to the charge of alliance with the Red hell. Political opposition, thereby, is given an inhumane overlay which then justifies the abrogation of all normally applied customs of civilized intercourse. A political policy is equated with moral right, and opposition to it with diabolical malevolence. Once such an equation is effectively made, society becomes a congerie of plots and counterplots, and the main role of government changes from that of the arbiter to that of the scourge of God.

The results of this process are no different now from what they ever were, except sometimes in the degree of cruelty inflicted, and not always even in that department. Normally the actions and deeds of a man were all that society felt comfortable in judging. The secret intent of an action was left to the ministers, priests, and rabbis to deal with. When diabolism rises, however, actions are the least important manifests of the true nature of a man. The Devil, as Reverend Hale said, is a wily one, and, until an hour before he fell, even God thought him beautiful in Heaven.

The analogy, however, seems to falter when one considers that, while there were no witches then, there are Communists and capitalists now, and in each camp there is certain proof that spies of each side are at work undermining the other. But this is a snobbish objection and not at all warranted by the facts. I have no doubt that people *were* communing with, and even worshiping, the Devil in Salem, and if the whole truth could be known in this case, as it is in others, we should discover a regular and conventionalized propitiation of the dark spirit. One certain evidence of this is the confession of Tituba, the slave of Reverend Parris, and another is the behavior of the children who were known to have indulged in sorceries with her.

There are accounts of similar *klatches* in Europe, where the daughters of the towns would assemble at night and, sometimes with fetishes, sometimes with a selected young man, give themselves to love, with some bastardly results. The Church, sharp-eyed as it must be when gods long dead are brought to life, condemned these orgies as witchcraft and interpreted them, rightly, as a resurgence of the Dionysiac forces it had crushed long before. Sex, sin, and the Devil were early linked, and so they continued to be in Salem, and are today. From all accounts there are no more puritanical mores in the world than those enforced by the Communists in Russia, where women's fashions, for instance, are as prudent and all-covering as any American Baptist would desire. The divorce laws lay a tremendous responsibility on the father for the care of his children. Even the laxity of divorce regulations in the early years of the revolution was undoubtedly a revulsion from the nineteenth-century Victorian immobility of marriage and the consequent hypocrisy that developed from it. If for no other reasons, a state so powerful, so jealous of the uniformity of its citizens, cannot long tolerate the atomization of the family. And yet, in American eyes at least, there remains the conviction that the Russian attitude toward women is lascivious. It is the Devil working again, just as he is working within the Slav who is shocked at the very idea of a woman's disrobing herself in a burlesque show. Our opposites are always robed in sexual sin, and it is from this unconscious conviction that demonology gains both its attractive sensuality and its capacity to infuriate and frighten.

Coming into Salem now, Reverend Hale conceives of himself much as a young doctor on his first call. His painfully acquired armory of symptoms, catchwords, and diagnostic procedures are now to be put to use at last. The road from Beverly is unusually busy this morning, and he has passed a hundred rumors that make him smile at the ignorance of the yeomanry in this most precise science. He feels himself allied with the best minds of Europe—kings, philosophers, scientists, and ecclesiasts of all churches. His goal is light, goodness and its preservation, and he knows the exaltation of the blessed whose intelligence, sharpened by minute examinations of enormous tracts, is finally called upon to face what may be a bloody fight with the Fiend himself.

He appears loaded down with half a dozen heavy books.

HALE: Pray you, someone take these!

PARRIS, *delighted:* Mr. Hale! Oh! it's good to see you again! *Taking some books:* My, they're heavy!

HALE, *setting down his books:* They must be; they are weighted with authority.

PARRIS, *a little scared:* Well, you do come prepared!

HALE: We shall need hard study if it comes to tracking down the Old Boy. *Noticing Rebecca:* You cannot be Rebecca Nurse?

REBECCA: I am, sir. Do you know me?

HALE: It's strange how I knew you, but I suppose you look as such a good soul should. We have all heard of your great charities in Beverly.

PARRIS: Do you know this gentleman? Mr. Thomas Putnam. And his good wife Ann.

HALE: Putnam! I had not expected such distinguished company, sir.

PUTNAM, *pleased:* It does not seem to help us today, Mr. Hale. We look to you to come to our house and save our child.

HALE: Your child ails too?

MRS. PUTNAM: Her soul, her soul seems flown away. She sleeps and yet she walks . . .

PUTNAM: She cannot eat.

HALE: Cannot eat! *Thinks on it. Then, to Proctor and Giles Corey:* Do you men have afflicted children?

PARRIS: No, no, these are farmers. John Proctor—

GILES COREY: He don't believe in witches.

PROCTOR, *to Hale:* I never spoke on witches one way or the other. Will you come, Giles?

GILES: No—no, John, I think not. I have some few queer questions of my own to ask this fellow.

PROCTOR: I've heard you to be a sensible man, Mr. Hale. I hope you'll leave some of it in Salem.

Proctor goes. Hale stands embarrassed for an instant.

PARRIS, *quickly:* Will you look at my daughter, sir? *Leads Hale to the bed.* She has tried to leap out the window; we discovered her this morning on the highroad, waving her arms as though she'd fly.

HALE, *narrowing his eyes:* Tries to fly.

PUTNAM: She cannot bear to hear the Lord's name, Mr. Hale; that's a sure sign of witchcraft afloat.

HALE, *holding up his hands:* No, no. Now let me instruct you. We cannot look to superstition in this. The Devil is precise; the marks of his presence are definite as stone, and I must tell you all that I shall not proceed unless you are prepared to believe me if I should find no bruise of hell upon her.

PARRIS: It is agreed, sir—it is agreed—we will abide by your judgment.

HALE: Good then. *He goes to the bed, looks down at Betty. To Parris:* Now, sir, what were your first warning of this strangeness?

PARRIS: Why, sir—I discovered her—*indicating Abigail*—and my niece and ten or twelve of the other girls, dancing in the forest last night.

HALE, *surprised:* You permit dancing?

PARRIS: No, no, it were secret—

MRS. PUTNAM, *unable to wait:* Mr. Parris's slave has knowledge of conjurin', sir.

PARRIS, *to Mrs. Putnam:* We cannot be sure of that, Goody Ann—

MRS. PUTNAM, *frightened, very softly:* I know it, sir. I sent my child—she should learn from Tituba who murdered her sisters.

REBECCA, *horrified:* Goody Ann! You sent a child to conjure up the dead?

MRS. PUTNAM: Let God blame me, not you, not you, Rebecca! I'll not have you judging me any more! *To Hale:* Is it a natural work to lose seven children before they live a day?

PARRIS: Sssh!

Rebecca, with great pain, turns her face away. There is a pause.

HALE: Seven dead in childbirth.

MRS. PUTNAM, *softly:* Aye. *Her voice breaks; she looks up at him. Silence. Hale is impressed. Parris looks to him. He goes to his books, opens one, turns pages, then reads. All wait, avidly.*

PARRIS, *hushed:* What book is that?

MRS. PUTNAM: What's there, sir?

HALE, *with a tasty love of intellectual pursuit:* Here is all the invisible world, caught, defined, and calculated. In these books the Devil stands stripped of all his brute disguises. Here are all your familiar spirits—your incubi and succubi; your witches that go by land, by air, and by sea; your wizards of the night and of the day. Have no fear now—we shall find him out if he has come among us, and I mean to crush him utterly if he has shown his face! *He starts for the bed.*

REBECCA: Will it hurt the child, sir?

HALE: I cannot tell. If she is truly in the Devil's grip we may have to rip and tear to get her free.

REBECCA: I think I'll go, then. I am too old for this. *She rises.*

PARRIS, *striving for conviction:* Why, Rebecca, we may open up the boil of all our troubles today!

REBECCA: Let us hope for that. I go to God for you, sir.

PARRIS, *with trepidation—and resentment:* I hope you do not mean we go to Satan here! *Slight pause.*

REBECCA: I wish I knew. *She goes out; they feel resentful of her note of moral superiority.*

PUTNAM, *abruptly:* Come, Mr. Hale, let's get on. Sit you here.

GILES: Mr. Hale, I have always wanted to ask a learned man—what signifies the readin' of strange books?

HALE: What books?

GILES: I cannot tell; she hides them.

HALE: Who does this?

GILES: Martha, my wife. I have waked at night many a time and found her in a corner, readin' of a book. Now what do you make of that?

HALE: Why, that's not necessarily—

GILES: It discomfits me! Last night—mark this—I tried and tried and could not say my prayers. And then she close her book and walks out of the house, and suddenly—mark this—I could pray again!

Old Giles must be spoken for, if only because his fate was to be so remarkable and so different from that of all the others. He was in his early eighties at this time, and was the most comical hero in the history. No man has ever been blamed for so much. If a cow was missed, the first thought was to look for her around Corey's house; a fire blazing up at night brought suspicion of arson to his door. He didn't give a hoot for public opinion, and only in his last years—after he had married Martha—did he bother much with the church. That she stopped his prayer is very probable, but he forgot to say that he'd only recently learned any prayers and it didn't take much to make him stumble over them. He was a crank and a nuisance, but withal a deeply innocent and brave man. In court, once, he was asked if it were true that he had been frightened by the strange behavior of a hog and had then said he knew it to be the Devil in an animal's shape. "What frighted you?" he was asked. He forgot everything but the word "frighted," and instantly replied, "I do not know that I ever spoke that word in my life."

HALE: Ah! The stoppage of prayer—that is strange. I'll speak further on that with you.

GILES: I'm not sayin' she's touched the Devil, now, but I'd admire to know what books she reads and why she hides them. She'll not answer me, y' see.

HALE: Aye, we'll discuss it. *To all:* Now mark me, if the Devil is in her you will witness some frightful wonders in this room, so please to keep your wits about you. Mr. Putnam, stand close in case she flies. Now, Betty, dear, will you sit up? *Putnam comes in closer, ready-handed. Hale sits Betty up, but she hangs limp in his hands.* Hmmm. *He observes her carefully. The others watch breathlessly.* Can you hear me? I am John Hale, minister of Beverly. I have come to help you, dear. Do you remember my two little girls in Beverly? *She does not stir in his hands.*

PARRIS, *in fright:* How can it be the Devil? Why would he choose my house to strike? We have all manner of licentious people in the village!

HALE: What victory would the Devil have to win a soul already bad? It is the best the Devil wants, and who is better than the minister?

GILES: That's deep, Mr. Parris, deep, deep!

PARRIS, *with resolution now:* Betty! Answer Mr. Hale! Betty!

HALE: Does someone afflict you, child? It need not be a woman, mind you, or a man. Perhaps some bird invisible to others comes to you—perhaps a pig, a mouse, or any beast at all. Is there some figure bids you fly? *The child remains limp in his hands. In silence he lays her back on the pillow. Now, holding out his hands toward her, he intones:* In nomine Domini Sabaoth sui filiique ite ad infernos. *She does not stir. He turns to Abigail, his eyes narrowing.* Abigail, what sort of dancing were you doing with her in the forest?

ABIGAIL: Why—common dancing is all.

PARRIS: I think I ought to say that I—I saw a kettle in the grass where they were dancing.

ABIGAIL: That were only soup.

HALE: What sort of soup were in this kettle, Abigail?

ABIGAIL: Why, it were beans—and lentils, I think, and—

HALE: Mr. Parris, you did not notice, did you, any living thing in the kettle? A mouse, perhaps, a spider, a frog—?

PARRIS, *fearfully:* I—do believe there were some movement—in the soup.

ABIGAIL: That jumped in, we never put it in!

HALE, *quickly:* What jumped in?

ABIGAIL: Why, a very little frog jumped—

PARRIS: A frog, Abby!

HALE, *grasping Abigail:* Abigail, it may be your cousin is dying. Did you call the Devil last night?

ABIGAIL: I never called him! Tituba, Tituba . . .

PARRIS, *blanched:* She called the Devil?

HALE: I should like to speak with Tituba.

PARRIS: Goody Ann, will you bring her up? *Mrs. Putnam exits.*

HALE: How did she call him?

ABIGAIL: I know not—she spoke Barbados.

HALE: Did you feel any strangeness when she called him? A sudden cold wind, perhaps? A trembling below the ground?

ABIGAIL: I didn't see no Devil! *Shaking Betty:* Betty, wake up. Betty! Betty!

HALE: You cannot evade me, Abigail. Did your cousin drink any of the brew in that kettle?

ABIGAIL: She never drank it!

HALE: Did you drink it?

ABIGAIL: No, sir!

HALE: Did Tituba ask you to drink it?

ABIGAIL: She tried, but I refused.

HALE: Why are you concealing? Have you sold yourself to Lucifer?

ABIGAIL: I never sold myself! I'm a good girl! I'm a proper girl!

Mrs. Putnam enters with Tituba, and instantly Abigail points at Tituba.

ABIGAIL: She made me do it! She made Betty do it!

TITUBA, *shocked and angry:* Abby!

ABIGAIL: She makes me drink blood!

PARRIS: Blood!!

MRS. PUTNAM: My baby's blood?

TITUBA: No, no, chicken blood. I give she chicken blood!

HALE: Woman, have you enlisted these children for the Devil?

TITUBA: No, no, sir, I don't truck with no Devil!

HALE: Why can she not wake? Are you silencing this child?

TITUBA: I love me Betty!

HALE: You have sent your spirit out upon this child, have you not? Are you gathering souls for the Devil?

ABIGAIL: She sends her spirit on me in church; she makes me laugh at prayer!

PARRIS: She have often laughed at prayer!

ABIGAIL: She comes to me every night to go and drink blood!

TITUBA: You beg *me* to conjure! She beg *me* make charm—

ABIGAIL: Don't lie! *To Hale:* She comes to me while I sleep; she's always making me dream corruptions!

TITUBA: Why you say that, Abby?

ABIGAIL: Sometimes I wake and find myself standing in the open doorway and not a stitch on my body! I always hear her laughing in my sleep. I hear her singing her Barbados songs and tempting me with—

TITUBA: Mister Reverend, I never—

HALE, *resolved now:* Tituba, I want you to wake this child.

TITUBA: I have no power on this child, sir.

HALE: You most certainly do, and you will free her from it now! When did you compact with the Devil?

TITUBA: I don't compact with no Devil!

PARRIS: You will confess yourself or I will take you out and whip you to your death, Tituba!

PUTNAM: This woman must be hanged! She must be taken and hanged!

TITUBA, *terrified, falls to her knees:* No, no, don't hang Tituba! I tell him I don't desire to work for him, sir.

PARRIS: The Devil?

HALE: Then you saw him! *Tituba weeps.* Now Tituba, I know that when we bind ourselves to Hell it is very hard to break with it. We are going to help you tear your-self free—

TITUBA, *frightened by the coming process:* Mister Reverend, I do believe somebody else be witchin' these children.

HALE: Who?

TITUBA: I don't know, sir, but the Devil got him numerous witches.

HALE: Does he! *It is a clue.* Tituba, look into my eyes. Come, look into me. *She raises her eyes to his fearfully.* You would be a good Christian woman, would you not, Tituba?

TITUBA: Aye, sir, a good Christian woman.

HALE: And you love these little children?

TITUBA: Oh, yes, sir, I don't desire to hurt little children.

HALE: And you love God, Tituba?

TITUBA: I love God with all my bein'.

HALE: Now, in God's holy name—

TITUBA: Bless Him. Bless Him. *She is rocking on her knees, sobbing in terror.*

HALE: And to His glory—

TITUBA: Eternal glory. Bless Him—bless God . . .

HALE: Open yourself, Tituba—open yourself and let God's holy light shine on you.

TITUBA: Oh, bless the Lord.

HALE: When the Devil comes to you does he ever come—with another person? *She stares up into his face.* Perhaps another person in the village? Someone you know.

PARRIS: Who came with him?

PUTNAM: Sarah Good? Did you ever see Sarah Good with him? Or Osburn?

PARRIS: Was it man or woman came with him?

TITUBA: Man or woman. Was—was woman.

PARRIS: What woman? A woman, you said. What woman?

TITUBA: It was black dark, and I—

PARRIS: You could see him, why could you not see her?

TITUBA: Well, they was always talking; they was always runnin' round and carryin' on—

PARRIS: You mean out of Salem? Salem witches?

TITUBA: I believe so, yes, sir.

Now Hale takes her hand. She is surprised.

HALE: Tituba. You must have no fear to tell us who they are, do you understand? We will protect you. The Devil can never overcome a minister. You know that, do you not?

TITUBA, *kisses Hale's hand:* Aye, sir, oh, I do.

HALE: You have confessed yourself to witchcraft, and that speaks a wish to come to Heaven's side. And we will bless you, Tituba.

TITUBA, *deeply relieved:* Oh, God bless you, Mr. Hale!

HALE, *with rising exaltation:* You are God's instrument put in our hands to discover the Devil's agents among us. You are selected, Tituba, you are chosen to help us cleanse our village. So speak utterly, Tituba, turn your back on him and face God—face God, Tituba, and God will protect you.

TITUBA, *joining with him:* Oh, God, protect Tituba!

HALE, *kindly:* Who came to you with the Devil? Two? Three? Four? How many?

Tituba pants, and begins rocking back and forth again, staring ahead.

TITUBA: There was four. There was four.

PARRIS, *pressing in on her:* Who? Who? Their names, their names!

TITUBA, *suddenly bursting out:* Oh, how many times he bid me kill you, Mr. Parris!

PARRIS: Kill me!

TITUBA, *in a fury:* He say Mr. Parris must be kill! Mr. Parris no goodly man, Mr. Parris mean man and no gentle man, and he bid me rise out of my bed and cut your throat! *They gasp.* But I tell him "No! I don't hate that man. I don't want kill that man." But he say, "You work for me, Tituba, and I make you free! I give you pretty dress to wear, and put you way high up in the air, and you gone fly back to Barbados!" And I say, "You lie, Devil, you lie!" And then he come one stormy night to me, and he say, "Look! I have *white* people belong to me." And I look—and there was Goody Good.

PARRIS: Sarah Good!

TITUBA, *rocking and weeping:* Aye, sir, and Goody Osburn.

MRS. PUTNAM: I knew it! Goody Osburn were midwife to me three times. I begged you, Thomas, did I not? I begged him not to call Osburn because I feared her. My babies always shriveled in her hands!

HALE: Take courage, you must give us all their names. How can you bear to see this child suffering? Look at her, Tituba. *He is indicating Betty on the bed.* Look at her God-given innocence; her soul is so tender; we must protect her, Tituba; the Devil is out and preying on her like a beast upon the flesh of the pure lamb. God will bless you for your help.

Abigail rises, staring as though inspired, and cries out.

ABIGAIL: I want to open myself! *They turn to her, startled. She is enraptured, as though in a pearly light.* I want the light of God, I want the sweet love of Jesus! I danced for the Devil; I saw him; I wrote in his book; I go back to Jesus; I kiss His hand. I saw Sarah Good with the Devil! I saw Goody Osburn with the Devil! I saw Bridget Bishop with the Devil!

As she is speaking, Betty is rising from the bed, a fever in her eyes, and picks up the chant.

BETTY, *staring too:* I saw George Jacobs with the Devil! I saw Goody Howe with the Devil!

PARRIS: She speaks! *He rushes to embrace Betty.* She speaks!

HALE: Glory to God! It is broken, they are free!

BETTY, *calling out hysterically and with great relief:* I saw Martha Bellows with the Devil!

ABIGAIL: I saw Goody Sibber with the Devil! *It is rising to a great glee.*

PUTNAM: The marshal, I'll call the marshal!

Paris is shouting a prayer of thanksgiving.

BETTY: I saw Alice Barrow with the Devil!

The curtain begins to fall.

HALE, *as Putnam goes out:* Let the marshal bring irons!

ABIGAIL: I saw Goody Hawkins with the Devil!

BETTY: I saw Goody Bibber with the Devil!

ABIGAIL: I saw Goody Booth with the Devil!

On their ecstatic cries—

Curtain

Act Two

The common room of Proctor's house, eight days later.

At the right is a door opening on the fields outside. A fireplace is at the left, and behind it a stairway leading upstairs. It is the low, dark, and rather long living room of the time. As the curtain rises, the room is empty. From above, Elizabeth is heard softly singing to the children. Presently the door opens and John Proctor enters, carrying his gun. He glances about the room as he comes toward the fireplace, then halts for an instant as he hears her singing. He continues on to the fireplace, leans the gun against the wall as he swings a pot out of the fire and smells it. Then he lifts out the ladle and tastes. He is not quite pleased. He reaches to a cupboard, takes a pinch of salt, and drops it into the pot. As he is tasting again, her footsteps are heard on the stair. He swings the pot into the fireplace and goes to a basin and washes his hands and face. Elizabeth enters.

ELIZABETH: What keeps you so late? It's almost dark.

PROCTOR: I were planting far out to the forest edge.

ELIZABETH: Oh, you're done then.

PROCTOR: Aye, the farm is seeded. The boys asleep?

ELIZABETH: They will be soon. *And she goes to the fireplace, proceeds to ladle up stew in a dish.*

PROCTOR: Pray now for a fair summer.

ELIZABETH: Aye.

PROCTOR: Are you well today?

ELIZABETH: I am. *She brings the plate to the table, and, indicating the food:* It is a rabbit.

PROCTOR, *going to the table:* Oh, is it! In Jonathan's trap?

ELIZABETH: No, she walked into the house this afternoon; I found her sittin' in the corner like she come to visit.

PROCTOR: Oh, that's a good sign walkin' in.

ELIZABETH: Pray God. It hurt my heart to strip her, poor rabbit. *She sits and watches him taste it.*

PROCTOR: It's well seasoned.

ELIZABETH, *blushing with pleasure:* I took great care. She's tender?

PROCTOR: Aye. *He eats. She watches him.* I think we'll see green fields soon. It's warm as blood beneath the clods.

ELIZABETH: That's well.

Proctor eats, then looks up.

PROCTOR: If the crop is good I'll buy George Jacob's heifer. How would that please you?

ELIZABETH: Aye, it would.

PROCTOR, *with a grin:* I mean to please you, Elizabeth.

ELIZABETH—*it is hard to say:* I know it, John.

He gets up, goes to her, kisses her. She receives it. With a certain disappointment, he returns to the table.

PROCTOR, *as gently as he can:* Cider?

ELIZABETH, *with a sense of reprimanding herself for having forgot:* Aye! *She gets up and goes and pours a glass for him. He now arches his back.*

PROCTOR: This farm's a continent when you go foot by foot droppin' seeds in it.

ELIZABETH, *coming with the cider:* It must be.

PROCTOR, *drinks a long draught, then, putting the glass down:* You ought to bring some flowers in the house.

ELIZABETH: Oh! I forgot! I will tomorrow.

PROCTOR: It's winter in here yet. On Sunday let you come with me, and we'll walk the farm together; I never see such a load of flowers on the earth. *With good feeling he goes and looks up at the sky through the open doorway.* Lilacs have a purple smell. Lilac is the smell of nightfall, I think. Massachusetts is a beauty in the spring!

ELIZABETH: Aye, it is.

There is a pause. She is watching him from the table as he stands there absorbing the night. It is as though she would speak but cannot. Instead, now, she takes up his plate and glass and fork and goes with them to the basin. Her back is turned to him. He turns to her and watches her. A sense of their separation rises.

PROCTOR: I think you're sad again. Are you?

ELIZABETH—*she doesn't want friction, and yet she must:* You come so late I thought you'd gone to Salem this afternoon.

PROCTOR: Why? I have no business in Salem.

ELIZABETH: You did speak of going, earlier this week.

PROCTOR—*he knows what she means:* I thought better of it since.

ELIZABETH: Mary Warren's there today.

PROCTOR: Why'd you let her? You heard me forbid her go to Salem any more!

ELIZABETH: I couldn't stop her.

PROCTOR, *holding back a full condemnation of her:* It is a fault, it is a fault, Elizabeth— you're the mistress here, not Mary Warren.

ELIZABETH: She frightened all my strength away.

PROCTOR: How may that mouse frighten you, Elizabeth? You—

ELIZABETH: It is a mouse no more. I forbid her go, and she raises up her chin like the daughter of a prince and says to me, "I must go to Salem, Goody Proctor; I am an official of the court!"

PROCTOR: Court! What court?

ELIZABETH: Aye, it is a proper court they have now. They've sent four judges out of Boston, she says, weighty magistrates of the General Court, and at the head sits the Deputy Governor of the Province.

PROCTOR, *astonished:* Why, she's mad.

ELIZABETH: I would to God she were. There be fourteen people in the jail now, she says. *Proctor simply looks at her, unable to grasp it.* And they'll be tried, and the court have power to hang them too, she says.

PROCTOR, *scoffing, but without conviction:* Ah, they'd never hang—

ELIZABETH: The Deputy Governor promise hangin' if they'll not confess, John. The town's gone wild, I think. She speak of Abigail, and I thought she were a saint, to hear her. Abigail brings the other girls into the court, and where she walks the crowd will part like the sea for Israel. And folks are brought before them, and if they scream and howl and fall to the floor—the person's clapped in the jail for bewitchin' them.

PROCTOR, *wide-eyed:* Oh, it is a black mischief.

ELIZABETH: I think you must go to Salem, John. *He turns to her.* I think so. You must tell them it is a fraud.

PROCTOR, *thinking beyond this:* Aye, it is, it is surely.

ELIZABETH: Let you go to Ezekiel Cheever—he knows you well. And tell him what she said to you last week in her uncle's house. She said it had naught to do with witchcraft, did she not?

PROCTOR, *in thought:* Aye, she did, she did. *Now, a pause.*

ELIZABETH, *quietly, fearing to anger him by prodding:* God forbid you keep that from the court, John. I think they must be told.

PROCTOR, *quietly, struggling with his thought:* Aye, they must, they must. It is a wonder they do believe her.

ELIZABETH: I would go to Salem now, John—let you go tonight.

PROCTOR: I'll think on it.

ELIZABETH, *with her courage now:* You cannot keep it, John.

PROCTOR, *angering:* I know I cannot keep it. I say I will think on it!

ELIZABETH, *hurt, and very coldly:* Good, then, let you think on it. *She stands and starts to walk out of the room.*

PROCTOR: I am only wondering how I may prove what she told me, Elizabeth. If the girl's a saint now, I think it is not easy to prove she's fraud, and the town gone so silly. She told it to me in a room alone—I have no proof for it.

ELIZABETH: You were alone with her?

PROCTOR, *stubbornly:* For a moment alone, aye.

ELIZABETH: Why, then, it is not as you told me.

PROCTOR, *his anger rising:* For a moment, I say. The others come in soon after.

ELIZABETH, *quietly—she has suddenly lost all faith in him:* Do as you wish, then. *She starts to turn.*

PROCTOR: Woman. *She turns to him.* I'll not have your suspicion any more.

ELIZABETH, *a little loftily:* I have no—

PROCTOR: I'll not have it!

ELIZABETH: Then let you not earn it.

PROCTOR, *with a violent undertone:* You doubt me yet?

ELIZABETH, *with a smile, to keep her dignity:* John, if it were not Abigail that you must go to hurt, would you falter now? I think not.

PROCTOR: Now look you—

ELIZABETH: I see what I see, John.

PROCTOR, *with solemn warning:* You will not judge me more, Elizabeth. I have good reason to think before I charge fraud on Abigail, and I will think on it. Let you look to your own improvement before you go to judge your husband any more. I have forgot Abigail, and—

ELIZABETH: And I.

PROCTOR: Spare me! You forget nothin' and forgive nothin'. Learn charity, woman. I have gone tiptoe in this house all seven month since she is gone. I have not moved from there to there without I think to please you, and still an everlasting funeral marches round your heart. I cannot speak but I am doubted, every moment judged for lies, as though I come into a court when I come into this house!

ELIZABETH: John, you are not open with me. You saw her with a crowd, you said. Now you—

PROCTOR: I'll plead my honesty no more, Elizabeth.

ELIZABETH—*now she would justify herself:* John, I am only—

PROCTOR: No more! I should have roared you down when first you told me your suspicion. But I wilted, and, like a Christian, I confessed. Confessed! Some dream I had must have mistaken you for God that day. But you're not, you're not, and let you remember it! Let you look sometimes for the goodness in me, and judge me not.

ELIZABETH: I do not judge you. The magistrate sits in your heart that judges you. I never thought you but a good man, John—*with a smile*—only somewhat bewildered.

PROCTOR, *laughing bitterly:* Oh, Elizabeth, your justice would freeze beer! *He turns suddenly toward a sound outside. He starts for the door as Mary Warren enters. As soon as he sees her, he goes directly to her and grabs her by her cloak, furious.* How do you go to Salem when I forbid it? Do you mock me? *Shaking her.* I'll whip you if you dare leave this house again!

Strangely, she doesn't resist him, but hangs limply by his grip.

MARY WARREN: I am sick, I am sick, Mr. Proctor. Pray, pray, hurt me not. *Her strangeness throws him off, and her evident pallor and weakness. He frees her.* My insides are all shuddery; I am in the proceedings all day, sir.

PROCTOR, *with draining anger—his curiosity is draining it:* And what of these proceedings here? When will you proceed to keep this house, as you are paid nine pound a year to do—and my wife not wholly well?

As though to compensate, Mary Warren goes to Elizabeth with a small rag doll.

MARY WARREN: I made a gift for you today, Goody Proctor. I had to sit long hours in a chair, and passed the time with sewing.

ELIZABETH, *perplexed, looking at the doll:* Why, thank you, it's a fair poppet.

MARY WARREN, *with a trembling, decayed voice:* We must all love each other now, Goody Proctor.

ELIZABETH, *amazed at her strangeness:* Aye, indeed we must.

MARY WARREN, *glancing at the room:* I'll get up early in the morning and clean the house. I must sleep now. *She turns and starts off.*

PROCTOR: Mary. *She halts.* Is it true? There be fourteen women arrested?

MARY WARREN: No, sir. There be thirty-nine now—*She suddenly breaks off and sobs and sits down, exhausted.*

ELIZABETH: Why, she's weepin'! What ails you, child?

MARY WARREN: Goody Osburn—will hang!

There is a shocked pause, while she sobs.

PROCTOR: Hang! *He calls into her face.* Hang, y'say?

MARY WARREN, *through her weeping:* Aye.

PROCTOR: The Deputy Governor will permit it?

MARY WARREN: He sentenced her. He must. *To ameliorate it:* But not Sarah Good. For Sarah Good confessed, y'see.

PROCTOR: Confessed! To what?

MARY WARREN: That she—*in horror at the memory*—she sometimes made a compact with Lucifer, and wrote her name in his black book—with her blood—and bound herself to torment Christians till God's thrown down—and we all must worship Hell forevermore.

Pause.

PROCTOR: But—surely you know what a jabberer she is. Did you tell them that?

MARY WARREN: Mr. Proctor, in open court she near to choked us all to death.

PROCTOR: How, choked you?

MARY WARREN: She sent her spirit out.

ELIZABETH: Oh, Mary, Mary, surely you—

MARY WARREN, *with an indignant edge:* She tried to kill me many times, Goody Proctor!

ELIZABETH: Why, I never heard you mention that before.

MARY WARREN: I never knew it before. I never knew anything before. When she come into the court I say to myself, I must not accuse this woman, for she sleep in ditches, and so very old and poor. But then—then she sit there, denying and denying, and I feel a misty coldness climbin' up my back, and the skin on my skull begin to creep, and I feel a clamp around my neck and I cannot breathe air; and then—*entranced*—I hear a voice, a screamin' voice, and it were my voice—and all at once I remembered everything she done to me!

PROCTOR: Why? What did she do to you?

MARY WARREN, *like one awakened to a marvelous secret insight:* So many time, Mr. Proctor, she come to this very door, beggin' bread and a cup of cider—and mark this: whenever I turned her away empty, she *mumbled.*

ELIZABETH: Mumbled! She may mumble if she's hungry.

MARY WARREN: But *what* does she mumble? You must remember, Goody Proctor. Last month—a Monday, I think—she walked away, and I thought my guts would burst for two days after. Do you remember it?

ELIZABETH: Why—I do, I think, but—

MARY WARREN: And so I told that to Judge Hathorne, and he asks her so. "Goody Osburn," says he, "what curse do you mumble that this girl must fall sick after turning you away?" And then she replies—*mimicking an old crone*—"Why, your excellence, no curse at all. I only say my commandments; I hope I may say my commandments," says she!

ELIZABETH: And that's an upright answer.

MARY WARREN: Aye, but then Judge Hathorne say, "Recite for us your commandments!"—*leaning avidly toward them*—and of all the ten she could not say a single one. She never knew no commandments, and they had her in a flat lie!

PROCTOR: And so condemned her?

MARY WARREN, *now a little strained, seeing his stubborn doubt:* Why, they must when she condemned herself.

PROCTOR: But the proof, the proof!

MARY WARREN, *with greater impatience with him:* I told you the proof. It's hard proof, hard as rock, the judges said.

PROCTOR, *pauses an instant, then:* You will not go to court again, Mary Warren.

MARY WARREN: I must tell you, sir, I will be gone every day now. I am amazed you do not see what weighty work we do.

PROCTOR: What work you do! It's strange work for a Christian girl to hang old women!

MARY WARREN: But, Mr. Proctor, they will not hang them if they confess. Sarah Good will only sit in jail some time—*recalling*—and here's a wonder for you; think on this. Goody Good is pregnant!

ELIZABETH: Pregnant! Are they mad? The woman's near to sixty!

MARY WARREN: They had Doctor Griggs examine her, and she's full to the brim. And smokin' a pipe all these years, and no husband either! But she's safe, thank God, for they'll not hurt the innocent child. But be that not a marvel? You must see it, sir, it's God's work we do. So I'll be gone every day for some time. I'm—I am an official of the court, they say, and I—*She has been edging toward offstage.*

PROCTOR: I'll official you! *He strides to the mantel, takes down the whip hanging there.*

MARY WARREN, *terrified, but coming erect, striving for her authority:* I'll not stand whipping any more!

ELIZABETH, *hurriedly, as Proctor approaches:* Mary, promise now you'll stay at home—

MARY WARREN, *backing from him, but keeping her erect posture, striving, striving for her way:* The Devil's loose in Salem, Mr. Proctor; we must discover where he's hiding!

PROCTOR: I'll whip the Devil out of you! *With whip raised he reaches out for her, and she streaks away and yells.*

MARY WARREN, *pointing at Elizabeth:* I saved her life today!

Silence. His whip comes down.

ELIZABETH, *softly:* I am accused?

MARY WARREN, *quaking:* Somewhat mentioned. But I said I never see no sign you ever sent your spirit out to hurt no one, and seeing I do live so closely with you, they dismissed it.

ELIZABETH: Who accused me?

MARY WARREN: I am bound by law, I cannot tell it. *To Proctor:* I only hope you'll not be so sarcastical no more. Four judges and the King's deputy sat to dinner with us but an hour ago. I—I would have you speak civilly to me, from this out.

PROCTOR, *in horror, muttering in disgust at her:* Go to bed.

MARY WARREN, *with a stamp of her foot:* I'll not be ordered to bed no more, Mr. Proctor! I am eighteen and a woman, however single!

PROCTOR: Do you wish to sit up? Then sit up.

MARY WARREN: I wish to go to bed!

PROCTOR, *in anger:* Good night, then!

MARY WARREN: Good night. *Dissatisfied, uncertain of herself, she goes out. Wide-eyed, both, Proctor and Elizabeth stand staring.*

ELIZABETH, *quietly:* Oh, the noose, the noose is up!

PROCTOR: There'll be no noose.

ELIZABETH: She wants me dead. I knew all week it would come to this!

PROCTOR, *without conviction:* They dismissed it. You heard her say—

ELIZABETH: And what of tomorrow? She will cry me out until they take me!

PROCTOR: Sit you down.

ELIZABETH: She wants me dead, John, you know it!

PROCTOR: I say sit down! *She sits, trembling. He speaks quietly, trying to keep his wits.* Now we must be wise, Elizabeth.

ELIZABETH, *with sarcasm, and a sense of being lost:* Oh, indeed, indeed!

PROCTOR: Fear nothing. I'll find Ezekiel Cheever. I'll tell him she said it were all sport.

ELIZABETH: John, with so many in the jail, more than Cheever's help is needed now, I think. Would you favor me with this? Go to Abigail.

PROCTOR, *his soul hardening as he senses . . . :* What have I to say to Abigail?

ELIZABETH, *delicately:* John—grant me this. You have a faulty understanding of young girls. There is a promise made in any bed—

PROCTOR, *striving against his anger:* What promise!

ELIZABETH: Spoke or silent, a promise is surely made. And she may dote on it now— I am sure she does—and thinks to kill me, then to take my place.

Proctor's anger is rising; he cannot speak.

ELIZABETH: It is her dearest hope, John, I know it. There be a thousand names; why does she call mine? There be a certain danger in calling such a name—I am no Goody Good that sleeps in ditches, nor Osburn, drunk and half-witted. She'd dare not call out such a farmer's wife but there be monstrous profit in it. She thinks to take my place, John.

PROCTOR: She cannot think it! *He knows it is true.*

ELIZABETH, *"reasonably":* John, have you ever shown her somewhat of contempt? She cannot pass you in the church but you will blush—

PROCTOR: I may blush for my sin.

ELIZABETH: I think she sees another meaning in that blush.

PROCTOR: And what see you? What see you, Elizabeth?

ELIZABETH, *"conceding":* I think you be somewhat ashamed, for I am there, and she so close.

PROCTOR: When will you know me, woman? Were I stone I would have cracked for shame this seven month!

ELIZABETH: Then go and tell her she's a whore. Whatever promise she may sense— break it, John, break it.

PROCTOR, *between his teeth:* Good, then. I'll go. *He starts for his rifle.*

ELIZABETH, *trembling, fearfully:* Oh, how unwillingly!

PROCTOR, *turning on her, rifle in hand:* I will curse her hotter than the oldest cinder in hell. But pray, begrudge me not my anger!

ELIZABETH: Your anger! I only ask you—

PROCTOR: Woman, am I so base? Do you truly think me base?

ELIZABETH: I never called you base.

PROCTOR: Then how do you charge me with such a promise? The promise that a stallion gives a mare I gave that girl!

ELIZABETH: Then why do you anger with me when I bid you break it?

PROCTOR: Because it speaks deceit, and I am honest! But I'll plead no more! I see now your spirit twists around the single error of my life, and I will never tear it free!

ELIZABETH, *crying out:* You'll tear it free—when you come to know that I will be your only wife, or no wife at all! She has an arrow in you yet, John Proctor, and you know it well!

Quite suddenly, as though from the air, a figure appears in the doorway. They start slightly. It is Mr. Hale. He is different now—drawn a little, and there is a quality of deference, even of guilt, about his manner now.

HALE: Good evening.

PROCTOR, *still in his shock:* Why, Mr. Hale! Good evening to you, sir. Come in, come in.

HALE, *to Elizabeth:* I hope I do not startle you.

ELIZABETH: No, no, it's only that I heard no horse—

HALE: You are Goodwife Proctor.

PROCTOR: Aye; Elizabeth.

HALE, *nods, then:* I hope you're not off to bed yet.

PROCTOR, *setting down his gun:* No, no. *Hale comes further into the room. And Proctor, to explain his nervousness:* We are not used to visitors after dark, but you're welcome here. Will you sit you down, sir?

HALE: I will. *He sits.* Let you sit, Goodwife Proctor.

She does, never letting him out of her sight. There is a pause as Hale looks about the room.

PROCTOR, *to break the silence:* Will you drink cider, Mr. Hale?

HALE: No, it rebels my stomach; I have some further traveling yet tonight. Sit you down, sir. *Proctor sits.* I will not keep you long, but I have some business with you.

PROCTOR: Business of the court?

HALE: No—no, I come of my own, without the court's authority. Hear me. *He wets his lips.* I know not if you are aware, but your wife's name is—mentioned in the court.

PROCTOR: We know it, sir. Our Mary Warren told us. We are entirely amazed.

HALE: I am a stranger here, as you know. And in my ignorance I find it hard to draw a clear opinion of them that come accused before the court. And so this afternoon, and now tonight, I go from house to house—I come now from Rebecca Nurse's house and—

ELIZABETH, *shocked:* Rebecca's charged!

HALE: God forbid such a one be charged. She is, however—mentioned somewhat.

ELIZABETH, *with an attempt at a laugh:* You will never believe, I hope, that Rebecca trafficked with the Devil.

HALE: Woman, it is possible.

PROCTOR, *taken aback:* Surely you cannot think so.

HALE: This is a strange time, Mister. No man may longer doubt the powers of the dark are gathered in monstrous attack upon this village. There is too much evidence now to deny it. You will agree, sir?

PROCTOR, *evading:* I—have no knowledge in that line. But it's hard to think so pious a woman be secretly a Devil's bitch after seventy year of such good prayer.

HALE: Aye. But the Devil is a wily one, you cannot deny it. However, she is far from accused, and I know she will not be. *Pause.* I thought, sir, to put some questions as to the Christian character of this house, if you'll permit me.

PROCTOR, *coldly, resentful:* Why, we—have no fear of questions, sir.

HALE: Good, then. *He makes himself more comfortable.* In the book of record that Mr. Parris keeps, I note that you are rarely in the church on Sabbath Day.

PROCTOR: No, sir, you are mistaken.

HALE: Twenty-six time in seventeen month, sir. I must call that rare. Will you tell me why you are so absent?

PROCTOR: Mr. Hale, I never knew I must account to that man for I come to church or stay at home. My wife were sick this winter.

HALE: So I am told. But you, Mister, why could you not come alone?

PROCTOR: I surely did come when I could, and when I could not I prayed in this house.

HALE: Mr. Proctor, your house is not a church; your theology must tell you that.

PROCTOR: It does, sir, it does; and it tells me that a minister may pray to God without he have golden candlesticks upon the altar.

HALE: What golden candlesticks?

PROCTOR: Since we built the church there were pewter candlesticks upon the altar; Francis Nurse made them, y'know, and a sweeter hand never touched the metal. But Parris came, and for twenty week he preach nothin' but golden candlesticks until he had them. I labor the earth from dawn of day to blink of night, and I tell you true, when I look to heaven and see my money glaring at his elbows—it hurt my prayer, sir, it hurt my prayer. I think, sometimes, the man dreams cathedrals, not clapboard meetin' houses.

HALE, *thinks, then:* And yet, Mister, a Christian on Sabbath Day must be in church. *Pause.* Tell me—you have three children?

PROCTOR: Aye. Boys.

HALE: How comes it that only two are baptized?

PROCTOR, *starts to speak, then stops, then, as though unable to restrain this:* I like it not that Mr. Parris should lay his hand upon my baby. I see no light of God in that man. I'll not conceal it.

HALE: I must say it, Mr. Proctor; that is not for you to decide. The man's ordained, therefore the light of God is in him.

PROCTOR, *flushed with resentment but trying to smile:* What's your suspicion, Mr. Hale?

HALE: No, no, I have no—

PROCTOR: I nailed the roof upon the church, I hung the door—

HALE: Oh, did you! That's a good sign, then.

PROCTOR: It may be I have been too quick to bring the man to book, but you cannot think we ever desired the destruction of religion. I think that's in your mind, is it not?

HALE, *not altogether giving way:* I—have—there is a softness in your record, sir, a softness.

ELIZABETH: I think, maybe, we have been too hard with Mr. Parris. I think so. But sure we never loved the Devil here.

HALE, *nods, deliberating this. Then, with the voice of one administering a secret test:* Do you know your Commandments, Elizabeth?

ELIZABETH, *without hesitation, even eagerly:* I surely do. There be no mark of blame upon my life, Mr. Hale. I am a convenanted Christian woman.

HALE: And you, Mister?

PROCTOR, *a trifle unsteadily:* I—am sure I do, sir.

HALE, *glances at her open face, then at John, then:* Let you repeat them, if you will.

PROCTOR: The Commandments.

HALE: Aye.

PROCTOR, *looking off, beginning to sweat:* Thou shalt not kill.

HALE: Aye.

PROCTOR, *counting on his fingers:* Thou shalt not steal. Thou shalt not covet thy neighbor's goods, nor make unto thee any graven image. Thou shalt not take the name of the Lord in vain; thou shalt have no other gods before me. *With some hesitation:* Thou shalt remember the Sabbath Day and keep it holy. *Pause. Then:* Thou shalt honor thy father and mother. Thou shalt not bear false witness. *He is stuck. He counts back on his fingers, knowing one is missing.* Thou shalt not make unto thee any graven image.

HALE: You have said that twice, sir.

PROCTOR, *lost:* Aye. *He is flailing for it.*

ELIZABETH, *delicately:* Adultery, John.

PROCTOR, *as though a secret arrow had pained his heart:* Aye. *Trying to grin it away— to Hale:* You see, sir, between the two of us we do know them all. *Hale only looks at Proctor, deep in his attempt to define this man. Proctor grows more uneasy.* I think it be a small fault.

HALE: Theology, sir, is a fortress; no crack in a fortress may be accounted small. *He rises; he seems worried now. He paces a little, in deep thought.*

PROCTOR: There be no love for Satan in this house, Mister.

HALE: I pray it, I pray it dearly. *He looks to both of them, an attempt at a smile on his face, but his misgivings are clear.* Well, then—I'll bid you good night.

ELIZABETH, *unable to restrain herself:* Mr. Hale. *He turns.* I do think you are suspecting me somewhat? Are you not?

HALE, *obviously disturbed—and evasive:* Goody Proctor, I do not judge you. My duty is to add what I may to the godly wisdom of the court. I pray you both good health and good fortune. *To John:* Good night, sir. *He starts out.*

ELIZABETH, *with a note of desperation:* I think you must tell him, John.

HALE: What's that?

ELIZABETH, *restraining a call:* Will you tell him?

Slight pause. Hale looks questioningly at John.

PROCTOR, *with difficulty:* I—I have no witness and cannot prove it, except my word be taken. But I know the children's sickness had naught to do with witchcraft.

HALE, *stopped, struck:* Naught to do—?

PROCTOR: Mr. Parris discovered them sportin' in the woods. They were startled and took sick.

Pause.

HALE: Who told you this?

PROCTOR, *hesitates, then:* Abigail Williams.

HALE: Abigail!

PROCTOR: Aye.

HALE, *his eyes wide:* Abigail Williams told you it had naught to do with witchcraft!

PROCTOR: She told me the day you came, sir.

HALE, *suspiciously:* Why—why did you keep this?

PROCTOR: I never knew until tonight that the world is gone daft with this nonsense.

HALE: Nonsense! Mister, I have myself examined Tituba, Sarah Good, and numerous others that have confessed to dealing with the Devil. They have *confessed* it.

PROCTOR: And why not, if they must hang for denyin' it? There are them that will swear to anything before they'll hang; have you never thought of that?

HALE: I have. I—I have indeed. *It is his own suspicion, but he resists it. He glances at Elizabeth, then at John.* And you—would you testify to this in court?

PROCTOR: I—had not reckoned with goin' into court. But if I must I will.

HALE: Do you falter here?

PROCTOR: I falter nothing, but I may wonder if my story will be credited in such a court. I do wonder on it, when such a steady-minded minister as you will suspicion such a woman that never lied, and cannot, and the world knows she cannot! I may falter somewhat, Mister; I am no fool.

HALE, *quietly—it has impressed him:* Proctor, let you open with me now, for I have a rumor that troubles me. It's said you hold no belief that there may even be witches in the world. Is that true, sir?

PROCTOR—*he knows this is critical, and is striving against his disgust with Hale and with himself for even answering:* I know not what I have said, I may have said it. I have wondered if there be witches in the world—although I cannot believe they come among us now.

HALE: Then you do not believe—

PROCTOR: I have no knowledge of it; the Bible speaks of witches, and I will not deny them.

HALE: And you, woman?

ELIZABETH: I—I cannot believe it.

HALE, *shocked:* You cannot!

PROCTOR: Elizabeth, you bewilder him!

ELIZABETH, *to Hale:* I cannot think the Devil may own a woman's soul, Mr. Hale, when she keeps an upright way, as I have. I am a good woman, I know it; and if you believe I may do only good work in the world, and yet be secretly bound to Satan, then I must tell you, sir, I do not believe it.

HALE: But, woman, you do believe there are witches in—

ELIZABETH: If you think that I am one, then I say there are none.

HALE: You surely do not fly against the Gospel, the Gospel—

PROCTOR: She believe in the Gospel, every word!

ELIZABETH: Question Abigail Williams about the Gospel, not myself!

Hale stares at her.

PROCTOR: She do not mean to doubt the Gospel, sir, you cannot think it. This be a Christian house, sir, a Christian house.

HALE: God keep you both; let the third child be quickly baptized, and go you without fail each Sunday in to Sabbath prayer; and keep a solemn, quiet way among you. I think—

Giles Corey appears in doorway.

GILES: John!

PROCTOR: Giles! What's the matter?

GILES: They take my wife.

Francis Nurse enters.

GILES: And his Rebecca!

PROCTOR, *to Francis:* Rebecca's in the *jail!*

FRANCIS: Aye, Cheever come and take her in his wagon. We've only now come from the jail, and they'll not even let us in to see them.

ELIZABETH: They've surely gone wild now, Mr. Hale!

FRANCIS, *going to Hale:* Reverend Hale! Can you not speak to the Deputy Governor? I'm sure he mistakes these people—

HALE: Pray calm yourself, Mr. Nurse.

FRANCIS: My wife is the very brick and mortar of the church, Mr. Hale—*indicating Giles*—and Martha Corey, there cannot be a woman closer yet to God than Martha.

HALE: How is Rebecca charged, Mr. Nurse?

FRANCIS, *with a mocking, half-hearted laugh:* For murder, she's charged! *Mockingly quoting the warrant:* "For the marvelous and supernatural murder of Goody Putnam's babies." What am I to do, Mr. Hale?

HALE, *turns from Francis, deeply troubled, then:* Believe me, Mr. Nurse, if Rebecca Nurse be tainted, then nothing's left to stop the whole green world from burning. Let you rest upon the justice of the court; the court will send her home, I know it.

FRANCIS: You cannot mean she will be tried in court!

HALE, *pleading:* Nurse, though our hearts break, we cannot flinch; these are new times, sir. There is a misty plot afoot so subtle we should be criminal to cling to old respects and ancient friendships. I have seen too many frightful proofs in court— the Devil is alive in Salem, and we dare not quail to follow wherever the accusing finger points!

PROCTOR, *angered:* How may such a woman murder children?

HALE, *in great pain:* Man, remember, until an hour before the Devil fell, God thought him beautiful in Heaven.

GILES: I never said my wife were a witch, Mr. Hale; I only said she were reading books!

HALE: Mr. Corey, exactly what complaint were made on your wife?

GILES: That bloody mongrel Walcott charge her. Y'see, he buy a pig of my wife four or five year ago, and the pig died soon after. So he come dancin' in for his money back. So my Martha, she says to him, "Walcott, if you haven't the wit to feed a pig properly, you'll not live to own many," she says. Now he goes to court and claims that from that day to this he cannot keep a pig alive for more than four weeks because my Martha bewitch them with her books!

Enter Ezekiel Cheever. A shocked silence.

CHEEVER: Good evening to you, Proctor.

PROCTOR: Why, Mr. Cheever. Good evening.

CHEEVER: Good evening, all. Good evening, Mr. Hale.

PROCTOR: I hope you come not on business of the court.

CHEEVER: I do, Proctor, aye. I am clerk of the court now, y'know.

Enter Marshal Herrick, a man in his early thirties, who is somewhat shamefaced at the moment.

GILES: It's a pity, Ezekiel, that an honest tailor might have gone to Heaven must burn in Hell. You'll burn for this, do you know it?

CHEEVER: You know yourself I must do as I'm told. You surely know that, Giles. And I'd as lief you'd not be sending me to Hell. I like not the sound of it, I tell you; I like not the sound of it. *He fears Proctor, but starts to reach inside his coat.* Now believe me, Proctor, how heavy be the law, all its tonnage I do carry on my back tonight. *He takes out a warrant.* I have a warrant for your wife.

PROCTOR, *to Hale:* You said she were not charged!

HALE: I know nothin' of it. *To Cheever:* When were she charged?

CHEEVER: I am given sixteen warrant tonight, sir, and she is one.

PROCTOR: Who charged her?

CHEEVER: Why, Abigail Williams charge her.

PROCTOR: On what proof, what proof?

CHEEVER, *looking about the room:* Mr. Proctor, I have little time. The court bid me search your house, but I like not to search a house. So will you hand me any poppets that your wife may keep here?

PROCTOR: Poppets?

ELIZABETH: I never kept no poppets, not since I were a girl.

CHEEVER, *embarrassed, glancing toward the mantel where sits Mary Warren's poppet:* I spy a poppet, Goody Proctor.

ELIZABETH: Oh! *Going for it:* Why, this is Mary's.

CHEEVER, *shyly:* Would you please to give it to me?

ELIZABETH, *handing it to him, asks Hale:* Has the court discovered a text in poppets now?

CHEEVER, *carefully holding the poppet:* Do you keep any others in this house?

PROCTOR: No, nor this one either till tonight. What signifies a poppet?

CHEEVER: Why, a poppet—*he gingerly turns the poppet over*—a poppet may signify— Now, woman, will you please to come with me?

PROCTOR: She will not! *To Elizabeth:* Fetch Mary here.

CHEEVER, *ineptly reaching toward Elizabeth:* No, no, I am forbid to leave her from my sight.

PROCTOR, *pushing his arm away:* You'll leave her out of sight and out of mind, Mister. Fetch Mary, Elizabeth. *Elizabeth goes upstairs.*

HALE: What signifies a poppet, Mr. Cheever?

CHEEVER, *turning the poppet over in his hands:* Why, they say it may signify that she— *He has lifted the poppet's skirt, and his eyes widen in astonished fear.* Why, this, this—

PROCTOR, *reaching for the poppet:* What's there?

CHEEVER: Why—*He draws out a long needle from the poppet*—it is a needle! Herrick, Herrick, it is a needle!

Herrick comes toward him.

PROCTOR, *angrily, bewildered:* And what signifies a needle!

CHEEVER, *his hands shaking:* Why, this go hard with her, Proctor, this—I had my doubts, Proctor, I had my doubts, but here's calamity. *To Hale, showing the needle:* You see it, sir, it is a needle!

HALE: Why? What meanin' has it?

CHEEVER, *wide-eyed, trembling:* The girl, the Williams girl, Abigail Williams, sir. She sat to dinner in Reverend Parris's house tonight, and without word nor warnin' she falls to the floor. Like a struck beast, he says, and screamed a scream that a bull would weep to hear. And he goes to save her, and, stuck two inches in the flesh of her belly, he draw a needle out. And demandin' of her how she come to be so stabbed, she—*to Proctor now*—testify it were your wife's familiar spirit pushed it in.

PROCTOR: Why, she done it herself! *To Hale:* I hope you're not takin' this for proof, Mister!

Hale, struck by the proof, is silent.

CHEEVER: 'Tis hard proof! *To Hale:* I find here a poppet Goody Proctor keeps. I have found it, sir. And in the belly of the poppet a needle's stuck. I tell you true, Proctor, I never warranted to see such proof of Hell, and I bid you obstruct me not, for I—

Enter Elizabeth with Mary Warren. Proctor, seeing Mary Warren, draws her by the arm to Hale.

PROCTOR: Here now! Mary, how did this poppet come into my house?

MARY WARREN, *frightened for herself, her voice very small:* What poppet's that, sir?

PROCTOR, *impatiently, pointing at the doll in Cheever's hand:* This poppet, this poppet.

MARY WARREN, *evasively, looking at it:* Why, I—I think it is mine.

PROCTOR: It is your poppet, is it not?

MARY WARREN, *not understanding the direction of this:* It—is, sir.

PROCTOR: And how did it come into this house?

MARY WARREN, *glancing about at the avid faces:* Why—I made it in the court, sir, and—give it to Goody Proctor tonight.

PROCTOR, *to Hale:* Now, sir—do you have it?

HALE: Mary Warren, a needle have been found inside this poppet.

MARY WARREN, *bewildered:* Why, I meant no harm by it, sir.

PROCTOR, *quickly:* You stuck that needle in yourself?

MARY WARREN: I—I believe I did, sir, I—

PROCTOR, *to Hale:* What say you now?

HALE, *watching Mary Warren closely:* Child, you are certain this be your natural memory? May it be, perhaps, that someone conjures you even now to say this?

MARY WARREN: Conjures me? Why, no, sir, I am entirely myself, I think. Let you ask Susanna Walcott—she saw me sewin' it in court. *Or better still:* Ask Abby, Abby sat beside me when I made it.

PROCTOR, *to Hale, of Cheever:* Bid him begone. Your mind is surely settled now. Bid him out, Mr. Hale.

ELIZABETH: What signifies a needle?

HALE: Mary—you charge a cold and cruel murder on Abigail.

MARY WARREN: Murder! I charge no—

HALE: Abigail were stabbed tonight; a needle were found stuck into her belly—

ELIZABETH: And she charges me?

HALE: Aye.

ELIZABETH, *her breath knocked out:* Why—! The girl is murder! She must be ripped out of the world!

CHEEVER, *pointing at Elizabeth:* You've heard that, sir! Ripped out of the world! Herrick, you heard it!

PROCTOR, *suddenly snatching the warrant out of Cheever's hands:* Out with you.

CHEEVER: Proctor, you dare not touch the warrant.

PROCTOR, *ripping the warrant:* Out with you!

CHEEVER: You've ripped the Deputy Governor's warrant, man!

PROCTOR: Damn the Deputy Governor! Out of my house!

HALE: Now, Proctor, Proctor!

PROCTOR: Get y'gone with them! You are a broken minister.

HALE: Proctor, if she is innocent, the court—

PROCTOR: If *she* is innocent! Why do you never wonder if Parris be innocent, or Abigail? Is the accuser always holy now? Were they born this morning as clean as God's fingers? I'll tell you what's walking Salem—vengeance is walking Salem. We are what we always were in Salem, but now the little crazy children are jangling the keys of the kingdom, and common vengeance writes the law! This warrant's vengeance! I'll not give my wife to vengeance!

ELIZABETH: I'll go, John—

PROCTOR: You will not go!

HERRICK: I have nine men outside. You cannot keep her. The law binds me, John, I cannot budge.

PROCTOR, *to Hale, ready to break him:* Will you see her taken?

HALE: Proctor, the court is just—

PROCTOR: Pontius Pilate! God will not let you wash your hands of this!

ELIZABETH: John—I think I must go with them. *He cannot bear to look at her.* Mary, there is bread enough for the morning; you will bake, in the afternoon. Help Mr. Proctor as you were his daughter—you owe me that, and much more. *She is fighting her weeping. To Proctor:* When the children wake, speak nothing of witchcraft—it will frighten them. *She cannot go on.*

PROCTOR: I will bring you home. I will bring you soon.

ELIZABETH: Oh, John, bring me soon!

PROCTOR: I will fall like an ocean on that court! Fear nothing, Elizabeth.

ELIZABETH, *with great fear:* I will fear nothing. *She looks about the room, as though to fix it in her mind.* Tell the children I have gone to visit someone sick.

She walks out the door, Herrick and Cheever behind her. For a moment, Proctor watches from the doorway. The clank of chain is heard.

PROCTOR: Herrick! Herrick, don't chain her! *He rushes out the door. From outside:* Damn you, man, you will not chain her! Off with them! I'll not have it! I will not have her chained!

There are other men's voices against his. Hale, in a fever of guilt and uncertainty, turns from the door to avoid the sight; Mary Warren bursts into tears and sits weeping. Giles Corey calls to Hale.

GILES: And yet silent, minister? It is fraud, you know it is fraud! What keeps you, man?

Proctor is half braced, half pushed into the room by two deputies and Herrick.

PROCTOR: I'll pay you, Herrick, I will surely pay you!

HERRICK, *panting:* In God's name, John, I cannot help myself. I must chain them all. Now let you keep inside this house till I am gone! *He goes out with his deputies.*

Proctor stands there, gulping air. Horses and a wagon creaking are heard.

HALE, *in great uncertainty:* Mr. Proctor—

PROCTOR: Out of my sight!

HALE: Charity, Proctor, charity. What I have heard in her favor, I will not fear to testify in court. God help me, I cannot judge her guilty or innocent—I know not. Only this consider: the world goes mad, and it profit nothing you should lay the cause to the vengeance of a little girl.

PROCTOR: You are a coward! Though you be ordained in God's own tears, you are a coward now!

HALE: Proctor, I cannot think God be provoked so grandly by such a petty cause. The jails are packed—our greatest judges sit in Salem now—and hangin's promised. Man, we must look to cause proportionate. Were there murder done, perhaps, and never brought to light? Abomination? Some secret blasphemy that stinks to Heaven? Think on cause, man, and let you help me to discover it. For there's your way, believe it, there is your only way, when such confusion strikes upon the world. *He goes to Giles and Francis.* Let you counsel among yourselves; think on your village and what may have drawn from heaven such thundering wrath upon you all. I shall pray God open up our eyes.

Hale goes out.

FRANCIS, *struck by Hale's mood:* I never heard no murder done in Salem.

PROCTOR—*he has been reached by Hale's words:* Leave me, Francis, leave me.

GILES, *shaken:* John—tell me, are we lost?

PROCTOR: Go home now, Giles. We'll speak on it tomorrow.

GILES: Let you think on it. We'll come early, eh?

PROCTOR: Aye. Go now, Giles.

GILES: Good night, then.

Giles Corey goes out. After a moment:

MARY WARREN, *in a fearful squeak of a voice:* Mr. Proctor, very likely they'll let her come home once they're given proper evidence.

PROCTOR: You're coming to the court with me, Mary. You will tell it in the court.

MARY WARREN: I cannot charge murder on Abigail.

PROCTOR, *moving menacingly toward her:* You will tell the court how that poppet come here and who stuck the needle in.

MARY WARREN: She'll kill me for sayin' that! *Proctor continues toward her.* Abby'll charge lechery on you, Mr. Proctor!

PROCTOR, *halting:* She's told you!

MARY WARREN: I have known it, sir. She'll ruin you with it, I know she will.

PROCTOR, *hesitating, and with deep hatred of himself:* Good. Then her saintliness is done with. *Mary backs from him.* We will slide together into our pit; you will tell the court what you know.

MARY WARREN, *in terror:* I cannot, they'll turn on me—

Proctor strides and catches her, and she is repeating, "I cannot, I cannot!"

PROCTOR: My wife will never die for me! I will bring your guts into your mouth but that goodness will not die for me!

MARY WARREN, *struggling to escape him:* I cannot do it, I cannot!

PROCTOR, *grasping her by the throat as though he would strangle her:* Make your peace with it! Now Hell and Heaven grapple on our backs, and all our old pretense is ripped away—make your peace! *He throws her to the floor, where she sobs, "I cannot, I cannot . . ."* And now, half to himself, staring, and turning to the open door: Peace. It is a providence, and no great change; we are only what we always were, but naked now. *He walks as though toward a great horror, facing the open sky.* Aye, naked! And the wind, God's icy wind, will blow!

And she is over and over again sobbing, "I cannot, I cannot, I cannot."

Curtain

Act Three

The vestry room of the Salem meeting house, now serving as the anteroom of the General Court.

As the curtain rises, the room is empty, but for sunlight pouring through two high windows in the back wall. The room is solemn, even forbidding. Heavy beams jut out, boards of random widths make up the walls. At the right are two doors leading into the meeting house proper, where the court is being held. At the left another door leads outside.

There is a plain bench at the left, and another at the right. In the center a rather long meeting table, with stools and a considerable armchair snugged up to it.

Through the partitioning wall at the right we hear a prosecutor's voice, Judge Hathorne's, asking a question; then a woman's voice, Martha Corey's, replying.

HATHORNE'S VOICE: Now, Martha Corey, there is abundant evidence in our hands to show that you have given yourself to the reading of fortunes. Do you deny it?

MARTHA COREY'S VOICE: I am innocent to a witch. I know not what a witch is.

HATHORNE'S VOICE: How do you know, then, that you are not a witch?

MARTHA COREY'S VOICE: If I were, I would know it.

HATHORNE'S VOICE: Why do you hurt these children?

MARTHA COREY'S VOICE: I do not hurt them. I scorn it!

GILES' VOICE, *roaring:* I have evidence for the court!

Voices of townspeople rise in excitement.

DANFORTH'S VOICE: You will keep your seat!
GILES' VOICE: Thomas Putnam is reaching out for land!
DANFORTH'S VOICE: Remove that man, Marshal!
GILES' VOICE: You're hearing lies, lies!

A roaring goes up from the people.

HATHORNE'S VOICE: Arrest him, excellency!
GILES' VOICE: I have evidence. Why will you not hear my evidence?

The door opens and Giles is half carried into the vestry room by Herrick.

GILES: Hands off, damn you, let me go!
HERRICK: Giles, Giles!
GILES: Out of my way, Herrick! I bring evidence—
HERRICK: You cannot go in there, Giles; it's a court!

Enter Hale from the court.

HALE: Pray be calm a moment.
GILES: You, Mr. Hale, go in there and demand I speak.
HALE: A moment, sir, a moment.
GILES: They'll be hangin' my wife!

Judge Hathorne enters. He is in his sixties, a bitter, remorseless Salem judge.

HATHORNE: How do you dare come roarin' into this court! Are you gone daft, Corey?
GILES: You're not a Boston judge yet, Hathorne. You'll not call me daft!

Enter Deputy Governor Danforth and, behind him, Ezekiel Cheever and Parris. On his appearance, silence falls. Danforth is a grave man in his sixties, of some humor and sophistication that does not, however, interfere with an exact loyalty to his position and his cause. He comes down to Giles, who awaits his wrath.

DANFORTH, *looking directly at Giles:* Who is this man?
PARRIS: Giles Corey, sir, and a more contentious—
GILES, *to Parris:* I am asked the question, and I am old enough to answer it! *To Danforth, who impresses him and to whom he smiles through his strain:* My name is Corey, sir, Giles Corey. I have six hundred acres, and timber in addition. It is my wife you be condemning now. *He indicates the courtroom.*
DANFORTH: And how do you imagine to help her cause with such contemptuous riot? Now be gone. Your old age alone keeps you out of jail for this.
GILES, *beginning to plead:* They be tellin' lies about my wife, sir, I—
DANFORTH: Do you take it upon yourself to determine what this court shall believe and what it shall set aside?
GILES: Your Excellency, we mean no disrespect for—
DANFORTH: Disrespect indeed! It is disruption, Mister. This is the highest court of the supreme government of this province, do you know it?
GILES, *beginning to weep:* Your Excellency, I only said she were readin' books, sir, and they come and take her out of my house for—
DANFORTH, *mystified:* Books! What books?

GILES, *through helpless sobs:* It is my third wife, sir; I never had no wife that be so taken with books, and I thought to find the cause of it, d'y'see, but it were no witch I blamed her for. *He is openly weeping.* I have broke charity with the woman, I have broke charity with her. *He covers his face, ashamed. Danforth is respectfully silent.*

HALE: Excellency, he claims hard evidence for his wife's defense. I think that in all justice you must—

DANFORTH: Then let him submit his evidence in proper affidavit. You are certainly aware of our procedure here, Mr. Hale. *To Herrick:* Clear this room.

HERRICK: Come now, Giles. *He gently pushes Corey out.*

FRANCIS: We are desperate, sir; we come here three days now and cannot be heard.

DANFORTH: Who is this man?

FRANCIS: Francis Nurse, Your Excellency.

HALE: His wife's Rebecca that were condemned this morning.

DANFORTH: Indeed! I am amazed to find you in such uproar. I have only good report of your character, Mr. Nurse.

HATHORNE: I think they must both be arrested in contempt, sir.

DANFORTH, *to Francis:* Let you write your plea, and in due time I will—

FRANCIS: Excellency, we have proof for your eyes; God forbid you shut them to it. The girls, sir, the girls are frauds.

DANFORTH: What's that?

FRANCIS: We have proof of it, sir. They are all deceiving you.

Danforth is shocked, but studying Francis.

HATHORNE: This is contempt, sir, contempt!

DANFORTH: Peace, Judge Hathorne. Do you know who I am, Mr. Nurse?

FRANCIS: I surely do, sir, and I think you must be a wise judge to be what you are.

DANFORTH: And do you know that near to four hundred are in the jails from Marblehead to Lynn, and upon my signature?

FRANCIS: I—

DANFORTH: And seventy-two condemned to hang by that signature?

FRANCIS: Excellency, I never thought to say it to such a weighty judge, but you are deceived.

Enter Giles Corey from left. All turn to see as he beckons in Mary Warren with Proctor. Mary is keeping her eyes to the ground; Proctor has her elbow as though she were near collapse.

PARRIS, *on seeing her, in shock:* Mary Warren! *He goes directly to bend close to her face.* What are you about here?

PROCTOR, *pressing Parris away from her with a gentle but firm motion of protectiveness:* She would speak with the Deputy Governor.

DANFORTH, *shocked by this, turns to Herrick:* Did you not tell me Mary Warren were sick in bed?

HERRICK: She were, Your Honor. When I go to fetch her to the court last week, she said she were sick.

GILES: She has been strivin' with her soul all week, Your Honor; she comes now to tell the truth of this to you.

DANFORTH: Who is this?

PROCTOR: John Proctor, sir. Elizabeth Proctor is my wife.

PARRIS: Beware this man, Your Excellency, this man is mischief.

HALE, *excitedly:* I think you must hear the girl, sir, she—

DANFORTH, *who has become very interested in Mary Warren and only raises a hand toward Hale:* Peace. What would you tell us, Mary Warren?

> *Proctor looks at her, but she cannot speak.*

PROCTOR: She never saw no spirits, sir.

DANFORTH, *with great alarm and surprise, to Mary:* Never saw no spirits!

GILES, *eagerly:* Never.

PROCTOR, *reaching into his jacket:* She has signed a deposition, sir—

DANFORTH, *instantly:* No, no, I accept no depositions. *He is rapidly calculating this; he turns from her to Proctor.* Tell me, Mr. Proctor, have you given out this story in the village?

PROCTOR: We have not.

PARRIS: They've come to overthrow the court, sir! This man is—

DANFORTH: I pray you, Mr. Parris. Do you know, Mr. Proctor, that the entire contention of the state in these trials is that the voice of Heaven is speaking through the children?

PROCTOR: I know that, sir.

DANFORTH, *thinks, staring at Proctor, then turns to Mary Warren:* And you, Mary Warren, how came you to cry out people for sending their spirits against you?

MARY WARREN: It were pretense, sir.

DANFORTH: I cannot hear you.

PROCTOR: It were pretense, she says.

DANFORTH: Ah? And the other girls? Susanna Walcott, and—the others? They are also pretending?

MARY WARREN: Aye, sir.

DANFORTH, *wide-eyed:* Indeed. *Pause. He is baffled by this. He turns to study Proctor's face.*

PARRIS, *in a sweat:* Excellency, you surely cannot think to let so vile a lie be spread in open court!

DANFORTH: Indeed not, but it strike hard upon me that she will dare come here with such a tale. Now, Mr. Proctor, before I decide whether I shall hear you or not, it is my duty to tell you this. We burn a hot fire here; it melts down all concealment.

PROCTOR: I know that, sir.

DANFORTH: Let me continue. I understand well, a husband's tenderness may drive him to extravagance in defense of a wife. Are you certain in your conscience, Mister, that your evidence is the truth?

PROCTOR: It is. And you will surely know it.

DANFORTH: And you thought to declare this revelation in the open court before the public?

PROCTOR: I thought I would, aye—with your permission.

DANFORTH, *his eyes narrowing:* Now, sir, what is your purpose in so doing?

PROCTOR: Why, I—I would free my wife, sir.

DANFORTH: There lurks nowhere in your heart, nor hidden in your spirit, any desire to undermine this court?

PROCTOR, *with the faintest faltering:* Why, no, sir.

CHEEVER, *clears his throat, awakening:* I—Your Excellency.

DANFORTH: Mr. Cheever.

CHEEVER: I think it be my duty, sir—*Kindly, to Proctor:* You'll not deny it, John. *To Danforth:* When we come to take his wife, he damned the court and ripped your warrant.

PARRIS: Now you have it!

DANFORTH: He did that, Mr. Hale?

HALE, *takes a breath:* Aye, he did.

PROCTOR: It were a temper, sir. I knew not what I did.

DANFORTH, *studying him:* Mr. Proctor.

PROCTOR: Aye, sir.

DANFORTH, *straight into his eyes:* Have you ever seen the Devil?

PROCTOR: No, sir.

DANFORTH: You are in all respects a Gospel Christian?

PROCTOR: I am, sir.

PARRIS: Such a Christian that will not come to church but once in a month!

DANFORTH, *restrained—he is curious:* Not come to church?

PROCTOR: I—I have no love for Mr. Parris. It is no secret. But God I surely love.

CHEEVER: He plow on Sunday, sir.

DANFORTH: Plow on Sunday!

CHEEVER, *apologetically:* I think it be evidence, John. I am an official of the court, I cannot keep it.

PROCTOR: I—I have once or twice plowed on Sunday. I have three children, sir, and until last year my land give little.

GILES: You'll find other Christians that do plow on Sunday if the truth be known.

HALE: Your Honor, I cannot think you may judge the man on such evidence.

DANFORTH: I judge nothing. *Pause. He keeps watching Proctor, who tries to meet his gaze.* I tell you straight, Mister—I have seen marvels in this court. I have seen people choked before my eyes by spirits; I have seen them stuck by pins and slashed by daggers. I have until this moment not the slightest reason to suspect that the children may be deceiving me. Do you understand my meaning?

PROCTOR: Excellency, does it not strike upon you that so many of these women have lived so long with such upright reputation, and—

PARRIS: Do you read the Gospel, Mr. Proctor?

PROCTOR: I read the Gospel.

PARRIS: I think not, or you should surely know that Cain were an upright man, and yet he did kill Abel.

PROCTOR: Aye, God tells us that. *To Danforth:* But who tells us Rebecca Nurse murdered seven babies by sending out her spirit on them? It is the children only, and this one will swear she lied to you.

Danforth considers, then beckons Hathorne to him. Hathorne leans in, and he speaks in his ear. Hathorne nods.

HATHORNE: Aye, she's the one.

DANFORTH: Mr. Proctor, this morning, your wife send me a claim in which she states that she is pregnant now.

PROCTOR: My wife pregnant!

DANFORTH: There be no sign of it—we have examined her body.

PROCTOR: But if she say she is pregnant, then she must be! That woman will never lie, Mr. Danforth.

DANFORTH: She will not?

PROCTOR: Never, sir, never.

DANFORTH: We have thought it too convenient to be credited. However, if I should tell you now that I will let her be kept another month; and if she begin to show her natural signs, you shall have her living yet another year until she is delivered—what say you to that? *John Proctor is struck silent.* Come now. You say your only purpose is to save your wife. Good, then, she is saved at least this year, and a year is long. What say you, sir? It is done now. *In conflict, Proctor glances at Francis and Giles.* Will you drop this charge?

PROCTOR: I—I think I cannot.

DANFORTH, *now an almost imperceptible hardness in his voice:* Then your purpose is somewhat larger.

PARRIS: He's come to overthrow this court, Your Honor!

PROCTOR: These are my friends. Their wives are also accused—

DANFORTH, *with a sudden briskness of manner:* I judge you not, sir. I am ready to hear your evidence.

PROCTOR: I come not to hurt the court; I only—

DANFORTH, *cutting him off:* Marshal, go into the court and bid Judge Stoughton and Judge Sewall declare recess for one hour. And let them go to the tavern, if they will. All witnesses and prisoners are to be kept in the building.

HERRICK: Aye, sir. *Very deferentially:* If I may say it, sir, I know this man all my life. It is a good man, sir.

DANFORTH—*it is the reflection on himself he resents:* I am sure of it, Marshal. *Herrick nods, then goes out.* Now, what deposition do you have for us, Mr. Proctor? And I beg you be clear, open as the sky, and honest.

PROCTOR, *as he takes out several papers:* I am no lawyer, so I'll—

DANFORTH: The pure in heart need no lawyers. Proceed as you will.

PROCTOR, *handing Danforth a paper:* Will you read this first, sir? It's a sort of testament. The people signing it declare their good opinion of Rebecca, and my wife, and Martha Corey. *Danforth looks down at the paper.*

PARRIS, *to enlist Danforth's sarcasm:* Their good opinion! *But Danforth goes on reading, and Proctor is heartened.*

PROCTOR: These are all landholding farmers, members of the church. *Delicately, trying to point out a paragraph:* If you'll notice, sir—they've known the women many years and never saw no sign they had dealings with the Devil.

Parris nervously moves over and reads over Danforth's shoulder.

DANFORTH, *glancing down a long list:* How many names are here?

FRANCIS: Ninety-one, Your Excellency.

PARRIS, *sweating:* These people should be summoned. *Danforth looks up at him questioningly.* For questioning.

FRANCIS, *trembling with anger:* Mr. Danforth, I gave them all my word no harm would come to them for signing this.

PARRIS: This is a clear attack upon the court!

HALE, *to Parris, trying to contain himself:* Is every defense an attack upon the court? Can no one—

PARRIS: All innocent and Christian people are happy for the courts in Salem! These people are gloomy for it. *To Danforth directly:* And I think you will want to know, from each and every one of them, what discontents them with you!

HATHORNE: I think they ought to be examined, sir.

DANFORTH: It is not necessarily an attack, I think. Yet—

FRANCIS: These are all covenanted Christians, sir.

DANFORTH: Then I am sure they may have nothing to fear. *Hands Cheever the paper.* Mr. Cheever, have warrants drawn for all of these—arrest for examination. *To Proctor:* Now, Mister, what other information do you have for us? *Francis is still standing, horrified.* You may sit, Mr. Nurse.

FRANCIS: I have brought trouble on these people; I have—

DANFORTH: No, old man, you have not hurt these people if they are of good conscience. But you must understand, sir, that a person is either with this court or he must be counted against it, there be no road between. This is a sharp time, now, a precise time—we live no longer in the dusky afternoon when evil mixed itself with good and befuddled the world. Now, by God's grace, the shining sun is up, and them that fear not light will surely praise it. I hope you will be one of those. *Mary Warren suddenly sobs.* She's not hearty, I see.

PROCTOR: No, she's not, sir. *To Mary, bending to her, holding her hand, quietly:* Now remember what the angel Raphael said to the boy Tobias. Remember it.

MARY WARREN, *hardly audible:* Aye.

PROCTOR: "Do that which is good, and no harm shall come to thee."

MARY WARREN: Aye.

DANFORTH: Come, man, we wait you.

Marshal Herrick returns, and takes his post at the door.

GILES: John, my deposition, give him mine.

PROCTOR: Aye. *He hands Danforth another paper.* This is Mr. Corey's deposition.

DANFORTH: Oh? *He looks down at it. Now Hathorne comes behind him and reads with him.*

HATHORNE, *suspiciously:* What lawyer drew this, Corey?

GILES: You know I never hired a lawyer in my life, Hathorne.

DANFORTH, *finishing the reading:* It is very well phrased. My compliments. Mr. Parris, if Mr. Putnam is in the court, will you bring him in? *Hathorne takes the deposition, and walks to the window with it. Parris goes into the court.* You have no legal training, Mr. Corey?

GILES, *very pleased:* I have the best, sir—I am thirty-three time in court in my life. And always plaintiff, too.

DANFORTH: Oh, then you're much put-upon.

GILES: I am never put-upon; I know my rights, sir, and I will have them. You know, your father tried a case of mine—might be thirty-five year ago, I think.

DANFORTH: Indeed.

GILES: He never spoke to you of it?

DANFORTH: No, I cannot recall it.

GILES: That's strange, he give me nine pound damages. He were a fair judge, your father. Y'see, I had a white mare that time, and this fellow come to borrow the mare—*Enter Parris with Thomas Putnam. When he sees Putnam, Giles' ease goes; he is hard.* Aye, there he is.

DANFORTH: Mr. Putnam, I have here an accusation by Mr. Corey against you. He states that you coldly prompted your daughter to cry witchery upon George Jacobs that is now in jail.

PUTNAM: It is a lie.

DANFORTH, *turning to Giles:* Mr. Putnam states your charge is a lie. What say you to that?

GILES, *furious, his fists clenched:* A fart on Thomas Putnam, that is what I say to that!

DANFORTH: What proof do you submit for your charge, sir?

GILES: My proof is there! *Pointing to the paper.* If Jacobs hangs for a witch he forfeit up his property—that's law! And there is none but Putnam with the coin to buy so great a piece. This man is killing his neighbors for their land!

DANFORTH: But proof, sir, proof.

GILES, *pointing at his deposition:* The proof is there! I have it from an honest man who heard Putnam say it! The day his daughter cried out on Jacobs, he said she'd given him a fair gift of land.

HATHORNE: And the name of this man?

GILES, *taken aback:* What name?

HATHORNE: The man that give you this information.

GILES, *hesitates, then:* Why, I—I cannot give you his name.

HATHORNE: And why not?

GILES, *hesitates, then bursts out:* You know well why not! He'll lay in jail if I give his name!

HATHORNE: This is contempt of the court, Mr. Danforth!

DANFORTH, *to avoid that:* You will surely tell us the name.

GILES: I will not give you no name. I mentioned my wife's name once and I'll burn in hell long enough for that. I stand mute.

DANFORTH: In that case, I have no choice but to arrest you for contempt of this court, do you know that?

GILES: This is a hearing; you cannot clap me for contempt of a hearing.

DANFORTH: Oh, it is a proper lawyer! Do you wish me to declare the court in full session here? Or will you give me good reply?

GILES, *faltering:* I cannot give you no name, sir, I cannot.

DANFORTH: You are a foolish old man. Mr. Cheever, begin the record. The court is now in session. I ask you, Mr. Corey—

PROCTOR, *breaking in:* Your Honor—he has the story in confidence, sir, and he—

PARRIS: The Devil lives on such confidences! *To Danforth:* Without confidences there could be no conspiracy, Your Honor!

HATHORNE: I think it must be broken, sir.

DANFORTH, *to Giles:* Old man, if your informant tells the truth let him come here openly like a decent man. But if he hide in anonymity I must know why. Now sir, the government and central church demand of you the name of him who reported Mr. Thomas Putnam a common murderer.

HALE: Excellency—

DANFORTH: Mr. Hale.

HALE: We cannot blink it more. There is a prodigious fear of this court in the country—

DANFORTH: Then there is a prodigious guilt in the country. Are *you* afraid to be questioned here?

HALE: I may only fear the Lord, sir, but there is fear in the country nevertheless.

DANFORTH, *angered now:* Reproach me not with the fear in the country; there is fear in the country because there is a moving plot to topple Christ in the country!

HALE: But it does not follow that everyone accused is part of it.

DANFORTH: No uncorrupted man may fear this court, Mr. Hale! None! *To Giles:* You are under arrest in contempt of this court. Now sit you down and take counsel with yourself, or you will be set in the jail until you decide to answer all questions.

Giles Corey makes a rush for Putnam. Proctor lunges and holds him.

PROCTOR: No, Giles!

GILES, *over Proctor's shoulder at Putnam:* I'll cut your throat, Putnam, I'll kill you yet!

PROCTOR, *forcing him into a chair:* Peace, Giles, peace. *Releasing him.* We'll prove ourselves. Now we will. *He starts to turn to Danforth.*

GILES: Say nothin' more, John. *Pointing at Danforth:* He's only playin' you! You means to hang us all!

Mary Warren bursts into sobs.

DANFORTH: This is a court of law, Mister. I'll have no effrontery here!

PROCTOR: Forgive him, sir, for his old age. Peace, Giles, we'll prove it all now. *He lifts up Mary's chin.* You cannot weep, Mary. Remember the angel, what he say to the boy. Hold to it, now; there is your rock. *Mary quiets. He takes out a paper, and turns to Danforth.* This is Mary Warren's deposition. I—I would ask you remember, sir, while you read it, that until two week ago she were no different than the other children are today. *He is speaking reasonably, restraining all his fears, his anger, his anxiety.* You saw her scream, she howled, she swore familiar spirits choked her; she even testified that Satan, in the form of women now in jail, tried to win her soul away, and then when she refused—

DANFORTH: We know all this.

PROCTOR: Aye, sir. She swears now that she never saw Satan; nor any spirit, vague or clear, that Satan may have sent to hurt her. And she declares her friends are lying now.

Proctor starts to hand Danforth the deposition, and Hale comes up to Danforth in a trembling state.

HALE: Excellency, a moment. I think this goes to the heart of the matter.

DANFORTH, *with deep misgivings:* It surely does.

HALE: I cannot say he is an honest man; I know him little. But in all justice, sir, a claim so weighty cannot be argued by a farmer. In God's name, sir, stop here; send him home and let him come again with a lawyer—

DANFORTH, *patiently:* Now look you, Mr. Hale—

HALE: Excellency, I have signed seventy-two death warrants; I am a minister of the Lord, and I dare not take a life without there be a proof so immaculate no slightest qualm of conscience may doubt it.

DANFORTH: Mr. Hale, you surely do not doubt my justice.

HALE: I have this morning signed away the soul of Rebecca Nurse, Your Honor. I'll not conceal it, my hand shakes yet as with a wound! I pray you, sir, *this* argument let lawyers present to you.

DANFORTH: Mr. Hale, believe me; for a man of such terrible learning you are most bewildered—I hope you will forgive me. I have been thirty-two year at the bar, sir, and I should be confounded were I called upon to defend these people. Let you consider, now—*To Proctor and the others:* And I bid you all do likewise. In an ordinary crime, how does one defend the accused? One calls up witnesses to prove his innocence. But witchcraft is *ipso facto,* on its face and by its nature, an invisible crime, is it not? Therefore, who may possibly be witness to it? The witch and the victim. None other. Now we cannot hope the witch will accuse herself; granted? Therefore, we must rely upon her victims—and they do testify, the children certainly do testify. As for the witches, none will deny that we are most eager for all their confessions. Therefore, what is left for a lawyer to bring out? I think I have made my point. Have I not?

HALE: But this child claims the girls are not truthful, and if they are not—

DANFORTH: That is precisely what I am about to consider, sir. What more may you ask of me? Unless you doubt my probity?

HALE, *defeated:* I surely do not, sir. Let you consider it, then.

DANFORTH: And let you put your heart to rest. Her deposition, Mr. Proctor.

Proctor hands it to him. Hathorne rises, goes beside Danforth, and starts reading. Parris comes to his other side. Danforth looks at John Proctor, then proceeds to read. Hale gets up, finds position near the judge, reads too. Proctor glances at Giles. Francis prays silently, hands pressed together. Cheever waits placidly, the sublime official, dutiful. Mary Warren sobs once. John Proctor touches her head reassuringly. Presently Danforth lifts his eyes, stands up, takes out a kerchief and blows his nose. The others stand aside as he moves in thought toward the window.

PARRIS, *hardly able to contain his anger and fear:* I should like to question—

DANFORTH—*his first real outburst, in which his contempt for Parris is clear:* Mr. Parris, I bid you be silent! *He stands in silence, looking out the window. Now, having established that he will set the gait:* Mr. Cheever, will you go into the court and bring the children here? *Cheever gets up and goes out upstage. Danforth now turns to Mary.* Mary Warren, how came you to this turnabout? Has Mr. Proctor threatened you for this deposition?

MARY WARREN: No, sir.

DANFORTH: Has he ever threatened you?

MARY WARREN, *weaker:* No, sir.

DANFORTH, *sensing a weakening:* Has he threatened you?

MARY WARREN: No, sir.

DANFORTH: Then you tell me that you sat in my court, callously lying, when you knew that people would hang by your evidence? *She does not answer.* Answer me!

MARY WARREN, *almost inaudibly:* I did, sir.

DANFORTH: How were you instructed in your life? Do you not know that God damns all liars? *She cannot speak.* Or is it now that you lie?

MARY WARREN: No, sir—I am with God now.

DANFORTH: You are with God now.

MARY WARREN: Aye, sir.

DANFORTH, *containing himself:* I will tell you this—you are either lying now, or you were lying in the court, and in either case you have committed perjury and you will go to jail for it. You cannot lightly say you lied, Mary. Do you know that?

MARY WARREN: I cannot lie no more. I am with God, I am with God.

But she breaks into sobs at the thought of it, and the right door opens, and enter Susanna Walcott, Mercy Lewis, Betty Parris, and finally Abigail. Cheever comes to Danforth.

CHEEVER: Ruth Putnam's not in the court, sir, nor the other children.

DANFORTH: These will be sufficient. Sit you down, children. *Silently they sit.* Your friend, Mary Warren, has given us a deposition. In which she swears that she never saw familiar spirits, apparitions, nor any manifest of the Devil. She claims as well that none of you have seen these things either. *Slight pause.* Now, children, this is a court of law. The law, based upon the Bible, and the Bible, writ by Almighty God, forbid the practice of witchcraft, and describe death as the penalty thereof. But likewise, children, the law and Bible damn all bearers of false witness. *Slight pause.* Now then. It does not escape me that this deposition may be devised to blind us; it may well be that Mary Warren has been conquered by Satan, who sends her here to distract our sacred purpose. If so, her neck will break for it. But if she speak true, I bid you now drop your guile and confess your pretense, for a quick confession will go easier with you. *Pause.* Abigail Williams, rise. *Abigail slowly rises.* Is there any truth in this?

ABIGAIL: No, sir.

DANFORTH, *thinks, glances at Mary, then back to Abigail:* Children, a very augur bit will now be turned into your souls until your honesty is proved. Will either of you change your positions now, or do you force me to hard questioning?

ABIGAIL: I have naught to change, sir. She lies.

DANFORTH, *to Mary:* You would still go on with this?

MARY WARREN, *faintly:* Aye, sir.

DANFORTH, *turning to Abigail:* A poppet were discovered in Mr. Proctor's house, stabbed by a needle. Mary Warren claims that you sat beside her in the court when she made it, and that you saw her make it and witnessed how she herself stuck her needle into it for safe-keeping. What say you to that?

ABIGAIL, *with a slight note of indignation:* It is a lie, sir.

DANFORTH, *after a slight pause:* While you worked for Mr. Proctor, did you see poppets in that house?

ABIGAIL: Goody Proctor always kept poppets.

PROCTOR: Your honor, my wife never kept no poppets. Mary Warren confesses it was her poppet.

CHEEVER: Your Excellency.

DANFORTH: Mr. Cheever.

CHEEVER: When I spoke with Goody Proctor in that house, she said she never kept no poppets. But she said she did keep poppets when she were a girl.

PROCTOR: She has not been a girl these fifteen years, Your Honor.

HATHORNE: But a poppet will keep fifteen years, will it not?

PROCTOR: It will keep if it is kept, but Mary Warren swears she never saw no poppets in my house, nor anyone else.

PARRIS: Why could there not have been poppets hid where no one ever saw them?

PROCTOR, *furious:* There might also be a dragon with five legs in my house, but no one has ever seen it.

PARRIS: We are here, Your Honor, precisely to discover what no one has ever seen.

PROCTOR: Mr. Danforth, what profit this girl to turn herself about? What may Mary Warren gain but hard questioning and worse?

DANFORTH: You are charging Abigail Williams with a marvelous cool plot to murder, do you understand that?

PROCTOR: I do, sir. I believe she means to murder.

DANFORTH, *pointing at Abigail, incredulously:* This child would murder your wife?

PROCTOR: It is not a child. Now hear me, sir. In the sight of the congregation she were twice this year put out of this meetin' house for laughter during prayer.

DANFORTH, *shocked, turning to Abigail:* What's this? Laughter during—!

PARRIS: Excellency, she were under Tituba's power at that time, but she is solemn now.

GILES: Aye, now she is solemn and goes to hang people!

DANFORTH: Quiet, man.

HATHORNE: Surely it have no bearing on the question, sir. He charges contemplation of murder.

DANFORTH: Aye. *He studies Abigail for a moment, then:* Continue, Mr. Proctor.

PROCTOR: Mary. Now tell the Governor how you danced in the woods.

PARRIS, *instantly:* Excellency, since I come to Salem this man is blackening my name. He—

DANFORTH: In a moment, sir. *To Mary Warren, sternly, and surprised:* What is this dancing?

MARY WARREN: I—*She glances at Abigail, who is staring down at her remorselessly. Then, appealing to Proctor:* Mr. Proctor—

PROCTOR, *taking it right up:* Abigail leads the girls to the woods, Your Honor, and they have danced there naked—

PARRIS: Your Honor, this—

PROCTOR, *at once:* Mr. Parris discovered them himself in the dead of night! There's the "child" she is!

DANFORTH—*it is growing into a nightmare, and he turns, astonished, to Parris:* Mr. Parris—

PARRIS: I can only say, sir, that I never found any of them naked, and this man is—

DANFORTH: But you discovered them dancing in the woods? *Eyes on Parris, he points at Abigail.* Abigail?

HALE: Excellency, when I first arrived from Beverly, Mr. Parris told me that.

DANFORTH: Do you deny it, Mr. Parris?

PARRIS: I do not, sir, but I never saw any of them naked.

DANFORTH: But she have *danced?*

PARRIS, *unwillingly:* Aye, sir.

Danforth, as though with new eyes, looks at Abigail.

HATHORNE: Excellency, will you permit me? *He points at Mary Warren.*

DANFORTH, *with great worry:* Pray, proceed.

HATHORNE: You say you never saw no spirits, Mary, were never threatened or af-flicted by any manifest of the Devil or the Devil's agents.

MARY WARREN, *very faintly:* No, sir.

HATHORNE, *with a gleam of victory:* And yet, when people accused of witchery con-fronted you in court, you would faint, saying their spirits came out of their bodies and choked you—

MARY WARREN: That were pretense, sir.

DANFORTH: I cannot hear you.

MARY WARREN: Pretense, sir.

PARRIS: But you did turn cold, did you not? I myself picked you up many times, and your skin were icy. Mr. Danforth, you—

DANFORTH: I saw that many times.

PROCTOR: She only pretended to faint, Your Excellency. They're all marvelous pre-tenders.

HATHORNE: Then can she pretend to faint now?

PROCTOR: Now?

PARRIS: Why not? Now there are no spirits attacking her, for none in this room is ac-cused of witchcraft. So let her turn herself cold now, let her pretend she is attacked now, let her faint. *He turns to Mary Warren.* Faint!

MARY WARREN: Faint?

PARRIS: Aye, faint. Prove to us how you pretended in the court so many times.

MARY WARREN, *looking to Proctor:* I—cannot faint now, sir.

PROCTOR, *alarmed, quietly:* Can you not pretend it?

MARY WARREN: I— *She looks about as though searching for the passion to faint.* I— have no *sense* of it now, I—

DANFORTH: Why? What is lacking now?

MARY WARREN: I—cannot tell, sir, I—

DANFORTH: Might it be that here we have no afflicting spirit loose, but in the court there were some?

MARY WARREN: I never saw no spirits.

PARRIS: Then see no spirits now, and prove to us that you can faint by your own will, as you claim.

MARY WARREN, *stares, searching for the emotion of it, and then shakes her head:* I— cannot do it.

PARRIS: Then you will confess, will you not? It were attacking spirits made you faint!

MARY WARREN: No, sir, I—

PARRIS: Your Excellency, this is a trick to blind the court!

MARY WARREN: It's not a trick! *She stands.* I—I used to faint because I—I thought I saw spirits.

DANFORTH: *Thought* you saw them!

MARY WARREN: But I did not, Your Honor.

HATHORNE: How could you think you saw them unless you saw them?

MARY WARREN: I—I cannot tell how, but I did. I—I heard the other girls screaming, and you, Your Honor, you seemed to believe them, and I— It were only sport in the beginning, sir, but then the whole world cried spirits, spirits, and I—I promise you, Mr. Danforth, I only thought I saw them but I did not.

Danforth peers at her.

PARRIS, *smiling, but nervous because Danforth seems to be struck by Mary Warren's story:* Surely Your Excellency is not taken by this simple lie.

DANFORTH, *turning worriedly to Abigail:* Abigail. I bid you now search your heart and tell me this—and beware of it, child, to God every soul is precious and His vengeance is terrible on them that take life without cause. Is it possible, child, that the spirits you have seen are illusion only, some deception that may cross your mind when—

ABIGAIL: Why, this—this—is a base question, sir.

DANFORTH: Child, I would have you consider it—

ABIGAIL: I have been hurt, Mr. Danforth; I have seen my blood runnin' out! I have been near to murdered every day because I done my duty pointing out the Devil's people—and this is my reward? To be mistrusted, denied, questioned like a—

DANFORTH, *weakening:* Child, I do not mistrust you—

ABIGAIL, *in an open threat:* Let *you* beware, Mr. Danforth. Think you to be so mighty that the power of Hell may not turn *your* wits? Beware of it! There is— *Suddenly, from an accusatory attitude, her face turns, looking into the air above—it is truly frightened.*

DANFORTH, *apprehensively:* What is it, child?

ABIGAIL, *looking about in the air, clasping her arms about her as though cold:* I—I know not. A wind, a cold wind, has come. *Her eyes fall on Mary Warren.*

MARY WARREN, *terrified, pleading:* Abby!

MERCY LEWIS, *shivering:* Your Honor, I freeze!

PROCTOR: They're pretending!

HATHORNE, *touching Abigail's hand:* She is cold, Your Honor, touch her!

MERCY LEWIS, *through chattering teeth:* Mary, do you send this shadow on me?

MARY WARREN: Lord, save me!

SUSANNA WALCOTT: I freeze, I freeze!

ABIGAIL, *shivering visibly:* It is a wind, a wind!

MARY WARREN: Abby, don't do that!

DANFORTH, *himself engaged and entered by Abigail:* Mary Warren, do you witch her? I say to you, do you send your spirit out?

With a hysterical cry Mary Warren starts to run. Proctor catches her.

MARY WARREN, *almost collapsing:* Let me go, Mr. Proctor, I cannot, I cannot—

ABIGAIL, *crying to Heaven:* Oh, Heavenly Father, take away this shadow!

Without warning or hesitation, Proctor leaps at Abigail and, grabbing her by the hair, pulls her to her feet. She screams in pain. Danforth, astonished, cries, "What are you about?" and Hathorne and Parris call, "Take your hands off her!" and out of it all comes Proctor's roaring voice.

PROCTOR: How do you call Heaven! Whore! Whore!

Herrick breaks Proctor from her.

HERRICK: John!

DANFORTH: Man! Man, what do you—

PROCTOR, *breathless and in agony:* It is a whore!

DANFORTH, *dumfounded:* You charge—?

ABIGAIL: Mr. Danforth, he is lying!

PROCTOR: Mark her! Now she'll suck a scream to stab me with but—

DANFORTH: You will prove this! This will not pass!

PROCTOR, *trembling, his life collapsing about him:* I have known her, sir. I have known her.

DANFORTH: You—you are a lecher?

FRANCIS, *horrified:* John, you cannot say such a—

PROCTOR: Oh, Francis, I wish you had some evil in you that you might know me! *To Danforth:* A man will not cast away his good name. You surely know that.

DANFORTH, *dumfounded:* In—in what time? In what place?

PROCTOR, *his voice about to break, and his shame great:* In the proper place—where my beasts are bedded. On the last night of my joy, some eight months past. She used to serve me in my house, sir. *He has to clamp his jaw to keep from weeping.* A man may think God sleeps, but God sees everything, I know it now. I beg you, sir, I beg you—see her what she is. My wife, my dear good wife, took this girl soon after, sir, and put her out on the highroad. And being what she is, a lump of vanity, sir— *He is being overcome.* Excellency, forgive me, forgive me. *Angrily against himself, he turns away from the Governor for a moment. Then, as though to cry out is his only means of speech left:* She thinks to dance with me on my wife's grave! And well she might, for I thought of her softly. God help me, I lusted, and there *is* a promise in such sweat. But it is a whore's vengeance, and you must see it; I set myself entirely in your hands. I know you must see it now.

DANFORTH, *blanched, in horror, turning to Abigail:* You deny every scrap and tittle of this?

ABIGAIL: If I must answer that, I will leave and I will not come back again!

Danforth seems unsteady.

PROCTOR: I have made a bell of my honor! I have rung the doom of my good name—you will believe me, Mr. Danforth! My wife is innocent, except she knew a whore when she saw one!

ABIGAIL, *stepping up to Danforth:* What look do you give me? *Danforth cannot speak.* I'll not have such looks! *She turns and starts for the door.*

DANFORTH: You will remain where you are! *Herrick steps into her path. She comes up short, fire in her eyes.* Mr. Parris, go into the court and bring Goodwife Proctor out.

PARRIS, *objecting:* Your Honor, this is all a—

DANFORTH, *sharply to Parris:* Bring her out! And tell her not one word of what's been spoken here. And let you knock before you enter. *Parris goes out.* Now we shall touch the bottom of this swamp. *To Proctor:* Your wife, you say, is an honest woman.

PROCTOR: In her life, sir, she have never lied. There are them that cannot sing, and them that cannot weep—my wife cannot lie. I have paid much to learn it, sir.

DANFORTH: And when she put this girl out of your house, she put her out for a harlot?

PROCTOR: Aye, sir.

DANFORTH: And knew her for a harlot?

PROCTOR: Aye, sir, she knew her for a harlot.

DANFORTH: Good then. *To Abigail:* And if she tell me, child, it were for harlotry, may God spread His mercy on you! *There is a knock. He calls to the door.* Hold! *To Abigail:* Turn your back. Turn your back. *To Proctor:* Do likewise. *Both turn their backs—Abigail with indignant slowness.* Now let neither of you turn to face Goody Proctor. No one in this room is to speak one word, or raise a gesture aye or nay. *He turns toward the door, calls:* Enter! *The door opens. Elizabeth enters with Parris. Parris leaves her. She stands alone, her eyes looking for Proctor.* Mr. Cheever, report this testimony in all exactness. Are you ready?

CHEEVER: Ready, sir.

DANFORTH: Come here, woman. *Elizabeth comes to him, glancing at Proctor's back.* Look at me only, not at your husband. In my eyes only.

ELIZABETH, *faintly:* Good, sir.

DANFORTH: We are given to understand that at one time you dismissed your servant, Abigail Williams.

ELIZABETH: That is true, sir.

DANFORTH: For what cause did you dismiss her? *Slight pause. Then Elizabeth tries to glance at Proctor.* You will look in my eyes only and not at your husband. The answer is in your memory and you need no help to give it to me. Why did you dismiss Abigail Williams?

ELIZABETH, *not knowing what to say, sensing a situation, wetting her lips to stall for time:* She—dissatisfied me. *Pause.* And my husband.

DANFORTH: In what way dissatisfied you?

ELIZABETH: She were— *She glances at Proctor for a cue.*

DANFORTH: Woman, look at me! *Elizabeth does.* Were she slovenly? Lazy? What disturbance did she cause?

ELIZABETH: Your Honor, I—in that time I were sick. And I—My husband is a good and righteous man. He is never drunk as some are, nor wastin' his time at the shovelboard, but always at his work. But in my sickness—you see, sir, I were a long time sick after my last baby, and I thought I saw my husband somewhat turning from me. And this girl— *She turns to Abigail.*

DANFORTH: Look at me.

ELIZABETH: Aye, sir. Abigail Williams— *She breaks off.*

DANFORTH: What of Abigail Williams?

ELIZABETH: I came to think he fancied her. And so one night I lost my wits, I think, and put her out on the highroad.

DANFORTH: Your husband—did he indeed turn from you?

ELIZABETH, *in agony:* My husband—is a goodly man, sir.

DANFORTH: Then he did not turn from you.

ELIZABETH, *starting to glance at Proctor:* He—

DANFORTH, *reaches out and holds her face, then:* Look at me! To your own knowledge, has John Proctor ever committed the crime of lechery? *In a crisis of indecision she cannot speak.* Answer my question! Is your husband a lecher!

ELIZABETH, *faintly:* No, sir.

DANFORTH: Remove her, Marshal.

PROCTOR: Elizabeth, tell the truth!

DANFORTH: She has spoken. Remove her!

PROCTOR, *crying out:* Elizabeth, I have confessed it!

ELIZABETH: Oh, God! *The door closes behind her.*

PROCTOR: She only thought to save my name!

HALE: Excellency, it is a natural lie to tell; I beg you, stop now before another is condemned! I may shut my conscience to it no more—private vengeance is working through this testimony! From the beginning this man has struck me true. By my oath to Heaven, I believe him now, and I pray you call back his wife before we—

DANFORTH: She spoke nothing of lechery, and this man has lied!

HALE: I believe him! *Pointing at Abigail:* This girl has always struck me false! She has—

Abigail, with a weird, wild, chilling cry, screams up to the ceiling.

ABIGAIL: You will not! Begone! Begone, I say!

DANFORTH: What is it, child? *But Abigail, pointing with fear, is now raising up her frightened eyes, her awed face, toward the ceiling—the girls are doing the same—and now Hathorne, Hale, Putnam, Cheever, Herrick, and Danforth do the same.* What's there? *He lowers his eyes from the ceiling, and now he is frightened; there is real tension in his voice.* Child! *She is transfixed—with all the girls, she is whimpering open-mouthed, agape at the ceiling.* Girls! Why do you—?

MERCY LEWIS, *pointing:* It's on the beam! Behind the rafter!

DANFORTH, *looking up:* Where!

ABIGAIL: Why—? *She gulps.* Why do you come, yellow bird?

PROCTOR: Where's a bird? I see no bird!

ABIGAIL, *to the ceiling:* My face? My face?

PROCTOR: Mr. Hale—

DANFORTH: Be quiet!

PROCTOR, *to Hale:* Do you see a bird?

DANFORTH: Be quiet!!

ABIGAIL, *to the ceiling, in a genuine conversation with the "bird," as though trying to talk it out of attacking her:* But God made my face; you cannot want to tear my face. Envy is a deadly sin, Mary.

MARY WARREN, *on her feet with a spring, and horrified, pleading:* Abby!

ABIGAIL, *unperturbed, continuing to the "bird":* Oh, Mary, this is a black art to change your shape. No, I cannot, I cannot stop my mouth; it's God's work I do.

MARY WARREN: Abby, I'm *here!*

PROCTOR, *frantically:* They're pretending, Mr. Danforth!

ABIGAIL—*now she takes a backward step, as though in fear the bird will swoop down momentarily:* Oh, please, Mary! Don't come down.

SUSANNA WALCOTT: Her claws, she's stretching her claws!

PROCTOR: Lies, lies.

ABIGAIL, *backing further, eyes still fixed above:* Mary, please don't hurt me!

MARY WARREN, *to Danforth:* I'm not hurting her!

DANFORTH, *to Mary Warren:* Why does she see this vision?

MARY WARREN: She sees nothin'!

ABIGAIL, *now staring full front as though hypnotized, and mimicking the exact tone of Mary Warren's cry:* She sees nothin'!

MARY WARREN, *pleading:* Abby, you mustn't!

ABIGAIL AND ALL THE GIRLS, *all transfixed:* Abby, you mustn't!

MARY WARREN, *to all the girls:* I'm here, I'm here!

GIRLS: I'm here, I'm here!

DANFORTH, *horrified:* Mary Warren! Draw back your spirit out of them!

MARY WARREN: Mr. Danforth!

GIRLS, *cutting her off:* Mr. Danforth!

DANFORTH: Have you compacted with the Devil? Have you?

MARY WARREN: Never, never!

GIRLS: Never, never!

DANFORTH, *growing hysterical:* Why can they only repeat you?

PROCTOR: Give me a whip—I'll stop it!

MARY WARREN: They're sporting. They—!

GIRLS: They're sporting!

MARY WARREN, *turning on them all hysterically and stamping her feet:* Abby, stop it!

GIRLS, *stamping their feet:* Abby, stop it!

MARY WARREN: Stop it!

GIRLS: Stop it!

MARY WARREN, *screaming it out at the top of her lungs, and raising her fists:* Stop it!!

GIRLS, *raising their fists:* Stop it!!

> *Mary Warren, utterly confounded, and becoming overwhelmed by Abigail's—and the girls'— utter conviction, starts to whimper, hands half raised, powerless, and all the girls begin whimpering exactly as she does.*

DANFORTH: A little while ago you were afflicted. Now it seems you afflict others; where did you find this power?

MARY WARREN, *staring at Abigail:* I—have no power.

GIRLS: I have no power.

PROCTOR: They're gulling you, Mister!

DANFORTH: Why did you turn about this past two weeks? You have seen the Devil, have you not?

HALE, *indicating Abigail and the girls:* You cannot believe them!

MARY WARREN: I—

PROCTOR, *sensing her weakening:* Mary, God damns all liars!

DANFORTH, *pounding it into her:* You have seen the Devil, you have made compact with Lucifer, have you not?

PROCTOR: God damns liars, Mary!

> *Mary utters something unintelligible, staring at Abigail, who keeps watching the "bird" above.*

DANFORTH: I cannot hear you. What do you say? *Mary utters again unintelligibly.* You will confess yourself or you will hang! *He turns her roughly to face him.* Do you know who I am? I say you will hang if you do not open with me!

PROCTOR: Mary, remember the angel Raphael—do that which is good and—

ABIGAIL, *pointing upward:* The wings! Her wings are spreading! Mary, please, don't, don't—!

HALE: I see nothing, Your Honor!

DANFORTH: Do you confess this power! *He is an inch from her face.* Speak!

ABIGAIL: She's going to come down! She's walking the beam!

DANFORTH: Will you speak!

MARY WARREN, *staring in horror:* I cannot!

GIRLS: I cannot!

PARRIS: Cast the Devil out! Look him in the face! Trample him! We'll save you, Mary, only stand fast against him and—

ABIGAIL, *looking up:* Look out! She's coming down!

She and all the girls run to one wall, shielding their eyes. And now, as though cornered, they let out a gigantic scream, and Mary, as though infected, opens her mouth and screams with them. Gradually Abigail and the girls leave off, until only Mary is left there, staring up at the "bird," screaming madly. All watch her, horrified by this evident fit. Proctor strides to her.

PROCTOR: Mary, tell the Governor what they— *He has hardly got a word out, when, seeing him coming for her, she rushes out of his reach, screaming in horror.*

MARY WARREN: Don't touch me—don't touch me! *At which the girls halt at the door.*

PROCTOR, *astonished:* Mary!

MARY WARREN, *pointing at Proctor:* You're the Devil's man!

He is stopped in his tracks.

PARRIS: Praise God!

GIRLS: Praise God!

PROCTOR, *numbed:* Mary, how—?

MARY WARREN: I'll not hang with you! I love God, I love God.

DANFORTH, *to Mary:* He bid you do the Devil's work?

MARY WARREN, *hysterically, indicating Proctor:* He come at me by night and every day to sign, to sign, to—

DANFORTH: Sign what?

PARRIS: The Devil's book? He come with a book?

MARY WARREN, *hysterically, pointing at Proctor, fearful of him:* My name, he want my name. "I'll murder you," he says, "if my wife hangs! We must go and overthrow the court," he says!

Danforth's head jerks toward Proctor, shock and horror in his face.

PROCTOR, *turning, appealing to Hale:* Mr. Hale!

MARY WARREN, *her sobs beginning:* He wake me every night, his eyes were like coals and his fingers claw my neck, and I sign, I sign . . .

HALE: Excellency, this child's gone wild!

PROCTOR, *as Danforth's wide eyes pour on him:* Mary, Mary!

MARY WARREN, *screaming at him:* No, I love God; I go your way no more. I love God, I bless God. *Sobbing, she rushes to Abigail.* Abby, Abby, I'll never hurt you more! *They all watch, as Abigail, out of her infinite charity, reaches out and draws the sobbing Mary to her, and then looks up to Danforth.*

DANFORTH, *to Proctor:* What are you? *Proctor is beyond speech in his anger.* You are combined with anti-Christ, are you not? I have seen your power; you will not deny it! What say you, Mister?

HALE: Excellency—

DANFORTH: I will have nothing from you, Mr. Hale! *To Proctor:* Will you confess yourself befouled with Hell, or do you keep that black allegiance yet? What say you?

PROCTOR, *his mind wild, breathless:* I say—I say—God is dead!

PARRIS: Hear it, hear it!

PROCTOR, *laughs insanely, then:* A fire, a fire is burning! I hear the boot of Lucifer, I see his filthy face! And it is my face, and yours, Danforth! For them that quail to bring men out of ignorance, as I have quailed, and as you quail now when you know in all your black hearts that this be fraud—God damns our kind especially, and we will burn, we will burn together!

DANFORTH: Marshal! Take him and Corey with him to the jail!

HALE, *starting across to the door:* I denounce these proceedings!

PROCTOR: You are pulling Heaven down and raising up a whore!

HALE: I denounce these proceedings, I quit this court! *He slams the door to the outside behind him.*

DANFORTH, *calling to him in a fury:* Mr. Hale! Mr. Hale!

Curtain

Act Four

A cell in Salem jail, that fall.

At the back is a high barred window; near it, a great, heavy door. Along the walls are two benches.

The place is in darkness but for the moonlight seeping through the bars. It appears empty. Presently footsteps are heard coming down a corridor beyond the wall, keys rattle, and the door swings open. Marshal Herrick enters with a lantern.

He is nearly drunk, and heavy-footed. He goes to a bench and nudges a bundle of rags lying on it.

HERRICK: Sarah, wake up! Sarah Good! *He then crosses to the other bench.*

SARAH GOOD, *rising in her rags:* Oh, Majesty! Comin', comin'! Tituba, he's here, His Majesty's come!

HERRICK: Go to the north cell; this place is wanted now. *He hangs his lantern on the wall. Tituba sits up.*

TITUBA: That don't look to me like His Majesty; look to me like the marshal.

HERRICK, *taking out a flask:* Get along with you now, clear this place. *He drinks, and Sarah Good comes and peers up into his face.*

SARAH GOOD: Oh, is it you, Marshal! I thought sure you be the Devil comin' for us. Could I have a sip of cider for me goin'-away?

HERRICK, *handing her the flask:* And where are you off to, Sarah?

TITUBA, *as Sarah drinks:* We goin' to Barbados, soon the Devil gits here with the feathers and the wings.

HERRICK: Oh? A happy voyage to you.

SARAH GOOD: A pair of bluebirds wingin' southerly, the two of us! Oh, it be a grand transformation, Marshal! *She raises the flask to drink again.*

HERRICK, *taking the flask from her lips:* You'd best give me that or you'll never rise off the ground. Come along now.

TITUBA: I'll speak to him for you, if you desires to come along, Marshal.

HERRICK: I'd not refuse it, Tituba; it's the proper morning to fly into Hell.

TITUBA: Oh, it be no Hell in Barbados. Devil, him be pleasureman in Barbados, him be singin' and dancin' in Barbados. It's you folks—you riles him up 'round here; it be too cold 'round here for that Old Boy. He freeze his soul in Massachusetts, but in Barbados he just as sweet and— *A bellowing cow is heard, and Tituba leaps up and calls to the window:* Aye, sir! That's him, Sarah!

SARAH GOOD: I'm here, Majesty! *They hurriedly pick up their rags as Hopkins, a guard, enters.*

HOPKINS: The Deputy Governor's arrived.

HERRICK, *grabbing Tituba:* Come along, come along.

TITUBA, *resisting him:* No, he comin' for me. I goin' home!

HERRICK, *pulling her to the door:* That's not Satan, just a poor old cow with a hatful of milk. Come along now, out with you!

TITUBA, *calling to the window:* Take me home, Devil! Take me home!

SARAH GOOD, *following the shouting Tituba out:* Tell him I'm goin', Tituba! Now you tell him Sarah Good is goin' too!

In the corridor outside Tituba calls on—"Take me home, Devil; Devil take me home!" and Hopkins' voice orders her to move on. Herrick returns and begins to push old rags and straw into a corner. Hearing footsteps, he turns, and enter Danforth and Judge Hathorne. They are in greatcoats and wear hats against the bitter cold. They are followed in by Cheever, who carries a dispatch case and a flat wooden box containing his writing materials.

HERRICK: Good morning, Excellency.

DANFORTH: Where is Mr. Parris?

HERRICK: I'll fetch him. *He starts for the door.*

DANFORTH: Marshal. *Herrick stops.* When did Reverend Hale arrive?

HERRICK: It were toward midnight, I think.

DANFORTH, *suspiciously:* What is he about here?

HERRICK: He goes among them that will hang, sir. And he prays with them. He sits with Goody Nurse now. And Mr. Parris with him.

DANFORTH: Indeed. That man have no authority to enter here, Marshal. Why have you let him in?

HERRICK: Why, Mr. Parris command me, sir. I cannot deny him.

DANFORTH: Are you drunk, Marshal?

HERRICK: No, sir; it is a bitter night, and I have no fire here.

DANFORTH, *containing his anger:* Fetch Mr. Parris.

HERRICK: Aye, sir.

DANFORTH: There is a prodigious stench in this place.

HERRICK: I have only now cleared the people out for you.

DANFORTH: Beware hard drink, Marshal.

HERRICK: Aye, sir. *He waits an instant for further orders. But Danforth, in dissatisfaction, turns his back on him, and Herrick goes out. There is a pause. Danforth stands in thought.*

HATHORNE: Let you question Hale, Excellency; I should not be surprised he have been preaching in Andover lately.

DANFORTH: We'll come to that; speak nothing of Andover. Parris prays with him. That's strange. *He blows on his hands, moves toward the window, and looks out.*

HATHORNE: Excellency, I wonder if it be wise to let Mr. Parris so continuously with the prisoners. *Danforth turns to him, interested.* I think, sometimes, the man has a mad look these days.

DANFORTH: Mad?

HATHORNE: I met him yesterday coming out of his house, and I bid him good morning—and he wept and went his way. I think it is not well the village sees him so unsteady.

DANFORTH: Perhaps he have some sorrow.

CHEEVER, *stamping his feet against the cold:* I think it be the cows, sir.

DANFORTH: Cows?

CHEEVER: There be so many cows wanderin' the highroads, now their masters are in the jails, and much disagreement who they will belong to now. I know Mr. Parris be arguin' with farmers all yesterday—there is great contention, sir, about the cows. Contention make him weep, sir; it were always a man that weep for contention. *He turns, as do Hathorne and Danforth, hearing someone coming up the corridor. Danforth raises his head as Parris enters. He is gaunt, frightened, and sweating in his greatcoat.*

PARRIS, *to Danforth, instantly:* Oh, good morning, sir, thank you for coming, I beg your pardon wakin' you so early. Good morning, Judge Hathorne.

DANFORTH: Reverend Hale have no right to enter this—

PARRIS: Excellency, a moment. *He hurries back and shuts the door.*

HATHORNE: Do you leave him alone with the prisoners?

DANFORTH: What's his business here?

PARRIS, *prayerfully holding up his hands:* Excellency, hear me. It is a providence. Reverend Hale has returned to bring Rebecca Nurse to God.

DANFORTH, *surprised:* He bids her confess?

PARRIS, *sitting:* Hear me. Rebecca have not given me a word this three month since she came. Now she sits with him, and her sister and Martha Corey and two or three others, and he pleads with them, confess their crimes and save their lives.

DANFORTH: Why—this is indeed a providence. And they soften, they soften?

PARRIS: Not yet, not yet. But I thought to summon you, sir, that we might think on whether it be not wise, to— *He dares not say it.* I had thought to put a question, sir, and I hope you will not—

DANFORTH: Mr. Parris, be plain, what troubles you?

PARRIS: There is news, sir, that the court—the court must reckon with. My niece, sir, my niece—I believe she has vanished.

DANFORTH: Vanished!

PARRIS: I had thought to advise you of it earlier in the week, but—

DANFORTH: Why? How long is she gone?

PARRIS: This be the third night. You see, sir, she told me she would stay a night with Mercy Lewis. And next day, when she does not return, I send to Mr. Lewis to inquire. Mercy told him she would sleep in *my* house for a night.

DANFORTH: They are both gone?!

PARRIS, *in fear of him:* They are, sir.

DANFORTH, *alarmed:* I will send a party for them. Where may they be?

PARRIS: Excellency, I think they be aboard a ship. *Danforth stands agape.* My daughter tells me how she heard them speaking of ships last week, and tonight I discover my— my strongbox is broke into. *He presses his fingers against his eyes to keep back tears.*

HATHORNE, *astonished:* She have robbed you?

PARRIS: Thirty-one pound is gone. I am penniless. *He covers his face and sobs.*

DANFORTH: Mr. Parris, you are a brainless man! *He walks in thought, deeply worried.*

PARRIS: Excellency, it profit nothing you should blame me. I cannot think they would run off except they fear to keep in Salem any more. *He is pleading.* Mark it, sir, Abigail had close knowledge of the town, and since the news of Andover has broken here—

DANFORTH: Andover is remedied. The court returns there on Friday, and will resume examinations.

PARRIS: I am sure of it, sir. But the rumor here speaks rebellion in Andover, and it—

DANFORTH: There is no rebellion in Andover!

PARRIS: I tell you what is said here, sir. Andover have thrown out the court, they say, and will have no part of witchcraft. There be a faction here, feeding on that news, and I tell you true, sir, I fear there will be riot here.

HATHORNE: Riot! Why at every execution I have seen naught but high satisfaction in the town.

PARRIS: Judge Hathorne—it were another sort that hanged till now. Rebecca Nurse is no Bridget that lived three year with Bishop before she married him. John Proctor is not Isaac Ward that drank his family to ruin. *To Danforth:* I would to God it were not so, Excellency, but these people have great weight yet in the town. Let Rebecca stand upon the gibbet and send up some righteous prayer, and I fear she'll wake a vengeance on you.

HATHORNE: Excellency, she is condemn a witch. The court have—

DANFORTH, *in deep concern, raising a hand to Hathorne:* Pray you. *To Parris:* How do you propose, then?

PARRIS: Excellency, I would postpone these hangin's for a time.

DANFORTH: There will be no postponement.

PARRIS: Now Mr. Hale's returned, there is hope, I think—for if he bring even one of these to God, that confession surely damns the others in the public eye, and none may doubt more that they are all linked to Hell. This way, unconfessed and claiming innocence, doubts are multiplied, many honest people will weep for them, and our good purpose is lost in their tears.

DANFORTH, *after thinking a moment, then going to Cheever:* Give me the list.

Cheever opens the dispatch case, searches.

PARRIS: It cannot be forgot, sir, that when I summoned the congregation for John Proctor's excommunication there were hardly thirty people come to hear it. That speak a discontent, I think, and—

DANFORTH, *studying the list:* There will be no postponement.

PARRIS: Excellency—

DANFORTH: Now, sir—which of these in your opinion may be brought to God? I will myself strive with him till dawn. *He hands the list to Parris, who merely glances at it.*

PARRIS: There is not sufficient time till dawn.

DANFORTH: I shall do my utmost. Which of them do you have hope for?

PARRIS, *not even glancing at the list now, and in a quavering voice, quietly:* Excellency—a dagger— *He chokes up.*

DANFORTH: What do you say?

PARRIS: Tonight, when I open my door to leave my house—a dagger clattered to the ground. *Silence. Danforth absorbs this. Now Parris cries out:* You cannot hang this sort. There is danger for me. I dare not step outside at night!

Reverend Hale enters. They look at him for an instant in silence.
He is steeped in sorrow, exhausted, and more direct than he ever was.

DANFORTH: Accept my congratulations, Reverend Hale; we are gladdened to see you returned to your good work.

HALE, *coming to Danforth now:* You must pardon them. They will not budge.

Herrick enters, waits.

DANFORTH, *conciliatory:* You misunderstand, sir; I cannot pardon these when twelve are already hanged for the same crime. It is not just.

PARRIS, *with failing heart:* Rebecca will not confess?

HALE: The sun will rise in a few minutes. Excellency, I must have more time.

DANFORTH: Now hear me, and beguile yourselves no more. I will not receive a single plea for pardon or postponement. Them that will not confess will hang. Twelve are already executed; the names of these seven are given out, and the village expects to see them die this morning. Postponement now speaks a floundering on my part; reprieve or pardon must cast doubt upon the guilt of them that died till now. While I speak God's law, I will not crack its voice with whimpering. If retaliation is your fear, know this—I should hang ten thousand that dared to rise against the law, and an ocean of salt tears could not melt the resolution of the statutes. Now draw yourselves up like men and help me, as you are bound by Heaven to do. Have you spoken with them all, Mr. Hale?

HALE: All but Proctor. He is in the dungeon.

DANFORTH, *to Herrick:* What's Proctor's way now?

HERRICK: He sits like some great bird; you'd not know he lived except he will take food from time to time.

DANFORTH, *after thinking a moment:* His wife—his wife must be well on with child now.

HERRICK: She is, sir.

DANFORTH: What think you, Mr. Parris? You have closer knowledge of this man; might her presence soften him?

PARRIS: It is possible, sir. He have not laid eyes on her these three months. I should summon her.

DANFORTH, *to Herrick:* Is he yet adamant? Has he struck at you again?

HERRICK: He cannot, sir, he is chained to the wall now.

DANFORTH, *after thinking on it:* Fetch Goody Proctor to me. Then let you bring him up.

HERRICK: Aye, sir. *Herrick goes. There is silence.*

HALE: Excellency, if you postpone a week and publish to the town that you are striving for their confessions, that speak mercy on your part, not faltering.

DANFORTH: Mr. Hale, as God have not empowered me like Joshua to stop this sun from rising, so I cannot withhold from them the perfection of their punishment.

HALE, *harder now:* If you think God wills you to raise rebellion, Mr. Danforth, you are mistaken.

DANFORTH, *instantly:* You have heard rebellion spoken in the town?

HALE: Excellency, there are orphans wandering from house to house; abandoned cattle bellow on the highroads, the stink of rotting crops hangs everywhere, and no man knows when the harlots' cry will end his life—and you wonder yet if rebellion's spoke? Better you should marvel how they do not burn your province!

DANFORTH: Mr. Hale, have you preached in Andover this month?

HALE: Thank God they have no need of me in Andover.

DANFORTH: You baffle me, sir. Why have you returned here?

HALE: Why, it is all simple. I come to do the Devil's work. I come to counsel Christians they should belie themselves. *His sarcasm collapses.* There is blood on my head! Can you not see the blood on my head!!

PARRIS: Hush! *For he has heard footsteps. They all face the door. Herrick enters with Elizabeth. Her wrists are linked by heavy chain, which Herrick now removes. Her clothes are dirty; her face is pale and gaunt. Herrick goes out.*

DANFORTH, *very politely:* Goody Proctor. *She is silent.* I hope you are hearty?

ELIZABETH, *as a warning reminder:* I am yet six month before my time.

DANFORTH: Pray be at your ease, we come not for your life. We—*uncertain how to plead, for he is not accustomed to it.* Mr. Hale, will you speak with the woman?

HALE: Goody Proctor, your husband is marked to hang this morning.

Pause.

ELIZABETH, *quietly:* I have heard it.

HALE: You know, do you not, that I have no connection with the court? *She seems to doubt it.* I come of my own, Goody Proctor. I would save your husband's life, for if he is taken I count myself his murderer. Do you understand me?

ELIZABETH: What do you want of me?

HALE: Goody Proctor, I have gone this three month like our Lord into the wilderness. I have sought a Christian way, for damnation's doubled on a minister who counsels men to lie.

HATHORNE: It is no lie, you cannot speak of lies.

HALE: It is a lie! They are innocent!

DANFORTH: I'll hear no more of that!

HALE, *continuing to Elizabeth:* Let you not mistake your duty as I mistook my own. I came into this village like a bridegroom to his beloved, bearing gifts of high religion; the very crowns of holy law I brought, and what I touched with my bright confidence, it died; and where I turned the eye of my great faith, blood flowed up. Beware, Goody Proctor—cleave to no faith when faith brings blood. It is mistaken law that leads you to sacrifice. Life, woman, life is God's most precious gift; no principle, however glorious, may justify the taking of it. I beg you, woman, prevail upon your husband to confess. Let him give his lie. Quail not before God's judgment in this, for it may well be God damns a liar less than he that throws his life away for pride. Will you plead with him? I cannot think he will listen to another.

ELIZABETH, *quietly:* I think that be the Devil's argument.

HALE, *with a climactic desperation:* Woman, before the laws of God we are as swine! We cannot read His will!

ELIZABETH: I cannot dispute with you, sir; I lack learning for it.

DANFORTH, *going to her:* Goody Proctor, you are not summoned here for disputation. Be there no wifely tenderness within you? He will die with the sunrise. Your husband. Do you understand it? *She only looks at him.* What say you? Will you contend with him? *She is silent.* Are you stone? I tell you true, woman, had I no other proof of your unnatural life, your dry eyes now would be sufficient evidence that you delivered up your soul to Hell! A very ape would weep at such calamity! Have the devil dried up any tear of pity in you? *She is silent.* Take her out. It profit nothing she should speak to him!

ELIZABETH, *quietly:* Let me speak with him, Excellency.

PARRIS, *with hope:* You'll strive with him? *She hesitates.*

DANFORTH: Will you plead for his confession or will you not?

ELIZABETH: I promise nothing. Let me speak with him.

A sound—the sibilance of dragging feet on stone. They turn. A pause. Herrick enters with John Proctor. His wrists are chained. He is another man, bearded, filthy, his eyes misty as though webs had overgrown them. He halts inside the doorway, his eye caught by the sight of Elizabeth. The emotion flowing between them prevents anyone from speaking for an instant. Now Hale, visibly affected, goes to Danforth and speaks quietly.

HALE: Pray, leave them, Excellency.

DANFORTH, *pressing Hale impatiently aside:* Mr. Proctor, you have been notified, have you not? *Proctor is silent, staring at Elizabeth.* I see light in the sky, Mister; let you counsel with your wife, and may God help you turn your back on Hell. *Proctor is silent, staring at Elizabeth.*

HALE, *quietly:* Excellency, let—

Danforth brushes past Hale and walks out. Hale follows. Cheever stands and follows, Hathorne behind. Herrick goes. Parris, from a safe distance, offers:

PARRIS: If you desire a cup of cider, Mr. Proctor, I am sure I—*Proctor turns an icy stare at him, and he breaks off. Parris raises his palms toward Proctor.* God lead you now. *Parris goes out.*

Alone. Proctor walks to her, halts. It is as though they stood in a spinning world. It is beyond sorrow, above it. He reaches out his hand as though toward an embodiment not quite real, and as he touches her, a strange soft sound, half laughter, half amazement, comes from his throat. He pats her hand. She covers his hand with hers. And then, weak, he sits. Then she sits, facing him.

PROCTOR: The child?

ELIZABETH: It grows.

PROCTOR: There is no word of the boys?

ELIZABETH: They're well. Rebecca's Samuel keeps them.

PROCTOR: You have not seen them?

ELIZABETH: I have not. *She catches a weakening in herself and downs it.*

PROCTOR: You are a—marvel, Elizabeth.

ELIZABETH: You—have been tortured?

PROCTOR: Aye. *Pause. She will not let herself be drowned in the sea that threatens her.* They come for my life now.

ELIZABETH: I know it.

Pause.

PROCTOR: None—have yet confessed?

ELIZABETH: There be many confessed.

PROCTOR: Who are they?

ELIZABETH: There be a hundred or more, they say. Goody Ballard is one; Isaiah Goodkind is one. There be many.

PROCTOR: Rebecca?

ELIZABETH: Not Rebecca. She is one foot in Heaven now; naught may hurt her more.

PROCTOR: And Giles?

ELIZABETH: You have not heard of it?

PROCTOR: I hear nothin', where I am kept.

ELIZABETH: Giles is dead.

He looks at her incredulously.

PROCTOR: When were he hanged?

ELIZABETH, *quietly, factually:* He were not hanged. He would not answer aye or nay to his indictment; for if he denied the charge they'd hang him surely, and auction out his property. So he stand mute, and died Christian under the law. And so his sons will have his farm. It is the law, for he could not be condemned a wizard without he answer the indictment, aye or nay.

PROCTOR: Then how does he die?

ELIZABETH, *gently:* They press him, John.

PROCTOR: Press?

ELIZABETH: Great stones they lay upon his chest until he plead aye or nay. *With a tender smile for the old man:* They say he give them but two words. "More weight," he says. And died.

PROCTOR: *numbed—a thread to weave into his agony:* "More weight."

ELIZABETH: Aye. It were a fearsome man, Giles Corey.

Pause.

PROCTOR, *with great force of will, but not quite looking at her:* I have been thinking I would confess to them, Elizabeth. *She shows nothing.* What say you? If I give them that?

ELIZABETH: I cannot judge you, John.

Pause.

PROCTOR, *simply—a pure question:* What would you have me do?

ELIZABETH: As you will, I would have it. *Slight pause:* I want you living, John. That's sure.

PROCTOR, *pauses, then with a flailing of hope:* Giles' wife? Have she confessed?

ELIZABETH: She will not.

Pause.

PROCTOR: It is a pretense. Elizabeth.

ELIZABETH: What is?

PROCTOR: I cannot mount the gibbet like a saint. It is a fraud. I am not that man. *She is silent.* My honesty is broke, Elizabeth; I am no good man. Nothing's spoiled by giving them this lie that were not rotten long before.

ELIZABETH: And yet you've not confessed till now. That speak goodness in you.

PROCTOR: Spite only keeps me silent. It is hard to give a lie to dogs. *Pause, for the first time he turns directly to her.* I would have your forgiveness, Elizabeth.

ELIZABETH: It is not for me to give, John, I am—

PROCTOR: I'd have you see some honesty in it. Let them that never lied die now to keep their souls. It is pretense for me, a vanity that will not blind God nor keep my children out of the wind. *Pause.* What say you?

ELIZABETH, *upon a heaving sob that always threatens:* John, it come to naught that I should forgive you, if you'll not forgive yourself. *Now he turns away a little, in great agony.* It is not my soul, John, it is yours. *He stands, as though in physical pain, slowly rising to his feet with a great immortal longing to find his answer. It is difficult to say, and she is on the verge of tears.* Only be sure of this, for I know it now: Whatever you will do, it is a good man does it. *He turns his doubting, searching gaze upon her.* I have read my heart this three month, John. *Pause.* I have sins of my own to count. It needs a cold wife to prompt lechery.

PROCTOR, *in great pain:* Enough, enough—

ELIZABETH, *now pouring out her heart:* Better you should know me!

PROCTOR: I will not hear it! I know you!

ELIZABETH: You take my sins upon you, John—

PROCTOR, *in agony:* No, I take my own, my own!

ELIZABETH: John, I counted myself so plain, so poorly made, no honest love could come to me! Suspicion kissed you when I did; I never knew how I should say my love. It were a cold house I kept! *In fright, she swerves, as Hathorne enters.*

HATHORNE: What say you, Proctor? The sun is soon up.

Proctor, his chest heaving, stares, turns to Elizabeth. She comes to him as though to plead, her voice quaking.

ELIZABETH: Do what you will. But let none be your judge. There be no higher judge under Heaven than Proctor is! Forgive me, forgive me, John—I never knew such goodness in the world! *She covers her face, weeping.*

Proctor turns from her to Hathorne; he is off the earth, his voice hollow.

PROCTOR: I want my life.

HATHORNE, *electrified, surprised:* You'll confess yourself?

PROCTOR: I will have my life.

HATHORNE, *with a mystical tone:* God be praised! It is a providence! *He rushes out the door, and his voice is heard calling down the corridor:* He will confess! Proctor will confess!

PROCTOR, *with a cry, as he strides to the door:* Why do you cry it? *In great pain he turns back to her.* It is evil, is it not? It is evil.

ELIZABETH, *in terror, weeping:* I cannot judge you, John, I cannot!

PROCTOR: Then who will judge me? *Suddenly clasping his hands:* God in Heaven, what is John Proctor, what is John Proctor? *He moves as an animal, and a fury is riding in him, a tantalized search.* I think it is honest, I think so; I am no saint. *As though she had denied this he calls angrily at her:* Let Rebecca go like a saint; for me it is fraud!

Voices are heard in the hall, speaking together in suppressed excitement.

ELIZABETH: I am not your judge, I cannot be. *As though giving him release:* Do as you will, do as you will!

PROCTOR: Would you give them such a lie? Say it. Would you ever give them this? *She cannot answer.* You would not; if tongs of fire were singeing you you would not! It is evil. Good, then—it is evil, and I do it!

Hathorne enters with Danforth, and, with them, Cheever, Parris, and Hale. It is a businesslike, rapid entrance, as though the ice had been broken.

DANFORTH, *with great relief and gratitude:* Praise to God, man, praise to God; you shall be blessed in Heaven for this. *Cheever has hurried to the bench with pen, ink, and paper. Proctor watches him.* Now then, let us have it. Are you ready, Mr. Cheever?

PROCTOR, *with a cold, cold horror at their efficiency:* Why must it be written?

DANFORTH: Why, for the good instruction of the village, Mister; this we shall post upon the church door! *To Parris, urgently:* Where is the marshal?

PARRIS, *runs to the door and calls down the corridor:* Marshal! Hurry!

DANFORTH: Now, then, Mister, will you speak slowly, and directly to the point, for Mr. Cheever's sake. *He is on record now, and is really dictating to Cheever, who writes.* Mr. Proctor, have you seen the Devil in your life? *Proctor's jaws lock.* Come, man, there is light in the sky; the town waits at the scaffold; I would give out this news. Did you see the Devil?

PROCTOR: I did.

PARRIS: Praise God!

DANFORTH: And when he come to you, what were his demand? *Proctor is silent. Danforth helps.* Did he bid you to do his work upon the earth?

PROCTOR: He did.

DANFORTH: And you bound yourself to his service? *Danforth turns, as Rebecca Nurse enters, with Herrick helping to support her. She is barely able to walk.* Come in, come in, woman!

REBECCA, *brightening as she sees Proctor:* Ah, John! You are well, then, eh?

Proctor turns his face to the wall.

DANFORTH: Courage, man, courage—let her witness your good example that she may come to God herself. Now hear it, Goody Nurse! Say on, Mr. Proctor. Did you bind yourself to the Devil's service?

REBECCA, *astonished:* Why, John!

PROCTOR, *through his teeth, his face turned from Rebecca:* I did.

DANFORTH: Now, woman, you surely see it profit nothin' to keep this conspiracy any further. Will you confess yourself with him?

REBECCA: Oh, John—God send his mercy on you!

DANFORTH: I say, will you confess yourself, Goody Nurse?

REBECCA: Why, it is a lie, it is a lie; how may I damn myself? I cannot, I cannot.

DANFORTH: Mr. Proctor. When the Devil came to you did you see Rebecca Nurse in his company? *Proctor is silent.* Come, man, take courage—did you ever see her with the Devil?

PROCTOR, *almost inaudibly:* No.

Danforth, now sensing trouble, glances at John and goes to the table, and picks up a sheet—the list of condemned.

DANFORTH: Did you ever see her sister, Mary Easty, with the Devil?

PROCTOR: No, I did not.

DANFORTH, *his eyes narrow on Proctor:* Did you ever see Martha Corey with the Devil?

PROCTOR: I did not.

DANFORTH, *realizing, slowly putting the sheet down:* Did you ever see anyone with the Devil?

PROCTOR: I did not.

DANFORTH: Proctor, you mistake me. I am not empowered to trade your life for a lie. You have most certainly seen some person with the Devil. *Proctor is silent.* Mr. Proctor, a score of people have already testified they saw this woman with the Devil.

PROCTOR: Then it is proved. Why must I say it?

DANFORTH: Why "must" you say it! Why, you should rejoice to say it if your soul is truly purged of any love for Hell!

PROCTOR: They think to go like saints. I like not to spoil their names.

DANFORTH, *inquiring, incredulous:* Mr. Proctor, do you think they go like saints?

PROCTOR, *evading:* This woman never thought she done the Devil's work.

DANFORTH: Look you, sir. I think you mistake your duty here. It matters nothing what she thought—she is convicted of the unnatural murder of children, and you for sending your spirit out upon Mary Warren. Your soul alone is the issue here, Mister, and you will prove its whiteness or you cannot live in a Christian country. Will you tell me now what persons conspired with you in the Devil's company? *Proctor is silent.* To your knowledge was Rebecca Nurse ever—

PROCTOR: I speak my own sins; I cannot judge another. *Crying out, with hatred:* I have no tongue for it.

HALE, *quickly to Danforth:* Excellency, it is enough he confess himself. Let him sign it, let him sign it.

PARRIS, *feverishly:* It is a great service, sir. It is a weighty name; it will strike the village that Proctor confess. I beg you, let him sign it. The sun is up, Excellency!

DANFORTH, *considers; then with dissatisfaction:* Come, then, sign your testimony. *To Cheever:* Give it to him. *Cheever goes to Proctor, the confession and a pen in hand. Proctor does not look at it.* Come, man, sign it.

PROCTOR, *after glancing at the confession:* You have all witnessed it—it is enough.

DANFORTH: You will not sign it?

PROCTOR: You have all witnessed it; what more is needed?

DANFORTH: Do you sport with me? You will sign your name or it is no confession, Mister! *His breast heaving with agonized breathing, Proctor now lays the paper down and signs his name.*

PARRIS: Praise be to the Lord!

Proctor has just finished signing when Danforth reaches for the paper. But Proctor snatches it up, and now a wild terror is rising in him, and a boundless anger.

DANFORTH, *perplexed, but politely extending his hand:* If you please, sir.

PROCTOR: No.

DANFORTH, *as though Proctor did not understand:* Mr. Proctor, I must have—

PROCTOR: No, no. I have signed it. You have seen me. It is done! You have no need for this.

PARRIS: Proctor, the village must have proof that—

PROCTOR: Damn the village! I confess to God, and God has seen my name on this! It is enough!

DANFORTH: No, sir, it is—

PROCTOR: You came to save my soul, did you not? Here! I have confessed myself; it is enough!

DANFORTH: You have not con—

PROCTOR: I have confessed myself! Is there no good penitence but it be public? God does not need my name nailed upon the church! God sees my name; God knows how black my sins are! It is enough!

DANFORTH: Mr. Proctor—

PROCTOR: You will not use me! I am no Sarah Good or Tituba, I am John Proctor! You will not use me! It is no part of salvation that you should use me!

DANFORTH: I do not wish to—

PROCTOR: I have three children—how may I teach them to walk like men in the world, an I sold my friends?

DANFORTH: You have not sold your friends—

PROCTOR: Beguile me not! I blacken all of them when this is nailed to the church the very day they hang for silence!

DANFORTH: Mr. Proctor, I must have good and legal proof that you—

PROCTOR: You are the high court, your word is good enough! Tell them I confessed myself; say Proctor broke his knees and wept like a woman; say what you will, but my name cannot—

DANFORTH, *with suspicion:* It is the same, is it not? If I report it or you sign to it?

PROCTOR—*he knows it is insane:* No, it is not the same! What others say and what I sign to is not the same!

DANFORTH: Why? Do you mean to deny this confession when you are free?

PROCTOR: I mean to deny nothing!

DANFORTH: Then explain to me, Mr. Proctor, why you will not let—

PROCTOR, *with a cry of his whole soul:* Because it is my name! Because I cannot have another in my life! Because I lie and sign myself to lies! Because I am not worth the dust on the feet of them that hang! How may I live without my name? I have given you my soul; leave me my name!

DANFORTH, *pointing at the confession in Proctor's hand:* Is that document a lie? If it is a lie I will not accept it! What say you? I will not deal in lies, Mister! *Proctor is motionless.* You will give me your honest confession in my hand, or I cannot keep you from the rope. *Proctor does not reply.* Which way do you go, Mister?

His breast heaving, his eyes staring, Proctor tears the paper and crumples it, and he is weeping in fury, but erect.

DANFORTH: Marshal!

PARRIS, *hysterically, as though the tearing paper were his life:* Proctor, Proctor!

HALE: Man, you will hang! You cannot!

PROCTOR, *his eyes full of tears:* I can. And there's your first marvel, that I can. You have made your magic now, for now I do think I see some shred of goodness in John Proctor. Not enough to weave a banner with, but white enough to keep it from such dogs. *Elizabeth, in a burst of terror, rushes to him and weeps against his hand.* Give them no tear! Tears pleasure them! Show honor now, show a stony heart and sink them with it! *He has lifted her, and kisses her now with great passion.*

REBECCA: Let you fear nothing! Another judgment waits us all!

DANFORTH: Hang them high over the town! Who weeps for these, weeps for corruption! *He sweeps out past them. Herrick starts to lead Rebecca, who almost collapses, but Proctor catches her, and she glances up at him apologetically.*

REBECCA: I've had no breakfast.

HERRICK: Come, man.

Herrick escorts them out, Hathorne and Cheever behind them. Elizabeth stands staring at the empty doorway.

PARRIS, *in deadly fear, to Elizabeth:* Go to him, Goody Proctor! There is yet time!

From outside a drumroll strikes the air. Parris is startled. Elizabeth jerks about toward the window.

PARRIS: Go to him! *He rushes out the door, as though to hold back his fate.* Proctor! Proctor!

Again, a short burst of drums.

HALE: Woman, plead with him! *He starts to rush out the door, and then goes back to her.* Woman! It is pride, it is vanity. *She avoids his eyes, and moves to the window. He drops to his knees.* Be his helper!—What profit him to bleed? Shall the dust praise him? Shall the worms declare his truth? Go to him, take his shame away!

ELIZABETH, *supporting herself against collapse, grips the bars of the window, and with a cry:* He have his goodness now. God forbid I take it from him!

The final drumroll crashes, then heightens violently. Hale weeps in frantic prayer, and the new sun is pouring in upon her face, and the drums rattle like bones in the morning air.

Curtain

Echoes Down the Corridor

Not long after the fever died, Parris was voted from office, walked out on the high-road, and was never heard of again.

The legend has it that Abigail turned up later as a prostitute in Boston.

Twenty years after the last execution, the government awarded compensation to the victims still living, and to the families of the dead. However, it is evident that some people still were unwilling to admit their total guilt, and also that the factionalism was still alive, for some beneficiaries were actually not victims at all, but informers.

Elizabeth Proctor married again, four years after Proctor's death.

In solemn meeting, the congregation rescinded the excommunications—this is March 1712. But they did so upon orders of the government. The jury, however, wrote a statement praying forgiveness of al who had suffered.

Certain farms which had belonged to the victims were left to ruin, and for more than a century no one would buy them or live on them.

To all intents and purposes, the power of theocracy in Massachusetts was broken.

1953

Saul Bellow 1915–2005

The son of immigrant parents from Russia, Saul Bellow grew up in a Jewish ghetto of Montreal, Canada, where he learned Yiddish, Hebrew, English, and French. In 1924 his family moved to Chicago, a city that often appears in his fiction. After earning a bachelor's degree from Northwestern University, in 1937 he entered the University of Wisconsin at Madison to study anthropology but left there in December to become a writer. Employed for a brief period with the Works Progress Administration Writers Project, he led a bohemian life until World War II, whereupon he served in the Merchant Marine. After the war, he taught at the University of Minnesota in Minneapolis and other schools, traveled in Europe, and lived in Paris for a period of time. From 1963 until his death he held academic positions at the University of Chicago and Boston University.

Bellow is usually considered to be one of America's most important contemporary writers; his work impresses one with its diversity of style, the profundity of its content, and its scope. Bellow published his first novel, *Dangling Man,* in 1944; it is a diary of a demoralized man who is left "dangling" with no real purpose as he waits to be drafted. Three years later, Bellow published *The Victim,* which borrows the technique of the Doppelgänger from Dostoevski's *The Eternal Husband.* In this second novel, he depicts the intense psy-

chological battle between the Jew Asa Leventhal and his "double," the Gentile Kirby Allbee.

In the late 1940s, Bellow became disenchanted with the "modernist" "victim literature" of his first two novels. Detached in tone, these restrained works followed "repressive" Flaubertian formal standards. With *The Adventures of Augie March* (1953), Bellow broke free from the "modernist" chains that bound him. In contrast to the two morose early novels, this openended, picaresque narrative with its flamboyant language, zany comedy, and exuberant hero affirms the potential of the individual, his imagination, and the worth of ordinary existence.

Bellow's subsequent novels develop the themes of *The Adventures of Augie March. Seize the Day* (1956) is a dark comedy that depicts the day of reckoning in the life of Tommy Wilhelm, "a loser" who is spiritually reborn at the very end of the work. *Henderson the Rain King* (1959) is the story of an eccentric, energetic millionaire who journeys to the heart of Africa and experiences fantastic adventures. *Herzog* (1964), an enormous critical and financial success, depicts the intense psychological struggles of a professor who is on the verge of a mental breakdown as a result of his divorce from his second wife and the betrayal of his best friend. *The Dean's December* (1982) confronts more directly than any of Bellow's other novels political and social problems; Bellow contrasts the near anarchy of the slums of Chicago with the authoritarianism of the Communist world and sees a "moral crisis" in both West and East. *Ravelstein* (2000) is a meditative and autobiographical novel that explores a variety of subjects but focuses on friendship, memory, and death.

Bellow also wrote short stories, some of which are collected in *Mosby's Memoirs and Other Stories* and *Him with His Foot in His Mouth and Other Stories,* a non-fiction book on Israel, *To Jerusalem and Back,* several plays, and a number of essays, some of which are collected in *It All Adds Up.* He received many awards for his writing, including the Nobel Prize for Literature in 1976.

Bellow was a master of narrative voice and perspective; he was a remarkable stylist who could move with ease from formal rhetoric to the language of the street. A great comic writer, perhaps America's greatest since Mark Twain, Bellow explored the tragicomic search of urban man for spiritual survival in a materialistic world hostile to the imagination and "higher meanings."

Allan Chavkin
Southwest Texas State University

PRIMARY WORKS

Dangling Man, 1944; *The Victim,* 1947; *The Adventures of Augie March,* 1953; *Seize the Day,* 1956; *Henderson the Rain King,* 1959; *Herzog,* 1964; *Mosby's Memoirs and Other Stories,* 1968; *Mr. Sammler's Planet,* 1970; *Humboldt's Gift,* 1975; *To Jerusalem and Back,* 1976; *The Dean's December,* 1982; *Him with His Foot in His Mouth and Other Stories,* 1984; *More Die of Heartbreak,* 1987; *A Theft,* 1989; *The Bellarosa Connection,* 1989; *Something to Remember Me By,* 1991; *It All Adds Up,* 1994; *The Actual,* 1997; *Ravelstein,* 2000.

Looking for Mr. Green

Whatsoever thy hand findeth to do, do it with thy might. . . .[1]

Hard work? No, it wasn't really so hard. He wasn't used to walking and stair-climbing, but the physical difficulty of his new job was not what George Grebe felt most. He was delivering relief checks in the Negro district, and although he was a native Chicagoan this was not a part of the city he knew much about—it needed a depression to introduce him to it. No, it wasn't literally hard work, not as reckoned in foot-pounds, but yet he was beginning to feel the strain of it, to grow aware of its peculiar difficulty. He could find the streets and numbers, but the clients were not where they were supposed to be, and he felt like a hunter inexperienced in the camouflage of his game. It was an unfavorable day, too—fall, and cold, dark weather, windy. But, anyway, instead of shells in his deep trenchcoat pocket he had the cardboard of checks, punctured for the spindles of the file, the holes reminding him of the holes in player-piano paper. And he didn't

[1]Ecclesiastes 9:10 "Whatsoever thy hand findeth to do, do it with thy might; for there is no work, nor device, nor knowledge, nor wisdom, in the grave, whither thou goest."

look much like a hunter, either; his was a city figure entirely, belted up in this Irish con-
spirator's coat. He was slender without being tall, stiff in the back, his legs looking
shabby in a pair of old tweed pants gone through and fringy at the cuffs. With this stiffness, he kept his head forward, so that his face was red from the sharpness of the
weather; and it was an indoors sort of face with gray eyes that persisted in some kind
of thought and yet seemed to avoid definiteness of conclusion. He wore sideburns that
surprised you somewhat by the tough curl of the blond hair and the effect of assertion
in their length. He was not so mild as he looked, nor so youthful; and nevertheless there
was no effort on his part to seem what he was not. He was an educated man; he was a
bachelor; he was in some ways simple; without lushing, he liked a drink; his luck had
not been good. Nothing was deliberately hidden.

He felt that his luck was better than usual today. When he had reported for work
that morning he had expected to be shut up in the relief office at a clerk's job, for he
had been hired downtown as a clerk, and he was glad to have, instead, the freedom of
the streets and welcomed, at least at first, the vigor of the cold and even the blowing
of the hard wind. But on the other hand he was not getting on with the distribution
of the checks. It was true that it was a city job; nobody expected you to push too hard
at a city job. His supervisor, that young Mr. Raynor, had practically told him that. Still,
he wanted to do well at it. For one thing, when he knew how quickly he could deliver
a batch of checks, he would know also how much time he could expect to clip for himself. And then, too, the clients would be waiting for their money. That was not the
most important consideration, though it certainly mattered to him. No, but he wanted
to do well, simply for doing-well's sake, to acquit himself decently of a job because he
so rarely had a job to do that required just this sort of energy. Of this peculiar energy
he now had a superabundance; once it had started to flow, it flowed all too heavily.
And, for the time being anyway, he was balked. He could not find Mr. Green.

So he stood in his big-skirted trenchcoat with a large envelope in his hand and
papers showing from his pocket, wondering why people should be so hard to locate
who were too feeble or sick to come to the station to collect their own checks. But
Raynor had told him that tracking them down was not easy at first and had offered
him some advice on how to proceed. "If you can see the postman, he's your first man
to ask, and your best bet. If you can't connect with him, try the stores and trades-
people around. Then the janitor and the neighbors. But you'll find the closer you
come to your man the less people will tell you. They don't want to tell you anything."

"Because I'm a stranger."

"Because you're white. We ought to have a Negro doing this, but we don't at the
moment, and of course you've got to eat, too, and this is public employment. Jobs
have to be made. Oh, that holds for me too. Mind you, I'm not letting myself out.
I've got three years of seniority on you, that's all. And a law degree. Otherwise, you
might be back of the desk and I might be going out into the field this cold day. The
same dough pays us both and for the same, exact, identical reason. What's my law
degree got to do with it? But you have to pass out these checks, Mr. Grebe, and it'll
help if you're stubborn, so I hope you are."

"Yes, I'm fairly stubborn."

Raynor sketched hard with an eraser in the old dirt of his desk, left-handed, and
said, "Sure, what else can you answer to such a question. Anyhow, the trouble you're
going to have is that they don't like to give information about anybody. They think

you're a plain-clothes dick or an installment collector, or summons-server or something like that. Till you've been seen around the neighborhood for a few months and people know you're only from the relief."

It was dark, ground-freezing, pre-Thanksgiving weather; the wind played hob with the smoke, rushing it down, and Grebe missed his gloves, which he had left in Raynor's office. And no one would admit knowing Green. It was past three o'clock and the postman had made his last delivery. The nearest grocer, himself a Negro, had never heard the name Tulliver Green, or said he hadn't. Grebe was inclined to think that it was true, that he had in the end convinced the man that he wanted only to deliver a check. But he wasn't sure. He needed experience in interpreting looks and signs and, even more, the will not to be put off or denied and even the force to bully if need be. If the grocer did know, he had got rid of him easily. But since most of his trade was with reliefers, why should he prevent the delivery of a check? Maybe Green, or Mrs. Green, if there was a Mrs. Green, patronized another grocer. And was there a Mrs. Green? It was one of Grebe's great handicaps that he hadn't looked at any of the case records. Raynor should have let him read files for a few hours. But he apparently saw no need for that, probably considering the job unimportant. Why prepare systematically to deliver a few checks?

But now it was time to look for the janitor. Grebe took in the building in the wind and gloom of the late November day—trampled, frost-hardened lots on one side; on the other, an automobile junk yard and then the infinite work of Elevated frames,[2] weak-looking, gaping with rubbish fires; two sets of leaning brick porches three stories high and a flight of cement stairs to the cellar. Descending, he entered the underground passage, where he tried the doors until one opened and he found himself in the furnace room. There someone rose toward him and approached, scraping on the coal grit and bending under the canvas-jacketed pipes.

"Are you the janitor?"

"What do you want?"

"I'm looking for a man who's supposed to be living here. Green."

"What Green?"

"Oh, you maybe have more than one Green?" said Grebe with new, pleasant hope. "This is Tulliver Green."

"I don't think I c'n help you, mister. I don't know any."

"A crippled man."

The janitor stood bent before him. Could it be that he was crippled? Oh, God! what if he was. Grebe's gray eyes sought with excited difficulty to see. But no, he was only very short and stooped. A head awakened from meditation, a strong-haired beard, low, wide shoulders. A staleness of sweat and coal rose from his black shirt and the burlap sack he wore as an apron.

"Crippled how?"

Grebe thought and then answered with the light voice of unmixed candor, "I don't know. I've never seen him." This was damaging, but his only other choice was to make a lying guess, and he was not up to it. "I'm delivering checks for the relief to

[2]The "El," or elevated railroad, which operates
on an elevated structure, as over streets.

shut-in cases. If he weren't crippled he'd come to collect himself. That's why I said crippled. Bedridden, chair-ridden—is there anybody like that?"

This sort of frankness was one of Grebe's oldest talents, going back to childhood. But it gained him nothing here.

"No suh. I've got four buildin's same as this that I take care of. I don' know all the tenants, leave alone the tenants' tenants. The rooms turn over so fast, people movin' in and out every day. I can't tell you."

The janitor opened his grimy lips but Grebe did not hear him in the piping of the valves and the consuming pull of air to flame in the body of the furnace. He knew, however, what he had said.

"Well, all the same, thanks. Sorry I bothered you. I'll prowl around upstairs again and see if I can turn up someone who knows him."

Once more in the cold air and early darkness he made the short circle from the cellarway to the entrance crowded between the brickwork pillars and began to climb to the third floor. Pieces of plaster ground under his feet; strips of brass tape from which the carpeting had been torn away marked old boundaries at the sides. In the passage, the cold reached him worse than in the street; it touched him to the bone. The hall toilets ran like springs. He thought grimly as he heard the wind burning around the building with a sound like that of the furnace, that this was a great piece of constructed shelter. Then he struck a match in the gloom and searched for names and numbers among the writings and scribbles on the walls. He saw WHOODY-DOODY GO TO JESUS, and zigzags, caricatures, sexual scrawls, and curses. So the sealed rooms of pyramids were also decorated, and the caves of human dawn.

The information on his card was, TULLIVER GREEN—APT 3D. There were no names, however, and no numbers. His shoulders drawn up, tears of cold in his eyes, breathing vapor, he went the length of the corridor and told himself that if he had been lucky enough to have the temperament for it he would bang on one of the doors and bawl out "Tulliver Green!" until he got results. But it wasn't in him to make an uproar and he continued to burn matches, passing the light over the walls. At the rear, in a corner off the hall, he discovered a door he had not seen before and he thought it best to investigate. It sounded empty when he knocked, but a young Negress answered, hardly more than a girl. She opened only a bit, to guard the warmth of the room.

"Yes suh?"

"I'm from the district relief station on Prairie Avenue. I'm looking for a man named Tulliver Green to give him his check. Do you know him?"

No, she didn't; but he thought she had not understood anything of what he had said. She had a dream-bound, dream-blind face, very soft and black, shut off. She wore a man's jacket and pulled the ends together at her throat. Her hair was parted in three directions, at the sides and transversely, standing up at the front in a dull puff.

"Is there somebody around here who might know?"

"I jus' taken this room las' week."

He observed that she shivered, but even her shiver was somnambulistic and there was no sharp consciousness of cold in the big smooth eyes of her handsome face.

"All right, miss, thank you. Thanks," he said, and went to try another place.

Here he was admitted. He was grateful, for the room was warm. It was full of people, and they were silent as he entered—ten people, or a dozen, perhaps more, sitting on benches like a parliament. There was no light, properly speaking, but a tempered darkness that the window gave, and everyone seemed to him enormous, the men padded out in heavy work clothes and winter coats, and the women huge, too, in their sweaters, hats, and old furs. And, besides, bed and bedding, a black cooking range, a piano piled towering to the ceiling with papers, a dining-room table of the old style of prosperous Chicago. Among these people Grebe, with his cold-heightened fresh color and his smaller stature, entered like a schoolboy. Even though he was met with smiles and good will, he knew, before a single word was spoken, that all the currents ran against him and that he would make no headway. Nevertheless he began. "Does anybody here know how I can deliver a check to Mr. Tulliver Green?"

"Green?" It was the man that had let him in who answered. He was in short sleeves, in a checkered shirt, and had a queer, high head, profusely overgrown and long as a shako;[3] the veins entered it strongly from his forehead. "I never heard mention of him. Is this where he live?"

"This is the address they gave me at the station. He's a sick man, and he'll need his check. Can't anybody tell me where to find him?"

He stood his ground and waited for a reply, his crimson wool scarf wound about his neck and drooping outside his trenchcoat, pockets weighted with the block of checks and official forms. They must have realized that he was not a college boy employed afternoons by a bill collector, trying foxily to pass for a relief clerk, recognized that he was an older man who knew himself what need was, who had had more than an average seasoning in hardship. It was evident enough if you looked at the marks under his eyes and at the sides of his mouth.

"Anybody know this sick man?"

"No suh." On all sides he saw heads shaken and smiles of denial. No one knew. And maybe it was true, he considered, standing silent in the earthen, musky human gloom of the place as the rumble continued. But he could never really be sure.

"What's the matter with this man?" said shako-head.

"I've never seen him. All I can tell you is that he can't come in person for his money. It's my first day in this district."

"Maybe they given you the wrong number?"

"I don't believe so. But where else can I ask about him?" He felt that this persistence amused them deeply, and in a way he shared their amusement that he should stand up so tenaciously to them. Though smaller, though slight, he was his own man, he retracted nothing about himself, and he looked back at them, gray-eyed, with amusement and also with a sort of courage. On the bench some man spoke in his throat, the words impossible to catch, and a woman answered with a wild, shrieking laugh, which was quickly cut off.

"Well, so nobody will tell me?"

"Ain't nobody who knows."

"At least, if he lives here, he pays rent to someone. Who manages the building?"

"Greatham Company. That's on Thirty-ninth Street."

---

[3]A military cap in the shape of a cylinder with a visor and a pompon or plume.

Grebe wrote it in his pad. But, in the street again, a sheet of wind-driven paper clinging to his leg while he deliberated what direction to take next, it seemed a feeble lead to follow. Probably this Green didn't rent a flat, but a room. Sometimes there were as many as twenty people in an apartment; the real-estate agent would know only the lessee. And not even the agent could tell you who the renters were. In some places the beds were even used in shifts, watchmen or jitney drivers or short-order cooks in night joints turning out after a day's sleep and surrendering their beds to a sister, a nephew, or perhaps a stranger, just off the bus. There were large numbers of newcomers in this terrific, blight-bitten portion of the city between Cottage Grove and Ashland, wandering from house to house and room to room. When you saw them, how could you know them? They didn't carry bundles on their backs or look picturesque. You only saw a man, a Negro, walking in the street or riding in the car, like everyone else, with his thumb closed on a transfer. And therefore how were you supposed to tell? Grebe thought the Greatham agent would only laugh at his question.

But how much it would have simplified the job to be able to say that Green was old, or blind, or consumptive. An hour in the files, taking a few notes, and he needn't have been at such a disadvantage. When Raynor gave him the block of checks he asked, "How much should I know about these people?" Then Raynor had looked as though he were preparing to accuse him of trying to make the job more important than it was. He smiled, because by then they were on fine terms, but nevertheless he had been getting ready to say something like that when the confusion began in the station over Staika and her children.

Grebe had waited a long time for this job. It came to him through the pull of an old schoolmate in the Corporation Counsel's office, never a close friend, but suddenly sympathetic and interested—pleased to show, moreover, how well he had done, how strongly he was coming on even in these miserable times. Well, he was coming through strongly, along with the Democratic administration itself. Grebe had gone to see him in City Hall, and they had had a counter lunch or beers at least once a month for a year, and finally it had been possible to swing the job. He didn't mind being assigned the lowest clerical grade, nor even being a messenger, though Raynor thought he did.

This Raynor was an original sort of guy and Grebe had taken to him immediately. As was proper on the first day, Grebe had come early, but he waited long, for Raynor was late. At last he darted into his cubicle of an office as though he had just jumped from one of those hurtling huge red Indian Avenue cars. His thin, rough face was wind-stung and he was grinning and saying something breathlessly to himself. In his hat, a small fedora, and his coat, the velvet collar a neat fit about his neck, and his silk muffler that set off the nervous twist of his chin, he swayed and turned himself in his swivel chair, feet leaving the ground; so that he pranced a little as he sat. Meanwhile he took Grebe's measure out of his eyes, eyes of an unusual vertical length and slightly sardonic. So the two men sat for a while, saying nothing, while the supervisor raised his hat from his miscombed hair and put it in his lap. His cold-darkened hands were not clean. A steel beam passed through the little make-shift room, from which machine belts once had hung. The building was an old factory.

"I'm younger than you; I hope you won't find it hard taking orders from me," said Raynor. "But I don't make them up, either. You're how old, about?"

"Thirty-five."

"And you thought you'd be inside doing paper work. But it so happens I have to send you out."

"I don't mind."

"And it's mostly a Negro load we have in this district."

"So I thought it would be."

"Fine. You'll get along. *C'est un bon boulot.*[4] Do you know French?"

"Some."

"I thought you'd be a university man."

"Have you been in France?" said Grebe.

"No, that's the French of the Berlitz School. I've been at it for more than a year, just as I'm sure people have been, all over the world, office boys in China and braves in Tanganyika. In fact, I damn well know it. Such is the attractive power of civilization. It's overrated, but what do you want? *Que voulez-vous?*[5] I get *Le Rire*[6] and all the spicy papers, just like in Tanganyika. It must be mystifying, out there. But my reason is that I'm aiming at the diplomatic service. I have a cousin who's a courier, and the way he describes it is awfully attractive. He rides in the *wagon-lits*[7] and reads books. While we—What did you do before?"

"I sold."

"Where?"

"Canned meat at Stop and Shop. In the basement."

"And before that?"

"Window shades, at Goldblatt's."

"Steady work?"

"No, Thursdays and Saturdays. I also sold shoes."

"You've been a shoe-dog too. Well. And prior to that? Here it is in your folder." He opened the record. "Saint Olaf's College, instructor in classical languages. Fellow, University of Chicago, 1926–27. I've had Latin, too. Let's trade quotations—'*Dum spiro spero.*'"

"'*Da dextram misero.*'"

"'*Alea jacta est.*'"

"'*Excelsior.*'"[8]

Raynor shouted with laughter, and other workers came to look at him over the partition. Grebe also laughed, feeling pleased and easy. The luxury of fun on a nervous morning.

When they were done and no one was watching or listening, Raynor said rather seriously, "What made you study Latin in the first place? Was it for the priesthood?"

"No."

"Just for the hell of it? For the culture? Oh, the things people think they can pull!" He made his cry hilarious and tragic. "I ran my pants off so I could study for the bar, and I've passed the bar, so I get twelve dollars a week more than you as a bonus for having seen life straight and whole. I'll tell you, as a man of culture, that even though nothing looks to be real, and everything stands for something else, and

---

[4]"It's a good job."
[5]"What do you want?"
[6]French comic journal.
[7]Train sleeping-cars.

[8]"While I breathe, I hope"; "Give your right hand to the wretched"; "The die is cast"; "Higher!"

that thing for another thing, and that thing for a still further one—there ain't any comparison between twenty-five and thirty-seven dollars a week, regardless of the last reality. Don't you think that was clear to your Greeks? They were a thoughtful people, but they didn't part with their slaves."

This was a great deal more than Grebe had looked for in his first interview with his supervisor. He was too shy to show all the astonishment he felt. He laughed a little, aroused, and brushed at the sunbeam that covered his head with its dust. "Do you think my mistake was so terrible?"

"Damn right it was terrible, and you know it now that you've had the whip of hard times laid on your back. You should have been preparing yourself for trouble. Your people must have been well off to send you to the university. Stop me, if I'm stepping on your toes. Did your mother pamper you? Did your father give in to you? Were you brought up tenderly, with permission to go and find out what were the last things that everything else stands for while everybody else labored in the fallen world of appearances?"

"Well, no, it wasn't exactly like that." Grebe smiled. *The fallen world of appearances!* no less. But now it was his turn to deliver a surprise. "We weren't rich. My father was the last genuine English butler in Chicago—"

"Are you kidding?"

"Why should I be?"

"In a livery?"

"In livery. Up on the Gold Coast."[9]

"And he wanted you to be educated like a gentleman?"

"He did not. He sent me to the Armour Institute to study chemical engineering. But when he died I changed schools."

He stopped himself, and considered how quickly Raynor had reached him. In no time he had your valise on the table and all your stuff unpacked. And afterward, in the streets, he was still reviewing how far he might have gone, and how much he might have been led to tell if they had not been interrupted by Mrs. Staika's great noise.

But just then a young woman, one of Raynor's workers, ran into the cubicle exclaiming, "Haven't you heard all the fuss?"

"We haven't heard anything."

"It's Staika, giving out with all her might. The reporters are coming. She said she phoned the papers, and you know she did."

"But what is she up to?" said Raynor.

"She brought her wash and she's ironing it here, with our current, because the relief won't pay her electric bill. She has her ironing board set up by the admitting desk, and her kids are with her, all six. They never are in school more than once a week. She's always dragging them around with her because of her reputation."

"I don't want to miss any of this," said Raynor, jumping up. Grebe, as he followed with the secretary, said, "Who is this Staika?"

"They call her the 'Blood Mother of Federal Street.' She's a professional donor at the hospitals. I think they pay ten dollars a pint. Of course it's no joke, but she makes a very big thing out of it and she and the kids are in the papers all the time."

[9]Lake Shore Drive, one of Chicago's richest areas.

A small crowd, staff and clients divided by a plywood barrier, stood in the narrow space of the entrance, and Staika was shouting in a gruff, mannish voice, plunging the iron on the board and slamming it on the metal rest.

"My father and mother came in a steerage, and I was born in our house, Robey by Huron. I'm no dirty immigrant. I'm a U.S. citizen. My husband is a gassed veteran from France with lungs weaker'n paper, that hardly can he go to the toilet by himself. These six children of mine, I have to buy the shoes for their feet with my own blood. Even a lousy little white Communion necktie, that a couple of drops of blood; a little piece of mosquito veil for my Vadja so she won't be ashamed in church for the other girls, they take my blood for it by Goldblatt. That's how I keep goin'. A fine thing if I had to depend on the relief. And there's plenty of people on the rolls—fakes! There's nothin' *they* can't get, that can go and wrap bacon at Swift and Armour any time. They're lookin' for them by the Yards. They never have to be out of work. Only they rather lay in their lousy beds and eat the public's money." She was not afraid, in a predominantly Negro station, to shout this way about Negroes.

Grebe and Raynor worked themselves forward to get a closer view of the woman. She was flaming with anger and with pleasure at herself, broad and huge, a golden-headed woman who wore a cotton cap laced with pink ribbon. She was bare-legged and had on black gym shoes, her Hoover apron was open and her great breasts, not much restrained by a man's undershirt, hampered her arms as she worked at the kid's dress on the ironing board. And the children, silent and white, with a kind of locked obstinacy, in sheepskins and lumberjackets, stood behind her. She had captured the station, and the pleasure this gave her was enormous. Yet her grievances were true grievances. She was telling the truth. But she behaved like a liar. The look of her small eyes was hidden, and while she raged she also seemed to be spinning and planning.

"They send me out college case workers in silk pants to talk me out of what I got comin'. Are they better'n me? Who told them? Fire them. Let 'em go and get married, and then you won't have to cut electric from people's budget."

The chief supervisor, Mr. Ewing, couldn't silence her and he stood with folded arms at the head of his staff, bald, bald-headed, saying to his subordinates like the ex-school principal he was, "Pretty soon she'll be tired and go."

"No she won't," said Raynor to Grebe. "She'll get what she wants. She knows more about the relief even then Ewing. She's been on the rolls for years, and she always gets what she wants because she puts on a noisy show. Ewing knows it. He'll give in soon. He's only saving face. If he gets bad publicity, the Commissioner'll have him on the carpet, downtown. She's got him submerged; she'll submerge everybody in time, and that includes nations and governments."

Grebe replied with his characteristic smile, disagreeing completely. Who would take Staika's orders, and what changes could her yelling ever bring about?

No, what Grebe saw in her, the power that made people listen, was that her cry expressed the war of flesh and blood, perhaps turned a little crazy and certainly ugly, on this place and this condition. And at first, when he went out, the spirit of Staika somehow presided over the whole district for him, and it took color from her; he saw her color, in the spotty curb fires, and the fires under the El, the straight alley of flamy gloom. Later, too, when he went into a tavern for a shot of rye, the sweat of beer, association with West Side Polish streets, made him think of her again.

He wiped the corners of his mouth with his muffler, his handkerchief being inconvenient to reach for, and went out again to get on with the delivery of his checks. The air bit cold and hard and a few flakes of snow formed near him. A train struck by and left a quiver in the frames and a bristling icy hiss over the rails.

Crossing the street, he descended a flight of board steps into a basement grocery, setting off a little bell. It was a dark, long store and it caught you with its stinks of smoked meat, soap, dried peaches, and fish. There was a fire wrinkling and flapping in the little stove, and the proprietor was waiting, an Italian with a long, hollow face and stubborn bristles. He kept his hands warm under his apron.

No, he didn't know Green. You knew people but not names. The same man might not have the same name twice. The police didn't know, either, and mostly didn't care. When somebody was shot or knifed they took the body away and didn't look for the murderer. In the first place, nobody would tell them anything. So they made up a name for the coroner and called it quits. And in the second place, they didn't give a goddamn anyhow. But they couldn't get to the bottom of a thing even if they wanted to. Nobody would get to know even a tenth of what went on among these people. They stabbed and stole, they did every crime and abomination you ever heard of, men and men, women and women, parents and children, worse than the animals. They carried on their own way, and the horrors passed off like a smoke. There was never anything like it in the history of the whole world.

It was a long speech, deepening with every word in its fantasy and passion and becoming increasingly senseless and terrible: a swarm amassed by suggestion and invention, a huge, hugging, despairing knot, a human wheel of heads, legs, bellies, arms, rolling through his shop.

Grebe felt that he must interrupt him. He said sharply, "What are you talking about! All I asked was whether you knew this man."

"That isn't even the half of it. I been here six years. You probably don't want to believe this. But suppose it's true?"

"All the same," said Grebe, "there must be a way to find a person."

The Italian's close-spaced eyes had been queerly concentrated, as were his muscles, while he leaned across the counter trying to convince Grebe. Now he gave up the effort and sat down on his stool. "Oh—I suppose. Once in a while. But I been telling you, even the cops don't get anywhere."

"They're always after somebody. It's not the same thing."

"Well, keep trying if you want. I can't help you."

But he didn't keep trying. He had no more time to spend on Green. He slipped Green's check to the back of the block. The next name on the list was FIELD, WINSTON.

He found the back-yard bungalow without the least trouble; it shared a lot with another house, a few feet of yard between. Grebe knew these two-shack arrangements. They had been built in vast numbers in the days before the swamps were filled and the streets raised, and they were all the same—a boardwalk along the fence, well under street level, three or four ball-headed posts for clotheslines, greening wood, dead shingles, and a long, long flight of stairs to the rear door.

A twelve-year-old boy let him into the kitchen, and there the old man was, sitting by the table in a wheel chair.

"Oh, it's d' Government man," he said to the boy when Grebe drew out his checks. "Go bring me my box of papers." He cleared a space on the table.

"Oh, you don't have to go to all that trouble," said Grebe. But Field laid out his papers: Social Security card, relief certification, letters from the state hospital in Manteno, and a naval discharge dated San Diego, 1920.

"That's plenty," Grebe said. "Just sign."

"You got to know who I am," the old man said. "You're from the Government. It's not your check, it's a Government check and you got no business to hand it over till everything is proved."

He loved the ceremony of it, and Grebe made no more objections. Field emptied his box and finished out the circle of cards and letters.

"There's everything I done and been. Just the death certificate and they can close book on me." He said this with a certain happy pride and magnificence. Still he did not sign; he merely held the little pen upright on the golden-green corduroy of his thigh. Grebe did not hurry him. He felt the old man's hunger for conversation.

"I got to get better coal," he said. "I send my little gran'son to the yard with my order and they fill his wagon with screening. The stove ain't made for it. It fall through the grate. The order says Franklin County egg-size coal."

"I'll report it and see what can be done."

"Nothing can be done, I expect. You know and I know. There ain't no little ways to make things better, and the only big thing is money. That's the only sunbeams, money. Nothing is black where it shines, and the only place you see black is where it ain't shining. What we colored have to have is our own rich. There ain't no other way."

Grebe sat, his reddened forehead bridged levelly by his close-cut hair and his cheeks lowered in the wings of his collar—the caked fire shone hard within the isinglass-and-iron frames but the room was not comfortable—sat and listened while the old man unfolded his scheme. This was to create one Negro millionaire a month by subscription. One clever, good-hearted young fellow elected every month would sign a contract to use the money to start a business employing Negroes. This would be advertised by chain letters and word of mouth, and every Negro wage earner would contribute a dollar a month. Within five years there would be sixty millionaires.

"That'll fetch respect," he said with a throat-stopped sound that came out like a foreign syllable. "You got to take and organize all the money that gets thrown away on the policy wheel and horse race. As long as they can take it away from you, they got no respect for you. Money, that's d' sun of human kind!" Field was a Negro of mixed blood, perhaps Cherokee, or Natchez; his skin was reddish. And he sounded, speaking about a golden sun in this dark room, and looked, shaggy and slab-headed, with the mingled blood of his face and broad lips, the little pen still upright in his hand, like one of the underground kings of mythology, old judge Minos[10] himself.

And now he accepted the check and signed. Not to soil the slip, he held it down with his knuckles. The table budged and creaked, the center of the gloomy, heathen midden[11] of the kitchen covered with bread, meat, and cans, and the scramble of papers.

---

[10]According to classical mythology, a ruler of Crete, who directed Daedalus to construct the Labyrinth, a vast maze to house the monstrous Minotaur.

[11]Refuse pile.

"Don't you think my scheme'd work?"

"It's worth thinking about. Something ought to be done, I agree."

"It'll work if people will do it. That's all. That's the only thing, any time. When they understand it in the same way, all of them."

"That's true," said Grebe, rising. His glance met the old man's.

"I know you got to go," he said. "Well, God bless you, boy, you ain't been sly with me. I can tell it in a minute."

He went back through the buried yard. Someone nursed a candle in a shed, where a man unloaded kindling wood from a sprawl-wheeled baby buggy and two voices carried on a high conversation. As he came up the sheltered passage he heard the hard boost of the wind in the branches and against the house fronts, and then, reaching the sidewalk, he saw the needle-eye red of cable towers in the open icy height hundreds of feet above the river and the factories—those keen points. From here, his view was obstructed all the way to the South Branch and its timber banks, and the cranes beside the water. Rebuilt after the Great Fire, this part of the city was, not fifty years later, in ruins again, factories boarded up, buildings deserted or fallen, gaps of prairie between. But it wasn't desolation that this made you feel, but rather a faltering of organization that set free a huge energy, an escaped, unattached, unregulated power from the giant raw place. Not only must people feel it but, it seemed to Grebe, they were compelled to match it. In their very bodies. He no less than others, he realized. Say that his parents had been servants in their time, whereas he was not supposed to be one. He thought that they had never done any service like this, which no one visible asked for, and probably flesh and blood could not even perform. Nor could anyone show why it should be performed; or see where the performance would lead. That did not mean that he wanted to be released from it, he realized with a grimly pensive face. On the contrary. He had something to do. To be compelled to feel this energy and yet have no task to do—that was horrible; that was suffering; he knew what that was. It was now quitting time. Six o'clock. He could go home if he liked, to his room, that is, to wash in hot water, to pour a drink, lie down on his quilt, read the paper, eat some liver paste on crackers before going out to dinner. But to think of this actually made him feel a little sick, as though he had swallowed hard air. He had six checks left, and he was determined to deliver at least one of these: Mr. Green's check.

So he started again. He had four or five dark blocks to go, past open lots, condemned houses, old foundations, closed schools, black churches, mounds, and he reflected that there must be many people alive who had once seen the neighborhood rebuilt and new. Now there was a second layer of ruins; centuries of history accomplished through human massing. Numbers had given the place forced growth; enormous numbers had also broken it down. Objects once so new, so concrete that it could have occurred to anyone they stood for other things, had crumbled. Therefore, reflected Grebe, the secret of them was out. It was that they stood for themselves by agreement, and were natural and not unnatural by agreement, and when the things themselves collapsed the agreement became visible. What was it, otherwise, that kept cities from looking peculiar? Rome, that was almost permanent, did not give rise to thoughts like these. And was it abidingly real? But in Chicago, where the cycles were so fast and the familiar died out, and again rose changed, and died again in thirty years, you saw the common agreement or covenant, and you were forced to think about appearances and realities. (He remembered Raynor and he smiled.

Raynor was a clever boy.) Once you had grasped this, a great many things became intelligible. For instance, why Mr. Field should conceive such a scheme. Of course, if people were to agree to create a millionaire, a real millionaire would come into existence. And if you wanted to know how Mr. Field was inspired to think of this, why, he had within sight of his kitchen window the chart, the very bones of a successful scheme—the El with its blue and green confetti of signals. People consented to pay dimes and ride the crash-box cars, and so it was a success. Yet how absurd it looked; how little reality there was to start with. And yet Yerkes,[12] the great financier who built it, had known that he could get people to agree to do it. Viewed as itself, what a scheme of a scheme it seemed, how close to an appearance. Then why wonder at Mr. Field's idea? He had grasped a principle. And then Grebe remembered, too, that Mr. Yerkes had established the Yerkes Observatory and endowed it with millions. Now how did the notion come to him in his New York museum of a palace or his Aegean-bound yacht to give money to astronomers? Was he awed by the success of his bizarre enterprise and therefore ready to spend money to find out where in the universe being and seeming were identical? Yes, he wanted to know what abides; and whether flesh is Bible grass;[13] and he offered money to be burned in the fire of suns. Okay, then, Grebe thought further, these things exist because people consent to exist with them—we have got so far—and also there is a reality which doesn't depend on consent but within which consent is a game. But what about need, the need that keeps so many vast thousands in position? You tell me that, you *private* little gentleman and *decent* soul—he used these words against himself scornfully. Why is the consent given to misery? And why so painfully ugly? Because there is *something* that is dismal and permanently ugly? Here he sighed and gave it up, and thought it was enough for the present moment that he had a real check in his pocket for a Mr. Green who must be real beyond question. If only his neighbors didn't think they had to conceal him.

This time he stopped at the second floor. He struck a match and found a door. Presently a man answered his knock and Grebe had the check ready and showed it even before he began. "Does Tulliver Green live here? I'm from the relief."

The man narrowed the opening and spoke to someone at his back.

"Does he live here?"

"Uh-uh. No."

"Or anywhere in this building? He's a sick man and he can't come for his dough." He exhibited the check in the light, which was smoky—the air smelled of charred lard—and the man held off the brim of his cap to study it.

[12]Charles Tyson Yerkes (1837-1905), American financier, who, by 1886, took control of the railway lines of the west and north sections of Chicago. By financial maneuvers and corrupt politics he acquired transportation franchises and constructed an empire. Yerkes's gift in 1892 to the University of Chicago resulted in the building of the Yerkes Observatory, which opened in 1897 in Williams Bay, Wisconsin. Dreiser's *The Financier, The Titan,* and *The Stoic* are based on Yerkes's life.

[13]See Isaiah 40:6–8.
"All flesh is grass,
And all the goodliness thereof is as the
    flower of the field;
The grass withereth, the flower fadeth;
Because the breath of the LORD bloweth
    upon it—
Surely the people is grass.
The grass withereth, the flower fadeth;
But the word of our God shall stand for
    ever."

"Uh-uh. Never seen the name."

"There's nobody around here that uses crutches?"

He seemed to think, but it was Grebe's impression that he was simply waiting for a decent interval to pass.

"No, suh. Nobody I ever see."

"I've been looking for this man all afternoon"—Grebe spoke out with sudden force—"and I'm going to have to carry this check back to the station. It seems strange not to be able to find a person to *give* him something when you're looking for him for a good reason. I suppose if I had bad news for him I'd find him quick enough."

There was a responsive motion in the other man's face. "That's right, I reckon."

"It almost doesn't do any good to have a name if you can't be found by it. It doesn't stand for anything. He might as well not have any," he went on, smiling. It was as much of a concession as he could make of his desire to laugh.

"Well, now, there's a little old knot-back man I see once in a while. He might be the one you lookin' for. Downstairs."

"Where? Right side or left? Which door?"

"I don't know which. Thin-face little knot-back with a stick."

But no one answered at any of the doors on the first floor. He went to the end of the corridor, searching by matchlight, and found only a stairless exit to the yard, a drop of about six feet. But there was a bungalow near the alley, an old house like Mr. Field's. To jump was unsafe. He ran from the front door, through the underground passage and into the yard. The place was occupied. There was a light through the curtains, upstairs. The name on the ticket under the broken, scoop-shaped mailbox was Green! He exultantly rang the bell and pressed against the locked door. Then the lock clicked faintly and a long staircase opened before him. Someone was slowly coming down—a woman. He had the impression in the weak light that she was shaping her hair as she came, making herself presentable, for he saw her arms raised. But it was for support that they were raised; she was feeling her way downward, down the wall, stumbling. Next he wondered about the pressure of her feet on the treads; she did not seem to be wearing shoes. And it was a freezing stairway. His ring had got her out of bed, perhaps, and she had forgotten to put them on. And then he saw that she was not only shoeless but naked; she was entirely naked, climbing down while she talked to herself, a heavy woman, naked and drunk. She blundered into him. The contact of her breasts, though they touched only his coat, made him go back against the door with a blind shock. See what he had tracked down, in his hunting game!

The woman was saying to herself, furious with insult, "So I cain't——k, huh? I'll show that son-of-a-bitch kin I, cain't I."

What should he do now? Grebe asked himself. Why, he should go. He should turn away and go. He couldn't talk to this woman. He couldn't keep her standing naked in the cold. But when he tried he found himself unable to turn away.

He said, "Is this where Mr. Green lives?"

But she was still talking to herself and did not hear him.

"Is this Mr. Green's house?"

At last she turned her furious drunken glance on him. "What do you want?"

Again her eyes wandered from him; there was a dot of blood in their enraged brilliance. He wondered why she didn't feel the cold.

"I'm from the relief."

"Awright, what?"

"I've got a check for Tulliver Green."

This time she heard and put out her hand.

"No, no, for *Mr.* Green. He's got to sign," he said. How was he going to get Green's signature tonight!

"I'll take it. He cain't."

He desperately shook his head, thinking of Mr. Field's precautions about identification. "I can't let you have it. It's for him. Are you Mrs. Green?"

"Maybe I is, and maybe I ain't. Who want to know?"

"Is he upstairs?"

"Awright. Take it up yourself, you goddamn fool."

Sure, he was a goddamn fool. Of course he could not go up because Green would probably be drunk and naked, too. And perhaps he would appear on the landing soon. He looked eagerly upward. Under the light was a high narrow brown wall. Empty! It remained empty!

"Hell with you, then!" he heard her cry. To deliver a check for coal and clothes, he was keeping her in the cold. She did not feel it, but his face was burning with frost and self-ridicule. He backed away from her.

"I'll come tomorrow, tell him."

"Ah, hell with you. Don' never come. What you doin' here in the nighttime? Don' come back." She yelled so that he saw the breadth of her tongue. She stood astride in the long cold box of the hall and held on to the banister and the wall. The bungalow itself was shaped something like a box, a clumsy, high box pointing into the freezing air with its sharp, wintry lights.

"If you are Mrs. Green, I'll give you the check," he said, changing his mind.

"Give here, then." She took it, took the pen offered with it in her left hand, and tried to sign the receipt on the wall. He looked around, almost as though to see whether his madness was being observed, and came near believing someone was standing on a mountain of used tires in the auto-junking shop next door.

"But are you Mrs. Green?" he now thought to ask. But she was already climbing the stairs with the check, and it was too late, if he had made an error, if he was now in trouble, to undo the thing. But he wasn't going to worry about it. Though she might not be Mrs. Green, he was convinced that Mr. Green was upstairs. Whoever she was, the woman stood for Green, whom he was not to see this time. Well, you silly bastard, he said to himself, so you think you found him. So what? Maybe you really did find him—what of it? But it was important that there was a real Mr. Green whom they could not keep him from reaching because he seemed to come as an emissary from hostile appearances. And though the self-ridicule was slow to diminish, and his face still blazed with it, he had, nevertheless, a feeling of elation, too. "For after all," he said, "he *could* be found!"

1951

Gwendolyn Brooks 1917–2000

Gwendolyn Brooks, born in Topeka, Kansas, considered herself a lifelong Chicagoan. When she began writing at age seven, her mother predicted, "You are going to be the *lady* Paul Laurence Dunbar." First published at eleven, by sixteen Brooks was contributing poetry weekly to the *Chicago Defender.* In *Report from Part One,* she describes a happy childhood spent in black neighborhoods with her parents and younger brother Raymond. "Duty-loving" Keziah Wims Brooks had been a fifth grade teacher; she played the piano, wrote music, and published a book of stories at eighty-six. David Anderson Brooks, son of a runaway slave, was a janitor with "rich artistic abilities." He sang, told stories, and worked hard to purchase a house and support his family. Both parents nurtured their daughter's precocious gifts. "I had always felt that to be black was good," Brooks said in her autobiography.

Her home environment supported her confidence and fostered her black musical heritage, which centered creatively in church. At church she met James Weldon Johnson and Langston Hughes. The latter became an inspiration and, later, a friend and mentor.

Following graduation from Wilson Junior College (now Kennedy-King) in 1936, Brooks worked for a month as a maid in a North Shore home and then spent four unhappy months as secretary to the spiritual adviser who became the prototype for Prophet Williams in "In the Mecca." In 1939 she married Henry Lowington Blakely II, a fellow member of Inez Cunningham Stark's poetry workshop in the South Side Community Art Center. In 1950 she won the Pulitzer Prize for Poetry with *Annie Allen,* the first black writer to be so honored. That award was followed by two Guggenheim Fellowships, election to membership in the National Institute of Arts and Letters, and selection as Consultant in Poetry to the Library of Congress.

Finely crafted, influenced by Langston Hughes, T. S. Eliot, Emily Dickinson, and Robert Frost—and later by the 1960s Black Arts movement, Brooks's poetry was always a social act. *A Street in Bronzeville* addresses the realities of segregation for black Americans at home and in World War II military service; *Annie Allen* ironically explores post-war anti-romanticism. *Maud Martha,* her prose masterpiece, sketches a bildungsroman of black womanhood; *The Bean Eaters* and later poems sound the urgencies of the Civil Rights movement. In 1967 she attended the Second Fisk University Writers' Conference and was deeply impressed with the activism of Amiri Baraka. Subsequently, although she had always experimented with various forms, her work opened more distinctly to free verse, a notable feature of *In the Mecca* (1968).

Returning to Chicago from the Fisk Conference, Brooks conducted a workshop with the Blackstone Rangers, a teen gang, who were succeeded by young writers like Carolyn M. Rodgers and Haki R. Madhubuti (then don l. lee). Her new Black Nationalist perspective impelled her commitment to black publishing. In 1969 she turned to Dudley Randall's Broadside Press for publication of *Riot,* followed by *Family Pictures* and *Aloneness,* and to Madhubuti's Third World Press for *The Tiger Who Wore White Gloves* and *To Disembark.* In 1971, she began publishing a literary annual, *The Black Position,* under her own aegis. Starting with *Primer for Blacks* in 1980, she took charge of her creative work. Although many of her earlier books now issue from Third World Press, *Children Coming Home* was published in 1991 by The David Company, her own imprint.

Brooks traveled widely and constantly, giving workshops and readings in schools, libraries, and prisons. Her visits to Africa in 1971 and 1974 deepened her sense of African heritage. Yet her poetry marks the rich confluence and continuity of a dual stream: the black sermonic tradition and black music—the spiritual, the blues, and jazz; and white antecedents like the ballad, the sonnet, and conventional and free forms. It suggests connections with Anglo-Saxon alliteration and strong-stressed verse, with the Homeric bard and the African griot. Brooks's heroic and prophetic voice surfaces in what she called "preachments." Brooks intended that her work "'call' all black people."

D. H. Melhem
Independent Scholar

PRIMARY WORKS

A Street in Bronzeville, 1945; *Annie Allen,* 1949; *Maud Martha,* 1953; *Bronzeville Boys and Girls,* 1956; *The Bean Eaters,* 1960; *Selected Poems,* 1963; *In the Mecca,* 1968; *Riot,* 1969; *Family Pictures,* 1970; *Aloneness,* 1971; *Jump Bad,* 1971; *The World of Gwendolyn Brooks,* 1971; *Report from Part One,* 1972; *Beckonings,* 1975; *A Capsule Course in Black Poetry Writing,* 1975; *Primer for Blacks,* 1980; *Young Poet's Primer,* 1980; *To Disembark,* 1981; *Mayor Harold Washington and Chicago, the* I Will *City,* 1983; *Very Young Poets,* 1983; *The Near-Johannesburg Boy and Other Poems,* 1986; *Blacks* (omnibus), 1987; *Gottschalk and the Grande Tarantelle,* 1988; *Winnie,* 1991; *Children Coming Home,* 1991; *Report from Part Two,* 1996.

The Sundays of Satin-Legs Smith

Inamoratas, with an approbation,
Bestowed his title. Blessed his inclination.

He wakes, unwinds, elaborately: a cat
Tawny, reluctant, royal. He is fat
5   And fine this morning. Definite. Reimbursed.

He waits a moment, he designs his reign,
That no performance may be plain or vain.
Then rises in a clear delirium.

He sheds, with his pajamas, shabby days.
10   And his desertedness, his intricate fear, the
Postponed resentments and the prim precautions.

Now, at his bath, would you deny him lavender
Or take away the power of his pine?
What smelly substitute, heady as wine,
15   Would you provide? life must be aromatic.

There must be scent, somehow there must be some.
Would you have flowers in his life? suggest
Asters? a Really Good geranium?
A white carnation? would you prescribe a Show
20 With the cold lilies, formal chrysanthemum
Magnificence, poinsettias, and emphatic
Red of prize roses? might his happiest
Alternative (you muse) be, after all,
A bit of gentle garden in the best
25 Of taste and straight tradition? Maybe so.
But you forget, or did you ever know,
His heritage of cabbage and pigtails,
Old intimacy with alleys, garbage pails,
Down in the deep (but always beautiful) South
30 Where roses blush their blithest (it is said)
And sweet magnolias put Chanel to shame.

No! He has not a flower to his name.
Except a feather one, for his lapel.
Apart from that, if he should think of flowers
35 It is in terms of dandelions or death.
Ah, there is little hope. You might as well—
Unless you care to set the world a-boil
And do a lot of equalizing things,
Remove a little ermine, say, from kings,
40 Shake hands with paupers and appoint them men,
For instance—certainly you might as well
Leave him his lotion, lavender and oil.

Let us proceed. Let us inspect, together
With his meticulous and serious love,
45 The innards of this closet. Which is a vault
Whose glory is not diamonds, not pearls,
Not silver plate with just enough dull shine.
But wonder-suits in yellow and in wine,
Sarcastic green and zebra-striped cobalt.
50 All drapes. With shoulder padding that is wide
And cocky and determined as his pride;
Ballooning pants that taper off to ends
Scheduled to choke precisely.
                      Here are hats
55 Like bright umbrellas; and hysterical ties
Like narrow banners for some gathering war.

People are so in need, in need of help.
People want so much that they do not know.
Below the tinkling trade of little coins

60 The gold impulse not possible to show
    Or spend. Promise piled over and betrayed.

    These kneaded limbs receive the kiss of silk.
    Then they receive the brave and beautiful
    Embrace of some of that equivocal wool.
65 He looks into his mirror, loves himself—
    The neat curve here; the angularity
    That is appropriate at just its place;
    The technique of a variegated grace.

    Here is all his sculpture and his art
70 And all his architectural design.
    Perhaps you would prefer to this a fine
    Value of marble, complicated stone.
    Would have him think with horror of baroque,
    Rococo. You forget and you forget.

75 He dances down the hotel steps that keep
    Remnants of last night's high life and distress.
    As spat-out purchased kisses and spilled beer.
    He swallows sunshine with a secret yelp.
    Passes to coffee and a roll or two.
80 Has breakfasted.
                        Out. Sounds about him smear,
    Become a unit. He hears and does not hear
    The alarm clock meddling in somebody's sleep;
    Children's governed Sunday happiness;
85 The dry tone of a plane; a woman's oath;
    Consumption's spiritless expectoration;
    An indignant robin's resolute donation
    Pinching a track through apathy and din;
    Restaurant vendors weeping; and the L
90 That comes on like a slightly horrible thought.

    Pictures, too, as usual, are blurred.
    He sees and does not see the broken windows
    Hiding their shame with newsprint; little girl
    With ribbons decking wornness, little boy
95 Wearing the trousers with the decentest patch,
    To honor Sunday; women on their way
    From "service," temperate holiness arranged
    Ably on asking faces; men estranged
    From music and from wonder and from joy
100 But far familiar with the guiding awe
    Of foodlessness.
                        He loiters.
                                Restaurant vendors

Weep, or out of them rolls a restless glee.
105 The Lonesome Blues, the Long-lost Blues, I Want A
Big Fat Mama. Down these sore avenues
Comes no Saint-Saëns, no piquant elusive Grieg,
And not Tschaikovsky's wayward eloquence
And not the shapely tender drift of Brahms.
110 But could he love them? Since a man must bring
To music what his mother spanked him for
When he was two: bits of forgotten hate,
Devotion: whether or not his mattress hurts:
The little dream his father humored: the thing
115 His sister did for money: what he ate
For breakfast—and for dinner twenty years
Ago last autumn: all his skipped desserts.

The pasts of his ancestors lean against
Him. Crowd him. Fog out his identity.
120 Hundreds of hungers mingle with his own,
Hundreds of voices advise so dexterously
He quite considers his reactions his,
Judges he walks most powerfully alone,
That everything is—simply what it is.

125 But movie-time approaches, time to boo
The hero's kiss, and boo the heroine
Whose ivory and yellow it is sin
For his eye to eat of. The Mickey Mouse,
However, is for everyone in the house.

130 Squires his lady to dinner at Joe's Eats.
His lady alters as to leg and eye,
Thickness and height, such minor points as these,
From Sunday to Sunday. But no matter what
Her name or body positively she's
135 In Queen Lace stockings with ambitious heels
That strain to kiss the calves, and vivid shoes
Frontless and backless, Chinese fingernails,
Earrings, three layers of lipstick, intense hat
Dripping with the most voluble of veils.
140 Her affable extremes are like sweet bombs
About him, whom no middle grace or good
Could gratify. He had no education
In quiet arts of compromise. He would
Not understand your counsels on control, nor
145 Thank you for your late trouble.

At Joe's Eats
You get your fish or chicken on meat platters.

With coleslaw, macaroni, candied sweets,
Coffee and apple pie. You go out full.
150 (The end is—isn't it?—all that really matters.)

And even and intrepid come
The tender boots of night to home.

Her body is like new brown bread
Under the Woolworth mignonette.[1]
155 *Her body is a honey bowl*
Whose waiting honey is deep and hot.
Her body is like summer earth,
Receptive, soft, and absolute . . .

1945

The Mother

Abortions will not let you forget.
You remember the children you got that you did not get.
The damp small pulps with a little or with no hair,
The singers and workers that never handled the air.
5 You will never neglect or beat
Them, or silence or buy with a sweet.
You will never wind up the sucking-thumb
Or scuttle off ghosts that come.
You will never leave them, controlling your luscious sigh,
10 Return for a snack of them, with gobbling mother-eye.

I have heard in the voices of the wind the voices of my dim killed
    children.
I have contracted. I have eased
My dim dears at the breasts they could never suck.
15 I have said, Sweets, if I sinned, if I seized
Your luck
And your lives from your unfinished reach,
If I stole your births and your names,
Your straight baby tears and your games,

[1] An herb, native to northern Africa; here it refers to a narrow bobbin lace, having a scattered small design on a ground somewhat like tulle and made especially by the French and the Flemish in the sixteenth through the nineteenth centuries.

20 Your stilted or lovely loves, your tumults, your marriages, aches,
       and your deaths,
If I poisoned the beginnings of your breaths,
Believe that even in my deliberateness I was not deliberate.
Though why should I whine,
25 Whine that the crime was other than mine?—
Since anyhow you are dead.
Or rather, or instead,
You were never made.
But that too, I am afraid,
30 Is faulty: oh, what shall I say, how is the truth to be said?
You were born, you had body, you died.
It is just that you never giggled or planned or cried.

Believe me, I loved you all.
Believe me, I knew you, though faintly, and I loved, I loved you
35 All.

                                       1945

We Real Cool

The Pool Players.
Seven at the Golden Shovel.

We real cool. We
Left school. We

Lurk late. We
Strike straight. We

5 Sing sin. We
Thin gin. We

Jazz June.[1] We
Die soon.

                 1960

---

[1] A reference to popular music and enjoying the summer of youth.

A Bronzeville Mother Loiters in Mississippi. Meanwhile, a Mississippi Mother Burns Bacon[1]

From the first it had been like a
Ballad. It had the beat inevitable. It had the blood.
A wildness cut up, and tied in little bunches,
Like the four-line stanzas of the ballads she had never quite
5 Understood—the ballads they had set her to, in school.

Herself: the milk-white maid, the "maid mild"
Of the ballad. Pursued
By the Dark Villain. Rescued by the Fine Prince.
The Happiness-Ever-After.
10 That was worth anything.
It was good to be a "maid mild."
That made the breath go fast.

Her bacon burned. She
Hastened to hide it in the step-on can, and
15 Drew more strips from the meat case. The eggs and sour-milk
        biscuits
Did well. She set out a jar
Of her new quince preserve.

. . . But there was a something about the matter of the Dark
20   Villain.
He should have been older, perhaps.
The hacking down of a villain was more fun to think about
When his menace possessed undisputed breadth, undisputed
        height,
25 And a harsh kind of vice.
And best of all, when his history was cluttered
With the bones of many eaten knights and princesses.

The fun was disturbed, then all but nullified
When the Dark Villain was a blackish child
30 Of fourteen, with eyes still too young to be dirty,
And a mouth too young to have lost every reminder
Of its infant softness.
That boy must have been surprised! For
These were grown-ups. Grown-ups were supposed to be wise.

---

[1]Both this poem and the next concern the murder of Emmett Louis Till, a fourteen-year-old Chicago youth who was murdered in Mississippi on August 28, 1955, because he had "wolf-whistled" at a white woman.

35 And the Fine Prince—and that other—so tall, so broad, so
Grown! Perhaps the boy had never guessed
That the trouble with grown-ups was that under the magnificent
    shell of adulthood, just under,
Waited the baby full of tantrums.
40 It occurred to her that there may have been something
Ridiculous in the picture of the Fine Prince
Rushing (rich with the breadth and height and
Mature solidness whose lack, in the Dark Villain, was impressing
    her,
45 Confronting her more and more as this first day after the trial
And acquittal wore on) rushing
With his heavy companion to hack down (unhorsed)
That little foe.
So much had happened, she could not remember now what that
50   foe had done
Against her, or if anything had been done.
The one thing in the world that she did know and knew
With terrifying clarity was that her composition
Had disintegrated. That, although the pattern prevailed,
55 The breaks were everywhere. That she could think
Of no thread capable of the necessary
Sew-work.

She made the babies sit in their places at the table.
Then, before calling Him, she hurried
60 To the mirror with her comb and lipstick. It was necessary
To be more beautiful than ever.
The beautiful wife.
For sometimes she fancied he looked at her as though
Measuring her. As if he considered, Had she been worth It?
65 Had *she* been worth the blood, the cramped cries, the little
    stuttering bravado,
The gradual dulling of those Negro eyes,
The sudden, overwhelming *little-boyness* in that barn?
Whatever she might feel or half-feel, the lipstick necessity was
70   something apart. He must never conclude
That she had not been worth It.

He sat down, the Fine Prince, and
Began buttering a biscuit. He looked at his hands.
He twisted in his chair, he scratched his nose.
75 He glanced again, almost secretly, at his hands.
More papers were in from the North, he mumbled. More
    meddling headlines.
With their pepper-words, "bestiality," and "barbarism," and
"Shocking."

80　The half-sneers he had mastered for the trial worked across
　　His sweet and pretty face.

　　What he'd like to do, he explained, was kill them all.
　　The time lost. The unwanted fame.
85　Still, it had been fun to show those intruders
　　A thing or two. To show that snappy-eyed mother,
　　That sassy, Northern, brown-black——

　　Nothing could stop Mississippi.
　　He knew that. Big Fella
90　Knew that.
　　And, what was so good, Mississippi knew that.
　　Nothing and nothing could stop Mississippi.
　　They could send in their petitions, and scar
　　Their newspapers with bleeding headlines. Their governors
95　Could appeal to Washington. . . .

　　"What I want," the older baby said, "is 'lasses on my jam."
　　Whereupon the younger baby
　　Picked up the molasses pitcher and threw
　　The molasses in his brother's face. Instantly
100　The Fine Prince leaned across the table and slapped
　　The small and smiling criminal.

　　She did not speak. When the Hand
　　Came down and away, and she could look at her child,
　　At her baby-child,
105　She could think only of blood.
　　Surely her baby's cheek
　　Had disappeared, and in its place, surely,
　　Hung a heaviness, a lengthening red, a red that had no end.
　　She shook her head. It was not true, of course.
110　It was not true at all. The
　　Child's face was as always, the
　　Color of the paste in her paste-jar.

　　She left the table, to the tune of the children's lamentations, which
　　　　were shriller
115　Than ever. She
　　Looked out of a window. She said not a word. *That*
　　Was one of the new Somethings—
　　The fear,
　　Tying her as with iron.

120　Suddenly she felt his hands upon her. He had followed her
　　To the window. The children were whimpering now.

Such bits of tots. And she, their mother,
Could not protect them. She looked at her shoulders, still
Gripped in the claim of his hands. She tried, but could not resist
125 the idea
That a red ooze was seeping, spreading darkly, thickly, slowly,
Over her white shoulders, her own shoulders,
And over all of Earth and Mars.

He whispered something to her, did the Fine Prince, something
130 About love, something about love and night and intention.

She heard no hoof-beat of the horse and saw no flash of the
  shining steel.
He pulled her face around to meet
His, and there it was, close close,
135 For the first time in all those days and nights.
His mouth, wet and red,
So very, very, very red,
Closed over hers.

Then a sickness heaved within her. The courtroom Coca-Cola,
140 The courtroom beer and hate and sweat and drone,
Pushed like a wall against her. She wanted to bear it.
But his mouth would not go away and neither would the
Decapitated exclamation points in that Other Woman's eyes.

She did not scream.
145 She stood there.
But a hatred for him burst into glorious flower,
And its perfume enclasped them—big,
Bigger than all magnolias.

The last bleak news of the ballad.
150 The rest of the rugged music.
The last quatrain.

               1960

The Last Quatrain
of the Ballad of Emmett Till

              after the murder,
              after the burial

Emmett's mother is a pretty-faced thing;
  the tint of pulled taffy.

5 She sits in a red room,
      drinking black coffee.
  She kisses her killed boy.
      And she is sorry.
  Chaos in windy grays
10   through a red prairie.

                    1960

Ulysses[1]

Religion

At home we pray every morning, we
get down on our knees in a circle,
holding hands, holding Love,
and we sing Hallelujah.

5 Then we go into the World.

Daddy *speeds,* to break bread with his Girl Friend.
Mommy's a Boss. And a lesbian.
(She too has a nice Girl Friend.)

My brothers and sisters and I come to school.
10 We bring knives pistols bottles, little boxes, and cans.

We talk to the man who's cool at the playground gate.
Nobody Sees us, nobody stops our sin.

Our teachers feed us geography.
We spit it out in a hurry.

15 Now we are coming home.

At home, we pray every evening, we
get down on our knees in a circle,
holding hands, holding Love.

And we sing Hallelujah.

                              1991

---

[1]The name of one of the twenty children who are the personae represented by each poem in the book. Ulysses is the Roman name for Odysseus, a famous Greek warrior whose adventures and return home after twenty years are recounted in Homer's epic poem, *The Odyssey.*

Robert Lowell, Jr. 1917–1977

Born to Charlotte Winslow and Robert Traill Spence Lowell in Boston, Robert Lowell was the great-grandnephew of James Russell Lowell and a distant cousin of Amy Lowell. He attended St. Marks School and then Harvard (1935–37), but completed his undergraduate education at Kenyon College in Ohio (his degree was *summa cum laude* in 1940). An avid student of poetry, he chose his friends from an artistic coterie and in 1940 married fiction writer Jean Stafford. During World War II, declaring himself a conscientious objector, Lowell was imprisoned in 1943–44. In 1947 he received a Guggenheim fellowship and the Pulitzer Prize for Poetry (for *Lord Weary's Castle*). He also was chosen Consultant in Poetry for the Library of Congress for 1947–48. In 1948 he and Stafford were divorced, and in 1949 he married critic Elizabeth Hardwick.

Lowell's life was devoted to poetry—writing and teaching—but it was marred by emotional breakdowns that required hospitalization. His periodic instability made relationships troublesome; he tended to find his greatest solace in friendships with other writers (Delmore Schwartz, John Berryman, Randall Jarrell, Elizabeth Bishop, William Carlos Williams, Anne Sexton, and the countless younger writers who studied with him at Boston University, Harvard, and the University of Iowa). His writing charted his cycles of change: from the rebellion of the elite Brahmin to the immersion in art experienced at Kenyon, where Lowell studied with John Crowe Ransom and developed his penchant for allusive, densely referential poetry. In 1940 he became a Catholic; in 1950 he left the church.

After giving a series of readings on the West Coast in 1957, Lowell became dissatisfied with his tightly structured poems, and began the process of self-exploration that led to his masterful autobiographical work. *Life Studies* and *For the Union Dead,* the latter of which drew together the autobiographical and Lowell's fascination with history, marked the apex of Lowell's influence on the poetry scene. He also had moved to New York, where he remained until his death. There he became politically active, marching against the Pentagon in 1967 and continuing to scrutinize his life against the canvas of world and national events.

In the early 1970s, Lowell and Hardwick divorced and Lowell married Lady Caroline Blackwood. He then divided his life between her home in England and periods of teaching at Harvard, a pattern that allowed him to explore the consequences of his New England roots and his need to cut himself off from that locale. When he died of a heart attack at age sixty, he was considered the most important and most influential poet of his generation.

Some critics reacted harshly to his last poetry, in which the occasion of his divorce from Hardwick and the separation of himself from his child became the subject of his art. And there is some limit to a reader's interest in seeing self-destruction portrayed in poetry. Like many of his peers, Lowell led a life of difficult and often broken human relationships, and his poems which chart those relationships are often less than great.

Linda Wagner-Martin
University of North Carolina at Chapel Hill

PRIMARY WORKS

Land of Unlikeness, 1944; *Lord Weary's Castle,* 1946; *The Mills of the Kavanaughs,* 1951; *Life Studies,* 1959; *Imitations,* 1961; *For the Union Dead,* 1964; *The Old Glory* (plays), 1965; *Selected Poems,* 1965; *Near the Ocean,* 1967; *Notebook 1967–68,* 1969; *The Dolphin,* 1973; *History,* 1973; *For Lizzie and Harriet,* 1973; *Selected Poems,* 1976; *Day by Day,* 1977; *The Collected Prose,* 1987.

Memories of West Street and Lepke[1]

Only teaching on Tuesdays, book-worming
in pajamas fresh from the washer each morning,
I hog a whole house on Boston's
"hardly passionate Marlborough Street,"[2]
5   where even the man
scavenging filth in the back alley trash cans,
has two children, a beach wagon, a helpmate,
and is a "young Republican."
I have a nine months' daughter,
10   young enough to be my granddaughter.
Like the sun she rises in her flame-flamingo infants' wear.

These are the tranquillized *Fifties,*
and I am forty. Ought I to regret my seedtime?
I was a fire-breathing Catholic C.O.,[3]
15   and made my manic statement,
telling off the state and president, and then
sat waiting sentence in the bull pen
beside a Negro boy with curlicues
of marijuana in his hair.

20   Given a year,
I walked on the roof of the West Street Jail, a short
enclosure like my school soccer court,
and saw the Hudson River once a day
through sooty clothesline entanglements
25   and bleaching khaki tenements.
Strolling, I yammered metaphysics with Abramowitz,
a jaundice-yellow ("it's really tan")
and fly-weight pacifist,
so vegetarian,
30   he wore rope shoes and preferred fallen fruit.
He tried to convert Bioff and Brown,
the Hollywood pimps, to his diet.
Hairy, muscular, suburban,
wearing chocolate double-breasted suits,
35   they blew their tops and beat him black and blue.
I was so out of things, I'd never heard

---

[1] After being sentenced in 1944 to a year and a
day for refusing to comply with the draft law,
Lowell was first sent to the West Street Jail in
Manhattan. The most famous prisoner there at
the time was Louis ("Lepke") Buchalter

(1897–1944), union racketeer, gang boss, and
murderer, who was awaiting execution.
[2] Description by Henry James.
[3] Conscientious objector.

of the Jehovah's Witnesses.
"Are you a C.O.?" I asked a fellow jailbird.
"No," he answered, "I'm a J.W."
40 He taught me the "hospital tuck,"
and pointed out the T shirted back
of *Murder Incorporated's* Czar Lepke,
there piling towels on a rack,
or dawdling off to his little segregated cell full
45 of things forbidden the common man:
a portable radio, a dresser, two toy American
flags tied together with a ribbon of Easter palm.
Flabby, bald, lobotomized,
he drifted in a sheepish calm,
50 where no agonizing reappraisal
jarred his concentration on the electric chair—
hanging like an oasis in his air
of lost connections. . . .

1959

Skunk Hour

(For Elizabeth Bishop)

Nautilus Island's[1] hermit
heiress still lives through winter in her Spartan cottage;
her sheep still graze above the sea.
Her son's a bishop. Her farmer
5 is first selectman in our village;
she's in her dotage.

Thirsting for
the hierarchic privacy
of Queen Victoria's century,
10 she buys up all
the eyesores facing her shore,
and lets them fall.

The season's ill—
we've lost our summer millionaire,

[1]In Maine.

15 who seemed to leap from an L.L. Bean[2]
    catalogue. His nine-knot yawl
    was auctioned off to lobstermen.
    A red fox stain covers Blue Hill.

    And now our fairy
20 decorator brightens his shop for fall;
    his fishnet's filled with orange cork,
    orange, his cobbler's bench and awl;
    there is no money in his work,
    he'd rather marry.

25 One dark night,
    my Tudor Ford climbed the hill's skull;
    I watched for love-cars. Lights turned down,
    they lay together, hull to hull,
    where the graveyard shelves on the town. . . .
30 My mind's not right.

    A car radio bleats,
    "Love, O careless Love. . . ." I hear
    my ill-spirit sob in each blood cell,
    as if my hand were at its throat. . . .
35 I myself am hell;
    nobody's here—

    only skunks, that search
    in the moonlight for a bite to eat.
    They march on their soles up Main Street:
40 white stripes, moonstruck eyes' red fire
    under the chalk-dry and spar spire
    of the Trinitarian Church.

    I stand on top
    of our back steps and breathe the rich air—
45 a mother skunk with her column of kittens swills the garbage pail.
    She jabs her wedge-head in a cup
    of sour cream, drops her ostrich tail,
    and will not scare.

                                                      1960

---

[2]Freeport, Maine, mail-order house.

For Theodore Roethke

1908–1963

All night you wallowed through my sleep,
then in the morning you were lost
in the Maine sky—close, cold and gray,
smoke and smoke-colored cloud.

5 Sheeplike, unsociable reptilian, two
hell-divers splattered squawking on the water,
loons devolving to a monochrome.
You honored nature,

helpless, elemental creature.
10 The black stump of your hand
just touched the waters under the earth,
and left them quickened with your name. . . .

Now, you honor the mother,
Omnipresent,
15 she made you nonexistent,
the ocean's anchor, our high tide.

1963

For the Union Dead

"Relinquunt Omnia Servare Rem Publicam."[1]

The old South Boston Aquarium stands
in a Sahara of snow now. It's broken windows are boarded.
The bronze weathervane cod has lost half its scales.
The airy tanks are dry.

5 Once my nose crawled like a snail on the glass;
my hand tingled

---

[1] "They give up all else to serve the republic."

to burst the bubbles
drifting from the noses of the cowed, compliant fish.

My hand draws back. I often sigh still
10   for the dark downward and vegetating kingdom
of the fish and reptile. One morning last March,
I pressed against the new barbed and galvanized

fence on the Boston Common. Behind their cage,
yellow dinosaur steamshovels were grunting
15   as they cropped up tons of mush and grass
to gouge their underworld garage.

Parking spaces luxuriate like civic
sandpiles in the heart of Boston.
A girdle of orange, Puritan-pumpkin colored girders
20   braces the tingling Statehouse,

shaking over the excavations, as it faces Colonel Shaw
and his bell-cheeked Negro infantry
on St. Gaudens' shaking Civil War relief,[2]
propped by a plank splint against the garage's earthquake.

25   Two months after marching through Boston,
half the regiment was dead;
at the dedication,
William James could almost hear the bronze Negroes breathe.

Their monument sticks like a fishbone
30   in the city's throat.
Its Colonel is as lean
as a compass-needle.

He has an angry wrenlike vigilance,
a greyhound's gentle tautness;
35   he seems to wince at pleasure,
and suffocate for privacy.

He is out of bounds now. He rejoices in man's lovely,
peculiar power to choose life and die—
when he leads his black soldiers to death,
40   he cannot bend his back.

---

[2]On the edge of Boston Common stands a monument honoring Colonel Robert Shaw (1837–1863) and the African American troops of the 54th Massachusetts by the sculptor Augustus Saint-Gaudens (1848–1907). Shaw was killed, with many of his men, in South Carolina on July 18, 1863.

On a thousand small town New England greens,
the old white churches hold their air
of sparse, sincere rebellion; frayed flags
quilt the graveyards of the Grand Army of the Republic.

45 The stone statues of the abstract Union Soldier
grow slimmer and younger each year—
wasp-waisted they doze over muskets
and muse through their sideburns . . .

Shaw's father wanted no monument
50 except the ditch,
where his son's body was thrown
and lost with his "niggers."

The ditch is nearer.
There are no statues for the last war here;
55 on Boylston Street, a commercial photograph
shows Hiroshima boiling

over a Mosler Safe, the "Rock of Ages"
that survived the blast. Space is nearer.
When I crouch to my television set,
60 the drained faces of Negro school-children rise like balloons.

Colonel Shaw
is riding on his bubble,
he waits
for the blessèd break.

65 The Aquarium is gone. Everywhere,
giant finned cars nose forward like fish;
a savage servility
slides by on grease.

1960

Near the Ocean

(For E.H.L.)[1]

The house is filled. The last heartthrob
thrills through her flesh. The hero stands,
stunned by the applauding hands,
and lifts her head to please the mob . . .
5 No, young and starry-eyed, the brother
and sister wait before their mother,
old iron-bruises, powder, "Child,
these breasts . . ." He knows. And if she's killed

his treadmill heart will never rest—
10 his wet mouth pressed to some slack breast,
or shifting over on his back . . .
the severed radiance filters back,
athirst for nightlife—gorgon head,
fished up from the Aegean dead,
15 with all its stranded snakes uncoiled,
here beheaded and despoiled.

We hear the ocean. Older seas
and deserts give asylum, peace
to each abortion and mistake.
20 Lost in the Near Eastern dreck,
the tyrant and tyrannicide
lie like the bridegroom and the bride;
the battering ram, abandoned, prone,
beside the apeman's phallic stone.

25 Betrayals! Was it the first night?
They stood against a black and white
inland New England backdrop. No dogs
there, horse or hunter, only frogs
chirring from the dark trees and swamps.
30 Elms watching like extinguished lamps.
Knee-high hedges of black sheep
encircling them at every step.

Some subway-green coldwater flat,
its walls tattooed with neon light,
35 then high delirious squalor, food

[1]Elizabeth Hardwick Lowell, the poet's former wife.

burned down with vodka . . . menstrual blood
caking the covers, when they woke
to the dry, childless Sunday walk,
saw cars on Brooklyn Bridge descend
40 through steel and coal dust to land's end.

Was it years later when they met,
and summer's coarse last-quarter drought
had dried the hardveined elms to bark—
lying like people out of work,
45 dead sober, cured, recovered, on
the downslope of some gritty green,
all access barred with broken glass;
and dehydration browned the grass?

Is it this shore? Their eyes worn white
50 as moons from hitting bottom? Night,
the sandfleas scissoring their feet,
the sandbed cooling to concrete,
one borrowed blanket, lights of cars
shining down at them like stars? . . .
55 Sand built the lost Atlantis . . . sand,
Atlantic ocean, condoms, sand.

Sleep, sleep. The ocean, grinding stones,
can only speak the present tense;
nothing will age, nothing will last,
60 or take corruption from the past.
A hand, your hand then! I'm afraid
to touch the crisp hair on your head—
Monster loved for what you are,
till time, that buries us, lay bare.

1967

Hisaye Yamamoto b. 1921

Hisaye Yamamoto once said that she "didn't have any imagination" and that she "just *embroidered* on things that happened, or that people told [her] happened." The statement, though spoken out of her wonted modesty, reveals the extent to which personal and historical circumstances form the grist to her fictional mill. Born in Redondo Beach, California, Yamamoto was a child of Japanese immigrants. She started writing when she was a teenager and contributed regularly to Japanese American newspapers. During World War II she was interned for three years in Poston, Arizona, where she served as a reporter and a columnist for the *Poston Chronicle* (the camp newspaper) and published a serialized mystery. After the war she worked from 1945 to 1948 for the *Los Angeles Tribune,* a black weekly. Soon afterward her short stories began to appear in national journals, and she received a John Hay Whitney Foundation Opportunity Fellowship (1950–51). She was also encouraged by Yvor Winters to accept a Stanford Writing Fellowship, but chose instead to work from 1953 to 1955 as a volunteer in a Catholic Worker rehabilitation farm on Staten Island founded by Dorothy Day. She returned to Los Angeles after marrying Anthony DeSoto.

Yamamoto was one of the first Japanese American writers to gain national recognition after the war, when anti-Japanese sentiment was still rampant. Four of her short stories were listed as "Distinctive Short Stories" in Martha Foley's *Best American Short Stories* collections: "The High-Heeled Shoes" (1948), "The Brown House" (1951), "Yoneko's Earthquake" (1951), and "Epithalamium" (1960). "Yoneko's Earthquake" was also chosen as one of the *Best American Short Stories: 1952.* In 1986 she received from the Before Columbus Foundation the American Book Award for Lifetime Achievement.

Because Yamamoto excels in depicting Japanese American communal life, it is helpful to see her fiction in historical and social context. Most Japanese immigrants came to America between 1885 and 1924. The first waves of immigrants consisted mainly of single young men who saw North America as a land of opportunity. After establishing themselves in the new country, some returned to Japan to seek wives, while others arranged their marriages by means of an exchange of photographs across the Pacific. Hence a large number of Japanese "picture brides" came to this country after the turn of the century to meet bridegrooms they had never seen in person. By 1930 the American-born Nisei (second generation) already outnumbered the Issei (first generation), and about half of the Japanese American population lived in rural areas in the western U.S. Japanese was the language generally spoken at home, so that many Nisei (including Yamamoto) spoke only Japanese until they entered kindergarten.

Despite the preoccupation with survival in America, a number of Issei maintained their interest in Japanese poetry. There were literary groups engaged in the traditional forms of *haiku, tanka,* and *senryu,* and numerous magazines devoted to Issei poetry. Nisei, on the other hand, mostly expressed themselves in the English sections of Japanese American newspapers. The vibrant Japanese American literary movement was disrupted by the advent of World War II, when over 110,000 Japanese Americans were incarcerated under the Japanese Relocation Act of 1942.

The pre-war and postwar experiences of many Japanese Americans are reflected in the work of Yamamoto, who persistently explores the relationship between Issei men and women and between immigrant parents and their children. Because of the prevalence of arranged marriages among the Issei, compatibility between couples could hardly be assumed. In "Seventeen Syllables" it is through the naive perceptions of a Nisei daughter—Rosie—that we glimpse the dark nuances of Issei silences. While intergenerational differences are not peculiar to Japanese Americans, the gap between the Issei and the Nisei is widened by language and cultural barriers. Rosie's inability to appreciate her mother's Japanese haiku bespeaks her more general incomprehension of her mother's life story. The child's partial understanding allows Yamamoto to tell the mother's story obliquely.

King-Kok Cheung
University of California at Los Angeles

PRIMARY WORKS

Seventeen Syllables and Other Stories, 1988.

Seventeen Syllables

The first Rosie knew that her mother had taken to writing poems was one evening when she finished one and read it aloud for her daughter's approval. It was about cats, and Rosie pretended to understand it thoroughly and appreciate it no end, partly because she hesitated to disillusion her mother about the quantity and quality of Japanese she had learned in all the years now that she had been going to Japanese school every Saturday (and Wednesday, too, in the summer). Even so, her mother must have been skeptical about the depth of Rosie's understanding, because she explained afterwards about the kind of poem she was trying to write.

See, Rosie, she said, it was a *haiku,* a poem in which she must pack all her meaning into seventeen syllables only, which were divided into three lines of five, seven, and five syllables. In the one she had just read, she had tried to capture the charm of a kitten, as well as comment on the superstition that owning a cat of three colors meant good luck.

"Yes, yes, I understand. How utterly lovely," Rosie said, and her mother, either satisfied or seeing through the deception and resigned, went back to composing.

The truth was that Rosie was lazy; English lay ready on the tongue but Japanese had to be searched for and examined, and even then put forth tentatively (probably to meet with laughter). It was so much easier to say yes, yes, even when one meant no, no. Besides, this was what was in her mind to say: I was looking through one of your magazines from Japan last night, Mother, and towards the back I found some *haiku* in English that delighted me. There was one that made me giggle off and on until I fell asleep—

> It is morning, and lo!
> I lie awake, comme il faut,
> sighing for some dough.

Now, how to reach her mother, how to communicate the melancholy song? Rosie knew formal Japanese by fits and starts, her mother had even less English, no French. It was much more possible to say yes, yes.

It developed that her mother was writing the *haiku* for a daily newspaper, the *Mainichi Shimbun,* that was published in San Francisco. Los Angeles, to be sure, was closer to the farming community in which the Hayashi family lived and several Japanese vernaculars were printed there, but Rosie's parents said they preferred the tone of the northern paper. Once a week, the *Mainichi* would have a section devoted to *haiku,* and her mother became an extravagant contributor, taking for herself the blossoming pen name, Ume Hanazono.

So Rosie and her father lived for awhile with two women, her mother and Ume Hanazono. Her mother (Tome Hayashi by name) kept house, cooked, washed, and, along with her husband and the Carrascos, the Mexican family hired for the harvest, did her ample share of picking tomatoes out in the sweltering fields and boxing them in tidy strata in the cool packing shed. Ume Hanazono, who came to life after the dinner dishes were done, was an earnest, muttering stranger who often neglected speaking when spoken to and stayed busy at the parlor table as late as midnight scribbling with pencil on scratch paper or carefully copying characters on good paper with her fat, pale green Parker.

The new interest had some repercussions on the household routine. Before, Rosie had been accustomed to her parents and herself taking their hot baths early and going to bed almost immediately afterwards, unless her parents challenged each other to a game of flower cards or unless company dropped in. Now if her father wanted to play cards, he had to resort to solitaire (at which he always cheated fearlessly), and if a group of friends came over, it was bound to contain someone who was also writing *haiku,* and the small assemblage would be split in two, her father entertaining the non-literary members and her mother comparing ecstatic notes with the visiting poet.

If they went out, it was more of the same thing. But Ume Hanazono's life span, even for a poet's, was very brief—perhaps three months at most.

One night they went over to see the Hayano family in the neighboring town to the west, an adventure both painful and attractive to Rosie. It was attractive because there were four Hayano girls, all lovely and each one named after a season of the year (Haru, Natsu, Aki, Fuyu), painful because something had been wrong with Mrs. Hayano ever since the birth of her first child. Rosie would sometimes watch Mrs. Hayano, reputed to have been the belle of her native village, making her way about a room, stooped, slowly shuffling, violently trembling (*always* trembling), and she would be reminded that this woman, in this same condition, had carried and given issue to three babies. She would look wonderingly at Mr. Hayano, handsome, tall, and strong, and she would look at her four pretty friends. But it was not a matter she could come to any decision about.

On this visit, however, Mrs. Hayano sat all evening in the rocker, as motionless and unobtrusive as it was possible for her to be, and Rosie found the greater part of the evening practically anaesthetic. Too, Rosie spent most of it in the girls' room, because Haru, the garrulous one, said almost as soon as the bows and other greetings were over, "Oh, you must see my new coat!"

It was a pale plaid of grey, sand, and blue, with an enormous collar, and Rosie, seeing nothing special in it, said, "Gee, how nice."

"Nice?" said Haru, indignantly. "Is that all you can say about it? It's gorgeous! And so cheap, too. Only seventeen-ninety-eight, because it was a sale. The saleslady said it was twenty-five dollars regular."

"Gee," said Rosie. Natsu, who never said much and when she said anything said it shyly, fingered the coat covetously and Haru pulled it away.

"Mine," she said, putting it on. She minced in the aisle between the two large beds and smiled happily. "Let's see how your mother likes it."

She broke into the front room and the adult conversation and went to stand in front of Rosie's mother, while the rest watched from the door. Rosie's mother was properly envious. "May I inherit it when you're through with it?"

Haru, pleased, giggled and said yes, she could, but Natsu reminded gravely from the door, "You promised me, Haru."

Everyone laughed but Natsu, who shamefacedly retreated into the bedroom. Haru came in laughing, taking off the coat. "We were only kidding, Natsu," she said. "Here, you try it on now."

After Natsu buttoned herself into the coat, inspected herself solemnly in the bureau mirror, and reluctantly shed it, Rosie, Aki, and Fuyu got their turns, and Fuyu, who was eight, drowned in it while her sisters and Rosie doubled up in amusement. They all went into the front room later, because Haru's mother quaveringly called to her to fix the tea and rice cakes and open a can of sliced peaches for everybody. Rosie noticed that her mother and Mr. Hayano were talking together at the little table— they were discussing a *haiku* that Mr. Hayano was planning to send to the *Mainichi,* while her father was sitting at one end of the sofa looking through a copy of *Life,* the new picture magazine. Occasionally, her father would comment on a photograph, holding it toward Mrs. Hayano and speaking to her as he always did—loudly, as though he thought someone such as she must surely be at least a trifle deaf also.

The five girls had their refreshments at the kitchen table, and it was while Rosie was showing the sisters her trick of swallowing peach slices without chewing (she chased each slippery crescent down with a swig of tea) that her father brought his empty teacup and untouched saucer to the sink and said, "Come on, Rosie, we're going home now."

"Already?" asked Rosie.

"Work tomorrow," he said.

He sounded irritated, and Rosie, puzzled, gulped one last yellow slice and stood up to go, while the sisters began protesting, as was their wont.

"We have to get up at five-thirty," he told them, going into the front room quickly, so that they did not have their usual chance to hang onto his hands and plead for an extension of time.

Rosie, following, saw that her mother and Mr. Hayano were sipping tea and still talking together, while Mrs. Hayano concentrated, quivering, on raising the handleless Japanese cup to her lips with both her hands and lowering it back to her lap. Her father, saying nothing, went out the door, onto the bright porch, and down the steps. Her mother looked up and asked, "Where is he going?"

"Where is he going?" Rosie said. "He said we were going home now."

"Going home?" Her mother looked with embarrassment at Mr. Hayano and his absorbed wife and then forced a smile. "He must be tired," she said.

Haru was not giving up yet. "May Rosie stay overnight?" she asked, and Natsu, Aki, and Fuyu came to reinforce their sister's plea by helping her make a circle around Rosie's mother. Rosie, for once having no desire to stay, was relieved when her mother, apologizing to the perturbed Mr. and Mrs. Hayano for her father's abruptness at the same time, managed to shake her head no at the quartet, kindly but adamant, so that they broke their circle and let her go.

Rosie's father looked ahead into the windshield as the two joined him. "I'm sorry," her mother said. "You must be tired." Her father, stepping on the starter, said nothing. "You know how I get when it's *haiku,*" she continued, "I forget what time it is." He only grunted.

As they rode homeward silently, Rosie, sitting between, felt a rush of hate for both—for her mother for begging, for her father for denying her mother. I wish this old Ford would crash, right now, she thought, then immediately, no, no, I wish my father would laugh, but it was too late: already the vision had passed through her mind of the green pick-up crumpled in the dark against one of the mighty eucalyptus trees they were just riding past, of the three contorted, bleeding bodies, one of them hers.

Rosie ran between two patches of tomatoes, her heart working more rambunctiously than she had ever known it to. How lucky it was that Aunt Taka and Uncle Gimpachi had come tonight, though, how very lucky. Otherwise she might not have really kept her half-promise to meet Jesus Carrasco. Jesus was going to be a senior in

September at the same school she went to, and his parents were the ones helping with the tomatoes this year. She and Jesus, who hardly remembered seeing each other at Cleveland High where there were so many other people and two whole grades between them, had become great friends this summer—he always had a joke for her when he periodically drove the loaded pick-up up from the fields to the shed where she was usually sorting while her mother and father did the packing, and they laughed a great deal together over infinitesimal repartee during the afternoon break for chilled watermelon or ice cream in the shade of the shed.

What she enjoyed most was racing him to see which could finish picking a double row first. He, who could work faster, would tease her by slowing down until she thought she would surely pass him this time, then speeding up furiously to leave her several sprawling vines behind. Once he had made her screech hideously by crossing over, while her back was turned, to place atop the tomatoes in her green-stained bucket a truly monstrous, pale green worm (it had looked more like an infant snake). And it was when they had finished a contest this morning, after she had pantingly pointed a green finger at the immature tomatoes evident in the lugs at the end of his row and he had returned the accusation (with justice), that he had startlingly brought up the matter of their possibly meeting outside the range of both their parents' dubious eyes.

"What for?" she had asked.

"I've got a secret I want to tell you," he said.

"Tell me now," she demanded.

"It won't be ready till tonight," he said.

She laughed. "Tell me tomorrow then."

"It'll be gone tomorrow," he threatened.

"Well, for seven hakes, what is it?" she had asked, more than twice, and when he had suggested that the packing shed would be an appropriate place to find out, she had cautiously answered maybe. She had not been certain she was going to keep the appointment until the arrival of mother's sister and her husband. Their coming seemed a sort of signal of permission, of grace, and she had definitely made up her mind to lie and leave as she was bowing them welcome.

So as soon as everyone appeared settled back for the evening, she announced loudly that she was going to the privy outside, "I'm going to the *benjo!*" and slipped out the door. And now that she was actually on her way, her heart pumped in such an undisciplined way that she could hear it with her ears. It's because I'm running, she told herself, slowing to a walk. The shed was up ahead, one more patch away, in the middle of the fields. Its bulk, looming in the dimness, took on a sinisterness that was funny when Rosie reminded herself that it was only a wooden frame with a canvas roof and three canvas walls that made a slapping noise on breezy days.

Jesus was sitting on the narrow plank that was the sorting platform and she went around to the other side and jumped backwards to seat herself on the rim of a packing stand. "Well, tell me," she said without greeting, thinking her voice sounded reassuringly familiar.

"I saw you coming out the door," Jesus said. "I heard you running part of the way, too."

"Uh-huh," Rosie said. "Now tell me the secret."

"I was afraid you wouldn't come," he said.

Rosie delved around on the chicken-wire bottom of the stall for number two tomatoes, ripe, which she was sitting beside, and came up with a left-over that felt edible. She bit into it and began sucking out the pulp and seeds. "I'm here," she pointed out.

"Rosie, are you sorry you came?"

"Sorry? What for?" she said. "You said you were going to tell me something."

"I will, I will," Jesus said, but his voice contained disappointment, and Rosie fleetingly felt the older of the two, realizing a brand-new power which vanished without category under her recognition.

"I have to go back in a minute," she said. "My aunt and uncle are here from Wintersburg. I told them I was going to the privy."

Jesus laughed. "You funny thing," he said. "You slay me!"

"Just because you have a bathroom *inside,*" Rosie said. "Come on, tell me."

Chuckling, Jesus came around to lean on the stand facing her. They still could not see each other very clearly, but Rosie noticed that Jesus became very sober again as he took the hollow tomato from her hand and dropped it back into the stall. When he took hold of her empty hand, she could find no words to protest; her vocabulary had become distressingly constricted and she thought desperately that all that remained intact now was yes and no and oh, and even these few sounds would not easily out. Thus, kissed by Jesus, Rosie fell for the first time entirely victim to a helplessness delectable beyond speech. But the terrible, beautiful sensation lasted no more than a second, and the reality of Jesus' lips and tongue and teeth and hands made her pull away with such strength that she nearly tumbled.

Rosie stopped running as she approached the lights from the windows of home. How long since she had left? She could not guess, but gasping yet, she went to the privy in back and locked herself in. Her own breathing deafened her in the dark, close space, and she sat and waited until she could hear at last the nightly calling of the frogs and crickets. Even then, all she could think to say was oh, my, and the pressure of Jesus' face against her face would not leave.

No one had missed her in the parlor, however, and Rosie walked in and through quickly, announcing that she was next going to take a bath. "Your father's in the bathhouse," her mother said, and Rosie, in her room, recalled that she had not seen him when she entered. There had been only Aunt Taka and Uncle Gimpachi with her mother at the table, drinking tea. She got her robe and straw sandals and crossed the parlor again to go outside. Her mother was telling them about the *haiku* competition in the *Mainichi* and the poem she had entered.

Rosie met her father coming out of the bathhouse. "Are you through Father?" she asked. "I was going to ask you to scrub my back."

"Scrub your own back," he said shortly, going toward the main house.

"What have I done now?" she yelled after him. She suddenly felt like doing a lot of yelling. But he did not answer, and she went into the bathhouse. Turning on the dangling light, she removed her denims and T-shirt and threw them in the big carton for dirty clothes standing next to the washing machine. Her other things she took with her into the bath compartment to wash after her bath. After she had scooped a basin of hot water from the square wooden tub, she sat on the grey cement of the floor and soaped herself at exaggerated leisure, singing "Red Sails in the Sunset" at the top of her voice and using da-da-da where she suspected her words. Then, standing up, still singing, for she was possessed by the notion that any attempt now to analyze would result in spoilage and she believed that the larger her volume the less she would be able to hear herself think, she obtained more hot water and poured it on until she was free of lather. Only then did she allow herself to step into the steaming vat, one leg first, then the remainder of her body inch by inch until the water no longer stung and she could move around at will.

She took a long time soaking, afterwards remembering to go around outside to stoke the embers of the tin-lined fireplace beneath the tub and to throw on a few more sticks so that the water might keep its heat for her mother, and when she finally returned to the parlor, she found her mother still talking *haiku* with her aunt and uncle, the three of them on another round of tea. Her father was nowhere in sight.

At Japanese school the next day (Wednesday, it was), Rosie was grave and giddy by turns. Preoccupied at her desk in the row for students on Book Eight, she made up for it at recess by performing wild mimicry for the benefit of her friend Chizuko. She held her nose and whined a witticism or two in what she considered was the manner of Fred Allen; she assumed intoxication and a British accent to go over the climax of the Rudy Vallee recording of the pub conversation about William Ewart Gladstone; she was the child Shirley Temple piping, "On the Good Ship Lollipop"; she was the gentleman soprano of the Four Inkspots trilling, "If I Didn't Care." And she felt reasonably satisfied when Chizuko wept and gasped, "Oh, Rosie, you ought to be in the movies!"

Her father came after her at noon, bringing her sandwiches of minced ham and two nectarines to eat while she rode, so that she could pitch right into the sorting when they got home. The lugs were piling up, he said, and the ripe tomatoes in them would probably have to be taken to the cannery tomorrow if they were not ready for the produce haulers tonight. "This heat's not doing them any good. And we've got no time for a break today."

It *was* hot, probably the hottest day of the year, and Rosie's blouse stuck damply to her back even under the protection of the canvas. But she worked as efficiently as a flawless machine and kept the stalls heaped, with one part of her mind listening in to the parental murmuring about the heat and the tomatoes and with another part planning the exact words she would say to Jesus when he drove up with the first load of the afternoon. But when at last she saw that the pick-up was coming, her hands went berserk and the tomatoes started falling in the wrong stalls, and her father said, "Hey, hey! Rosie, watch what you're doing!"

"Well, I have to go to the *benjo,*" she said, hiding panic.

"Go in the weeds over there," he said, only half-joking.

"Oh, Father!" she protested.

"Oh, go on home," her mother said. "We'll make out for awhile."

In the privy Rosie peered through a knothole toward the fields, watching as much as she could of Jesus. Happily she thought she saw him look in the direction of the house from time to time before he finished unloading and went back toward the patch where his mother and father worked. As she was heading for the shed, a very presentable black car purred up the dirt driveway to the house and its driver motioned to her. Was this the Hayashi home, he wanted to know. She nodded. Was she a Hayashi? Yes, she said, thinking that he was a good-looking man. He got out of the car with a huge, flat package and she saw that he warmly wore a business suit. "I have something here for your mother then," he said, in a more elegant Japanese than she was used to.

She told him where her mother was and he came along with her, patting his face with an immaculate white handkerchief and saying something about the coolness of San Francisco. To her surprised mother and father, he bowed and introduced himself as, among other things, the *haiku* editor of the *Mainichi Shimbun,* saying that since he had been coming as far as Los Angeles anyway, he had decided to bring her the first prize she had won in the recent contest.

"First prize?" her mother echoed, believing and not believing, pleased and overwhelmed. Handed the package with a bow, she bobbed her head up and down numerous times to express her utter gratitude.

"It is nothing much," he added, "but I hope it will serve as a token of our great appreciation for your contributions and our great admiration of your considerable talent."

"I am not worthy," she said, falling easily into his style. "It is I who should make some sign of my humble thanks for being permitted to contribute."

"No, no, to the contrary," he said, bowing again.

But Rosie's mother insisted, and then saying that she knew she was being unorthodox, she asked if she might open the package because her curiosity was so great. Certainly she might. In fact, he would like her reaction to it, for personally, it was one of his favorite *Hiroshiges.*

Rosie thought it was a pleasant picture, which looked to have been sketched with delicate quickness. There were pink clouds, containing some graceful calligraphy, and a sea that was a pale blue except at the edges, containing four sampans with indications of people in them. Pines edged the water and on the far-off beach there was a cluster of thatched huts towered over by pine-dotted mountains of grey and blue. The frame was scalloped and gilt.

After Rosie's mother pronounced it without peer and somewhat prodded her father into nodding agreement, she said Mr. Kuroda must at least have a cup of tea after coming all this way, and although Mr. Kuroda did not want to impose, he soon agreed that a cup of tea would be refreshing and went along with her to the house, carrying the picture for her.

"Ha, your mother's crazy!" Rosie's father said, and Rosie laughed uneasily as she resumed judgment on the tomatoes. She had emptied six lugs when he broke into an imaginary conversation with Jesus to tell her to go and remind her mother of the tomatoes, and she went slowly.

Mr. Kuroda was in his shirtsleeves expounding some *haiku* theory as he munched a rice cake, and her mother was rapt. Abashed in the great man's presence, Rosie stood next to her mother's chair until her mother looked up inquiringly, and then she started to whisper the message, but her mother pushed her gently away and reproached, "You are not being very polite to our guest."

"Father says the tomatoes . . ." Rosie said aloud, smiling foolishly.

"Tell him I shall only be a minute," her mother said, speaking the language of Mr. Kuroda.

When Rosie carried the reply to her father, he did not seem to hear and she said again, "Mother says she'll be back in a minute."

"All right, all right," he nodded, and they worked again in silence. But suddenly, her father uttered an incredible noise, exactly like the cork of a bottle popping, and the next Rosie knew, he was stalking angrily toward the house, almost running in fact, and she chased after him crying, "Father! Father! What are you going to do?"

He stopped long enough to order her back to the shed. "Never mind!" he shouted, "Get on with the sorting!"

And from the place in the fields where she stood, frightened and vacillating, Rosie saw her father enter the house. Soon Mr. Kuroda came out alone, putting on his coat. Mr. Kuroda got into his car and backed out down the driveway onto the highway. Next her father emerged, also alone, something in his arms (it was the picture, she realized), and, going over to the bathhouse woodpile, he threw the picture on the ground and picked up the axe. Smashing the picture, glass and all (she heard the explosion faintly), he reached over for the kerosene that was used to encourage the bath fire and poured it over the wreckage. I am dreaming, Rosie said to herself, I am dreaming, but her father, having made sure that his act of cremation was irrevocable, was even then returning to the fields.

Rosie ran past him and toward the house. What had become of her mother? She burst into the parlor and found her mother at the back window watching the dying fire. They watched together until there remained only a feeble smoke under the blazing sun. Her mother was very calm.

"Do you know why I married your father?" she said without turning.

"No," said Rosie. It was the most frightening question she had ever been called upon to answer. Don't tell me now, she wanted to say, tell me tomorrow, tell me next week, don't tell me today. But she knew she would be told now, that the telling would combine with the other violence of the hot afternoon to level her life, her world to the very ground.

It was like a story out of the magazines illustrated in sepia, which she had consumed so greedily for a period until the information had somehow reached her that those wretchedly unhappy autobiographies, offered to her as the testimonials of living men and women, were largely inventions: Her mother, at nineteen, had come to America and married her father as an alternative to suicide.

At eighteen she had been in love with the first son of one of the well-to-do families in her village. The two had met whenever and wherever they could, secretly, because it would not have done for his family to see him favor her—her father had no money; he was a drunkard and a gambler besides. She had learned she was with child; an excellent match had already been arranged for her lover. Despised by her family, she had given premature birth to a stillborn son, who would be seventeen now. Her family did not turn her out, but she could no longer project herself in any direction without refreshing in them the memory of her indiscretion. She wrote to Aunt Taka, her favorite sister in America, threatening to kill herself if Aunt Taka would not send for her. Aunt Taka hastily arranged a marriage with a young man of whom she knew, but lately arrived from Japan, a young man of simple mind, it was said, but of kindly heart. The young man was never told why his unseen betrothed was so eager to hasten the day of meeting.

The story was told perfectly, with neither groping for words nor untoward passion. It was as though her mother had memorized it by heart, reciting it to herself so many times over that its nagging vileness had long since gone.

"I had a brother then?" Rosie asked, for this was what seemed to matter now; she would think about the other later, she assured herself, pushing back the illumination which threatened all that darkness that had hitherto been merely mysterious or even glamorous. "A half-brother?"

"Yes."

"I would have liked a brother," she said.

Suddenly, her mother knelt on the floor and took her by the wrists. "Rosie," she said urgently, "Promise me you will never marry!" Shocked more by the request than the revelation, Rosie stared at her mother's face. Jesus, Jesus, she called silently, not certain whether she was invoking the help of the son of the Carrascos or of God, until there returned sweetly the memory of Jesus' hand, how it had touched her and where. Still her mother waited for an answer, holding her wrists so tightly that her hands were going numb. She tried to pull free. Promise, her mother whispered fiercely, promise. Yes, yes, I promise, Rosie said. But for an instant she turned away, and her mother, hearing the familiar glib agreement, released her. Oh, you, you, you, her eyes and twisted mouth said, you fool. Rosie, covering her face, began at last to cry, and the embrace and consoling hand came much later than she expected.

1949

Grace Paley 1922–2007

Grace Paley was born to Isaac and Mary Goodside, Russian Jewish immigrants full of secular and socialist ideas gleaned from the intellectual ferment that preceded the Russian Revolution of 1917. Although her father, a doctor, influenced her love of Russian literature, both parents encouraged her intellectual precocity and political activism.

For a while Paley attended Hunter College and New York University, but a consuming interest in ordinary lives, a resistance to institutional authority, caused her to drop out. In 1942 at the age of twenty she married Jess Paley, a photographer, and later bore a son and a daughter. After they were divorced, Paley married Robert Nichols, a poet and playwright. Despite the vicissitudes inherent in raising children and working at marginal jobs, she found time to perfect her writing craft. Three small short story collections, *The Little Disturbances of Man,* 1959; *Enor-*

mous Changes at the Last Minute, 1974; and *Later the Same Day,* 1985 have established her reputation as a unique, virtually inimitable contemporary writer. In 1961 she was awarded a Guggenheim fellowship in fiction, and in 1970 received both a National Council on the Arts grant and a National Institute of Arts and Letters award for short story writing.

The titles of Paley's collections suggest the stories' themes: the irrepressible life force underlying the daily lives of New York working-class men and women; human courage in the face of aging and loss; the willingness to take risks which ensure the possibility of change within their lifetimes. Paley's readers will discover more: loose vignettes artfully fragmented, the precise metaphors of a poet, characters created through conversations articulated with an impeccable ear for the varied tones, rhythms, and cadences of New York speech. Paley's style creates small worlds, allowing readers to see what William Blake in another context called "the world in a grain of sand." Above all, Paley's is an extraordinary narrative voice, sassy, ironic, always authoritative, insistently faithful to pacifist and feminist ideals.

Paley's abiding love for independent-minded children extended later to include their feisty mothers resisting boorish husbands; involving themselves in love affairs, playground politics, and an activism ranging from the fight for drug-free schools, to vehement opposition to the Vietnam War, and the ongoing resistance to nuclear proliferation. Until her death she remained engaged politically and personally, an iconoclast loudly debunking patriarchal institutions denying life-affirming choice. All of her stories embody this engagement.

In fact "The Expensive Moment" is best summarized as *expansive,* to include women beyond the confines of Vesey Street, namely, Xie Feng, sent as a delegate to a woman's convention from mainland China during a lull in the Cold War and after the Cultural Revolution. Ruthie, who has been to China, met Xie Feng in China; the latter understands her fears about Rachel, since Xie Feng's children were left against her will with harsh grandparents. As Faith and Xie Feng wander throughout the urban, ethnic neighborhood where Faith recapitulates for her friend's benefit, the places where she has come of age, loved, married, divorced, fought to make life safer and saner for her children, they are joined by Ruthie. All three women bond in mutual concern over their children and are united by the nagging question of whether in violent and dangerous times they have raised them to be resilient, compassionate, and responsible human beings.

Rose Yalow Kamel
Philadelphia College of Pharmacy
and Science

PRIMARY WORKS

The Little Disturbances of Man. Stories of Men and Women at Love, 1959; *Enormous Changes at the Last Minute,* 1974; *Later the Same Day,* 1985; *Leaning Forward,* 1985; *Long Walks and Intimate Talks,* 1991; *New and Collected Poems,* 1992; *Collected Stories,* 1994; *Just as I Thought,* 1998; *Begin Again: The Collected Poems of Grace Paley,* 2000.

The Expensive Moment

Faith did not tell Jack.

At about two in the afternoon she went to visit Nick Hegstraw, the famous sinologist.[1] He was not famous in the whole world. He was famous in their neighborhood and in the adjoining neighborhoods, north, south, and east. He was studying China, he said, in order to free us all of distance and mystery. But because of foolish remarks that were immediately published, he had been excluded from wonderful visits to China's new green parlor. He sometimes felt insufficiently informed. Hundreds of people who knew nothing about Han and Da tung visited, returned, wrote articles; one friend with about seventy-five Chinese words had made a three-hour documentary. Well, sometimes he did believe in socialism and sometimes only in the

[1]One who makes a study of the Chinese language and its civilization.

Late T'ang. It's hard to stand behind a people and culture in revolutionary transition when you are constantly worried about their irreplaceable and breakable artifacts.

He was noticeably handsome, the way men are every now and then, with a face full of good architectural planning. (Good use of face space, Jack said.) In the hardware store or in line at the local movie, women and men would look at him. They might turn away saying, Not my type, or, Where have I seen him before? TV? Actually they had seen him at the vegetable market. As an unmarried vegetarian sinologist he bought bagfuls of broccoli and waited with other eaters for snow peas from California at $4.79 a pound.

Are you lovers? Ruth asked.

Oh God, no. I'm pretty monogamous when I'm monogamous. Why are you laughing?

You're lying. Really, Faith, why did you describe him at such length? You don't usually do that.

But the fun of talking, Ruthy. What about that? It's as good as fucking lots of times. Isn't it?

Oh boy, Ruth said, if it's that good, then it's got to be that bad.

At lunch Jack said, Ruth is not a Chinese cook. She doesn't mince words. She doesn't sauté a lot of imperial verbs and docile predicates like some women.

Faith left the room. Someday, she said, I'm never coming back.

But I love the way Jack talks, said Ruth. He's a true gossip like us. And another thing, he's the only one who ever asks me anymore about Rachel.

Don't trust him, said Faith.

After Faith slammed the door, Jack decided to buy a pipe so he could smoke thoughtfully in the evening. He wished he had a new dog or a new child or a new wife. He had none of these things because he only thought about them once in ten days and then only for about five minutes. The interest in sustained shopping or courtship had left him. He was a busy man selling discount furniture in a rough neighborhood during the day, and reading reading reading, thinking writing grieving all night the bad world-ending politics which were using up the last years of his life. Oh, come back, come back, he cried. Faith! At least for supper.

On this particular afternoon, Nick (the sinologist) said, How are your children? Fine, she said. Tonto is in love and Richard has officially joined the League for Revolutionary Youth.

Ah, said Nick. L.R.Y. I spoke at one of their meetings last month. They threw half a pizza pie at me.

Why? What'd you say? Did you say something terrible? Maybe it's an anti-agist coalition of New Left pie throwers and Old Left tomato throwers.

It's not a joke, he said. And it's not funny. And besides, that's not what I want to talk about. He then expressed opposition to the Great Leap Forward[2] and the

---

[2]Under Chairman Mao Tse Tung's leadership, the Chinese Communist Party from 1958–1960 forcibly decentralized and collectivized the peasantry. Using manpower, not machinery, to irrigate channels and build dikes, the Great Leap Forward caused mass starvation.

Cultural Revolution.[3] He did this by walking back and forth muttering, Wrong. Wrong. Wrong.

Faith, who had just read *Fanshen* at his suggestion, accepted both. But he worried about great art and literature, its way of rising out of the already risen. Faith, sit down, he said. Where were the already risen nowadays? Driven away from their typewriters and calligraphy pens by the Young Guards—like all the young, wild with a dream of wildness.

Faith said, Maybe it's the right now rising. Maybe the already risen don't need anything more. They just sit there in their lawn chairs and appreciate the culture of the just rising. They may even like to do that. The work of creation is probably too hard when you are required because of having already risen to be always distinguishing good from bad, great from good . . .

Nick would not even laugh at serious jokes. He decided to show Faith with mocking examples how wrong she was. None of the examples convinced her. In fact, they seemed to support an opposing position. Faith wondered if his acquisitive mind was not sometimes betrayed by a poor filing system.

Here they are anyway:

Working hard in the fields of Shanxi is John Keats,[4] brilliant and tubercular. The sun beats on his pale flesh. The water in which he is ankle-deep is colder than he likes. The little green shoots are no comfort to him despite their light-green beauty. He is thinking about last night—this lunar beauty, etc. When he gets back to the commune he learns that they have been requested by the province to write poems. Keats is discouraged. He's thinking, This lunar beauty, this lunar beauty . . . The head communard, a bourgeois leftover, says, Oh, what can ail thee, pale individualist?[5] He laughs, then says, Relax, comrade. Just let politics take command. Keats does this, and soon, smiling his sad intelligent smile, he says, Ah . . .

> This lunar beauty
> > touches Shanxi province
> in the year of the bumper crops
> > the peasants free of the landlords
> stand in the fields
> > they talk of this and that
> > and admire
> the harvest moon.

Meanwhile, all around him peasants are dampening the dry lead pencil points with their tongues.

Faith interrupted. She hoped someone would tell them how dangerous lead was. And industrial pollution.

[3]The decade 1966–1976 saw a split with the Communist Party between Mao and intellectual reformers called revisionists. Mao's Red Guards rampaged through cities and villages, seized power, and destroyed old ideas, customs, and habits. Those perceived as intellectuals or middle-class were publicly humiliated; some were killed or committed suicide; others failed at or forced to become manual laborers.

[4]English Romantic poet, 1795–1821, who died of tuberculosis. Keat's "Ode to Psyche" focused on Keats's inner life and imaginative power, which the Maoist Cultural Revolution would have considered decadent.

[5]Paley parodies the Maoist rejection of Keats's "La Belle Dame sans Merci."

For godsakes, said Nick, and continued. One peasant writes:

This morning the paddy
　　looked like the sea
At high tide we will
　　harvest the rice
This is because of Mao Zedong
　　whose love for the peasants
has fed the urban proletariat.

That's enough. Do you get it? Yes, Faith said. Something like this? And sang.

On the highway to Communism
the little children put plum blossoms
in their hair and dance
on the new-harvested wheat

She was about to remember another poem from her newly invented memory, but Nick said, Faith, it's already 3:30, so—full of the play of poems they unfolded his narrow daybed to a comfortable three-quarter width. Their lovemaking was ordinary but satisfactory. Its difference lay only in difference. Of course, if one is living a whole life in passionate affection with another, this differentness on occasional afternoons is often enough.

＊　　＊　　＊

And besides that, almost at once on rising to tea or coffee, Faith asked, Nick, why do they have such a rotten foreign policy? The question had settled in her mind earlier, resting just under the light inflammation of desire.

It was not the first time she had asked this question, nor was Nick the last person who answered.

Nick: For godsakes, don't you understand anything about politics?

Richard: Yeah, and why does Israel trade probably every day with South Africa?

Ruth (*Although her remarks actually came a couple of years later*): Cuba carries on commercial negotiations with Argentina. No?

The boys at supper: Tonto (*Softly, with narrowed eyes*): Why did China recognize Pinochet[6] just about ten minutes after the coup in Chile?

Richard (*Tolerantly explaining*): Asshole, because Allende didn't know how to run a revolution, that's why.

Jack reminded them that the U.S.S.R. may have had to overcome intense ideological repugnance in order to satisfy her old longing for South African industrial diamonds.

Faith thought, But if you think like that forever you can be sad forever. You can be cynical, you can go around saying no hope, you can say import-export, you can

---

[6]Ugarte Pinochet, b. 1915. A right-wing Chilean army general who seized power from the democratically elected president Salvadore Allende who presided over Chile 1970–1973.

mumble all day, World Bank. So she tried thinking: The beauty of trade, the caravans crossing Africa and Asia, the roads to Peru through the terrible forests of Guatemala, and then especially the village markets of underdeveloped countries, plazas behind churches under awnings and tents, not to mention the Orlando Market around the corner; also the Free Market, which costs so much in the world, and what about the discount house of Jack, Son of Jake.

Oh sure, Richard said, the beauty of trade. I'm surprised at you, Ma, the beauty of trade—those Indians going through Guatemala with leather thongs cutting into their foreheads holding about a ton of beauty on their backs. Beauty, he said.

He rested for about an hour. Then he continued. I'm surprised at you Faith, really surprised. He blinked his eyes a couple of times. Mother, he said, have you ever read any political theory? No. All those dumb peace meetings you go to. Don't they ever talk about anything but melting up a couple of really great swords?

He'd become so pale.

Richard, she said. You're absolutely white. You seem to have quit drinking orange juice.

This simple remark made him leave home for three days.

But first he looked at her with either contempt or despair.

Then, because the brain at work pays no attention to time and speedily connects and chooses, she thought: Oh, long ago I looked at my father. What kind of face is that? he had asked. She was leaning against their bedroom wall. She was about fourteen. Fifteen? A lot you care, she said. A giant war is coming out of Germany[7] and all you say is Russia. Bad old Russia. I'm the one that's gonna get killed. You? he answered. Ha ha! A little girl sitting in safe America is going to be killed. Ha ha!

And what about the looks those other boys half a generation ago had made her accept. Ruth had called them put-up-or-shut-up looks. She and her friends had walked round and round the draft boards with signs that said I COUNSEL DRAFT REFUSAL. Some of those young fellows were calm and holy, and some were fierce and grouchy. But not one of them was trivial, and neither was Richard.

Still, Faith thought, what if history should seize him as it had actually taken Ruth's daughter Rachel when her face was still as round as an apple; a moment in history, the expensive moment when everyone his age is called but just a few are chosen by conscience or passion or even only love of one's own agemates, and they are the ones who smash an important nosecone (as has been recently done) or blow up some building full of oppressive money or murderous military plans; but, oh, what if a human creature (maybe rotten to the core but a living person still) is in it? What if they disappear then to live in exile or in the deepest underground and you don't see them for ten years or have to travel to Cuba or Canada or farther to look at their changed faces? Then you think sadly, I could have worked harder at raising that child, the one that was once mine. I could have raised him to become a brilliant economist or finish graduate school and be a lawyer or a doctor maybe. He could have done a lot of good, just as much *that* way, healing or defending the underdog.

But Richard had slipped a note under the door before he left. In his neat handwriting it said: "Trade. Shit. It's production that's beautiful. That's what's beautiful. And the producers. They're beautiful."

---

[7]The child "Faith" is referring to World War II.

What's the use, said Ruth when she and Faith sat eating barley soup in the Art Foods Deli. You're always wrong. She looked into the light beyond the plate-glass window. It was unusual for her to allow sadness. Faith took her hand and kissed it. She said, Ruthy darling. Ruth leaned across the table to hug her. The soup spoon fell to the floor, mixing barley and sawdust.

But look, Ruth said, Joe got this news clipping at the office from some place in Minnesota. "Red and green acrylic circles were painted around telephone poles and trees ringing the Dakota State Prison last night. It was assumed that the Red and the Green were planning some destructive act. These circles were last seen in Arizona. Two convicts escaped from that prison within a week. Red and green circles were stenciled on the walls of their cells. The cost for removing these signatures will probably go as high as $4,300."

What for? said Faith.

For? asked Ruth. They were political prisoners. Someone has to not forget them. The green is for ecology.

Nobody leaves that out nowadays.

Well, they shouldn't, said Ruth.

This Rachel of Ruth and Joe's had grown from girl to woman in far absence, making little personal waves from time to time in the newspapers or in rumor which would finally reach her parents on the shores of their always waiting—that is, the office mailbox or the eleven o'clock news.

One day Ruth and Joe were invited to a cultural event. This was because Joe was a cultural worker. He had in fact edited *The Social Ordure,* a periodical which published everything Jack wrote. He and Ruth had also visited China and connected themselves in print to some indulgent views of the Gang of Four, from which it had been hard to disengage. Ruth was still certain that the bad politics and free life of Jiang Qing would be used for at least a generation to punish ALL Chinese women.

But isn't that true everywhere, said Faith. If you say a simple thing like, "There are only eight women in Congress," or if you say the word "patriarchy," someone always says, Yeah? look at Margaret Thatcher, or look at Golda Meir.[8]

I love Golda Meir.

You do? Oh! said Faith.

But the evening belonged to the Chinese artists and writers who had been rehabilitated while still alive. All sorts of American cultural workers were invited. Some laughed to hear themselves described in this way. They were accustomed to being called "dreamer poet realist postmodernist." They might have liked being called "cultural dreamer," but no one had thought of that yet.

Many of these Chinese artists (mostly men and some women) flew back and forth from American coast to coast so often (sometimes stopping in Iowa City) that they were no longer interested in window seats but slept on the aisle or across the fat center where the armrests can be adjusted . . . while the great deep dipping Rockies, the Indian Black Hills, the Badlands, the good and endless plains moved slowly west under the gently trembling jet. They never bother anymore to dash to the windows

[8]Golda Meir, 1898–1978. Israeli premier, 1969–1974.

at the circling of New York as the pattern holds and the lights of our city engage and eliminate the sky.

Ruth said she would personally bring Nick to the party since China was still too annoyed to have invited him. It wasn't fair for a superficial visitor like herself to be present when a person like Nick, with whole verses of his obsession falling out of his pockets, was excluded.

That's O.K., Ruth. You don't have to ask him, Faith said. Don't bother on my account. I don't even see him much anymore.

How come?

I don't know. Whenever I got to like one of his opinions he'd change it, and he never liked any of mine. Also, I couldn't talk to you about it, so it never got thick enough. I mean woofed and warped. Anyway, it hadn't been Nick, she realized. He was all right, but it was travel she longed for—somewhere else—the sexiness of the unknown parts of far imaginable places.

Sex? Ruth said. She bit her lips. Wouldn't it be interesting if way out there Rachel was having a baby?

God, yes, of course! Wonderful! Oh, Ruthy, Faith said, remembering babies, those round, staring, day-in day-out companions of her youth.

Well, Faith asked, what was he like, Nick—the poet Ai Qing? What'd he say?

He has a very large head, Nick said. The great poet raised from exile.

Was Ding Ling there? The amazing woman, the storyteller, Ding Ling?

They're not up to her yet, Nick said. Maybe next year.

Well, what did Bien Tselin say? Faith asked. Nick, tell me.

Well, he's very tiny. He looks like my father did when he was old.

Yes, but what did they say?

Do you have any other questions? he asked. I'm thinking about something right now. He was writing in his little book—thoughts, comments, maybe even new songs for Chinese modernization—which he planned to publish as soon as possible. He thought Faith could read them then.

Finally he said, They showed me their muscles. There were other poets there. They told some jokes but not against us. They laughed and nudged each other. They talked Chinese, you know. I don't know why they were so jolly. They kept saying, Do not think that we have ceased to be Communists. We are Communists. They weren't bitter. They acted interested and happy.

Ruthy, Faith said, please tell me what they said.

Well, one of the women, Faith, about our age, she said the same thing. She also said the peasants were good to her. But the soldiers were bad. She said the peasants in the countryside helped her. They knew she felt lonely and frightened. She said she loved the Chinese peasant. That's exactly the way she said it, like a little speech: I'll never forget and I will always love the Chinese peasant. It's the one thing Mao was right about—of course he was also a good poet. But she said, well, you can imagine— she said, the children . . . When the entire working office was sent down to the country-side to dig up stones, she left her daughters with her mother. Her mother was old-fashioned, especially about girls. It's not so hard to be strong about oneself.

Some months later, at a meeting of women's governmental organizations spon-sored by the UN, Faith met the very same Chinese woman who'd talked to Ruth. She remembered Ruth well. Yes, the lady who hasn't seen her daughter in eight years. Oh, what a sadness. Who would forget that woman. I have known a few. My name is Xie Feng, she said. Now you say it.

The two women said each other's strange name and laughed. The Chinese woman said, Faith in what? Then she gathered whatever strength and aggression she'd needed to reach this country; she added the courtesy of shyness, breathed deep, and said, Now I would like to see how you live. I have been to meetings, one after another and day after day. But what is a person's home like? How do you live?

Faith said, Me? My house? You want to see my house? In the mirror that evening brushing her teeth, she smiled at her smiling face. She had been invited to be hospitable to a woman from half the world away who'd lived a life beyond foreignness and had experienced extreme history.

The next day they drank tea in Faith's kitchen out of Chinese cups that Ruth had brought from her travels. Misty terraced hills were painted on these cups and a little oil derrick inserted among them.

Faith showed her the boys' bedroom. The Chinese woman took a little camera out of her pocket. You don't mind? she asked. This is the front room, said Faith. It's called the living room. This is our bedroom. That's a picture of Jack giving a paper at the Other Historian meeting and that picture is Jack with two guys who've worked in his store since they were all young. The skinny one just led a strike against Jack and won. Jack says they were right.

I see—both principled men, said the Chinese woman.

They walked around the block a couple of times to get the feel of a neighborhood. They stopped for strudel at the Art Foods. It was half past two and just in time to see the children fly out of the school around the corner. The littlest ones banged against the legs of teachers and mothers. Here and there a father rested his length against somebody's illegally parked car. They stopped to buy a couple of apples. This is my Chinese friend from China, Faith said to Eddie the butcher, who was smoking a cigar, spitting and smiling at the sunlight of an afternoon break. So many peaches, so many oranges, the woman said admiringly to Eddie.

They walked west to the Hudson River. It's called the North River but it's really our Lordly Hudson. This is a good river, but very quiet, said the Chinese woman as they stepped onto the beautiful, green, rusting, slightly crumpled, totally unused pier and looked at New Jersey. They returned along a street of small houses and Faith pointed up to the second-floor apartment where she and Jack had first made love. Ah, the woman said, do you notice that in time you love the children more and the man less? Faith said, Yes! but as soon as she said it, she wanted to run home and find Jack and kiss his pink ears and his 243 last hairs, to call out, Old friend, don't worry, you are loved. But before she could speak of this, Tonto flew by on his financially rewarding messenger's bike, screaming, Hi, Mom, *nee hau, nee hau.* He has a Chinese girlfriend this week. He says that means hello. My other son is at a meeting. She didn't say it was the L.R.Y.'s regular beep-the-horn-if-you-support-Mao meeting. She showed her the church basement where she and Ruth and Ann and Louise and their group of mostly women and some men had made leaflets, offered sanctuary to draft resisters. They would probably do so soon again. Some young people looked up from a light board, saw a representative of the Third World, and smiled peacefully. They walked east and south to neighborhoods where our city, in fields of garbage and broken brick, stands desolate, her windows burnt and blind. Here, Faith said, the people suffer and struggle, their children turn round and round in one place, growing first in beauty, then in rage.

Now we are home again. And I will tell you about my life, the Chinese woman said. Oh yes, please, said Faith, very embarrassed. Of course the desire to share the facts and places of her life had come from generosity, but it had come from self-centeredness too.

Yes, the Chinese woman said. Things are a little better now. They get good at home, they get a little bad, then improve. And the men, you know, they were very bad. But now they are a little better, not all, but some, a few. May I ask you, do you worry that your older boy is in a political group that isn't liked? What will be his trade? Will he go to university? My eldest is without skills to this day. Her school years happened in the time of great confusion and running about. My youngest studies well. Ah, she said, rising. Hello. Good afternoon.

Ruth stood in the doorway. Faith's friend, the listener and the answerer, listening.

We were speaking, the Chinese woman said. About the children, how to raise them. My youngest sister is permitted to have a child this year, so we often talk thoughtfully. This is what we think: Shall we teach them to be straightforward, honorable, kind, brave, maybe shrewd, self-serving a little? What is the best way to help them in the real world? We don't know the best way. You don't want them to be cruel, but you want them to take care of themselves wisely. Now my own children are nearly grown. Perhaps it's too late. Was I foolish? I didn't know in those years how to do it.

Yes, yes, said Faith. I know what you mean. Ruthy?

Ruth remained quiet.

Faith waited a couple of seconds. Then she turned to the Chinese woman. Oh, Xie Feng, she said. Neither did I.

1985

John Okada 1923–1971

Born and raised in Seattle, Washington, John Okada received two B.A. degrees (in English and Library Science) from the University of Washington and an M.A. degree (in English) from Columbia University. He served as a sergeant in the U.S. Air Force during World War II. He died, of a heart attack, in obscurity.

When *No-No Boy* came out in 1957 it received little attention. According to its publisher, Charles Tuttle, even the Japanese American community rejected the book. Perhaps the community did not want to be reminded of the demeaning in-

ternment experience with its lingering effects: uncertain identity, fragmented family, split community, hostile society. The novel was rediscovered by a group of Asian American writers in the 1970s.

Since the rediscovery Okada has been acclaimed as one of the greatest Asian American writers, and *No-No Boy* as one of the first Japanese American novels. The book reveals the many wrenching experiences Japanese Americans faced in the wake of Pearl Harbor, after which they were confined in various relocation camps. In 1943 internees were administered a "loyalty questionnaire" containing two un-settling questions: whether or not the in-ternee would be willing to serve in the American armed forces and whether or not the internee would forswear allegiance to Japan. Ichiro, the protagonist of the novel, answered "No-No" and refused the draft. His double negative was understandable and sensible given the circumstances. He was not eager to serve a government that treated him as an enemy by interning him—an American—in an American camp. He could not forswear an allegiance that he had never felt. Other personal con-siderations also made it difficult for Ichiro to answer affirmatively: his mother was fa-natically pro-Japan; his father was arrested for nationality alone. (At the time Japanese immigrants were not allowed to become naturalized American citizens.)

Yet his sensible response was deemed treasonous. For his two "No's," Ichiro was imprisoned for two years. When he is re-leased after the war, he feels guilty, ashamed, and hostile toward his parents. To exacerbate matters, his peers treat him with great disdain: one former friend spits on him; his younger brother—ashamed of Ichiro's decision—arranges to have Ichiro beaten and quits high school to join the army himself.

One exception is Kenji, who remains Ichiro's friend. Kenji himself has fought in the war and won many medals—but lost a leg. The wound continues to fester so that periodically more inches have to be ampu-tated from the stump. He dies after one of the operations. The excerpt (Chapter 6) is about Kenji's last visit to his family before the fatal operation. We feel at once the family's distress at Kenji's physical condi-tion and the acceptance that things could not have been otherwise: the desire to be recognized as an American was so great that no cost seemed too high.

Kenji acts as a foil to Ichiro through-out the novel. Ichiro is despised by his peers; Kenji is idolized. The war breaks Ichiro's family apart; Kenji's is brought closer together. Ichiro undergoes gnawing despair and persistent mental anguish for not joining the war; Kenji receives what is to be a terminal wound and continuous physical pain for having done so. Despite their opposite choices the No-No Boy and the veteran alike suffer intensely.

The novel is not just about these two characters, however. Nor is it confined to the Japanese American predicament. As the excerpt (especially the Club Oriental episode) illustrates, racism creeps into nu-merous segments of American society; it is not just a matter of whites against Asians or whites against blacks. A group that suffers discrimination from another may in turn inflict racist treatment on a third: Asians discriminated against by whites may, for example, look down on blacks. Discrimi-nation occurs even within one racial group: foreign-born and American-born Japanese may scorn one another. Ichiro's inner con-flict reflects the conflict of the country at large. In the course of the novel his indi-vidual guilt dissolves in the collective guilt of America.

King-Kok Cheung
University of California–Los Angeles

PRIMARY WORKS

No-No Boy, 1957.

from No-No Boy

Chapter Six

Home for Kenji was an old frame, two-story, seven-room house which the family rented for fifty dollars a month from a Japanese owner who had resettled in Chicago after the war and would probably never return to Seattle. It sat on the top of a steep, unpaved hill and commanded an uninspiring view of clean, gray concrete that was six lanes wide and an assortment of boxy, flat store buildings and spacious super gas-stations.

Kenji eased the car over into the left-turn lane and followed the blinking green arrow toward the hill. At its foot, he braked the car almost to a full stop before carefully starting up, for the sharp angle of the hill and the loose dirt necessitated skill and caution.

As he labored to the top, he saw his father sitting on the porch reading a newspaper. Before he could depress the horn ring, the man looked up and waved casually. He waved back and steered the Oldsmobile into the driveway.

When he walked around the side of the house and came up front, the father said "Hello, Ken" as matter-of-factly as if he had seen his son a few hours previously, and returned his attention to the newspaper to finish the article he had been reading.

"Who's home, Pop?" he asked, holding out the bag.

"Nobody," said the father, taking the present and looking into the bag. It held two fifths of good blended whisky. He was a big man, almost six feet tall and strong. As a painter and paper hanger he had no equal, but he found it sufficient to work only a few days a week and held himself to it, for his children were all grown and he no longer saw the need to drive himself. He smiled warmly and gratefully: "Thank you."

"Sure, Pop. One of these days, I'll bring home a case."

"Last me two days. Better bring a truckful," he said, feigning seriousness.

They laughed together comfortably, the father because he loved his son and the son because he both loved and respected his father, who was a moderate and good man. They walked into the house, the father making the son precede him.

In the dining room the father deposited the two new bottles with a dozen others in the china cabinet. "I'm fixed for a long time," he said. "That's a good feeling."

"You're really getting stocked up," said Kenji.

"The trust and faith and love of my children," he said proudly. "You know I don't need clothes or shaving lotion in fancy jars or suitcases or pajamas, but whisky I can use. I'm happy."

"Are you, Pop?"

The father sat down opposite his son at the polished mahogany table and took in at a glance the new rugs and furniture and lamps and the big television set with the radio and phonograph all built into one impressive, blond console. "All I did was feed you and clothe you and spank you once in a while. All of a sudden, you're all grown up. The government gives you money, Hisa and Toyo are married to fine boys, Hana and Tom have splendid jobs, and Eddie is in college and making more money in a part-time job than I did for all of us when your mother died. No longer do I have to work all the time, but only two or three days a week and I have more money than I can spend. Yes, Ken, I am happy and I wish your mother were here to see all this."

"I'm happy too, Pop." He shifted his legs to make himself comfortable and winced unwillingly.

Noticing, the father screwed his face as if the pain were in himself, for it was. Before the pain turned to sorrow, before the suffering for his son made his lips quiver as he held back the tears, he hastened into the kitchen and came back with two jigger-glasses.

"I am anxious to sample your present," he said jovially, but his movements were hurried as he got the bottle from the cabinet and fumbled impatiently with the seal.

Kenji downed his thankfully and watched his father take the other glass and sniff the whisky appreciatively before sipping it leisurely. He lifted the bottle toward his son.

"No more, Pop," refused Kenji. "That did it fine."

The father capped the bottle and put it back. He closed the cabinet door and let his hand linger on the knob as if ashamed of himself for having tried to be cheerful when he knew that the pain was again in his son and the thought of death hovered over them.

"Pop."

"Yes?" He turned slowly to face his son.

"Come on. Sit down. It'll be all right."

Sitting down, the father shook his head, saying: "I came to America to become a rich man so that I could go back to the village in Japan and be somebody. I was greedy and ambitious and proud. I was not a good man or an intelligent one, but a young fool. And you have paid for it."

"What kind of talk is that?" replied Kenji, genuinely grieved. "That's not true at all."

"That is what I think nevertheless. I am to blame."

"It'll be okay, Pop. Maybe they won't even operate."

"When do you go?"

"Tomorrow morning."

"I will go with you."

"No." He looked straight at his father.

In answer, the father merely nodded, acceding to his son's wish because his son was a man who had gone to war to fight for the abundance and happiness that pervaded a Japanese household in America and that was a thing he himself could never fully comprehend except to know that it was very dear. He had long forgotten when it was that he had discarded the notion of a return to Japan but remembered only that it was the time when this country which he had no intention of loving had suddenly begun to become a part of him because it was a part of his children and he saw and felt it in their speech and joys and sorrows and hopes and he was a part of them. And in the dying of the foolish dreams which he had brought to America, the richness of the life that was possible in this foreign country destroyed the longing for a past that really must not have been as precious as he imagined or else he would surely not have left it. Where else could a man, left alone with six small children, have found it possible to have had so much with so little? He had not begged or borrowed or gone to the city for welfare assistance. There had been times of hunger and despair and seeming hopelessness, but did it not mean something now that he could look around and feel the love of the men and women who were once only children?

And there was the one who sat before him, the one who had come to him and said calmly that he was going into the army. It could not be said then that it mattered not that he was a Japanese son of Japanese parents. It had mattered. It was because he was Japanese that the son had to come to his Japanese father and simply state that he had decided to volunteer for the army instead of being able to wait until such time as the army called him. It was because he was Japanese and, at the same time, had to prove to the world that he was not Japanese that the turmoil was in his soul and urged him to enlist. There was confusion, but, underneath it, a conviction that he loved America and would fight and die for it because he did not wish to live anyplace else. And the father, also confused, understood what the son had not said and gave his consent. It was not a time for clear thinking because the sense of loyalty had become dispersed and the shaken faith of an American interned in an American concentration camp was indeed a flimsy thing. So, on this steadfast bit of conviction that remained, and knowing not what the future held, this son had gone to war to prove that he deserved to enjoy those rights which should rightfully have been his.

And he remembered that a week after Kenji had gone to a camp in Mississippi, the neighbor's son, an American soldier since before Pearl Harbor, had come to see his family which was in a camp enclosed by wire fencing and had guards who were American soldiers like himself. And he had been present when the soldier bitterly spoke of how all he did was dump garbage and wash dishes and take care of the latrines. And the soldier swore and ranted and could hardly make himself speak of the time when the president named Roosevelt had come to the camp in Kansas and all the American soldiers in the camp who were Japanese had been herded into a warehouse and guarded by other American soldiers with machine guns until the president named Roosevelt had departed. And he had gone to his own cubicle with the seven steel cots and the potbellied stove and the canvas picnic-chairs from Sears Roebuck and cried for Kenji, who was now a soldier and would not merely turn bitter and swear if the army let him do only such things as the soldier had spoken of, but would be driven to protest more violently because he was the quiet one with the deep feelings whose anger was a terrible thing. But, with training over, Kenji had written that he was going to Europe, and the next letter was from Italy, where the Americans were fighting the Germans, and he found relief in the knowledge, partly because Kenji was fighting and he knew that was what his son wished and partly because the enemy was German and not Japanese.

He thought he remembered that he had not wanted Kenji to go into the army. But when he was asked, he had said yes. And so this son had come back after long months in a hospital with one good leg and another that was only a stick where the other good one had been. Had he done right? Should he not have forbidden him? Should he not have explained how it was not sensible for Japanese to fight a war against Japanese? If what he had done was wrong, how was it so and why?

"Would you," he said to his son, "have stayed out of the army if I had forbidden it?"

Kenji did not answer immediately, for the question came as a surprise to disturb the long, thought-filled silence. "I don't think so, Pop," he started out hesitantly. He paused, delving into his mind for an explanation, then said with great finality: "No, I would have gone anyway."

"Of course," said the father, finding some assurance in the answer.

Kenji pushed himself to a standing position and spoke gently: "You're not to blame, Pop. Every time we get to talking like this, I know you're blaming yourself. Don't do it. Nobody's to blame, nobody."

"To lose a leg is not the worst thing, but, to lose a part of it and then a little more and a little more again until . . . Well, I don't understand. You don't deserve it." He shrugged his shoulders wearily against the weight of his terrible anguish.

"I'm going up to take a nap." He walked a few steps and turned back to his father. "I'll go upstairs and lie down on the bed and I won't sleep right away because the leg will hurt a little and I'll be thinking. And I'll think that if things had been different, if you had been different, it might have been that I would also not have been the same and maybe you would have kept me from going into the war and I would have stayed out and had both my legs. But, you know, every time I think about it that way, I also have to think that, had such been the case, you and I would probably not be sitting down and having a drink together and talking or not talking as we wished. If my leg hurts, so what? We're buddies, aren't we? That counts. I don't worry about anything else."

Up in his room, he stretched out on his back on the bed and thought about what he had said to his father. It made a lot of sense. If, in the course of things, the pattern called for a stump of a leg that wouldn't stay healed, he wasn't going to decry the fact, for that would mean another pattern with attendant changes which might not be as perfectly desirable as the one he cherished. Things are as they should be, he assured himself, and, feeling greatly at peace, sleep came with surprising ease.

After Kenji had left him, the father walked down the hill to the neighborhood Safeway and bought a large roasting chicken. It was a fat bird with bulging drumsticks and, as he headed back to the house with both arms supporting the ingredients of an ample family feast, he thought of the lean years and the six small ones and the pinched, hungry faces that had been taught not to ask for more but could not be taught how not to look hungry when they were in fact quite hungry. And it was during those years that it seemed as if they would never have enough.

But such a time had come. It had come with the war and the growing of the children and it had come with the return of the thoughtful son whose terrible wound paid no heed to the cessation of hostilities. Yet, the son had said he was happy and the father was happy also for, while one might grieve for the limb that was lost and the pain that endured, he chose to feel gratitude for the fact that the son had come back alive even if only for a brief while.

And he remembered what the young sociologist had said in halting, pained Japanese at one of the family-relations meetings he had attended while interned in the relocation center because it was someplace to go. The instructor was a recent college graduate who had later left the camp to do graduate work at a famous Eastern school. He, short fellow that he was, had stood on an orange crate so that he might be better heard and seen by the sea of elderly men and women who had been attracted to the mess hall because they too had nothing else to do and nowhere else to go. There had been many meetings, although it had early become evident that lecturer and audience were poles apart, and if anything had been accomplished it was that the meetings helped to pass the time, and so the instructor continued to blast away at the unyielding wall of indifference and the old people came to pass an hour or two. But it was on this particular night that the small sociologist, struggling for the words painstakingly and not always correctly selected from his meager knowledge of the Japanese language, had managed to impart a message of great truth. And this message was that the old Japanese, the fathers and mothers, who sat courteously attentive, did not know their own sons and daughters.

"How many of you are able to sit down with your own sons and own daughters and enjoy the companionship of conversation? How many, I ask? If I were to say none of you, I would not be far from the truth." He paused, for the grumbling was swollen with anger and indignation, and continued in a loud, shouting voice before it could engulf him: "You are not displeased because of what I said but because I have hit upon the truth. And I know it to be true because I am a Nisei and you old ones are like my own father and mother. If we are children of America and not the sons and daughters of our parents, it is because you have failed. It is because you have been stupid enough to think that growing rice in muddy fields is the same as growing a giant fir tree. Change, now, if you can, even if it may be too late, and become companions to your children. This is America, where you have lived and worked and suffered for thirty and forty years. This is not Japan. I will tell you what it is like to be an American boy or girl. I will tell you what the relationship between parents and children is in an American family. As I speak, compare what I say with your own families." And so he had spoken and the old people had listened and, when the meeting was over, they got up and scattered over the camp toward their assigned cubicles. Some said they would attend no more lectures; others heaped hateful abuse upon the young fool who dared to have spoken with such disrespect; and then there was the elderly couple, the woman silently following the man, who stopped at another mess hall, where a dance was in progress, and peered into the dimly lit room and watched the young boys and girls gliding effortlessly around to the blaring music from a phonograph. Always before, they had found something to say about the decadent ways of an amoral nation, but, on this evening, they watched longer than usual and searched longingly to recognize their own daughter, whom they knew to be at the dance but who was only an unrecognizable shadow among the other shadows. . . .

Halting for a moment to shift the bag, Kenji's father started up the hill with a smile on his lips. He was glad that the market had had such a fine roasting chicken. There was nothing as satisfying as sitting at a well-laden table with one's family whether the occasion was a holiday or a birthday or a home-coming of some member or, yes, even if it meant someone was going away.

Please come back, Ken, he said to himself, please come back and I will have for you the biggest, fattest chicken that ever graced a table, American or otherwise.

Hanako, who was chubby and pleasant and kept books for three doctors and a dentist in a downtown office, came home before Tom, who was big and husky like his father and had gone straight from high school into a drafting job at an aircraft plant. She had seen the car in the driveway and smelled the chicken in the oven and, smiling sympathetically with the father, put a clean cloth on the table and took out the little chest of Wm. & Rogers Silverplate.

While she was making the salad, Tom came home bearing a bakery pie in a flat, white box. "Hello, Pop, Sis," he said, putting the box on the table. "Where's Ken?"

"Taking a nap," said Hanako.

"Dinner about ready?" He sniffed appreciatively and rubbed his stomach in approval.

"Just about," smiled his sister.

"Psychic, that's what I am."

"What?"

"I say I'm psychic. I brought home a lemon meringue. Chicken and lemon meringue. Boy! Don't you think so?"

"What's that?"

"About my being psychic."

"You're always bringing home lemon meringue. Coincidence, that's all."

"How soon do we eat?"

"I just got through telling you—in a little while," she replied a bit impatiently.

"Good. I'm starved. I'll wash up and rouse the boy." He started to head for the stairs but turned back thoughtfully. "What's the occasion?" he asked.

"Ken has to go to the hospital again," said the father kindly. "Wash yourself at the sink and let him sleep a while longer. We will eat when he wakes up."

"Sure," said Tom, now sharing the unspoken sadness and terror which abided in the hearts of his father and sister. He went to the sink and, clearing it carefully of the pots and dishes, washed himself as quietly as possible.

It was a whole hour before Kenji came thumping down the stairs. It was the right leg, the good one, that made the thumps which followed the empty pauses when the false leg was gently lowered a step. When he saw the family sitting lazily around the table, he knew they had waited for him.

"You shouldn't have waited," he said, a little embarrassed. "I slept longer than I intended."

"We're waiting for the chicken," lied the father. "Takes time to roast a big one."

Hanako agreed too hastily: "Oh, yes, I've never known a chicken to take so long. Ought to be just about ready now." She trotted into the kitchen and, a moment later, shouted back: "It's ready. Mmmm, can you smell it?"

"That's all I've been doing," Tom said with a famished grin. "Let's get it out here."

"Sorry I made you wait," smiled Kenji at his brother.

Tom, regretting his impatience, shook his head vigorously. "No, it's the bird, like Pop said. You know how he is. Always gets 'em big and tough. This one's made of cast iron." He followed Hanako to help bring the food from the kitchen.

No one said much during the first part of the dinner. Tom ate ravenously. Hanako seemed about to say something several times but couldn't bring herself to speak. The father kept looking at Kenji without having to say what it was that he felt for his son. Surprisingly, it was Tom who broached the subject which was on all their minds.

"What the hell's the matter with those damn doctors?" He slammed his fork angrily against the table.

"Tom, please," said Hanako, looking deeply concerned.

"No, no, no," he said, gesturing freely with his hands, "I won't please shut up. If they can't fix you up, why don't they get somebody who can? They're killing you. What do they do when you go down there? Give you aspirins?" Slumped in his chair, he glared furiously at the table.

The father grasped Tom's arm firmly. "If you can't talk sense, don't."

"It's okay, Tom. This'll be a short trip. I think it's just that the brace doesn't fit right."

"You mean that?" He looked hopefully at Kenji.

"Sure. That's probably what it is. I'll only be gone a few days. Doesn't really hurt so much, but I don't want to take any chances."

"Gee, I hope you're right."

"I ought to know. A few more trips and they'll make me head surgeon down there."

"Yeah," Tom smiled, not because of the joke, but because he was grateful for having a brother like Kenji.

"Eat," reminded the father, "baseball on television tonight, you know."

"I'll get the pie," Hanako said and hastened to the kitchen.

"Lemon meringue," said Tom hungrily, as he proceeded to clean up his plate.

The game was in its second inning when they turned the set on, and they had hardly gotten settled down when Hisa and Toyo came with their husbands and children.

Tom grumbled good naturedly and, giving the newcomers a hasty nod, pulled up closer to the set, preparing to watch the game under what would obviously be difficult conditions.

Hats and coats were shed and piled in the corner and everyone talked loudly and excitedly, as if they had not seen each other for a long time. Chairs were brought in from the dining room and, suddenly, the place was full and noisy and crowded and comfortable.

The father gave up trying to follow the game and bounced a year-old granddaughter on his knee while two young grandsons fought to conquer the other knee. The remaining three grandchildren were all girls, older, more well-behaved, and they huddled on the floor around Tom to watch the baseball game.

Hisa's husband sat beside Kenji and engaged him in conversation, mostly about fishing and about how he'd like to win a car in the Salmon Derby because his was getting old and a coupe wasn't too practical for a big family. He had the four girls and probably wouldn't stop until he hit a boy and things weren't so bad, but he couldn't see his way to acquiring a near-new used car for a while. And then he got up and went to tell the same thing to his father-in-law, who was something of a fisherman himself. No sooner had he moved across the room than Toyo's husband, who was soft-spoken and mild but had been a captain in the army and sold enough insurance to keep two cars in the double garage behind a large brick house in a pretty good neighborhood, slid into the empty space beside Kenji and asked him how he'd been and so on and talked about a lot of other things when he really wanted to talk to Kenji about the leg and didn't know how.

Then came the first lull when talk died down and the younger children were showing signs of drowsiness and everyone smiled thoughtfully and contentedly at one another. Hanako suggested refreshments, and when the coffee and milk and pop and cookies and ice cream were distributed, everyone got his second wind and immediately discovered a number of things which they had forgotten to discuss.

Kenji, for the moment alone, looked at all of them and said to himself: Now's as good a time as any to go. I won't wait until tomorrow. In another thirty minutes Hana and Toyo and the kids and their fathers will start stretching and heading for their hats and coats. Then someone will say "Well, Ken" in a kind of hesitant way and, immediately, they will all be struggling for something to say about my going to Portland because Hana called them and told them to come over because I'm going down there again and that's why they'll have to say something about it. If I had said to Pop that I was going the day after tomorrow, we would have had a big feast with everyone here for it tomorrow night. I don't want that. There's no need for it. I don't want Toyo to cry and Hana to dab at her eyes and I don't want everyone standing around trying to say goodbye and not being able to make themselves leave because maybe they won't see me again.

He started to get up and saw Hanako looking at him. "I'm just going to get a drink," he said.

"Stay, I'll get it," she replied.

"No. It'll give me a chance to stretch." He caught his father's eye and held it for a moment.

Without getting his drink, he slipped quietly out to the back porch and stood and waited and listened to the voices inside.

He heard Hisa's husband yell something to one of his girls and, the next minute, everyone was laughing amusedly. While he was wondering what cute deviltry the guilty one had done, his father came through the kitchen and out to stand beside him.

"You are going."

Kenji looked up and saw the big shoulders sagging wearily. "I got a good rest, Pop. This way, I'll be there in the morning and it's easier driving at night. Not so many cars, you know."

"It's pretty bad this time, isn't it?"

"Yes," he said truthfully, because he could not lie to his father, "it's not like before, Pop. It's different this time. The pain is heavier, deeper. Not sharp and raw like the other times. I don't know why. I'm scared."

"If . . . if . . ." Throwing his arm around his son's neck impulsively, the father hugged him close. "You call me every day. Every day, you understand?"

"Sure, Pop. Explain to everyone, will you?" He pulled himself free and looked at his father nodding, unable to speak.

Pausing halfway down the stairs, he listened once more for the voices in the house.

Hoarsely, in choked syllables, his father spoke to him: "Every day, Ken, don't forget. I will be home."

"Bye, Pop." Feeling his way along the dark drive with his cane, he limped to the car. Behind the wheel, he had to sit and wait until the heaviness had lifted from his chest and relieved the mistiness of his eyes. He started the motor and turned on the headlights and their brilliant glare caught fully the father standing ahead. Urged by an overwhelming desire to rush back to him and be with him for a few minutes longer, Kenji's hand fumbled for the door handle. At that moment, the father raised his arm once slowly in farewell. Quickly, he pulled back out of the driveway and was soon out of sight of father and home and family.

He fully intended to drive directly to the grocery store to get Ichiro, but found himself drawn to the Club Oriental. Parking in the vacant lot where only the previous night Ichiro had experienced his humiliation, he limped through the dark alley to the club.

It was only a little after ten, but the bar and tables were crowded. Ignoring several invitations to sit at tables of acquaintances, he threaded his way to the end of the bar and had only to wait a moment before Al saw him and brought the usual bourbon and water.

Not until he was on his third leisurely drink did he manage to secure a stool. It was between strangers, and for that he was grateful. He didn't want to talk or be talked to. Through the vast mirror ahead, he studied the faces alongside and behind him. By craning a bit, he could even catch an occasional glimpse of couples on the dance floor.

It's a nice place, he thought. When a fellow goes away, he likes to take something along to remember and this is what I'm taking. It's not like having a million bucks and sitting in the Waldorf with a long-stemmed beauty, but I'm a small guy with small wants and this is my Waldorf. Here, as long as I've got the price of a drink, I can sit all night and be among friends. I can relax and drink and feel sad or happy or high and nobody much gives a damn, since they feel the same way. It's a good feeling, a fine feeling.

He followed Al around with his eyes until the bartender looked back at him and returned the smile.

The help knows me and likes me.

Swinging around on the stool, he surveyed the crowd and acknowledged a number of greetings and nods.

I've got a lot of friends here and they know and like me.

Jim Eng, the slender, dapper Chinese who ran the place, came out of the office with a bagful of change and brought it behind the bar to check the register. As he did so, he grinned at Kenji and inquired about his leg.

Even the management's on my side. It's like a home away from home only more precious because one expects home to be like that. Not many places a Jap can go to and feel so completely at ease. It must be nice to be white and American and to be able to feel like this no matter where one goes to, but I won't cry about that. There's been a war and, suddenly, things are better for the Japs and the Chinks and—

There was a commotion at the entrance and Jim Eng slammed the cash drawer shut and raced toward the loud voices. He spoke briefly to someone in the office, probably to find out the cause of the disturbance, and then stepped outside. As he did so, Kenji caught sight of three youths, a Japanese and two Negroes.

After what sounded like considerable loud and excited shouting, Jim Eng stormed back in and resumed his task at the register though with hands shaking.

When he had calmed down a little, someone inquired: "What's the trouble?"

"No trouble," he said in a high-pitched voice which he was endeavoring to keep steady. "That crazy Jap boy Floyd tried to get in with two niggers. That's the second time he tried that. What's the matter with him?"

A Japanese beside Kenji shouted out sneeringly: "Them ignorant cotton pickers make me sick. You let one in and before you know it, the place will be black as night."

"Sure," said Jim Eng, "sure. I got no use for them. Nothing but trouble they make and I run a clean place."

"Hail Columbia," said a small, drunken voice.

"Oh, you Japs and Chinks, I love you all," rasped out a brash redhead who looked as if she had come directly from one of the burlesque houses without changing her make-up. She struggled to her feet, obviously intending to launch into further oratory.

Her escort, a pale, lanky Japanese screamed "Shut up!" and, at the same time, pulled viciously at her arm, causing her to tumble comically into the chair.

Everyone laughed, or so it seemed, and quiet and decency and cleanliness and honesty returned to the Club Oriental.

Leaving his drink unfinished, Kenji left the club without returning any of the farewells which were directed at him.

He drove aimlessly, torturing himself repeatedly with the question which plagued his mind and confused it to the point of madness. Was there no answer to the bigotry and meanness and smallness and ugliness of people? One hears the voice of the Negro or Japanese or Chinese or Jew, a clear and bell-like intonation of the common struggle for recognition as a complete human being and there is a sense of unity and purpose which inspires one to hope and optimism. One encounters obstacles, but the wedge of the persecuted is not without patience and intelligence and humility, and the opposition weakens and wavers and disperses. And the one who is the Negro or Japanese or Chinese or Jew is further fortified and gladdened with the knowledge that the democracy is a democracy in fact for all of them. One has hope, for he has reason to hope, and the quest for completeness seems to be a thing near at hand, and then . . .

the woman with the dark hair and large nose who has barely learned to speak English makes a big show of vacating her bus seat when a Negro occupies the other half. She stamps indignantly down the aisle, hastening away from the contamination which is only in her contaminated mind. The Negro stares silently out of the window, a proud calmness on his face, which hides the boiling fury that is capable of murder.

and then . . .

a sweet-looking Chinese girl is at a high-school prom with a white boy. She has risen in the world, or so she thinks, for it is evident in her expression and manner. She does not entirely ignore the other Chinese and Japanese at the dance, which would at least be honest, but worse, she flaunts her newly found status in their faces with haughty smiles and overly polite phrases.

and then . . .

there is the small Italian restaurant underneath a pool parlor, where the spaghetti and chicken is hard to beat. The Japanese, who feels he is better than the Chinese because his parents made him so, comes into the restaurant with a Jewish companion, who is a good Jew and young and American and not like the kike bastards from the countries from which they've been kicked out, and waits patiently for the waiter. None of the waiters come, although the place is quite empty and two of them are talking not ten feet away. All his efforts to attract them failing, he stalks toward them. The two, who are supposed to wait on the tables but do not, scurry into the kitchen. In a moment they return with the cook, who is also the owner, and he tells the Japanese that the place is not for Japs and to get out and go back to Tokyo.

and then . . .

the Negro who was always being mistaken for a white man becomes a white man and he becomes hated by the Negroes with whom he once hated on the same side. And the young Japanese hates the not-so-young Japanese who is more Japanese than himself, and the not-so-young, in turn, hates the old Japanese who is all Japanese and, therefore, even more Japanese than he . . .

1957

James Baldwin 1924–1987

Perhaps more than any other writer who came to prominence after 1950, James Baldwin represented the process by which a person at odds with the country of his birth seeks to reconcile him- or herself to it, and to a status as less than a first-class citizen. Through the essays that became his trademark, Baldwin pricked the conscience of an America that had distorted the original conceptions of democracy. He encouraged Americans to retrieve those seeds and bring them to fruition. Through his life and his art, Baldwin repeatedly bore witness to the injustices heaped upon black Americans, and consistently urged healing of the social fabric before it is torn beyond repair.

Born to Emma Berdis Jones (a single mother) in Harlem, New York, Baldwin would make art of the pain of illegitimacy and the problems he had with his stepfather, David Baldwin, whom his mother married when he was three. As his mother bore eight more children, Baldwin cared for them, and tried to escape the anger of his stepfather by excelling in school. Relationships between parents and children, particularly between fathers and sons, formed the theme of many of Baldwin's works, including "Sonny's Blues" and others of his stories collected in Going to Meet

the Man, 1965. The religious fanaticism of his stepfather also became a dominant subject for his fiction.

Influenced by Harriet Beecher Stowe's Uncle Tom's Cabin, Charles Dickens, and Horatio Alger, Baldwin read voraciously. In fact, he read through the Harlem libraries, and moved into other territories within the city. He edited the junior high newspaper, and shared editorial duties on the Magpie at DeWitt Clinton High School, a predominantly white Bronx secondary school. When Baldwin was 14, he underwent a religious conversion which led to ministerial duties until he was 17. The whole religious experience was partly to defy his stepfather, but it too recurred throughout his later writing.

Although Baldwin published some scattered pieces in the 1940s, he made his debut in 1953 with Go Tell It on the Mountain, a chronicle of three generations of a black family plagued by slavery and internal strife. Young John Grimes, in the present generation of the novel, serves as Baldwin's fictional creation of his crisis of the spirit. He dealt in subsequent fiction with homosexuality (among white characters), racial and sexual identities, problems of the Civil Rights movement, life in Harlem, and religion. While his fiction was well received, the essay may be Baldwin's strength, and his collections of essays were sometimes better sellers than his novels.

Of Baldwin's plays, two continue the religious and political themes of his other works. *The Amen Corner* focuses upon the influence of the church in the lives of black Americans; *Blues for Mister Charlie* is loosely based on the case of Emmett Till, the fourteen-year-old black boy who was killed in Mississippi in 1955 for allegedly whistling at a white woman.

Although Baldwin was quite active in the Civil Rights movement, he participated only by returning to the States in the 1950s and 1960s from France, a country to which he had bought a one-way ticket in 1948. After that time, he moved back and forth, never staying in the States for an extended period. Whatever his vantage point, Baldwin continued to prod Americans into better behavior, for he genuinely loved the country that was less willing than he would have wished to return that love.

Trudier Harris
University of North Carolina–Chapel Hill

PRIMARY WORKS

Go Tell It on the Mountain, 1953; *Notes of a Native Son,* 1955; *Giovanni's Room,* 1956; *Nobody Knows My Name,* 1961; *Another Country,* 1962; *The Fire Next Time,* 1963; *Blues for Mister Charlie,* 1964; *Nothing Personal* (with Richard Avedon), 1964; *Going to Meet the Man,* 1965; *Tell Me How Long the Train's Been Gone,* 1968; *The Amen Corner,* 1968; *No Name in the Street,* 1972; *A Dialogue* (with Nikki Giovanni), 1973; *If Beale Street Could Talk,* 1974; *The Devil Finds Work,* 1976; *Just Above My Head,* 1979; *Jimmy's Blues,* 1983; *The Evidence of Things Not Seen,* 1985.

Sonny's Blues

I read about it in the paper, in the subway, on my way to work. I read it, and I couldn't believe it, and I read it again. Then perhaps I just stared at it, at the newsprint spelling out his name, spelling out the story. I stared at it in the swinging lights of the subway car, and in the faces and bodies of the people, and in my own face, trapped in the darkness which roared outside.

It was not to be believed and I kept telling myself that, as I walked from the subway station to the high school. And at the same time I couldn't doubt it. I was scared, scared for Sonny. He became real to me again. A great block of ice got settled in my belly and kept melting there slowly all day long, while I taught my classes algebra. It was a special kind of ice. It kept melting, sending trickles of ice water all up and down my veins, but it never got less. Sometimes it hardened and seemed to expand until I felt my guts were going to come spilling out or that I was going to choke or scream. This would always be at a moment when I was remembering some specific thing Sonny had once said or done.

When he was about as old as the boys in my classes his face had been bright and open, there was a lot of copper in it; and he'd had wonderfully direct brown eyes, and great gentleness and privacy. I wondered what he looked like now. He had been picked up the evening before, in a raid on an apartment downtown, for peddling and using heroin.

I couldn't believe it: but what I mean by that is that I couldn't find any room for it anywhere inside me. I had kept it outside me for a long time. I hadn't wanted to know. I had had suspicions, but I didn't name them, I kept putting them away. I told myself that Sonny was wild, but he wasn't crazy. And he'd always been a good boy, he hadn't ever turned hard or evil or disrespectful, the way kids can, so quick, especially in Harlem. I didn't want to believe that I'd ever see my brother going down, coming to nothing, all that light in his face gone out, in the condition I'd already seen so many others. Yet it had happened and here I was, talking about algebra to a lot of boys who might, every one of them for all I knew, be popping off needles every time they went to the head. Maybe it did more for them than algebra could.

I was sure that the first time Sonny had ever had horse,[1] he couldn't have been much older than these boys were now. These boys, now, were living as we'd been living then, they were growing up with a rush and their heads bumped abruptly against the low ceiling of their actual possibilities. They were filled with rage. All they really knew were two darknesses, the darkness of their lives, which was now closing in on them, and the darkness of the movies, which had blinded them to that other darkness, and in which they now, vindictively, dreamed, at once more together than they were at any other time, and more alone.

When the last bell rang, the last class ended, I let out my breath. It seemed I'd been holding it for all that time. My clothes were wet—I may have looked as though I'd been sitting in a steam bath, all dressed up all afternoon. I sat alone in the classroom a long time. I listened to the boys outside, downstairs, shouting and cursing and laughing. Their laughter struck me for perhaps the first time. It was not the joyous laughter which—God knows why—one associates with children. It was mocking and insular, its intent was to denigrate. It was disenchanted, and in this, also, lay the authority of their curses. Perhaps I was listening to them because I was thinking about my brother and in them I heard my brother. And myself.

One boy was whistling a tune, at once very complicated and very simple, it seemed to be pouring out of him as though he were a bird, and it sounded very cool and moving through all that harsh, bright air, only just holding its own through all those other sounds.

I stood up and walked over to the window and looked down into the courtyard. It was the beginning of the spring and the sap was rising in the boys. A teacher passed through them every now and again, quickly, as though he or she couldn't wait to get out of that courtyard, to get those boys out of their sight and off their minds. I started collecting my stuff. I thought I'd better get home and talk to Isabel.

The courtyard was almost deserted by the time I got downstairs. I saw this boy standing in the shadow of a doorway, looking just like Sonny. I almost called his name. Then I saw that it wasn't Sonny, but somebody we used to know, a boy from around our block. He'd been Sonny's friend. He'd never been mine, having been too young for me, and, anyway, I'd never liked him. And now, even though he was a grown-up man, he still hung around that block, still spent hours on the street corners, was always high and raggy. I used to run into him from time to time and he'd

---

[1]Heroin.

often work around to asking me for a quarter or fifty cents. He always had some real good excuse too, and I always gave it to him, I don't know why.

But now, abruptly I hated him. I couldn't stand the way he looked at me, partly like a dog, partly like a cunning child. I wanted to ask him what the hell he was doing in the school courtyard.

He sort of shuffled over to me, and he said, "I see you got the papers. So you already know about it."

"You mean about Sonny? Yes, I already know about it. How come they didn't get you?"

He grinned. It made him repulsive and it also brought to mind what he'd looked like as a kid. "I wasn't there. I stay away from them people."

"Good for you." I offered him a cigarette and I watched him through the smoke. "You come all the way down here just to tell me about Sonny?"

"That's right." He was sort of shaking his head and his eyes looked strange, as though they were about to cross. The bright sun deadened his damp dark brown skin and it made his eyes look yellow and showed up the dirt in his kinked hair. He smelled funky. I moved a little way away from him and I said, "Well, thanks. But I already know about it and I got to get home."

"I'll walk you a little ways," he said. We started walking. There were a couple of kids still loitering in the courtyard and one of them said goodnight to me and looked strangely at the boy beside me.

"What're you going to do?" he asked me. "I mean, about Sonny?"

"Look. I haven't seen Sonny for over a year. I'm not sure I'm going to do anything. Anyway, what the hell *can* I do?"

"That's right," he said quickly, "ain't nothing you can do. Can't much help old Sonny no more, I guess."

It was what I was thinking and so it seemed to me he had no right to say it.

"I'm surprised at Sonny, though," he went on—he had a funny way of talking, he looked straight ahead as though he were talking to himself—"I thought Sonny was a smart boy, I thought he was too smart to get hung."

"I guess he thought so too," I said sharply, "and that's how he got hung. And how about you? You're pretty goddamn smart, I bet."

Then he looked directly at me, just for a minute. "I ain't smart," he said. "If I was smart, I'd have reached for a pistol a long time ago."

"Look. Don't tell *me* your sad story, if it was up to me, I'd give you one." Then I felt guilty—guilty, probably, for never having supposed that the poor bastard *had* a story of his own, much less a sad one, and I asked, quickly, "What's going to happen to him now?"

He didn't answer this. He was off by himself some place. "Funny thing," he said, and from his tone we might have been discussing the quickest way to get to Brooklyn, "when I saw the papers this morning, the first thing I asked myself was if I had anything to do with it. I felt sort of responsible."

I began to listen more carefully. The subway station was on the corner, just before us, and I stopped. He stopped, too. We were in front of a bar and he ducked slightly, peering in, but whoever he was looking for didn't seem to be there. The juke box was blasting away with something black and bouncy and I half watched the barmaid as she danced her way from the juke box to her place behind the bar.

And I watched her face as she laughingly responded to something someone said to her, still keeping time to the music. When she smiled one saw the little girl, one sensed the doomed, still struggling woman beneath the battered face of the semi-whore.

"I never *give* Sonny nothing," the boy said finally, "but a long time ago I come to school high and Sonny asked me how it felt." He paused, I couldn't bear to watch him, I watched the barmaid, and I listened to the music which seemed to be causing the pavement to shake. "I told him it felt great." The music stopped, the barmaid paused and watched the juke box until the music began again. "It did."

All this was carrying me some place I didn't want to go. I certainly didn't want to know how it felt. It filled everything, the people, the houses, the music, the dark, quicksilver barmaid, with menace, and this menace was their reality.

"What's going to happen to him now?" I asked again.

"They'll send him away some place and they'll try to cure him." He shook his head. "Maybe he'll even think he's kicked the habit. Then they'll let him loose"—he gestured, throwing his cigarette into the gutter. "That's all."

"What do you mean that's *all*?"

But I knew what he meant.

"I *mean*, that's *all*." He turned his head and looked at me, pulling down the corners of his mouth. "Don't you know what I mean?" he asked, softly.

"How the hell *would* I know what you mean?" I almost whispered it, I don't know why.

"That's right," he said to the air, "how would *he* know what I mean?" He turned toward me again, patient and calm, and yet I somehow felt him shaking, shaking as though he were going to fall apart. I felt that ice in my guts again, the dread I'd felt all afternoon; and again I watched the barmaid, moving about the bar, washing glasses, and singing. "Listen. They'll let him out and then it'll just start all over again. That's what I mean."

"You mean—they'll let him out. And then he'll just start working his way back in again. You mean he'll never kick the habit. Is that what you mean?"

"That's right," he said cheerfully. "*You* see what I mean."

"Tell me," I said at last, "why does he want to die? He must want to die, he's killing himself, why does he want to die?"

He looked at me in surprise. He licked his lips. "He don't want to die. He wants to live. Don't nobody want to die, ever."

Then I wanted to ask him—too many things. He could not have answered, or if he had, I could not have borne the answers. I started walking. "Well, I guess it's none of my business."

"It's going to be rough on old Sonny," he said. We reached the subway station. "This is your station?" he asked. I nodded. I took one step down. "Damn!" he said suddenly. I looked up at him. He grinned again. "Damn it if I didn't leave all my money home. You ain't got a dollar on you, have you? Just for a couple of days, is all."

All at once something inside gave and threatened to come pouring out of me. I didn't hate him any more. I felt that in another moment I'd start crying like a child.

"Sure," I said. "Don't sweat." I looked in my wallet and didn't have a dollar, I only had five. "Here," I said. "That hold you?"

He didn't look at it—he didn't want to look at it. A terrible closed look came over his face, as though he were keeping the number on the bill a secret from him and me. "Thanks," he said, and now he was dying to see me go. "Don't worry about Sonny. Maybe I'll write him or something."

"Sure," I said. "You do that. So long."

"Be seeing you," he said. I went on down the steps.

*   *   *

And I didn't write Sonny or send him anything for a long time. When I finally did, it was just after my little girl died, he wrote me back a letter which made me feel like a bastard.

Here's what he said:

Dear brother,

You don't know how much I needed to hear from you. I wanted to write you many a time but I dug how much I must have hurt you and so I didn't write. But now I feel like a man who's been trying to climb up out of some deep, real deep and funky hole and just saw the sun up there, outside. I got to get outside.

I can't tell you much about how I got here. I mean I don't know how to tell you. I guess I was afraid of something or I was trying to escape from something and you know I have never been very strong in the head (smile). I'm glad Mama and Daddy are dead and can't see what's happened to their son and I swear if I'd known what I was doing I would never have hurt you so, you and a lot of other fine people who were nice to me and who believed in me.

I don't want you to think it had anything to do with me being a musician. It's more than that. Or maybe less than that. I can't get anything straight in my head down here and I try not to think about what's going to happen to me when I get outside again. Sometime I think I'm going to flip and *never* get outside and sometime I think I'll come straight back. I tell you one thing, though, I'd rather blow my brains out than go through this again. But that's what they all say, so they tell me. If I tell you when I'm coming to New York and if you could meet me, I sure would appreciate it. Give my love to Isabel and the kids and I was sure sorry to hear about little Gracie. I wish I could be like Mama and say the Lord's will be done, but I don't know it seems to me that trouble is the one thing that never does get stopped and I don't know what good it does to blame it on the Lord. But maybe it does some good if you believe it.

Your brother,
Sonny

Then I kept in constant touch with him and I sent him whatever I could and I went to meet him when he came back to New York. When I saw him many things I thought I had forgotten came flooding back to me. This was because I had begun, finally, to wonder about Sonny, about the life that Sonny lived inside. This life, whatever it was, had made him older and thinner and it had deepened the distant stillness in which he had always moved. He looked very unlike my baby brother. Yet, when he smiled, when we shook hands, the baby brother I'd never known looked out from the depths of his private life, like an animal waiting to be coaxed into the light.

"How you been keeping?" he asked me.

"All right. And you?"

"Just fine." He was smiling all over his face. "It's good to see you again."

"It's good to see you."

The seven years' difference in our ages lay between us like a chasm: I wondered if these years would ever operate between us as a bridge. I was remembering, and it made it hard to catch my breath, that I had been there when he was born; and I had heard the first words he had ever spoken. When he started to walk, he walked from our mother straight to me. I caught him just before he fell when he took the first steps he ever took in this world.

"How's Isabel?"

"Just fine. She's dying to see you."

"And the boys?"

"They're fine, too. They're anxious to see their uncle."

"Oh, come on. You know they don't remember me."

"Are you kidding? Of course they remember you."

He grinned again. We got into a taxi. We had a lot to say to each other, far too much to know how to begin.

As the taxi began to move, I asked, "You still want to go to India?"

He laughed. "You still remember that. Hell, no. This place is Indian enough for me."

"It used to belong to them," I said.

And he laughed again. "They damn sure knew what they were doing when they got rid of it."

Years ago, when he was around fourteen, he'd been all hipped on the idea of going to India. He read books about people sitting on rocks, naked, in all kinds of weather, but mostly bad, naturally, and walking barefoot through hot coals and arriving at wisdom. I used to say that it sounded to me as though they were getting away from wisdom as fast as they could. I think he sort of looked down on me for that.

"Do you mind," he asked, "if we have the driver drive alongside the park? On the west side—I haven't seen the city in so long."

"Of course not," I said. I was afraid that I might sound as though I were humoring him, but I hoped he wouldn't take it that way.

So we drove along, between the green of the park and the stony, lifeless elegance of hotels and apartment buildings, toward the vivid, killing streets of our childhood. These streets hadn't changed, though housing projects jutted up out of them now like rocks in the middle of a boiling sea. Most of the houses in which we had grown up had vanished, as had the stores from which we had stolen, the basements in which we had first tried sex, the rooftops from which we had hurled tin cans and bricks. But houses exactly like the houses of our past yet dominated the landscape, boys exactly like the boys we once had been found themselves smothering in these houses, came down into the streets for light and air and found themselves encircled by disaster. Some escaped the trap, most didn't. Those who got out always left something of themselves behind, as some animals amputate a leg and leave it in the trap. It might be said, perhaps, that I had escaped, after all, I was a school teacher; or that Sonny had, he hadn't lived in Harlem for years. Yet, as the cab moved uptown through streets which seemed, with a rush, to darken with dark people, and as I covertly studied Sonny's face, it came to me that what we both were seeking through our separate cab windows was that part of ourselves which had been left behind. It's always at the hour of trouble and confrontation that the missing member aches.

We hit 110th Street and started rolling up Lenox Avenue. And I'd known this avenue all my life, but it seemed to me again, as it had seemed on the day I'd first heard about Sonny's trouble, filled with a hidden menace which was its very breath of life.

"We almost there," said Sonny.

"Almost." We were both too nervous to say anything more.

We live in a housing project. It hasn't been up long. A few days after it was up it seemed uninhabitably new, now, of course, it's already rundown. It looks like a parody of the good, clean, faceless life—God knows the people who live in it do their best to make it a parody. The beat-looking grass lying around isn't enough to make their lives green, the hedges will never hold out the streets, and they know it. The big windows fool no one, they aren't big enough to make space out of no space. They don't bother with the windows, they watch the TV screen instead. The playground is most popular with the children who don't play at jacks, or skip rope, or roller skate, or swing, and they can be found in it after dark. We moved in partly because it's not too far from where I teach, and partly for the kids; but it's really just like the houses in which Sonny and I grew up. The same things happen, they'll have the same things to remember. The moment Sonny and I started into the house I had the feeling that I was simply bringing him back into the danger he had almost died trying to escape.

Sonny has never been talkative. So I don't know why I was sure he'd be dying to talk to me when supper was over the first night. Everything went fine, the oldest boy remembered him, and the youngest boy liked him, and Sonny had remembered to bring something for each of them; and Isabel, who is really much nicer than I am, more open and giving, had gone to a lot of trouble about dinner and was genuinely glad to see him. And she's always been able to tease Sonny in a way that I haven't. It was nice to see her face so vivid again and to hear her laugh and watch her make Sonny laugh. She wasn't, or, anyway, she didn't seem to be, at all uneasy or embarrassed. She chatted as though there were no subject which had to be avoided and she got Sonny past his first, faint stiffness. And thank God she was there, for I was filled with that icy dread again. Everything I did seemed awkward to me, and everything I said sounded freighted with hidden meaning. I was trying to remember everything I'd heard about dope addiction and I couldn't help watching Sonny for signs. I wasn't doing it out of malice. I was trying to find out something about my brother. I was dying to hear him tell me he was safe.

"Safe!" my father grunted, whenever Mama suggested trying to move to a neighborhood which might be safer for children. "Safe, hell! Ain't no place safe for kids, nor nobody."

He always went on like this, but he wasn't, ever, really as bad as he sounded, not even on weekends, when he got drunk. As a matter of fact, he was always on the lookout for "something a little better," but he died before he found it. He died suddenly, during a drunken weekend in the middle of the war, when Sonny was fifteen. He and

Sonny hadn't ever got on too well. And this was partly because Sonny was the apple of his father's eye. It was because he loved Sonny so much and was frightened for him, that he was always fighting with him. It doesn't do any good to fight with Sonny. Sonny just moves back, inside himself, where he can't be reached. But the principal reason that they never hit it off is that they were so much alike. Daddy was big and rough and loud-talking, just the opposite of Sonny, but they both had—that same privacy.

Mama tried to tell me something about this, just after Daddy died. I was home on leave from the army.

This was the last time I ever saw my mother alive. Just the same, this picture gets all mixed up in my mind with pictures I had of her when she was younger. The way I always see her is the way she used to be on a Sunday afternoon, say, when the old folks were talking after the big Sunday dinner. I always see her wearing pale blue. She'd be sitting on the sofa. And my father would be sitting in the easy chair, not far from her. And the living room would be full of church folks and relatives. There they sit, in chairs all around the living room, and the night is creeping up outside, but nobody knows it yet. You can see the darkness growing against the window-panes and you hear the street noises every now and again, or maybe the jangling beat of a tambourine from one of the churches close by, but it's real quiet in the room. For a moment nobody's talking, but every face looks darkening, like the sky outside. And my mother rocks a little from the waist, and my father's eyes are closed. Everyone is looking at something a child can't see. For a minute they've forgotten the children. Maybe a kid is lying on the rug, half asleep. Maybe somebody's got a kid in his lap and is absent-mindedly stroking the kid's head. Maybe there's a kid, quiet and big-eyed, curled up in a big chair in the corner. The silence, the darkness coming, and the darkness in the faces frightens the child obscurely. He hopes that the hand which strokes his forehead will never stop—will never die. He hopes that there will never come a time when the old folks won't be sitting around the living room, talking about where they've come from, and what they've seen, and what's happened to them and their kinfolk.

But something deep and watchful in the child knows that this is bound to end, is already ending. In a moment someone will get up and turn on the light. Then the old folks will remember the children and they won't talk any more that day. And when light fills the room, the child is filled with darkness. He knows that every time this happens he's moved just a little closer to that darkness outside. The darkness outside is what the old folks have been talking about. It's what they've come from. It's what they endure. The child knows that they won't talk any more because if he knows too much about what's happening to *them,* he'll know too much too soon, about what's going to happen to *him.*

The last time I talked to my mother, I remember I was restless. I wanted to get out and see Isabel. We weren't married then and we had a lot to straighten out between us.

There Mama sat, in black, by the window. She was humming an old church song, *Lord you brought me from a long ways off.* Sonny was out somewhere. Mama kept watching the streets.

"I don't know," she said, "if I'll ever see you again, after you go off from here. But I hope you'll remember the things I tried to teach you."

"Don't talk like that," I said, and smiled. "You'll be here a long time yet."

She smiled, too, but she said nothing. She was quiet for a long time. And I said, "Mama, don't you worry about nothing. I'll be writing all the time, and you be getting the checks. . . ."

"I want to talk to you about your brother," she said, suddenly. "If anything happens to me he ain't going to have nobody to look out for him."

"Mama," I said, "ain't nothing going to happen to you *or* Sonny. Sonny's all right. He's a good boy and he's got good sense."

"It ain't a question of his being a good boy," Mama said, "nor of his having good sense. It ain't only the bad ones, nor yet the dumb ones that gets sucked under." She stopped, looking at me. "Your Daddy once had a brother," she said, and she smiled in a way that made me feel she was in pain. "You didn't never know that, did you?"

"No," I said, "I never knew that," and I watched her face.

"Oh, yes," she said, "your Daddy had a brother." She looked out of the window again. "I know you never saw your Daddy cry. But *I* did—many a time, through all these years."

I asked her, "What happened to his brother? How come nobody's ever talked about him?"

This was the first time I ever saw my mother look old.

"His brother got killed," she said, "when he was just a little younger than you are now. I knew him. He was a fine boy. He was maybe a little full of the devil, but he didn't mean nobody no harm."

Then she stopped and the room was silent, exactly as it had sometimes been on those Sunday afternoons. Mama kept looking out into the streets.

"He used to have a job in the mill," she said, "and, like all young folks, he just liked to perform on Saturday nights. Saturday nights, him and your father would drift around to different places, go to dances and things like that, or just sit around with people they knew, and your father's brother would sing, he had a fine voice, and play along with himself on his guitar. Well, this particular Saturday night, him and your father was coming home from some place, and they were both a little drunk and there was a moon that night, it was bright like day. Your father's brother was feeling kind of good, and he was whistling to himself, and he had his guitar slung over his shoulder. They was coming down a hill and beneath them was a road that turned off from the highway. Well, your father's brother, being always kind of frisky, decided to run down this hill, and he did, with that guitar banging and clanging behind him, and he ran across the road, and he was making water behind a tree. And your father was sort of amused at him and he was still coming down the hill, kind of slow. Then he heard a car motor and that same minute his brother stepped from behind the tree, into the road, in the moonlight. And he started to cross the road. And your father started to run down the hill, he says he don't know why. This car was full of white men. They was all drunk, and when they seen your father's brother they let out a great whoop and holler and they aimed the car straight at him. They was having fun, they just wanted to scare him, the way they do sometimes, you know. But they was drunk. And I guess the boy, being drunk, too, and scared, kind of lost his head. By the time he jumped it was too late. Your father says he heard his brother scream when the car rolled over him, and he heard the wood of that guitar when it give, and he heard them strings go flying, and he heard them white men shouting, and the car kept on a-going and it ain't stopped till this day. And, time your father got down the hill, his brother weren't nothing but blood and pulp."

Tears were gleaming on my mother's face. There wasn't anything I could say.

"He never mentioned it," she said, "because I never let him mention it before you children. Your Daddy was like a crazy man that night and for many a night thereafter. He says he never in his life seen anything as dark as that road after the lights of that car had gone away. Weren't nothing, weren't nobody on that road, just your Daddy and his brother and that busted guitar. Oh, yes. Your Daddy never did really get right again. Till the day he died he weren't sure but that every white man he saw was the man that killed his brother."

She stopped and took out her handkerchief and dried her eyes and looked at me.

"I ain't telling you all this," she said, "to make you scared or bitter or to make you hate nobody. I'm telling you this because you got a brother. And the world ain't changed."

I guess I didn't want to believe this. I guess she saw this in my face. She turned away from me, toward the window again, searching those streets.

"But I praise my Redeemer," she said at last, "that He called your Daddy home before me. I ain't saying it to throw no flowers at myself, but, I declare, it keeps me from feeling too cast down to know I helped your father get safely through this world. Your father always acted like he was the roughest, strongest man on earth. And everybody took him to be like that. But if he hadn't had *me* there—to see his tears!"

She was crying again. Still I couldn't move. I said, "Lord, Lord, Mama, I didn't know it was like that."

"Oh, honey," she said, "there's a lot that you don't know. But you are going to find it out." She stood up from the window and came over to me. "You got to hold on to your brother," she said, "and don't let him fall, no matter what it looks like is happening to him and no matter how evil you gets with him. You going to be evil with him many a time. But don't you forget what I told you, you hear?"

"I won't forget," I said. "Don't you worry, I won't forget. I won't let nothing happen to Sonny."

My mother smiled as though she were amused at something she saw in my face. Then, "You may not be able to stop nothing from happening. But you got to let him know you's *there*."

Two days later I was married, and then I was gone. And I had a lot of things on my mind and I pretty well forgot my promise to Mama until I got shipped home on a special furlough for her funeral.

And, after the funeral, with just Sonny and me alone in the empty kitchen, I tried to find out something about him.

"What do you want to do?" I asked him.

"I'm going to be a musician," he said.

For he had graduated, in the time I had been away, from dancing to the juke box to finding out who was playing what, and what they were doing with it, and he had bought himself a set of drums.

"You mean, you want to be a drummer?" I somehow had the feeling that being a drummer might be all right for other people but not for my brother Sonny.

"I don't think," he said, looking at me very gravely, "that I'll ever be a good drummer. But I think I can play a piano."

I frowned. I'd never played the role of the older brother quite so seriously before, had scarcely ever, in fact, *asked* Sonny a damn thing. I sensed myself in the presence of something I didn't really know how to handle, didn't understand. So I made my frown a little deeper as I asked: "What kind of musician do you want to be?"

He grinned. "How many kinds do you think there are?"

"Be *serious*," I said.

He laughed, throwing his head back, and then looked at me. "I *am* serious."

"Well, then, for Christ's sake, stop kidding around and answer a serious question. I mean, do you want to be a concert pianist, or want to play classical music and all that, or—or what?" Long before I finished he was laughing again. "For Christ's *sake,* Sonny!"

He sobered, but with difficulty. "I'm sorry. But you sound so—*scared!*" and he was off again.

"Well, you may think it's funny now, baby, but it's not going to be so funny when you have to make your living at it, let me tell you *that.*" I was furious because I knew he was laughing at me and I didn't know why.

"No," he said, very sober now, and afraid, perhaps, that he'd hurt me, "I don't want to be a classical pianist. That isn't what interests me. I mean"—he paused, looking hard at me, as though his eyes would help me to understand, and then gestured helplessly, as though perhaps his hand would help—"I mean, I'll have a lot of studying to do, and I'll have to study *everything,* but, I mean, I want to play *with*—jazz musicians." He stopped. "I want to play jazz," he said.

Well, the word had never before sounded as heavy, as real, as it sounded that afternoon in Sonny's mouth. I just looked at him and I was probably frowning a real frown by this time. I simply couldn't see why on earth he'd want to spend his time hanging around nightclubs, clowning around on bandstands, while people pushed each other around a dance floor. It seemed—beneath him, somehow. I had never thought about it before, had never been forced to, but I suppose I had always put jazz musicians in a class with what Daddy called "goodtime people."

"Are you *serious?*"

"Hell, *yes,* I'm serious."

He looked more helpless than ever, and annoyed, and deeply hurt.

I suggested helpfully: "You mean—like Louis Armstrong?"

His face closed as though I'd struck him. "No. I'm not talking about none of that old-time, down home crap."

"Well, look Sonny, I'm sorry, don't get mad. I just don't altogether get it, that's all. Name somebody—you know, a jazz musician you admire."

"Bird."

"Who?"

"Bird! Charlie Parker! Don't they teach you nothing in the god-damn army?" I lit a cigarette. I was surprised and then a little amused to discover that I was trembling. "I've been out of touch," I said. "You'll have to be patient with me. Now. Who's this Parker character?"

"He's just one of the greatest jazz musicians alive," said Sonny, sullenly, his hands in his pockets, his back to me. "Maybe *the* greatest," he added, bitterly, "that's probably why *you* never heard of him."

"All right," I said, "I'm ignorant. I'm sorry. I'll go out and buy all the cat's records right away, all right?"

"It don't," said Sonny, with dignity, "make any difference to me. I don't care what you listen to. Don't do me no favors."

I was beginning to realize that I'd never seen him so upset before. With another part of my mind I was thinking that this would probably turn out to be one of those things kids go through and that I shouldn't make it seem important by pushing it too hard. Still, I didn't think it would do any harm to ask: "Doesn't all this take a lot of time? Can you make a living at it?"

He turned back to me and half leaned, half sat, on the kitchen table. "Everything takes time," he said, "and—well, yes, sure, I can make a living at it. But what I don't seem to be able to make you understand is that it's the only thing I want to do."

"Well, Sonny," I said gently, "you know people can't always do exactly what they *want* to do—"

"*No,* I don't know that," said Sonny, surprising me. "I think people *ought* to do what they want to do, what else are they alive for?"

"You are getting to be a big boy," I said desperately, "it's time you started thinking about your future."

"I'm thinking about my future," said Sonny, grimly. "I think about it all the time."

I gave up. I decided, if he didn't change his mind, that we could always talk about it later. "In the meantime," I said, "you got to finish school." We had already decided that he'd have to move in with Isabel and her folks. I knew this wasn't the ideal arrangement because Isabel's folks are inclined to be dicty[2] and they hadn't especially wanted Isabel to marry me. But I didn't know what else to do. "And we have to get you fixed up at Isabel's."

There was a long silence. He moved from the kitchen table to the window. "That's a terrible idea. You know it yourself."

"Do you have a *better* idea?"

He just walked up and down the kitchen for a minute. He was as tall as I was. He had started to shave. I suddenly had the feeling that I didn't know him at all.

He stopped at the kitchen table and picked up my cigarettes. Looking at me with a kind of mocking, amused defiance, he put one between his lips. "You mind?"

"You smoking already?"

He lit the cigarette and nodded, watching me through the smoke. "I just wanted to see if I'd have the courage to smoke in front of you." He grinned and blew a great cloud of smoke to the ceiling. "It was easy." He looked at my face. "Come on, now. I bet you was smoking at my age, tell the truth."

I didn't say anything but the truth was on my face, and he laughed. But now there was something very strained in his laugh. "Sure. And I bet that ain't all you was doing."

He was frightening me a little. "Cut the crap," I said. "We already decided that you was going to go and live at Isabel's. Now what's got into you all of a sudden?"

"*You* decided it," he pointed out. "*I* didn't decide nothing." He stopped in front of me, leaning against the stove, arms loosely folded. "Look, brother. I don't want to

[2]Snobbish.

stay in Harlem no more, I really don't." He was very earnest. He looked at me, then over toward the kitchen window. There was something in his eyes I'd never seen before, some thoughtfulness, some worry all his own. He rubbed the muscle of one arm. "It's time I was getting out of here."

"Where do you want to *go,* Sonny?"

"I want to join the army. Or the navy, I don't care. If I say I'm old enough, they'll believe me."

Then I got mad. It was because I was so scared. "You must be crazy. You goddamn fool, what the hell do you want to go and join the *army* for?"

"I just told you. To get out of Harlem."

"Sonny, you haven't even finished *school.* And if you really want to be a musician, how do you expect to study if you're in the *army?*"

He looked at me, trapped, and in anguish. "There's ways. I might be able to work out some kind of deal. Anyway, I'll have the G.I. Bill when I come out."

"*If* you come out." We stared at each other. "Sonny, please. Be reasonable. I know the setup is far from perfect. But we got to do the best we can."

"I ain't learning nothing in school," he said. "Even when I go." He turned away from me and opened the window and threw his cigarette out into the narrow alley. I watched his back. "At least, I ain't learning nothing you'd want me to learn." He slammed the window so hard I thought the glass would fly out, and turned back to me. "And I'm sick of the stink of these garbage cans!"

"Sonny," I said, "I know how you feel. But if you don't finish school now, you're going to be sorry later that you didn't." I grabbed him by the shoulders. "And you only got another year. It ain't so bad. And I'll come back and I swear I'll help you do *whatever* you want to do. Just try to put up with it till I come back. Will you please do that? For me?"

He didn't answer and he wouldn't look at me.

"Sonny. You hear me?"

He pulled away. "I hear you. But you never hear anything *I* say."

I didn't know what to say to that. He looked out of the window and then back at me. "OK," he said, and sighed. "I'll try."

Then I said, trying to cheer him up a little, "They got a piano at Isabel's. You can practice on it."

And as a matter of fact, it did cheer him up for a minute. "That's right," he said to himself. "I forgot that." His face relaxed a little. But the worry, the thoughtfulness, played on it still, the way shadows play on a face which is staring into the fire.

But I thought I'd never hear the end of that piano. At first, Isabel would write me, saying how nice it was that Sonny was so serious about his music and how, as soon as he came in from school, or wherever he had been when he was supposed to be at school, he went straight to that piano and stayed there until suppertime. And, after supper, he went back to that piano and stayed there until everybody went to bed. He was at the piano all day Saturday and all day Sunday. Then he bought a record player and started playing records. He'd play one record over and over again, all day long sometimes, and he'd improvise along with it on the piano. Or he'd play one section of the record, one chord, one change, one progression, then he'd do it on the piano. Then back to the record. Then back to the piano.

Well, I really don't know how they stood it. Isabel finally confessed that it wasn't like living with a person at all, it was like living with sound. And the sound didn't make any sense to her, didn't make any sense to any of them—naturally. They began, in a way, to be afflicted by this presence that was living in their home. It was as though Sonny were some sort of god, or monster. He moved in an atmosphere which wasn't like theirs at all. They fed him and he ate, he washed himself, he walked in and out of their door; he certainly wasn't nasty or unpleasant or rude, Sonny isn't any of those things; but it was as though he were all wrapped up in some cloud, some fire, some vision all his own; and there wasn't any way to reach him.

At the same time, he wasn't really a man yet, he was still a child, and they had to watch out for him in all kinds of ways. They certainly couldn't throw him out. Neither did they dare to make a great scene about that piano because even they dimly sensed, as I sensed, from so many thousands of miles away, that Sonny was at that piano playing for his life.

But he hadn't been going to school. One day a letter came from the school board and Isabel's mother got it—there had, apparently, been other letters but Sonny had torn them up. This day, when Sonny came in, Isabel's mother showed him the letter and asked where he'd been spending his time. And she finally got it out of him that he'd been down in Greenwich Village, with musicians and other characters, in a white girl's apartment. And this scared her and she started to scream at him and what came up, once she began—though she denies it to this day—was what sacrifices they were making to give Sonny a decent home and how little he appreciated it.

Sonny didn't play the piano that day. By evening, Isabel's mother had calmed down but then there was the old man to deal with, and Isabel herself. Isabel says she did her best to be calm but she broke down and started crying. She says she just watched Sonny's face. She could tell, by watching him, what was happening with him. And what was happening was that they penetrated his cloud, they had reached him. Even if their fingers had been a thousand times more gentle than human fingers ever are, he could hardly help feeling that they had stripped him naked and were spitting on that nakedness. For he also had to see that his presence, that music, which was life or death to him, had been torture for them and that they had endured it, not at all for his sake, but only for mine. And Sonny couldn't take that. He can take it a little better today than he could then but he's still not very good at it and, frankly, I don't know anybody who is.

The silence of the next few days must have been louder than the sound of all the music ever played since time began. One morning, before she went to work, Isabel was in his room for something and she suddenly realized that all of his records were gone. And she knew for certain that he was gone. And he was. He went as far as the navy would carry him. He finally sent me a postcard from some place in Greece and that was the first I knew that Sonny was still alive. I didn't see him any more until we were both back in New York and the war had long been over.

He was a man by then, of course, but I wasn't willing to see it. He came by the house from time to time, but we fought almost every time we met. I didn't like the way he carried himself, loose and dreamlike all the time, and I didn't like his friends, and his music seemed to be merely an excuse for the life he led. It sounded just that weird and disordered.

Then we had a fight, a pretty awful fight, and I didn't see him for months. By and by I looked him up, where he was living, in a furnished room in the Village, and I tried to make it up. But there were lots of other people in the room and Sonny just lay on his bed, and he wouldn't come downstairs with me, and he treated these other people as though they were his family and I weren't. So I got mad and then he got mad, and then I told him that he might just as well be dead as live the way he was living. Then he stood up and he told me not to worry about him any more in life, that he *was* dead as far as I was concerned. Then he pushed me to the door and the other people looked on as though nothing were happening, and he slammed the door behind me. I stood in the hallway, staring at the door. I heard somebody laugh in the room and then the tears came to my eyes. I started down the steps, whistling to keep from crying, I kept whistling to myself, *You going to need me, baby, one of these cold, rainy days.*

I read about Sonny's trouble in the spring. Little Grace died in the fall. She was a beautiful little girl. But she only lived a little over two years. She died of polio and she suffered. She had a slight fever for a couple of days, but it didn't seem like anything and we just kept her in bed. And we would certainly have called the doctor, but the fever dropped, she seemed to be all right. So we thought it had just been a cold. Then, one day, she was up, playing, Isabel was in the kitchen fixing lunch for the two boys when they'd come in from school, and she heard Grace fall down in the living room. When you have a lot of children you don't always start running when one of them falls, unless they start screaming or something. And, this time, Grace was quiet. Yet, Isabel says that when she heard that *thump* and then that silence, something happened in her to make her afraid. And she ran to the living room and there was little Grace on the floor, all twisted up, and the reason she hadn't screamed was that she couldn't get her breath. And when she did scream, it was the worst sound, Isabel says, that she'd ever heard in all her life, and she still hears it sometimes in her dreams. Isabel will sometimes wake me up with a low, moaning, strangled sound and I have to be quick to awaken her and hold her to me and where Isabel is weeping against me seems a mortal wound.

I think I may have written Sonny the very day that little Grace was buried. I was sitting in the living room in the dark, by myself, and I suddenly thought of Sonny. My trouble made his real.

One Saturday afternoon, when Sonny had been living with us, or, anyway, been in our house, for nearly two weeks, I found myself wandering aimlessly about the living room, drinking from a can of beer, and trying to work up the courage to search Sonny's room. He was out, he was usually out whenever I was home, and Isabel had taken the children to see their grandparents. Suddenly I was standing still in front of the living room window, watching Seventh Avenue. The idea of searching Sonny's room made me still. I scarcely dared to admit to myself what I'd be searching for. I didn't know what I'd do if I found it. Or if I didn't.

On the sidewalk across from me, near the entrance to a barbecue joint, some people were holding an old-fashioned revival meeting. The barbecue cook, wearing a dirty white apron, his *conked* hair reddish and metallic in the pale sun, and a cigarette between his lips, stood in the doorway, watching them. Kids and older people paused in their errands and stood there, along with some older men and a couple of very tough-looking women who watched everything that happened on the avenue, as though they owned it, or were maybe owned by it. Well, they were watching this, too. The revival was being carried on by three sisters in black, and a brother. All they had were their voices and their Bibles and a tambourine. The brother was testifying and while he testified two of the sisters stood together, seeming to say, amen, and the third sister walked around with the tambourine outstretched and a couple of people dropped coins into it. Then the brother's testimony ended and the sister who had been taking up the collection dumped the coins into her palm and transferred them to the pocket of her long black robe. Then she raised both hands, striking the tambourine against the air, and then against one hand, and she started to sing. And the two other sisters and the brother joined in.

It was strange, suddenly, to watch, though I had been seeing these street meetings all my life. So, of course, had everybody else down there. Yet, they paused and watched and listened and I stood still at the window. *"Tis the old ship of Zion,"* they sang, and the sister with the tambourine kept a steady, jangling beat, *"it has rescued many a thousand!"* Not a soul under the sound of their voices was hearing this song for the first time, not one of them had been rescued. Nor had they seen much in the way of rescue work being done around them. Neither did they especially believe in the holiness of the three sisters and the brother, they knew too much about them, knew where they lived, and how. The woman with the tambourine, whose voice dominated the air, whose face was bright with joy, was divided by very little from the woman who stood watching her, a cigarette between her heavy, chapped lips, her hair a cuckoo's nest, her face scarred and swollen from many beatings, and her black eyes glittering like coal. Perhaps they both knew this, which was why, when, as rarely, they addressed each other, they addressed each other as Sister. As the singing filled the air the watching, listening faces underwent a change, the eyes focusing on something within; the music seemed to soothe a poison out of them; and time seemed, nearly, to fall away from the sullen, belligerent, battered faces, as though they were fleeing back to their first condition, while dreaming of their last. The barbecue cook half shook his head and smiled, and dropped his cigarette and disappeared into his joint. A man fumbled in his pockets for change and stood holding it in his hand impatiently, as though he had just remembered a pressing appointment further up the avenue. He looked furious. Then I saw Sonny, standing on the edge of the crowd. He was carrying a wide, flat notebook with a green cover, and it made him look, from where I was standing, almost like a schoolboy. The coppery sun brought out the copper in his skin, he was very faintly smiling, standing very still. Then the singing stopped, the tambourine turned into a collection plate again. The furious man dropped in his coins and vanished, so did a couple of the women, and Sonny dropped some change in the plate, looking directly at the woman with a little smile. He started across the avenue, toward the house. He has a slow, loping walk, something like the way Harlem hipsters walk, only he's imposed on this his own half-beat. I had never really noticed it before.

I stayed at the window, both relieved and apprehensive. As Sonny disappeared from my sight, they began singing again. And they were still singing when his key turned in the lock.

"Hey," he said.

"Hey, yourself. You want some beer?"

"No. Well, maybe." But he came up to the window and stood beside me, look-ing out. "What a warm voice," he said.

They were singing *If I could only hear my mother pray again!*

"Yes," I said, "and she can sure beat that tambourine."

"But what a terrible song," he said, and laughed. He dropped his notebook on the sofa and disappeared into the kitchen. "Where's Isabel and the kids?"

"I think they went to see their grandparents. You hungry?"

"No." He came back into the living room with his can of beer. "You want to come some place with me tonight?"

I sensed, I don't know how, that I couldn't possibly say no. "Sure. Where?"

He sat down on the sofa and picked up his notebook and started leafing through it. "I'm going to sit in with some fellows in a joint in the Village."

"You mean, you're going to play, tonight?"

"That's right." He took a swallow of his beer and moved back, to the window. He gave me a sidelong look. "If you can stand it."

"I'll try," I said.

He smiled to himself and we both watched as the meeting across the way broke up. The three sisters and the brother, heads bowed, were singing *God be with you till we meet again.* The faces around them were very quiet. Then the song ended. The small crowd dispersed. We watched the three women and the lone man walk slowly up the avenue.

"When she was singing before," said Sonny, abruptly, "her voice reminded me for a minute of what heroin feels like sometimes—when it's in your veins. It makes you feel sort of warm and cool at the same time. And distant. And—and sure." He sipped his beer, very deliberately not looking at me. I watched his face. "It makes you feel—in control. Sometimes you've got to have that feeling."

"Do you?" I sat down slowly in the easy chair.

"Sometimes." He went to the sofa and picked up his notebook again. "Some people do."

"In order," I asked, "to play?" And my voice was very ugly, full of contempt and anger.

"Well"—he looked at me with great, troubled eyes, as though, in fact, he hoped his eyes would tell me things he could never otherwise say—"they *think* so. And *if* they think so—!"

"And what do *you* think?" I asked.

He sat on the sofa and put his can of beer on the floor. "I don't know," he said, and I couldn't be sure if he were answering my question or pursuing his thoughts. His face didn't tell me. "It's not so much to *play.* It's to *stand* it, to be able to make it at all. On any level." He frowned and smiled: "In order to keep from shaking to pieces."

"But these friends of yours," I said, "they seem to shake themselves to pieces pretty goddamn fast."

"Maybe." He played with the notebook. And something told me that I should curb my tongue, that Sonny was doing his best to talk, that I should listen. "But of course you only know the ones that've gone to pieces. Some don't—or at least they haven't *yet* and that's just about all *any* of us can say." He paused. "And then there are some who just live, really, in hell, and they know it and they see what's happening, and they go right on. I don't know." He sighed, dropped the notebook, folded his arms. "Some guys, you can tell from the way they play, they on something *all* the time. And you can see that, well, it makes something real for them. But of course," he picked up his beer from the floor and sipped it and put the can down again, "they *want* to, too, you've got to see that. Even some of them that say they don't—*some,* not all."

"And what about you?" I asked—I couldn't help it. "What about you? Do *you* want to?"

He stood up and walked to the window and remained silent for a long time. Then he sighed. "Me," he said. Then: "While I was downstairs before, on my way here, listening to that woman sing, it struck me all of a sudden how much suffering she must have had to go through—to sing like that. It's *repulsive* to think you have to suffer that much."

I said: "But there's no way not to suffer—is there, Sonny?"

"I believe not," he said and smiled, "but that's never stopped anyone from trying." He looked at me. "Has it?" I realized, with this mocking look, that there stood between us, forever, beyond the power of time or forgiveness, the fact that I had held silence—so long!—when he had needed human speech to help him. He turned back to the window. "No, there's no way not to suffer. But you try all kinds of ways to keep from drowning in it, to keep on top of it, and to make it seem—well, like *you.* Like you did something, all right, and now you're suffering for it. You know?" I said nothing. "Well you know," he said, impatiently, "why *do* people suffer? Maybe it's better to do something to give it a reason, *any* reason."

"But we just agreed," I said, "that there's no way not to suffer. Isn't it better, then, just to—take it?"

"But nobody just takes it," Sonny cried, "that's what I'm telling you! *Everybody* tries not to. You're just hung up on the *way* some people try—it's not *your* way!"

The hair on my face began to itch, my face felt wet. "That's not true," I said, "that's not true. I don't give a damn what other people do, I don't even care how they suffer. I just care how *you* suffer." And he looked at me. "Please believe me," I said. "I don't want to see you—die—trying not to suffer."

"I won't," he said, flatly, "die trying not to suffer. At least, not any faster than anybody else."

"But there's no need," I said, trying to laugh, "is there? in killing yourself."

I wanted to say more, but I couldn't. I wanted to talk about will power and how life could be—well, beautiful. I wanted to say that it was all within; but was it? or, rather, wasn't that exactly the trouble? And I wanted to promise that I would never fail him again. But it would all have sounded—empty words and lies.

So I made the promise to myself and prayed that I would keep it.

"It's terrible sometimes, inside," he said, "that's what's the trouble. You walk these streets, black and funky and cold, and there's not really a living ass to talk to, and there's nothing shaking, and there's no way of getting it out—that storm inside. You can't talk it and you can't make love with it, and when you finally try to get with it and play it, you realize *nobody's* listening. So *you've* got to listen. You got to find a way to listen."

And then he walked away from the window and sat on the sofa again, as though all the wind had suddenly been knocked out of him. "Sometimes you'll do *anything* to play, even cut your mother's throat." He laughed and looked at me. "Or your brother's." Then he sobered. "Or your own." Then: "Don't worry. I'm all right now and I think I'll *be* all right. But I can't forget—where I've been. I don't mean just the physical place I've been, I mean where I've *been*. And *what* I've been."

"What have you been, Sonny?" I asked.

He smiled—but sat sideways on the sofa, his elbow resting on the back, his fingers playing with his mouth and chin, not looking at me. "I've been something I didn't recognize, didn't know I could be. Didn't know anybody could be." He stopped, looking inward, looking helplessly young, looking old. "I'm not talking about it now because I feel *guilty* or anything like that—maybe it would be better if I did, I don't know. Anyway, I can't really talk about it. Not to you, not to anybody," and now he turned and faced me. "Sometimes, you know and it was actually when I was most *out* of the world. I felt that I was in it, that I was *with* it, really, and I could play or I didn't really have to *play*, it just came out of me, it was there. And I don't know how I played, thinking about it now, but I know I did awful things, those times, sometimes, to people. Or it wasn't that I *did* anything to them—it was that they weren't real." He picked up the beer can; it was empty; he rolled it between his palms: "And other times—well, I needed a fix, I needed to find a place to lean, I needed to clear a space to *listen*—and I couldn't find it, and I —went crazy, I did terrible things to *me*, I was terrible *for* me." He began pressing the beer can between his hands, I watched the metal begin to give. It glittered, as he played with it, like a knife, and I was afraid he would cut himself, but I said nothing. "Oh well. I can never tell you. I was all by myself at the bottom of something, stinking and sweating and crying and shaking, and I smelled it, you know? *my* stink, and I thought I'd die if I couldn't get away from it and yet, all the same, I knew that everything I was doing was just locking me in with it. And I didn't know," he paused, still flattening the beer can, "I didn't know, I still *don't* know, something kept telling me that maybe it was good to smell your own stink, but I didn't think that *that* was what I'd been trying to do—and—who can stand it?" and he abruptly dropped the ruined beer can, looking at me with a small, still smile, and then rose, walking to the window as though it were the lodestone rock. I watched his face, he watched the avenue. "I couldn't tell you when Mama died—but the reason I wanted to leave Harlem so bad was to get away from drugs. And then, when I ran away, that's what I was running from—really. When I came back, nothing had changed, *I* hadn't changed, I was just—older." And he stopped drumming with his fingers on the windowpane. The sun had vanished, soon darkness would fall. I watched his face. "It can come again," he said, almost as though speaking to himself. Then he turned to me. "It can come again," he repeated. "I just want you to know that."

"All right," I said, at last. "So it can come again, All right."

He smiled, but the smile was sorrowful. "I had to try to tell you," he said.

"Yes," I said. "I understand that."

"You're my brother," he said, looking straight at me, and not smiling at all.

"Yes," I repeated, "yes. I understand that."

He turned back to the window, looking out. "All that hatred down there," he said, "all that hatred and misery and love. It's a wonder it doesn't blow the avenue apart."

We went to the only nightclub on a short, dark street, downtown. We squeezed through the narrow, chattering, jam-packed bar to the entrance of the big room, where the bandstand was. And we stood there for a moment, for the lights were very dim in this room and we couldn't see. Then, "Hello, boy," said a voice and an enormous black man, much older than Sonny or myself, erupted out of all that atmospheric lighting and put an arm around Sonny's shoulder. "I been sitting right here," he said, "waiting for you."

He had a big voice, too, and heads in the darkness turned toward us.

Sonny grinned and pulled a little away, and said, "Creole, this is my brother. I told you about him."

Creole shook my hand. "I'm glad to meet you, son," he said, and it was clear that he was glad to meet me *there,* for Sonny's sake. And he smiled, "You got a real musician in *your* family," and he took his arm from Sonny's shoulder and slapped him, lightly, affectionately, with the back of his hand.

"Well. Now I've heard it all," said a voice behind us. This was another musician, and a friend of Sonny's, a coal-black, cheerful-looking man, built close to the ground. He immediately began confiding to me, at the top of his lungs, the most terrible things about Sonny, his teeth gleaming like a lighthouse and his laugh coming up out of him like the beginning of an earthquake. And it turned out that everyone at the bar knew Sonny, or almost everyone; some were musicians, working there, or nearby, or not working, some were simply hangers-on, and some were there to hear Sonny play. I was introduced to all of them and they were all very polite to me. Yet, it was clear that, for them, I was only Sonny's brother. Here, I was in Sonny's world. Or, rather: his kingdom. Here, it was not even a question that his veins bore royal blood.

They were going to play soon and Creole installed me, by myself, at a table in a dark corner. Then I watched them, Creole, and the little black man, and Sonny, and the others, while they horsed around, standing just below the bandstand. The light from the bandstand spilled just a little short of them and, watching them laughing and gesturing and moving about, I had the feeling that they, nevertheless, were being most careful not to step into that circle of light too suddenly: that if they moved into the light too suddenly, without thinking, they would perish in flame. Then, while I watched, one of them, the small, black man, moved into the light and crossed the bandstand and started fooling around with his drums. Then—being funny and being, also, extremely ceremonious—Creole took Sonny by the arm and led him to the piano. A woman's voice called Sonny's name and a few hands started clapping. And Sonny, also being funny and being ceremonious, and so touched, I think, that he could have cried, but neither hiding it nor showing it, riding it like a man, grinned, and put both hands to his heart and bowed from the waist.

Creole then went to the bass fiddle and a lean, very bright-skinned brown man jumped up on the bandstand and picked up his horn. So there they were, and the atmosphere on the bandstand and in the room began to change and tighten. Someone stepped up to the microphone and announced them. Then there were all kinds of murmurs. Some people at the bar shushed others. The waitress ran around, frantically getting in the last orders, guys and chicks got closer to each other, and the lights on the bandstand, on the quartet, turned to a kind of indigo. Then they all looked different there. Creole looked about him for the last time, as though he were making certain that all his chickens were in the coop, and then he—jumped and struck the fiddle. And there they were.

All I know about music is that not many people ever really hear it. And even then, on the rare occasions when something opens within, and the music enters, what we mainly hear, or hear corroborated, are personal, private, vanishing evocations. But the man who creates the music is hearing something else, is dealing with the roar rising from the void and imposing order on it as it hits the air. What is evoked in him, then, is of another order, more terrible because it has no words, and triumphant, too, for that same reason. And his triumph, when he triumphs, is ours. I just watched Sonny's face. His face was troubled, he was working hard, but he wasn't with it. And I had the feeling that, in a way, everyone on the bandstand was waiting for him, both waiting for him and pushing him along. But as I began to watch Creole, I realized that it was Creole who held them all back. He had them on a short rein. Up there, keeping the beat with his whole body, wailing on the fiddle, with his eyes half closed, he was listening to everything, but he was listening to Sonny. He was having a dialogue with Sonny. He wanted Sonny to leave the shoreline and strike out for the deep water. He was Sonny's witness that deep water and drowning were not the same thing—he had been there, and he knew. And he wanted Sonny to know. He was waiting for Sonny to do the things on the keys which would let Creole know that Sonny was in the water.

And, while Creole listened, Sonny moved, deep within, exactly like someone in torment. I had never before thought of how awful the relationship must be between the musician and his instrument. He has to fill it, this instrument, with the breath of life, his own. He has to make it do what he wants it to do. And a piano is just a piano. It's made out of so much wood and wires and little hammers and big ones, and ivory. While there's only so much you can do with it, the only way to find this out is to try; to try and make it do everything.

And Sonny hadn't been near a piano for over a year. And he wasn't on much better terms with his life, not the life that stretched before him now. He and the piano stammered, started one way, got scared, stopped; started another way, panicked, marked time, started again; then seemed to have found a direction, panicked again, got stuck. And the face I saw on Sonny I'd never seen before. Everything had been burned out of it, and, at the same time, things usually hidden were being burned in, by the fire and fury of the battle which was occurring in him up there.

Yet, watching Creole's face as they neared the end of the first set, I had the feeling that something had happened, something I hadn't heard. Then they finished, there was scattered applause, and then, without an instant's warning, Creole started into something else, it was almost sardonic, it was *Am I Blue.* And, as though he commanded, Sonny began to play. Something began to happen. And Creole let out the reins. The dry, low, black man said something awful on the drums, Creole answered, and the drums talked back. Then the horn insisted, sweet and high, slightly detached perhaps, and Creole listened, commenting now and then, dry, and driving, beautiful and calm and old. Then they all came together again, and Sonny was part of the family again. I could tell this from his face. He seemed to have found, right there beneath his fingers, a damn brand-new piano. It seemed that he couldn't get over it. Then, for awhile, just being happy with Sonny, they seemed to be agreeing with him that brand-new pianos certainly were a gas.

Then Creole stepped forward to remind them that what they were playing was the blues. He hit something in all of them, he hit something in me, myself, and the music tightened and deepened, apprehension began to beat the air. Creole began to tell us what the blues were all about. They were not about anything very new. He and his boys up there were keeping it new, at the risk of ruin, destruction, madness, and death, in order to find new ways to make us listen. For, while the tale of how we suffer, and how we are delighted, and how we may triumph is never new, it always must be heard. There isn't any other tale to tell, it's the only light we've got in all this darkness.

And this tale, according to that face, that body, those strong hands on those strings, has another aspect in every country, and a new depth in every generation. Listen, Creole seemed to be saying, listen. Now these are Sonny's blues. He made the little black man on the drums know it, and the bright, brown man on the horn. Creole wasn't trying any longer to get Sonny in the water. He was wishing him Godspeed. Then he stepped back, very slowly, filling the air with the immense suggestion that Sonny speak for himself.

Then they all gathered around Sonny and Sonny played. Every now and again one of them seemed to say, amen. Sonny's fingers filled the air with life, his life. But that life contained so many others. And Sonny went all the way back, he really began with the spare, flat statement of the opening phrase of the song. Then he began to make it his. It was very beautiful because it wasn't hurried and it was no longer a lament. I seemed to hear with what burning he had made it his, with what burning we had yet to make it ours, how we could cease lamenting. Freedom lurked around us and I understood, at last, that he could help us to be free if we would listen, that he would never be free until we did. Yet, there was no battle in his face now. I heard what he had gone through, and would continue to go through until he came to rest in earth. He had made it his: that long line, of which we knew only Mama and Daddy. And he was giving it back, as everything must be given back, so that, passing through death, it can live forever. I saw my mother's face again, and felt, for the first time, how the stones of the road she had walked on must have bruised her feet. I saw the moonlit road where my father's brother died. And it brought something else back to me, and carried me past it, I saw my little girl again and felt Isabel's tears again, and I felt my own tears begin to rise. And I was yet aware that this was only a moment, that the world waited outside, as hungry as a tiger, and that trouble stretched above us, longer than the sky.

Then it was over. Creole and Sonny let out their breath, both soaking wet, and grinning. There was a lot of applause and some of it was real. In the dark, the girl came by and I asked her to take drinks to the bandstand. There was a long pause, while they talked up there in the indigo light and after awhile I saw the girl put a Scotch and milk on top of the piano for Sonny. He didn't seem to notice it, but just before they started playing again he sipped from it and looked toward me, and nodded. Then he put it back on top of the piano. For me, then, as they began to play again, it glowed and shook above my brother's head like the very cup of trembling.

1957

Flannery O'Connor 1925–1964

Grotesque, Catholic, Southern—each of these labels has been affixed to Flannery O'Connor's writing, yet none fully captures its scope. For her work is all of these and more.

She did often make use of the grotesque, for instance, but its use was not, as one critic claimed, gratuitous. She wanted to push the reader to experience a sense of something beyond the ordinary, a sense of the mystery of life. She wanted to shock the reader into recognizing the distortions of modern life that we have come to consider natural: "for the almost-blind you draw large and startling figures," she has noted in an essay.

O'Connor's writing was also fueled by her Roman Catholic beliefs. The something beyond the ordinary that she wanted the reader to experience, starkly, unsentimentally, was a sense of the sacred. But the reader of her fiction doesn't need to be Catholic to appreciate the extra-ordinary, to experience the mystery of life.

This Catholicism probably contributed to O'Connor's sense of living in a fallen world. And she also probably absorbed such a sense of having fallen from past grandeur by growing up white in the post–Civil-War South. Yet her characters are not so much fallen aristocrats as poor or middle-class whites, who often don't realize what their lives are lacking. Her portrayal of these characters, their thoughts, their speech, is true, funny, powerful—and devastating.

Like most of her characters, Mary Flannery O'Connor grew up in the South—in Georgia. The only child of Edward Francis O'Connor and Regina Cline O'Connor, she lived in Savannah her first thirteen years. Then her father was diagnosed as having disseminated lupus erythematosis, a disease of the immune system, a disease so debilitating that he could not continue his real-estate work. The family moved to Milledgeville, to the house where O'Connor's mother had grown up, a house that had been the governor's mansion when Milledgeville was the capital of Georgia a century before. O'Connor's father died three years later. The following year, when O'Connor was seventeen, she entered Georgia State College for Women, now Georgia College. There she majored in social science (she would later satirize social scientists mercilessly) and published cartoons in the school newspaper (since *The New Yorker* wouldn't publish them).

In 1945 O'Connor left Georgia to study creative writing at the Writers' Workshop of the State University of Iowa (now the University of Iowa), where she wrote a series of short stories and earned a master's degree in fine arts. She then embarked on her first novel, working on it at Yaddo, an artists' colony in upstate New York, in an apartment in New York City, and while boarding with friends in Ridgefield, Connecticut. Heading home for Christmas in 1950, O'Connor suffered an attack of lupus, the disease that had killed her father.

Severely weakened—she was too weak to climb stairs—O'Connor, with her mother and uncle, moved to the family farm near Milledgeville. Cortisone drugs kept the lupus largely under control but weakened O'Connor's bones. During the next thirteen years she hobbled about with a cane or crutches, raised peafowl, and wrote for two or three hours a day. Sometimes she was well enough to travel within or beyond Georgia to give a speech or a reading or to accept an honorary degree; once she even traveled as far as Lourdes and Rome. But mostly she lived quietly on the farm—until surgery in February 1964 reactivated the lupus; she died in August, at the age of 39.

O'Connor completed two novels, *Wise Blood* and *The Violent Bear It Away*, but is better remembered for her two volumes of short stories, *A Good Man Is Hard to Find* and the posthumous *Everything That Rises Must Converge.* Several other volumes have been published since her death: a complete collection of stories and also collections of essays *(Mystery and Manners),* letters (including *The Habit of Being),* and book reviews (including *The Presence of Grace).*

"A Good Man Is Hard to Find" is typical of many of O'Connor's stories, with its jolting disruption of the mundane, its satire, its toughness. Yet even more than O'Connor's other work, this story provokes extreme reactions: it is funny but also horrifying.

Beverly Lyon Clark
Wheaton College

PRIMARY WORKS

Wise Blood, 1952; *A Good Man Is Hard to Find, and Other Stories,* 1955; *The Violent Bear It Away,* 1960; *Everything That Rises Must Converge,* 1965; *Mystery and Manners: Occasional Prose,* 1969; *The Complete Stories,* 1971; *The Habit of Being: The Letters of Flannery O'Connor,* 1979; *The Presence of Grace, and Other Book Reviews,* 1983; *Collected Works,* 1988.

A Good Man Is Hard to Find[1]

The grandmother didn't want to go to Florida. She wanted to visit some of her connections in east Tennessee and she was seizing at every chance to change Bailey's mind. Bailey was the son she lived with, her only boy. He was sitting on the edge of his chair at the table, bent over the orange sports section of the *Journal.* "Now look here, Bailey," she said, "see here, read this," and she stood with one hand on her thin hip and the other rattling the newspaper at his bald head. "Here this fellow that calls himself the Misfit is aloose from the Federal Pen and headed toward Florida and you read here what it says he did to these people. Just you read it. I wouldn't take my children in any direction with a criminal like that aloose in it. I couldn't answer to my conscience if I did."

Bailey didn't look up from his reading so she wheeled around then and faced the children's mother, a young woman in slacks, whose face was as broad and innocent as a cabbage and was tied around with a green head-kerchief that had two points on the top like rabbit's ears. She was sitting on the sofa, feeding the baby his apricots out of a jar. "The children have been to Florida before," the old lady said. "You all ought to take them somewhere else for a change so they would see different parts of the world and be broad. They never have been to east Tennessee."

The children's mother didn't seem to hear but the eight-year-old boy, John Wesley, a stocky child with glasses, said, "If you don't want to go to Florida, why dontcha stay at home?" He and the little girl, June Star, were reading the funny papers on the floor.

"She wouldn't stay at home to be queen for a day," June Star said without raising her yellow head.

[1]Also the title of a blues song, composed by Eddie Green in 1918.

"Yes and what would you do if this fellow, The Misfit, caught you?" the grandmother asked.

"I'd smack his face," John Wesley said.

"She wouldn't stay at home for a million bucks," June Star said. "Afraid she'd miss something. She has to go everywhere we go."

"All right, Miss," the grandmother said. "Just remember that the next time you want me to curl your hair."

June Star said her hair was naturally curly.

The next morning the grandmother was the first one in the car, ready to go. She had her big black valise that looked like the head of a hippopotamus in one corner, and underneath it she was hiding a basket with Pitty Sing,[2] the cat, in it. She didn't intend for the cat to be left alone in the house for three days because he would miss her too much and she was afraid he might brush against one of the gas burners and accidentally asphyxiate himself. Her son, Bailey, didn't like to arrive at a motel with a cat.

She sat in the middle of the back seat with John Wesley and June Star on either side of her. Bailey and the children's mother and the baby sat in front and they left Atlanta at eight forty-five with the mileage on the car at 55890. The grandmother wrote this down because she thought it would be interesting to say how many miles they had been when they got back. It took them twenty minutes to reach the outskirts of the city.

The old lady settled herself comfortably, removing her white cotton gloves and putting them up with her purse on the shelf in front of the back window. The children's mother still had on slacks and still had her head tied up in a green kerchief, but the grandmother had on a navy blue straw sailor hat with a bunch of white violets on the brim and a navy blue dress with a small white dot in the print. Her collars and cuffs were white organdy trimmed with lace and at her neckline she had pinned a purple spray of cloth violets containing a sachet. In case of an accident, anyone seeing her dead on the highway would know at once that she was a lady.

She said she thought it was going to be a good day for driving, neither too hot nor too cold, and she cautioned Bailey that the speed limit was fifty-five miles an hour and that the patrolmen hid themselves behind billboards and small clumps of trees and sped out after you before you had a chance to slow down. She pointed out interesting details of the scenery: Stone Mountain; the blue granite that in some places came up to both sides of the highway; the brilliant red clay banks slightly streaked with purple; and the various crops that made rows of green lace-work on the ground. The trees were full of silver-white sunlight and the meanest of them sparkled. The children were reading comic magazines and their mother had gone back to sleep.

"Let's go through Georgia fast so we won't have to look at it much," John Wesley said.

"If I were a little boy," said the grandmother, "I wouldn't talk about my native state that way. Tennessee has the mountains and Georgia has the hills."

"Tennessee is just a hillbilly dumping ground," John Wesley said, "and Georgia is a lousy state too."

---

[2] Alludes to one of the three little maids from school in the Gilbert and Sullivan comic opera *The Mikado* (1885). Pitti-Sing helps mislead the Mikado, the Emperor of Japan, into believing that a requested beheading has taken place; fortunately it has not, for the man who would have been executed turns out to be the Mikado's son.

"You said it," June Star said.

"In my time," said the grandmother, folding her thin veined fingers, "children were more respectful of their native states and their parents and everything else. People did right then. Oh look at the cute little pickaninny!" she said and pointed to a Negro child standing in the door of a shack. "Wouldn't that make a picture, now?" she asked and they all turned and looked at the little Negro out of the back window. He waved.

"He didn't have any britches on," June Star said.

"He probably didn't have any," the grandmother explained. "Little niggers in the country don't have things like we do. If I could paint, I'd paint that picture," she said.

The children exchanged comic books.

The grandmother offered to hold the baby and the children's mother passed him over the front seat to her. She set him on her knee and bounced him and told him about the things they were passing. She rolled her eyes and screwed up her mouth and stuck her leathery thin face into his smooth bland one. Occasionally he gave her a faraway smile. They passed a large cotton field with five or six graves fenced in the middle of it, like a small island. "Look at the graveyard!" the grandmother said, pointing it out. "That was the old family burying ground. That belonged to the plantation."

"Where's the plantation?" John Wesley asked.

"Gone With the Wind,"[3] said the grandmother. "Ha. Ha."

When the children finished all the comic books they had brought, they opened the lunch and ate it. The grandmother ate a peanut butter sandwich and an olive and would not let the children throw the box and the paper napkins out the window. When there was nothing else to do they played a game by choosing a cloud and making the other two guess what shape it suggested. John Wesley took one the shape of a cow and June Star guessed a cow and John Wesley said, no, an automobile, and June Star said he didn't play fair, and they began to slap each other over the grandmother.

The grandmother said she would tell them a story if they would keep quiet. When she told a story, she rolled her eyes and waved her head and was very dramatic. She said once when she was a maiden lady she had been courted by a Mr. Edgar Atkins Teagarden from Jasper, Georgia. She said he was a very good-looking man and a gentleman and that he brought her a watermelon every Saturday afternoon with his initials cut in it, E.A.T. Well, one Saturday, she said, Mr. Teagarden brought the watermelon and there was nobody at home and he left it on the front porch and returned in his buggy to Jasper, but she never got the watermelon, she said, because a nigger boy ate it when he saw the initials, E.A.T.! This story tickled John Wesley's funny bone and he giggled and giggled but June Star didn't think it was any good. She said she wouldn't marry a man that just brought her a watermelon on Saturday. The grandmother said she would have done well to marry Mr. Teagarden because he was a gentleman and had bought Coca-Cola stock when it first came out and that he had died only a few years ago, a very wealthy man.

[3]Alludes to the best-selling novel (1936) by Margaret Mitchell; also made into an Academy Award-winning movie (1939).

They stopped at The Tower for barbecued sandwiches. The Tower was a part stucco and part wood filling station and dance hall set in a clearing outside of Timothy. A fat man named Red Sammy Butts ran it and there were signs stuck here and there on the building and for miles up and down the highway saying, TRY RED SAMMY'S FAMOUS BARBECUE. NONE LIKE FAMOUS RED SAMMY'S! RED SAM! THE FAT BOY WITH THE HAPPY LAUGH. A VETERAN! RED SAMMY'S YOUR MAN!

Red Sammy was lying on the bare ground outside The Tower with his head under a truck while a gray monkey about a foot high, chained to a small chinaberry tree, chattered nearby. The monkey sprang back into the tree and got on the highest limb as soon as he saw the children jump out of the car and run toward him.

Inside, The Tower was a long dark room with a counter at one end and tables at the other and dancing space in the middle. They all sat down at a board table next to the nickelodeon and Red Sam's wife, a tall burnt-brown woman with hair and eyes lighter than her skin, came and took their order. The children's mother put a dime in the machine and played "The Tennessee Waltz," and the grandmother said that tune always made her want to dance. She asked Bailey if he would like to dance but he only glared at her. He didn't have a naturally sunny disposition like she did and trips made him nervous. The grandmother's brown eyes were very bright. She swayed her head from side to side and pretended she was dancing in her chair. June Star said play something she could tap to so the children's mother put in another dime and played a fast number and June Star stepped out onto the dance floor and did her tap routine.

"Ain't she cute?" Red Sam's wife said, leaning over the counter. "Would you like to come be my little girl?"

"No I certainly wouldn't," June Star said. "I wouldn't live in a broken-down place like this for a million bucks!" and she ran back to the table.

"Ain't she cute?" the woman repeated, stretching her mouth politely.

"Aren't you ashamed?" hissed the grandmother.

Red Sam came in and told his wife to quit lounging on the counter and hurry up with these people's order. His khaki trousers reached just to his hip bones and his stomach hung over them like a sack of meal swaying under his shirt. He came over and sat down at a table nearby and let out a combination sigh and yodel. "You can't win," he said. "You can't win," and he wiped his sweating red face off with a gray handkerchief. "These days you don't know who to trust," he said. "Ain't that the truth?"

"People are certainly not nice like they used to be," said the grandmother.

"Two fellers come in here last week," Red Sammy said, "driving a Chrysler. It was a old beat-up car but it was a good one and these boys looked all right to me. Said they worked at the mill and you know I let them fellers charge the gas they bought? Now why did I do that?"

"Because you're a good man!" the grandmother said at once.

"Yes'm, I suppose so," Red Sam said as if he were struck with this answer.

His wife brought the orders, carrying the five plates all at once without a tray, two in each hand and one balanced on her arm. "It isn't a soul in this green world of God's that you can trust," she said. "And I don't count nobody out of that, not nobody," she repeated, looking at Red Sammy.

"Did you read about that criminal, The Misfit, that's escaped?" asked the grandmother.

"I wouldn't be a bit surprised if he didn't attact this place right here," said the woman. "If he hears about it being here, I wouldn't be none surprised to see him. If he hears it's two cent in the cash register, I wouldn't be a tall surprised if he . . ."

"That'll do," Red Sam said. "Go bring these people their Co'-Colas," and the woman went off to get the rest of the order.

"A good man is hard to find," Red Sammy said. "Everything is getting terrible. I remember the day you could go off and leave your screen door unlatched. Not no more."

He and the grandmother discussed better times. The old lady said that in her opinion Europe was entirely to blame for the way things were now. She said the way Europe acted you would think we were made of money and Red Sam said it was no use talking about it, she was exactly right. The children ran outside into the white sunlight and looked at the monkey in the lacy chinaberry tree. He was busy catching fleas on himself and biting each one carefully between his teeth as if it were a delicacy.

They drove off again into the hot afternoon. The grandmother took cat naps and woke up every few minutes with her own snoring. Outside of Toombsboro she woke up and recalled an old plantation that she had visited in this neighborhood once when she was a young lady. She said the house had six white columns across the front and that there was an avenue of oaks leading up to it and two little wooden trellis arbors on either side in front where you sat down with your suitor after a stroll in the garden. She recalled exactly which road to turn off to get to it. She knew that Bailey would not be willing to lose any time looking at an old house, but the more she talked about it, the more she wanted to see it once again and find out if the little twin arbors were still standing. "There was a secret panel in this house," she said craftily, not telling the truth but wishing that she were, "and the story went that all the family silver was hidden in it when Sherman[4] came through but it was never found . . ."

"Hey!" John Wesley said. "Let's go see it! We'll find it! We'll poke all the woodwork and find it! Who lives there? Where do you turn off at? Hey Pop, can't we turn off there?"

"We never have seen a house with a secret panel!" June Star shrieked. "Let's go to the house with the secret panel! Hey Pop, can't we go see the house with the secret panel!"

"It's not far from here, I know," the grandmother said. "It wouldn't take over twenty minutes."

Bailey was looking straight ahead. His jaw was as rigid as a horseshoe. "No," he said.

The children began to yell and scream that they wanted to see the house with the secret panel. John Wesley kicked the back of the front seat and June Star hung over her mother's shoulder and whined desperately into her ear that they never had any fun even on their vacation, that they could never do what THEY wanted to do. The baby began to scream and John Wesley kicked the back of the seat so hard that his father could feel the blows in his kidney.

"All right!" he shouted and drew the car to a stop at the side of the road. "Will you all shut up? Will you all just shut up for one second? If you don't shut up, we won't go anywhere."

[4]Northern Civil War general, best known for his march through Georgia (starting in Tennessee), destroying houses and plantations on his way to the sea.

"It would be very educational for them," the grandmother murmured.

"All right," Bailey said, "but get this: this is the only time we're going to stop for anything like this. This is the one and only time."

"The dirt road that you have to turn down is about a mile back," the grandmother directed. "I marked it when we passed."

"A dirt road," Bailey groaned.

After they had turned around and were headed toward the dirt road, the grandmother recalled other points about the house, the beautiful glass over the front doorway and the candle-lamp in the hall. John Wesley said that the secret panel was probably in the fireplace.

"You can't go inside this house," Bailey said. "You don't know who lives there."

"While you all talk to the people in front, I'll run around behind and get in a window," John Wesley suggested.

"We'll all stay in the car," his mother said.

They turned onto the dirt road and the car raced roughly along in a swirl of pink dust. The grandmother recalled the times when there were no paved roads and thirty miles was a day's journey. The dirt road was hilly and there were sudden washes in it and sharp curves on dangerous embankments. All at once they would be on a hill, looking down over the blue tops of trees for miles around, then the next minute, they would be in a red depression with the dust-coated trees looking down on them.

"This place had better turn up in a minute," Bailey said, "or I'm going to turn around."

The road looked as if no one had traveled on it in months.

"It's not much farther," the grandmother said and just as she said it, a horrible thought came to her. The thought was so embarrassing that she turned red in the face and her eyes dilated and her feet jumped up, upsetting her valise in the corner. The instant the valise moved, the newspaper top she had over the basket under it rose with a snarl and Pitty Sing, the cat, sprang onto Bailey's shoulder.

The children were thrown to the floor and their mother, clutching the baby, was thrown out the door onto the ground; the old lady was thrown into the front seat. The car turned over once and landed right-side-up in a gulch off the side of the road. Bailey remained in the driver's seat with the cat—gray-striped with a broad white face and an orange nose—clinging to his neck like a caterpillar.

As soon as the children saw they could move their arms and legs, they scrambled out of the car, shouting, "We've had an ACCIDENT!" The grandmother was curled up under the dashboard, hoping she was injured so that Bailey's wrath would not come down on her all at once. The horrible thought she had had before the accident was that the house she had remembered so vividly was not in Georgia but in Tennessee.

Bailey removed the cat from his neck with both hands and flung it out the window against the side of a pine tree. Then he got out of the car and started looking for the children's mother. She was sitting against the side of a red gutted ditch, holding the screaming baby, but she only had a cut down her face and a broken shoulder. "We've had an ACCIDENT!" the children screamed in a frenzy of delight.

"But nobody's killed," June Star said with disappointment as the grandmother limped out of the car, her hat still pinned to her head but the broken front brim standing up at a jaunty angle and the violet spray hanging off the side. They all sat down in the ditch, except the children, to recover from the shock. They were all shaking.

"Maybe a car will come along," said the children's mother hoarsely.

"I believe I have injured an organ," said the grandmother, pressing her side, but no one answered her. Bailey's teeth were clattering. He had on a yellow sport shirt with bright blue parrots designed in it and his face was as yellow as the shirt. The grandmother decided that she would not mention that the house was in Tennessee.

The road was about ten feet above and they could see only the tops of the trees on the other side of it. Behind the ditch they were sitting in there were more woods, tall and dark and deep. In a few minutes they saw a car some distance away on top of a hill, coming slowly as if the occupants were watching them. The grandmother stood up and waved both arms dramatically to attract their attention. The car continued to come on slowly, disappeared around a bend and appeared again, moving even slower, on top of the hill they had gone over. It was a big black battered hearse-like automobile. There were three men in it.

It came to a stop just over them and for some minutes, the driver looked down with a steady expressionless gaze to where they were sitting, and didn't speak. Then he turned his head and muttered something to the other two and they got out. One was a fat boy in black trousers and a red sweat shirt with a silver stallion embossed on the front of it. He moved around on the right side of them and stood staring, his mouth partly open in a kind of loose grin. The other had on khaki pants and a blue striped coat and a gray hat pulled down very low, hiding most of his face. He came around slowly on the left side. Neither spoke.

The driver got out of the car and stood by the side of it, looking down at them. He was an older man than the other two. His hair was just beginning to gray and he wore silver-rimmed spectacles that gave him a scholarly look. He had a long creased face and didn't have on any shirt or undershirt. He had on blue jeans that were too tight for him and he was holding a black hat and a gun. The two boys also had guns.

"We've had an ACCIDENT!" the children screamed.

The grandmother had the peculiar feeling that the bespectacled man was someone she knew. His face was as familiar to her as if she had known him all her life but she could not recall who he was. He moved away from the car and began to come down the embankment, placing his feet carefully so that he wouldn't slip. He had on tan and white shoes and no socks, and his ankles were red and thin. "Good afternoon," he said. "I see you all had you a little spill."

"We turned over twice!" said the grandmother.

"Oncet," he corrected. "We seen it happen. Try their car and see will it run, Hiram," he said quietly to the boy with the gray hat.

"What you got that gun for?" John Wesley asked. "Whatcha gonna do with that gun?"

"Lady," the man said to the children's mother, "would you mind calling them children to sit down by you? Children make me nervous. I want all you all to sit down right together there where you're at."

"What are you telling US what to do for?" June Star asked.

Behind them the line of woods gaped like a dark open mouth. "Come here," said the mother.

"Look here now," Bailey began suddenly, "we're in a predicament! We're in . . ."

The grandmother shrieked. She scrambled to her feet and stood staring. "You're The Misfit!" she said. "I recognized you at once!"

"Yes'm," the man said, smiling slightly as if he were pleased in spite of himself to be known, "but it would have been better for all of you, lady, if you hadn't of reckernized me."

Bailey turned his head sharply and said something to his mother that shocked even the children. The old lady began to cry and The Misfit reddened.

"Lady," he said, "don't you get upset. Sometimes a man says things he don't mean. I don't reckon he meant to talk to you thataway."

"You wouldn't shoot a lady, would you?" the grandmother said and removed a clean handkerchief from her cuff and began to slap at her eyes with it.

The Misfit pointed the toe of his shoe into the ground and made a little hole and then covered it up again. "I would hate to have to," he said.

"Listen," the grandmother almost screamed, "I know you're a good man. You don't look a bit like you have common blood. I know you must come from nice people!"

"Yes mam," he said, "finest people in the world." When he smiled he showed a row of strong white teeth. "God never made a finer woman than my mother and my daddy's heart was pure gold," he said. The boy with the red sweat shirt had come around behind them and was standing with his gun at his hip. The Misfit squatted down on the ground. "Watch them children, Bobby Lee," he said. "You know they make me nervous." He looked at the six of them huddled together in front of him and he seemed to be embarrassed as if he couldn't think of anything to say. "Ain't a cloud in the sky," he remarked, looking up at it. "Don't see no sun but don't see no cloud neither."

"Yes, it's a beautiful day," said the grandmother. "Listen," she said, "you shouldn't call yourself The Misfit because I know you're a good man at heart. I can just look at you and tell."

"Hush!" Bailey yelled. "Hush! Everybody shut up and let me handle this!" He was squatting in the position of a runner about to sprint forward but he didn't move.

"I pre-chate that, lady," The Misfit said and drew a little circle in the ground with the butt of his gun.

"It'll take a half a hour to fix this here car," Hiram called, looking over the raised hood of it.

"Well, first you Bobby Lee get him and that little boy to step over yonder with you," The Misfit said, pointing to Bailey and John Wesley. "The boys want to ast you something," he said to Bailey. "Would you mind stepping back in them woods there with them?"

"Listen," Bailey began, "we're in a terrible predicament! Nobody realizes what this is," and his voice cracked. His eyes were as blue and intense as the parrots in his shirt and he remained perfectly still.

The grandmother reached up to adjust her hat brim as if she were going to the woods with him but it came off in her hand. She stood staring at it and after a second she let it fall on the ground. Hiram pulled Bailey up by the arm as if he were assisting an old man. John Wesley caught hold of his father's hand and Bobby Lee followed. They went off toward the woods and just as they reached the dark edge, Bailey turned and supporting himself against a gray naked pine trunk, he shouted, "I'll be back in a minute, Mamma, wait on me!"

"Come back this instant!" his mother shrilled but they all disappeared into the woods.

"Bailey Boy!" the grandmother called in a tragic voice but she found she was looking at The Misfit squatting on the ground in front of her. "I just know you're a good man," she said desperately. "You're not a bit common!"

"Nome, I ain't a good man," The Misfit said after a second as if he had considered her statement carefully, "but I ain't the worst in the world neither. My daddy said I was a different breed of dog from my brothers and sisters. 'You know,' Daddy said, 'it's some that can live their whole life without asking about it and it's others has to know why it is, and this boy is one of the latters. He's going to be into everything!'" He put on his black hat and looked up suddenly and then away deep into the woods as if he were embarrassed again. "I'm sorry I don't have on a shirt before you ladies," he said, hunching his shoulders slightly. "We buried our clothes that we had on when we escaped and we're just making do until we can get better. We borrowed these from some folks we met," he explained.

"That's perfectly all right," the grandmother said. "Maybe Bailey has an extra shirt in his suitcase."

"I'll look and see terrectly," The Misfit said.

"Where are they taking him?" the children's mother screamed.

"Daddy was a card himself," The Misfit said. "You couldn't put anything over on him. He never got in trouble with the Authorities though. Just had the knack of handling them."

"You could be honest too if you'd only try," said the grandmother. "Think how wonderful it would be to settle down and live a comfortable life and not have to think about somebody chasing you all the time."

The Misfit kept scratching in the ground with the butt of his gun as if he were thinking about it. "Yes'm, somebody is always after you," he murmured.

The grandmother noticed how thin his shoulder blades were just behind his hat because she was standing up looking down on him. "Do you ever pray?" she asked.

He shook his head. All she saw was the black hat wiggle between his shoulder blades. "Nome," he said.

There was a pistol shot from the woods, followed closely by another. Then silence. The old lady's head jerked around. She could hear the wind move through the tree tops like a long satisfied insuck of breath. "Bailey Boy!" she called.

"I was a gospel singer for a while," The Misfit said. "I been most everything. Been in the arm service, both land and sea, at home and abroad, been twict married, been an undertaker, been with the railroads, plowed Mother Earth, been in a tornado, seen a man burnt alive oncet," and he looked up at the children's mother and the little girl who were sitting close together, their faces white and their eyes glassy. "I even seen a woman flogged," he said.

"Pray, pray," the grandmother began, "pray, pray . . ."

"I never was a bad boy that I remember of," The Misfit said in an almost dreamy voice, "but somewheres along the line I done something wrong and got sent to the penitentiary. I was buried alive," and he looked up and held her attention to him by a steady stare.

"That's when you should have started to pray," she said, "What did you do to get sent to the penitentiary that first time?"

"Turn to the right, it was a wall," The Misfit said, looking up again at the cloudless sky. "Turn to the left, it was a wall. Look up it was a ceiling, look down it was a floor. I forget what I done, lady. I set there and set there, trying to remember what it was I done and I ain't recalled it to this day. Oncet in a while, I would think it was coming to me, but it never come."

"Maybe they put you in by mistake," the old lady said vaguely.

"Nome," he said. "It wasn't no mistake. They had the papers on me."

"You must have stolen something," she said.

The Misfit sneered slightly. "Nobody had nothing I wanted," he said. "It was a head-doctor at the penitentiary said what I had done was kill my daddy but I known that for a lie. My daddy died in nineteen ought nineteen of the epidemic flu and I never had a thing to do with it. He was buried in the Mount Hopewell Baptist churchyard and you can go there and see for yourself."

"If you would pray," the old lady said, "Jesus would help you."

"That's right," The Misfit said.

"Well then, why don't you pray?" she asked trembling with delight suddenly.

"I don't want no hep," he said. "I'm doing all right by myself."

Bobby Lee and Hiram came ambling back from the woods. Bobby Lee was dragging a yellow shirt with bright blue parrots in it.

"Thow me that shirt, Bobby Lee," The Misfit said. The shirt came flying at him and landed on his shoulder and he put it on. The grandmother couldn't name what the shirt reminded her of. "No, lady," The Misfit said while he was buttoning it up, "I found out the crime don't matter. You can do one thing or you can do another, kill a man or take a tire off his car, because sooner or later you're going to forget what it was you done and just be punished for it."

The children's mother had begun to make heaving noises as if she couldn't get her breath. "Lady," he asked, "would you and that little girl like to step off yonder with Bobby Lee and Hiram and join your husband?"

"Yes, thank you," the mother said faintly. Her left arm dangled helplessly and she was holding the baby, who had gone to sleep, in the other. "Hep that lady up, Hiram," The Misfit said as she struggled to climb out of the ditch, "and Bobby Lee, you hold onto that little girl's hand."

"I don't want to hold hands with him," June Star said. "He reminds me of a pig."

The fat boy blushed and laughed and caught her by the arm and pulled her off into the woods after Hiram and her mother.

Alone with The Misfit, the grandmother found that she had lost her voice. There was not a cloud in the sky nor any sun. There was nothing around her but woods. She wanted to tell him that he must pray. She opened and closed her mouth several times before anything came out. Finally she found herself saying, "Jesus. Jesus," meaning, Jesus will help you, but the way she was saying it, it sounded as if she might be cursing.

"Yes'm," The Misfit said as if he agreed. "Jesus thown everything off balance. It was the same case with Him as with me except He hadn't committed any crime and they could prove I had committed one because they had the papers on me. Of course," he said, "they never shown me my papers. That's why I sign myself now. I said long ago, you get you a signature and sign everything you do and keep a copy of it. Then you'll know what you done and you can hold up the crime to the punishment and see do they match and in the end you'll have something to prove you ain't been treated right. I call myself The Misfit," he said, "because I can't make what all I done wrong fit what all I gone through in punishment."

There was a piercing scream from the woods, followed closely by a pistol report. "Does it seem right to you, lady, that one is punished a heap and another ain't punished at all?"

"Jesus!" the old lady cried. "You've got good blood! I know you wouldn't shoot a lady! I know you come from nice people! Pray! Jesus, you ought not to shoot a lady. I'll give you all the money I've got!"

"Lady," The Misfit said, looking beyond her far into the woods, "there never was a body that give the undertaker a tip."

There were two more pistol reports and the grandmother raised her head like a parched old turkey hen crying for water and called, "Bailey Boy, Bailey Boy!" as if her heart would break.

"Jesus was the only One that ever raised the dead," The Misfit continued, "and He shouldn't have done it. He thown everything off balance. If He did what He said, then it's nothing for you to do but thow away everything and follow Him, and if He didn't, then it's nothing for you to do but enjoy the few minutes you got left the best way you can—by killing somebody or burning down his house or doing some other meanness to him. No pleasure but meanness," he said and his voice had become almost a snarl.

"Maybe He didn't raise the dead," the old lady mumbled, not knowing what she was saying and feeling so dizzy that she sank down in the ditch with her legs twisted under her.

"I wasn't there so I can't say He didn't," The Misfit said. "I wisht I had of been there," he said, hitting the ground with his fist. "It ain't right I wasn't there because if I had of been there I would of known. Listen lady," he said in a high voice, "if I had of been there I would of known and I wouldn't be like I am now." His voice seemed about to crack and the grandmother's head cleared for an instant. She saw the man's face twisted close to her own as if he were going to cry and she murmured, "Why you're one of my babies. You're one of my own children!" She reached out and touched him on the shoulder. The Misfit sprang back as if a snake had bitten him and shot her three times through the chest. Then he put his gun down on the ground and took off his glasses and began to clean them.

Hiram and Bobby Lee returned from the woods and stood over the ditch, looking down at the grandmother who half sat and half lay in a puddle of blood with her legs crossed under her like a child's and her face smiling up at the cloudless sky.

Without his glasses, The Misfit's eyes were red-rimmed and pale and defenseless-looking. "Take her off and thow her where you thown the others," he said, picking up the cat that was rubbing itself against his leg.

"She was a talker, wasn't she?" Bobby Lee said, sliding down the ditch with a yodel.

"She would of been a good woman," The Misfit said, "if it had been somebody there to shoot her every minute of her life."

"Some fun!" Bobby Lee said.

"Shut up, Bobby Lee," The Misfit said. "It's no real pleasure in life."

1953

A Sheaf of Poetry and Prose from the Beat Movement

When Lawrence Ferlinghetti published Allen Ginsberg's long poem "Howl" at his San Francisco–based City Lights Books in 1956, the first widely circulated text of the anti-establishment Beat culture was born. *Howl and Other Poems* appeared in the highly visible white and black pocketbook format that was to showcase works by Jack Kerouac, Gregory Corso, Robert Creeley, Ginsberg, Ferlinghetti himself, and many others. The concept of a group identity may have begun at a 1955 poetry reading at the Six Gallery in San Francisco. Kenneth Rexroth was master of ceremonies, and readers were—besides Ginsberg—Philip Lamantia, Michael McClure, Gary Snyder, Lew Welsh, and Philip Whalen.

Responding to the restrictive and conservative post–World War II culture (the soporific 1950s), this group of poets—which often included Denise Levertov, Charles Olson, Robert Duncan, Neal Cassady, William Everson, and others—forced on the reading public an awareness of other cultures: drug experiences, lives in prison and mental institutions, homosexual and lesbian sexualities, liberal politics, spiritualism not necessarily housed in suburban Protestant environs. Admittedly intended to shock in some cases, the works—poetry, prose, and matrices of both—were descended from writers as disparate as Whitman, Rimbaud, William Carlos Williams, Antonin Artaud, William Burroughs, and other American writers not yet acknowledged as significant writers. One of the foremost characteristics of writing of the Beats was a sense of humor, long absent from United States writing, and a belief that spiritual life (*beat* meaning "beatific, holy") was essential to a person's existence.

Allen Ginsberg 1926–1997

Allen Ginsberg brought not only a new self-consciousness to American poetry but a rare sense of humor. While poets contemporary with him—W. D. Snodgrass, Robert Lowell, Theodore Roethke, and somewhat later Anne Sexton and Sylvia Plath—were mining the personal to unearth images that would speak for an "Every person" understanding, Ginsberg was exploring the psyche with a shrewd sense of humor. His dialogue with Walt Whitman, "A Supermarket in California," views the suburban scene of lush plenty with a wry vision that brings the elements of poetry and life together in a completely new perspective.

Ginsberg is best known for his first long-lined poem, "Howl," written after he left Columbia University and the New York avant-garde and moved to California. "Howl" lamented the 1950s wastes—good minds buried under layers of convention, stifling restrictions on art and sexual expression—reversing Whitman's catalogs of praise to chart uncountable griefs. Its irony and its all-too-real truths gave Ginsberg an immediate audience once City Lights published the poem, with a foreword by William Carlos Williams.

Though Ginsberg quickly became identified with the homosexual drug culture, his roots more directly stretched back to his New Jersey home, where his knowledge of social inequities and cultural frustrations mirrored that of his older Rutherford neighbor, Williams. His next major poem, "Kaddish," a lament for the health of his brilliant Jewish mother, Naomi Levy, reflected much of that social coercion, intensified with cultural alienation and social response to mental instability.

Ginsberg was born in 1926 to Naomi and Louis Ginsberg, in Newark, where his father was a high school teacher and a poet. Before graduating from Columbia University in 1949, Ginsberg held jobs as a dishwasher, spot welder, copy boy on the *New York World-Telegram,* and reporter for a New Jersey paper. After he graduated with his A.B. degree, he traveled to California to find William Burroughs, who wrote from the tradition of prophetic, inspired voices (Ginsberg had had visions in which he saw William Blake, and he thought of himself as a seer in his art). After his comparative successes in California, determined to live on his income from writing—no small endeavor—Ginsberg spent part of 1963 in India, traveling with his lover Peter Orlovsky. He returned to the States to participate in a poetry festival at University of British Columbia, bringing with him a mantra-like chant that from then on enhanced the delivery of his poetry.

In 1963 Ginsberg was a Guggenheim Fellow; in 1969 he received a National Institute of Arts and Letters award and in 1973 the National Book Award for *The Fall of America: Poems of These States.* In 1979 he received the National Arts Club Medal of Honor for Literature. Although he read frequently on university campuses and remained a spokesperson for the avant-garde, Ginsberg developed a comparatively mild profile during the last decade of his life. He returned to New Jersey, where he lived on a small farm, accessible to his friends and admirers, writing a remarkably constant poetry that hammered away at the problems faced not only by the United States but by most of the world cultures. The "insane demands" he spoke of in his 1956 poem "America" are still rampant, and Ginsberg proved to be prophetic once more as he described himself as staying with the country, trying to work through its aberrations to find some of its truth. In that endeavor, too, he echoed the efforts of William Carlos Williams. Though never accepted by the culture he was so critical of, Ginsberg never expatriated himself from it; he rather preached, and sang, and chanted, lessons he thought might be helpful to its greatest dilemmas.

Linda Wagner-Martin
University of North Carolina–Chapel Hill

PRIMARY WORKS

Howl and Other Poems, 1956; *Kaddish and Other Poems 1958–60,* 1961; *Empty Mirror: Early Poems,* 1961; *Reality Sandwiches: 1953–1960,* 1963; *Wichita Vortex Sutra,* 1967; *Planet News,* 1968; *Iron Horse,* 1972; *The Fall of America: Poems of These States, 1965–1971,* 1973; *Mind Breaths: Poems, 1972–1977,* 1978; *Collected Poems 1947–1980,* 1984; *Howl* (facsimile), 1986; *White Shroud, Poems 1980–1985,* 1986; *Cosmopolitan Greetings: Poems 1986–1992,* 1995; *Death and Fame: Poems, 1993–1997,* 1999.

A Supermarket in California

What thoughts I have of you tonight, Walt Whitman, for I
walked down the sidestreets under the trees with a headache
self-conscious looking at the full moon.

In my hungry fatigue, and shopping for images, I went into
the neon fruit supermarket, dreaming of your enumerations!

What peaches and what penumbras! Whole families
shopping at night! Aisles full of husbands! Wives in the
avocados, babies in the tomatoes!—and you, Garcia Lorca,[1]
what were you doing down by the watermelons?

I saw you, Walt Whitman, childless, lonely old grubber,
poking among the meats in the refrigerator and eyeing the
grocery boys.

I heard you asking questions of each: Who killed the pork
chops? What price bananas? Are you my Angel?

I wandered in and out of the brilliant stacks of cans
following you, and followed in my imagination by the store
detective.

We strode down the open corridors together in our solitary
fancy tasting artichokes, possessing every frozen delicacy, and
never passing the cashier.

Where are we going, Walt Whitman? The doors close in an
hour. Which way does your beard point tonight?

(I touch your book and dream of our odyssey in the
supermarket and feel absurd.)

Will we walk all night through solitary streets? The trees
add shade to shade, lights out in the houses, we'll both be
lonely.

Will we stroll dreaming of the lost America of love past
blue automobiles in driveways, home to our silent cottage?

Ah, dear father, graybeard, lonely old courage-teacher, what
America did you have when Charon[2] quit poling his ferry and
you got out on a smoking bank and stood watching the boat
disappear on the black waters of Lethe?

1956

---

[1] Spanish poet and playwright Federico García
Lorca (1899–1936), who was murdered at the
start of the Spanish Civil War.

[2] In Greek myth, Charon ferried the shades
of the dead to Hades over Lethe, river of
forgetfulness.

Howl

for Carl Solomon[1]

I

I saw the best minds of my generation destroyed by madness,
　　starving hysterical naked,
dragging themselves through the negro streets at dawn looking for
　　an angry fix,
5　angelheaded hipsters burning for the ancient heavenly connection
　　to the starry dynamo in the machinery of night,
who poverty and tatters and hollow-eyed and high sat up smoking
　　in the supernatural darkness of cold-water flats floating across
　　the tops of cities contemplating jazz,
10　who bared their brains to Heaven under the El[2] and saw
　　Mohammedan angels staggering on tenement roofs
　　illuminated,
who passed through universities with radiant cool eyes
　　hallucinating Arkansas and Blake-light[3] tragedy among the
15　　scholars of war,
who were expelled from the academies for crazy & publishing
　　obscene odes on the windows of the skull,[4]
who cowered in unshaven rooms in underwear, burning their
　　money in wastebaskets and listening to the Terror through the
20　　wall,
who got busted in their pubic beards returning through Laredo
　　with a belt of marijuana for New York,
who ate fire in paint hotels or drank turpentine in Paradise Alley,[5]
　　death, or purgatoried their torsos night after night
25　with dreams, with drugs, with waking nightmares, alcohol and cock
　　and endless balls,
incomparable blind streets of shuddering cloud and lightning in
　　the mind leaping toward poles of Canada & Paterson,
　　illuminating all the motionless world of Time between,
30　Peyote solidities of halls, backyard green tree cemetery dawns,
　　wine drunkenness over the rooftops, storefront boroughs of
　　teahead joyride neon blinking traffic light, sun and moon and

---

[1] Friend of Ginsberg and fellow psychiatric patient in 1949.
[2] The elevated railway.
[3] Refers to English poet William Blake (1757–1827).

[4] Ginsberg was expelled from Columbia for writing an obscenity on his windowpane.
[5] A slum courtyard on the East Side.

tree vibrations in the roaring winter dusks of Brooklyn, ashcan
   rantings and kind king light of mind,
35 who chained themselves to subways for the endless ride from
   Battery to holy Bronx on benzedrine until the noise of wheels
   and children brought them down shuddering mouth-wracked
   and battered bleak of brain all drained of brilliance in the
   drear light of Zoo,
40 who sank all night in submarine light of Bickford's[6] floated out
   and sat through the stale beer afternoon in desolate
   Fugazzi's,[7] listening to the crack of doom on the hydrogen
   jukebox,
   who talked continuously seventy hours from park to pad to bar to
45   Bellevue[8] to museum to the Brooklyn Bridge,
   a lost battalion of platonic conversationalists jumping down the
   stoops off fire escapes off windowsills off Empire State out of
   the moon,
   yacketayakking screaming vomiting whispering facts and memories
50   and anecdotes and eyeball kicks and shocks of hospitals and
   jails and wars,
   whole intellects disgorged in total recall for seven days and nights
   with brilliant eyes, meat for the Synagogue cast on the
   pavement,
55 who vanished into nowhere Zen New Jersey leaving a trail of
   ambiguous picture postcards of Atlantic City Hall,
   suffering Eastern sweats and Tangerian bone-grindings and
   migraines of China under junk-withdrawal in Newark's bleak
   furnished room,
60 who wandered around and around at midnight in the railroad yard
   wondering where to go, and went, leaving no broken hearts,
   who lit cigarettes in boxcars boxcars boxcars racketing through
   snow toward lonesome farms in grandfather night,
   who studied Plotinus Poe St. John of the Cross[9] telepathy and bop
65   kaballa[10] because the cosmos instinctively vibrated at their feet
   in Kansas,
   who loned it through the streets of Idaho seeking visionary indian
   angels who were visionary indian angels,
   who thought they were only mad when Baltimore gleamed in
70   supernatural ecstasy,
   who jumped in limousines with the Chinaman of Oklahoma on the
   impulse of winter midnight streetlight smalltown rain,

---

[6]Cafeteria.
[7]Bar in Greenwich Village.
[8]New York City public hospital.
[9]Plotinus (205–270) Roman philosopher;

Edgar Allan Poe (1809–1849); St. John of the
Cross (1542–1591) Spanish poet.
[10]Cf. Cabala: esoteric interpretation of Hebrew
scriptures.

who lounged hungry and lonesome through Houston seeking jazz
or sex or soup, and followed the brilliant Spaniard to
75   converse about America and Eternity, a hopeless task, and so
took ship to Africa,
who disappeared into the volcanoes of Mexico leaving behind
nothing but the shadow of dungarees and the lava and ash of
poetry scattered in fireplace Chicago,
80 who reappeared on the West Coast investigating the F.B.I. in
beards and shorts with big pacifist eyes sexy in their dark skin
passing out incomprehensible leaflets,
who burned cigarette holes in their arms protesting the narcotic
tobacco haze of Capitalism,
85 who distributed Supercommunist pamphlets in Union Square
weeping and undressing while the sirens of Los Alamos wailed
them down, and wailed down Wall, and the Staten Island
ferry also wailed,
who broke down crying in white gymnasiums naked and trembling
90   before the machinery of other skeletons,
who bit detectives in the neck and shrieked with delight in
policecars for committing no crime but their own wild
cooking pederasty and intoxication,
who howled on their knees in the subway and were dragged off
95   the roof waving genitals and manuscripts,
who let themselves be fucked in the ass by saintly motorcyclists,
and screamed with joy,
who blew and were blown by those human seraphim, the sailors,
caresses of Atlantic and Caribbean love,
100 who balled in the morning in the evenings in rosegardens and the
grass of public parks and cemeteries scattering their semen
freely to whomever come who may,
who hiccupped endlessly trying to giggle but wound up with a sob
behind a partition in a Turkish Bath when the blonde &
105   naked angel came to pierce them with a sword,
who lost their loveboys to the three old shrews of fate the one
eyed shrew of the heterosexual dollar the one eyed shrew that
winks out of the womb and the one eyed shrew that does
nothing but sit on her ass and snip the intellectual golden
110   threads of the craftsman's loom,
who copulated ecstatic and insatiate with a bottle of beer a
sweetheart a package of cigarettes a candle and fell off the
bed, and continued along the floor and down the hall and
ended fainting on the wall with a vision of ultimate cunt and
115   come eluding the last gyzm of consciousness,
who sweetened the snatches of a million girls trembling in the
sunset, and were red eyed in the morning but prepared to
sweeten the snatch of the sunrise, flashing buttocks under
barns and naked in the lake,

120   who went out whoring through Colorado in myriad stolen night-
        cars, N.C.,[11] secret hero of these poems, cocksman and
        Adonis of Denver—joy to the memory of his innumerable lays
        of girls in empty lots & diner backyards, moviehouses' rickety
        rows, on mountaintops in caves or with gaunt waitresses in
125   familiar roadside lonely petticoat upliftings & especially secret
        gas-station solipsisms of johns, & hometown alleys too,
     who faded out in vast sordid movies, were shifted in dreams, woke
        on a sudden Manhattan, and picked themselves up out of
        basements hungover with heartless Tokay and horrors of
130   Third Avenue iron dreams & stumbled to unemployment
        offices,
     who walked all night with their shoes full of blood on the
        snowbank docks waiting for a door in the East River to open
        to a room full of steamheat and opium,
135   who created great suicidal dramas on the apartment cliff-banks of
        the Hudson under the wartime blue floodlight of the moon &
        their heads shall be crowned with laurel in oblivion,
     who ate the lamb stew of the imagination or digested the crab at
        the muddy bottom of the rivers of Bowery,
140   who wept at the romance of the streets with their pushcarts full of
        onions and bad music,
     who sat in boxes breathing in the darkness under the bridge, and
        rose up to build harpsichords in their lofts,
     who coughed on the sixth floor of Harlem crowned with flame
145   under the tubercular sky surrounded by orange crates of
        theology,
     who scribbled all night rocking and rolling over lofty incantations
        which in the yellow morning were stanzas of gibberish,
     who cooked rotten animals lung heart feet tail borscht & tortillas
150   dreaming of the pure vegetable kingdom,
     who plunged themselves under meat trucks looking for an egg,
     who threw their watches off the roof to cast their ballot for
        Eternity outside of Time, & alarm clocks fell on their heads
        every day for the next decade,
155   who cut their wrists three times successively unsuccessfully, gave
        up and were forced to open antique stores where they thought
        they were growing old and cried,
     who were burned alive in their innocent flannel suits on Madison
        Avenue amid blasts of leaden verse & the tanked-up clatter of
160   the iron regiments of fashion & the nitroglycerine shrieks of
        the fairies of advertising & the mustard gas of sinister

---

[11]Neal Cassady, friend of Ginsberg and Jack
Kerouac.

intelligent editors, or were run down by the drunken taxicabs
of Absolute Reality,

who jumped off the Brooklyn Bridge this actually happened and
165 walked away unknown and forgotten into the ghostly daze of
Chinatown soup alleyways & firetrucks, not even one free
beer,

who sang out of their windows in despair, fell out of the subway
window, jumped in the filthy Passaic, leaped on negroes, cried
170 all over the street, danced on broken wineglasses barefoot
smashed phonograph records of nostalgic European 1930's
German jazz finished the whiskey and threw up groaning into
the bloody toilet, moans in their ears and the blast of colossal
steamwhistles,

175 who barreled down the highways of the past journeying to each
other's hotrod-Golgotha[12] jail-solitude watch or Birmingham
jazz incarnation,

who drove crosscountry seventytwo hours to find out if I had a
vision or you had a vision or he had a vision to find out
180 Eternity,

who journeyed to Denver, who died in Denver, who came back to
Denver & waited in vain, who watched over Denver &
brooded & loned in Denver and finally went away to find out
the Time, & now Denver is lonesome for her heroes,

185 who fell on their knees in hopeless cathedrals praying for each
other's salvation and light and breasts, until the soul
illuminated its hair for a second,

who crashed through their minds in jail waiting for impossible
criminals with golden heads and the charm of reality in their
190 hearts who sang sweet blues to Alcatraz,

who retired to Mexico to cultivate a habit, or Rocky Mount to
tender Buddha or Tangiers to boys or Southern Pacific to the
black locomotive or Harvard to Narcissus to Woodlawn[13] to
the daisychain or grave,

195 who demanded sanity trials accusing the radio of hypnotism &
were left with their insanity & their hands & a hung jury,

who threw potato salad at CCNY lecturers on Dadaism and
subsequently presented themselves on the granite steps of the
madhouse with shaven heads and harlequin speech of suicide,
200 demanding instantaneous lobotomy,

and who were given instead the concrete void of insulin metrasol
electricity hydrotherapy psychotherapy occupational therapy
pingpong & amnesia,

who in humorless protest overturned only one symbolic pingpong
205 table, resting briefly in catatonia,

---

[12]Scene of Jesus' crucifixion.
[13]Bronx cemetery.

returning years later truly bald except for a wig of blood, and tears
and fingers, to the visible madman doom of the wards of the
madtowns of the East,
Pilgrim State's Rockland's and Greystone's[14] foetid halls, bickering
210   with the echoes of the soul, rocking and rolling in the
midnight solitude-bench dolmen-realms of love, dream of life
a nightmare, bodies turned to stone as heavy as the moon,
with mother finally ******, and the last fantastic book flung out of
the tenement window, and the last door closed at 4 AM and
215   the last telephone slammed at the wall in reply and the last
furnished room emptied down to the last piece of mental
furniture, a yellow paper rose twisted on a wire hanger in the
closet, and even that imaginary, nothing but a hopeful little
bit of hallucination—
220 ah, Carl, while you are not safe I am not safe, and now you're
really in the total animal soup of time—
and who therefore ran through the icy streets obsessed with a
sudden flash of the alchemy of the use of the ellipse the
catalog the meter & the vibrating plane,
225 who dreamt and made incarnate gaps in Time & Space through
images juxtaposed, and trapped the archangel of the soul
between 2 visual images and joined the elemental verbs and
set the noun and dash of consciousness together jumping with
sensation of Pater Omnipotens Aeterna Deus[15]
230 to recreate the syntax and measure of poor human prose and stand
before you speechless and intelligent and shaking with shame,
rejected yet confessing out the soul to conform to the rhythm
of thought in his naked and endless head,
the madman bum and angel beat in Time, unknown, yet putting
235   down here what might be left to say in time come after death,
and rose incarnate in the ghostly clothes of jazz in the goldhorn
shadow of the band and blew the suffering of America's
naked mind for love into an eli eli lamma lamma sabacthani[16]
saxophone cry that shivered the cities down to the last radio
240 with the absolute heart of the poem of life butchered out of their
own bodies good to eat a thousand years.

---

[14]Mental hospitals in New York and New Jersey.

[15]Latin: "Omnipotent Father Eternal God," from a letter of French painter Paul Cézanne (1839–1906).

[16]Hebrew: "My God, my God, why hast thou forsaken me?" Christ's words on the cross (Matthew 27:46).

II

What sphinx of cement and aluminum bashed open their skulls
and ate up their brains and imagination?
Moloch![17] Solitude! Filth! Ugliness! Ashcans and unobtainable
245   dollars! Children screaming under the stairways! Boys
sobbing in armies! Old men weeping in the parks!
Moloch! Moloch! Nightmare of Moloch! Moloch the loveless!
Mental Moloch! Moloch the heavy judger of men!
Moloch the incomprehensible prison! Moloch the crossbone
250   soulless jailhouse and Congress of sorrows! Moloch whose
buildings are judgement! Moloch the vast stone of war!
Moloch the stunned governments!
Moloch whose mind is pure machinery! Moloch whose blood is
running money! Moloch whose fingers are ten armies!
255   Moloch whose breast is a cannibal dynamo! Moloch whose
ear is a smoking tomb!
Moloch whose eyes are a thousand blind windows! Moloch whose
skyscrapers stand in the long streets like endless Jehovahs!
Moloch whose factories dream and croak in the fog!
260   Moloch whose smokestacks and antennae crown the cities!
Moloch whose love is endless oil and stone! Moloch whose soul is
electricity and banks! Moloch whose poverty is the
specter of genius! Moloch whose fate is a cloud of sexless
hydrogen! Moloch whose name is the Mind!
265 Moloch in whom I sit lonely! Moloch in whom I dream Angels!
Crazy in Moloch! Cocksucker in Moloch! Lacklove and
manless in Moloch!
Moloch who entered my soul early! Moloch in whom I am a
consciousness without a body! Moloch who frightened me
270   out of my natural ecstasy! Moloch whom I abandon!
Wake up in Moloch! Light streaming out of the sky!
Moloch! Moloch! Robot apartments! invisible suburbs!
skeleton treasuries! blind capitals! demonic industries!
spectral nations! invincible madhouses! granite cocks!
275   monstrous bombs!
They broke their backs lifting Moloch to Heaven! Pavements,
trees, radios, tons! lifting the city to Heaven which exists
and is everywhere about us!
Visions! omens! hallucinations! miracles! ecstasies! gone down
280   the American river!
Dreams! adorations! illuminations! religions! the whole
boatload of sensitive bullshit!

---

[17]Semitic god to whom children were sacrificed.

Breakthroughs! over the river! flips and crucifixions! gone down
    the flood! Highs! Epiphanies! Despairs! Ten years'
285   animal screams and suicides! Minds! New loves! Mad
    generation! down on the rocks of Time!
Real holy laughter in the river! They saw it all! the wild eyes!
    the holy yells! They bade farewell! They jumped off the
    roof! to solitude! waving! carrying flowers! Down to
290   the river! into the street!

III

Carl Solomon! I'm with you in Rockland
    where you're madder than I am
I'm with you in Rockland
    where you must feel very strange
295 I'm with you in Rockland
    where you imitate the shade of my mother
I'm with you in Rockland
    where you've murdered your twelve secretaries
I'm with you in Rockland
300   where you laugh at this invisible humor
I'm with you in Rockland
    where we are great writers on the same dreadful typewriter
I'm with you in Rockland
    where your condition has become serious and is reported on
305   the radio
I'm with you in Rockland
    where the faculties of the skull no longer admit the worms
    of the senses
I'm with you in Rockland
310   where you drink the tea of the breasts of the spinsters of
    Utica
I'm with you in Rockland
    where you pun on the bodies of your nurses the harpies of
    the Bronx
315 I'm with you in Rockland
    where you scream in a straightjacket that you're losing the
    game of the actual pingpong of the abyss
I'm with you in Rockland
    where you bang on the catatonic piano the soul is innocent
320   and immortal it should never die ungodly in an armed
    madhouse
I'm with you in Rockland
    where fifty more shocks will never return your soul to its
    body again from its pilgrimage to a cross in the void

325 I'm with you in Rockland
> where you accuse your doctors of insanity and plot the
> Hebrew socialist revolution against the fascist national
> Golgotha[18]

I'm with you in Rockland
330 where you split the heavens of Long Island and resurrect
> your living human Jesus from the superhuman tomb

I'm with you in Rockland
> where there are twentyfive-thousand mad comrades all
> together singing the final stanzas of the Internationale

335 I'm with you in Rockland
> where we hug and kiss the United States under our
> bedsheets   the United States that coughs all night and won't
> let us sleep

I'm with you in Rockland
340 where we wake up electrified out of the coma by our own
> souls' airplanes roaring over the roof they've come to drop
> angelic bombs   the hospital illuminates itself   imaginary
> walls collapse   O skinny legions run outside   O starry-
> spangled shock of mercy the eternal war is here   O victory
345 forget your underwear we're free

I'm with you in Rockland
> in my dreams you walk dripping from a sea-journey on the
> highway across America in tears to the door of my cottage
> in the Western night

1955–56

America

America I've given you all and now I'm nothing.
America two dollars and twentyseven cents January 17, 1956.
I can't stand my own mind.
America when will we end the human war?
5 Go fuck yourself with your atom bomb.
I don't feel good don't bother me.
I won't write my poem till I'm in my right mind.
America when will you be angelic?
When will you take off your clothes?

[18]Same as Calvary, the hill where Jesus was crucified.

10   When will you look at yourself through the grave?
     When will you be worthy of your million Trotskyites?[1]
     America why are your libraries full of tears?
     America when will you send your eggs to India?
     I'm sick of your insane demands.
15   When can I go into the supermarket and buy what I need with my
         good looks?
     America after all it is you and I who are perfect not the next
         world.
     Your machinery is too much for me.
20   You made me want to be a saint.
     There must be some other way to settle this argument.
     Burroughs[2] is in Tangiers I don't think he'll come back it's sinister.
     Are you being sinister or is this some form of practical joke?
     I'm trying to come to the point.
25   I refuse to give up my obsession.
     America stop pushing I know what I'm doing.
     America the plum blossoms are falling.
     I haven't read the newspapers for months, everyday somebody goes
         on trial for murder.
30   America I feel sentimental about the Wobblies.[3]
     America I used to be a communist when I was a kid I'm not sorry.
     I smoke marijuana every chance I get.
     I sit in my house for days on end and stare at the roses in the
         closet.
35   When I go to Chinatown I get drunk and never get laid.
     My mind is made up there's going to be trouble.
     You should have seen me reading Marx.
     My psychoanalyst thinks I'm perfectly right.
     I won't say the Lord's Prayer.
40   I have mystical visions and cosmic vibrations.
     America I still haven't told you what you did to Uncle Max after
         he came over from Russia.

     I'm addressing you.
     Are you going to let your emotional life be run by Time
45   Magazine?
     I'm obsessed by Time Magazine.
     I read it every week.
     Its cover stares at me every time I slink past the corner candystore.
     I read it in the basement of the Berkeley Public Library.

---

[1]Communist idealists, followers of Leon Trot-
sky (1879–1940).
[2]William Burroughs (1914–1997), author of
Naked Lunch.

[3]Nickname for Industrial Workers of the World,
a militant labor organization strong in the 1910s.

50 It's always telling me about responsibility. Businessmen are serious.
        Movie producers are serious. Everybody's serious but me.
    It occurs to me that I am America.
    I am talking to myself again.

    Asia is rising against me.
55 I haven't got a chinaman's chance.
    I'd better consider my national resources.
    My national resources consist of two joints of marijuana millions of
        genitals an unpublished private literature that goes 1400 miles
        an hour and twentyfive-thousand mental institutions.
60 I say nothing about my prisons nor the millions of underprivileged
        who live in my flowerpots under the light of five hundred
        suns.
    I have abolished the whorehouses of France, Tangiers is the next
        to go.
65 My ambition is to be President despite the fact that I'm a
        Catholic.

    America how can I write a holy litany in your silly mood?
    I will continue like Henry Ford my strophes are as individual as
        his automobiles more so they're all different sexes.
70 America I will sell you strophes $2500 apiece $500 down on your
        old strophe
    America free Tom Mooney[4]
    America save the Spanish Loyalists[5]
    America Sacco & Vanzetti[6] must not die.
75 America I am the Scottsboro boys.[7]
    America when I was seven momma took me to Communist Cell
        meetings they sold us garbanzos a handful per ticket a ticket
        cost a nickel and the speeches were free everybody was
        angelic and sentimental about the workers it was all so sincere
80   you have no idea what a good thing the party was in 1935
        Scott Nearing was a grand old man a real mensch Mother
        Bloor made my cry I once saw Israel Amter[8] plain. Everybody
        must have been a spy.
    America you don't really want to go to war.

---

[4]Labor leader sentenced to death for killings in 1916; the sentence was commuted and he was eventually pardoned.
[5]Opponents of Franco's Fascists in the Spanish Civil War.
[6]Anarchists executed in Massachusetts for murder (1927) in a case that aroused much controversy.

[7]Nine blacks falsely convicted in Alabama for the rape of two white women (1931). The defense was undertaken by the Communist Party, and the case became a cause for liberals and radicals, who believed it to be a miscarriage of justice.
[8]Nearing, Bloor, and Amter were active in Socialist and radical causes.

85 America it's them bad Russians
Them Russians them Russians and them Chinamen. And them Russians.
The Russia wants to eat us alive. The Russia's power mad. She wants to take our cars from out our garages.
90 Her wants to grab Chicago. Her needs a Red Reader's Digest. Her wants our auto plants in Siberia. Him big bureaucracy running our fillingstations.
That no good. Ugh. Him make Indians learn read. Him need big black niggers. Hah. Her make us all work sixteen hours a day.
95 Help.
America this is quite serious.
America this is the impression I get from looking in the television set.
America is this correct?
100 I'd better get right down to the job.
It's true I don't want to join the Army or turn lathes in precision parts factories, I'm nearsighted and psychopathic anyway.
America I'm putting my queer shoulder to the wheel.

1956

Jack Kerouac 1922–1969

Jack Kerouac transformed his life into a modern myth, one that appeals anew to each generation discovering his classic *On the Road* (1957). While romanticizing his cross-country travels and writing frankly about the sex, drugs, and drinking that took up so much of his time, Kerouac also infused his books with a literary consciousness and brooding spirituality, proof that he was smarter and deeper than detractors such as Truman Capote (who claimed Kerouac's writing was mere "typing") wanted him to be.

Though known as a novelist of the open road, he also wrote at length about his childhood in Lowell, Massachusetts, the provincial New England mill town where he was born Jean Louis Lebris de Kerouac to French Canadian immigrant parents in 1922. Lowell is the basis for the town in *The Town and the City* (1950), his first and most traditional novel, modeled

after the work of Thomas Wolfe, and it provides the mystical atmosphere for several of his other novels, including *Visions of Gerard* (1963), the account of his nine-year-old brother Gerard's illness and death. This book effectively blends the Catholicism of his youth with the Buddhist principles informing his later years; its free-flowing style epitomizes the "spontaneous prose" that grew out of the author's faith in "the unspeakable visions of the individual."

After graduating from Lowell High School, Kerouac earned a football scholarship to Columbia College by way of a year at the Horace Mann Preparatory School in New York. At Horace Mann he enjoyed a charmed life as an athlete and scholar. His subsequent years at Columbia did not go so smoothly. An injury derailed his football career, and he eventually dropped out of school and enlisted in the U.S. Navy and later the Merchant Marine. In the midst of this indecisive time, he made the friends with whom he would instigate the literary trend and liberal lifestyle known as the Beat movement.

Allen Ginsberg and William S. Burroughs (a Harvard graduate) were brilliant, driven, and often self-tormented, like Kerouac himself. In New York City's jazz clubs and gay bars and among the criminal elements of Times Square they found a bracing alternative to workaday jobs and conventional family life. The hustler Herbert Huncke introduced them to "beat," a slang term for a drug deal gone bad. Kerouac applied the musically resonant word to his down-and-out but spiritually questing ("beatific") peers. In 1948 he told his friend John Clellon Holmes that their post-war generation of outsiders evinced "a weariness with all the forms, all the conventions of the world. . . . So I guess you might say we're a beat generation."

The following year, Kerouac took to the road with Neal Cassady, a charismatic con man who personified all things beat. The model for Dean Moriarty in *On the Road* and Cody in *Visions of Cody* (1972), Cassady lived as spontaneously as Kerouac wanted to write. In *On the Road*, he applauds the fictional counterparts of Cassady and Ginsberg, "the ones who are mad to live, mad to talk, mad to be saved, desirous of everything at the same time, the ones who never yawn or say a commonplace thing."

After the publication of *On the Road* and *The Dharma Bums* (1958), the successful follow-up novel based on his friendship with the poet Gary Snyder, Kerouac drifted on a sea of distracting fame. Though he continued to publish both prose and poetry, his drinking and often outlandish behavior cost him the critical recognition that he craved. He died of stomach hemorrhaging at age forty-seven in St. Petersburg, Florida, in the company of his mother and his third wife, Stella Sampas Kerouac of Lowell.

Kerouac embodied many of the contradictions and paradoxes that have long animated American society. He was a homebody and vagabond, bottle-swigging hedonist and Thoreau-quoting hermit, all-American hero and hard-luck hobo. All of these personas show up in his compelling, recklessly honest writing.

Hilary Holladay
University of Massachusetts, Lowell

PRIMARY WORKS

The Town and the City, 1950; *On the Road*, 1957; *The Dharma Bums*, 1958; *The Subterraneans*, 1958; *Doctor Sax: Faust Part Three*, 1959; *Maggie Cassidy*, 1959; *Mexico City Blues*, 1959; *The Scripture of the Golden Eternity*, 1960; *Tristessa*, 1960; *Lonesome Traveler*, 1960; *Book of Dreams*, 1961; *Pull My Daisy*, 1961; *Big Sur*, 1962; *Visions of Gerard*, 1963; *Desolation Angels*, 1965; *Satori in Paris*, 1966; *Vanity of Duluoz: An Adventurous Education*, 1968; *Scattered Poems*, 1971; *Pic*, 1971; *Visions of Cody*, 1972; *Heaven and Other Poems*, 1977; *Pomes All Sizes*, 1992; *Old Angel Midnight*, 1993; *Good Blonde & Others*, 1993; *Some of the Dharma*, 1997; *Selected Letters: 1940–1956*, 1995; *Selected Letters: 1957–1969*, 1999; *Atop an Underwood: Early Stories and Other Writings*, 1999; *Book of Sketches*, 2006; *Windblown World (Journals)*, 2006.

The Vanishing American Hobo

The American hobo has a hard time hoboing nowadays due to the increase in police surveillance of highways, railroad yards, sea shores, river bottoms, embankments and the thousand-and-one hiding holes of industrial night.——In California, the pack rat, the original old type who goes walking from town to town with supplies and bedding on his back, the "Homeless Brother," has practically vanished, along with the ancient gold-panning desert rat who used to walk with hope in his heart through struggling Western towns that are now so prosperous they dont want old bums any more.——"Man dont want no pack rats here even though they founded California" said an old man hiding with a can of beans and an Indian fire in a river bottom outside Riverside California in 1955.——Great sinister tax-paid police cars (1960 models with humorless searchlights) are likely to bear down at any moment on the hobo in his idealistic lope to freedom and the hills of holy silence and holy privacy.——There's nothing nobler than to put up with a few inconveniences like snakes and dust for the sake of absolute freedom.

I myself was a hobo but only of sorts, as you see, because I knew someday my literary efforts would be rewarded by social protection——I was not a real hobo with no hope ever except that secret eternal hope you get sleeping in empty boxcars flying up the Salinas Valley in hot January sunshine full of Golden Eternity toward San Jose where mean-looking old bo's 'll look at you from surly lips and offer you something to eat and a drink too——down by the tracks or in the Guadaloupe Creekbottom.

The original hobo dream was best expressed in a lovely little poem mentioned by Dwight Goddard in his *Buddhist Bible:*

> *Oh for this one rare occurrence*
> *Gladly would I give ten thousand pieces of gold!*
> *A hat is on my head, a bundle on my back,*
> *And my staff, the refreshing breeze and the full moon.*

In America there has always been (you will notice the peculiarly Whitmanesque tone of this poem, probably written by old Goddard) a definite special idea of foot-walking freedom going back to the days of Jim Bridger and Johnny Appleseed and carried on today by a vanishing group of hardy old timers still seen sometimes waiting in a desert highway for a short bus ride into town for panhandling (or work) and grub, or wandering the Eastern part of the country hitting Salvation Armies and moving on from town to town and state to state toward the eventual doom of big-city skid rows when their feet give out.——Nevertheless not long ago in California I did see (deep in the gorge by a railroad track outside San Jose buried in eucalyptus leaves and the blessed oblivion of vines) a bunch of cardboard and jerrybuilt huts at evening in front of one of which sat an aged man puffing his 15¢ Granger tobacco in his corncob pipe (Japan's mountains are full of free huts and old men who cackle over root brews waiting for Supreme Enlightenment which is only obtainable through occasional complete solitude.)

In America camping is considered a healthy sport for Boy Scouts but a crime for mature men who have made it their vocation.——Poverty is considered a virtue among the monks of civilized nations——in America you spend a night in the calaboose if you're caught short without your vagrancy change (it was fifty cents last I heard of, Pard——what now?)

In Brueghel's time children danced around the hobo, he wore huge and raggy clothes and always looked straight ahead indifferent to the children, and the families didnt mind the children playing with the hobo, it was a natural thing.——But today mothers hold tight their children when the hobo passes through town, because of what newspapers made the hobo to be——the rapist, the strangler, child-eater.—— Stay away from strangers, they'll give you poison candy. Though the Brueghel hobo and the hobo today are the same, the children are different.——Where is even the Chaplinesque hobo? The old Divine Comedy hobo? The hobo is Virgil, he lead-eth.——The hobo enters the child's world (like in the famous painting by Brueghel of a huge hobo solemnly passing through the washtub village being barked at and laughed at by children, St. Pied Piper) but today it's an adult world, it's not a child's world.——Today the hobo's made to slink——everybody's watching the cop heroes on TV.

Benjamin Franklin was like a hobo in Pennsylvania; he walked through Philly with three big rolls under his arms and a Massachusetts halfpenny on his hat.—— John Muir was a hobo who went off into the mountains with a pocketful of dried bread, which he soaked in creeks.

Did Whitman terrify the children of Louisiana when he walked the open road?

What about the Black Hobo? Moonshiner? Chicken snatcher? Remus? The black hobo in the South is the last of the Brueghel bums, children pay tribute and stand in awe making no comment. You see him coming out of the piney barren with an old unspeakable sack. Is he carrying coons? Is he carrying Br'er Rabbit? Nobody knows what he's carrying.

The Forty Niner, the ghost of the plains, Old Zacatecan Jack the Walking Saint, the prospector, the spirits and ghosts of hoboism are gone——but they (the prospectors) wanted to fill their unspeakable sacks with gold.——Teddy Roosevelt, political hobo——Vachel Lindsay, troubadour hobo, seedy hobo——how many pies for one of *his* poems? The hobo lives in a Disneyland, Pete-the-Tramp land, where everything is human lions, tin men, moondogs with rubber teeth, orange-and-purple paths, emerald castles in the distance looming, kind philosophers of witches.——No witch ever cooked a hobo.——The hobo has two watches you can't buy in Tiffany's, on one wrist the sun, on the other wrist the moon, both bands are made of sky.

> *Hark! Hark! The dogs do bark,*
> *The beggars are coming to town;*
> *Some in rags, some in tags,*
> *And some in velvet gowns.*

The Jet Age is crucifying the hobo because how can he hop a freight jet? Does Louella Parsons look kindly upon hobos, I wonder? Henry Miller would allow the hobos to swim in his swimming pool.——What about Shirley Temple, to whom the hobo gave the Bluebird? Are the young Temples bluebirdless?

Today the hobo has to hide, he has fewer places to hide, the cops are looking for him, *calling all cars, calling all cars, hobos seen in the vicinity of Bird-in-Hand*——Jean Valjean weighed with his sack of candelabra, screaming to youth, "There's your *sou*, your *sou!*" Beethoven was a hobo who knelt and listened to the light, a deaf hobo who could not hear other hobo complaints.——Einstein the hobo with his ratty turtleneck sweater made of lamb, Bernard Baruch the disillusioned hobo sitting on a park bench with voice-catcher plastic in his ear waiting for John Henry, waiting for somebody very mad, waiting for the Persian epic.——

Sergei Esenin was a great hobo who took advantage of the Russian Revolution to rush around drinking potato juice in the backward villages of Russia (his most famous poem is called *Confessions of a Bum*) who said at the moment they were storming the Czar "Right now I feel like pissing through the window at the moon." It is the egoless hobo that will give birth to a child someday——Li Po was a mighty hobo.——ego is the greatest hobo——Hail Hobo Ego! Whose monument someday will be a golden tin coffee can.

Jesus was a strange hobo who walked on water.——

Buddha was also a hobo who paid no attention to the other hobo.——

Chief Rain-In-The-Face, weirder even.——

W. C. Fields——his red nose explained the meaning of the triple world, Great Vehicle, Lesser Vehicle, Diamond Vehicle.

The hobo is born of pride, having nothing to do with a community but with himself and other hobos and maybe a dog.——Hobos by the railroad embankments cook at night huge tin cans of coffee.——Proud was the way the hobo walked through a town by the back doors where pies were cooling on window sills, the hobo was a mental leper, he didnt need to beg to eat, strong Western bony mothers knew his tinkling beard and tattered toga, *come and get it!* But proud be proud, still there was some annoyance because sometimes when she called *come and get it,* hordes of hobos came, ten or twenty at a time, and it was kind of hard to feed that many, sometimes hobos were inconsiderate, but not always, but when they were, they no longer held their pride, they became bums——they migrated to the Bowery in New York, to Scollay Square in Boston, to Pratt Street in Baltimore, to Madison Street in Chicago, to 12th Street in Kansas City, to Larimer Street in Denver, to South Main Street in Los Angeles, to downtown Third Street in San Francisco, to Skid Road in Seattle ("blighted areas" all)——

The Bowery is the haven for hobos who came to the big city to make the big time by getting pushcarts and collecting cardboard.——Lots of Bowery bums are Scandinavian, lots of them bleed easily because they drink too much.——When winter comes bums drink a drink called smoke, it consists of wood alcohol and a drop of iodine and a scab of lemon, this they gulp down and wham! they hibernate all winter so as not to catch cold, because they dont live anywhere, and it gets very cold outside in the city in winter.——Sometimes hobos sleep arm-in-arm to keep warm, right on the sidewalk. Bowery Mission veterans say that the beer-drinking bums are the most belligerent of the lot.

Fred Bunz is the great Howard Johnson's of the bums——it is located on 277 Bowery in New York. They write the menu in soap on the windows.——You see the bums reluctantly paying fifteen cents for pig brains, twenty-five cents for goulash, and shuffling out in thin cotton shirts in the cold November night to go and make the lunar Bowery with a smash of broken bottle in an alley where they stand against a wall like naughty boys.——Some of them wear adventurous rainy hats picked up by the track in Hugo Colorado or blasted shoes kicked off by Indians in the dumps of Juarez, or coats from the lugubrious salon of the seal and fish.——Bum hotels are white and tiled and seem as though they were upright johns.——Used to be bums told tourists that they once were successful doctors, now they tell tourists they were once guides for movie stars or directors in Africa and that when TV came into being they lost their safari rights.

In Holland they dont allow bums, the same maybe in Copenhagen. But in Paris you can be a bum——in Paris bums are treated with great respect and are rarely refused a few francs.——There are various kinds of classes of bums in Paris, the high-class bum has a dog and a baby carriage in which he keeps all his belongings, and that usually consists of old *France Soirs,* rags, tin cans, empty bottles, broken dolls.—— This bum sometimes has a mistress who follows him and his dog and carriage around.——The lower bums dont own a thing, they just sit on the banks of the Seine picking their nose at the Eiffel Tower.——

The bums in England have English accents, and it makes them seem strange—— they don't understand bums in Germany.——America is the motherland of bum-dom.——

American hobo Lou Jenkins from Allentown Pennsylvania was interviewed at Fred Bunz's on The Bowery.——"What you wanta know all this info for, what you want?"

"I understand that you've been a hobo travelin' around the country."

"How about givin' a fella few bits for some wine before we talk."

"Al, go get the wine."

"Where's this gonna be in, the *Daily News?*"

"No, in a book."

"What are you young kids doing here, I mean where's the drink?"

"Al's gone to the liquor store——You wanted Thunderbird, wasnt it?"

"Yair."

Lou Jenkins then grew worse——"How about a few bits for a flop tonight?"

"Okay, we just wanta ask you a few questions like why did you leave Allentown?"

"My wife.——My wife,——Never get married. You'll never live it down. You mean to say it's gonna be in a book hey what I'm sayin'?"

"Come on say something about bums or something.——"

"Well whattaya wanta know about bums? Lot of 'em around, kinda tough these days, no money——lissen, how about a good meal?"

"See you in the Sagamore." (Respectable bums' cafeteria at Third and Cooper Union.)

"Okay kid, thanks a lot."——He opens the Thunderbird bottle with one expert flip of the plastic seal.——Glub, as the moon rises resplendent as a rose he swallows with big ugly lips thirsty to gulp the throat down, Sclup! and down goes the drink and his eyes be-pop themselves and he licks tongue on top lip and says "H-a-h!" And he shouts "Dont forget my name is spelled Jenkins, J-e-n-k-y-n-s.——"

Another character——"You say that your name is Ephram Freece of Pawling New York?"

"Well, no, my name is James Russell Hubbard."

"You look pretty respectable for a bum."

"My grandfather was a Kentucky colonel."

"Oh?"

"Yes."

"Whatever made you come here to Third Avenue?"

"I really cant do it, I dont care, I cant be bothered, I feel nothing, I dont care any more. I'm sorry but——somebody stole my razor blade last night, if you can lay some money on me I'll buy myself a Schick razor."

"Where will you plug it in? Do you have such facilities?"

"A Schick injector."

"Oh."

"And I always carry this book with me——*The Rules of St. Benedict.* A dreary book, but well I got another book in my pack. A dreary book too I guess."

"Why do you read it then?"

"Because I found it——I found it in Bristol last year."

"What are you interested in? You like interested in something?"

"Well, this other book I got there is er, yee, er, a big strange book——you shouldnt be interviewing me. Talk to that old nigra fella over there with the harmonica——I'm no good for nothing, all I want is to be left alone——"

"I see you smoke a pipe."

"Yeah——Granger tobacco. Want some?"

"Will you show me the book?"

"No I aint got it with me, I only got this with me."——He points to his pipe and tobacco.

"Can you say something?"

"Lightin flash."

The American Hobo is on the way out as long as sheriffs operate with as Louis-Ferdinand Céline said, "One line of crime and nine of boredom," because having nothing to do in the middle of the night with everybody gone to sleep they pick on the first human being they see walking.——They pick on lovers on the beach even. They just dont know what to do with themselves in those five-thousand-dollar police cars with the twoway Dick Tracy radios except pick on anything that moves in the night and in the daytime on anything that seems to be moving independently of gasoline, power, Army or police.——I myself was a hobo but I had to give it up around 1956 because of increasing television stories about the abominableness of strangers with packs passing through by themselves independently——I was surrounded by three squad cars in Tucson Arizona at 2 A.M. as I was walking pack-on-back for a night's sweet sleep in the red moon desert:

"Where you goin'?"

"Sleep."

"Sleep where?"

"On the sand."

"Why?"

"Got my sleeping bag."

"Why?"

"Studyin' the great outdoors."

"Who are you? Let's see your identification."

"I just spent a summer with the Forest Service."

"Did you get paid?"

"Yeah."

"Then why dont you go to a hotel?"

"I like it better outdoors and it's free."

"Why?"

"Because I'm studying hobo."

"What's so good about that?"

They wanted an *explanation* for my hoboing and came close to hauling me in but I was sincere with them and they ended up scratching their heads and saying "Go ahead if that's what you want."——They didnt offer me a ride four miles out to the desert.

And the sheriff of Cochise allowed me to sleep on the cold clay outside Bowie Arizona only because he didnt know about it.——

There's something strange going on, you cant even be alone any more in the primitive wilderness ("primitive areas" so-called), there's always a helicopter comes and snoops around, you need camouflage.——Then they begin to demand that you observe strange aircraft for Civil Defense as though you knew the difference between regular strange aircraft and any kind of strange aircraft.——As far as I'm concerned the only thing to do is sit in a room and get drunk and give up your hoboing and your camping ambitions because there aint a sheriff or fire warden in any of the new fifty states who will let you cook a little meal over some burning sticks in the tule brake or the hidden valley or anyplace any more because he has nothing to do but pick on what he sees out there on the landscape moving independently of the gasoline power army police station.——I have no ax to grind: I'm simply going to another world.

Ray Rademacher, a fellow staying at the Mission in the Bowery, said recently, "I wish things was like they was when my father was known as Johnny the Walker of the White Mountains.——He once straightened out a young boy's bones after an accident, for a meal, and left. The French around there called him '*Le Passant.*'" (He who passes through.)

The hobos of America who can still travel in a healthy way are still in good shape, they can go hide in cemeteries and drink wine under cemetery groves of trees and micturate and sleep on cardboards and smash bottles on the tombstones and not care and not be scared of the dead but serious and humorous in the cop-avoiding night and even amused and leave litters of their picnic between the grizzled slabs of Imagined Death, cussing what they think are real days, but Oh the poor bum of the skid row! There he sleeps in the doorway, back to wall, head down, with his right hand palm-up as if to receive from the night, the other hand hanging, strong, firm, like Joe Louis hands, pathetic, made tragic by unavoidable circumstance——the hand like a beggar's upheld with the fingers forming a suggestion of what he deserves and desires to receive, shaping the alms, thumb almost touching finger tips, as though on the tip of the tongue he's about to say in sleep and with that gesture what he couldnt say awake: "Why have you taken this away from me, that I cant draw my breath in the peace and sweetness of my own bed but here in these dull and nameless rags on this humbling stoop I have to sit waiting for the wheels of the city to roll," and further, "I dont want to show my hand but in sleep I'm helpless to straighten it, yet take this opportunity to see my plea, I'm alone, I'm sick, I'm dying——see my hand up-tipped, learn the secret of my human heart, give me the thing, give me your hand, take me to the emerald mountains beyond the city, take me to the safe place, be kind, be nice, smile——I'm too tired now of everything else, I've had enough, I give up, I quit, I want to go home, take me home O brother in the night——take me home, lock me in safe, take me to where all is peace and amity, to the family of life, my mother, my father, my sister, my wife and you my brother and you my friend——but no hope, no hope, no hope, I wake up and I'd give a million dollars to be in my own bed——O Lord save me——" In evil roads behind gas tanks where murderous dogs snarl from behind wire fences cruisers suddenly leap out like getaway cars but from a crime more secret, more baneful than words can tell.

The woods are full of wardens.

1960

Lawrence Ferlinghetti b. 1919

A prominent voice of the Beat poetry movement of the 1950s whose primary aim was to bring poetry back to the people, Lawrence Ferlinghetti has greatly extended that specific objective in his prolific career as editor and publisher of the renowned City Lights Books press in San Francisco. His literary production has embraced many areas: translation, fiction writing, travelogues, playwriting, film narration, and essays. Yet his impact and importance remain as a poet and as a voice of dissent which is reflected in his describing his politics as "an enemy of the State."

Following graduation from the University of North Carolina and service in World War II, Ferlinghetti received a master's degree from Columbia University in 1948 and a doctorate from the Sorbonne in 1951. From 1951 to 1953, when he settled in San Francisco, he taught French in an adult education program. In 1953 he became co-owner of the City Lights Bookshop, the first all-paperback bookstore in the country, and by 1955 had founded and become editor of the City Lights Books publishing house. City Lights served as a meeting place for Beat writers. His press published and promoted Beat writings, and he himself encouraged them, in the case of Diane di Prima, writing the introduction for her first collection, *This Kind of Bird Flies Backward.*

Ferlinghetti's publication of Allen Ginsberg's *Howl* in 1956 led to his arrest on obscenity charges. The trial that followed (he was acquitted) drew national attention to the Beat movement and established Ferlinghetti as its prominent voice. In fact, Ferlinghetti own *A Coney Island of the Mind,* was, along with *Howl,* the most popular poetry book of the 1950s. Often concerned with political and social issues, Ferlinghetti's poetry set out to dispute the literary elite's definition of art and the artist's role in the world. Though imbued with the commonplace, his poetry cannot be dismissed as polemic or personal protest, for it stands on his craftsmanship, thematics, and grounding in tradition.

Ferlinghetti described his one novel, *Her,* as "a surreal semi-autobiographical blackbook." It deals with a young man's search for his identity, although its free-association experimentation proved baffling to critics.

Known for his political poetry, he explains his commitment in art as well as life by saying "Only the dead are disengaged." Well aware of the incongruity of his social dissent with his success as a publisher, Ferlinghetti, in an interview for the Los Angeles *Times,* remarked on "the enormous capacity of society to ingest its own most dissident elements. . . . It happens to everyone successful within the system. I'm ingested myself."

Helen Barolini
Independent scholar

PRIMARY WORKS

Pictures of the Gone World, 1955, 1973, 1995; *A Coney Island of the Mind,* 1958; *Her* (novel), 1960; *Starting from San Francisco,* 1961, 1967; *Unfair Arguments with Existence,* 1963; *Routines,* 1964; *Tyrannus Nix?,* 1969; *The Secret Meaning of Things,* 1969; *The Mexican Night: Travel Journal,* 1970; *Back Roads to Far Places,* 1971; *Love Is No Stone on the Moon: Automatic Poem,* 1971; *Open Eye, Open Heart,* 1973; *Who Are We Now?,* 1976; *Landscapes of Living and Dying,* 1979; *Literary San Francisco,* 1980; *Endless Life: Selected Poems,* 1981; *Over All the Obscene Boundaries,* 1984; *The Canticle of Jack Kerouac,* 1987; *Love in the Days of Rage,* 1988; *European Poems and Transitions,* 1988; *Ascending over Ohio,* 1989; *A Buddha in the Woodpile,* 1993; *These Are My Rivers: New and Selected Poems,* 1993; *A Far Rockaway of the Heart,* 1997; *How to Paint Sunlight: Lyric Poems and Others 1997–2000,* 2001; *San Francisco Poems,* 2001; *Americus: Part 1,* 2004; *Poetry as Insurgent Art,* 2007.

I Am Waiting

I am waiting for my case to come up
and I am waiting
for a rebirth of wonder
and I am waiting for someone
5 to really discover America
and wail
and I am waiting
for the discovery
of a new symbolic western frontier
10 and I am waiting
for the American Eagle
to really spread its wings
and straighten up and fly right
and I am waiting
15 for the Age of Anxiety
to drop dead
and I am waiting
for the war to be fought
which will make the world safe
20 for anarchy
and I am waiting
for the final withering away
of all governments
and I am perpetually awaiting
25 a rebirth of wonder

I am waiting for the Second Coming
and I am waiting
for a religious revival
to sweep thru the state of Arizona

30 and I am waiting
    for the Grapes of Wrath to be stored
    and I am waiting
    for them to prove
    that God is really American
35 and I am seriously waiting
    for Billy Graham and Elvis Presley
    to exhange roles seriously
    and I am waiting
    to see God on television
40 piped onto church altars
    if only they can find
    the right channel
    to tune in on
    and I am waiting
45 for the Last Supper to be served again
    with a strange new appetizer
    and I am perpetually awaiting
    a rebirth of wonder

    I am waiting for my number to be called
50 and I am waiting
    for the living end
    and I am waiting
    for dad to come home
    his pockets full
55 of irradiated silver dollars
    and I am waiting
    for the atomic tests to end
    and I am waiting happily
    for things to get much worse
60 before they improve
    and I am waiting
    for the Salvation Army to take over
    and I am waiting
    for the human crowd
65 to wander off a cliff somewhere
    clutching its atomic umbrella
    and I am waiting
    for Ike to act
    and I am waiting
70 for the meek to be blessed
    and inherit the earth
    without taxes
    and I am waiting
    for forests and animals
75 to reclaim the earth as theirs

and I am waiting
for a way to be devised
to destroy all nationalisms
without killing anybody
80 and I am waiting
for linnets and planets to fall like rain
and I am waiting for lovers and weepers
to lie down together again
in a new rebirth of wonder

85 I am waiting for the Great Divide to be crossed
and I am anxiously waiting
for the secret of eternal life to be discovered
by an obscure general practitioner
and save me forever from certain death
90 and I am waiting
for life to begin
and I am waiting
for the storms of life
to be over
95 and I am waiting
to set sail for happiness
and I am waiting
for a reconstructed Mayflower
to reach America
100 with its picture story and tv rights
sold in advance to the natives
and I am waiting
for the lost music to sound again
in the Lost Continent
105 in a new rebirth of wonder

I am waiting for the day
that maketh all things clear
and I am waiting
for Ole Man River
110 to just stop rolling along
past the country club
and I am waiting
for the deepest South
to just stop Reconstructing itself
115 in its own image
and I am waiting
for a sweet desegregated chariot
to swing low
and carry me back to Ole Virginie
120 and I am waiting
for Ole Virginie to discover
just why Darkies are born

and I am waiting
for God to lookout
125 from Lookout Mountain
and see the Ode to the Confederate Dead
as a real farce
and I am awaiting retribution
for what America did
130 to Tom Sawyer
and I am waiting retribution
for what America did
to Tom Sawyer
and I am perpetually awaiting
135 a rebirth of wonder

I am waiting for Tom Swift to grow up
and I am waiting
for the American Boy
to take off Beauty's clothes
140 and get on top of her
and I am waiting
for Alice in Wonderland
to retransmit to me
her total dream of innocence
145 and I am waiting
for Childe Roland to come
to the final darkest tower
and I am waiting
for Aphrodite
150 to grow live arms
at a final disarmament conference
in a new rebirth of wonder

I am waiting
to get some intimations
155 of immortality
by recollecting my early childhood
and I am waiting
for the green mornings to come again
youth's dumb green fields come back again
160 and I am waiting
for some strains of unpremeditated art
to shake my typewriter
and I am waiting to write
the great indelible poem
165 and I am waiting
for the last long careless rapture
and I am perpetually waiting
for the fleeing lovers on the Grecian Urn
to catch each other up at last

170 and embrace
and I am waiting
perpetually and forever
a renaissance of wonder

                    1958

Dove Sta Amore . . .

Dove sta amore
Where lies love
Dove sta amore
Here lies love
5 The ring dove love
In lyrical delight
Hear love's hillsong
Love's true willsong
Love's low plainsong
10 Too sweet painsong
In passages of night
Dove sta amore
Here lies love
The ring dove love
15 Dove sta amore
Here lies love

                    1958

The Old Italians Dying

For years the old Italians have been dying
all over America
For years the old Italians in faded felt hats
have been sunning themselves and dying
5 You have seen them on the benches
in the park in Washington Square
the old Italians in their black high button shoes
the old men in their old felt fedoras
                    with stained hatbands
10 have been dying and dying
                    day by day

You have seen them
every day in Washington Square San Francisco
the slow bell
15 tolls in the morning
in the Church of Peter & Paul
in the marzipan church on the plaza
toward ten in the morning the slow bell tolls
in the towers of Peter & Paul
20 and the old men who are still alive
sit sunning themselves in a row
on the wood benches in the park
and watch the processions in and out
funerals in the morning
25 weddings in the afternoon
slow bell in the morning Fast bell at noon
In one door out the other
the old men sit there in their hats
and watch the coming & going
30 You have seen them
the ones who feed the pigeons
        cutting the stale bread
           with their thumbs & penknives
the ones with old pocketwatches
35 the old ones with gnarled hands
              and wild eyebrows
the ones with the baggy pants
         with both belt & suspenders
the grappa drinkers with teeth like corn
40 the Piemontesi the Genovesi the Sicilianos
       smelling of garlic & pepperonis
the ones who loved Mussolini
the old fascists
the ones who loved Garibaldi
45 the old anarchists reading *L'Umanita Nova*
the ones who loved Sacco & Vanzetti
They are almost all gone now
They are sitting and waiting their turn
and sunning themselves in front of the church
50 over the doors of which is inscribed
a phrase which would seem to be unfinished
from Dante's *Paradiso*
about the glory of the One
        who moves everything . . .
55 The old men are waiting
for it to be finished
for their glorious sentence on earth
        to be finished
the slow bell tolls & tolls

60 the pigeons strut about
    not even thinking of flying
    the air too heavy with heavy tolling
    The black hired hearses draw up
    the black limousines with black windowshades
65 shielding the widows
    the widows with the long black veils
    who will outlive them all
    You have seen them
    madre di terra, madre di mare
70 The widows climb out of the limousines
    The family mourners step out in stiff suits
    The widows walk so slowly
    up the steps of the cathedral
    fishnet veils drawn down
75 leaning hard on darkcloth arms
    Their faces do not fall apart
    They are merely drawn apart
    They are still the matriarchs
    outliving everyone
80 the old dagos dying out
    in Little Italys all over America
    the old dead dagos
    hauled out in the morning sun
    that does not mourn for anyone
85 One by one Year by year
    they are carried out
    The bell
    never stops tolling
    The old Italians with lapstrake faces
90 are hauled out of the hearses
    by the paid pallbearers
    in mafioso mourning coats & dark glasses
    The old dead men are hauled out
    in their black coffins like small skiffs
95 They enter the true church
    for the first time in many years
    in these carved black boats
             ready to be ferried over
    The priests scurry about
100   as if to cast off the lines
    The other old men
           still alive on the benches
    watch it all with their hats on

    You have seen them sitting there
105 waiting for the bocci ball to stop rolling

waiting for the bell
      to stop tolling & tolling
for the slow bell
      to be finished tolling
110 telling the unfinished *Paradiso* story
as seen in an unfinished phrase
      on the face of a church
as seen in a fisherman's face
in a black boat without sails
115 making his final haul

1979

Brenda (Bonnie) Frazer b. 1939

Bonnie Frazer has lived along a border of American mainstream culture, dropping out for writing and hipster adventure and dropping in for work and family life several times over. Similarly, her writing probes a fault line of literary invention, the point at which confession borders fiction. Writing of the people and panoramas of the road, amalgamating art and life in her tales, combining personal confession with artistic composition, Frazer expresses quintessential Beat literary impulses.

Frazer was born in Washington, D.C., in 1939. After studying briefly at Sweet Briar College, in 1959 she met the Beat poet Ray Bremser and married him three weeks later. In 1961, she, Bremser, and their baby daughter, Rachel, fled to Mexico to evade New Jersey prison authorities, who were pursuing Bremser for parole violation. A year later Frazer, who had given up her child for adoption in Mexico and resorted to prostitution to survive, produced *Troia: Mexican Memoirs* (under the name Bonnie Bremser) from letters to Ray while he was again in prison in New Jersey. Bremser, along with the book's editor, Michael Perkins, arranged the letters into a narrative, and *Troia* was published at his insistence in 1969. It came out in Great Britain under the title *For Love of Ray* in

1971. Frazer eventually left both Bremser and the Beat counterculture, obtained a master's degree in soil science, and worked for the U.S. Department of Agriculture as a soil surveyor to support herself and her children. Frazer is now retired and lives in Michigan, where she has returned to writing, expanding her narrative of life in the Beat movement. *Troia* is Frazer's major published work, and it advances the movement's signature aesthetics while integrating female sexuality, consciousness, and desire, as well as motherhood and a woman's artistic ambition, into the Beat literary and cultural domain.

Troia's composition and character follow Beat aesthetics of immersion in memory and imagination, and reliance on spontaneous expression and free association. Frazer wrote *Troia* in two-page daily installments, writing letters to Ray of memories of the previous year in emulation of Kerouac's methods for composing poetry and prose. However, Frazer's poetics modify Beat avant-garde ideals by demanding that sexual freedom and freedom of expression be permitted equally to women as to men. "Troia" means sexual adventurer, and this story of a woman's experience on the road violates long-held patriarchal constraints on women's lives and conduct, echoing contemporaneous claims of second-wave feminism for female equality and sexual self-determination. *Troia* alters the male-centered road tale with domestic elements, bringing to Beat generation legends a mobile female protagonist whose picaresque adventures defy the male model by the presence of her baby. Through its focus on motherhood and gender, *Troia* critiques hipster marriage and sexual politics, just as the narrator jettisons the guilt and shame associated with her sexual promiscuity, open prostitution, and relinquishment of her child. Modifying *On the Road, Troia* explicitly asks what existential and sexual adventuring can mean for women under laws of male dominance and ideas of women as caretakers and sexual objects. A revolutionary text of women's liberation, *Troia* is an original, radical example of antiestablishment Beat generation writing.

Ronna C. Johnson
Tufts University

PRIMARY WORK

Troia: Mexican Memoirs, 1969.

from Troia: Mexican Memoirs

Once across, we were quickly tired of Matamoros and purchased tickets to Mexico City. Transportes Del Norte, maroon buses, nothing to complain of in these first class accommodations, we had enough money to get safely to Mexico City from where we were somehow to get safely to Veracruz, where we were to find our refuge . . . had I already exchanged one fear for another? Had the cold damp night of Matamoros put another chill into my heart? Was my fear at this time all composed of not being able to handle external circumstances, afraid I would not be able to keep Rachel healthy, or at least not crying, (and that was a feat I didn't often succeed in,) and not to be able to satisfy Ray—what was happening in his head, something similar? And it all was so extremely personal, this service of responsibility, that the failure of it and maybe the success I have not had much chance to experience up to this point was a very lonely thing; we were not really helping each other too much now. Each of us was just clinging as well as possible to what shreds of strength were left in the confidential self. The bus ride to Mexico City, full of this, I am constantly with the baby on my lap, broken hearted at every spell of crying, the frustration of not being a very good mother really—trying to groove, trying to groove under the circumstances—and in spite of it I have impressions of dark shrouded nights of passage through the hills, of an oasis of light in a restaurant stop. 2 A.M. with everyone sitting around the narrow lighted room—with a sense of it being the only lighted room for fifty miles around—eating eggs Mexican style for the first time. Ray got his *huevos rancheros* and me eggs scrambled with fried beans and this was sort of a prelude to our Mexican trip. . . .

The trip—maroon bus awaits us beside the low immigration building, near the broken-down bridge—beer cans clatter in the dusty road afternoon no sunlight but the approaching lowering clouds of a thunderstorm spreading out over the sky into gray vastness of a depressing stand-still underneath any tree; lonely your reality here in Matamoros, the streets which carry through the center of town growing in importance to the four central parallels which cut out the square of the plaza, where afternoon bistek eaters and shoe-shine boys eye each other from across the unpaved streets; these same streets spread outward into the still mathematically correct city layout but sidewalks disappear and houses rise in midst of a block shacked upwards from a broken down fence entryway by eroded paths; a house may take any shape or position within a block and weeds of menacing aspect care little for the store on the corner so drawn into its cache of paper candies and orange soda signs it has shrunk to the stature of a poverty-struck doll house—the incredible ironies of Mexico—the wild-flung filth of Matamoros. Leaving town on the bus, mud hole crossroads fifty yards wide of rutting and industry—some International Harvester or reaping machine showroom with its economic splendor surveying the city; it will grow on, and the sky disapproves. Pass Sta. Teresa, a cafe faces east on the flat land. Look across to the Gulf, and nothing looks back, save the mesquite bushes, a mangy dog chases a couple of not promising cows across a landscape you would not expect to carry even that much vision of life. Seen from the air, Transportes Del Norte carries on, a vision of good service, sixty people burning up the dust on the first stretch of the roads which do indeed all lead to Mexico City—San Fernando, Tres Palos, Encinal. The sun shines briefly as I change the baby's diaper and we have a cup of coffee and head back to the bus. Santandar Jimeniz, we do not know yet that from here dots one of those "almost" roads perpendicular to the route of travelling civilization. A road which grows out of the solid surety of modern highway dotting in weak secrecy into the plain to Abasolo where another almost not to be seen road, goes nowhere, but goes—we want to see where all the roads go, since then, but this first trip just get us there and quick, get us there where we are going, and we don't know yet that nothing waits but the bottom waiting to be scraped in our own whimsical and full-of-love fashion—got to get there and quick—damn the crying and wet diapers and laps full of Gerbers on the bus, of leg cramps and not much to view—Padilla, Guemez, Ciudad Victoria, chicken salad sandwiches and the unknown feeling of a waterfall. In all of these places we stop, passing through, rushing downward, seeking our level, slowly dying, get it over, let's get there. Ciudad Monte, non-stop Valles, passing in the night the bus driver picks up on lack of sleep, answers on the wheeling whispering pavement. We take our first curves into the hills, the roads start to swing—Tamazunchale, lights seen across a valley, Jacala, pencil marks on maps of future excitement. We turn East in the night approaching Ixmiquilpan, herald Indian feathers, the driver mutters incoherent names over the sleeping passageway, the bus careens as we shoot through Actopan, come another and final turning point at Pachuca. The driver announces the last lap and everyone stirs and gets excited at the news, not realizing it is more than 3 hours of approach to Mexico City. I look out and God drops from his hand the myriad stars and constellations I have never seen before, plumb to the horizon flat landed out beneath the giant horoscopic screen of Mexican heaven. . . .

Two o'clock *en la mañana*, we arrive in Mexico City and the bus leaves us off at ADO and not at the Transportes Del Norte bus terminal. In a swelter of homeless appearing people whom we don't recognize there are many who are waiting for the morning bus perhaps, and though they look disreputable something will eventually be brought out of their packs to make them proud—like us, our records, our chevrons at that point I guess, on our way to make the scene at P's and it couldn't be too soon for me. I was cold, tired and ready for the new day to dawn with everything O.K., as usual. Taxi drivers, *caldo* eaters of the night, our soon-to-be-compadres of doubtful reckonings on Mexico City taxi meters. When the meter registers two pesos, the passenger somehow must pay four and even more surprisingly we find out this is not just tourist graft and that the taxi in Mexico is one of the cheapest rides anywhere with privacy like a king; cheapest except for the bus ride, if you are game, but that is more rollercoaster thrills. . . .

Ray was perhaps responding to the illusion of everything being beautiful. He always was ahead of me in that respect, and I do respect, although it in fact leaves me behind. He decided to stay in Mexico City for twenty-four hours more while it is decided for me that I will travel to Veracruz by bus with N and the baby. Ah bitter, I was not about to accept with grace my maidenly burdened-by-baby responsibility at this particular time. I should have put my foot down instead of being shuffled because see what it did in rebellion (sure! almost sure! suspecting something really wrong since Matamoros—that Ray had already set his eye on something that didn't include me—what could it be—my perceptions were not sharp) and my survival reflexes were working overtime, I guess. But I go—midway between holding the baby on the eight hour bus trip, the night quickly sets in and I decide to try my seductive powers on N, and the mistaken blue jeans, not to survive this episode, did indeed entice his hand where it should have by any standards stayed away from, the baby on my lap, we arrive in Mexico, me zipping up alone, my lonely pleasure, had I known I could have got in any restroom by my own mechanics—damn N.

If I could only do more than grab at a passing branch over my head, but the trouble with that is everything up until now has taken place fast on the go, the screeching terror of speed of everything falling out from underneath you—the recurring dream of bridges falling and falling away from beneath your very feet into rushing water, the resulting social shock, but more than that, knowing what it is to fall for the last time forever.

1969

Joyce Johnson b. 1934

With the 1983 publication of *Minor Characters,* Joyce Johnson's memoir of her experiences as a young writer in the New York Beat scene of the 1950s, women associated with the movement became visible. Johnson's writing of women's lives in the era just before second-wave feminism epitomizes the "cool" Beat style of cerebral detachment. All her works—two memoirs, three novels, a letters collection, and a nonfiction book—bear her signature tone and style: restrained, ironic, witty inflections; an understated scrutiny that refuses easy compromise; a Beat weariness of inflated claims that is still open to possibilities of redemption and relief. Her observant, lucid prose shows that Johnson, recalling the maxim of her model, Henry James, is a writer on whom nothing has been lost; aloof acuity is her Beat style.

Johnson was born Joyce Glassman in 1934 in New York City and left Barnard College in 1954 one course short of graduation, found a job in publishing, and began to focus on becoming a novelist. She earned a book contract in her early twenties—before becoming involved with Jack Kerouac in 1957—and, as Joyce Glassman, published her first novel, *Come and Join the Dance,* in 1962. Johnson's second novel came out in 1978 after a hiatus from writing during which she was widowed, then remarried, and had a child and began her publishing career as an editor at such houses as William Morrow, Dial, Atlantic Monthly, and McGraw-Hill. Johnson writes regularly for magazines and newspapers and continues to produce her own books; the most recent, *Missing Men* (2004), is a memoir of her life before and after the Beat generation heyday.

Her novels, and especially her hipster protagonists, reconfigure dominant Beat themes and, through depictions of women's sexual self-determination, challenge sexist constructions of female inferiority and marginality. Johnson's *Come and Join the Dance,* the first Beat novel by and about a woman, insists that women of the fifties had deeper ambitions that the M-R-S degree. It fills in Beat generation narratives with hipster women's existential and personal ethics and aesthetics, beliefs, and conduct. *Bad Connections* (1978) portrays the turmoil of the white, middle-class protagonist as she struggles to maintain a home for her child and participate in sixties liberation movements. *In the Night Café* (1989) returns to Beat themes and venues through its young female heroine, who is married to a destructive and talented abstract painter in the fifties. These three novels form a trilogy about hipster New York that offsets the Beat men's famous tales by representing women in the movement.

In a similar vein, *Minor Characters* recounts Beat history through women Johnson knew—her close friends, colleagues, and fellow writers, including the self-destructive poet Elise Cowen; Edie Parker, Kerouac's first wife; Joan Vollmer Adams Burroughs, murdered by William S. Burroughs in 1951; the sculptor Mary Frank; and late-blooming poet Hettie Jones. Johnson tells of these bohemian women's struggles to write and to be recognized, raise children, produce art, and survive on the subsistence economies and downward mobility of Beat culture. Johnson's remarkable 1957–1958 correspondence with Kerouac, published in *Door Wide Open* (2000), testifies to the real-life trials of women's exclusion from the full social and political life, and in the art of the letter evinces the wellsprings of the trademark Beat confessionalism that informs all her work.

Ronna C. Johnson
Tufts University

PRIMARY WORKS

Come and Join the Dance, 1962; *Bad Connections,* 1978; *Minor Characters,* 1983; *In the Night Café,* 1989; *What Lisa Knew: The Truth and Lies of the Steinberg Case,* 1991; *Door Wide Open,* 2000; *Missing Men,* 2004.

from Door Wide Open

July 26, 1957

Dear Jack,

Yes, yes I will come to Mexico!

I wish you hadn't been afraid to write me. I know you have to do what you have to do, and that isn't being a bum—don't put yourself down like that. Elise wrote me that you'd left, but her letter was so vague that it sounded as though you were in some terrible trouble and had decided to disappear, and I've spent a sad week, wanting so much to write you not to disappear and not know where to write—so that it was just too much to get your letter. I walked out of the hotel with it in my hand, ordered on enormous breakfast that I couldn't eat, and *flew* downtown in the IRT, which I think I imagined as somehow bound for Mexico that minute. Yes, and I bought a learning-Spanish-phonetically-thru-pictures type book and can already say Yo soy muchacha, a sentence which I am sure will come in very handy eventually. I wish it were September.

It worries me, Jack, to think of you with $33 to your name while Viking's machinery works out a way of feeding you. And I've really got all this money—so would you like some in the meanwhile? Let me know, and I'll send you a money order or whatever.

I got a review copy of ON THE ROAD, read it, and think it's a great, beautiful book. I think you write with the same power and freedom that Dean Moriarty drives a car. Well, it's terrific, and very moving and affirmative. Don't know why, but it made me remember Mark Twain. Ed Stringham has read it too and thinks it "one of the best books since World War II" and is going to write you a long letter and tell you all this, much more coherently than I can.

Saw [Sheila] off to Europe Wednesday on a little white ship not much bigger than a ferry boat, full of waving singing young kids. Everybody smiling and throwing streamers, [Sheila] too, but I didn't know how she felt. It's funny the way you and Allen and Peter came to town this winter and shook us all up. Just think—we had been here all our lives, and now suddenly Elise is in Frisco, [Sheila] in Paris, and I'm going to Mexico—most peculiar. I feel rather friendless in New York at present, miss talking to Elise a lot, especially. She called me collect from San Francisco this week because she needed money and we tried to talk but couldn't hear each other and kept screaming "Wh-a-a-t? Wh-a-a-t." But then I remember walking with you at night through the Brooklyn docks and seeing the white steam rising from the ships against the black sky and how beautiful it was and I'd never seen it before—imagine!—but if I'd walked through it with anyone else, I wouldn't have seen it either, because I wouldn't have felt safe in what my mother would categorically call "a bad neighborhood," I would have been thinking "Where's the subway?" and missed everything. But with you—I felt as though nothing could touch me, and if anything happened, the Hell with it. You don't know what narrow lives girls have, how few real adventures there are for them; misadventures, yes, like abortions and little men following them in subways, but seldom anything like seeing ships at night. So that's why we've all taken off like this, and that's also part of why I love you.

Take care.

Love,
Joyce

P.S. When you write next maybe you could say something about the Mexican climate, whether it ever gets cold, so I'll know what to bring with me. As you've probably gathered by now, I'm incredibly vague about geography.

from Minor Characters

In a "dream letter" from John Clellon Holmes recorded by Allen Ginsberg in 1954 are the words: "The social organization which is most true of itself to the artist is the boy gang." To which Allen, awakening, writing into his journal, added sternly, "Not society's perfum'd marriage."

The messages of the real Holmes seem to have remained consistent with those of the dream one. Even in 1977, after years of a stable and sustaining second marriage, after all the messages of Women's Liberation that so battered the consciousness of the seventies, Holmes wrote in his preface to a new edition of *Go:* "Did we really resemble these feverish young men, these centerless young women, awkwardly reaching out for love, for hope, for comprehension of their lives and times?" And whereas he scrupulously matches each of the male characters in his roman à clef to their originals, the "girls" are variously "amalgams of several people"; "accurate to the young women of the time"; "a type rather than an individual." He can't quite remember them—they were mere anonymous passengers on the big Greyhound bus of experience. Lacking centers, how could they burn with the fever that infected his young men? What they did, I guess, was fill up the seats.

It's a crisp September morning, the beginning of yet another academic year. The grey-haired, craggy-faced, perhaps self-consciously Lincolnesque professor enters the small classroom where his girl students await him. There's a proper hush as he takes his place behind the oak table, circa 1910, lays out his sharpened pencils, his roll book containing their names, his two slim volumes of something or other—must be the latest in criticism. Intimidated in advance, the girl students study this man's glamorously American Gothic features, looking for signs of humor or mercy. Can he be gotten around? They will be judged by this Professor X, the big fish in the rather smallish pond that is the Barnard English Department.

Picture this middle-aged man, who no doubt wishes he were standing before a class at Harvard—*that* would count for something. There will be few compensations for the spirit here, much less the eye, in teaching this new frumpy lot of young females—rumpled, pasty girls who've dived into the laundry bag for something to wear to class. Only one slouching beauty with a tangle of auburn hair and a glory of freckles, as well as—perhaps he notices immediately—extraordinary knees, can possibly redeem this semester for him.

He wrenches his gaze away from her and begins. Ha! Let's try this question on 'em, he thinks. He rises to his full six feet, the more to heighten the little drama of this opening moment.

"Well"—his tone is as dry as the crackers in the American cultural barrel—"how many of you girls want to be writers?"

He watches with sardonic amusement as one hand flies up confusedly, then another, till all fifteen are flapping. Here and there an engagement ring sparkles.

The air is thick with the uneasiness of the girl students. Why is Professor X asking this? He knows his course is required of all creative-writing majors.

"Well, I'm sorry to see this," says Professor X, the Melville and Hawthorne expert. "Very sorry. Because"—there's a steel glint in his cold eye—"first of all, if you were going to be writers, you wouldn't be enrolled in this class. You couldn't even be enrolled in school. You'd be hopping freight trains, riding through America."

The received wisdom of 1953.

The young would-be writers in this room have understood instantly that of course there is no hope. One by one their hands have all come down.

I was one of those who'd raised hers.

The social organization which is most true of itself to the artist is the girl gang.

Why, everyone would agree, that's absolutely absurd! . . .

. . .

I moved out of 116th Street on Independence Day, 1955—a date I'd chosen not for its symbolism but because it was the first day of a long weekend. I'd taken a tiny maid's room in an apartment on Amsterdam Avenue five blocks away, to which I planned to move all my things, going back and forth with my mother's shopping cart.

I got up early that morning and started putting books into shopping bags. When I thought my parents would be awake, I walked into their room. They were dozing in their twin beds, an oscillating fan whirring between them. I said, "I have something to tell you. I'm moving out today." I felt sick to my stomach, as if I had murdered these two mild people. I could see their blood on the beige summer covers.

Two weeks earlier I'd found the room. With the first paychecks from my new job, I'd bought an unpainted rocking chair, a small desk, two sheets, and a poster of Picasso's *Blue Boy*—the furnishings of my first freedom. I knew children did not own furniture.

All this had been accomplished in secret, like the arrangements for a coup d'état. I wouldn't speak until it was time to leave. There was nothing to discuss. I was terribly afraid of being talked out of it.

"I need to borrow the cart," I said to my mother, "for my clothes and books."

"Don't think—" she said. "Don't think you can just come around here for dinner any time you want."

All day long I dragged the cart back and forth over the hot red brick sidewalks of the Columbia campus. No one shouted. No one stood at the door on 116th Street and tried to bar my way. In the stillness of their house, my parents moved slowly around the rooms as if injured.

I was done by evening. On my way out for the last time, I wrote my address on a piece of paper and left it on the kitchen table. From my new apartment, I called Elise and Sheila, who were sharing a place in Yorkville. "I really did it, I guess," I said.

Everyone knew in the 1950s why a girl from a nice family left home. The meaning of her theft of herself from her parents was clear to all—as well as what she'd be up to in that room of her own.

On 116th Street the superintendent knew it. He'd seen my comings and goings with the cart. He spread the word among the neighbors that the Glassmans' daughter was "bad." His imagination rendered me pregnant. He wrote my parents a note to that effect. My mother called and, weeping over the phone, asked if this was true.

The crime of sex was like guilt by association—not visible to the eye of the outsider, but an act that could be rather easily conjectured. Consequences would make it manifest.

I, too, knew why I'd left—better than anyone. It was to be with Alex. He was the concrete embodiment of my more abstract desire to be "free." By which I meant—if I'd been pressed to admit it—sexually free. The desire for this kind of freedom subsumed every other. For this I was prepared to make my way in the world at the age of nineteen, incurring all the risks of waifdom on fifty dollars a week. In fact, fifty dollars seemed a lot to me, since I'd never had more than ten dollars in my pocket all at once. I opened a charge account at Lord and Taylor. . . .

My boss, Naomi Burton, who'd hired me despite my lack of a B.A., took an interest in me. I was talented, she told me. I could become a literary agent myself if I worked for her for a few more years. She persuaded me to show her a story I'd written at Barnard and published in the college literary magazine. "You're a writer," she said. "You should try your hand at a novel." She rang up a friend of hers, an editor named Hiram Haydn who ran a famous novel workshop at the New School for Social Research, and asked him to let me into the course.

It was thrilling but terrifying—as if I were really in danger of fulfilling the destiny my mother had wanted for me, which I had gone to such lengths to avoid. It seemed to be happening to a person outside the person I really was. I'd hidden from my mother's eyes the story Naomi Burton was sending Hiram Haydn—a story I'd written over and over again in various forms ever since my high-school days—about a thirteen-year-old girl whose mother confides in her one day her bitter disappointment with her marriage.

1983

Gary Snyder b. 1930

Gary Snyder has said that his work "has been driven by the insight that all is connected and interdependent—nature, societies; rocks, stars." Growing up on a small farm north of Seattle, Washington, he was devoted to hiking and camping. At Reed College he wrote poetry, majored in literature and anthropology, read Chinese and Indian Buddhist philosophy, and prepared a thesis on a Native American myth of the Northwest coast. After studying linguistics and anthropology for a term at Indiana University, he broke off his academic career—ending also the marriage with Alison Gass that had begun at Reed—and went to San Francisco. He spent two summers as a forest-fire lookout—at Crater Mountain and Sourdough Mountain—and then entered the University of California in 1953 as a student of Oriental languages, preparing himself to go to Asia.

The American West and ancient China came together in his translations from "Cold Mountain," by the Zen hermit Han Shan. In 1955, having met Kenneth Rexroth, Jack Kerouac, and Allen Ginsberg, he took part in the poetry reading at the Six Gallery that launched the "San Francisco Renaissance." A lively if rather superficial portrait of him, as Japhy Ryder, is central to Kerouac's novel *The Dharma Bums*.

In 1956 Snyder went to Japan, where he learned Japanese and studied Zen Buddhism with Miura Isshu. Over the next twelve years he spent much time there, continuing his studies with Oda Sesso. He also had brief interludes of work in a ship's engine-room, travel through India with

Ginsberg and Peter Orlovsky, teaching at Berkeley, and reading his poetry on American college campuses. From 1960 to 1965 he was married to Joanne Kyger. In 1967, while living at Banyan Ashram on Suwa-No-Se Island off the coast of Kyushu, Japan, he married Masa Uehara. After their son Kai was born the following year, the family came to the United States, where a second son, Gen, was born in 1969. In 1971 Snyder built a home in the foothills of the Sierra Mountains in California, where the family lived together for many years. In 1988, Snyder and Masa Uehara separated, and he was joined at "Kitkitdizze" by Carole Korda, whom he married in 1991.

During the last two decades—in poetry, prose, political action, and personal example—Snyder has been an advocate for ecological awareness. With *Earth House Hold* and *Turtle Island* (awarded the Pulitzer Prize for Poetry in 1975) his vision of cosmic interdependence or community assumed forceful and comprehensive literary form. Since 1985 he has been teaching at the University of California at Davis.

Snyder's poetry recovers values important to Thoreau and Whitman but does so in ways that have been influenced by the darker perspective of Robinson Jeffers, the pan-sexuality of D. H. Lawrence, the imagist discipline of Ezra Pound and William Carlos Williams, related disciplines in Japanese and Chinese poetry, the structural use of myth in the long poem from *The Waste Land* to *Paterson* and *The Maximus Poems,* the sound-shaping and shamanism in oral poetry, and the analytical insights of depth psychology, anthropology, and biology. All this is grounded in the serious practice of Zen. The poetics of *Riprap* is a craft of placing verbal details to make a path for the attention. That of the early *Myths & Texts* and of *Mountains and Rivers Without End,* a text composed over a forty-year period, involves the counterpointing of personal experience, meditation, exploration of myth, and song. In *Regarding Wave* his attention turned more sharply to words—their sounds, etymologies, proliferating meanings—as offering a field of generative energies like those that shape the cosmos itself. With urgency and detachment, seriousness and humor, Snyder continues as poet and essayist to explore the primal activities through which we participate in the "Great Family" whose habitation is Mind.

Thomas R. Whitaker
Yale University

PRIMARY WORKS

Riprap, 1959; *Myths & Texts,* 1960; *Riprap, and Cold Mountain Poems,* 1965; *A Range of Poems,* 1966; *The Back Country,* 1968; *Earth House Hold: Technical Notes & Queries to Fellow Dharma Revolutionaries,* 1969; *Regarding Wave,* 1969, 1970; *Turtle Island,* 1974; *The Old Ways: Six Essays,* 1977; *Axe Handles,* 1983; *Passage Through India,* 1984; *Left Out in the Rain: New Poems 1947–1985,* 1986; *The Practice of the Wild: Essays,* 1990; *No Nature: New and Selected Poems,* 1992; *A Place in Space: Ethics, Aesthetics, and Watersheds: New and Selected Prose,* 1995; *Mountains and Rivers Without End,* 1996; *The Gary Snyder Reader: Prose, Poetry, and Translations, 1952–1998,* 1999; *Look Out: A Selection of New Writings,* 2002; *Danger on Peaks,* 2005; *Back on the Fire: Essays,* 2007.

Riprap[1]

Lay down these words
Before your mind like rocks.
        placed solid, by hands
In choice of place, set
5 Before the body of the mind
        in space and time:
Solidity of bark, leaf, or wall
        riprap of things:
Cobble of milky way,
10   straying planets,
These poems, people,
        lost ponies with
Dragging saddles—
        and rocky sure-foot trails.
15 The worlds like an endless
        four-dimensional
Game of *Go.*[2]
        ants and pebbles
In the thin loam, each rock a word
20   a creek-washed stone
Granite: ingrained
        with torment of fire and weight
Crystal and sediment linked hot
        all change, in thoughts,
25 As well as things.

                   1959

Vapor Trails

Twin streaks twice higher than cumulus,
Precise plane icetracks in the vertical blue
Cloud-flaked light-shot shadow-arcing
Field of all future war, edging off to space.

---

[1]Snyder's own annotation: "a cobble of stone laid on steep slick rock to make a trail for horses in the mountains."

[2]A Japanese game played with black and white stones on a board marked with nineteen vertical and nineteen horizontal lines to make 361 intersections.

5 Young expert U.S. pilots waiting
The day of criss-cross rockets
And white blossoming smoke of bomb,
The air world torn and staggered for these
Specks of brushy land and ant-hill towns—

10   I stumble on the cobble rockpath,
Passing through temples,
Watching for two-leaf pine
    —spotting that design.
in Daitoku-ji[1]

1951

Wave

Grooving clam shell,
    streakt through marble,
      sweeping down ponderosa pine bark-scale
        rip-cut tree grain
5   sand-dunes, lava
            flow
Wave   wife.
      woman—wyfman[1]—
"veiled; vibrating; vague"
10 sawtooth ranges pulsing;
      veins on the back of the hand.

Forkt out; birdsfoot-alluvium
    wash

      great dunes rolling
15 Each inch rippld, every grain a wave.

Leaning against sand cornices til they blow away

    —wind, shake
still thorns of cholla, ocotillo
sometimes I get stuck in thickets—

---

[1]The Japanese site of the poem's experience.
[1]Anglo-Saxon: "female human being," an early
form of "woman."

20 Ah, trembling spreading radiating wyf
        racing zebra
    catch me and fling me wide
To the dancing grain of things
               of my mind!

                 1969

It Was When

We harked up the path in the dark
    to the bamboo house
        green strokes down my back
        arms over your doubled hips
5   under cow-breath thatch
        bent   cool
             breasts brush my chest
—and Naga walked in with a candle,
    "I'm sleepy"

10 Or jungle ridge by a snag—
        banyan canyon—a Temminck's Robin
          whirled down the waterfall gorge
    in zazen,[1] a poncho spread out on the stones.
        below us the overturning
15   silvery
        brush-bamboo slopes—
rainsqualls came up on us naked
        brown nipples in needles of ocean-
        cloud
20   rain.

Or the night in the farmhouse
    with Franco on one side, or Pon
    Miko's head against me, I swung you
        around and came into you
25   careless and joyous,
        late
        when Antares[2] had set

---

[1]The practice in Zen Buddhism of sitting cross-legged in sustained contemplation.

[2]A bright red star in the constellation Scorpio.

Or out on the boulders
        south beach at noon
30   rockt by surf
    burnd under by stone
    burnd over by sun
            saltwater caked
  skin   swing
35   hips on my eyes
                burn   between;

That we caught: sprout
    took grip in your womb and it held.
    new power in your breath called its place.
40   blood of the moon   stoppt;
    you pickt your steps well.

Waves
    and the
        prevalent easterly
45   breeze.
    whispering into you,
        through us,
            the grace.

                  1969

Albert Saijo b. 1926

Albert Saijo is best known to readers by a different name. In *Big Sur* (1962), Jack Kerouac refers to his friend George Baso as a "Zen master," one whose "answers come like an old man's." As the inspiration for the fictional Baso, Saijo often served as the racially visible alternative that the beats sought throughout the 1950s and 1960s in, among many things, Zen Buddhism. He is sprinkled in many of the beats' longer meditations on their physical and psychic journeys, and Saijo's name emerges from shadow occasionally in letters from major figures of the beat movement. But even as he seemed to embody for his fellow beats the ambivalent status of what Jane Iwamura calls the "Oriental Monk," Saijo maintained a relative literary silence during the move-ment's heyday. Nevertheless, he played a pivotal role in the beat movement, and his reflective and sometimes critical poetic vision was informed, but not subsumed, by the machinations of beat culture.

Born on February 4, 1926, to a minister and a Japanese schoolteacher, the young Saijo was born in the United States and grew up near Los Angeles. Like other Japanese Americans living on the West Coast, Saijo was interned early in World War II. His family was removed to the Heart Mountain Relocation Center in northern Wyoming, where he completed high school and was immediately drafted into the U.S. Army. As a member of the famed and later cele-brated all-Nisei 442nd Regimental Combat Unit, Saijo participated in missions in Italy and France until the end of the war in Europe. He returned to the United States and eventually to Los Angeles, where he began to study Zen Buddhism and earned a degree from the University of Southern California.

In the 1950s, Saijo moved to the San Francisco Bay area, where he met beat poets and Zen practitioners in San Francisco. As Kerouac, Gary Snyder, and Lew Welch deepened their interest in Zen Buddhism, they often turned to Saijo's expertise. Saijo helped Snyder establish Marin-An, a meditation hall, or floating *zendo,* in 1958 and lived with fellow beats Welch and Phillip Walen at Hyphen House in San Francisco. Saijo traveled with Kerouac and Welch on a cross-country road trip that later was chronicled in the collectively assembled *Trip Trap* (1973), an extended haiku about the three men's experiences between San Francisco and New York. But Saijo also spent much time in the High Sierras, an experience that formed the basis of his first book, *The Backpacker* (1972). A primer on the West Coast wilderness, *The Backpacker* is at turns a practical guide to surviving in the wild and a meditation on the visionary possibilities of escaping the stultifying environment of industrialized society.

In his seventies, Saijo published his first book of poetry, *Outspeaks: A Rhapsody* (1997), which he describes as a kind of "slanguage." Printed entirely in capital letters, Saijo's style is jarring, perhaps to reveal the exuberant, even explosive, possibilities of language and culture that simmer under the surface of someone considered a Zen master by his former associates. Still, his poetics of shock (which should not be misconstrued as expressions of utter autonomy) leads him at one point to sit "ON THE FLOOR CUZ CHAIRS SEEMED A FORM OF REPRESSION." In other moments, Saijo turns himself into the Bodhisattva, a figure on the brink of achieving the state of nirvana, or ascending to the level of Buddha, but who remains in human form. A fitting, perhaps wistful (and grumpy), recasting of his role as Zen master to the more famous beats might well be that of helping others, over and over, off a sinking ship. And that may be his legacy.

James Kyung-Jin Lee
University of California, Santa Barbara

PRIMARY WORKS

The Backpacker, 1972; *Trip, Trap* (with Jack Kerouac and Lew Welch), 1973; *Outspeaks: A Rhapsody,* 1997.

Bodhisattva Vows

BODHISATTVA VOWS TO BE THE LAST ONE OFF THE SINKING SHIP—YOU SIGN UP & FIND OUT IT'S FOREVER—PASSENGER LIST ENDLESS—SHIP NEVER EMPTIES—SHIP KEEPS SINKING BUT DOESN'T GO QUITE UNDER—ON BOARD ANGST PANIC & DESPERATION HOLD SWAY—TURNS OUT BODHISATTVAHOOD IS A FUCKING JOB LIKE ANY OTHER BUT DIFFERENT IN THAT THERE'S NO WEEKENDS HOLIDAYS VACATIONS NO GOLDEN YEARS OF RETIREMENT—YOU'RE SPENDING ALL YOUR TIME & ENERGY GETTING OTHER PEOPLE OFF THE

SINKING SHIP INTO LIFEBOATS BOUND GAILY FOR NIRVANA WHILE
THERE YOU ARE SINKING—& OF COURSE YOU HAD TO GO & GIVE
YOUR LIFEJACKET AWAY—SO NOW LET US BE CHEERFUL AS WE
SINK—OUR SPIRIT EVER BUOYANT AS WE SINK

1972

from Trip Trap (with Lew Welch and Jack Kerouac)

Lew's Haiku

I turned into
   a gas station
—The engine stopped

In the desert
5   sun, a yellow
Caboose

1973

Albert

Seems like stealing
   candy
from a baby,
   this road

5 The new moon
   is
the toenail of God

1973

Albert

It's us humans
   give things
Back and front

1973

Jack & Lew

Mormons who had
narrow little wagons
have left us
very wide streets
5   and
temples
with
no
nails

1973

Lew

I always take
more keen,
I cook it in a rifle
and shoot myself

1973

Albert
Fucking with the Muse in Texas

The country is blond
and flat.
For fifty miles
couldn't think
5   of anything but that whore
in Chicago and the tub
of oysters

1973

Your Head

Backpacking into wilderness is a change, and a vivid change at that. It is a nearly total separation from the normal context of your life. The supportive context. The context within which you know who you are. This is my home. This is my family. This is my job. This is the newspaper I read. These are the things I like and dislike. Suddenly you are not home but in the middle of wilderness. The first reaction is generally one of exhilaration, even euphoria. If this is your first trip, you may also feel some uncertainty, since you don't know what to expect. Then there's that heavy pack and that rough walking. It's no joke. It's strenuous. It can be toilsome and irritating.

Should you have taken this trail? Does your friend and guide—say this is your first trip—know what he's doing? You're beginning to feel the altitude. Your head feels like your skull is too small. Isn't the pace a little fast? There must be an easier trail. The heel of one foot is starting to get sore and you realize that you haven't broken in your boots enough. Stop. A blister already. The trail begins to ascend. Are you really expected to climb that wall? Your pack seems to be getting heavier. You feel like a beast of burden. And it's hot besides. The mosquitoes gather to you like cows to a feeding trough. You begin to yearn for the familiar context of who you know yourself to be. What are you doing out here anyhow?

This negative chain of thought might be avoided if you were to start out with a different attitude. Perhaps the trip could be thought of as a pilgrimage. Like the pilgrimage to the Virgin of Guadalupe where the pilgrims make their way on their knees, or by one full-length prostration after another. Like the pilgrimage of Harding and Caldwell up the Wall of the Early Morning Light in Yosemite. Or like the pilgrimage of Lama Govinda to Kailasa. Well, is wilderness a shrine? And is backpacking a form of devotion?

As you descend a trail and look at the faces of the people coming up, you get the feeling that you are all involved in some mystery or vaster allegory, in which you are all devotees of a space. A space not even outside, perhaps. What you might be doing is a pilgrimage to a more authentic outback inside yourself. But is there an inside and an outside? And you thought you were just backpacking?

Don't let yourself get bogged down in a negative space. When you're doing a tough stretch, you need to boost your body with a certain psychic drive. Do your mantra, if you have a mantra. Take a rosary and say it as you walk. If you have a koan, work on it. Isn't walking a form of meditation?

Say you're climbing a pass and find it rough going. You're thinking of how far you've come and of the thousand feet you still have to go. Take it a step at a time. As a psychic booster, you might think of each step as bringing you one step closer to the time and place of your death. Not in a morbid sense, but in the sense that your life is a journey from one place to another place, and that this wilderness trip is a short segment of that journey, a thing you have to do, a place you have to come to in order to reach the next place. You can't hold back. You've got to go on. If you weren't supposed to be in wilderness, you wouldn't be there. It is a step-by-step revelation of your fate. Let each step be whole, conscious and clear. Keep your head wide open. You get to the top of the pass, or top of the mountain—so where are you?

Here is that cirque with lake. You made it. Now to find your spot and set out your camp.

1972

Malcolm X 1925–1965

In Omaha, Nebraska, Malcolm X was born Malcolm Little, the son of Earl and Louise Little. Earl Little followed Marcus Garvey, who instilled racial pride among masses of African Americans. Little died at a relatively young age, leaving his wife and eight children in extreme poverty. "We would be so hungry," Malcolm X later reported, "we were dizzy." Malcolm Little quit school at age fifteen and moved to Harlem where, he recalled he became a thief and a drug dealer.

At age twenty, Little entered prison and began to educate himself. When he learned about the Nation of Islam (or Black Muslims), led by Elijah Muhammad, he became an eager convert. He accepted Elijah Muhammad's doctrine that white people were devils and rejoiced in a new-found racial identity. Leaving prison, he met Elijah Muhammad and replaced his own last name with "X," which stands for the African name his ancestors lost when brought to the United States in slave ships.

Malcolm X became an extremely popular evangelist for the Nation of Islam, recruiting new members and emphasizing African American pride. With brilliant fables, analogies, and turns of speech, he elevated the spirits of urban blacks trapped by segregation. He condemned hypocritical whites for preaching love and democracy while treating blacks as subhuman. In "Message to the Grass Roots," he criticized African Americans for their submission to whites:

As long as the white man sent you to Korea, you bled. He sent you to Germany, you bled. He sent you to the South Pacific to fight the Japanese, you bled. You bleed for white people, but when it comes to seeing your own churches being bombed and little black girls murdered, you haven't got any blood. You bleed when the white man says bleed; you bite when the white man says bite; and you bark when the white man says bark. I hate to say this about us, but it's true.

Malcolm X also castigated Martin Luther King, Jr., but his fiery, uncompromising militance helped prepare whites to accept King's message, which, by contrast, seemed moderate and palatable.

"The Ballot or the Bullet" is an address delivered in 1964, shortly after Malcolm X announced his break with the Nation of Islam. He had learned of Elijah Muhammad's flaws and became bitterly disenchanted with the man who "had virtually raised me from the dead." Recovering from disillusionment, he made a pilgrimage to Mecca, met white followers of Islam, and became more accepting of some whites. After returning to the United States, he formed the Organization of Afro-American Unity. In 1965, however, black assailants murdered him in a hail of gunfire.

Mourned by Harlemites and praised by portions of the Third World press, Malcolm X had been damned by the established American media. The New York Times, for example, had branded him an "irresponsible demagogue." The eloquent Malcolm X, however, had the last word. He had dictated his life story to Alex Haley. The posthumous Autobiography of Malcolm X portrays a person capable of the most startling self-transformation: from a starving child, to a parasitic criminal, to an angry but uplifting orator, to a notably more tolerant leader worthy of a world stage. Though challenged over some of its details, the best-selling Autobiography of Malcolm X brilliantly portrays American race relations.

Keith D. Miller
Arizona State University

PRIMARY WORKS

Autobiography of Malcolm X (with Alex Haley), 1964; *Malcolm X Speaks,* 1965; *By Any Means Necessary,* 1970; *The End of White World Supremacy: Four Speeches,* 1971; *The Last Speeches,* 1989.

from The Autobiography of Malcolm X

from Chapter 19: 1965

I kept having all kinds of troubles trying to develop the kind of Black Nationalist organization I wanted to build for the American Negro. Why Black Nationalism? Well, in the competitive American society, how can there ever be any white-black solidarity before there is first some black solidarity? If you will remember, in my childhood I had been exposed to the Black Nationalist teachings of Marcus Garvey—which, in fact, I had been told had led to my father's murder. Even when I was a follower of Elijah Muhammad, I had been strongly aware of how the Black Nationalist political, economic and social philosophies had the ability to instill within black men the racial dignity, the incentive, and the confidence that the black race needs today to get up off its knees, and to get on its feet, and get rid of its scars, and to take a stand for itself.

One of the major troubles that I was having in building the organization that I wanted—an all-black organization whose ultimate objective was to help create a society in which there could exist honest white-black brotherhood—was that my earlier public image, my old so-called "Black Muslim" image, kept blocking me. I was trying to gradually reshape that image. I was trying to turn a corner, into a new regard by the public, especially Negroes: I was no less angry than I had been, but at the same time the true brotherhood I had seen in the Holy World had influenced me to recognize the anger can blind human vision.

Every free moment I could find, I did a lot of talking to key people whom I knew around Harlem, and I made a lot of speeches, saying: "True Islam taught me that it takes *all* of the religious, political, economic, psychological, and racial ingredients, or characteristics, to make the Human Family and the Human Society complete.

"Since I learned the *truth* in Mecca, my dearest friends have come to include *all* kinds—some Christians, Jews, Buddhists, Hindus, agnostics, and even atheists! I have friends who are called Capitalists, Socialists, and Communists! Some of my friends are moderates, conservatives, extremists—some are even Uncle Toms! My friends today are black, brown, red, yellow, and *white!*"

I said to Harlem street audiences that only when mankind would submit to the One God who created all—only then would mankind even approach the "peace" of which so much *talk* could be heard . . . but toward which so little *action* was seen.

I said that on the American racial level, we had to approach the black man's struggle against the white man's racism as a human problem, that we had to forget hypocritical politics and propaganda. I said that both races, as human beings, had the obligation, the responsibility, of helping to correct America's human problem.

The well-meaning white people, I said, had to combat, actively and directly, the racism in other white people. And the black people had to build within themselves much greater awareness that along with equal rights there had to be the bearing of equal responsibilities.

I knew, better than most Negroes, how many white people truly wanted to see American racial problems solved. I knew that many whites were as frustrated as Negroes. I'll bet I got fifty letters some days from white people. The white people in meeting audiences would throng around me, asking me, after I had addressed them somewhere, "What *can* a sincere white person do?"

When I say that here now, it makes me think about the little co-ed I told you about, the one who flew from her New England college down to New York and came up to me in the Nation of Islam's restaurant in Harlem, and I told her that there was "nothing" she could do. I regret that I told her that. I wish that now I knew her name, or where I could telephone her, or write to her, and tell her what I tell white people now when they present themselves as being sincere, and ask me, one way or another, the same thing that she asked.

The first thing I tell them is that at least where my own particular Black Nationalist organization, the Organization of Afro-American Unity, is concerned, they can't join us. I have these very deep feelings that white people who want to join black organizations are really just taking the escapist way to salve their consciences. By visibly hovering near us, they are "proving" that they are "with us." But the hard truth is this isn't helping to solve America's racist problem. The Negroes aren't the racists. Where the really sincere white people have got to do their "proving" of themselves is not among the black victims, but on the battle lines of where America's racism really is—and that's in their own home communities; America's racism is among their own fellow whites. That's where the sincere whites who really mean to accomplish something have got to work.

Aside from that, I mean nothing against any sincere whites, when I say that as members of black organizations, generally whites' very presence subtly renders the black organization automatically less effective. Even the best white members will slow down the Negroes' discovery of what they need to do, and particularly of what they can do—for themselves, working by themselves, among their own kind, in their own communities.

I sure don't want to hurt anybody's feelings, but in fact I'll even go so far as to say that I never really trust the kind of white people who are always so anxious to hang around Negroes, or to hang around in Negro communities. I don't trust the kind of whites who love having Negroes always hanging around them. I don't know—this feeling may be a throwback to the years when I was hustling in Harlem and all of those red-faced, drunk whites in the after-hours clubs were always grabbing hold of some Negroes and talking about "I just want you to know you're just as good as I am—" And then they got back in their taxicabs and black limousines and went back downtown to the places where they lived and worked, where no blacks except servants had better get caught. But, anyway, I know that every time that whites join a black organization, you watch, pretty soon the blacks will be leaning on the whites to support it, and before you know it a black may be up front with a title, but the whites, because of their money, are the real controllers.

I tell sincere white people, "Work in conjunction with us—each of us working among our own kind." Let sincere white individuals find all other white people they can who feel as they do—and let them form their own all-white groups, to work trying to convert other white people who are thinking and acting so racist. Let sincere whites go and teach non-violence to white people!

We will completely respect our white co-workers. They will deserve every credit. We will give them every credit. We will meanwhile be working among our own kind, in our own black communities—showing and teaching black men in ways that other black men can—that the black man has got to help himself. Working separately, the sincere white people and sincere black people actually will be together.

In our mutual sincerity we might be able to show a road to the salvation of America's very soul. It can only be salvaged if human rights and dignity, in full, are extended to black men. Only such real, meaningful actions as those which are sincerely motivated from a deep sense of humanism and moral responsibility can get at the basic causes that produce the racial explosions in America today. Otherwise, the racial explosions are only going to grow worse. Certainly nothing is ever going to be solved by throwing upon me and other so-called black "extremists" and "demagogues" the blame for the racism that is in America.

Sometimes, I have dared to dream to myself that one day, history may even say that my voice—which disturbed the white man's smugness, and his arrogance, and his complacency—that my voice helped to save America from a grave, possibly even a fatal catastrophe.

The goal has always been the same, with the approaches to it as different as mine and Dr. Martin Luther King's non-violent marching, that dramatizes the brutality and the evil of the white man against defenseless blacks. And in the racial climate of this country today, it is anybody's guess which of the "extremes" in approach to the black man's problems might *personally* meet a fatal catastrophe first—"non-violent" Dr. King, or so-called "violent" me.

Anything I do today, I regard as urgent. No man is given but so much time to accomplish whatever is his life's work. My life in particular never has stayed fixed in one position for very long. You have seen how throughout my life, I have often known unexpected drastic changes.

I am only facing the facts when I know that any moment of any day, or any night, could bring me death. This is particularly true since the last trip that I made abroad. I have seen the nature of things that are happening, and I have heard things from sources which are reliable.

To speculate about dying doesn't disturb me as it might some people. I never have felt that I would live to become an old man. Even before I was a Muslim—when I was a hustler in the ghetto jungle, and then a criminal in prison, it always stayed on my mind that I could die a violent death. In fact, it runs in my family. My father and most of his brothers died by violence—my father because of what he believed in. To come right down to it, if I take the kind of things in which I believe, then add to that the kind of temperament that I have, plus the one hundred percent dedication I have to whatever I believe in—these are ingredients which make it just about impossible for me to die of old age.

I have given to this book so much of whatever time I have because I feel, and I hope, that if I honestly and fully tell my life's account, read objectively it might prove to be a testimony of some social value.

I think that an objective reader may see how in the society to which I was exposed as a black youth here in America, for me to wind up in a prison was really just about inevitable. It happens to so many thousands of black youth.

I think than an objective reader may see how when I heard "The white man is the devil," when I played back what had been my own experiences, it was inevitable that I would respond positively: then the next twelve years of my life were devoted and dedicated to propagating that phrase among the black people.

I think, I hope, that the objective reader, in following my life—the life of only one ghetto-created Negro—may gain a better picture and understanding than he has previously had of the black ghettoes which are shaping the lives and the thinking of almost all of the 22 million Negroes who live in America.

Thicker each year in these ghettoes is the kind of teenager that I was—with the wrong kinds of heroes, and the wrong kinds of influences. I am not saying that all of them become the kind of parasite that I was. Fortunately, by far most do not. But still, the small fraction who do add up to an annual total of more and more costly, dangerous youthful criminals. The F.B.I. not long ago released a report of a shocking rise in crime each successive year since the end of World War II—ten to twelve percent each year. The report did not say so in so many words, but I am saying that the majority of that crime increase in annually spawned in the black ghettoes which the American racist society permits to exist. In the 1964 "long, hot summer" riots in major cities across the United States, the socially disinherited black ghetto youth were always at the forefront.

In this year, 1965, I am certain that more—and worse—riots are going to erupt, in yet more cities, in spite of the conscience-salving Civil Rights Bill. The reason is that the *cause* of these riots, the racist malignancy in America, has been too long unattended.

I believe that it would be almost impossible to find anywhere in America a black man who has lived further down in the mud of human society than I have; or a black man who has been any more ignorant than I have been; or a black man who has suffered more anguish during his life than I have. But it is only after the deepest darkness that the greatest joy can come; it is only after slavery and prison that the sweetest appreciation of freedom can come.

For the freedom of my twenty-two million black brothers and sisters here in America, I do believe that I have fought the best that I knew how, and the best that I could, with the shortcomings that I have had. I know that my shortcomings are many.

My greatest lack has been, I believe, that I don't have the kind of academic education I wish I had been able to get—to have been a lawyer, perhaps. I do believe that I might have made a good lawyer. I have always loved verbal battle, and challenge. You can believe me that if I had the time right now, I would not be one bit ashamed to go back into any New York City public school and start where I left off at the ninth grade, and go on through a degree. Because I don't begin to be academically equipped for so many of the interest that I have. For instance, I love languages. I wish I were an accomplished linguist. I don't know anything more frustrating than to be around people talking something you can't understand. Especially when they are people who look just like you. In Africa, I heard original mother tongues, such as Hausa, and Swahili, being spoken, and there I was standing like some little boy, waiting for someone to tell me what had been said; I never will forget how ignorant I felt.

Aside from the basic African dialects, I would try to learn Chinese, because it looks as if Chinese will be the most powerful political language of the future. And already I have begun studying Arabic, which I think is going to be the most power-ful spiritual language of the future.

I would just like to study. I mean ranging study, because I have a wide-open mind. I'm interested in almost any subject you can mention. I know this is the rea-son I have come to really like, as individuals, some of the hosts of radio or television panel programs I have been on, and to respect their minds—because even if they have been almost steadily in disagreement with me on the race issue, they still kept their minds open and objective about the truths of things happening in this world. Irv Kupcinet in Chicago, and Barry Farber, Barry Gray and Mike Wallace in New York—people like them. They also let me see that they respected my mind—in a way I know they never realized. The way I knew was that often they would invite my opin-ion on subjects off the race issue. Sometimes, after the programs, we would sit around and talk about all kinds of things, current events and other things, for an hour or more. You see, most whites, even when they credit a Negro with some intel-ligence, will still feel that all he can talk about is the race issue; most whites never feel that Negroes can contribute anything to other areas of thought, and ideas. You just notice how rarely you will ever hear whites asking any Negroes what they thing about the problem of world health, or the space race to land men on the moon.

Every morning when I wake up, now, I regard it as having another borrowed day. In any city, wherever I go, making speeches, holding meetings of my organiza-tion, or attending to other business, black men are watching every move I make, awaiting their chance to kill me. I have said publicly many times that I know that they have their orders. Anyone who chooses not to believe what I am saying doesn't know the Muslims in the Nation of Islam.

But I am also blessed with faithful followers who are, I believe, as dedicated to me as I once was to Mr. Elijah Muhammad. Those who would hunt a man need to remember that a jungle also contains those who hunt the hunters.

I know, too, that I could suddenly die at the hands of some white racists. Or I could die at the hands of some Negro hired by the white man. Or it could be some brainwashed Negro acting on his own idea that by eliminating me he would be help-ing out the white man, because I talk about the white man the way I do.

Anyway, now, each day I live as if I am already dead, and I tell you what I would like for you to do. when I *am* dead—I say it that way because from the things I *know*, I do not expect to live long enough to read this book in its finished form—I want you to just watch and see if I'm not right in what I say: that the white man, in his press, is going to identifying me with "hate."

He will make use of me dead, as he has made use of me alive, as a convenient symbol of "hatred"—and that will help him to escape facing the truth that all I have been doing is holding up a mirror to reflect, to show, the history of unspeakable crimes that his race has committed against my race.

You watch. I will be labeled as, at best, an "irresponsible" black man. I have al-ways felt about this accusation that the black "leader" whom white men consider to be "responsible" is invariably the black "leader" who never gets any results. You only get action as a black man if you are regarded by the white man as "irresponsible." In fact, this much I had learned when I was just a little boy. And since I have been some kind of a "leader" of black people here in the racist society of America, I have been more reassured each time the white man resisted me, or attacked me harder—because each time made me more certain that I was on the right track in the American black man's best interests. The racist white man's opposition automatically made me know that I did offer the black man something worthwhile.

Yes, I have cherished my "demagogue" role. I know that societies often have killed the people who have helped to change those societies. And if I can die having brought any light, having exposed any meaningful truth that will help to destroy the racist cancer that is malignant in the body of America—then, all of the credit is due to Allah. Only the mistakes have been mine.

Robert Creeley 1926–2005

Robert Creeley has been widely recognized as a central figure in contemporary American writing. Creeley grew up on a small farm in West Acton, Massachusetts, where his mother worked as a public health nurse. After graduating from Holderness School in New Hampshire, he attended Harvard, drove an ambulance in India for the American Field Service, returned to Harvard, and then left without a degree in 1947. By that time he had married Ann MacKinnon, with whom he tried subsistence farming for a while near Littleton, New Hampshire. In 1949 he began to correspond with Cid Corman (the later editor of *Origin*) and in 1950 with Charles Olson, who continued to be a mentor. The Creeleys soon moved to southern France and then to Mallorca—the scene of his later novel, *The Island*. In 1954 Creeley joined Olson at Black Mountain College, North Carolina, where he received a B.A., taught, and edited *Black Mountain Review*. After a divorce he left Black Mountain for the West, settling in Albuquerque, where he taught at a boys' school. In 1957 he married Bobbie Hall, who over the next two decades would provide many occasions for poems. After two years as a tutor in Guatemala, and an M.A. from the University of New Mexico, Creeley became an instructor of English at that institution in 1961. During the 1950s he had published widely with little magazines and presses. In the 1960s he gained a national reputation; and he has continued to teach and read his poetry at various universities. A divorce from Bobbie was followed in 1977 by marriage to Penelope Highton. Since 1978, he has been Gray Professor of Poetry and Letters at the State University of New York at Buffalo, and, more recently, Capen Professor of Poetry and Humanities. He was New York State Poet for 1989–1991.

Creeley's poetry has been shaped by his New England childhood, his early admiration for Wallace Stevens, Paul Valéry, and classical poetry, his wide reading in European love poetry, his years of discussion with Charles Olson, his assimilation of the Whitman tradition as modified by William Carlos Williams, Ezra Pound, and Hart Crane—and also by his own experimental openness, his remarkable ear, his obsessive self-examination, and his firm sense of the poem as an act of responsibility. He has a classicist's respect for given poetic forms and also a Projectivist's insistence that form must be an extension of freshly perceived content. Though his poems may at first seem thin or abstract, they express with honesty and precision a quite specific interior drama: the struggle of consciousness to articulate its movements in response to an ungraspable and "broken" world. Whether arising from occasions of loss, perplexity, ironic reflection, gratitude, or brief ecstasy, the poems render that drama in their groping diction, tortured syntax, wry echoes and rhymes, strategic line-breaks, and stammering pace. Since the writing of *Pieces* Creeley often constructed from brief poems or prose notations a larger form that might register the difficult passage of such a consciousness through its continuing present. *Memory Gardens* modulates his lifelong concerns into a more quietly elegiac and meditative mode, and *Windows* engages more fully both the "inside" and the "outside" worlds.

Thomas R. Whitaker
Yale University

PRIMARY WORKS

The Gold Diggers, 1954; *Four Poems from A Form of Women*, 1959; *For Love: Poems 1950-1960*, 1962; *The Island*, 1963; *Words*, 1967; *The Charm: Early and Uncollected Poems*, 1967; *Pieces*, 1969; *A Quick Graph: Collected Notes & Essays*, 1970; *A Day Book*, 1972; *Listen*, 1972; *A Sense of Measure*, 1973; *Contexts of Poetry: Interviews 1961–1972*, 1973; *Thirty Things*, 1974; *Away*, 1976; *Presences*, 1976; *Mabel: A Story*, 1976; *Hello: A Journal*, 1978; *Later*, 1979; *Was That a Real Poem and Other Essays*, 1979; *The Collected Poems 1945–1975*, 1982; *Echoes*, 1982; *Mirrors*, 1983; *Going On: Selected Poems 1958–1980*, 1983; *The Collected Prose*, 1984; *Memory Gardens*, 1986; *The Company*, 1988; *The Collected Essays*, 1989; *Windows*, 1990; *Selected Poems*, 1991; *Life & Death*, 1998; *Personal*, 1998; *Day Book of a Virtual Poet*, 1998; *So There: Poems 1976–1983*, 1998; *Just in Time: Poems 1984–1994*, 2001; *Collected Prose*, 2001; *On Earth: Last Poems and an Essay*, 2006.

Hart Crane

for Slater Brown[1]

1

He had been stuttering, by the edge
of the street, one foot still
on the sidewalk, and the other
in the gutter . . .

5   like a bird, say, wired to flight, the
wings, pinned to their motion, stuffed.

The words, several, and for each, several
senses.
        "It is very difficult to sum up
10   briefly . . ."
        It always was.

---

[1] A friend of Hart Crane who also became a friend of Creeley.

(Slater, let me come home.
The letters have proved insufficient.
The mind cannot hang to them as it could
15 to the words.

There are ways beyond
what I have here to work with,
what my head cannot push to any kind
of conclusion.

20 But my own ineptness
cannot bring them to hand,
the particulars of those times
we had talked.)

"Men kill themselves because they are
25 afraid of death, he says . . ."

The push
        beyond and
into

Respect, they said he respected the
30 ones with the learning, lacking it
himself
        (Waldo Frank[2] & his
6 languages)
                What had seemed
35 important
While Crane sailed to Mexico I was writing
(so that one betrayed
                himself)

He slowed
40   (without those friends to keep going, to
keep up), stopped
                dead and the head could not
go further
                without those friends
45 . . . *And so it was I entered the broken world*[3]

Hart Crane.

        Hart

                            1962

[2]Critic, novelist, and friend of Hart Crane.
[3]Quoted from Crane's late poem "The Broken
Tower."

I Know a Man

As I sd to my
friend, because I am
always talking,—John, I

sd, which was not his
5   name, the darkness surrounds us, what

can we do against
it, or else, shall we &
why not, buy a goddam big car,

10   drive, he sd, for
christ's sake, look
out where yr going.

                      1962

For Love

for Bobbie[1]

Yesterday I wanted to
speak of it, that sense above
the others to me
important because all

5   that I know derives
from what it teaches me.
Today, what is it that
is finally so helpless,

different, despairs of its own
10   statement, wants to
turn away, endlessly
to turn away.

If the moon did not . . .
no, if you did not
15   I wouldn't either, but
what would I not

---

[1]Creeley's second wife.

do, what prevention, what
thing so quickly stopped.
That is love yesterday
20 or tomorrow, not

now. Can I eat
what you give me. I
have not earned it. Must
I think of everything
25 as earned. Now love also
becomes a reward so
remote from me I have
only made it with my mind.

Here is tedium,
30 despair, a painful
sense of isolation and
whimsical if pompous

self-regard. But that image
is only of the mind's
35 vague structure, vague to me
because it is my own.

Love, what do I think
to say. I cannot say it.
What have you become to ask,
40 what have I made you into,

companion, good company,
crossed legs with skirt, or
soft body under
the bones of the bed.

45 Nothing says anything
but that which it wishes
would come true, fears
what else might happen in

some other place, some
50 other time not this one.
A voice in my place, an
echo of that only in yours,

Let me stumble into
not the confession but
55 the obsession I begin with
now. For you

also (also)
some time beyond place, or
place beyond time, no
60 mind left to

say anything at all,
that face gone, now.
Into the company of love[2]
it all returns.

1962

Words

You are always
with me,
there is never
a separate

5 place. But if
in the twisted
place I
cannot speak,

not indulgence
10 or fear only,
but a tongue
rotten with what

it tastes—There is
a memory
15 of water, of
food, when hungry.

Some day
will not be
this one, then
20 to say

words like a
clear, fine

[2]A phrase from Hart Crane's "The Broken
Tower."

ash sifts,
like dust,
25 from nowhere.

1967

America

America, you ode for reality![1]
Give back the people you took.

Let the sun shine again
on the four corners of the world

5 you thought of first but do not
own, or keep like a convenience.

People are your own word, you
invented that locus and term.

Here, you said and say, is
10 where we are. Give back

what we are, these people you made,
us, and nowhere but you to be.

1969

Frank O'Hara 1926–1966

Joe LeSueur, a playwright and Frank O'Hara's roommate for nearly a decade, wrote in a memoir, "as far as I could tell, writing poetry was something Frank did in his spare time. . . . For that reason, I didn't realize right away that if you took poetry as much for granted as you did breathing it might mean you felt that it was essential to your life."[1] For many readers, the enormous appeal of Frank O'Hara's work—and he is among the most appealing of all American poets—is that he combines a seemingly effortlessness of expression with a life-sustaining intensity of purpose. The poems were often dashed off almost always on the typewriter—*The Lunch Poems,* for example, got their title because they were written on O'Hara's lunch hour—but they

---

[1] Cf. Walt Whitman, in Preface to *Leaves of Grass:* "The United States themselves are essentially the greatest poem."

[1] Joe LeSueur, "Four Apartments" in *Homage to Frank O'Hara,* eds. Bill Berkson and Joe LeSueur. New York: Big Sky, 1978, p. 47.

came out of the wholeness of O'Hara's experience and emotions. As funny as they often are, they always indicate a shrewd awareness of people, places, and history. And although O'Hara is one of the most joyous poets America has produced, a darkness always hovers below the surface, accentuating the brightness above.

Frank O'Hara was born in Baltimore, Maryland, and grew up in Worcester, Massachusetts. He attended Harvard University, where he studied music, and the graduate school of the University of Michigan. But he is most associated with New York City and the Long Island coast, especially Fire Island, where he died in a freak accident—run over by a jeep on an island where cars are banned. With John Ashbery (a friend from his undergraduate days), James Schuyler, and Kenneth Koch, O'Hara formed the central core of what has been dubbed the New York School. Although what primarily bound these poets was personal friendship, they do have certain poetic similarities that unite them: (1) They all emphasize the immediacy of the individual poetic voice rather than the impersonal presentation of images. (2) They playfully combine elements from high and low culture, incorporating into their works the most mundane aspects of urban life and such features of popular culture as comic strip characters, Hollywood movies, and popular songs. (3) They fearlessly court the comic, the slapstick, the vulgar, and the sentimental. (4) They experiment with surrealism, although the dream-like often dissolves into the quite ordinary.

O'Hara, Ashbery, and Schuyler are also united by their involvement in the visual arts. All three worked at various times for *Art News,* writing articles and reviews. O'Hara worked first as a ticket taker, then as a curator for the Museum of Modern Art, organizing major exhibitions by the end of his life. O'Hara was a personal friend of many important artists, including Larry Rivers, Willem de Kooning, Grace Hartigan, and Fairfield Porter. The directness and energy that many of these artists wished to bring to painting, O'Hara sought to register in his own work.

One of the typical modes in which O'Hara worked was what he called the "I do this I do that" poem. Many lesser poets have attempted to imitate O'Hara's seemingly documentary style, but few have caught his eye for detail, his ear for the music of American English, or his sensitivity to the wide fluctuation of mood. O'Hara was also among the earliest poets to write unself-consciously of his homosexual relationships. His love poems—and he wrote many of them—have a frankness, a joy, and a pathos that would seem more revolutionary if they did not appear so natural and easy.

David Bergman
Towson University

PRIMARY WORKS

A City Winter and Other Poems, 1952; *Meditations in an Emergency,* 1957; *Jackson Pollack,* 1959; *Lunch Poems,* 1964; *Collected Poems,* 1971; *Art Chronicles 1954–1966,* 1975; *Early Writing,* 1977; *Poems Retrieved 1951-1966,* 1977; *Selected Plays,* 1978; *Standing Still and Walking in New York,* 1983; *Collected Poems of Frank O'Hara,* 1995; *Poems Retrieved,* 1996; *Amorous Nightmares of Delay: Selected Plays,* 1997.

My Heart

I'm not going to cry all the time
nor shall I laugh all the time,
I don't prefer one "strain" to another.
I'd have the immediacy of a bad movie,
5 not just a sleeper,[1] but also the big,
overproduced first-run kind. I want to be
at least as alive as the vulgar. And if
some aficionado[2] of my mess says "That's
not like Frank!", all to the good! I
10 don't wear brown and grey suits all the time,
do I? No. I wear workshirts to the opera,
often. I want my feet to be bare,
I want my face to be shaven, and my heart—
you can't plan on the heart, but
15 the better part of it, my poetry, is open.

1970

The Day Lady Died[1]

It is 12:20 in New York a Friday
three days after Bastille day,[2] yes
it is 1959 and I go get a shoeshine
because I will get off the 4:19 in Easthampton,[3]
5 at 7:15 and then go straight to dinner
and I don't know the people who will feed me

I walk up the muggy street beginning to sun
and have a hamburger and a malted and buy
an ugly NEW WORLD WRITING to see what the poets
10 in Ghana are doing these days

               I go on to the bank

[1]A "sleeper" is film jargon for an unexpectedly successful movie, usually a low-budget film that proves to be of artistic and commercial value.

[2]An aficionado is a person devoted to someone, or his or her works; a fan.

[1]The poem is a homage to the great blues singer Billie Holiday (1915–1959), whose nickname, "Lady Day," is alluded to in the title.

[2]Bastille Day, July 14, is French Independence Day.

[3]Easthampton is a town on the south shore of Long Island, and a stop on the Long Island Railroad. O'Hara is going to visit Patsy Southgate and her husband at the time, Mike Goldberg (they are referred to in lines 15 and 20, and Mike Goldberg is the painter referred to in "Why I Am Not a Painter"). They lived in Southampton, a nearby community, where "Getting Up Ahead of Someone (Sun)" is set. The Hamptons have now become a rather exclusive area, but in the 1950s, they were a group of farming communities and an inexpensive place for artists to live and work.

and Miss Stillwagon (first name Linda I once heard)
doesn't even look up my balance for once in her life
and in the GOLDEN GRIFFIN I get a little Verlaine,[4]
15 for Patsy with drawings by Bonnard,[5] although I do
think of Hesiod, trans. Richmond Lattimore,[6] or
Brendan Behan's new play,[7] or *Le Balcon* or *Les Nègres*
of Genet,[8] but I don't, I stick with Verlaine
after practically going to sleep with quandariness

20 and for Mike I just stroll into the PARK LANE
Liquor Store and ask for a bottle of Strega and
then I go back where I came from to 6th Avenue
and the tobacconist in the Ziegfeld Theatre and
casually ask for a carton of Gauloises and a carton
25 of Picayunes[9] and a NEW YORK POST with her face on it

and I am sweating a lot by now and thinking of
leaning on the john door in the 5 SPOT
while she whispered a song along the keyboard
to Mal Waldron[10] and everyone and I stopped breathing

1964

Why I Am Not a Painter

I am not a painter, I am a poet.
Why? I think I would rather be
a painter, but I am not. Well,

for instance, Mike Goldberg[1]
5 is starting a painting. I drop in.
"Sit down and have a drink" he
says. I drink; we drink. I look

[4]Paul Verlaine (1844–1896) was one of the great French poets of the nineteenth century.
[5]Pierre Bonnard (1867–1947) was one of the major French post-Impressionist painters. He illustrated Verlaine's *Parallelement* in 1902.
[6]Hesiod was an ancient Greek poet. Richmond Lattimore, a prolific Greek translator, published his *Hesiod* in 1959.
[7]Brendan Behan (1923–1964) was a controversial Irish playwright, author of *The Quare Fellow* (1956) and *The Hostage* (1958).
[8]Jean Genêt (1910–1986) was one of France's greatest twentieth-century writers. His plays *Le Balcon* (The Balcony) and *Les Negres* (The

Blacks), produced in the 1950s, created enormous controversy because of their sexual, racial, and political subject matter.
[9]Gauloises and Picayunes are brands of French cigarettes. The emphasis on French culture stands in contrast to Billie Holiday, the subject of the poem. The effect is to suggest how far away O'Hara's thoughts are from Holiday until he sees her face in the newspaper.
[10]Mal Waldron (1925–2002) was Billie Holiday's pianist.
[1]Mike Goldberg (b. 1924) was a painter who worked with O'Hara on several projects.

up. "You have SARDINES in it."
"Yes, it needed something there."
10   "Oh." I go and the days go by
and I drop in again. The painting
is going on, and I go, and the days
go by. I drop in. The painting is
finished. "Where's SARDINES?"
15   All that's left is just
letters, "It was too much," Mike says.

But me? One day I am thinking of
a color: orange. I write a line
about orange. Pretty soon it is a
20   whole page of words, not lines.
Then another page. There should be
so much more, not of orange, of
words, of how terrible orange is
and life. Days go by. It is even in
25   prose, I am a real poet. My poem
is finished and I haven't mentioned
orange yet. It's twelve poems, I call
it ORANGES. And one day in a gallery
I see Mike's painting, called SARDINES.

1971

Poem

"À la recherche de Gertrude Stein"[1]

When I am feeling depressed and anxious sullen[2]
all you have to do is take your clothes off
and all is wiped away revealing life's tenderness
that we are flesh and breathe and are near us
5   as you are really as you are I become as I
really am alive and knowing vaguely what is
and what is important to me above the intrusions
of incident and accidental relationships

[1]*A la recherche de Gertrude Stein*" is French for "in remembrance of Gertrude Stein" (1874–1946), the American expatriate writer, whose experimental works and involvement with painters mirrors O'Hara's own career. The phrase alludes to Marcel Proust's multi-volume novel *A la recherche du temps perdu,* often translated as *Remembrance of Things Past.*
[2]The opening line recalls the opening of Shakespeare's sonnet "When in disgrace with fortune and men's eyes," which, according to Patsy Southgate, was O'Hara's favorite Shakespeare sonnet.

which have nothing to do with my life
10 when I am in your presence I feel life is strong
and will defeat all its enemies and all of mine
and all of yours and yours in you and mine in me
sick logic and feeble reasoning are cured
by the perfect symmetry of your arms and legs
15 spread out making an eternal circle together
creating a golden pillar beside the Atlantic
the faint line of hair dividing your torso
gives my mind rest and emotions their release
into the infinite air where since once we are
20 together we always will be in this life come what may

1965

John Ashbery b. 1927

John Ashbery was born in Rochester, New York, and attended Harvard University, where he met the poets Frank O'Hara and Kenneth Koch. Later, these college friends moved to New York City, where they formed the core of the so-called New York School, noted for its use of popular imagery, surrealistic turns of thought, and high-spirited humor. After college Ashbery worked for Oxford University Press and McGraw-Hill. "The Instruction Manual" dates from those days.

In 1956, awarded a Fulbright fellowship, Ashbery moved to France and worked as an art journalist, a profession he followed for the next thirty years, writing for such magazines as *Art International, New York,* and *Newsweek.* In 1965, he returned to New York to become executive editor of *Art News.* In 1974, he joined the faculty of Brooklyn College, where he served as Distinguished Professor. He now teaches at Bard College, where he is the Charles P. Stevenson Professor of Languages and Literature.

Ashbery is one of the few poets who has been able to gain the admiration of both experimental artists and conservative academicians, winning virtually all the major literary prizes this country has to offer. In "Farm Implements and Rutabagas in a Landscape," for example, he sets his outrageous installment of Popeye in the form of a sestina, one of the most difficult poetic forms. Thus the poem combines untraditional subject matter with highly traditional form.

Many of Ashbery's chief preoccupations are also traditional ones, which he treats in an unusually charged and avant-garde manner. One important theme running through virtually all of his work is "mutability," a central theme of the English Renaissance and American Transcendentalists. For older writers and thinkers, the mutable or changeable world of human and natural affairs is contrasted to the eternal, fixed world of the spirit and ideas. Some poets, including Wallace Stevens— one of the strongest influences on Ashbery—prefer the mutable to the eternal.

Yet another topic informed by the theme of mutability is the self: is our consciousness fixed and unitary or fluid and multiple? Many poems try to catch the mind even as it changes shape, for what is empathy but the power to take on another person's consciousness, or the imagination but the ability to transform the experiences around us into something very different? Reality for Ashbery is not a hard, fixed, or certain entity but an awareness brimming with impressions, memories, and desires which are constantly transformed, repeated, blurred, and blotted out.

David Bergman
Towson University

PRIMARY WORKS

Some Trees, 1956; *The Tennis Court Oath*, 1962; *Rivers and Mountains*, 1966; *A Nest of Ninnies*, 1969 (novel with James Schuyler); *The Double Dream of Spring*, 1970; *Three Poems*, 1972; *The Vermont Notebook*, 1975; *Self Portrait in a Convex Mirror*, 1975; *Houseboat Days*, 1978; *Three Plays*, 1978; *As We Know*, 1979; *Shadow Train*, 1981; *A Wave*, 1984; *Selected Poems*, 1985; *April Galleons*, 1987; *Reported Sightings: Art Chronicles 1957–87*, 1989; *Flow Chart*, 1991; *Hotel L'Autreamont*, 1993; *Three Books*, 1993; *And the Stars Were Shining*, 1994; *Can You Hear, Bird*, 1995; *The Mooring of Starting Out: The First Five Books of Poetry*, 1997; *Wakefulness*, 1998; *Girls on the Run*, 1999; *Other Traditions*, 2000; *Your Name Here*, 2000; *The Vermont Notebook*, 2001; *Chinese Whispers*, 2002; *Where Shall I Wander*, 2005; *A Worldly Country*, 2007.

The Instruction Manual

As I sit looking out of a window of the building
I wish I did not have to write the instruction manual on the uses
    of a new metal.
I look down into the street and see people, each walking with an
5   inner peace,
And envy them—they are so far away from me!
Not one of them has to worry about getting out this manual on
    schedule.
And, as my way is, I begin to dream, resting my elbows on the
10   desk and leaning out of the window a little,
Of dim Guadalajara![1] City of rose-colored flowers!
City I wanted most to see, and most did not see, in Mexico!
But I fancy I see, under the press of having to write the
    instruction manual,
15   Your public square, city, with its elaborate little bandstand!
The band is playing *Scheherazade* by Rimsky-Korsakov.[2]
Around stand the flower girls, handing out rose- and lemon-
    colored flowers,
Each attractive in her rose-and-blue striped dress (Oh! such shades
20   of rose and blue),

[1] Guadalajara is the second largest city in Mexico, 275 miles west-northwest of Mexico City. Mariachi bands originated in Guadalajara.
[2] Rimsky-Korsakov (1844–1908) was one of the finest Russian composers of his time. *Schehera-* *zade* (1888) was composed for the Russian Ballet and celebrates the dancing-girl who preserved her life by weaving the thousand-and-one stories of the *Arabian Nights*.

And nearby is the little white booth where women in green serve
    you green and yellow fruit.
The couples are parading; everyone is in a holiday mood.
First, leading the parade, is a dapper fellow
25 Clothed in deep blue. On his head sits a white hat
And he wears a mustache, which has been trimmed for the
    occasion.
His dear one, his wife, is young and pretty; her shawl is rose,
    pink, and white.
30 Her slippers are patent leather, in the American fashion,
And she carries a fan, for she is modest, and does not want the
    crowd to see her face too often.
But everybody is so busy with his wife or loved one
I doubt they would notice the mustachioed man's wife.
35 Here come the boys! They are skipping and throwing little things
    on the sidewalk
Which is made of gray tile. One of them, a little older, has a
    toothpick in his teeth.
He is silenter than the rest, and affects not to notice the pretty
40   young girls in white.
But his friends notice them, and shout their jeers at the laughing girls.
Yet soon all this will cease, with the deepening of their years,
And love bring each to the parade grounds for another reason.
45 But I have lost sight of the young fellow with the toothpick.
Wait—there he is—on the other side of the bandstand,
Secluded from his friends, in earnest talk with a young girl
Of fourteen or fifteen. I try to hear what they are saying
But it seems they are just mumbling something—shy words of
50   love, probably.
She is slightly taller than he, and looks quietly down into his
    sincere eyes.
She is wearing white. The breeze ruffles her long fine black hair
    against her olive cheek.
55 Obviously she is in love. The boy, the young boy with the
    toothpick, he is in love too;
His eyes show it. Turning from this couple,
I see there is an intermission in the concert.
The paraders are resting and sipping drinks through straws
60 (The drinks are dispensed from a large glass crock by a lady in
    dark blue),
And the musicians mingle among them, in their creamy white
    uniforms, and talk
About the weather, perhaps, or how their kids are doing at school.

65 Let us take this opportunity to tiptoe into one of the side streets.
Here you may see one of those white houses with green trim
That are so popular here. Look—I told you!

It is cool and dim inside, but the patio is sunny.
An old woman in gray sits there, fanning herself with a palm leaf
70   fan.
She welcomes us to her patio, and offers us a cooling drink.
"My son is in Mexico City," she says? "He would welcome you
     too
If he were here. But his job is with a bank there.
75 Look, here is a photograph of him."
And a dark-skinned lad with pearly teeth grins out at us from the
     worn leather frame.
We thank her for her hospitality, for it is getting late
And we must catch a view of the city, before we leave, from a
80   good high place.
That church tower will do—the faded pink one, there against the
     fierce blue of the sky. Slowly we enter.
The caretaker, an old man dressed in brown and gray, asks us how
     long we have been in the city, and how we like it here.
85 His daughter is scrubbing the steps—she nods to us as we pass
     into the tower.
Soon we have reached the top, and the whole network of the city
     extends before us.
There is the rich quarter, with its houses of pink and white, and
90   its crumbling, leafy terraces.
There is the poorer quarter, its homes a deep blue.
There is the market, where men are selling hats and swatting flies
And there is the public library, painted several shades of pale
     green and beige.
95 Look! There is the square we just came from, with the
     promenaders.
There are fewer of them, now that the heat of the day has
     increased,
But the young boy and girl still lurk in the shadows of the
100   bandstand.
And there is the home of the little old lady—
She is still sitting in the patio, fanning herself.
How limited, but how complete withal, has been our experience of
     Guadalajara!
105 We have seen young love, married love, and the love of an aged
     mother for her son.
We have heard the music, tasted the drinks, and looked at colored
     houses.
What more is there to do, except stay? And that we cannot do.
110 And as a last breeze freshens the top of the weathered old tower, I
     turn my gaze
Back to the instruction manual which has made me dream of
     Guadalajara.

             1956

Farm Implements and Rutabagas in a Landscape[1]

The first of the undecoded messages read: "Popeye sits in
    thunder,[2]
Unthought of. From that shoebox of an apartment,
From livid curtain's hue, a tangram emerges: a country."
5 Meanwhile the Sea Hag was relaxing on a green couch: "How
    pleasant
To spend one's vacation *en la casa de Popeye*,"[3] she scratched
Her cleft chin's solitary hair. She remembered spinach

And was going to ask Wimpy if he had bought any spinach.
10 "M'love," he intercepted, "the plains are decked out in thunder
Today, and it shall be as you wish." He scratched
The part of his head under his hat. The apartment
Seemed to grow smaller. "But what if no pleasant
Inspiration plunge us now to the stars? *For this is my country.*"

15 Suddenly they remembered how it was cheaper in the country.
Wimpy was thoughtfully cutting open a number 2 can of spinach
When the door opened and Swee'pea crept in. "How pleasant!"
But Swee'pea looked morose. A note was pinned to his bib.
    "Thunder
20 And tears are unavailing," it read. "Henceforth shall Popeye's
    apartment
Be but remembered space, toxic or salubrious, whole or
    scratched."

Olive came hurtling through the window; its geraniums scratched
25 Her long thigh. "I have news!" she gasped. "Popeye, forced as
    you know to flee the country

---

[1]When he was an editor for *Art News,* Ashbery and the poet James Schuyler amused themselves by inventing funny titles for imaginary paintings and prints.

[2]Popeye was the main character in a comic strip created by Segar and transformed into animated films by Max Fleisher. In the 1930s, Popeye rivaled Mickey Mouse in popularity. In an interview, Ashbery explained: "I go back to my earliest impressions a great deal when writing poetry. All poets do, I think. To me, it was always a great event. On Saturday night we got colored comics."

[3]Spanish for "in Popeye's house." Ashbery explains: "The reason that the Spanish phrase is in the poem is because [Popeye is] now published in New York only in *El Diaro,* the Spanish-language paper. . . . I just liked the way it looks, and the fact of the characters speaking Spanish, seems so funny. I used to follow it also in French newspapers, where Popeye's dislocations of the English language are reproduced charmingly in French. . . . I tend to dislocate the language myself."

One musty gusty evening, by the schemes of his wizened, duplicate
    father, jealous of the apartment
And all that it contains, myself and spinach
30 In particular, heave bolts of loving thunder
At his own astonished becoming, rupturing the pleasant

Arpeggio of our years. No more shall pleasant
Rays of the sun refresh your sense of growing old, nor the
    scratched
35 Tree-trunks and mossy foliage, only immaculate darkness and
    thunder."
She grabbed Swee'pea. "I'm taking the brat to the country."
"But you can't do that—he hasn't even finished his spinach."
Urged the Sea Hag, looking fearfully around at the apartment.

40 But Olive was already out of earshot. Now the apartment
Succumbed to a strange new hush. "Actually it's quite pleasant
Here," thought the Sea Hag. "If this is all we need fear from
    spinach
Then I don't mind so much. Perhaps we could invite Alice the
45   Goon over"—she scratched
One dug pensively—"but Wimpy is such a country
Bumpkin, always burping like that." Minute at first, the thunder

Soon filled the apartment. It was domestic thunder,
The color of spinach. Popeye chuckled and scratched
50 his balls: it sure was pleasant to spend a day in the country.

                                                   1970

As You Came from the Holy Land

of western New York state[1]
were the graves all right in their bushings
was there a note of panic in the late August air
because the old man had peed in his pants again
5 was there turning away from the late afternoon glare

---

[1]Western New York State may be a "holy land" for Ashbery because it is his birthplace, the area where Joseph Smith in 1827 discovered the mystical tablets that form the basis of the Mormon religion, and the location of the Oneida Community, a Utopian society founded in 1847 by John Humphrey Noyes.

as though it too could be wished away
was any of this present
and how could this be
the magic solution to what you are in now
10 whatever has held you motionless
like this so long through the dark season
until now the women come out in navy blue
and the worms come out of the compost to die
it is the end of any season

15 you reading there so accurately
sitting not wanting to be disturbed
as you came from that holy land
what other signs of earth's dependency were upon you
what fixed sign at the crossroads
20 what lethargy in the avenues
where all is said in a whisper
what tone of voice among the hedges
what tone under the apple trees
the numbered land stretches away
25 and your house is built in tomorrow
but surely not before the examination
of what is right and will befall
not before the census
and the writing down of names

30 remember you are free to wander away
as from other times other scenes that were taking place
the history of someone who came too late
the time is ripe now and the adage
is hatching as the seasons change and tremble
35 it is finally as though that thing of monstrous interest
were happening in the sky
but the sun is setting and prevents you from seeing it

out of night the token emerges
its leaves like birds alighting all at once under a tree
40 taken up and shaken again
put down in weak rage
knowing as the brain does it can never come about
not here not yesterday in the past
only in the gap of today filling itself
45 as emptiness is distributed
in the idea of what time it is
when that time is already past

1975

Cynthia Ozick b. 1928

For Cynthia Ozick, literature is seductive: stories "arouse"; they "enchant"; they "transfigure." Ozick describes herself in "early young-womanhood" as "a worshipper of literature," drawn to the world of the imagination "with all the rigor and force and stunned ardor of religious belief." Yet the pleasure of attraction is tempered by danger. Adoration of art can become a form of idolatry—a kind of "aesthetic paganism" that for her is incompatible with Judaism because it betrays the biblical commandment against graven images. Art can also "tear away from humanity," and Ozick worries that the beauty of language can distract from art's moral function of judging and interpreting the world. These tensions—between art and idolatry, between aestheticism and moral seriousness, between the attraction of surfaces and the weight of history—lie at the heart of Ozick's fiction and essays. Indeed, Ozick is often considered a writer of oppositions, many of which are reflected in her efforts to translate what she calls a "Jewish sensibility" into the English language. "I suppose you might say that I am myself an oxymoron," she explains, "but in the life of story-writing, there are no boundaries."

Cynthia Ozick was born in New York City on April 17, 1928, to Russian Jewish immigrants, William and Celia Regelson Ozick. Her childhood was spent in the Pelham Bay section of the Bronx, where her parents worked long hours to maintain a pharmacy during the Depression. She recalls these years as an idyllic time of reading and dreaming of writing; she also remembers being made to feel "hopelessly stupid" at school and being subjected to overt anti-Semitism. After graduating from Hunter High School, Ozick went on to complete a B.A. at New York University and an M.A. in English Literature at Ohio State University, where she wrote a thesis on the late novels of Henry James. James

became a kind of obsession for her, both inspiring and inhibiting her burgeoning writing career. For nearly seven years she struggled to write a long, "philosophical" novel entitled *Mercy, Pity, Peace, and Love,* which she finally abandoned after writing 300,000 words. During this time, Ozick moved back to New York, married Bernard Hallote, and began working as an advertising copywriter. She also wrote short stories and labored for six more years on what became her first novel, *Trust,* published soon after the birth of her daughter Rachel in 1965. At this time, she also began the intensive study of Jewish philosophy, history, and literature that eventually transformed her writing.

Although slow to come into her own as a writer, Ozick is now prolific and widely acclaimed. She has been recognized through numerous awards and grants, including a National Endowment for the Arts Fellowship, a Guggenheim Fellowship, the American Academy and Institute of Arts and Letters Strauss Livings grant, and the Jewish Book Council Award. Three of her essays have been republished in the annual collection of *Best American Essays,* five of her stories have been chosen to appear in *Best American Short Stories,* and three have received first prize in the O. Henry Prize Stories competition. Perhaps best known for her fiction and essays, Ozick also writes and translates poetry, and she has recently written a play based on two of her short stories, "The Shawl" (1981) and "Rosa" (1984) (later published together in a single volume).

In characteristically contradictory terms, Ozick has described herself—as a first-generation American Jew—to be "perfectly at home and yet perfectly insecure, perfectly acculturated and yet perfectly marginal." However, unlike many Jewish American writers who were the children of immigrants, Ozick does not write about the sociological experiences of assimilation and subsequent generational conflict. Rather, her sense of being simultaneously inside and outside the dominant culture is manifested in a real faith in "the thesis of American pluralism," a pluralism that accommodates particularist and diverse impulses. Perhaps somewhat paradoxically, one of Ozick's greatest contributions to American literature is her unwavering effort to remain "centrally Jewish" in her concerns by perpetuating the stories and histories of Jewish texts and traditions. "The Shawl," reprinted here, reflects Ozick's commitment to Jewish memory, as well as her long-standing fears about the dangers of artistic representation. Although many of Ozick's works address the historical and psychological consequences of the Holocaust, "The Shawl" is an exception: only here does she attempt to render life in the concentration camps directly. She has explained her reluctance to write fiction about the events of the Holocaust by insisting instead that "we ought to absorb the documents, the endless, endless data. . . . I want the documents to be enough; I don't want to tamper or invent or imagine. And yet I have done it. I can't not do it. It comes, it invades." The imaginative origin of "The Shawl" was, in fact, a historical text: the story evolved out of one evocative sentence in William Shirer's *The Rise and Fall of the Third Reich* about babies being thrown against electrified fences.

In an extraordinarily compressed and almost incantatory prose, Ozick depicts such horrifyingly familiar images of Nazi brutality as forced marches, starvation, dehumanization, and murder, while nevertheless managing to convey her ambivalence about using metaphoric language to represent an experience that is nearly unimaginable. The story makes clear that speech itself is dangerous: despite Rosa's desire to hear her child's voice, Magda is safe only as long as she is mute. The consequence of her cry—the only dialogue in the story—is death. Through a series of paradoxical images that combine the fantastical and the realistic, Ozick demonstrates that in writing and thinking about the unnatural world of a death camp, all expectations must be subverted: here, a baby's first tooth is an "elfin tombstone"; a breast is a "dead volcano"; a starved belly is "fat, full and round"; and a shawl can be "magic," sheltering and nourishing a child as an extension of the mother's body. Yet neither motherhood nor magic can save lives here; that which protects is also that which causes death. By overturning the natural order and unsettling the reader's ability to "know," Ozick makes the powerful point that the "reality" of the Holocaust is fundamentally inaccessible and that conventional means of understanding simply do not apply.

Tresa Grauer
University of Pennsylvania

PRIMARY WORKS

Trust, 1966; *The Pagan Rabbi, and Other Stories,* 1971; *Bloodshed and Three Novellas,* 1976; *Levitation: Five Fictions,* 1982; *Art & Ardor: Essays,* 1983; *The Cannibal Galaxy,* 1983; *The Messiah of Stockholm,* 1987; *The Shawl,* 1988; *Metaphor & Memory: Essays,* 1989; *Epodes: First Poems,* 1992; *Blue Light: A Play,* 1994; *Fame & Folly: Essays,* 1996; *Portrait of the Artist as a Bad Character,* 1996; *The Putter-Messer papers,* 1997; *SHE: Portrait of the Essay as a Warm Body,* 1998; *Quarrel and Quandary: Essays,* 2000; *Heir to the Glimmering World,* 2004; *The Din in the Head: Essays,* 2006; *Dictation: A Quartet,* 2008.

The Shawl

Stella, cold, cold, the coldness of hell. How they walked on the roads together, Rosa with Magda curled up between sore breasts, Magda wound up in the shawl. Sometimes Stella carried Magda. But she was jealous of Magda. A thin girl of fourteen, too small, with thin breasts of her own, Stella wanted to be wrapped in a shawl, hidden away, asleep, rocked by the march, a baby, a round infant in arms. Magda took Rosa's nipple, and Rosa never stopped walking, a walking cradle. There was not enough milk; sometimes Magda sucked air; then she screamed. Stella was ravenous. Her knees were tumors on sticks, her elbows chicken bones.

Rosa did not feel hunger; she felt light, not like someone walking but like someone in a faint, in trance, arrested in a fit, someone who is already a floating angel, alert and seeing everything, but in the air, not there, not touching the road. As if teetering on the tips of her fingernails. She looked into Magda's face through a gap in the shawl: a squirrel in a nest, safe, no one could reach her inside the little house of the shawl's windings. The face, very round, a pocket mirror of a face: but it was not Rosa's bleak complexion, dark like cholera, it was another kind of face altogether, eyes blue as air, smooth feathers of hair nearly as yellow as the Star sewn into Rosa's coat. You could think she was one of *their* babies.

Rosa, floating, dreamed of giving Magda away in one of the villages. She could leave the line for a minute and push Magda into the hands of any woman on the side of the road. But if she moved out of line they might shoot. And even if she fled the line for half a second and pushed the shawl-bundle at a stranger, would the woman take it? She might be surprised, or afraid; she might drop the shawl, and Magda would fall out and strike her head and die. The little round head. Such a good child, she gave up screaming, and sucked now only for the taste of the drying nipple itself. The neat grip of the tiny gums. One mite of a tooth tip sticking up in the bottom gum, how shining, an elfin tombstone of white marble gleaming there. Without complaining, Magda relinquished Rosa's teats, first the left, then the right; both were cracked, not a sniff of milk. The duct-crevice extinct, a dead volcano, blind eye, chill hole, so Magda took the corner of the shawl and milked it instead. She sucked and sucked, flooding threads with wetness. The shawl's good flavor, milk of linen.

It was a magic shawl, it could nourish an infant for three days and three nights. Magda did not die, she stayed alive, although very quiet. A peculiar smell, of cinnamon and almonds, lifted out of her mouth. She held her eyes open every moment, forgetting how to blink or nap, and Rosa and sometimes Stella studied their blueness. On the road they raised one burden of a leg after another and studied Magda's face. "Aryan," Stella said, in a voice grown as thin as a string; and Rosa thought how Stella gazed at Magda like a young cannibal. And the time that Stella said "Aryan," it sounded to Rosa as if Stella had really said "Let us devour her."

But Magda lived to walk. She lived that long, but she did not walk very well, partly because she was only fifteen months old, and partly because the spindles of her legs could not hold up her fat belly. It was fat with air, full and round. Rosa gave almost all her food to Magda, Stella gave nothing; Stella was ravenous, a growing child herself, but not growing much. Stella did not menstruate. Rosa did not menstruate. Rosa was ravenous, but also not; she learned from Magda how to drink the taste of a finger in one's mouth. They were in a place without pity, all pity was annihilated in Rosa, she looked at Stella's bones without pity. She was sure that Stella was waiting for Magda to die so she could put her teeth into the little thighs.

Rosa knew Magda was going to die very soon; she should have been dead already, but she had been buried away deep inside the magic shawl, mistaken there for the shivering mound of Rosa's breasts; Rosa clung to the shawl as if it covered only herself. No one took it away from her. Magda was mute. She never cried. Rosa hid her in the barracks, under the shawl, but she knew that one day someone would inform; or one day someone, not even Stella, would steal Magda to eat her. When Magda began to walk Rosa knew that Magda was going to die very soon, something would happen. She was afraid to fall asleep; she slept with the weight of her thigh on Magda's body; she was afraid she would smother Magda under her thigh. The weight of Rosa was becoming less and less; Rosa and Stella were slowly turning into air.

Magda was quiet, but her eyes were horribly alive, like blue tigers. She watched. Sometimes she laughed—it seemed a laugh, but how could it be? Magda had never seen anyone laugh. Still, Magda laughed at her shawl when the wind blew its corners, the bad wind with pieces of black in it, that made Stella's and Rosa's eyes tear. Magda's eyes were always clear and tearless. She watched like a tiger. She guarded her shawl. No one could touch it; only Rosa could touch it. Stella was not allowed. The shawl was Magda's own baby, her pet, her little sister. She tangled herself up in it and sucked on one of the corners when she wanted to be very still.

Then Stella took the shawl away and made Magda die.

Afterward Stella said: "I was cold."

And afterward she was always cold, always. The cold went into her heart: Rosa saw that Stella's heart was cold. Magda flopped onward with her little pencil legs scribbling this way and that, in search of the shawl; the pencils faltered at the barracks opening, where the light began. Rosa saw and pursued. But already Magda was in the square outside the barracks, in the jolly light. It was the roll-call arena. Every morning Rosa had to conceal Magda under the shawl against a wall of the barracks and go out and stand in the arena with Stella and hundreds of others, sometimes for hours, and Magda, deserted, was quiet under the shawl, sucking on her corner. Every day Magda was silent, and so she did not die. Rosa saw that today Magda was going to die, and at the same time a fearful joy ran in Rosa's two palms, her fingers were on fire, she was astonished, febrile: Magda, in the sunlight, swaying on her pencil legs, was howling. Ever since the drying up of Rosa's nipples, ever since Magda's last scream on the road, Magda had been devoid of any syllable; Magda was a mute. Rosa believed that something had gone wrong with her vocal cords, with her windpipe, with the cave of her larynx; Magda was defective, without a voice; perhaps she was deaf; there might be something amiss with her intelligence; Magda was dumb. Even the laugh that came when the ash-stippled wind made a clown out of Magda's shawl was only the air-blown showing of her teeth. Even when the lice, head lice and body lice, crazed her so that she became as wild as one of the big rats that plundered the barracks at daybreak looking for carrion, she rubbed and scratched and kicked and bit and rolled without a whimper. But now Magda's mouth was spilling a long viscous rope of clamor.

"Maaaa—"

It was the first noise Magda had ever sent out from her throat since the drying up of Rosa's nipples.

"Maaaa . . . aaa!"

Again! Magda was wavering in the perilous sunlight of the arena, scribbling on such pitiful little bent shins. Rosa saw. She saw that Magda was grieving for the loss of her shawl, she saw that Magda was going to die. A tide of commands hammered in Rosa's nipples: Fetch, get, bring! But she did not know which to go after first, Magda or the shawl. If she jumped out into the arena to snatch Magda up, the howling would not stop, because Magda would still not have the shawl; but if she ran back into the barracks to find the shawl, and if she found it, and if she came after Magda holding it and shaking it, then she would get Magda back, Magda would put the shawl in her mouth and turn dumb again.

Rosa entered the dark. It was easy to discover the shawl. Stella was heaped under it, asleep in her thin bones. Rosa tore the shawl free and flew—she could fly, she was only air—into the arena. The sunheat murmured of another life, of butterflies in summer. The light was placid, mellow. On the other side of the steel fence, far away, there were green meadows speckled with dandelions and deep-colored violets; beyond them, even farther, innocent tiger lilies, tall, lifting their orange bonnets. In the barracks they spoke of "flowers," of "rain": excrement, thick turd-braids, and the slow stinking maroon waterfall that slunk down from the upper bunks, the stink mixed with a bitter fatty floating smoke that greased Rosa's skin. She stood for an instant at the margin of the arena. Sometimes the electricity inside the fence would seem to hum; even Stella said it was only an imagining, but Rosa heard real sounds in the wire; grainy sad voices. The farther she was from the fence, the more clearly the voices crowded at her. The lamenting voices strummed so convincingly, so passionately, it was impossible to suspect them of being phantoms. The voices told her to hold up the shawl, high; the voices told her to shake it, to whip with it, to unfurl it like a flag. Rosa lifted, shook, whipped, unfurled. Far off, very far, Magda leaned across her air-fed belly, reaching out with the rods of her arms. She was high up, elevated, riding someone's shoulder. But the shoulder that carried Magda was not coming toward Rosa and the shawl, it was drifting away, the speck of Magda was moving more and more into the smoky distance. Above the shoulder a helmet glinted. The light tapped the helmet and sparkled it into a goblet. Below the helmet a black body like a domino and a pair of black boots hurled themselves in the direction of the electrified fence. The electric voices began to chatter wildly. "Maamaa, maaamaaa," they all hummed together. How far Magda was from Rosa now, across the whole square, past a dozen barracks, all the way on the other side! She was no bigger than a moth.

All at once Magda was swimming through the air. The whole of Magda traveled through loftiness. She looked like a butterfly touching a silver vine. And the moment Magda's feathered round head and her pencil legs and balloonish belly and zigzag arms splashed against the fence, the steel voices went mad in their growling, urging Rosa to run and run to the spot where Magda had fallen from her flight against the electrified fence; but of course Rosa did not obey them. She only stood, because if she ran they would shoot, and if she tried to pick up the sticks of Magda's body they would shoot, and if she let the wolf's screech ascending now through the ladder of her skeleton break out, they would shoot; so she took Magda's shawl and filled her own mouth with it, stuffed it in and stuffed it in, until she was swallowing up the wolf's screech and tasting the cinnamon and almond depth of Magda's saliva; and Rosa drank Magda's shawl until it dried.

1981

Edward Albee b. 1928

Albee's association with the theater began early. Two weeks after his birth in Washington, D.C., Albee was adopted by the wealthy owner of a chain of vaudeville theaters, Reed Albee, and his wife, Frances. Theater people came and went during Albee's childhood, many visiting the family at their lavish house in Larchmont. The young Albee attended the theater in New York City and began writing both poetry and plays. He continued writing throughout his fitful academic career—he was dismissed from two prep schools before graduating from Choate and was later dismissed from Trinity College while a sophomore. At twenty-two, Albee left home and lived in Manhattan during the 1950s—working as an office boy, a salesman, and a Western Union delivery boy. The constants in his life were writing and theater-going.

According to a story that has by now become legend, Albee wrote *The Zoo Story* just before his thirtieth birthday on a wobbly table in his kitchen in the space of three weeks. The play then followed a circuitous route that ended with its being produced at the Schiller Theater Werkstatt in Berlin in 1959. That play received American production, on a double bill with Beckett's *Krapp's Last Tape,* in January 1960; *The Sandbox* was produced in April of that year at The Jazz Gallery in New York City. With *The Death of Bessie Smith,* these plays comprise Albee's first works for theater.

The Sandbox treats characters that were to appear later in his *The American Dream.* The materialistic, and mechanistic, married couple—intent on killing off the wife's troublesome, aging mother—create a seaside idyll that must end with the death of the 86-year-old woman. Working within clichés of both language and social behavior, Albee maps the nastiness of the inhuman "Mommy" and "Daddy." Replete with suggestions of sexual impotence that controls social power, the very brief play (requiring only fourteen minutes to perform) packs a world of content into its few lines. In this play, the son of the couple becomes the Angel of Death; in *The American Dream* he is a much more active agent of social coercion.

Albee's first full-length play and biggest box office success, *Who's Afraid of Virginia Woolf?,* was produced in 1962, preceded by *The American Dream* (1961) and followed by *Tiny Alice* (1964), *A Delicate Balance* (1966), *Box* and *Quotations from Chairman Mao Tse-tung* (1968), *All Over* (1971), *Seascape* (1975), and others. Each play is marked by Albee's inventive handling of dialogue. While colloquial, his language is pared to essentials. Albee plays with words—from the puns in *Tiny Alice* to the long sentences filled with qualifiers in *A Delicate Balance.* Clichés, revivified for the theatrical purpose at hand, appear frequently.

Albee's earliest plays remain among the best-known American drama of this century, dealing with human loneliness, the inability or unwillingness of people to connect with others, and about the illusions people maintain in order to ignore the emotional sterility of their lives. Although Albee's worldview is existential, his focus is psychological, not metaphysical. He is not an absurdist playwright either stylistically or thematically, but rather part of the continuing American (and English) experimentation with basically realistic theater.

Carol A. Burns
Southern Illinois University

PRIMARY WORKS

The American Dream and *The Zoo Story*, 1961; *Who's Afraid of Virginia Woolf?*, 1962; *Sandbox* and *The Death of Bessie Smith*, 1964; *Tiny Alice*, 1965; *Malcolm, from the Novel by James Purdy*, 1966; *A Delicate Balance*, 1966; *Everything in the Garden, from the Play by Giles Cooper*, 1968; *Box and Quotations from Chairman Mao Tse Tung: Two Inter-related Plays*, 1969; *All Over*, 1970; *Seascape*, 1975; *Counting the Ways and Listening*, 1977; *The Lady from Dubuque*, 1980; *Selected Plays of Edward Albee*, 1987; *Finding the Sun*, 1994; *Three Tall Women*, 1995; *Edward Albee's Marriage Play*, 1995; *The Play about the Baby*, 1998; *The Goat: or, Who Is Sylvia?*, 2002; *Occupant*, 2002; *Knock! Knock! Who's There?*, 2003; *Me, Myself and I*, 2007.

The Sandbox

A Brief Play, in Memory of My Grandmother (1876–1959)

Players

THE YOUNG MAN, 25, *a good-looking, well-built boy in a bathing suit*
MOMMY, 55, *a well-dressed, imposing woman*
DADDY, 60, *a small man; gray, thin*
GRANDMA, 86, *a tiny, wizened woman with bright eyes*
THE MUSICIAN, *no particular age, but young would be nice*

NOTE.   *When, in the course of the play,* MOMMY *and* DADDY *call each other by these names, there should be no suggestion of regionalism. These names are of empty affection and point up the pre-senility and vacuity of their characters.*

SCENE.   *A bare stage, with only the following: Near the footlights, far stage right, two simple chairs set side by side, facing the audience; near the footlights, far stage left, a chair facing stage right with a music stand before it; farther back, and stage center, slightly elevated and raked, a large child's sandbox with a toy pail and shovel; the background is the sky, which alters from brightest day to deepest night.*

　　At the beginning, it is brightest day; the YOUNG MAN *is alone on stage to the rear of the sandbox, and to one side. He is doing calisthenics; he does calisthenics until quite at the very end of the play. These calisthenics, employing the arms only, should suggest the beating and fluttering of wings. The* YOUNG MAN *is, after all, the Angel of Death.*

　MOMMY *and* DADDY *enter from stage left,* MOMMY *first.*

MOMMY (*motioning to* DADDY) Well, here we are; this is the beach.
DADDY (*whining*) I'm cold.
MOMMY (*dismissing him with a little laugh*) Don't be silly; it's as warm as toast. Look at that nice young man over there: *he* doesn't think it's cold. (*Waves to the* YOUNG MAN) Hello.
YOUNG MAN (*with an endearing smile*) Hi!
MOMMY (*looking about*) This will do perfectly . . . don't you think so, Daddy? There's sand there . . . and the water beyond. What do you think, Daddy?

DADDY (*vaguely*) Whatever you say, Mommy.

MOMMY (*with the same little laugh*) Well, of course . . . whatever I say. Then, it's settled, is it?

DADDY (*shrugs*) She's *your* mother, not mine.

MOMMY I know she's my mother. What do you take me for? (*A pause*) All right, now; let's get on with it. (*She shouts into the wings, stage-left*) You! Out there! You can come in now. (*The* MUSICIAN *enters, seats himself in the chair, stage-left, places music on the music stand, is ready to play.* MOMMY *nods approvingly.*) Very nice; very nice. Are you ready, Daddy? Let's go get Grandma.

DADDY Whatever you say, Mommy.

MOMMY (*leading the way out, stage-left*) Of course, whatever I say. (*To the* MUSICIAN) You can begin now. (*The* MUSICIAN *begins playing;* MOMMY *and* DADDY *exit; the* MUSICIAN, *all the while playing, nods to the* YOUNG MAN.)

YOUNG MAN (*with the same endearing smile*): Hi! (*After a moment,* MOMMY *and* DADDY *re-enter, carrying* GRANDMA. *She is borne in by their hands under her armpits; she is quite rigid; her legs are drawn up; her feet do not touch the ground; the expression on her ancient face is that of puzzlement and fear.*)

DADDY Where do we put her?

MOMMY (*the same little laugh*) Wherever I say, of course. Let me see . . . well . . . all right, over there . . . in the sandbox. (*Pause*) Well, what are you waiting for, Daddy? . . . The sandbox! (*Together they carry* GRANDMA *over to the sandbox and more or less dump her in.*)

GRANDMA (*righting herself to a sitting position; her voice a cross between a baby's laugh and cry*) Ahhhhhh! Graaaaa!

DADDY (*dusting himself*) What do we do now?

MOMMY (*to the* MUSICIAN) You can stop now. (*The* MUSICIAN *stops.*) (*Back to* DADDY) What do you mean, what do we do now? We go over there and sit down, of course. (*To the* YOUNG MAN) Hello there.

YOUNG MAN (*again smiling*) Hi! (MOMMY *and* DADDY *move to the chairs, stage-right, and sit down. A pause.*)

GRANDMA (*same as before*) Ahhhhhh! Ah-haaaaaa! Graaaaaa!

DADDY Do you think . . . do you think she's . . . comfortable?

MOMMY (*impatiently*) How would I know?

DADDY (*pause*) What do we do now?

MOMMY (*as if remembering*) We . . . wait. We . . . sit here . . . and we wait . . . that's what we do.

DADDY (*after a pause*) Shall we talk to each other?

MOMMY (*with that little laugh; picking something off her dress*) Well, *you* can talk, if you want to . . . if you can think of anything to say . . . if you can think of anything new.

DADDY (*thinks*) No . . . I suppose not.

MOMMY (*with a triumphant laugh*) Of course not!

GRANDMA (*banging the toy shovel against the pail*) Haaaaaa! Ah-haaaaaa!

MOMMY (*out over the audience*) Be quiet Grandma . . . just be quiet, and wait. (GRANDMA *throws a shovelful of sand at* MOMMY.) (*Still out over the audience*) She's throwing sand at me! You stop that, Grandma; you stop throwing sand at Mommy! (*To* DADDY) She's throwing sand at me. (DADDY *looks around at* GRANDMA, *who screams at him.*)

GRANDMA GRAAAAA!

MOMMY Don't look at her. Just . . . sit here . . . be very still . . . and wait. (*To the* MUSICIAN) You . . . uh . . . you go ahead and do whatever it is you do. (*The* MUSICIAN *plays.* MOMMY *and* DADDY *are fixed, staring out beyond the audience.* GRANDMA *looks at them, looks at the* MUSICIAN, *looks at the sandox, throws down the shovel.*)

GRANDMA Ah-haaaaaa! Graaaaaa! (*Looks for reaction; gets none. Now . . . directly to the audience*) Honestly! What a way to treat an old woman! Drag her out of the house . . . stick her in a car . . . bring her out here from the city . . . dump her in a pile of sand . . . and leave her here to set. I'm eighty-six years old! I was married when I was seventeen. To a farmer. He died when I was thirty. (*To the* MUSICIAN) Will you stop that, please? (*The* MUSICIAN *stops playing.*) I'm a feeble old woman . . . how do you expect anybody to hear me over that peep! peep! peep! (*To herself*) There's no respect around here. (*To the* YOUNG MAN) There's no respect around here!

YOUNG MAN (*same smile*) Hi!

GRANDMA (*after a pause, a mild double-take, continues, to the audience*) My husband died when I was thirty (*indicates* MOMMY), and I had to raise that big cow over there all by my lonesome. You can imagine what *that was like.* Lordy! (*To the* YOUNG MAN) Where'd they get *you?*

YOUNG MAN Oh . . . I've been around for a while.

GRANDMA I'll bet you have! Heh, heh, heh. Will you look at you!

YOUNG MAN (*flexing his muscles*) Isn't that something? (*Continues his calisthenics.*)

GRANDMA Boy, oh boy; I'll say. Pretty good.

YOUNG MAN (*sweetly*) I'll say.

GRANDMA Where ya from?

YOUNG MAN Southern California.

GRANDMA (*nodding*) Figgers; figgers. What's your name, honey?

YOUNG MAN I don't know . . .

GRANDMA (*to the audience*) Bright, too!

YOUNG MAN I mean . . . I mean, they haven't given me one yet . . . the studio . . .

GRANDMA (*giving him the once-over*) You don't say . . . you don't say. Well . . . uh, I've got to talk some more . . . don't you go 'way.

YOUNG MAN Oh, no.

GRANDMA (*turning her attention back to the audience*) Fine; fine. (*Then, once more, back to the* YOUNG MAN) You're . . . you're an actor, hunh?

YOUNG MAN (*beaming*) Yes. I am.

GRANDMA (*to the audience again; shrugs*) I'm smart that way. *Anyhow,* I had to raise . . . *that* over there all by my lonesome; and what's next to her there . . . that's what she married. Rich? I tell you . . . money, money, money. They took me off the farm . . . which was real decent of them . . . and they moved me into the big town house with *them* . . . fixed a nice place for me under the stove . . . gave me an army blanket . . . and my own dish . . . my very own dish! So, what have I got to complain about? Nothing, of course! I'm not complaining. (*She looks up at the sky, shouts to someone off stage*) Shouldn't it be getting dark now, dear? (*The lights dim; night comes on. The* MUSICIAN *begins to play; it becomes deepest night. There are spotlights on all the players, including the* YOUNG MAN, *who is, of course, continuing his calisthenics.*)

DADDY (*stirring*) It's nighttime.

MOMMY Shhhh. Be still . . . wait.

DADDY (*whining*) It's so hot.

MOMMY Shhhhhh. Be still . . . wait.

GRANDMA (*to herself*) That's better. Night. (*To the* MUSICIAN) Honey, do you play all through this part? (*The* MUSICIAN *nods.*) Well, keep it nice and soft; that's a good boy. (*The* MUSICIAN *nods again; plays softly.*) That's nice. (*There is an off-stage rumble.*)

DADDY (*starting*) What was that?

MOMMY (*beginning to weep*) It was nothing.

DADDY It was . . . it was . . . thunder . . . or a wave breaking . . . or something.

MOMMY (*whispering, through her tears*) It was an off-stage rumble . . . and you know what *that* means . . .

DADDY I forget . . .

MOMMY (*barely able to talk*) It means the time has come for poor Grandma . . . and I can't bear it!

DADDY (*vacantly*) I . . . I suppose you've got to be brave.

GRANDMA (*mocking*) That's right, kid; be brave. You'll bear up; you'll get over it. (*Another off-stage rumble . . . louder.*)

MOMMY Ohhhhhhhhhh . . . poor Grandma . . . poor Grandma . . .

GRANDMA (*to* MOMMY) I'm fine! I'm all right! It hasn't happened yet! (*A violent off-stage rumble. All the lights go out, save the spot on the* YOUNG MAN; *the* MUSICIAN *stops playing.*)

MOMMY Ohhhhhhhhh . . . Ohhhhhhhhhh . . . (*Silence.*)

GRANDMA Don't put the lights up yet . . . I'm not ready; I'm not quite ready. (*Silence*) All right, dear . . . I'm about done. (*The lights come up again, to the brightest day; the* MUSICIAN *begins to play.* GRANDMA *is discovered, still in the sandbox, lying on her side, propped up on an elbow, half covered, busily shoveling sand over herself.*)

GRANDMA (*muttering*) I don't know how I'm supposed to do anything with this goddam toy shovel . . .

DADDY Mommy! It's daylight!

MOMMY (*brightly*) So it is! Well! Our long night is over. We must put away our tears, take off our mourning . . . and face the future. It's our duty.

GRANDMA (*still shoveling; mimicking*) . . . take off our mourning . . . face the future . . . Lordy! (MOMMY *and* DADDY *rise, stretch.* MOMMY *waves to the* YOUNG MAN.)

YOUNG MAN (*with that smile*) Hi! (GRANDMA *plays dead.*[!] MOMMY *and* DADDY *go over to look at her; she is a little more than half buried in the sand; the toy shovel is in her hands, which are crossed on her breast.*)

MOMMY (*before the sandbox; shaking her head*) Lovely! It's . . . it's hard to be sad . . . she looks . . . so happy. (*With pride and conviction*) It pays to do things well. (*To the* MUSICIAN) All right, you can stop now, if you want to. I mean, stay around for a swim, or something; it's all right with us. (*She sighs heavily*) Well, Daddy . . . off we go.

DADDY Brave Mommy!

MOMMY Brave Daddy! (*They exit, stage-left.*)

GRANDMA (*after they leave; lying quite still*) It pays to do things well . . . Boy, oh boy! (*She tries to sit up*) . . . well, kids . . . (*but she finds she can't*) . . . I . . . I can't get up. I . . . I can't move . . . (*The* YOUNG MAN *stops his calisthenics, nods to the* MUSICIAN, *walks over to* GRANDMA, *kneels down by the sandbox.*)

GRANDMA I . . . can't move . . .

YOUNG MAN Shhhhh . . . be very still . . .

GRANDMA I . . . I can't move . . .

YOUNG MAN Uh . . . ma'am; I . . . I have a line here.

GRANDMA Oh, I'm sorry, sweetie; you go right ahead.

YOUNG MAN I am . . . uh . . .

GRANDMA Take your time, dear.

YOUNG MAN (*prepares; delivers the line like a real amateur*) I am the Angel of Death. I am . . . uh . . . I am come for you.

GRANDMA What . . . wha . . . (*then, with resignation*) . . . ohhhh . . . ohhhh, I see. (*The* YOUNG MAN *bends over, kisses* GRANDMA *gently on the forehead.*)

GRANDMA (*her eyes closed, her hands folded on her breast again, the shovel between her hands, a sweet smile on her face*) Well . . . that was very nice, dear . . .

YOUNG MAN (*still kneeling*) Shhhhh . . . be still . . .

GRANDMA What I meant was . . . you did that very well, dear . . .

YOUNG MAN (*blushing*) . . . oh . . .

GRANDMA No; I mean it. You've got that . . . you've got a quality.

YOUNG MAN (*with his endearing smile*) Oh . . . thank you; thank you very much . . . ma'am.

GRANDMA (*slowly; softly—as the* YOUNG MAN *puts his hands on top of* GRANDMA'S) You're . . . you're welcome . . . dear.

(*Tableau. The* MUSICIAN *continues to play as the curtain slowly comes down.*)

Philip Levine b. 1928

A self-described anarchist, Philip Levine considers himself "an intensely political person, but a man without a party." He was born in Detroit in 1928 and remembers the "very strong familial setting" of his youth. In his early years, he was unaware of the world outside his home. He lived with his Russian-born Jewish parents and two brothers; his grandparents lived downstairs, and his aunt lived nearby. In 1933 (the year is the title of one of Levine's most powerful collections), when he was five, his father died, and the family's relatively comfortable existence ended.

Part of his upbringing involved a sense of persecution in a period when fascism was gaining strength in Europe and Father Charles Coughlin was broadcasting weekly anti-Semitic radio programs in Detroit. The Spanish Civil War, which began when Levine was eight, is a recurrent topic in his work. When he was a junior in high school, he read Wilfred Owen, a poet who chronicled World War I and whose writings confirmed Levine's beliefs about the insanity of war. Levine worked in a number of blue-collar jobs in the automobile industry. Levine began to write poetry while attending

Wayne State University at night, and his early work is influenced by his modernist predecessors.

Levine left Detroit for California in 1957 and does not romanticize his native city, which fell on hard times in the late twentieth century as trends in car manufacturing changed. Yet Levine has remained an urban poet with a strong affection for people, especially the working class. He regards storytelling as one of the primary motivators in his work. His verse stories tend to reflect the dignity of working-class characters and the realities of their lives. He is careful to draw a distinction between anarchy and antigovernment terrorism. The government is "the enemy" in his work because of its potential to oppress powerless individuals and rob them of their agency. He writes, "I don't believe in the validity of governments, laws, charters, all that hide us from our essential oneness."

Levine has published sixteen volumes of poetry since his first in 1963 and is the recipient of major awards, including two Guggenheim fellowships and the Pulitzer Prize. Occasionally referred to as America's "proletariat poet" because of his focus on working-class subjects and his belief that property is theft, Levine has been a consistent and important voice on the American literary scene for nearly half a century. He regards poetry not as something mystical so much as the product of work. As he puts it, "I'm not a 'special case.' I'm a man who is more articulate than most people and one who found something called poetry quite early in life, grew to it, determined to make it, and because of his stubbornness is . . . still trying."

D. Quentin Miller
Suffolk University

PRIMARY WORKS

On the Edge, 1963; Not This Pig, 1968; Pili's Wall, 1971; Red Dust, 1971; They Feed They Lion, 1972; 1933, 1974; The Names of the Lost, 1976; Ashes: Poems New and Old, 1979; Seven Years from Somewhere, 1979; One for the Rose, 1981; Selected Poems, 1984; Sweet Will, 1985; A Walk with Tom Jefferson, 1988, New Selected Poems, 1991; What Work Is, 1991; The Simple Truth, 1994; Unselected Poems, 1997; The Mercy, 2000; Breath, 2004.

Coming Home, *Detroit,* 1968

A winter Tuesday, the city pouring fire,
Ford Rouge sulfurs the sun, Cadillac, Lincoln,
Chevy gray. The fat stacks
of breweries hold their tongues. Rags,
5 papers, hands, the stems of birches
dirtied with words.
                          Near the freeway
you stop and wonder what came off,
recall the snowstorm where you lost it all,
10 the wolverine, the northern bear, the wolf
caught out, ice and steel raining
from the foundries in a shower

of human breath. On sleds in the false sun
the new material rests. One brown child
15 stares and stares into your frozen eyes
until the lights change and you go
forward to work. The charred faces, the eyes
boarded up, the rubble of innards, the cry
of wet smoke hanging in your throat,
20 the twisted river stopped at the color of iron.
We burn this city every day.

1972

The Rats

Because of the great press
of steel on steel
I cannot hear the shadows hunched
under the machines. When the power
5 fails, the machines stop,
and the lights go out
I am listening to myself,
to my breathing and to
the noise my breathing makes.

10 They are moving, the shadows,
out of time, out
of sight, somewhere out
there in the darkness, and
when the lights
15 come back they are no longer
where they were.

Someone who never stood
next to me has poisoned
the shadows. They are dead
20 in the stairwell or under
the floorboards, darker
than ever and more compact
and moving in the sweet air
sweetening the air I breathe.

25 Later I will be in
the parking lot looking

for my car or I will remember
I have no car and it
will be tomorrow or years
30 from then.

                It will be now.
I will have been talking
sitting across from where
you sit at ease on
35 the outrageous, impeccable sofa
I have admired,
and in that quiet that comes
in speech I will hear them
moving at last and see them
40 moving toward you in the light
bringing their great sweetness.

                        1980

The Everlasting Sunday

Waiting for it
in line to punch out
or punch in.
Bowed my head
5 into the cold grey
soup of the wash trough,
talked with men
who couldn't talk, marked
my bread with the black
10 print of my thumb
and ate it.

Nine-foot lengths
of alloy tubing between
my gloved hands
15 sliding, and the plop
of the cutter, and again
the tube drawing. Above
like swords, bundles
of steel sliding
20 in the blackened vaults,
and I, a lone child,
counting out.

Now to awaken,
pace the wood floor.
25 Through the torn shade
the moon between
the poplars riding
toward morning. My
dark suit, my stiffened
30 shirt stained
with God knows what,
my tie, my silvered
underwear guarding
the sad bed.

35 Naked, my hard arms
are thin as a girl's,
my body's hairs tipped
with frost. This house,
this ark of sleeping men,
40 bobs in the silence. I feel
my fingers curl
but not in anger,
the floor warms,
my eyes fill with light.
45 When was I young?

                    1980

The Simple Truth

I bought a dollar and a half's worth of small red potatoes,
took them home, boiled them in their jackets
and ate them for dinner with a little butter and salt.
Then I walked through the dried fields
5 on the edge of town. In middle June the light
hung on in the dark furrows at my feet,
and in the mountain oaks overhead the birds
were gathering for the night, the jays and mockers
squawking back and forth, the finches still darting
10 into the dusty light. The woman who sold me
the potatoes was from Poland; she was someone
out of my childhood in a pink spangled sweater and sunglasses
praising the perfection of all her fruits and vegetables
at the road-side stand and urging me to taste
15 even the pale, raw sweet corn trucked all the way,

she swore, from New Jersey. "Eat, eat," she said,
"Even if you don't I'll say you did."
                                    Some things
you know all your life. They are so simple and true
20 they must be said without elegance, meter and rhyme,
they must be laid on the table beside the salt shaker,
the glass of water, the absence of light gathering
in the shadows of picture frames, they must be
naked and alone, they must stand for themselves.
25 My friend Henri and I arrived at this together in 1965
before I went away, before he began to kill himself,
and the two of us to betray our love. Can you taste
what I'm saying? It is onions or potatoes, a pinch
of simple salt, the wealth of melting butter, it is obvious,
30 it stays in the back of your throat like a truth
you never uttered because the time was always wrong,
it stays there for the rest of your life, unspoken,
made of that dirt we call earth, the metal we call salt,
in a form we have no words for, and you live on it.

                                                    1995

The Lesson

Early in the final industrial century
on the street where I was born lived
a doctor who smoked black shag
and walked his dog each morning
5 as he muttered to himself in a language
only the dog knew. The doctor had saved
my brother's life, the story went, reached
two stained fingers down his throat
to extract a chicken bone and then
10 bowed to kiss the ring-encrusted hand
of my beautiful mother, a young widow
on the lookout for a professional.
Years before, before the invention of smog,
before Fluid Drive, the eight-hour day,
15 the iron lung, I'd come into the world
in a shower of industrial filth raining
from the bruised sky above Detroit.
Time did not stop. Mother married
a bland wizard in clutch plates

20 and drive shafts. My uncles went off
    to their world wars, and I began a career
    in root vegetables. Each morning,
    just as the dark expired, the corner church
    tolled its bells. Beyond the church
25 an oily river ran both day and night
    and there along its banks I first conversed
    with the doctor and Waldo, his dog.
    "Young man," he said in words
    resembling English, "you would dress
30 heavy for autumn, scarf, hat, gloves.
    Not to smoke," he added, "as I do."
    Eleven, small for my age but ambitious,
    I took whatever good advice I got,
    though I knew then what I know
35 now: the past, not the future, was mine.
    If I told you he and I became pals
    even though I barely understood him,
    would you doubt me? Wakened before dawn
    by the Catholic bells, I would dress
40 in the dark—remembering scarf, hat, gloves—
    to make my way into the deserted streets
    to where Waldo and his master ambled
    the riverbank. Sixty-four years ago,
    and each morning is frozen in memory,
45 each a lesson in what was to come.
    What was to come? you ask. This world
    as we have it, utterly unknowable,
    utterly unacceptable, utterly unlovable,
    the world we waken to each day
50 with or without bells. The lesson was
    in his hands, one holding a cigarette,
    the other buried in blond dog fur, and in
    his words thick with laughter, hushed,
    incomprehensible, words that were sound
55 only without sense, just as these must be.
    Staring into the moist eyes of my maestro,
    I heard the lost voices of creation running
    over stones as the last darkness sifted upward,
    voices saddened by the milky residue
60 of machine shops and spangled with first light,
    discordant, harsh, but voices nonetheless.

                                  2004

Paule Marshall b. 1929

Paule Marshall, née Valenza Pauline Burke, was born in Brooklyn, New York. Her parents, Ada and Samuel Burke, were emigrants from Barbados, West Indies. At the age of nine, Marshall made an extended visit to the native land of her parents and discovered for herself the quality of life peculiar to that tropical isle. Although she then wrote a series of poems reflecting her impressions, creative writing did not become a serious pursuit until much later in her young adult life. The selection included here is a mature reminiscence and symbolic expansion of that childhood visit.

A quiet and retiring child ("living her old days first," her mother used to say), Marshall was an avid reader who spent countless hours in her neighborhood library. This, it seems, was at least a partial escape from the pressures of growing up, for the author admits going through a painful childhood period in which she rejected her West Indian heritage. Easily identified by the heavy silver bangles which girls from "the islands" wore on their wrists, she felt even more estranged from her classmates when she returned from Barbados with a noticeable accent. During early adolescence, reading also helped ease the longing for her father who, having become a devoted follower of Father Divine, left home to live in the Harlem "kingdom."

Marshall had been attending Hunter College, majoring in social work, when illness necessitated a one-year stay in a sanatorium in upstate New York. There, in a tranquil lake setting, she wrote letters so vividly describing the surroundings that a friend encouraged her to think of a career in writing. Upon her release from the sanatorium, she transferred to Brooklyn College, changed her major to English Literature, and graduated Phi Beta Kappa in 1953. Her first marriage, in 1957, was to Kenneth Marshall, with whom she had a son, Evan Keith. She divorced in 1963 and in 1970 wed a second time to Haitian businessman, Nourry Ménard.

Formerly a researcher and staff writer for *Our World* magazine, located in New York City, Marshall traveled on assignment to Brazil and to the West Indies. Once her literary career had been launched, she contributed short stories and articles to numerous magazines and anthologies and began lecturing at several colleges and universities within the United States and abroad. The recipient of several prestigious awards, including the John D. and Catherine T. MacArthur Fellowship, Marshall continues to write and to teach. She currently is a professor of English and creative writing at Virginia Commonwealth University and resides in Richmond, Virginia.

While clearly influenced by the literary giants (black and white), Marshall attributes her love of language and storytelling to her mother and other Bajan (Barbadian) women who, sitting around the kitchen table, effortlessly created narrative art. In her informative essay, "From the Poets in the Kitchen," the author explains the process as a transformation of standard English into "an idiom, an instrument that more adequately described them—changing around the syntax and imposing their own rhythm and accent so that the sentences were more pleasing to their ears. . . .

And to make it more vivid, more in keeping with their expressive quality, they brought to bear a raft of metaphors, parables, Biblical quotations, sayings and the like.

Marshall goes on to provide examples like the following:

"The sea ain' got no back door," ...
*meaning that it wasn't like a house where if
there was a fire you could run out the back.
Meaning that it was not to be trifled with.
And meaning perhaps in a larger sense that
man should treat all of nature with caution
and respect.*

This is the legacy that the artist proudly
claims, and she makes of it a distinctive
stylistic device which combines forms of
Western origin with the style and function of traditional African oral narrative.
In short, she manipulates verbal structures
so that they accommodate new patterns
and rhythms, and this gives to the written
word a stamp of cultural authenticity.

Marshall's artistic vision evolves in a
clear progression as she moves, through
her creations, from an American to an
African American/African Caribbean and,
finally, a Pan-African sensibility. Indeed,
the chronological order of her publications
suggests an underlying design to follow the
"middle passage" in reverse. That is, she
examines the experience of blacks not in
transit from Africa to the New World, but
from the New World toward Africa. Thus,
her first major work, *Brown Girl, Brownstones,* considers the coming of age of a
young West Indian girl and simultaneously
explores the black emigrant experience in
America. *Soul Clap Hands and Sing,* a collection of novellas, is a lyrical depiction of
the lives of four aging men coming to grips
with the decline of Western values. The geographical setting changes from Brooklyn
to Barbados to British Guiana and then to
Brazil. Marshall next moves, in *The Chosen
Place, the Timeless People,* to an imaginary
Caribbean island that, on one side, faces
the continent of Africa. In this epic novel,
she traces the development and perpetuation of colonialism. In *Praisesong for the
Widow,* the artist shows increasing reliance
on African images as she presents the portrait of an elderly black American widow
who, on a cruise to Grenada, confronts her
African heritage. In her novel *Daughters,*
Marshall moves her geographical setting
back and forth between the Caribbean and
the United States to suggest the bicultural
ties of her protagonist as well as the political strategies affecting both nations.
She further establishes the centrality of
women in transforming self, community,
and nation.

Throughout her fiction, Marshall is
preoccupied with black cultural history.
Additionally, her emphasis on black female
characters addresses contemporary feminist issues from an Afrocentric perspective. She insists that African peoples take a
"journey back" through time to understand the political, social, and economic
structures upon which contemporary societies are based. As her vision expands to
include oppressed peoples (men and
women) all over the world, she develops a
sensibility which values cultural differences while it celebrates the triumph of the
human spirit.

Dorothy L. Denniston
Brown University

PRIMARY WORKS

Brown Girl, Brownstones, 1959; *Soul Clap Hands and Sing,* 1961; *The Chosen Place, the Timeless People,* 1969; *Praisesong for the Widow,* 1983; *Reena and Other Short Stories,* 1983; *Daughters,* 1991; *The Fisher King: A Novel,* 2001.

To Da-duh: In Memoriam

This is the most autobiographical of the stories, a reminiscence largely of a visit I paid to my grandmother (whose nickname was Da-duh) on the island of Barbados when I was nine. Ours was a complex relationship—close, affectionate yet rivalrous. During the year I spent with her a subtle kind of power struggle went on between us. It was as if we both knew, at a level beyond words, that I had come into the world not only to love her and to continue her line but to take her very life in order that I might live.

Years later, when I got around to writing the story, I tried giving the contest I had sensed between us a wider meaning. I wanted the basic theme of youth and old age to suggest rivalries, dichotomies of a cultural and political nature, having to do with the relationship of western civilization and the Third World.

Apart from this story, Da-duh also appears in one form or another in my other work as well. She's the old hairdresser, Mrs. Thompson, in BROWN GIRL, BROWNSTONES, *who offers Selina total, unquestioning love. She's Leesy Walkes and the silent cook, Carrington, "whose great breast . . . had been used it seemed to suckle the world" in* THE CHOSEN PLACE, THE TIMELESS PEOPLE. *She's Aunt Vi in "Reena" and Medford, the old family retainer in "British Guiana" from* SOUL CLAP HANDS AND SING. *And she's Avey Johnson's Great-aunt Cuney in* PRAISESONG FOR THE WIDOW. *Da-duh turns up everywhere.*

She's an ancestor figure, symbolic for me of the long line of black women and men—African and New World—who made my being possible, and whose spirit I believe continues to animate my life and work. I wish to acknowledge and celebrate them. I am, in a word, an unabashed ancestor worshipper.

> *". . . Oh Nana! all of you is not involved in this evil business*
> *Death,*
> *Nor all of us in life."*
> —FROM "AT MY GRANDMOTHER'S GRAVE," BY LEBERT BETHUNE

I did not see her at first I remember. For not only was it dark inside the crowded disembarkation shed in spite of the daylight flooding in from outside, but standing there waiting for her with my mother and sister I was still somewhat blinded from the sheen of tropical sunlight on the water of the bay which we had just crossed in the landing boat, leaving behind us the ship that had brought us from New York lying in the offing. Besides, being only nine years of age at the time and knowing nothing of islands I was busy attending to the alien sights and sounds of Barbados, the unfamiliar smells.

I did not see her, but I was alerted to her approach by my mother's hand which suddenly tightened around mine, and looking up I traced her gaze through the gloom in the shed until I finally made out the small, purposeful, painfully erect figure of the old woman headed our way.

Her face was drowned in the shadow of an ugly rolled-brim brown felt hat, but the details of her slight body and of the struggle taking place within it were clear enough—an intense, unrelenting struggle between her back which was beginning to bend ever so slightly under the weight of her eighty-odd years and the rest of her which sought to deny those years and hold that back straight, keep it in line. Moving swiftly toward us (so swiftly it seemed she did not intend stopping when she reached us but would sweep past us out the doorway which opened onto the sea and like Christ walk upon the water!)[1] she was caught between the sunlight at her end of the building and the darkness inside—and for a moment she appeared to contain them both: the light in the long severe old-fashioned white dress she wore which brought the sense of a past that was still alive into our bustling present and in the snatch of white at her eye; the darkness in her black high-top shoes and in her face which was visible now that she was closer.

It was as stark and fleshless as a death mask, that face. The maggots might have already done their work, leaving only the framework of bone beneath the ruined skin and deep wells at the temple and jaw. But her eyes were alive, unnervingly so for one so old, with a sharp light that flicked out of the dim clouded depths like a lizard's tongue to snap up all in her view. Those eyes betrayed a child's curiosity about the world, and I wondered vaguely seeing them, and seeing the way the bodice of her ancient dress had collapsed in on her flat chest (what had happened to her breasts?), whether she might not be some kind of child at the same time that she was a woman, with fourteen children, my mother included, to prove it. Perhaps she was both, both child and woman, darkness and light, past and present, life and death—all the opposites contained and reconciled in her.

"My Da-duh," my mother said formally and stepped forward. The name sounded like thunder fading softly in the distance.

"Child," Da-duh said, and her tone, her quick scrutiny of my mother, the brief embrace in which they appeared to shy from each other rather than touch, wiped out the fifteen years my mother had been away and restored the old relationship. My mother, who was such a formidable figure in my eyes, had suddenly with a word been reduced to my status.

"Yes, God is good," Da-duh said with a nod that was like a tic. "He has spared me to see my child again."

We were led forward then, apologetically because not only did Da-duh prefer boys but she also liked her grandchildren to be "white," that is, fair-skinned; and we had, I was to discover, a number of cousins, the outside children[2] of white estate managers and the like, who qualified. We, though, were as black as she.

My sister being the oldest was presented first. "This one takes after the father," my mother said and waited to be reproved.

Frowning, Da-duh tilted my sister's face toward the light. But her frown soon gave way to a grudging smile, for my sister with her large mild eyes and little broad winged nose, with our father's high-cheeked Barbadian cast to her face, was pretty.

"She's goin' be lucky," Da-duh said and patted her once on the cheek. "Any girl child that takes after the father does be lucky."

She turned then to me. But oddly enough she did not touch me. Instead leaning close, she peered hard at me, and then quickly drew back. I thought I saw her hand start up as though to shield her eyes. It was almost as if she saw not only me, a thin truculent child who it was said took after no one but myself, but something in me which for some reason she found disturbing, even threatening. We looked silently at each other for a long time there in the noisy shed, our gaze locked. She was the first to look away.

"But Adry," she said to my mother and her laugh was cracked, thin, apprehensive. "Where did you get this one here with this fierce look?"

[1]Biblical allusion, Matthew 14:22–33.   [2]Children born outside marriage.

"We don't know where she came out of, my Da-duh," my mother said, laughing also. Even I smiled to myself. After all I had won the encounter. Da-duh had recognized my small strength—and this was all I ever asked of the adults in my life then.

"Come, soul," Da-duh said and took my hand. "You must be one of those New York terrors you hear so much about."

She led us, me at her side and my sister and mother behind, out of the shed into the sunlight that was like a bright driving summer rain and over to a group of people clustered beside a decrepit lorry. They were our relatives, most of them from St. Andrews although Da-duh herself lived in St. Thomas, the women wearing bright print dresses, the colors vivid against their darkness, the men rusty black suits that encased them like straitjackets. Da-duh, holding fast to my hand, became my anchor as they circled round us like a nervous sea, exclaiming, touching us with their calloused hands, embracing us shyly. They laughed in awed bursts: "But look Adry got big-big children!"/"And see the nice things they wearing, wrist watch and all!"/ "I tell you, Adry has done all right for sheself in New York. . . ."

Da-duh, ashamed at their wonder, embarrassed for them, admonished them the while. "But oh Christ," she said, "why you all got to get on like you never saw people from 'Away' before? You would think New York is the only place in the world to hear wunna. That's why I don't like to go anyplace with you St. Andrews people, you know. You all ain't been colonized."[3]

We were in the back of the lorry finally, packed in among the barrels of ham, flour, cornmeal and rice and the trunks of clothes that my mother had brought as gifts. We made our way slowly through Bridgetown's clogged streets, part of a funereal procession of cars and open-sided buses, bicycles and donkey carts. The dim little limestone shops and offices along the way marched with us, at the same mournful pace, toward the same grave ceremony—as did the people, the women balancing huge baskets on top their heads as if they were no more than hats they wore to shade them from the sun. Looking over the edge of the lorry I watched as their feet slurred the dust. I listened, and their voices, raw and loud and dissonant in the heat, seemed to be grappling with each other high overhead.

Da-duh sat on a trunk in our midst, a monarch amid her court. She still held my hand, but it was different now. I had suddenly become her anchor, for I felt her fear of the lorry with its asthmatic motor (a fear and distrust, I later learned, she held of all machines)[4] beating like a pulse in her rough palm.

As soon as we left Bridgetown behind though, she relaxed, and while the others around us talked she gazed at the canes standing tall on either side of the winding marl road. "C'dear,"[5] she said softly to herself after a time. "The canes this side are pretty enough."

They were too much for me. I thought of them as giant weeds that had overrun the island, leaving scarcely any room for the small tottering houses of sunbleached pine we passed or the people, dark streaks as our lorry hurtled by. I suddenly feared that we were journeying, unaware that we were, toward some dangerous place where

[3]Malapropism.
[4]The same dread of the mechanical appears in Leesy Walkes, a character in Marshall's *The Chosen Place, the Timeless People* (1969). Here the author symbolically establishes the conflict engendered when Western technology encroaches upon Da-duh's edenic garden.
[5]A form of address spoken with a hard "C." Loosely translated as "Come dear" or "Good dear."

the canes, grown as high and thick as a forest, would close in on us and run us through with their stiletto blades. I longed then for the familiar: for the street in Brooklyn where I lived, for my father who had refused to accompany us ("Blowing out good money on foolishness," he had said of the trip), for a game of tag with my friends under the chestnut tree outside our aging brownstone house.

"Yes, but wait till you see St. Thomas canes," Da-duh was saying to me. "They's canes father, bo," she gave a proud arrogant nod. "Tomorrow, God willing, I goin' take you out in the ground and show them to you."

True to her word Da-duh took me with her the following day out into the ground. It was a fairly large plot adjoining her weathered board and shingle house and consisting of a small orchard, a good-sized canepiece and behind the canes, where the land sloped abruptly down, a gully. She had purchased it with Panama money[6] sent her by her eldest son, my uncle Joseph, who had died working on the canal. We entered the ground along a trail no wider than her body and as devious and complex as her reasons for showing me her land. Da-duh strode briskly ahead, her slight form filled out this morning by the layers of sacking petticoats she wore under her working dress to protect her against the damp. A fresh white cloth, elaborately arranged around her head, added to her height, and lent her a vain, almost roguish air.

Her pace slowed once we reached the orchard, and glancing back at me occasionally over her shoulder, she pointed out the various trees.

"This here is a breadfruit," she said. "That one yonder is a papaw. Here's a guava. This is a mango. I know you don't have anything like these in New York. Here's a sugar apple." (The fruit looked more like artichokes than apples to me.) "This one bears limes. . . ." She went on for some time, intoning the names of the trees as though they were those of her gods. Finally, turning to me, she said, "I know you don't have anything this nice where you come from." Then, as I hesitated: "I said I know you don't have anything this nice where you come from. . . ."

"No," I said and my world did seem suddenly lacking.

Da-duh nodded and passed on. The orchard ended and we were on the narrow cart road that led through the canepiece, the canes clashing like swords above my cowering head. Again she turned and her thin muscular arms spread wide, her dim gaze embracing the small field of canes, she said—and her voice almost broke under the weight of her pride, "Tell me, have you got anything like these in that place where you were born?"

"No."

"I din' think so. I bet you don't even know that these canes here and the sugar you eat is one and the same thing. That they does throw the canes into some damn machine at the factory and squeeze out all the little life in them to make sugar for you all so in New York to eat. I bet you don't know that."

"I've got two cavities and I'm not allowed to eat a lot of sugar."

But Da-duh didn't hear me. She had turned with an inexplicably angry motion and was making her way rapidly out of the canes and down the slope at the edge of the field which led to the gully below. Following her apprehensively down the incline amid a stand of banana plants whose leaves flapped like elephants ears in the wind,

[6]Because of poor economic conditions in Barbados, many islanders worked abroad and sent money home to support their families.

I found myself in the middle of a small tropical wood—a place dense and damp and gloomy and tremulous with the fitful play of light and shadow as the leaves high above moved against the sun that was almost hidden from view. It was a violent place, the tangled foliage fighting each other for a chance at the sunlight, the branches of the trees locked in what seemed an immemorial struggle, one both necessary and inevitable. But despite the violence, it was pleasant, almost peaceful in the gully, and beneath the thick undergrowth the earth smelled like spring.

This time Da-duh didn't even bother to ask her usual question, but simply turned and waited for me to speak.

"No," I said, my head bowed. "We don't have anything like this in New York."

"Ah," she cried, her triumph complete. "I din' think so. Why, I've heard that's a place where you can walk till you near drop and never see a tree."

"We've got a chestnut tree in front of our house," I said.

"Does it bear?" She waited. "I ask you, does it bear?"

"Not anymore," I muttered. "It used to, but not anymore."

She gave the nod that was like a nervous twitch. "You see," she said, "Nothing can bear there." Then, secure behind her scorn, she added, "But tell me, what's this snow like that you hear so much about?"

Looking up, I studied her closely, sensing my chance, and then I told her, describing at length and with as much drama as I could summon not only what snow in the city was like, but what it would be like here, in her perennial summer kingdom.

". . . And you see all these trees you got here," I said. "Well, they'd be bare. No leaves, no fruit, nothing. They'd be covered in snow. You see your canes. They'd be buried under tons of snow. The snow would be higher than your head, higher than your house, and you wouldn't be able to come down into this here gully because it would be snowed under. . . ."

She searched my face for the lie, still scornful but intrigued. "What a thing, huh?" she said finally, whispering it softly to herself.

"And when it snows you couldn't dress like you are now," I said. "Oh no, you'd freeze to death. You'd have to wear a hat and gloves and galoshes and ear muffs so your ears wouldn't freeze and drop off, and a heavy coat. I've got a Shirley Temple coat with fur on the collar. I can dance. You wanna see?"

Before she could answer I began, with a dance called the Truck which was popular back then in the 1930's. My right forefinger waving, I trucked around the nearby trees and around Da-duh's awed and rigid form. After the Truck I did the Suzy-Q, my lean hips swishing, my sneakers sidling zigzag over the ground. "I can sing," I said and did so, starting with "I'm Gonna Sit Right Down and Write Myself a Letter," then without pausing, "Tea For Two," and ending with "I Found a Million Dollar Baby in a Five and Ten Cent Store."

For long moments afterwards Da-duh stared at me as if I were a creature from Mars, an emissary from some world she did not know but which intrigued her and whose power she both felt and feared. Yet something about my performance must have pleased her, because bending down she slowly lifted her long skirt and then, one by one, the layers of petticoats until she came to a drawstring purse dangling at the end of a long strip of cloth tied round her waist. Opening the purse she handed me a penny. "Here," she said half-smiling against her will. "Take this to buy yourself a sweet at the shop up the road. There's nothing to be done with you, soul."

From then on, whenever I wasn't taken to visit relatives, I accompanied Da-duh out into the ground, and alone with her amid the canes or down in the gully I told her about New York. It always began with some slighting remark on her part: "I know they don't have anything this nice where you come from," or "Tell me, I hear those foolish people in New York does do such and such. . . ." But as I answered, recreating my towering world of steel and concrete and machines for her, building the city out of words, I would feel her give way. I came to know the signs of her surrender: the total stillness that would come over her little hard dry form, the probing gaze that like a surgeon's knife sought to cut through my skull to get at the images there, to see if I were lying; above all, her fear, a fear nameless and profound, the same one I had felt beating in the palm of her hand that day in the lorry.

Over the weeks I told her about refrigerators, radios, gas stoves, elevators, trolley cars, wringer washing machines, movies, airplanes, the cyclone at Coney Island, subways, toasters, electric lights: "At night, see, all you have to do is flip this little switch on the wall and all the lights in the house go on. Just like that. Like magic. It's like turning on the sun at night."

"But tell me," she said to me once with a faint mocking smile, "do the white people have all these things too or it's only the people looking like us?"

I laughed. "What d'ya mean," I said. "The white people have even better." Then: "I beat up a white girl in my class last term."

"Beating up white people!" Her tone was incredulous.

"How you mean!" I said, using an expression of hers. "She called me a name."

For some reason Da-duh could not quite get over this and repeated in the same hushed, shocked voice, "Beating up white people now! Oh, the lord, the world's changing up so I can scarce recognize it anymore."

One morning toward the end of our stay, Da-duh led me into a part of the gully that we had never visited before, an area darker and more thickly overgrown than the rest, almost impenetrable. There in a small clearing amid the dense bush, she stopped before an incredibly tall royal palm which rose cleanly out of the ground, and drawing the eye up with it, soared high above the trees around it into the sky. It appeared to be touching the blue dome of sky, to be flaunting its dark crown of fronds right in the blinding white face of the late morning sun.

Da-duh watched me a long time before she spoke, and then she said, very quietly, "All right, now, tell me if you've got anything this tall in that place you're from."

I almost wished, seeing her face, that I could have said no. "Yes," I said. "We've got buildings hundreds of times this tall in New York. There's one called the Empire State Building that's the tallest in the world. My class visited it last year and I went all the way to the top. It's got over a hundred floors. I can't describe how tall it is. Wait a minute. What's the name of that hill I went to visit the other day, where they have the police station?"

"You mean Bissex?"

"Yes, Bissex. Well, the Empire State Building is way taller than that."

"You're lying now!" she shouted, trembling with rage. Her hand lifted to strike me.

"No, I'm not," I said. "It really is, if you don't believe me I'll send you a picture postcard of it soon as I get back home so you can see for yourself. But it's way taller than Bissex."

All the fight went out of her at that. The hand poised to strike me fell limp to her side, and as she stared at me, seeing not me but the building that was taller than the highest hill she knew, the small stubborn light in her eyes (it was the same amber as the flame in the kerosene lamp she lit at dusk) began to fail. Finally, with a vague gesture that even in the midst of her defeat still tried to dismiss me and my world, she turned and started back through the gully, walking slowly, her steps groping and uncertain, as if she were suddenly no longer sure of the way, while I followed triumphant yet strangely saddened behind.

The next morning I found her dressed for our morning walk but stretched out on the Berbice chair in the tiny drawing room where she sometimes napped during the afternoon heat, her face turned to the window beside her. She appeared thinner and suddenly indescribably old.

"My Da-duh," I said.

"Yes, nuh," she said. Her voice was listless and the face she slowly turned my way was, now that I think back on it, like a Benin mask the features drawn and almost distorted by an ancient abstract sorrow.

"Don't you feel well?" I asked.

"Girl, I don't know."

"My Da-duh, I goin' boil you some bush tea," my aunt, Da-duh's youngest child, who lived with her, called from the shed roof kitchen.

"Who tell you I need bush tea?" she cried, her voice assuming for a moment its old authority. "You can't even rest nowadays without some malicious person looking for you to be dead. Come girl," she motioned me to a place beside her on the old-fashioned lounge chair, "give us a tune."

I sang for her until breakfast at eleven, all my brash irreverent Tin Pan Alley songs, and then just before noon we went out into the ground. But it was a short, dispirited walk. Da-duh didn't even notice that the mangoes were beginning to ripen and would have to be picked before the village boys got to them. And when she paused occasionally and looked out across the canes or up at her trees it wasn't as if she were seeing them but something else. Some huge, monolithic shape had imposed itself, it seemed, between her and the land, obstructing her vision. Returning to the house she slept the entire afternoon on the Berbice chair.

She remained like this until we left, languishing away the mornings on the chair at the window gazing out at the land as if it were already doomed; then, at noon, taking the brief stroll with me through the ground during which she seldom spoke, and afterwards returning home to sleep till almost dusk sometimes.

On the day of our departure she put on the austere, ankle length white dress, the black shoes and brown felt hat (her town clothes she called them), but she did not go with us to town. She saw us off on the road outside her house and in the midst of my mother's tearful protracted farewell, she leaned down and whispered in my ear, "Girl, you're not to forget now to send me the picture of that building, you hear."

By the time I mailed her the large colored picture postcard of the Empire State building she was dead. She died during the famous '37 strike which began shortly after we left. On the day of her death England sent planes flying low over the island in a show of force—so low, according to my aunt's letter, that the downdraft from them shook the ripened mangoes from the trees in Da-duh's orchard. Frightened, everyone in the village fled into the canes. Except Da-duh. She remained in the house at the window so my aunt said, watching as the planes came swooping and screaming like monstrous birds down over the village, over her house, rattling her trees and flattening the young canes in her field. It must have seemed to her lying there that they did not intend pulling out of their dive, but like the hardback beetles which hurled themselves with suicidal force against the walls of the house at night, those menacing silver shapes would hurl themselves in an ecstasy of self-immolation onto the land, destroying it utterly.

When the planes finally left and the villagers returned they found her dead on the Berbice chair at the window.

She died and I lived, but always, to this day even, within the shadow of her death. For a brief period after I was grown I went to live alone, like one doing penance, in a loft above a noisy factory in downtown New York and there painted seas of sugar-cane and huge swirling Van Gogh suns and palm trees striding like brightly-plumed Tutsi warriors across a tropical landscape, while the thunderous tread of the machines downstairs jarred the floor beneath my easel, mocking my efforts.

1967

Adrienne Rich b. 1929

The daughter of Helen Jones and Arnold Rich, a professor of pathology at Johns Hopkins University, Adrienne Rich grew up in Baltimore. Her father, an exacting tutor, required that his daughter master complex poetic meters and rhyme schemes. Her mother, who had been a concert pianist before marriage, conveyed to her child a love of the lyrical as well as the rhythmic.

Educated at Radcliffe College, Rich graduated Phi Beta Kappa and shortly after won distinction when her first book of poems, *A Change of World,* won the Yale Younger Poets award and was published with a laudatory preface by W. H. Auden. After traveling and writing in Europe on a Guggenheim fellowship, Rich married Alfred Conrad, an economics professor at Harvard. As a wife and the mother of three sons during the 1950s, Rich was expected to conform to a life of domestic femininity, which meant that she had little time for serious writing. Her *Snapshots of a Daughter-in-Law* conveys the anger and confusion she felt during those years of confinement. In her 1963 book of verse, Rich smashes the icons of domesticity: the coffee pot and raked gardens.

The conflict and distress experienced by creative, intellectual women in a culture that too often devalues female experience is a recurring theme in Rich's poetry. In the fifty years of her career, her poems and her essays chronicle the evolution of feminist consciousness and illuminate the phases of her personal growth from self-analysis and individual accomplishment to lesbian/feminist activism and the collective shaping of a feminist vision of community that is perhaps strangely rooted in the Puritan ideal of the city on a hill. The personal and political converge in her belief that politics is "not something 'out there' but something 'in here' and of the essense of [her] condition."

Adrienne Rich is a poet whose work has influenced the lives of many of her readers. She acknowledges that it is a profound responsibility and privilege to be a poet whose work is read by so many. As a radical feminist, Rich has written poetry that is politically charged, refusing to accept the criticism that art and activism are antithetical. Her poems combine lyricism and tightly constructed lines characterized by the use of elegant assonance, consonance, slant rhyme, and onomatopoeia, with quotations and slogans from antiwar and feminist statements.

Influenced by the open styles of Pound, Williams, and Levertov, and the confessional mode of Lowell, Plath, Sexton, and Berryman, Rich has created a poetic voice that is distinctive and powerful. Her unusual combination of artistic excellence and committed activism has been internationally praised, and she has won numerous awards including the 1974 National Book Award, the 1986 Ruth Lilly Poetry Prize, the 1997 Tanning Prize, the 1999 Lannan Foundation's Lifetime Achievement Award, as well as two Guggenheim fellowships and a MacArthur fellowship. As a poet who has committed herself to writing poetry that will change lives, Rich has observed in *Lies, Secrets, and Silences,* her collected essays, "Poetry is, among other things, a criticism of language. Poetry is above all a concentration of the power of language, which is the power of our ultimate relationship to everything in the universe."

Wendy Martin
Claremont Graduate University

PRIMARY WORKS

A Change of World, 1951; *Snapshots of a Daughter-in-Law,* 1963; *Necessities of Life,* 1966; *Leaflets,* 1969; *The Will to Change,* 1971; *Diving into the Wreck: Poems 1971–1972,* 1973; *Poems Selected and New,* 1975; *Of Woman Born: Motherhood as Experience and Institution,* 1976, 1986; *The Dream of a Common Language: Poems 1974–1977,* 1978; *On Lies, Secrets, and Silence: Selected Prose 1966–1978,* 1979; *A Wild Patience Has Taken Me This Far: Poems 1978–1981,* 1981; *Sources,* 1983; *The Fact of a Doorframe: Poems Selected and New 1950–1984,* 1984; *Your Native Land, Your Life,* 1986; *Blood, Bread and Poetry: Selected Prose 1979–1985,* 1986; *Time's Power: Poems 1985–1988,* 1989; *Women and Honor: Some Notes on Lying,* 1990; *An Atlas of the Difficult World: Poems 1988–1991,* 1991; *What Is Found There?: Notebooks on Poetry and Politics,* 1993; *Collected Early Poems, 1950–1970,* 1995; *Dark Fields of the Republic: Poems, 1991–1995,* 1995; *Selected Poems,* 1996; *Midnight Salvage: Poems, 1995–1998,* 1999; *Arts of the Possible: Essays and Conversation,* 2001; *Fox: Poems 1998–2000,* 2001; *Selected Poems,* 2004; *Telephone Ringing in the Labyrinth,* 2007.

Diving into the Wreck

First having read the book of myths,
and loaded the camera,
and checked the edge of the knife-blade,
I put on
5   the body-armor of black rubber
the absurd flippers
the grave and awkward mask.
I am having to do this
not like Cousteau[1] with his
10   assiduous team
aboard the sun-flooded schooner
but here alone.

---

[1] Jacques Cousteau (1910–1997). French underwater explorer and environmentalist.

There is a ladder.
The ladder is always there
15 hanging innocently
close to the side of the schooner.
We know what it is for,
we who have used it.
Otherwise
20 it's a piece of maritime floss
some sundry equipment.

I go down.
Rung after rung and still
the oxygen immerses me
25 the blue light
the clear atoms
of our human air.
I go down.
My flippers cripple me,
30 I crawl like an insect down the ladder
and there is no one
to tell me when the ocean
will begin.

First the air is blue and then
35 it is bluer and then green and then
black I am blacking out and yet
my mask is powerful
it pumps my blood with power
the sea is another story
40 the sea is not a question of power
I have to learn alone
to turn my body without force
in the deep element.

And now: it is easy to forget
45 what I came for
among so many who have always
lived here
swaying their crenellated fans
between the reefs
50 and besides
you breathe differently down here.

I came to explore the wreck.
The words are purposes.
The words are maps.
55 I came to see the damage that was done
and the treasures that prevail.

I stroke the beam of my lamp
slowly along the flank
of something more permanent
60 than fish or weed

the thing I came for:
the wreck and not the story of the wreck
the thing itself and not the myth
the drowned face always staring
65 toward the sun
the evidence of damage
worn by salt and sway into this threadbare beauty
the ribs of the disaster
curving their assertion
70 among the tentative haunters.

This is the place.
And I am here, the mermaid whose dark hair
streams black, the merman in his armored body
We circle silently
75 about the wreck
we dive into the hold.
I am she: I am he
whose drowned face sleeps with open eyes
whose breasts still bear the stress
80 whose silver, copper, vermeil cargo lies
obscurely inside barrels
half-wedged and left to rot
we are the half-destroyed instruments
that once held to a course
85 the water-eaten log
the fouled compass

We are, I am, you are
by cowardice or courage
the one who find our way
90 back to this scene
carrying a knife, a camera
a book of myths
in which
our names do not appear.

1973

From a Survivor

The pact that we made was the ordinary pact
of men & women in those days

I don't know who we thought we were
that our personalities
5 could resist the failures of the race

Lucky or unlucky, we didn't know
the race had failures of that order
and that we were going to share them

Like everybody else, we thought of ourselves as special

10 Your body is as vivid to me
as it ever was: even more

since my feeling for it is clearer:
I know what it could and could not do

it is no longer
15 the body of a god
or anything with power over my life

Next year it would have been 20 years
and you are wastefully dead[1]
who might have made the leap
20 we talked, too late, of making

which I live now
not as a leap
but a succession of brief, amazing movements

each one making possible the next

                                    1973

---

[1]Adrienne Rich's husband, Alfred Conrad,
committed suicide in 1970.

Power

Living   in the earth-deposits   of our history

Today a backhoe divulged   out of a crumbling flank of earth
one bottle   amber   perfect   a hundred-year-old
cure for fever   or melancholy   a tonic
5 for living on this earth   in the winters of this climate

Today I was reading about Marie Curie:[1]
she must have known she suffered   from radiation sickness
her body bombarded for years   by the element
she had purified
10 It seems she denied to the end
the source of the cataracts on her eyes
the cracked and suppurating skin   of her finger-ends
till she could no longer hold   a test-tube or a pencil

She died   a famous woman   denying
15 her wounds
denying
her wounds   came   from the same source as her power

1978

Not Somewhere Else, but Here

Courage   Her face in the leaves   the polygons
of the paving   Her   out of touch
Courage to breathe   The death of October
Spilt wine   The unbuilt house   The unmade life
5 Graffiti   without memory   grown conventional
scrawling the least wall   *god loves you   voice of the ghetto*
Death of the city   Her face
sleeping   Her quick stride   Her
running   Search for a private space   The city
10 caving in from within   The lessons badly
learned   Or not at all   The unbuilt world

[1]Marie Curie (1867–1934) won a Nobel Prize
for her research on radioactive elements. She
died of leukemia.

This one love flowing   Touching other
lives   Spilt love   The least wall caving

To have enough courage   The life that must be lived
15 in terrible October
Sudden immersion in yellows   streaked blood   The fast rain
Faces   Inscriptions   Trying to teach
unlearnable lessons   October   This one love
Repetitions   from other lives   The deaths
20 that must be lived   Denials   Blank walls
Our quick stride side by side   Her fugue
Bad air in the tunnels   *voice of the ghetto   god loves you*
My face   pale in the window   anger is pale
the blood shrinks to the heart
25 the head severed   it does not pay to feel

Her face   The fast rain tearing   Courage
to feel this   To tell of this   to be alive
Trying to learn   unteachable lessons

The fugue   Blood in my eyes   The careful sutures
30 ripped open   The hands that touch me   Shall it be said
I am not alone
Spilt love   seeking its level   flooding other
lives   that must be lived   not somewhere else
but here   seeing through blood   nothing is lost

1974

Coast to Coast

There are days when housework seems the only
outlet   old funnel I've poured caldrons through
old servitude   In grief and fury bending
to the accustomed tasks   the vacuum cleaner plowing
5 realms of dust   the mirror scoured   grey webs
behind framed photographs   brushed away
the grey-seamed sky enormous in the west
snow gathering in corners   of the north

Seeing through the prism
10 you who gave it me
You, bearing ceaselessly
yourself   the witness

Rainbow dissolves the Hudson   This chary, stinting
skin of late winter   ice   forming and breaking up
15   The unprotected seeing it through
with their ordinary valor
        Rainbow composed of ordinary light
February-flat
grey-white of a cheap enamelled pan
20   breaking into veridian, azure, violet
You write: *Three and a half weeks lost from writing . . .*
I think of the word *protection*
who it is we try to protect   and why
        Seeing through the prism   Your face, fog-hollowed   burning
25   cold of eucalyptus hung with butterflies
lavender of rockbloom
O and your anger uttered in silence word and stammer
shattering the fog   lances of sun
piercing the grey Pacific   unanswerable tide
30   carving itself in clefts and fissures of the rock
Beauty of your breasts   your hands
turning a stone a shell a week a prism   in coastal light
traveller and witness
the passion of the speechless
35   driving your speech
protectless

If you can read and understand this poem
send something back: a burning strand of hair
a still-warm, still-liquid drop of blood
40   *a shell*
thickened from being battered year on year
send something back.

1981

Frame

Winter twilight. She comes out of the laboratory, last class of the day
a pile of notebooks slung in her knapsack, coat
zipped high against the already swirling
5   evening sleet. The wind is wicked and the
busses slower than usual. On her mind
is organic chemistry and the issue
of next month's rent and will it be possible to
bypass the professor with the coldest eyes

10   to get a reference for graduate school,
     and whether any of them, even those who smile
     can see, looking at her, a biochemist
     or a marine biologist, which of the faces
     can she trust to see her at all, either today
15   or in any future. The busses are worm-slow in the
     quickly gathering dark. *I don't know her. I am*
     standing though somewhere just outside the frame
     of all this, trying to see. At her back
     the newly finished building suddenly looks
20   like shelter, it has glass doors, lighted halls
     presumably heat. The wind is wicked. She throws a
     glance down the street, sees no bus coming and runs
     up the newly constructed steps into the newly
     constructed hallway. *I am standing all this time*
25   *just beyond the frame, trying to see.* She runs
     her hand through the crystals of sleet about to melt
     on her hair. She shifts the weight of the books
     on her back. It isn't warm here exactly but it's
     out of that wind. Through the glass
30   door panels she can watch for the bus through the thickening
     weather. Watching so, she is not
     watching for the white man who watches the building
     who has been watching her. This is Boston 1979.
     I am standing somewhere at the edge of the frame
35   *watching the man, we are both white, who watches the building*
     telling her to move on, get out of the hallway.
     I can hear nothing because I am not supposed to be
     present but I can see her gesturing
     out toward the street at the wind-raked curb
40   *I see her drawing her small body up*
     against the implied charges. The man
     goes away. Her body is different now.
     It is holding together with more than a hint of fury
     and more than a hint of fear. She is smaller, thinner
45   more fragile-looking than I am. *But I am not supposed to be*
     there. I am just outside the frame
     of this action when the anonymous white man
     returns with a white police officer. Then she starts
     to leave into the windraked night but already
50   the policeman is going to work, the handcuffs are on her
     wrists he is throwing her down his knee has gone into
     her breast he is dragging her down the stairs *I am unable*
     to hear a sound of all this all that I know is what
     I can see from this position there is no soundtrack
55   *to go with this and I understand at once*
     it is meant to be in silence that this happens
     in silence that he pushes her into the car

banging her head in silence that she cries out
in silence that she tries to explain she was only
60 waiting for a bus
in silence that he twists the flesh of her thigh
with his nails in silence that her tears begin to flow
that she pleads with the other policeman as if
he could be trusted to see her at all
65 in silence that in the precinct she refuses to give her name
in silence that they throw her into the cell
in silence that she stares him
straight in the face in silence that he sprays her
in her eyes with Mace in silence that she sinks her teeth
70 into his hand in silence that she is charged
with trespass assault and battery in
silence that at the sleet-swept corner her bus
passes without stopping and goes on
in silence. *What I am telling you*
75 *is told by a white woman who they will say*
was never there. I say I am there.

1981

Cluster: E Pluribus Unum Cluster—
Landmark Legislation

The United States exists and has flourished for more than two hundred years largely because of the strength of its legal foundations. The U.S. Constitution delineates the rights of citizens and serves as the basis for key aspects of their civil identity. But the Constitution was not intended to be a sacred text that could never be altered. It is regarded as a starting point for legal challenges that have been and will continue to be argued in courts. The U.S. Supreme Court arrives at decisions that affect our culture in profound and sometimes subtle ways.

We have selected four important legislative decisions that span the time period covered in Volume E of *The Heath Anthology of American Literature*. These are just a few of the many decisions that have affected history, political identity, and therefore literature. Since the late 1970s, a vital intersection of academic disciplines has developed—the law and literature movement. There are many advantages to reading legal texts with literary texts. Most obviously, the events that form the backdrop of literary texts are frequently related to legal decisions, so the law provides a valuable context for literary understanding. But studying legal texts also reaffirms the ways that such texts themselves affect the reader. Trials are narratives, not just supplements to the way we read narrative.

Students of nineteenth-century American literature benefit greatly from an understanding of the legal assumptions of slavery. In *Dred Scott v. Sandford* (1857), the U.S. Supreme Court ruled that, according to the Constitution, black people, whether slave or free, could not be citizens and "had no rights which the white man was bound to respect." The Dred Scott decision essentially upheld slavery. This public legal statement gives a new weight and meaning to the slaves' claim to self-determination in slave narratives or as they were depicted in novels like *Uncle Tom's Cabin*. Reading the Dred Scott decision helps us to understand that Supreme Court decisions are not permanent. They exist for a time, sometimes are resisted and occasionally are overturned. However, such an overturning sometimes takes a revolution, in this case a social one. The civil rights of black citizens were not fully recognized until passage of the Civil Rights Act of 1964 and the Voting Rights Act of 1965—more than a century after the Dred Scott decision and then by Congress, not the Supreme Court.

The first two decisions in this cluster are connected to the Civil Rights and Voting Rights acts. The first is the 1954 U.S. Supreme Court decision known as *Brown v. Board of Education*, included here in its entirety. The decision ended segregation in schools and served as the precedent for many other decisions that essentially ended the practice of segregation in all public places, overturning decades of laws (known as Jim Crow laws) that were set up after Reconstruction to enforce the second-class status of African Americans. The second document included here is an abridged version of the Supreme Court's 1967 decision in *Loving v. Virginia*. In *Loving*, the justices looked at the laws in some states (including the Commonwealth of Virginia) that made it illegal for blacks and whites to marry each other. Their decision overturned the case that had enabled Virginia's laws to exist for a decade or more after *Brown*.

The third decision is one that virtually all students have heard of—*Roe v. Wade*, the 1973 Supreme Court decision in which the justices found that most laws banning abortions at that time violated women's constitutional right to privacy. The ruling made it legal for women to obtain abortions until the point when a fetus becomes viable. This case has been controversial for nearly four decades, and it has been upheld repeatedly by the Supreme Court, most recently in 2008. The decision is controversial because of disagreements about the definition of when human life begins, women's right to choose to continue or terminate a pregnancy, and women's right to obtain an abortion that is both legal and medically safe. *Roe v. Wade* has given a substantial amount of agency to women that had previously been denied to them and has had a positive effect on public health. The case has also highlighted deep divisions in U.S. society along religious and political lines. Because of the length of the decision, we have included only the introduction and conclusion here.

The final piece of legal writing in this cluster is much longer. It is not a legal decision but an act passed by Congress. The Uniting and Strengthening America by Providing Appropriate Tools Required to Intercept and Obstruct Terrorism Act (also known by its anagram, "USA PATRIOT Act") was passed in the immediate aftermath of the terror attacks on September 11, 2001, and was ostensibly designed to secure our nation and to prevent other attacks. While few citizens and politicians are opposed to the ostensible goals of the Patriot Act, its provisions have proved to be controversial. The U.S. military, for instance, has been able to detain terror suspects indefinitely at the military base at Guantanamo Bay, Cuba, without charging them with a crime, without following other processes dictated by the Geneva Convention, and without respecting rights guaranteed by the U.S. Constitution to U.S. citizens. Moreover, the U.S. government has gained what some citizens consider an intrusive amount of power when it comes to surveillance. In the name of safety and intelligence gathering, the free and open nature of living in American society has been diminished. The Patriot Act is perhaps not the cause of this diminishment, but it can be seen as legal underwriting for it. Because of its length, we have included only excerpts of the Library of Congress's summary of the act.

As you read the documents that follow, you may find yourself empowered as a citizen and as a critical reader. The numbers and abbreviations following case names in the decisions provide the reader with information for finding the decision in that case, not unlike the footnotes you include in your research in college writing. These legal decisions have shaped the culture that produced the literature you are studying, and they have also affected your identity as a U.S. citizen.

D. Quentin Miller
Suffolk University

United States Supreme Court

Brown v. Board of Education, 347 U.S. 483 (1954)

Appeal from the United States District Court for the District of Kansas

Syllabus

Segregation of white and Negro children in the public schools of a State solely on the basis of race, pursuant to state laws permitting or requiring such segregation, denies to Negro children the equal protection of the laws guaranteed by the Fourteenth Amendment—even though the physical facilities and other "tangible" factors of white and Negro schools may be equal.

(a) The history of the Fourteenth Amendment is inconclusive as to its intended effect on public education.

(b) The question presented in these cases must be determined not on the basis of conditions existing when the Fourteenth Amendment was adopted, but in the light of the full development of public education and its present place in American life throughout the Nation.

(c) Where a State has undertaken to provide an opportunity for an education in its public schools, such an opportunity is a right which must be made available to all on equal terms.

(d) Segregation of children in public schools solely on the basis of race deprives children of the minority group of equal educational opportunities, even though the physical facilities and other "tangible" factors may be equal.

(e) The "separate but equal" doctrine adopted in *Plessy v. Ferguson,* 163 U.S. 537, has no place in the field of public education.

(f) The cases are restored to the docket for further argument on specified questions relating to the forms of the decrees.

Opinion

Mr. Chief Justice Warren delivered the opinion of the Court.

These cases come to us from the States of Kansas, South Carolina, Virginia, and Delaware. They are premised on different facts and different local conditions, but a common legal question justifies their consideration together in this consolidated opinion.

In each of the cases, minors of the Negro race, through their legal representatives, seek the aid of the courts in obtaining admission to the public schools of their community on a nonsegregated basis. In each instance, they had been denied admission to schools attended by white children under laws requiring or permitting segregation according to race. This segregation was alleged to deprive the plaintiffs of the equal protection of the laws under the Fourteenth Amendment. In each of the cases other than the Delaware case, a three-judge federal district court denied relief to the plaintiffs on the so-called "separate but equal" doctrine announced by this Court in *Plessy v. Ferguson,* 163 U.S. 537. Under that doctrine, equality of treatment is accorded when the races are provided substantially equal facilities, even though these facilities be separate. In the Delaware case, the Supreme Court of Delaware adhered to that doctrine, but ordered that the plaintiffs be admitted to the white schools because of their superiority to the Negro schools.

The plaintiffs contend that segregated public schools are not "equal" and cannot be made "equal," and that hence they are deprived of the equal protection of the laws. Because of the obvious importance of the question presented, the Court took jurisdiction. Argument was heard in the 1952 Term, and reargument was heard this Term on certain questions propounded by the Court.

Reargument was largely devoted to the circumstances surrounding the adoption of the Fourteenth Amendment in 1868. It covered exhaustively consideration of the Amendment in Congress, ratification by the states, then-existing practices in racial segregation, and the views of proponents and opponents of the Amendment. This discussion and our own investigation convince us that, although these sources cast some light, it is not enough to resolve the problem with which we are faced. At best, they are inconclusive. The most avid proponents of the post-War Amendments undoubtedly intended them to remove all legal distinctions among "all persons born or naturalized in the United States." Their opponents, just as certainly, were antagonistic to both the letter and the spirit of the Amendments and wished them to have the most limited effect. What others in Congress and the state legislatures had in mind cannot be determined with any degree of certainty.

An additional reason for the inconclusive nature of the Amendment's history with respect to segregated schools is the status of public education at that time. In the South, the movement toward free common schools, supported by general taxation, had not yet taken hold. Education of white children was largely in the hands of private groups. Education of Negroes was almost nonexistent, and practically all of the race were illiterate. In fact, any education of Negroes was forbidden by law in some states. Today, in contrast, many Negroes have achieved outstanding success in the arts and sciences, as well as in the business and professional world. It is true that public school education at the time of the Amendment had advanced further in the North, but the effect of the Amendment on Northern States was generally ignored in the congressional debates. Even in the North, the conditions of public education did not approximate those existing today. The curriculum was usually rudimentary; ungraded schools were common in rural areas; the school term was but three months a year in many states, and compulsory school attendance was virtually unknown. As a consequence, it is not surprising that there should be so little in the history of the Fourteenth Amendment relating to its intended effect on public education.

In the first cases in this Court construing the Fourteenth Amendment, decided shortly after its adoption, the Court interpreted it as proscribing all state-imposed discriminations against the Negro race. The doctrine of "separate but equal" did not make its appearance in this Court until 1896 in the case of *Plessy v. Ferguson,* supra, involving not education but transportation. American courts have since labored with the doctrine for over half a century. In this Court, there have been six cases involving the "separate but equal" doctrine in the field of public education. In *Cumming v. County Board of Education,* 175 U.S. 528, and *Gong Lum v. Rice,* 275 U.S. 78, the validity of the doctrine itself was not challenged. In more recent cases, all on the graduate school level, inequality was found in that specific benefits enjoyed by white students were denied to Negro students of the same educational qualifications. *Missouri ex rel. Gaines v. Canada,* 305 U.S. 337; *Sipuel v. Oklahoma,* 332 U.S. 631; *Sweatt v. Painter,* 339 U.S. 629; *McLaurin v. Oklahoma State Regents,* 339 U.S. 637. In none of these cases was it necessary to reexamine the doctrine to grant relief to the Negro plaintiff. And in *Sweatt v. Painter,* supra, the Court expressly reserved decision on the question whether *Plessy v. Ferguson* should be held inapplicable to public education.

In the instant cases, that question is directly presented. Here, unlike *Sweatt v. Painter,* there are findings below that the Negro and white schools involved have been equalized, or are being equalized, with respect to buildings, curricula, qualifications and salaries of teachers, and other "tangible" factors. Our decision, therefore, cannot turn on merely a comparison of these tangible factors in the Negro and white schools involved in each of the cases. We must look instead to the effect of segregation itself on public education.

In approaching this problem, we cannot turn the clock back to 1868, when the Amendment was adopted, or even to 1896, when *Plessy v. Ferguson* was written. We must consider public education in the light of its full development and its present place in American life throughout the Nation. Only in this way can it be determined if segregation in public schools deprives these plaintiffs of the equal protection of the laws.

Today, education is perhaps the most important function of state and local governments. Compulsory school attendance laws and the great expenditures for education both demonstrate our recognition of the importance of education to our democratic society. It is required in the performance of our most basic public responsibilities, even service in the armed forces. It is the very foundation of good citizenship. Today it is a principal instrument in awakening the child to cultural values, in preparing him for later professional training, and in helping him to adjust normally to his environment. In these days, it is doubtful that any child may reasonably be expected to succeed in life if he is denied the opportunity of an education. Such an opportunity, where the state has undertaken to provide it, is a right which must be made available to all on equal terms.

We come then to the question presented: Does segregation of children in public schools solely on the basis of race, even though the physical facilities and other "tangible" factors may be equal, deprive the children of the minority group of equal educational opportunities? We believe that it does.

In *Sweatt v. Painter,* supra, in finding that a segregated law school for Negroes could not provide them equal educational opportunities, this Court relied in large part on "those qualities which are incapable of objective measurement but which make for greatness in a law school." In *McLaurin v. Oklahoma State Regents,* supra, the Court, in requiring that a Negro admitted to a white graduate school be treated like all other students, again resorted to intangible considerations: ". . . his ability to study, to engage in discussions and exchange views with other students, and, in general, to learn his profession." Such considerations apply with added force to children in grade and high schools. To separate them from others of similar age and qualifications solely because of their race generates a feeling of inferiority as to their status in the community that may affect their hearts and minds in a way unlikely ever to be undone. The effect of this separation on their educational opportunities was well stated by a finding in the Kansas case by a court which nevertheless felt compelled to rule against the Negro plaintiffs:

> Segregation of white and colored children in public schools has a detrimental effect upon the colored children. The impact is greater when it has the sanction of the law, for the policy of separating the races is usually interpreted as denoting the inferiority of the negro group. A sense of inferiority affects the motivation of a child to learn. Segregation with the sanction of law, therefore, has a tendency to [retard] the educational and mental development of negro children and to deprive them of some of the benefits they would receive in a racial[ly] integrated school system.

Whatever may have been the extent of psychological knowledge at the time of *Plessy v. Ferguson,* this finding is amply supported by modern authority. Any language in *Plessy v. Ferguson* contrary to this finding is rejected.

We conclude that, in the field of public education, the doctrine of "separate but equal" has no place. Separate educational facilities are inherently unequal. Therefore, we hold that the plaintiffs and others similarly situated for whom the actions have been brought are, by reason of the segregation complained of, deprived of the equal protection of the laws guaranteed by the Fourteenth Amendment. This disposition makes unnecessary any discussion whether such segregation also violates the Due Process Clause of the Fourteenth Amendment.

Because these are class actions, because of the wide applicability of this decision, and because of the great variety of local conditions, the formulation of decrees in these cases presents problems of considerable complexity. On reargument, the consideration of appropriate relief was necessarily subordinated to the primary question—the constitutionality of segregation in public education. We have now announced that such segregation is a denial of the equal protection of the laws. In order that we may have the full assistance of the parties in formulating decrees, the cases will be restored to the docket, and the parties are requested to present further argument on Questions 4 and 5 previously propounded by the Court for the reargument this Term. The Attorney General of the United States is again invited to participate. The Attorneys General of the states requiring or permitting segregation in public education will also be permitted to appear as amici curiae upon request to do so by September 15, 1954, and submission of briefs by October 1, 1954.

It is so ordered.

1954

U.S. Supreme Court

Loving v. Virginia, 388 U.S. 1 (1967)

Appeal from the Supreme Court of Appeals of Virginia

Opinion of the Court

Mr. Chief Justice Warren delivered the opinion of the Court.

This case presents a constitutional question never addressed by this Court: whether a statutory scheme adopted by the State of Virginia to prevent marriages between persons solely on the basis of racial classifications violates the Equal Protection and Due Process Clauses of the Fourteenth Amendment. For reasons which seem to us to reflect the central meaning of those constitutional commands, we conclude that these statutes cannot stand consistently with the Fourteenth Amendment.

In June, 1958, two residents of Virginia, Mildred Jeter, a Negro woman, and Richard Loving, a white man, were married in the District of Columbia pursuant to its laws. Shortly after their marriage, the Lovings returned to Virginia and established their marital abode in Caroline County. At the October Term, 1958, of the Circuit Court of Caroline County, a grand jury issued an indictment charging the Lovings with violating Virginia's ban on interracial marriages. On January 6, 1959, the Lovings pleaded guilty to the charge, and were sentenced to one year in jail; however, the trial judge suspended the sentence for a period of 25 years on the condition that the Lovings leave the State and not return to Virginia together for 25 years. He stated in an opinion that:

> Almighty God created the races white, black, yellow, malay and red, and he placed them on separate continents. And, but for the interference with his arrangement, there would be no cause for such marriage. The fact that he separated the races shows that he did not intend for the races to mix.

After their convictions, the Lovings took up residence in the District of Columbia. On November 6, 1963, they filed a motion in the state trial court to vacate the judgment and set aside the sentence on the ground that the statutes which they had violated were repugnant to the Fourteenth Amendment. The motion not having been decided by October 28, 1964, the Lovings instituted a class action in the United States District Court for the Eastern District of Virginia requesting that a three-judge court be convened to declare the Virginia anti-miscegenation statutes unconstitutional and to enjoin state officials from enforcing their convictions. On January 22, 1965, the state trial judge denied the motion to vacate the sentences, and the Lovings perfected an appeal to the Supreme Court of Appeals of Virginia. On February 11, 1965, the three-judge District Court continued the case to allow the Lovings to present their constitutional claims to the highest state court.

The Supreme Court of Appeals upheld the constitutionality of the anti-miscegenation statutes and, after modifying the sentence, affirmed the convictions.

The Lovings appealed this decision, and we noted probable jurisdiction on December 12, 1966, 385 U.S. 986.

The two statutes under which appellants were convicted and sentenced are part of a comprehensive statutory scheme aimed at prohibiting and punishing interracial marriages. The Lovings were convicted of violating Section 258 of the Virginia Code:

Leaving State to evade law. *If any white person and colored person shall go out of this State, for the purpose of being married, and with the intention of returning, and be married out of it, and afterwards return to and reside in it, cohabiting as man and wife, they shall be punished as provided in Section 20-59, and the marriage shall be governed by the same law as if it had been solemnized in this State. The fact of their cohabitation here as man and wife shall be evidence of their marriage.*

Section 259, which defines the penalty for miscegenation, provides:

Punishment for marriage. *If any white person intermarry with a colored person, or any colored person intermarry with a white person, he shall be guilty of a felony and shall be punished by confinement in the penitentiary for not less than one nor more than five years.*

Other central provisions in the Virginia statutory scheme are Section 20-57, which automatically voids all marriages between "a white person and a colored person" without any judicial proceeding, and Sections 20-54 and 1-14 which, respectively, define "white persons" and "colored persons and Indians" for purposes of the statutory prohibitions. The Lovings have never disputed in the course of this litigation that Mrs. Loving is a "colored person" or that Mr. Loving is a "white person" within the meanings given those terms by the Virginia statutes.

Virginia is now one of 16 States which prohibit and punish marriages on the basis of racial classifications. Penalties for miscegenation arose as an incident to slavery, and have been common in Virginia since the colonial period. The present statutory scheme dates from the adoption of the Racial Integrity Act of 1924, passed during the period of extreme nativism which followed the end of the First World War. The central features of this Act, and current Virginia law, are the absolute prohibition of a "white person" marrying other than another "white person," a prohibition against issuing marriage licenses until the issuing official is satisfied that the applicants' statements as to their race are correct, certificates of "racial composition" to be kept by both local and state registrars, and the carrying forward of earlier prohibitions against racial intermarriage.

I

In upholding the constitutionality of these provisions in the decision below, the Supreme Court of Appeals of Virginia referred to its 1965 decision in *Naim v. Naim,* 197 Va. 80, 87 S.E.2d 749, as stating the reasons supporting the validity of these laws. In *Naim,* the state court concluded that the State's legitimate purposes were "to preserve the racial integrity of its citizens," and to prevent "the corruption of blood," "a mongrel breed of citizens," and "the obliteration of racial pride," obviously an endorsement of the doctrine of White Supremacy. Id. at 90, 87 S.E.2d at 756. The court also reasoned that marriage has traditionally been subject to state regulation without federal intervention, and, consequently, the regulation of marriage should be left to exclusive state control by the Tenth Amendment.

While the state court is no doubt correct in asserting that marriage is a social relation subject to the State's police power, *Maynard v. Hill,* 125 U.S. 190 (1888), the State does not contend in its argument before this Court that its powers to regulate marriage are unlimited notwithstanding the commands of the Fourteenth Amendment. Nor could it do so in light of *Meyer v. Nebraska,* 262 U.S. 390 (1923), and *Skinner v. Oklahoma,* 316 U.S. 535 (1942). Instead, the State argues that the meaning of the Equal Protection Clause, as illuminated by the statements of the Framers, is only that state penal laws containing an interracial element as part of the definition of the offense must apply equally to whites and Negroes in the sense that members of each race are punished to the same degree. . . .

. . . The clear and central purpose of the Fourteenth Amendment was to eliminate all official state sources of invidious racial discrimination in the States. . . .

There can be no question but that Virginia's miscegenation statutes rest solely upon distinctions drawn according to race. The statutes proscribe generally accepted conduct if engaged in by members of different races. . . . Over the years, this Court has consistently repudiated "[d]istinctions between citizens solely because of their ancestry" as being "odious to a free people whose institutions are founded upon the doctrine of equality." *Hirabayashi v. United States,* 320 U.S. 81, 100 (1943). At the very least, the Equal Protection Clause demands that racial classifications, especially suspect in criminal statutes, be subjected to the "most rigid scrutiny," *Korematsu v. United States,* 323 U.S. 214, 216 (1944), and, if they are ever to be upheld, they must be shown to be necessary to the accomplishment of some permissible state objective, independent of the racial discrimination which it was the object of the Fourteenth Amendment to eliminate. Indeed, two members of this Court have already stated that they "cannot conceive of a valid legislative purpose . . . which makes the color of a person's skin the test of whether his conduct is a criminal offense.". . .

There is patently no legitimate overriding purpose independent of invidious racial discrimination which justifies this classification. The fact that Virginia prohibits only interracial marriages involving white persons demonstrates that the racial classifications must stand on their own justification, as measures designed to maintain White Supremacy. We have consistently denied the constitutionality of measures which restrict the rights of citizens on account of race. There can be no doubt that restricting the freedom to marry solely because of racial classifications violates the central meaning of the Equal Protection Clause.

II

These statutes also deprive the Lovings of liberty without due process of law in violation of the Due Process Clause of the Fourteenth Amendment. The freedom to marry has long been recognized as one of the vital personal rights essential to the orderly pursuit of happiness by free men.

Marriage is one of the "basic civil rights of man," fundamental to our very existence and survival. *Skinner v. Oklahoma,* 316 U.S. 535, 541 (1942). See also *Maynard v. Hill,* 125 U.S. 190 (1888). To deny this fundamental freedom on so unsupportable a basis as the racial classifications embodied in these statutes, classifications so directly subversive of the principle of equality at the heart of the Fourteenth Amendment, is surely to deprive all the State's citizens of liberty without due process of law. The Fourteenth Amendment requires that the freedom of choice to marry not be restricted by invidious racial discriminations. Under our Constitution, the freedom to marry, or not marry, a person of another race resides with the individual, and cannot be infringed by the State.

These convictions must be reversed.

It is so ordered.

1967

U.S. Supreme Court

Roe v. Wade, 410 U.S. 113 (1973)

Appeal from the United States District Court for the Northern District of Texas

Opinion of the Court

Mr. Justice Blackmun delivered the opinion of the Court.

This Texas federal appeal and its Georgia companion, *Doe v. Bolton, . . .* present constitutional challenges to state criminal abortion legislation. The Texas statutes under attack here are typical of those that have been in effect in many States for approximately a century. The Georgia statutes, in contrast, have a modern cast and are a legislative product that, to an extent at least, obviously reflects the influences of recent attitudinal change, of advancing medical knowledge and techniques, and of new thinking about an old issue.

We forthwith acknowledge our awareness of the sensitive and emotional nature of the abortion controversy, of the vigorous opposing views, even among physicians, and of the deep and seemingly absolute convictions that the subject inspires. One's philosophy, one's experiences, one's exposure to the raw edges of human existence, one's religious training, one's attitudes toward life and family and their values, and the moral standards one establishes and seeks to observe, are all likely to influence and to color one's thinking and conclusions about abortion.

In addition, population growth, pollution, poverty, and racial overtones tend to complicate and not to simplify the problem.

Our task, of course, is to resolve the issue by constitutional measurement, free of emotion and of predilection. We seek earnestly to do this, and, because we do, we have inquired into, and in this opinion place some emphasis upon, medical and medical-legal history and what that history reveals about man's attitudes toward the abortion procedure over the centuries. We bear in mind, too, Mr. Justice Holmes' admonition in his now-vindicated dissent in *Lochner v. New York,* 198 U.S. 45, 76 (1905):

> *[The Constitution] is made for people of fundamentally differing views, and the accident of our finding certain opinions natural and familiar or novel and even shocking ought not to conclude our judgment upon the question whether statutes embodying them conflict with the Constitution of the United States.*

I

The Texas statutes that concern us here are Articles 1191–1194 and 1196 of the State's Penal Code. These make it a crime to "procure an abortion," as therein defined, or to attempt one, except with respect to "an abortion procured or attempted by medical advice for the purpose of saving the life of the mother." Similar statutes are in existence in a majority of the States.

Texas first enacted a criminal abortion statute in 1854. Texas Laws 1854, Chapter 49, Section 1, set forth in 3 H. Gammel, *Laws of Texas* 1502 (1898). This was soon modified into language that has remained substantially unchanged to the present time. See Texas Penal Code of 1857, Chapter 7, Articles 531–536; G. Paschal, *Laws of Texas,* Articles 2192–2197 (1866); Texas Rev. Stat., Chapter 8, Articles 536–541 (1879); Texas Rev. Crim. Stat., Articles 1071–1076 (1911). The final article in each of these compilations provided the same exception, as does the present Article 1196, for an abortion by "medical advice for the purpose of saving the life of the mother."

II

Jane Roe, a single woman who was residing in Dallas County, Texas, instituted this federal action in March 1970 against the District Attorney of the county. She sought a declaratory judgment that the Texas criminal abortion statutes were unconstitutional on their face, and an injunction restraining the defendant from enforcing the statutes.

Roe alleged that she was unmarried and pregnant; that she wished to terminate her pregnancy by an abortion "performed by a competent, licensed physician, under safe, clinical conditions"; that she was unable to get a "legal" abortion in Texas because her life did not appear to be threatened by the continuation of her pregnancy; and that she could not afford to travel to another jurisdiction in order to secure a legal abortion under safe conditions. She claimed that the Texas statutes were unconstitutionally vague and that they abridged her right of personal privacy, protected by the First, Fourth, Fifth, Ninth, and Fourteenth Amendments. By an amendment to her complaint Roe purported to sue "on behalf of herself and all other women" similarly situated.

James Hubert Hallford, a licensed physician, sought and was granted leave to intervene in Roe's action. In his complaint he alleged that he had been arrested previously for violations of the Texas abortion statutes and that two such prosecutions were pending against him. He described conditions of patients who came to him seeking abortions, and he claimed that for many cases he, as a physician, was unable to determine whether they fell within or outside the exception recognized by Article 1196. He alleged that, as a consequence, the statutes were vague and uncertain, in violation of the Fourteenth Amendment, and that they violated his own and his patients' rights to privacy in the doctor-patient relationship and his own right to practice medicine, rights he claimed were guaranteed by the First, Fourth, Fifth, Ninth, and Fourteenth Amendments.

John and Mary Doe, a married couple, filed a companion complaint to that of Roe. They also named the District Attorney as defendant, claimed like constitutional deprivations, and sought declaratory and injunctive relief. The Does alleged that they were a childless couple; that Mrs. Doe was suffering from a "neural-chemical" disorder; that her physician had "advised her to avoid pregnancy until such time as her condition has materially improved" (although a pregnancy at the present time would not present "a serious risk" to her life); that, pursuant to medical advice, she had discontinued use of birth control pills; and that if she should become pregnant, she would want to terminate the pregnancy by an abortion performed by a competent, licensed physician under safe, clinical conditions. By an amendment to their complaint, the Does purported to sue "on behalf of themselves and all couples similarly situated."

The two actions were consolidated and heard together by a duly convened three-judge district court. The suits thus presented the situations of the pregnant single woman, the childless couple, with the wife not pregnant, and the licensed practicing physician, all joining in the attack on the Texas criminal abortion statutes. Upon the filing of affidavits, motions were made for dismissal and for summary judgment. The court held that Roe and members of her class, and Dr. Hallford, had standing to sue and presented justiciable controversies, but that the Does had failed to allege facts sufficient to state a present controversy and did not have standing. It concluded that, with respect to the requests for a declaratory judgment, abstention was not warranted. On the merits, the District Court held that the "fundamental right of single women and married persons to choose whether to have children is protected by the Ninth Amendment, through the Fourteenth Amendment," and that the Texas criminal abortion statutes were void on their face because they were both unconstitutionally vague and constituted an overbroad infringement of the plaintiffs' Ninth Amendment rights. The court then held that abstention was warranted with respect to the requests for an injunction. It therefore dismissed the Does' complaint, declared the abortion statutes void, and dismissed the application for injunctive relief. . . .

The plaintiffs Roe and Doe and the intervenor Hallford, pursuant to 28 U.S.C. Section 1253, have appealed to this Court from that part of the District Court's judgment denying the injunction. The defendant District Attorney has purported to cross-appeal, pursuant to the same statute, from the court's grant of declaratory relief to Roe and Hallford. Both sides also have taken protective appeals to the United States Court of Appeals for the Fifth Circuit. That court ordered the appeals held in abeyance pending decision here. We postponed decision on jurisdiction to the hearing on the merits. 402 U.S. 941 (1971).

III

It might have been preferable if the defendant, pursuant to our Rule 20, had presented to us a petition for certiorari before judgment in the Court of Appeals with respect to the granting of the plaintiffs' prayer for declaratory relief. Our decisions in *Mitchell v. Donovan*, 398 U.S. 427 (1970), and *Gunn v. University Committee*, 399 U.S. 383 (1970), are to the effect that Section 1253 does not authorize an appeal to this Court from the grant or denial of declaratory relief alone. We conclude, nevertheless, that those decisions do not foreclose our review of both the injunctive and the declaratory aspects of a case of this kind when it is properly here, as this one is, on appeal under Section 1253 from specific denial of injunctive relief, and the arguments as to both aspects are necessarily identical. See *Carter v. Jury Comm'n*, 396 U.S. 320 (1970); *Florida Lime Growers v. Jacobsen*, 362 U.S. 73, 80–81 (1960). It would be destructive of time and energy for all concerned were we to rule otherwise. . . .

XI

To summarize and to repeat:

1. A state criminal abortion statute of the current Texas type, that excepts from criminality only a lifesaving procedure on behalf of the mother, without regard to pregnancy stage and without recognition of the other interests involved, is violative of the Due Process Clause of the Fourteenth Amendment.

   (a) For the stage prior to approximately the end of the first trimester, the abortion decision and its effectuation must be left to the medical judgment of the pregnant woman's attending physician.

   (b) For the stage subsequent to approximately the end of the first trimester, the State, in promoting its interest in the health of the mother, may, if it chooses, regulate the abortion procedure in ways that are reasonably related to maternal health.

   (c) For the stage subsequent to viability, the State in promoting its interest in the potentiality of human life may, if it chooses, regulate, and even proscribe, abortion except where it is necessary, in appropriate medical judgment, for the preservation of the life or health of the mother.

2. The State may define the term "physician," as it has been employed in the preceding paragraphs of this Part XI of this opinion, to mean only a physician currently licensed by the State, and may proscribe any abortion by a person who is not a physician as so defined.

In *Doe v. Bolton*, . . . procedural requirements contained in one of the modern abortion statutes are considered. That opinion and this one, of course, are to be read together.

This holding, we feel, is consistent with the relative weights of the respective interests involved, with the lessons and examples of medical and legal history, with the lenity of the common law, and with the demands of the profound problems of the present day. The decision leaves the State free to place increasing restrictions on abortion as the period of pregnancy lengthens, so long as those restrictions are tailored to the recognized state interests. The decision vindicates the right of the physician to administer medical treatment according to his professional judgment up to the points where important state interests provide compelling justifications for intervention. Up to those points, the abortion decision in all its aspects is inherently, and primarily, a medical decision, and basic responsibility for it must rest with the physician. If an individual practitioner abuses the privilege of exercising proper medical judgment, the usual remedies, judicial and intra-professional, are available.

XII

Our conclusion that Article 1196 is unconstitutional means, of course, that the Texas abortion statutes, as a unit, must fall. The exception of Article 1196 cannot be struck down separately, for then the State would be left with a statute proscribing all abortion procedures no matter how medically urgent the case.

Although the District Court granted appellant Roe declaratory relief, it stopped short of issuing an injunction against enforcement of the Texas statutes. The Court has recognized that different considerations enter into a federal court's decision as to declaratory relief, on the one hand, and injunctive relief, on the other. *Zwickler v. Koota,* 389 U.S. 241, 252–255 (1967); *Dombrowski v. Pfister,* 380 U.S. 479 (1965). We are not dealing with a statute that, on its face, appears to abridge free expression, an area of particular concern under Dombrowski and refined in *Younger v. Harris,* 401 U.S., at 50.

We find it unnecessary to decide whether the District Court erred in withholding injunctive relief, for we assume the Texas prosecutorial authorities will give full credence to this decision that the present criminal abortion statutes of that State are unconstitutional.

The judgment of the District Court as to intervenor Hallford is reversed, and Dr. Hallford's complaint in intervention is dismissed. In all other respects, the judgment of the District Court is affirmed. Costs are allowed to the appellee.

It is so ordered.

1973

U.S. House of Representatives

The USA Patriot Act

H.R. 3162: The Uniting and Strengthening America by Providing Appropriate Tools Required to Intercept and Obstruct Terrorism (USA PATRIOT) Act of 2001. Summary as of October 24, 2001: Passed House without amendment.

Title I: Enhancing Domestic Security against Terrorism

Establishes in the Treasury the Counterterrorism Fund.

(Sec. 102) Expresses the sense of Congress that: (1) the civil rights and liberties of all Americans, including Arab Americans, must be protected, and that every effort must be taken to preserve their safety; (2) any acts of violence or discrimination against any Americans be condemned; and (3) the Nation is called upon to recognize the patriotism of fellow citizens from all ethnic, racial, and religious backgrounds.

(Sec. 103) Authorizes appropriations for the Federal Bureau of Investigation's (FBI) Technical Support Center.

(Sec. 104) Authorizes the Attorney General to request the Secretary of Defense to provide assistance in support of Department of Justice (DOJ) activities relating to the enforcement of Federal criminal code (code) provisions regarding the use of weapons of mass destruction during an emergency situation involving a weapon (currently, chemical weapon) of mass destruction.

(Sec. 105) Requires the Director of the U.S. Secret Service to take actions to develop a national network of electronic crime task forces throughout the United States to prevent, detect, and investigate various forms of electronic crimes, including potential terrorist attacks against critical infrastructure and financial payment systems.

(Sec. 106) Modifies provisions relating to presidential authority under the International Emergency Powers Act to: (1) authorize the President, when the United States is engaged in armed hostilities or has been attacked by a foreign country or foreign nationals, to confiscate any property subject to U.S. jurisdiction of a foreign person, organization, or country that he determines has planned, authorized, aided, or engaged in such hostilities or attacks (the rights to which shall vest in such agency or person as the President may designate); and (2) provide that, in any judicial review of a determination made under such provisions, if the determination was based on classified information such information may be submitted to the reviewing court ex parte and in camera.

Title II: Enhanced Surveillance Procedures

Amends the Federal criminal code to authorize the interception of wire, oral, and electronic communications for the production of evidence of: (1) specified chemical weapons or terrorism offenses; and (2) computer fraud and abuse.

(Sec. 203) Amends rule 6 of the Federal Rules of Criminal Procedure (FRCrP) to permit the sharing of grand jury information that involves foreign intelligence or counterintelligence with Federal law enforcement, intelligence, protective, immigration, national defense, or national security officials (such officials), subject to specified requirements.

Authorizes an investigative or law enforcement officer, or an attorney for the Government, who, by authorized means, has obtained knowledge of the contents of any wire, oral, or electronic communication or evidence derived therefrom to disclose such contents to such officials to the extent that such contents include foreign intelligence or counterintelligence.

Directs the Attorney General to establish procedures for the disclosure of information (pursuant to the code and the FRCrP) that identifies a United States person, as defined in the Foreign Intelligence Surveillance Act of 1978 (FISA).

Authorizes the disclosure of foreign intelligence or counterintelligence obtained as part of a criminal investigation to such officials.

(Sec. 204) Clarifies that nothing in code provisions regarding pen registers shall be deemed to affect the acquisition by the Government of specified foreign intelligence information, and that procedures under FISA shall be the exclusive means by which electronic surveillance and the interception of domestic wire and oral (current law) and electronic communications may be conducted.

(Sec. 205) Authorizes the Director of the FBI to expedite the employment of personnel as translators to support counter-terrorism investigations and operations without regard to applicable Federal personnel requirements. Requires: (1) the Director to establish such security requirements as necessary for such personnel; and (2) the Attorney General to report to the House and Senate Judiciary Committees regarding translators.

(Sec. 206) Grants roving surveillance authority under FISA after requiring a court order approving an electronic surveillance to direct any person to furnish necessary information, facilities, or technical assistance in circumstances where the Court finds that the actions of the surveillance target may have the effect of thwarting the identification of a specified person.

(Sec. 207) Increases the duration of FISA surveillance permitted for non-U.S. persons who are agents of a foreign power.

(Sec. 208) Increases (from seven to 11) the number of district court judges designated to hear applications for and grant orders approving electronic surveillance. Requires that no fewer than three reside within 20 miles of the District of Columbia.

(Sec. 209) Permits the seizure of voice-mail messages under a warrant.

(Sec. 210) Expands the scope of subpoenas for records of electronic communications to include the length and types of service utilized, temporarily assigned network addresses, and the means and source of payment (including any credit card or bank account number).

(Sec. 211) Amends the Communications Act of 1934 to permit specified disclosures to Government entities, except for records revealing cable subscriber selection of video programming from a cable operator.

(Sec. 212) Permits electronic communication and remote computing service providers to make emergency disclosures to a governmental entity of customer electronic communications to protect life and limb.

(Sec. 213) Authorizes Federal district courts to allow a delay of required notices of the execution of a warrant if immediate notice may have an adverse result and under other specified circumstances.

(Sec. 214) Prohibits use of a pen register or trap and trace devices in any investigation to protect against international terrorism or clandestine intelligence activities that is conducted solely on the basis of activities protected by the first amendment to the U.S. Constitution.

(Sec. 215) Authorizes the Director of the FBI (or designee) to apply for a court order requiring production of certain business records for foreign intelligence and international terrorism investigations. Requires the Attorney General to report to the House and Senate Intelligence and Judiciary Committees semi-annually.

(Sec. 216) Amends the code to: (1) require a trap and trace device to restrict recoding or decoding so as not to include the contents of a wire or electronic communication; (2) apply a court order for a pen register or trap and trace devices to any person or entity providing wire or electronic communication service in the United

States whose assistance may facilitate execution of the order; (3) require specified records kept on any pen register or trap and trace device on a packet-switched data network of a provider of electronic communication service to the public; and (4) allow a trap and trace device to identify the source (but not the contents) of a wire or electronic communication.

(Sec. 217) Makes it lawful to intercept the wire or electronic communication of a computer trespasser in certain circumstances.

(Sec. 218) Amends FISA to require an application for an electronic surveillance order or search warrant to certify that a significant purpose (currently, the sole or main purpose) of the surveillance is to obtain foreign intelligence information.

(Sec. 219) Amends rule 41 of the FRCrP to permit Federal magistrate judges in any district in which terrorism-related activities may have occurred to issue search warrants for searches within or outside the district.

(Sec. 220) Provides for nationwide service of search warrants for electronic evidence.

(Sec. 221) Amends the Trade Sanctions Reform and Export Enhancement Act of 2000 to extend trade sanctions to the territory of Afghanistan controlled by the Taliban.

(Sec. 222) Specifies that: (1) nothing in this Act shall impose any additional technical obligation or requirement on a provider of a wire or electronic communication service or other person to furnish facilities or technical assistance; and (2) a provider of such service, and a landlord, custodian, or other person who furnishes such facilities or technical assistance, shall be reasonably compensated for such reasonable expenditures incurred in providing such facilities or assistance. . . .

Subtitle B: Enhanced Immigration Provisions

Amends the Immigration and Nationality Act to broaden the scope of aliens ineligible for admission or deportable due to terrorist activities to include an alien who: (1) is a representative of a political, social, or similar group whose political endorsement of terrorist acts undermines U.S. antiterrorist efforts; (2) has used a position of prominence to endorse terrorist activity, or to persuade others to support such activity in a way that undermines U.S. antiterrorist efforts (or the child or spouse of such an alien under specified circumstances); or (3) has been associated with a terrorist organization and intends to engage in threatening activities while in the United States.

(Sec. 411) Includes within the definition of "terrorist activity" the use of any weapon or dangerous device.

Redefines "engage in terrorist activity" to mean, in an individual capacity or as a member of an organization, to: (1) commit or to incite to commit, under circumstances indicating an intention to cause death or serious bodily injury, a terrorist activity; (2) prepare or plan a terrorist activity; (3) gather information on potential targets for terrorist activity; (4) solicit funds or other things of value for a terrorist activity or a terrorist organization (with an exception for lack of knowledge); (5) solicit any individual to engage in prohibited conduct or for terrorist organization membership (with an exception for lack of knowledge); or (6) commit an act that the actor knows, or reasonably should know, affords material support, including a safe house, transportation, communications, funds, transfer of funds or other material financial benefit, false documentation or identification, weapons (including chemical, biological, or radiological weapons), explosives, or training for the commission of a terrorist activity; to any individual who the actor knows or reasonably should know has committed or plans to commit a terrorist activity; or to a terrorist organization (with an exception for lack of knowledge).

Defines "terrorist organization" as a group: (1) designated under the Immigration and Nationality Act or by the Secretary of State; or (2) a group of two or more individuals, whether related or not, which engages in terrorist-related activities.

Provides for the retroactive application of amendments under this Act. Stipulates that an alien shall not be considered inadmissible or deportable because of a relationship to an organization that was not designated as a terrorist organization prior to enactment of this Act. States that the amendments under this section shall apply to all aliens in exclusion or deportation proceedings on or after the date of enactment of this Act.

Directs the Secretary of State to notify specified congressional leaders seven days prior to designating an organization as a terrorist organization. Provides for organization redesignation or revocation.

(Sec. 412) Provides for mandatory detention until removal from the United States (regardless of any relief from removal) of an alien certified by the Attorney General as a suspected terrorist or threat to national security. Requires release of such alien after seven days if removal proceedings have not commenced, or the alien has not been charged with a criminal offense. Authorizes detention for additional periods of up to six months of an alien not likely to be deported in the reasonably foreseeable future only if release will threaten U.S. national security or the safety of the community or any person. Limits judicial review to habeas corpus proceedings in the U.S. Supreme Court, the U.S. Court of Appeals for the District of Columbia, or any district court with jurisdiction to entertain a habeas corpus petition. Restricts to the U.S. Court of Appeals for the District of Columbia the right of appeal of any final order by a circuit or district judge.

(Sec. 413) Authorizes the Secretary of State, on a reciprocal basis, to share criminal- and terrorist-related visa lookout information with foreign governments.

(Sec. 414) Declares the sense of Congress that the Attorney General should: (1) fully implement the integrated entry and exit data system for airports, seaports, and land border ports of entry with all deliberate speed; and (2) begin immediately establishing the Integrated Entry and Exit Data System Task Force. Authorizes appropriations.

Requires the Attorney General and the Secretary of State, in developing the integrated entry and exit data system, to focus on the use of biometric technology and the development of tamper-resistant documents readable at ports of entry.

(Sec. 415) Amends the Immigration and Naturalization Service Data Management Improvement Act of 2000 to include the Office of Homeland Security in the Integrated Entry and Exit Data System Task Force.

(Sec. 416) Directs the Attorney General to implement fully and expand the foreign student monitoring program to include other approved educational institutions like air flight, language training, or vocational schools.

(Sec. 417) Requires audits and reports on implementation of the mandate for machine readable passports.

(Sec. 418) Directs the Secretary of State to: (1) review how consular officers issue visas to determine if consular shopping is a problem; and (2) if it is a problem, take steps to address it, and report on them to Congress.

Subtitle C: Preservation of Immigration Benefits for Victims of Terrorism

Authorizes the Attorney General to provide permanent resident status through the special immigrant program to an alien (and spouse, child, or grandparent under specified circumstances) who was the beneficiary of a petition filed on or before September 11, 2001, to grant the alien permanent residence as an employer-sponsored immigrant or of an application for labor certification if the petition or application was rendered null because of the disability of the beneficiary or loss of employment due to physical damage to, or destruction of, the business of the petitioner or applicant as a direct result of the terrorist attacks on September 11, 2001 (September attacks), or because of the death of the petitioner or applicant as a direct result of such attacks.

(Sec. 422) States that an alien who was legally in a nonimmigrant status and was disabled as a direct result of the September attacks may remain in the United States until his or her normal status termination date or September, 11, 2002. Includes in such extension the spouse or child of such an alien or of an alien who was killed in such attacks. Authorizes employment during such period.

Extends specified immigration-related deadlines and other filing requirements for an alien (and spouse and child) who was directly prevented from meeting such requirements as a result of the September attacks respecting: (1) nonimmigrant status and status revision; (2) diversity immigrants; (3) immigrant visas; (4) parolees; and (5) voluntary departure.

(Sec. 423) Waives, under specified circumstances, the requirement that an alien spouse (and child) of a U.S. citizen must have been married for at least two years prior to such citizen's death in order to maintain immediate relative status if such citizen died as a direct result of the September attacks. Provides for: (1) continued family-sponsored immigrant eligibility for the spouse, child, or unmarried son or daughter of a permanent resident who died as a direct result of such attacks; and (2) continued eligibility for adjustment of status for the spouse and child of an employment-based immigrant who died similarly.

(Sec. 424) Amends the Immigration and Nationality Act to extend the visa categorization of "child" for aliens with petitions filed on or before September 11, 2001, for aliens whose 21st birthday is in September 2001 (90 days), or after September 2001 (45 days).

(Sec. 425) Authorizes the Attorney General to provide temporary administrative relief to an alien who, as of September, 10, 2001, was lawfully in the United States and was the spouse, parent, or child of an individual who died or was disabled as a direct result of the September attacks.

(Sec. 426) Directs the Attorney General to establish evidentiary guidelines for death, disability, and loss of employment or destruction of business in connection with the provisions of this subtitle.

(Sec. 427) Prohibits benefits to terrorists or their family members.

Title V: Removing Obstacles to Investigating Terrorism

Authorizes the Attorney General to pay rewards from available funds pursuant to public advertisements for assistance to DOJ to combat terrorism and defend the Nation against terrorist acts, in accordance with procedures and regulations established or issued by the Attorney General, subject to specified conditions, including a prohibition against any such reward of $250,000 or more from being made or offered without the personal approval of either the Attorney General or the President.

(Sec. 502) Amends the State Department Basic Authorities Act of 1956 to modify the Department of State rewards program to authorize rewards for information leading to: (1) the dismantling of a terrorist organization in whole or significant part; and (2) the identification or location of an individual who holds a key leadership position in a terrorist organization. Raises the limit on rewards if the Secretary State determines that a larger sum is necessary to combat terrorism or defend the Nation against terrorist acts.

(Sec. 503) Amends the DNA Analysis Backlog Elimination Act of 2000 to qualify a Federal terrorism offense for collection of DNA for identification.

(Sec. 504) Amends FISA to authorize consultation among Federal law enforcement officers regarding information acquired from an electronic surveillance or physical search in terrorism and related investigations or protective measures.

(Sec. 505) Allows the FBI to request telephone toll and transactional records, financial records, and consumer reports in any investigation to protect against international terrorism or clandestine intelligence activities only if the investigation is not conducted solely on the basis of activities protected by the first amendment to the U.S. Constitution.

(Sec. 506) Revises U.S. Secret Service jurisdiction with respect to fraud and related activity in connection with computers. Grants the FBI primary authority to investigate specified fraud and computer-related activity for cases involving espionage, foreign counter-intelligence, information protected against unauthorized disclosure for reasons of national defense or foreign relations, or restricted data, except for offenses affecting Secret Service duties.

(Sec. 507) Amends the General Education Provisions Act and the National Education Statistics Act of 1994 to provide for disclosure of educational records to the Attorney General in a terrorism investigation or prosecution.

Title VI: Providing for Victims of Terrorism, Public Safety Officers, and Their Families

Subtitle A: Aid to Families of Public Safety Officers

Provides for expedited payments for: (1) public safety officers involved in the prevention, investigation, rescue, or recovery efforts related to a terrorist attack; and

(2) heroic public safety officers. Increases Public Safety Officers Benefit Program payments.

Subtitle B: Amendments to the Victims of Crime Act of 1984

Amends the Victims of Crime Act of 1984 to: (1) revise provisions regarding the allocation of funds for compensation and assistance, location of compensable crime, and the relationship of crime victim compensation to means-tested Federal benefit programs and to the September 11th victim compensation fund; and (2) establish an antiterrorism emergency reserve in the Victims of Crime Fund.

Title VII: Increased Information Sharing for Critical Infrastructure Protection

Amends the Omnibus Crime Control and Safe Streets Act of 1968 to extend Bureau of Justice Assistance regional information sharing system grants to systems that enhance the investigation and prosecution abilities of participating Federal, State, and local law enforcement agencies in addressing multi-jurisdictional terrorist conspiracies and activities. Authorizes appropriations.

Title VIII: Strengthening the Criminal Laws against Terrorism

Amends the Federal criminal code to prohibit specific terrorist acts or otherwise destructive, disruptive, or violent acts against mass transportation vehicles, ferries, providers, employees, passengers, or operating systems.

(Sec. 802) Amends the Federal criminal code to: (1) revise the definition of "international terrorism" to include activities that appear to be intended to affect the conduct of government by mass destruction; and (2) define "domestic terrorism" as activities that occur primarily within U.S. jurisdiction, that involve criminal acts dangerous to human life, and that appear to be intended to intimidate or coerce a civilian population, to influence government policy by intimidation or coercion, or to affect government conduct by mass destruction, assassination, or kidnapping.

(Sec. 803) Prohibits harboring any person knowing or having reasonable grounds to believe that such person has committed or to be about to commit a terrorism offense.

(Sec. 804) Establishes Federal jurisdiction over crimes committed at U.S. facilities abroad.

(Sec. 805) Applies the prohibitions against providing material support for terrorism to offenses outside of the United States.

(Sec. 806) Subjects to civil forfeiture all assets, foreign or domestic, of terrorist organizations.

(Sec. 808) Expands: (1) the offenses over which the Attorney General shall have primary investigative jurisdiction under provisions governing acts of terrorism transcending national boundaries; and (2) the offenses included within the definition of the Federal crime of terrorism.

(Sec. 809) Provides that there shall be no statute of limitations for certain terrorism offenses if the commission of such an offense resulted in, or created a foreseeable risk of, death or serious bodily injury to another person.

(Sec. 810) Provides for alternative maximum penalties for specified terrorism crimes.

(Sec. 811) Makes: (1) the penalties for attempts and conspiracies the same as those for terrorism offenses; (2) the supervised release terms for offenses with terrorism predicates any term of years or life; and (3) specified terrorism crimes Racketeer Influenced and Corrupt Organizations statute predicates.

(Sec. 814) Revises prohibitions and penalties regarding fraud and related activity in connection with computers to include specified cyber-terrorism offenses.

(Sec. 816) Directs the Attorney General to establish regional computer forensic laboratories, and to support existing laboratories, to develop specified cyber-security capabilities.

(Sec. 817) Prescribes penalties for knowing possession in certain circumstances of biological agents, toxins, or delivery systems, especially by certain restricted persons. . . .

2001

Source: THOMAS, Library of Congress.

Martin Luther King, Jr. 1929–1968

The son and grandson of Baptist preachers, Martin Luther King, Jr., grew up in a middle-class home in Atlanta. He graduated with a B.A. from Morehouse College, completed ministerial studies at Crozer Theological Seminary, and earned a Ph.D. at Boston University.

After King became a pastor in Montgomery, Alabama, Rosa Parks was arrested for refusing to yield her bus seat to a white man. Her jailing spurred Jo Ann Robinson and the Women's Political Council to initiate the Montgomery Bus Boycott, a yearlong nonviolent protest in that city. King's eloquent leadership of that struggle earned him the national spotlight. By outlawing bus segregation in Montgomery, the Supreme Court gave King an important victory.

After others launched the lunch counter sit-ins of 1960 and the Freedom Rides of 1961, King directed a well-publicized racial protest in Birmingham, Alabama. National television cameras recorded scenes of nonviolent black marchers, including children, being attacked by the fire hoses and police dogs of Birmingham's city government. Arrested, King penned his "Letter from Birmingham Jail." Winning the battle for American public opinion, he successfully pushed business leaders to outlaw segregation in downtown Birmingham.

In August 1963, two hundred fifty thousand protesters heard King deliver "I Have a Dream" at the Lincoln Memorial in Washington, D.C. This electrifying address helped build momentum for the Civil Rights Act of 1964, a sweeping measure that banned racial discrimination in hotels, restaurants, and other public accommodations. King won the Nobel Peace Prize in that same year. In 1965 his march from Selma, Alabama, to Montgomery prompted passage of the Voting Rights Act, which guaranteed African Americans the right to vote.

In 1967 King condemned American participation in the Vietnam War. A previously sympathetic press vilified him for this stance, which also earned the contempt of a once-friendly president.

King also railed against poverty. Planning his most ambitious protest, he envisioned thousands of blacks, Hispanics, Indians, and poor whites converging on the nation's capital. A strike by garbage workers in Memphis diverted him from this effort. After galvanizing supporters with "I've Been to the Mountaintop," he was assassinated the next day.

Unfortunately, King's fame has obscured the contributions of James Farmer, Ella Baker, John Lewis, Fannie Lou Hamer, and others, who, like King, mastered Gandhian strategy in the quest for racial justice.

But King's fiery yet magisterial language convinced whites to tear down the walls of legalized segregation. He triumphed by reviving the slaves' vivid identification with the biblical Hebrews trapped in Egyptian bondage, a strategy especially evident in "I've Been to the Mountaintop." Trained by African American folk preachers, he adopted their assumption that language is a shared treasure, not private property. King often borrowed sermons without acknowledgment from Harry Emerson Fosdick and other liberal preachers. This borrowed material appears in scores of King's published and unpublished addresses and essays, including "Letter from Birmingham Jail," "I Have a Dream," the Nobel Prize Address, and "I've Been to the Mountaintop." By synthesizing black and white pulpit traditions, King persuaded whites to hear the slaves' cry, "Let my people go!"

Keith D. Miller
Arizona State University

PRIMARY WORKS

Stride Toward Freedom: The Montgomery Story, 1958; *Strength to Love,* 1963; *Why We Can't Wait,* 1965; *Where Do We Go from Here? Chaos or Community,* 1967; *A Testament of Hope: The Essential Writings of Martin Luther King, Jr.,* 1986; *The Papers of Martin Luther King, Jr.,* vols. 1–4, 1992, 1994, 1997, 2000.

I Have a Dream

I am happy to join with you today in what will go down in history as the greatest demonstration for freedom in the history of our nation.

Five score years ago a great American in whose symbolic shadow we stand today signed the Emancipation Proclamation.[1] This momentous decree came as a great beacon light of hope to millions of Negro slaves who had been seared in the flames of withering injustice. It came as a joyous daybreak to end the long night of their captivity. But one hundred years later the Negro still is not free. One hundred years later the life of the Negro is still sadly crippled by the manacles of segregation and the chains of discrimination. One hundred years later the Negro lives on a lonely island of poverty in the midst of a vast ocean of material prosperity. One hundred years later the Negro is still languished in the corners of American society and finds himself in exile in his own land. So we've come here today to dramatize a shameful condition.

In a sense we've come to our nation's capital to cash a check. When the architects of our Republic wrote the magnificent words of the Constitution and the Declaration of Independence, they were signing a promissory note to which every American was to fall heir. This note was a promise that all men—yes, black men as well as white men—would be guaranteed the unalienable rights of life, liberty and the pursuit of happiness.[2] It is obvious today that America has defaulted on this promissory note insofar as her citizens of color are concerned. Instead of honoring this sacred obligation, America has given the Negro people a bad check, a check which has come back marked "insufficient funds."

But we refuse to believe that the bank of justice is bankrupt. We refuse to believe that there are insufficient funds in the great vaults of opportunity of this nation. So we've come to cash this check, a check that will give us upon demand the riches of freedom and the security of justice.

We have also come to this hallowed spot to remind America of the fierce urgency of now. This is no time to engage in the luxury of cooling off or to take the tranquilizing drug of gradualism. Now is the time to make real the promises of democracy. Now is the time to rise from the dark and desolate valley of segregation to the sunlit path of racial justice. Now is the time to lift our nation from the quicksands of racial injustice to the solid rock of brotherhood.

---

[1] King delivered this speech on the steps of the Lincoln Memorial, which houses a giant marble statue of Abraham Lincoln, whose Emancipation Proclamation freed American slaves. "Five score years ago . . ." echoes the beginning of Lincoln's famous Gettysburg Address.

[2] The phrase "unalienable rights of life, liberty, and the pursuit of happiness" appears in the Declaration of Independence, written by Thomas Jefferson.

Now is the time to make justice a reality for all of God's children. It would be fatal for the nation to overlook the urgency of the moment. This sweltering summer of the Negro's legitimate discontent[3] will not pass until there is an invigorating autumn of freedom and equality—nineteen sixty-three is not an end but a beginning. Those who hope that the Negro needed to blow off steam and will now be content will have a rude awakening if the nation returns to business as usual.

There will be neither rest nor tranquility in America until the Negro is granted his citizenship rights. The whirlwinds of revolt will continue to shake the foundations of our nation until the bright day of justice emerges.

But there is something that I must say to my people who stand on the worn threshold which leads into the palace of justice. In the process of gaining our rightful place we must not be guilty of wrongful deeds. Let us not seek to satisfy our thirst for freedom by drinking from the cup of bitterness and hatred.

We must forever conduct our struggle on the high plane of dignity and discipline. We must not allow our creative protests to degenerate into physical violence. Again and again we must rise to the majestic heights of meeting physical force with soul force.[4] The marvelous new militancy which has engulfed the Negro community must not lead us to a distrust of all white people, for many of our white brothers, as evidenced by their presence here today, have come to realize that their destiny is tied up with our destiny. They have come to realize that their freedom is inextricably bound to our freedom. We cannot walk alone. And as we walk we must make the pledge that we shall always march ahead. We cannot turn back.

There are those who are asking the devotees of civil rights, "When will you be satisfied?"

We can never be satisfied as long as the Negro is the victim of the unspeakable horrors of police brutality.

We can never be satisfied as long as our bodies, heavy with the fatigue of travel, cannot gain lodging in the motels of the highways and the hotels of the cities.[5]

We cannot be satisfied as long as the Negro's basic mobility is from a smaller ghetto to a larger one.[6] We can never be satisfied as long as our children are stripped of their selfhood and robbed of their dignity by signs stating "For Whites Only."

We cannot be satisfied as long as the Negro in Mississippi cannot vote and the Negro in New York believes he has nothing for which to vote.

No, no, we are not satisfied, and we will not be satisfied until justice rolls down like waters and righteousness like a mighty stream.[7]

I am not unmindful that some of you have come here out of great trials and tribulations. Some of you have come fresh from narrow jail cells.[8] Some of you have come from areas where your quest for freedom left you battered by the storms of

---

[3]King turns inside out Shakespeare's "Now is the winter of our discontent/Made glorious summer by this sun of York. . . ." See *Richard III,* Act I, Scene I.

[4]Following the example of Gandhi, King consistently practiced and preached nonviolence, even though his opponents often resorted to violence against him.

[5]Throughout the South most motels and hotels were reserved for whites only.

[6]Throughout much of the nation blacks experienced racial discrimination in housing.

[7]This statement includes a renowned biblical declaration from the Hebrew prophet Amos ("Let justice roll down . . ."). See Amos 5:24.

[8]Violating local laws, King and other civil rights protesters voluntarily went to jail to dramatize their cause.

persecution and staggered by the winds of police brutality. You have been the veterans of creative suffering.

Continue to work with the faith that unearned suffering is redemptive. Go back to Mississippi, go back to Alabama, go back to South Carolina, go back to Georgia, go back to Louisiana, go back to the slums and ghettos of our Northern cities, knowing that somehow this situation can and will be changed. Let us not wallow in the valley of despair.

I say to you today, my friends, so even though we face the difficulties of today and tomorrow, I still have a dream. It is a dream deeply rooted in the American dream. I have a dream that one day this nation will rise up, live out the true meaning of its creed: "We hold these truths to be self-evident, that all men are created equal."[9]

I have a dream that one day on the red hills of Georgia sons of former slaves and the sons of former slave-owners will be able to sit down together at the table of brotherhood. I have a dream that one day even the state of Mississippi, a state sweltering with the heat of injustice, sweltering with the heat of oppression, will be transformed into an oasis of freedom and justice.

I have a dream that my four little children will one day live in a nation where they will not be judged by the color of their skin but by the content of their character. I have a dream today. I have a dream that one day down in Alabama, with its vicious racists, with its governor having his lips dripping with the words of interposition and nullification,[10] one day right there in Alabama little black boys and black girls will be able to join hands with little white boys and white girls as sisters and brothers.

I have a dream today. I have a dream that one day every valley shall be exalted, every hill and mountain shall be made low. The rough places will be made plain, and the crooked places will be made straight. And the glory of the Lord shall be revealed, and all flesh shall see it together.[11] This is our hope. This is the faith that I go back to the South with. With this faith we will be able to hew out of the mountain of despair a stone of hope. With this faith we will be able to transform the jangling discords of our nation into a beautiful symphony of brotherhood. With this faith we will be able to work together, to pray together, to struggle together, to go to jail together, to stand up for freedom together, knowing that we will be free one day.

This will be the day, this will be the day when all of God's children will be able to sing with new meaning, "My country, 'tis of thee, sweet land of liberty, of thee I sing. Land where my fathers died, land of the pilgrim's pride, from every mountainside, let freedom ring."[12] And if America is to be a great nation, this must become true. So let freedom ring from the prodigious hilltops of New Hampshire. Let freedom ring from the mighty mountains of New York. Let freedom ring from the

[9]"We hold these truths . . ." is the most famous sentence of the Declaration of Independence.

[10]Governor George Wallace of Alabama attempted to interpose state authority to nullify federal orders to integrate his state.

[11]This passage incorporates visionary language from the Hebrew prophet Isaiah ("Every valley shall be exalted . . .") that reappears in the Christian New Testament. Handel includes it in the *Messiah,* a popular, long piece of Christian music. See Isaiah 40:4 and Luke 3:5. Biblical quotations remind listeners of King's status as a minister.

[12]These are the opening lines of "America," our unofficial national anthem. King's use of the phrase "Let freedom ring" seems to extend the lyrics of the song.

heightening Alleghenies of Pennsylvania. Let freedom ring from the snowcapped Rockies of Colorado. Let freedom ring from the curvaceous slopes of California.

But not only that. Let freedom ring from Stone Mountain of Georgia. Let freedom ring from Lookout Mountain of Tennessee. Let freedom ring from every hill and molehill of Mississippi, from every mountainside.[13] Let freedom ring.

And when this happens, when we allow freedom [to] ring—when we let it ring from every village and every hamlet, from every state and every city, we will be able to speed up that day when all of God's children, black men and white men, Jews and Gentiles, Protestants and Catholics, will be able to join hands and sing in the words of the old Negro spiritual, "Free at last, Free at last, Thank God a-mighty, We are free at last."

1963

Letter from Birmingham Jail

April 16, 1963

My Dear Fellow Clergymen:

While confined here in the Birmingham city jail, I came across your recent statement calling my present activities "unwise and untimely." Seldom do I pause to answer criticism of my work and ideas. If I sought to answer all the criticisms that cross my desk, my secretaries would have little time for anything other than such correspondence in the course of the day, and I would have no time for constructive work. But since I feel that you are men of genuine good will and that your criticisms are sincerely set forth, I want to try to answer your statement in what I hope will be patient and reasonable terms.

I think I should indicate why I am here in Birmingham, since you have been influenced by the view which argues against "outsiders coming in." I have the honor of serving as president of the Southern Christian Leadership Conference, an organization operating in every southern state, with headquarters in Atlanta, Georgia. We have some eighty-five affiliated organizations across the South, and one of them is the Alabama Christian Movement for Human Rights. Frequently we share staff, educational, and financial resources with our affiliates. Several months ago the affiliate here in Birmingham asked us to be on call to engage in a nonviolent direct-action program if such were deemed necessary. We readily consented, and when the hour came we lived

---

[13]King borrowed and adapted the "Let freedom ring "litany from a speech at the 1952 Republican Convention by Archibald Carey, an African American minister from Chicago and friend of King.

up to our promise. So I, along with several members of my staff, am here because I was invited here. I am here because I have organizational ties here.

But more basically, I am in Birmingham because injustice is here. Just as the prophets of the eighth century b.c. left their villages and carried their "thus saith the Lord" far beyond the boundaries of their home towns, and just as the Apostle Paul[1] left his village of Tarsus and carried the gospel of Jesus Christ to the far corners of the Greco-Roman world, so am I compelled to carry the gospel of freedom beyond my own home town. Like Paul, I must constantly respond to the Macedonian call for aid.

Moreover, I am cognizant of the interrelatedness of all communities and states. I cannot sit idly by in Atlanta and not be concerned about what happens in Birmingham. Injustice anywhere is a threat to justice everywhere. We are caught in an inescapable network of mutuality, tied in a single garment of destiny. Whatever affects one directly, affects all indirectly. Never again can we afford to live with the narrow, provincial, "outside agitator" idea. Anyone who lives inside the United States can never be considered an outsider anywhere within its bounds.

You deplore the demonstrations taking place in Birmingham. But your statement, I am sorry to say, fails to express an similar concern for the conditions that brought about the demonstrations. I am sure that none of you would want to rest content with the superficial kind of social analysis that deals merely with the effects and does not grapple with underlying causes. It is unfortunate that demonstrations are taking place in Birmingham, but it is even more unfortunate that the city's white power structure left the Negro community with no alternative.

In any nonviolent campaign there are four basic steps: collection of the facts to determine whether injustices exist; negotiation; self-purification; and direct action. We have gone through all these steps in Birmingham. There can be no gainsaying the fact that racial injustice engulfs this community. Birmingham is probably the most thoroughly segregated city in the United States. Its ugly record of brutality is widely known. Negroes have experienced grossly unjust treatment in the courts. There have been more unsolved bombings of Negro homes and churches in Birmingham than in any other city in the nation. These are the hard brutal facts of the case. On the basis of these conditions, Negro leaders sought to negotiate with the city fathers. But the latter consistently refused to engage in good-faith negotiation.

Then, last September, came the opportunity to talk with leaders of Birmingham's economic community. In the course of the negotiations, certain promises were made by the merchants—for example, to remove the stores' humiliating racial signs. On the basis of these promises, the Reverend Fred Shuttlesworth[2] and the leaders of the Alabama Christian Movement for Human Rights agreed to a moratorium on all demonstrations. As the weeks and months went by, we realized that we were the victims of a broken promise. A few signs, briefly removed, returned; the others remained.

---

[1]*Paul:* Saint Paul, originally Saul of Tarsus, was a follower of Jesus who went on a mission after seeing a vision that the Macedonian people needed his help. Martin Luther King is also following in Paul's tradition as a writer of inspirational letters.

[2]*Reverend Fred Shuttlesworth:* Fred Shuttlesworth (b. 1922) was a civil rights activist who fought against segregation.

As in so many past experiences, our hopes had been blasted, and the shadows of deep disappointment settled upon us. We had no alternative except to prepare for direct action, whereby we would present our very bodies as a means of laying our case before the conscience of the local and the national community. Mindful of the difficulties involved, we decided to undertake a process of self-purification. We began a series of workshops on nonviolence, and we repeatedly asked ourselves: "Are you able to accept blows without retaliating?" "Are you able to endure the ordeal of jail?" We decided to schedule our direct-action program for the Easter season, realizing that except for Christmas, this is the main shopping period of the year. Knowing that a strong economic-withdrawal program would be the by-product of direct action, we felt that this would be the best time to bring pressure to bear on the merchants for the needed change.

Then it occurred to us that Birmingham's mayoral election was coming up in March, and we speedily decided to postpone action until after election day. When we discovered that the Commissioner of Public Safety, Eugene "Bull" Connor, had piled up enough votes to be in the run-off, we decided again to postpone action until the day after the run-off so that the demonstration could not be used to cloud the issues. Like many others, we waited to see Mr. Connor defeated, and to this end we endured postponement after postponement. Having aided in this community need, we felt that our direct-action program could be delayed no longer.

You may well ask, "Why direct action? Why sit-ins, marches, and so forth? Isn't 10 negotiation a better path?" You are quite right in calling for negotiation. Indeed, this is the very purpose of direct action. Nonviolent direct action seeks to create such a crisis and foster such a tension that a community which has constantly refused to negotiate is forced to confront the issue. It seeks so to dramatize the issue that it can no longer be ignored. My citing the creation of tension as part of the work of the non-violent resister may sound rather shocking. But I must confess that I am not afraid of the word "tension." I have earnestly opposed violent tension, but there is a type of constructive, non-violent tension which is necessary for growth. Just as Socrates felt that it was necessary to create a tension in the mind so that individuals could rise from the bondage of myths and half truths to the unfettered realm of creative analysis and objective appraisal, so must we see the need for nonviolent gadflies to create the kind of tension in society that will help men rise from the dark depths of prejudice and racism to the majestic heights of understanding and brotherhood.

The purpose of our direct-action program is to create a situation so crisis-packed that it will inevitably open the door to negotiation. I therefore concur with you in your call for negotiation. Too long has our beloved Southland been bogged down in a tragic effort to live in monologue rather than dialogue.

One of the basic points in your statement is that the action that I and my associates have taken in Birmingham is untimely. Some have asked: "Why didn't you give the new city administration time to act?" The only answer that I can give to this query is that the new Birmingham administration most be prodded about as much as the outgoing one, before it will act. We are sadly mistaken if we feel that the election of Albert Boutwell as mayor will bring the millennium to Birmingham. While Mr. Boutwell is a much more gentle person than Mr. Connor, they are both segregationists, dedicated to maintenance of the status quo. I have hoped that Mr. Boutwell will be reasonable enough to see the futility of massive resistance to desegregation. But he will not see this without pressure from devotees of civil rights. My friends, I must say to you that we have not made a single gain in civil rights without determined legal and nonviolent pressure. Lamentably, it is an historical fact that privileged groups seldom give up their privileges voluntarily. Individuals may see the moral light and voluntarily give up their unjust posture; but, as Reinhold Niebuhr[3] has reminded us, groups tend to be more immoral than individuals.

We know through painful experience that freedom is never voluntarily given by the oppressor; it must be demanded by the oppressed. Frankly, I have yet to engage in a direct-action campaign that was "well timed" in the view of those who have not suffered unduly from the disease of segregation. For years now I have heard the word "Wait!" It rings in the ear of every Negro with piercing familiarity. This "Wait" has almost always meant "Never." We must come to see, with one of our distinguished jurists, that "justice too long delayed is justice denied."

We have waited for more than 340 years for our constitutional and God-given rights. The nations of Asia and Africa are moving with jet-like speed toward gaining political independence, but we still creep at horse-and-buggy pace toward gaining a cup of coffee at a lunch counter. Perhaps it is easy for those who have never felt the stinging darts of segregation to say, "Wait." But when you have seen vicious mobs lynch your mothers and fathers at will and drown your sisters and brothers at whim; when you have seen hate-filled policemen curse, kick, and even kill your black brothers and sisters; when you see the vast majority of your twenty million Negro brothers smothering in an airtight cage of poverty in the midst of an affluent society; when you suddenly find your tongue twisted and your speech stammering as you seek to explain to your six-year-old daughter why she can't go to the public amusement park that has just been advertised on television, and see tears welling up in her eyes when she is told that Funtown is closed to colored children, and see ominous clouds of inferiority beginning to form in her little mental sky, and see her beginning to distort her personality by developing an unconscious bitterness toward white people; when you have to concoct an answer for a five-year-old son who is asking, "Daddy, why do white people treat colored people so mean?"; when you take a cross-country drive and find it necessary to sleep night after night in the uncomfortable corners of your automobile because no motel will accept you; when you are humiliated day in and day out by nagging signs reading "white" and "colored"; when your first name becomes "nigger," and your middle name becomes "boy" (however old you are) and your last name becomes "John," and your wife and mother are never given the respected title "Mrs."; when you are harried by day and haunted by night by the fact that you are a Negro, living constantly at tiptoe stance, never quite knowing what to expect next, and are plagued with inner fears and outer resentments; when you are forever fighting a degenerating sense of "nobodiness"—then you will understand why we find it difficult to wait. There comes a time when the cup of endurance runs over, and men are no longer willing to be plunged into the abyss of despair. I hope, sirs, you can understand our legitimate and unavoidable impatience.

---

[3]*Reinhold Niebuhr:* Reinhold Niebuhr (1892–1971) was a Protestant theologian and philosopher who attempted to reconcile Christianity and pacifism with the need to fight against injustice.

You express a great deal of anxiety over our willingness to break laws. This is certainly a legitimate concern. Since we so diligently urge people to obey the Supreme Court's decision of 1954 outlawing segregation in the public schools, at first glance it may seem rather paradoxical for us consciously to break laws. One may well ask: "How can you advocate breaking some laws and obeying others?" The answer lies in the fact that there are two types of laws: just and unjust. I would be the first to advocate obeying just laws. One has not only a legal but a moral responsibility to obey just laws. Conversely, one has a moral responsibility to disobey unjust laws. I would agree with St. Augustine that "an unjust law is no law at all."

Now, what is the difference between the two? How does one determine whether a law is just or unjust? A just law is a man-made code that squares with the moral law or the law of God. An unjust law is a code that is out of harmony with the moral law. To put it in the terms of St. Thomas Aquinas: An unjust law is a human law that is not rooted in eternal law and natural law. Any law that uplifts human personality is just. Any law that degrades human personality is unjust. All segregation statutes are unjust because segregation distorts the soul and damages the personality. It gives the segregator a false sense of superiority and the segregated a false sense of inferiority. Segregation, to use the terminology of the Jewish philosopher Martin Buber, substitutes an "I-it" relationship for an "I-thou" relationship and ends up relegating persons to the status of things. Hence segregation is not only politically, economically, and sociologically unsound, it is morally wrong and sinful. Paul Tillich has said that sin is separation. Is not segregation an existential expression of man's tragic separation, his awful estrangement, his terrible sinfullness? Thus it is that I can urge men to obey the 1954 decision of the Supreme Court, for it is morally right; and I can urge them to disobey segregation ordinances, for they are morally wrong.

Let us consider a more concrete example of just and unjust laws. An unjust law is a code that a numerical or power majority group compels a minority group to obey but does not make binding on itself. This is *difference* made legal. By the same token, a just law is a code that a majority compels a minority to follow and that it is willing to follow itself. This is *sameness* made legal.

Let me give another explanation. A law is unjust if it is inflicted on a minority that, as a result of being denied the right to vote, had no part in enacting or devising the law. Who can say that the legislature of Alabama which set up that state's segregation laws was democratically elected? Throughout Alabama all sorts of devious methods are used to prevent Negroes from becoming registered voters, and there are some counties in which, even though Negroes constitute a majority of the population, not a single Negro is registered. Can any law enacted under such circumstances be considered democratically structured?

Sometimes a law is just on its face and unjust in its application. For instance, I have been arrested on a charge of parading without a permit. Now, there is nothing wrong in having an ordinance which requires a permit for a parade. But such ordinance becomes unjust when it is used to maintain segregation and to deny citizens the First Amendment privilege of peaceful assembly and protest.

I hope you are able to see the distinction I am trying to point out. In no sense do I advocate evading or defying the law, as would the rabid segregationist. That would lead to anarchy. One who breaks an unjust law must do so openly, lovingly, and with a willingness to accept the penalty. I submit that an individual who breaks a law that conscience tells him is unjust, and who willingly accepts the penalty of imprisonment in order to arouse the conscience of the community over its injustice, is in reality expressing the highest respect for law.

Of course, there is nothing new about this kind of civil disobedience. It was evidenced sublimely in the refusal of Shadrach, Meshach, and Abednego to obey the laws of Nebuchadnezzar,[4] on the ground that a higher moral law was at stake. It was practiced superbly by the early Christians, who were willing to face hungry lions and the excruciating pain of chopping blocks rather than submit to certain unjust laws of the Roman Empire. To a degree, academic freedom is a reality today because Socrates practiced civil disobedience. In our own nation, the Boston Tea Party represented a massive act of civil disobdience.

We should never forget that everything Adolf Hitler did in Germany was "legal" and everything the Hungarian freedom fighters did in Hungary was "illegal." It was "illegal" to aid and comfort a Jew in Hitler's Germany. Even so, I am sure that, had I lived in Germany at the time, I would have aided and comforted my Jewish brothers. If today I lived in a Communist country where certain principles dear to the Christian faith are suppressed, I would openly advocate disobeying that country's antireligious laws.

I must make two honest confessions to you, my Christian and Jewish brothers. First, I must confess that over the past few years I have been gravely disappointed with the white moderate. I have almost reached the regrettable conclusion that the Negro's great stumbling block in his stride toward freedom is not the White Citizen's Counciler or the Ku Klux Klanner, but the white moderate, who is more devoted to "order" than to justice, who prefer a negative peace which is the absence of tension to a positive peace which is the presence of justice; who constantly says, "I agree with you in the goal you seek, but I cannot agree with your methods of direct action"; who paternalistically believes he can set the timetable for another man's freedom; who lives by a mythical concept of time and who constantly advises the Negro to wait for a "more convenient season." Shallow understanding from people of good will is more frustrating than absolute misunderstanding from people of ill will. Lukewarm acceptance is much more bewildering than outright rejection.

I had hoped that the white moderate would understand that law and order exist for the purpose of establishing justice and that when they fail in this purpose they become the dangerously structured dams that block the flow of social progress. I had hoped that the white moderate would understand that the present tension in the South is a necessary phase of the transition from an obnoxious negative peace, in which the Negro passively accepted his unjust plight, to a substantive and positive peace, in which all men will respect the dignity and worth of human personality. Actually, we who engage in nonviolent direct action are not the creators of tension. We bring it out in the open, where it can be seen and dealt with. Like a boil that can never be cured so long as it is covered up but must be opened with all its ugliness to the natural medicines of air and light, injustices must be exposed, with all the tension

[4]*Nebuchadnezzar:* A leader of Babylon who helped build his empire through conquests of Jerusalem and Judah. In the Book of Daniel, he ordered Shadrach, Meshach, and Abednego to worship a golden idol, and when they refused, he threw them into a furnace, but they were miraculously unharmed.

its exposure creates, to the light of human conscience and the air of national opinion, before it can be cured.

In your statement you assert that our actions, even though peaceful, must be condemned because they precipitate violence. But is this a logical assertion? Isn't this like condemning a robbed man because his possession of money precipitated the evil act of robbery? Isn't this like condemning Socrates because his unswerving commitment to truth and his philosophical inquiries precipitated the act by the misguided populace in which they made him drink hemlock? Isn't this like condemning Jesus because his unique God-consciousness and never-ceasing devotion to God's will precipitated the evil act of crucifixion? We must come to see that, as the federal courts have consistently affirmed, it is wrong to urge an individual to cease his efforts to gain his basic constitutional rights because the quest may precipitate violence. Society must protect the robbed and punish the robber.

I had also hoped that the white moderate would reject the myth concerning time in relation to the struggle for freedom. I have just received a letter from a white brother in Texas. He writes: "All Christians know that the colored people will receive equal rights eventually, but it is possible that you are in too great a religious hurry. It has taken Christianity almost two thousand years to accomplish what it has. The teachings of Christ take time to come to earth." Such an attitude stems from a tragic misconception of time, from the strangely irrational notion that there is something in the very flow of time that will inevitably cure all ills. Actually, time itself is neutral; it can be used either destructively or constructively. More and more I feel that the people of ill will have used time much more effectively than have the people of good will. We will have to repent in this generation not merely for the hateful words and actions of the bad people, but for the appalling silence of the good people. Human progress never rolls in on wheels inevitability; it comes through the tireless efforts of men willing to be co-workers with God, and without this hard work, time itself becomes an ally of the forces of social stagnation. We must use time creatively, in the knowledge that the time is always ripe to do right. Now is the time to make real the promise of democracy and transform our pending national elegy into a creative psalm of brotherhood. Now is the time to lift our national policy from the quicksand of racial injustice to the solid rock of human dignity.

You speak of our activity in Birmingham as extreme. At first I was rather disappointed that fellow clergymen would see my nonviolent efforts as those of an extremist. I began thinking about the fact that I stand in the middle of two opposing forces in the Negro community. One is a force of complacency made up in part of Negroes who, as a result of long years of oppression, are so drained of self-respect and a sense of "somebodiness" that they have adjusted to segregation; and in part of a few middle-class Negroes who, because of a degree of academic and economic security and because in some ways they profit by segregation, have become insensitive to the problems of the masses. The other force is one of bitterness and hatred, and it comes perilously close to advocating violence. It is expressed in the various black nationalist groups that are springing up across the nation, the largest and best known being Elijah Muhammad's Muslim movement. Nourished by the Negro's frustration over the continued existence of racial discrimination, this movement is made up of people who have lost faith in America, who have absolutely repudiated Christianity, and who have concluded that the white man is an incorrigible "devil."

I have tried to stand between these two forces, saying that we need emulate neither the "do-nothingism" of the complacent nor the hatred and despair of the black nationalist. For there is the more excellent way of love and nonviolent protest. I am grateful to God that, through the influence of the Negro church, the way of nonviolence became an integral part of our struggle.

If this philosophy had not emerged, by now many streets of the South would, I am convinced, be flowing with blood. And I am further convinced that if our white brothers dismiss as "rabble rousers" and "outside agitators" those of us who employ nonviolent direct action, and if they refuse to support our nonviolent efforts, millions of Negroes will, out of frustration and despair, seek solace and security in black nationalist ideologies—a development that would inevitably lead to a frightening racial nightmare.

Oppressed people cannot remain oppressed forever. The yearning for freedom 30 eventually manifests itself, and that is what has happened to the American Negro. Something within has reminded him of his birthright of freedom, and something without has reminded him that it can be gained. Consciously or unconsciously, he has been caught up by the Zeitgeist,[5] and with his black brothers of Africa and his brown and yellow brothers of Asia, South America, and the Caribbean, the United States Negro is moving with a sense of great urgency toward the promised land of racial justice. If one recognizes this vital urge that has engulfed the Negro community, one should readily understand why public demonstrations are taking place. The Negro has many pent-up resentments and latent frustrations, and he must release them. So let him march; let him make prayer pilgrimages to the city hall, let him go on freedom rides—and try to understand why he must do so. If his repressed emotions are not released in nonviolent ways, they will seek expression through violence; this is not a threat but a fact of history. So I have not said to my people, "Get rid of your discontent." Rather, I have tried to say that this normal and healthy discontent can be channeled into the creative outlet of nonviolent direct action. And now this approach is being termed extremist.

But though I was initially disappointed at being categorized as an extremist, as I continued to think about the matter I gradually gained a measure of satisfaction from the label. Was not Jesus an extremist for love: "Love your enemies, bless them that curse you, do good to them that hate you, and pray for them which despitefully use you, and persecute you." Was not Amos an extremist for justice: "Let justice roll down like waters and righteousness like an ever-flowing stream." Was not Paul an extremist for the Christian gospel: "I bear in my body the marks of the Lord Jesus." Was not Martin Luther[6] an extremist: "Here I stand; I cannot do otherwise, so help me God." And John Bunyan:[7] "I will stay in jail to the end of my days before I make a butchery of my conscience." And Abraham Lincoln: "This nation cannot survive half slave and half free." And Thomas Jefferson: "We hold these truths to be self-

[5]*Zeitgeist:* Spirit of the times (German).
[6]*Martin Luther:* Martin Luther (1483–1546) was a German monk and religious dissident whose "95 Theses" nailed to a church door in 1517 marked the beginning of the Protestant Reformation in Europe.

[7]*John Bunyan:* John Bunyan (1628–1688) was an English writer and preacher who wrote *Pilgrim's Progress* (published in 1678 and 1684), a highly influential Christian allegory.

evident, that all men are created equal. . . ." So the question is not whether we will be extremists, but what kind of extremists we will be. Will we be extremists for hate or for love? Will we be extremists for the preservation of injustice or for the extension of justice? In that dramatic scene on Calvary's hill three men were crucified. We must never forget that all three were crucified for the same crime—the crime of extremism. Two were extremists for immorality, and thus fell below their environment. The other, Jesus Christ, was an extremist for love, truth, and goodness, and thereby rose above his environment. Perhaps the South, the nation, and the world are in dire need of creative extremists.

I had hoped that the white moderate would see this need. Perhaps I was too optimistic; perhaps I expected too much. I suppose I should have realized that few members of the oppressor race can understand the deep groans and passionate yearnings of the oppressed race, and still fewer have the vision to see that injustice must be rooted out by strong, persistent, and determined action. I am thankful, however, that some of our white brothers in the South have grasped the meaning of this social revolution and committed themselves to it. They are still all too few in quantity, but they are big in quality. Some—such as Ralph McGill, Lillian Smith, Harry Golden, James McBride Dabbs, Ann Braden, and Sarah Patton Boyle—have written about our struggle in eloquent and prophetic terms. Others have marched with us down nameless streets of the South. They have languished in filthy, roach-infested jails, suffering the abuse and brutality of policemen who view them as "dirty nigger-lovers." Unlike so many of their moderate brothers and sisters, they have recognized the urgency of the moment and sensed the need for powerful "action" antidotes to combat the disease of segregation.

Let me take note of my other major disappointment. I have been so greatly disappointed with the white church and its leadership. Of course, there are some notable exceptions. I am not unmindful of the fact that each of you has taken some significant stands on this issue. I commend you, Reverend Stallings, for your Christian stand on this past Sunday, in welcoming Negroes to your worship service on a non-segregated basis. I commend the Catholic leaders of this state for integrating Spring Hill College[8] several years ago.

But despite these notable exceptions, I must honestly reiterate that I have been disappointed with the church. I do not say this as one of those negative critics who can always find something wrong with the church. I say this as a minister of the gospel, who loves the church; who was nurtured in its bosom; who has been sustained by its spiritual blessings and who will remain true to it as long as the cord of life shall lengthen.

When I was suddenly catapulted into the leadership of the bus protest in Montgomery, Alabama, a few years ago, I felt we would be supported by the white church. I felt that the white ministers, priests, and rabbis of the South would be among our strongest allies. Instead, some have been outright opponents, refusing to understand the freedom movement and misrepresenting its leaders; all too many others have been more cautious than courageous and have remained silent behind the anesthetizing security of stained-glass windows.

35

---

[8]*Spring Hill College:* The first Catholic Jesuit college in the South, Spring Hill College (located in Mobile, Alabama) was desegregated in 1954, just before the United States Supreme Court's landmark decision banning segregation.

In spite of my shattered dreams, I came to Birmingham with the hope that the white religious leadership of this community would see the justice of our cause and, with deep moral concerns, would serve as the channel through which our just grievances could reach the power structure. I had hoped that each of you would understand. But again I have been disappointed. . . .

There was a time when the church was very powerful—in the time when the early Christians rejoiced at being deemed worthy to suffer for what they believed. In those days the church was not merely a thermometer that recorded the ideas and principles of popular opinion; it was a thermostat that transformed the mores of society. Whenever the early Christians entered a town, the people in power became disturbed and immediately sought to convict the Christians for being "disturbers of the peace" and "outside agitators." But the Christians pressed on, in the conviction that they were a "colony of heaven," called to obey God rather than man. Small in number, they were big in commitment. They were too God intoxicated to be "astronomically intimidated." By their effort and example they brought an end to such ancient evils as infanticide and gladiatorial contests.

Things are different now. So often the contemporary church is a weak, ineffectual voice with an uncertain sound. So often it is an archdefender of the status quo. Far from being disturbed by the presence of the church, the power structure of the average community is consoled by the church's silent—and often even vocal—sanction of things as they are.

But the judgment of God is upon the church as never before. If today's church does not recapture the sacrificial spirit of the early church, it will lose its authenticity, forfeit the loyalty of millions, and be dismissed as an irrelevant social club with no meaning for the twentieth century. Every day I meet young people whose disappointment with the church has turned into outright disgust.

Perhaps I have once again been too optimistic. Is organized religion too inextri- 40 cably bound to the status quo to save our nation and the world? Perhaps I must turn my faith to the inner spiritual church, the church within the church, as the true ekklesia and the hope of the world. But again I am thankful to God that some noble souls from the ranks of organized religion have broken loose from the paralyzing chains of conformity and joined us as active partners in the struggle for freedom. They have left their secure congregations and walked the streets of Albany, Georgia, with us. They have gone down the highways of the South on torturous rides for freedom. Yes, they have gone to jail with us. Some have been dismissed from their churches, have lost the support of their bishops and fellow ministers. But they have acted in the faith that right defeated is strong than evil triumphant. Their witness has been the spiritual salt that has preserved the true meaning of the gospel in these troubled times. They have carved a tunnel of hope through the dark mountain of disappointment.

I hope the church as a whole will meet the challenge of this decisive hour. But even if the church does not come to the aid of justice, I have no despair about the future. I have no fear about the outcome of our struggle in Birmingham, even if our motives are at present misunderstood. We will reach the goal of freedom in Birmingham and all over the nation, because the goal of America is freedom. Abused and scorned though we may be, our destiny is tied up with America's destiny. Before the pilgrims landed at Plymouth, we were here. Before the pen of Jefferson etched the majestic words of the Declaration of Independence across the pages of history, we were here. For more than two centuries our forebears labored in this country without wages; they made cotton king; they built the homes of their masters while suffering gross injustice and shameful humiliation—and yet out of a bottomless vitality they continued to thrive and develop. If the inexpressible cruelties of slavery could not stop us, the opposition we now face will surely fail. We will win our freedom because the sacred heritage of our nation and the eternal will of God are embodied in our echoing demands.

Before closing I feel impelled to mention one other point in your statement that has troubled me profoundly. You warmly commended the Birmingham police force for keeping "order" and "preventing violence." I doubt that you would have so warmly commended the police force if you had seen its dogs sinking their teeth into unarmed, non-violent Negroes. I doubt that you would so quickly commend the policemen if you were to observe their ugly and inhumane treatment of Negroes here in the city jail; if you were to watch them push and curse old Negro women and young Negro girls; if you were to see them slap and kick old Negro men and young boys; if you were to observe them, as they did on two occasions, refuse to give us food because we wanted to sing our grace together. I cannot join you in your praise of the Birmingham police department.

It is true that the police have exercised a degree of discipline in handling the demonstrations. In this sense they have conducted themselves rather "nonviolently" in public. But for what purpose? To preserve the evil system of segregation. Over the past few years I have consistently preached that nonviolence demands that the means we use must be as pure as the ends we seek. I have tried to make clear that it is wrong to use immoral means to attain moral ends. But now I must affirm that it is just as wrong, or perhaps even more so, to use moral means to preserve immoral ends. Perhaps Mr. Connor and his policemen have been rather nonviolent in public, as was Chief Pritchett in Albany, Georgia, but they have used the moral means of nonviolence to maintain the immoral end of racial injustice. As T. S. Eliot has said, "The last temptation is the greatest treason: To do the right deed for the wrong reason."

I wish you had commended the Negro sit-inners and demonstrators of Birmingham for their sublime courage, their willingness to suffer, and their amazing discipline in the midst of great provocation. One day the South will recognize its real heroes. They will be the James Merediths,[9] with the noble sense of purpose that enables them to face jeering and hostile mobs, and with the agonizing loneliness that characterizes the life of the pioneer. They will be old, oppressed, battered Negro women, symbolized in a seventy-two-year-old woman in Montgomery, Alabama, who rose up with a sense of dignity and with her people decided not to ride segregated buses, and who responded with ungrammatical profundity to one who inquired about her weariness: "My feets is tired, but my soul is at rest." They will be the young high school and college students, the young ministers of the gospel and a host of their elders, courageously and nonviolently sitting in at lunch counters and willingly going to jail for conscience' sake. One day the South will know that when these disinherited children of God sat down at lunch counters, they were in reality standing up for

---

[9]*James Merediths:* James Meredith (b. 1933) was an African American student whose enrollment in the University of Mississippi in 1962 set off riots at the campus in Oxford, Mississippi.

what is best in the American dream and for the most sacred values in our Judaeo-Christian heritage, thereby bringing our nation back to those great wells of democracy which were dug deep by the founding fathers in their formulation of the Constitution and the Declaration of Independence.

Never before have I written so long a letter. I'm afraid it is much too long to take 45 your precious time. I can assure you that it would have been much shorter if I had been writing from a comfortable desk, but what else can one do when he is alone in a narrow jail cell, other than write long letters, think long thoughts, and pray long prayers?

If I have said anything in this letter that overstates the truth and indicates an unreasonable impatience, I beg you to forgive me. If I have said anything that understates the truth and indicates my having a patience that allows me to settle for anything less than brotherhood, I beg God to forgive me.

I hope this letter finds you strong in the faith. I also hope that circumstances will soon make it possible for me to meet each of you, not as an integrationist or a civil rights leader but as a fellow clergyman and a Christian brother. Let us all hope that the dark clouds of racial prejudice will soon pass away and the deep fog of misunderstanding will be lifted from our fear-drenched communities, and in some not too distant tomorrow the radiant stars of love and brotherhood will shine over our great nation with all their scintillating beauty.

Yours in the cause of Peace and Brotherhood,
Martin Luther King, Jr.
1963

A Sheaf of Vietnam Conflict Poetry and Prose

In a modest attempt to focus attention on literature responding to the United States–Vietnam military conflict, this section includes prose by Michael Herr, Tim O'Brien, Norman Mailer, and Lee Ly Hayslip and poetry by Yusef Komunyakaa, Denise Levertov, and Robert Bly. Komunyakaa came to prominence during the 1990s; Bly was one of the leaders of the very active "Poets and Writers Against Vietnam," along with Muriel Rukeyser, Denise Levertov, W. S. Merwin, James Wright, Hayden Carruth, Adrienne Rich, Galway Kinnell, Robert Lowell, Allen Ginsberg, and others. Mailer's *Armies of the Night,* his meditative account of one of those crucial actions, has become a classic. The works by Tim O'Brien and Yusef Komunyakaa express veterans' view of the horrors of actual combat.

As Michael Bibby has reminded us, this literature is central to our view of mid-century American life, "considering that the Vietnam war was the longest overseas military conflict in U.S. history and that practically every working writer from 1965 to 1975 had something to say about it . . ." (see Bibby's 1996 *Hearts and Minds: Bodies, Poetry, and Resistance in the Vietnam Era*).

Michael Herr b. 1940

Among the most private of contemporary writers, Michael Herr has revealed little of his personal life. He was born and raised in Syracuse, New York, and attended Syracuse University. He then moved to New York City, where he worked in the editorial offices of *Holiday* magazine and produced articles and film criticism for such periodicals as *Mademoiselle* and the *New Leader.* In 1967, he persuaded Harold Hayes, the editor of *Esquire* magazine, to send him to Vietnam. He stayed there for over a year and witnessed some of the most intense fighting of the war. For a writer, Herr's situation in Vietnam was ideal: he had no specific assignment, he was relatively free to travel where he liked, and he was unencumbered by deadlines. Herr initially intended to write a monthly column from Vietnam but soon realized the idea was "horrible." In fact, Herr published only a few Vietnam pieces in *Esquire* and did not get his war experiences into a book until 1977.

After the war, Herr lived in New York for a time. After finishing *Dispatches,* he collaborated on the screenplay for *Apocalypse Now* and, more recently, for *Full Metal Jacket.* At last report, Herr lives in London.

Dispatches is perhaps the most brilliant American literary treatment of the Vietnam War. Ostensibly journalistic, *Dispatches* is more properly regarded as a painstakingly executed product of the author's imagination, if not quite a novel then certainly a literary work whose most dominant and satisfying qualities are novelistic. *Dispatches* is organized tautly, provides rich characterization, and evinces an extraordinary style thoroughly compatible with its subject. As Herr tells it, the Vietnam War was very much a 1960s spectacle: part John Wayne movie, part rock-and-roll concert, part redneck riot, part media event, and part bad drug trip. Herr's style, so perfectly grounded in the popular culture of the time, pulls at the reader with great power and unmistakable authenticity. After a particularly terrible battle, a young Marine glared at Herr, knowing he was a writer, and snarled: "Okay, man, you go on, you go on out of here, you cocksucker, but I mean it, you tell it! You tell it, man." And so Herr did.

The excerpt from *Dispatches* printed here comes from the beginning of the first section, called "Breathing In." Herr immediately establishes the hallucinatory quality of the war, against which he depicts the violence and remarkable array of characters. Herr's field of vision is broad but always at its center are the "grunts," the infantrymen who invariably carried themselves through the war with dignity and a carefully cultivated and life-sustaining combination of humor and cynicism.

Raymund Paredes
University of California–Los Angeles

PRIMARY WORKS

Dispatches, 1977; *The Big Room,* 1986 (with Guy Peellaert); *Walter Winchell,* 1990; *Kubrick,* 2000.

from Dispatches

I

Going out at night the medics gave you pills, Dexedrine breath like dead snakes kept too long in a jar. I never saw the need for them myself, a little contact or anything that even sounded like contact would give me more speed than I could bear. Whenever I heard something outside of our clenched little circle I'd practically flip, hoping to God that I wasn't the only one who'd noticed it. A couple of rounds fired off in the dark a kilometer away and the Elephant would be there kneeling on my chest, sending me down into my boots for a breath. Once I thought I saw a light moving in the jungle and I caught myself just under a whisper saying, "I'm not ready for this, I'm not ready for this." That's when I decided to drop it and do something else with my nights. And I wasn't going out like the night ambushers did, or the Lurps, long-range recon patrollers who did it night after night for weeks and months, creeping up on VC base camps or around moving columns of North Vietnamese. I was living too close to my bones as it was, all I had to do was accept it. Anyway, I'd save the pills for later, for Saigon and the awful depressions I always had there.

I knew one 4th Division Lurp who took his pills by the fistful, downs from the left pocket of his tiger suit and ups from the right, one to cut the trail for him and the other to send him down it. He told me that they cooled things out just right for him, that he could see that old jungle at night like he was looking at it through a starlight scope. "They sure give you the range," he said.

This was his third tour. In 1965 he'd been the only survivor in a platoon of the Cav wiped out going into the Ia Drang Valley. In '66 he'd come back with the Special Forces and one morning after an ambush he'd hidden under the bodies of his team while the VC walked all around them with knives, making sure. They stripped the bodies of their gear, the berets too, and finally went away, laughing. After that, there was nothing left for him in the war except the Lurps.

"I just can't hack it back in the World," he said. He told me that after he'd come back home the last time he would sit in his room all day, and sometimes he'd stick a hunting rifle out the window, leading people and cars as they passed his house until the only feeling he was aware of was all up in the tip of that one finger. "It used to put my folks real uptight," he said. But he put people uptight here too, even here.

"No man, I'm sorry, he's just too crazy for me," one of the men in his team said. "All's you got to do is look in his eyes, that's the whole fucking story right there."

"Yeah, but you better do it quick," someone else said. "I mean, you don't want to let him catch you at it."

But he always seemed to be watching for it, I think he slept with his eyes open, and I was afraid of him anyway. All I ever managed was one quick look in, and that was like looking at the floor of an ocean. He wore a gold earring and a headband torn from a piece of camouflage parachute material, and since nobody was about to tell him to get his hair cut it fell below his shoulders, covering a thick purple scar. Even at division he never went anywhere without at least a .45 and a knife, and he thought I was a freak because I wouldn't carry a weapon.

"Didn't you ever meet a reporter before?" I asked him.

"Tits on a bull," he said. "Nothing personal."

But what a story he told me, as one-pointed and resonant as any war story I ever heard, it took me a year to understand it:

"Patrol went up the mountain. One man came back. He died before he could tell us what happened."

I waited for the rest, but it seemed not to be that kind of story; when I asked him what had happened he just looked like he felt sorry for me, fucked if he'd waste time telling stories to anyone dumb as I was.

His face was all painted up for night walking now like a bad hallucination, not like the painted faces I'd seen in San Francisco only a few weeks before, the other extreme of the same theater. In the coming hours he'd stand as faceless and quiet in the jungle as a fallen tree, and God help his opposite numbers unless they had at least half a squad along, he was a good killer, one of our best. The rest of his team were gathered outside the tent, set a little apart from the other division units, with its own Lurp-designated latrine and its own exclusive freeze-dry rations, three-star war food, the same chop they sold at Abercrombie & Fitch. The regular division troops would almost shy off the path when they passed the area on their way to and from the mess tent. No matter how toughened up they became in the war, they still looked innocent compared to the Lurps. When the team had grouped they walked in a file down the hill to the lz across the strip to the perimeter and into the treeline.

I never spoke to him again, but I saw him. When they came back in the next morning he had a prisoner with him, blindfolded and with his elbows bound sharply behind him. The Lurp area would definitely be off limits during the interrogation, and anyway, I was already down at the strip waiting for a helicopter to come and take me out of there.

"Hey, what're you guys, with the USO? Aw, we thought you was with the USO 'cause your hair's so long." Page took the kid's picture, I got the words down and

Flynn laughed and told him we were the Rolling Stones. The three of us traveled around together for about a month that summer. At one lz the brigade chopper came in with a real foxtail hanging off the aerial, when the commander walked by us he almost took an infarction.

"Don't you men salute officers?"

"We're not men," Page said. "We're correspondents."

When the commander heard that, he wanted to throw a spontaneous operation for us, crank up his whole brigade and get some people killed. We had to get out on the next chopper to keep him from going ahead with it, amazing what some of them would do for a little ink. Page liked to augment his field gear with freak paraphernalia, scarves and beads, plus he was English, guys would stare at him like he'd just come down off a wall on Mars. Sean Flynn could look more incredibly beautiful than even his father, Errol, had thirty years before as Captain Blood, but sometimes he looked more like Artaud coming out of some heavy heart-of-darkness trip, overloaded on the information, the input! The input! He'd give off a bad sweat and sit for hours, combing his mustache through with the saw blade of his Swiss Army knife. We packed grass and tape: Have You Seen Your Mother Baby Standing in the Shadows, Best of the Animals, Strange Days, Purple Haze, Archie Bell and the Drells, "C'mon now everybody, do the Tighten Up. . . ." Once in a while we'd catch a chopper straight into one of the lower hells, but it was a quiet time in the war, mostly it was lz's and camps, grunts hanging around, faces, stories.

"Best way's to just keep moving, one of them told us. "Just keep moving, stay in motion, you know what I'm saying?"

We knew. He was a moving-target-survivor subscriber, a true child of the war, because except for the rare times when you were pinned or stranded the system was geared to keep you mobile, if that was what you thought you wanted. As a technique for staying alive it seemed to make as much sense as anything, given naturally that you went there to begin with and wanted to see it close; it started out sound and straight but it formed a cone as it progressed, because the more you moved the more you saw, the more you saw the more besides death and mutilation you risked, and the more you risked of that the more you would have to let go of one day as a "survivor." Some of us moved around the war like crazy people until we couldn't see which way the run was even taking us anymore, only the war all over its surface with occasional, unexpected penetration. As long as we could have choppers like taxis it took real exhaustion or depression near shock or a dozen pipes of opium to keep us even apparently quiet, we'd still be running around inside our skins like something was after us, ha ha, La Vida Loca.

In the months after I got back the hundreds of helicopters I'd flown in began to draw together until they'd formed a collective meta-chopper, and in my mind it was the sexiest thing going; saver-destroyed, provider-waster, right hand-left hand, nimble, fluent, canny and human; hot steel, grease, jungle-saturated canvas webbing, sweat cooling and warming up again, cassette rock and roll in one ear and door-gun fire in the other, fuel, heat, vitality and death, death itself, hardly an intruder. Men on the crews would say that once you'd carried a dead person he would always be there, riding with you. Like all combat people they were incredibly superstitious and invariably self-dramatic, but it was (I knew) unbearably true that close exposure to the dead sensitized you to the force of their presence and made for long reverberations; long. Some people were so delicate that one look was enough to wipe them away; but even bone-dumb grunts seemed to feel that something weird and extra was happening to them.

Helicopters and people jumping out of helicopters, people so in love they'd run to get on even when there wasn't any pressure. Choppers rising straight out of small cleared jungle spaces, wobbling down onto city rooftops, cartons of rations and ammunition thrown off, dead and wounded loaded on. Sometimes they were so plentiful and loose that you could touch down at five or six places in a day, look around, hear the talk, catch the next one out. There were installations as big as cities with 30,000 citizens, once we dropped in to feed supply to one man. God knows what kind of Lord Jim phoenix numbers he was doing in there, all he said to me was, "You didn't see a thing, right Chief? You weren't even here." There were posh fat air-conditioned camps like comfortable middle-class scenes with the violence tacit, "far away"; camps named for commanders' wives, LZ Thelma, LZ Betty Lou; number-named hilltops in trouble where I didn't want to stay; trail, paddy, swamp, deep hairy bush, scrub, swale, village, even city, where the ground couldn't drink up what the action spilled, it made you careful where you walked.

Sometimes the chopper you were riding in would top a hill and all the ground in front of you as far as the next hill would be charred and pitted and still smoking, and something between your chest and your stomach would turn over. Frail gray smoke where they'd burned off the rice fields around a free-strike zone, brilliant white smoke from phosphorus ("Willy Peter/Make you a buh liever"), deep black smoke from 'palm, they said that if you stood at the base of a column of napalm smoke it would such the air right out of your lungs. Once we fanned over a little ville that had just been airstruck and the words of a song by Wingy Manone that I'd heard when I was a few years old snapped into my head, "Stop the War, These Cats Is Killing Themselves." Then we dropped, hovered, settled down into purple lz smoke, dozens of children broke from their hootches to run in toward the focus of our landing, the pilot laughing and saying, "Vietnam, man, Bomb 'em and feed 'em, bomb 'em and feed 'em."

Flying over jungle was almost pure pleasure, doing it on foot was nearly all pain. I never belonged in there. Maybe it really was what its people had always called it, Beyond; at the very least it was serious, I gave up things to it I probably never got back. ("Aw, jungle's okay. If you know her you can live in her real good, if you don't she'll take you down in an hour. Under.") Once in some thick jungle corner with some grunts standing around, a correspondent said, "Gee, you must really see some beautiful sunsets in here," and they almost pissed themselves laughing. But you could fly up and into hot tropic sunsets that would change the way you thought about light forever. You could also fly out of places that were so grim they turned to black and white in your head five minutes after you'd gone.

That could be the coldest one in the world, standing at the edge of a clearing watching the chopper you'd just come in on taking off again, leaving you there to think about what it was going to be for you now: if this was a bad place, the wrong place, maybe even the last place, and whether you'd made a terrible mistake this time.

There was a camp at Soc Trang where a man at the lz said, "If you come looking for a story this is your lucky day, we got Condition Red here," and before the sound of the chopper had faded out, I knew I had it too.

"That's affirmative," the camp commander said, "we are *definitely* expecting rain. Glad to see you." He was a young captain, he was laughing and taping a bunch of sixteen clips together bottom to bottom for faster reloading, "grease." Everyone there was busy at it, cracking crates, squirreling away grenades, checking mortar pieces, piling rounds, clicking banana clips into automatic weapons that I'd never even seen before. They were wired into their listening posts out around the camp, into each other, into themselves, and when it got dark it got worse. The moon came up nasty and full, a fat moist piece of decadent fruit. It was soft and saffron-misted when you looked up at it, but its light over the sandbags and into the jungle was harsh and bright. We were all rubbing Army-issue nightfighter cosmetic under our eyes to cut the glare and the terrible things it made you see. (Around midnight, just for something to do, I crossed to the other perimeter and looked at the road running engineer-straight toward Route 4 like a yellow frozen ribbon out of sight and I saw it move, the whole road.) There were a few sharp arguments about who the light really favored, attackers or defenders, men were sitting around with Cinemascope eyes and jaws stuck out like they could shoot bullets, moving and antsing and shifting around inside their fatigues. "No sense us getting too relaxed, Charlie don't relax, just when you get good and comfortable is when he comes over and takes a giant shit on you." That was the level until morning, I smoked a pack an hour all night long, and nothing happened. Ten minutes after daybreak I was down at the lz asking about choppers.

A few days later Sean Flynn and I went up to a big firebase in the Americal TAOR that took it all the way over to another extreme, National Guard weekend. The colonel in command was so drunk that day that he could barely get his words out, and when he did, it was to say things like, "We aim to make good and god-dammit sure that if *those guys* try *anything cute* they won't catch us with our pants down." The main mission there was to fire H&I, but one man told us that their record was the worst in the whole Corps, probably the whole country, they'd ha-rassed and interdicted a lot of sleeping civilians and Korean Marines, even a couple of Americal patrols, but hardly any Viet Cong. (The colonel kept calling it "artiller-ary." The first time he said it Flynn and I looked away from each other, the second time we blew beer through our noses, but the colonel fell in laughing right away and more than covered us.) No sandbags, exposed shells, dirty pieces, guys going around giving us that look, "We're cool, how come you're not?" At the strip Sean was talk-ing to the operator about it and the man got angry. "Oh yeah? Well fuck *you,* how tight do you think you want it? There ain't been any veecees around here in three months."

"So far so good," Sean said. "Hear anything on that chopper yet?"

But sometimes everything stopped, nothing flew, you couldn't even find out why. I got stuck for a chopper once in some lost patrol outpost in the Delta where the sergeant chain-ate candy bars and played country-and-western tapes twenty hours a day until I heard it in my sleep, some sleep, *Up on Wolverton Mountain* and *Lone-some as the bats and the bears in Miller's Cave* and *I fell into a burning ring of fire,* surrounded by strungout rednecks who weren't getting much sleep either because they couldn't trust one of their 400 mercenary troopers or their own handpicked perimeter guards or anybody else except maybe Baby Ruth and Johnny Cash, they'd been waiting for it so long now they were afraid they wouldn't know it when they finally got it, *and it burns burns burns. . . .* Finally on the fourth day a helicopter came in to deliver meat and movies to the camp and I went out on it, so happy to get back to Saigon that I didn't crash for two days.

Airmobility, dig it, you weren't going anywhere. It made you feel safe, it made you feel Omni, but it was only a stunt, technology. Mobility was just mobility, it saved lives or took them all the time (saved mine I don't know how many times, maybe dozens, maybe none), what you really needed was a flexibility far greater than anything the technology could provide, some generous, spontaneous gift for accepting surprises, and I didn't have it. I got to hate surprises, control freak at the crossroads, if you were one of those people who always thought they had to know what was coming next, the war could cream you. It was the same with your ongoing attempts at getting used to the jungle or the blow-you-out climate or the saturating strangeness of the place which didn't lessen with exposure so often as it fattened and darkened in accumulating alienation. It was great if you could adapt, you had to try, but it wasn't the same as making a discipline, going into your own reserves and developing a real war metabolism, slow yourself down when your heart tried to punch its way through your chest, get swift when everything went to stop and all you could feel of your whole life was the entropy whipping through it. Unlovable terms.

The ground was always in play, always being swept. Under the ground was his, above it was ours. We have the air, we could get up in it but not disappear in *to* it, we could run but we couldn't hide, and he could do each so well that sometimes it looked like he was doing them both at once, while our finder just went limp. All the same, one place or another it was always going on, rock around the clock, we had the days and he had the nights. You could be in the most protected space in Vietnam and still know that your safety was provisional, that early death, blindness, loss of legs, arms or balls, major and lasting disfigurement—the whole rotten deal—could come in on the freaky-fluky as easily as in the so-called expected ways, you heard so many of those stories it was a wonder anyone was left alive to die in firefights and mortar-rocket attacks. After a few weeks, when the nickel had jarred loose and dropped and I saw that everyone around me was carrying a gun, I also saw that any one of them could go off at any time, putting you where it wouldn't matter whether it had been an accident or not. The roads were mined, the trails booby-trapped, satchel charges and grenades blew up jeeps and movie theaters, the VC got work inside all the camps as shoeshine boys and laundresses and honey-dippers, they'd starch your fatigues and burn your shit and then go home and mortar your area. Saigon and Cholon and Danang held such hostile vibes that you felt you were being dry-sniped every time someone looked at you, and choppers fell out of the sky like fat poisoned birds a hundred times a day. After a while I couldn't get on one without thinking that I must be out of my fucking mind.

Fear and motion, fear and standstill, no preferred cut there, no way even to be clear about which was really worse, the wait or the delivery. Combat spared far more men than it wasted, but everyone suffered the time between contact, especially when they were going out every day looking for it; bad going on foot, terrible in trucks and APC's, awful in helicopters, the worst, traveling so fast toward something so frightening. I can remember times when I went half dead with my fear of the motion, the speed and direction already fixed and pointed one way. It was painful enough just flying "safe" hops between firebases and lz's; if you were ever on a helicopter that had been hit by ground fire your deep, perpetual chopper anxiety was guaranteed. At least actual contact when it was happening would draw long ragged strands of energy out of you, it was juicy, fast and refining, and traveling toward it was hollow, dry, cold and steady, it never let you alone. All you could do was look around at the other people on board and see if they were as scared and numbed out as you were. If it looked like they weren't you thought they were insane, if it looked like they were it made you feel a lot worse.

I went through that thing a number of times and only got a fast return on my fear once, a too classic hot landing with the heat coming from the trees about 300 yards away, sweeping machine-gun fire that sent men head down into swampy water, running on their hands and knees toward the grass where it wasn't blown flat by the rotor blades, not much to be running for but better than nothing. The helicopter pulled up before we'd all gotten out, leaving the last few men to jump twenty feet down between the guns across the paddy and the gun on the chopper door. When we'd all reached the cover of the wall and the captain had made a check, we were amazed to see that no one had even been hurt, except for one man who'd sprained both his ankles jumping.. Afterwards, I remembered that I'd been down in the muck worrying about leeches. I guess you could say that I was refusing to accept the situation.

"Boy, you sure get offered some shitty choices," a Marine once said to me, and I couldn't help but feel that what he really meant was that you didn't get offered any at all. Specifically, he was just talking about a couple of C-ration cans, "dinner," but considering his young life you couldn't blame him for thinking that if he knew one thing for sure, it was that there was no one anywhere who cared less about what *he* wanted. There wasn't anybody he wanted to thank for his food, but he was grateful that he was still alive to eat it, that the mother-fucker hadn't scarfed him up first. He hadn't been anything but tired and scared for six months and he'd lost a lot, mostly people, and seen far too much, but he was breathing in and breathing out, some kind of choice all by itself.

He had one of those faces, I saw that face at least a thousand times at a hundred bases and camps, all the youth sucked out of the eyes, the color drawn from the skin, cold white lips, you knew he wouldn't wait for any of it to come back. Life had made him old, he'd live it out old. All those faces, sometimes it was like looking into faces at a rock concert, locked in, the event had them; or like students who were very heavily advanced, serious beyond what you'd call their years if you didn't know for yourself what the minutes and hours of those years were made up of. Not just like all the ones you saw who looked like they couldn't drag their asses through another day of it. (How do you feel when a nineteen-year-old kid tells you from the bottom of his heart that he's gotten too old for this kind of shit?) Not like the faces of the dead or wounded either, they could look more released than overtaken. These were the faces of boys whose whole lives seemed to have backed up on them, they'd be a few feet away but they'd be looking back at you over a distance you knew you'd never really cross. We'd talk, sometimes fly together, guys going out on R&R, guys escorting bodies, guys who'd flipped over into extremes of peace or violence. Once I flew with a kid who was going home, he looked back down once at the ground where he'd spent the year and spilled his whole load of tears. Sometimes you even flew with the dead.

Once I jumped on a chopper that was full of them. The kid in the op shack had said that there would be a body on board, but he'd been given some wrong information. "How bad do you want to get to Danang?" he'd asked me, and I'd said, "Bad."

When I saw what was happening I didn't want to get on, but they'd made a divert and a special landing for me, I had to go with the chopper I'd drawn, I was afraid of looking squeamish. (I remember, too, thinking that a chopper full of dead men was far less likely to get shot down than one full of living.) They weren't even in bags. They'd been on a truck near one of the firebases in the DMZ that was firing support for Khe Sanh, and the truck had hit a Command-detonated mine, then they'd been rocketed. The Marines were always running out of things, even food, ammo and medicine, it wasn't so strange that they'd run out of bags too. The men had been wrapped around in ponchos, some of them carelessly fastened with plastic straps, and loaded on board. There was a small space cleared for me between one of them and the door gunner, who looked pale and so tremendously furious that I thought he was angry with me and I couldn't look at him for a while. When we went up the wind blew through the ship and made the ponchos shake and tremble until the one next to me blew back in a fast brutal flap, uncovering the face. They hadn't even closed his eyes for him.

The gunner started hollering as loud as he could, "Fix it! Fix it!," maybe he thought the eyes were looking at him, but there wasn't anything I could do. My hand went there a couple of times and I couldn't, and then I did. I pulled the poncho tight, lifted his head carefully and tucked the poncho under it, and then I couldn't believe that I'd done it. All during the ride the gunner kept trying to smile, and when we landed at Dong Ha he thanked me and ran off to get a detail. The pilots jumped down and walked away without looking back once, like they'd never seen that chopper before in their lives. I flew the rest of the way to Danang in a general's plane.

1977

Tim O'Brien b. 1946

After a small-town Minnesota childhood and a college education at Macalaster (class president, summa cum laude, Phi Beta Kappa), Tim O'Brien was drafted into the U.S. Army in 1968 and served one year as an infantryman in the American conflict in Vietnam. The war, which appears in all seven of his published books, constitutes a central focus of his uncollected writings; yet in interviews O'Brien repeatedly objects to being labeled a Vietnam War writer: "It's like calling Toni Morrison a black writer or Shakespeare a king writer." His concerns as a writer resonate beyond the battlefield: the subjective nature of experience, the life of the imagination, the grip of the past, control and its loss, love, betrayal, obsession, language, guilt, rage, death, moral ambiguity, mental and emotional instability, and storytelling as a means of coping with it all. Nevertheless, his personal experience of that war, along with his midwestern background, provided him a site for his literary explorations of the human condition in late-twentieth-century American life.

Three of his books—one work of nonfiction and two works of fiction—deal directly with the war experience: *If I Die in a Combat Zone, Box Me Up and Ship Me Home* (1973), *Going After Cacciato* (1978), and *The Things They Carried* (1990). *Going After Cacciato,* his third book and second novel, won the National Book Award. The book takes place largely in the mind of Paul Berlin as he keeps himself awake on guard duty by remembering actual events and fancifully imagining what might have been. Berlin imagines his squad chasing the deserting Cacciato all the way to Paris, and his imagination transforms this initial act of *what if* into a tale that includes an echo of Alice in Wonderland and a Socratic exchange on the morality of the war, a tale that dramatizes Berlin's own desire to escape the war and to deny his own culpability. O'Brien's intellectual approach to the war is significantly informed by his political science graduate study at Harvard in the early 1970s; his unfinished doctoral dissertation is titled "Case Studies in American Military Interventions."

O'Brien's fourth work of fiction, *The Things They Carried,* is a collection of previously published and new stories, brought together, revised, and arranged to make a thematically unified work much like Hemingway's *In Our Time* and Joyce's *Dubliners.* The story printed here, "In the Field," comes from this book. Several of its stories are narrated by a character named "Tim O'Brien," who remains distinct from the author. The presence of "Tim O'Brien"

underscores one of the novel's major conceits: the difference between "happening-truth" and "story-truth," or what actually happened versus what we say happened as factual events are received through our limited perspective and then transformed by memory, by the nature of storytelling, and by quasi-willful acts of reinvention for psychic survival.

O'Brien's other novels, including *Tomcat in Love* (1997), turn from war to romantic love between men and women as another source of conflict, ambiguity, shame, and haunting history. *Northern Lights* (1975), his first and by his own judgment his worst novel, pits two brothers— one a recently returned veteran—against one another, against the women in their lives, and against mother nature. Set in the future of 1995, *The Nuclear Age* (1985) presents a man struggling with his wife's adultery and his own obsession with nuclear war while simultaneously reliving a turbulent past of being in love with a militant anti-war activist. Paul Wade, the protagonist of *In the Lake of the Woods* (1994), is a politician who just lost an election after the newspapers exposed his presence during the atrocities against Vietnamese civilians at My Lai, and who wakes one morning to find that his wife has vanished.

What happens to Paul Wade's wife? What happens to bring about Kiowa's death in the following story? Tim O'Brien's fiction frequently resists answering the *what happens* questions to emphasize that who we are is far more manifold, layered, and mysterious than such questions pretend.

Alex Vernon
Hendrix College

PRIMARY SOURCES

If I Die in a Combat Zone, Box Me Up and Ship Me Home, 1973, rev. 1983; *Northern Lights,* 1975; *Going After Cacciato,* 1978, rev. 1989; *The Nuclear Age,* 1985, 1993; *The Things They Carried,* 1990; *In the Lake of the Woods,* 1994; *Tomcat in Love,* 1997; *July, July,* 2002.

In the Field

At daybreak the platoon of eighteen soldiers formed into a loose rank and began wading side by side through the deep muck of the shit field. They moved slowly in the rain. Leaning forward, heads down, they used the butts of their weapons as probes, wading across the field to the river and then turning and wading back again. They were tired and miserable; all they wanted now was to get it finished. Kiowa was gone. He was under the mud and water, folded in with the war, and their only thought was to find him and dig him out and then move on to someplace dry and warm. It had been a hard night. Maybe the worst ever. The rains had fallen without stop, and the Song Tra Bong had overflowed its banks, and the muck had now risen thigh-deep in the field along the river. A low, gray mist hovered over the land. Off to the west there was thunder, soft little moaning sounds, and the monsoons seemed to be a lasting element of the war. The eighteen soldiers moved in silence. First Lieutenant Jimmy Cross went first, now and then straightening out the rank, closing up the gaps. His uniform was dark with mud; his arms and face were filthy. Early in the morning he had radioed in the MIA report, giving the name and circumstances, but he was now determined to find his man, no matter what, even if it meant flying in slabs of concrete and damming up the river and draining the entire field. He would not lose a member of his command like this. It wasn't right. Kiowa had been a fine soldier and a fine human being, a devout Baptist, and there was no way Lieutenant Cross would allow such a good man to be lost under the slime of a shit field.

Briefly, he stopped and watched the clouds. Except for some occasional thunder it was a deeply quiet morning, just the rain and the steady sloshing sounds of eighteen men wading through the thick waters. Lieutenant Cross wished the rain would let up. Even for an hour, it would make things easier.

But then he shrugged. The rain was the war and you had to fight it.

Turning, he looked out across the field and yelled at one of his men to close up the rank. Not a man, really—a boy. The young soldier stood off by himself at the center of the field in knee-deep water, reaching down with both hands as if chasing some object just beneath the surface. The boy's shoulders were shaking. Jimmy Cross yelled again but the young soldier did not turn or look up. In his hooded poncho, everything caked with mud, the boy's face was impossible to make out. The filth seemed to erase identities, transforming the men into identical copies of a single soldier, which was exactly how Jimmy Cross had been trained to treat them, as interchangeable units of command. It was difficult sometimes, but he tried to avoid that sort of thinking. He had no military ambitions. He preferred to view his men not as units but as human beings. And Kiowa had been a splendid human being, the very best, intelligent and gentle and quiet-spoken. Very brave, too. And decent. The kid's father taught Sunday school in Oklahoma City, where Kiowa had been raised to believe in the promise of salvation under Jesus Christ, and this conviction had always been present in the boy's smile, in his posture toward the world, in the way he never went anywhere without an illustrated New Testament that his father had mailed to him as a birthday present back in January.

A crime, Jimmy Cross thought.

Looking out toward the river, he knew for a fact that he had made a mistake setting up here. The order had come from higher, true, but still he should've exercised some field discretion. He should've moved to higher ground for the night, should've radioed in false coordinates. There was nothing he could do now, but still it was a mistake and a hideous waste. He felt sick about it. Standing in the deep waters of the field, First Lieutenant Jimmy Cross began composing a letter in his head to the kid's father, not mentioning the shit field, just saying what a fine soldier Kiowa had been, what a fine human being, and how he was the kind of son that any father could be proud of forever.

The search went slowly. For a time the morning seemed to brighten, the sky going to a lighter shade of silver, but then the rains came back hard and steady. There was the feel of permanent twilight.

At the far left of the line, Azar and Norman Bowker and Mitchell Sanders waded along the edge of the field closest to the river. They were tall men, but at times the muck came to midthigh, other times to the crotch.

Azar kept shaking his head. He coughed and shook his head and said, "Man, talk about irony. I bet if Kiowa was here, I bet he'd just laugh. Eating shit—it's your classic irony."

"Fine," said Norman Bowker. "Now pipe down."

Azar sighed. "Wasted in the waste," he said. "A shit field. You got to admit, it's pure world-class irony."

The three men moved with slow, heavy steps. It was hard to keep balance. Their boots sank into the ooze, which produced a powerful downward suction, and with each step they would have to pull up hard to break the hold. The rain made quick dents in the water, like tiny mouths, and the stink was everywhere.

When they reached the river, they shifted a few meters to the north and began wading back up the field. Occasionally they used their weapons to test the bottom, but mostly they just searched with their feet.

"A classic case," Azar was saying. "Biting the dirt, so to speak, that tells the story."

"Enough," Bowker said.

"Like those old cowboy movies. One more redskin bites the dust."

"I'm serious, man. Zip it shut."

Azar smiled and said, "Classic."

The morning was cold and wet. They had not slept during the night, not even for a few moments, and all three of them were feeling the tension as they moved across the field toward the river. There was nothing they could do for Kiowa. Just find him and slide him aboard a chopper. Whenever a man died it was always the same, a desire to get it over with quickly, no fuss or ceremony, and what they wanted now was to head for a ville and get under a roof and forget what had happened during the night.

Halfway across the field Mitchell Sanders stopped. He stood for a moment with his eyes shut, feeling along the bottom with a foot, then he passed his weapon over to Norman Bowker and reached down into the muck. After a second he hauled up a filthy green rucksack.

The three men did not speak for a time. The pack was heavy with mud and water, dead-looking. Inside were a pair of moccasins and an illustrated New Testament.

"Well," Mitchell Sanders finally said, "the guy's around here somewhere."

"Better tell the LT."

"Screw him."

"Yeah, but—"

"Some lieutenant," Sanders said. "Camps us in a toilet. Man don't *know* shit."

"Nobody knew," Bowker said.

"Maybe so, maybe not. Ten billion places we could've set up last night, the man picks a latrine."

Norman Bowker stared down at the rucksack. It was made of dark green nylon with an aluminum frame, but now it had the curious look of flesh.

"It wasn't the LT's fault," Bowker said quietly.

"Whose then?"

"Nobody's. Nobody knew till afterward."

Mitchell Sanders made a sound in his throat. He hoisted up the rucksack, slipped into the harness, and pulled the straps tight. "All right, but this much for sure. The man knew it was raining. He knew about the river. One plus one. Add it up, you get exactly what happened."

Sanders glared at the river.

"Move it," he said. "Kiowa's waiting on us."

Slowly then, bending against the rain, Azar and Norman Bowker and Mitchell Sanders began wading again through the deep waters, their eyes down, circling out from where they had found the rucksack.

First Lieutenant Jimmy Cross stood fifty meters away. He had finished writing the letter in his head, explaining things to Kiowa's father, and now he folded his arms and watched his platoon crisscrossing the wide field. In a funny way, it reminded him of the municipal golf course in his hometown in New Jersey. A lost ball, he thought. Tired players searching through the rough, sweeping back and forth in long systematic patterns. He wished he were there right now. On the sixth hole. Looking out across the water hazard that fronted the small flat green, a seven iron in his hand, calculating wind and distance, wondering if he should reach instead for an eight. A tough decision, but all you could ever lose was a ball. You did not lose a player. And you never had to wade out into the hazard and spend the day searching through the slime.

Jimmy Cross did not want the responsibility of leading these men. He had never wanted it. In his sophomore year at Mount Sebastian College he had signed up for the Reserve Officer Training Corps without much thought. An automatic thing: because his friends had joined, and because it was worth a few credits, and because it seemed preferable to letting the draft take him. He was unprepared. Twenty-four years old and his heart wasn't in it. Military matters meant nothing to him. He did not care one way or the other about the war, and he had no desire to command, and even after all these months in the bush, all the days and nights, even then he did not know enough to keep his men out of a shit field.

What he should've done, he told himself, was follow his first impulse. In the late afternoon yesterday, when they reached the night coordinates, he should've taken one look and headed for higher ground. He should've known. No excuses. At one edge of the field was a small ville, and right away a couple of old mama-sans had trotted out to warn him. Number ten, they'd said. Evil ground. Not a good spot for good GIs. But it was a war, and he had his orders, so they'd set up a perimeter and crawled under their ponchos and tried to settle in for the night. The rain never stopped. By midnight the Song Tra Bong had overflowed its banks. The field turned to slop, everything soft and mushy. He remembered how the water kept rising, how a terrible stink began to bubble up out of the earth. It was a dead-fish smell, partly, but something else, too, and then later in the night Mitchell Sanders had crawled through the rain and grabbed him hard by the arm and asked what he was doing setting up in a shit field. The village toilet, Sanders said. He remembered the look on Sanders's face. The guy stared for a moment and then wiped his mouth and whispered, "Shit," and then crawled away into the dark.

A stupid mistake. That's all it was, a mistake, but it had killed Kiowa.

Lieutenant Jimmy Cross felt something tighten inside him. In the letter to Kiowa's father he would apologize point-blank. Just admit to the blunders.

He would place the blame where it belonged. Tactically, he'd say, it was indefensible ground from the start. Low and flat. No natural cover. And so late in the night, when they took mortar fire from across the river, all they could do was snake down under the slop and lie there and wait. The field just exploded. Rain and slop and shrapnel, it all mixed together, and the field seemed to boil. He would explain this to Kiowa's father. Carefully, not covering up his own guilt, he would tell how the mortar rounds made craters in the slush, spraying up great showers of filth, and how the craters then collapsed on themselves and filled up with mud and water, sucking things down, swallowing things, weapons and entrenching tools and belts of ammunition, and how in this way his son Kiowa had been combined with the waste and the war.

My own fault, he would say.

Straightening up, First Lieutenant Jimmy Cross rubbed his eyes and tried to get his thoughts together. The rain fell in a cold, sad drizzle.

Off toward the river he again noticed the young soldier standing alone at the center of the field. The boy's shoulders were shaking. Maybe it was something in the posture of the soldier, or the way he seemed to be reaching for some invisible object beneath the surface, but for several moments Jimmy Cross stood very still, afraid to move, yet knowing he had to, and then he murmured to himself, "My fault," and he nodded and waded out across the field toward the boy.

The young soldier was trying hard not to cry.

He, too, blamed himself. Bent forward at the waist, groping with both hands, he seemed to be chasing some creature just beyond reach, something elusive, a fish or a frog. His lips were moving. Like Jimmy Cross, the boy was explaining things to an absent judge. It wasn't to defend himself. The boy recognized his own guilt and wanted only to lay out the full causes.

Wading sideways a few steps, he leaned down and felt along the soft bottom of the field.

He pictured Kiowa's face. They'd been close buddies, the tightest, and he remembered how last night they had huddled together under their ponchos, the rain cold and steady, the water rising to their knees, but how Kiowa had just laughed it off and said they should concentrate on better things. And so for a long while they'd talked about their families and hometowns. At one point, the boy remembered, he'd been showing Kiowa a picture of his girlfriend. He remembered switching on his flashlight. A stupid thing to do, but he did it anyway, and he remembered Kiowa leaning in for a look at the picture— "Hey, she's *cute*," he'd said—and then the field exploded all around them.

Like murder, the boy thought. The flashlight made it happen. Dumb and dangerous. And as a result his friend Kiowa was dead.

That simple, he thought.

He wished there were some other way to look at it, but there wasn't. Very simple and very final. He remembered two mortar rounds hitting close by. Then a third, even closer, and off to his left he'd heard somebody scream. The voice was ragged and clotted up, but he knew instantly that it was Kiowa.

He remembered trying to crawl toward the screaming. No sense of direction, though, and the field seemed to suck him under, and everything was black and wet and swirling, and he couldn't get his bearings, and then another round hit nearby, and for a few moments all he could do was hold his breath and duck down beneath the water.

Later, when he came up again, there were no more screams. There was an arm and a wristwatch and part of a boot. There were bubbles where Kiowa's head should've been.

He remembered grabbing the boot. He remembered pulling hard, but how the field seemed to pull back, like a tug-of-war he couldn't win, and how finally he had to whisper his friend's name and let go and watch the boot slide away. Then for a long time there were things he could not remember. Various sounds, various smells. Later he'd found himself lying on a little rise, face-up, tasting the field in his mouth, listening to the rain and explosions and bubbling sounds. He was alone. He'd lost everything. He'd lost Kiowa and his weapon and his flashlight and his girlfriend's picture. He remembered this. He remembered wondering if he could lose himself.

Now, in the dull morning rain, the boy seemed frantic. He waded quickly from spot to spot, leaning down and plunging his hands into the water. He did not look up when Lieutenant Jimmy Cross approached.

"Right here," the boy was saying. "Got to be right here."

Jimmy Cross remembered the kid's face but not the name. That happened sometimes. He tried to treat his men as individuals but sometimes the names just escaped him.

He watched the young soldier shove his hands into the water. "Right *here*," he kept saying. His movements seemed random and jerky.

Jimmy Cross waited a moment, then stepped closer. "Listen," he said quietly, "the guy could be anywhere."

The boy glanced up. "Who could?"

"Kiowa. You can't expect—"

"Kiowa's *dead*."

"Well, yes."

The young soldier nodded. "So what about Billie?"

"Who?"

"My girl. What about her? This picture, it was the only one I had. Right here, I lost it."

Jimmy Cross shook his head. It bothered him that he could not come up with a name.

"Slow down," he said. "I don't—"

"Billie's *picture*. I had it all wrapped up, I had it in plastic, so it'll be okay if I can . . . Last night we were looking at it, me and Kiowa. Right here. I know for sure it's right here somewhere."

Jimmy Cross smiled at the boy. "You can ask her for another one. A better one."

"She won't *send* another one. She's not even my *girl* anymore, she won't . . . Man, I got to find it."

The boy yanked his arm free.

He shuffled sideways and stooped down again and dipped into the muck with both hands. His shoulders were shaking. Briefly, Lieutenant Cross wondered where the kid's weapon was, and his helmet, but it seemed better not to ask.

He felt some pity come on him. For a moment the day seemed to soften. So much hurt, he thought. He watched the young soldier wading through the water, bending down and then standing and then bending down again, as if something might finally be salvaged from all the waste.

Jimmy Cross silently wished the boy luck.

Then he closed his eyes and went back to working on the letter to Kiowa's father.

Across the field Azar and Norman Bowker and Mitchell Sanders were wading alongside a narrow dike at the edge of the field. It was near noon now.

Norman Bowker found Kiowa. He was under two feet of water. Nothing showed except the heel of a boot.

"That's him?" Azar said.

"Who else?"

"I don't know." Azar shook his head. "I don't know."

Norman Bowker touched the boot, covered his eyes for a moment, then stood up and looked at Azar.

"So where's the joke?" he said.

"No joke."

"Eating shit. Let's hear that one."

"Forget it."

Mitchell Sanders told them to knock it off. The three soldiers moved to the dike, put down their packs and weapons, then waded back to where the boot was showing. The body lay partly wedged under a layer of mud beneath the water. It was hard to get traction; with each movement the muck would grip their feet and hold tight. The rain had come back harder now. Mitchell Sanders reached down and found Kiowa's other boot, and they waited a moment, then Sanders sighed and said, "Okay," and they took hold of the two boots and pulled up hard. There was only a slight give. They tried again, but this time the body did not move at all. After the third try they stopped and looked down for a while. "One more time," Norman Bowker said. He counted to three and they leaned back and pulled.

"Stuck," said Mitchell Sanders.

"I see that. Christ."

They tried again, then called over Henry Dobbins and Rat Kiley, and all five of them put their arms and backs into it, but the body was jammed in tight.

Azar moved to the dike and sat holding his stomach. His face was pale.

The others stood in a circle, watching the water, then after a time somebody said, "We can't just *leave* him there," and the men nodded and got out their entrenching tools and began digging. It was hard, sloppy work. The mud seemed to flow back faster than they could dig, but Kiowa was their friend and they kept at it anyway.

Slowly, in little groups, the rest of the platoon drifted over to watch. Only Lieutenant Jimmy Cross and the young soldier were still searching the field.

"What we should do, I guess," Norman Bowker said, "is tell the LT."

Mitchell Sanders shook his head. "Just mess things up. Besides, the man looks happy out there, real content. Let him be."

After ten minutes they uncovered most of Kiowa's lower body. The corpse was angled steeply into the muck, upside down, like a diver who plunged headfirst off a high tower. The men stood quietly for a few seconds. There was a feeling of awe. Mitchell Sanders finally nodded and said, "Let's get it done," and they took hold of the legs and pulled up hard, then pulled again, and after a moment Kiowa came sliding to the surface. A piece of his shoulder was missing; the arms and chest and face were cut up with shrapnel. He was covered with bluish green mud. "Well," Henry Dobbins said, "it could be worse," and Dave Jensen said, "How, man? Tell me *how*." Carefully, trying not to look at the body, they carried Kiowa over to the dike and laid him down. They used towels to clean off the scum. Rat Kiley went through the kid's pockets, placed his personal effects in a plastic bag, taped the bag to Kiowa's wrist, then used the radio to call in a dustoff.

Moving away, the men found things to do with themselves, some smoking, some opening up cans of C rations, a few just standing in the rain.

For all of them it was a relief to have it finished. There was the promise now of finding a hootch somewhere, or an abandoned pagoda, where they could strip down and wring out their fatigues and maybe start a hot fire. They felt bad for Kiowa. But they also felt a kind of giddiness, a secret joy, because they were alive, and because even the rain was preferable to being sucked under a shit field, and because it was all a matter of luck and happenstance.

Azar sat down on the dike next to Norman Bowker.

"Listen," he said. "Those jumb jokes—I didn't mean anything."

"We all say things."

"Yeah, but when I saw the guy, it made me feel—I don't know—like he was listening."

"He wasn't."

"I guess not. But I felt sort of guilty almost, like if I'd kept my mouth shut none of it would've ever happened. Like it was my fault."

Norman Bowker looked out across the wet field.

"Nobody's fault," he said. "Everybody's."

* * *

Near the center of the field First Lieutenant Jimmy Cross squatted in the muck, almost entirely submerged. In his head he was revising the letter to Kiowa's father. Impersonal this time. An officer expressing an officer's condolences. No apologies were necessary, because in fact it was one of those freak things, and the war was full of freaks, and nothing could ever change it anyway. Which was the truth, he thought. The exact truth.

Lieutenant Cross went deeper into the muck, the dark water at his throat, and tried to tell himself it was the truth.

Beside him, a few steps off to the left, the young soldier was still searching for his girlfriend's picture. Still remembering how he had killed Kiowa.

The boy wanted to confess. He wanted to tell the lieutenant how in the middle of the night he had pulled out Billie's picture and passed it over to Kiowa and then switched on the flashlight, and how Kiowa had whispered, "Hey, she's *cute,*" and how for a second the flashlight had made Billie's face sparkle, and how right then the field had exploded all around them. The flashlight had done it. Like a target shining in the dark.

The boy looked up at the sky, then at Jimmy Cross.

"Sir?" he said.

The rain and mist moved across the field in broad, sweeping sheets of gray. Close by, there was thunder.

"Sir," the boy said, "I got to explain something."

But Lieutenant Jimmy Cross wasn't listening. Eyes closed, he let himself go deeper into the waste, just letting the field take him. He lay back and floated.

When a man died, there had to be blame. Jimmy Cross understood this. You could blame the war. You could blame the idiots who made the war. You could blame Kiowa for going to it. You could blame the rain. You could blame the river. You could blame the field, the mud, the climate. You could blame the enemy. You could blame the mortar rounds. You could blame people who were too lazy to read a newspaper, who were bored by the daily body counts, who switched channels at the mention of politics. You could blame whole nations. You could blame God. You could blame the munitions makers or Karl Marx or a trick of fate or an old man in Omaha who forgot to vote.

In the field, though, the causes were immediate. A moment of carelessness or bad judgment or plain stupidity carried consequences that lasted forever.

For a long while Jimmy Cross lay floating. In the clouds to the east there was the sound of a helicopter, but he did not take notice. With his eyes still closed, bobbing in the field, he let himself slip away. He was back home in New Jersey. A golden afternoon on the golf course, the fairways lush and green, and he was teeing it up on the first hole. It was a world without responsibility. When the war was over, he thought, maybe then he would write a letter to Kiowa's father. Or maybe not. Maybe he would just take a couple of practice swings and knock the ball down the middle and pick up his clubs and walk off into the afternoon.

1990

Norman Mailer 1923–2007

Norman Kingsley Mailer was born in Long Branch, New Jersey, and raised in Brooklyn, New York. He entered Harvard at the age of sixteen. There he majored in aeronautical engineering but soon became fascinated by literature, especially the work of Steinbeck, Farrell, and Dos Passos. Active in Harvard literary groups, he won *Story* magazine's College Award in 1941.

In 1944, drafted into the U.S. Army, he served as a rifleman with the 112th Cavalry out of San Antonio, Texas, an alien milieu for an unprepossessing Jewish boy from Brooklyn. He served for eighteen months in the Philippines and Japan, from which experience grew his first novel, *The Naked and the Dead.* An enormous popular and critical success, this book made Mailer a celebrity at the age of twenty-five and set in motion a complex series of public responses.

Controversy dogged Mailer through his personal and professional life. The father of nine children, he was married six times and at the center of numerous political storms. His sometimes bizarre behavior during his youth and early middle age (fistfights, arrests, above all the non-fatal stabbing of his second wife, Adele Morales, in 1960), coupled with his involvement in political life (co-founding the *Village Voice* in 1956, running for mayor of New York City in 1969, being arrested for civil disobedience during the 1967 March on the Pentagon), made him a convenient target for the media. Simultaneously his work and its critical reception proceeded through various stages.

The Armies of the Night (1968), for which Mailer won both the Pulitzer Prize for general nonfiction and the National Book Award for Arts and Letters, recounts his vision of the March on the Pentagon. This book is paradigmatic of various lines of development in his life and work. In this "nonfiction novel," subtitled *History as a Novel: The Novel as History,* Mailer's fictional voice, his political activism, and his flamboyant public image converge.

After *The Naked and the Dead,* a powerful but derivative naturalistic novel, Mailer developed an existential fictional voice that peaked in *An American Dream* (1965). This controversial novel treats allegorically the protagonist's murder of his wife, presenting a sophisticated and profoundly disturbing vision of the violence endemic in America.

Although Mailer remained paradoxical and flamboyant, *The Armies of the Night* forced the literary establishment to take him seriously once again. In the more than forty years since this book, he matured as an artist, producing a large body of important work and becoming a truly major figure in American letters. In 1979 he won his second Pulitzer Prize, for *The Executioner's Song,* the "true-life novel" of the murderer Gary Gilmore, which led to further criticism of Mailer's obsession with (some say glamorizing of) American violence. The year 1991 saw the publication of the massive *Harlot's Ghost,* steeped in Mailer's obsessive themes of sexuality, violence, and existential choice.

If his work did not cease to engender intense reactions, the former *enfant terrible* unquestionably mellowed personally and grew into the role of senior statesman of American letters. Happily married to his sixth wife, Norris Church, Mailer seemed to have found tranquillity. As president of PEN, an international organization of writers, he led the fight for freedom of expression. And in every arena of American life, he left his distinctive and indelible mark.

Barry H. Leeds
Central Connecticut State University

PRIMARY WORKS

The Naked and the Dead, 1948; *Barbary Shore,* 1951; *The Deer Park,* 1955; *The White Negro,* 1958; *Advertisements for Myself,* 1959; *Deaths for the Ladies and Other Disasters,* 1962; *The Presidential Papers,* 1963; *An American Dream,* 1965; *Cannibals and Christians,* 1966; *Why Are We in Vietnam?,* 1967; *Short Fiction of Norman Mailer,* 1967; *Miami and the Siege of Chicago,* 1968; *The Armies of the Night,* 1968; *Of a Fire on the Moon,* 1970; *The Prisoner of Sex,* 1971; *St. George and the Godfather,* 1972; *Essential Errands,* 1972; *Marilyn,* 1973; *The Faith of Graffiti,* 1974; *The Fight,* 1975; *Some Honorable Men,* 1976; *Genius and Lust,* 1976; *The Executioner's Song,* 1979; *Of Women and Their Elegance,* 1980; *Pieces and Pontifications,* 1982; *Ancient Evenings,* 1983; *Tough Guys Don't Dance,* 1984; *The Last Night,* 1984; *Harlot's Ghost,* 1991; *Oswald: An American Mystery,* 1995; *Portrait of Picasso as a Young Man,* 1996; *The Gospel According to the Son,* 1997; *The Time of Our Time,* 1998; *The Spooky Art: Some Thoughts on Writing,* 2003; *The Castle in the Forest,* 2007.

from The Armies of the Night

. . . "We are gathered here"—shades of Lincoln in hippieland—"to make a move on Saturday to invest the Pentagon and halt and slow down its workings, and this will be at once a symbolic act and a real act"—he was roaring—"for real heads may possibly get hurt, and soldiers will be there to hold us back, and some of us may be arrested"—how, wondered the wise voice at the rear of this roaring voice, could one ever leave Washington now without going to jail?—"some blood conceivably will be shed. If I were the man in the government responsible for controlling this March, I would not know what to do." Sonorously—"I would not wish to arrest too many or hurt anyone for fear the repercussions in the world would be too large for my bureaucrat's heart to bear—it's so full of shit." Roars and chills from the audience again. He was off into obscenity. It gave a heartiness like the blood of beef tea to his associations. There was no villainy in obscenity for him, just paradoxically, characteristically—his love for America: he had first come to love America when he served in the U.S. Army, not the America of course of the flag, the patriotic unendurable fix of the television programs and the newspapers, no, long before he was ever aware of the institutional oleo of the most suffocating American ideas he had come to love what editorial writers were fond of calling the democratic principle with its faith in the common man. He found that principle and that man in the Army, but what none of the editorial writers ever mentioned was that that noble common man was obscene as an old goat, and his obscenity was what saved him. The sanity of said common democratic man was in his humor, his humor was in his obscenity. And his philosophy as well—a reductive philosophy which looked to restore the hard edge of proportion to the overblown values overhanging each small military existence—viz: being forced to salute an overconscientious officer with your back stiffened into an exaggerated posture. "That Lieutenant is chicken-shit," would be the platoon verdict, and a blow had somehow been struck for democracy and the sanity of good temper. Mailer once heard a private end an argument about the merits of a general by saying, "his spit don't smell like ice cream either," only the private was not speaking of spit.

Mailer thought enough of the line to put it into *The Naked and the Dead,* along with a good many other such lines the characters in his mind and his memory of the Army had begun to offer him. The common discovery of America was probably that Americans were the first people on earth to live for their humor; nothing was so important to Americans as humor. In Brooklyn, he had taken this for granted, at Harvard he had thought it was a by-product of being at Harvard, but in the Army he discovered that the humor was probably in the veins and the roots of the local history of every state and county in America—the truth of the way it really felt over the years passed on a river of obscenity from small-town storyteller to storyteller there down below the bankers and the books and the educators and the legislators—so Mailer never felt more like an American than when he was naturally obscene—all the gifts of the American language came out in the happy play of obscenity upon concept, which enabled one to go back to concept again. What was magnificent about the word shit is that it enabled you to use the word noble: a skinny Southern cracker with a beatific smile on his face saying in the dawn in a Filipino rice paddy, "Man, I just managed to take me a noble shit." Yeah, that was Mailer's America. If he was going to love something in the country, he would love that. So after years of keeping obscene language off to one corner of his work, as if to prove after *The Naked and the Dead* that he had many an arrow in his literary quiver, he had come back to obscenity again in the last year—he had kicked goodbye in his novel *Why Are We In Vietnam?* to the old literary corset of good taste, letting his sense of language play on obscenity as freely as it wished, so discovering that everything he knew about the American language (with its incommensurable resources) went flying in and out of the line of his prose with the happiest beating of wings—it was the first time his style seemed at once very American to him and very literary in the best way, at least as he saw the best way. But the reception of the book had been disappointing. Not because many of the reviews were bad (he had learned, despite all sudden discoveries of sorrow, to live with that as one lived with smog) no, what was disappointing was the crankiness across the country. Where fusty conservative old critics had once defended the obscenity in *The Naked and the Dead,* they, or their sons, now condemned it in the new book, and that *was* disappointing. The country was not growing up so much as getting a premature case of arthritis.

At any rate, he had come to the point where he liked to use a little obscenity in his public speaking. Once people got over the shock, they were sometimes able to discover that the humor it provided was not less powerful than the damage of the pain. Of course he did not do it often and tried not to do it unless he was in good voice—Mailer was under no illusion that public speaking was equal to candid conversation; an obscenity uttered in a voice too weak for its freight was obscene, since obscenity probably resides in the quick conversion of excitement to nausea—which is why Lyndon Johnson's speeches are called obscene by some. The excitement of listening to the American President alters abruptly into the nausea of wandering down the blind alleys of his voice.

This has been a considerable defense of the point, but then the point was at the center of his argument and it could be put thus: the American corporation executive, who was after all the foremost representative of Man in the world today, was perfectly capable of burning unseen women and children in the Vietnamese jungles, yet felt a large displeasure and fairly final disapproval at the generous use of obscenity in literature and in public. . . .

In a little more than a half hour, the students were done. Now began the faculty. They too came up one by one, but now there was no particular sense offered of an internal organization. Unlike the students, they had not debated these matters in open forum for months, organized, proselyted, or been overcome by argument, no, most of them had served as advisers to the students, had counseled them, and been picked up, many of them, and brought along by the rush of this moral stream much as a small piece of river bank might separate from the shore and go down the line of the flood. It must have been painful for these academics. They were older, certainly less suited for jail, aware more precisely of how and where their careers would be diverted or impeded, they had families many of them, they were liberal academics, technologues, they were being forced to abdicate from the machines they had chosen for their life. Their decision to turn in draft cards must have come for many in the middle of the night; for others it must have come even last night, or as they stood here debating with themselves. Many of them seemed to stand irresolutely near the steps for long periods, then move up at last. Rogoff, standing next to Mailer, hugging his thin chest in the October air, now cold, finally took out his card and, with a grin at Mailer, said, "I guess I'm going to turn this in. But you know the ridiculous part of it is that I'm 4-F."[1] So they came up one by one, not in solidarity, but as individuals, each breaking the shield or the fence or the mold or the home or even the construct of his own security. And as they did this, a deep gloom began to work on Mailer, because a deep modesty was on its way to him, he could feel himself becoming more and more of a modest man as he stood there in the cold with his hangover, and he hated this because modesty was an old family relative, he had been born to a modest family, had been a modest boy, a modest young man, and he hated that, he loved the pride and the arrogance and the confidence and the egocentricity he had acquired over the years, that was his force and his luxury and the iron in his greed, the richest sugar of his pleasure, the strength of his competitive force, he had lived long enough to know that the intimation one was being steeped in a new psychical condition (like this oncoming modest grace) was never to be disregarded, permanent new states could come into one on just so light a breeze. He stood in the cold watching the faculty men come up, yes always one by one, and felt his hangover which had come in part out of his imperfectly swallowed contempt for them the night before, and in part out of his fear, yes now he saw it, fear of the consequences of this weekend in Washington, for he had known from the beginning it could disrupt his life for a season or more and in some way the danger was there it could change him forever. He was forty-four years old, and it had taken him most of those forty-four years to begin to be able to enjoy his pleasures where he found them, rather than worry about his pleasures which eluded him—it was obviously no time to embark on ventures which would eventually give one more than a few years in jail. Yet, there was no escape. As if some final cherished rare innocence of childhood still preserved intact in him was brought finally to the surface and there expired, so he lost at that instant the last secret delight he retained in life as a game where finally you never got hurt if you played the game well enough. For years he had envisioned himself in some final cataclysm,[2] as an underground leader in the city, or a guerrilla with a gun in the hills,

---

[1] Military term for individuals who are medically unfit for service.　　[2] A violent upheaval.

and had scorned the organizational aspects of revolution, the speeches, mimeograph machines, the hard dull forging of new parties and programs, the dull maneuvering to keep power, the intolerable obedience required before the over-all intellectual necessities of each objective period, and had scorned it, yes, had spit at it, and perhaps had been right, certainly had been right, such revolutions were the womb and cradle of technology land, no the only revolutionary truth was a gun in the hills, and that would not be his, he would be too old by then, and too incompetent, yes, too incompetent said the new modesty, and too showboat, too lacking in essential judgment—besides, he was too well-known! He would pay for the pleasures of his notoriety in the impossibility of disguise. No gun in the hills, no taste for organization, no, he was a figurehead, and therefore he was expendable, said the new modesty—not a future leader, but a future victim: *there* would be his real value. He could go to jail for protest, and spend some years if it came to it, possibly his life, for if the war went on, and America put its hot martial tongue across the Chinese border, well, jail was the probable perspective, detention camps, dissociation centers, liquidation alleys, that would be his portion, and it would come about the time he had learned how to live.

The depth of this gloom and this modesty came down on Mailer, and he watched the delegation take the bag into the Department of Justice with 994 cards contained inside, and listened to the speeches while they waited, and was eventually called up himself to make a speech, and made a modest one in a voice so used by the stentorian demonstrations of the night before that he was happy for the mike since otherwise he might have communicated in a whisper. He said a little of what he had thought while watching the others: that he had recognized on this afternoon that the time had come when Americans, many Americans, would have to face the possibility of going to jail for their ideas, and this was a prospect with no cheer because prisons were unattractive places where much of the best in oneself was slowly extinguished, but it could be there was no choice. The war in Vietnam was an obscene war, the worst war the nation had ever been in, and so its logic might compel sacrifice from those who were not so accustomed. And, out of hardly more than a sense of old habit and old anger, he scolded the press for their lies, and their misrepresentation, for their guilt in creating a psychology over the last twenty years in the average American which made wars like Vietnam possible; then he surrendered the mike and stepped down and the applause was pleasant.

. . . out from that direction came the clear bitter-sweet excitation of a military trumpet resounding in the near distance, one peal which seemed to go all the way back through a galaxy of bugles to the cries of the Civil War and the first trumpet note to blow the attack. The ghosts of old battles were wheeling like clouds over Washington today.

The trumpet sounded again. It was calling the troops. "Come here," it called from the steps of Lincoln Memorial over the two furlongs of the long reflecting pool, out to the swell of the hill at the base of Washington Monument, "come here, come here, come here. The rally is on!" And from the north and the east, from the direction of the White House and the Smithsonian and the Capitol, from Union Station and the Department of Justice the troops were coming in, the volunteers were answering the call. They came walking up in all sizes, a citizens' army not ranked yet by height, an army of both sexes in numbers almost equal, and of all ages, although most were young. Some were well-dressed, some were poor, many were conventional in appearance, as often were not. The hippies were there in great number, perambulating down the hill, many dressed like the legions of Sgt. Pepper's Band,[3] some were gotten up like Arab shieks, or in Park Avenue's doormen's greatcoats, others like Rogers and Clark of the West, Wyatt Earp, Kit Carson, Daniel Boone in buckskin, some had grown mustaches to look like *Have Gun, Will Travel*—Paladin's[4] surrogate was here!—and wild Indians with feathers, a hippie gotten up like Batman, another like Claude Rains in *The Invisible Man*—his face wrapped in a turban of bandages and he wore a black satin top hat. A host of these troops wore capes, beat-up khaki capes, slept on, used as blankets, towels, improvised duffel bags; or fine capes, orange linings, or luminous rose linings, the edges ragged, near a tatter, the threads ready to feather, but a musketeer's hat on their head. One hippie may have been dressed like Charles Chaplin; Buster Keaton and W.C. Fields[5] could have come to the ball; there were Martians and Moon-men and a knight unhorsed who stalked about in the weight of real armor. There were to be seen a hundred soldiers in Confederate gray, and maybe there were two or three hundred hippies in officer's coats of Union dark-blue. They had picked up their costumes where they could, in surplus stores, and Blow-your-mind shops, Digger free emporiums, and psychedelic caches of Hindu junk. There were soldiers in Foreign Legion uniforms, and tropical bush jackets, San Quentin and Chino, California striped shirt and pants, British copies of Eisenhower jackets, hippies dressed like Turkish shepherds and Roman senators, gurus, and samurai in dirty smocks. They were close to being assembled from all the intersections between history and the comic books, between legend and television, the Biblical archetypes and the movies. The sight of these troops, this army with a thousand costumes, fulfilled to the hilt our General's oldest idea of war which is that every man should dress as he pleases if he is going into battle, for that is his right, and variety never hurts the zest of the hardiest workers in every battalion (here today by thousands in plain hunting jackets, corduroys or dungarees, ready for assault!) if the sight of such masquerade lost its usual happy connotation of masked ladies and starving children outside the ball, it was not only because of the shabbiness of the costumes (up close half of them must have been used by hippies for everyday wear) but also because the aesthetic at last was in the politics—the dress ball was going into battle. Still, there were nightmares beneath the gaiety of these middle-class runaways, these Crusaders, going out to attack the hard core of technology land with less training than armies were once offered by a medieval assembly ground. The nightmare was in the echo of those trips which had fractured their sense of past and present. If nature was a veil whose tissue had been ripped by static, screams of jet motors, the highway grid of the suburbs, smog, defoliation, pollution of streams, overfertilization of earth, anti-fertilization of women, and the radiation of two decades of near blind atom busting, then perhaps the history of the past was another tissue, spiritual, no doubt, without physical embodiment, unless its embodiment was in the cuneiform hieroglyphics of the chromosome (so much like primitive writing!) but that tissue of past history, whether traceable in the flesh, or merely palpable in the collective underworld of the

---

[3]Fictional band made famous by the British rock group, The Beatles.

[4]Various fictional and non-fictional American folk heroes.

[5]American comedians and early stars of film.

dream, was nonetheless being bombed by the use of LSD as outrageously as the atoll of Eniwetok, Hiroshima, Nagasaki, and the scorched foliage of Vietnam. The history of the past was being exploded right into the present: perhaps there were now lacunae in the firmament of the past, holes where once had been the psychic reality of an era which was gone. Mailer was haunted by the nightmare that the evils of the present not only exploited the present, but consumed the past, and gave every promise of demolishing whole territories of the future. The same villains who, promiscuously, wantonly, heedlessly, had gorged on LSD and consumed God knows what essential marrows of history, wearing indeed the history of all eras on their back as trophies of this gluttony, were now going forth (conscience-struck?) to make war on those other villains, corporation-land villains, who were destroying the promise of the present in their self-righteousness and greed and secret lust (often unknown to themselves) for some sexo-technological variety of neo-fascism.[6]

Mailer's final allegiance, however, was with the villains who were hippies. They would never have looked to blow their minds and destroy some part of the past if the authority had not brainwashed the mood of the present until it smelled like deodorant. (To cover the odor of burning flesh in Vietnam?) So he continued to enjoy the play of costumes, but his pleasure was now edged with a hint of the sinister. Not inappropriate for battle. He and Lowell,[7] were still in the best of moods. The morning was so splendid—it spoke of a vitality in nature which no number of bombings in space nor innerspace might ever subdue; the rustle of costumes warming up for the war spoke of future redemptions as quickly as they reminded of hog-swillings from the past, and the thin air! wine of Civil War apples in the October air! edge of excitement and awe—how would this day end? No one could know. Incredible spectacle now gathering—tens of thousands traveling hundreds of miles to attend a symbolic battle. In the capital of technology land beat a primitive drum. New drum of the Left! And the Left had been until this year the secret unwitting accomplice of every increase in the power of the technicians, bureaucrats, and labor leaders who ran the governmental military-industrial complex of super-technology land. . . .

6: A Confrontation by the River

It was not much of a situation to study. The MPs stood in two widely spaced ranks. The first rank was ten yards behind the rope, and each MP in that row was close to twenty feet from the next man. The second rank, similarly spaced, was ten yards behind the first rank and perhaps thirty yards behind them a cluster appeared, every fifty yards or so, of two or three U.S. Marshals in white helmets and dark blue suits. They were out there waiting. Two moods confronted one another, two separate senses of a private silence.

It was not unlike being a boy about to jump from one garage roof to an adjoining garage roof. The one thing not to do was wait. Mailer looked at Macdonald[8] and

[6]A new or recent form of fascism, a type of right-wing dictatorship.

[7]Robert Lowell, major American poet (1917–1977).

[8]Dwight Macdonald, major American critic (1906–1982).

Lowell. "Let's go," he said. Not looking again at them, not pausing to gather or dissipate resolve, he made a point of stepping neatly and decisively over the low rope. Then he headed across the grass to the nearest MP he saw.

It was as if the air had changed, or light had altered; he felt immediately much more alive—yes, bathed in air—and yet disembodied from himself, as if indeed he were watching himself in a film where this action was taking place. He could feel the eyes of the people behind the rope watching him, could feel the intensity of their existence as spectators. And as he walked forward, he and the MP looked at one another with the naked stricken lucidity which comes when absolute strangers are for the moment absolutely locked together.

The MP lifted his club to his chest as if to bar all passage. To Mailer's great surprise—he had secretly expected the enemy to be calm and strong, why should they not? they had every power, all the guns—to his great surprise, the MP was trembling. He was a young Negro, part white, who looked to have come from some small town where perhaps there were not many other Negroes; he had at any rate no Harlem smoke, no devil swish, no black, no black power for him, just a simple boy in an Army suit with a look of horror in his eye, "Why, why did it have to happen to me?" was the message of the petrified marbles in his face.

"Go back," he said hoarsely to Mailer.

"If you don't arrest me, I'm going to the Pentagon."

"No. Go back."

The thought of a return—"since they won't arrest me, what can I do?"—over these same ten yards was not at all suitable.

As the MP spoke, the raised club quivered. He did not know if it quivered from the desire of the MP to strike him, or secret military wonder was he now possessed of a moral force which implanted terror in the arms of young soldiers? Some unfamiliar current, now gyroscopic, now a sluggish whirlpool, was evolving from that quiver of the club, and the MP seemed to turn slowly away from his position confronting the rope, and the novelist turned with him, each still facing the other until the axis of their shoulders was now perpendicular to the rope, and still they kept turning in this psychic field, not touching, the club quivering, and then Mailer was behind the MP, he was free of him, and he wheeled around and kept going in a half run to the next line of MPs and then on the push of a sudden instinct, sprinted suddenly around the nearest MP in the second line, much as if he were a back cutting around the nearest man in the secondary to break free—that was actually his precise thought—and had a passing perception of how simple it was to get past the MPs. They looked petrified. Striken faces as he went by. They did not know what to do. It was his dark pinstripe suit, his vest, the maroon and blue regimental tie, the part in his hair, the barrel chest, the early paunch—he must have looked like a banker himself, a banker, gone ape! And then he saw the Pentagon to his right across the field, not a hundred yards away, and a little to his left, the marshals, and he ran on a jog toward them, and came up, and they glared at him and shouted, "Go back."

He had a quick impression of hard-faced men with gray eyes burning some transparent fuel for flame, and said, "I won't go back. If you don't arrest me, I'm going on to the Pentagon," and knew he meant it, some absolute certainty had come to him, and then two of them leaped on him at once in the cold clammy murderous fury of all cops at the existential moment of making their bust—all cops who secretly expect to be struck at that instant for their sins—and a supervising force came to his voice, and he roared, to his own distant pleasure in new achievement and new authority—"Take your hands off me, can't you see? I'm not resisting arrest," and one then let go of him, and the other stopped trying to pry his arm into a lock, and contented himself with a hard hand under his armpit, and they set off walking across the field at a rabid intent quick rate, walking parallel to the wall of the Pentagon, fully visible on his right at last, and he was arrested, he had succeeded in that, and without a club on his head, the mountain air in his lungs as thin and fierce as smoke, yes, the livid air of tension on this livid side promised a few events of more interest than the routine wait to be free, yes he was more than a visitor, he was in the land of the enemy now, he would get to see their face. . . .

But now a tall U.S. Marshal who had the body and insane look of a very good rangy defensive end in professional football—that same hard high-muscled build, same coiled spring of wrath, same livid conviction that everything opposing the team must be wrecked, sod, turf, grass, uniforms, helmets, bodies, yes even bite the football if it will help—now leaped into the truck and jumped between them. "Shut up," he said, "or I'll wreck both of you." He had a long craggy face somewhere in the physiognomical land between Steve McQueen and Robert Mitchum, but he would never have made Hollywood, for his skin was pocked with the big boiling craters of a red lunar acne, and his eyes in Cinemascope would have blazed an audience off their seat for such gray-green flame could only have issued from a blowtorch. Under his white Marshal's helmet, he was one impressive piece of gathered wrath.

Speaking to the Marshal at this point would have been dangerous. The Marshal's emotions had obviously been marinating for a week in the very special bile waters American Patriotism reserves for its need. His feelings were now caustic as a whip—too gentle the simile!—he was in agonies of frustration because the honor of his profession kept him from battering every prisoner's head to a Communist pulp. Mailer looked him over covertly to see what he could try if the Marshal went to work on him. All reports: negative. He would not stand a chance with this Marshal—there seemed no place to hit him where he'd be vulnerable; stone larynx, leather testicles, ice cubes for eyes. And he had his Marshal's club in his hand as well. Brother! Bring back the Nazi!

Whether the Marshal had been once in the Marine Corps, or in Vietnam, or if half his family were now in Vietnam, or if he just hated the sheer New York presumption of that slovenly, drug-ridden weak contaminating America-hating army of termites outside this fortress' walls, he was certainly any upstanding demonstrator's nightmare. Because he was full of American rectitude and was fearless, and savage, savage as the exhaust left in the wake of a motorcycle club, gasoline and cheap perfume were one end of his spectrum, yeah, this Marshal loved action, but he was also in that no man's land between the old frontier and the new ranch home—as they, yes *they*—the enemies of the Marshal—tried to pass bills to limit the purchase of hunting rifles, so did *they* try to kill America, inch by inch, all the forces of evil, disorder, mess and chaos in the world, and *cowardice!* and city ways, and slick shit, and despoliation of national resources, all the subtle invisible creeping paralyses of Communism which were changing America from a land where blood was red to a land where water was foul—yes in this Marshal's mind—no lesser explanation could suffice for the Knight of God light in the flame of his eye—the evil was without,

America was threatened by a foreign disease and the Marshal was threatened to the core of his sanity by any one of the first fifty of Mailer's ideas which would insist that the evil was within, that the best in America was being destroyed by what in itself seemed next best, yes American heroism corrupted by American know-how—no wonder murder stood out in his face as he looked at the novelist—for the Marshal to lose his sanity was no passing psychiatric affair: think rather of a rifleman on a tower in Texas and a score of his dead on the street.[9]. . .

It may be obvious by now that a history of the March on the Pentagon which is not unfair will never be written, any more than a history which could prove dependable in details!

As it grew dark there was the air of carnival as well. The last few thousand Marchers to arrive from Lincoln Memorial did not even bother to go to the North Parking Area, but turned directly to the Mall and were cheered by the isolated detachments who saw them from a ledge of the wall at the plaza. Somewhere, somebody lit his draft card, and as it began to burn he held it high. The light of the burning card traveled through the crowd until it found another draft card someone else was ready to burn and this was lit, and then another in the distance. In the gathering dark it looked like a dusting of fireflies over the great shrub of the Mall.

By now, however, the way was open again to the North Parking. The chartered buses were getting ready to leave. That portion of this revolution which was Revolution on Excursion Ticket was now obliged to leave. Where once there had been thirty thousand people in the Mall, there were now suddenly twenty thousand people, ten thousand people, less. As the busses ground through the interlockings of their gears and pulled out into a mournful wheezing acceleration along the road, so did other thousands on the Mall look at one another and decide it was probably time to catch a cab or take the long walk back to Washington—they were in fact hungry for a meal. So the Mall began to empty, and the demonstrators on the steps must have drawn a little closer. The mass assault was over.

A few thousand, however, were left, and they were the best. The civil disobedience might be far from done. On the Mall, since the oncoming night was cold, bonfires were lit. On the stairs, a peace pipe was passed. It was filled with hashish. Soon the demonstrators were breaking out marijuana, handing it back and forth, offering it even to the soldiers here and there. The Army after all had been smoking marijuana since Korea, and in Vietnam—by all reports—were gorging on it. The smell of the drug, sweet as the sweetest leaves of burning tea, floated down to the Mall where its sharp bite of sugar and smoldering grass pinched the nose, relaxed the neck. Soon most of the young on the Mall were smoking as well. Can this be one of the moments when the Secretary of Defense looks out from his window in the Pentagon at the crowd on the Mall and studies their fires below? They cannot be unreminiscent of other campfires in Washington and Virginia little more than a century ago.[10]

. . . this passage through the night was a rite of passage, and these disenchanted heirs of the Old Left, this rabble of American Vietcong, and hippies, and pacifists, and whoever else was left were afloat on a voyage whose first note had been struck with the first sound of the trumpet Mailer had heard crossing Washington Monu-

---

[9]A reference to Charles Whitman, who shot numerous pedestrians from atop a Texas clock tower on August 1, 1966.

[10]An allusion to the Civil War.

ment in the morning. "Come here, come here, come here," the trumpet had said, and now eighteen hours later, in the false dawn, the echo of far greater rites of passage in American history, the light reflected from the radiance of greater more heroic hours may have come nonetheless to shine along the inner space and the caverns of the freaks, some hint of a glorious future may have hung in the air, some refrain from all the great American rites of passage when men and women manacled themselves to a lost and painful principle and survived a day, a night, a week, a month, a year, a celebration of Thanksgiving—the country had been founded on a rite of passage. Very few had not emigrated here without the echo of that rite, even if it were no more (and no less!) than eight days in the stink, bustle, fear, and propinquity of steerage on an ocean crossing (or the eighty days of dying on a slave ship) each generation of Americans had forged their own rite, in the forest of the Alleghenies and the Adirondacks, at Valley Forge, at New Orleans in 1812, with Rogers and Clark or at Sutter's Mill, at Gettysburg, the Alamo, the Klondike, the Argonne, Normandy, Pusan,[11]—the engagement at the Pentagon was a pale rite of passage next to these, and yet it was probably a true one, for it came to the spoiled children of a dead de-animalized middle class who had chosen most freely, out of the incomprehensible mysteries of moral choice, to make an attack and then hold a testament before the most authoritative embodiment of the principle that America was right, America was might, America was the true religious war of Christ against the Communist. So it became a rite of passage for these tender drug-vitiated jargon-mired children, they endured through a night, a black dark night which began in joy, near foundered in terror, and dragged on through empty apathetic hours while glints of light came to each alone. Yet the rite of passage was invoked, the moral ladder was climbed, they were forever different in the morning than they had been before the night, which is the meaning of a rite of passage, one has voyaged through a channel of shipwreck and temptation, and so some of the vices carried from another nether world into life itself (on the day of one's birth) may have departed, or fled, or quit; some part of the man has been born again, and is better, just as some hardly so remarkable area of the soul may have been in some miniscule sweet fashion reborn on the crossing of the marchers over Arlington Memorial Bridge, for the worst of them and the most timid were moving nonetheless to a confrontation they could only fear, they were going to the land of the warmakers. Not so easy for the timid when all is said.

11: The Metaphor Delivered

Whole crisis of Christianity in America that the military heroes were on one side, and the unnamed saints on the other! Let the bugle blow. The death of America rides in on the smog. America—the land where a new kind of man was born from the idea that God was present in every man not only as compassion but as power, and so the country belonged to the people; for the will of the people—if the locks of their life could be given the art to turn—was then the will of God. Great and dangerous idea! If the locks did not turn, then the will of the people was the will of the Devil. Who by now could know where was what? Liars controlled the locks.

[11]References to various major American battles and explorations.

Brood on that country who expresses our will. She is America, once a beauty of magnificence unparalleled, now a beauty with a leprous skin. She is heavy with child—no one knows if legitimate—and languishes in a dungeon whose walls are never seen. Now the first contractions of her fearsome labor begin—it will go on: no doctor exists to tell the hour. It is only known that false labor is not likely on her now, no, she will probably give birth, and to what?—the most fearsome totalitarianism the world has ever known? or can she, poor giant, tormented lovely girl, deliver a babe of a new world brave and tender, artful and wild? Rush to the locks. God writhes in his bonds. Rush to the locks. Deliver us from our curse. For we must end on the road to that mystery where courage, death, and the dream of love give promise of sleep.

1968

Robert Bly b. 1926

Few American poets have explored so many facets of the creative—and the human—experience as Robert Bly. After graduating from Harvard, he returned to the Minnesota of his childhood and became one of the leading midcentury poets. Along with James Wright and William Stafford, Bly was the pre-eminent poet of nature, simplicity, and the reality of human experience. In a line of descent from William Carlos Williams, with overtones of the exact language drawn from Wallace Stevens, these poets forced readers back to an encounter with the truly human that had sometimes been obscured in the highly formalist poetry of Richard Eberhart, Richard Wilbur, and even Robert Lowell. Despite his geographically remote location, Bly influenced what was happening in United States poetry through his editing of a series of respected (if idiosyncratic) little magazines—first *The Fifties,* then *The Sixties.* His reviews, signed "Crunk," were read avidly.

Like Williams before him, Bly assumed a posture of stability: his address didn't change, his keen appreciation for the poetry of others was a given, and he was open to friendships with people who might have been seen as his competitors—such as his relationship with James Wright. Also, like the best of the world's poets, Bly was immensely influential in bringing readers, as well as other poets, to appreciate the work of non-English writers. From early in his career through the present, Bly has translated, published, and proselytized about the writings of Vallejo, Neruda, Machado, Jimánez, Rilke, Ponge, Tranströmer, Lagerlöf, Kabir, and (since his translations in 1981) Maulana Jalal al-Din Rumi, a thirteenth-century Persian poet.

Bly's poetry became one of search. Not only was he poised to become a leading poet for ecological preservation—given his immersion in the beauties and violence of the natural world—but he was intent on finding the richest poetic traditions from which to draw. His skill with translating was enhanced by his willingness to work with native speakers, or scholars, of the languages of the poems: Bly's contributions to what the art of translation could become have yet to be appreciated. But what gave Bly's career its most public visibility was U.S. involvement in the Vietnam conflict. Two of his best-known poems, "Counting Small-Boned Bodies" (which stresses the macho superiority of U.S. physical size dominating the stature of the Vietnamese soldiers) and "The Teeth Mother Naked at Last" (which presents his Jungian understanding of the divided female principle—welcoming mother set against destructive female), were published as anti-war works. (With Denise Levertov, Muriel Rukeyser, and many other writers, Bly was an active proponent of Writers and Artists Against the Vietnam War.)

Bly's later publishing history continues to promote the psychological exploration of the human consciousness. Not only his poetry, but his series of popular books that began with *Iron John* in 1990, insists on the ways men (in this stridently gendered world) must come to terms with their conflicted—or, perhaps, richly ambivalent—psyches. As a spokesperson for the archetypal, the Jungian, and the mystical, Bly travels and speaks widely: he may well be America's most visible poet. Such visibility draws mixed responses, but at heart, Robert Bly continues to be the poet we welcomed so heartily at the time of the publication of his first collection, *Silence in the Snowy Fields*.

Linda Wagner-Martin
University of North Carolina–Chapel Hill

PRIMARY WORKS

Silence in the Snowy Fields, 1962; *The Light Around the Body,* 1967; *Forty Poems Touching on Recent American History,* 1970; *The Sea and the Honeycomb,* 1971; *Jumping Out of Bed,* 1973; *Sleepers Joining Hands,* 1973; *For the Stomach: Selected Poems,* 1974; *Old Man Rubbing His Eyes,* 1975; *The Morning Glory,* 1975; *This Body Is Made of Camphor and Gopherwood,* 1977; *The Kabir Book,* 1977; *This Tree Will Be Here for a Thousand Years,* 1979; *News of the Universe,* 1980; *Talking All Morning,* 1980; *The Man in the Black Coat Turns,* 1981; *Loving a Woman in Two Worlds,* 1985; *Selected Poems,* 1986; *American Poetry: Wilderness and Domesticity,* 1990; *Iron John: A Book About Men,* 1990; *What Have I Ever Lost by Dying: Collected Prose Poems,* 1992; *Gratitude to Old Teachers,* 1993; *Meditations on the Insatiable Soul,* 1994; *The Sibling Society,* 1996; *Morning Poems,* 1997; *Holes the Crickets Have Eaten in Blankets: A Sequence of Poems,* 1997; *The Maiden King: The Reunion of Masculine and Feminine,* 1998; *Eating the Honey of Words,* 1999; *The Night Abraham Called to the Stars,* 2001; *My Sentence Was a Thousand Years of Joy,* 2005; *The Urge to Travel Long Distances,* 2005; *Turkish Pears in August,* 2007.

Counting Small-Boned Bodies

Let's count the bodies over again.

If we could only make the bodies smaller,
The size of skulls,
We could make a whole plain white with skulls in the moonlight!

5 If we could only make the bodies smaller,
Maybe we could get
A whole year's kill in front of us on a desk!

If we could only make the bodies smaller,
We could fit
10 A body into a finger-ring, for a keepsake forever.

1967

The Teeth Mother Naked at Last

I

Massive engines lift beautifully from the deck.
Wings appear over the trees, wings with eight hundred rivets.

Engines burning a thousand gallons of gasoline a minute sweep over
    the huts with dirt floors.

The chickens feel the new fear deep in the pits of their beaks.
5 Buddha with Padma Sambhava.

Meanwhile, out on the China Sea,
immense gray bodies are floating,
born in Roanoke,
the ocean on both sides expanding, "buoyed on the dense marine."

10 Helicopters flutter overhead. The death-
bee is coming. Super Sabres
like knots of neurotic energy sweep
around and return.
This is Hamilton's triumph.
15 This is the advantage of a centralized bank.
B-52s come from Guam. All the teachers
die in flames. The hopes of Tolstoy fall asleep in the ant heap.
Do not ask for mercy.

Now the time comes to look into the past-tunnels,
20 the hours given and taken in school,
the scuffles in coatrooms,
foam leaps from his nostrils,
now we come to the scum you take from the mouths of the dead,
now we sit beside the dying, and hold their hands, there is hardly time
    for good-bye,
25 the staff sergeant from North Carolina is dying—you hold his hand,
he knows the mansions of the dead are empty, he has an empty place
inside him, created one night when his parents came home drunk,
he uses half his skin to cover it,
as you try to protect a balloon from sharp objects . . .

30 Artillery shells explode. Napalm canisters roll end over end.
800 steel pellets fly through the vegetable walls.
The six-hour infant puts his fists instinctively to his eyes to keep out
    the light.
But the room explodes,

the children explode.
35 Blood leaps on the vegetable walls.

Yes, I know, blood leaps on the walls—
Don't cry at that—
Do you cry at the wind pouring out of Canada?
Do you cry at the reeds shaken at the edge of the sloughs?
40 *The Marine battalion enters.*
This happens when the seasons change,
This happens when the leaves begin to drop from the trees too early
"Kill them: I don't want to see anything moving."
This happens when the ice begins to show its teeth in the ponds
45 This happens when the heavy layers of lake water press down on the
      fish's head, and send him deeper, where his tail swirls slowly, and
      his brain passes him pictures of heavy reeds, of vegetation fallen
      on vegetation. . . .
Hamilton saw all this in detail:

*"Every banana tree slashed, every cooking utensil smashed, every
    mattress cut."*

Now the Marine knives sweep around like sharp-edged jets; how
    beautifully they slash open the rice bags,
the mattresses . . .
50 ducks are killed with $150 shotguns.

Old women watch the soldiers as they move.

II

Excellent Roman knives slip along the ribs.

A stronger man starts to jerk up the strips of flesh.

"Let's hear it again, you believe in the Father, the Son, and the Holy Ghost?"

55 A long scream unrolls.

More.

*"From the political point of view, democratic institutions are being built
    in Vietnam, wouldn't you agree?"*

A green parrot shudders under the fingernails.
Blood jumps in the pocket.
60 The scream lashes like a tail.

"Let us not be deterred from our task by the voices of dissent. . . ."

The whines of the jets
pierce like a long needle.

As soon as the President finishes his press conference, black wings
    carry off the words,
65 bits of flesh still clinging to them.

       * * *

The ministers lie, the professors lie, the television lies, the priests
    lie. . . .
These lies mean that the country wants to die.
Lie after lie starts out into the prairie grass,
like enormous caravans of Conestoga wagons. . . .

70 And a long desire for death flows out, guiding the enormous caravans
    from beneath,
stringing together the vague and foolish words.
It is a desire to eat death,
to gobble it down,
to rush on it like a cobra with mouth open

75 It's a desire to take death inside,
to feel it burning inside, pushing out velvety hairs,
like a clothes brush in the intestines—

This is the thrill that leads the President on to lie

       * * *

Now the Chief Executive enters; the press conference begins:
80 First the President lies about the date the Appalachian Mountains rose.
Then he lies about the population of Chicago, then he lies about the
    weight of the adult eagle, then about the acreage of the Everglades

He lies about the number of fish taken every year in the Arctic, he has
    private information about which city *is* the capital of Wyoming, he
    lies about the birthplace of Attila the Hun.

He lies about the composition of the amniotic fluid, and he insists
    that Luther was never a German, and that only the Protestants sold
    indulgences,

That Pope Leo X *wanted* to reform the church, but the "liberal
    elements" prevented him,
85 that the Peasants' War was fomented by Italians from the North.

And the Attorney General lies about the time the sun sets.

* * *

These lies are only the longing we all feel to die.
It is the longing for someone to come and take you by the hand to
    where they all are sleeping:
where the Egyptian pharaohs are asleep, and your own mother,
90 and all those disappeared children, who used to go around with you
    in the rings at grade school. . . .

Do not be angry at the President—he is longing to take in his hand
the locks of death hair—
to meet his own children dead, or unborn. . . .
He is drifting sideways toward the dusty places

III

95 This is what it's like for a rich country to make war
this is what it's like to bomb huts (afterwards described as "structures")
this is what it's like to kill marginal farmers (afterwards described as
    "Communists")

this is what it's like to watch the altimeter needle going mad

Baron 25, this is 81. Are there any friendlies in the area? 81 from 25,
negative on the friendlies. I'd like you to take out as many structures
as possible located in those trees within 200 meters east and west of
my smoke mark.

100 diving, the green earth swinging, cheeks hanging back, red pins
    blossoming ahead of us, 20-millimeter cannon fire, leveling off, rice
    fields shooting by like telephone poles, smoke rising, hut roofs
    loom up huge as landing fields, slugs going in, half the huts on fire,
    small figures running, palm trees burning, shooting past, up again; . . .
    blue sky . . . cloud mountains

This is what it's like to have a gross national product.

It's because the aluminum window shade business is doing so well in
    the United States that we roll fire over entire villages
It's because a hospital room in the average American city now costs
    $90 a day that we bomb hospitals in the North

It's because the milk trains coming into New Jersey hit the right
    switches every day that the best Vietnamese men are cut in two by
    American bullets that follow each other like freight cars

105 This is what it's like to send firebombs down from air-conditioned
    cockpits.

This is what it's like to be told to fire into a reed hut with an
    automatic weapon.

It's because we have new packaging for smoked oysters that bomb
    holes appear in the rice paddies

It is because we have so few women sobbing in back rooms,
because we have so few children's heads torn apart by high-velocity
    bullets,
110 Because we have so few tears falling on our own hands
that the Super Sabre turns and screams down toward the earth.

It's because taxpayers move to the suburbs that we transfer
    populations.
The Marines use cigarette lighters to light the thatched roofs of huts
because so many Americans own their own homes.

IV

115 I see a car rolling toward a rock wall.
The treads in the face begin to crack.
We all feel like tires being run down roads under heavy cars.

The teen-ager imagines herself floating through the Seven Spheres.
Oven doors are found
120 open.
Soot collects over the doorframe, has children, takes courses,
goes mad, and dies.

There is a black silo inside our bodies, revolving fast.
Bits of black paint are flaking off,
125 where the motorcycles roar, around and around,
rising higher on the silo walls,
the bodies bent toward the horizon,
driven by angry women dressed in black.

      * * *

I know that books are tired of us.
130 I *know* they are chaining the Bible to chairs.
Books don't want to remain in the same room with us anymore.

New Testaments are escaping . . . dressed as women . . . they go off
    after dark.
And Plato! Plato . . . Plato wants to go backwards. . . .
He wants to hurry back up the river of time, so he can end as some
    blob of sea flesh rotting on an Australian beach.

V

135 Why are they dying? I have written this so many times.
They are dying because the President has opened a Bible again.
They are dying because gold deposits have been found among the
  Shoshoni Indians.

They are dying because money follows intellect!
And intellect is like a fan opening in the wind—

140 The Marines think that unless they die the rivers will not move.
They are dying so that the mountain shadows will continue to fall east
  in the afternoon,
so that the beetle can move along the ground near the fallen twigs.

VI

But if one of those children came near that we have set on fire,
came toward you like a gray barn, walking,
145 you would howl like a wind tunnel in a hurricane,
you would tear at your shirt with blue hands,
you would drive over your own child's wagon trying to back up,
the pupils of your eyes would go wild—

If a child came by burning, you would dance on a lawn,
150 trying to leap into the air, digging into your cheeks,
you would ram your head against the wall of your bedroom
like a bull penned too long in his moody pen—

If one of those children came toward me with both hands
in the air, fire rising along both elbows,
155 I would suddenly go back to my animal brain,
I would drop on all fours, screaming,
my vocal chords would turn blue, so would yours,
it would be two days before I could play with my own children again.

VII

I want to sleep awhile in the rays of the sun slanting over the snow.
160 Don't wake me.
Don't tell me how much grief there is in the leaf with its natural oils.
Don't tell me how many children have been born with stumpy hands
  all those years we lived in St. Augustine's shadow.

Tell me about the dust that falls from the yellow daffodil shaken in
  the restless winds.

Tell me about the particles of Babylonian thought that still pass
    through the earthworm every day.
165 Don't tell me about "the frightening laborers who do not read books."

Now the whole nation starts to whirl,
the end of the Republic breaks off,
Europe comes to take revenge,
the mad beast covered with European hair rushes through the mesa
    bushes in Mendocino County,
170 pigs rush toward the cliff,
the waters underneath part: in one ocean luminous globes float up
    (in them hairy and ecstatic men—)
in the other, the teeth mother, naked at last.

Let us drive cars
up
175 the light beams
to the stars . . .

And return to earth crouched inside the drop of sweat
that falls
from the chin of the Protestant tied in the fire.

1970

Yusef Komunyakaa b. 1947

Born in Bogalusa, Louisiana, the oldest of five children, Komunyakaa is the son of a carpenter and of a mother who bought a set of encyclopedias for her children. When he was sixteen, he discovered James Baldwin's essays and decided to become a writer.

From 1965 to 1968, Komunyakaa served a tour of duty in Vietnam as an information specialist, editing a military newspaper called the *Southern Cross*. In Vietnam he won the Bronze Star. After military service, he enrolled at the University of Colorado (double major in English and sociology) and began writing poetry. Upon graduation in 1980, he studied further at both Colorado State University (where he received an M.A. in creative writing) and the University of California, Irvine (where he received an M.F.A.) and taught at various universities before moving to New Orleans.

While teaching at the University of New Orleans, in 1985, he married Australian novelist Mandy Sayer. Only then, nearly twenty years after his Vietnam experiences, did Komunyakaa write his important war poems, published in 1988 as *Dien Cai Dau*.

The violence of war, the pain of identifying with the Vietnamese, and the anguish of returning to the States had seldom been so eloquently and hauntingly expressed. By 1994, when these poems were included in *Neon Vernacular: New and Selected Poems, 1977–1989*. Komunyakaa had won two creative writing fellowships from the National Endowment for the Arts and the San Francisco Poetry Center Award, and he had held the Lilly Professorship of Poetry at Indiana University. *Neon Vernacular* received the Pulitzer Prize for Poetry, as well as the Kingsley-Tufts Poetry Award from the Claremont Graduate School, and as a result his earlier eight collections of work have been re-evaluated.

In 1998 his poetry collection *Thieves of Paradise* was a finalist for the 1999 National Book Critics Circle Award, and that same year saw the publication of his recording, *Love Notes from the Madhouse.* In 2000, Radicloni Clytus edited a book of Komunyakaa's prose, *Blue Notes: Essays, Interviews, and Commentaries,* for the University of Michigan Press series. In an essay from that collection, "Control Is the Mainspring," the poet writes, "I learned that the body and the mind are indeed connected: good writing is physical and mental. I welcomed the knowledge of this because I am from a working-class people who believe that physical labor is sacred and spiritual." This combination of the realistic and the spiritual runs throughout Komunyakaa's poems, whether they are about his childhood, the father-son relationship, the spiritual journey each of us takes—alone, and in whatever circumstances life hands us— and the various conflicts of war. He has become an important poet for our times.

Linda Wagner-Martin
University of North Carolina–Chapel Hill

PRIMARY WORKS

Dedications and Other Darkhorses, 1977; *Lost in the Bonewheel Factory,* 1979; *Copacetic,* 1984; *I Apologize for the Eyes in My Head,* 1986; *Toys in the Field,* 1987; *Dien Cai Dau,* 1988; *February in Sydney,* 1989; *Magic City,* 1992; *Neon Vernacular,* 1994; *Thieves of Paradise,* 1998; *Blue Notes: Essays, Interviews, and Commentaries,* ed. Radicloni Clytus, 2000; *Talking Dirty to the Gods,* 2000; *Pleasure Dome,* 2000; *Taboo,* 2004; *Gilgamesh,* 2006.

Tu Do Street[1]

Music divides the evening.
I close my eyes & can see
men drawing lines in the dust.
America pushes through the membrane
5 of mist & smoke, & I'm a small boy
again in Bogalusa.[2] *White Only*
signs & Hank Snow.[3] But tonight
I walk into a place where bar girls
fade like tropical birds. When
10 I order a beer, the mama-san
behind the counter acts as if she
can't understand, while her eyes
skirt each white face, as Hank Williams[4]
calls from the psychedelic jukebox.

---

[1]Tu Do Street: street packed with bars and brothels at the center of Saigon, capital of South Vietnam; American Army headquarters during the Vietnam War, 1956–1975.
[2]Bogalusa: the Louisiana town where the poet grew up.

[3]Hank Snow: country singer on Nashville's *Grand Ole Opry* program.
[4]Hank Williams: American composer, singer, guitarist; one of the most influential figures in country music.

15 We have played Judas where
    only machine-gun fire brings us
    together. Down the street
    black GIs hold to their turf also.
    An off-limits sign pulls me
20 deeper into alleys, as I look
    for a softness behind these voices
    wounded by their beauty & war.
    Back in the bush at Dak To[5]
    & Khe Sanh,[6] we fought
25 the brothers of these women
    we now run to hold in our arms.
    There's more than a nation
    inside us, as black & white
    soldiers touch the same lovers
30 minutes apart, tasting
    each other's breath,
    without knowing these rooms
    run into each other like tunnels
    leading to the underworld.

1988

Prisoners

    Usually at the helipad
    I see them stumble-dance
    across the hot asphalt
    with crokersacks over their heads,
5 moving toward the interrogation huts,
    thin-framed as box kites
    of sticks & black silk
    anticipating a hard wind
    that'll tug & snatch them
10 out into space. I think
    some must be laughing
    under their dust-colored hoods,
    knowing rockets are aimed
    at Chu Lai[1]—that the water's

[5]Dak To: site of one of the most violent battles of the war in November 1967; located in northwest South Vietnam.
[6]Khe Sanh: location of U.S. Marine base near the Laotian border; attacked by North Vietnamese Army on January 21, 1968, and kept under siege until April 7.
[1]Chu Lai: northern coastal town fifty miles south of Danang; in 1965, the site of a major U.S. amphibious operation.

15 evaporating & soon the nail
will make contact with metal.
How can anyone anywhere love
these half-broken figures
bent under the sky's brightness?
20 The weight they carry
is the soil we tread night & day.
Who can cry for them?
I've heard the old ones
are the hardest to break.
25 An arm twist, a combat boot
against the skull, a .45
jabbed into the mouth, nothing
works. When they start talking
with ancestors faint as camphor
30 smoke in pagodas, you know
you'll have to kill them
to get an answer.
Sunlight throws
scythes against the afternoon.
35 Everything's a heat mirage; a river
tugs at their slow feet.
I stand alone & amazed,
with a pill-happy door gunner
signaling for me to board the Cobra.[2]
40 I remember how one day
I almost bowed to such figures
walking toward me, under
a corporal's ironclad stare.
I can't say why.
45 From a half-mile away
trees huddle together,
& the prisoners look like
marionettes hooked to strings of light.

1988

Thanks

Thanks for the tree
between me & a sniper's bullet.
I don't know what made the grass

---

[2]Cobra: brand of U.S. helicopter.

    sway seconds before the Viet Cong
5 raised his soundless rifle.
    Some voice always followed,
    telling me which foot
    to put down first.
    Thanks for deflecting the ricochet
10 against that anarchy of dusk.
    I was back in San Francisco
    wrapped up in a woman's wild colors,
    causing some dark bird's love call
    to be shattered by daylight
15 when my hands reached up
    & pulled a branch away
    from my face. Thanks
    for the vague white flower
    that pointed to the gleaming metal
20 reflecting how it is to be broken
    like mist over the grass,
    as we played some deadly
    game for blind gods.
    What made me spot the monarch
25 writhing on a single thread
    tied to a farmer's gate,
    holding the day together
    like an unfingered guitar string,
    is beyond me. Maybe the hills
30 grew weary & leaned a little in the heat.
    Again, thanks for the dud
    hand grenade tossed at my feet
    outside Chu Lai. I'm still
    falling through its silence.
35 I don't know why the intrepid
    sun touched the bayonet,
    but I know that something
    stood among those lost trees
    & moved only when I moved.

                  1988

Facing It

My black face fades,
hiding inside the black granite.
I said I wouldn't,
dammit: No tears.

5 I'm stone. I'm flesh.
   My clouded reflection eyes me
   like a bird of prey, the profile of night
   slanted against morning. I turn
   this way—the stone lets me go.
10 I turn that way—I'm inside
   the Vietnam Veterans Memorial
   again, depending on the light
   to make a difference.
   I go down the 58,022 names,
15 half-expecting to find
   my own in letters like smoke.
   I touch the name Andrew Johnson;
   I see the booby trap's white flash.
   Names shimmer on a woman's blouse
20 but when she walks away
   the names stay on the wall.
   Brushstrokes flash, a red bird's
   wings cutting across my stare.
   The sky. A plane in the sky.
25 A white vet's image floats
   closer to me, then his pale eyes
   look through mine. I'm a window.
   He's lost his right arm
   inside the stone. In the black mirror
30 a woman's trying to erase names:
   No, she's brushing a boy's hair.

                1988

Fog Galleon

   Horse-headed clouds, flags
   & pennants tied to black
   Smokestacks in swamp mist.
   From the quick green calm
5 Some nocturnal bird calls
   Ship ahoy, ship ahoy!
   I press against the taxicab
   Window. I'm back here, interfaced
   With a dead phosphorescence;
10 The whole town smells
   Like the world's oldest anger.
   Scabrous residue hunkers down under
   Sulfur & dioxide, waiting

For sunrise, like cargo
15 On a phantom ship outside Gaul.
Cool glass against my cheek
Pulls me from the black schooner
On a timeless sea—everything
Dwarfed beneath the papermill
20 Lights blinking behind the cloudy
Commerce of wheels, of chemicals
That turn workers into pulp
When they fall into vats
Of steamy serenity.

1993

Denise Levertov 1923–1997

Denise Levertov, one of America's fore-most contemporary poets, was born in Es-sex, England; was privately educated except for ballet school and a wartime nursing program; served as a nurse during World War II; and emigrated to the United States in 1948. She taught at Vassar, Drew, City College of New York, M.I.T., Tufts University, and Brandeis University, and retired as a full professor at Stanford University in 1994. Levertov was a scholar at the Radcliffe Institute for Independent Study, received the Lenore Marshall Prize for poetry, a Guggenheim Fellowship, the Elmer Holmes Bobst Award, and was a member of the American Institute of Arts & Letters.

Levertov was influenced by the poetry and poetic theory of William Carlos Williams. And though she was earlier considered an "aesthetic compatriot" of some of the poets of the Black Mountain School, she did not consider herself part of any particular "school" of poetry. She brought her own unmistakably distinctive voice to poems concerned with several dimensions of the human experience: love, motherhood, nature, war, the nuclear arms race, mysticism, poetry, and the role of the poet. Levertov cites a William Carlos Williams verse in her essay "Poetry, Prophecy, Survival": "It is

difficult/to get news from poems/yet men die miserably every day/for lack/of what is found there." She tells us in this essay that people turn to poems for "some kind of illumination, for revelations that help them to survive, to survive in spirit not only in body." She believed that these revelations are usually not of the unheard of but of what lies around us, unseen and forgotten—like "Flowers of Sophia" in her 1996 volume of poetry. And she believed that poems and/or dreams, as she poignantly muses in "Dream Instruction," can "illuminate what we feel but don't *know* we feel until it is articulated."

"Poetry, Prophecy, Survival" reiterates a theme that Levertov articulated on several occasions throughout her career: the poet or artist's call "to summon the divine." She speaks clearly of this "vocation" in "The Origins of a Poem" and "The Sense of Pilgrimage" essays in *The Poet in the World* (1973); in "On the Edge of Darkness: What Is Political Poetry?" in *Light up the Cave* (1981); and in "A Poet's View" (1984). Levertov's awareness of the truly awesome nature of the poet's task is evident in "A Poet's View":

To believe, as an artist, in inspiration or the intuitive, to know that without Imagi-

nation . . . no amount of acquired craft or scholarship or of brilliant reasoning will suffice, is to live with a door of one's life open to the transcendent, the numinous. Not every artist, clearly, acknowledges that fact—yet all, in the creative act, experience mystery. The concept of 'inspiration' presupposes a power that enters the individual and is not a personal attribute; and it is linked to a view of the artist's life as one of obedience to a vocation.[1]

Levertov's poems, most notably those after *The Jacob's Ladder* in 1958, reflect her serious commitment to this concept. In "Dream Instruction," one observes the poet's sensitive awareness of the rich depth of her inheritance and the important influence of the "cultural ambiance" of her family—those other "travellers/gone into dark." The Hasidic ancestry of her father, Paul Levertoff, his being steeped in Jewish, and, after his conversion, Christian scholarship and mysticism, and the Welsh intensity and lyric feeling for nature of her mother, Beatrice Levertoff, are significant parts of the poet's finest works.

An interest in humanitarian politics came early into Levertov's life. Her father was active in protesting Mussolini's invasion of Abyssinia; both he and her sister Olga protested Britain's lack of support for

Spain. Long before these events, her mother canvassed on behalf of the League of Nations Union; and all three worked on behalf of German and Austrian refugees from 1933 onward. (One is not surprised, then, to find among her later poems wrenching reflections on the Gulf War.) This strong familial blend of the mystical with a firm commitment to social issues undoubtedly contributed to Levertov's being placed in the American visionary tradition. Rather than deliberately attempting to integrate social and political themes with lyricism, her approach was to fuse them, believing as she did that they are not antithetical. And as is evident in her poetry of her last years, though Levertov's range of subject matter remained by no means exclusively "engaged," she believed, as she tells us in "Making Peace," that "each act of living/[is] one of its words, each word/a vibration of light—facets/of the forming crystal." So she, along with other such poets as Pablo Neruda and Muriel Rukeyser, confronted social and political issues of our time. Levertov was named the sixty-first winner of the Academy of American Poets Fellowship in 1995.

Joan F. Hallisey
Regis College

PRIMARY WORKS

The Double Image, 1946; *Here and Now,* 1957; *The Jacob's Ladder,* 1958; *Overland to the Islands,* 1958; *With Eyes at the Back of Our Heads,* 1959; *O Taste and See,* 1964; *The Sorrow Dance,* 1966; *Relearning the Alphabet,* 1970; *To Stay Alive,* 1971; *The Poet in the World,* 1973; *Footprints,* 1975; *The Freeing of the Dust,* 1975; *Life in the Forest,* 1978; *Collected Earlier Poems 1940–1960,* 1979; *Light up the Cave,* 1982; *Candles in Babylon,* 1982; *Poems 1960–1967,* 1983; *Oblique Prayers,* 1984; *Breathing the Water,* 1987; *Poems 1968–1972,* 1987; *The Menaced World,* 1985; *A Door in the Hive,* 1989; *Batterers,* 1990; *Evening Train,* 1992; *New and Selected Essays,* 1992; *Tesserae: Memories and Suppositions,* 1995; *Sands in the Well,* 1996; *Stream & the Sapphire,* 1997; *The Great Unknowing,* 1999; *Poems 1972–1982,* 2001; *Selected Poems,* 2002.

---

[1]See *New and Selected Essays,* 1992, p. 241.

Overheard over S. E. Asia

'White phosphorus, white phosphorus,
mechanical snow,
where are you falling?'

'I am falling impartially on roads and roofs,
5 on bamboo thickets, on people.
My name recalls rich seas on rainy nights,
each drop that hits the surface eliciting
luminous response from a million algae.
My name is a whisper of sequins. Ha!
10 Each of them is a disk of fire,
I am the snow that burns.
                I fall
wherever men send me to fall—
but I prefer flesh, so smooth, so dense:
15 I decorate it in black, and seek
the bone.'

The theater of war. Offstage
a cast of thousands weeping.

Left center, well-lit, a mound
20 of unburied bodies,

or parts of bodies. Right,
near some dead bamboo that serves as wings,

a whole body, on which
a splash of napalm is working.

25 Enter the Bride.

She has one breast, one eye,
half of her scalp is bald.

She hobbles towards center front.
Enter the Bridegroom,

30 a young soldier, thin, but without
visible wounds. He sees her.

Slowly at first, then faster and faster,
he begins to shudder, to shudder,

to ripple with shudders.   Curtain.

1970

In Thai Binh (Peace) Province

for Muriel and Jane

I've used up all my film on bombed hospitals,
bombed village schools, the scattered
lemon-yellow cocoons at the bombed silk-factory,

and for the moment all my tears too
5 are used up, having seen today
yet another child with its feet blown off,
          a girl, this one, eleven years old,
patient and bewildered in her home, a fragile
small house of mud bricks among rice fields.

10 So I'll use my dry burning eyes
to photograph within me
dark sails of the river boats,
warm slant of afternoon light
apricot on the brown, swift, wide river,
15 village towers—church and pagoda—on the far shore,
and a boy and small bird both
perched, relaxed, on a quietly grazing
buffalo.   Peace within the
                    long war.

20 It is that life, unhurried, sure, persistent,
I must bring home when I try to bring
the war home.
                    Child, river, light.

Here the future, fabled bird
25 that has migrated away from America,
nests, and breeds, and sings,

common as any sparrow.

                                        1974

Fragrance of Life, Odor of Death

All the while among
the rubble even, and in
the hospitals, among the wounded,
        not only beneath
5   lofty clouds

            in temples
        by the shores of lotus-dreaming
        lakes

a fragrance:
10 flowers, incense, the earth-mist rising
of mild daybreak in the delta—good smell
of life.

It's in America
where no bombs ever
15 have screamed down smashing
the buildings, shredding the people's bodies,
tossing the fields of Kansas or Vermont or Maryland into
                    the air
to land wrong way up, a gash of earth-guts . . .
20 it's in America, everywhere, a faint seepage,
I smell death.

                Hanoi–Boston–Maine, November 1972

A Poem at Christmas, 1972,
during the Terror-Bombing of North Vietnam

Now I have lain awake imagining murder.
At first my pockets were loaded with rocks, with knives,
wherever I ran windows smashed, but I was swift
                              and unseen,
5   I was saving the knives until I reached
certain men . . .
                    Yes, Kissinger's smile faded,
he clutched his belly, he reeled . . .
But as the night
10 wore on, what I held
hidden—under a napkin perhaps,
            I as a waitress at the inaugural dinner—
was a container of napalm:
and as I threw it in Nixon's face
15 and his crowd leapt back from the flames with crude
                                    yells of horror,
and some came rushing to seize me:
            quick as thought I had ready
a round of those small bombs designed
20 to explode at the pressure of a small child's weight,
and these instantly
dealt with the feet of Nixon's friends and henchmen,
who fell in their own blood
while the foul smoke of his body-oils
25 blackened the hellish room . . .
It was of no interest
to imagine further. Instead,
the scene recommenced.
Each time around, fresh details,
30 variations of place and weapon.
All night to imagining murder.
O, to kill
the killers!

It is
35 to this extremity

the infection of their evil

thrusts us . . .

1974

Le Ly Hayslip (b. 1949)

Le Ly Hayslip, born in 1949 as Phung Thi Le Ly in the village of Ky La, South Vietnam, is a memoirist. Hayslip married an American engineer in 1972, during the waning days of U.S. involvement in Vietnam, and emigrated to the United States. She wrote two autobiographical books, *When Heaven and Earth Changed Places* (1989) and *Child of War, Woman of Peace* (1993), which were published when memories of the divisive Vietnam War were still vivid for many Americans. While American authors had produced a voluminous literature about Vietnam, it was centered on the experiences of Americans and of men. Hayslip addressed the silences in this literature by speaking from the perspective of a Vietnamese woman. In doing so, she became the first Vietnamese American writer to gain national prominence.

When Heaven and Earth Changed Places, cowritten with Jay Wurts, established her reputation. The book is a highly readable account that intercuts stories of Hayslip's youth in South Vietnam with a narrative about her eventual return to a reunified Vietnam in 1986. Hayslip's life was influenced by both French colonization, which ended in 1954, and the conflict that the Vietnamese call the American War (1964–73). As a young peasant girl in the south, Hayslip finds herself caught between the guerrilla forces of the National Liberation Front, commonly known as the Vietcong, and the U.S. Army with its South Vietnamese allies. After fleeing the war-torn countryside to the relative safety of Da Nang, the teenage Hayslip is impregnated by the man who has hired her to be his maid. This begins a long string of relationships that continues throughout her young life and into the second volume of her autobiography, *Child of War, Woman of Peace.* Written with her oldest son, James Hayslip, this book is divided between her life in suburban San Diego as a struggling immigrant mother of three boys and her second return to her native land. In postwar Vietnam, she reunites with her mother, sisters, and older brother, who had fought on the Communist side, and concludes her narrative with a call to her readers to forgive their enemies.

This narrative of forgiveness, in conjunction with Hayslip's representation of herself as a successful American immigrant, has helped the popularity of her book with American readers. The appeal of her writing can be measured by the adaption of her books by the director Oliver Stone into the movie *Heaven and Earth* (1993) (Stone is well known for his Vietnam War film *Platoon*). Since then, a younger generation of Vietnamese American writers that includes Monique Truong and le thi diem thuy has joined Hayslip, but her works remain valuable for their unique perspective. Hayslip's books are based on the experiences of peasants, who comprise the overwhelming majority of Vietnamese, presenting stories that are both rarely heard by U.S. audiences and rarely told by Vietnamese American writers.

Viet Thanh Nguyen
University of Southern California

PRIMARY WORKS

When Heaven and Earth Changed Places, 1989; *Child of War, Woman of Peace,* 1993.

from When Heaven and Earth Changed Places

from 7. A Different View

My wartime "souvenir" business lasted almost two years. During this time, my mother tried to look after Hung while she fretted over her two other Danang daughters, our various aunts and uncles who lived in the area, and, whenever possible, my father in Ky La. Because I was preoccupied with my business—making money to pay for our needs, saving for emergencies and for better times—I spent very little time at home. Because of our joint neglect, little Hung came to look like a typical Danang street urchin. His skin always suffered from one rash or another and his belly ballooned like a pregnant woman's from eating sand to comfort his feelings. I felt bad for my baby but I didn't know what to do. If I stayed home, we would lose our house and be forced to live again on the street or on the charity of others. Besides, my mother had raised six strong children already. If she couldn't keep Hung healthy, how could I do any better?

There seemed no solution until one day I learned from a girlfriend that a new American firebase had been set up outside Ky La. Because I now felt safer around Americans than ever before, this seemed an ideal time to go back to the village, visit my father—as I had longed to do for years—and see if it might be possible for Hung to live and grow up in the house where I myself had been raised. Failing that, of course, I could always make some sales.

I left my mother at sunrise praying for my safety. Both she and Ba had tried to discourage me from making the trip—saying there were rumors that my father had been beaten and that danger was everywhere—but they understood neither the risks I had already taken in my business nor the fact that I now knew Americans to be a bit less brutal and more trustworthy than either the Vietnamese or Viet Cong forces. To avoid combatants on either side, I traced the route I had taken in the storm almost three years before, through the swamps, jungle, hills, and brush country from Danang to Marble Mountain to Ky La but this time the weather was fine and I had plenty of time to think about my father and what to do when I got home. When I arrived, however, the village I remembered no longer existed.

Half of Ky La had been leveled to give the Americans a better "killing zone" when defending the village. Their camp, which was a complex of bunkers and trenches with tin roofs, sandbags, radio antennas, and tents, lorded over the village from a hilltop outside of town. Around its slopes, homeless peasants and little kids poked through the American garbage in hopes of finding food or something to sell. In the distance, through a screen of withered trees (which had been defoliated now by chemicals as well as bombs), I could see that Bai Gian had not been rebuilt, and that the few remaining temples, pagodas, and wayside shrines—even my old schoolhouse and the guardsmen's awful prison—had been wiped away by the hand of war. Beautiful tropical forests had been turned into a bomb-cratered desert. It was as if the American giant, who had for so long been taunted and annoyed by the Viet Cong ants, had finally come to stamp its feet—to drive the painted, smiling Buddha from his house and substitute instead the khaki, glowering God of Abraham.

With the sickening feeling that I was now a stranger in my own homeland, I crossed the last few yards to my house with a lump in my throat and a growing sense of dread. Houses could be rebuilt and damaged dikes repaired—but the loss of our temples and shrines meant the death of our culture itself. It meant that a generation of children would grow up without fathers to teach them about their ancestors or the rituals of worship. Families would lose records of their lineage and with them the umbilicals to the very root of our society—not just old buildings and books, but *people* who once lived and loved like them. Our ties to our past were being severed, setting us adrift on a sea of borrowed Western materialism, disrespect for the elderly, and selfishness. The war no longer seemed like a fight to see which view would prevail. Instead, it had become a fight to see just how much and how far the Vietnam of my ancestors would be transformed. It was as if I was standing by the cradle of a dying child and speculating with its aunts and uncles on what the doomed baby would have looked like had it grown up. By tugging on their baby so brutally, both parents had wound up killing it. Even worse, the war now attacked Mother Earth—the seedbed of us all. This, to me, was the highest crime—the frenzied suicide of cannibals. How shall one mourn a lifeless planet?

Inside, the neat, clean home of my childhood was a hovel. What few furnishings and tools were left after the battles had been looted or burned for fuel. Our household shrine, which always greeted new arrivals as the centerpiece of our family's pride, was in shambles. Immediately I saw the bag of bones and torn sinew that was my father lying in his bed. Our eyes met briefly but there was no sign of recognition in his dull face. Instead, he rolled away from me and asked:

"Where is your son?"

I crossed the room and knelt by his bed. I was afraid to touch him for fear of disturbing his wounds or tormenting his aching soul even more. He clutched his side as if his ribs hurt badly and I could see that his face was bruised and swollen.

"I am alone," I answered, swallowing back my tears. "Who did this to you?"

"Dich." (The enemy.) It was a peasant's standard answer.

I went to the kitchen and made some tea from a few dried leaves. It was as if my father knew he was dying and did not wish the house or its stores to survive him. If one must die alone, it should be in an empty place without wasting a thing.

When I returned, he was on his back. I held his poor, scabbed head and helped him drink some tea. I could see he was dehydrated, being unable to draw water from the well or get up to drink it even when neighbors brought some to the house.

"Where were you taken? What was the charge?" I asked.

"It doesn't matter." My father drank gratefully and lay back on the bed. "The Americans came to examine our family bunker. Because it was so big, they thought Viet Cong might be hiding inside and ordered me to go in first. When I came out and told them no one was there, they didn't believe me and threw in some grenades. One of them didn't go off right away and the two Americans who went in afterward were killed. They were just boys—" My father coughed up blood. "I don't blame them for being angry. That's what war is all about, isn't it? Bad luck. Bad karma."

"So they beat you up?"

"They pinned a paper on my back that said 'VC' and took me to Hoa Cam District for interrogation. I don't have to tell you what happened after that. I'm just lucky to be alive."

As sad as I felt about my father's misfortune, growing fury now burned inside me. There was no reason to beat this poor man almost to death because of a soldier's tragic mistake.

I made my father as comfortable as possible and climbed the hill to the American fortress with my bucket of merchandise, intent on making a different kind of sale.

"Honcho?" I asked the first soldier I saw on the trail. I didn't understand his answer, but eventually I made myself understood well enough to impress him with my harmlessness: "You buy? Very nice? No *bum-bum!* See captain. Where honcho?"

Eventually I made my way to an officer who poked around my bucket, which by now had been searched four or five times by Americans for explosives. When he finally understood I wanted to talk to him about more than the price of bracelets, he called for the camp's Vietnamese translator.

"Thank god!" I said, bowing politely to the frowning Republican soldier who was not from the Central Coast. I explained the situation quickly to him in Vietnamese. I told him there had been a terrible mistake and that my father lay badly wounded in our house down the hill. I told him I wanted the Americans to take him to a hospital where he would be cared for and to help repair his house when he came back. I told him I knew the Americans were required to do all these things by their own regulations.

The Republican translator only laughed at me. "Look, missy," he said, "the Americans do what they damn well please around here. They don't take orders from anybody, especially little Vietnamese girls. Now, if you're smart, you'll take your father and get the hell out of here!"

"But you didn't even translate what I said to the captain!" I protested. "Come on—give the American a chance to speak for himself!"

"Look—" the translator exploded. "You'd better get out of here now or I'll denounce you as VC! If you have a complaint, go to the district headquarters like everyone else! Put your request through channels—and be prepared to spend some money. Now run along before I get mad!"

I gathered my things and went back down the hill. Although some GIs tried to wave me over, I was too upset to make a sale. I just wanted to help my father and keep things from getting worse.

Because the Americans so dominated the area, I felt comparatively safe staying near my house and tending to my father. Unlike the Republicans, who commandeered civilian houses for their quarters, the Americans kept their distance and so managed to avoid a lot of friction with the peasants. I no longer tried to sell anything (the villagers still hated anyone who dealt with the invaders) and pretended I didn't speak English when their troops stopped me from time to time. Although people going to the toilet or gathering firewood were still shot occasionally by jumpy soldiers, things remained blessedly quiet. It had been months since a major Viet Cong attack and a new, if smaller, generation of children now played in Ky La's streets. More dangerous were the Koreans who now patrolled the American sector. Because a child from our village once walked into their camp and exploded a Viet Cong bomb wired to his body, the Koreans took terrible retribution against the children themselves (whom they saw simply as little Viet Cong). After the incident, some Korean soldiers went to a school, snatched up some boys, threw them into a well, and tossed a grenade in afterward as an example to the others. To the villagers, these Koreans were like the Moroccans—tougher and meaner than the white soldiers they supported. Like the Japanese of World War II, they seemed to have no conscience and went about their duties as ruthless killing machines. No wonder they found my country a perfect place to ply their terrible trade.

I discovered that most of the kids I grew up with (those who had not been killed in the fighting) had married or moved away. Girls my age, if they had not yet married, were considered burdens on their family—old maids who consumed food without producing children. They also attracted the unsavory attention of soldiers, which always led to trouble. One reason so many of our young women wound up in the cities was because the shortage of available men made them liabilities to their families. At least a dutiful grown-up daughter could work as a housekeeper, nanny, hostess, or prostitute and send back money to the family who no longer wanted her. Many families, too, had been uprooted—like the refugees from Bai Gian or those who had been moved so that their houses could be bulldozed to provide a better fire zone for the Americans. For every soldier who went into battle, a hundred civilians moved ahead of him—to get out of the way; or behind him—following in his wake the way leaves are pulled along in a cyclone, hoping to live off his garbage, his money, and when all else failed, his mercy.

This is not to say that rubble and refugees were the only by-products of our war. Hundreds of thousands of tons of rice and countless motorbikes, luxury cars, TVs, stereos, refrigerators, air conditioners, and crates of cigarettes, liquor, and cosmetics were imported for the Vietnamese elite and the Americans who supported them. This created a new class of privileged people—wealthy young officers, officials, and war profiteers—who supplanted the elderly as objects of veneration. Consequently, displaced farmers—old people, now, as well as young—became their servants, working as maids to the madams or bootblacks for fuzz-cheeked GIs. It was a common sight to see old people prostrate themselves before these young demigods, crying *lay ong*— I beg you, sir!—where before such elderly people paid homage to no one but their ancestors. It was a world turned on its head.

Of those villagers who remained in Ky La, many were disfigured from the war, suffering amputated limbs, jagged scars, or the diseases that followed malnutrition or took over a body no longer inhabited by a happy human spirit.

Saddest of all these, perhaps, was Ong Xa Quang, a once-wealthy man who had been like a second father to me in the village. Quang was a handsome, good-natured man who sent two sons north in 1954. Of his two remaining sons, one was drafted by the Republican army and the other, much later, joined the Viet Cong. His two daughters married men who also went north, and so were left widows for at least the duration of the war. When I went to visit Quang I found his home and his life in ruins. He had lost both legs to an American mine, and every last son had been killed in battle. His wife now neglected him (she wasn't home when I called) because he was so much trouble to care for and he looked malnourished and on the verge of starvation. Still, he counted himself lucky. Fate had spared his life while it took the lives of so many others around him. All his suffering was part of his life's education—but for what purpose, he admitted he was still not wise enough to know. Nonetheless, Quang said I should remember everything he told me, and to forget none of the details of the tragedies I myself had seen and was yet to see. I gave him a daughter's tearful hug and left, knowing I would probably never see him alive again.

I walked to the hill behind my house where my father had taken me when I was a little girl—the hill where he told me about my destiny and duty as a Phung Thi woman. I surveyed the broken dikes and battered crops and empty animal pens of my once flourishing village. I saw the ghosts of my friends and relatives going about their work and a generation of children who would never be born playing in the muddy fields and dusty streets. I wondered about the martyrs and heroes of our ancient legends—shouldn't they be here to throw back the invaders and punish the Vietnamese on both sides who were making our country not just a graveyard, but a sewer of corruption and prison of fear? Could a god who made such saints as well as ordinary people truly be a god if he couldn't feel our suffering with us? For that matter, what use was god at all when people, not deities, seemed to cause our problems on earth?

I shut my eyes and called on my spirit sense to answer but I heard no reply. It was as if life's cycle was no longer birth, growth, and death but only endless dying brought about by endless war. I realized that I, along with so many of my countrymen, had been born into war and that my soul knew nothing else. I tried to imagine people somewhere who knew only peace—what a paradise! How many souls in that world were blessed with the simple privilege of saying good-bye to their loved ones before they died? And how many of those loved ones died with the smile of a life well lived on their lips—knowing that their existence added up to something more than a number in a "body count" or another human brick on a towering wall of corpses? Perhaps such a place was America, although American wives and mothers, too, were losing husbands and sons every day in the evil vortex between heaven and hell that my country had become.

I sat on the hill for a very long time, like a vessel waiting to be filled up with rain—soft wisdom from heaven—but the sun simply drifted lower in the west and the insects buzzed and the tin roofs of the American camps shimmered in the heat and my village and the war sat heavily—unmoved and unmovable like an oppressive gravestone—on my land and in my heart. I got up and dusted off my pants. It was time to feed my father.

Back home, I told him about my visit to "our hilltop." I said I now regretted fleeing Ky La. Perhaps it would have been better to stay and fight—to fight the Americans with the Viet Cong or the Viet Cong with the Republicans or to fight both together by myself and with anyone else who would join me.

My father stopped eating and looked at me intently. "Bay Ly, you were born to be a wife and mother, not a killer. That is your duty. For as long as you live, you must remember what I say. You and me—we weren't born to make enemies. Don't make vengeance your god, because such gods are satisfied only by human sacrifice."

"But there has been so much suffering—so much destruction!" I replied, again on the verge of tears, "Shouldn't someone be punished?"

"Are you so smart that you truly know who's to blame? If you ask the Viet Cong, they'll blame the Americans. If you ask the Americans, they'll blame the North. If you ask the North, they'll blame the South. If you ask the South, they'll blame the Viet Cong. If you ask the monks, they'll blame the Catholics, or tell you our ancestors did something terrible and so brought this endless suffering on our heads. So tell me, who would you punish? The common soldier on both sides who's only doing his duty? Would you ask the French or Americans to repay our Vietnamese debt?"

"But generals and politicians give orders—orders to kill and destroy. And our own people cheat each other as if there's nothing to it. I know—I've seen it! And nobody has the right to destroy Mother Earth!"

"Well then, Bay Ly, go out and do the same, eh? Kill the killers and cheat the cheaters. That will certainly stop the war, won't it? Perhaps that's been our problem all along—not enough profiteers and soldiers!"

Despite my father's reasoning, my anger and confusion were so full-up that they burst forth, not with new arguments, but tears. He took me in his arms. "Shhh—listen, little peach blossom, when you see all those young Americans out there being killed and wounded in our war—in a war that fate or luck or god has commanded us to wage for our redemption and education—you must thank them, at least in your heart, for helping to put us back on our life's course. Don't wonder about right and wrong. Those are weapons as deadly as bombs and bullets. Right is the goodness you carry in your heart—love for your ancestors and your baby and your family for everything that lives. Wrong is anything that comes between you and that love. Go back to your little son. Raise him the best way you can. That is the battle you were born to fight. That is the victory you must win."

1989

New World Disorder: Recent Literature

The writers represented in the first half of this volume are likely to have responded to a single question at some point in their lives: "Where were you when President Kennedy was shot?" Most writers in the second half of this volume are likely to have responded to a similar question: "Where were you on 9/11?" The questions describe events nearly four decades apart, but they are surprisingly similar: Both try to connect individual experience with a national tragedy. Both describe violent, senseless events as markers of history. Both events signaled more violence to come. And very few people saw them coming.

The terror attacks of September 11, 2001, made Americans more fearful and less confident about their position of global prominence. After the dismantling of the Soviet Union in the late 1980s and early 1990s, there appeared to be only one superpower left standing. America's long period of prosperity continued into the 1990s, fueled to a large degree by the computer industry and the development of the Internet. As this new technology developed, the world seemed smaller than ever. The information superhighway made it possible to travel anywhere (virtually). It knows no borders. It has also opened up new markets for trade. Combined with economic prosperity and military strength, superfast communication is a formidable force.

After the disintegration of the Soviet Union realigned the globe in 1989 and 1990, then-president George Herbert Walker Bush described a "new world order" and delivered these words on September 11, 1991, while the United States was facing off with Iraq in the Persian Gulf War—ten years to the day before the 9/11 attacks. What had been an even competition with a powerful adversary had turned into a lopsided game.

The years of the Clinton presidency (essentially the 1990s) secured that sense of a new world order as venture capitalists and even modest middle-class investors became rich. When terrorists flew planes into the buildings that symbolized our nation's wealth (the World Trade Center) and military might (the Pentagon), it seemed like the new world order had been demolished and that disorder had taken its place.

The attacks of 9/11 were gruesome, sickening, unjustifiable, and difficult to comprehend. As Americans gain historical distance from it, we might begin to see how it brings into focus a number of themes that were hidden from plain view in the decades leading up to it. The American war in Vietnam, for instance, sparked controversy both at home and abroad because many people thought the United States was getting involved in a conflict that did not directly involve it. (See the Sheaf of Vietnam Conflict Poetry and Prose in this volume.) The same controversy surrounded the Persian Gulf War in the early 1990s—the United States provided military support to its Middle Eastern ally Kuwait when neighboring Iraq invaded the tiny nation. America's global trade interests and its willingness to use its military power to control conflicts distant from its borders clearly provoked anger in less-powerful nations and factions abroad.

Domestic tremors also foreshadowed the terror attacks. The random violence of 9/11 was massive, but random violence itself was nothing new in the United States. John Kennedy's assassination was just one of a number of shootings of famous men, including Kennedy's brother Robert (a presidential hopeful); black activists Medgar Evers, Malcolm X and Martin Luther King, Jr.; rock stars John Lennon and Marvin Gaye in the 1980s; and fashion designer Gianni Versace in the 1990s.

And famous people were not the only victims of widespread, random violence. The Charles Manson and "Son of Sam" murders of the early 1970s were serial killings that had ordinary citizens in Los Angeles and New York watching their neighbors and bolting their doors. Terrifying school shootings have plagued the nation and claimed many young lives. In the 1990s, religious cults and so-called militias engaged in armed standoffs with the U.S. government agents, resulting in deaths in Ruby Ridge, Idaho, and Waco, Texas. Another antigovernment radical, Timothy McVeigh, drove a truckload of explosives into a federal building in Oklahoma City in 1995, killing 168 people, including nineteen children.

Although the 9/11 terror attacks were not related to all this domestic violence, random violence that resulted in the murder of innocents became woven into the American fabric in the late twentieth century. A nation never becomes completely desensitized to violence, but it can easily cease trying to explain violence and to resign itself to the notion that chaos reigns. The late twentieth- and early twenty-first centuries in America have proved to be chaotic times.

Writers are particularly sensitive to this chaos, and it is reflected in the work of many postmodern writers. There is no commonly accepted definition of *postmodernism,* though its chief practitioners share a few traits. The works of John Barth, Donald Barthelme, Thomas Pynchon, Ishmael Reed, and Don DeLillo, all represented in this volume, are classic examples of postmodern fiction and poetry. They are characterized by a willingness to accept randomness and

chaos as principles of contemporary life and therefore of the literature that reflects it. Critics have used chaos theory and systems theory to analyze the fiction of Barthelme, Pynchon, and DeLillo, all of whom are preoccupied with the tendency for systems to overwhelm the agency of individuals. Reed and Barth are perhaps less concerned with the world of physics and more concerned with the history of literature. All five writers, and many, many other postmodernists, consistently point to their own fictions as fiction, revealing (often humorously) the inner workings of their stories or novels. Barth's story "Lost in the Funhouse," included in this volume, is one of the most famous examples of such postmodern self-reflexiveness and self-consciousness.

Postmodern literature both embraces and reflects the chaos of the contemporary world. The rational logic of cause and effect is difficult to discern in these works. The reader can come away disoriented and wondering whether stability is possible in the real world or in works of fiction. Many postmodern works create their own world, but others play with the history and legends of the world we think we know.

Don DeLillo, for instance, has written novels about John F. Kennedy's assassination (*Libra*) and 9/11 (*Falling Man,* the beginning of which is reprinted here). Writers like DeLillo, E. L. Doctorow, and Toni Morrison tend to use history as the basis for their fiction, and other writers included here, such as John Updike and Philip Roth, have dabbled in this mode, often termed *historiography.* DeLillo claims he was inspired to write *Libra,* about JFK's assassin, Lee Harvey Oswald, after stumbling across an old newspaper clipping. Morrison was similarly inspired to write her masterpiece *Beloved* when she read about Margaret Garner, an escaped slave who killed one of her children to prevent the girl's being returned to slavery.

Although Morrison's work reflects many traits of postmodernism, her career is also significant for other trends it signals in contemporary American literature. As the most recent American recipient of the Nobel Prize in literature (in 1993) and the first African American recipient of that award, Morrison is in the vanguard of minority writers in the United States who finally began to gain proper recognition for their achievements as the twentieth century came to a close.

Our sheaf on multiethnic aesthetics and politics of the 1960s and 1970s raises questions about the formal differences and political intentions of literature written by minority writers. As postmodernism was beginning to solidify as something that could be recognized and defined in the 1960s, American writers of racial and ethnic minorities were modifying, reacting to, rejecting, or embracing postmodern techniques for their own ends.

Yet it is limiting to connect all the writers in the late twentieth and early twenty-first centuries to postmodernism. As has always been true, some prominent writers produce work that is traditional or that does not fit neatly into any definition of postmodernism. The significance of many multiethnic voices in the final part of this volume is that they document experiences that had been invisible or difficult to see in earlier historical periods. On the other hand, difference is a postmodern characteristic. Following the cultural turbulence of the 1960s, America was better prepared than it had ever been to comprehend its own diversity, especially where literature was concerned.

Race and ethnicity are only two dimensions of the word *diversity*, however. Gender is another. Morrison's prominence is also significant because she is a woman. The most prominent black writers of the midtwentieth century (Richard Wright, Ralph Ellison, James Baldwin, and Amiri Baraka) were men. The female African American experience is given deep consideration in the works of Morrison, Toni Cade Bambara, Alice Walker, Rita Dove,

and many others in the latter half of this volume.

In addition to the rise to prominence of African American women, Asian and Hispanic/Latino writers also take a much more visible role during this period, reflecting new patterns of immigration and demographic changes in the late twentieth century. Hispanic and Latino writers flourish especially in the genre of poetry. The establishment of the Nuyorican Poets' Café in the East Village section of Manhattan was one catalyst for this phenomenon. Puerto Ricans became the largest new immigrant group in New York City in the 1960s, and such prominent poets as Pedro Pietri and Tato Laviera (included in this volume) were active participants in the café, which is still vibrant and features poetry performances and "slams"— quasi-competitions between poets.

The Nuyorican Poets' Café was the foundation for a number of similar Hispanic and Latino intellectual gathering places in cities across the country. When Quinto Sol Publications was established in Berkeley, California, in 1967, its sole mission was to publish Mexican American writing, and it provided a forum for publication that complemented such performance spaces as the Nuyorican Poets' Café.

This particular ethnic group—first- or second-generation immigrants from Spanish-speaking countries—has grown so diverse in recent years that it may no longer be useful to classify them together. The sensibility and style of the nonfiction writers Richard Rodriguez and Gloria Anzaldúa, for instance, are markedly different, though both essentially wrestle with deep questions of identity based on the degree to which they have assimilated into Anglo-American culture. Anzaldúa resists this assimilation, to the point that she preserves Spanish language within her largely English prose. Rodriguez has a complex relationship to the American culture he has mostly embraced. An immigrant "success story" who attended prestigious schools on scholarship, he has written of his rise to literary fame with pride but also with some guilt at sacrificing certain aspects of his parents' native Mexican culture, such as language, in his drive for education and wealth. These two writers illustrate an ongoing debate about the importance of preserving one's heritage in a nation that continues to demand that its immigrants assimilate, especially when it comes to language. The poetic exchange between Sandra María Esteves and Luz María Umpierre, included here, is in fact a direct poetic debate that crystallizes some of these issues of identity, especially as they relate to gender.

Gender identity is especially important across race and ethnicity lines during this period. Following the liberation achieved by the feminist movement in the 1960s and 1970s, the roles and expectations of American women in general had changed dramatically. The works of Anzaldúa, Morrison, and Walker are deeply concerned with this change, as is virtually every other female writer in this section. The stories by Joyce Carol Oates and Bobbie Ann Mason contemplate these questions from the points of view of young women who are not especially well suited to deal with them.

One consistent motif in women's writing during this period is an examination of the circumstances and meaning of one's sexual awakening—as in the play *How I Learned to Drive* by Paula Vogel—and a curiosity about how one's sexual experiences connect or fail to connect to one's public gender identity. Questions of gender identity are also related to the expectations of one's family, often a favorite subject of ethnic writers. See, for example, the works included here by Edwidge Danticat, Maxine Hong Kingston, Gish Jen, Bharati Mukherjee, and Jhumpa Lahiri.

The last four of these writers are among the most prominent writers of Asian origin in the United States, signaling another notable change in late twentieth-century American literature. Immigrants from the most populous continent have changed the demographics of the United States, especially (but certainly not exclusively) on the west coast. Three of the major U.S. military conflicts of the past seventy-five years—against Japan in World War II, North Korea in the Korean War, and North Vietnam in the Vietnam War—have been against Asian adversaries. As a result, Asian immigrants have had to face residual prejudices, which have been reinforced by racist stereotypes in Hollywood movies.

Recently, Asian immigrants have dealt with an unusual stereotype. Because of their statistical tendency to excel in school and business settings, Asians have come to be regarded as the model minority and therefore are susceptible to a kind of pressure to succeed on white America's terms that might result in a painful identity conflict. The works by Kingston, Jen, Mukherjee, Chang-Rae Lee, and Li-Young Lee included here all reveal a radical intergenerational shift related to the difficulty of preserving Asian culture—language, custom, stories, food—in an American setting.

As American demographics shifted in the late twentieth century, American literature recognized the contributions of the various immigrant groups mentioned above, as well as others such as Paule Marshall and Jamaica Kincaid from the Caribbean and Naomi Shihab Nye, who lived in Jerusalem with her Palestinian father as a child. But one of the most prominent minority groups in this contemporary volume of American literature is, ironically, the only group of nonimmigrants. Native American literature has also flourished and gained widespread attention in the past half century, beginning with the publication of N. Scott Momaday's *House Made of Dawn* in 1968. Momaday's novel won the Pulitzer Prize for fiction that year, and since then many writers with Native American ancestry have earned the attention of critics, students, and general readers, including Gerald Vizenor,

Leslie Marmon Silko, Louise Erdrich, and Sherman Alexie in fiction and Wendy Rose and Joy Harjo in poetry.

Although it is difficult to generalize about this substantial body of work, it is fair to say that it demonstrates a deep and painful sense of loss of ancient traditions and beliefs and that it depicts the impoverishment and despair of contemporary reservations. The ravishment of the environment is another recurrent theme in Native American literature, and it is especially evident in Silko's work. Our cluster on ecocriticism and its relationship to spirituality helps to clarify this dimension in these works and in contemporary literature more generally.

It is clear even from this brief overview that chaos or heterogeneity reign in contemporary literature, but it is not necessarily true that "things fall apart," as the Irish modernist poet W. B. Yeats says in his poem "The Second Coming," because "the center cannot hold." The central assumptions of western civilization have always been less stable than they might appear. The very notion of what constitutes literature changes from time to time. Our inclusion of excerpts of the increasingly popular form known as graphic narrative demonstrates that American culture has become increasingly image oriented, and literature has adapted, putting forth important figures such as Art Speigelman, whose allegorical graphic novel *Maus* has become a popular text in college courses. Younger readers who came of age around the time of September 11, 2001, regard literature differently than earlier generations of readers did. For these young readers, chaos, violence, diversity, and a resistance to stereotypical gender roles are nothing new. But the notion that literature is a vital cultural force that seeks to articulate and examine these phenomena might be.

Rolando Hinojosa-Smith b. 1929

Rolando Hinojosa-Smith, son of a Mexican American father and an Anglo-American mother, is a product of the Mexican-U.S. border's cultural synthesis. He grew up in the southern Rio Grande valley of Texas, where Spanish and English still compete for dominance. His paternal family roots in Texas go back to the 1740s, predating the U.S. annexation by a century. Justifiably, there is no sense of immigration in him, but rather one of legitimate ownership and belonging. After serving in the Korean conflict and then completing a doctorate in Spanish literature, he held several teaching assignments, including Chairman of Chicano Studies at Minnesota. In the early 1980s he switched academic departments to become a professor of English and Creative Writing at the University of Texas at Austin.

Hinojosa's books form a multi-volumed story that, through the life of two cousins, relates the history of a fictional South Texas county of Belkin. His main preoccupation is the survival of what he calls Texas-Mexican Border Culture despite constant repression by the economically dominant Anglo-Texans in league with some traitorous Mexican Americans. History itself becomes a battleground for conflicting versions of the past, and the Tex-Mex communal oral tradition is revealed as more reliable than the official written texts, the latter being controlled by the Anglo-American colonizers, who manipulate historical records, as they do the legal and academic systems, to assure a favorable status quo. His work resembles a vast detective novel, with social protest overtones, in which the neglected truth of Texas history is sought through the fragmented memories of numerous witnesses. The villains and criminals are the invaders and their stooges, the Texas Rangers. The original Mexican inhabitants are the plaintiffs; and the narrator, who constantly cedes the word to others, is like an investigative reporter gathering evidence to slowly piece together into an indictment of oppression.

Concern for the oral tradition explains both Hinojosa's conversational tone and the constant intercalations of documents, testimony, and transcriptions of oral memoirs. Writing must remain faithful to the people it reflects and to their traditional form of expression, the spoken word. His texts engage the dominant culture's repressive writing, juxtaposing it to oral versions. Hence, the framing newspaper notes that not only persist in repeating what the oral evidence disproves, but reveal, through the errata, the written media's callous indifference to Chicanos. This conflict between the written and the oral, as well as the need to make writing embody suppressed traditions, is a key to understanding not only Chicano writing, but that of many marginal groups as they begin to produce a literature.

Juan Bruce-Novoa
University of California at Irvine

PRIMARY WORKS

Estampas del Valle y otras obras/Sketches of the Valley and Other Works, 1973; *Klail City y sus alrededores/Klail City,* 1976; *Generaciones y semblanzas,* 1977; *Korean Love Songs,* 1978; *Mi querido Rafa,* 1981; *Rites and Witnesses,* 1982; *Partners in Crime,* 1985; *Claros varones de Belkin/Fair Gentlemen of Belken County,* 1986; *Becky and Her Friends,* 1990; *The Useless Servants,* 1993; *Ask a Policeman,* 1998; *We Happy Few,* 2006.

Sometimes It Just Happens That Way; That's All

Excerpt from the *Klail City Enterprise-News* (March 15, 1970)

Klail City. (Special) Baldemar Cordero, 30, of 169 South Hidalgo Street, is in the city jail following a row in a bar in the city's Southside. Cordero is alleged to have fatally stabbed Arnesto Tamez, also 30, over the affections of one of the "hostesses" who works there.

No bail had been set at press time.

One of Those Things

This cassette recording of Balde Cordero's statements has been reproduced faithfully using conventional spelling where necessary. What matters here is the content, not the form. March 16, 1970, Klail City Workhouse.

What can I tell you? The truth's the truth, and there's no dodging it, is there? It's a natural fact: I killed Ernesto Tamez, and I did it right there at the *Aquí me quedo*.[1] And how can I deny it? But don't come asking me for no details; not just yet, anyway, 'cause I'm not all that sure just how it did happen—and that's God's truth, and no one else's, as we say. That's right; Neto Tamez is gone and like the Bible says: I can see, and I can hear.

But that's the way it goes, I guess. He's laid out there somewhere, and just yesterday late afternoon it was that me and my brother-in-law, Beto Castañeda, he married my sister Marta, you know . . . well, there we were, the two of us drinking, laughing, cuttin' up, and just having ourselves a time, when up pops Ernesto Tamez just like Old Nick himself: swearing and cursing like always, and I got the first blast, but I let it go like I usually . . . like I always do . . . Oh, well . . . Anyway, he kept it up, but it didn't bother me none; and that's the truth, too.

You knew Tamez, didn't you? What am I saying? Of course, you did. Remember that time at Félix Champión's place? Someone came up and broke a bottle of beer, full, too; broke it right backside Ernesto's head, someone did. Ol' Ernesto'd broken a mirror, remember? He'd taken this beer bottle and just let go at that mirror, he did. Well'p, I sure haven't forgotten, and I always kept my eyes open; no telling what he'd do next. I wouldn't step aside, of course, but I wouldn't turn my attention away from him, see?

Well, it was like I said: there we were, Beto and me, we'd hoist a few until we'd run out of cash, or we'd get beer bent, but that was it: none o' that cadging free drinks for us; when we got the money, we drink. When we don't, we don't, and that's it.

Now, I've known Tamez—the whole family, in fact—since primary school and when they lived out in Rebaje; there was Joaquín—he's the oldest, and he wound up marrying or had to anyway, Jovita de Anda. You know her? Now, before she married

---

[1] Here I'll stay.

Joaquín, Jovita was about as hard to catch as a cold in the month of February. She straightened out, though; and fast, too. Then there's Emilio; he's the second in line; he got that permanent limp o' his after he slipped and then fell off a refrigerator car that was standing off the old Mo-Pac line over by that pre-cooler run by Chico Fernández. The last one's Bertita; she's the only girl in the family, and she married one of those hard workin' Leal boys. Took her out of Klail City faster 'n anything you ever saw: he set himself up out in West Texas—Muleshoe, I think it was—and being the worker he was, why, he turned many a shiny penny: Good for him is what I say: he earned it. Bertita's no bargain, I'll say that, but she wasn't a bad woman, either. Ernesto was something, though; from the beginning. I'll tell you this much: I put up with a lot—and took a lot, too. For years. But sometimes something happens, you know. And when it does, well . . .

There's no room for lying, Hinojosa; you've known me, and you've known my folks for a long time . . . Well, as I was saying, Beto and I started drinking at the *San Diego,* from there we showed up at the *Diamond*—the *old Diamond* over on Third—stayed there a while, and we were still on our feet, so we made for the *Blue Bar* after that. We would've stayed there, too, 'cept for the Reyna brothers who showed up. There's usually trouble for somebody when they're around, and that's no secret, no, sir. What they do is they'll drink a beer or two, at the most, but that's about it, 'cause they only drink to cover up the grass they've been popping . . . But you know that already . . . Cops that don't know 'em come up, smell the brew, and they figure the Reynas are drunk, not high. But everybody else knows; don Manuel, for one, he knows. Anyway, as soon as the Reynas showed up at the *Blue Bar,* Beto and I moved on; that's the way to avoid trouble; get out of there, 'cause trouble'll cross your way, and fast. As for Anselmo Reyna, well, I guess he learned his when I looked him down at the *Diamond* that one time; he learned his, all right. But there they were at the *Blue Bar,* higher'n a cat's back, so we got out o' there, and then went on over to the *Aquí me quedo.*

That's really something, isn't it? I mean, if the Reynas hadn't-a showed up at the *Blue Bar,* why, nothing would've happened later on, right? But that's not right either, is it? 'Cause when something's bound to happen, it'll happen; and right on schedule, too. Shoot! That was going to be Ernesto's last night in the Valley, and I was chosen to see to it: just like that. One. Two. Three. No two ways is there? . . . Although . . . well, I mean, it boils down to this: I killed a human being. Who'd-a thought it?

It's funny, Hinojosa . . . I kind of remember the why but not the when of it all. I mean, I've been sworn at, cussed at, but I always let that kind of stuff go by, know what I mean? But then, too . . . to actually have someone come-right-up-to-you like this here, come right up to you, see, point blank kind-a, and, and, ah, added to which I'd been drinking some and Ernesto there had been breaking 'em for me for a long time, and me, remembering a lot o' past crap he'd dumped on me, and him being a coward and all, yeah, he was, always counting on his brothers for everything, so . . . there it was—we went after it. Finally. After all these years.

Later on it I think it was that Beto told me about the blood and about how it just jumped out and got on my arms, and shirt, 'n face, and all over . . . Beto also said I didn't blink an eye or anything; I just stood there, he said. All I remember now is that I didn't hear a word; nothing. Not the women, or the screaming . . . Nothing; not even the guys who came a-running. Nothing. I could see 'em, though, but that's all.

Sometime later, I don't know when or for how long, but sometime later, I walked on out to the street and stood on the curb there, and noticed a family in a house across the way just sitting down and watching TV; they looked peaceful there, y'-know what I mean? Innocent-like. Why, they had no idea . . . of what had . . . and here I was, why, I'd been just as innocent a few minutes before . . . You, ah, you understand what I'm saying? . . . I'll say this, though, that talk about life and death is something serious. I mean, it's . . . it's . . . Shoot, I don't even know *what* I'm tryin' to say here . . .

Did I ever tell you that Ernesto—and this was in front of a lot o' people, now—did I ever tell you he cut in every chance he got? Just like that. He'd cut in on a girl I was dancing with, or just take her away from me. All the time. Over at *El Farol* and the other places . . . Well, he did. One other time, he told a dance girl that I had come down with a dose of the clap. Can you beat that? He was always up to something—and then something happened, and I killed him. Justlikethat. Not because of that one thing, no. Jesus! It just happens, that's all. One o'those things, I guess . . . Maybe I shouldn't've waited so long; maybe I should've cut his water off sooner, and then perhaps this wouldn't've happened . . . Ahhhh, who'm I kidding? What's done's done, and that's it.

Well, last night just tore it for me, though; he swore right at me—no mistake there—and he laughed at me, too. And then, like talking into a microphone, he said I didn't have the balls to stand up to him. Right there, in front of everybody again. Now, I had put up with a lot of crap, and I have. From friends, too, 'cause I can then swear or say some things myself, but it's all part of the game—but not with him. Ever. I didn't say a word. Not one; I sure didn't. I just looked at him, but I didn't move or do or say anything; I'm telling you I just stood there. Damfool probably thought I was afraid of him. Well, that was his mistake, and now mine, too, I guess. He kept it up—wouldn't stop, not for a minute. Then, to top it off, he brings one of the dance girls over and says to her, to me, to everybody there, that he'd looked me down a hundred times or more; looked me down, and that I had taken it—'cause I was scared. Chicken, he said. The dance girl, she didn't know what to say, what to do; she was half-scared, and embarrassed, too, I'll warrant . . . But she just stood there as he held on to her . . . by the wrist . . . I think the music stopped or something. I remember, or I think I do, anyway, that there was a buzz or a buzzer going off somewhere, like I was wearing a beehive instead of that hat of mine. Does that make sense? I heard that buzzing, see, and the hissing, raspy voice of that damfool, and then I saw that fixed, idiotic smile o' that dance girl, and then—suddenly, yeah—in a rush, see; suddenly a scream, a yell, a, a shriek-like, and I saw Ernesto sliding, slippin' sort-a, in a heap . . . and falling away . . . falling, eh?

Now, I do recall I took a deep breath, and the buzzing sort-a-stopped and I remember walking outside, to the sidewalk, and then I spotted that family I told you about, the one watching TV. And standing there, I looked at my left hand: I was carrying that pearl-handled knife that Pa Albino had given me when I was up in Michigan.

I went back inside the place, 'n then I went out again. I didn't even think of running away. What for? And where ? Everybody knew me. Shoot. The second time I walked back in, I noticed that the cement floor had been hosed down, scrubbed clean. Not a trace-a blood either, not on the floor, or anywhere. They'd taken Ernesto out back, where they keep the warm beer and the snacks, next to the toilet there. When don Manuel came in, I gave him the knife, and then I went to the sidewalk, to the side of the place . . . I got sick, and then I couldn't stop coughing. I finally got in don Manuel's car, 'n I waited for him. When he got through in there, he brought me here . . . straight to jail . . . That old man probably went home to see my Ma, right? Well . . .

Anyway, early this morning, one of his kids brought me some coffee, and he waited until I finished the pot. You know . . . I've tried to fix, to set down in my mind, when it was that I buried my knife in that damfool. But I just can't remember . . . I just can't, you know . . . And try as I may, too. It could be I just don't *want* to remember, right?

Anyway, Beto was here just before you came in . . . He's on his way to the District Attorney's office to give a deposition, he says. I'll tell you how I feel right now: I feel bad. I can't say how I'll feel later on, but for now, I do, I feel really bad, you know. That stuff about no use crying over spilled milk and all that, that's just talk, and nothing more. I feel terrible. I killed a . . . and when I think about it, real slow, I feel bad . . . Real bad . . .

I was wrong—dead wrong, I know; but if Ernesto was to insult me again, I'd probably go after him again. The truth is . . . The truth is one never learns.

Look, I'm not trying to tire you out on this—I keep saying the same thing over and over, but that's all I can talk about. But thanks for coming over. And thanks for the cigarettes, okay? Look, maybe—just maybe, now—maybe one of these days I'll know why I killed him—but he was due and bound to get it someday, wasn't he? All I did was to hurry it up a bit . . . You see? There I go again . . .

Oh, and before I forget, will you tell Mr. Royce that I won't be in tomorrow . . . and remind him I got one week's pay coming to me. Will you see to that?

I'll see you, Hinojosa . . . and thanks, okay?

Marta, and What She Knows

Cassette dated March 17, 1970.

. . . what happened was that when Pa Albino died up in Michigan as a result of that accident at the pickle plant, Balde decided we'd all spend the winter there in Michigan till we heard about the settlement one way or 'nother. Right off, then, that contractor who brought us up from the Valley, he tried to skin us there and then and so Balde had to threaten him so he'd do right by us. So, with what little we got out of him, Balde hired us a lawyer to sue Turner Pickle Company. He was a young one that lawyer, but a good one: he won the case, and that pickle company, well, they had to pay up for damages, as they call them. Now, when that was settled, we paid what we owed there in Saginaw, and with what we had left from that, well, we used it to see us through the winter months there while we looked around for another contractor to bring us back or to live up in Michigan while some work or other turned up. By this time, Beto was calling on me but not in a formal way. You see, we, Ma and I, we were still in mourning on account o' Pa, and . . . well, you know how that is . . .

You've known Balde since he was a kid, and, as Pa used to say: What can I tell you? Ma's been laid up with paralysis for years, but with all that, she's never missed a trip up North. Well, there we were with other mexicano families from Texas, stuck up in Saginaw, Michigan and waiting for winter to set in and looking for work. Any type of work; whatever it was, it didn't matter. Balde was the first one to land a job: he got himself hired on as a night man at the bay port there. Not too much after that, he put in a good word for Beto, and that way they worked together. Later on, but you know this, Beto and I got married. At that time, Balde must've been twenty-seven years old, and he could have had his pick of any Valley girl there or anywhere else, but because of Ma's condition, and the lack-a money, 'n first one thing and then 'nother, well, you know how that goes sometimes. So, we've been back in the Valley for some two years now, and I guess Balde stopped looking. But you know him; he's a good man; he was raised solid, and no one begrudges the beer or two or whatever many he has on Saturdays: he won't fight, and that's it. He won't say why he won't fight, but I, Ma 'n me, we know why: we'd be hurting, that's why. I'll tell you this, too: he's put up with a lot. A lot . . . but that's because he's always thinking o' Ma and me, see?

Once, and just the once, and by chance, too, I did hear that Balde laid it to one of the Reyna brothers, and no holds barred from what I heard . . . but this wasn't ever brought up here at the house.

You know, it's really hard to say what I felt or even *how* I felt when I first heard about what had happened to Neto Tamez. At first I couldn't . . . I couldn't bring myself to believe it, to picture it . . . I . . . I just couldn't imagine that my brother Balde . . . that he would kill someone. I'm not saying this 'cause he's a saint or something like that, no, not a-tall. But I will say this: it must've been something terrible; horrible, even. Something he just couldn't swallow; put up with. It cost him; I mean, Balde had to hold back for a long time, and he held back, for a long time . . . Holding it in all that time just got to him. It must have.

And, too, it could be that Ernesto went too far that time; too far. Beto had told me, or tried to, in his way, he tried to tell me about some of the stuff Neto Tamez was doing, or saying, and all of it against Balde; trouble is that Beto's not much of a talker, and he keeps everything inside, too, just like Balde does . . . As far as me getting any news out o' Balde, well . . . all he ever brought home was a smile on his face. I'll say this, though, once in a while he'd be as serious and as quiet as anything you'd ever want to see; I wasn't about to ask him anything, no sir, I wasn't about to do that. At any rate, what with tending to Ma here, caring for both of the men of the house, and you add the wash and the cooking, and the sewing, and what not, hooh! I've got enough to do here without worrying about gossip.

I'm not pretending to be an angel here either, but what I do know is all secondhand. What I picked up from Beto or from some of my women friends who'd call, or from what I could pick up here and there from Balde. I'm telling you what I could piece out or what I would come up with by adding two and two together, but I don't really know; like I told you, I don't have that much to go on.

Now, the whole world and its first cousin know that Neto Tamez was always picking and backbiting and just making life miserable for him . . . Well, everybody else knows how Balde put up with it, too. I'll say again that if Balde didn't put a muzzle on him right away, it was because Balde was thinking-a Ma 'n me. And that's the truth. What people don't know is why Neto did what he did against my brother.

Listen to this: back when we were in junior high, Neto Tamez would send me love notes; yes, back then. And he'd follow me home, too. To top this, he'd bully some kids to act as his messenger boys. Yes, he would. Now, I'd never paid attention to him, mind you, and I never gave him any ground to do so, either. The girls'd tell me that Neto wouldn't even let other boys come near me 'n he acted as if he owned me or something like that. This happened a long time ago, a-course, and I'd never breathe a word of it to Balde; but! the very first time I learned that Neto Tamez was giving my brother a hard time, I knew or thought I knew why he was doing it. I don't really know if Balde knew or not, though, but like Beto says: anything's possible.

Some girlfriends of mine once told me that at *La Golondrina* and *El farolito,* you know, those kind-a places . . . Anyway, the girls said that Neto insulted Balde right in front of everybody; a lotta times, too. You know, he'd cut in or just up and walk away with whatever girl Balde had at the time . . . or Neto'd say something nasty, anything, anything to make Balde's life a complete misery. On and on, see? Now, I'm not saying Neto Tamez would actually follow him from place to place, no, I'm not saying that at all; but what I *am* saying is that Neto'd never lose the opportunity . . . I mean the opportunity to push 'n shove, embarrass him until Balde would just have to get up and leave the place, see? You've got to keep in mind that living in the same town, in the same neighborhood, almost, and then to have to put up with all sorts of garbage, why, that's enough to tempt and drive a saint to madness. I swear it would, and Balde's no saint. So many's the time Balde'd come home, not say a word, and drinking or not, he'd come in, kiss Ma as he always did, and he'd sit and talk a while and then go out to the porch and have himself a smoke. Why, compared to Balde, my Beto's a walking-talking chatterbox . . .

The Tamezes are a peculiar bunch of people, you know. When they used to live out in Rebaje, it looked as if they were forever into something with someone, the neighbors, anybody. I remember the time Joaquín had to get married to Jovita de Anda; don Servando Tamez barred all the doors to the house, and then he wouldn't let the de Andas in; they couldn't even attend the wedding, and that was *it*. They say that old Mister de Anda . . . don Marcial . . . the little candyman? Well, they say he cried and just like a baby 'cause he wouldn't get to see his only daughter get married. I remember, too, that Emilio, one leg shorter 'n the other by that time, was marching up and down in front of their house like he was a soldier or something . . .

It was a good thing that poor doña Tula Tamez had passed away and was buried up in Bascom by that time, 'cause she'd-a been mortified with the goings on in that house . . . I swear. About the only thing to come out-a that house was Bertita, and oh! did she have a case on Balde. For years, too. She finally married Ramiro Leal; you know him, do you? His folks own the tortilla machine . . .

Well, anyway, yesterday, just about the time you went to see Balde at the jail-house, don Manuel Guzmán showed up here. He said he'd come just to say hello to Ma, but that was just an excuse: what he really said was for us not to worry about the law and the house. Isn't that something? Why, I've seen that man dole out kicks, head buttings, and a haymaker or two to every troublemaker here in Klail, and then, bright 'n early, one of his kids'll bring coffee to whoever it is that winds up in jail that weekend. I'll say this, too, though: the streets in Klail have never been safer, and I know that for a fact. Anyway, just as he was about to leave, don Manuel told me that

Ma 'n me that we could draw our groceries from the Torres' grocery store down the way. Don Manuel and Pa Albino go back a long time, you know; from the Revolution, I think.

Things are going to get tight around here without Balde, but Ma 'n me we still have Beto here, and . . . My only hope is that the Tamezes don't come looking for Beto 'cause that'll really put us under without a man in the house. Beto's at the Court House just now; he had to go and make a statement, they said.

Oh, Mr. Hinojosa, I just don't know where all of this is going to take us . . . But God'll provide . . . He's got to.

ROMEO HINOJOSA

Attorney at Law

420 South Cerralvo   Tel. 843-1640

The following is a deposition, in English, made by Beto Castañeda, today, March 17, 1970, in the office of Mr. Robert A. Chapman, Assistant District Attorney for Belken County.

The aforementioned officer of the court gave me a copy of the statement as part of the testimony in the trial of *The State of Texas v. Cordero* set for August 23 of this year in the court of Judge Harrison Phelps who presides in the 139th District Court.

Romeo Hinojosa

Romeo Hinojosa

March 17, 1970

A Deposition Freely Given

on this seventeenth day of March, 1970, by Mr. Gilberto Castañeda in room 218 of the Belken County Court House was duly taken, witnessed, and signed by Miss Helen Chacón, a legal interpreter and acting assistant deputy recorder for said County, as part of a criminal investigation assigned to Robert A. Chapman, assistant district attorney for the same County.

It is understood that Mr. Castañeda is acting solely as a deponent and is not a party to any civil or criminal investigation, proceeding, or violation which may be alluded to in this deposition.

"Well, my name is Gilberto Castañeda, and I live at 169 South Hidalgo Street here in Klail. It is not my house; it belong to my mother-in-law, but I have live there since I marry Marta (Marta Cordero Castañeda, 169 South Hidalgo Street, Klail City) about three years ago.

"I am working at the Royce-Fedders tomato packing shed as a grader. My brother-in-law, Balde Cordero, work there too. He pack tomatoes and don't get pay for the hour, he get pay for what he pack and since I am a grader I make sure he get the same class tomato and that way he pack faster; he just get a tomato with the right hand, and he wrap it with the left. He pack a lug of tomatoes so fast you don't see it, and he does it fast because I am a good grader.

"Balde is a good man. His father, don Albino, my father-in-law who die up in Saginaw, Michigan when Marta and I, you know, go together . . . well, Balde is like don Albino, you understand? A good man. A right man. Me, I stay an orphan and when the Mejías take me when my father and my mother die in that train wreck— near Flora? don Albino tell the Mejías I must go to the school. I go to First Ward Elementary where Mr. Gold is principal. In First Ward I am a friend of Balde and there I meet Marta too. Later, when I grow up I don't visit the house too much because of Marta, you know what I mean? Anyway, Balde is my friend and I have know him very well . . . maybe more than nobody else. He's a good man.

"Well, last night Balde and I took a few beers in some of the places near where we live. We drink a couple here and a couple there, you know, and we save the *Aquí me quedo* on South Missouri for last. It is there that I tell Balde a joke about the drunk guy who is going to his house and he hear the clock in the corner make two sounds. You know that one? Well, this drunk guy he hear the clock go bong-bong and he say that the clock is wrong for it give one o'clock two time. Well, Balde think that is funny . . . Anyway, when I tell the joke in Spanish it's better. Well, there we were drinking a beer when Ernesto Tamez comes. Ernesto Tamez is like a woman, you know? Everytime he get in trouble he call his family to help him . . . that is the way it is with him. Well, that night he bother Balde again. More than one time Balde has stop me when Tamez begin to insult. That Balde is a man of patience. This time Ernesto bring a *vieja* (woman) and Balde don't say nothing, nothing, nothing. What happens is that things get spooky, you know. Ernesto talking and *burlándose de él* (ridiculing him) and at the same time he have the poor woman by the arm. And then something happen. I don't know what happen, but something and fast.

"I don't know. I really don't know. It all happen so fast; the knife, the blood squirt all over my face and arms, the woman try to get away, a loud really loud scream, not a *grito* (local Mexican yell) but more a woman screaming, you know what I mean? and then Ernesto fall on the cement.

"Right there I look at Balde and his face is like a mask in asleep, you understand? No angry, no surprise, nothing. In his left hand he have the knife and he shake his head before he walk to the door. Look, it happen so fast no one move for a while. Then Balde come in and go out of the place and when don Manuel (Manuel Guzmán, constable for precinct 21) come in, Balde just hand over the knife. Lucas Barrón, you know, El Chorreao (a nickname) well, he wash the blood and sweep the floor before don Manuel get there. Don Manuel just shake his head and tell Balde to go to the car and wait. Don Manuel he walk to the back to see Ernesto and on the way out one of the women, I think it is *la güera Balín* (Amelia Cortez, 23, no known address, this city), try to make a joke, but don Manuel he say *no estés chingando* (shut the hell up, or words to that effect) and after that don Manuel go about his own business. Me, I go to the door but all I see is Balde looking at a house across the street and he don't even know I come to say goodbye. Anyway, this morning a little boy of don Manuel say for me to come here and here I am."

Further deponent sayeth not.
Sworn to before me, this
17th day of March, 1970

Helen Chacón

/s/ _____

Helen Chacón
Acting Asst. Deputy Recorder
Belken County

Gilberto Castañeda

/s/ _____

Gilberto Castañeda

1983

Excerpt from the *Klail City Enterprise-News* (August 24, 1970)

Klail City. (Special). Baldemar Cordero, 30, of 169 South Hidalgo Street, drew a 15 year sentence to the Huntsville State Prison in Judge Harrison Phelps' 139th District Court for the murder of Ernesto Tamez last Spring.

Cordero is alleged to have fatally stabbed Ernesto Tanez, also 30, over the affections of one of the "hostesses" who works there.

No appeal had been made at press time.

John Barth b. 1930

John Barth's birth on May 22, 1930, in Cambridge, a small "southern" town on the Eastern Shore of Maryland, established his claim to one of the strongest literary heritages in twentieth-century America, the modernist tradition that took root in the American South through the novels that William Faulkner and Thomas Wolfe wrote during the 1920s and 1930s. Despite an early focus on music, Barth, who in 1953 became a college writing teacher, absorbed this tradition well enough to give his first two novels, *The Floating Opera* (1956) and *The End of the Road* (1958), the strong sense of place and fate commonly found in modern southern fiction.

Barth's first two books, however, also exhibited a playfulness closer to the improvisations of modern jazz, his earlier passion, and to the black humor emerging in the fifties, than to modern southern fiction. The novels parodied the existential movement, the dominant tendency of European writing during the late modernist period; *The Floating Opera* expresses Barth's comic response to Camus's earnest and familiar defense of suicide while *The End of the Road* pushes Sartre's views of commitment and protean freedom to sardonic extremes. In short, Barth was already experimenting with one of his favorite devices, the practice of framing seemingly exhausted literary modes by reworking them from radically different perspectives to renew them and thereby replenish the literary tradition. Eventually, his use of parody and frames would be his major contribution to the (then) undetected emergence of postmodernism, the dominant cultural development of the second half of the twentieth century and a movement in which Barth is regarded as the major American literary practitioner and advocate.

Barth's *The Sot-Weed Factor* (1960), taking a clue from a short work of fiction, "Pierre Menard, Author of Don Quixote," by Jorge Luis Borges (the modern writer from whom he appears to have learned most), continued his parodies of established modes of writing by creating a gigantic eighteenth-century Anglo-southern novel out of comic characters and themes appropriate to the mid-twentieth century. In *Giles Goat-Boy, or The Revised New Syllabus* (1966), the novelist took a decisive step toward postmodernism when he freed himself from both memory and history by creating an imaginary university parodying the universe in which earthlings found themselves during the cold war.

The experiments collected in 1968 in *Lost in the Funhouse* mark Barth's emergence as leader of the American wing of the movement called postmodernism. As a contribution to the postmodern, the title story, reprinted below, generates special excitement, for it is difficult to imagine a more self-referential metafiction. Here the author frames a seemingly heart-felt parody of a story about a boy from a small town as he comes of age, a subject typical of the southern modernists, with the fatalistic thoughts of a beginning or blocked writer who struggles to obey the best-intended formulas of creative writing classes. Writer's block became a major theme, and likely a metaphor for contemporary culture, in such later works as *Chimera* (a masterpiece of the postmodern in America, published in 1972) and *Letters: A Novel* (1979).

After the seemingly (perhaps deliberately) botched experiment with narration and point of view in *Sabbatical: A Romance* (1982), Barth's jazz-like powers of improvisation returned full force in his joy-filled megafiction *The Tidewater Tales* (1987), while the temporal pastiche of *The Last Voyage of Somebody the Sailor* (1991) throws the assumptions of modern realist fiction into confusion by making the adventures of Sinbad seem to the audience that hears them examples of traditional realism, and competing journalistic accounts of modern events appear to be sheer fiction. *On with the Story: Stories* (1996) complements the *Lost in the Funhouse* collection in its attempt to jump-start experimental postmodern fiction, which in the 1990s was losing ground to several retro tendencies. *The Friday Book* and *Further Fridays,* Barth's essays and non-fiction gathered together in 1984 and 1995, may be the best year-by-year record in existence of the emergence—from modernism, existentialism, black humor, and "irrealism"—of American literary postmodernism.

Julius Rowan Raper
University of North Carolina at Chapel Hill

PRIMARY WORKS

The Floating Opera, 1956 [rev. 1967]; *The End of the Road,* 1958 [rev. 1967]; *The Sot-Weed Factor,* 1960 [rev. 1967]; *Giles Goat-Boy, or The Revised New Syllabus,* 1966; *Lost in the Funhouse: Fiction for Print, Tape, Live Voice,* 1968; *Chimera,* 1972; *LETTERS: A Novel,* 1979; *Sabbatical: A Romance,* 1982; *The Friday Book: Essays and Other Nonfiction,* 1984; *The Tidewater Tales: A Novel,* 1987; *The Last Voyage of Somebody the Sailor,* 1991; *Once Upon a Time: A Floating Opera,* 1994; *Further Fridays: Essays, Lectures, and Other Nonfiction, 1984–94,* 1995; *On with the Story: Stories,* 1996; *The Book of Ten Nights and a Night,* 2004; *Where Three Roads Meet,* 2005; *The Development,* 2008.

Lost in the Funhouse

For whom is the funhouse fun? Perhaps for lovers. For Ambrose it is *a place of fear and confusion.* He has come to the seashore with his family for the holiday, *the occasion of their visit is Independence Day, the most important secular holiday of the United States of America.* A single straight underline is the manuscript mark for italic type, *which in turn* is the printed equivalent to oral emphasis of words and phrases as well as the customary type for titles of complete works, not to mention. Italics are also employed, in fiction stories especially, for "outside," intrusive, or artificial voices, such as radio announcements, the texts of telegrams and newspaper articles, et cetera. They should be used *sparingly.* If passages originally in roman type are italicized by someone repeating them, it's customary to acknowledge the fact. *Italics mine.*

Ambrose was "at that awkward age." His voice came out high-pitched as a child's if he let himself get carried away; to be on the safe side, therefore, he moved and spoke with *deliberate calm* and *adult gravity.* Talking soberly of unimportant or irrelevant matters and listening consciously to the sound of your own voice are useful habits for maintaining control in this difficult interval. *En route* to Ocean City he sat in the back seat of the family car with his brother Peter, age fifteen, and Magda G_____, age fourteen, a pretty girl an exquisite young lady, who lived not far from them on B_____ Street in the town of D_____, Maryland. Initials, blanks, or both were often substituted for proper names in nineteenth-century fiction to enhance the illusion of reality. It is as if the author felt it necessary to delete the names for reasons of tact or legal liability. Interestingly, as with other aspects of realism, it is an *illusion* that is being enhanced, by purely artificial means. Is it likely, does it violate the principle of verisimilitude, that a thirteen-year-old boy could make such a sophisticated observation? A girl of fourteen is *the psychological coeval* of a boy of fifteen or sixteen; a thirteen-year-old boy, therefore, even one precocious in some other respects, might be three years *her emotional junior.*

Thrice a year—on Memorial, Independence, and Labor Days—the family visits Ocean City for the afternoon and evening. When Ambrose and Peter's father was their age, the excursion was made by train, as mentioned in the novel *The 42nd Parallel* by John Dos Passos. Many families from the same neighborhood used to travel together, with dependent relatives and often with Negro servants; schoolfuls of children swarmed through the railway cars; everyone shared everyone else's Maryland fried chicken, Virginia ham, deviled eggs, potato salad, beaten biscuits, iced tea. Nowadays (that is, in 19——, the year of our story) the journey is made by automobile—more comfortably and quickly though without the extra fun though without the *camaraderie* of a general excursion. It's all part of the deterioration of American life, their father declares; Uncle Karl supposes that when the boys take *their* families to Ocean City for the holidays they'll fly in Autogiros. Their mother, sitting in the middle of the front seat like Magda in the second, only with her arms on the seat-back behind the men's shoulders, wouldn't want the good old days back again, the steaming trains and stuffy long dresses; on the other hand she can do without Autogiros, too, if she has to become a grandmother to fly in them.

Description of physical appearance and mannerisms is one of several standard methods of characterization used by writers of fiction. It is also important to "keep the senses operating"; when a detail from one of the five senses, say visual, is "crossed" with a detail from another, say auditory, the reader's imagination is oriented to the scene, perhaps unconsciously. This procedure may be compared to the way surveyors and navigators determine their positions by two or more compass bearings, a process known as triangulation. The brown hair on Ambrose's mother's forearms gleamed in the sun like. Though right-handed, she took her left arm from the seat-back to press the dashboard cigar lighter for Uncle Karl. When the glass bead in its handle glowed red, the lighter was ready for use. The smell of Uncle Karl's cigar smoke reminded one of. The fragrance of the ocean came strong to the picnic ground where they always stopped for lunch, two miles inland from Ocean City. Having to pause for a full hour almost within the sound of the breakers was difficult for Peter and Ambrose when they were younger; even at their present age it was not easy to keep their anticipation, *stimulated by the briny spume,* from turning into short temper. The Irish author James Joyce, in his unusual novel entitled *Ulysses,* now available in this country, uses the adjectives *snot-green* and *scrotum-tightening* to describe the sea. Visual, auditory, tactile, olfactory, gustatory. Peter and Ambrose's father, while steering their black 1936 LaSalle sedan with one hand, could with the other remove the first cigarette from a white pack of Lucky Strikes and, more remarkably, light it with a match forefingered from its book and thumbed against the flint paper without being detached. The matchbook cover merely advertised U.S. War Bonds and Stamps. A fine metaphor, simile, or other figure of speech, in addition to its obvious "first-order" relevance to the thing it describes, will be seen upon reflection to have a second order of significance: it may be drawn from the *milieu* of the action, for example, or be particularly appropriate to the sensibility of the narrator, even hinting to the reader things of which the narrator is unaware; or it may cast further and subtler lights upon the thing it describes, sometimes ironically qualifying the more evident sense of the comparison.

To say that Ambrose's and Peter's mother was *pretty* is to accomplish nothing; the reader may acknowledge the proposition, but his imagination is not engaged. Besides, Magda was also pretty, yet in an altogether different way. Although she lived on B_____ Street she had very good manners and did better than average in school. Her figure was very well developed for her age. Her right hand lay casually on the plush upholstery of the seat, very near Ambrose's left leg, on which his own hand rested. The space between their legs, between her right and his left leg, was out of the line of sight of anyone sitting on the other side of Magda, as well as anyone glancing into the rearview mirror. Uncle Karl's face resembled Peter's—rather, vice versa. Both had dark hair and eyes, short husky statures, deep voices. Magda's left hand was probably in a similar position on her left side. The boy's father is difficult to describe; no particular feature of his appearance or manner stood out. He wore glasses and was principal of a T_____ County grade school. Uncle Karl was a masonry contractor.

Although Peter must have known as well as Ambrose that the latter, because of his position in the car, would be the first to see the electrical towers of the power plant at V_____, the halfway point of their trip, he leaned forward and slightly toward the center of the car and pretended to be looking for them through the flat pinewoods and tuckahoe creeks along the highway. For as long as the boys could remember, "looking for the Towers" had been a feature of the first half of their excursions to Ocean City, "looking for the standpipe" of the second. Though the game was childish, their mother preserved the tradition of rewarding the first to see the Towers with a candybar or piece of fruit. She insisted now that Magda play the game; the prize, she said, was "something hard to get nowadays." Ambrose decided not to join in; he sat far back in his seat. Magda, like Peter, leaned forward. Two sets of straps were discernible through the shoulders of her sun dress; the inside right one, a brassiere-strap, was fastened or shortened with a small safety pin. The right armpit of her dress, presumably the left as well, was damp with perspiration. The simple strategy for being first to espy the Towers, which Ambrose had understood by the age of four, was to sit on the right-hand side of the car. Whoever sat there, however, had also to put up with the worst of the sun, and so Ambrose, without mentioning the matter, chose sometimes the one and sometimes the other. Not impossibly Peter had never caught on to the trick, or thought that his brother hadn't simply because Ambrose on occasion preferred shade to a Baby Ruth or tangerine.

The shade-sun situation didn't apply to the front seat, owing to the windshield; if anything the driver got more sun, since the person on the passenger side not only was shaded below by the door and dashboard but might swing down his sunvisor all the way too.

"Is that them?" Magda asked. Ambrose's mother teased the boys for letting Magda win, insinuating that "somebody [had] a girlfriend." Peter and Ambrose's father reached a long thin arm across their mother to butt his cigarette in the dashboard ashtray, under the lighter. The prize this time for seeing the Towers first was a banana. Their mother bestowed it after chiding their father for wasting a half-smoked cigarette when everything was so scarce. Magda, to take the prize, moved her hand from so near Ambrose's that he could have touched it as though accidentally. She offered to share the prize, things like that were so hard to find; but everyone insisted it was hers alone. Ambrose's mother sang an iambic trimeter couplet from a popular song, femininely rhymed:

> *"What's good is in the Army;*
> *What's left will never harm me."*

Uncle Karl tapped his cigar ash out the ventilator window; some particles were sucked by the slipstream back into the car through the rear window on the passenger side. Magda demonstrated her ability to hold a banana in one hand and peel it with her teeth. She still sat forward; Ambrose pushed his glasses back onto the bridge of his nose with his left hand, which he then negligently let fall to the seat cushion immediately behind her. He even permitted the single hair, gold, on the second joint of his thumb to brush the fabric of her skirt. Should she have sat back at that instant, his hand would have been caught under her.

Plush upholstery prickles uncomfortably through gabardine slacks in the July sun. The function of the *beginning* of a story is to introduce the principal characters, establish their initial relationships, set the scene for the main action, expose the background of the situation if necessary, plant motifs and foreshadowings where appropriate, and initiate the first complication or whatever of the "rising action." Actually, if one imagines a story called "The Funhouse," or "Lost in the Funhouse," the details of the drive to Ocean City don't seem especially relevant. The *beginning* should recount the events between Ambrose's first sight of the funhouse early in the afternoon and his entering it with Magda and Peter in the evening. The *middle* would narrate all relevant events from the time he goes in to the time he loses his way; middles have the double and contradictory function of delaying the climax while at the same time preparing the reader for it and fetching him to it. Then the *ending* would tell what Ambrose does while he's lost, how he finally finds his way out, and what everybody makes of the experience. So far there's been no real dialogue, very little sensory detail, and nothing in the way of a *theme*. And a long time has gone by already without anything happening; it makes a person wonder. We haven't even reached Ocean City yet: we will never get out of the funhouse.

The more closely an author identifies with the narrator, literally or metaphorically, the less advisable it is, as a rule, to use the first-person narrative viewpoint. Once three years previously the young people *aforementioned* played Niggers and Masters in the backyard; when it was Ambrose's turn to be Master and theirs to be Niggers Peter had to go serve his evening papers; Ambrose was afraid to punish Magda alone but she led him to the whitewashed Torture Chamber between the woodshed and the privy in the Slaves Quarters; there she knelt sweating among bamboo rakes and dusty Mason jars, pleadingly embraced his knees, and while bees droned in the lattice as if on an ordinary summer afternoon, purchased clemency at a surprising price set by herself. Doubtless she remembered nothing of this event; Ambrose on the other hand seemed unable to forget the least detail of his life. He even recalled how, standing beside himself with awed impersonality in the reeky heat, he'd stared the while at an empty cigar box in which Uncle Karl kept stone-cutting chisels: beneath the words *El Producto,* a laureled, loose-toga'd lady regarded the sea from a marble bench; beside her, forgotten or not yet turned to, was a five-stringed lyre. Her chin reposed on the back of her right hand; her left depended negligently from the bench-arm. The lower half of scene and lady was peeled away; the words EXAMINED BY_____ were inked there into the wood. Nowadays cigar boxes are made of pasteboard. Ambrose wondered what Magda would have done, Ambrose wondered what Magda would do when she sat back on his hand as he resolved she should. Be angry. Make a teasing joke of it. Give no sign at all. For a long time she leaned forward, playing cow-poker with Peter against Uncle Karl and Mother and watching for the first sign of Ocean City. At nearly the same instant, picnic ground and Ocean City standpipe hove into view; an Amoco filling station on their side of the road cost Mother and Uncle Karl fifty cows and the game; Magda bounced back, clapping her right hand on Mother's right arm; Ambrose moved clear "in the nick of time."

At this rate our hero, at this rate our protagonist will remain in the funhouse forever. Narrative ordinarily consists of alternating dramatization and summarization. One symptom of nervous tension, paradoxically, is repeated and violent yawning; neither Peter nor Magda nor Uncle Karl nor Mother reacted in this manner. Although they were no longer small children, Peter and Ambrose were each given a dollar to spend on boardwalk amusements in addition to what money of their own they'd brought along. Magda too, though she protested she had ample spending money. The boys' mother made a little scene out of distributing the bills; she pretended that her sons and Magda were small children and cautioned them not to spend the sum too quickly or in one place. Magda promised with a merry laugh and, having both hands free, took the bill with her left. Peter laughed also and pledged in a falsetto to be a good boy. His imitation of a child was not clever. The boys' father was tall and thin, balding, fair-complexioned. Assertions of that sort are not effective; the reader may acknowledge the proposition, but. We should be much farther along than we are; something has gone wrong; not much of this preliminary rambling seems relevant. Yet everyone begins in the same place; how is it that most go along without difficulty but a few lose their way?

"Stay out from under the boardwalk," Uncle Karl growled from the side of his mouth. The boys' mother pushed his shoulder *in mock annoyance.* They were all standing before Fat May the Laughing Lady who advertised the funhouse. Larger than life, Fat May mechanically shook, rocked on her heels, slapped her thighs while recorded laughter—uproarious, female—came amplified from a hidden loudspeaker. It chuckled, wheezed, wept; tried in vain to catch its breath; tittered, groaned, exploded raucous and anew. You couldn't hear it without laughing yourself, no matter how you felt. Father came back from talking to a Coast-Guardsman on duty and reported that the surf was spoiled with crude oil from tankers recently torpedoed offshore. Lumps of it, difficult to remove, made tarry tidelines on the beach and stuck on swimmers. Many bathed in the surf nevertheless and came out speckled; others paid to use a municipal pool and only sunbathed on the beach. We would do the latter. We would do the latter. We would do the latter.

Under the boardwalk, matchbook covers, grainy other things. What is the story's theme? Ambrose is ill. He perspires in the dark passages; candied apples-on-a-stick, delicious-looking, disappointing to eat. Funhouses need men's and ladies' room at intervals. Others perhaps have also vomited in corners and corridors; may even have had bowel movements liable to be stepped in in the dark. The word *fuck* suggests suction and/or and/or flatulence. Mother and Father; grandmothers and grandfathers on both sides; great-grandmothers and great-grandfathers on four sides, et cetera. Count a generation as thirty years: in approximately the year when Lord Baltimore was granted charter to the province of Maryland by Charles I, five hundred twelve women—English, Welsh, Bavarian, Swiss—of every class and character, received into themselves the penises the intromittent organs of five hundred twelve men, ditto, in every circumstance and posture, to conceive the five hundred twelve ancestors of the two hundred fifty-six ancestors of the et cetera et cetera et cetera et cetera et cetera et cetera et cetera et cetera of the author, of the narrator, of this story, *Lost in the Funhouse.* In alleyways, ditches, canopy beds, pinewoods, bridal suites, ship's cabins, coach-and-fours, coaches-and-four, sultry toolsheds; on the cold sand under boardwalks, littered with *El Producto* cigar butts, treasured with Lucky Strike cigarette stubs, Coca-Cola caps, gritty turds, cardboard lollipop sticks, matchbook covers warning that A Slip of the Lip Can Sink a Ship. The shluppish whisper, continuous as seawash round the globe, tidelike falls and rises with the circuit of dawn and dusk.

Magda's teeth. She *was* left-handed. Perspiration. They've gone all the way, through, Magda and Peter, they've been waiting for hours with Mother and Uncle Karl while Father searches for his lost son; they draw french-fried potatoes from a paper cup and shake their heads. They've named the children they'll one day have and bring to Ocean City on holidays. Can spermatozoa properly be thought of as male animalcules when there are no female spermatozoa? They grope through hot, dark windings, past Love's Tunnel's fearsome obstacles. Some perhaps lose their way.

Peter suggested then and there that they do the funhouse; he had been through it before, so had Magda, Ambrose hadn't and suggested, his voice cracking on account of Fat May's laughter, that they swim first. All were chuckling, couldn't help it; Ambrose's father, Ambrose's and Peter's father came up grinning like a lunatic with two boxes of syrup-coated popcorn, one for Mother, one for Magda; the men were to help themselves. Ambrose walked on Magda's right: being by nature left-handed, she carried the box in her left hand. Up front the situation was reversed.

"What are you limping for?" Magda inquired of Ambrose. He supposed in a husky tone that his foot had gone to sleep in the car. Her teeth flashed. "Pins and needles?" It was the honeysuckle on the lattice of the former privy that drew the bees. Imagine being stung there. How long is this going to take?

The adults decided to forgo the pool; but Uncle Karl insisted they change into swimsuits and do the beach. "He wants to watch the pretty girls," Peter teased, and ducked behind Magda from Uncle Karl's pretended wrath. "You've got all the pretty girls you need right here," Magda declared, and Mother said: "Now that's the gospel truth." Magda scolded Peter, who reached over her shoulder to sneak some popcorn. "Your brother and father aren't getting any." Uncle Karl wondered if they were going to have fireworks that night, what with the shortages. It wasn't the shortages, Mr. M_____ replied; Ocean City had fireworks from pre-war. But it was too risky on account of the enemy submarines, some people thought.

"Don't seem like Fourth of July without fireworks," said Uncle Karl. The inverted tag in dialogue writing is still considered permissible with proper names or epithets, but sounds old-fashioned with personal pronouns. "We'll have 'em again soon enough," predicted the boys' father. Their mother declared she could do without fireworks: they reminded her too much of the real thing. Their father said all the more reason to shoot off a few now and again. Uncle Karl asked *rhetorically* who needed reminding, just look at people's hair and skin.

"The oil, yes," said Mrs. M_____.

Ambrose had a pain in his stomach and so didn't swim but enjoyed watching the others. He and his father burned red easily. Magda's figure was exceedingly well developed for her age. She too declined to swim, and got mad, and became angry when Peter attempted to drag her into the pool. She always swam, he insisted; what did she mean not swim? Why did a person come to Ocean City?

"Maybe I want to lay here with Ambrose," Magda teased.

Nobody likes a pedant.

"Aha," said Mother. Peter grabbed Magda by one ankle and ordered Ambrose to grab the other. She squealed and rolled over on the beach blanket. Ambrose pretended to help hold her back. Her tan was darker than even Mother's and Peter's. "Help out, Uncle Karl!" Peter cried. Uncle Karl went to seize the other ankle. Inside the top of her swimsuit, however, you could see the line where the sunburn ended and, when she hunched her shoulders and squealed again, one nipple's auburn edge. Mother made them behave themselves. "*You* should certainly know," she said to Uncle Karl. Archly. "That when a lady says she doesn't feel like swimming, a gentleman doesn't ask questions." Uncle Karl said excuse *him;* Mother winked at Magda; Ambrose blushed; stupid Peter kept saying "Phooey on *feel like!*" and tugging at Magda's ankle; then even he got the point, and cannonballed with a holler into the pool.

"I swear," Magda said, in mock *in feigned* exasperation.

The diving would make a suitable literary symbol. To go off the high board you had to wait in a line along the poolside and up the ladder. Fellows tickled girls and goosed one another and shouted to the ones at the top to hurry up, or razzed them for bellyfloppers. Once on the springboard some took a great while posing or clowning or deciding on a dive or getting up their nerve; others ran right off. Especially among the younger fellows the idea was to strike the funniest pose or do the craziest stunt as you fell, a thing that got harder to do as you kept on and kept on. But whether you hollered *Geronimo!* or *Sieg heil!*, held your nose or "rode a bicycle," pretended to be shot or did a perfect jackknife or changed your mind halfway down and ended up with nothing, it was over in two seconds, after all that wait. Spring, pose, splash. Spring, neat-o, splash. Spring, aw fooey, splash.

The grown-ups had gone on; Ambrose wanted to converse with Magda; she was remarkably well developed for her age; it was said that that came from rubbing with a turkish towel, and there were other theories. Ambrose could think of nothing to say except how good a diver Peter was, who was showing off for her benefit. You could pretty well tell by looking at their bathing suits and arm muscles how far along the different fellows were. Ambrose was glad he hadn't gone in swimming, the cold water shrank you up so. Magda pretended to be uninterested in the diving; she probably weighed as much as he did. If you knew your way around in the funhouse like your own bedroom, you could wait until a girl came along and then slip away without ever getting caught, even if her boyfriend was right with her. She'd think *he* did it! It would be better to be the boyfriend, and act outraged, and tear the funhouse apart.

Not act; *be.*

"He's a master diver," Ambrose said. In feigned admiration. "You really have to slave away at it to get that good." What would it matter anyhow if he asked her right out whether she remembered, even teased her with it as Peter would have?

There's no point in going farther; this isn't getting anybody anywhere; they haven't even come to the funhouse yet. Ambrose is off the track, in some new or old part of the place that's not supposed to be used; he strayed into it by some one-in-a-million chance, like the time the roller-coaster car left the tracks in the nineteen-teens against all the laws of physics and sailed over the boardwalk in the dark. And they can't locate him because they don't know where to look. Even the designer and operator have forgotten this other part, that winds around on itself like a whelk shell. That winds around the right part like the snakes on Mercury's caduceus. Some people, perhaps, don't "hit their stride" until their twenties, when the growing-up business is over and women appreciate other things besides wisecracks and teasing and strutting. Peter didn't have one-tenth the imagination *he* had, not one-tenth. Peter did this naming-their-children thing as a joke, making up names like Aloysius and Murgatroyd, but Ambrose knew *exactly* how it would feel to be married and have children of your own, and be a loving husband and father, and go comfortably to work in the mornings and to bed with your wife at night, and wake up with her there. With a breeze coming through the sash and birds and mockingbirds singing in the Chinese-cigar trees. His eyes watered, there aren't enough ways to say that. He would be quite famous in his line of work. Whether Magda was his wife or not, one evening when he was wise-lined and gray at the temples he'd smile gravely, at a fashionable dinner party, and remind her of his youthful passion. The time they went with his family to Ocean City; the *erotic fantasies* he used to have about her. How long ago it seemed, and childish! Yet tender, too, *n'est-ce pas?* Would she have imagined that the world-famous whatever remembered how many strings were on the lyre on the bench beside the girl on the label of the cigar box he'd stared at in the toolshed at age ten while she, age eleven. Even then he had felt *wise beyond his years;* he'd stroked her hair and said in his deepest voice and correctest English, as to a dear child: "I shall never forget this moment."

But though he had breathed heavily, groaned as if ecstatic, what he'd really felt throughout was an odd detachment, as though someone else were Master. Strive as he might to be transported, he heard his mind take notes upon the scene: *This is what they call* passion. *I am experiencing it.* Many of the digger machines were out of order in the penny arcades and could not be repaired or replaced for the duration. Moreover the prizes, made now in USA, were less interesting than formerly, pasteboard items for the most part, and some of the machines wouldn't work on white pennies. The gypsy fortune-teller machine might have provided a foreshadowing of the climax of this story if Ambrose had operated it. It was even dilapidateder than most: the silver coating was worn off the brown metal handles, the glass windows around the dummy were cracked and taped, her kerchiefs and silks long-faded. If a man lived by himself, he could take a department-store mannequin with flexible joints and modify her in certain ways. *However:* by the time he was that old he'd have a real woman. There was a machine that stamped your name around a white-metal coin with a star in the middle: A_____. His son would be the second, and when the lad reached thirteen or so he would put a strong arm around his shoulder and tell him calmly: "It is perfectly normal. We have all been through it. It will not last for-ever." Nobody knew how to be what they were right. He'd smoke a pipe, teach his son how to fish and softcrab, assure him he needn't worry about himself. Magda would certainly give, Magda would certainly yield a great deal of milk, although guilty of occasional solecisms. It don't taste so bad. Suppose the lights came on now!

The day wore on. You think you're yourself, but there are other persons in you. Ambrose gets hard when Ambrose doesn't want to, *and obversely.* Ambrose watches them disagree; Ambrose watches him watch. In the funhouse mirror-room you can't see yourself go on forever, because no matter how you stand, your head gets in the way. Even if you had a glass periscope, the image of your eye would cover up the thing you really wanted to see. The police will come; there'll be a story in the papers. That must be where it happened. Unless he can find a surprise exit, an unofficial backdoor or escape hatch opening on an alley, say, and then stroll up to the family in front of the funhouse and ask where everybody's been; *he's* been out of the place for ages. That's just where it happened, in that last lighted room: Peter and Magda found the right exit; he found one that you weren't supposed to find and strayed off into the works somewhere. In a perfect funhouse you'd be able to go only one way, like the divers off the highboard; getting lost would be impossible; the doors and halls would work like minnow traps or the valves in veins.

On account of German U-boats, Ocean City was "browned out": streetlights were shaded on the seaward side; shop-windows and boardwalk amusement places were kept dim, not to silhouette tankers and Liberty-ships for torpedoing. In a short story about Ocean City, Maryland, during World War II, the author could make use of the image of sailors on leave in the penny arcades and shooting galleries, sighting through the crosshairs of toy machine guns at swastika'd subs, while out in the black Atlantic a U-boat skipper squints through his periscope at real ships outlined by the glow of penny arcades. After dinner the family strolled back to the amusement end of the boardwalk. The boys' father had burnt red as always and was masked with Noxzema, a minstrel in reverse. The grownups stood at the end of the boardwalk where the Hurricane of '33 had cut an inlet from the ocean to Assawoman Bay.

"Pronounced with a long *o,*" Uncle Karl reminded Magda with a wink. His short sleeves were rolled up; Mother punched his brown biceps with the arrowed heart on it and said his mind was naughty. Fat May's laugh came suddenly from the funhouse, as if she'd just got the joke; the family laughed too at the coincidence. Ambrose went under the boardwalk to search for out-of-town matchbook covers with the aid of his pocket flashlight; he looked out from the edge of the North American continent and wondered how far their laughter carried over the water. Spies in rubber rafts; survivors in lifeboats. If the joke had been beyond his understanding, he could have said: "*The laughter was over his head.*" And let the reader see the serious wordplay on second reading.

He turned the flashlight on and then off at once even before the woman whooped. He sprang away, heart athud, dropping the light. What had the man grunted? Perspiration drenched and chilled him by the time he scrambled up to the family. "See anything?" his father asked. His voice wouldn't come; he shrugged and violently brushed sand from his pants legs.

"Let's ride the old flying horses!" Magda cried. I'll never be an author. It's been forever already, everybody's gone home, Ocean City's deserted, the ghost-crabs are tickling across the beach and down the littered cold streets. And the empty halls of clapboard hotels and abandoned funhouses. A tidal wave; an enemy air raid; a monster-crab swelling like an island from the sea. *The inhabitants fled in terror.* Magda clung to his trouser leg; he alone knew the maze's secret. "He gave his life that we might live," said Uncle Karl with a scowl of pain, as he. The fellow's hands had been tattooed; the woman's legs, the woman's fat white legs had. *An astonishing coincidence.* He yearned to tell Peter. He wanted to throw up for excitement. They hadn't even chased him. He wished he were dead.

One possible ending would be to have Ambrose come across another lost person in the dark. They'd match their wits together against the funhouse, struggle like Ulysses past obstacle after obstacle, help and encourage each other. Or a girl. By the time they found the exit they'd be closest friends, sweethearts if it were a girl; they'd know each other's inmost souls, be bound together *by the cement of shared adventure;* then they'd emerge into the light and it would turn out that his friend was a Negro. A blind girl. President Roosevelt's son. Ambrose's former archenemy.

Shortly after the mirror room he'd groped along a musty corridor, his heart already misgiving him at the absence of phosphorescent arrows and other signs. He'd found a crack of light—not a door, it turned out, but a seam between the plyboard wall panels—and squinting up to it, espied a small old man, *in appearance not unlike* the photographs at home of Ambrose's late grandfather, nodding upon a stool beneath a bare, speckled bulb. A crude panel of toggle- and knife-switches hung beside the open fuse box near his head; elsewhere in the little room were wooden levers and ropes belayed to boat cleats. At the time, Ambrose wasn't lost enough to rap or call; later he couldn't find that crack. Now it seemed to him that he'd possibly dozed off for a few minutes somewhere along the way; certainly he was exhausted from the afternoon's sunshine and the evening's problems; he couldn't be sure he hadn't dreamed part or all of the sight. Had an old black wall fan droned like bees and shimmied two flypaper streamers? Had the funhouse operator—gentle, somewhat sad and tired-appearing, in expression not unlike the photographs at home of Ambrose's late Uncle Konrad—murmured in his sleep? Is there really such a person as Ambrose, or is he a figment of the author's imagination? Was it Assawoman Bay or Sinepuxent? Are there other errors of fact in this fiction? Was there another sound besides the little slap slap of thigh on ham, like water sucking at the chineboards of a skiff?

When you're lost, the smartest thing to do is stay put till you're found, hollering if necessary. But to holler guarantees humiliation as well as rescue; keeping silent permits some saving of face—you can act surprised at the fuss when your rescuers find you and swear you weren't lost, if they do. What's more you might find your own way yet, *however belatedly.*

"Don't tell me your foot's still asleep!" Magda exclaimed as the three young people walked from the inlet to the area set aside for ferris wheels, carrousels, and other carnival rides, they having decided in favor of the vast and ancient merry-go-round instead of the funhouse. What a sentence, everything was wrong from the outset. People don't know what to make of him, he doesn't know what to make of himself, he's only thirteen, *athletically and socially inept,* not astonishingly bright, but there are antennae; he has . . . some sort of receivers in his head; things speak to him, he understands more than he should, the world winks at him through its objects, grabs grinning at his coat. Everybody else is in on some secret he doesn't know; they've forgotten to tell him. Through simple *procrastination* his mother put off his baptism until this year. Everyone else had it done as a baby; he'd assumed the same of himself, as had his mother, so she claimed, until it was time for him to join Grace Methodist-Protestant and the oversight came out. He was mortified, but pitched sleepless through his private catechizing, intimidated by the ancient mysteries, a thirteen year old would never say that, resolved to experience conversion like St. Augustine. When the water touched his brow and Adam's sin left him, he contrived by a strain like defecation to bring tears into his eyes—but felt nothing. There was some simple, radical difference about him; he hoped it was genius, feared it was madness, devoted himself to amiability and inconspicuousness. Alone on the seawall near his house he was seized by the terrifying transports he'd thought to find in toolshed, in Communion-cup. The grass was alive! The town, the river, himself, were not imaginary; time roared in his ears like wind; the world was *going on!* This part ought to be dramatized. The Irish author James Joyce once wrote. Ambrose M_____ is going to scream.

There is no *texture of rendered sensory detail,* for one thing. The faded distorting mirrors beside Fat May; the impossibility of choosing a mount when one had but a single ride on the great carrousel; the *vertigo attendant on his recognition* that Ocean City was worn out, the place of fathers and grandfathers, straw-boatered men and parasoled ladies survived by their amusements. Money spent, the three paused at Peter's insistence beside Fat May to watch the girls get their skirts blown up. The object was to tease Magda, who said: "I swear, Peter M_____, you've got a one-track mind! Amby and me aren't *interested* in such things." In the tumbling-barrel, too, just inside the Devil's-mouth entrance to the funhouse, the girls were upended and their boyfriends and others could see up their dresses if they cared to. Which was the whole point, Ambrose realized. Of the entire funhouse! If you looked around, you noticed that almost all the people on the boardwalk were paired off into couples except the small children; in a way, that was the whole point of Ocean City! If you had X-ray eyes and could see everything going on at that instant under the boardwalk and in all the hotel rooms and cars and alleyways, you'd realize that all that normally *showed,* like restaurants and dance halls and clothing and test-your-strength machines, was merely preparation and intermission. Fat May screamed.

Because he watched the goings-on from the corner of his eye, it was Ambrose who spied the half-dollar on the boardwalk near the tumbling-barrel. Losers weepers. The first time he'd heard some people moving through a corridor not far away, just after he'd lost sight of the crack of light, he'd decided not to call to them, for fear they'd guess he was scared and poke fun; it sounded like roughnecks; he'd hoped they'd come by and he could follow in the dark without their knowing. Another time he'd heard just one person, unless he imagined it, bumping along as if on the other side of the plywood; perhaps Peter coming back for him, or Father, or Magda lost too. Or the owner and operator of the funhouse. He'd called out once, as though merrily: "Anybody know where the heck we are?" But the query was too stiff, his voice cracked, when the sounds stopped he was terrified: maybe it was a queer who waited for fellows to get lost, or a longhaired filthy monster that lived in some cranny of the funhouse. He stood rigid for hours it seemed like, scarcely respiring. His future was shockingly clear, in outline. He tried holding his breath to the point of unconsciousness. There ought to be a button you could push to end your life absolutely without pain; disappear in a flick, like turning out a light. He would push it instantly! He despised Uncle Karl. But he despised his father too, for not being what he was supposed to be. Perhaps his father hated *his* father, and so on, and his son would hate him, and so on. Instantly!

Naturally he didn't have nerve enough to ask Magda to go through the funhouse with him. With incredible nerve and to everyone's surprise he invited Magda, quietly and politely, to go through the funhouse with him. "I warn you, I've never been through it before," he added, *laughing easily;* "but I reckon we can manage somehow. The important thing to remember, after all, is that it's meant to be a *fun*house; that is, a place of amusement. If people really got lost or injured or too badly frightened in it, the owner'd go out of business. There'd even be lawsuits. No character in a work of fiction can make a speech this long without interruption or acknowledgment from the other characters."

Mother teased Uncle Karl: "Three's a crowd, I always heard." But actually Ambrose was relieved that Peter now had a quarter too. Nothing was what it looked like. Every instant, under the surface of the Atlantic Ocean, millions of living animals devoured one another. Pilots were falling in flames over Europe; women were being forcibly raped in the South Pacific. His father should have taken him aside and said: "There is a simple secret to getting through the funhouse, as simple as being first to see the Towers. Here it is. Peter does not know it; neither does your Uncle Karl. You and I are different. Not surprisingly, you've often wished you weren't. Don't think I haven't noticed how unhappy your childhood has been! But you'll understand, when I tell you, why it had to be kept secret until now. And you won't regret not being like your brother and your uncle. *On the contrary!*" If you knew all the stories behind all the people on the boardwalk, you'd see that *nothing* was what it looked like. Husbands and wives often hated each other; parents didn't necessarily love their children; et cetera. A child took things for granted because he had nothing to compare his life to and everybody acted as if things were as they should be. Therefore each saw himself as the hero of the story, when the truth might turn out to be that he's the villain, or the coward. And there wasn't one thing you could do about it!

Hunchbacks, fat ladies, fools—that no one chose what he was was unbearable. In the movies he'd meet a beautiful young girl in the funhouse; they'd have hairsbreadth escapes from real dangers; he'd do and say the right things; she also; in the end they'd be lovers; their dialogue lines would match up; he'd be perfectly at ease; she'd not only like him well enough, she'd think he was *marvelous;* she'd lie awake thinking about *him,* instead of vice versa—the way *his* face looked in different lights and how he stood and exactly what he'd said—and yet that would be only one small episode in his wonderful life, among many many others. Not a *turning point* at all. What had happened in the toolshed was nothing. He hated, he loathed his parents! One reason for not writing a lost-in-the-funhouse story is that either everybody's felt what Ambrose feels, in which case it goes without saying, or else no normal person feels such things, in which case Ambrose is a freak. "Is anything more tiresome, in fiction, than the problems of sensitive adolescents?" And it's all too long and rambling, as if the author. For all a person knows the first time through, the end could be just around any corner; perhaps, *not impossibly* it's been within reach any number of times. On the other hand he may be scarcely past the start, with everything yet to get through, an intolerable idea.

Fill in: His father's raised eyebrows when he announced his decision to do the funhouse with Magda. Ambrose understands now, but didn't then, that his father was wondering whether he knew what the funhouse was *for*—especially since he didn't object, as he should have, when Peter decided to come along too. The ticket-woman, witchlike, mortifying him when inadvertently he gave her his name-coin instead of the half-dollar, then unkindly calling Magda's attention to the birthmark on his temple: "Watch out for him, girlie, he's a marked man!" She wasn't even cruel, he understood, only vulgar and insensitive. Somewhere in the world there was a young woman with such splendid understanding that she'd see him entire, like a poem or story, and find his words so valuable after all that when he confessed his apprehensions she would explain why they were in fact the very things that made him precious to her . . . and to Western Civilization! There was no such girl, the simple truth being. Violent yawns as they approached the mouth. Whispered advice from an old-timer on a bench near the barrel: "Go crabwise and ye'll get an eyeful with-out upsetting!" Composure vanished at the first pitch: Peter hollered joyously, Magda tumbled, shrieked, clutched her skirt; Ambrose scrambled crabwise, tight-lipped with terror, was soon out, watched his dropped name-coin slide among the couples. Shame-faced he saw that to get through expeditiously was not the point; Peter feigned assistance in order to trip Magda up, shouted "I see Christmas!" when her legs went flying. The old man, his latest betrayer, cacked approval. A dim hall then of black-thread cobwebs and recorded gibber: he took Magda's elbow to steady her against revolving discs set in the slanted floor to throw your feet out from under, and explained to her in a calm, deep voice his theory that each phase of the funhouse was triggered either automatically, by a series of photoelectric devices, or else man-ually by operators stationed at peepholes. But he lost his voice thrice as the discs unbalanced him; Magda was anyhow squealing; but at one point she clutched him about the waist to keep from falling, and her right cheek pressed for a moment against his belt-buckle. Heroically he drew her up, it was his chance to clutch her close as if for support and say: "I love you." He even put an arm lightly about the small of her back before a sailor-and-girl pitched into them from behind, sorely treading his left big toe and knocking Magda asprawl with them. The sailor's girl was a string-haired hussy with a loud laugh and light blue drawers; Ambrose realized that he wouldn't have said "I love you" anyhow, and was smitten with self-contempt. How much better it would be to be that common sailor! A wiry little Seaman 3rd, the fellow squeezed a girl to each side and stumbled hilarious into the mirror room, closer to Magda in thirty seconds than Ambrose had got in thirteen years. She gig-gled at something the fellow said to Peter; she drew her hair from her eyes with a movement so womanly it struck Ambrose's heart; Peter's smacking her backside then seemed particularly coarse. But Magda made a pleased indignant face and cried, "All right for *you,* mister!" and pursued Peter into the maze without a backward glance. The sailor followed after, leisurely, drawing his girl against his hip; Ambrose under-stood not only that they were all so relieved to be rid of his burdensome company that they didn't even notice his absence, but that he himself shared their relief. Step-ping from the treacherous passage at last into the mirror-maze, he saw once again, more clearly than ever, how readily he deceived himself into supposing he was a per-son. He even foresaw, wincing at his dreadful self-knowledge, that he would repeat the deception, at ever-rarer intervals, all his wretched life, so fearful were the alter-natives. Fame, madness, suicide; perhaps all three. It's not believable that so young a boy could articulate that reflection, and in fiction the merely true must always yield to the plausible. Moreover, the symbolism is in places heavy-footed. Yet Ambrose M_____ understood, as few adults do, that the famous loneliness of the great was no popular myth but a general truth—furthermore, that it was as much cause as effect.

All the preceding except the last few sentences is exposition that should've been done earlier or interspersed with the present action instead of lumped together. No reader would put up with so much with such *prolixity.* It's interesting that Ambrose's father, though presumably an intelligent man (as indicated by his role as grade-school principal), neither encouraged nor discouraged his sons at all in any way—as if he either didn't care about them or cared all right but didn't know how to act. If this fact should contribute to one of them's becoming a celebrated but wretchedly unhappy scientist, was it a good thing or not? He too might someday face the question; it would be useful to know whether it had tortured his father for years, for example, or never once crossed his mind.

In the maze two important things happened. First, our hero found a name-coin someone else had lost or discarded: AMBROSE, suggestive of the famous lightship and of his late grandfather's favorite dessert, which his mother used to prepare on special occasions out of coconut, oranges, grapes, and what else. Second, as he wondered at the endless replication of his image in the mirrors, second, as he *lost himself in the reflection* that the necessity for an observer makes perfect observation impossible, better make him eighteen at least, yet that would render other things unlikely, he heard Peter and Magda chuckling somewhere together in the maze. "Here!" "No, here!" they shouted to each other; Peter said, "Where's Amby?" Magda murmured. "Amb?" Peter called. In a pleased, friendly voice. He didn't reply. The truth was, his brother was a *happy-go-lucky youngster* who'd've been better off with a regular brother of his own, but who seldom complained of his lot and was generally cordial. Ambrose's throat ached; there aren't enough different ways to say that. He stood quietly while the two young people giggled and thumped through the glittering maze, hurrah'd their discovery of its exit, cried out in joyful alarm at what next beset them. Then he set his mouth and followed after, as he supposed, took a wrong turn, strayed into the pass *wherein he lingers yet.*

The action of conventional dramatic narrative may be represented by a diagram called Freitag's Triangle:

or more accurately by a variant of that diagram:

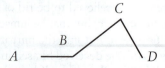

in which *AB* represents the exposition, *B* the introduction of conflict, *BC* the "rising action," complication, or development of the conflict, *C* the climax, or turn of the action, *CD* the dénouement, or resolution of the conflict. While there is no reason to regard this pattern as an absolute necessity, like many other conventions it became conventional because great numbers of people over many years learned by trial and error that it was effective; one ought not to forsake it, therefore, unless one wishes to forsake as well the effect of drama or has clear cause to feel that deliberate violation of the "normal" pattern can better can better effect that effect. This can't go on much longer; it can go on forever. He died telling stories to himself in the dark; years later, when that vast unsuspected area of the funhouse came to light, the first expedition found his skeleton in one of its labyrinthine corridors and mistook it for part of the entertainment. He died of starvation telling himself stories in the dark; but unbeknownst unbeknownst to him, an assistant operator of the funhouse, happening to overhear him, crouched just behind the plyboard partition and wrote down his every word. The operator's daughter, an exquisite young woman with a figure unusually well developed for her age, crouched just behind the partition and transcribed his every word. Though she had never laid eyes on him, she recognized that here was one of Western Culture's truly great imaginations, the eloquence of whose suffering would be an inspiration to unnumbered. And her heart was torn between her love for the misfortunate young man (yes, she loved him, though she had never laid though she knew him only—but how well!—through his words, and the deep, calm voice in which he spoke them) between her love et cetera and her womanly intuition that only in suffering and isolation could he give voice et cetera. Lone dark dying. Quietly she kissed the rough plyboard, and a tear fell upon the page. Where she had written in shorthand *Where she had written in shorthand* Where she had written in shorthand *Where she* et cetera. A long time ago we should have passed the apex of Freitag's Triangle and made brief work of the *dénouement;* the plot doesn't rise by meaningful steps but winds upon itself, digresses, retreats, hesitates, sighs, collapses, expires. The climax of the story must be its protagonist's discovery of a way to get through the funhouse. But he has found none, may have ceased to search.

What relevance does the war have to the story? Should there be fireworks outside or not?

Ambrose wandered, languished, dozed. Now and then he fell into his habit of rehearsing to himself the unadventurous story of his life, narrated from the third-person point of view, from his earliest memory parenthesis of maple leaves stirring in the summer breath of tidewater Maryland end of parenthesis to the present moment. Its principal events, on this telling, would appear to have been *A, B, C,* and *D.*

He imagined himself years hence, successful, married, at ease in the world, the trials of his adolescence far behind him. He has come to the seashore with his family for the holiday: how Ocean City has changed! But at one seldom at one ill-frequented end of the boardwalk a few derelict amusements survive from times gone by: the great carrousel from the turn of the century, with its monstrous griffins and mechanical concert band; the roller coaster rumored since 1916 to have been condemned; the mechanical shooting gallery in which only the image of our enemies changed. His own son laughs with Fat May and wants to know what a funhouse is; Ambrose hugs the sturdy lad close and smiles around his pipestem at his wife.

The family's going home. Mother sits between Father and Uncle Karl, who teases him good-naturedly who chuckles over the fact that the comrade with whom he'd fought his way shoulder to shoulder through the funhouse had turned out to be a blind Negro girl—to their mutual discomfort, as they'd opened their souls. But such are the walls of custom, which even. Whose arm is where? How must it feel. He dreams of a funhouse vaster by far than any yet constructed; but by then they may be out of fashion, like steamboats and excursion trains. Already quaint and seedy: the draperied ladies on the frieze of the carrousel are his father's father's moon-cheeked dreams; if he thinks of it more he will vomit his apple-on-a-stick.

He wonders: will he become a regular person? Something has gone wrong; his vaccination didn't take; at the Boy-Scout initiation campfire he only pretended to be deeply moved, as he pretends to this hour that it is not so bad after all in the fun-house, and that he has a little limp. How long will it last? He envisions a truly aston-ishing funhouse, incredibly complex yet utterly controlled from a great central switchboard like the console of a pipe organ. Nobody had enough imagination. He could design such a place himself, wiring and all, and he's only thirteen years old. He would be its operator: panel lights would show what was up in every cranny of its cunning of its multifarious vastness; a switch-flick would ease this fellow's way, com-plicate that's, to balance things out; if anyone seemed lost or frightened, all the op-erator had to do was.

He wishes he had never entered the funhouse. But he has. Then he wishes he were dead. But he's not. Therefore he will construct funhouses for others and be their secret operator—though he would rather be among the lovers for whom fun-houses are designed.

1968

Donald Barthelme 1931–1989

Born in Philadelphia but raised in Houston, Texas, Barthelme began writing stories and poems in high school and continued writing (journalism as well as fiction and poetry) at the University of Houston. After army service in Japan and Korea, he returned to the university and worked as a reporter locally. He then became director of Houston's Contemporary Arts Museum.

In 1962 he moved to New York and soon found his own voice and style. He became a regular contributor to the *New Yorker,* and began to find in his fiction the innovation that was occurring in film and graphic art. He was influenced by the French Symbolists, and worked frequently with myth and spatial techniques (perhaps because of the visionary influence of his father, an architect). His vision was comic, surreal, macabre; and his play with language—giving the reader the unexpected, the grotesque, and above all the fragmented—marked him as a postmodernist even before that classification existed.

With a montage style reminiscent of that of Dos Passos, Barthelme drew phrases and lines from advertising, songs, and stereotyped phrases of the times; and created from those borrowings new structures and new perspectives. His first novel, *Snow White,* retold the classic fairytale, but with wit and acerbity that surprised readers of the 1960s. Structural experimentation in *The Dead Fathers* made that novel another treasure house of narrative technique, and brought a patina of fashion to a more serious theme. But even more than a montage of materials, "At the End of the Mechanical Age" represents a parody of fictional traditions and the various structures of storytelling they employ. By juxtaposing such structures, Barthelme exposes—to both scrutiny and laughter—the historical consciousness of the modern age. When biblical or creation myths jostle with "true romance" materials, then the modernist belief that we stand at the end of a long historical process, and thereby derive a certain cultural and social advantage, is given the lie. At the same time the themes of divorce, repression, and secular self-doubt enter the mix, as they do in the tradition of nineteenth-century realist novels, but in a telegraphed way that some critics see as one of the hallmarks of Barthelme's style. He not only parodies his characters and their concerns, he also mocks the very possibilities and burdens of storytelling itself. Because he calls into question the mechanics of this central cultural activity, and by extension the ability of language to represent reality, he is often credited with influencing many aspects of postmodernism.

Charles Molesworth
Queens College, CUNY

PRIMARY WORKS

Come Back, Dr. Caligari (stories), 1964; *Snow White,* 1967; *Unspeakable Practices, Unnatural Acts* (stories), 1968; *City Life* (stories), 1970; *Sadness,* 1972; *Guilty Pleasures,* 1974; *The Dead Father,* 1975; *Amateurs* (stories), 1976; *Great Days* (stories), 1979; *Sixty Stories,* 1981; *Overnight to Many Distant Cities,* 1983; *Paradise,* 1986; *Forty Stories,* 1989; *The King,* 1990; *The Teachings of Don B.: The Satires, Parodies, Fables, Illustrated Stories, and Plays of Donald Barthelme,* 1992.

At the End of the Mechanical Age

I went to the grocery store to buy some soap. I stood for a long time before the soaps in their attractive boxes, RUB and FAB and TUB and suchlike, I couldn't decide so I closed my eyes and reached out blindly and when I opened my eyes I found her hand in mine.

Her name was Mrs. Davis, she said, and TUB was best for important cleaning experiences, in her opinion. So we went to lunch at a Mexican restaurant which as it happened she owned, she took me into the kitchen and showed me her stacks of handsome beige tortillas and the steam tables which were shiny-brite. I told her I wasn't very good with women and she said it didn't matter, few men were, and that nothing mattered, now that Jake was gone, but I would do as an interim project and sit down and have a Carta Blanca. So I sat down and had a cool Carta Blanca, God was standing in the basement reading the meters to see how much grace had been used up in the month of June. Grace is electricity, science has found, it is not *like* electricity, it *is* electricity and God was down in the basement reading the meters in His blue jump suit with the flashlight stuck in the back pocket.

"The mechanical age is drawing to a close," I said to her.

"Or has already done so," she replied.

"It was a good age," I said. "I was comfortable in it, relatively. Probably I will not enjoy the age to come quite so much. I don't like its look."

"One must be fair. We don't know yet what kind of an age the next one will be. Although I feel in my bones that it will be an age inimical to personal well-being and comfort, and that is what I like, personal well-being and comfort."

"Do you suppose there is something to be done?" I asked her.

"Huddle and cling," said Mrs. Davis. "We can huddle and cling. It will pall, of course, everything palls, in time . . ."

Then we went back to my house to huddle and cling, most women are two different colors when they remove their clothes especially in summer but Mrs. Davis was all one color, an ocher. She seemed to like huddling and clinging, she stayed for many days. From time to time she checked the restaurant keeping everything shiny-brite and distributing sums of money to the staff, returning with tortillas in sacks, cases of Carta Blanca, buckets of guacamole, but I paid her for it because I didn't want to feel obligated.

There was a song I sang her, a song of great expectations.

"Ralph is coming," I sang, "Ralph is striding in his suit of lights over moons and mountains, over parking lots and fountains, toward your silky side. Ralph is coming, he has a coat of many colors and all major credit cards and he is striding to meet you and culminate your foggy dreams in an explosion of blood and soil, at the end of the mechanical age. Ralph is coming preceded by fifty running men with spears and fifty dancing ladies who are throwing leaf spinach out of little baskets, in his path. Ralph is perfect," I sang, "but he is also full of interesting tragic flaws, and he can drink fifty running men under the table without breaking his stride and he can have congress with fifty dancing ladies without breaking his stride, even his socks are ironed, so natty is Ralph, but he is also right down in the mud with the rest of us, he markets the mud at high prices for specialized industrial uses and he is striding, striding, striding, toward your waiting heart. Of course you may not like him, some people are awfully picky . . .*

Ralph is coming," I sang to her, *"he is striding over dappled plains and crazy rivers and he will change your life for the better, probably, you will be fainting with glee at the simple touch of his grave gentle immense hand although I am aware that some people can't stand prosperity, Ralph is coming, I hear his hoofsteps on the drumhead of history, he is striding as he has been all his life toward you, you, you."*

"Yes," Mrs. Davis said, when I had finished singing, "that is what I deserve, all right. But probably I will not get it. And in the meantime, there is you."

* * *

God then rained for forty days and forty nights, when the water tore away the front of the house we got into the boat, Mrs. Davis liked the way I maneuvered the boat off the trailer and out of the garage, she was provoked into a memoir of Jake.

"Jake was a straight-ahead kind of man," she said, "he was simpleminded and that helped him to be the kind of man that he was." She was staring into her Scotch-and-floodwater rather moodily I thought, debris bouncing on the waves all around us but she paid no attention. "That is the type of man I like," she said, "a strong and simple-minded man. The case-study method was not Jake's method, he went right through the middle of the line and never failed to gain yardage, no matter what the game was. He had a lust for life, and life had a lust for him. I was inconsolable when Jake passed away." Mrs. Davis was drinking the Scotch for her nerves, she had no nerves of course, she was nerveless and possibly heartless also but that is another question, gutless she was not, she had a gut and a very pretty one ocher in color but that was another matter. God was standing up to His neck in the raging waters with a smile of incredible beauty on His visage, He seemed to be enjoying His creation, the disaster, the waters all around us were raging louder now, raging like a mighty tractor-trailer tailgating you on the highway.

Then Mrs. Davis sang to me, a song of great expectations.

"Maude is waiting for you," Mrs. Davis sang to me, *"Maude is waiting for you in all her seriousness and splendor, under her gilded onion dome, in that city which I cannot name at this time, Maude waits. Maude is what you lack, the profoundest of your lacks. Your every yearn since the first yearn has been a yearn for Maude, only you did not know it until I, your dear friend, pointed it out. She is going to heal your scrappy and generally unsatisfactory life with the balm of her Maudeness, luckiest of dogs, she waits only for you. Let me give you just one instance of Maude's inhuman sagacity. Maude named the tools. It was Maude who thought of calling the rattail file a rattail file. It was Maude who christened the needle-nose pliers. Maude named the rasp. Think of it. What else could a rasp be but a rasp? Maude in her wisdom went right to the point, and called it rasp. It was Maude who named the maul. Similarly the sledge, the wedge, the ball-peen hammer, the adz, the shim, the hone, the strop. The hand-saw, the hacksaw, the bucksaw, and the fretsaw were named by Maude, peering into each saw and intuiting at once its specialness. The scratch awl, the scuffle hoe, the prick punch and the countersink—I could go on and on. The tools came to Maude, tool by tool in a long respectful line, she gave them their names. The vise. The gimlet. The cold chisel. The reamer, the router, the gouge. The plumb bob. How could she have thought up the rough justice of these wonderful cognomens? Looking languidly at a pair of tin snips, and then deciding to call them tin snips—what a burst of glory! And I haven't even cited the bush hook, the grass snath, or the plumber's snake, or the*

C-clamp, or the nippers, or the scythe. What a tall achievement, naming the tools! And this is just one of Maude's contributions to our worldly estate, there are others. What delights will come crowding," Mrs. Davis sang to me, *"delight upon delight, when the epithalamium is ground out by the hundred organ grinders who are Maude's constant attendants, on that good-quality day of her own choosing, which you have desperately desired all your lean life, only you weren't aware of it until I, your dear friend, pointed it out. And Maude is young but not too young,"* Mrs. Davis sang to me, *"she is not too old either, she is just right and she is waiting for you with her tawny limbs and horse sense, when you receive Maude's nod your future and your past will begin."*

There was a pause, or pall.

"Is that true," I asked, "that song?"

"It is a metaphor," said Mrs. Davis, "it has metaphorical truth."

"And the end of the mechanical age," I said, "is that a metaphor?"

"The end of the mechanical age," said Mrs. Davis, "is in my judgment an actuality straining to become a metaphor. One must wish it luck, I suppose. One must cheer it on. Intellectual rigor demands that we give these damned metaphors every chance, even if they are inimical to personal well-being and comfort. We have a duty to understand everything, whether we like it or not—a duty I would scant if I could."

At that moment the water jumped into the boat and sank us.

* * *

At the wedding Mrs. Davis spoke to me kindly.

"Tom," she said, "you are not Ralph, but you are all that is around at the moment. I have taken in the whole horizon with a single sweep of my practiced eye, no giant figure looms there and that is why I have decided to marry you, temporarily, with Jake gone and an age ending. It will be a marriage of convenience all right, and when Ralph comes, or Maude nods, then our arrangement will automatically self-destruct, like the tinted bubble that it is. You were very kind and considerate, when we were drying out, in the tree, and I appreciated that. That counted for something. Of course kindness and consideration are not what the great songs, the Ralph-song and the Maude-song, promise. They are merely flaky substitutes for the terminal experience. I realize that and want you to realize it. I want to be straight with you. That is one of the most admirable things about me, that I am always straight with people, from the sweet beginning to the bitter end. Now I will return to the big house where my handmaidens will proceed with the robing of the bride."

It was cool in the meadow by the river, the meadow Mrs. Davis had selected for the travesty, I walked over to the tree under which my friend Blackie was standing, he was the best man, in a sense.

"This disgusts me," Blackie said, "this hollow pretense and empty sham and I had to come all the way from Chicago."

God came to the wedding and stood behind a tree with just part of His effulgence showing, I wondered whether He was planning to bless this makeshift construct with His grace, or not. It's hard to imagine what He was thinking of in the beginning when He planned everything that was ever going to happen, planned everything exquisitely right down to the tiniest detail such as what I was thinking at this very moment, my thought about His thought, planned the end of the mechanical age and detailed the new age to follow, and then the bride emerged from the house with her train, all ocher in color and very lovely.

"And do you, Anne," the minister said, "promise to make whatever mutually satisfactory accommodations necessary to reduce tensions and arrive at whatever previously agreed-upon goals both parties have harmoniously set in the appropriate planning sessions?"

"I do," said Mrs. Davis.

"And do you, Thomas, promise to explore all differences thoroughly with patience and inner honesty ignoring no fruitful avenues of discussion and seeking at all times to achieve rapprochement while eschewing advantage in conflict situations?"

"Yes," I said.

"Well, now we are married," said Mrs. Davis, "I think I will retain my present name if you don't mind, I have always been Mrs. Davis and your name is a shade graceless, no offense, dear."

"O.K.," I said.

Then we received the congratulations and good wishes of the guests, who were mostly employees of the Mexican restaurant, Raul was there and Consuelo, Pedro, and Pepe came crowding around with outstretched hands and Blackie came crowding around with outstretched hands, God was standing behind the caterer's tables looking at the enchiladas and chalupas and chile con queso and chicken mole as if He had never seen such things before but that was hard to believe.

I started to speak to Him as all of the world's great religions with a few exceptions urge, from the heart, I started to say "Lord, Little Father of the Poor, and all that, I was just wondering now that an age, the mechanical age, is ending and a new age beginning or so they say, I was just wondering if You could give me a hint, sort of, not a Sign, I'm not asking for a Sign, but just the barest hint as to whether what we have been told about Your nature and our nature is, forgive me and I know how You feel about doubt or rather what we have been told you feel about it, but if You could just let drop the slightest indication as to whether what we have been told is authentic or just a bunch of apocryphal heterodoxy—"

But He had gone away with an insanely beautiful smile on His lighted countenance, gone away to read the meters and get a line on the efficacy of grace in that area, I surmised, I couldn't blame Him, my question had not been so very elegantly put, had I been able to express it mathematically He would have been more interested, maybe, but I have never been able to express anything mathematically.

After the marriage Mrs. Davis explained marriage to me.

Marriage, she said, an institution deeply enmeshed with the mechanical age.

Pairings smiled upon by law were but reifications of the laws of mechanics, inspired by unions of a technical nature, such as nut with bolt, wood with wood screw, aircraft with Plane-Mate.

Permanence or impermanence of the bond a function of (1) materials and (2) technique.

Growth of literacy a factor, she said.

Growth of illiteracy also.

The center will not hold if it has been spot-welded by an operator whose deepest concern is not with the weld but with his lottery ticket.

God interested only in grace—keeping things humming.

Blackouts, brownouts, temporary dimmings of household illumination all portents not of Divine displeasure but of Divine indifference to executive-development programs at middle-management levels.

He likes to get out into the field Himself, she said. With His flashlight. He is doing the best He can.

We two, she and I, no exception to general ebb/flow of world juice and its concomitant psychological effects, she said.

Bitter with the sweet, she said.

* * *

After the explanation came the divorce.

"Will you be wanting to contest the divorce?" I asked Mrs. Davis.

"I think not," she said calmly, "although I suppose one of us should, for the fun of the thing. An uncontested divorce always seems to me contrary to the spirit of divorce."

"That is true," I said, "I have had the same feeling myself, not infrequently."

After the divorce the child was born. We named him A.F. of L. Davis and sent him to that part of Russia where people live to be one hundred and ten years old. He is living there still, probably, growing in wisdom and beauty. Then we shook hands, Mrs. Davis and I, and she set out Ralphward, and I, Maudeward, the glow of hope not yet extinguished, the fear of pall not yet triumphant, standby generators ensuring the flow of grace to all of God's creatures at the end of the mechanical age.

1977

Toni Morrison b. 1931

Since winning the Nobel Prize for Literature in 1993, Toni Morrison has become an industry. As much a household name as some of the writers in the Black Arts movement of the 1960s, Morrison is author, critic, lecturer, teacher, and public servant. Since she made her debut on the literary scene with the publication of *The Bluest Eye* in 1970, she has been a model worthy of emulation and a paragon of success. Her nine novels to date make her one of the most prolific African American women novelists, and her international reputation makes her one of the best-known American writers. Critically acclaimed for her deft use of language and lyrical writing, Morrison also counts among her honors the National Book Critics' Circle Award as well as the Pulitzer Prize.

Now known as Toni Morrison, Chloe Anthony Wofford was born in Lorain, Ohio, on February 18, 1931, to Rahmah Willis Wofford and George Wofford, both migrants from the South. Her storytelling home environment enabled Morrison to enter first grade as the only child in her class who already knew how to read, a skill that she would cultivate as an adolescent by reading Russian novels, *Madame Bovary,* and works by Jane Austen. She graduated with honors from Lorain High School and entered Howard University, where she changed her name to Toni (people had trouble pronouncing Chloe) and traveled through the South during summer break with the Howard University Players. She earned a B.A. in English with a minor in classics in 1953. In 1955, she earned a master's degree in English from Cornell University with a now frequently referenced thesis on suicide in the works of Virginia Woolf and William Faulkner.

Morrison has retained close contacts with academia and has held several teaching appointments, including ones at Texas Southern University (1955–1957) and Howard University (1957–1964). She began to write in 1957, after she returned to Howard as an instructor in English; she joined a group of ten black writers in Washington, D.C. It was there that she met and married Harold Morrison, a Jamaican architect. The couple had two sons, Harold Ford and Kevin Slade, before they divorced in 1964. Morrison returned briefly to her parents' home in Ohio before getting an editing job with a textbook subsidiary of Random House in Syracuse, New York, where she moved in 1965.

From 1969 to 1970, Morrison was an instructor at the State University of New York at Purchase. From 1975 to 1977, she served as Distinguished Visiting Professor at Yale University and as Distinguished Visiting Lecturer at Bard College from 1979 to 1980. Named Albert Schweitzer Professor of the Humanities at the State University of New York at Albany, she left Random House to assume that position in 1984. She held it until 1989, when she moved to Princeton University to accept her second endowed professorship, that of Robert F. Goheen Professor of the Council of the Humanities, from which illustrious position she teaches courses in African American studies and creative writing.

Her richly rewarded creative output and public service, including a stint as co-chairperson of the Schomburg Library's Commission for the Preservation of Black Culture and a term on the board of the Center for the Study of Southern Culture, have earned Morrison an unmatched reputation among African American women writers as well as among American writers in general.

Trudier Harris
University of North Carolina–Chapel Hill

PRIMARY WORKS

The Bluest Eye, 1970; *Sula,* 1974; *The Black Book,* 1974 (with Middleton Harris); *Song of Solomon,* 1977; *Tar Baby,* 1981; *Beloved,* 1987; *Playing in the Dark: Whiteness and the Literary Imagination,* 1992; *Jazz,* 1992; *The Dancing Mind,* 1996; *Paradise,* 1998; *Love,* 2003; *A Mercy,* 2008.

Recitatif

My mother danced all night and Roberta's was sick. That's why we were taken to St. Bonny's. People want to put their arms around you when you tell them you were in a shelter, but it really wasn't bad. No big long room with one hundred beds like Bellevue. There were four to a room, and when Roberta and me came, there was a shortage of state kids, so we were the only ones assigned to 406 and could go from bed to bed if we wanted to. And we wanted to, too. We changed beds every night and for the whole four months we were there we never picked one out as our own permanent bed.

It didn't start out that way. The minute I walked in and the Big Bozo introduced us, I got sick to my stomach. It was one thing to be taken out of your own bed early in the morning—it was something else to be stuck in a strange place with a girl from a whole other race. And Mary, that's my mother, she was right. Every now and then she would stop dancing long enough to tell me something important and one of the things she said was that they never washed their hair and they smelled funny. Roberta sure did. Smell funny, I mean. So when the Big Bozo (nobody ever called her Mrs. Itkin, just like nobody ever said St. Bonaventure)—when she said, "Twyla, this is Roberta. Roberta, this is Twyla. Make each other welcome," I said. "My mother won't like you putting me in here."

"Good," said Bozo. "Maybe then she'll come and take you home."

How's that for mean? If Roberta had laughed I would have killed her, but she didn't. She just walked over to the window and stood with her back to us.

"Turn around," said Bozo. "Don't be rude. Now Twyla. Roberta. When you hear a loud buzzer, that's the call for dinner. Come down to the first floor. Any fights and no movie." And then, just to make sure we knew what we would be missing: *"The Wizard of Oz."*

Roberta must have thought I meant that my mother would be mad about my being put in a shelter. Not about rooming with her, because as soon as Bozo left she came over to me and said, "Is your mother sick too?"

"No," I said. "She just likes to dance all night."

"Oh." She nodded her head and I liked the way she understood things so fast. So for the moment it didn't matter that we looked like salt and pepper standing there and that's what the other kids called us sometimes. We were eight years old and got F's all the time. Me because I couldn't remember what I read or what the teacher said. And Roberta because she couldn't read at all and didn't even listen to the teacher. She wasn't good at anything except jacks, at which she was a killer: pow scoop pow scoop pow scoop.

We didn't like each other all that much at first, but nobody else wanted to play with us because we weren't real orphans with beautiful dead parents in the sky. We were dumped. Even the New York City Puerto Ricans and the upstate Indians ignored us. All kinds of kids were in there, black ones, white ones, even two Koreans. The food was good, thought. At least I thought so. Roberta hated it and left whole pieces of things on her plate: Spam, Salisbury steak—even Jell-O with fruit cocktail in it, and she didn't care if I ate what she wouldn't. Mary's idea of supper was popcorn and a can of Yoo-Hoo. Hot mashed potatoes and two weenies was like Thanksgiving for me.

It really wasn't bad, St. Bonny's. The big girls on the second floor pushed us around now and then. But that was all. They wore lipstick and eyebrow pencil and wobbled their knees while they watched TV. Fifteen, sixteen, even, some of them were. They were put-out girls, scared runaways most of them. Poor little girls who fought their uncles off but looked tough to us, and mean. God, did they look mean. The staff tried to keep them separate from the younger children, but sometimes they caught us watching them in the orchard where they played radios and danced with each other. They'd light out after us and pull our hair or twist our arms. We were scared of them, Roberta and me, but neither of us wanted the other one to know it. So we got a good list of dirty names we could shout back when we ran from them through the orchard. I used to dream a lot and almost always the orchard was there. Two acres, four maybe, of these little apple trees. Hundreds of them. Empty and crooked like beggar women when I first came to St. Bonny's but fat with flowers when I left. I don't know why I dreamt about that orchard so much. Nothing really happened there. Nothing all that important, I mean. Just the big girls dancing and playing the radio. Roberta and me watching. Maggie fell down there once. The kitchen woman with legs like parentheses. And the big girls laughed at her. We should have helped her up, I know, but we were scared of those girls with lipstick and eyebrow pencil. Maggie couldn't talk. The kids said she had her tongue cut out, but I think she was just born that way: mute. She was old and sandy-colored and she worked in the kitchen. I don't know if she was nice or not. I just remember her legs like parentheses and how she rocked when she walked. She worked from early in the morning till two o'clock, and if she was late, if she had too much cleaning and didn't get out till two-fifteen or so, she'd cut through the orchard so she wouldn't miss her bus and have to wait another hour. She wore this really stupid little hat—a kid's hat with ear flaps—and she wasn't much taller than we were. A really awful little hat. Even for a mute, it was dumb—dressing like a kid and never saying anything at all.

"But what about if somebody tries to kill her?" I used to wonder about that. "Or what if she wants to cry? Can she cry?"

"Sure," Roberta said. "But just tears. No sounds come out."

"She can't scream?"

"Nope. Nothing."

"Can she hear?"

"I guess."

"Let's call her," I said. And we did.

"Dummy! Dummy!" She never turned her head.

"Bow legs! Bow legs!" Nothing. She just rocked on, the chin straps of her baby-boy hat swaying from side to side. I think we were wrong. I think she could hear and didn't let on. And it shames me even now to think there was somebody in there after all who heard us call her those names and couldn't tell on us.

We got along all right, Roberta and me. Changed beds every night, got F's in civics and communication skills and gym. The Bozo was disappointed in us, she said. Out of 130 of us state cases, 90 were under twelve. Almost all were real orphans with beautiful dead parents in the sky. We were the only ones dumped and the only ones with F's in three classes including gym. So we got along—what with her leaving whole pieces of things on her plate and being nice about not asking questions.

I think it was the day before Maggie fell down that we found out our mothers were coming to visit us on the same Sunday. We had been at the shelter twenty-eight days (Roberta twenty-eight and a half) and this was their first visit with us. Our mothers would come at ten o'clock in time for chapel, then lunch with us in the teacher's lounge. I thought if my dancing mother met her sick mother it might be good for her. And Roberta thought her sick mother would get a bang out of a dancing one. We got excited about it and curled each other's hair. After breakfast we sat on the bed watching the road from the window. Roberta's socks were still wet. She washed them the night before and put them on the radiator to dry. They hadn't, but she put them on anyway because their tops were so pretty—scalloped in pink. Each of us had a purple construction-paper basket that we had made in craft class. Mine had a yellow crayon rabbit on it. Roberta's had eggs with wiggly lines of color. Inside were cellophane grass and just the jelly beans because I'd eaten the two marshmallow eggs they gave us. The Big Bozo came herself to get us. Smiling she told us we looked very nice and to come downstairs. We were so surprised by the smile we'd never seen before, neither of us moved.

"Don't you want to see your mommies?"

I stood up first and spilled the jelly beans all over the floor. Bozo's smile disappeared while we scrambled to get the candy up off the floor and put it back in the grass.

She escorted us downstairs to the first floor, where the other girls were lining up to file into the chapel. A bunch of grown-ups stood to one side. Viewers mostly. The old biddies who wanted servants and the fags who wanted company looking for children they might want to adopt. Once in a while a grandmother. Almost never anybody young or anybody whose face wouldn't scare you in the night. Because if any of the real orphans had young relatives they wouldn't be real orphans. I saw Mary right away. She had on those green slacks I hated and hated even more now because didn't she know we were going to chapel? And that fur jacket with the pocket linings so ripped she had to pull to get her hands out of them. But her face was pretty— like always—and she smiled and waved like she was the little girl looking for her mother, not me.

I walked slowly, trying not to drop the jelly beans and hoping the paper handle would hold. I had to use my last Chiclet because by the time I finished cutting everything out, all the Elmer's was gone. I am left-handed and the scissors never worked for me. It didn't matter, though; I might just as well have chewed the gum. Mary dropped to her knees and grabbed me, mashing the basket, the jelly beans, and the grass into her ratty fur jacket.

"Twyla, baby. Twyla, baby!"

I could have killed her. Already I heard the big girls in the orchard the next time saying, "Twyyyyla, baby!" But I couldn't stay mad at Mary while she was smiling and hugging me and smelling of Lady Esther dusting powder. I wanted to stay buried in her fur all day.

To tell the truth I forgot about Roberta. Mary and I got in line for the traipse into chapel and I was feeling proud because she looked so beautiful even in those ugly green slacks that made her behind stick out. A pretty mother on earth is better than a beautiful dead one in the sky even if she did leave you all alone to go dancing.

I felt a tap on my shoulder, turned, and saw Roberta smiling. I smiled back, but not too much lest somebody think this visit was the biggest thing that ever happened in my life. Then Roberta said, "Mother, I want you to meet my roommate, Twyla. And that's Twyla's mother."

I looked up it seemed for miles. She was big. Bigger than any man and on her chest was the biggest cross I'd ever seen. I swear it was six inches long each way. And in the crook of her arm was the biggest Bible ever made.

Mary, simpleminded as ever, grinned and tried to yank her hand out of the pocket with the raggedy lining—to shake hands, I guess. Roberta's mother looked down at me and then looked down at Mary too. She didn't say anything, just grabbed Roberta with her Bible-free hand and stepped out of line, walking quickly to the rear of it. Mary was still grinning because she's not too swift when it comes to what's really going on. Then this light bulb goes off in her head and she says "That bitch!" really loud and us almost in the chapel now. Organ music whining; the Bonny Angels singing sweetly. Everybody in the world turned around to look. And Mary would have kept it up—kept calling names if I hadn't squeezed her hand as hard as I could. That helped a little, but she still twitched and crossed and uncrossed her legs all through service. Even groaned a couple of times. Why did I think she would come there and act right? Slacks. No hat like the grandmothers and viewers, and groaning all the while. When we stood for hymns she kept her mouth shut. Wouldn't even look at the words on the page. She actually reached in her purse for a mirror to check her lipstick. All I could think of was that she really needed to be killed. The sermon lasted a year, and I knew the real orphans were looking smug again.

We were supposed to have lunch in the teachers' lounge, but Mary didn't bring anything, so we picked fur and cellophane grass off the mashed jelly beans and ate them. I could have killed her. I sneaked a look at Roberta. Her mother had brought chicken legs and ham sandwiches and oranges and a whole box of chocolate-covered grahams. Roberta drank milk from a thermos while her mother read the Bible to her.

Things are not right. The wrong food is always with the wrong people. Maybe that's why I got into waitress work later—to match up the right people with the right food. Roberta just let those chicken legs sit there, but she did bring a stack of grahams up to me later when the visit was over. I think she was sorry that her mother would not shake my mother's hand. And I liked that and I liked the fact that she didn't say a word about Mary groaning all the way through the service and not bringing any lunch.

Roberta left in May when the apple trees were heavy and white. On her last day we went to the orchard to watch the big girls smoke and dance by the radio. It didn't matter that they said, "Twyyyyla, baby." We sat on the ground and breathed. Lady Esther. Apple blossoms. I still go soft when I smell one or the other. Roberta was going home. The big cross and the big Bible was coming to get her and she seemed sort of glad and sort of not. I thought I would die in that room of four beds without her and I knew Bozo had plans to move some other dumped kid in there with me. Roberta promised to write every day, which was really sweet of her because she couldn't read a lick so how could she write anybody? I would have drawn pictures and sent them to her but she never gave me her address. Little by little she faded. Her wet socks with the pink scalloped tops and her big serious-looking eyes—that's all I could catch when I tried to bring her to mind.

I was working behind the counter at the Howard Johnson's on the Thruway just before the Kingston exit. Not a bad job. Kind of a long ride from Newburgh, but okay once I got there. Mine was the second shift, eleven to seven. Very light until a Greyhound checked in for breakfast around six-thirty. At that hour the sun was all the way clear of the hills behind the restaurant. The place looked better at night—more like shelter—but I loved it when the sun broke in, even if it did show all the cracks in the vinyl and the speckled floor looked dirty no matter what the mop boy did.

It was August and a bus crowd was just unloading. They would stand around a long while: going to the john, and looking at gifts and junk-for-sale machines, reluctant to sit down so soon. Even to eat. I was trying to fill the coffeepots and get them all situated on the electric burners when I saw her. She was sitting in a booth smoking a cigarette with two guys smothered in head and facial hair. Her own hair was so big and wild I could hardly see her face. But the eyes. I would know them anywhere. She had on a powder-blue halter and shorts outfit and earrings the size of bracelets. Talk about lipstick and eyebrow pencil. She made the big girls look like nuns. I couldn't get off the counter until seven o'clock but I kept watching the booth in case they got up to leave before that. My replacement was on time for a change, so I counted and stacked my receipts as fast as I could and signed off. I walked over to the booth, smiling and wondering if she would remember me. Or even if she wanted to remember me. Maybe she didn't want to be reminded of St. Bonny's or have anybody know she was ever there. I know I never talked about it to anybody.

I put my hands in my apron pockets and leaned against the back of the booth facing them.

"Roberta? Roberta Fisk?"

She looked up. "Yeah?"

"Twyla."

She squinted for a second and then said, "Wow."

"Remember me?"

"Sure. Hey. Wow."

"It's been awhile," I said, and gave a smile to the two hairy guys.

"Yeah. Wow. You work here?"

"Yeah," I said. "I live in Newburgh."

"Newburgh? No kidding?" She laughed then, a private laugh that included the guys, and they laughed with her. What could I do but laugh too and wonder why I was standing there with my knees showing out from under that uniform. Without looking I could see the blue-and-white triangle on my head, my hair shapeless in a net, my ankles thick in white oxfords. Nothing could have been less sheer than my stockings. There was this silence that came down right after I laughed. A silence it was her turn to fill up. With introductions, maybe, to her boyfriends or an invitation to sit down and have a Coke. Instead she lit a cigarette off the one she'd just finished and said, "We're on our way to the Coast. He's got an appointment with Hendrix." She gestured casually toward the boy next to her.

"Hendrix? Fantastic," I said. "Really fantastic. What's she doing now?"

Roberta coughed on her cigarette and the two guys rolled their eyes up at the ceiling.

"Hendrix. Jimi Hendrix, asshole. He's only the biggest—Oh, wow. Forget it."

I was dismissed without anyone saying good-bye, so I thought I would do it for her.

"How's your mother?" I asked. Her grin cracked her whole face. She swallowed. "Fine," she said. "How's yours?"

"Pretty as a picture," I said and turned away. The backs of my knees were damp. Howard Johnson's really was a dump in the sunlight.

James is as comfortable as a house slipper. He liked my cooking and I liked his big loud family. They have lived in Newburgh all of their lives and talk about it the way people do who have always known a home. His grandmother has a porch swing older than his father and when they talk about streets and avenues and buildings they call them names they no longer have. They still call the A&P Rico's because it stands on property once a mom-and-pop store owned by Mr. Rico. And they call the new community college Town Hall because it once was. My mother-in-law puts up jelly and cucumbers and buys butter wrapped in cloth from a dairy. James and his father talk about fishing and baseball and I can see them all together on the Hudson in a raggedy skiff. Half the population of Newburgh is on welfare now, but to my husband's family it was still some upstate paradise of a time long past. A time of ice houses and vegetable wagons, coal furnaces and children weeding gardens. When our son was born my mother-in-law gave me the crib blanket that had been hers.

But the town they remembered had changed. Something quick was in the air. Magnificent old houses, so ruined they had become shelter for squatters and rent risks, were bought and renovated. Smart IBM people moved out of their suburbs back into the city and put shutters up and herb gardens in their backyards. A brochure came in the mail announcing the opening of a Food Emporium. Gourmet food, it said—and listed items the rich IBM crowd would want. It was located in a new mall at the edge of town and I drove out to shop there one day—just to see. It was late in June. After the tulips were gone and the Queen Elizabeth roses were open everywhere. I trailed my cart along the aisle tossing in smoked oysters and Robert's sauce and things I knew would sit in my cupboard for years. Only when I found some Klondike ice cream bars did I feel less guilty about spending Jame's fireman's salary so foolishly. My father-in-law ate them with the same gusto little Joseph did.

Waiting in the checkout line I heard a voice say, "Twyla!"

The classical music piped over the aisles had affected me and the woman leaning toward me was dressed to kill. Diamonds on her hands, a smart white summer dress. "I'm Mrs. Benson," I said.

"Ho. Ho. The Big Bozo," she sang.

For a split second I didn't know what she was talking about. She had a bunch of asparagus and two cartons of fancy water.

"Roberta!"

"Right."

"For heaven's sake. Roberta."

"You look great," she said.

"So do you. Where are you? Here? In Newburgh?"

"Yes. Over in Annandale."

I was opening my mouth to say more when the cashier called my attention to her empty counter.

"Meet you outside." Roberta pointed her finger and went into the express line.

I placed the groceries and kept myself from glancing around to check Roberta's progress. I remembered Howard Johnson's and looking for a chance to speak only to be greeted with a stingy "wow." But she was waiting for me and her huge hair was sleek now, smooth around a small, nicely shaped head. Shoes, dress, everything lovely and summery and rich. I was dying to know what happened to her, how she got from Jimi Hendrix to Annandale, a neighborhood full of doctors and IBM executives. Easy, I thought. Everything is so easy for them. They think they own the world.

"How long," I asked her. "How long have you been here?"

"A year. I got married to a man who lives here. And you, you're married too, right? Benson, you said."

"Yeah. James Benson."

"And is he nice?"

"Oh, is he nice?"

"Well, is he?" Roberta's eyes were steady as though she really meant the question and wanted an answer.

"He's wonderful, Roberta. Wonderful."

"So you're happy."

"Very."

"That's good," she said and nodded her head. "I always hoped you'd be happy. Any kids? I know you have kids."

"One. A boy. How about you?"

"Four."

"Four?"

She laughed. "Step kids. He's a widower."

"Oh."

"Got a minute? Let's have coffee."

I thought about the Klondikes melting and the inconvenience of going all the way to my car and putting the bags in the trunk. Served me right for buying all that stuff I didn't need. Roberta was ahead of me.

"Put them in my car. It's right here."

And then I saw the dark blue limousine.

"You married a Chinaman?"

"No." She laughed. "He's the driver."

"Oh, my. If the Big Bozo could see you now."

We both giggled. Really giggled. Suddenly, in just a pulse beat, twenty years disappeared and all of it came rushing back. The big girls (whom we called gar girls—Roberta's misheard word for the evil stone faces described in a civics class) there dancing in the orchard, the ploppy mashed potatoes, the double weenies, the Spam with pineapple. We went into the coffee shop holding on to one another and I tried to think why we were glad to see each other this time and not before. Once, twelve years ago, we passed like strangers. A black girl and white girl meeting in a Howard Johnson's on the road and having nothing to say. One in a blue-and-white triangle waitress hat, the other on her way to see Hendrix. Now we were behaving like sisters separated for much too long. Those four short months were nothing in time. Maybe it was the thing itself. Just being there, together. Two little girls who knew what nobody else in the world knew—how not to ask questions. How to believe what had to be believed. There was politeness in that reluctance and generosity as well. Is your mother sick too? No, she dances all night. Oh—and an understanding nod.

We sat in a booth by the window and fell into recollection like veterans.

"Did you ever learn to read?"

"Watch." She picked up the menu. "Special of the day. Cream of corn soup. Entrées. Two dots and a wiggly line. Quiche. Chef salad, scallops. . . ."

I was laughing and applauding when the waitress came up.

"Remember the Easter baskets?"

"And how we tried to *introduce* them?"

"Your mother with that cross like two telephone poles."

"And yours with those tight slacks."

We laughed so loudly heads turned and made the laughter hard to suppress.

"What happened to the Jimi Hendrix date?"

Roberta made a blow-out sound with her lips.

"When he died I thought about you."

"Oh, you heard about him finally?"

"Finally. Come on. I was a small-town waitress."

"And I was a small-town country dropout. God, were we wild. I still don't know how I got out of there alive."

"But you did."

"I did. I really did. Now I'm Mrs. Kenneth Norton."

"Sounds like a mouthful."

"It is."

"Servants and all?"

Roberta held up two fingers.

"Ow! What does he do?"

"Computers and stuff. What do I know?"

"I don't remember a hell of a lot from those days, but Lord, St. Bonny's is as clear as daylight. Remember Maggie? The day she fell down and those gar girls laughed at her?"

Roberta looked up from her salad and stared at me. "Maggie didn't fall," she said.

"Yes, she did. You remember."

"No, Twyla. They knocked her down. Those girls pushed her down and tore her clothes. In the orchard."

"I don't—that's not what happened."

"Sure it is. In the orchard. Remember how scared we were?"

"Wait a minute. I don't remember any of that."

"And Bozo was fired."

"You're crazy. She was there when I left. You left before me."

"I went back. You weren't there when they fired Bozo."

"What?"

"Twice. Once for a year when I was about ten, another for two months when I was fourteen. That's when I ran away."

"You ran away from St. Bonny's?"

"I had to. What do you want? Me dancing in that orchard?"

"Are you sure about Maggie?"

"Of course I'm sure. You've blocked it, Twyla. It happened. Those girls had behavior problems, you know."

"Didn't they, though. But why can't I remember the Maggie thing?"

"Believe me. It happened. And we were there."

"Who did you room with when you went back?" I asked her as if I would know her. The Maggie thing was troubling me.

"Creeps. They tickled themselves in the night."

My ears were itching and I wanted to go home suddenly. This was all very well but she couldn't just comb her hair, wash her face, and pretend everything was hunky-dory. After the Howard Johnson's snub. And no apology. Nothing.

"Were you on dope or what that time at Howard Johnson's?" I tried to make my voice sound friendlier than I felt.

"Maybe, a little. I never did drugs much. Why?"

"I don't know, you acted sort of like you didn't want to know me then."

"Oh, Twyla, you know how it was in those days: black—white. You know how everything was."

But I didn't know. I thought it was just the opposite. Busloads of blacks and whites came into Howard Johnson's together. They roamed together then: students, musicians, lovers, protesters. You got to see everything at Howard Johnson's, and blacks were very friendly with whites in those days. But sitting there with nothing on my plate but two hard tomato wedges wondering about the melting Klondikes it seemed childish remembering the slight. We went to her car and, with the help of the driver, got my stuff into my station wagon.

"We'll keep in touch this time," she said.

"Sure," I said. "Sure. Give me a call."

"I will," she said, and then, just as I was sliding behind the wheel, she leaned into the window. "By the way. Your mother. Did she ever stop dancing?"

I shook my head. "No. Never."

Roberta nodded.

"And yours? Did she ever get well?"

She smiled a tiny sad smile. "No. She never did. Look, call me, okay?"

"Okay," I said, but I knew I wouldn't. Roberta had messed up my past somehow with that business about Maggie. I wouldn't forget a thing like that. Would I?

Strife came to us that fall. At least that's what the paper called it. Strife. Racial strife. The word made me think of a bird—a big shrieking bird out of 1,000,000,000 B.C. Flapping its wings and cawing. Its eye with no lid always bearing down on you. All day it screeched and at night it slept on the rooftops. It woke you in the morning, and from the Today show to the eleven o'clock news it kept you an awful company. I couldn't figure it out from one day to the next. I knew I was supposed to feel something strong, but I didn't know what, and James wasn't any help. Joseph was on the list of kids to be transferred from the junior high school to another one at some far-out-of-the-way place and I thought it was a good thing until I heard it was a bad thing. I mean I didn't know. All the schools seemed dumps to me, and the fact that one was nicer looking didn't hold much weight. But the papers were full of it and then the kids began to get jumpy. In August, mind you. Schools weren't even open yet. I thought Joseph might be frightened to go over there, but he didn't seem scared so I forgot about it, until I found myself driving along Hudson Street out there by the school they were trying to integrate and saw a line of women marching. And who do you suppose was in line, big as life, holding a sign in front of her bigger than her mother's cross. MOTHERS HAVE RIGHTS TOO! it said.

I drove on and then changed my mind. I circled the block, slowed down, and honked my horn.

Roberta looked over and when she saw me she waved. I didn't wave back, but I didn't move either. She handed her sign to another woman and came over to where I was parked.

"Hi."

"What are you doing?"

"Picketing. What's it look like?"

"What for?"

"What do you mean. 'What for?' They want to take my kids and send them out of the neighborhood. They don't want to go."

"So what if they go to another school? My boy's being bussed too, and I don't mind. Why should you?"

"It's not about us, Twyla. Me and you. It's about our kids."

"What's more *us* than that?"

"Well, it is a free country."

"Not yet, but it will be."

"What the hell does that mean? I'm not doing anything to you."

"You really think that?"

"I know it."

"I wonder what made me think you were different."

"I wonder what made me think you were different."

"Look at them," I said. "Just look. Who do they think they are? Swarming all over the place like they own it. And now they think they can decide where my child goes to school. Look at them, Roberta. They're Bozos."

Roberta turned around and looked at the women. Almost all of them were standing still now, waiting. Some were even edging toward us. Roberta looked at me out of some refrigerator behind her eyes. "No, they're not. They're just mothers."

"And what am I? Swiss cheese?"

"I used to curl your hair."

"I hated your hands in my hair."

The women were moving. Our faces looked mean to them of course and they looked as though they could not wait to throw themselves in front of a police car or, better yet, into my car and drage me away by my ankles. Now they surrounded my car and gently, gently began to rock it. I swayed back and forth like a sideways yo-yo. Automatically I reached for Roberta, like the old days in the orchard when they saw us watching them and we had to get out of there, and if one of us fell the other pulled her up and if one of us was caught the other stayed to kick and scratch, and neither would leave the other behind. My arm shot out of the car window but no receiving hand was there. Roberta was looking at me sway from side to side in the car and her face was still. My purse slid from the car seat down under the dashboard. The four policemen who had been drinking Tab in their car finally got the message and strolled over, forcing their way through the women. Quietly, firmly they spoke, "Okay, ladies. Back in line off the streets."

Some of them went away willingly; others had to be urged away from the car doors and the hood. Roberta didn't move. She was looking steadily at me. I was fumbling to turn on the ignition, which wouldn't catch because the gearshift was still in drive. The seats of the car were a mess because the swaying had thrown my grocery coupons all over and my purse was sprawled on the floor.

"Maybe I am different now, Twyla. But you're not. You're the same little state kid who kicked a poor old black lady when she was down on the ground. You kicked a black lady and you have the nerve to call me a bigot."

The coupons were everywhere and the guts of my purse were bunched under the dashboard. What was she saying? Black? Maggie wasn't black.

"She wasn't black," I said.

"Like hell she wasn't, and you kicked her. We both did. You kicked a black lady who couldn't even scream."

"Liar!"

"You're the liar! Why don't you just go on home and leave us alone, huh?"

She turned away and I skidded away from the curb.

The next morning I went into the garage and cut the side out of the carton our portable TV had come in. It wasn't nearly big enough, but after a while I had a decent sign: red spray-painted letters on a white background—AND SO DO CHILDREN****. I meant just to go down to the school and tack it up somewhere so those cows on the picket line across the street could see it, but when I got there, some ten or so others had assembled—protesting the cows across the street. Police permits and everything. I got in line and we strutted in time on our side while Roberta's group strutted on theirs. That first day we were all dignified, pretending the other side didn't exist. The second day there was name calling and finger gestures. But that was about all. People changed signs form time to time, but Roberta never did and neither did I. Actually my sign didn't make sense without Roberta's. "And so do children what?" one of the women on my side asked me. Have rights, I said, as though it was obvious.

Roberta didn't acknowledge my presence in any way, and I got to thinking maybe she didn't know I was there. I began to pace myself in line, jostling people one minute and lagging behind the next, so Roberta and I could reach the end of our respective lines at the same time and there would be a moment in our turn when we would face each other. Still, I couldn't tell whether she saw me and knew my sign was for her. The next day I went early before we were scheduled to assemble. I waited until she got there before I exposed my new creation. As soon as she hoisted her mothers have rights too I began to wave my new one, which said, HOW WOULD YOU KNOW? I know she saw that one, but I had gotten addicted now. My signs got crazier each day, and the women on my side decided that I was a kook. They couldn't make heads or tails out of my brilliant screaming posters.

I brought a painted sign in queenly red with huge black letters that said, IS YOUR MOTHER WELL? Roberta took her lunch break and didn't come back for the rest of the day or any day after. Two days later I stopped going too and couldn't have been missed because nobody understood my signs anyway.

It was a nasty six weeks. Classes were suspended and Joseph didn't go to anybody's school until October. The children—everybody's children—soon got bored with that extended vacation they thought was going to be so great. They looked at TV until their eyes flattened. I spent a couple of mornings tutoring my son, as the other mothers said we should. Twice I opened a text from last year that he had never turned in. Twice he yawned in my face. Other mothers organized living room sessions so the kids would keep up. None of the kids could concentrate, so they drifted back to The Price Is Right and The Brady Bunch. When the school finally opened there were fights once or twice and some sirens roared through the streets everyone once in a while. There were a lot of photographers from Albany. And just when ABC was about to send up a news crew, the kids settled down like nothing in the world had happened. Joseph hung my how would you know? sign in his bedroom. I don't know what became of and so do children****. I think my father-in-law cleaned some fish on it. He was always puttering around in our garage. Each of his five children lived in Newburgh, and he acted as though he had five extra homes.

I couldn't help looking for Roberta when Joseph graduated from high school, but I didn't see her. It didn't trouble me much what she had said to me in the car. I mean the kicking part. I know I didn't do that, I couldn't do that. But I was puzzled by her telling me Maggie was black. When I thought about it I actually couldn't be certain. She wasn't pitch-black, I knew, or I would have remembered that. What I remember was the kiddie hat and the semicircle legs. I tried to reassure myself about the race thing for a long time until it dawned on me that the truth was already there, and Roberta knew it. I didn't kick her; I didn't join in with the gar girls and kick that lady, but I sure did want to. We watched and never tried to help her and never called for help. Maggie was my dancing mother. Deaf, I thought, and dumb. Nobody inside. Nobody who would hear you if you cried in the night. Nobody who could tell you anything important that you could use. Rocking, dancing, swaying as she walked. And when the gar girls pushed her down and started roughhousing, I knew she wouldn't scream, couldn't—just like me—and I was glad about that.

We decided not to have a tree, because Christmas would be at my mother-in-law's house, so why have a tree at both places? Joseph was as SUNY New Palz and we had to economize, we said. But at the last minute, I changed my mind. Nothing could be that bad. So I rushed around town looking for a tree, something small but wide. By the time I found a place, it was snowing and very late. I dawdled like it was the most important purchase in the world and the tree man was fed up with me. Finally I chose one and had it tied onto the trunk of the car. I drove away slowly because the sand trucks were not out yet and the streets could be murder at the beginning of a snowfall. Downtown the streets were wide and rather empty except for a cluster of people coming out of the Newburgh Hotel. The one hotel in town that wasn't built out of cardboard and Plexiglas. A party, probably. The men huddled in the snow were dressed in tails and the women had on furs. Shiny things glittered from underneath their coats. It made me tired to look at them. Tired, tired, tired. On the next corner was a small diner with loops and loops of paper bells in the window. I stopped the car and went in. Just for a cup of coffee and twenty minutes of peace before I went home and tried to finish everything before Christmas Eve.

"Twyla?"

There she was. In a silvery evening gown and dark fur coat. A man and another woman were with her, the man fumbling for change to put in the cigarette machine. The woman was humming and tapping the counter with her fingernails. They all looked a little bit drunk.

"Well. It's you."

"How are you?"

I shrugged. "Pretty good. Frazzled. Christmas and all."

"Regular?" called the woman from the counter.

"Fine," Roberta called back and then, "Wait for me in the car."

She slipped into the booth beside me. "I have to tell you something, Twyla. I made up my mind if I ever saw you again, I'd tell you."

"I'd just as soon not hear anything, Roberta. It doesn't matter now, anyway."

"No," she said. "Not about that."

"Don't be long," said the woman. She carried two regulars to go and the man peeled his cigarette pack as they left.

"It's about St. Bonny's and Maggie."

"Oh, please."

"Listen to me. I really did think she was black. I didn't make that up. I really thought so. But now I can't be sure. I just remember her as old, so old. And because she couldn't talk—well, you know, I thought she was crazy. She'd been brought up in an institution like my mother was and like I thought I would be too. And you were right. We didn't kick her. It was the gar girls. Only them. But, well, I wanted to. I really wanted them to hurt her. I said we did it, too. You and me, but that's not true. And I don't want you to carry that around. It was just that I wanted to do it so bad that day—wanting to is doing it."

Her eyes were watery from the drinks she'd had, I guess. I know it's that way with me. One glass of wine and I start bawling over the littlest thing.

"We were kids, Roberta."

"Yeah. Yeah. I know, just kids."

"Eight."

"Eight."

"And lonely."

"Scared, too."

She wiped her cheeks with the heel of her hand and smiled. "Well, that's all I wanted to say."

I nodded and couldn't think of any way to fill the silence that went from the diner past the paper bells on out into the snow. It was heavy now. I thought I'd better wait for the sand trucks before starting home.

"Thanks, Roberta."

"Sure."

"Did I tell you? My mother, she never did stop dancing."

"Yes. You told me. And mine, she never got well." Roberta lifted her hands from the tabletop and covered her face with her palms. When she took them away she really was crying. "Oh, shit, Twyla. Shit, shit, shit. What the hell happened to Maggie?"

1995

Anne Sexton 1928–1974

Anne Gray Harvey Sexton was born in Newton, Massachusetts, the third daughter of Mary Gray and Ralph Harvey. Sexton's great-uncle had been governor of Maine, and her grandfather, editor of Maine's *Lewiston Evening Journal,* was a respected journalist. The family's primary emphasis by the time of Sexton's birth was mercantile; Sexton's father and, later, her husband were both wool merchants. The Harveys lived in Boston suburbs during the year and on Squirrel Island, Maine, during summers. Her childhood was both privileged and difficult. Sexton felt she could not fulfill her family's expectations, which were both high and vague. She was implicitly expected to marry at the right time and to behave decorously—neither of which she did—but not necessarily to distinguish herself professionally or intellectually.

Anne Harvey was a spirited and demanding child, a romantic and popular adolescent, an undistinguished student (she attended a finishing school for women

in Boston). In 1948 she eloped with Alfred Sexton, to whom she remained married until 1973. Shortly after the births of each of her two daughters (in 1953 and 1955), Sexton was hospitalized for the recurring emotional disturbances that continued to plague her for the rest of her life. After a suicide attempt in 1956, on the advice of her doctor, she began writing poetry. In 1957, Sexton enrolled in John Holmes's poetry workshop, Boston, where she met Maxine Kumin, her closest personal friend. In 1958–59 she was a student in Robert Lowell's writing seminar at Boston University, where she met Sylvia Plath.

Her first collection, *To Bedlam and Part Way Back* (1960), was controversial and established Sexton's reputation as a confessional poet. Popularity and something approaching notoriety accompanied Sexton's poetic career. She received numerous awards, including a nomination for the National Book Award; fellowships from the American Academy of Arts and

Letters, the Ford Foundation, and the Guggenheim Foundation; several honorary doctorates; and in 1967, the Pulitzer Prize for *Live or Die*. She taught at Harvard and Radcliffe, lectured at Breadloaf Writers' Conference, held the Crashaw Chair at Colgate University, and was a full professor at Boston University by 1972. Her celebrated readings on the poetry circuit were criticized as the flamboyant, dramatic performances they were. When Sexton killed herself in 1974, she was still professionally successful and productive. Diane Wood Middlebrook's *Anne Sexton: A Biography* tells readers much more about a life that seems, but clearly is not, fully disclosed in the poetry.

Sexton used the personal to speak to cultural concerns, many of which apply to women's conflicts and transitions in modern American society. If Lowell and Snodgrass are the fathers of confessional poetry, Sexton is perhaps its first mother. The gender distinction is worth making. Snodgrass gave her "permission," as she phrased it, to write about loss, neurosis, even madness, but no one had extended the permission to write about such experiences from a female point of view. For that bold stroke there was no precedent. Many feminist poets and critics find in her work a set of resonant and enabling myths, as well as a critique of those that disabled Sexton herself.

Sexton's early work was preoccupied with formal structure and lyric discipline, while the later work became what critics have variously called surreal, mythic, or visionary. Anne Sexton's poems articulate some of the deepest dilemmas of her contemporaries about their—our—most fundamental wishes and fears.

Diana Hume George
The Pennsylvania State University/
Behrend College

PRIMARY WORKS

To Bedlam and Part Way Back, 1960; *All My Pretty Ones,* 1962; *Selected Poems,* 1964; *Live or Die,* 1966; *Love Poems,* 1969; *Transformations,* 1971; *The Book of Folly,* 1972; *The Death Notebooks,* 1974; *The Awful Rowing Toward God,* 1975; *45 Mercy Street,* 1976; *Anne Sexton: A Self-Portrait in Letters,* 1977; *Words for Dr. Y: Uncollected Poems with Three Stories,* 1978; *The Complete Poems,* 1981; *No Evil Star: Selected Essays, Interviews, and Prose,* 1985; *Selected Poems of Anne Sexton,* 1988.

Her Kind

I have gone out, a possessed witch,
haunting the black air, braver at night;
dreaming evil, I have done my hitch
over the plain houses, light by light:
5 lonely thing, twelve-fingered, out of mind.
A woman like that is not a woman, quite.
I have been her kind.

I have found the warm caves in the woods,
filled them with skillets, carvings, shelves,

10 closets, silks, innumerable goods;
    fixed the suppers for the worms and the elves:
    whining, rearranging the disaligned.
    A woman like that is misunderstood.
    I have been her kind.

15 I have ridden in your cart, driver,
    waved my nude arms at villages going by,
    learning the last bright routes, survivor
    where your flames still bite my thigh
    and my ribs crack where your wheels wind.
20 A woman like that is not ashamed to die.
    I have been her kind.

                                        1960

Housewife

Some women marry houses.
It's another kind of skin; it has a heart,
a mouth, a liver and bowel movements.
The walls are permanent and pink.
5 See how she sits on her knees all day,
faithfully washing herself down.
Men enter by force, drawn back like Jonah
into their fleshy mothers.
A woman *is* her mother.
10 That's the main thing.

                                        1962

Young

A thousand doors ago
when I was a lonely kid
in a big house with four
garages and it was summer
5 as long as I could remember,
I lay on the lawn at night,
clover wrinkling under me,
the wise stars bedding over me,

my mother's window a funnel
10 of yellow heat running out,
my father's window, half shut,
an eye where sleepers pass,
and the boards of the house
were smooth and white as wax
15 and probably a million leaves
sailed on their strange stalks
as the crickets ticked together
and I, in my brand new body,
which was not a woman's yet,
20 told the stars my questions
and thought God could really see
the heat and the painted light,
elbows, knees, dreams, goodnight.

1961

Somewhere in Africa

Must you leave, John Holmes,[1] with the prayers and psalms
you never said, said over you? Death with no rage
to weigh you down? Praised by the mild God, his arm
over the pulpit, leaving you timid, with no real age,
5 whitewashed by belief, as dull as the windy preacher!
Dead of a dark thing, John Holmes, you've been lost
in the college chapel, mourned as father and teacher,
mourned with piety and grace under the University Cross.

Your last book unsung, your last hard words unknown,
10 abandoned by science, cancer blossomed in your throat,
rooted like bougainvillea into your gray backbone,
ruptured your pores until you wore it like a coat.

The thick petals, the exotic reds, the purples and whites
covered up your nakedness and bore you up with all
15 their blind power. I think of your last June nights
in Boston, your body swollen but light, your eyes small

[1]John Holmes was a mid-twentieth century American poet who died in 1962. In 1957, Sexton enrolled in his poetry workshop at the Boston Center for Adult Education, where she also met Maxine Kumin and George Starbuck. The group continued meeting for several years after the initial workshop. Sexton's troubled, ambivalent relationship with her first teacher produced two of her poems, "Somewhere in Africa" and "For John, Who Begs Me Not to Enquire Further."

as you let the nurses carry you into a strange land.
. . . If this is death and God is necessary let him be hidden
from the missionary, the well-wisher and the glad hand.
20 Let God be some tribal female who is known but forbidden.

Let there be this God who is a woman who will place you
upon her shallow boat, who is a woman naked to the waist,
moist with palm oil and sweat, a woman of some virtue
and wild breasts, her limbs excellent, unbruised and chaste.

25 Let her take you. She will put twelve strong men at the oars
for you are stronger than mahogany and your bones fill
the boat high as with fruit and bark from the interior.
She will have you now, you whom the funeral cannot kill.

John Holmes, cut from a single tree, lie heavy in her hold
30 and go down that river with the ivory, the copra and the gold.

1966

Sylvia Plath 1932–1963

Sylvia Plath was the precocious child of well-educated Boston parents, Otto and Aurelia Schoeber Plath. Otto, who taught German and zoology at Boston University, died when Sylvia was eight of complications following the amputation of his leg. An authority on bees, he had been ill the previous four years from untreated diabetes mellitus. Finances were slim so Sylvia's mother returned to teaching, and to help care for the children, her maternal grandparents moved into the Plath home, where they remained until their deaths. In order to take a position at Boston University herself, Aurelia moved the family to Wellesley.

Plath's childhood and adolescence were a series of high academic achievements. She published poetry, fiction, and journalism in a number of places even before attending Smith College on a partial scholarship. An English major at Smith, she continued her consistent prize winning, but she was also very much a woman of the 1950s, plagued with thoughts that she had

to marry and have children, or else she would never be a "complete" female. Some of her conflicts over direction (career vs. marriage, sexual experience vs. chastity) combined with a strain of depression in her paternal line to cause a breakdown in the summer of 1953, shortly after she had served as a *Mademoiselle* College Board editor. The outpatient electroconvulsive shock treatments she received then probably led to her subsequent suicide attempt in August 1953, and she spent the next four months under psychiatric care before returning to Smith. In June 1955, she graduated *summa cum laude* and got an M.A. on a Fulbright Fellowship at Cambridge, England.

On June 16, 1956, she married Ted Hughes, eventually to become Poet Laureate of England. In 1957 they returned to the States where Plath taught freshman English at Smith. She and Hughes then lived for another year in Boston, establishing themselves as professional writers; late in 1959 they returned to England. In the next three years, Plath bore two children, published *The Colossus and Other Poems*, established a home in Devon, separated from Hughes, and was living with her children in a flat in Yeats's house in London when she committed suicide, just a few weeks after *The Bell Jar* had been published. In 1965 *Ariel*, the collection of some of her last poems, appeared.

Plath's poems show a steadily developing sense of her own voice, speaking of subjects that—before the 1960s—were seldom considered appropriate for poetry: anger, macabre humor, defiance, contrasted with a rarer joy and a poignant understanding of women's various roles. "Three Women," which is set in a maternity ward, *The Bell Jar*, and many of her late 1962 poems were unlike any of the expert literature she had so carefully imitated—until the last years of her life. Her breaking out of the conventional patterns set an example that shaped a great deal of poetry for the next forty years—reliance on metaphor, quick shifts from image to image, a frantic yet always controlled pace that mirrored the tensions of her single-parent life during 1962. In contrast to late poems like "Daddy" and "Lady Lazarus," Plath's final poems were icily mystic, solemn, and resigned. The full range of her work is evident in the 1981 *Collected Poems*, which won the Pulitzer Prize for Poetry in 1982.

Linda Wagner-Martin
University of North Carolina at Chapel Hill

PRIMARY WORKS

The Colossus, 1960; *The Bell Jar*, 1963 (published under "Victoria Lucas"); *Ariel*, 1965; *Crossing the Water*, 1971; *Winter Trees*, 1972; *Johnny Panic and the Bible of Dreams and Other Prose Writings*, 1977; *The Collected Poems*, 1981; *The Journals of Sylvia Plath*, 1982.

For a Fatherless Son

You will be aware of an absence, presently,
Growing beside you, like a tree,
A death tree, color gone, an Australian gum tree—
Balding, gelded by lightning—an illusion,
5 And a sky like a pig's backside, an utter lack of attention.

But right now you are dumb.
And I love your stupidity,
The blind mirror of it. I look in
And find no face but my own, and you think that's funny.
10 It is good for me

To have you grab my nose, a ladder rung.
One day you may touch what's wrong—
The small skulls, the smashed blue hills, the godawful hush.
Till then your smiles are found money.

1962

Daddy

You do not do, you do not do
Any more, black shoe
In which I have lived like a foot
For thirty years, poor and white,
5   Barely daring to breathe or Achoo.

Daddy, I have had to kill you.
You died before I had time——
Marble-heavy, a bag full of God,
Ghastly statue with one gray toe
10 Big as a Frisco seal[1]

And a head in the freakish Atlantic
Where it pours bean green over blue
In the waters off beautiful Nauset.[2]
I used to pray to recover you.
15 Ach, du.[3]

In the German tongue, in the Polish town
Scraped flat by the roller
Of wars, wars, wars.
But the name of the town is common.
20 My Polack friend

Says there are a dozen or two.
So I never could tell where you
Put your foot, your root,
I never could talk to you.
25 The tongue stuck in my jaw.

It stuck in a barb wire snare.
Ich, ich, ich, ich,[4]
I could hardly speak.
I thought every German was you.
30 And the language obscene

An engine, an engine
Chuffing me off like a Jew.
A Jew to Dachau, Auschwitz, Belsen.[5]

[1]San Francisco Seal Rocks.
[2]Cape Cod harbor.
[3]German: Ah, you.
[4]German: I.
[5]Nazi concentration camps of Holocaust.

I began to talk like a Jew.
35 I think I may well be a Jew.

The snows of the Tyrol,[6] the clear beer of Vienna
Are not very pure or true.
With my gipsy ancestress and my weird luck
And my Taroc[7] pack and my Taroc pack
40 I may be a bit of a Jew.

I have always been scared of *you*,
With your Luftwaffe,[8] your gobbledygoo.
And your neat mustache
And your Aryan[9] eye, bright blue.
45 Panzer-man, panzer-man,[10] O You——

Not God but a swastika
So black no sky could squeak through.
Every woman adores a Fascist,
The boot in the face, the brute
50 Brute heart of a brute like you.

You stand at the blackboard, daddy,
In the picture I have of you,
A cleft in your chin instead of your foot
But no less a devil for that, no not
55 Any less the black man who

Bit my pretty red heart in two.
I was ten when they buried you.
At twenty I tried to die
And get back, back, back to you.
60 I thought even the bones would do.

But they pulled me out of the sack,
And they stuck me together with glue.
And then I knew what to do.
I made a model of you,
65 A man in black with a Meinkampf[11] look

And a love of the rack and the screw.
And I said I do, I do.

---

[6] Austrian alps.
[7] Tarot fortune-telling cards.
[8] Nazi air force.
[9] Caucasian gentile, the Nazi ideal race.

[10] Panzer is German for armor: Nazi World War II armored divisions.
[11] Hitler's manifesto, "My Battle."

So daddy, I'm finally through.
The black telephone's off at the root,
70 The voices just can't worm through.

If I've killed one man, I've killed two——
The vampire who said he was you
And drank my blood for a year,
Seven years, if you want to know.
75 Daddy, you can lie back now.

There's a stake in your fat black heart
And the villagers never liked you.
They are dancing and stamping on you.
They always *knew* it was you.
80 Daddy, daddy, you bastard, I'm through.

                                        1965

Lady Lazarus

I have done it again.
One year in every ten
I manage it——

A sort of walking miracle, my skin
5 Bright as a Nazi lampshade,
My right foot

A paperweight,
My face a featureless, fine
Jew linen.

10 Peel off the napkin
O my enemy.
Do I terrify?——

The nose, the eye pits, the full set of teeth?
The sour breath
15 Will vanish in a day.

Soon, soon the flesh
The grave cave ate will be
At home on me

And I a smiling woman.
20 I am only thirty.
And like the cat I have nine times to die.

This is Number Three.
What a trash
To annihilate each decade.

25 What a million filaments.
The peanut-crunching crowd
Shoves in to see

Them unwrap me hand and foot——
The big strip tease.
30 Gentlemen, ladies

These are my hands,
My knees.
I may be skin and bone,

Nevertheless, I am the same, identical woman.
35 The first time it happened I was ten.
It was an accident.

The second time I meant
To last it out and not come back at all.
I rocked shut

40 As a seashell.
They had to call and call
And pick the worms off me like sticky pearls.

Dying
Is an art, like everything else.
45 I do it exceptionally well.

I do it so it feels like hell.
I do it so it feels real.
I guess you could say I've a call.

It's easy enough to do it in a cell.
50 It's easy enough to do it and stay put.
It's the theatrical

Comeback in broad day
To the same place, the same face, the same brute
Amused shout:

55   "A miracle!"
    That knocks me out.
    There is a charge

    For the eyeing of my scars, there is a charge
    For the hearing of my heart——
60   It really goes.

    And there is a charge, a very large charge
    For a word or a touch
    Or a bit of blood

    Or a piece of my hair or my clothes.
65   So, so, Herr Doktor.
    So, Herr Enemy.

    I am your opus,
    I am your valuable,
    The pure gold baby

70   That melts to a shriek.
    I turn and burn.
    Do not think I underestimate your great concern.

    Ash, ash—
    You poke and stir.
75   Flesh, bone, there is nothing there——

    A cake of soap,
    A wedding ring,
    A gold filling.

    Herr God, Herr Lucifer,
80   Beware
    Beware.

    Out of the ash
    I rise with my red hair
    And I eat men like air.

                      1965

Stings

Bare-handed, I hand the combs.
The man in white smiles, bare-handed,
Our cheesecloth gauntlets neat and sweet,
The throats of our wrists brave lilies.
5 He and I

Have a thousand clean cells between us,
Eight combs of yellow cups,
And the hive itself a teacup,
White with pink flowers on it,
10 With excessive love I enameled it

Thinking "Sweetness, sweetness."
Brood cells gray as the fossils of shells
Terrify me, they seem so old.
What am I buying, wormy mahogany?
15 Is there any queen at all in it?

If there is, she is old,
Her wings torn shawls, her long body
Rubbed of its plush——
Poor and bare and unqueenly and even shameful.
20 I stand in a column

Of winged, unmiraculous women,
Honey-drudgers.
I am no drudge
Though for years I have eaten dust
25 And dried plates with my dense hair.

And seen my strangeness evaporate,
Blue dew from dangerous skin.
Will they hate me,
These women who only scurry,
30 Whose news is the open cherry, the open clover?

It is almost over.
I am in control.
Here is my honey-machine,
It will work without thinking,
35 Opening, in spring, like an industrious virgin

To scour the creaming crests
As the moon, for its ivory powders, scours the sea.

A third person is watching.
He has nothing to do with the bee-seller or with me.
40 Now he is gone

In eight great bounds, a great scapegoat.
Here is his slipper, here is another,
And here the square of white linen
He wore instead of a hat.
45 He was sweet,

The sweat of his efforts a rain
Tugging the world to fruit.
The bees found him out,
Molding onto his lips like lies,
50 Complicating his features.

They thought death was worth it, but I
Have a self to recover, a queen.
Is she dead, is she sleeping?
Where has she been,
55 With her lion-red body, her wings of glass?

Now she is flying
More terrible than she ever was, red
Scar in the sky, red comet
Over the engine that killed her——
60 The mausoleum, the wax house.

1965

Fever 103°

Pure? What does it mean?
The tongues of hell
Are dull, dull as the triple

Tongues of dull, fat Cerberus
5 Who wheezes at the gate. Incapable
Of licking clean

The aguey tendon, the sin, the sin.
The tinder cries.
The indelible smell

10   Of a snuffed candle!
Love, love, the low smokes roll
From me like Isadora's scarves, I'm in a fright

One scarf will catch and anchor in the wheel.
Such yellow sullen smokes
15   Make their own element. They will not rise,

But trundle round the globe
Choking the aged and the meek,
The weak

Hothouse baby in its crib,
20   The ghastly orchid
Hanging its hanging garden in the air,

Devilish leopard!
Radiation turned it white
And killed it in an hour.

25   Greasing the bodies of adulterers
Like Hiroshima ash and eating in.
The sin. The sin.

Darling, all night
I have been flickering, off, on, off, on.
30   The sheets grow heavy as a lecher's kiss.

Three days. Three nights.
Lemon water, chicken
Water, water make me retch.

I am too pure for you or anyone.
35   Your body
Hurts me as the world hurts God. I am a lantern——

My head a moon
Of Japanese paper, my gold beaten skin
Infinitely delicate and infinitely expensive.

40   Does not my heat astound you. And my light.
All by myself I am a huge camellia
Glowing and coming and going, flush on flush.

I think I am going up,
I think I may rise——
45   The beads of hot metal fly, and I, love, I

Am a pure acetylene
Virgin
Attended by roses,

By kisses, by cherubim,
50 By whatever these pink things mean.
Not you, nor him

Not him, nor him
(My selves dissolving, old whore petticoats)——
To Paradise.

1965

John Updike b. 1932

Born in Shillington, Pennsylvania, John Updike was the only child of Wesley R. and Linda Grace (Hoyer) Updike. His father was a high-school mathematics teacher and his mother later became a freelance writer. Young Updike received a full scholarship to Harvard University, where he was elected president of the *Lampoon,* the campus humor magazine. Upon graduating *summa cum laude* in 1954, he attended the Ruskin School of Drawing and Fine Art in Oxford, England. Since 1955 he has written for the *New Yorker* magazine, first as a reporter and then as a regular contributor of stories, poems, and reviews. He has published more than fifty books and has received numerous honors, including the National Book Award, the Pulitzer Prize, and election to the prestigious American Academy of Arts and Letters. Divorced and remarried, he now lives in Massachusetts.

Over the years, Updike has become something of a celebrity, appearing on talk shows and magazine covers. His short stories have been dramatized for television; his novel *The Witches of Eastwick* was a Book-of-the-Month Club selection and was later released as a Warner Brothers film starring Jack Nicholson. Updike's work is assigned in college literature courses and has generated a substantial body of scholarly criticism. He is a rarity among serious writers, having secured both popular success and academic acclaim.

Remarkably versatile—writing novels, children's books, short story and poetry collections, a play, and eight anthologies of nonfiction prose—he is most highly regarded as a fiction writer. He draws heavily upon his own life for subject matter but transcends the particulars of personal experience, achieving a broadly encompassing vision of the contemporary American situation.

With a few exceptions, his novels and stories can be grouped into three overlapping categories: the "Olinger" fiction, the "Rabbit" novels, and the "suburban" books. Chief among the early works set in fictional Olinger, Pennsylvania (based on Updike's hometown), is *The Centaur,* a loving tribute to his father. The tetralogy comprising *Rabbit, Run; Rabbit Redux; Rabbit Is Rich;* and *Rabbit at Rest* focuses on Harry Angstrom, a blue-collar protagonist whom some critics have identified as Updike's alter-ego. Other works—*Couples, Marry Me,* and the many stories about Richard and Joan Maple, for example—

document the tensions of upper-middle-class suburbia, often depicting divorce and its aftermath.

Common to all of Updike's works is a concern with individual moral responsibility and guilt, coupled with a clearcut indictment of current values and a quixotic yearning to recapture the simpler and presumably purer American past. A consciously religious writer, he repeatedly creates confused, unfulfilled characters unable to reconcile the opposed demands of the self and the social contract, particularly in the context of interpersonal relationships. Parents and children, husbands and wives, lovers and friends encounter difficulties because they cannot strike a balance between license and repression. Usually this failure is linked to sexual avidity, and the resulting dilemmas are played out against a depressing background of vulgar materialism. Updike's overriding theme is that of cultural disintegration, the abrogation of the Protestant ethic.

He is not, however, simply a diagnostician of social ills. His books will endure for their historical accuracy but also as *belles-lettres*—works of art. Although a novelist of the everyday, Updike fashions sparkling metaphors that invest his rather commonplace topics with fresh vitality. This keenness derives also from the striking specificity and exactitude that typify his presentation of sensory detail. He tells the reader not only what to see but what to hear, what to taste, what to smell—a technique that he may have learned from the example of James Joyce. At his best, Updike can evoke a moment as vividly as anyone writing today. And although his content is highly contemporary (including frequent forays into explicitly sexual depiction), he is in many respects a throwback to the nineteenth-century novelists of manners, capturing social nuances while plumbing the depths of his characters' motivations and interrelationships. As the critic Charles Thomas Samuels said, "Updike offers the novel's traditional pleasures."

This selection, the title story from his 1987 short story collection, is an excellent example of Updike at the top of his form.

George J. Searles
Mohawk Valley Community College

PRIMARY WORKS

The Carpentered Hen, 1958; *The Poorhouse Fair,* 1959; *The Same Door,* 1959; *Rabbit, Run,* 1960; *The Magic Flute,* 1962; *Pigeon Feathers,* 1962; *The Centaur,* 1963; *Telephone Poles,* 1963; *Olinger Stories,* 1964; *The Ring,* 1964; *Assorted Prose,* 1965; *A Child's Calendar,* 1965; *Of the Farm,* 1965; *Verse,* 1965; *The Music School,* 1966; *Couples,* 1968; *Bottom's Dream,* 1969; *Midpoint,* 1969; *Bech: A Book,* 1970; *Rabbit Redux,* 1971; *Museums and Women,* 1972; *Buchanan Dying,* 1974; *A Month of Sundays,* 1975; *Picked-Up Pieces,* 1975; *Marry Me,* 1976; *Tossing and Turning,* 1977; *The Coup,* 1978; *Problems,* 1979; *Too Far to Go,* 1979; *Rabbit Is Rich,* 1980; *Bech Is Back,* 1982; *Hugging the Shore,* 1983; *The Witches of Eastwick,* 1984; *Facing Nature,* 1985; *Roger's Version,* 1986; *Trust Me,* 1987; *S.,* 1988; *Just Looking,* 1989; *Self-Consciousness,* 1989; *Rabbit at Rest,* 1990; *Odd Jobs,* 1991; *Memories of the Ford Administration,* 1992; *Collected Poems, 1953-1993,* 1993; *Brazil,* 1994; *The Afterlife and Other Stories,* 1994; *Rabbit Angstrom: The Four Novels,* 1995; *In the Beauty of the Lilies,* 1996; *Golf Dreams: Writings on Golf,* 1996; *A Helpful Alphabet of Friendly Objects,* 1996; *Toward the End of Time,* 1997; *Bech at Bay,* 1998; *More Matter,* 1999; *Gertrude and Claudius,* 2000; *Licks of Love,* 2000; *Americana and Other Poems,* 2001; *Seek My Face,* 2002; *Villages,* 2004; *Still Looking,* 2005; *Terrorist,* 2006; *Due Considerations,* 2007; *The Widows of Eastwick,* 2008.

Trust Me

When Harold was three or four, his father and mother took him to a swimming pool. This was strange, for his family rarely went places, except to the movie house two blocks from their house. Harold had no memory of ever seeing his parents in bathing suits again, after this unhappy day. What he did remember was this:

His father, nearly naked, was in the pool, treading water. Harold was standing shivering on the wet tile edge, suspended above the abysmal odor of chlorine, hypnotized by the bright, lapping agitation of this great volume of unnaturally blue-green water. His mother, in a black bathing suit that made her flesh appear very white, was off in a corner of his mind. His father was asking him to jump. "C'mon, Hassy, jump," he was saying, in his mild, encouraging voice. "It'll be all right. Jump right into my hands." The words echoed in the flat acoustics of the water and tile and sunlight, heightening Harold's sense of exposure, his awareness of his own white skin. His father seemed eerily stable and calm in the water, and the child idly wondered, as he jumped, what the man was standing on.

Then the blue green water was all around him, dense and churning, and when he tried to take a breath a fist was shoved into his throat. He saw his own bubbles rising in front of his face, a multitude of them, rising as he sank; he sank it seemed for a very long time, until something located him in the darkening element and seized him by the arm.

He was in the air again, on his father's shoulder, still fighting for breath. They were out of the pool. His mother swiftly came up to the two of them and, with a deftness remarkable in one so angry, slapped his father on the face, loudly, next to Harold's ear. The slap seemed to resonate all over the pool area, and to be heard by all the other bathers; but perhaps this was the acoustics of memory. His sense of public embarrassment amid sparkling nakedness—of every strange face turned toward him as he passed from his father's wet arms into his mother's dry ones—survived his recovery of breath. His mother's anger seemed directed at him as much as at his father. His feet were now on grass. Standing wrapped in a towel near his mother's knees while the last burning fragments of water were coughed from his lungs, Harold felt eternally disgraced.

He never knew what happened: by the time he asked, so many years had passed that his father had forgotten. "Wasn't that a crying shame," the old man said, with his mild mixture of mournfulness and comedy. "Sink or swim, and you sank." Perhaps Harold had leaped a moment before it was expected, or had proved unexpectedly heavy, and had thus slipped through his father's grasp. Unaccountably, all through his growing up he continued to trust his father; it was his mother he distrusted, her swift sure-handed anger.

He didn't learn to swim until college, and even then he passed the test by frog-kicking the length of the pool on his back, with the instructor brandishing a thick stick to grasp if he panicked and began to sink. The chemical scent of a pool always frightened him: blue-green dragon breath.

His children, raised in an amphibious world of summer camps and country clubs, easily became swimmers. They tried to teach him how to dive. "You must keep your head *down*, Dad. That's why you keep getting belly-whoppers."

"I'm scared of not coming up," he confessed. What he especially did not like, under water, was the sight of bubbles rising around his face.

His first wife dreaded flying. Yet they flew a great deal. "Either that," he told her, "or resign from the twentieth century." They flew to California, and while they were there two planes collided over the Grand Canyon. They flew out of Boston the day after starlings had blocked the engines of an Electra and caused it to crash into the harbor with such force that people were cut in two by their safety belts. They flew over Africa, crossing the equator at night, the land beneath them an inky chasm lit by a few sparks of tribal fire. They landed on dusty runways, with the cabin doors banging. He promised her, her fear was so acute, that she would never have to fly with him again. At last, their final African flight took them up from the Ethiopian Plateau, across the pale width of the Libyan Desert, to the edge of the Mediterranean, and on to Rome.

The Pan Am plane out of Rome was the most comforting possible—a jumbo jet wide as a house, stocked with American magazines and snacks, its walls dribbling music, with only a few passengers. The great plane lifted off, and he relaxed into a *Newsweek,* into the prospect of a meal, a nap, and a homecoming. Harold's wife asked, after ten minutes, "Why aren't we climbing?"

He looked out the window, and it was true—the watery world below them was not diminishing; he could distinctly see small boats and the white tips of breaking waves. The stewardesses were moving up and down the aisle with unusual speed, with unusual expressions on their glamorous faces. Harold looked at the palms of his hands; they had become damp and mottled, as during nausea. However hard he stared, the sea beneath the wings did not fall away. Sun sparkled on its surface; a tiny sailboat tacked.

The pilot's voice crackled into being above them. "Folks, there's a little warning light come on for one of our starboard engines, and in conformance with our policy of absolute security we're going to circle around and return to the Rome airport."

During the bank and return, which seemed to take an extremely long time, the stewardesses buckled themselves into rear seats, the man across the aisle kept reading *L'Osservatore,* and Harold's wife, a faithful student of safety instructions, removed her high-heeled shoes and took the pins out of her hair. So again he marvelled at the deft dynamism of women in crises.

He held her damp hand in his and steadily gazed out of the window, pressing the sea down with his vision, stiff-arming it with his will to live. If he blinked, they would fall. One little boat at a time, the plane edged back to Rome. The blue sea visually interlocked with the calm silver edge of the wing: Olympian surfaces serenely oblivious of the immense tension between them. He had often felt, through one of these scratched oval windows, something falsely reassuring in the elaborate order of the rivets pinning the aluminum sheets together. *Trust me,* the metallic code spelled out; in his heart Harold, like his wife, had refused, and this refusal in him formed a hollow space terror could always flood.

The 747 landed smoothly back in Rome and, after an hour's delay, while mechanics persuaded the warning light to go off, resumed the flight to America. At home, their scare became a story, a joke. He kept his promise, though, that she would never have to fly with him again; within a year, they separated.

During the time of separation Harold seemed to be slinging his children from one rooftop to another, silently begging them to trust him. It was as when, years before, he had adjusted his daughter's braces in her mouth with a needle-nose pliers. She had come to him in pain, a wire gouging the inside of her cheek. But then, with his clumsy fingers in her mouth, her eyes widened with fear of worse pain. He gaily accused her. "You don't trust me." The gaiety of his voice revealed a crucial space, a gap between their situations: it would be his blunder, but her pain. Another's pain is not our own. Religion, he supposed, seeks to close this gap, but each generation's torturers keep it open. Without it, compassion would crush us; the space of indifference is where we breathe. Harold had heard this necessary indifference in the pilot's voice drawling "Folks," and in his father's voice urging "Jump." He heard it in his own reassurances as he bestowed them. "Sweetie, I know you're feeling pressure now, but if you'll just hold *still* . . . there's this little sharp end—oops. Well, you wriggled."

He took his girl friend to the top of a mountain. Harold hadn't had a girl friend for many years and had to relearn the delicate blend of protectiveness and challengingness that is courtship. She was, Priscilla, old enough to have her own children, and old enough to feel fragile on skis. She had spent the day on the baby slope, practicing turns and gradually gaining confidence, while Harold ranged far and wide on the mountain, in the company of her children. As the afternoon drew to an end, he swooped down upon her in a smart spray of snow. She begged him, "Ride the baby chair, so I can show you my snowplow."

"If you can snowplow here, you can come down from the top of the mountain." Harold told her.

"Really?" Her cheeks were pink, from her day on the baby slope. She wore a white knit hat. Her eyes were baby blue.

"Absolutely. We'll come down on the novice trail."

She trusted him. But on the chair lift, as the slope beneath them increased and the windswept iciness of the higher trails became apparent, a tremulous doubt entered into her face, and he realized, with that perversely joyful inner widening the torturer feels, that he had done the wrong thing. The lift rumbled onward, ever higher. "Can I really ski this?" Priscilla asked, with a child's beautiful willingness to be reassured. In the realms of empathy, he was again standing on the edge of that swimming pool. The evil-smelling water was a long way down.

He told her, "You won't be skiing this part. Look at the view. It's gorgeous."

She turned, rigid in the chair as it swayed across a chasm. With obedient eyes she gazed at the infinite blue-green perspectives of wooded mountain and frozen lake. The parking lot below seemed a little platter tessellated with cars. The lift cable irresistibly slithered; the air dropped in temperature. The pines around them had grown stunted and twisted. Mist licked off the ice; they were in the clouds. Priscilla was trembling all over, and at the top could scarcely stand on her skis.

"I can't do it," she announced.

"Do what I do," Harold said. He quickly slid to a few yards below her. "Put your weight first on one ski, then the other. Don't look at the steepness, just think of your weight shifting."

She leaned her weight backward, away from the slope, and fell down. Tears welled in her eyes; he feared they would freeze and make her blind. He gathered all his love into his voice and rolled it toward her, to melt her recalcitrance, her terror. "Just do your snowplow. Don't think about where you are."

"There isn't any snow," she said. "Just ice."

"It's not icy at the edges."

"There are *trees* at the edges."

"Come on, honey. The light's getting flat."

"We'll freeze to death."

"Don't be silly, the ski patrol dusts the trails last thing. Put your weight on your downhill ski and let yourself turn. You *must.* Goddamn it, it's *sim*ple."

"Simple for *you,*" Priscilla said. She followed his directions and began gingerly to slide. She hit a small mogul and fell again. She began to scream. She tried to throw her ski poles, but the straps held them to her wrists. She kicked her feet like an infant in a tantrum, and one ski binding released. "I *hate* you," she cried. "I can't do it, I *can't* do it! I was so *proud* on the baby slope, all I wanted was for you to *watch me*—watch me for one lousy minute, that was all I asked you to do. You *knew* I wasn't ready for this. *Why* did you bring me up here, *why?*"

"I thought you were," he said weakly. "Ready. I wanted to show you the view." His father had wanted to give him the joy of the water, no doubt.

Dusk was coming to the mountain. Teen-aged experts bombed past in an avalanche of heedless color, with occasional curious side-glances. Harold and Priscilla agreed to take off their skis and walk down. It took an hour, and cost him a blister on each heel. The woods around them, perceived at so unusually slow a speed, wore a magical frozen strangeness, the ironical calm of airplane rivets. Her children were waiting at the edge of the emptying parking lot with tears in their eyes. "I tried to give her a treat," he explained to them, "but your mother doesn't trust me."

During this same perilous period, Harold attended his son's seventeenth birthday party, in the house he had left. As he was rushing to catch the evening train that would take him back to his apartment in the city, he noticed a fresh pan of brownies cooling on the stove. This was odd, because birthday cake had already been served. He asked his son, "What are these?"

The boy smiled cherubically. "Hash brownies. Have one, Dad. You can eat it on the train."

"It won't do anything funny to me?"

"Naa. It's just something the other kids cooked up for me as a joke. It's more the idea of it; they won't do anything."

Harold as a child had had a sweet tooth, a taste for starch; he took one of the bigger of the brownies and gobbled it in the car as his son drove him to the railroad station. In the train, he leaned his head against the black glass and entertained the rueful thoughts of a separated man. Slowly he came to realize that his mouth was very dry and his thoughts were not only repeating themselves but had taken on an intense, brightly colored form in his head. They were squeezed one on top of another, like strata of shale, and were vividly polychrome, like campaign ribbons. When he swung down from the train onto the platform of the city station, one side of him had grown much larger than the other, so he had to lean sharply or fall down. His body did not so much support as accompany him, in several laggard sections. Walking in what felt like a procession to the subway entrance, through a throng of hooded strangers and across a street of swollen cars, he reasoned what had happened: he had eaten a hash brownie.

One half of his brain kept shouting prudent advice to the other: *Look both ways. Take out a dollar. No, wait, here's a token. Put it in the slot. Wait for the No. 16, don't take Symphony. Don't panic.* Every process seemed to take a very long time, while his ribbonlike thoughts multiplied and shuttled with the speed of a computer. These thoughts kept adding up to nonsense, the other half of his brain noticed, while it called instructions and congratulations throughout his homeward progress. The people in the subway car stared at him as if they could hear this loud interior conversation going on. But he felt safe behind his face, as if behind a steel mask. Wheels beneath him screeched. A code of colored lights flew past the windows.

He was in the air again, walking the three blocks from the subway to his apartment. Something in his throat burned. He felt nauseated, and kept selecting hedges and trash cans to vomit in, if it came to that, which it did not, quite. It seemed the confirmation of a gigantically abstruse theorem that his key fit in the lock of his door and that beyond the door lay a room full of dazzlingly familiar furniture. He picked up the telephone, which had the sheen and two-dimensional largeness of an image on a billboard, and called Priscilla.

"Hi, love."

Her voice rose in pitch. "What's happened to you, Harold?"

"Do I sound different?"

"Very." Her voice was sharp as porcupine quills, black and white tips. "What did they do to you?" *They*—his children, his ex-wife.

"They fed me a hash brownie. Jimmy said I wouldn't feel anything, but on the train in, my thoughts got very little and intense, and on the way from the station I had to keep coaching myself on how to get from there to here." The protective, trustworthy half of his brain congratulated him on how cogent he sounded.

But something was displeasing to Priscilla. She cried, "Oh, that's disgusting! I don't think it's funny, I don't think *any* of you are funny."

"Any of who?"

"You know who."

"I don't." Though he did. He looked at his palms; they were mottled. "Sweetie, I feel like throwing up. Help me."

"I can't," Priscilla said, and hung up. The click sounded like a slap, the same echoing slap that had once exploded next to his ear. Except that his father had become his son, and his mother was his girl friend. This much remained true: it had not been his fault, and in surviving he was somehow blamed.

The palms of his hands, less mottled, looked pale and wrinkled, like uncomfortable pillows. In his shirt pocket Harold found tucked the dollar bill rejected at the subway turnstile, extremely long ago. While waiting for Priscilla to relent and call back, he turned to its back side, examined the mystical eye above the truncated pyramid, and read, over and over, the slogan printed above the ONE.

1979

Ernest J. Gaines b. 1933

Ernest J. Gaines was born in Pointe Coupee Parish on "The Quarters" of River Lake Plantation, a few miles from New Roads, Louisiana. "Until I was fifteen years old," Gaines recounts, "I had been raised by an aunt, Miss Augusteen Jefferson, a lady who had never walked a day in her life," but who, as he says in the dedication to *The Autobiography of Miss Jane Pittman,* "taught me the importance of standing." As a boy Gaines worked in the cane fields "where all my people before me worked."

In 1948 Gaines left Louisiana to join his mother and stepfather in Vallejo, California. There, as a teenager, he began to "read all the Southern writers I could find in the Vallejo library; then I began to read any writer who wrote about nature or about people who worked the land—anyone who would say something about dirt and trees, clear streams, and open sky." After a two-year stint in the army Gaines took his B.A. degree from San Francisco State College in 1957. He then won a Wallace Stegner Creative Writing Fellowship at Stanford and also received the Joseph Henry Jackson Literary Award there in 1959.

Gaines's novels and short fiction are set in an imaginary Louisiana that evokes and re-creates the world of his childhood and the changes he has observed on his many returns to Louisiana. Although he has a drawer full of San Francisco-inspired fiction, Gaines's published work is exclusively about Louisiana. "I wanted," he says of his intention as a writer, "to smell that Louisiana earth, feel that Louisiana sun, sit under the shade of one of those Louisiana oaks, search for pecans in that Louisiana grass in one of those Louisiana yards next to one of those Louisiana bayous, not far from a Louisiana river. I wanted to see on paper those Louisiana black children walking to school on cold days while yellow Louisiana buses passed them by. I wanted to see on paper those black parents going to work before the sun came up and coming back home to look after their children after the sun went down. I wanted to see on paper the true reason why those black fathers left home—not because they were trifling or shiftless—but because they were tired of putting up with certain conditions. I wanted to see on paper the small country churches (schools during the week), and I wanted to hear those simple religious songs, those simple prayers—that true devotion. (It was Faulkner, I think, who said that if God were to stay alive in the country, the blacks would have to keep Him so.) And I wanted to hear that Louisiana dialect—that combination of English, Creole, Cajun, Black. For me there's no more beautiful sound anywhere."

Through the act of writing Gaines re-experiences Louisiana. Once there in imagination, he puts on paper the historical but alterable society which exists in the midst of nature's abiding reality. The instrument behind the passage of the spoken word to the page is the writer's healing human voice. Like his storytellers, Gaines breaks down the barriers between his voice and the voices of his characters. As a writer for his people, Gaines keeps faith with the oral tradition—a tradition of responsibility and change, and, despite violent opposition, a tradition of citizenship.

"The Sky Is Gray" and the other stories in Gaines's *Bloodline* mediate two complementary facts of life: first, that very little changes in his remote parish between the Civil War and his departure after World War II; and, second, that even rural Louisiana could not resist the racial upheaval of the 1950s and 1960s. According to Gaines's speech-driven donnée of fiction, for the writer to be free, his characters must be free, and an independent, individual voice is the first test of freedom.

John F. Callahan
Lewis and Clark College

PRIMARY WORKS

Catherine Carmier, 1964; *Of Love and Dust,* 1967; *Bloodline,* 1968; *The Autobiography of Miss Jane Pittman,* 1971; *In My Father's House,* 1978; *A Gathering of Old Men,* 1983; *A Lesson Before Dying,* 1993; *Mozart and Leadbelly,* 2005.

The Sky Is Gray

1

Go'n be coming in a few minutes. Coming round that bend down there full speed. And I'm go'n get out my handkerchief and wave it down, and we go'n get on it and go.

I keep on looking for it, but Mama don't look that way no more. She's looking down the road where we just come from. It's a long old road, and far 's you can see you don't see nothing but gravel. You got dry weeds on both sides, and you got trees on both sides, and fences on both sides, too. And you got cows in the pastures and they standing close together. And when we was coming out here to catch the bus I seen the smoke coming out of the cows' noses.

I look at my mama and I know what she's thinking. I been with Mama so much, just me and her, I know what she's thinking all the time. Right now it's home—Auntie and them. She's thinking if they got enough wood—if she left enough there to keep them warm till we get back. She's thinking if it go'n rain and if any of them go'n have to go out in the rain. She's thinking 'bout the hog—if he go'n get out, and if Ty and Val be able to get him back in. She always worry like that when she leaves the house. She don't worry too much if she leave me there with the smaller ones, 'cause she know I'm go'n look after them and look after Auntie and everything else. I'm the oldest and she say I'm the man.

I look at my mama and I love my mama. She's wearing that black coat and that black hat and she's looking sad. I love my mama and I want put my arm round her and tell her. But I'm not supposed to do that. She say that's weakness and that's cry-baby stuff, and she don't want no crybaby round her. She don't want you to be scared, either. 'Cause Ty's scared of ghosts and she's always whipping him. I'm scared of the dark, too, but I make 'tend I ain't. I make 'tend I ain't 'cause I'm the oldest, and I got to set a good sample for the rest. I can't ever be scared and I can't ever cry. And that's why I never said nothing 'bout my teeth. It's been hurting me and hurting me close to a month now, but I never said it. I didn't say it 'cause I didn't want act like a crybaby, and 'cause I know we didn't have enough money to go have it pulled. But, Lord, it been hurting me. And look like it wouldn't start till at night when you was trying to get yourself little sleep. Then soon 's you shut your eyes—ummm-ummm, Lord, look like it go right down to your heartstring.

"Hurting, hanh?" Ty'd say.

I'd shake my head, but I wouldn't open my mouth for nothing. You open your mouth and let that wind in, and it almost kill you.

I'd just lay there and listen to them snore. Ty there, right 'side me, and Auntie and Val over by the fireplace. Val younger than me and Ty, and he sleeps with Auntie. Mama sleeps round the other side with Louis and Walker.

I'd just lay there and listen to them, and listen to that wind out there, and listen to that fire in the fireplace. Sometimes it'd stop long enough to let me get little rest. Sometimes it just hurt, hurt, hurt. Lord, have mercy.

2

Auntie knowed it was hurting me. I didn't tell nobody but Ty, 'cause we buddies and he ain't go'n tell nobody. But some kind of way Auntie found out. When she asked me, I told her no, nothing was wrong. But she knowed it all the time. She told me to mash up a piece of aspirin and wrap it in some cotton and jugg it down in that hole. I did it, but it didn't do no good. It stopped for a little while, and started right back again. Auntie wanted to tell Mama, but I told her, "Uh-uh." 'Cause I knowed we didn't have any money, and it just was go'n make her mad again. So Auntie told Monsieur Bayonne, and Monsieur Bayonne came over to the house and told me to kneel down 'side him on the fireplace. He put his finger in his mouth and made the Sign of the Cross on my jaw. The tip of Monsieur Bayonne's finger is some hard, 'cause he's always playing on that guitar. If we sit outside at night we can always hear Monsieur Bayonne playing on his guitar. Sometimes we leave him out there playing on the guitar.

Monsieur Bayonne made the Sign of the Cross over and over on my jaw, but that didn't do no good. Even when he prayed and told me to pray some, too, that tooth still hurt me.

"How you feeling?" he say.

"Same," I say.

He kept on praying and making the Sign of the Cross and I kept on praying, too.

"Still hurting?" he say.

"Yes, sir."

Monsieur Bayonne mashed harder and harder on my jaw. He mashed so hard he almost pushed me over on Ty. But then he stopped.

"What kind of prayers you praying, boy?" he say.

"Baptist," I say.

"Well, I'll be—no wonder that tooth still killing him. I'm going one way and he pulling the other. Boy, don't you know any Catholic prayers?"

"I know 'Hail Mary,'" I say.

"Then you better start saying it."

"Yes, sir."

He started mashing on my jaw again, and I could hear him praying at the same time. And, sure enough, after while it stopped hurting me.

Me and Ty went outside where Monsieur Bayonne's two hounds was and we started playing with them. "Let's go hunting," Ty say. "All right," I say; and we went on back in the pasture. Soon the hounds got on a trail, and me and Ty followed them all 'cross the pasture and then back in the woods, too. And then they cornered this little old rabbit and killed him, and me and Ty made them get back, and we picked up the rabbit and started on back home. But my tooth had started hurting me again.

It was hurting me plenty now, but I wouldn't tell Monsieur Bayonne. That night I didn't sleep a bit, and first thing in the morning Auntie told me to go back and let Monsieur Bayonne pray over me some more. Monsieur Bayonne was in his kitchen making coffee when I got there. Soon 's he seen me he knowed what was wrong.

"All right, kneel down there 'side that stove," he say. "And this time make sure you pray Catholic. I don't know nothing 'bout that Baptist, and I don't want know nothing 'bout him."

3

Last night Mama say, "Tomorrow we going to town."

"It ain't hurting me no more," I say. "I can eat anything on it."

"Tomorrow we going to town," she say.

And after she finished eating, she got up and went to bed. She always go to bed early now. 'Fore Daddy went in the Army, she used to stay up late. All of us sitting out on the gallery or round the fire. But now, look like soon 's she finish eating she go to bed.

This morning when I woke up, her and Auntie was standing 'fore the fireplace. She say: "Enough to get there and get back. Dollar and a half to have it pulled. Twenty-five for me to go, twenty-five for him. Twenty-five for me to come back, twenty-five for him. Fifty cents left. Guess I get little piece of salt meat with that."

"Sure can use it," Auntie say. "White beans and no salt meat ain't white beans."

"I do the best I can," Mama say.

They was quiet after that, and I made 'tend I was still asleep.

"James, hit the floor," Auntie say.

I still made 'tend I was asleep. I didn't want them to know I was listening.

"All right," Auntie say, shaking me by the shoulder. "Come on. Today's the day."

I pushed the cover down to get out, and Ty grabbed it and pulled it back.

"You, too, Ty," Auntie say.

"I ain't getting no teef pulled," Ty say.

"Don't mean it ain't time to get up," Auntie say. "Hit it, Ty."

Ty got up grumbling.

"James, you hurry up and get in your clothes and eat your food," Auntie say. "What time y'all coming back?" she say to Mama.

"That 'leven o'clock bus," Mama say. "Got to get back in that field this evening."

"Get a move on you, James," Auntie say.

I went in the kitchen and washed my face, then I ate my breakfast. I was having bread and syrup. The bread was warm and hard and tasted good. And I tried to make it last a long time.

Ty came back there grumbling and mad at me.

"Got to get up," he say. "I ain't having no teefes pulled. What I got to be getting up for?"

Ty poured some syrup in his pan and got a piece of bread. He didn't wash his hands, neither his face, and I could see that white stuff in his eyes.

"You the one getting your teef pulled," he say. "What I got to get up for. I bet if I was getting a teef pulled, you wouldn't be getting up. Shucks; syrup again. I'm getting tired of this old syrup. Syrup, syrup, syrup. I'm go'n take with the sugar diabetes. I want me some bacon sometime."

"Go out in the field and work and you can have your bacon," Auntie say. She stood in the middle door looking at Ty. "You better be glad you got syrup. Some people ain't got that—hard 's time is."

"Shucks," Ty say. "How can I be strong."

"I don't know too much 'bout your strength," Auntie say; "but I know where you go'n be hot at, you keep that grumbling up. James, get a move on you; your mama waiting."

I ate my last piece of bread and went in the front room. Mama was standing 'fore the fireplace warming her hands. I put on my coat and my cap, and we left the house.

4

I look down there again, but it still ain't coming. I almost say, "It ain't coming yet," but I keep my mouth shut. 'Cause that's something else she don't like. She don't like for you to say something just for nothing. She can see it ain't coming, I can see it ain't coming, so why say it ain't coming. I don't say it, I turn and look at the river that's back of us. It's so cold the smoke's just raising up from the water. I see a bunch of pool-doos not too far out—just on the other side the lilies. I'm wondering if you can eat pool-doos. I ain't too sure, 'cause I ain't never ate none. But I done ate owls and blackbirds, and I done ate redbirds, too. I didn't want kill the redbirds, but she made me kill them. They had two of them back there. One in my trap, one in Ty's trap. Me and Ty was go'n play with them and let them go, but she made me kill them 'cause we needed the food.

"I can't," I say. "I can't."

"Here," she say. "Take it."

"I can't," I say. "I can't. I can't kill him, Mama, please."

"Here," she say. "Take this fork, James."

"Please, Mama, I can't kill him," I say.

I could tell she was go'n hit me. I jerked back, but I didn't jerk back soon enough.

"Take it," she say.

I took it and reached in for him, but he kept on hopping to the back.

"I can't, Mama," I say. The water just kept on running down my face. "I can't," I say.

"Get him out of there," she say.

I reached in for him and he kept on hopping to the back. Then I reached in farther, and he pecked me on the hand.

"I can't, Mama," I say.

She slapped me again.

I reached in again, but he kept on hopping out my way. Then he hopped to one side and I reached there. The fork got him on the leg and I heard his leg pop. I pulled my hand out 'cause I had hurt him.

"Give it here," she say, and jerked the fork out my hand.

She reached in and got the little bird right in the neck. I heard the fork go in his neck, and I heard it go in the ground. She brought him out and helt him right in front of me.

"That's one," she say. She shook him off and gived me the fork. "Get the other one."

"I can't, Mama," I say. "I'll do anything, but don't make me do that."

She went to the corner of the fence and broke the biggest switch over there she could find. I knelt 'side the trap, crying.

"Get him out of there," she say.

"I can't, Mama."

She started hitting me 'cross the back. I went down on the ground, crying.

"Get him," she say.

"Octavia?" Auntie say.

'Cause she had come out of the house and she was standing by the tree looking at us.

"Get him out of there," Mama say.

"Octavia," Auntie say, "explain to him. Explain to him. Just don't beat him. Explain to him."

But she hit me and hit me and hit me.

I'm still young—I ain't no more than eight; but I know now; I know why I had to do it. (They was so little though. They was so little. I 'member how I picked the feathers off them and cleaned them and helt them over the fire. Then we all ate them. Ain't had but a little bitty piece each, but we all had a little bitty piece, and everybody just looked at me 'cause they was so proud.) Suppose she had to go away? That's why I had to do it. Suppose she had to go away like Daddy went away? Then who was go'n look after us? They had to be somebody left to carry on. I didn't know it then, but I know it now. Auntie and Monsieur Bayonne talked to me and made me see.

5

Time I see it I get out my handkerchief and start waving. It's still 'way down there, but I keep waving anyhow. Then it come up and stop and me and Mama get on. Mama tell me go sit in the back while she pay. I do like she say, and the people look at me. When I pass the little sign that say "White" and "Colored," I start looking for a seat. I just see one of them back there, but I don't take it, 'cause I want my mama to sit down herself. She comes in the back and sit down, and I lean on the seat. They got seats in the front, but I know I can't sit there, 'cause I have to sit back of the sign. Anyhow, I don't want sit there if my mama go'n sit back here.

They got a lady sitting 'side my mama and she looks at me and smiles little bit. I smile back, but I don't open my mouth, 'cause the wind'll get in and make that tooth ache. The lady take out a pack of gum and reach me a slice, but I shake my head. The lady just can't understand why a little boy'll turn down gum, and she reach me a slice again. This time I point to my jaw. The lady understands and smiles little bit, and I smile little bit, but I don't open my mouth, though.

They got a girl sitting 'cross from me. She got on a red overcoat and her hair's plaited in one big plait. First, I make 'tend I don't see her over there, but then I start looking at her little bit. She make 'tend she don't see me, either, but I catch her looking that way. She got a cold, and every now and then she h'ist that little handkerchief to her nose. She ought to blow it, but she don't. Must think she's too much a lady or something.

Every time she h'ist that little handkerchief, the lady 'side her say something in her ear. She shakes her head and lays her hands in her lap again. Then I catch her kind of looking where I'm at. I smile at her little bit. But think she'll smile back? Uh-uh. She just turn up her little old nose and turn her head. Well, I show her both of us can turn us head. I turn mine too and look out at the river.

The river is gray. The sky is gray. They have pool-doos on the water. The water is wavy, and the pool-doos go up and down. The bus go round a turn, and you got plenty trees hiding the river. Then the bus go round another turn, and I can see the river again.

I look toward the front where all the white people sitting. Then I look at that little old gal again. I don't look right at her, 'cause I don't want all them people to know I love her. I just look at her little bit, like I'm looking out that window over there. But she knows I'm looking that way, and she kind of look at me, too. The lady sitting 'side her catch her this time, and she leans over and says something in her ear.

"I don't love him nothing," that little old gal says out loud.

Everybody back there hear her mouth, and all of them look at us and laugh.

"I don't love you, either," I say. "So you don't have to turn up your nose, Miss."

"You the one looking," she say.

"I wasn't looking at you," I say. "I was looking out that window, there."

"Out that window, my foot," she say. "I seen you. Everytime I turned round you was looking at me."

"You must of been looking yourself if you seen me all them times," I say.

"Shucks," she say, "I got me all kind of boyfriends."

"I got girlfriends, too," I say.

"Well, I just don't want you getting your hopes up," she say.

I don't say no more to that little old gal 'cause I don't want have to bust her in the mouth. I lean on the seat where Mama sitting, and I don't even look that way no more. When we get to Bayonne, she jugg her little old tongue out at me. I make 'tend I'm go'n hit her, and she duck down 'side her mama. And all the people laugh at us again.

6

Me and Mama get off and start walking in town. Bayonne is a little bitty town. Baton Rouge is a hundred times bigger than Bayonne. I went to Baton Rouge once—me, Ty, Mama, and Daddy. But that was 'way back yonder, 'fore Daddy went in the Army. I wonder when we go'n see him again. I wonder when. Look like he ain't ever coming back home. . . . Even the pavement all cracked in Bayonne. Got grass shooting right out the sidewalk. Got weeds in the ditch, too; just like they got at home.

It's some cold in Bayonne. Look like it's colder than it is home. The wind blows in my face, and I feel that stuff running down my nose. I sniff. Mama says use that handkerchief. I blow my nose and put it back.

We pass a school and I see them white children playing in the yard. Big old red school, and them children just running and playing. Then we pass a café, and I see a bunch of people in there eating. I wish I was in there 'cause I'm cold. Mama tells me keep my eyes in front where they belong.

We pass stores that's got dummies, and we pass another café, and then we pass a shoe shop, and that bald-head man in there fixing on a shoe. I look at him and I butt into that white lady, and Mama jerks me in front and tells me stay there.

We come up to the courthouse, and I see the flag waving there. This flag ain't like the one we got at school. This one here ain't got but a handful of stars.[1] One at school got a big pile of stars—one for every state. We pass it and we turn and there it is—the dentist office. Me and Mama go in, and they got people sitting everywhere you look. They even got a little boy in there younger than me.

Me and Mama sit on that bench, and a white lady come in there and ask me what my name is. Mama tells her and the white lady goes on back. Then I hear somebody hollering in there. Soon 's that little boy hear him hollering, he starts hollering, too. His mama pats him and pats him, trying to make him hush up, but he ain't thinking 'bout his mama.

The man that was hollering in there comes out holding his jaw. He is a big old man and he's wearing overalls and a jumper.

"Got it, hanh?" another man asks him.

The man shakes his head—don't want open his mouth.

"Man, I thought they was killing you in there," the other man says. "Hollering like a pig under a gate."

The man don't say nothing. He just heads for the door, and the other man follows him.

"John Lee," the white lady says. "John Lee Williams."

The little boy juggs his head down in his mama's lap and holler more now. His mama tells him go with the nurse, but he ain't thinking 'bout his mama. His mama tells him again, but he don't even hear her. His mama picks him up and takes him in there, and even when the white lady shuts the door I can still hear little old John Lee.

"I often wonder why the Lord let a child like that suffer," a lady says to my mama. The lady's sitting right in front of us on another bench. She's got on a white dress and a black sweater. She must be a nurse or something herself, I reckon.

"Not us to question," a man says.

"Sometimes I don't know if we shouldn't," the lady says.

"I know definitely we shouldn't," the man says. The man looks like a preacher. He's big and fat and he's got on a black suit. He's got a gold chain, too.

"Why?" the lady says.

"Why anything?" the preacher says.

"Yes," the lady says. "Why anything?"

"Not us to question," the preacher says.

The lady looks at the preacher a little while and looks at Mama again.

---

[1] Up through the 1940s and beyond, the Confederate flag with its stars and bars was displayed outside public schools, courthouses, and other official buildings in many southern states.

"And look like it's the poor who suffers the most," she says. "I don't understand it."

"Best not to even try," the preacher says. "He works in mysterious ways— wonders to perform."

Right then little John Lee bust out hollering, and everybody turn they head to listen.

"He's not a good dentist," the lady says. "Dr. Robillard is much better. But more expensive. That's why most of the colored people come here. The white people go to Dr. Robillard. Y'all from Bayonne?"

"Down the river," my mama says. And that's all she go'n say, 'cause she don't talk much. But the lady keeps on looking at her, and so she says, "Near Morgan."

"I see," the lady says.

7

"That's the trouble with the black people in this country today," somebody else says. This one here's sitting on the same side me and Mama's sitting, and he is kind of sitting in front of that preacher. He looks like a teacher or somebody that goes to college. He's got on a suit, and he's got a book that he's been reading. "We don't question is exactly our problem," he says. "We should question and question and question—question everything."

The preacher just looks at him a long time. He done put a toothpick or something in his mouth, and he just keeps on turning it and turning it. You can see he don't like that boy with that book.

"Maybe you can explain what you mean," he says.

"I said what I meant," the boy says. "Question everything. Every stripe, every star, every word spoken. Everything."

"It 'pears to me that this young lady and I was talking 'bout God, young man," the preacher says.

"Question Him, too," the boy says.

"Wait," the preacher says. "Wait now."

"You heard me right," the boy says. "His existence as well as everything else. Everything."

The preacher just looks across the room at the boy. You can see he's getting madder and madder. But mad or no mad, the boy ain't thinking 'bout him. He looks at that preacher just 's hard 's the preacher looks at him.

"Is this what they coming to?" the preacher says. "Is this what we educating them for?"

"You're not educating me," the boy says. "I wash dishes at night so that I can go to school in the day. So even the words you spoke need questioning."

The preacher just looks at him and shakes his head.

"When I come in this room and seen you there with your book, I said to myself, 'There's an intelligent man.' How wrong a person can be."

"Show me one reason to believe in the existence of a God," the boy says.

"My heart tells me," the preacher says.

"'My heart tells me,'" the boy says. "'My heart tells me.' Sure, 'My heart tells me.' And as long as you listen to what your heart tells you, you will have only what the white man gives you and nothing more. Me, I don't listen to my heart. The purpose of the heart is to pump blood throughout the body, and nothing else."

"Who's your paw, boy?" the preacher says.

"Why?"

"Who is he?"

"He's dead."

"And your mom?"

"She's in Charity Hospital with pneumonia. Half killed herself, working for nothing."

"And 'cause he's dead and she's sick, you mad at the world?"

"I'm not mad at the world. I'm questioning the world. I'm questioning it with cold logic, sir. What do words like Freedom, Liberty, God, White, Colored mean? I want to know. That's why *you* are sending us to school, to read and to ask questions. And because we ask these questions, you call us mad. No sir, it is not us who are mad."

"You keep saying 'us'?"

"'Us.' Yes—us. I'm not alone."

The preacher just shakes his head. Then he looks at everybody in the room—everybody. Some of the people look down at the floor, keep from looking at him. I kind of look 'way myself, but soon 's I know he done turn his head, I look that way again.

"I'm sorry for you," he says to the boy.

"Why?" the boy says. "Why not be sorry for yourself? Why are you so much better off than I am? Why aren't you sorry for these other people in here? Why not be sorry for the lady who had to drag her child into the dentist office? Why not be sorry for the lady sitting on that bench over there? Be sorry for them. Not for me. Some way or other I'm going to make it."

"No, I'm sorry for you," the preacher says.

"Of course, of course," the boy says, nodding his head. "You're sorry for me because I rock that pillar you're leaning on."

"You can't ever rock the pillar I'm leaning on, young man. It's stronger than anything man can ever do."

"You believe in God because a man told you to believe in God," the boy says. "A white man told you to believe in God. And why? To keep you ignorant so he can keep his feet on your neck."

"So now we the ignorant?" the preacher says.

"Yes," the boy says. "Yes." And he opens his book again.

The preacher just looks at him sitting there. The boy done forgot all about him. Everybody else make 'tend they done forgot the squabble, too.

Then I see that preacher getting up real slow. Preacher's a great big old man and he got to brace himself to get up. He comes over where the boy is sitting. He just stands there a little while looking down at him, but the boy don't raise his head.

"Get up, boy," preacher says.

The boy looks up at him, then he shuts his book real slow and stands up. Preacher just hauls back and hit him in the face. The boy falls back 'gainst the wall, but he straightens himself up and looks right back at that preacher.

"You forgot the other cheek," he says.

The preacher hauls back and hit him again on the other side. But this time the boy braces himself and don't fall.

"That hasn't changed a thing," he says.

The preacher just looks at the boy. The preacher's breathing real hard like he just run up a big hill. The boy sits down and opens his book again.

"I feel sorry for you," the preacher says. "I never felt so sorry for a man before."

The boy makes 'tend he don't even hear that preacher. He keeps on reading his book. The preacher goes back and gets his hat off the chair.

"Excuse me," he says to us. "I'll come back some other time. Y'all, please excuse me."

And he looks at the boy and goes out the room. The boy h'ist his hand up to his mouth one time to wipe 'way some blood. All the rest of the time he keeps on reading. And nobody else in there say a word.

8

Little John Lee and his mama come out the dentist office, and the nurse calls somebody else in. Then little bit later they come out, and the nurse calls another name. But fast 's she calls somebody in there, somebody else comes in the place where we sitting, and the room stays full.

The people coming in now, all of them wearing big coats. One of them says something 'bout sleeting, another one says he hope not. Another one says he think it ain't nothing but rain. 'Cause, he says, rain can get awful cold this time of year.

All round the room they talking. Some of them talking to people right by them, some of them talking to people clear 'cross the room, some of them talking to anybody'll listen. It's a little bitty room, no bigger than us kitchen, and I can see everybody in there. The little old room's full of smoke, 'cause you got two old men smoking pipes over by that side door. I think I feel my tooth thumping me some, and I hold my breath and wait. I wait and wait, but it don't thump me no more. Thank God for that.

I feel like going to sleep, and I lean back 'gainst the wall. But I'm scared to go to sleep. Scared 'cause the nurse might call my name and I won't hear her. And Mama might go to sleep, too, and she'll be mad if neither one of us heard the nurse.

I look up at Mama. I love my mama. I love my mama. And when cotton come I'm go'n get her a new coat. And I ain't go'n get a black one, either. I think I'm go'n get her a red one.

"They got some books over there," I say. "Want read one of them?"

Mama looks at the books, but she don't answer me.

"You got yourself a little man there," the lady says.

Mama don't say nothing to the lady, but she must've smiled, 'cause I seen the lady smiling back. The lady looks at me a little while, like she's feeling sorry for me.

"You sure got that preacher out here in a hurry," she says to that boy.

The boy looks up at her and looks in his book again. When I grow up I want be just like him. I want clothes like that and I want keep a book with me, too.

"You really don't believe in God?" the lady says.

"No," he says.

"But why?" the lady says.

"Because the wind is pink," he says.

"What?" the lady says.

The boy don't answer her no more. He just reads in his book.

"Talking 'bout the wind is pink," that old lady says. She's sitting on the same bench with the boy and she's trying to look in his face. The boy makes 'tend the old lady ain't even there. He just keeps on reading. "Wind is pink," she says again. "Eh, Lord, what children go'n be saying next?"

The lady 'cross from us bust out laughing.

"That's a good one," she says. "The wind is pink. Yes sir, that's a good one."

"Don't you believe the wind is pink?" the boy says. He keeps his head down in the book.

"Course I believe it, honey," the lady says. "Course I do." She looks at us and winks her eye. "And what color is grass, honey?"

"Grass? Grass is black."

She bust out laughing again. The boy looks at her.

"Don't you believe grass is black?" he says.

The lady quits her laughing and looks at him. Everybody else looking at him, too. The place quiet, quiet.

"Grass is green, honey," the lady says. "It was green yesterday, it's green today, and it's go'n be green tomorrow."

"How do you know it's green?"

"I know because I know."

"You don't know it's green," the boy says. "You believe it's green because someone told you it was green. If someone had told you it was black you'd believe it was black."

"It's green," the lady says. "I know green when I see green."

"Prove it's green," the boy says.

"Sure, now," the lady says. "Don't tell me it's coming to that."

"It's coming to just that," the boy says. "Words mean nothing. One means no more than the other."

"That's what it all coming to?" that old lady says. That old lady got on a turban and she got on two sweaters. She got a green sweater under a black sweater. I can see the green sweater 'cause some of the buttons on the other sweater's missing.

"Yes ma'am," the boy says. "Words mean nothing. Action is the only thing. Doing. That's the only thing."

"Other words, you want the Lord to come down here and show Hisself to you?" she says.

"Exactly, ma'am," he says.

"You don't mean that, I'm sure?" she says.

"I do, ma'am," he says.

"Done, Jesus," the old lady says, shaking her head.

"I didn't go 'long with that preacher at first," the other lady says; "but now—I don't know. When a person say the grass is black, he's either a lunatic or something's wrong."

"Prove to me that it's green," the boy says.

"It's green because the people say it's green."

"Those same people say we're citizens of these United States," the boy says.

"I think I'm a citizen," the lady says.

"Citizens have certain rights," the boy says. "Name me one right that you have. One right, granted by the Constitution, that you can exercise in Bayonne."

The lady don't answer him. She just looks at him like she don't know what he's talking 'bout. I know I don't.

"Things changing," she says.

"Things are changing because some black men have begun to think with their brains and not their hearts," the boy says.

"You trying to say these people don't believe in God?"

"I'm sure some of them do. Maybe most of them do. But they don't believe that God is going to touch these white people's hearts and change things tomorrow. Things change through action. By no other way."

Everybody sit quiet and look at the boy. Nobody says a thing. Then the lady 'cross the room from me and Mama just shakes her head.

"Let's hope that not all your generation feel the same way you do," she says.

"Think what you please, it doesn't matter," the boy says. "But it will be men who listen to their heads and not their hearts who will see that your children have a better chance than you had."

"Let's hope they ain't all like you, though," the old lady says. "Done forgot the heart absolutely."

"Yes ma'am, I hope they aren't all like me," the boy says. "Unfortunately, I was born too late to believe in your God. Let's hope that the ones who come after will have your faith—if not in your God, then in something else, something definitely that they can lean on. I haven't anything. For me, the wind is pink, the grass is black."

9

The nurse comes in the room where we all sitting and waiting and says the doctor won't take no more patients till one o'clock this evening. My mama jumps up off the bench and goes up to the white lady.

"Nurse, I have to go back in the field this evening," she says.

"The doctor is treating his last patient now," the nurse says. "One o'clock this evening."

"Can I at least speak to the doctor?" my mama asks.

"I'm his nurse," the lady says.

"My little boy's sick," my mama says. "Right now his tooth almost killing him."

The nurse looks at me. She's trying to make up her mind if to let me come in. I look at her real pitiful. The tooth ain't hurting me at all, but Mama say it is, so I make 'tend for her sake.

"This evening," the nurse says, and goes on back in the office.

"Don't feel 'jected, honey," the lady says to Mama. "I been round them a long time—they take you when they want to. If you was white, that's something else; but we the wrong color."

Mama don't say nothing to the lady, and me and her go outside and stand 'gainst the wall. It's cold out there. I can feel that wind going through my coat. Some of the other people come out of the room and go up the street. Me and Mama stand there a little while and we start walking. I don't know where we going. When we come to the other street we just stand there.

"You don't have to make water, do you?" Mama says.

"No, ma'am," I say.

We go on up the street. Walking real slow. I can tell Mama don't know where she's going. When we come to a store we stand there and look at the dummies. I look at a little boy wearing a brown overcoat. He's got on brown shoes, too. I look at my old shoes and look at his'n again. You wait till summer, I say.

Me and Mama walk away. We come up to another store and we stop and look at them dummies, too. Then we go on again. We pass a café where the white people in there eating. Mama tells me keep my eyes in front where they belong, but I can't help from seeing them people eat. My stomach starts to growling 'cause I'm hungry. When I see people eating, I get hungry; when I see a coat, I get cold.

A man whistles at my mama when we go by a filling station. She makes 'tend she don't even see him. I look back and I feel like hitting him in the mouth. If I was bigger, I say; if I was bigger, you'd see.

We keep on going. I'm getting colder and colder, but I don't say nothing. I feel that stuff running down my nose and I sniff.

"That rag," Mama says.

I get it out and wipe my nose. I'm getting cold all over now—my face, my hands, my feet, everything. We pass another little café, but this'n for white people, too, and we can't go in there, either. So we just walk. I'm so cold now I'm 'bout ready to say it. If I knowed where we was going I wouldn't be so cold, but I don't know where we going. We go, we go, we go. We walk clean out of Bayonne. Then we cross the street and we come back. Same thing I seen when I got off the bus this morning. Same old trees, same old walk, same old weeds, same old cracked pave—same old everything.

I sniff again.

"That rag," Mama says.

I wipe my nose real fast and jugg that handkerchief back in my pocket 'fore my hand gets too cold. I raise my head and I can see David's hardware store. When we come up to it, we go in. I don't know why, but I'm glad.

It's warm in there. It's so warm in there you don't ever want to leave. I look for the heater, and I see it over by them barrels. Three white men standing round the heater talking in Creole. One of them comes over to see what my mama want.

"Got any axe handles?" she says.

Me, Mama and the white man start to the back, but Mama stops me when we come up to the heater. She and the white man go on. I hold my hands over the heater and look at them. They go all the way to the back, and I see the white man pointing to the axe handles 'gainst the wall. Mama takes one of them and shakes it like she's trying to figure how much it weighs. Then she rubs her hand over it from one end to the other end. She turns it over and looks at the other side, then she shakes it again, and shakes her head and puts it back. She gets another one and she does it just like she did the first one, then she shakes her head. Then she gets a brown one and do it that, too. But she don't like this one, either. Then she gets another one, but 'fore she shakes it or anything, she looks at me. Look like she's trying to say something to me, but I don't know what it is. All I know is I done got warm now and I'm feeling right smart better. Mama shakes this axe handle just like she did the others, and shakes her head and says something to the white man. The white man just looks at his pile of axe handles, and when Mama pass him to come to the front, the white man just scratch his head and follows her. She tells me come on and we go on out and start walking again.

We walk and walk, and no time at all I'm cold again. Look like I'm colder now 'cause I can still remember how good it was back there. My stomach growls and I suck it in to keep Mama from hearing it. She's walking right 'side me, and it growls so loud you can hear it a mile. But Mama don't say a word.

10

When we come up to the courthouse, I look at the clock. It's got quarter to twelve. Mean we got another hour and a quarter to be out here in the cold. We go and stand 'side a building. Something hits my cap and I look up at the sky. Sleet's falling.

I look at Mama standing there. I want stand close 'side her, but she don't like that. She say that's crybaby stuff. She say you got to stand for yourself, by yourself.

"Let's go back to that office," she says.

We cross the street. When we get to the dentist office I try to open the door, but I can't. I twist and twist, but I can't. Mama pushes me to the side and she twist the knob, but she can't open the door, either. She turns 'way from the door. I look at her, but I don't move and I don't say nothing. I done seen her like this before and I'm scared of her.

"You hungry?" she says. She says it like she's mad at me, like I'm the cause of everything.

"No, ma'am," I say.

"You want eat and walk back, or you rather don't eat and ride?"

"I ain't hungry," I say.

I ain't just hungry, but I'm cold, too. I'm so hungry and cold I want to cry. And look like I'm getting colder and colder. My feet done got numb. I try to work my toes, but I don't even feel them. Look like I'm go'n die. Look like I'm go'n stand right here and freeze to death. I think 'bout home. I think 'bout Val and Auntie and Ty and Louis and Walker. It's 'bout twelve o'clock and I know they eating dinner now. I can hear Ty making jokes. He done forgot 'bout getting up early this morning and right now he's probably making jokes. Always trying to make somebody laugh. I wish I was right there listening to him. Give anything in the world if I was home round the fire.

"Come on," Mama says.

We start walking again. My feet so numb I can't hardly feel them. We turn the corner and go on back up the street. The clock on the courthouse starts hitting for twelve.

The sleet's coming down plenty now. They hit the pave and bounce like rice. Oh, Lord; oh, Lord, I pray. Don't let me die, don't let me die, don't let me die, Lord.

11

Now I know where we going. We going back of town where the colored people eat. I don't care if I don't eat. I been hungry before. I can stand it. But I can't stand the cold.

I can see we go'n have a long walk. It's 'bout a mile down there. But I don't mind. I know when I get there I'm go'n warm myself. I think I can hold out. My hands numb in my pockets and my feet numb, too, but if I keep moving I can hold out. Just don't stop no more, that's all.

The sky's gray. The sleet keeps on falling. Falling like rain now—plenty, plenty. You can hear it hitting the pave. You can see it bouncing. Sometimes it bounces two times 'fore it settles.

We keep on going. We don't say nothing. We just keep on going, keep on going.

I wonder what Mama's thinking. I hope she ain't mad at me. When summer come I'm go'n pick plenty cotton and get her a coat. I'm go'n get her a red one.

I hope they'd make it summer all the time. I'd be glad if it was summer all the time—but it ain't. We got to have winter, too. Lord, I hate the winter. I guess everybody hate the winter.

I don't sniff this time. I get out my handkerchief and wipe my nose. My hands's so cold I can hardly hold the handkerchief.

I think we getting close, but we ain't there yet. I wonder where everybody is. Can't see a soul but us. Look like we the only two people moving round today. Must be too cold for the rest of the people to move round in.

I can hear my teeth. I hope they don't knock together too hard and make that bad one hurt. Lord, that's all I need, for that bad one to start off.

I hear a church bell somewhere. But today ain't Sunday. They must be ringing for a funeral or something.

I wonder what they doing at home. They must be eating. Monsieur Bayonne might be there with his guitar. One day Ty played with Monsieur Bayonne's guitar and broke one of the strings. Monsieur Bayonne was some mad with Ty. He say Ty wasn't go'n ever 'mount to nothing. Ty can go just like Monsieur Bayonne when he ain't there. Ty can make everybody laugh when he starts to mocking Monsieur Bayonne.

I used to like to be with Mama and Daddy. We used to be happy. But they took him in the Army. Now, nobody happy no more. . . . I be glad when Daddy comes home.

Monsieur Bayonne say it wasn't fair for them to take Daddy and give Mama nothing and give us nothing. Auntie say, "Shhh, Etienne. Don't let them hear you talk like that." Monsieur Bayonne say, "It's God truth. What they giving his children? They have to walk three and a half miles to school hot or cold. That's anything to give for a paw? She's got to work in the field rain or shine just to make ends meet. That's anything to give for a husband?" Auntie say, "Shhh, Etienne, shhh." "Yes, you right," Monsieur Bayonne say. "Best don't say it in front of them now. But one day they go'n find out. One day." "Yes, I suppose so," Auntie say. "Then what, Rose Mary?" Monsieur Bayonne say. "I don't know, Etienne," Auntie say. "All we can do is us job, and leave everything else in His hand . . ."

We getting closer, now. We getting closer. I can even see the railroad tracks.

We cross the tracks, and now I see the café. Just to get in there, I say. Just to get in there. Already I'm starting to feel little better.

12

We go in. Ahh, it's good. I look for the heater; there 'gainst the wall. One of them little brown ones. I just stand there and hold my hands over it. I can't open my hands too wide 'cause they almost froze.

Mama's standing right 'side me. She done unbuttoned her coat. Smoke rises out of the coat, and the coat smells like a wet dog.

I move to the side so Mama can have more room. She opens out her hands and rubs them together. I rub mine together, too, 'cause this keep them from hurting. If you let them warm too fast, they hurt you sure. But if you let them warm just little bit at a time, and you keep rubbing them, they be all right every time.

They got just two more people in the café. A lady back of the counter, and a man on this side the counter. They been watching us ever since we come in.

Mama gets out the handkerchief and count up the money. Both of us know how much money she's got there. Three dollars. No, she ain't got three dollars, 'cause she had to pay us way up here. She ain't got but two dollars and a half left. Dollar and a half to get my tooth pulled, and fifty cents for us to go back on, and fifty cents worth of salt meat.

She stirs the money round with her finger. Most of the money is change 'cause I can hear it rubbing together. She stirs it and stirs it. Then she looks at the door. It's still sleeting. I can hear it hitting 'gainst the wall like rice.

"I ain't hungry, Mama," I say.

"Got to pay them something for they heat," she says.

She takes a quarter out the handkerchief and ties the handkerchief up again. She looks over her shoulder at the people, but she still don't move. I hope she don't spend the money. I don't want her spending it on me. I'm hungry, I'm almost starving I'm so hungry, but I don't want her spending the money on me.

She flips the quarter over like she's thinking. She's must be thinking 'bout us walking back home. Lord, I sure don't want walk home. If I thought it'd do any good to say something, I'd say it. But Mama makes up her own mind 'bout things.

She turns 'way from the heater right fast, like she better hurry up and spend the quarter 'fore she change her mind. I watch her go toward the counter. The man and the lady look at her, too. She tells the lady something and the lady walks away. The man keeps on looking at her. Her back's turned to the man, and she don't even know he's standing there.

The lady puts some cakes and a glass of milk on the counter. Then she pours up a cup of coffee and sets it 'side the other stuff. Mama pays her for the things and come on back where I'm standing. She tells me sit down at the table 'gainst the wall.

The milk and the cakes's for me; the coffee's for Mama. I eat slow and I look at her. She's looking outside at the sleet. She's looking real sad. I say to myself, I'm go'n make all this up one day. You see, one day, I'm go'n make all this up. I want say it now; I want tell her how I feel right now; but Mama don't like for us to talk like that.

"I can't eat all this," I say.

They ain't got but just three little old cakes there. I'm so hungry right now, the Lord knows I can eat a hundred times three, but I want my mama to have one.

Mama don't even look my way. She knows I'm hungry, she knows I want it. I let it stay there a little while, then I get it and eat it. I eat just on my front teeth, though, 'cause if cake touch that back tooth I know what'll happen. Thank God it ain't hurt me at all today.

After I finish eating I see the man go to the juke box. He drops a nickel in it, then he just stand there a little while looking at the record. Mama tells me keep my eyes in front where they belong. I turn my head like she say, but then I hear the man coming toward us.

"Dance, pretty?" he says.

Mama gets up to dance with him. But 'fore you know it, she done grabbed the little man in the collar and done heaved him 'side the wall. He hit the wall so hard he stop the juke box from playing.

"Some pimp," the lady back of the counter says. "Some pimp."

The little man jumps up off the floor and starts toward my mama. 'Fore you know it, Mama done sprung open her knife and she's waiting for him.

"Come on," she says. "Come on. I'll gut you from your neighbo to your throat. Come on."

I go up to the little man to hit him, but Mama makes me come and stand 'side her. The little man looks at me and Mama and goes on back to the counter.

"Some pimp," the lady back of the counter says. "Some pimp." She starts laughing and pointing at the little man. "Yes sir, you a pimp, all right. Yes sir-ree."

13

"Fasten that coat, let's go," Mama says.

"You don't have to leave," the lady says.

Mama don't answer the lady, and we right out in the cold again. I'm warm right now—my hands, my ears, my feet—but I know this ain't go'n last too long. It done sleet so much now you got ice everywhere you look.

We cross the railroad tracks, and soon's we do, I get cold. That wind goes through this little old coat like it ain't even there. I got on a shirt and a sweater under the coat, but that wind don't pay them no mind. I look up and I can see we got a long way to go. I wonder if we go'n make it 'fore I get too cold.

We cross over to walk on the sidewalk. They got just one sidewalk back here, and it's over there.

After we go just a little piece, I smell bread cooking. I look, then I see a baker shop. When we get closer, I can smell it more better. I shut my eyes and make 'tend I'm eating. But I keep them shut too long and I butt up 'gainst a telephone post. Mama grabs me and see if I'm hurt. I ain't bleeding or nothing and she turns me loose.

I can feel I'm getting colder and colder, and I look up to see how far we still got to go. Uptown is 'way up yonder. A half mile more, I reckon. I try to think of something. They say think and you won't get cold. I think of that poem, "Annabel Lee."[2] I ain't been to school in so long—this bad weather—I reckon they done passed "Annabel Lee" by now. But passed it or not, I'm sure Miss Walker go'n make me re-

[2]An elegiac poem by Edgar Allan Poe often required to be memorized and recited by grade school pupils.

cite it when I get there. That woman don't never forget nothing. I ain't never seen nobody like that in my life.

I'm still getting cold. "Annabel Lee" or no "Annabel Lee," I'm still getting cold. But I can see we getting closer. We getting there gradually.

Soon 's we turn the corner, I see a little old white lady up in front of us. She's the only lady on the street. She's all in black and she's got a long black rag over her head.

"Stop," she says.

Me and mama stop and look at her. She must be crazy to be out in all this bad weather. Ain't got but a few other people out there, and all of them's men.

"Y'll done ate?" she says.

"Just finish," Mama says.

"Y'all must be cold then?" she says.

"We headed for the dentist," Mama says. "We'll warm up when we get there."

"What dentist?" the old lady says. "Mr. Bassett?"

"Yes, ma'am," Mama says.

"Come on in," the old lady says. "I'll telephone him and tell him y'all coming."

Me and Mama follow the old lady in the store. It's a little bitty store, and it don't have much in there. The old lady takes off her head rag and folds it up.

"Helena?" somebody calls from the back.

"Yes, Alnest?" the old lady says.

"Did you see them?"

"They're here. Standing beside me."

"Good. Now you can stay inside."

The old lady looks at Mama. Mama's waiting to hear what she brought us in here for. I'm waiting for that, too.

"I saw y'all each time you went by," she says. "I came out to catch you, but you were gone."

"We went back of town," Mama says.

"Did you eat?"

"Yes, ma'am."

The old lady looks at Mama a long time, like she's thinking Mama might be just saying that. Mama looks right back at her. The old lady looks at me to see what I have to say. I don't say nothing. I sure ain't going 'gainst my mama.

"There's food in the kitchen," she says to Mama. "I've been keeping it warm."

Mama turns right around and starts for the door.

"Just a minute," the old lady says. Mama stops. "The boy'll have to work for it. It isn't free."

"We don't take no handout," Mama says.

"I'm not handing out anything," the old lady says. "I need my garbage moved to the front. Ernest has a bad cold and can't go out there."

"James'll move it for you," Mama says.

"Not unless you eat," the old lady says. "I'm old, but I have my pride, too, you know."

Mama can see she ain't go'n beat this old lady down, so she just shakes her head.

"All right," the old lady says. "Come into the kitchen."

She leads the way with that rag in her hand. The kitchen is a little bitty little old thing, too. The table and the stove just 'bout fill it up. They got a little room to the side. Somebody in there laying 'cross the bed—'cause I can see one of his feet. Must be the person she was talking to: Ernest or Alnest—something like that.

"Sit down," the old lady says to Mama. "Not you," she says to me. "You have to move the cans."

"Helena?" the man says in the other room.

"Yes, Alnest?" the old lady says.

"Are you going out there again?"

"I must show the boy where the garbage is, Alnest," the old lady says.

"Keep that shawl over your head," the old man says.

"You don't have to remind me, Alnest. Come, boy," the old lady says.

We go out in the yard. Little old back yard ain't no bigger than the store or the kitchen. But it can sleet here just like it can sleet in any big back yard. And 'fore you know it, I'm trembling.

"There," the old lady says, pointing to the cans. I pick up one of the cans and set it right back down. The can's so light, I'm go'n see what's inside of it.

"Here," the old lady says. "Leave that can alone."

I look back at her standing there in the door. She's got that black rag wrapped round her shoulders, and she's pointing one of her little old fingers at me.

"Pick it up and carry it to the front," she says. I go by her with the can, and she's looking at me all the time. I'm sure the can's empty. I'm sure she could've carried it herself—maybe both of them at the same time. "Set it on the sidewalk by the door and come back for the other one," she says.

I go and come back, and Mama looks at me when I pass her. I get the other can and take it to the front. It don't feel a bit heavier than that first one. I tell myself I ain't go'n be nobody's fool, and I'm go'n look inside this can to see just what I been hauling. First, I look up the street, then down the street. Nobody coming. Then I look over my shoulder toward the door. That little old lady done slipped up there quiet 's mouse, watching me again. Look like she knowed what I was go'n do.

"Ehh, Lord," she says. "Children, children. Come in here, boy, and go wash your hands."

I follow her in the kitchen. She points toward the bathroom, and I go in there and wash up. Little bitty old bathroom, but it's clean, clean. I don't use any of her towels; I wipe my hands on my pants legs.

When I come back in the kitchen, the old lady done dished up the food. Rice, gravy, meat—and she even got some lettuce and tomato in a saucer. She even got a glass of milk and a piece of cake there, too. It looks so good, I almost start eating 'fore I say my blessing.

"Helena?" the old man says.

"Yes, Alnest?"

"Are they eating?"

"Yes," she says.

"Good," he says. "Now you'll stay inside."

The old lady goes in there where he is and I can hear them talking. I look at Mama. She's eating slow like she's thinking. I wonder what's the matter now. I reckon she's thinking 'bout home.

The old lady comes back in the kitchen.

"I talked to Dr. Bassett's nurse," she says. "Dr. Bassett will take you as soon as you get there."

"Thank you, ma'am," Mama says.

"Perfectly all right," the old lady says. "Which one is it?"

Mama nods toward me. The old lady looks at me real sad. I look sad, too.

"You're not afraid, are you?" she says.

"No, ma'am," I say.

"That's a good boy," the old lady says. "Nothing to be afraid of. Dr. Bassett will not hurt you."

When me and Mama get through eating, we thank the old lady again.

"Helena, are they leaving?" the old man says.

"Yes, Alnest."

"Tell them I say good-bye."

"They can hear you, Alnest."

"Good-bye both mother and son," the old man says. "And may God be with you."

Me and Mama tell the old man good-bye, and we follow the old lady in the front room. Mama opens the door to go out, but she stops and comes back in the store.

"You sell salt meat?" she says.

"Yes."

"Give me two bits worth."

"That isn't very much salt meat," the old lady says.

"That's all I have," Mama says.

The old lady goes back of the counter and cuts a big piece off the chunk. Then she wraps it up and puts it in a paper bag.

"Two bits," she says.

"That looks like awful lot of meat for a quarter," Mama says.

"Two bits," the old lady says. "I've been selling salt meat behind this counter twenty-five years. I think I know what I'm doing."

"You got a scale there," Mama says.

"What?" the old lady says.

"Weigh it," Mama says.

"What?" the old lady says. "Are you telling me how to run my business?"

"Thanks very much for the food," Mama says.

"Just a minute," the old lady says.

"James," Mama says to me. I move toward the door.

"Just one minute, I said," the old lady says.

Me and Mama stop again and look at her. The old lady takes the meat out of the bag and unwraps it and cuts 'bout half of it off. Then she wraps it up again and juggs it back in the bag and gives the bag to Mama. Mama lays the quarter on the counter.

"Your kindness will never be forgotten," she says. "James," she says to me.

We go out, and the old lady comes to the door to look at us. After we go a little piece I look back, and she's still there watching us.

The sleet's coming down heavy, heavy now, and I turn up my coat collar to keep my neck warm. My mama tells me turn it right back down.

"You not a bum," she says. "You a man."

1968

Philip Roth b. 1933

Philip Roth is one of the most prolific and persistent American novelists of the past half century. His early fiction was highly controversial, both for its critique of post–World War II American Jewish identity and for its explicit sexual content. Although his work earned a number of critical prizes such as the National Book Award and the Pulitzer Prize, he remained a controversial figure through the 1980s. Since then he has published a startling amount of fiction that has earned him a place among elite American writers. In a 2006 *New York Times Book Review* retrospective of the best twenty-five novels of the previous twenty-five years, six were written by Roth. His willingness to dig beneath the surface of the American reality to explore its contradictions, difficulties, and invariable agony, mixed with humor, has earned him the status of one of the most important fiction writers of his time.

Roth was born in Newark, New Jersey, in 1933, and his birthplace often serves as the setting for his fiction. He earned his B.A. from Bucknell University in Pennsylvania and an M.A. from the University of Chicago, where he taught fiction for a time. He has lived in near-seclusion in a restored farmhouse in Connecticut since the mid-1980s. His first book, *Goodbye, Columbus* (1959), contained a novella as well as five short stories, including "You Can't Tell a Man by the Song He Sings." This book earned Roth his first National Book Award, but it also initiated the controversy associated with the first half of his career. In particular, American Jews were upset by the depiction of a character in the story "Defender of the Faith" who apparently uses his religion as an excuse to shirk military duties. Roth's depiction of the well-to-do Patimkin family in the novella *Goodbye, Columbus* also calls into question the notion of suburban, middle-class American success, couched again in terms of the Jewish experience.

Roth's 1969 novel, *Portnoy's Complaint,* eclipsed the controversy of his first book, however. Humorous from some perspectives, offensive from others, this novel uses psychoanalysis and masturbation as consistent touchstones in the life of a man consumed with the meaning of being an American Jew.

Although Roth's legacy rests to some degree on these two books, it could be argued that his breakthrough occurred with the publication of the novel *My Life as a Man* in 1974. Here Roth created a fictional protagonist named Nathan Zuckerman who is the author's close alter ego. Zuckerman has proved to be one of the longest-lived recurrent characters in contemporary fiction. Through him Roth has been able to find his own voice and his own subject matter. Zuckerman has been both a character and a chronicler of contemporary America, at times dispassionate and at times a sharp critic.

The early Zuckerman books were initially collected in *Zuckerman Bound* (1985), but Zuckerman has also resurfaced in the critically acclaimed American trilogy *American Pastoral* (1997), *I Married a Communist* (1998), and *The Human Stain* (2000). These mature works combine recent American history, social commentary, and human drama to paint a rich and complex portrait of what it means to be a late twentieth-century American. In *The Human Stain,* a psychologically damaged Vietnam War veteran, who is likely responsible for the death of his former wife and her lover, asks Zuckerman what kind of books he writes, and he answers succinctly: "I write about people like you [and] their problems."

It makes sense that Roth's most enduring character is a writer because his work has always revealed a preoccupation with work. The story that follows, "You Can't Tell a Man by the Song He Sings," reveals that same preoccupation and includes a number of Roth's other themes—

the fragility of social respectability, the ability of the government to monitor and control individuals, the individual's will to resist such control, and the human proclivity to misjudge others. Roth's characteristic humor is also apparent here, as is his pre-disposition to focus on the male experience, often with baseball as a backdrop.

D. Quentin Miller
Suffolk University

PRIMARY WORKS

Goodbye, Columbus, 1959; *Letting Go,* 1962; *When She Was Good,* 1967; *Portnoy's Complaint,* 1969; *Our Gang,* 1971; *The Breast,* 1972; *The Great American Novel,* 1973; *My Life as a Man,* 1974; *The Professor of Desire,* 1977; *The Ghost Writer,* 1979; *Zuckerman Unbound,* 1981; *The Anatomy Lesson,* 1983; *The Counterlife,* 1986; *The Facts: A Novelist's Autobiography,* 1988; *Deception: A Novel,* 1990; *Patrimony: A True Story,* 1991; *Operation Shylock: A Confession,* 1993; *Sabbath's Theater,* 1995; *The Prague Orgy,* 1996; *American Pastoral,* 1997; *I Married a Communist,* 1998; *The Human Stain,* 2000; *The Dying Animal,* 2001; *The Plot against America,* 2004; *Everyman,* 2006; *Exit, Ghost,* 2007; *Indignation,* 2008.

You Can't Tell a Man by the Song He Sings

It was in a freshman high school class called "Occupations" that, fifteen years ago, I first met the ex-con, Alberto Pelagutti. The first week my new classmates and I were given "a battery of tests" designed to reveal our skills, deficiencies, tendencies, and psyches. At the end of the week, Mr. Russo, the Occupations teacher, would add the skills, subtract the deficiencies, and tell us what jobs best suited our talents; it was all mysterious but scientific. I remember we first took a "Preference Test": "Which would you prefer to do, this, that, or the other thing . . ." Albie Pelagutti sat one seat behind me and to my left, and while this first day of high school I strolled happily through the test, examining ancient fossils here, defending criminals there, Albie, like the inside of Vesuvius, rose, fell, pitched, tossed, and swelled in his chair. When he finally made a decision, he made it. You could hear his pencil drive the *x* into the column opposite the activity in which he thought it wisest to prefer to engage. His agony reinforced the legend that had preceded him: he was seventeen; had just left Jamesburg Reformatory; this was his third high school, his third freshman year; but now—I heard another *x* driven home—he had decided "to go straight."

Halfway through the hour Mr. Russo left the room. "I'm going for a drink," he said. Russo was forever at pains to let us know what a square-shooter he was and that, unlike other teachers we might have had, he would not go out the front door of the classroom to sneak around to the back door and observe how responsible we were. And sure enough, when he returned after going for a drink, his lips were wet; when he came back from the men's room, you could smell the soap on his hands. "Take your time, boys," he said, and the door swung shut behind him.

His black wingtipped shoes beat down the marble corridor and five thick fingers dug into my shoulder. I turned around; it was Pelagutti. "What?" I said. "Number twenty-six," Pelagutti said, "What's the answer?" I gave him the truth: "Anything." Pelagutti rose halfway over his desk and glared at me. He was a hippopotamus, big, black, and smelly; his short sleeves squeezed tight around his monstrous arms as though they were taking his own blood pressure—which at that moment was sky-bound: "What's the answer!" Menaced, I flipped back three pages in my question booklet and reread number twenty-six. "Which would you prefer to do: (1) Attend a World Trade Convention. (2) Pick cherries. (3) Stay with and read to a sick friend. (4) Tinker with automobile engines." I looked blank-faced back to Albie, and shrugged my shoulders. "It doesn't matter—there's no right answer. Anything." He almost rocketed out of his seat. "Don't give me that crap! What's the answer!" Strange heads popped up all over the room—thin-eyed glances, hissing lips, shaming grins—and I realized that any minute Russo, wet-lipped, might come back and my first day in high school I would be caught cheating. I looked again at number twenty-six; then back to Albie; and then propelled—as I always was towards him—by anger, pity, fear, love, vengeance, and an instinct for irony that was at the time delicate as a mallet, I whispered, "Stay and read to a sick friend." The volcano subsided, and Albie and I had met.

We became friends. He remained at my elbow throughout the testing, then throughout lunch, then after school. I learned that Albie, as a youth, had done all the things I, under direction, had not: he had eaten hamburgers in strange diners; he had gone out after cold showers, wet-haired, into winter weather; he had been cruel to animals; he had trafficked with whores; he had stolen, he had been caught, and he had paid. But now he told me, as I unwrapped my lunch in the candy store across the school, "No, I'm through crappin' around. I'm gettin' an education. I'm gonna—" and I think he picked up the figure from a movie musical he had seen the previous afternoon while the rest of us were in English class—"I'm gonna put my best foot forward." The following week when Russo read the results of the testing it appeared that Albie's feet were not only moving forward but finding strange, wonderful paths. Russo sat at his desk, piles of tests stacked before him like ammunition, charts and diagrams mounted huge on either side, and delivered our destinies. Albie and I were going to be lawyers.

Of all that Albie confessed to me that first week, one fact in particular fastened on my brain: I soon forgot the town in Sicily where he was born; the occupation of his father (he either made ice or delivered it); the year and model of the cars he had stolen. I did not forget though that Albie had apparently been the star of the James-burg Reformatory baseball team. When I was selected by the gym teacher, Mr. Hopper, to captain one of my gym class's softball teams (we played softball until the World Series was over, then switched to touch football), I knew that I had to get Pelagutti on my side. With those arms he could hit the ball a mile.

The day teams were to be selected Albie shuffled back and forth at my side, while in the lockerroom I changed into my gym uniform—jockstrap, khaki-colored shorts, T-shirt, sweat socks, and sneakers. Albie had already changed: beneath his khaki gym shorts he did not wear a support but retained his lavender undershorts; they hung down three inches below the outer shorts and looked like a long fancy hem. Instead of a T-shirt he wore a sleeveless undershirt; and beneath his high, tar-black sneakers he wore thin black silk socks with slender arrows embroidered up the sides. Naked he might, like some centuries-dead ancestor, have tossed lions to their death in the Colosseum; the outfit, though I didn't tell him, detracted from his dignity.

As we left the lockerroom and padded through the dark basement corridor and up onto the sunny September playing field, he talked continually, "I didn't play sports when I was a kid, but I played at Jamesburg and baseball came to me like nothing." I nodded my head. "What you think of Pete Reiser?" he asked. "He's a pretty good man," I said. "What you think of Tommy Henrich?" "I don't know," I answered, "he's dependable, I guess." As a Dodger fan I preferred Reiser to the Yankees' Henrich; and besides, my tastes have always been a bit baroque, and Reiser, who repeatedly bounced off outfield walls to save the day for Brooklyn, had won a special trophy in the Cooperstown of my heart. "Yeh," Albie said, "I like all them Yankees."

I didn't have a chance to ask Albie what he meant by that, for Mr. Hopper, bronzed, smiling, erect, was flipping a coin; I looked up, saw the glint in the sun, and I was calling "heads." It landed tails and the other captain had first choice. My heart flopped over when he looked at Albie's arms, but calmed when he passed on and chose first a tall, lean, first-baseman type. Immediately I said, "I'll take Pelagutti." You don't very often see smiles like the one that crossed Albie Pelagutti's face that moment: you would think I had paroled him from a life sentence.

The game began. I played shortstop—left-handed—and batted second; Albie was in center field and, at his wish, batted fourth. Their first man grounded out, me to the first baseman. The next batter hit a high, lofty fly ball to center field. The moment I saw Albie move after it I knew Tommy Henrich and Pete Reiser were only names to him; all he knew about baseball he'd boned up on the night before. While the ball hung in the air, Albie jumped up and down beneath it, his arms raised upward directly above his head; his wrists were glued together, and his two hands flapped open and closed like a butterfly's wings, begging the ball toward him.

"C'mon," he was screaming to the sky, "c'mon you bastard . . ." And his legs bicycle-pumped up and down, up and down. I hope the moment of my death does not take as long as it did for that damn ball to drop. It hung, it hung, Albie cavorting beneath like a Holy Roller. And then it landed, smack into Albie's chest. The runner was rounding second and heading for third while Albie twirled all around, looking, his arms down now, stretched out, as though he were playing ring-around-a-rosy with two invisible children. "Behind you, Pelagutti!" I screamed. He stopped moving. "What?" he called back to me. I ran halfway out to center field. "Behind you—relay it!" And then, as the runner rounded third, I had to stand there defining "relay" to him.

At the end of the first half of the first inning we came to bat behind, 8–0—eight home runs, all relayed in too late by Pelagutti.

Out of a masochistic delight I must describe Albie at the plate: first, he *faced* the pitcher; then, when he swung at the ball—and he did, at every one—it was not to the side but down, as though he were driving a peg into the ground. Don't ask if he was right-handed or left-handed. I don't know.

While we changed out of our gym uniforms I was silent. I boiled as I watched Pelagutti from the corner of my eye. He kicked off those crazy black sneakers and pulled his pink gaucho shirt on over his undershirt—there was still a red spot above the U front of the undershirt where the first fly ball had hit him. Without removing his gym shorts he stuck his feet into his gray trousers—I watched as he hoisted the trousers over the red splotches where ground balls had banged off his shins, past the red splotches where pitched balls had smacked his knee caps and thighs.

Finally I spoke. "Damn you, Pelagutti, you wouldn't know Pete Reiser if you fell over him!" He was stuffing his sneakers into his locker; he didn't answer. I was talking to his mountainous pink shirt back. "Where do you come off telling me you played for that prison team?" He mumbled something. "What?" I said. "I did," he grumbled. "Bullshit!" I said. He turned and, black-eyed, glared at me: "I did!" "That must've been some team!" I said. We did not speak as we left the lockerroom. As we passed the gym office on our way up to Occupations, Mr. Hopper looked up from his desk and winked at me. Then he motioned his head at Pelagutti to indicate that he knew I'd picked a lemon, but how could I have expected a bum like Pelagutti to be an All-American boy in the first place? Then Mr. Hopper turned his sun-lamped head back to his desk.

"Now," I said to Pelagutti as we turned at the second floor landing, "now I'm stuck with you for the rest of the term." He shuffled ahead of me without answering; his oxlike behind should have had a tail on it to flick the flies away—it infuriated me. "You goddamn liar!" I said.

He spun around as fast as an ox can. "You ain't stuck with nobody." We were at the top of the landing headed into the locker-lined corridor; the kids who were piling up the stairs behind stopped, listened. "No you ain't, you snot-ass!" And I saw five hairy knuckles coming right at my mouth. I moved but not in time, and heard a crash inside the bridge of my nose. I felt my hips dip back, my legs and head come forward, and, curved like the letter *c*, I was swept fifteen feet backward before I felt cold marble beneath the palms of my hands. Albie stepped around me and into the Occupations room. Just then I looked up to see Mr. Russo's black wingtipped shoes enter the room. I'm almost sure he had seen Albie blast me but I'll never know. Nobody, including Albie and myself, ever mentioned it again. Perhaps it had been a mistake for me to call Albie a liar, but if he had starred at baseball, it was in some league I did not know.

By way of contrast I want to introduce Duke Scarpa, another ex-con who was with us that year. Neither Albie nor the Duke, incidentally, was a typical member of my high school community. Both lived at the other end of Newark, "down neck," and they had reached us only after the Board of Education had tried Albie at two other schools and the Duke at four. The Board hoped finally, like Marx, that the higher culture would absorb the lower.

Albie and Duke had no particular use for each other; where Albie had made up his mind to go straight, one always felt that the Duke, in his oily quietness, his boneless grace, was planning a job. Yet, though affection never lived between them, Duke wandered after Albie and me, aware, I suspect, that if Albie despised him it was because he was able to read his soul—and that such an associate was easier to abide than one who despises you because he does not know your soul at all. Where Albie was a hippopotamus, an ox, Duke was reptilian. Me? I don't know; it is easy to spot the animal in one's fellows.

During lunch hour, the Duke and I used to spar with each other in the hall outside the cafeteria. He did not know a hook from a jab and disliked having his dark skin roughened or his hair mussed; but he so delighted in moving, bobbing, coiling, and uncoiling, that I think he would have paid for the privilege of playing the serpent with me. He hypnotized me, the Duke; he pulled some slimy string inside me—where Albie Pelagutti sought and stretched a deeper and, I think, a nobler cord.

But I make Albie sound like peaches-and-cream. Let me tell you what he and I did to Mr. Russo.

Russo believed in his battery of tests as his immigrant parents (and Albie's, and maybe Albie himself) believed in papal infallibility. If the tests said Albie was going to be a lawyer then he was going to be a lawyer. As for Albie's past, it seemed only to increase Russo's devotion to the prophecy: he approached Albie with salvation in his eyes. In September, then, he gave Albie a biography to read, the life of Oliver Wendell Holmes; during October, once a week, he had the poor fellow speak impromptu before the class; in November he had him write a report on the Constitution, which I wrote; and then in December, the final indignity, he sent Albie and me (and two others who displayed a legal bent) to the Essex County Court House where he could see "real lawyers in action."

It was a cold, windy morning and as we flicked our cigarettes at the Lincoln statue on the courtyard plaza, and started up the long flight of white cement steps, Albie suddenly did an about-face and headed back across the plaza and out to Market Street. I called to him but he shouted back that he had seen it all before, and then he was not walking, but running towards the crowded downtown streets, pursued not by police, but by other days. It wasn't that he considered Russo an ass for having sent him to visit the Court House—Albie respected teachers too much for that; rather I think he felt Russo had tried to rub his nose in it.

No surprise, then, when the next day after gym Albie announced his assault on the Occupations teacher; it was the first crime he had planned since his decision to go straight back in September. He outlined the action to me and indicated that I should pass the details on to the other members of the class. As liaison between Albie and the well-behaved, healthy nonconvicts like myself who made up the rest of the class, I was stationed at the classroom door and as each member passed in I unfolded the plot into his ear: "As soon after ten-fifteen as Russo turns to the blackboard, you bend over to tie your shoelace." If a classmate looked back at me puzzled, I would motion to Pelagutti hulking over his desk; the puzzled expression would vanish and another accomplice would enter the room. The only one who gave me any trouble was the Duke. He listened to the plan and then scowled back at me with the look of a man who's got his own syndicate, and, in fact, has never even heard of yours.

Finally the bell rang; I closed the door behind me and moved noiselessly to my desk. I waited for the clock to move to a quarter after; it did; and then Russo turned to the board to write upon it the salary range of aluminum workers. I bent to tie my shoelaces—beneath all the desks I saw other upside-down grinning faces. To my left behind me I heard Albie hissing; his hands fumbled about his black silk socks, and the hiss grew and grew until it was a rush of Sicilian, muttered, spewed, vicious. The exchange was strictly between Russo and himself. I looked to the front of the classroom, my fingers knotting and unknotting my shoelaces, the blood pumping now to my face. I saw Russo's legs turn. What a sight he must have seen—where there had been twenty-five faces, now there was nothing. Just desks. "Okay," I heard Russo say, "okay." And then he gave a little clap with his hands. "That's enough now, fellas. The joke is over. Sit up." And then Albie's hiss traveled to all the blood-pinked ears below the desks; it rushed about us like a subterranean stream—"Stay down!"

While Russo asked us to get up we stayed down. And we did not sit up until Albie told us to; and then under his direction we were singing—

> Don't sit under the apple tree
> With anyone else but me,
> Anyone else but me,
> Anyone else but me,
> Oh, no, no, don't sit under the apple tree . . .

And then in time to the music we clapped. What a noise!

Mr. Russo stood motionless at the front of the class, listening, astonished. He wore a neatly pressed dark blue pin-striped suit, a tan tie with a collie's head in the center, and a tieclasp with the initials R.R. engraved upon it; he had on the black wingtipped shoes; they glittered. Russo, who believed in neatness, honesty, punctuality, planned destinies—who believed in the future, in Occupations! And next to me, behind me, inside me, all over me—Albie! We looked at each other, Albie and I, and my lungs split with joy: *"Don't sit under the apple tree—"* Albie's monotone boomed out, and then a thick liquid crooner's voice behind Albie bathed me in sound: it was the Duke's; he clapped to a tango beat.

Russo leaned for a moment against a visual aids chart—"Skilled Laborers: Salaries and Requirements"—and then scraped back his chair and plunged down into it, so far down it looked to have no bottom. He lowered his big head to the desk and his shoulders curled forward like the ends of wet paper; and that was when Albie pulled his coup. He stopped singing "Don't Sit Under the Apple Tree"; we all stopped. Russo looked up at the silence; his eyes black and baggy, he stared at our leader, Alberto Pelagutti. Slowly Russo began to shake his head from side to side: this was no Capone, this was a Garibaldi! Russo waited, I waited, we all waited. Albie slowly rose, and began to sing *"Oh, say can you see, by the dawn's early light, what so proudly we hailed—"* And we all stood and joined him. Tears sparkling on his long black lashes, Mr. Robert Russo dragged himself wearily up from his desk, beaten, and as the Pelagutti basso boomed disastrously behind me, I saw Russo's lips begin to move, *"the bombs bursting in air, gave proof—"* God, did we sing!

Albie left school in June of that year—he had passed only Occupations—but our comradeship, that strange vessel, was smashed to bits at noon one day a few months earlier. It was a lunch hour in March, the Duke and I were sparring in the hall outside the cafeteria, and Albie, who had been more hospitable to the Duke since the day his warm, liquid voice had joined the others—Albie had decided to act as our referee, jumping between us, separating our clinches, warning us about low blows, grabbing out for the Duke's droopy crotch, in general having a good time. I remember that the Duke and I were in a clinch; as I showered soft little punches to his kidneys he squirmed in my embrace. The sun shone through the window behind him, lighting up his hair like a nest of snakes. I fluttered his sides, he twisted, I breathed hard through my nose, my eyes registered on his snaky hair, and suddenly Albie wedged between and knocked us apart—the Duke plunged sideways, I plunged forward, and my fist crashed through the window that Scarpa had been using as his corner. Feet pounded;

in a second a wisecracking, guiltless, chewing crowd was gathered around me, just me. Albie and the Duke were gone. I cursed them both, the honorless bastards! The crowd did not drift back to lunch until the head dietitian, a huge, varicose-veined matron in a laundry-stiff white uniform had written down my name and led me to the nurse's office to have the glass picked out of my knuckles. Later in the afternoon I was called for the first and only time to the office of Mr. Wendell, the Principal.

Fifteen years have passed since then and I do not know what has happened to Albie Pelagutti. If he is a gangster he was not one with notoriety or money enough for the Kefauver Committee[1] to interest itself in several years ago. When the Crime Committee reached New Jersey I followed their investigations carefully but never did I read in the papers the name Alberto Pelagutti or even Duke Scarpa—though who can tell what name the Duke is known by now. I do know, however, what happened to the Occupations teacher, for when another Senate Committee swooped through the state a while back it was discovered that Robert Russo—among others—had been a Marxist while attending Montclair State Teachers' College circa 1935. Russo refused to answer some of the Committee's questions, and the Newark Board of Education met, chastened, and dismissed him. I read now and then in the Newark *News* that Civil Liberties Union attorneys are still trying to appeal his case, and I have even written a letter to the Board of Education swearing that if anything subversive was ever done to my character, it wasn't done by my ex-high school teacher, Russo; if he was a Communist I never knew it. I could not decide whether or not to include in the letter a report of the "Star-Spangled Banner" incident: who knows what is and is not proof to the crotchety ladies and chainstore owners who sit and die on Boards of Education?

And if (to alter an Ancient's text) a man's history is his fate, who knows whether the Newark Board of Education will ever attend to a letter written to them by me. I mean, have fifteen years buried that afternoon I was called to see the Principal?

. . . He was a tall, distinguished gentleman and as I entered his office he rose and extended his hand. The same sun that an hour earlier had lit up snakes in the Duke's hair now slanted through Mr. Wendell's blinds and warmed his deep green carpet. "How do you do?" he said. "Yes," I answered, non sequiturly, and ducked my bandaged hand under my unbandaged hand. Graciously he said, "Sit down, won't you?" Frightened, unpracticed, I performed an aborted curtsy and sat. I watched Mr. Wendell go to his metal filing cabinet, slide one drawer open, and take from it a large white index card. He set the card on his desk and motioned me over so I might read what was typed on the card. At the top, in caps, was my whole name—last, first, and middle; below the name was a Roman numeral one, and beside it, "Fighting in corridor; broke window (3/19/42)." Already documented. And on a big card with plenty of space.

I returned to my chair and sat back as Mr. Wendell told me that the card would follow me through life. At first I listened, but as he talked on and on the drama went out of what he said, and my attention wandered to his filing cabinet. I began to imagine the cards inside, Albie's card and the Duke's, and then I understood—just short of forgiveness—why the two of them had zoomed off and left me to pay penance for the window by myself. Albie, you see, had always known about the filing cabinet and these index cards; I hadn't; and Russo, poor Russo, has only recently found out.

1958

[1]A U.S. Senate committee that investigated organized crime in 1950 and 1951.

N. Scott Momaday (Kiowa) b. 1934

N. Scott Momaday often attributes the diversity of his forms of expression to his rich cultural inheritance and varied life experiences. From his father's family he received Kiowa storytelling traditions and a love of the Rainy Mountain area of Oklahoma. His mother, whose paternal great-grandmother was Cherokee, gave him admiration for literature written in English and the example of how a willful act of imagination could create an "Indian" identity. As Momaday recounts in *The Names,* during his childhood he lived in non-Indian communities, as well as with several Southwestern tribes, especially the Jemez Pueblo. He attended reservation, public, and parochial schools, a Virginia military academy, the University of New Mexico (political science), the University of Virginia (to study law briefly), and Stanford, where he received his M.A. and Ph.D. and was strongly influenced by his mentor Yvor Winters. Momaday's teaching career includes professorships at Berkeley, Stanford, and the University of Arizona. He has been recognized by both non-Indian and Indian worlds with a Guggenheim Fellowship, a Pulitzer Prize (for *House Made of Dawn*), and membership in the Kiowa Gourd Clan.

The tendency toward divers forms of expression is obvious in most of Momaday's works. In *The Names* he used fictional, as well as traditional, autobiographical techniques. The poems in *The Gourd Dancer, In the Presence of the Sun,* and *In the Bear's House* range from forms close to American Indian oral traditions ("The Delight Song of Tsoai-talee") to poems utilizing highly structured written conventions ("Before an Old Painting of the Crucifiction") to free or open verse ("Comparatives") and dialogues ("The Bear-God Dialogues"). *House Made of Dawn,* a powerful novel

about an alienated Jemez Pueblo World War II veteran, is told from different viewpoints and exhibits styles as direct as Hemingway's, as dense as Faulkner's, and as resonant as the songs of the Navajo Nightway ceremony, the source of the novel's title. Several of his works—most notably *In the Presence of the Sun* and *Circle of Wonder*—combine written and visual expressions. His second novel, *Ancient Child,* juxtaposes ancient Kiowa bear narratives, a contemporary artist's male mid-life crisis story, and Billy the Kid fantasies.

It is *The Way to Rainy Mountain,* however, that more than any other of his works demonstrates Momaday's ability to break through generic boundaries. In his essay "The Man Made of Words" (available in *The Remembered Earth,* ed. Geary Hobson, 1979/1981), Momaday describes the composition process that began with his desire to comprehend his Kiowa identity and with the collecting from Kiowa elders of stories. To all but a few of these brief tribal and family stories he added short historical and personal "commentaries." Momaday then arranged twenty-four of these three-voice sections into three divisions ("The Setting Out," "The Going On," "The Closing In") to suggest several physical and spiritual journeys, the two most obvious being the migration and history of the Kiowa and the gradual development of his Kiowa identity. The three divisions were framed by two poems and three lyric essays (Prologue, Introduction, Epilogue) that combine mythic, historic, and personal perspectives.

The following selections, taken from each of the three divisions of *Rainy Mountain,* suggest the nature of the form and themes—themes that reappear in most of Momaday's works: celebrating the importance of the imagination, memory, and oral traditions; seeing the land as a crucial aspect of identity; acknowledging the power of American Indian concepts of sacredness, beauty, and harmony; and revering a sense of language that encompasses economy, power, delight, and wonder.

Kenneth M. Roemer
University of Texas at Arlington

PRIMARY WORKS

House Made of Dawn, 1968; *The Way to Rainy Mountain*, 1969; *The Gourd Dancer*, 1976; *The Names: A Memoir*, 1976; *The Ancient Child*, 1989; *In the Presence of the Sun*, 1992; *Circle of Wonder: A Native American Christmas Story*, 1994; *The Man Made of Words*, 1997; *In the Bear's House*, 1999.

from The Way to Rainy Mountain

Headwaters

Noon in the intermountain plain:
There is scant telling of the marsh—
A log, hollow and weather-stained,
An insect at the mouth, and moss—
Yet waters rise against the roots,
Stand brimming to the stalks. What moves?
What moves on this archaic force
Was wild and welling at the source.

Prologue

The journey began one day long ago on the edge of the northern Plains. It was carried on over a course of many generations and many hundreds of miles. In the end there were many things to remember, to dwell upon and talk about.

"You know, everything had to begin. . . ." For the Kiowas the beginning was a struggle for existence in the bleak northern mountains. It was there, they say, that they entered the world through a hollow log. The end, too, was a struggle, and it was lost. The young Plains culture of the Kiowas withered and died like grass that is burned in the prairie wind. There came a day like destiny; in every direction, as far as the eye could see, carrion lay out in the land. The buffalo was the animal representation of the sun, the essential and sacrificial victim of the Sun Dance. When the wild herds were destroyed, so too was the will of the Kiowa people; there was nothing to sustain them in spirit. But these are idle recollections, the mean and ordinary agonies of human history. The interim was a time of great adventure and nobility and fulfillment.

Tai-me came to the Kiowas in a vision born of suffering and despair.[1] "Take me with you," Tai-me said, "and I will give you whatever you want." And it was so. The great adventure of the Kiowas was a going forth into the heart of the continent. They began a long migration from the headwaters of the Yellowstone River eastward to the Black Hills and south to the Wichita Mountains. Along the way they acquired horses, the religion of the Plains, a love and possession of the open land. Their nomadic soul was set free. In alliance with the Comanches they held dominion in the southern Plains for a hundred years. In the course of that long migration they had come of age as a people. They had conceived a good idea of themselves; they had dared to imagine and determine who they were.

In one sense, then, the way to Rainy Mountain is preeminently the history of an idea, man's idea of himself, and it has old and essential being in language. The verbal tradition by which it has been preserved has suffered a deterioration in time. What remains is fragmentary: mythology, legend, lore, and hearsay—and of course the idea itself, as crucial and complete as it ever was. That is the miracle.

The journey herein recalled continues to be made anew each time the miracle comes to mind, for that is peculiarly the right and responsibility of the imagination. It is a whole journey, intricate with motion and meaning; and it is made with the whole memory, that experience of the mind which is legendary as well as historical, personal as well as cultural. And the journey is an evocation of three things in particular: a landscape that is incomparable, a time that is gone forever, and the human spirit, which endures. The imaginative experience and the historical express equally the traditions of man's reality. Finally, then, the journey recalled is among other things the revelation of one way in which these traditions are conceived, developed, and interfused in the human mind. There are on the way to Rainy Mountain many landmarks, many journeys in the one. From the beginning the migration of the Kiowas was an expression of the human spirit, and that expression is most truly made in terms of wonder and delight: "There were many people, and oh, it was beautiful. That was the beginning of the Sun Dance. It was all for Tai-me, you know, and it was a long time ago."[2]

from **Introduction**[3]

Houses are like sentinels in the plain, old keepers of the weather watch. There, in a very little while, wood takes on the appearance of great age. All colors wear soon away in the wind and rain, and then the wood is burned gray and the grain appears

---

[1]The Tai-me (or Tai-may) appears primarily in two manifestations in this book: as the legendary being who appeared to the Kiowas during "bad times," offering to help them, and as the revered Sun Dance doll, "less than 2 feet in length, representing a human figure dressed in a robe of white feathers" (*The Way to Rainy Mountain,* Sec. 10).
[2]These words, spoken by an old Kiowa woman, Ko-sahn, are repeated near the conclusion of

the Epilogue, which is included in this excerpt.
[3]The following paragraphs conclude the Introduction. They are preceded by Momaday's moving descriptions of the Rainy Mountain area of southwestern Oklahoma, of his tribe's migration from mountainous western Montana, and of his own retracing of that journey, which concluded with his pilgrimage to his grandmother's (Aho's) house and her grave.

and the nails turn red with rust. The windowpanes are black and opaque; you imagine there is nothing within, and indeed there are many ghosts, bones given up to the land. They stand here and there against the sky, and you approach them for a longer time than you expect. They belong in the distance; it is their domain.

Once there was a lot of sound in my grandmother's house, a lot of coming and going, feasting and talk. The summers there were full of excitement and reunion. The Kiowas are a summer people; they abide the cold and keep to themselves, but when the season turns and the land becomes warm and vital they cannot hold still; an old love of going returns upon them. The aged visitors who came to my grandmother's house when I was a child were made of lean and leather, and they bore themselves upright. They wore great black hats and bright ample shirts that shook in the wind. They rubbed fat upon their hair and wound their braids with strips of colored cloth. Some of them painted their faces and carried the scars of old and cherished enmities. They were an old council of warlords, come to remind and be reminded of who they were. Their wives and daughters served them well. The women might indulge themselves; gossip was at once the mark and compensation of their servitude. They made loud and elaborate talk among themselves, full of jest and gesture, fright and false alarm. They went abroad in fringed and flowered shawls, bright beadwork and German silver. They were at home in the kitchen, and they prepared meals that were banquets.

There were frequent prayer meetings, and great nocturnal feasts. When I was a child I played with my cousins outside, where the lamplight fell upon the ground and the singing of the old people rose up around us and carried away into the darkness. There were a lot of good things to eat, a lot of laughter and surprise. And afterwards, when the quiet returned, I lay down with my grandmother and could hear the frogs away by the river and feel the motion of the air.

Now there is a funeral silence in the rooms, the endless wake of some final word. The walls have closed in upon my grandmother's house. When I returned to it in mourning, I saw for the first time in my life how small it was. It was late at night, and there was a white moon, nearly full. I sat for a long time on the stone steps by the kitchen door. From there I could see out across the land; I could see the long row of trees by the creek, the low light upon the rolling plains, and the stars of the Big Dipper. Once I looked at the moon and caught sight of a strange thing. A cricket had perched upon the handrail, only a few inches away from me. My line of vision was such that the creature filled the moon like a fossil. It had gone there, I thought, to live and die, for there, of all places, was its small definition made whole and eternal. A warm wind rose up and purled like the longing within me.

The next morning I awoke at dawn and went out on the dirt road to Rainy Mountain. It was already hot, and the grasshoppers began to fill the air. Still, it was early in the morning, and the birds sang out of the shadows. The long yellow grass on the mountain shone in the bright light, and a scissortail hied above the land. There, where it ought to be, at the end of a long and legendary way, was my grandmother's grave. Here and there on the dark stones were ancestral names. Looking back once, I saw the mountain and came away.

IV

They lived at first in the mountains. They did not yet know of Tai-me, but this is what they knew: There was a man and his wife. They had a beautiful child, a little girl whom they would not allow to go out of their sight. But one day a friend of the family came and asked if she might take the child outside to play. The mother guessed that would be all right, but she told the friend to leave the child in its cradle and to place the cradle in a tree. While the child was in the tree, a redbird came among the branches. It was not like any bird that you have seen; it was very beautiful, and it did not fly away. It kept still upon a limb, close to the child. After a while the child got out of its cradle and began to climb after the redbird. And at the same time the tree began to grow taller, and the child was borne up into the sky. She was then a woman, and she found herself in a strange place. Instead of a redbird, there was a young man standing before her. The man spoke to her and said: "I have been watching you for a long time, and I knew that I would find a way to bring you here. I have brought you here to be my wife." The woman looked all around; she saw that he was the only living man there. She saw that he was the sun.

There the land itself ascends into the sky. These mountains lie at the top of the continent, and they cast a long rain shadow on the sea of grasses to the east. They arise out of the last North American wilderness, and they have wilderness names: Wasatch, Bitterroot, Bighorn, Wind River.[4]

I have walked in a mountain meadow bright with Indian paintbrush, lupine, and wild buckwheat, and I have seen high in the branches of a lodgepole pine the male pine grosbeak, round and rose-colored, its dark, striped wings nearly invisible in the soft, mottled light. And the uppermost branches of the tree seemed very slowly to ride across the blue sky.

---

[4]These mountain ranges are located in Wyoming, Utah, Idaho, and Montana.

XVI

There was a strange thing, a buffalo with horns of steel. One day a man came upon it in the plain, just there where once upon a time four trees stood close together. The man and the buffalo began to fight. The man's hunting horse was killed right away, and the man climbed one of the trees. The great bull lowered its head and began to strike the tree with its black metal horns, and soon the tree fell. But the man was quick, and he leaped to the safety of the second tree. Again the bull struck with its unnatural horns, and the tree soon splintered and fell. The man leaped to the third tree and all the while he shot arrows at the beast; but the arrows glanced away like sparks from its dark hide. At last there remained only one tree and the man had only one arrow. He believed then that he would surely die. But something spoke to him and said: "Each time the buffalo prepares to charge, it spreads its cloven hooves and strikes the ground. Only there in the cleft of the hoof is it vulnerable; it is there you must aim." The buffalo went away and turned, spreading its hooves, and the man drew the arrow to his bow. His aim was true and the arrow struck deep into the soft flesh of the hoof. The great bull shuddered and fell, and its steel horns flashed once in the sun.

Forty years ago the townspeople of Carnegie, Oklahoma, gathered about two old Kiowa men who were mounted on work horses and armed with bows and arrows. Someone had got a buffalo, a poor broken beast in which there was no trace left of the wild strain. The old men waited silently amid the laughter and talk; then, at a signal, the buffalo was let go. It balked at first, more confused, perhaps, than afraid, and the horses had to be urged and then brought up short. The people shouted, and at last the buffalo wheeled and ran. The old men gave chase, and in the distance they were lost to view in a great, red cloud of dust. But they ran that animal down and killed it with arrows.

One morning my father and I walked in Medicine Park, on the edge of a small herd of buffalo. It was late in the spring, and many of the cows had newborn calves. Nearby a calf lay in the tall grass; it was red-orange in color, delicately beautiful with new life. We approached, but suddenly the cow was there in our way, her great dark head low and fearful-looking. Then she came at us, and we turned and ran as hard as we could. She gave up after a short run, and I think we had not been in any real danger. But the spring morning was deep and beautiful and our hearts were beating fast and we knew just then what it was to be alive.

XVII

Bad women are thrown away. Once there was a handsome young man. He was wild and reckless, and the chief talked to the wind about him. After that, the man went hunting. A great whirlwind passed by, and he was blind. The Kiowas have no need of a blind man; they left him alone with his wife and child. The winter was coming on and food was scarce. In four days the man's wife grew tired of caring for him. A herd of buffalo came near, and the man knew the sound. He asked his wife to hand him a bow and an arrow. "You must tell me," he said, "when the buffalo are directly in front of me." And in that way he killed a bull, but his wife said that he had missed. He asked for another arrow and killed another bull, but again his wife said that he had missed. Now the man was a hunter, and he knew the sound an arrow makes when it strikes home, but he said nothing. Then his wife helped herself to the meat and ran away with her child. The man was blind; he ate grass and kept himself alive. In seven days a band of Kiowas found him and took him to their camp. There in the firelight a woman was telling a story. She told of how her husband had been killed by enemy warriors. The blind man listened, and he knew her voice. That was a bad woman. At sunrise they threw her away.

In the Kiowa calendars[5] there is graphic proof that the lives of women were hard, whether they were "bad women" or not. Only the captives, who were slaves, held lower status. During the Sun Dance of 1843, a man stabbed his wife in the breast because she accepted Chief Dohasan's invitation to ride with him in the ceremonial procession. And in the winter of 1851–52, Big Bow stole the wife of a man who was away on a raiding expedition. He brought her to his father's camp and made her wait outside in the bitter cold while he went in to collect his things. But his father knew what was going on, and he held Big Bow and would not let him go. The woman was made to wait in the snow until her feet were frozen.

Mammedaty's[6] grandmother, Kau-au-ointy, was a Mexican captive, taken from her homeland when she was a child of eight or ten years. I never knew her, but I have been to her grave at Rainy Mountain.

KAU-AU-OINTY
BORN 1834
DIED 1929
AT REST

She raised a lot of eyebrows, they say, for she would not play the part of a Kiowa woman. From slavery she rose up to become a figure in the tribe. She owned a great herd of cattle, and she could ride as well as any man. She had blue eyes.

---

[5]Kiowa history was kept on pictorial calendars. For example, see James Mooney's *Calendar History of the Kiowa Indians* (rpt. 1979).

[6]Momaday's paternal grandfather.

XXIV

East of my grandmother's house, south of the pecan grove, there is buried a woman in a beautiful dress. Mammedaty used to know where she is buried, but now no one knows. If you stand on the front porch of the house and look eastward towards Carnegie, you know that the woman is buried somewhere within the range of your vision. But her grave is unmarked. She was buried in a cabinet, and she wore a beautiful dress. How beautiful it was! It was one of those fine buckskin dresses, and it was decorated with elk's teeth and beadwork. That dress is still there, under the ground.

Aho's high moccasins are made of softest, cream-colored skins. On each in-step there is a bright disc of beadwork—an eight-pointed star, red and pale blue on a white field—and there are bands of beadwork at the soles and ankles. The flaps of the leggings are wide and richly ornamented with blue and red and green and white and lavender beads.

East of my grandmother's house the sun rises out of the plain. Once in his life a man ought to concentrate his mind upon the remembered earth, I believe. He ought to give himself up to a particular landscape in his experience, to look at it from as many angles as he can, to wonder about it, to dwell upon it. He ought to imagine that he touches it with his hands at every season and listens to the sounds that are made upon it. He ought to imagine the creatures there and all the faintest motions of the wind. He ought to recollect the glare of noon and all the colors of the dawn and dusk.

Epilogue

During the first hours after midnight on the morning of November 13, 1833, it seemed that the world was coming to an end. Suddenly the stillness of the night was broken; there were brilliant flashes of light in the sky, light of such intensity that people were awakened by it. With the speed and density of a driving rain, stars were falling in the universe. Some were brighter than Venus; one was said to be as large as the moon.

That most brilliant shower of Leonid meteors has a special place in the memory of the Kiowa people. It is among the earliest entries in the Kiowa calendars, and it marks the beginning as it were of the historical period in the tribal mind. In the preceding year Tai-me had been stolen by a band of Osages, and although it was later returned, the loss was an almost unimaginable tragedy; and in 1837 the Kiowas made the first of their treaties with the United States. The falling stars seemed to image the sudden and violent disintegration of an old order.

But indeed the golden age of the Kiowas had been short-lived, ninety or a hundred years, say, from about 1740. The culture would persist for a while in decline, until about 1875, but then it would be gone, and there would be very little material evidence that it had ever been. Yet it is within the reach of memory still, though tenuously now, and moreover it is even defined in a remarkably rich and living verbal tradition which demands to be preserved for its own sake. The living memory and the verbal tradition which transcends it were brought together for me once and for all in the person of Ko-sahn.

A hundred-year-old woman came to my grandmother's house one afternoon in July. Aho was dead; Mammedaty had died before I was born. There were very few Kiowas left who could remember the Sun Dances; Ko-sahn was one of them; she was a grown woman when my grandparents came into the world. Her body was twisted and her face deeply lined with age. Her thin white hair was held in place by a cap of black netting, though she wore braids as well, and she had but one eye. She was dressed in the manner of a Kiowa matron, a dark, full-cut dress that reached nearly to the ankles, full, flowing sleeves, and a wide, apron-like sash. She sat on a bench in the arbor so concentrated in her great age that she seemed extraordinarily small. She was quiet for a time—she might almost have been asleep—and then she began to speak and to sing. She spoke of many things, and once she spoke of the Sun Dance:

My sisters and I were very young; that was a long time ago. Early one morning they came to wake us up. They had brought a great buffalo in from the plain. Everyone went out to see and to pray. We heard a great many voices. One man said that the lodge was almost ready. We were told to go there, and someone gave me a piece of cloth. It was very beautiful. Then I asked what I ought to do with it, and they said that I must tie it to the Tai-me tree. There were other pieces of cloth on the tree, and so I put mine there as well.

When the lodge frame was finished, a woman—sometimes a man—began to sing. It was like this:

Everything is ready.
Now the four societies must go out.
They must go out and get the leaves,
   the branches for the lodge.

And when the branches were tied in place, again there was singing:

Let the boys go out.
Come on, boys, now we must get the earth.

The boys began to shout. Now they were not just ordinary boys, not all of them; they were those for whom prayers had been made, and they were dressed in different ways. There was an old, old woman. She had something on her back. The boys went out to see. The old woman had a bag full of earth on her back. It was a certain kind of sandy earth. That is what they must have in the lodge. The dancers must dance upon the sandy earth. The old woman held a digging tool in her hand. She turned towards the south and pointed with her lips. It was like a kiss, and she began to sing:

We have brought the earth,
Now it is time to play;
As old as I am, I still have the feeling of play.
That was the beginning of the Sun Dance. The dancers treated themselves with buffalo medicine, and slowly they began to take their steps . . . And all the people were around, and they wore splendid things—beautiful buckskin and beads. The chiefs wore necklaces,

*and their pendants shone like the sun. There were many people, and oh, it was beautiful!
That was the beginning of the Sun Dance. It was all for Tai-me, you know, and it was a
long time ago.*

It was—all of this and more—a quest, a going forth upon the way to Rainy Mountain. Probably Ko-sahn too is dead now. At times, in the quiet of evening, I think she
must have wondered, dreaming, who she was. Was she become in her sleep that old
purveyor of the sacred earth, perhaps, that ancient one who, old as she was, still had
the feeling of play? And in her mind, at times, did she see the falling stars?

Rainy Mountain Cemetery

*Most is your name the name of this dark stone.
Deranged in death, the mind to be inheres
Forever in the nominal unknown,
The wake of nothing audible he hears
Who listens here and now to hear your name.*

*The early sun, red as a hunter's moon,
Runs in the plain. The mountain burns and shines;
And silence is the long approach of noon
Upon the shadow that your name defines—
And death this cold, black density of stone.*

1969

Audre Lorde 1934–1992

Audre Lorde, a black, lesbian, feminist, warrior poet, was the youngest of three daughters born to Linda and Frederic Byron Lorde, who immigrated to New York City from Granada, the West Indies. Lorde's parents came to the United States with two plans. First they hoped to reap the financial rewards of hard work, and then they planned to return to their island home in grand style. But with the stock-market crash of 1929, they were forced to abandon both dreams.

As a child, Lorde was inarticulate; in fact, she didn't speak until she was five years old. Even when she began talking, she spoke in poetry; that is, she would re-cite a poem in order to express herself. Hence, poetry literally became her language of communication, and she believed that "the sensual content of life was masked and cryptic, but attended in well-coded phrases." She also learned to see herself as "a reflection of [her] mother's secret poetry as well as of her hidden anger." Giving expression to this reflection has been the impetus for much of her work.

Lorde attended Hunter High School and received the B.A. in 1959 from Hunter College and the M.L.S. in 1961 from Columbia University. In 1962 she married Edwin Ashley Rollins and gave birth to two children: Elizabeth and Jonathan. The marriage ended in divorce. In 1968 Lorde decided to become a full-time poet, leaving her job as head librarian of the City University of New York to become a poet-in-residence at Tougaloo College in Mississippi. Before her death, Lorde was Poet and Professor of English at Hunter College of the City University of New York.

Lorde insisted that she wrote to fulfill her responsibility "to speak the truth as [she felt] it, and to attempt to speak it with as much precision and beauty as possible." She described her life's work in terms of survival and teaching, two themes that dominate her prose and verse. Her power and high productivity arose from her living out these ambitions by confronting her own mortality, her own fear and the opposition of those who tried to silence her.

All of her work resonates with courage, in which she advises us "Not to be afraid of difference. To be real, tough, loving." "Even if you are afraid," she adds, "do it anyway because we learn to work when we are tired, so we can learn to work when we are afraid." In Lorde's later works her vision arises from celebrating the legends of strong black women, especially her mother. In *Zami: A New Spelling of My Name* she combines autobiography, history, and myth to create a new literary form that she calls, "biomythography." *Zami* and *Our Dead Behind Us,* especially, signify the "strong triad of grandmother mother daughter," and "recreate in words the women who helped give [her] substance." They are her "mattering core"; they invigorate Lorde's visions of life and art with power.

Claudia Tate
George Washington University

PRIMARY WORKS

The First Cities, 1970; *Cables to Rage,* 1973; *From a Land Where Other People Live,* 1973 (nominated for the National Book Award in 1974); *New York Head Shop and Museum,* 1974; *Coal,* 1976; *Between Ourselves,* 1976; *The Black Unicorn,* 1978; *The Erotic as Power,* 1978; *The Cancer Journals,* 1980 (received a 1981 Book Award from the American Library Association Gay Caucus); *Zami: A New Spelling of My Name,* 1982; *Chosen Poems: Old and New,* 1982; *Sister Outsider,* 1984; *Our Dead Behind Us,* 1986; *Apartheid USA,* 1986; *I Am Your Sister,* 1986; *Need: A Chorale for Black Woman Voices,* 1990; *A Burst of Light: Essays,* 1992; *Undersong: Chosen Poems, Old and New,* 1992; *The Marvelous Arithmetics of Distance,* 1993; *The Collected Poems,* 1997.

Power

The difference between poetry and rhetoric
is being
ready to kill
yourself
5   instead of your children.

I am trapped on a desert of raw gunshot wounds
and a dead child dragging his shattered black
face off the edge of my sleep
blood from his punctured cheeks and shoulders

10 is the only liquid for miles and my stomach
churns at the imagined taste while
my mouth splits into dry lips
without loyalty or reason
thirsting for the wetness of his blood
15 as it sinks into the whiteness
of the desert where I am lost
without imagery or magic
trying to make power out of hatred and destruction
trying to heal my dying son with kisses
20 only the sun will bleach his bones quicker.

The policeman who shot down a 10-year-old in Queens
stood over the boy with his cop shoes in childish blood
and a voice said "Die you little motherfucker" and
there are tapes to prove that. At his trial
25 this policeman said in his own defense
"I didn't notice the size or nothing else
only the color," and
there are tapes to prove that, too.

Today that 37-year-old white man with 13 years of police forcing
30 has been set free
by 11 white men who said they were satisfied
justice had been done
and one black woman who said
"They convinced me" meaning
35 they had dragged her 4'10" black woman's frame
over the hot coals of four centuries of white male approval
until she let go the first real power she ever had
and lined her own womb with cement
to make a graveyard for our children.

40 I have not been able to touch the destruction within me.
But unless I learn to use
the difference between poetry and rhetoric
my power too will run corrupt as poisonous mold
or lie limp and useless as an unconnected wire
45 and one day I will take my teenaged plug
and connect it to the nearest socket
raping an 85-year-old white woman
who is somebody's mother
and as I beat her senseless and set a torch to her bed
50 a greek chorus will be singing in 3/4 time
"Poor thing. She never hurt a soul. What beasts they are."

1978

Walking Our Boundaries

This first bright day has broken
the back of winter.
We rise from war
to walk across the earth
5   around our house
both stunned that sun can shine so brightly
after all our pain
Cautiously we inspect our joint holding.
A part of last year's garden still stands
10 bracken
one tough missed okra pod clings to the vine
a parody of fruit cold-hard and swollen
underfoot
one rotting shingle
15 is becoming loam.

I take your hand beside the compost heap
glad to be alive and still
with you
we talk of ordinary articles
20 with relief
while we peer upward
each half-afraid
there will be no tight buds started
on our ancient apple tree
25 so badly damaged by last winter's storm
knowing
it does not pay to cherish symbols
when the substance
lies so close at hand
30 waiting to be held
your hand
falls off the apple bark
like casual fire
along my back
35 my shoulders are dead leaves
waiting to be burned
to life.

The sun is watery warm
our voices
40 seem too loud for this small yard
too tentative for women
so in love

the siding has come loose in spots
our footsteps hold this place
45 together
as our place
our joint decisions make the possible
whole.
I do not know when
50 we shall laugh again
but next week
we will spade up another plot
for this spring's seeding.

1978

Never Take Fire from a Woman

My sister and I
have been raised to hate
genteelly
each other's silences
5 sear up our tongues
like flame
we greet each other
with respect
meaning
10 from a watchful distance
while we dream of lying
in the tender of passion
to drink from a woman
who smells like love.

1978

The Art of Response

The first answer was incorrect
the second was
sorry   the third trimmed its toenails

on the Vatican steps
5 the fourth went mad
the fifth
nursed a grudge until it bore twins
that drank poisoned grape juice in Jonestown
the sixth   wrote a book about it
10 the seventh
argued a case before the Supreme Court
against taxation on Girl Scout Cookies
the eighth held a news conference
while four Black babies
15 and one other   picketed New York City
for a hospital bed to die in
the ninth and tenth swore
Revenge on the Opposition
and the eleventh dug their graves
20 next to Eternal Truth
the twelfth
processed funds from a Third World country
that provides doctors for Central Harlem
the thirteenth
25 refused
the fourteenth sold cocaine and shamrocks
near a toilet in the Big Apple circus
the fifteenth
changed the question.

                                      1986

Stations

Some women love
to wait
for life   for a ring
in the June light   for a touch
5 of the sun to heal them   for another
woman's voice   to make them whole
to untie their hands
put words in their mouths
form to their passages   sound
10 to their screams   for some other sleeper
to remember   their future   their past.

Some women wait for their right
train   in the wrong station
in the alleys of morning
15 for the noon to holler
the night come down.

Some women wait for love
to rise up
the child of their promise
20 to gather from earth
what they do not plant
to claim pain for labor
to become
the tip of an arrow   to aim
25 at the heart of now
but it never stays.

Some women wait for visions
that do not return
where they were not welcome
30 naked
for invitations to places
they always wanted
to visit
to be repeated.

35 Some women wait for themselves
around the next corner
and call the empty spot peace
but the opposite of living
is only not living
40 and the stars do not care.

Some women wait for something
to change   and nothing
does change
so they change
45 themselves.

                    1986

The Master's Tools Will Never Dismantle the Master's House[1]

I agreed to take part in a New York University Institute for the Humanities conference a year ago, with the understanding that I would be commenting upon papers dealing with the role of difference within the lives of american women: difference of race, sexuality, class, and age. The absence of these considerations weakens any feminist discussion of the personal and the political.

It is a particular academic arrogance to assume any discussion of feminist theory without examining our many differences, and without a significant input from poor women, Black and Third World women, and lesbians. And yet, I stand here as a Black lesbian feminist, having been invited to comment within the only panel at this conference where the input of Black feminists and lesbians is represented. What this says about the vision of this conference is sad, in a country where racism, sexism, and homophobia are inseparable. To read this program is to assume that lesbian and Black women have nothing to say about existentialism, the erotic, women's culture and silence, developing feminist theory, or heterosexuality and power. And what does it mean in personal and political terms when even the two Black women who did present here were literally found at the last hour? What does it mean when the tools of a racist patriarchy are used to examine the fruits of that same patriarchy? It means that only the most narrow perimeters of change are possible and allowable.

The absence of any consideration of lesbian consciousness or the consciousness of Third World women leaves a serious gap within this conference and within the papers presented here. For example, in a paper on material relationships between women, I was conscious of an either/or model of nurturing which totally dismissed my knowledge as a Black lesbian. In this paper there was no examination of mutuality between women, no systems of shared support, no interdependence as exists between lesbians and women-identified women. Yet it is only in the patriarchal model of nurturance that women "who attempt to emancipate themselves pay perhaps too high a price for the results," as this paper states.

For women, the need and desire to nurture each other is not pathological but redemptive, and it is within that knowledge that our real power is rediscovered. It is this real connection which is so feared by a patriarchal world. Only within a patriarchal structure is maternity the only social power open to women.

Interdependency between women is the way to a freedom which allows the *I* to *be*, not in order to be used, but in order to be creative. This is a difference between the passive *be* and the active *being*.

Advocating the mere tolerance of difference between women is the grossest reformism. It is a total denial of the creative function of difference in our lives. Difference must be not merely tolerated, but seen as a fund of necessary polarities between which our creativity can spark like a dialectic. Only then does the necessity for

[1]Comments at "The Personal and the Political Panel," Second Sex Conference, New York, September 29, 1979.

interdependency become unthreatening. Only within that interdependency of different strengths, acknowledged and equal, can the power to seek new ways of being in the world generate, as well as the courage and sustenance to act where there are no charters.

Within the interdependence of mutual (nondominant) differences lies that security which enables us to descend into the chaos of knowledge and return with true visions of our future, along with the concomitant power to effect those changes which can bring that future into being. Difference is that raw and powerful connection from which our personal power is forged.

As women, we have been taught either to ignore our differences, or to view them as causes for separation and suspicion rather than as forces for change. Without community there is no liberation, only the most vulnerable and temporary armistice between an individual and her oppression. But community must not mean a shedding of our differences, nor the pathetic pretense that these differences do not exist.

Those of us who stand outside the circle of this society's definition of acceptable women; those of us who have been forged in the crucibles of difference—those of us who are poor, who are lesbians, who are Black, who are older—know that *survival is not an academic skill*. It is learning how to stand alone, unpopular and sometimes reviled, and how to make common cause with those others identified as outside the structures in order to define and seek a world in which we can all flourish. It is learning how to take our differences and make them strengths. *For the master's tools will never dismantle the master's house.* They may allow us temporarily to beat him at his own game, but they will never enable us to bring about genuine change. And this fact is only threatening to those women who still define the master's house as their only source of support.

Poor women and women of Color know there is a difference between the daily manifestations of marital slavery and prostitution because it is our daughters who line 42nd Street. If white american feminist theory need not deal with the differences between us, and the resulting difference in our oppressions, then how do you deal with the fact that the women who clean your houses and tend your children while you attend conferences on feminist theory are, for the most part, poor women and women of Color? What is the theory behind racist feminism?

In a world of possibility for us all, our personal visions help lay the groundwork for political action. The failure of academic feminists to recognize difference as a crucial strength is a failure to reach beyond the first patriarchal lesson. In our world, divide and conquer must become define and empower.

Why weren't other women of Color found to participate in this conference? Why were two phone calls to me considered a consultation? Am I the only possible source of names of Black feminists? And although the Black panelist's paper ends on an important and powerful connection of love between women, what about interracial cooperation between feminists who don't love each other?

In academic feminist circles, the answer to these questions is often, "We did not know who to ask." But that is the same evasion of responsibility, the same cop-out, that keeps Black women's art out of women's exhibitions, Black women's work out of most feminist publications except for the occasional "Special Third World Women's Issue," and Black women's texts off your reading lists. But as Adrienne Rich pointed out in a recent talk, white feminists have educated themselves about such an enormous amount over the past ten years, how come you haven't also educated yourselves about Black women and the differences between us—white and Black—when it is key to our survival as a movement?

Women of today are still being called upon to stretch across the gap of male ignorance and to educate men as to our existence and our needs. This is an old and primary tool of all oppressors to keep the oppressed occupied with the master's concerns. Now we hear that it is the task of women of Color to educate white women—in the face of tremendous resistance—as to our existence, our differences, our relative roles in our joint survival. This is a diversion of energies and a tragic repetition of racist patriarchal thought.

Simone de Beauvoir once said: "It is in the knowledge of the genuine conditions of our lives that we must draw our strength to live and our reasons for acting."

Racism and homophobia are real conditions of all our lives in this place and time. *I urge each one of us here to reach down into that deep place of knowledge inside herself and touch that terror and loathing of any difference that lives there. See whose face it wears.* Then the personal as the political can begin to illuminate all our choices.

1979

Cluster: Aesthetics and Politics of the 1960s and 1970s—Black, Brown, Yellow, Red

For all the revolutionary zeal that informed the content and manner in which U.S. writers of color composed works of deliberate difference, Russell Leong reminds us that authors during this period turned most often to the poetic form for its sheer practicality. "Poems are portable," Leong reflected about two decades after the emergence of "movement aesthetics." "They are easily held, do not require a light projector, a picture frame, a wind or percussion instrument to carry their images or produce their sounds." All that the poet required to produce this kind of writing was to put pen to paper and an audience ready and willing to listen and see anew what it already implicitly knew—that people have stories and are ready to tell them anywhere and everywhere despite the fetters of industry, institution, and technology.

This call to a poetic expression (and, by extension, a general creative expression) that is readily accessible to everyone nonetheless was perhaps an impossible goal. It demanded simultaneously that the poet craft different slants of light *and* maintain a watchful relationship with the people whose stories the poet distilled into new, dynamic arrangements.

Leong calls the artists of this generation simply storytellers who "live in communities where they write for family and friends. The relationship between the teller and listener is neighborly, because the teller of the stories must also listen. Storytellers, in their work, utilize the beliefs, feelings, and common dialects of those around them." A sense of responsibility informed the practical nature of movement aesthetics and led to writings that moved bodies as much as they moved hearts.

These writers witnessed the tectonic upheavals that permeated the decades of the 1960s and 1970s. The lines that society had drawn to regulate how people walked through the world were being redrawn or broken. No sooner had the United States begun to recover from the assassination of President John F. Kennedy in 1963 than the country witnessed the fall of others—Malcolm X, Martin Luther King, Jr., Robert Kennedy. Meanwhile, the water hoses that had been turned on peaceful protesters in Selma in the early part of the decade were soon directed at burning cars and storefronts. In the summers of 1965 and 1967 the urban fires of revolt reminded some Americans—and informed others—of the despair and misery that plagued communities of color throughout U.S. cities.

And unlike politicians and police officers, who struggled to keep pace with such foment, artists scrambled to find the language to walk with the national ferment and perhaps even become its prophets. But how would they find the poetic word or line that improved on the one already heard on the streets? "Burn, baby, burn!" Established writers like former beat-turned-black-nationalist LeRoi Jones/Amiri Baraka convened conferences, and Gwendolyn Brooks recalibrated her stanzas to the vibrant syncopation of the times to move closer to the spirit of the movement. But Larry Neal's reflections on the black aesthetic might best articulate the movement writers' desire to bring together politics and aesthetics, responsibility, and creativity: the black aesthetic, as he puts it, is "[m]ore concerned with the vibration of the Word than the Word itself."

It wasn't just black artists who wanted to feel the vibration of the word. Others sensed the reverberations, too. Vine Deloria wrote of the difficulties that Native Americans face because their history has been controlled by European Americans who see only the stereotyped and misunderstood versions of real Native Americans.

While black aesthetic practitioners looked to the collective history of African Americans and the mythos of Africa as sources of creative and political unity, Asian Americans decided to stop listening to the siren song touting their status as "model minorities"—those minorities whose exemplary behavior implicitly scorned the calls for immediate social change by other groups. What this meant most immediately was that Asian Americans looked in the mirror and did not see a white reflection, as the anonymous, presumably female, writer of "White Male Qualities" satirically suggests.

This rejection of whiteness would not be completed overnight, nor was such renunciation done without humor. Like the author of "White Male Qualities," Ron Tanaka inveighs against the extent to which an Asian American culture must first shed itself of its allegiance to white standards. Because Tanaka's untitled polemic is written primarily in blank verse, a centuries-old Anglo-American poetic form, it allows us to read the struggle against "Western standards" or "White qualities" as one that

is much more deep seated, complex, and fraught than simple reversals or rejections. This kind of ambiguity between content and form makes the movement aesthetic, and the struggle to find "voice," perhaps more fun, as Wing Tek Lum's slicing of the proverbial American apple pie suggests.

Appeals for unity were made in the artistic communities of color during this period. Present also were those who asserted alternative visions and who maintained that the movement demanded stories and poetics to fight not only racism and classism but also sexism, homophobia, and their intersections.

The "Black Feminist Statement" of the Combahee River Collective signals a moment in the history of feminist theory when a politics and poetics of "intersectional analysis" dispelled the notion that social change required a hierarchy of oppression. Maybe, as Rita Sánchez discovers in her "Chicana Writer Breaking Out of Silence," the practicality of organizing around and writing about those made most marginal by U.S. society is the true calling of poetry. Maybe the most revolutionary legacy of the movement and its aesthetics is the confidence that her capacity and willingness to write herself into history and community can indeed speak for an entire people and change the world.

James Kyung-Jin Lee
University of California, Santa Barbara

Larry Neal 1937–1981

Some Reflections on the Black Aesthetic

This outline below is a rough overview of some categories and elements that constituted a "Black Aesthetic" outlook. All of these categories need further elaboration, so I am working on a larger essay that will tie them all together.

Mythology	*formal manifestation*	1. RACE MEMORY
Spirit worship, Orishas, ancestors, African Gods. Syncretism/ catholic voodoo, macumba, Holy Ghost, Jesus as somebody you might know, like a personal deity. River spirits.	Samba, Calypso, Batucada, Cha-Cha, juba, gospel songs, jubilees, work song, spirituals.	(Africa, Middle Passage) Rhythm as an expression of race memory; rhythm as a basic creative principle; rhythm as an existence; creative force as vector of existence. Swinging.
		2. MIDDLE PASSAGE (Diaspora) Race memory: terror, landlessness, claustrophobia: "America is a prison . . ." Malcolm X.
Neo-Mythology	*formal manifestation*	3. TRANSMUTATION AND SYNTHESIS
Shamans: Preachers, poets, blues singers, musicians, mack-daddies, and politicians.	All aspects of Black dance styles in the New World. Pelvic. Dress and walk.	Funky Butt, Stomps, Jump Jim Crow, Buck n' Wing, Jigs, Snake, Grind, slow drag, jitterbug, twist, Watusi, fish, swim, boogaloo, etc. Dance to the *after* beat. Dance as race memory; transmitted through the collective folk consciousness.

Neo-Mythology
Legba, Oshun,
Yemaya, Urzulie,
Soul Momma, Evil
women, Good loving
women, woman as primarily
need/man as doer. Blues
singer as poet and moral
judge; bad man Earth
centered, but directed
cosmologically. Folk poet,
philosopher, priest, priestess,
conjurer, preacher,
teacher, hustler, seer,
soothsayer . . .

4. BLUES GOD/TONE AS MEANING AND MEMORY

Sound as racial memory, primeval. Life breath. Word is perceived as energy or force. Call and response Blues perceived as an emanation outside of man, but yet a manifestation of his being/reality. Same energy source as Gospel, field holler, but delineated in narrative song. The African voice transplanted. This God must be the meanest and the strongest. He survives and persists Once perceived as an evil force: ". . . and I (Dude Botley) got to thinking about how many thousand of people (Buddy) Bolden had made happy and all of them women who used to idolize him. 'Where are they now?' I say to myself. Then I hear Bolden's cornet. I look through the crack and there he is, relaxed back in the chair, blowing that silver cornet softly, just above a whisper, and I see he's got his hat over the bell of the horn. I put my ear close to the keyhole. I thought I heard Bolden play the blues before, and play hymns at funerals, but what he is playing now is real strange and I listen carefully, because he's playing something that, for a while sounds like the blues, then like a hymn. I cannot make out the tune, but after awhile I catch on. He is mixing up the blues with the hymns. He plays the blues real sad and the hymn sadder than the blues and then the blues sadder than the hymn. That is the first time that I had ever heard hymns and blues cooked up together. A strange cold feeling comes over me; I get sort of scared because I know the Lord don't like that mixing the Devil's music with his music. . . . It sounded like a battle between the Good Lord and the Devil. Something tells me to listen and see who wins. If Bolden stops on the hymn, the Good Lord wins; if he stops on the blues, the Devil wins."

HISTORY AS UNITARY MYTH

Shango, Nat Turner, Denmark, Vesey, Brer' Rabbit, High John the Conqueror, Jack Johnson, Ray Robinson, Signifying Monkey, Malcolm X, Adam Clayton Powell, Garvey, DuBois, Hon. Elijah Muhammed, Martin L. King, Rap Brown, Rev. Franklin, Charlie Parker, Duke Ellington, James Brown, Bessie Smith, Moms Mabley, King Pleasure, Maefilt Johnson, Son House. Louis Armstrong. . . . Voodoo again/Ishmael Reed's Hoodoo. Islamic suffis. Third World's destiny. The East as the Womb and the Tomb. Fanon's Third World, Bandung Humanism. Revolution is the operational mythology. Symbol change. Expanded metaphors as in the poetry of Curtis Lyle and Stanley Crouch; or L. Barrett's *Song for MuMu* . . . Nigger styles and masks such as Rinehart in the *Invisible Man.* Style as in James P. Johnson description of stride pianists in the twenties. Bobby Blue Bland wearing a dashiki and a process. All of this links up with the transmutation of African styles and the revitalization of these styles on the West.

5. BLACK ARTS MOVEMENT/BLACK ART AESTHETIC

Feeling/contemporary and historical. Energy intensifies. Non-matrixed art forms: Coltrane, Ornette, Sun Ra. More concerned with the vibrations of the Word, than with the Word itself. Like signifying.

The Black Nation as Poem. Ethical stance as aesthetic. The synthesis of the above presented outline. The integral unity of culture, politics, and art. Spiritual. Despises alienation in the European sense. Art consciously committed; art addressed primarily to Black and Third World people. Black attempts to realize the world as art by making Man more compatible to it and it more compatible to Man. Styles itself from nigger rhythms to cosmic sensibility. Black love, conscious and affirmed. Change.

1972

Anonymous

White Male Qualities

I intend to marry a White man. But what were my attitudes leading up to our decision to marry?

My parents have tried to encourage me to marry an Oriental, but they also wanted me to marry a man of my own choosing. I have met many Oriental men, and they seem to lack many qualities that I would need in any man I would marry. My fiancee possesses all these qualities and many more. It seems that they are all the White stereotype qualities that are important to White middle and upper class mothers. His qualities: 1) tall, 2) handsome, 3) manly, 4) self-confident, 5) well-poised, 6) protective, 7) domineering, 8) affectionate, and 9) imaginative. These are all Prince Charming characteristics that all White women instill in their daughters for the ideal mate.

My future-husband seems to possess all of them, and he's also White.

It seems that Oriental girls who marry White men are looking for this stereotype and will not settle for the short, ugly, unconfident, clumsy, arrogant Oriental man that we are all plagued with.

Oriental women also have stereotypes—small, long black hair, gentle, obedient, loving, soft, very womanly, quiet, and beautiful.

None of these are derogatory, but all complimentary. Women like to be thought of in this way.

In the pre-marital relationship between an Oriental couple, the boy will first woo the girl by taking her out on expensive dates; once he knows she will be his girl friend, he takes her for granted, causing many heartaches for her; but necessary for him, to show his masculinity.

The Oriental man seems to have a very distorted picture of masculinity. More and more Asian American girls are seeing that there is a better life—dating the White male. He treats her as the woman she really is, and doesn't have a hangup about proving his masculinity.

The Oriental girl is unique to a White male, because of her Oriental face, her Oriental body; but the Oriental boy seems to like those girls who evoke little of their Orientalness.

One of my old boyfriends was a Japanese American and he seemed to dislike all and any interest exhibited about Yellow identity. He wanted to continue to pretend he was White.

My fiancee wants me to retain all my cultural ties. Perhaps he sees me as a little Japanese doll in kimono, but at least I know what I am. We want to have children, and he wants them all to have black hair. He would also like me to learn to make all Japanese dishes and specialties from my grandmother.

I am much more Oriental now, marrying him.

One of my girl friends mentioned that although she doesn't like the idea of stereotypes, she doesn't really mind it with White men. They seem to appreciate one much more. She feels much better adjusted not dating Orientals.

It seems to me that Sanseis marrying Sanseis will grow up to be exactly like their parents, not better, not worse. I have much higher aspirations for myself and family. I want my children to be free of all hangups. My fiancee and I don't dwell upon my being Japanese and he being white—we think much more about being a man and woman.

Another aspect that may be brought into this project could be the attitudes concerning sex. I think most Orientals have hangups about sex. More than our White counterparts. The cultural ties to duty and honor may have a lot to do with this.

After an Oriental boy has seduced his girl friend, she will expect to marry him, and he begins to take her for granted. He has proved his masculinity, and for once, she feels truly loved.

If an Oriental girl were seduced by a White boy friend, she would probably enjoy the relationship much more and not dwell upon marriage.

Oriental girls have two forms of behavior, one for Oriental boys, and one for White boys. When they find the one that is typically them, as I did—they make their decision.

I have been lucky in my decision—my parents want me to marry for love and happiness, and not for preservation of the blood.

They will let me go ahead and marry him. They trust my judgment completely, and realize that I am just as they raised me—with White ideals.

I feel that if I make any contributions to the community, they will be better for having married him.

1970

Reprinted from *GIDRA* (January 1970).

Wing Tek Lum b. 1946

Minority Poem

For George Lee

Why
we're just as American
as apple pie—
that is, if you count
the leftover peelings
lying on the kitchen counter
which the cook has forgotten about
or doesn't know
quite what to do with
except hope that the maid
when she cleans off the chopping block
will chuck them away
into a garbage can she'll take out
on leaving for the night.

1973

Ron Tanaka 1944–2007

I Hate My Wife for Her Flat Yellow Face

I hate my wife for her flat yellow face
and her fat cucumber legs, but mostly
for her lack of elegance and lack of
intelligence compared to judith gluck.

"Minority Poem" appeared in *East/West,*
April 4, 1973, San Francisco.

I married my wife, daughter of a rich
east los angeles banker, for money,
of course, I thought I deserved better, but
suffering is something else altogether.

She married me for love but she can't love
me, since no one who went to Fresno State
knows anything about Warhol or Ginsberg or
Viet Nam. She has no jewish friends.

She's like a stupid water buffalo from
the old country, slowly plodding between
muddy furrows, and that's all she knows of
love beneath my curses and sometimes blows.

I thought I could love her at first, that she
could teach me to be myself again, free
from years of bopping round LA ghettos,
western civilization and the playmate of the month

since she was raised a buddhist with all
the arts of dancing, arranging and the
serving of tea, and I thought I saw in my
arrogance some long forgotten warrior prince.

But I wanted to be an anglican
too much and listened too long to dylan
or maybe it was the playmate of the
month or poetry and judith gluck.

So I hate my gentle wife for her flat
yellow face and her soft cucumber legs
bearing the burden of the love she has
borne for centuries, centuries before
                        anglicans and dylans
                        playmates and rock
                        before
                        me or judith gluck

1969

Reprinted from *GIDRA* (September 1969).

Combahee River Collective*

A Black Feminist Statement

We are a collective of Black feminists who have been meeting together since 1974.[1] During that time we have been involved in the process of defining and clarifying our politics, while at the same time doing political work within our own group and in coalition with other progressive organizations and movements. The most general statement of our politics at the present time would be that we are actively committed to struggling against racial, sexual, heterosexual, and class oppression and see as our particular task the development of integrated analysis and practice based upon the fact that the major systems of oppression are interlocking. The synthesis of these oppressions creates the conditions of our lives. As Black women we see Black feminism as the logical political movement to combat the manifold and simultaneous oppressions that all women of color face.

We will discuss four major topics in the paper that follows: (1) the genesis of contemporary black feminism; (2) what we believe, i.e., the specific province of our politics; (3) the problems in organizing Black feminists, including a brief history of our collective; and (4) Black feminist issues and practice.

1. The Genesis of Contemporary Black Feminism

Before looking at the recent development of Black feminism we would like to affirm that we find our origins in the historical reality of Afro-American women's continuous life-and-death struggle for survival and liberation. Black women's extremely negative relationship to the American political system (a system of white male rule) has always been determined by our membership in two oppressed racial and sexual castes. As Angela Davis points out in "Reflections on the Black Woman's Role in the Community of Slaves," Black women have always embodied, if only in their physical manifestation, an adversary stance to white male rule and have actively resisted its inroads upon them and their communities in both dramatic and subtle ways. There have always been Black women activists—some known, like Sojourner Truth, Harriet Tubman, Frances E. W. Harper, Ida B. Wells Barnett, and Mary Church Terrell, and thousands upon thousands unknown—who had a shared awareness of how their sexual identity combined with their racial identity to make their whole life situation and the focus of their political struggles unique. Contemporary Black feminism is the outgrowth of countless generations of personal sacrifice, militancy, and work by our mothers and sisters.

---

*The Combahee River Collective is a Black feminist group in Boston whose name comes from the guerrilla action conceptualized and led by Harriet Tubman on June 2, 1863, in the Port Royal region of South Carolina. This action freed more than 750 slaves and is the only military campaign in American history planned and led by a woman.

[1] This statement is dated April 1977.

A Black feminist presence has evolved most obviously in connection with the second wave of the American women's movement beginning in the late 1960s. Black, other Third World, and working women have been involved in the feminist movement from its start, but both outside reactionary forces and racism and elitism within the movement itself have served to obscure our participation. In 1973 Black feminists, primarily located in New York, felt the necessity of forming a separate Black feminist group. This became the National Black Feminist Organization (NBFO).

Black feminist politics also have an obvious connection to movements for Black liberation, particularly those of the 1960s and 1970s. Many of us were active in those movements (civil rights, Black nationalism, the Black Panthers), and all of our lives were greatly affected and changed by their ideology, their goals, and the tactics used to achieve their goals. It was our experience and disillusionment within these liberation movements, as well as the experience on the periphery of the white male left, that led to the need to develop a politics that was antiracist, unlike those of white women, and antisexist, unlike those of Black and white men.

There is also undeniably a personal genesis for Black feminism, that is, the political realization that comes from the seemingly personal experiences of individual Black women's lives. Black feminists and many more Black women who do not define themselves as feminists have all experienced sexual oppression as a constant factor in our day-to-day existence. As children we realized that we were different from boys and that we were treated differently. For example, we were told in the same breath to be quiet both for the sake of being "ladylike" and to make us less objectionable in the eyes of white people. As we grew older we became aware of the threat of physical and sexual abuse by men. However, we had no way of conceptualizing what was so apparent to us, what we *knew* was really happening.

Black feminists often talk about their feelings of craziness before becoming conscious of the concepts of sexual politics, patriarchal rule, and most importantly, feminism, the political analysis and practice that we women use to struggle against our oppression. The fact that racial politics and indeed racism are pervasive factors in our lives did not allow us, and still does not allow most Black women, to look more deeply into our own experiences and, from that sharing and growing consciousness, to build a politics that will change our lives and inevitably end our oppression. Our development must also be tied to the contemporary economic and political position of Black people. The post World War II generation of Black youth was the first to be able to minimally partake of certain educational and employment options, previously closed completely to Black people. Although our economic position is still at the very bottom of the American capitalistic economy, a handful of us have been able to gain certain tools as a result of tokenism in education and employment which potentially enable us to more effectively fight our oppression.

A combined antiracist and antisexist position drew us together initially, and as we developed politically we addressed ourselves to hetero-sexism and economic oppression under capitalism.

2. What We Believe

Above all else, our politics initially sprang from the shared belief that Black women are inherently valuable, that our liberation is a necessity not as an adjunct to somebody else's but because of our need as human persons for autonomy. This may seem so obvious as to sound simplistic, but it is apparent that no other ostensibly progressive movement has ever considered our specific oppression as a priority or worked seriously for the ending of that oppression. Merely naming the pejorative stereotypes attributed to Black women (e.g., mammy, matriarch, Sapphire, whore, bulldagger), let alone cataloguing the cruel, often murderous, treatment we receive, indicates how little value has been placed upon our lives during four centuries of bondage in the Western hemisphere. We realize that the only people who care enough about us to work consistently for our liberation is us. Our politics evolve from a healthy love for ourselves, our sisters and our community which allows us to continue our struggle and work.

This focusing upon our own oppression is embodied in the concept of identity politics. We believe that the most profound and potentially the most radical politics come directly out of our own identity, as opposed to working to end somebody else's oppression. In the case of Black women this is a particularly repugnant, dangerous, threatening, and therefore revolutionary concept because it is obvious from looking at all the political movements that have preceded us that anyone is more worthy of liberation than ourselves. We reject pedestals, queenhood, and walking ten paces behind. To be recognized as human, levelly human, is enough.

We believe that sexual politics under patriarchy is as pervasive in Black women's lives as are the politics of class and race. We also often find it difficult to separate race from class from sex oppression because in our lives they are most often experienced simultaneously. We know that there is such a thing as racial-sexual oppression which is neither solely racial nor solely sexual, e.g., the history of rape of Black women by white men as a weapon of political repression.

Although we are feminists and lesbians, we feel solidarity with progressive Black men and do not advocate the fractionalization that white women who are separatists demand. Our situation as Black people necessitates that we have solidarity around the fact of race, which white women of course do not need to have with white men, unless it is their negative solidarity as racial oppressors. We struggle together with Black men against racism, while we also struggle with Black men about sexism.

We realize that the liberation of all oppressed peoples necessitates the destruction of the political-economic systems of capitalism and imperialism as well as patriarchy. We are socialists because we believe the work must be organized for the collective benefit of those who do the work and create the products, and not for the profit of the bosses. Material resources must be equally distributed among those who create these resources. We are not convinced, however, that a socialist revolution that is not also a feminist and antiracist revolution will guarantee our liberation. We have arrived at the necessity for developing an understanding of class relationships that takes into account the specific class position of Black women who are generally marginal in the labor force, while at this particular time some of us are temporarily viewed as doubly desirable tokens at white-collar and professional levels. We need to articulate the real class situation of persons who are not merely raceless, sexless workers, but for whom racial and sexual oppression are significant determinants in their working/economic lives. Although we are in essential agreement with Marx's theory as it applied to the very specific economic relationships he analyzed, we know that his analysis must be extended further in order for us to understand our specific economic situation as Black women.

A political contribution which we feel we have already made is the expansion of the feminist principle that the personal is political. In our consciousness-raising sessions, for example, we have in many ways gone beyond white women's revelations because we are dealing with the implications of race and class as well as sex. Even our Black women's style of talking/testifying in Black language about what we have experienced has a resonance that is both cultural and political. We have spent a great deal of energy delving into the cultural and experiential nature of our oppression out of necessity because none of these matters has ever been looked at before. No one before has ever examined the multilayered texture of Black women's lives. An example of this kind of revelation/conceptualization occurred at a meeting as we discussed the ways in which our early intellectual interests had been attacked by our peers, particularly Black males. We discovered that all of us, because we were "smart" had also been considered "ugly," i.e., "smart-ugly." "Smart-ugly" crystallized the way in which most of us had been forced to develop our intellects at great cost to our "social" lives. The sanctions in the Black and white communities against Black women thinkers is comparatively much higher than for white women, particularly ones from the educated middle and upper classes.

As we have already stated, we reject the stance of lesbian separatism because it is not a viable political analysis or strategy for us. It leaves out far too much and far too many people, particularly Black men, women, and children. We have a great deal of criticism and loathing for what men have been socialized to be in this society: what they support, how they act, and how they oppress. But we do not have the misguided notion that it is their maleness, per se—i.e., their biological maleness—that makes them what they are. As Black women we find any type of biological determinism a particularly dangerous and reactionary basis upon which to build a politic. We must also question whether lesbian separatism is an adequate and progressive political analysis and strategy, even for those who practice it, since it is so completely denies any but the sexual sources of women's oppression, negating the facts of class and race.

3. Problems in Organizing Black Feminists

During our years together as a Black feminist collective we have experienced success and defeat, joy and pain, victory and failure. We have found that it is very difficult to organize around Black feminist issues, difficult even to announce in certain contexts that we *are* Black feminists. We have tried to think about the reasons for our difficulties, particularly since the white women's movement continues to be strong and to grow in many directions. In this section we will discuss some of the general reasons for the organizing problems we face and also talk specifically about the stages in organizing in our own collective.

The major source of difficulty in our political work is that we are not just trying to fight oppression on one front or even two, but instead to address a whole range of oppressions. We do not have racial, sexual, heterosexual, or class privilege to rely upon, nor do we have even the minimal access to resources and power that groups who possess any one of these types of privilege have.

The psychological toll of being a Black woman and the difficulties this presents in reaching political consciousness and doing political work can never be underestimated.

There is a very low value placed upon Black women's psyches in this society, which is both racist and sexist. As an early group member once said, "We are all damaged people merely by virtue of being Black women." We are dispossessed psychologically and on every other level, and yet we feel the necessity to struggle to change the condition of all Black women. In "A Black Feminist's Search for Sisterhood," Michele Wallace arrives at this conclusion:

> We exist as women who are Black who are feminists, each stranded for the moment, working independently because there is not yet an environment in this society remotely congenial to our struggle—because, being on the bottom, we would have to do what no one else has done: we would have to fight the world.[2]

Wallace is pessimistic but realistic in her assessment of Black feminists' position, particularly in her allusion to the nearly classic isolation most of us face. We might use our position at the bottom, however, to make a clear leap into revolutionary action. If Black women were free, it would mean that everyone else would have to be free since our freedom would necessitate the destruction of all the systems of oppression.

Feminism is, nevertheless, very threatening to the majority of Black people because it calls into question some of the most basic assumptions about our existence, i.e., that sex should be a determinant of power relationships. Here is the way male and female voices were defined in a Black nationalist pamphlet from the early 1970's.

> We understand that it is and has been traditional that the man is the head of the house. He is the leader of the house/nation because his knowledge of the world is broader, his awareness is greater, his understanding is fuller and his application of this information is wiser . . . After all, it is only reasonable that the man be the head of the house because he is able to defend and protect the development of his home . . . Women cannot do the same things as men—they are made by nature to function differently. Equality of men and women is something that cannot happen even in the abstract world. Men are not equal to other men, i.e. ability, experience or even understanding. The value of men and women can be seen as in the value of gold and silver—they are not equal but both have great value. We must realize that men and women are a complement to each other because there is no house/family without a man and his wife. Both are essential to the development of any life.[3]

The material conditions of most Black women would hardly lead them to upset both economic and sexual arrangements that seem to represent some stability in their lives. Many Black women had a good understanding of both sexism and racism, but because of the everyday constrictions of their lives cannot risk struggling against them both.

The reaction of Black men to feminism has been notoriously negative. They are, of course, even more threatened than Black women by the possibility that Black feminists might organize around our own needs. They realize that they might not only lose valuable and hard-working allies in their struggles but that they might also be

---

[2]Michele Wallace, "A Black Feminist's Search for Sisterhood," *Village Voice,* July 28, 1975, pp. 6–7.

[3]The Mumininas of the Committee for Unified Newark, "Mwanamke Mwanachi" (The Nationalist Woman), Newark, N.J., c. 1971, pp. 4–5.

The Atomic Bombing of Hiroshima (1945). On August 6, 1945, the *Enola Gay,* a B-29 bomber, dropped a 9,700-pound uranium bomb on the Japanese city of Hiroshima, which had a population of almost 300,000 civilians and 43,000 soldiers. About 70,000 people probably died immediately. With the effects of radioactive fallout, the five-year death total may have reached or even exceeded 200,000. On August 9, another bomb was dropped on Nagasaki, and one day later Japan surrendered unconditionally, ending World War II. America had achieved victory but at a tremendous cost.

Jackson Pollock, *One: Number 31, 1950* **(c. 1950).** Jackson Pollock (1912–1956) created three wall-size paintings in 1950. In 1947, he began experimenting with the technique of laying a canvas on the floor and dribbling or pouring paint directly onto its surface. Often photographed creating huge paintings, Pollock saw himself as a medium. He commented, "[T]he painting has a life of its own. I try to let it come through."

Edward Hopper, *Western Motel* **(1957).** Edward Hopper (1882–1967) captures the loneliness and isolation of American life in this image of a woman sitting on a bed next to a motel window. A car waits outside, and beyond is a stark and bleak landscape. Suitcases occupy the bottom left corner of the painting. As with all of Hopper's paintings, the light is rich and beautiful, but the viewer is left with a sense of rootlessness and transience. The woman is caught, momentarily still, but she will soon move outside the frame, into the car, and down the road to, presumably, another lonely motel.

One of four different styles of the Jubilee

One of four different styles of the Levittowner

Levittown IN 1957

One of five different styles of the Pennsylvanian

One of four different styles of the Country Clubber

Levittown in 1957. Levittown, Pennsylvania, was the second of the mass-produced planned communities built after World War II by the developer Levitt & Sons. (The first was built on Long Island in New York State from 1947 to 1951, and the third and fourth were built in New Jersey and Puerto Rico.) The Pennsylvania town was built from 1951 to 1957 and included churches, schools, swimming pools, and a shopping center. About 70,000 residents lived there, mostly veterans and their families. The houses cost from about $8,000 to $18,000 and were fully equipped and landscaped. Veterans could buy them for no money down (others paid a $90 downpayment). Homeowners paid a monthly mortgage payment of about $60 to the Veterans Administration or the Federal Housing Administration.

Martin Luther King, Jr., giving a speech in Washington, D.C., in 1963. On August 28, 1963, more than 200,000 people of all races gathered at the Lincoln Memorial to demand equal justice for all citizens under the law. Martin Luther King, Jr. (1929–1968) delivered his "I Have a Dream" speech at this gathering.

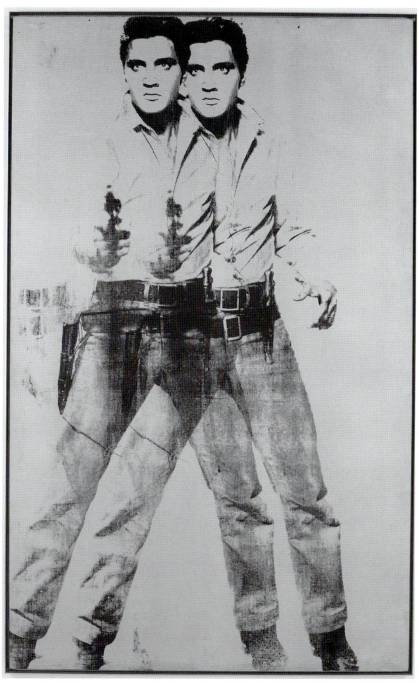

Andy Warhol, *Double Elvis* **(1963).** Andy Warhol (born Andrew Warhola, 1928–1984) comments on Americans' fixation on celebrity images as he manipulates a photograph of Elvis appropriately dressed as a cowboy, perhaps as seen in one of his movies. Elvis takes his place along with Warhol's paintings of Marilyn Monroe, the Campbell soup cans, and other American icons.

Malcolm X. Malcolm X (born Malcolm Little, 1925–1965) was an important figure in the Nation of Islam, a group that promoted black nationalism in the early 1960s. He was an articulate and persuasive advocate for African American identity, integrity, and independence.

Allen Ginsberg reading "Howl" in Washington Square in 1966. Allen Ginsberg (1926–1997) reading "Howl" in Washington Square in 1966. The writing of the beats (*beat* meaning "beatific, holy" with connotations of music as well as fatigue) was intended to be shared with an audience in a performance that unites poet and listeners. After a visit to India, Ginsberg brought back a mantra-like chant that enhanced the delivery of his poetry. He became a kind of prophet, shedding light on America's aberrations in his poetry.

Huynh Cong (Nick) Ut, *Vietnam Napalm, Trang Bang* (1972). Ever since Matthew Brady displayed his Civil War photos in his New York gallery, photography has transformed perceptions of war. In the past, paintings depicted fallen heroes and brave generals leading their troops. Photography is much more democratic. The Vietnam War was the most photographed war to that date. Photojournalists flocked to the tiny country, and many soldiers documented personal experiences with their own cameras. This photo by Nick Ut (b. 1951) sheds light on the effects of war on the innocent bystanders who are outside the heroic frames.

View of the earth as seen by the *Apollo 17* crew traveling toward the moon (1972). This image has been interpreted many different ways. When it was taken in 1972, Americans saw the earth as part of a larger universe—"the last frontier"—that was just beginning to be explored. From a twenty-first-century perspective, with the resources of the earth in peril, we view this globe as a delicate ecosystem that is under attack.

9/11 Tribute. The Tribute in Light viewed in 2004 from Jersey City on the anniversary of the September 11, 2001, attacks. Created as a memorial in 2002, the Tribute is a temporary art installation of 88 search lights that are located next to the World Trade Center site. The tribute was repeated in 2003 and has been recreated each year on September 11.

forced to change their habitually sexist ways of interacting with and oppressing Black women. Accusations that Black feminism divides the Black struggles are powerful deterrents to the growth of an autonomous Black women's movement.

Still, hundreds of women have been active at different times during the three-year existence of our group. And every Black woman who came, came out of a strongly-felt need for some level of possibility that did not previously exist in her life.

When we first started meeting early in 1974 after the NBFO first eastern regional conference, we did not have a strategy for organizing, or even a focus. We just wanted to see what we had. After a period of months of not meeting, we began to meet again late in the year and started doing an intense variety of consciousness-raising. The overwhelming feeling that we had is that after years and years we had finally found each other. Although we were not doing political work as a group, individuals continued their involvement in Lesbian politics, sterilization abuse and abortion rights work, Third World Women's International Women's Day activities, and support activity for the trials of Dr. Kenneth Edelin, Joan Little, and Inéz García. During our first summer, when membership had dropped off considerably, those of us remaining devoted serious discussions to the possibility of opening a refuge for battered women in a Black community. (There was no refuge in Boston at that time.) We also decided around that time to become an independent collective since we had serious disagreements with NBFO's bourgeois-feminist stance and their lack of a clear political focus.

We also were contacted at that time by socialist feminists, with whom we had worked on abortion rights activities, who wanted to encourage us to attend the National Socialist Feminist Conference in Yellow Springs. One of our members did attend and despite the narrowness of the ideology that was promoted at that particular conference, we became more aware of the need for us to understand our own economic situation and to make our own economic analysis.

In the fall, when some members returned, we experienced several months of comparative inactivity and internal disagreements which were first conceptualized as a Lesbian-straight split but which were also the result of class and political differences. During the summer those of us who were still meeting had determined the need to do political work and to move beyond consciousness-raising and serving exclusively as an emotional support group. At the beginning of 1976, when some of the women who had not wanted to do political work and who also had voiced disagreements stopped attending of their own accord, we again looked for a focus. We decided at that time, with the addition of new members, to become a study group. We had always shared our reading with each other, and some of us had written papers on Black feminism for group discussion a few months before this decision was made. We began functioning as a study group and also began discussing the possibility of starting a Black feminist publication. We had a retreat in the late spring which provided a time for both political discussion and working our interpersonal issues. Currently we are planning to gather together a collection of Black feminist writing. We feel that it is absolutely essential to demonstrate the reality of our politics to other Black women and believe that we can do this through writing and distributing our work. The fact that individual Black feminists are living in isolation all over the country, that our own numbers are small, and that we have some skills in writing, printing, and publishing makes us want to carry out these kinds of projects as a means of organizing Black feminists as we continue to do political work in coalition with other groups.

4. Black Feminist Issues and Projects

During our time together we have identified and worked on many issues of particular relevance to Black women. The inclusiveness of our politics makes us concerned with any situation that impinges upon the lives of women, Third World and working people. We are of course particularly committed to working on those struggles in which race, sex and class are simultaneous factors in oppression. We might, for example, become involved in workplace organizing at a factory that employs Third World women or picket a hospital that is cutting back on already inadequate health care to a Third World community, or set up a rape crisis center in a Black neighborhood. Organizing around welfare and daycare concerns might also be a focus. The work to be done and the countless issues that this work represents merely reflect the pervasiveness of our oppression.

Issues and projects that collective members have actually worked on are sterilization abuse, abortion rights, battered women, rape and health care. We have also done many workshops and educationals on black feminism on college campuses, at women's conferences, and most recently for high school women. One issue that is of major concern to us and that we have begun to publicly address is racism in the white women's movement. As black feminists we are made constantly and painfully aware of how little effort white women have made to understand and combat their racism, which requires among other things that they have a more than superficial comprehension of race, color, and black history and culture. Eliminating racism in the white women's movement is by definition work for white women to do, but we will continue to speak to and demand accountability on this issue.

In the practice of our politics we do not believe that the end always justifies the means. Many reactionary and destructive acts have been done in the name of achieving "correct" political goals. As feminists we do not want to mess over people in the name of politics. We believe in collective process and a nonhierarchical distribution of power with our own group and in our vision of a revolutionary society. We are committed to a continual examination of our politics as they develop through criticism and self-criticism as an essential aspect of our practice. As black feminists and lesbians we know that we have a very definite revolutionary task to perform and we are ready for the lifetime of work and struggle before us.

1977

Rita Sánchez b. 1952

Chicana Writer Breaking Out of the Silence

The Chicana writer, by the fact that she is even writing in today's society, is making a revolutionary act. Embodied in the act of writing is her voice against others' definitions of who she is and what she should be. There is, in her open expression and in the very nature of this act of opening up, a refusal to submit to a quality of silence that has been imposed upon her for centuries. In the act of writing, the Chicana is saying "No," and by doing so she becomes the revolutionary, a source of change, and a real force for humanization.

By becoming a writer, the Chicana has to have already rebelled against a socialization process that would have her remain merely the silent helpmate. Everything in her society, the schools, the church, the home, has sought this goal for her: she must be sheltered from the evils, noise, confusion, from the realities of the outside world, from sex to politics, even at times from intellectual dialogue, to be considered acceptable. In short, she should make no intrusion into adult or male conversation. Now, the Chicana, by voicing her own brand of expression has rejected the latter in favor of telling anyone who wishes to read her work, hear her voice, exactly what she is not, and who she, in fact, is.

Courageously, La Chicana writer, by understanding the condition of colonization under which she was born, the images of betrayal that surround her, and the forces of racism that still exist for her, has exhibited her strength by the very denial of these impositions. By her refusal to accept the myths, misinterpretations and the stereotypes of herself as presented by another, she has transcended the bounds of tradition, made a choice to determine her own life, and finally, has become the revolutionary voice. The reality of her history reveals La Mujer Chicana as the central core and basis of Chicana struggle. The Cuban film, *Lucia,* depicts the epic struggle of an entire people, and at the center: La Mujer. The rape of a woman in this story symbolized the colonization of the country. La Mujer has suffered the violation, but has emerged as the visionary who awakens her people. The Chicana is the same woman.

In her act of self expression shared in writing with others like herself she is saying what she feels and who she is; every time she puts down on paper her words; and every time those words are read by another Chicana, she has defined further who we Chicanas truly are. Her voice, in expressing a Chicana view, comes closer to expressing a collective Chicana voice. We, her readers, through reading what she has to say, through reading about her, are reading about ourselves and our own experiences. This phenomenon takes place simply because by writing she has put a name to what we have felt—a name to the feelings of anger, pain, love, joy, sympathy, strength, celebration. Every poem, essay, story becomes more than a work of art in this vital combination of writer and reader. Each work becomes an expression of life. The Chicana

From *De Colores,* vol. 3, no. 3, 1977, pp. 31–37.

writer, like the revolutionary, is a creator and the result is twofold. She becomes the creator of a work of art and the creator of a destiny.

Although the Chicana voice is only recently emerging in writing, her presence, like the presence of the river in [Rodolfo] Anaya's *Bless Me, Ultima,* has always surrounded us; and when this presence reveals itself, finally, as it does to the protagonist, Antonio, it is an awesome revelation, one, like life itself, to be both revered and heeded. At first, what appears to be only a silence, in reality carries with it an underlying depth, strength, and volume, constantly moving, constantly alive; it is unable to be stopped and is not to be taken lightly.

In this sense the new Chicana poet, writer, the new voice you are hearing is not new at all. It has encompassed us since time immemorial only to have revealed itself in a more profound and real way. In Dorinda Moreno's *La Mujer en Pie de Lucha,* poet Viola Correa reveals the drama and fervor of this startling reality of the Chicana presence coming to life, in her poem, "la Nueva Chicana." This voice does not come from the elite, the women with the college degrees or titles, nor is it clad like one may have expected Jesus to have been clad, with royal robes. Her grandeur is of a different kind. Her presence is clothed in the voice of *tu hermana, tu madre, tu tia* [your sister, your mother, your aunt]. And by coming to us in this way, the voice is even more real to us; it comes from midst ourselves and not from above, as poets often do. More significantly, it comes from out of our own very real struggles: the picket lines, the factories, the fields, the *barrios,* the streets, *la casa* [the home].

The Chicana voice of today is reflective of the Aztec poets long ago. It binds us to a beauty of the past. Antonia Castañeda, co-editor of *Literature Chicana,* one of the first Chicanas to teach *"La Mujer de la Raza"* at the University of Washington, speaks of the depth of a Chicano collective voice as it comes to us from a long-ago voice of the Aztec poet, Temilotzín. Temilotzín, in his poetry, speaks not only for himself, but to all the people. *Literatura Chicana* says that his mission is to create flower and song while seeking *humanidad* [humanity] with the community. Antonia Casteñeda translates, *"en prestamos los unos a los otros,"* to mean, literally, that we are on loan to one another. The Chicana presence, the Chicana voice reaffirms this concept when she speaks. In so doing, she is reaching out to all Chicanas, "with song to encircle the community."

Writing, breaking the silence, subjective as it may appear, becomes a monumental and collective act because it signifies overcoming, freeing oneself from the confines and conditions of history. The collective act may not even be expressed in the words themselves, but is manifest in the act of writing down these words. Writing is the tool which allows the Chicana to implement action, critical thought, change. It signifies a voice, a dimension beyond just a presence. It allows us a voice that reaches out to yet another, spurring critical questions while creating empathy. By this process involving writer and reader, both participants are breaking out of silence, no longer are they mere presences, but instruments for change, visionaries awakening the people.

All of Chicana literature crys out to make the world, to make relationships human again. Although living in our own communities has sheltered us in a sense from the atrocities of the outside world, we are still confronted with the technocratic society that surrounds us. And in many ways, this society is worse than the physical poverty we might have known in our communities. It is more destructive because it leaves us spiritually poor. It attempts to strip us of those elements with which we grew up within our communities that allowed us to hold on to our humanidad [humanity]; our language, our culture, our family unity. Our responses of anger are against such dehumanization; they are a reaction against a kind of violence that already exists.

More and more the Chicana woman is emerging out of a traditionally imposed silence. Her already awesome presence becomes more awesome when it speaks. It becomes the conscience of the people; from one who is a participant in history. It is the writing process that will facilitate the goal we seek: that in writing, our effects may be far-reaching and that it will bring each one of us to our fullest human potential.

As long as we remain silent, no voice exists. Our right to speak, to voice ourselves is stripped from us; if you do not hear us, no voice exists and no one will notice our absence.

Verónica Cunningham through poetry admonishes our silence. If we do not speak out, the indictment is of ourselves and we must harbor the guilt of our own rape. If, in our silence, we make no rebellion our sentence, she says, will be our own silence; in itself, the worst possible punishment. Importantly, she begins this indictment with "I" and in so doing, her poem becomes all-encompassing. But she speaks to all women who would remain silent: "Chicana, Black, Asian, White, any woman, any age, child, sister, wife, aunt, or friend." As long as you are silent you are yourself guilty:

> You women are guilty of
> being victim, guilty of being raped
> And you are guilty of laying
>   yourself down
> to your courts of justice
> and your sentence has been silence . . .

Chicanas are being called upon today to put their thoughts down in writing, to share their emotions with others, thus beginning the process, the chain reaction that might spur others to self-expression and creativity. Our depth as Chicana women must be shared, in fact, is urgently needed so that others might hear the prophetic voice. This sharing is essential; it is the spirit of our people. This process creates a new awakening, a breaking out of silence, a revolutionary act. The burden is finally on us, on all Chicanas to break out of silence, to be present to all others who may themselves benefit from a voice, one that is both fearless and the penetrating conscience of the people.

1977

Vine DeLoria 1933–2005

from Custer Died for Your Sins

1 Indians Today, the Real and the Unreal

Indians are like the weather. Everyone knows all about the weather, but none can change it. When storms are predicted, the sun shines. When picnic weather is announced, the rain begins. Likewise, if you count on the unpredictability of Indian people, you will never be sorry.

One of the finest things about being an Indian is that people are always interested in you and your "plight." Other groups have difficulties, predicaments, quandaries, problems, or troubles. Traditionally we Indians have a "plight."

Our foremost plight is our transparency. People can tell just by looking at us what we want, what should be done to help us, how we feel, and what a "real" Indian is really like. Indian life, as it relates to the real world, is a continuous attempt not to disappoint people who know us. Unfulfilled expectations cause grief and we have already had our share.

Because people can see right through us, it becomes impossible to tell the truth from fiction or fact from mythology. Experts paint us as they would like us to be. Often we paint ourselves as we wish we were or as we might have been.

The more we try to be ourselves the more we are forced to defend what we have never been. The American public feels most comfortable with the mythical Indians of stereotype-land who were always THERE. These Indians are fierce, they wear feathers and grunt. Most of us don't fit this idealized figure since we grunt only when overeating, which is seldom.

To be an Indian in modern American society is in a very real sense to be unreal and ahistorical. In this book we will discuss the other side—the unrealities that face *us* as Indian people. It is this unreal feeling that has been welling up inside us and threatens to make this decade the most decisive in history for Indian people. In so many ways, Indian people are re-examining themselves in an effort to redefine a new social structure for their people. Tribes are reordering their priorities to account for the obvious discrepancies between their goals and the goals whites have defined for them.

Indian reactions are sudden and surprising. One day at a conference we were singing "My Country 'Tis of Thee" and we came across the part that goes:

> *Land where our fathers died*
> *Land of the Pilgrims' pride . . .*

Some of us broke out laughing when we realized that our fathers undoubtedly died trying to keep those Pilgrims from stealing our land. In fact, many of our fathers died because the Pilgrims killed them as witches. We didn't feel much kinship with those Pilgrims, regardless of who they did in.

We often hear "give it back to the Indians" when a gadget fails to work. It's a terrible thing for a people to realize that society has set aside all non-working gadgets for their exclusive use.

During my three years as Executive Director of the National Congress of American Indians it was a rare day when some white didn't visit my office and proudly proclaim that he or she was of Indian descent.

Cherokee was the most popular tribe of their choice and many people placed the Cherokees anywhere from Maine to Washington State. Mohawk, Sioux, and Chippewa were next in popularity. Occasionally I would be told about some mythical tribe from lower Pennsylvania, Virginia, or Massachusetts which had spawned the white standing before me.

At times I became quite defensive about being a Sioux when these white people had a pedigree that was so much more respectable than mine. But eventually I came to understand their need to identify as partially Indian and did not resent them. I would confirm their wildest stories about their Indian ancestry and would add a few tales of my own hoping that they would be able to accept themselves someday and leave us alone.

Whites claiming Indian blood generally tend to reinforce mythical beliefs about Indians. All but one person I met who claimed Indian blood claimed it on their grandmother's side. I once did a projection backward and discovered that evidently most tribes were entirely female for the first three hundred years of white occupation. No one, it seemed, wanted to claim a male Indian as a forebear.

It doesn't take much insight into racial attitudes to understand the real meaning of the Indian-grandmother complex that plagues certain whites. A male ancestor has too much of the aura of the savage warrior, the unknown primitive, the instinctive animal, to make him a respectable member of the family tree. But a young Indian princess? Ah, there was royalty for the taking. Somehow the white was linked with a noble house of gentility and culture if his grandmother was an Indian princess who ran away with an intrepid pioneer. And royalty has always been an unconscious but all-consuming goal of the European immigrant.

The early colonists, accustomed to life under benevolent despots, projected their understanding of the European political structure onto the Indian tribe in trying to explain its political and social structure. European royal houses were closed to ex-convicts and indentured servants, so the colonists made all Indian maidens princesses, then proceeded to climb a social ladder of their own creation. Within the next generation, if the trend continues, a large portion of the American population will eventually be related to Powhattan.

While a real Indian grandmother is probably the nicest thing that could happen to a child, why is a remote Indian princess grandmother so necessary for many whites? Is it because they are afraid of being classed as foreigners? Do they need some blood tie with the frontier and its dangers in order to experience what it means to be an American? Or is it an attempt to avoid facing the guilt they bear for the treatment of the Indian?

The phenomenon seems to be universal. Only among the Jewish community, which has a long tribal-religious tradition of its own, does the mysterious Indian grandmother, the primeval princess, fail to dominate the family tree. Otherwise, there's not much to be gained by claiming Indian blood or publicly identifying as an Indian.

The white believes that there is a great danger the lazy Indian will eventually corrupt God's hardworking people. He is still suspicious that the Indian way of life is dreadfully wrong. There is, in fact, something *un-American* about Indians for most whites.

I ran across a classic statement of this attitude one day in a history book which was published shortly after the turn of the century. Often have I wondered how many Senators, Congressmen, and clergymen of the day accepted the attitudes of that book as a basic fact of life in America. In no uncertain terms did the book praise God that the Indian had not yet been able to corrupt North America as he had South America:

> It was perhaps fortunate for the future of America that the Indians of the North rejected civilization. Had they accepted it the whites and Indians might have intermarried to some extent as they did in Mexico. That would have given us a population made up in a measure of shiftless half-breeds.

I never dared to show this passage to my white friends who had claimed Indian blood, but I often wondered why they were so energetic if they did have some of the bad seed in them.

Those whites who dare not claim Indian blood have an asset of their own. They *understand* Indians.

Understanding Indians is not an esoteric art. All it takes is a trip through Arizona or New Mexico, watching a documentary on TV, having known *one* in the service, or having read a popular book on *them*.

There appears to be some secret osmosis about Indian people by which they can magically and instantaneously communicate complete knowledge about themselves to these interested whites. Rarely is physical contact required. Anyone and everyone who knows an Indian or who is *interested,* immediately and thoroughly understands them.

You can verify this great truth at your next party. Mention Indians and you will find a person who saw some in a gas station in Utah, or who attended the Gallup ceremonial celebration, or whose Uncle Jim hired one to cut logs in Oregon, or whose church had a missionary come to speak last Sunday on the plight of Indians and the mission of the church.

There is no subject on earth so easily understood as that of the American Indian. Each summer, work camps disgorge teenagers on various reservations. Within one month's time the youngsters acquire a knowledge of Indians that would astound a college professor.

Easy knowledge about Indians is a historical tradition. After Columbus "discovered" America he brought back news of a great new world which he assumed to be India and, therefore, filled with Indians. Almost at once European folklore devised a complete explanation of the new land and its inhabitants which feature the Fountain of Youth, the Seven Cities of Gold, and other exotic attractions. The absence of elephants apparently did not tip off the explorers that they weren't in India. By the time they realized their mistake, instant knowledge of Indians was a cherished tradition.

Missionaries, after learning some of the religious myths of tribes they encountered, solemnly declared that the inhabitants of the new continent were the Ten Lost Tribes of Israel. Indians thus received a religious-historical identity far greater than they wanted to deserved. But it was an impossible identity. Their failure to measure up to Old Testament standards doomed them to a fall from grace and they were soon relegated to the status of a picturesque species of wildlife.

Like the deer and the antelope, Indians seemed to play rather than get down to the serious business of piling up treasures upon the earth where thieves break through and steal. Scalping, introduced prior to the French and Indian War by the English,* confirmed the suspicion that Indians were wild animals to be hunted and skinned. Bounties were set and an Indian scalp became more valuable than beaver, otter, marten, and other animal pelts.

American blacks had become recognized as a species of human being by amendments to the Constitution shortly after the Civil War. Prior to emancipation they had been counted as three-fifths of a person in determining population for representation in the House of Representatives. Early Civil Rights bills nebulously state that other people shall have the same rights as "white people," indicating there *were* "other people." But Civil Rights bills passed during and after the Civil War systematically excluded Indian people. For a long time an Indian was not presumed capable of initiating an action in a court of law, of owning property, or of giving testimony against whites in court. Nor could an Indian vote or leave his reservation. Indians were America's captive people without any defined rights whatsoever.

Then one day the white man discovered that the Indian tribes still owned some 135 million acres of land. To his horror he learned that much of it was very valuable. Some was good grazing land, some was farm land, some mining land, and some covered with timber.

Animals could be herded together on a piece of land, but they could not sell it. Therefore it took no time at all to discover that Indians were really people and should have the right to sell their lands. Land was the means of recognizing the Indian as a human being. It was the method whereby land could be stolen legally and not blatantly.

Once the Indian was thus acknowledged, it was fairly simple to determine what his goals were. If, thinking went, the Indian was just like the white, he must have the

---

*Notice, for example the following proclamation:

"Given at the Council Chamber in Boston this third day of November 1755 in the twenty-ninth year of the Reign of our Sovereign Lord George the Second by the Grace of God of Great Britain, France, and Ireland, King Defender of the Faith.

By His Honour's command
J. Willard, Secry.
God Save the King

"Whereas the tribe of Penobscot Indians have repeatedly in a perfidious manner acted contrary to their solemn submission unto his Majesty long since made and frequently renewed.

"I have, therefore, at the desire of the House of Representatives . . . thought fit to issue this Proclamation and to declare the Penobscot Tribe of Indians to be enemies, rebels and traitors to his Majesty. . . . And I do hereby require his Majesty's subjects of the Province to embrace all opportunities of pursuing, captivating, killing and destroy-all and every of the aforesaid Indians.

"And whereas the General Court of this Province have voted that a bounty . . . be granted and allowed to be paid out of the Province Treasury . . . the premiums of bounty following viz:

"For every scalp of a male Indian brought in as evidence of their being killed as aforesaid, forty pounds.

"For every scalp of such female Indian or male Indian under the age of twelve years that shall be killed and brought in as evidence of their being killed as aforesaid, twenty pounds."

same outlook as the white. So the future was planned for the Indian people in public and private life. First in order was allotting them reservations so that they could sell their lands. God's foreordained plan to repopulate the continent fit exactly with the goals of the tribes as they were defined by their white friends.

It is fortunate that we were never slaves. We gave up land instead of life and labor. Because the Negro labored, he was considered a draft animal. Because the Indian occupied large areas of land, he was considered a wild animal. Had we given up anything else, or had anything else to give up, it is certain that we would have been considered some other thing.

Whites have had different attitudes toward the Indians and the blacks since the Republic was founded. Whites have always refused to give non-whites the respect which they have been found to legally possess. Instead there has always been a contemptuous attitude that although the law says one thing, "we all know better."

Thus whites steadfastly refused to allow blacks to enjoy the fruits of full citizenship. They systematically closed schools, churches, stores, restaurants, and public places to blacks or made insulting provisions for them. For one hundred years every program of public and private white America was devoted to the exclusion of the black. It was, perhaps, embarrassing to be rubbing shoulders with one who had not so long before been defined as a field animal.

The Indian suffered the reverse treatment. Law after law was passed requiring him to conform to white institutions. Indian children were kidnapped and forced into boarding schools thousands of miles from their homes to learn the white man's ways. Reservations were turned over to different Christian denominations for governing. Reservations were for a long time church operated. Everything possible was done to ensure that Indians were forced into American life. The wild animal was made into a household pet whether or not he wanted to be one.

Policies for both black and Indian failed completely. Blacks eventually began the Civil Rights movement. In doing so they assured themselves some rights in white society. Indians continued to withdraw from the overtures of white society. Indians continued to withdraw from the overtures of white society and tried to maintain their own communities and activities.

Actually both groups had little choice. Blacks, trapped in a world of white symbols, retreated into themselves. And people thought comparable Indian withdrawal unnatural because they expected Indians to behave like whites.

The white world of abstract symbols became a nightmare for Indian people. The words of the treaties, clearly stating that Indians should have "free and undisturbed" use of their lands under the protection of the federal government, were cast aside by the whites as if they didn't exist. The Sioux once had a treaty plainly stating that it would take the signature or marks of three-fourths of the adult males to amend it. Yet through force the government obtained only 10 percent of the required signatures and declared the new agreement valid.

Indian solutions to problems which had been defined by the white society were rejected out of hand and obvious solutions discarded when they called for courses of action that were not proper in white society. When Crow Dog assassinated Spotted Tail the matter was solved under traditional Sioux customs. Yet an outraged public, furious because Crow Dog had not been executed, pressured for the Seven Major Crimes Act for the federal government to assume nearly total criminal jurisdiction over the reservations. Thus foreign laws and customs using the basic concepts of justice came to dominate Indian life. If, Indians reasoned, justice is for society's benefit, why isn't our justice accepted? Indians became convinced they were the world's stupidest people.

Words and situations never seemed to fit together. Always, it seemed, the white man chose a course of action that did not work. The white man preached that it was good to help the poor, yet he did nothing to assist the poor in his society. Instead he put constant pressure on the Indian people to hoard their worldly goods, and when they failed to accumulate capital but freely gave to the poor, the white man reacted violently. . . .

1969

Amiri Baraka (LeRoi Jones) b. 1934

Amiri Baraka, born Everett LeRoy Jones to Coyt LeRoy and Anna Lois Jones in Newark, New Jersey, grew up in a middle-class environment. He attended a predominantly black elementary school, but his college-prep high school, from which he graduated with honors in 1951, was mainly white. About 1951, the first of his name changes occurred with the spelling of his middle name from "LeRoy" to "LeRoi." From 1952 to 1954 he attended Howard University, where he studied with Sterling Brown and Nathan Scott. After he flunked out of school, he enlisted in the U.S. Air Force until 1957. These were years of intellectual commitment and poetry writing. In 1957, however, he was dishonorably discharged because of suspicions of communism and such "suspicious activities" as voracious reading, journal-keeping, poetry writing, and subscribing to avant-garde journals.

Free to live the avant-garde life that had become his preference, Baraka moved to New York's Greenwich Village. Among his associates there were Charles Olson, Frank O'Hara, and Allen Ginsberg. In 1958 he married Hettie Cohn, a Jewish woman also much a part of the Beat scene, and together they edited *Yugen,* a literary journal which published the work of Kerouac, Ginsberg, and many others.

The next decade was marked by a significant change from things aesthetic to things political. His 1960 visit to Cuba marks the genesis of political awareness of blackness and a new frame of reference: the third world. Although the year after his trip saw the inauguration of another avant-garde journal, this time co-edited with poet Diane di Prima, and the publication of his first volume of poetry, by 1964 the tensions inherent along the spectrum of early poetic asceticism and racial didacticism become apparent in the poems of *The Dead Lecturer,* as well as his play *Dutchman,* for which he won an Obie Award for its off-Broadway production.

Radically affected by the assassination of Malcolm X in 1965, Baraka left Hettie and the bohemian life of the Village and moved to Harlem, where he established the Black Arts Repertory Theater/School. In 1966, returning to Newark, he founded a similar venture, Spirit House, and married Sylvia Robinson, a black woman. Again a change of name signaled a reshaping of identity: LeRoi Jones became Imamu Amiri Baraka, as he was known through the racial upheavals of the '60s. By the early '70s he had dropped the title "Imamu," yet another indication of a shift: this one from black nationalism to international socialism, a stance obviously not tolerant of titles. His published poetry of the late '70s reflects this shift in thought.

In 1979 he joined the African Studies Department at SUNY Stony Brook, was promoted to associate professor with tenure in 1982, and to full professor in 1984 following the publication of *Autobiography* and *Daggers and Javelins.* He continues to work on *Wise/Whys,* an African American poetic-historical odyssey.

The sense of flux and process, of intensity and explosion, of rebellion and reconstruction, and always the *SOUND* of it, are everywhere present in his poetry and in his prose. *Dutchman,* included here, has come to be seen as his signature work.

Marcellette Williams
University of Massachusetts–Amherst

PRIMARY WORKS

Preface to a Twenty Volume Suicide Note . . ., 1961; *Blues People: Negro Music in White America*, 1963; *Dutchman* and *The Slave*, 1964; *The Dead Lecturer*, 1964; *Home: Social Essays*, 1966; *The Baptism* and *The Toilet*, 1967; *Black Music*, 1967; *Tales*, 1967; *Black Magic*, 1969; *In Our Terribleness*, 1970; *It's Nation Time*, 1970; *Jello*, 1970; *Raise, Race, Rays, Raze: Essays Since 1965*, 1971; *Spirit Reach*, 1972; *The Floating Bear*, 1973; *Hard Facts*, 1975; *The Motion of History and Other Plays*, 1978; *Selected Poetry of Amiri Baraka/LeRoi Jones*, 1979; *Selected Plays and Prose of Amiri Baraka/LeRoi Jones*, 1979; *The Autobiography of LeRoi Jones/Amiri Baraka*, 1984; *Daggers and Javelins: Essays, 1974–1979*, 1984; *The Music: Reflections on Jazz and Blues*, 1987; *The LeRoi Jones/Amiri Baraka Reader*, 1991; *Transbluesency: Selected Poems*, 1995; *Funk Lore: New Poems*, 1996; *The Fiction of LeRoi Jones/Amiri Baraka*, 2000; *Somebody Blew Up America*, 2001; *Tales of the Out and the Gone*, 2006.

An Agony. As now.

I am inside someone
who hates me. I look
out from his eyes. Smell
what fouled tunes come in
5   to his breath. Love his
wretched women.

Slits in the metal, for sun. Where
my eyes sit turning, at the cool air
the glance of light, or hard flesh
10   rubbed against me, a woman, a man,
without shadow, or voice, or meaning.

This is the enclosure (flesh,
where innocence is a weapon. An
abstraction. Touch. (Not mine.
15   Or yours, if you are the soul I had
and abandoned when I was blind and had
my enemies carry me as a dead man
(if he is beautiful, or pitied.

It can be pain. (As now, as all his
20   flesh hurts me.) It can be that. Or
pain. As when she ran from me into
that forest.

Or pain, the mind
silver spiraled whirled against the
25   sun, higher than even old men thought

God would be. Or pain. And the other. The
yes. (Inside his books, his fingers. They
are withered yellow flowers and were never
beautiful.) The yes. You will, lost soul, say
30 "beauty." Beauty, practiced, as the tree. The
slow river. A white sun in its wet sentences.

Or, the cold men in their gale. Ecstasy. Flesh
or souls. The yes. (Their robes blown. Their bowls
empty. They chant at my heels, not at yours.) Flesh
35 or soul, as corrupt. Where the answer moves too quickly.
Where the God is a self, after all.)

Cold air blown through narrow blind eyes. Flesh,
white hot metal. Glows as the day with its sun.
It is a human love, I live inside. A bony skeleton
40 you recognize as words or simple feeling.

But it has no feeling. As the metal, is hot, it is not,
given to love.

It burns the thing
inside it. And that thing
45 screams.

1964

Ka 'Ba[1]

A closed window looks down
on a dirty courtyard, and black people
call across or scream across or walk across
defying physics in the stream of their will

5 Our world is full of sound
Our world is more lovely than anyone's
tho we suffer, and kill each other
and sometimes fail to walk the air

We are beautiful people
10 with african imaginations

---

[1]Relating to the sacred Islamic shrine in Mecca.

full of masks and dances and swelling chants
with african eyes, and noses, and arms,
though we sprawl in grey chains in a place
full of winters, when what we want is sun.
15 We have been captured,
brothers. And we labor
to make our getaway, into
the ancient image, into a new

correspondence with ourselves
20 and our black family. We need magic
now we need the spells, to raise up
return, destroy, and create. What will be

the sacred words?

1969

Black People: This Is Our Destiny

The road runs straight with no turning, the circle
runs complete as it is in the storm of peace, the all
embraced embracing in the circle complete turning road
straight like a burning straight with the circle complete
5 as in a peaceful storm, the elements, the niggers' voices
harmonized with creation on a peak in the holy black man's
eyes that we rise, whose race is only direction up, where
we go to meet the realization of makers knowing who we are
and the war in our hearts but the purity of the holy world
10 that we long for, knowing how to live, and what life is, and
who God is, and the many revolutions we must spin through in our
seven adventures in the endlessness of all existing feeling, all
existing forms of life, the gases, the plants, the ghost minerals
the spirits the souls the light in the stillness where the storm
15 the glow the nothing in God is complete except there is nothing
to be incomplete the pulse and change of rhythm, blown flight
to be anything at all . . . vibration holy nuance beating against
itself, a rhythm a playing re-understood now by one of the 1st race
the primitives the first men who evolve again to civilize the
20 world

1969

A Poem Some People Will Have to Understand

Dull unwashed windows of eyes
and buildings of industry. What
industry do I practice? A slick
colored boy, 12 miles from his
5   home. I practice no industry.
I am no longer a credit
to my race. I read a little,
scratch against silence slow spring
afternoons.
10   I had thought, before, some years ago
that I'd come to the end of my life.
              Watercolor ego. Without the preciseness
a violent man could propose.
              But the wheel, and the wheels,
15   won't let us alone. All the fantasy
              and justice, and dry charcoal winters
All the pitifully intelligent citizens
              I've forced myself to love.

              We have awaited the coming of a natural
20   phenomenon. Mystics and romantics, knowledgeable
              workers
              of the land.

              But none has come.
              (Repeat)
25   but none has come.

Will the machinegunners please step forward?

                                              1969

Numbers, Letters

If you're not home, where
are you? Where'd you go? What
were you doing when gone? When
you come back, better make it good.
5 What was you doing down there, freakin' off[1]

---

[1]Going crazy.

with white women, hangin' out
with Queens, say it straight, to be
understood straight, put it flat and real
in the street where the sun comes and the
10 moon comes and the cold wind in winter
waters your eyes. Say what you mean, dig
it out put it down, and be strong
about it.

I cant say who I am
15 unless you agree I'm real

I cant be anything I'm not
Except these words pretend
to life not yet explained,
so here's some feeling for you
20 see how you like it, what it
reveals, and that's me.

Unless you agree I'm real
that I can feel
whatever beats hardest
25 at our black souls

I am real, and I can't say who
I am. Ask me if I know, I'll say
yes, I might say no. Still, ask.

I'm Everett LeRoi Jones, 30 yrs old.
30 A black nigger in the universe. A long breath singer,
wouldbe dancer, strong from years of fantasy
and study. All this time then, for what's happening
now. All that spilling of white ether, clocks in ghostheads
lips drying and rewet, eyes opening and shut, mouths churning.

35 I am a meditative man. And when I say something it's all of me
saying, and all the things that make me, have formed me, colored me
this brilliant reddish night. I will say nothing that I feel is
lie, or unproven by the same ghostclocks, by the same riders
always move so fast with the word slung over their backs or
40 in saddlebags, charging down Chinese roads. I carry some words,
some feeling, some life in me. My heart is large as my mind
this is a messenger calling, over here, over here, open your eyes
and your ears and your souls; today is the history we must learn
to desire. There is no guilt in love

1969

Dutchman

Characters

CLAY, *twenty-year-old Negro*
LULA, *thirty-year-old white woman*
RIDERS OF COACH, *white and black*
YOUNG NEGRO
CONDUCTOR

In the flying underbelly of the city. Steaming hot, and summer on top, outside. Underground. The subway heaped in modern myth.

Opening scene is a man sitting in a subway seat, holding a magazine but looking vacantly just above its wilting pages. Occasionally he looks blankly toward the window on his right. Dim lights and darkness whistling by against the glass. (Or paste the lights, as admitted props, right on the subway windows. Have them move, even dim and flicker. But give the sense of speed. Also stations, whether the train is stopped or the glitter and activity of these stations merely flashes by the windows.)

The man is sitting alone. That is, only his seat is visible, though the rest of the car is outfitted as a complete subway car. But only his seat is shown. There might be, for a time, as the play begins, a loud scream of the actual train. And it can recur throughout the play, or continue on a lower key once the dialogue starts.

The train slows after a time, pulling to a brief stop at one of the stations. The man looks idly up, until he sees a woman's face staring at him through the window; when it realizes that the man has noticed the face, it begins very premeditatedly to smile. The man smiles too, for a moment, without a trace of self-consciousness. Almost an instinctive though undesirable response. Then a kind of awkwardness or embarrassment sets in, and the man makes to look away, is further embarrassed, so he brings back his eyes to where the face was, but by now the train is moving again, and the face would seem to be left behind by the way the man turns his head to look back through the other windows at the slowly fading platform. He smiles then; more comfortably confident, hoping perhaps that his memory of this brief encounter will be pleasant. And then he is idle again.

Scene I

Train roars. Lights flash outside the windows.

LULA *enters from the rear of the car in bright, skimpy summer clothes and sandals. She carries a net bag full of paper books, fruit, and other anonymous articles. She is wearing sunglasses, which she pushes up on her forehead from time to time.* LULA *is a tall, slender, beautiful woman with long red hair hanging straight down her back, wearing only loud lipstick in somebody's good taste. She is eating an apple, very daintily. Coming down the car toward* CLAY.

She stops beside CLAY's *seat and hangs languidly from the strap, still managing to eat the apple. It is apparent that she is going to sit in the seat next to* CLAY, *and that she is only waiting for him to notice her before she sits.*

CLAY *sits as before, looking just beyond his magazine, now and again pulling the magazine slowly back and forth in front of his face in a hopeless effort to fan himself. Then he sees the woman hanging there beside him and he looks up into her face, smiling quizzically.*

LULA: Hello.
CLAY: Uh, hi're you?
LULA: I'm going to sit down. . . . O.K.?
CLAY: Sure.
LULA:

[*Swings down onto the seat, pushing her legs straight out as if she is very weary*]

Oooof! Too much weight.
CLAY: Ha, doesn't look like much to me.

[*Leaning back against the window, a little surprised and maybe stiff*]

LULA: It's so anyway.

[*And she moves her toes in the sandals, then pulls her right leg up on the left knee, better to inspect the bottoms of the sandals and the back of her heel. She appears for a second not to notice that* CLAY *is sitting next to her or that she has spoken to him just a second before.* CLAY *looks at the magazine, then out the black window. As he does this, she turns very quickly toward him*]

Weren't you staring at me through the window?
CLAY:

[*Wheeling around and very much stiffened*]

What?
LULA: Weren't you staring at me through the window? At the last stop?
CLAY: Staring at you? What do you mean?
LULA: Don't you know what staring means?
CLAY: I saw you through the window . . . if that's what it means. I don't know if I was staring. Seems to me you were staring through the window at me.
LULA: I was. But only after I'd turned around and saw you staring through that window down in the vicinity of my ass and legs.
CLAY: Really?
LULA: Really. I guess you were just taking those idle potshots. Nothing else to do. Run your mind over people's flesh.
CLAY: Oh boy. Wow, now I admit I was looking in your direction. But the rest of that weight is yours.

LULA: I suppose.

CLAY: Staring through train windows is weird business. Much weirder than staring very sedately at abstract asses.

LULA: That's why I came looking through the window . . . so you'd have more than that to go on. I even smiled at you.

CLAY: That's right.

LULA: I even got into this train, going some other way than mine. Walked down the aisle . . . searching you out.

CLAY: Really? That's pretty funny.

LULA: That's pretty funny. . . . God, you're dull.

CLAY: Well, I'm sorry, lady, but I really wasn't prepared for party talk.

LULA: No, you're not. What are you prepared for?

[Wrapping the apple core in a Kleenex and dropping it on the floor]

CLAY:

[Takes her conversation as pure sex talk. He turns to confront her squarely with this idea]

I'm prepared for anything. How about you?

LULA:

[Laughing loudly and cutting it off abruptly]

What do you think you're doing?

CLAY: What?

LULA: You think I want to pick you up, get you to take me somewhere and screw me, huh?

CLAY: Is that the way I look?

LULA: You look like you been trying to grow a beard. That's exactly what you look like. You look like you live in New Jersey with your parents and are trying to grow a beard. That's what. You look like you've been reading Chinese poetry and drinking lukewarm sugarless tea.

[Laughs, uncrossing and recrossing her legs]

You look like death eating a soda cracker.

CLAY:

[Cocking his head from one side to the other, embarrassed and trying to make some comeback, but also intrigued by what the woman is saying . . . even the sharp city coarseness of her voice, which is still a kind of gentle sidewalk throb]

Really? I look like all that?

LULA: Not all of it.

[She feints a seriousness to cover an actual somber tone]

    I lie a lot.

[Smiling]

    It helps me control the world.

CLAY:

[Relieved and laughing louder than the humor]

    Yeah, I bet.

LULA: But it's true, most of it, right? Jersey? Your bumpy neck?

CLAY: How'd you know all that? Huh? Really, I mean about Jersey . . . and even the beard. I met you before? You know Warren Enright?

LULA: You tried to make it with your sister when you were ten.

[CLAY leans back hard against the back of the seat, his eyes opening now, still trying to look amused]

    But I succeeded a few weeks ago.

[She starts to laugh again]

CLAY: What're you talking about? Warren tell you that? You're a friend of Georgia's?

LULA: I told you I lie. I don't know your sister. I don't know Warren Enright.

CLAY: You mean you're just picking these things out of the air?

LULA: Is Warren Enright a tall skinny black black boy with a phony English accent?

CLAY: I figured you knew him.

LULA: But I don't. I just figured you would know somebody like that.

[Laughs]

CLAY: Yeah, yeah.

LULA: You're probably on your way to his house now.

CLAY: That's right.

LULA:

[Putting her hand on CLAY's closest knee, drawing it from the knee up to the thigh's hinge, then removing it, watching his face very closely and continuing to laugh, perhaps more gently than before]

    Dull, dull, dull. I bet you think I'm exciting.

CLAY: You're O.K.

LULA: Am I exciting you now?

CLAY: Right. That's not what's supposed to happen?

LULA: How do I know?

[She returns her hand, without moving it, then takes it away and plunges it in her bag to draw out an apple]

You want this?

CLAY: Sure.

LULA:

[She gets one out of the bag for herself]

Eating apples together is always the first step. Or walking up uninhabited Seventh Avenue in the twenties on weekends.

[Bites and giggles, glancing at CLAY and speaking in loose sing-song]

Can get you involved . . . boy! Get us involved. Um-huh.

[Mock seriousness]

Would you like to get involved with me, Mister Man?

CLAY:

[Trying to be as flippant as LULA, whacking happily at the apple]

Sure. Why not? A beautiful woman like you. Huh, I'd be a fool not to.

LULA: And I bet you're sure you know what you're talking about.

[Taking him a little roughly by the wrist, so he cannot eat the apple, then shaking the wrist]

I bet you're sure of almost everything anybody ever asked you about . . . right?

[Shakes his wrist harder]

Right?

CLAY: Yeah, right. . . . Wow, you're pretty strong, you know? Whatta you, a lady wrestler or something?

LULA: What's wrong with lady wrestlers? And don't answer because you never knew any. Huh.

[Cynically]

That's for sure. They don't have any lady wrestlers in that part of Jersey. That's for sure.

CLAY: Hey, you still haven't told me how you know so much about me.

LULA: I told you I didn't know anything about *you* . . . you're a well-known type.

CLAY: Really?

LULA: Or at least I know the type very well. And your skinny English friend too.

CLAY: Anonymously?

LULA:

[Settles back in seat, single-mindedly finishing her apple and humming snatches of rhythm and blues song]

What?

CLAY: Without knowing us specifically?

LULA: Oh boy.

[Looking quickly at Clay]

What a face. You know, you could be a handsome man.

CLAY: I can't argue with you.

LULA:

[Vague, off-center response]

What?

CLAY:

[Raising his voice, thinking the train noise has drowned part of his sentence]

I can't argue with you.

LULA: My hair is turning gray. A gray hair for each year and type I've come through.

CLAY: Why do you want to sound so old?

LULA: But it's always gentle when it starts.

[Attention drifting]

Hugged against tenements, day or night.

CLAY: What?

LULA:

[Refocusing]

Hey, why don't you take me to that party you're going to?

CLAY: You must be a friend of Warren's to know about the party.

LULA: Wouldn't you like to take me to the party?

[Imitates clinging vine]

Oh, come on, ask me to your party.

CLAY: Of course I'll ask you to come with me to the party. And I'll bet you're a friend of Warren's.

LULA: Why not be a friend of Warren's? Why not?

[Taking his arm]

Have you asked me yet?

CLAY: How can I ask you when I don't know your name?

LULA: Are you talking to my name?

CLAY: What is it, a secret?

LULA: I'm Lena the Hyena.[1]

CLAY: The famous woman poet?

LULA: Poetess! The same!

CLAY: Well, you know so much about me . . . what's my name?

LULA: Morris the Hyena.

CLAY: The famous woman poet?

LULA: The same.

[Laughing and going into her bag]

You want another apple?

CLAY: Can't make it, lady. I only have to keep one doctor away a day.

LULA: I bet your name is . . . something like . . . uh, Gerald or Walter. Huh?

CLAY: God, no.

LULA: Lloyd, Norman? One of those hopeless colored names creeping out of New Jersey. Leonard? Gag. . . .

CLAY: Like Warren?

LULA: Definitely. Just exactly like Warren. Or Everett.

CLAY: Gag. . . .

LULA: Well, for sure, it's not Willie.

CLAY: It's Clay.

LULA: Clay? Really? Clay what?

CLAY: Take your pick. Jackson, Johnson, or Williams.

LULA: Oh, really? Good for you. But it's got to be Williams. You're too pretentious to be a Jackson or Johnson.

CLAY: Thass right.

LULA: But Clay's O.K.

CLAY: So's Lena.

LULA: It's Lula.

CLAY: Oh?

LULA: Lula the Hyena.

---

[1]Character in Al Capp's comic strip, *Li'l Abner* (1934–1977). The ugliest woman who ever lived, Lena drove anyone who looked at her instantly mad, so no sane person could reliably describe her. She was the subject of a famous national drawing contest sponsored by Capp in 1945.

CLAY: Very good.
LULA:

[Starts laughing again]

Now you say to me, "Lula, Lula, why don't you go to this party with me tonight?" It's your turn, and let those be your lines.
CLAY: Lula, why don't you go to this party with me tonight, Huh?
LULA: Say my name twice before you ask, and no huh's.
CLAY: Lula, Lula, why don't you go to this party with me tonight?
LULA: I'd like to go, Clay, but how can you ask me to go when you barely know me?
CLAY: That is strange, isn't it?
LULA: What kind of reaction is that? You're supposed to say, "Aw, come on, we'll get to know each other better at the party."
CLAY: That's pretty corny.
LULA: What are you into anyway?

[Looking at him half sullenly but still amused]

What thing are you playing at, Mister? Mister Clay Williams?

[Grabs his thigh, up near the crotch]

What are *you* thinking about?
CLAY: Watch it now, you're gonna excite me for real.
LULA:

[Taking her hand away and throwing her apple core through the window]

I bet.

[She slumps in the seat and is heavily silent]

CLAY: I thought you knew everything about me? What happened?

[LULA looks at him, then looks slowly away, then over where the other aisle would be. Noise of the train. She reaches in her bag and pulls out one of the paper books. She puts it on her leg and thumbs the pages listlessly. CLAY cocks his head to see the title of the book. Noise of the train. LULA flips pages and her eyes drift. Both remain silent]

Are you going to the party with me, Lula?
LULA:

[Bored and not even looking]

I don't even know you.
CLAY: You said you know my type.

LULA:

[Strangely irritated]

Don't get smart with me, Buster. I know you like the palm of my hand.

CLAY: The one you eat the apples with?

LULA: Yeh. And the one I open doors late Saturday evening with. That's my door. Up at the top of the stairs. Five flights. Above a lot of Italians and lying Americans. And scrape carrots with. Also . . .

[Looks at him]

the same hand I unbutton my dress with, or let my skirt fall down. Same hand. Lover.

CLAY: Are you angry about anything? Did I say something wrong?

LULA: Everything you say is wrong.

[Mock smile]

That's what makes you so attractive. Ha. In that funnybook jacket with all the buttons.

[More animate, taking hold of his jacket]

What've you got that jacket and tie on in all this heat for? And why're you wearing a jacket and tie like that? Did your people ever burn witches or start revolutions over the price of tea? Boy, those narrow shoulder clothes come from a tradition you ought to feel oppressed by. A three-button suit. What right do you have to be wearing a three-button suit and striped tie? Your grandfather was a slave, he didn't go to Harvard.

CLAY: My grandfather was a night watchman.

LULA: And you went to a colored college where everybody thought they were Averell Harriman.[2]

CLAY: All except me.

LULA: And who did you think you were? Who do you think you are now?

CLAY:

[Laughs as if to make light of the whole trend of the conversation]

Well, in college I thought I was Baudelaire.[3] But I've slowed down since.

LULA: I bet you never once thought you were a black nigger.

---

[2]Wealthy U.S. businessman and public official (1891–1986). Harriman was undersecretary of state in 1964, when *Dutchman* was first performed.

[3]Charles Baudelaire (1821–1867), French poet and critic unappreciated during his lifetime (he was fined for "offenses against public morals" after the publication of one book), now considered a landmark French literary figure.

[*Mock serious, then she howls with laughter.* CLAY *is stunned but after initial reaction, he quickly tries to appreciate the humor.* LULA *almost shrieks*]

A black Baudelaire.

CLAY: That's right.

LULA: Boy, are you corny. I take back what I said before. Everything you say is not wrong. It's perfect. You should be on television.

CLAY: You act like you're on television already.

LULA: That's because I'm an actress.

CLAY: I thought so.

LULA: Well, you're wrong. I'm no actress. I told you I always lie. I'm nothing, honey, and don't you ever forget it.

[*Lighter*]

Although my mother was a Communist. The only person in my family ever to amount to anything.

CLAY: My mother was a Republican.

LULA: And your father voted for the man[4] rather than the party.[5]

CLAY: Right!

LULA: Yea for him. Yea, yea for him.

CLAY: Yea!

LULA: And yea for America where he is free to vote for the mediocrity of his choice! Yea!

CLAY: Yea!

LULA: And yea for both your parents who even though they differ about so crucial a matter as the body politic still forged a union of love and sacrifice that was destined to flower at the birth of the noble Clay . . . what's your middle name?

CLAY: Clay.

LULA: A union of love and sacrifice that was destined to flower at the birth of the noble Clay Clay Williams. Yea! And most of all yea yea for you, Clay Clay. The Black Baudelaire! Yes!

[*And with knifelike cynicism*]

My Christ. My Christ.

CLAY: Thank you, ma'am.

LULA: May the people accept you as a ghost of the future. And love you, that you might not kill when you can.

CLAY: What?

LULA: You're a murderer, Clay, and you know it.

---

[4]Slang for "the white man," or the system of institutionalized racism that oppresses black Americans.

[5]The International Communist Party, which recruited heavily among the American black population in the mid-twentieth century by promising complete racial equality.

[*Her voice darkening with significance*]

    You know goddamn well what I mean.

CLAY: I do?

LULA: So we'll pretend the air is light and full of perfume.

CLAY:

[*Sniffing at her blouse*]

    It is.

LULA: And we'll pretend the people cannot see you. That is, the citizens. And that you are free of your own history. And I am free of my history. We'll pretend that we are both anonymous beauties smashing along through the city's entrails.

[*She yells as loud as she can*]

    GROOVE!

Black

Scene II

Scene is the same as before, though now there are other seats visible in the car. And throughout the scene other people get on the subway. There are maybe one or two seated in the car as the scene opens, though neither CLAY *nor* LULA *notices them.* CLAY's *tie is open.* LULA *is hugging his arm.*

CLAY: The party!

LULA: I know it'll be something good. You can come in with me, looking casual and significant. I'll be strange, haughty, and silent, and walk with long slow strides.

CLAY: Right.

LULA: When you get drunk, pat me once, very lovingly on the flanks, and I'll look at you cryptically, licking my lips.

CLAY: It sounds like something we can do.

LULA: You'll go around talking to young men about your mind, and to old men about your plans. If you meet a very close friend who is also with someone like me, we can stand together, sipping our drinks and exchanging codes of lust. The atmosphere will be slithering in love and half-love and very open moral decision.

CLAY: Great. Great.

LULA: And everyone will pretend they don't know your name, and then . . .

[*She pauses heavily*]

    later, when they have to, they'll claim a friendship that denies your sterling character.

CLAY:

[Kissing her neck and fingers]

And then what?

LULA: Then? Well, then we'll go down the street, late night, eating apples and winding very deliberately toward my house.

CLAY: Deliberately?

LULA: I mean, we'll look in all the shopwindows, and make fun of the queers. Maybe we'll meet a Jewish Buddhist and flatten his conceits over some very pretentious coffee.

CLAY: In honor of whose God?

LULA: Mine.

CLAY: Who is . . . ?

LULA: Me . . . and you?

CLAY: A corporate Godhead.

LULA: Exactly. Exactly.

[Notices one of the other people entering]

CLAY: Go on with the chronicle. Then what happens to us?

LULA:

[A mild depression, but she still makes her description triumphant and increasingly direct]

To my house, of course.

CLAY: Of course.

LULA: And up the narrow steps of the tenement.[6]

CLAY: You live in a tenement?

LULA: Wouldn't live anywhere else. Reminds me specifically of my novel form of insanity.

CLAY: Up the tenement stairs.

LULA: And with my apple-eating hand I push open the door and lead you, my tender big-eyed prey, into my . . . God, what can I call it . . . into my hovel.

CLAY: Then what happens?

LULA: After the dancing and games, after the long drinks and long walks, the real fun begins.

CLAY: Ah, the real fun.

[Embarrassed, in spite of himself]

Which is . . . ?

---

[6]Apartment house, but with connotations of overcrowding, poor sanitation, safety hazards, and discomfort. Generally used to refer to the housing of impoverished urban immigrants during the early twentieth century.

LULA:

[Laughs at him]

Real fun in the dark house. Hah! Real fun in the dark house, high up above the street and the ignorant cowboys. I lead you in, holding your wet hand gently in my hand . . .
CLAY: Which is not wet?
LULA: Which is dry as ashes.
CLAY: And cold?
LULA: Don't think you'll get out of your responsibility that way. It's not cold at all. You Fascist![7] Into my dark living room. Where we'll sit and talk endlessly, endlessly.
CLAY: About what?
LULA: About what? About your manhood, what do you think? What do you think we've been talking about all this time?
CLAY: Well, I didn't know it was that. That's for sure. Every other thing in the world but that.

[Notices another person entering, looks quickly, almost involuntarily up and down the car, seeing the other people in the car]

Hey, I didn't even notice when those people got on.
LULA: Yeah, I know.
CLAY: Man, this subway is slow.
LULA: Yeah, I know.
CLAY: Well, go on. We were talking about my manhood.
LULA: We still are. All the time.
CLAY: We were in your living room.
LULA: My dark living room. Talking endlessly.
CLAY: About my manhood.
LULA: I'll make you a map of it. Just as soon as we get to my house.
CLAY: Well, that's great.
LULA: One of the things we do while we talk. And screw.
CLAY:

[Trying to make his smile broader and less shaky]

We finally got there.
LULA: And you'll call my rooms black as a grave. You'll say, "This place is like Juliet's tomb."[8]

---

[7]An adherent of Fascism, a totalitarian political system organized around fidelity to a dictatorial leader, social and economic centralization, and the violent suppression of resistance.
[8]From William Shakespeare's *Romeo and Juliet.* Because her parents opposed her marriage to Romeo, Juliet feigned death with a sleeping potion in order to be reunited with him, thus spending several days alive in her family's tomb.

CLAY:

[Laughs]

I might.

LULA: I know. You've probably said it before.

CLAY: And is that all? The whole grand tour?

LULA: Not all. You'll say to me very close to my face, many, many times, you'll say, even whisper, that you love me.

CLAY: Maybe I will.

LULA: And you'll be lying.

CLAY: I wouldn't lie about something like that.

LULA: Hah. It's the only kind of thing you will lie about. Especially if you think it'll keep me alive.

CLAY: Keep you alive? I don't understand.

LULA:

[Bursting out laughing, but too shrilly]

Don't understand? Well, don't look at me. It's the path I take, that's all. Where both feet take me when I set them down. One in front of the other.

CLAY: Morbid. Morbid. You sure you're not an actress? All that self-aggrandizement.

LULA: Well, I told you I wasn't an actress . . . but I also told you I lie all the time. Draw your own conclusions.

CLAY: Morbid. Morbid. You sure you're not an actress? All scribed? There's no more?

LULA: I've told you all I know. Or almost all.

CLAY: There's no funny parts?

LULA: I thought it was all funny.

CLAY: But you mean peculiar, not ha-ha.

LULA: You don't know what I mean.

CLAY: Well, tell me the almost part then. You said almost all. What else? I want the whole story.

LULA:

[Searching aimlessly through her bag. She begins to talk breathlessly, with a light and silly tone]

All stories are whole stories. All of 'em. Our whole story . . . nothing but change. How could things go on like that forever? Huh?

[Slaps him on the shoulder, begins finding things in her bag, taking them out and throwing them over her shoulder into the aisle]

Except I do go on as I do. Apples and long walks with deathless intelligent lovers. But you mix it up. Look out the window, all the time. Turning pages.

Change change change. Till, shit, I don't know you. Wouldn't, for that matter. You're too serious. I bet you're even too serious to be psychoanalyzed. Like all those Jewish poets from Yonkers,[9] who leave their mothers looking for other mothers, or others' mothers, on whose baggy tits they lay their fumbling heads. Their poems are always funny, and all about sex.

CLAY: They sound great. Like movies.

LULA: But you change.

[Blankly]

And things work on you till you hate them.

[More people come into the train. They come closer to the couple, some of them not sitting, but swinging drearily on the straps, staring at the two with uncertain interest]

CLAY: Wow. All these people, so suddenly. They must all come from the same place.

LULA: Right. That they do.

CLAY: Oh? You know about them too?

LULA: Oh yeah. About them more than I know about you. Do they frighten you?

CLAY: Frighten me? Why should they frighten me?

LULA: 'Cause you're an escaped nigger.

CLAY: Yeah?

LULA: 'Cause you crawled through the wire and made tracks to my side.

CLAY: Wire?

LULA: Don't they have wire around plantations?

CLAY: You must be Jewish. All you can think about is wire.[10] Plantations didn't have any wire. Plantations were big open whitewashed places like heaven, and everybody on 'em was grooved to be there. Just strummin' and hummin' all day.

LULA: Yes, yes.

CLAY: And that's how the blues was born.

LULA: Yes, yes. And that's how the blues was born.

[Begins to make up a song that becomes quickly hysterical. As she sings she rises from her seat, still throwing things out of her bag into the aisle, beginning a rhythmical shudder and twistlike wiggle, which she continues up and down the aisle, bumping into many of the standing people and tripping over the feet of those sitting. Each time she runs into a person she lets out a very vicious piece of profanity, wiggling and stepping all the time]

---

[9]Suburb of Manhattan in southern Westchester County, New York.

[10]Reference to the barbed wire fences surrounding Nazi concentration camps during the Holocaust.

And that's how the blues was born. Yes. Yes. Son of a bitch, get out of the way. Yes. Quack. Yes. Yes. And that's how the blues was born. Ten little niggers sitting on a limb, but none of them ever looked like him.[11]

[Points to CLAY, *returns toward the seat, with her hands extended for him to rise and dance with her]*

And that's how blues was born. Yes. Come on, Clay. Let's do the nasty. Rub bellies. Rub bellies.

CLAY:

[Waves his hands to refuse. He is embarrassed, but determined to get a kick out of the proceedings]

Hey, what was in those apples? Mirror, mirror on the wall, who's the fairest one of all? Snow White,[12] baby, and don't you forget it.

LULA:

[Grabbing for his hands, which he draws away]

Come on, Clay. Let's rub bellies on the train. The nasty. The nasty. Do the gritty grind, like your ol' rag-head mammy. Grind till you lose your mind. Shake it, shake it, shake it, shake it! OOOOweeee! Come on, Clay. Let's do the choo-choo train shuffle, the navel scratcher.

CLAY: Hey, you coming on like the lady who smoked up her grass skirt.

LULA:

[Becoming annoyed that he will not dance, and becoming more animated as if to embarrass him still further]

Come on, Clay . . . let's do the thing. Uhh! Uhh! Clay! Clay! You middle-class black bastard. Forget your social-working mother for a few seconds and let's knock stomachs. Clay, you liver-lipped white man. You would-be Christian. You ain't no nigger, you're just a dirty white man. Get up, Clay. Dance with me, Clay.

CLAY: Lula! Sit down, now. Be cool.

LULA:

[Mocking him, in wild dance]

Be cool. Be cool. That's all you know . . . shaking that wildroot cream-oil on your knotty head, jackets buttoning up to your chin, so full of white man's

---

[11]Parody of a British nursery rhyme, "Ten Little Niggers" (also known as "Ten Little Indians"), in which each of the ten is sequentially killed—for example, "Ten little niggers going out to dine/One choked his little self and then there were nine." In Lula's version, all ten are lynching victims who were hanged from a tree limb.

[12]Slang reference to cocaine.

words. Christ. God. Get up and scream at these people. Like scream meaningless shit in these hopeless faces.

[She screams at people in train, still dancing]

Red trains cough Jewish underwear for keeps! Expanding smells of silence. Gravy snot whistling like sea birds. Clay. Clay, you got to break out. Don't sit there dying the way they want you to die. Get up.

CLAY: Oh, sit the fuck down.

[He moves to restrain her]

Sit down, goddamn it.

LULA:

[Twisting out of his reach]

Screw yourself, Uncle Tom.[13] Thomas Woolly-head.

[Begins to dance a kind of jig, mocking CLAY with loud forced humor]

There is Uncle Tom . . . I mean, Uncle Thomas Woolly-Head. With old white matted mane. He hobbles on his wooden cane. Old Tom. Old Tom. Let the white man hump his ol' mama, and he jes' shuffle off in the woods and hide his gentle gray head. Ol' Thomas Woolly-Head.

[Some of the other riders are laughing now. A drunk gets up and joins LULA in her dance, singing, as best he can, her "song." CLAY gets up out of his seat and visibly scans the faces of the other riders]

CLAY: Lula! Lula!

[She is dancing and turning, still shouting as loud as she can. The drunk too is shouting, and waving his hands wildly]

Lula . . . you dumb bitch. Why don't you stop it?

[He rushes half stumbling from his seat, and grabs one of her flailing arms]

LULA: Let me go! You black son of a bitch.

[She struggles against him]

Let me go! Help!

---

[13]Slang term for a servile black man, taken from the docile, pious black slave and title charac- ter of Harriet Beecher Stowe's 1852 novel *Uncle Tom's Cabin.*

[CLAY *is dragging her towards her seat, and the drunk seeks to interfere. He grabs* CLAY *around the shoulders and begins wrestling with him.* CLAY *clubs the drunk to the floor without releasing* LULA, *who is still screaming.* CLAY *finally gets her to the seat and throws her into it*]

CLAY: Now you shut the hell up.

[*Grabbing her shoulders*]

Just shut up. You don't know what you're talking about. You don't know anything. So just keep your stupid mouth closed.

LULA: You're afraid of white people. And your father was. Uncle Tom Big Lip!

CLAY:

[*Slaps her as hard as he can, across the mouth.* LULA's *head bangs against the back of the seat. When she raises it again,* CLAY *slaps her again*]

Now shut up and let me talk.

[*He turns toward the other riders, some of whom are sitting on the edge of their seats. The drunk is on one knee, rubbing his head, and singing softly the same song. He shuts up too when he sees* CLAY *watching him. The others go back to newspapers or stare out the windows*]

Shit, you don't have any sense, Lula, nor feelings either. I could murder you now. Such a tiny ugly throat. I could squeeze it flat, and watch you turn blue, on a humble. For dull kicks. And all these weak-faced ofays[14] squatting around here, staring over their papers at me. Murder them too. Even if they expected it. That man there . . .

[*Points to well-dressed man*]

I could rip that *Times* right out of his hand, as skinny and middle-classed as I am, I could rip that paper out of his hand and just as easily rip out his throat. It takes no great effort. For what? To kill you soft idiots? You don't understand anything but luxury.

LULA: You fool!

CLAY:

[*Pushing her against the seat*]

I'm not telling you again, Tallulah Bankhead![15] Luxury. In your face and your fingers. You telling me what I ought to do.

[14]Derogatory black slang for white people.

[15]Flamboyant American stage and film actress (1903–1968), notorious for glamorous parties, heavy drinking, chain smoking, and public nudity.

[Sudden scream frightening the whole coach]

Well, don't! Don't you tell me anything! If I'm a middle-class fake white man . . . let me be. And let me be in the way I want.

[Through his teeth]

I'll rip your lousy breasts off! Let me be who I feel like being. Uncle Tom. Thomas. Whoever. It's none of your business. You don't know anything except what's there for you to see. An act. Lies. Device. Not the pure heart, the pumping black heart. You don't ever know that. And I sit here, in this buttoned-up suit, to keep myself from cutting all your throats. I mean wantonly. You great liberated whore! You fuck some black man, and right away you're an expert on black people. What a lotta shit that is. The only thing you know is that you come if he bangs you hard enough. And that's all. The belly rub? You wanted to do the belly rub? Shit, you don't even know how. You don't know how. That ol' dipty-dip shit you do, rolling your ass like an elephant. That's not my kind of belly rub. Belly rub is not Queens. Belly rub is dark places, with big hats and overcoats held up with one arm. Belly rub hates you. Old bald-headed four-eyed ofays popping their fingers . . . and don't know yet what they're doing. They say, "I love Bessie Smith."[16] And don't even understand that Bessie Smith is saying, "Kiss my ass, kiss my black unruly ass." Before love, suffering, desire, anything you can explain, she's saying, and very plainly, "Kiss my black ass." And if you don't know that, it's you that's doing the kissing.

Charlie Parker?[17] Charlie Parker. All the hip white boys scream for Bird. And Bird saying, "Up your ass, feeble-minded ofay! Up your ass." And they sit there talking about the tortured genius of Charlie Parker. Bird would've played not a note of music if he just walked up to East Sixty-seventh Street and killed the first ten white people he saw. Not a note! And I'm the great would-be poet. Yes. That's right! Poet. Some kind of bastard literature . . . all it needs is a simple knife thrust. Just let me bleed you, you loud whore, and one poem vanished. A whole people of neurotics, struggling to keep from being sane. And the only thing that would cure the neurosis would be your murder. Simple as that. I mean if I murdered you, then other white people would begin to understand me. You understand? No. I guess not. If Bessie Smith had killed some white people she wouldn't have needed that music. She could have talked very straight and plain about the world. No metaphors. No grunts. No wiggles in the dark of her soul.

---

[16]Legendary American blues singer and enormously influential musician (1895–1937) who achieved stardom in the 1920s with both black and white audiences.

[17]Known as "Bird," brilliant jazz saxophonist (1920–1955) who pioneered bebop and im-provisational forms, changing popular music forever. Almost as well known for his lifelong drug use as for his music, Parker collaborated with nearly every major jazz musician of the mid-twentieth century before his untimely death at 34.

Just straight two and two are four. Money. Power. Luxury. Like that. All of them. Crazy niggers turning their backs on sanity. When all it needs is that simple act. Murder. Just murder! Would make us all sane.

[Suddenly weary]

Ahhh. Shit. But who needs it? I'd rather be a fool. Insane. Safe with my words, and no deaths, and clean, hard thoughts, urging me to new conquests. My people's madness. Hah! That's a laugh. My people. They don't need me to claim them. They got legs and arms of their own. Personal insanities. Mirrors. They don't need all those words. They don't need any defense. But listen, though, one more thing. And you tell this to your father, who's probably the kind of man who needs to know at once. So he can plan ahead. Tell him not to preach so much rationalism and cold logic to these niggers. Let them alone. Let them sing curses at you in code and see your filth as simple lack of style. Don't make the mistake, through some irresponsible surge of Christian charity, of talking too much about the advantages of Western rationalism, or the great intellectual legacy of the white man, or maybe they'll begin to listen. And then, maybe one day, you'll find they actually do understand exactly what you are talking about, all these fantasy people. All these blues people. And on that day, as sure as shit, when you really believe you can "accept" them into your fold, as half-white trusties late of the subject peoples. With no more blues, except the very old ones, and not a watermelon in sight, the great missionary heart will have triumphed, and all of those ex-coons will be stand-up Western men, with eyes for clean hard useful lives, sober, pious and sane, and they'll murder you. They'll murder you, and have very rational explanations. Very much like your own. They'll cut your throats, and drag you out to the edge of your cities so the flesh can fall away from your bones, in sanitary isolation.

LULA:

[Her voice takes on a different, more businesslike quality]

I've heard enough.

CLAY:

[Reaching for his books]

I bet you have. I guess I better collect my stuff and get off this train. Looks like we won't be acting out that little pageant you outlined before.

LULA: No. We won't. You're right about that, at least.

[She turns to look quickly around the rest of the car]

All right!

[The others respond]

CLAY:

[Bending across the girl to retrieve his belongings]

Sorry, baby, I don't think we could make it.

[As he is bending over her, the girl brings up a small knife and plunges it into CLAY's chest. Twice. He slumps across her knees, his mouth working stupidly]

LULA: Sorry is right.

[Turning to the others in the car who have already gotten up from their seats]

Sorry is the rightest thing you've said. Get this man off me! Hurry, now!

[The others come and drag CLAY's body down the aisle]

Open the door and throw his body out.

[They throw him off]

And all of you get off at the next stop.

[LULA busies herself straightening her things. Getting everything in order. She takes out a notebook and makes a quick scribbling note. Drops it in her bag. The train apparently stops and all the others get off, leaving her alone in the coach.

Very soon a young Negro of about twenty comes into the coach, with a couple of books under his arm. He sits a few seats in back of LULA. When he is seated she turns and gives him a long slow look. He looks up from his book and drops the book on his lap. Then an old Negro conductor comes into the car, doing a sort of restrained soft shoe, and half mumbling the words of some song. He looks at the young man, briefly, with a quick greeting]

CONDUCTOR: Hey, brother!
YOUNG MAN: Hey.

[The conductor continues down the aisle with his little dance and the mumbled song. LULA turns to stare at him and follows his movements down the aisle. The conductor tips his hat when he reaches her seat, and continues out the car]

Curtain

1964

Sonia Sanchez b. 1934

Born in Birmingham, Alabama, Sanchez has taught creative writing and African American literature in at least eight universities across the United States. Now a professor of English at Temple University, she has performed her poems and given poetry workshops in Australia, England, Cuba, Nicaragua, and Africa, as well as the States. No other American figure blends the roles of mother, teacher, poet, and political activist more sincerely and energetically than Sanchez.

Her poems manifest the spiritual link between art and politics. If her earlier poems are to be appreciated, the reader must forget all conceptions of what the "poem" is, and listen attentively to Sanchez's attacks on the Euro-American political, social, and aesthetic establishments. Her work is intentionally non-intellectual, unacademic, and anti-middle-class. "To blk/record buyers" is characteristic of her work which aims at teaching blacks to know themselves, to be self-reliant, and strong. In this poem she attacks the Righteous Brothers for their aping a style which originated with black performers such as James Brown. What appears to be a list of the activities in the black urban community contains over three hundred years of black history. Sex, language and retorts, drinking, mocking war materials, crime, and religion are the placeboes blacks have used for comfort. Sanchez's poem ends with the "AAAH, AAAH, AAAH, yeah" which both affirms her point and echoes the style of popular artists like Aretha Franklin and James Brown.

Sanchez's language comes out of her immediate surroundings and accents her characters' lifestyles. Her refusal to use standard, academic English is a part of a political statement which undermines the use of language as a tool for oppression.

Two of her more important thematic concerns are her interest in the relationship between black men and black women, and her interest in black children. Two of her books are written for the young: *It's a New Day* and *A Sound Investment.* In these texts, too, Sanchez's purpose is to teach black people to know themselves, to be themselves, and to love themselves.

By the time of the publication of *It's a New Day,* Sanchez had become a member of Elijah Muhammad's Muslim community. Her Islamic ideology infuses her fourth and fifth books of poetry, *Love Poems* and *Blues Book for Blue Black Magical Women;* there she expresses her spiritual, mystical nature. And from this influence, her poetry becomes more mystical, more suggestive and abstract. While she experiments with the spatial possibilities in her earlier collections, *Homegirls & Handgrenades,* her sixth volume of poetry, introduces several prose-poems such as the very moving "Just Don't Never Give Up on Love" that looks like prose, but has many of the characteristics of poetry. *Under a Soprano Sky,* Sanchez's last collection to date, demonstrates both the fact that she has perfectly honed her skills at repetition, hyperbole, and invective, and that she has become more captivated by the sounds of language and the use of metaphor and imagery.

Joyce Ann Joyce
Chicago State University

PRIMARY WORKS

Homecoming, 1969; *Liberation Poem,* 1970; *We a BaddDDD People,* 1970; *Ima Talken bout the Nation of Islam,* 1972; *A Blues Book for Blue Black Magical Women,* 1973; *Love Poems,* 1973; *I've Been a Woman: New and Selected Poems,* 1981; *Homegirls & Handgrenades,* 1984; *Under a Soprano Sky,* 1987; *Wounded in the House of a Friend,* 1995; *Does Your House Have Lions?,* 1997; *Like Singing Coming Off the Drums: Love Poems,* 1998; *Shake Loose My Skin: New and Selected Poems,* 1999; *Ash,* 2001.

to blk/record/buyers

    don't play me no
    righteous bros.
               white people
    ain't rt bout nothing
5 no mo.
         don't tell me bout
    foreign dudes
           cuz no blk/
    people are grooving on a
10 sunday afternoon.
             they either
    making out/
          signifying/
                drinking/
15 making molotov cocktails/
                 stealing
    or rather more taking their goods
    from the honky thieves who
    ain't hung up
20   on no pacifist/jesus/
               cross/   but.
    play blk/songs
         to drown out the
    shit/screams of honkies.   AAAH.
25 AAAH AAAH yeah.   brothers.
      andmanymoretogo.

                     1969

Masks

(blacks don't have the intellectual capacity to succeed.)
                            —WILLIAM COORS

    the river runs toward day
    and never stops.
    so life receives the lakes
    patrolled by one-eyed pimps
5 who wash their feet in our blue whoredom

    the river floods
    the days grow short

we wait to change our masks
we wait for warmer days and
10   fountains without force
we wait for seasons without power.

today
ah today
only the shrill sparrow seeks the sky
15   our days are edifice.
we look toward temples that give birth to sanctioned flesh.

               o bring the white mask
               full of the chalk sky.

entering the temple
20   on this day of sundays
i hear the word spoken
by the unhurried speaker
who speaks of unveiled eyes.

               o bring the chalk mask
25   full of altitudes.

straight in this chair
tall in an unrehearsed role
i rejoice
and the spirit sinks in twilight of
30   distant smells.

               o bring the mask
               full of drying blood.

fee, fie, fo, fum,
i smell the blood
35   *of an englishman*

o my people
wear the white masks
for they speak without speaking
and hear words of forgetfulness.

40   o my people.

                             1984

Just Don't Never Give Up on Love

Feeling tired that day, I came to the park with the children. I saw her as I rounded the corner, sitting old as stale beer on the bench, ruminating on some uneventful past. And I thought, "Hell. No rap from the roots today. I need the present. On this day. This Monday. This July day buckling me under her summer wings, I need more than old words for my body to squeeze into."

I sat down at the far end of the bench, draping my legs over the edge, baring my back to time and time unwell spent. I screamed to the children to watch those curves threatening their youth as they rode their 10-speed bikes against mid-western rhythms.

I opened my book and began to write. They were coming again, those words insistent as his hands had been, pounding inside me, demanding their time and place. I relaxed as my hands moved across the paper like one possessed.

I wasn't sure just what it was I heard. At first I thought it was one of the boys calling me so I kept on writing. They knew the routine by now. Emergencies demanded a presence. A facial confrontation. No long distance screams across trees and space and other children's screams. But the sound pierced the pages and I looked around, and there she was inching her bamboo-creased body toward my back, coughing a beaded sentence off her tongue.

"Guess you think I ain't never loved, huh girl? Hee. Hee. Guess that what you be thinking, huh?"

I turned. Startled by her closeness and impropriety, I stuttered, "I, I, I, Whhhaat dooooo you mean?"

"Hee. Hee. Guess you think I been old like this fo'ever, huh?" She leaned toward me, "Huh? I was so pretty that mens brought me breakfast in bed. Wouldn't let me hardly do no work at all."

"That's nice ma'am. I'm glad to hear that." I returned to my book. I didn't want to hear about some ancient love that she carried inside her. I had to finish a review for the journal. I was already late. I hoped she would get the hint and just sit still. I looked at her out of the corner of my eyes.

"He could barely keep hisself in changing clothes. But he was pretty. My first husband looked like the sun. I used to say his name over and over again 'til it hung from my ears like diamonds. Has you ever loved a pretty man, girl?"

I raised my eyes, determined to keep a distance from this woman disturbing my day.

"No ma'am. But I've seen many a pretty man. I don't like them though cuz they keep their love up high in a linen closet and I'm too short to reach it."

Her skin shook with laughter.

"Girl you gots some spunk about you after all. C'mon over here next to me. I wants to see yo' eyes up close. You looks so uneven sittin' over there."

Did she say uneven? Did this old buddah splintering death say uneven? Couldn't she see that I had one eye shorter than the other; that my breath was painted on porcelain; that one breast crocheted keloids under this white blouse?

I moved toward her though. I scooped up the years that had stripped me to the waist and moved toward her. And she called to me to come out, come out wherever you are young woman, playing hide and go seek with scarecrow men. I gathered myself up at the gateway of her confessionals.

"Do you know what it mean to love a pretty man, girl?" She crooned in my ear. "You always running behind a man like that girl while he cradles his privates. Ain't no joy in a pretty yellow man, cuz he always out pleasurin' and givin' pleasure."

I nodded my head as her words sailed in my ears. Here was the pulse of a woman whose black ass shook the world once.

She continued. "A woman crying all the time is pitiful. Pitiful I says. I wuz pitiful sitting by the window every night like a cow in the fields chewin' on cud. I wanted to cry out, but not even God hisself could hear me. I tried to cry out til my mouth wuz split open at the throat. I 'spoze there is a time all womens has to visit the slaughter house. My visit lasted five years."

Touching her hands, I felt the summer splintering in prayer, touching her hands, I felt my bones migrating in red noise. I asked, "When did you see the butterflies again?"

Her eyes wandered like quicksand over my face. Then she smiled, "Girl don't you know yet that you don't never give up on love? Don't you know you has in you the pulse of winds? The noise of dragon flies?" Her eyes squinted close and she said, "One of them mornings he woke up callin' me and I wuz gone. I wuz gone running with the moon over my shoulders. I looked no which way at all. I had inside me 'nough knives and spoons to cut/scoop out the night. I wuz a tremblin' as I met the mornin'."

She stirred in her 84-year-old memory. She stirred up her body as she talked. "They's men and mens. Some good. Some bad. Some breathing death. Some breathing life. William wuz my beginnin'. I come to my second husband spittin' metal and he just pick me up and fold me inside him. I wuz christen' with his love."

She began to hum. I didn't recognize the song; it was a prayer. I leaned back and listened to her voice rustling like silk. I heard cathedrals and sonnets; I heard tents and revivals and a black woman spilling black juice among her ruins.

"We all gotta salute death one time or 'nother girl. Death be waitin' out doors trying to get inside. William died at his job. Death just turned 'round and snatched him right off the street."

Her humming became the only sound in the park. Her voice moved across the bench like a mutilated child. And I cried. For myself. For this woman talkin' about love. For all the women who have ever stretched their bodies out anticipating civilization and finding ruins.

The crashing of the bikes was anticlimactic. I jumped up, rushed toward the accident. Man. Little man. Where you bicycling to so very fast? Man. Second little man. Take it slow. It all passes so fast any how.

As I walked the boys and their bikes toward the bench, I smiled at this old woman waiting for our return.

"I want you to meet a great lady, boys."

"Is she a writer, too, ma?"

"No honey. She's a lady who has lived life instead of writing about it."

"After we say hello can we ride a little while longer? Please!"

"Ok. But watch your manners now and your bones afterwards."

"These are my sons, Ma'am."

"How you do sons? I'm Mrs. Rosalie Johnson. Glad to meet you."

The boys shook her hand and listened for a minute to her words. Then they rode off, spinning their wheels on a city neutral with pain.

As I stood watching them race the morning, Mrs. Johnson got up.

"Don't go," I cried. "You didn't finish your story."

"We'll talk by-and-by. I comes out here almost everyday. I sits here on the same bench everyday. I'll probably die sittin' here one day. As good a place as any I 'magine."

"May I hug you, ma'am? You've helped me so much today. You've given me strength to keep on looking."

"No. Don't never go looking for love girl. Just wait. It'll come. Like the rain fallin' from the heaven, it'll come. Just don't never give up on love."

We hugged; then she walked her 84-year-old walk down the street. A black woman. Echoing gold. Carrying couplets from the sky to crease the ground.

1984

A Letter to Dr. Martin Luther King

Dear Martin,

Great God, what a morning, Martin!

The sun is rolling in from faraway places. I watch it reaching out, circling these bare trees like some reverent lover. I have been standing still listening to the morning, and I hear your voice crouched near hills, rising from the mountain tops, breaking the circle of dawn.

You would have been 54 today.

As I point my face toward a new decade, Martin, I want you to know that the country still crowds the spirit. I want you to know that we still hear your footsteps setting out on a road cemented with black bones. I want you to know that the stuttering of guns could not stop your light from crashing against cathedrals chanting piety while hustling the world.

Great God, what a country, Martin!

The decade after your death docked like a spaceship on a new planet. Voyagers all we were. We were the aliens walking up the '70s, a holocaust people on the move looking out from dark eyes. A thirsty generation, circling the peaks of our country for more than a Pepsi taste. We were youngbloods, spinning hip syllables while saluting death in a country neutral with pain.

And our children saw the mirage of plenty spilling from capitalistic sands.
And they ran toward the desert.
And the gods of sand made them immune to words that strengthen the breast.
And they became scavengers walking on the earth.
And you can see them playing. Hide-and-go-seek robbers. Native sons. Running

on their knees. Reinventing slavery on asphalt. Peeling their umbilical cords for a gold chain.

And you can see them on Times Square, in N.Y.C., Martin, selling their 11-, 12-year-old, 13-, 14-year-old bodies to suburban forefathers.

And you can see them on Market Street in Philadelphia bobbing up bellywise, young fishes for old sharks.

And no cocks are crowing on those mean streets.

Great God, what a morning it'll be someday, Martin!

That decade fell like a stone on our eyes. Our movements. Rhythms. Loves. Books. Delivered us from the night, drove out the fears keeping some of us hoarse. New births knocking at the womb kept us walking.

We crossed the cities while a backlash of judges tried to turn us into moles with blackrobed words of reverse racism. But we knew. And our knowing was like a sister's embrace. We crossed the land where famine was fed in public. Where black stomachs exploded on the world's dais while men embalmed their eyes and tongues in gold. But we knew. And our knowing squatted from memory.

Sitting on our past, we watch the new decade dawning. These are strange days, Martin, when the color of freedom becomes disco fever; when soap operas populate our Zulu braids; as the world turns to the conservative right and general hospitals are closing in Black neighborhoods and the young and the restless are drugged by early morning reefer butts. And houses tremble.

These are dangerous days, Martin, when cowboy-riding presidents corral Blacks (and others) in a common crown of thorns; when nuclear-toting generals recite an alphabet of blood; when multinational corporations assassinate ancient cultures while inaugurating new civilizations. Comeout comeout wherever you are. Black country. Waiting to be born . . .

But, Martin, on this, your 54th birthday—with all the reversals—we have learned that black is the beginning of everything.

> *it was black in the universe before the sun;*
> *it was black in the mind before we opened our eyes;*
> *it was black in the womb of our mother;*
> *black is the beginning,*
> *and if we are the beginning we will be forever.*

Martin. I have learned too that fear is not a Black man or woman. Fear cannot disturb the length of those who struggle against material gains for self-aggrandizement. Fear cannot disturb the good of people who have moved to a meeting place where the pulse pounds out freedom and justice for the universe.

Now is the changing of the tides, Martin. You forecast it where leaves dance on the wings of man. Martin. Listen. On this your 54th year, listen and you will hear the earth delivering up curfews to the missionaries and assassins. Listen. And you will hear the tribal songs:

> *Ayeeee   Ayooooo   Ayeee*
> *Ayeeee   Ayooooo   Ayeee*
> *Malcolm . . .*
> *Robeson . . .*
> *Lumumba . . .*

> *Fannie Lou . . .*
> *Garvey . . .*
> *Johnbrown . . .*
> *Tubman . . .*
> *Mandela . . .*
> *(free Mandela,*
> *free Mandela)*
> *Assata . . .*
> *Ke wa rona*[1]
> *Ke wa rona*
> *Ke wa rona*
> *Ke wa rona*
> *Ke wa rona*
> *Ke wa rona*
> *Ke wa rona*
> *Ke wa rona*

As we go with you to the sun,
as we walk in the dawn, turn our eyes
Eastward and let the prophecy come true
and let the prophecy come true.
    Great God, Martin, what a morning it will be!

1984

Father and Daughter

    we talk of light things you and I in this
    small house. no winds stir here among
    flame orange drapes that drape our genesis
    And snow melts into rivers. The young
5 grandchild reviews her impudence that
    makes you laugh and clap for more allure.
    Ah, how she twirls the emerald lariat.
    When evening comes your eyes transfer
    to space you have not known and taste the blood
10 breath of a final flower. Past equal birth,
    the smell of salt begins another flood:
    your land is in the ashes of the South.
    perhaps the color of our losses:
    perhaps the memory that dreams nurse:
15 old man, we do not speak of crosses.

1985

---

[1]He is ours.

Tomás Rivera 1935–1984

The son of Mexican citizens who migrated to Texas in the 1920s, Tomás Rivera was born in Crystal City, Texas, in the agricultural region called the "Winter Garden." Rivera's parents worked as farm laborers in the 1930s and '40s and throughout Rivera's childhood were a part of the migrant stream that took Mexican workers from south Texas into Oklahoma and Missouri and then into the vegetable fields of Michigan and Minnesota.

Rivera's working-class background provided the basis for his writing. He too worked as a migrant farm laborer through the 1950s, even during his junior college years in Texas. On graduation from Southwest Texas State University with a degree in English, Rivera faced the realities of life in the Southwest. Unable to find work as an English teacher because he was Mexican American, he returned to Southwest Texas State to earn a master's degree in English and administration. He then received a doctorate in Spanish literature at the University of Oklahoma in 1969. After a few years of teaching, Rivera became vice president for administration at the University of Texas at San Antonio and, later, executive vice president at the University of Texas at El Paso. At the time of his death, he was chancellor of the University of California, Riverside.

. . . y no se lo tragó la tierra/ And the Earth Did Not Devour Him (1971) is a milestone in Mexican American literary history, set explicitly within the social and political contexts of the agricultural laborer's life in the years after World War II. Winner in 1970 of the first Quinto Sol Prize for literature, the most prestigious literary award in the early years of Chicano literature, Rivera's novel, from which the present selections are drawn, became a primary element of the new Mexican American literary history.

In the original South Texas Spanish, Rivera's prose is tight and lean, the vocabulary and syntax rigorously controlled and set within the world of the Chicano migrant farmworker. Like Faulkner's *As I Lay Dying,* Rivera's narrative is not expository. In documenting the life of the farmworker and trying to keep its significant place in contemporary American history alive, *Tierra* offers a complex narrative of subjective impressions purposely disjointed from simple chronology. "The Lost Year" is the first half of the frame story that brackets the twelve sections of Rivera's novel. The following selections, including the titular chapter, ". . . And the Earth Did Not Devour Him," and the penultimate chapter, "When We Arrive," depict crucial moments of dawning self-consciousness and collective solidarity. The links between the chapters follow a stream-of-consciousness thread, bereft of traditional narrative causality, relating the seasonal events in an allegorical year of the life of the anonymous migrant farmworker child.

In a 1980 interview, Rivera situated his work squarely within the Mexican American's struggle for social and political justice: "In . . . *Tierra* . . . I wrote about [the life of] the migrant worker in [the] ten year period [between 1945 and 1955]. . . . I began to see that my role . . . would be to document that period of time, but giving it some kind of spiritual strength or spiritual history" (Bruce-Novoa, *Chicano Authors: Inquiry by Interview,* 1980:148). Written during the period 1967–1968, at the height of the politicization of the Chicano labor struggles and the takeover of political power in Crystal City by Mexican Americans of the radical La Raza Unida party, Rivera's stories have a sense of political urgency. They also present the anguish of spiritual alienation and the reality of economic and social injustice. Rivera's narrator, born into a world of absence and loss, seeks to discover his identity and to inscribe his name and that of his community in the text of history. The characters of Rivera's stories are not the pragmatic subjects who populate the myth of American individualism, nor are they romanticized symbols of the worker engaged in a world-wide struggle. Rather, his characters are rooted in the reality of south Texas social and economic history, lived out and em-bodied in the form of the community of *la raza* (the people).

Ramón Saldívar
Stanford University

PRIMARY WORK

. . . *y no se lo tragó la tierra/And the Earth Did Not Devour Him*, 1971; *The Harvest: Short Stories*, 1989; *The Searchers: Collected Poetry*, 1990; *The Complete Works*, 1991.

from . . . y no se lo tragó la tierra/And the Earth Did Not Devour Him

The Lost Year

That year was lost to him. At times he tried to remember and, just about when he thought everything was clearing up some, he would be at a loss for words. It almost always began with a dream in which he would suddenly awaken and then realize that he was really asleep. Then he wouldn't know whether what he was thinking had happened or not.

It always began when he would hear someone calling him by his name but when he turned his head to see who was calling, he would make a complete turn, and there he would end up—in the same place. This was why he never could discover who was calling him nor why. And then he even forgot the name he had been called.

One time he stopped at mid-turn and fear suddenly set in. He realized that he had called himself. And thus the lost year began.

He tried to figure out when that time he had come to call "year" had started. He became aware that he was always thinking and thinking, and from this there was no way out. Then he started thinking about how he never thought, and this was when his mind would go blank and he would fall asleep. But before falling asleep he saw and heard many things . . .

And the Earth Did Not Devour Him

The first time he felt hate and anger was when he saw his mother crying for his uncle and his aunt. They both had caught tuberculosis and had been sent to different sanitariums. So, between the brothers and sisters, they had distributed the children among themselves and had taken care of them as best they could. Then the aunt died, and soon thereafter they brought the uncle back from the sanitarium, but he was already spitting blood. That was when he saw his mother crying every little while. He became angry because he was unable to do anything against anyone. Today he felt the same. Only today it was for his father.

"You all should've come home right away, m'ijo. Couldn't you see that your Daddy was sick? You should have known that he was sunstruck. Why didn't you come home?"

"I don't know. Us being so soaked with sweat, we didn't feel so hot, but I guess that when you're sunstruck it's different. But I did tell him to sit down under the tree that's at the edge of the rows, but he didn't want to. And that was when he started throwing up. Then we saw he couldn't hoe anymore and we dragged him and put him under a tree. He didn't put up a fuss at that point. He just let us take him. He didn't even say a word."

"Poor viejo, my poor viejo. Last night he hardly slept. Didn't you hear him outside the house. He squirmed in bed all night with cramps. God willing, he'll get well. I've been giving him cool lemonade all day, but his eyes still look glassy. If I'd gone to the fields yesterday, I tell you, he wouldn't have gotten sick. My poor viejo, he's going to have cramps all over his body for three days and three nights at the least. Now, you all take care of yourselves. Don't overwork yourselves so much. Don't pay any mind to that boss if he tries to rush you. Just don't do it. He thinks its so easy since he's not the one who's out there, stooped."

He became even angrier when he heard his father moan outside the chicken coop. He wouldn't stay inside because he said it made him feel very nervous. Outside where he could feel the fresh air was where he got some relief. And also when the cramps came he could roll over on the grass. Then he thought about whether his father might die from the sunstroke. At times he heard his father start to pray and ask for God's help. At first he had faith that he would get well soon but by the next day he felt the anger growing inside of him. And all the more when he heard his mother and his father clamoring for God's mercy. That night, well past midnight, he had been awakened by his father's groans. His mother got up and removed the scapularies from around his neck and washed them. Then she lit some candles. But nothing happened. It was like his aunt and uncle all over again.

"What's to be gained from doing all that, Mother? Don't tell me you think it helped my aunt and uncle any. How come we're like this, like we're buried alive? Either the germs eat us alive or the sun burns us up. Always some kind of sickness. And every day we work and work. For what? Poor Dad, always working so hard. I think he was born working. Like he says, barely five years old and already helping his father plant corn. All the time feeding the earth and the sun, only to one day, just like that, get knocked down by the sun. And there you are, helpless. And them, begging for God's help . . . why, God doesn't care about us . . . No, better not say it, what if Dad gets worse. Poor Dad, I guess that at least gives him some hope."

His mother noticed how furious he was, and that morning she told him to calm down, that everything was in God's hands and that with God's help his father was going to get well.

"Oh, Mother, do you really believe that? I am certain that God has no concern for us. Now you tell me, is Dad evil or mean-hearted? You tell me if he has ever done any harm to anyone."

"Of course not."

"So there you have it. You see? And my aunt and uncle? You explain. And the poor kids, now orphans, never having known their parents. Why did God have to take them away? I tell you, God could care less about the poor. Tell me, why must we live here like this? What have we done to deserve this? You're so good and yet you have to suffer so much."

"Oh, please, m'ijo, don't talk that way. Don't speak against the will of God. Don't talk that way, please, m'ijo. You scare me. It's as if already the blood of Satan runs through your veins."

"Well, maybe. That way at least I could get rid of this anger. I'm so tired of thinking about it. Why? Why you? Why Dad? Why my uncle? Why my aunt? Why their kids? Tell me, Mother, why? Why us, buried in the earth like animals with no hope for anything? You know the only hope we have is coming out here every year. And like you yourself say, only death brings rest. I think that's the way my aunt and uncle felt and that's how Dad must feel too."

"That's how it is m'ijo. Only death brings us rest."

"But why us?"

"Well, they say that . . ."

"Don't say it. I know what you're going to tell me—that the poor go to heaven."

That day started out cloudy and he could feel the morning coolness brushing his eyelashes as he and his brothers and sisters began the day's labor. Their mother had to stay home to care for her husband. Thus, he felt responsible for hurrying on his brothers and sisters. During the morning, at least for the first few hours, they endured the heat but by ten-thirty the sun had suddenly cleared the skies and pressed down against the world. They began working more slowly because of the weakness, dizziness and suffocation they felt when they worked too fast. Then they had to wipe the sweat from their eyes every little while because their vision would get blurred.

"If you start blacking out, stop working, you hear me? Or go a little slower. When we reach the edge we'll rest a bit to get our strength back. It's gonna be hot today. If only it'd stay just a bit cloudy like this morning, then nobody would complain. But no, once the sun bears down like this not even one little cloud dares to appear out of fear. And the worst of it is we'll finish up here by two and then we have to go over to that other field that's nothing but hills. It's okay at the top of the hill but down in the lower part of the slopes it gets to be real suffocating. There's no breeze there. Hardly any air goes through. Remember?"

"Yeah."

"That's where the hottest part of the day will catch us. Just drink plenty of water every little while. It don't matter if the boss gets mad. Just don't get sick. And if you can't go on, tell me right away, all right? We'll go home. Y'all saw what happened to Dad when he pushed himself too hard. The sun has no mercy, it can eat you alive."

Just as they had anticipated, they had moved on to the other field by early afternoon. By three o'clock they were all soaking with sweat. Not one part of their clothing was dry. Every little while they would stop. At times they could barely breathe, then they would black out and they would become fearful of getting sunstruck, but they kept on working.

"How do y'all feel?"

"Man, it's so hot! But we've got to keep on. 'Til six, at least. Except this water doesn't cut our thirst any. Sure wish I had a bottle of cool water, real cool, fresh from the well, or a coke, ice-cold."

* * *

"Are you crazy? That'd sure make you sunsick right now. Just don't work so fast. Let's see if we can make it until six. What do you think?"

At four o'clock the youngest became ill. He was only nine years old, but since he was paid the same as a grown up he tried to keep up with the rest. He began vomiting. He sat down, then he laid down. Terrified, the other children ran to where he lay and looked at him. It appeared that he had fainted and when they opened his eyelids they saw his eyes were rolled back. The next youngest child started crying but right away he told him to stop and help him carry his brother home. It seemed he was having cramps all over his little body. He lifted him and carried him by himself, and he began asking himself again, *why?*

"Why Dad and then my little brother? He's only nine years old. Why? He has to work like a mule buried in the earth. Dad, Mom, and my little brother here, what are they guilty of?"

Each step that he took towards the house resounded with the question, *why?* About halfway to the house he began to get furious. Then he started crying out of rage. His little brothers and sisters did not know what to do, and they, too, started crying, but out of fear. Then he started cursing. And without even realizing it, he said what he had been wanting to say for a long time. He cursed God. Upon doing this he felt that fear instilled in him by the years and by his parents. For a second he saw the earth opening up to devour him. Then he felt his footsteps against the earth, compact, more solid than ever. Then his anger swelled up again, and he vented it by cursing God. He looked at his brother, he no longer appeared as sick. He didn't know whether his brothers and sisters had understood the enormity of his curse.

That night he did not fall asleep until very late. He felt at peace as never before. He felt as though he had become detached from everything. He no longer worried about his father nor his brother. All that he awaited was the new day, the freshness of the morning. By daybreak his father was doing better. He was on his way to recovery. And his little brother, too; the cramps had almost completely subsided. Frequently he felt a sense of surprise upon recalling what he had done the previous afternoon. He thought of telling his mother, but he decided to keep it secret. All he told her was the earth did not devour anyone, nor did the sun.

He left for work and encountered a very cool morning. There were clouds in the sky and for the first time he felt capable of doing and undoing anything that he pleased. He looked down at the earth and kicked it hard and said.

"Not yet, you can't swallow me up yet. Someday, yes. But I'll never know it."

When We Arrive

At about four o'clock in the morning the truck broke down. All night they stood hypnotized by the high-pitched whir of the tires turning against the pavement. When the truck stopped they awakened. The silence alone told them something was wrong. All along the way the truck had been overheating and then when they stopped and checked the motor they saw that it had practically burned up. It just wouldn't go anymore. They would have to wait there until daybreak and then ask for a lift to the next town. Inside the trailer the people awakened and then struck up several conversations. Then, in the darkness, their eyes had gradually begun to close and all became so silent that all that could be heard was the chirping of the crickets. Some were sleeping, others were thinking.

"Good thing the truck stopped here. My stomach's been hurting a lot for some time but I would've had to wake up a lot of people to get to the window and ask them to stop. But you still can't hardly see anything. Well, I'm getting off, see if I can find a field or a ditch. Must've been that chile I ate, it was so hot but I hated to let it go to waste. I hope my vieja is doing all right in there, carrying the baby and all."

"This driver that we have this year is a good one. He keeps on going. He doesn't stop for anything. Just gases up and lets go. We've been on the road over twenty-four hours. We should be close to Des Moines. Sure wish I could sit down for just a little while at least. I'd get out and lie down on the side of the road but there's no telling if there's snakes or some other kind of animal. Just before I fell asleep on my feet it felt like my knees were going to buckle. But, I guess your body gets used to it right away 'cause it doesn't seem so hard anymore. But the kids must feel real tired standing like this all the way and with nothing to hold on to. Us grownups can at least hold on to this center bar that supports the canvas. And to think we're not as crowded as other times. I think there must be forty of us at the most. I remember that one time I traveled with that bunch of wetbacks, there were more than sixty of us. We couldn't even smoke."

"What a stupid woman! How could she be so dumb as to throw that diaper out the front of the truck. It came sliding along the canvas and good thing I had my glasses on or else I would've gotten my eyes full of shit too! What a stupid woman! How could she do that? She should've known that crap would be blown towards all of us standing up back here. Why the hell couldn't she just wait until we got to a gas station and dump the shit there!"

"That Negrito's eyes just about popped out when I ordered those fifty-four hamburgers. At two o'clock in the morning . . . And since I walked into the restaurant alone and I'm sure he didn't see the truck pull up loaded with people. His eyes just popped wide open . . . 'at two o'clock in the morning, hamburgers? Fifty-four of them? Man, you must eat one hell of a lot.' It's that the people hadn't eaten and the driver asked for just one of us to get out and order for everyone. That Negrito was astounded. He couldn't believe what I ordered, that I wanted fifty-four hamburgers. At two o'clock in the morning you can eat that many hamburgers very easily, especially when you're starving."

"This is the last fuckin' year I come out here. As soon as we get to the farm I'm getting the hell out. I'll go look for a job in Minneapolis. I'll be damned if I go back to Texas. Out here you can at least make a living at a decent job. I'll look for my uncle, see if he can find me a job at the hotel where he works as a bellboy. Who knows, maybe they'll give me a break there or at some other hotel. And then the gringas, that's just a matter of finding them."

"If things go well this year maybe we'll buy us a car so we won't have to travel this way, like cattle. The girls are pretty big now and I know they feel embarrassed. Sometimes

they have some good buys at the gas stations out there. I'll talk to my compadre, he knows some of the car salesmen. I'll get one I like, even if it's old. I'm tired of coming out here in a truck like this. My compadre drove back a good little car last year. If we do well with the onion crop, I'll buy me one that's at least half-way decent. I'll teach my boy how to drive and he can take it all the way to Texas. As long as he doesn't get lost like my nephew. They didn't stop to ask for directions and ended up in New Mexico instead of Texas. Or I'll get Mundo to drive it and I won't charge him for gas. I'll see if he wants to."

"With the money Mr. Thompson loaned me we have enough to buy food for at least two months. By then we should have the money from the beet crop. Just hope we don't get too much in debt. He loaned me two-hundred dollars but by the time you pay for the trip practically half of it is gone, and now that they've started charging me half-fare for the children . . . And then when we return, I have to pay him back double. Four-hundred dollars. That's too much interest, but what can you do? When you need it, you need it. Some people have told me to report him because that's way too much interest, but now he's even got the deed to the house. I'm just hoping that things go okay for us with the beet crop or else we'll be left to the wind, homeless. We have to save enough to pay him back the four-hundred. And then we'll see if we have something left. And these kids, they need to start going to school. I don't know. I hope it goes okay for us, if not I don't know how we're going to do it. I just pray to God that there's work."

"Fuckin' life, this goddamn fuckin' life! This fuckin' sonofabitchin' life for being dumb! dumb! dumb! We're nothing but a bunch of goddam assholes! To hell with this goddamn motherfuckin' life! This is the last time I go through this, standing up all the way like a goddamn animal. As soon as we get there I'm headed for Minneapolis. Somehow I'll find me something to do where I don't have to work like a fuckin' mule. Fuckin' life! One of these days they'll fuckin' pay for this. Sonofabitch! For being such a goddam asshole!"

"Poor viejo. He must be real tired now, standing up the whole trip. I saw him nodding off a little while ago. And with no way to help him, what with these two in my arms. How I wish we were there already so we could lie down, even if it's on the hard floor. These children are nothing but trouble. I hope I'll be able to help him out in the fields, but I'm afraid that this year, what with these kids, I won't be able to do anything. I have to breastfeed them every little while and then they're still so little. If only they were just a bit older. I'm still going to try my best to help him out. At least along his row so he won't feel so overworked. Even if it's just for short whiles. My poor viejo . . . the children are still so little and already he wishes they could start school. I just hope I'll be able to help him. God willing, I'll be able to help him."

"What a great view of the stars from here! It looks like they're coming down and touching the tarp of the truck. It's almost like there aren't any people inside. There's hardly any traffic at this hour. Every now and then a trailer passes by. The silence of the morning twilight makes everything look like it's made of satin. And now, what do I wipe myself with? Why couldn't it always be early dawn like this? We're going to be here till midday for sure. By the time they find help in the town and then by the time they fix the motor . . . If only it could stay like early dawn, then nobody would complain.

I'm going to keep my eyes on the stars till the last one disappears. I wonder how many more people are watching the same star? And how many more might there be wondering how many are looking at the same star? It's so silent it looks like it's the stars the crickets are calling to."

"Goddam truck. It's nothing but trouble. When we get there everybody will just have to look out for themselves. All I'm doing is dropping them off with the growers and I'm getting the hell out. Besides, we don't have a contract. They'll find themselves somebody to take them back to Texas. Somebody's bound to come by and pick them up. You can't make money off beets anymore. My best bet is to head back to Texas just as soon as I drop these people off and then see how things go hauling watermelons. The melon season's almost here. All I need now is for there not to be anyone in this goddam town who can fix the truck. What the hell will I do then? So long as the cops don't come by and start hassling me about moving the truck from here. Boy, that town had to be the worst. We didn't even stop and still the cop caught up with us just to tell us that he didn't want us staying there. I guess he just wanted to show off in front of the town people. But we didn't even stop in their goddam town. When we get there, as soon as I drop them off, I'll turn back. Each one to fend for himself."

"When we get there I'm gonna see about getting a good bed for my vieja. Her kidneys are really bothering her a lot nowadays. Just hope we don't end up in a chicken coop like last year, with that cement floor. Even though you cover it with straw, once the cold season sets in, you just can't stand it. That was why my rheumatism got so bad, I'm sure of that."

"When we arrive, when we arrive, the real truth is that I'm tired of arriving. Arriving and leaving, it's the same thing because we no sooner arrive and . . . the real truth of the matter . . . I'm tired of arriving. I really should say when we don't arrive because that's the real truth. We never arrive."

"When we arrive, when we arrive . . ."

Little by little the crickets ceased their chirping. It seemed as though they were becoming tired and the dawn gradually affirmed the presence of objects, ever so carefully and very slowly, so that no one would take notice of what was happening. And the people were becoming people. They began getting out of the trailer and they huddled around and commenced to talk about what they would do when they arrived.

1971

Lucille Clifton b. 1936

Thelma Lucille Sayles Clifton was born in Depew, New York, and educated at Fredonia State Teachers College, Fredonia, New York, and at Howard University. Although she began writing at a young age, Clifton devoted her early adult life to raising her family. In the midst of her life with her husband, Fred, and six children under the age of ten, she published her first collection of poetry, *Good Times,* in 1969. Since that time, she has published eight additional collections of poetry, a memoir, a compilation of her early work, and more than sixteen books for young readers—including the popular Everett Anderson series. Presently Distinguished Professor of Humanities at St. Mary's College in Maryland, Clifton has taught at Coppin State College, Goucher College, American University, and the University of California at Santa Cruz, among other colleges and universities. Her awards and distinctions include the University of Massachusetts Press Juniper Prize for Poetry; two National Endowment for the Arts Fellowships for creative writing; a nomination for the Pulitzer Prize for Poetry for *Two-Headed Woman* and a second Pulitzer Prize nomination for both *Good Woman: Poems and a Memoir 1969–1980* and *Next: New Poems;* an Emmy Award from the American Academy of Television Arts and Sciences; Poet Laureate of the State of Maryland; and a 1996 Lannan Literary Award for Poetry.

The themes and language of Clifton's poetry are shaped by her concern with family history and relationships, with community, with racial history, and with the possibilities of reconciliation and transcendence. In *Good Times* she uses direct, unadorned language to capture the rhythms and values of urban African American working-class life. Throughout this collection Clifton consciously pits her spare, economical language against the pervasive and negative images of black urban life, insis-

tently reminding her readers of the humanity concealed underneath social and economic statistics. Like Langston Hughes and Gwendolyn Brooks, she sees virtue and dignity in the lives of ordinary African Americans, giving them faces, names, and histories, and validating their existence. In the face of the daily realities of urban life, Clifton records both the adversity and the small triumphs, always maintaining a strong-willed sense of optimism and spiritual resilience. One source of this equanimity, of this poise in the face of adversity and tragedy, derives from Clifton's strong sense of rootedness in the legacy of her family history—particularly of her great-great-grandmother Caroline, a woman kidnapped to America from Dahomey, and Caroline's daughter, Lucille, who bore the distinction of being the first black woman lynched in Virginia. These two women in particular conjure up images of survival and endurance on the one hand, and avenging spirits on the other. By locating herself within this family history, Clifton not only lays claim to an African past—a recurrent feature of many of her poems—she also defines herself as a poet whose task is to keep historical memory alive. At the same time that Clifton accepts the weight of this history, however, she refuses to be trapped or defeated by it. Like a blues singer's lyrics, Clifton's poems confront the chaos, disorder, and pain of human experience to transcend these conditions and to reaffirm her humanity.

The optimism that shapes Clifton's poetry is nourished by her deep spiritual beliefs. While she often invokes Christian motifs and biblical references in her poems, she draws freely upon other values and beliefs as well. "The black God, Kali/a woman God and terrible/with her skulls and breasts" often appears in her poems, as do references to African goddesses like Yemoja, the Yoruba water-deity, and to

Native American beliefs. More specifically, Clifton's invocation of the "two-headed woman" of African American folk belief, with its overtones of Hoodoo and conjure, makes plain her commitment to other ways of knowing and understanding the world. Certainly the spiritual dimension of her poetry has deepened since the death of her husband, Fred Clifton, in 1984. Whether her poetry is exploring the biological changes within her own body or imagining the death of the Sioux chief Crazy Horse,

Lucille Clifton's world is both earthy and spiritual. In her capacity as both witness and seer, she looks through the madness and sorrow of the world, locating moments of epiphany in the mundane and ordinary. And her poetry invariably moves toward those moments of calm and tranquillity, of grace, which speak to the continuity of the human spirit.

James A. Miller
George Washington University

PRIMARY WORKS

Good Times, 1969; *Good News About the Earth*, 1972; *An Ordinary Woman*, 1974; *Generations*, 1976; *Two-Headed Woman*, 1980; *Next: New Poems*, 1987; *Good Woman: Poems and A Memoir 1969–1980*, 1987; *Quilting: Poems 1987–1990*, 1991; *The Book of Light*, 1993; *The Terrible Stories: Poems*, 1996; *Blessing the Boats: New and Collected Poems, 1998–2000*, 2000; *Mercy*, 2004; also children's books.

the thirty eighth year

the thirty eighth year
of my life,
plain as bread
round as a cake
5 an ordinary woman.

an ordinary woman.

i had expected to be
smaller than this,
more beautiful,
10 wiser in afrikan ways,
more confident,
i had expected
more than this.

i will be forty soon.
15 my mother once was forty.

my mother died at forty four,
a woman of sad countenance
leaving behind a girl

awkward as a stork.
20 my mother was thick,
her hair was a jungle and
she was very wise
and beautiful
and sad.

25 i have dreamed dreams
for you mama
more than once.
i have wrapped me
in your skin
30 and made you live again
more than once.
i have taken the bones you hardened
and built daughters
and they blossom and promise fruit
35 like afrikan trees.
i am a woman now.
an ordinary woman.

in the thirty eighth
year of my life,
40 surrounded by life,
a perfect picture of
blackness blessed,
i had not expected this
loneliness.

45 if it is western,
if it is the final
europe in my mind,
if in the middle of my life
i am turning the final turn
50 into the shining dark
let me come to it whole
and holy
not afraid
not lonely
55 out of my mother's life
into my own.
into my own.

i had expected more than this.
i had not expected to be
60 an ordinary woman.

1974

i am accused of tending to the past

i am accused of tending to the past
as if i made it,
as if i sculpted it
with my own hands. i did not.
5 this past was waiting for me
when i came,
a monstrous unnamed baby,
and i with my mother's itch
took it to breast
10 and named it
History.
she is more human now,
learning language everyday,
remembering faces, names and dates.
15 when she is strong enough to travel
on her own, beware, she will.

1991

at the cemetery, walnut grove plantation, south carolina, 1989

among the rocks
at walnut grove
your silence drumming
in my bones,
5 tell me your names.

nobody mentioned slaves
and yet the curious tools
shine with your fingerprints.
nobody mentioned slaves
10 but somebody did this work
who had no guide, no stone,
who moulders under rock.

tell me your names,
tell me your bashful names
15 and i will testify.

the inventory lists ten slaves
but only men were recognized.

among the rocks
at walnut grove
20 some of these honored dead
were dark
some of these dark
were slaves
some of these slaves
25 were women
some of them did this
honored work.
tell me your names
foremothers, brothers,
30 tell me your dishonored names.
here lies
here lies
here lies
here lies
35 hear

1991

reply

[from a letter written to Dr. W.E.B. Dubois by Alvin Borgquest of Clark University in Massachusetts and dated April 3, 1905:

"We are pursuing an investigation here on the subject of crying as an expression of the emotions, and should like very much to learn about its peculiarities among the colored people. We have been referred to you as a person competent to give us information on the subject. We desire especially to know about the following salient aspects: 1. Whether the Negro sheds tears . . ."]

reply

he do
she do
they live
5 they love
they try
they tire
they flee

they fight
10 they bleed
they break
they moan
they mourn
they weep
15 they die
they do
they do
they do

      1991

in white america

1   i come to read them poems

i come to read them poems,
a fancy trick i do
like juggling with balls of light.
i stand, a dark spinner,
5 in the grange hall,
in the library, in the
smaller conference room,
and toss and catch as if by magic,
my eyes bright, my mouth smiling,
10 my singed hands burning.

2   the history

1800's in this town
fourteen longhouses were destroyed
by not these people here.
not these people
15 burned the crops and chopped down
all the peach trees.
not these people. these people
preserve peaches, even now.

3   the tour

"this was a female school.
20 my mother's mother graduated
second in her class.

they were taught embroidery,
and chenille and filigree,
ladies' learning. yes,
25 we have a liberal history here."
smiling she pats my darky hand.

4   the hall

in this hall
dark women
scrubbed the aisles
30 between the pews
on their knees.
they could not rise
to worship.
in this hall
35 dark women
my sisters and mothers

though i speak with the tongues
of men and of angels and
have not charity . . .

40 in this hall
dark women,
my sisters and mothers,
i stand
and let the church say
45 let the church say
let the church say
AMEN.

5   the reading

i look into none of my faces
and do the best i can.
50 the human hair between us
stretches but does not break.
i slide myself along it and
love them, love them all.

6   it is late

it is late
55 in white america.

         i stand
         in the light of the
         7–11
         looking out toward
   60   the church
         and for a moment only
         i feel the reverberation
         of myself
         in white america
   65   a black cat
         in the belfry
         hanging
         and
         ringing.

                              1987

June Jordan b. 1936

Like many of the finest writers in the
African American literary tradition, June
Jordan has proven her skill in several genres. Poet, essayist, playwright, novelist, and
composer, she is also a seasoned political
activist and teacher. Currently a professor
of African American studies and women's
studies at the University of California at
Berkeley, she has also taught at City College of New York, Sarah Lawrence College, and Yale University. Born July 9,
1936, in Harlem, Jordan began writing poetry at the age of seven after her family had
moved into a brownstone in Brooklyn's
now well-known Bedford-Stuyvesant.

Although her parents, particularly her
father, introduced her to the poetry of
Shakespeare, Edgar Allan Poe, and Paul
Laurence Dunbar, and although the writing of T. S. Eliot and Emily Dickinson is
also reflected in her work, she later studied
the poetry of Langston Hughes, Margaret
Walker, and Robert Hayden. Jordan's poetry is unique. Because of the diversity of
these early influences and because of the
ingenious way in which she weaves her political activism and her personal experi-

ences as a black bisexual woman into the
fabric of her art, her poetry defines its own
place in African-American literary history,
despite the commonalities she shares with
Audre Lorde and Alexis Deveaux.

Jordan's work is heavily influenced by
important and sometimes devastating events
from her life: her father's disappointment
that she was not a boy, his extreme discipline while she was growing up, her
mother's suicide, an early marriage that
failed, and her having been raped. Jordan's
essays and poetry chart the connections she
finds among the personal, the literary, the
political, and the global. In a 1981 *Essence*
interview with Alexis Deveaux, Jordan said
of "Poem about My Rights," which she
wrote in response to having been raped, "I
tried to show as clearly as I could that the
difference between South Africa and rape
and my mother trying to change my face
and my father wanting me to be a boy was
not an important difference to me. *It all violates self-determination.*"

This relationship that Jordan addresses
between her personal experiences and those
of others throughout the world, particularly

those in oppressed cultures, defines the depth and range of her art. The titles of her essay collections—*Civil Wars* (1981), *On Call: Political Essays* (1985), *Moving Towards Home: Political Essays* (1989), and *Technical Difficulties: African-American Notes on the State of the Union* (1992),— suggest the connection she makes between the personal, the global, and the political. Her essays as well as her poetry are rooted in her blackness, her bisexuality, and in the honest, fearless way in which she attacks racism and all its related illnesses.

Her travels to Nicaragua, her teaching experience (including children's writing workshops), her work as a freelance journalist, as a research associate and writer for Mobilization for Youth, and her studying architecture at the Donnell Library in Manhattan are all manifest in her poems. In 1969 Jordan won the Prix de Rome in Environmental Design for the way in which she transformed architectural design into fiction in her novel for adolescents *His Own Where,* later published in 1971. She has also written three other books primarily for children.

Although Jordan published three early collections of poetry—*Who Look at Me* (1969), *Some Changes* (1971), and *New Days: Poems of Exile and Return* (1974)— the 1977 *Things That I Do in the Dark: Selected Poetry* contains most of this early work. Prefaced by the poem, "These po-ems they are things that I do in the dark," this rich collection addresses everything and everybody from her son Christopher to her father Granville Ivanhoe Jordan, her mother, marriage, former President Lyndon Johnson, Malcolm X, bisexuality, and Senator Daniel Patrick Moynihan. Both *Living Room: New Poems* (1985) and *Naming Our Own Destiny* (1989), Jordan's recent collections, show her skill at using titles to illuminate her purpose. The poems in both books address the physical/emotional/spiritual space the oppressed in the United States, Lebanon, Nicaragua, and South Africa need in order to become self-determining. "Moving Towards Home," the last poem in *Living Room,* captures the essence of Jordan's irony and repetition; her ability to use a word seemingly out of context, such as her use of *redeem* near the end of this poem. Translated into Arabic, Spanish, French, Swedish, German, and Japanese, "Moving Towards Home" affirms the international status of Jordan's poetry. Yet all too little is known of her work as a dramatist. She is the author of at least three full-length plays, including the autobiographical *All These Blessings,* completed in 1988. Her work as a dramatist remains virtually unexplored.

Joyce Ann Joyce
Chicago State University

PRIMARY WORKS

Who Look at Me, 1969; *Some Changes,* 1971; *New Days: Poems of Exile and Return,* 1974; *Things That I Do in the Dark: Selected Poetry,* 1977; *Passion: New Poems, 1977–1980,* 1980; *Civil Wars,* 1981; *On Call: Political Essays,* 1985; *Living Room: New Poems,* 1985; *Lyrical Campaigns: Selected Poems,* 1989; *Naming Our Destiny: New and Selected Poems,* 1989; *Moving Towards Home: Political Essays,* 1989; *Technical Difficulties: African-American Notes on the State of the Union,* 1992; *Haruko: Love Poems,* 1994; *Kissing God Goodbye: Poems 1991–1997,* 1997; *Affirmative Acts: Political Essays,* 1998; *Soldier: A Poet's Childhood,* 2000; *Some of Us Do Not Die: New and Selected Essays,* 2002.

Poem about My Rights

Even tonight and I need to take a walk and clear
my head about this poem about why I can't
go out without changing my clothes my shoes
my body posture my gender identity my age
5   my status as a woman alone in the evening/
alone on the streets/alone not being the point/
the point being that I can't do what I want
to do with my own body because I am the wrong
sex the wrong age the wrong skin and
10 suppose it was not here in the city but down on the beach/
or far into the woods and I wanted to go
there by myself thinking about God/or thinking
about children or thinking about the world/all of it
disclosed by the stars and the silence:
15 I could not go and I could not think and I could not
stay there
alone
as I need to be
alone because I can't do what I want to do with my own
20 body and
who in the hell set things up
like this
and in France they say if the guy penetrates
but does not ejaculate then he did not rape me
25 and if after stabbing him if after screams if
after begging the bastard and if even after smashing
a hammer to his head if even after that if he
and his buddies fuck me after that
then I consented and there was
30 no rape because finally you understand finally
they fucked me over because I was wrong I was
wrong again to be me being me where I was/wrong
to be who I am
which is exactly like South Africa
35 penetrating into Namibia penetrating into
Angola and does that mean I mean how do you know if
Pretoria ejaculates what will the evidence look like the
proof of the monster jackboot ejaculation on Blackland
and if
40 after Namibia and if after Angola and if after Zimbabwe
and if after all of my kinsmen and women resist even to
self-immolation of the villages and if after that
we lose nevertheless what will the big boys say will they
claim my consent:

45 Do You Follow Me: We are the wrong people of
the wrong skin on the wrong continent and what
in the hell is everybody being reasonable about
and according to the *Times* this week
back in 1966 the C.I.A. decided that they had this problem
50 and the problem was a man named Nkrumah so they
killed him and before that it was Patrice Lumumba
and before that it was my father on the campus
of my Ivy League school and my father afraid
to walk into the cafeteria because he said he
55 was wrong the wrong age the wrong skin the wrong
gender identity and he was paying my tuition and
before that
it was my father saying I was wrong saying that
I should have been a boy because he wanted one/a
60 boy and that I should have been lighter skinned and
that I should have had straighter hair and that
I should not be so boy crazy but instead I should
just be one/a boy and before that
it was my mother pleading plastic surgery for
65 my nose and braces for my teeth and telling me
to let the books loose to let them loose in other
words
I am very familiar with the problems of the C.I.A.
and the problems of South Africa and the problems
70 of Exxon Corporation and the problems of white
America in general and the problems of the teachers
and the preachers and the F.B.I. and the social
workers and my particular Mom and Dad/I am very
familiar with the problems because the problems
75 turn out to be
me
I am the history of rape
I am the history of the rejection of who I am
I am the history of the terrorized incarceration of
80 my self
I am the history of battery assault and limitless
armies against whatever I want to do with my mind
and my body and my soul and
whether it's about walking out at night
85 or whether it's about the love that I feel or
whether it's about the sanctity of my vagina or
the sanctity of my national boundaries
or the sanctity of my leaders or the sanctity
of each and every desire
90 that I know from my personal and idiosyncratic
and indisputably single and singular heart

I have been raped
be-
cause I have been wrong the wrong sex the wrong age
95 the wrong skin the wrong nose the wrong hair the
wrong need the wrong dream the wrong geographic
the wrong sartorial I
I have been the meaning of rape
I have been the problem everyone seeks to
100 eliminate by forced
penetration with or without the evidence of slime and/
but let this be unmistakable this poem
is not consent I do not consent
to my mother to my father to the teachers to
105 the F.B.I. to South Africa to Bedford-Stuy
to Park Avenue to American Airlines to the hardon
idlers on the corners to the sneaky creeps in
cars
I am not wrong: Wrong is not my name
110 My name is my own my own my own
and I can't tell you who the hell set things up like this
but I can tell you that from now on my resistance
my simple and daily and nightly self-determination
may very well cost you your life

1989

To Free Nelson Mandela

Every night Winnie Mandela
Every night the waters of the world
turn to the softly burning
light of the moon

5 Every night Winnie Mandela
Every night

Have they killed the twelve-year-old girl?
Have they hung the poet?
Have they shot down the students?
10 Have they splashed the clinic the house
and the faces of the children
with blood?

Every night Winnie Mandela
Every night the waters of the world

15 turn to the softly burning
light of the moon

They have murdered Victoria Mxenge
They have murdered her
victorious now
20 that the earth recoils from that crime
of her murder now
that the very dirt shudders from the falling blood
the thud of bodies fallen
into the sickening
25 into the thickening
crimes of apartheid

Every night
Every night Winnie Mandela

Every night Winnie Mandela
30 Every night the waters of the world
turn to the softly burning
light of the moon

At last the bullets boomerang
At last the artifice of exile explodes
35 At last no one obeys the bossman of atrocities

At last the carpenters the midwives

the miners the weavers the anonymous
housekeepers the anonymous
street sweepers
40 the diggers of the ditch
the sentries the scouts the ministers
the mob the pallbearers the practical
nurse
the diggers of the ditch
45 the banned
the tortured
the detained
the everlastingly insulted
the twelve-year-old girl and her brothers at last
50 the diggers of the ditch
despise the meal without grace
the water without wine
the trial without rights
the work without rest
55 at last the diggers of the ditch

begin the living funeral
for death

Every night Winnie Mandela
Every night

60 Every night Winnie Mandela
Every night the waters of the world
turn to the softly burning
light of the moon

Every night Winnie Mandela
65 Every night

1989

Moving towards Home

"Where is Abu Fadi," she wailed.
"Who will bring me my loved one?"
   —NEW YORK TIMES 9/20/82

I do not wish to speak about the bulldozer and the
red dirt
not quite covering all of the arms and legs
Nor do I wish to speak about the nightlong screams
5 that reached
the observation posts where soldiers lounged about
Nor do I wish to speak about the woman who shoved
her baby
into the stranger's hands before she was led away
10 Nor do I wish to speak about the father whose sons
were shot
through the head while they slit his own throat before
the eyes
of his wife
15 Nor do I wish to speak about the army that lit continuous
flares into the darkness so that the others could see
the backs of their victims lined against the wall
Nor do I wish to speak about the piled up bodies and
the stench
20 that will not float

Nor do I wish to speak about the nurse again and
again raped
before they murdered her on the hospital floor
Nor do I wish to speak about the rattling bullets that
25   did not
halt on that keening trajectory
Nor do I wish to speak about the pounding on the
doors and
the breaking of windows and the hauling of families into
30   the world of the dead
I do not wish to speak about the bulldozer and the
red dirt
not quite covering all of the arms and legs
because I do not wish to speak about unspeakable events
35   that must follow from those who dare
"to purify" a people
those who dare
"to exterminate" a people
those who dare
40   to describe human beings as "beasts with two legs"
those who dare
"to mop up"
"to tighten the noose"
"to step up the military pressure"
45   "to ring around" civilian streets with tanks
those who dare
to close the universities
to abolish the press
to kill the elected representatives
50   of the people who refuse to be purified
those are the ones from whom we must redeem
the words of our beginning
because I need to speak about home
I need to speak about living room
55   where the land is not bullied and beaten into
a tombstone
I need to speak about living room
where the talk will take place in my language
I need to speak about living room
60   where my children will grow without horror
I need to speak about living room where the men
of my family between the ages of six and sixty-five
are not
marched into a roundup that leads to the grave
65   I need to talk about living room
where I can sit without grief without wailing aloud

for my loved ones
where I must not ask where is Abu Fadi
because he will be there beside me
70   I need to talk about living room
because I need to talk about home

I was born a Black woman
and now
I am become a Palestinian
75   against the relentless laughter of evil
there is less and less living room
and where are my loved ones?

It is time to make our way home.

1985

Rudolfo A. Anaya b. 1937

Bless Me, Ultima (1972), Rudolfo Anaya's first novel, is the single literary work most responsible not only for introducing American readers to Mexican American experience but for suggesting something of its vast imaginative potential. *Bless Me, Ultima* compelled its readers to discard the traditional American stereotype of Mexican American culture as a minor regional phenomenon, a curious, even degraded blend of customs and values drawn haphazardly from either side of the United States–Mexico border. Anaya delineated instead a distinctive culture rooted in the rich traditions of pre-Columbian aboriginal America and golden-age Spain. To be sure, Anaya's fictional terrain was a highly individualized and relatively remote region of east-central New Mexico; nevertheless, *Bless Me, Ultima* had the effect of validating Mexican American culture from California to Texas and beyond.

Like many first novels, *Bless Me, Ultima* contains various autobiographical elements. Anaya is himself from east-central New Mexico, having been born in Pastura. He attended school in nearby Santa Rosa and later in Albuquerque where he has lived most of his adult life. He earned several degrees in English and guidance and counseling and taught for seven years in the Albuquerque public schools. Anaya had become director of counseling at the University of Albuquerque when *Bless Me, Ultima* appeared. Two years later, in 1974, Anaya joined the faculty of the University of New Mexico where he maintains an appointment as professor of English.

Since *Bless Me, Ultima,* Anaya has published a steady sequence of novels, short stories, plays, and even a travel book entitled *A Chicano in China.* Despite the subject of this last book, Anaya retains his fascination with New Mexico, its clash and blending of cultures and its unique qualities as a setting for the engagement of fundamental religious and moral questions. His most recent works perfectly illustrate the range of his interest in his native state. The drama "Matachines" explores the cultural meaning of a ritual dance combining Moorish, Spanish, and Indian elements; the novel *Alburquerque* (spelled as in the original Spanish) concerns a young man's search for his father against the backdrop of a city losing its cultural moorings and beset by urban problems. None of Anaya's subsequent writing has matched either the appeal or the power of his first novel.

Bless Me, Ultima focuses on the experiences of Antonio Marez as he begins school at the conclusion of World War II. As the last of four sons in the family, Antonio carries the burden of his parents' increasingly desperate hopes. His mother, of a sedentary, tradition-bound clan of farmers, wishes Antonio to become a priest to absolve the indiscretions of one of her forebears. The father, equally alert to tradition, wants his son to maintain the *vaquero* customs of his family, most notably their fierce independence and self-reliance. As the battlelines for the control of Antonio's destiny are drawn, the revered Ultima appears to nurture the boy in her own extraordinary way. Ultima is a *curandera*, a folk healer who joins the Marez household ostensibly to merely live out the rest of her days. Under Ultima's tutelage, Antonio flourishes and begins preparations to fulfill his true destiny: to write, record, and thus preserve the traditions of his father's and mother's families alike.

Bless Me, Ultima is a novel rich in folklore. Anaya appropriates legends such as *La Llorona* (the crying woman), folk medicine, and superstition to convey a feeling of Mexican American culture in rural New Mexico. For Antonio, the folklore transmitted to him by Ultima serves as the very core of his cultural identity.

In the passage from *Bless Me, Ultima* presented here, Antonio recalls events surrounding his first communion. Even as a very young boy, Antonio has doubts about the Catholic church, its morbid emphasis on sinfulness, the unintelligibility of some of its practices, its inability to justify God's treatment of his friend Florence who, just a boy himself, has already lost his parents and watched helplessly as his older sisters drifted into prostitution. Already, Antonio finds himself attracted to the stories of the Golden Carp, a local, pagan symbol of benevolence. But for all his growing doubts, Antonio is still very much the product of his mother's religious training and so, for now, he acquiesces and participates in the church's rituals.

Raymund A. Paredes
University of California, Los Angeles

PRIMARY WORKS

Bless Me, Ultima, 1972; *Heart of Aztlan,* 1976; *Tortuga,* 1979; *The Silence of the Llano: Short Stories,* 1982; *The Legend of La Llorona,* 1984; *The Adventures of Juan Chicaspatas,* 1985; *A Chicano in China,* 1986; *Lord of the Dawn: The Legend of Quetzalcóatl,* 1987; *The Season of La Llorona* (play), 1987; *Matachines* (play), 1992; *Alburquerque,* 1992; *The Anaya Reader,* 1995; *Zia Summer,* 1995; *Rio Grande Fall,* 1996; *Jalamanta: A Message from the Desert,* 1996; *Shaman Winter,* 1998; *The Curse of the Chupacabra,* 2003; *The Man Who Could Fly and Other Stories,* 2006.

from Bless Me, Ultima

Dieciocho

Ash Wednesday. There is no other day like Ash Wednesday. The proud and the meek, the arrogant and the humble are all made equal on Ash Wednesday. The healthy and the sick, the assured and the sick in spirit, all make their way to church in the gray morning or in the dusty afternoon. They line up silently, eyes downcast, bony fingers counting the beads of the rosary, lips mumbling prayers. All are repentant, all are preparing themselves for the shock of the laying of the ashes on the forehead and the priest's agonizing words, "Thou art dust, and to dust thou shalt return."

The annointment is done, and the priest moves on, only the dull feeling of helplessness remains. The body is not important. It is made of dust; it is made of ashes. It is food for the worms. The winds and the waters dissolve it and scatter it to the four corners of the earth. In the end, what we care most for lasts only a brief lifetime, then there is eternity. Time forever. Millions of worlds are born, evolve, and pass away into nebulous, unmeasured skies; and there is still eternity. Time always. The body becomes dust and trees and exploding fire, it becomes gaseous and disappears, and still there is eternity. Silent, unopposed, brooding, forever . . .

But the soul survives. The soul lives on forever. It is the soul that must be saved, because the soul endures. And so when the burden of being nothing lifts from one's thoughts the idea of the immortality of the soul is like a light in a blinding storm. Dear God! the spirit cries out, my soul will live forever!

And so we hurried to catechism! The trying forty days of Lent lay ahead of us, then the shining goal, Easter Sunday and first holy communion! Very little else mattered in my life. School work was dull and uninspiring compared to the mysteries of religion. Each new question, each new catechism chapter, each new story seemed to open up a thousand facets concerning the salvation of my soul. I saw very little of Ultima, or even of my mother and father. I was concerned with myself. I knew that eternity lasted forever, and a soul because of one mistake could spend that eternity in hell.

The knowledge of this was frightful. I had many dreams in which I saw myself or different people burning in the fires of hell. One person especially continually haunted my nightmares. It was Florence. Inevitably it was he whom I saw burning in the roaring inferno of eternal damnation.

But why? I questioned the hissing fires, Florence knows all the answers!

But he does not accept, the flames lisped back.

"Florence," I begged him that afternoon, "try to answer."

He smiled. "And lie to myself," he answered.

"Don't lie! Just answer!" I shouted with impatience.

"You mean, when the priest asks where is God, I am to say God is everywhere: He is the worms that await the summer heat to eat Narciso, He shares the bed with Tenorio and his evil daughters—"

"Oh, God!" I cried in despair.

Samuel came up and touched me on the shoulder. "Perhaps things would not be so difficult if he believed in the golden carp," he said softly.

"Does Florence know?" I asked.

"This summer he shall know," Samuel answered wisely.

"What's that all about?" Ernie asked.

"Nothing," I said.

"Come on!" Abel shouted, "bell's ringing—"

It was Friday and we ran to attend the ritual of the Stations of the Cross. The weather was beginning to warm up but the winds still blew, and the whistling of the wind and the mournful cou-rouing of the pigeons and the burning incense made the agony of Christ's journey very sad. Father Byrnes stood at the first station and prayed to the bulto on the wall that showed Christ being sentenced by Pilate. Two high-school altar boys accompanied the priest, one to hold the lighted candle and the other to hold the incense burner. The hushed journeyers with Christ answered the priest's prayer. Then there was an interlude of silence while the priest and his attendants moved to the second station, Christ receiving the cross.

Horse sat by me. He was carving his initials into the back of the seat in front of us. Horse never prayed all of the stations, he waited until the priest came near, then he prayed the one he happened to be sitting by. I looked at the wall and saw that today he had picked to sit by the third fall of Christ.

The priest genuflected and prayed at the first fall of Christ. The incense was thick and sweet. Sometimes it made me sick inside and I felt faint. Next Friday would be Good Friday. Lent had gone by fast. There would be no stations on Good Friday, and maybe no catechism. By then we would be ready for confession Saturday and then the receiving of the sacrament on the most holy of days, Easter Sunday.

"What's Immmm-ack-que-let Con-sep-shion?" Abel asked. And Father Byrnes moved to the station where Christ meets his mother. I tried to concentrate. I felt sympathy for the Virgin.

"Immaculate Conception," Lloyd whispered.

"Yeah?"

"The Virgin Mary—"

"But what does it mean?"

"Having babies without—"

"What?"

I tried to shut my ears, I tried to hear the priest, but he was moving away, moving to where Simon helped Christ carry the cross. Dear Lord, I will help.

"I don't know—" Everybody giggled.

"Shhh!" Agnes scowled at us. The girls always prayed with bowed heads throughout the stations.

"A man and a woman, it takes a man and a woman," Florence nodded.

But the Virgin! I panicked, the Virgin Mary was the mother of God! The priest had said she was a mother through a miracle.

The priest finished the station where Veronica wiped the bloodied face of Christ, and he moved to Christ's second fall. The face of Christ was imprinted on the cloth. Besides the Virgin's blue robe, it was the holiest cloth on earth. The cross was heavy, and when He fell the soldiers whipped Him and struck Him with clubs. The people laughed. His agony began to fill the church and the women moaned their prayers, but the kids would not listen.

"The test is Saturday morning—"

Horse left his carving and looked up. The word "test" made him nervous.

"I, I, I'll pass," he nodded. Bones growled.

"Everybody will pass," I said, trying to be reassuring.

"Florence doesn't believe!" Rita hissed behind us.

"Shhhh! The priest is turning." Father Byrnes was at the back of the church, the seventh station. Now he would come down this side of the aisle for the remaining seven. Christ was speaking to the women.

Maybe that's why they prayed so hard, Christ spoke to them.

In the bell tower the pigeons cou-rouing made a mournful sound.

The priest was by us now. I could smell the incense trapped in his frock, like the fragrance of Ultima's herbs was part of her clothes. I bowed my head. The burning incense was sweet and suffocating; the glowing candle was hypnotizing. Horse had looked at it too long. When the priest moved on Horse leaned on me. His face was white.

"A la chingada," he whispered, "voy a tirar tripas—"

The priest was at the station of the Crucifixion. The hammer blows were falling on the nails that ripped through the flesh. I could almost hear the murmuring of the crowd as they craned their necks to see. But today I could not feel the agony.

"Tony—" Horse was leaning on me and gagging.

I struggled under his weight. People turned to watch me carrying the limp Horse up the aisle. Florence left his seat to help me and together we dragged Horse outside. He threw up on the steps of the church.

"He watched the candle too long," Florence said.

"Yes," I answered.

Horse smiled weakly. He wiped the hot puke from his lips and said, "ah la veca, I'm going to try that again next Friday—"

We managed to get through the final week of catechism lessons. The depression that comes with fasting and strict penance deepened as Lent drew to its completion. On Good Friday there was no school. I went to church with my mother and Ultima. All of the saints' statues in the church were covered with purple sheaths. The church was packed with women in black, each one stoically suffering the three hours of the Crucifixion with the tortured Christ. Outside the wind blew and cut off the light of the sun with its dust, and the pigeons cried mournfully in the tower. Inside the prayers were like muffled cries against a storm which seemed to engulf the world. There seemed to be no one to turn to for solace. And when the dying Christ cried, "My God, my God, why hast Thou forsaken me?" the piercing words seemed to drive through to my heart and make me feel alone and lost in a dying universe.

Good Friday was forlorn, heavy and dreary with the death of God's son and the accompanying sense of utter hopelessness.

But on Saturday morning our spirits lifted. We had been through the agony and now the ecstasy of Easter was just ahead. Then too we had our first confession to look forward to in the afternoon. In the morning my mother took me to town and bought me a white shirt and dark pants and jacket. It was the first suit I ever owned, and I smiled when I saw myself in the store mirror. I even got new shoes. Everything was new, as it should be for the first communion.

My mother was excited. When we returned from town she would not allow me to go anywhere or do anything. Every five minutes she glanced at the clock. She did not want me to be late for confession.

"It's time!" she finally called, and with a kiss she sent me scampering down the goat path, to the bridge where I raced the Vitamin Kid and lost, then waited to walk to church with Samuel.

"You ready?" I asked. He only smiled. At the church all the kids were gathered around the steps, waiting for the priest to call us.

"Did you pass?" everyone asked. "What did the priest ask you?" He had given each one of us a quiz, asking us to answer questions on the catechism lessons or to recite prayers.

"He asked me how many persons in one God?" Bones howled.

"Wha'daya say?"

"Four! Four! Four!" Bones cried. Then he shook his head vigorously. "Or five! I don't know."

"And you passed?" Lloyd said contemptuously.

"I got my suit, don't I?" Bones growled. He would fight anyone who said he didn't pass.

"Okay, okay, you passed," Lloyd said to avoid a fight.

"Whad' did he ask you, Tony?"

"I had to recite the Apostles' Creed and tell what each part meant, and I had to explain where we get original sin—"

"¡Oh sí!" "¡Ah la veca!" "¡Chingada!"

"Bullshit!" Horse spit out the grass he had been chewing.

"Tony could do it," Florence defended me, "if he wanted to."

"Yeah, Tony knows more about religion and stuff like that than anyone—"

"Tony's gonna be a priest!"

"Hey, let's practice going to confession and make Tony the priest!" Ernie shouted.

"Yeahhhhh!" Horse reared up. Bones snarled and grabbed my pant leg in his teeth.

"Tony be the priest! Tony be the priest!" they began to chant.

"No, no," I begged, but they surrounded me. Ernie took off his sweater and draped it around me. "His priest's dress!" he shouted, and the others followed. They took off their jackets and sweaters and tied them around my waist and neck. I looked in vain for help but there was none.

"Tony is the priest, Tony is the priest, yah-yah-yah-ya-ya!" they sang and danced around me. I grew dizzy. The weight of the jackets on me was heavy and suffocating.

"All right!" I cried to appease them, "I shall be your priest!" I looked at Samuel. He had turned away.

"Yea-aaaaaaaaye!" A great shout went up. Even the girls drew closer to watch.

"Hail to our priest!" Lloyd said judiciously.

"Do it right!" Agnes shouted.

"Yeah! Me first! Do it like for reals!" Horse shouted and threw himself at my feet.

"Everybody quiet!" Ernie held up his hands. They all drew around the kneeling Horse and myself, and the wall provided the enclosure but not the privacy of the confessional.

"Bless me, father—" Horse said, but as he concentrated to make the sign of the cross he forgot his lines. "Bless me, father—" he repeated desperately.

"You have sinned," I said. It was very quiet in the enclosure.

"Yes," he said. I remembered hearing the confession of the dying Narciso.

"It's not right to hear another person's confession," I said, glancing at the expectant faces around me.

"Go on!" Ernie hissed and hit me on the back. Blows fell on my head and shoulders. "Go on!" they cried. They really wanted to hear Horse's confession.

"It's only a game!" Rita whispered.

"How long has it been since your last confession?" I asked Horse.

"Always," he blurted out, "since I was born!"

"What are your sins?" I asked. I felt hot and uncomfortable under the weight of the jackets.

"Tell him only your worst one," Rita coaxed the Horse. "Yeah!" all the rest agreed.

The Horse was very quiet, thinking. He had grabbed one of my hands and he clutched it tightly, as if some holy power was going to pass through it and absolve him of his sins. His eyes rolled wildly, then he smiled and opened his mouth. His breath fouled the air.

"I know! I know!" he said excitedly, "one day when Miss Violet let me go to the bathroom I made a hole in the wall! With a nail! Then I could see into the girls' bathroom! I waited a long time! Then one of the girls came and sat down, and I could see everything! Her ass! Everything! I could even hear the pee!" he cried out.

"Horse, you're dirty!" June exclaimed. Then the girls looked shyly at each other and giggled.

"You have sinned," I said to Horse. Horse freed my hand and began rubbing at the front of his pants.

"There's more!" he cried, "I saw a teacher!"

"No!"

"Yes! Yes!" He rubbed harder.

"Who?" one of the girls asked.

"Mrs. Harrington!" Everyone laughed. Mrs. Harrington weighed about two hundred pounds. "It was biggggggggg—!" he exploded and fell trembling on the ground.

"Give him a penance!" the girls chanted and pointed accusing fingers at the pale Horse. "You are dirty, Horse," they cried, and he whimpered and accepted their accusations.

"For your penance say a rosary to the Virgin," I said weakly. I didn't feel good. The weight of the jackets was making me sweat, and the revelation of Horse's confession and the way the kids were acting was making me sick. I wondered how the priest could shoulder the burden of all the sins he heard.

. . . the weight of the sins will sink the town into the lake of the golden carp . . .

I looked for Samuel. He was not joining in the game. Florence was calmly accepting the sacriligious game we were playing, but then it didn't matter to him, he didn't believe.

"Me next! Me next!" Bones shouted. He let go of my leg and knelt in front of me. "I got a better sin than Horse! Bless me, father! Bless me, father! Bless me, father!" he repeated. He kept making the sign of the cross over and over. "I got a sin! I got to confess! I saw a high school boy and a girl fucking in the grass by the Blue Lake!" He smiled proudly and looked around.

"Ah, I see them every night under the railroad bridge," the Vitamin Kid scoffed.

"What do you mean?" I asked Bones.

"Naked! Jumping up and down!" he exclaimed.

"You lie, Bones!" Horse shouted. He didn't want his own sin bettered.

"No I don't!" Bones argued. "I don't lie, father, I don't lie!" he pleaded.

"Who was it?" Rita asked.

"It was Larry Saiz, and that dumb gabacha whose father owns the Texaco station—please father, it's my sin! I saw it! I confess!" He squeezed my hand very hard.

"Okay, Bones, okay," I nodded my head, "it's your sin."

"Give me a penance!" he growled.

"A rosary to the Virgin," I said to be rid of him.

"Like Horse?" he shouted.

"Yes."

"But my sin was bigger!" he snarled and leaped for my throat. "Whaggggghhh—" he threw me down and would have strangled me if the others hadn't pulled him away.

"Another rosary for daring to touch the priest!" I shouted in self-defense and pointed an accusing finger at him. That made him happy and he settled down.

"Florence next!" Abel cried.

"Nah, Florence ain't goin' make it anyway," Lloyd argued.

"That's enough practice," I said and started to take off the cumbersome costume, but they wouldn't let me.

"Abel's right," Ernie said emphatically, "Florence needs the practice! He didn't make it because he didn't practice!"

"He didn't make it because he doesn't believe!" Agnes taunted.

"Why doesn't he believe?" June asked.

"Let's find out!" "Make him tell!" "¡Chingada!"

They grabbed tall Florence before he could bolt away and made him kneel in front of me.

"No!" I protested.

"Confess him!" they chanted. They held him with his arms pinned behind his back. I looked down at him and tried to let him know we might as well go along with the game. It would be easier that way.

"What are your sins?" I asked.

"I don't have any," Florence said softly.

"You do, you bastard!" Ernie shouted and pulled Florence's head back.

"You have sins," Abel agreed.

"Everybody has sins!" Agnes shouted. She helped Ernie twist Florence's head back. Florence tried to struggle but he was pinned by Horse and Bones and Abel. I tried to pull their hands away from him to relieve the pain I saw in his face, but the trappings of the priest's costume entangled me and so I could do very little.

"Tell me one sin," I pleaded with Florence. His face was very close to mine now, and when he shook his head to tell me again that he didn't have sins I saw a frightening truth in his eyes. He was telling the truth! He did not believe that he had ever sinned against God! "Oh my God!" I heard myself gasp.

"Confess your sins or you'll go to hell!" Rita cried out. She grabbed his blonde hair and helped Ernie and Agnes twist his head.

"Confess! Confess!" they cried. Then with one powerful heave and a groan Florence shook off his tormentors. He was long and sinewy, but because of his mild manner we had always underestimated his strength. Now the girls and Ernie and even Horse fell off him like flies.

"I have not sinned!" he shouted, looking me square in the eyes, challenging me, the priest. His voice was like Ultima's when she had challenged Tenorio, or Narciso's when he had tried to save Lupito.

"It is God who has sinned against me!" his voice thundered, and we fell back in horror at the blasphemy he uttered.

"Florence," I heard June whimper, "don't say that—"

Florence grinned. "Why? Because it is the truth?" he questioned. "Because you refuse to see the truth, or to accept me because I do not believe in your lies! I say God has sinned against me because he took my father and mother from me when I most needed them, and he made my sisters whores— He has punished all of us without just cause, Tony," his look pierced me, "He took Narciso! And why? What harm did Narciso ever do—"

"We shouldn't listen to him," Agnes had the courage to interrupt Florence, "we'll have to confess what we heard and the priest will be mad."

"The priest was right in not passing Florence, because he doesn't believe!" Rita added.

"He shouldn't even be here if he is not going to believe in the laws we learn," Lloyd said.

"Give him a penance! Make him ask for forgiveness for those terrible things he said about God!" Agnes insisted. They were gathering behind me now, I could feel their presence and their hot, bitter breath. They wanted me to be their leader; they wanted me to punish Florence.

"Make his penance hard," Rita leered.

"Make him kneel and we'll all beat him," Ernie suggested.

"Yeah, beat him!" Bones said wildly.

"Stone him!"

"Beat him!"

"Kill him!"

They circled around me and advanced on Florence, their eyes flashing with the thought of the punishment they would impose on the non-believer. It was then that the fear left me, and I knew what I had to do. I spun around and held out my hands to stop them.

"No!" I shouted, "there will be no punishment, there will be no penance! His sins are forgiven!" I turned and made the sign of the cross. "Go in peace, my son," I said to Florence.

"No!" they shouted, "don't let him go free!"

"Make him do penance! That's the law!"

"Punish him for not believing in God!"

"I am the priest!" I shouted back, "and I have absolved him of his sins!" I was facing the angry kids and I could see that their hunger for vengeance was directed at me, but I didn't care, I felt relieved. I had stood my ground for what I felt to be right and I was not afraid. I thought that perhaps it was this kind of strength that allowed Florence to say he did not believe in God.

"You are a bad priest, Tony!" Agnes lashed out at me.

"We do not want you for our priest!" Rita followed.

"Punish the priest!" they shouted and they engulfed me like a wave. They were upon me, clawing, kicking, tearing off the jackets, defrocking me. I fought back but it was useless. They were too many. They spread me out and held me pinned down to the hard ground. They had torn my shirt off so the sharp pebbles and stickers cut into my back.

"Give him the Indian torture!" someone shouted.

"Yeah, the Indian torture!" they chanted.

They held my arms while Horse jumped on my stomach and methodically began to pound with his fist on my chest. He used his sharp knuckles and aimed each blow directly at my breastbone. I kicked and wiggled and struggled to get free from the incessant beating, but they held me tight and I could not throw them off.

"No! No!" I shouted, but the raining blows continued. The blows of the knuckles coming down again and again on my breastbone were unbearable, but Horse knew no pity, and there was no pity on the faces of the others.

"God!" I cried, "God!" But the jarring blows continued to fall. I jerked my head from side to side and tried to kick or bite, but I could not get loose. Finally I bit my lips so I wouldn't cry, but my eyes filled with tears anyway. They were laughing and pointing down at the red welt that raised on my chest where the Horse was pounding.

"Serves him right," I heard, "he let the sinner go—"

Then, after what seemed an eternity of torture, they let me go. The priest was calling from the church steps, so they ran off to confession. I slowly picked myself up and rubbed the bruises on my chest. Florence handed me my shirt and jacket.

"You should have given me a penance," he said.

"You don't have to do any penance," I answered. I wiped my eyes and shook my head. Everything in me seemed loose and disconnected.

"Are you going to confession?" he asked.

"Yes," I answered and finished buttoning my shirt.

"You could never be their priest," he said.

I looked at the open door of the church. There was a calm in the wind and the bright sunlight made everything stark and harsh. The last of the kids went into the church and the doors closed.

"No," I nodded. "Are you going to confession?" I asked him.

"No," he muttered. "Like I said, I only wanted to be with you guys—I cannot eat God," he added.

"I have to," I whispered. I ran up the steps and entered the dark, musky church. I genuflected at the font of holy water, wet my fingertips, and made the sign of the cross. The lines were already formed on either side of the confessional, and the kids were behaving and quiet. Each one stood with bowed head, preparing himself to confess all of his sins to Father Byrnes. I walked quietly around the back pew and went to the end of one line. I made the sign of the cross again and began to say my prayers. As each kid finished his confession the line shuffled forward. I closed my eyes and tried not to be distracted by anything around me. I thought hard of all the sins I had ever committed, and I said as many prayers as I could remember. I begged God forgiveness for my sins over and over. After a long wait, Agnes, who had been in front of me came out of the confessional. She held the curtain as I stepped in, then she let it drop and all was dark. I knelt on the rough board and leaned against the small window. I prayed. I could hear whisperings from the confessional on the other side. My eyes grew accustomed to the gloom and I saw a small crucifix nailed to the side of the window. I kissed the feet of the hanging Jesus. The confessional smelled of old wood. I thought of the million sins that had been revealed in this small, dark space.

Then abruptly my thoughts were scattered. The small wooden door of the window slid open in front of me, and in the dark I could make out the head of Father Byrnes. His eyes were closed, his head bowed forward. He mumbled something in Latin then put his hand on his forehead and waited.

I made the sign of the cross and said, "Forgive me, Father, for I have sinned," and I made my first confession to him.

1972

Thomas Pynchon b. 1937

Very few American writers, while still alive, have been accorded the somewhat dubious honor of having their last name turned into an adjective. Even fewer have seen this resultant adjective become a buzzword in highbrow popular culture, a process that associates their name with everything from film and literature to advertising campaigns, pop music, and underground publications. Thomas Ruggles Pynchon, Jr., came into the collective consciousness of late-twentieth- and early-twenty-first-century American culture largely through the use (and abuse) of the labels "Pynchonian" and "Pynchonesque," which sprang up after the publication of his mammoth novel *Gravity's Rainbow*. These two adjectives connote extreme intellectualism, an encyclopedic frame of reference, paranoia, spiraling conspiracy theories, reclusiveness, dark humor, or a combination of all these. Perhaps unfairly, these have also been the dominant themes in criticism of Pynchon's work.

Few biographical details are known. Pynchon was born on Long Island in Oyster Bay, New York, on May 8, 1937. His family is descended from the Puritan Pyncheons who provided Nathaniel Hawthorne

with material for *The House of Seven Gables*. After a brief stint in the U.S. Navy, he attended Cornell University, where he majored in engineering before switching to English; he took classes from Vladimir Nabokov and befriended Richard Fariña, whose 1966 novel *Been Down So Long It Looks like Up to Me* anticipated many themes that Pynchon would later treat. Having passed up an opportunity to go to graduate school, he worked as a technical writer for Boeing Aircraft in Seattle from 1960 to 1962. His subsequent public biography consists almost entirely of his publication history.

Pynchon's first novel *V.*, published in 1963, won the Faulkner First Novel Award. In 1966 *The Crying of Lot 49*, a shorter but no less complex novel, garnered the Rosenthal Memorial Award. *Gravity's Rainbow*, published in 1973, nearly won the Pulitzer Prize until several jurors rejected it on the grounds of "obscenity and obscurity." In 1975 Pynchon was awarded the Howells Medal of the American Academy but turned it down without giving a reason. His literary output for the remainder of the 1970s and 80s was limited to *Slow Learner*, a collection of five short stories ("Entropy" among them) originally published between 1959 and 1964, and a small number of essays and reviews.

It is generally believed that Pynchon lived in Aptos, a small town in northern California, for much of the 1980s, during which he produced his novel *Vineland* (1990) and possibly wrote a series of letters to a small local newspaper using the pseudonym Wanda Tinasky. He has apparently lived in New York City since that time. He is married to his literary agent Melanie Jackson; they have one son. His most recent novel is *Against the Day,* published in 2006.

Whatever the facts of his life may be, Pynchon's small but important body of work (six novels and a collection of short stories over the course of more than forty years) has had a profound effect on the development of American literature. Many readers have been tempted to categorize Pynchon's individual works as products of a certain place and time, especially *The Crying of Lot 49* and *Vineland,* which are often criticized for being generational pieces "about" California in the 1960s and 80s, respectively. Examination of his entire body of work, though, leads to an understanding of both the depth of Pynchon's encyclopedic erudition and his wide-ranging cultural satire.

"Entropy" initially appeared in the *Kenyon Review* in the spring of 1960. Pynchon himself evinced considerable disdain for the story in the introduction to *Slow Learner:* "The story is a fine example of a procedural error beginning writers are always cautioned against. It is simply wrong to begin with a theme, symbol or other ab- stract unifying agent, and then to try to force characters and events to conform to it." Despite this harsh self-criticism, the story represents his first extensive treatment of the concept of entropy in its thermodynamic, informational, and cosmic forms. This theme recurs notably in the "Whole Sick Crew" episodes of *V.* and throughout *The Crying of Lot 49,* most tellingly in the "Maxwell's Demon" portions.

"Entropy" does not have the intricately organized and at times maddeningly allusive structure of *Gravity's Rainbow,* but it is possible to see Pynchon's authorial voice taking shape in this story. The blending of near-farcical comic elements with a dark, even brooding satirical impulse leaves the reader with an ambiguous message, another hallmark of his later works. Critics disagree about whether Pynchon is more sympathetic to Meatball Mulligan, who attempts to make order out of chaos despite the unavoidable force of entropy, or to Callisto, who walls himself off from the outside world and seems to have resigned himself to its "heat-death." One's interpretation largely determines whether the dual endings of the story represent an affirmation of life like that of the Beats (whose works and language Pynchon cites as an early influence) or an acquiescence to the inevitability of death, a theme that existentialist philosophers/novelists such as Albert Camus and Jean-Paul Sartre had popularized during Pynchon's adolescence.

Derek C. Maus
University of North Carolina–Chapel Hill

PRIMARY WORKS

V., 1963; *The Crying of Lot 49,* 1966; *Gravity's Rainbow,* 1973; *Slow Learner,* 1984; *Vineland,* 1990; *Mason & Dixon,* 1997; *Against the Day,* 2006.

Entropy

Boris has just given me a summary of his views. He is a weather prophet. The weather will continue bad, he says. There will be more calamities, more death, more despair. Not the slightest indication of a change anywhere. . . . We must get into step, a lockstep toward the prison of death. There is no escape. The weather will not change.

—Tropic of Cancer

Downstairs, Meatball Mulligan's lease-breaking party was moving into its 40th hour. On the kitchen floor, amid a litter of empty champagne fifths, were Sandor Rojas and three friends, playing spit in the ocean and staying awake on Heidseck and benzedrine pills. In the living room Duke, Vincent, Krinkles and Paco sat crouched over a 15-inch speaker which had been bolted into the top of a wastepaper basket, listening to 27 watts' worth of *The Heroes' Gate at Kiev*. They all wore hornrimmed sunglasses and rapt expressions, and smoked funny-looking cigarettes which contained not, as you might expect, tobacco, but an adulterated form of *cannabis sativa*. This group was the Duke di Angelis quartet. They recorded for a local label called Tambú and had to their credit one 10" LP entitled *Songs of Outer Space*. From time to time one of them would flick the ashes from his cigarette into the speaker cone to watch them dance around. Meatball himself was sleeping over by the window, holding an empty magnum to his chest as if it were a teddy bear. Several government girls, who worked for people like the State Department and NSA, had passed out on couches, chairs and in one case the bathroom sink.

This was in early February of '57 and back then there were a lot of American expatriates around Washington, D.C., who would talk, every time they met you, about how someday they were going to go over to Europe for real but right now it seemed they were working for the government. Everyone saw a fine irony in this. They would stage, for instance, polyglot parties where the newcomer was sort of ignored if he couldn't carry on simultaneous conversations in three or four languages. They would haunt Armenian delicatessens for weeks at a stretch and invite you over for bulghour and lamb in tiny kitchens whose walls were covered with bullfight posters. They would have affairs with sultry girls from Andalucía or the Midi who studied economics at Georgetown. Their Dôme was a collegiate Rathskeller out on Wisconsin Avenue called the Old Heidelberg and they had to settle for cherry blossoms instead of lime trees when spring came, but in its lethargic way their life provided, as they said, kicks.

At the moment, Meatball's party seemed to be gathering its second wind. Outside there was rain. Rain splatted against the tar paper on the roof and was fractured into a fine spray off the noses, eyebrows and lips of wooden gargoyles under the eaves, and ran like drool down the windowpanes. The day before, it had snowed and the day before that there had been winds of gale force and before that the sun had made the city glitter bright as April, though the calendar read early February. It is a curious season in Washington, this false spring. Somewhere in it are Lincoln's

Birthday and the Chinese New Year, and a forlornness in the streets because cherry blossoms are weeks away still and, as Sarah Vaughan has put it, spring will be a little late this year. Generally crowds like the one which would gather in the Old Heidelberg on weekday afternoons to drink Würtzburger and to sing Lili Marlene (not to mention The Sweetheart of Sigma Chi) are inevitably and incorrigibly Romantic. And as every good Romantic knows, the soul *(spiritus, ruach, pneuma)* is nothing, substantially, but air; it is only natural that warpings in the atmosphere should be recapitulated in those who breathe it. So that over and above the public components—holidays, tourist attractions—there are private meanderings, linked to the climate as if this spell were a *stretto* passage in the year's fugue: haphazard weather, aimless loves, unpredicted commitments: months one can easily spend *in* fugue, because oddly enough, later on, winds, rains, passions of February and March are never remembered in that city, it is as if they had never been.

The last bass notes of *The Heroes' Gate* boomed up through the floor and woke Callisto from an uneasy sleep. The first thing he became aware of was a small bird he had been holding gently between his hands, against his body. He turned his head sidewise on the pillow to smile down at it, at its blue hunched-down head and sick, lidded eyes, wondering how many more nights he would have to give it warmth before it was well again. He had been holding the bird like that for three days: it was the only way he knew to restore its health. Next to him the girl stirred and whimpered, her arm thrown across her face. Mingled with the sounds of the rain came the first tentative, querulous morning voices of the other birds, hidden in philodendrons and small fan palms: patches of scarlet, yellow and blue laced through this Rousseau-like fantasy, this hothouse jungle it had taken him seven years to weave together. Hermetically sealed, it was a tiny enclave of regularity in the city's chaos, alien to the vagaries of the weather, of national politics, of any civil disorder. Through trial-and-error Callisto had perfected its ecological balance, with the help of the girl its artistic harmony, so that the swayings of its plant life, the stirrings of its birds and human inhabitants were all as integral as the rhythms of a perfectly-executed mobile. He and the girl could no longer, of course, be omitted from that sanctuary; they had become necessary to its unity. What they needed from outside was delivered. They did not go out.

"Is he all right," she whispered. She lay like a tawny question mark facing him, her eyes suddenly huge and dark and blinking slowly. Callisto ran a finger beneath the feathers at the base of the bird's neck; caressed it gently. "He's going to be well, I think. See: he hears his friends beginning to wake up." The girl had heard the rain and the birds even before she was fully awake. Her name was Aubade: she was part French and part Annamese, and she lived on her own curious and lonely planet, where the clouds and the odor of poincianas, the bitterness of wine and the accidental fingers at the small of her back or feathery against her breasts came to her reduced inevitably to the terms of sound: of music which emerged at intervals from a howling darkness of discordancy. "Aubade," he said, "go see." Obedient, she arose; padded to the window, pulled aside the drapes and after a moment said: "It is 37. Still 37." Callisto frowned. "Since Tuesday, then," he said. "No change." Henry Adams, three generations before his own, had stared aghast at Power; Callisto found himself now in much the same state over Thermodynamics, the inner life of that power, realizing like his predeccessor that the Virgin and the dynamo stand as much for love as for power; that the two are indeed identical; and that love therefore not only makes the world go round but also makes the boccie ball spin, the nebula precess. It was this latter or sidereal element which disturbed him. The cosmologists had predicted an eventual heat-death for the universe (something like Limbo: form and motion abolished, heat-energy identical at every point in it); the meteorologists, day-to-day, staved it off by contradicting with a reassuring array of varied temperatures.

But for three days now, despite the changeful weather, the mercury had stayed at 37 degrees Fahrenheit. Leery at omens of apocalypse, Callisto shifted beneath the covers. His fingers pressed the bird more firmly, as if needing some pulsing or suffering assurance of an early break in the temperature.

It was that last cymbal crash that did it. Meatball was hurled wincing into consciousness as the synchronized wagging of heads over the wastebasket stopped. The final hiss remained for an instant in the room, then melted into the whisper of rain outside. "Aarrgghh," announced Meatball in the silence, looking at the empty magnum. Krinkles, in slow motion, turned, smiled and held out a cigarette. "Tea time, man," he said. "No, no," said Meatball. "How many times I got to tell you guys. Not at my place. You ought to know, Washington is lousy with Feds." Krinkles looked wistful. "Jeez, Meatball," he said, "you don't want to do nothing no more." "Hair of dog," said Meatball. "Only hope. Any juice left?" He began to crawl toward the kitchen. "No champagne, I don't think," Duke said. "Case of tequila behind the icebox." They put on an Earl Bostic side. Meatball paused at the kitchen door, glowering at Sandor Rojas. "Lemons," he said after some thought. He crawled to the refrigerator and got out three lemons and some cubes, found the tequila and set about restoring order to his nervous system. He drew blood once cutting the lemons and had to use two hands squeezing them and his foot to crack the ice tray but after about ten minutes he found himself, through some miracle, beaming down into a monster tequila sour. "That looks yummy," Sandor Rojas said. "How about you make me one." Meatball blinked at him. *"Kitchi lofass a shegitbe,"* he replied automatically, and wandered away into the bathroom. "I say," he called out a moment later to no one in particular. "I say, there seems to be a girl or something sleeping in the sink." He took her by the shoulders and shook. "Wha," she said. "You don't look too comfortable," Meatball said. "Well," she agreed. She stumbled to the shower, turned on the cold water and sat down crosslegged in the spray. "That's better," she smiled.

"Meatball," Sandor Rojas yelled from the kitchen. "Somebody is trying to come in the window. A burglar, I think. A second-story man." "What are you worrying about," Meatball said. "We're on the third floor." He loped back into the kitchen. A shaggy woebegone figure stood out on the fire escape, raking his fingernails down the windowpane. Meatball opened the window. "Saul," he said.

"Sort of wet out," Saul said. He climbed in, dripping. "You heard, I guess."

"Miriam left you," Meatball said, "or something, is all I heard."

There was a sudden flurry of knocking at the front door. "Do come in," Sandor Rojas called. The door opened and there were three coeds from George Washington, all of whom were majoring in philosophy. They were each holding a gallon of Chianti. Sandor leaped up and dashed into the living room. "We heard there was a party," one blonde said. "Young blood," Sandor shouted. He was an ex-Hungarian freedom fighter who had easily the worst chronic case of what certain critics of the middle class have called Don Giovannism in the District of Columbia. *Purche porti la gonnella, voi sapete quel che fa.* Like Pavlov's dog: a contralto voice or a whiff of Arpège and Sandor would begin to salivate. Meatball regarded the trio blearily as they filed into the kitchen; he shrugged. "Put the wine in the icebox," he said "and good morning."

Aubade's neck made a golden bow as she bent over the sheets of foolscap, scribbling away in the green murk of the room. "As a young man at Princeton," Callisto was dictating, nestling the bird against the gray hairs of his chest, "Callisto had learned a mnemonic device for remembering the Laws of Thermodynamics: you can't win, things are going to get worse before they get better, who says they're going to get better. At the age of 54, confronted with Gibbs' notion of the universe, he suddenly realized that undergraduate cant had been oracle, after all. That spindly maze of equations became, for him, a vision of ultimate, cosmic heat-death. He had known all along, of course, that nothing but a theoretical engine or system ever runs at 100% efficiency; and about the theorem of Clausius, which states that the entropy of an isolated system always continually increases. It was not, however, until Gibbs and Boltzmann brought to this principle the methods of statistical mechanics that the horrible significance of it all dawned on him: only then did he realize that the isolated system—galaxy, engine, human being, culture, whatever—must evolve spontaneously toward the Condition of the More Probable. He was forced, therefore, in the sad dying fall of middle age, to a radical reevaluation of everything he had learned up to then; all the cities and seasons and casual passions of his days had now to be looked at in a new and elusive light. He did not know if he was equal to the task. He was aware of the dangers of the reductive fallacy and, he hoped, strong enough not to drift into the graceful decadence of an enervated fatalism. His had always been a vigorous, Italian sort of pessimism: like Machiavelli, he allowed the forces of *virtù* and *fortuna* to be about 50/50; but the equations now introduced a random factor which pushed the odds to some unutterable and indeterminate ratio which he found himself afraid to calculate." Around him loomed vague hothouse shapes; the pitifully small heart fluttered against his own. Counterpointed against his words the girl heard the chatter of birds and fitful car honkings scattered along the wet morning and Earl Bostic's alto rising in occasional wild peaks through the floor. The architectonic purity of her world was constantly threatened by such hints of anarchy: gaps and excrescences and skew lines, and a shifting or tilting of planes to which she had continually to readjust lest the whole structure shiver into a disarray of discrete and meaningless signals. Callisto had described the process once as a kind of "feedback": she crawled into dreams each night with a sense of exhaustion, and a desperate resolve never to relax that vigilance. Even in the brief periods when Callisto made love to her, soaring above the bowing of taut nerves in haphazard double-stops would be the one singing string of her determination.

"Nevertheless," continued Callisto, "he found in entropy or the measure of disorganization for a closed system an adequate metaphor to apply to certain phenomena in his own world. He saw, for example, the younger generation responding to Madison Avenue with the same spleen his own had once reserved for Wall Street: and in American 'consumerism' discovered a similar tendency from the least to the most probable, from differentiation to sameness, from ordered individuality to a kind of chaos. He found himself, in short, restating Gibbs' prediction in social terms, and envisioned a heat-death for his culture in which ideas, like heat-energy, would no longer be transferred, since each point in it would ultimately have the same quantity of energy; and intellectual motion would, accordingly, cease." He glanced up suddenly. "Check it now," he said. Again she rose and peered out at the thermometer. "37," she said. "The rain has stopped." He bent his head quickly and held his lips against a quivering wing. "Then it will change soon," he said, trying to keep his voice firm.

Sitting on the stove Saul was like any big rag doll that a kid has been taking out some incomprehensible rage on. "What happened," Meatball said. "If you feel like talking, I mean."

"Of course I feel like talking," Saul said. "One thing I did, I slugged her."

"Discipline must be maintained."

"Ha, ha. I wish you'd been there. Oh Meatball, it was a lovely fight. She ended up throwing a *Handbook of Chemistry and Physics* at me, only it missed and went through the window, and when the glass broke I reckon something in her broke too. She stormed out of the house crying, out in the rain. No raincoat or anything."

"She'll be back."

"No."

"Well." Soon Meatball said: "It was something earth-shattering, no doubt. Like who is better, Sal Mineo or Ricky Nelson."

"What it was about," Saul said, "was communication theory. Which of course makes it very hilarious."

"I don't know anything about communication theory."

"Neither does my wife. Come right down to it, who does? That's the joke."

When Meatball saw the kind of smile Saul had on his face he said: "Maybe you would like tequila or something."

"No. I mean, I'm sorry. It's a field you can go off the deep end in, is all. You get where you're watching all the time for security cops: behind bushes, around corners, MUFFET is top secret."

"Wha."

"Multi-unit factorial field electronic tabulator."

"You were fighting about that."

"Miriam has been reading science fiction again. That and *Scientific American*. It seems she is, as we say, bugged at this idea of computers acting like people. I made the mistake of saying you can just as well turn that around, and talk about human behavior like a program fed into an IBM machine."

"Why not," Meatball said.

"Indeed, why not. In fact it is sort of crucial to communication, not to mention information theory. Only when I said that she hit the roof. Up went the balloon. And I can't figure out *why*. If anybody should know why, I should. I refuse to believe the government is wasting taxpayers' money on me, when it has so many bigger and better things to waste it on."

Meatball made a moue. "Maybe she thought you were acting like a cold, dehumanized amoral scientist type."

"My god," Saul flung up an arm. "Dehumanized. How much more human can I get? I worry, Meatball, I do. There are Europeans wandering around North Africa these days with their tongues torn out of their heads because those tongues have spoken the wrong words. Only the Europeans thought they were the right words."

"Language barrier," Meatball suggested.

Saul jumped down off the stove. "That," he said, angry, "is a good candidate for sick joke of the year. No, ace, it is *not* a barrier. If it is anything it's a kind of leakage. Tell a girl: 'I love you.' No trouble with two-thirds of that, it's a closed circuit. Just you and she. But that nasty four-letter word in the middle, *that's* the one you have to look out for. Ambiguity. Redundancy. Irrelevance, even. Leakage. All this is noise. Noise screws up your signal, makes for disorganization in the circuit."

Meatball shuffled around. "Well, now, Saul," he muttered, "you're sort of, I don't know, expecting a lot from people. I mean, you know. What it is is, most of the things we say, I guess, are mostly noise."

"Ha! Half of what you just said, for example."

"Well, you do it too."

"I know." Saul smiled grimly. "It's a bitch, ain't it?"

"I bet that's what keeps divorce lawyers in business. Whoops."

"Oh I'm not sensitive. Besides," frowning, "you're right. You find I think that most 'successful' marriages—Miriam and me, up to last night—are sort of founded on compromises. You never run at top efficiency, usually all you have is a minimum basis for a workable thing. I believe the phrase is Togetherness."

"Aarrgghh."

"Exactly. You find that one a bit noisy, don't you. But the noise content is different for each of us because you're a bachelor and I'm not. Or wasn't. The hell with it."

"Well sure," Meatball said, trying to be helpful, "you were using different words. By 'human being' you meant something that you can look at like it was a computer. It helps you think better on the job or something. But Miriam meant something entirely—"

"The hell with it."

Meatball fell silent. "I'll take that drink," Saul said after a while.

The card game had been abandoned and Sandor's friends were slowly getting wasted on tequila. On the living room couch, one of the coeds and Krinkles were engaged in amorous conversation. "No," Krinkles was saying, "no, I can't put Dave *down.* In fact I give Dave a lot of credit, man. Especially considering his accident and all." The girl's smile faded. "How terrible," she said. "What accident?" "Hadn't you heard?" Krinkles said. "When Dave was in the army, just a private E-2, they sent him down to Oak Ridge on special duty. Something to do with the Manhattan Project. He was handling hot stuff one day and got an overdose of radiation. So now he's got to wear lead gloves all the time." She shook her head sympathetically. "What an awful break for a piano-player."

Meatball had abandoned Saul to a bottle of tequila and was about to go to sleep in a closet when the front door flew open and the place was invaded by five enlisted personnel of the U.S. Navy, all in varying stages of abomination. "This is the place," shouted a fat, pimply seaman apprentice who had lost his white hat. "This here is the hoorhouse that chief was telling us about." A stringy-looking 3rd class boatswain's mate pushed him aside and cased the living room. "You're right, Slab," he said. "But it don't look like much, even for Stateside. I seen better tail in Naples, Italy." "How much, hey," boomed a large seaman with adenoids, who was holding a Mason jar full of white lightning. "Oh, my god," said Meatball.

Outside the temperature remained constant at 37 degrees Fahrenheit. In the hothouse Aubade stood absently caressing the branches of a young mimosa, hearing a motif of sap-rising, the rough and unresolved anticipatory theme of those fragile pink blossoms which, it is said, insure fertility. That music rose in a tangled tracery: arabesques of order competing fugally with the improvised discords of the party downstairs, which peaked sometimes in cusps and ogees of noise. That precious signal-to-noise ratio, whose delicate balance required every calorie of her strength, seesawed inside the small tenuous skull as she watched Callisto, sheltering the bird. Callisto was trying to confront any idea of the heat-death now, as he nuzzled the feathery lump in his hands. He sought correspondences. Sade, of course. And Temple Drake, gaunt and hopeless in her little park in Paris, at the end of *Sanctuary.* Final equilibrium. *Nightwood.* And the tango. Any tango, but more than any perhaps the sad sick dance in Stravinsky's *L'Histoire du Soldat.* He thought back: what had tango music been for them after the war, what meanings had he missed in all the stately coupled automatons in the *cafés-dansants,* or in the metronomes which had ticked behind the eyes of his own partners? Not even the clean constant winds of Switzerland could cure the *grippe espagnole:* Stravinsky had had it, they all had had it. And how many musicians were left after Passchendaele, after the Marne? It came down in this case to seven: violin, double-bass. Clarinet, bassoon. Cornet, trombone. Tympani. Almost as if any tiny troupe of saltimbanques had set about conveying the same information as a full pit-orchestra. There was hardly a full complement left in Europe. Yet with violin and tympani Stravinsky had managed to communicate in that tango the same exhaustion, the same airlessness one saw in the slicked-down youths who were trying to imitate Vernon Castle, and in their mistresses, who simply did not care. *Ma maîtresse.* Celeste. Returning to Nice after the second war he had found that café replaced by a perfume shop which catered to American tourists. And no secret vestige of her in the cobblestones or in the old pension next door; no perfume to match her breath heavy with the sweet Spanish wine she always drank. And so instead he had purchased a Henry Miller novel and left for Paris, and read the book on the train so that when he arrived he had been given at least a little forewarning. And saw that Celeste and the others and even Temple Drake were not all that had changed. "Aubade," he said, "my head aches." The sound of his voice generated in the girl an answering scrap of melody. Her movement toward the kitchen, the towel, the cold water, and his eyes following her formed a weird and intricate canon; as she placed the compress on his forehead his sigh of gratitude seemed to signal a new subject, another series of modulations.

"No," Meatball was still saying, "no, I'm afraid not. This is not a house of ill repute. I'm sorry, really I am." Slab was adamant. "But the chief said," he kept repeating. The seaman offered to swap the moonshine for a good piece. Meatball looked around frantically, as if seeking assistance. In the middle of the room, the Duke di Angelis quartet were engaged in a historic moment. Vincent was seated and the others standing: they were going through the motions of a group having a session, only without instruments. "I say," Meatball said. Duke moved his head a few times, smiled faintly, lit a cigarette, and eventually caught sight of Meatball. "Quiet, man," he whispered. Vincent began to fling his arms around, his fists clenched; then, abruptly, was still, then repeated the performance. This went on for a few minutes while Meatball sipped his drink moodily. The navy had withdrawn to the kitchen. Finally at some invisible signal the group stopped tapping their feet and Duke grinned and said, "At least we ended together."

Meatball glared at him. "I say," he said. "I have this new conception, man," Duke said. "You remember your namesake. You remember Gerry."

"No," said Meatball. "I'll remember April, if that's any help."

"As a matter of fact," Duke said, "it was Love for Sale. Which shows how much you know. The point is, it was Mulligan, Chet Baker and that crew, way back then, out yonder. You dig?"

"Baritone sax," Meatball said. "Something about a baritone sax."

"But no piano, man. No guitar. Or accordion. You know what that means."

"Not exactly," Meatball said.

"Well first let me just say, that I am no Mingus, no John Lewis. Theory was never my strong point. I mean things like reading were always difficult for me and all—"

"I know," Meatball said drily. "You got your card taken away because you changed key on Happy Birthday at a Kiwanis Club picnic."

"Rotarian. But it occurred to me, in one of these flashes of insight, that if that first quartet of Mulligan's had no piano, it could only mean one thing."

"No chords," said Paco, the baby-faced bass.

"What he is trying to say," Duke said, "is no root chords. Nothing to listen to while you blow a horizontal line. What one does in such a case is, one *thinks* the roots."

A horrified awareness was dawning on Meatball. "And the next logical extension," he said.

"Is to think everything," Duke announced with simple dignity. "Roots, line, everything."

Meatball looked at Duke, awed. "But," he said.

"Well," Duke said modestly, "there are a few bugs to work out."

"But," Meatball said.

"Just listen," Duke said. "You'll catch on." And off they went again into orbit, presumably somewhere around the asteroid belt. After a while Krinkles made an embouchure and started moving his fingers and Duke clapped his hand to his forehead. "Oaf!" he roared. "The new head we're using, you remember, I wrote last night?" "Sure," Krinkles said, "the new head. I come in on the bridge. All your heads I come in then." "Right," Duke said. "So why—" "Wha," said Krinkles, "16 bars, I wait, I come in—" "16?" Duke said. "No. No, Krinkles. Eight you waited. You want me to sing it? A cigarette that bears a lipstick's traces, an airline ticket to romantic places." Krinkles scratched his head. "These Foolish Things, you mean." "Yes," Duke said, "yes, Krinkles. Bravo." "Not I'll Remember April," Krinkles said. *"Minghe morte,"* said Duke. "I *figured* we were playing it a little slow," Krinkles said. Meatball chuckled. "Back to the old drawing board," he said. "No, man," Duke said, "back to the airless void." And they took off again, only it seemed Paco was playing in G sharp while the rest were in E flat, so they had to start all over.

In the kitchen two of the girls from George Washington and the sailors were singing Let's All Go Down and Piss on the Forrestal. There was a two-handed, bilingual *morra* game on over by the icebox. Saul had filled several paper bags with water and was sitting on the fire escape, dropping them on passersby in the street. A fat government girl in a Bennington sweatshirt, recently engaged to an ensign attached to the Forrestal, came charging into the kitchen, head lowered, and butted Slab in the stomach. Figuring this was as good an excuse for a fight as any, Slab's buddies piled in. The *morra* players were nose-to-nose, screaming *trois, sette* at the tops of their lungs. From the shower the girl Meatball had taken out of the sink announced that she was drowning. She had apparently sat on the drain and the water was now up to her neck. The noise in Meatball's apartment had reached a sustained, ungodly crescendo.

Meatball stood and watched, scratching his stomach lazily. The way he figured, there were only about two ways he could cope: (a) lock himself in the closet and maybe eventually they would all go away, or (b) try to calm everybody down, one by one. (a) was certainly the more attractive alternative. But then he started thinking about that closet. It was dark and stuffy and he would be alone. He did not feature being alone. And then this crew off the good ship Lollipop or whatever it was might take it upon themselves to kick down the closet door, for a lark. And if that happened he would be, at the very least, embarrassed. The other way was more a pain in the neck, but probably better in the long run.

So he decided to try and keep his lease-breaking party from deteriorating into total chaos: he gave wine to the sailors and separated the *morra* players; he introduced the fat government girl to Sandor Rojas, who would keep her out of trouble; he helped the girl in the shower to dry off and get into bed; he had another talk with Saul; he called a repairman for the refrigerator, which someone had discovered was on the blink. This is what he did until nightfall, when most of the revellers had passed out and the party trembled on the threshold of its third day.

Upstairs Callisto, helpless in the past, did not feel the faint rhythm inside the bird begin to slacken and fail. Aubade was by the window, wandering the ashes of her own lovely world; the temperature held steady, the sky had become a uniform darkening gray. Then something from downstairs—a girl's scream, an overturned chair, a glass dropped on the floor, he would never know what exactly—pierced that private time-warp and he became aware of the faltering, the constriction of muscles, the tiny tossing of the bird's head; and his own pulse began to pound more fiercely, as if trying to compensate. "Aubade," he called weakly, "he's dying." The girl, flowing and rapt, crossed the hothouse to gaze down at Callisto's hands. The two remained like that, poised, for one minute, and two, while the heartbeat ticked a graceful diminuendo down at last into stillness. Callisto raised his head slowly. "I held him," he protested, impotent with the wonder of it, "to give him the warmth of my body. Almost as if I were communicating life to him, or a sense of life. What has happened? Has the transfer of heat ceased to work? Is there no more . . ." He did not finish.

"I was just at the window," she said. He sank back, terrified. She stood a moment more, irresolute; she had sensed his obsession long ago, realized somehow that that constant 37 was now decisive. Suddenly then, as if seeing the single and unavoidable conclusion to all this she moved swiftly to the window before Callisto could speak; tore away the drapes and smashed out the glass with two exquisite hands which came away bleeding and glistening with splinters; and turned to face the man on the bed and wait with him until the moment of equilibrium was reached, when 37 degrees Fahrenheit should prevail both outside and inside, and forever, and the hovering, curious dominant of their separate lives should resolve into a tonic of darkness and the final absence of all motion.

1960

Nicholasa Mohr b. 1938

Nicholasa Mohr is one of the most widely published Puerto Rican writers in the United States. Born to parents who came to New York City with the massive migration during World War II, Mohr grew up in the Bronx and studied art at the Students' Art League. She became a well-known graphic artist. Her art agent once asked her to write about growing up Puerto Rican and female in the Bronx, perhaps expecting sensationalist tales of crime, drugs, and gang activity. The stories Mohr wrote were quite different, and she had difficulties getting editors interested in publishing her work. *Nilda,* her first novel, appeared in 1974.

Somewhat autobiographical, *Nilda* relates life in the Bronx through the eyes of a ten-year-old girl who is a second-generation Puerto Rican. Mohr's protagonist uses her imagination and her fantasies to sustain herself through the hardships of her cultural and economic circumstances. As in this book, Mohr chooses to use a child's perspective for much of her writing. *Felita* and *Going Home* are, in fact, aimed at an adolescent audience. They relate Felita's experiences growing up in El Barrio and on a return trip to Puerto Rico, where she discovers differences between the values of her family and community in New York and the values of her relatives and of Puerto Rican society at large.

Rituals of Survival: A Woman's Portfolio is one of Mohr's most interesting publications. It consists of six vignettes about adult Puerto Rican women, each one representing various lifestyles, ages, and circumstances. Their common bond is their need to survive as individuals and as women free from restricting social and cultural expectations. In "A Thanksgiving Celebration," reproduced here, Amy, the young widowed mother of four children, resorts to her ingenuity and storytelling traditions inherited from her grandmother, in order to give meaning to Thanksgiving Day. All of Mohr's characters have to struggle with the sexual roles imposed on them by the Hispanic culture, with the *machista* attitudes of the men in their lives, and with the expectations set on them by their families.

Although Nicholasa Mohr has been called a "meat-and-potatoes" writer, because of her simple style and the emphasis she places on the humanity of her characters, who are likely to be everyday people with everyday conflicts to surmount, her storytelling is clear, direct, and powerful. That it found publication in the adolescent reader market does not detract from its importance as a voice of a people sometimes marginalized by economic and social stratifications. Mohr's work has been important because it has, often for the first time in English, presented and preserved family and household rituals from the Puerto Rican culture. It has also recorded the conflicts and ambivalences of a young Puerto Rican girl growing up in El Barrio of New York. As Mohr once said, "In American literature, I, as a Puerto Rican child, did not exist . . . and I as a Puerto Rican woman do not exist now." Her prose has established a precedent for young Puerto Rican women writers to continue to explore, question, and critique their lives in a bicultural world. Most important, Mohr has rescued readers' images of Barrio life from stereotypes of *puertorriqueños* as gang members or criminals. Her work has received several prizes, among them the 1974 Jane Addams Children's Book Award and *The New York Times* Outstanding Book of the Year. She was also a National Book Award finalist.

Frances R. Aparicio
University of Illinois at Chicago

PRIMARY WORKS

Nilda, 1974; *El Bronx Remembered,* 1976; *In Nueva York,* 1977; *Felita,* 1979; *Rituals of Survival: A Woman's Portfolio,* 1985; *Going Home,* 1986; *All for the Better: A Story of El Barrio,* 1993; *The Song of El Coqui and Other Tales of Puerto Rico,* 1995; *The Magic Shell,* 1995; *A Matter of Pride and Other Stories,* 1997.

from Rituals of Survival

A Thanksgiving Celebration (Amy)

Amy sat on her bed thinking. Gary napped soundly in his crib, which was placed right next to her bed. The sucking sound he made as he chewed on his thumb interrupted her thoughts from time to time. Amy glanced at Gary and smiled. He was her constant companion now; he shared her bedroom and was with her during those frightening moments when, late into the night and early morning, she wondered if she could face another day just like the one she had safely survived. Amy looked at the small alarm clock on the bedside table. In another hour or so it would be time to wake Gary and give him his milk, then she had just enough time to shop and pick up the others, after school.

She heard the plopping sound of water dropping into a full pail. Amy hurried into the bathroom, emptied the pail into the toilet, then replaced it so that the floor remained dry. Last week she had forgotten, and the water had overflowed out of the pail and onto the floor, leaking down into Mrs. Wynn's bathroom. Now, Mrs. Wynn was threatening to take her to small claims court, if the landlord refused to fix the damage done to her bathroom ceiling and wallpaper. All right, Amy shrugged, she would try calling the landlord once more. She was tired of the countless phone calls to plead with them to come and fix the leak in the roof.

"Yes, Mrs. Guzman, we got your message and we'll send somebody over. Yes, just as soon as we can . . . we got other tenants with bigger problems, you know. We are doing our best, we'll get somebody over; you gotta be patient . . ."

Time and again they had promised, but no one had ever showed up. And it was now more than four months that she had been forced to live like this. Damn, Amy walked into her kitchen, they never refuse the rent for that, there's somebody ready any time! Right now, this was the best she could do. The building was still under rent control and she had enough room. Where else could she go? No one in a better neighborhood would rent to her, not the way things were.

She stood by the window, leaning her side against the molding, and looked out. It was a crisp sunny autumn day, mild for the end of November. She remembered it was the eve of Thanksgiving and felt a tightness in her chest. Amy took a deep breath, deciding not to worry about that right now.

Rows and rows of endless streets scattered with abandoned buildings and small houses stretched out for miles. Some of the blocks were almost entirely leveled, except for clumps of partial structures charred and blackened by fire. From a distance they looked like organic masses pushing their way out of the earth. Garbage, debris, shattered glass, bricks and broken, discarded furniture covered the ground. Rusting carcasses of cars that had been stripped down to the shell shone and glistened a bright orange under the afternoon sun.

There were no people to be seen nor traffic, save for a group of children jumping on an old filthy mattress that had been ripped open. They were busy pulling the stuffing out of the mattress and tossing it about playfully. Nearby, several stray dogs searched the garbage for food. One of the boys picked up a brick, then threw it at the dogs, barely missing them. Reluctantly, the dogs moved on.

Amy sighed and swallowed, it was all getting closer and closer. It seemed as if only last month, when she had looked out of this very window, all of that was much further away; in fact, she recalled feeling somewhat removed and safe. Now the decay was creeping up to this area. The fire engine sirens screeching and screaming in the night reminded her that the devastation was constant, never stopping even for a night's rest. Amy was fearful of living on the top floor. Going down four flights to safety with the kids in case of a fire was another source of worry for her. She remembered how she had argued with Charlie when they had first moved in.

"All them steps to climb with Michele and Carlito, plus carrying the carriage for Carlito, is too much."

"Come on baby," Charlie had insisted "it's only temporary. The rent's cheaper and we can save something towards buying our own place. Come on . . ."

That was seven years ago. There were two more children now, Lisabeth and Gary; and she was still here, without Charlie.

"Soon it'll come right to this street and to my doorstep. God Almighty!" Amy whispered. It was like a plague: a disease for which there seemed to be no cure, no prevention. Gangs of youngsters occupied empty store fronts and basements; derelicts, drunk or wasted on drugs, positioned themselves on street corners and in empty doorways. Every day she saw more abandoned and burned-out sections.

As Amy continued to look out, a feeling that she had been in this same situation before, a long time ago, startled her. The feeling of deja vu so real to her, reminded Amy quite vividly of the dream she had had last night. In that dream, she had been standing in the center of a circle of little girls. She herself was very young and they were all singing a rhyme. In a soft whisper, Amy sang the rhyme: "London Bridge is falling down, falling down, falling down, London Bridge is falling down, my fair lady . . ." She stopped and saw herself once again in her dream, picking up her arms and chanting, "wave your arms and fly away, fly away, fly away . . ."

She stood in the middle of the circle waving her arms, first gently, then more forcefully, until she was flapping them. The other girls stared silently at her. Slowly, Amy had felt herself elevated above the circle, higher and higher until she could barely make out the human figures below. Waving her arms like the wings of a bird, she began to fly. A pleasant breeze pushed her gently, and she glided along, passing through soft white clouds into an intense silence. Then she saw it. Beneath her, huge areas were filled with crumbling buildings and large caverns; miles of destruction spread out in every direction. Amy had felt herself suspended in this silence for a moment and then she began to fall. She flapped her arms and legs furiously, trying to clutch at the air, hoping for a breeze, something to get her going again, but there was nothing. Quickly she fell, faster and faster, as the ground below her swirled and turned, coming closer and closer, revealing destroyed, burned buildings, rubble and a huge dark cavern. In a state of hysteria, Amy had fought against the loss of control and helplessness, as her body descended into the large black hole and had woken up with a start just before she hit bottom.

Amy stepped away from the window for a moment, almost out of breath as she recollected the fear she had felt in her dream. She walked over to the sink and poured herself a glass of water.

"That's it, Europe and the war," she said aloud. "In the movies, just like my dream."

Amy clearly remembered how she had sat as a very little girl in a local movie theatre with her mother and watched horrified at the scenes on the screen. Newsreels showed entire cities almost totally devastated. Exactly as it had been in her dream, she recalled seeing all the destruction caused by warfare. Names like "Munich, Nuremburg, Berlin" and "the German people" identified the areas. Most of the streets were empty, except for the occasional small groups of people who rummaged about, searching among the ruins and huge piles of debris, sharing the spoils with packs of rats who scavenged at a safe distance. Some people pulled wagons and baby carriages loaded with bundles and household goods. Others carried what they owned on their backs.

Amy remembered turning to her mother, asking, "What was going on? Mami, who did this? Why did they do it? Who are those people living there?"

"The enemy, that's who," her mother had whispered emphatically. "Bad people who started the war against our country and did terrible things to other people and to us. That's where your papa was for so long, fighting in the army. Don't you remember, Amy?"

"What kinds of things, Mami? Who were the other people they did bad things to?"

"Don't worry about them things. These people got what they deserved. Besides, they are getting help from us, now that we won the war. There's a plan to help them, even though they don't deserve no help from us."

Amy had persisted, "Are there any little kids there? Do they go to school? Do they live in them holes?"

"Shh . . . let me hear the rest of the news . . ." her mother had responded, annoyed. Amy had sat during the remainder of the double feature, wondering where those people lived and all about the kids there. And she continued to wonder and worry for several days, until one day she forgot all about it.

Amy sipped from the glass she held, then emptied most of the water back into the sink. She sat and looked around at her small kitchen. The ceiling was peeling and flakes of paint had fallen on the kitchen table. The entire apartment was in urgent need of a thorough plastering and paint job. She blinked and shook her head, and now? Who are we now? What have I done? Who is the enemy? Is there a war? Are we at war? Amy suppressed a loud chuckle.

"Nobody answered my questions then, and nobody's gonna answer them now," she spoke out loud.

Amy still wondered and groped for answers about Charlie. No one could tell her what had really happened . . . how he had felt and what he was thinking before he died. Almost two years had gone by, but she was still filled with an overwhelming sense of loneliness. That day was just like so many other days; they were together, planning about the kids, living from one crisis to the next, fighting, barely finding the time to make love without being exhausted; then late that night, it was all over. Charlie's late again, Amy had thought, and didn't even call me. She was angry when she heard the doorbell. He forgot the key again. Dammit, Charlie! You would forget your head if it weren't attached to you!

They had stood there before her; both had shown her their badges, but only one had spoken.

"Come in . . . sit down, won't you."

"You better sit down, miss." The stranger told her very calmly and soberly that Charlie was dead.

"On the Bruckner Boulevard Expressway . . . head on collision . . . dead on arrival . . . didn't suffer too long . . . nobody was with him, but we found his wallet."

Amy had protested and argued—No way! They were lying to her. But after a while she knew they brought the truth to her, and Charlie wasn't coming back.

Tomorrow would be the second Thanksgiving without him and one she could not celebrate. Celebrate with what? Amy stood and walked over and opened the refrigerator door. She had enough bread, a large pitcher of powdered milk which she had flavored with Hershey's cocoa and powdered sugar. There was plenty of peanut butter and some graham crackers she had kept fresh by sealing them in a plastic bag. For tonight she had enough chopped meat and macaroni. But tomorrow? What could she buy for tomorrow?

Amy shut the refrigerator door and reached over to the money tin set way back on one of the shelves. Carefully she took out the money and counted every cent. There was no way she could buy a turkey, even a small one. She still had to manage until the first; she needed every penny just to make it to the next check. Things were bad, worse than they had ever been. In the past, when things were rough, she had turned to Charlie and sharing had made it all easier. Now there was no one. She resealed the money tin and put it away.

Amy had thought of calling the lawyers once more. What good would that do? What can they do for me? Right now . . . today!

"These cases take time before we get to trial. We don't want to take the first settlement they offer. That wouldn't do you or the children any good. You have a good case, the other driver was at fault. He didn't have his license or the registration, and we have proof he was drinking. His father is a prominent judge who doesn't want that kind of publicity. I know . . . yes, things are rough, but just hold on a little longer. We don't want to accept a poor settlement and risk your future and the future of your children, do we?" Mr. Silverman of Silverman, Knapp and Ullman was handling the case personally. "By early Spring we should be making a date for trial . . . just hang in there a bit longer . . ." And so it went every time she called: the promise that in just a few more months she could hope for relief, some money, enough to live like people.

Survivor benefits had not been sufficient, and since they had not kept up premium payments on Charlie's G.I. insurance policy, she had no other income. Amy was given a little more assistance from the Aid to Dependent Children agency. Somehow she had managed so far.

The two food stores that extended her credit were still waiting for Amy to settle overdue accounts. In an emergency she could count on a few friends; they would lend her something, but not for this, not for Thanksgiving dinner.

She didn't want to go to Papo and Mary's again. She knew her brother meant well, and that she always had an open invitation. They're good people, but we are five more mouths to feed, plus they've been taking care of Papa all these years, ever since Mami died. Enough is enough. Amy shut her eyes. I want my own dinner this year, just for my family, for me and the kids.

If I had the money, I'd make a dinner tomorrow and invite Papa and Lou Ann from downstairs and her kids. She's been such a good friend to us. I'd get a gallon of cider and a bottle of wine . . . a large cake at the bakery by Alexander's, some dried fruits and nuts . . . even a holiday centerpiece for the table. Yes, it would be my dinner for us and my friends. I might even invite Jimmy. She hadn't seen Jimmy for a long time. Must be over six months . . . almost a year? He worked with Charlie at the plant. After Charlie's death, Jimmy had come by often, but Amy was not ready to see another man, not just then, so she discouraged him. From time to time, she thought of Jimmy and hoped he would visit her again.

Amy opened her eyes and a sinking feeling flowed through her, as she looked down at the chips of paint spread out on the kitchen table. Slowly, Amy brushed them with her hand, making a neat pile.

These past few months, she had seriously thought of going out to work. Before she had Michele, she had worked as a clerk-typist for a large insurance company, but that was almost ten years ago. She would have to brush up on her typing and math. Besides, she didn't know if she could earn enough to pay for a sitter. She couldn't leave the kids alone; Gary wasn't even three and Michele had just turned nine. Amy had applied for part-time work as a teacher's aide, but when she learned that her check from Aid to Dependent Children could be discontinued, she withdrew her application. Better to go on like this until the case comes to trial.

Amy choked back the tears. I can't let myself get like this. I just can't! Lately, she had begun to find comfort at the thought of never waking up again. What about my kids, then? I must do something. I have to. Tomorrow is going to be for us, just us, our day.

Her thoughts went back to her own childhood and the holiday dinners with her family. They had been poor, but there was always food. We used to have such good times. Amy remembered the many stories her grandmother used to tell them. She spoke about her own childhood on a farm in a rural area of Puerto Rico. Her grandmother's stories were about the animals, whom she claimed to know personally and very well. Amy laughed, recalling that most of the stories her grandmother related were too impossible to be true, such as a talking goat who saved the town from a flood, and the handsome mouse and beautiful lady beetle who fell in love, got married and had the biggest and fanciest wedding her grandmother had ever attended. Her grandmother was very old and had died before Amy was ten. Amy had loved her best, more than her own parents, and she still remembered the old woman quite clearly.

"Abuelita,[1] did them things really happen? How come them animals talked? Animals don't talk. Everybody knows that."

"Oh, but they do talk! And yes, everything I tell you is absolutely the truth. I believe it and you must believe it too." The old woman had been completely convincing. And for many years Amy had secretly believed that when her grandmother was a little girl, somewhere in a special place, animals talked, got married and were heroes.

"Abuelita," Amy whispered, "I wish you were here and could help me now."

---

[1]Abuelita, grandmother in Spanish. The diminutive form expresses warmth and affection.

And then she thought of it. Something special for tomorrow. Quickly, Amy took out the money tin, counting out just the right amount of money she needed. She hesitated for a moment. What if it won't work and I can't convince them? Amy took a deep breath. Never mind, I have to try, I must. She counted out a few more dollars. I'll work it all out somehow. Then she warmed up Gary's milk and got ready to leave.

Amy heard the voices of her children with delight. Shouts and squeals of laughter bounced into the kitchen as they played in the living room. Today they were all happy, anticipating their mother's promise of a celebration. Recently, her frequent moods of depression and short temper had frightened them. Privately, the children had blamed themselves for their mother's unhappiness, fighting with each other in helpless confusion. The children welcomed their mother's energy and good mood with relief.

Lately Amy had begun to realize that Michele and Carlito were constantly fighting. Carlito was always angry and would pick on Lisabeth. Poor Lisabeth, she's always so sad. I never have time for her and she's not really much older than Gary. This way of life has been affecting us all . . . but not today. Amy worked quickly. The apartment was filled with an air of festivity. She had set the kitchen table with a paper tablecloth, napkins and paper cups to match. These were decorated with turkeys, pilgrims, Indian corn and all the symbols of the Thanksgiving holiday. Amy had also bought a roll of orange paper streamers and decorated the kitchen chairs. Each setting had a name-card printed with bright magic markers. She had even managed to purchase a small holiday cake for dessert.

As she worked, Amy fought moments of anxiety and fear that threatened to weaken her sense of self-confidence. What if they laugh at me? Dear God in heaven, will my children think I'm a fool? But she had already spent the money, cooked and arranged everything; she had to go ahead. If I make it through this day, Amy nodded, I'll be all right.

She set the food platter in the center of the table and stepped back. A mound of bright yellow rice, flavored with a few spices and bits of fatback, was surrounded by a dozen hardboiled eggs that had been colored a bright orange. Smiling, Amy felt it was all truly beautiful; she was ready for the party.

"All right," Amy walked into the living room. "We're ready!" The children quickly followed her into the kitchen.

"Oooh, Mommy," Lisabeth shouted, "everything looks so pretty."

"Each place has got a card with your own name, so find the right seat." Amy took Gary and sat him down on his special chair next to her.

"Mommy," Michele spoke, "is this the whole surprise?"

"Yes," Amy answered, "just a minute, we also have some cider." Amy brought a small bottle of cider to the table.

"Easter eggs for Thanksgiving?" Carlito asked.

"Is that what you think they are, Carlito?" Amy asked. "Because they are not Easter eggs."

The children silently turned to one another, exchanging bewildered looks.

"What are they?" Lisabeth asked.

"Well," Amy said, "these are . . . turkey eggs, that's what. What's better than a turkey on Thanksgiving day? Her eggs, right?" Amy continued as all of them watched her. "You see, it's not easy to get these eggs. They're what you call a delicacy.

But I found a special store that sells them, and they agreed to sell me a whole dozen for today."

"What store is that, Mommy?" Michele asked. "Is it around here?"

"No. They don't have stores like that here. It's special, way downtown."

"Did the turkey lay them eggs like that? That color?" Carlito asked.

"I want an egg," Gary said pointing to the platter.

"No, no . . . I just colored them that way for today, so everything goes together nicely, you know . . ." Amy began to serve the food. "All right, you can start eating."

"Well then, what's so special about these eggs? What's the difference between a turkey egg and an egg from a chicken?" Carlito asked.

"Ah, the taste, Carlito, just wait until you have some." Amy quickly finished serving everyone. "You see, these eggs are hard to find because they taste so fantastic." She chewed a mouthful of egg. "Ummm . . . fantastic, isn't it?" She nodded at them.

"Wonderful, Mommy," said Lisabeth. "It tastes real different."

"Oh yeah," Carlito said, "you can taste it right away. Really good."

Everyone was busy eating and commenting on how special the eggs tasted. As Amy watched her children, a sense of joy filled her, and she knew it had been a very long time since they had been together like this, close and loving.

"Mommy, did you ever eat these kinds of eggs before?" asked Michele.

"Yes, when I was little" she answered. "My grandmother got them for me. You know, I talked about my abuelita before. When I first ate them, I couldn't get over how good they tasted, just like you." Amy spoke with assurance, as they listened to every word she said. "Abuelita lived on a farm when she was very little. That's how come she knew all about turkey eggs. She used to tell me the most wonderful stories about her life there."

"Tell us!"

"Yeah, please Mommy, please tell us."

"All right, I'll tell you one about a hero who saved her whole village from a big flood. He was . . . a billy goat."

"Mommy," Michele interrupted, "a billy goat?"

"That's right, and you have to believe what I'm going to tell you. All of you have to believe me. Because everything I'm going to say is absolutely the truth. Promise? All right, then, in the olden days, when my grandmother was very little, far away in a small town in Puerto Rico . . ."

Amy continued, remembering stories that she had long since forgotten. The children listened, intrigued by what their mother had to say. She felt a calmness within. Yes, Amy told herself, today's for us, for me and the kids.

1985

Raymond Carver 1938–1988

Raymond Carver's characters have been called diminished and lost. Carver's study in character represents a cold look at the complicated inner lives of the working poor in the United States during the 1970s and 1980s: at any time, anyone might lose everything; not only material positions are lost but also trust, love, and truth. Carver may occasionally be naturalistic, but he is never nostalgic or romantic about life near the edge.

Carver lived much of his life in the same desperate straits as his characters. His father was a laborer with grand dreams and a deadly attraction to alcohol. Carver himself was married and raising two children before his twentieth birthday. He worked a variety of jobs that would never be presented as a career path on a résumé—picking tulips, pumping gas, sweeping up, delivering packages. He recalled, "Once I even considered, for a few minutes anyway—the job application form there in front of me—becoming a bill collector!" He and his wife declared bankruptcy several times. He inherited his father's drinking problem.

In 1958 with two small children, he and his wife moved to Chico, California. They borrowed $125 from the druggist who employed Carver as a delivery man. With that money, Carver enrolled in Chico State and took his first writing class from John Gardner, at that time a young, unknown, and unpublished novelist. Encouraged by Gardner and later by the editor Gordon Lish, Carver began to take himself seriously as a writer. He began to publish regularly in little magazines, but not until 1968 did his first book, a collection of poems, appear, in a limited edition. Eight years later his first collection of stories, *Will You Please Be Quiet, Please?* was published. Readers did not realize that Carver had stopped writing a couple of years before the book's publication.

In June 1977 Carver's life changed drastically. He stopped drinking, he was awarded a Guggenheim Fellowship, and he met the poet and short-story writer Tess Gallagher, who was to become his companion and eventually his second wife.

To the consternation of many editors, Carver was a rewriter of his own work. At least one of his stories has appeared with as many as three different titles and a slight rewriting at each publication. In an essay called "On Rewriting" he writes, "I like to mess with my stories. I'd rather tinker with a story after writing it, and then tinker some more, changing this, changing that, than have to write the story in the first place." Even his successful stories were not exempted from his rewriting. "The Bath," a widely praised story from *What We Talk About When We Talk About Love* and winner of the Carlos Fuentes Fiction Award, reappeared in a much longer form in *Cathedral* as "A Small, Good Thing." Writing in the *Washington Post,* Jonathan Yardley said, "The first version is beautifully crafted and admirably concise, but lacking in genuine compassion; the mysterious caller is not so much a human being as a mere voice, malign and characterless. But in the second version that voice becomes a person, one whose own losses are, in different ways, as crippling and heartbreaking as the one suffered by the grieving parents." Although many do not agree with Yardley, it is obvious that Carver found a different kind of strength in *Cathedral.*

Yet there is new controversy about Carver's rewriting and his relationship to his editors, particularly Lish. Recent publications in *The New Yorker*—the story "Beginners" (which became "What We Talk About When We Talk About Love" after extensive editing by Lish), the accompanying article, and an online piece that displays Lish's edits in detail—show that Carver's rewriting may have been both an attempt to recover his stories as well as an enlargement of earlier minimalist works. As soon as some legal issues are resolved, we will be able to take a closer look at Carver's process, intentions, and art and evaluate better the relationship between Carver and Lish.

Until his death from lung cancer in 1988 at the age of fifty, Carver continued to write poems and stories. His last book was a collection of poems called *A New Path to the Waterfall.*

Paul Jones
University of North Carolina–Chapel Hill

PRIMARY WORKS

Will You Please be Quiet, Please? 1976; *Furious Seasons,* 1977; *What We Talk About When We Talk About Love,* 1981; *Fires: Essays, Poems, and Stories, 1966–1982,* 1983; *Cathedral,* 1984; *Dostoevsky: The Screenplay,* 1985; *Where Water Comes Together With Other Water,* 1985; *Ultramarine,* 1986; *Saints,* 1987; *Where I'm Calling From: New and Selected Stories,* 1988; *A New Path to the Waterfall,* 1989; *No Heroics, Please: Uncollected Writings,* 1992; *Carnations: A One-Act Play,* 1992; *Short Cuts: Selected Stories,* 1993; *All of Us: The Collected Poems,* 1998; *Call If You Need Me: The Uncollected Fiction & Prose,* 2001.

What We Talk about When We Talk about Love

My friend Mel McGinnis was talking. Mel McGinnis is a cardiologist, and sometimes that gives him the right.

The four of us were sitting around his kitchen table drinking gin. Sunlight filled the kitchen from the big window behind the sink. There were Mel and me and his second wife, Teresa—Terri, we called her—and my wife, Laura. We lived in Albuquerque then. But we were all from somewhere else.

There was an ice bucket on the table. The gin and tonic water kept going around, and we somehow got on the subject of love. Mel thought real love was nothing less than spiritual love. He said he'd spent five years in a seminary before quitting to go to medical school. He said he still looked back on those years in the seminary as the most important years in his life.

Terri said the man she lived with before she lived with Mel loved her so much he tried to kill her. Then Terri said, "He beat me up one night. He dragged me around the living room by my ankles. He kept saying, 'I love you, I love you, you bitch.' He went on dragging me around the living room. My head kept knocking on things." Terry looked around the table. "What do you do with love like that?"

She was a bone-thin woman with a pretty face, dark eyes, and brown hair that hung down her back. She liked necklaces made of turquoise, and long pendant earrings.

"My God, don't be silly. That's not love, and you know it," Mel said. "I don't know what you'd call it, but I sure know you wouldn't call it love."

"Say what you want to, but I know it was," Terri said. "It may sound crazy to you, but it's true just the same. People are different, Mel. Sure, sometimes he may have acted crazy. Okay. But he loved me. In his own way maybe, but he loved me. There was love there, Mel. Don't say there wasn't."

Mel let out his breath. He held the glass and turned to Laura and me. "The man threatened to kill me," Mel said. He finished his drink and reached for the gin bottle. "Terri's a romantic. Terri's of the kick-me-so-I'll-know-you-love-me school. Terri, hon, don't look that way." Mel reached across the table and touched Terri's cheek with his fingers. He grinned at her.

"Now he wants to make up," Terri said.

"Make up what?" Mel said. "What is there to make up? I know what I know. That's all."

"How'd we get started on this subject, anyway?" Terri said. She raised her glass and drank from it. "Mel always has love on his mind," she said. "Don't you, honey?" She smiled, and I thought that was the last of it.

"I just wouldn't call Ed's behavior love. That's all I'm saying, honey," Mel said. "What about you guys?" Mel said to Laura and me. "Does that sound like love to you?"

"I'm the wrong person to ask," I said. "I didn't even know the man. I've only heard his name mentioned in passing. I wouldn't know. You have to know the particulars. But I think what you're saying is that love is an absolute."

Mel said, "The kind of love I'm talking about is. The kind of love I'm talking about, you don't try to kill people."

Laura said, "I don't know anything about Ed, or anything about the situation. But who can judge anyone else's situation?"

I touched the back of Laura's hand. She gave me a quick smile. I picked up Laura's hand. It was warm, the nails polished, perfectly manicured, I encircled the broad wrist with my fingers, and I held her.

"When I left, he drank rat poison," Terri said. She clasped her arms with her hands. "They took him to the hospital in Santa Fe. That's where we lived then, about ten miles out. They saved his life. But his gums went crazy from it. I mean they pulled away from his teeth. After that, his teeth stood out like fangs. My God," Terri said. She waited a minute, then let go of her arms and picked up her glass.

"What people won't do!" Laura said.

"He's out of the action now," Mel said. "He's dead."

Mel handed me the saucer of limes. I took a section, squeezed it over my drink, and stirred the ice cubes with my finger.

"It gets worse," Terri said. "He shot himself in the mouth. But he bungled that too. Poor Ed," she said. Terri shook her head.

"Poor Ed nothing," Mel said. "He was dangerous."

Mel was forty-five years old. He was tall and rangy with curly soft hair. His face and arms were brown from the tennis he played. When he was sober, his gestures, all his movements, were precise, very careful.

"He did love me though, Mel. Grant me that, can't you?"

"What do you mean, he bungled it?" I said.

Laura leaned forward with her glass. She put her elbows on the table and held her glass in both hands. She glanced from Mel to Terri and waited with a look of bewilderment on her open face, as if amazed that such things happened to people you were friendly with.

"How'd he bungle it when he killed himself?" I said.

"I'll tell you what happened," Mel said. "He took this twenty-two pistol he'd bought to threaten Terri and me with. Oh, I'm serious, the man was always threatening. You should have seen the way we lived in those days. Like fugitives. I even bought a gun myself. Can you believe it? A guy like me? But I did. I bought one for self-defense and carried it in the glove compartment. Sometimes I'd have to leave the apartment in the middle of the night. To go to the hospital, you know? Terri and I weren't married then, and my first wife had the house and the kids, the dog, everything, and Terri and I were living in this apartment here. Sometimes, as I say, I'd get a call in the middle of the night and have to go in to the hospital at two or three in the morning. It'd be dark out there in the parking lot, and I'd break into a sweat before I could even get to my car. I never knew if he was going to come up out of the shrubbery or from behind a car and start shooting. I mean, the man was crazy. He was capable of wiring a bomb, anything. He used to call my service at all hours and say he needed to talk to the doctor, and when I'd return the call, he'd say, 'Son of a bitch, your days are numbered.' Little things like that. It was scary, I'm telling you."

"I still feel sorry for him," Terri said.

"It sounds like a nightmare," Laura said. "But what exactly happened after he shot himself?"

Laura is a legal secretary. We'd met in a professional capacity. Before we knew it, it was a courtship. She's thirty-five, three years younger than I am. In addition to being in love, we like each other and enjoy one another's company. She's easy to be with.

"What happened?" Laura said.

Mel said, "He shot himself in the mouth in his room. Someone heard the shot and told the manager. They came in with a passkey, saw what had happened, and called an ambulance. I happened to be there when they brought him in, alive but past recall. The man lived for three days. His head swelled up to twice the size of a normal head. I'd never seen anything like it, and I hope I never do again. Terri wanted to go in and sit with him when she found out about it. We had a fight over it. I didn't think she should see him like that. I didn't think she should see him, and I still don't."

"Who won the fight?" Laura said.

"I was in the room with him when he died," Terri said. "He never came up out of it. But I sat with him. He didn't have anyone else."

"He was dangerous," Mel said. "If you call that love, you can have it."

"It was love," Terri said. "Sure, it's abnormal in most people's eyes. But he was willing to die for it. He did die for it."

"I sure as hell wouldn't call it love," Mel said. "I mean, no one knows what he did it for. I've seen a lot of suicides, and I couldn't say anyone ever knew what they did it for."

Mel put his hands behind his neck and tilted his chair back. "I'm not interested in that kind of love," he said. "If that's love, you can have it."

Terri said, "We were afraid. Mel even made a will out and wrote to his brother in California who used to be a Green Beret. Mel told him who to look for if something happened to him."

Terri drank from her glass. She said, "But Mel's right—we lived like fugitives. We were afraid. Mel was, weren't you, honey? I even called the police at one point, but they were no help. They said they couldn't do anything until Ed actually did something. Isn't that a laugh?" Terri said.

She poured the last of the gin into her glass and waggled the bottle. Mel got up from the table and went to the cupboard. He took down another bottle.

"Well, Nick and I know what love is," Laura said. "For us, I mean," Laura said. She bumped my knee with her knee. "You're supposed to say something now," Laura said, and turned her smile on me.

For an answer, I took Laura's hand and raised it to my lips. I made a big production out of kissing her hand. Everyone was amused.

"We're lucky," I said.

"You guys," Terri said. "Stop that now. You're making me sick. You're still on the honeymoon, for God's sake. You're still gaga, for crying out loud. Just wait. How long have you been together now? How long has it been? A year? Longer than a year?"

"Going on a year and a half," Laura said, flushed and smiling.

"Oh, now," Terri said. "Wait awhile."

She held her drink and gazed at Laura.

"I'm only kidding," Terri said.

Mel opened the gin and went around the table with the bottle.

"Here, you guys," he said. "Let's have a toast. I want to propose a toast. A toast to love. To true love," Mel said.

We touched glasses.

"To love," we said.

Outside in the backyard, one of the dogs began to bark. The leaves of the aspen that leaned past the window ticked against the glass. The afternoon sun was like a presence in this room, the spacious light of ease and generosity. We could have been anywhere, somewhere enchanted. We raised our glasses again and grinned at each other like children who had agreed on something forbidden.

"I'll tell you what real love is," Mel said. "I mean, I'll give you a good example. And then you can draw your own conclusions." He poured more gin into his glass. He added an ice cube and a sliver of lime. We waited and sipped our drinks. Laura and I touched knees again. I put a hand on her warm thigh and left it there.

"What do any of us really know about love?" Mel said. "It seems to me we're just beginners at love. We say we love each other and we do, I don't doubt it. I love Terri and Terri loves me, and you guys love each other too. You know the kind of love I'm talking about now. Physical love, that impulse that drives you to someone special, as well as love of the other person's being, his or her essence, as it were. Carnal love and, well, call it sentimental love, the day-to-day caring about the other person. But sometimes I have a hard time accounting for the fact that I must have loved my first wife too. But I did, I know I did. So I suppose I am like Terri in that regard. Terri and Ed." He thought about it and then he went on. "There was a time when I thought I loved my first wife more than life itself. But now I hate her guts. I do. How do you explain that? What happened to that love? What happened to it, is what I'd like to know. I wish someone could tell me. Then there's

Ed. Okay, we're back to Ed. He loves Terri so much he tries to kill her and winds up killing himself." Mel stopped talking and swallowed from his glass. "You guys have been together eighteen months and you love each other. It shows all over you. You glow with it. But you both loved other people before you met each other. You've both been married before, just like us. And you probably loved other people before that too, even. Terri and I have been together five years, been married for four. And the terrible thing, the terrible thing is, but the good thing too, the saving grace, you might say, is that if something happened to one of us—excuse me for saying this—but if something happened to one of us tomorrow, I think the other one, the other person, would grieve for a while, you know, but then the surviving party would go out and love again, have someone else soon enough. All this, all of this love we're talking about, it would just be a memory. Maybe not even a memory. Am I wrong? Am I way off base? Because I want you to set me straight if you think I'm wrong. I want to know. I mean, I don't know anything, and I'm the first one to admit it."

"Mel, for God's sake," Terri said. She reached out and took hold of his wrist. "Are you getting drunk? Honey? Are you drunk?"

"Honey, I'm just talking," Mel said. "All right? I don't have to be drunk to say what I think. I mean, we're all just talking, right?" Mel said. He fixed his eyes on her.

"Sweetie, I'm not criticizing," Terri said.

She picked up her glass.

"I'm not on call today," Mel said. "Let me remind you of that. I am not on call," he said.

"Mel, we love you," Laura said.

Mel looked at Laura. He looked at her as if he could not place her, as if she was not the woman she was.

"Love you too, Laura," Mel said. "And you, Nick, love you too. You know something?" Mel said. "You guys are our pals," Mel said.

He picked up his glass.

Mel said, "I was going to tell you about something. I mean, I was going to prove a point. You see, this happened a few months ago, but it's still going on right now, and it ought to make us feel ashamed when we talk like we know what we're talking about when we talk about love."

"Come on now," Terri said. "Don't talk like you're drunk if you're not drunk."

"Just shut up for once in your life," Mel said very quietly. "Will you do me a favor and do that for a minute? So as I was saying, there's this old couple who had this car wreck out on the interstate. A kid hit them and they were all torn to shit and nobody was giving them much chance to pull through."

Terri looked at us and then back at Mel. She seemed anxious, or maybe that's too strong a word.

Mel was handing the bottle around the table.

"I was on call that night," Mel said. "It was May or maybe it was June. Terri and I had just sat down to dinner when the hospital called. There'd been this thing out on the interstate. Drunk kid, teenager, plowed his dad's pickup into this camper with this old couple in it. They were up in the mid-seventies, that couple. The kid—eighteen, nineteen, something—he was DOA. Taken the steering wheel through his sternum. The old couple, they were alive, you understand. I mean, just barely. But they had everything. Multiple fractures, internal injuries, hemorrhaging, contusions, lacerations, the works, and they each of them had themselves concussions. They were in a bad way, believe me. And, of course, their age was two strikes against them. I'd say she was worse off than he was. Ruptured spleen along with everything else. Both kneecaps broken. But they'd been wearing their seatbelts and, God knows, that's what saved them for the time being."

"Folks, this is an advertisement for the National Safety Council," Terri said. "This is your spokesman, Dr. Melvin R. McGinnis, talking." Terri laughed. "Mel," she said, "sometimes you're just too much. But I love you, hon," she said.

"Honey, I love you," Mel said.

He leaned across the table. Terri met him halfway. They kissed.

"Terri's right," Mel said as he settled himself again. "Get those seatbelts on. But seriously, they were in some shape, those oldsters. By the time I got down there, the kid was dead, as I said. He was off in a corner, laid out on a gurney. I took one look at the old couple and told the ER nurse to get me a neurologist and an orthopedic man and a couple of surgeons down there right away."

He drank from his glass. "I'll try to keep this short," he said. "So we took the two of them up to the OR and worked like fuck on them most of the night. They had these incredible reserves, those two. You see that once in a while. So we did everything that we could be done, and toward morning we're giving them a fifty-fifty chance, maybe less than that for her. So here they are, still alive the next morning. So, okay, we move them into the ICU, which is where they both kept plugging away at it for two weeks, hitting it better and better on all the scopes. So we transfer them out to their own room."

Mel stopped talking. "Here," he said, "let's drink this cheapo gin the hell up. Then we're going to dinner, right? Terri and I know a new place. That's where we'll go to this new place we know about. But we're not going until we finish up this cut-rate, lousy gin."

Terri said, "We haven't actually eaten there yet. But it looks good. From the outside, you know."

"I like food," Mel said. "If I had it to do over again, I'd be a chef, you know? Right, Terri?" Mel said.

He laughed. He fingered the ice in his glass.

"Terri knows," he said. "Terri can tell you. But let me say this. If I could come back again in a different life, a different time and all, you know what? I'd like to come back as a knight. You were pretty safe wearing all that armor. It was all right being a knight until gunpowder and muskets and pistols came along."

"Mel would like to ride a horse and carry a lance," Terri said.

"Carry a woman's scarf with you everywhere," Laura said.

"Or just a woman," Mel said.

"Shame on you," Laura said.

Terri said, "Suppose you came back as a serf. The serfs didn't have it so good in those days," Terri said.

"The serfs never had it good," Mel said. "But I guess even the knights were vessels to someone. Isn't that the way it worked? But then everyone is always a vessel to someone. Isn't that right, Terri? But what I liked about knights, besides their ladies, was that they had that suit of armor, you know, and they couldn't get hurt very easy. No cars in those days, you know? No drunk teenagers to tear into your ass."

"Vassals," Terri said.

"What?" Mel said.

"Vassals," Terri said. "They were called vassals, not vessels."

"Vassals, vessels," Mel said. "what the fuck's the difference? You know what I meant anyway. All right," Mel said, "So I'm not educated. I learned my stuff. I'm a heart surgeon, sure, but I'm just a mechanic. I go in and I fuck around and I fix things. Shit," Mel said.

"Modesty doesn't become you," Terri said.

"He's just a humble sawbones," I said. "But sometimes they suffocated in all that armor, Mel. They'd even have heart attacks if it got too hot and they were too tired and worn out. I read somewhere that they'd fall off their horses and not be able to get up because they were too tired to stand with all that armor on them. They got trampled by their own horses sometimes."

"That's terrible," Mel said. "That's a terrible thing, Nicky. I guess they'd just lay there and wait until somebody came along and made a shish kebab out of them."

"Some other vessel," Terri said.

"That's right," Mel said. "Some vassal would come along and spat the bastard in the name of love. Or whatever the fuck it was they fought over in those days."

"Same things we fight over these days," Terri said.

Laura said, "Nothing's changed."

The color was still high in Laura's cheeks. Her eyes were bright. She brought her glass to her lips.

Mel poured himself another drink. He looked at the label closely as if studying a long row of numbers. Then he slowly put the bottle down on the table and slowly reached for the tonic water.

"What about the old couple?" Laura said. "You didn't finish that story you started."

Laura was having a hard time lighting her cigarette. Her matches kept going out.

The sunshine inside the room was different now, changing, getting thinner. But the leaves outside the window were still shimmering, and I stared at the pattern they made on the panes and on the Formica counter. They weren't the same patterns, of course.

"What about the old couple?" I said.

"Older but wiser," Terri said.

Mel stared at her.

Terri said, "Go on with your story, hon. I was only kidding. Then what happened?"

"Terri, sometimes," Mel said.

"Please, Mel," Terri said. "Don't always be so serious, sweetie. Can't you take a joke?"

"Where's the joke?" Mel said.

He held his glass and gazed steadily at his wife.

"What happened?" Laura said.

Mel fastened his eyes on Laura. He said, "Laura, if I didn't have Terri and if I didn't love her so much, and if Nick wasn't my best friend, I'd fall in love with you. I'd carry you off, honey," he said.

"Tell your story," Terri said. "Then we'll go to that new place, okay?"

"Okay," Mel said. "Where was I?" he said. He stared at the table and then he began again.

"I dropped in to see each of them every day, sometimes twice a day if I was up doing other calls anyway. Casts and bandages, head to foot, the both of them. You know, you've seen it in the movies. That's just the way they looked, just like in the movies. Little eye-holes and nose-holes and mouth-holes. And she had to have her legs slung up on top of it. Well, the husband was very depressed for the longest while. Even after he found out that his wife was going to pull through, he was still very depressed. Not about the accident, though. I mean, the accident was one thing, but it wasn't everything. I'd get up to his mouth-hole, you know, and he'd say no, it wasn't the accident exactly but it was because he couldn't see her through his eye-holes. He said that was what was making him feel so bad. Can you imagine? I'm telling you, the man's heart was breaking because he couldn't turn his goddamn head and *see* his goddamn wife."

Mel looked around the table and shook his head at what he was going to say.

"I mean, it was killing the old fart just because he couldn't *look* at the fucking woman."

We all looked at Mel.

"Do you see what I'm saying?" he said.

Maybe we were a little drunk by then. I know it was hard keeping things in focus. The light was draining out of the room, going back through the window where it had come from. Yet nobody made a move to get up from the table to turn on the overhead light.

"Listen," Mel said. "Let's finish this fucking gin. There's about enough left here for one shooter all around. Then let's go eat. Let's go to the new place."

"He's depressed," Terri said. "Mel, why don't you take a pill?"

Mel shook his head. "I've taken everything there is."

"We all need a pill now and then," I said.

"Some people are born needing them," Terri said.

She was using her finger to rub at something on the table. Then she stopped rubbing.

"I think I want to call my kids," Mel said. "Is that all right with everybody? I'll call my kids," he said.

Terri said, "What if Marjorie answers the phone? You guys, you've heard us on the subject of Marjorie? Honey, you know you don't want to talk to Marjorie. It'll make you feel even worse."

"I don't want to talk to Marjorie," Mel said. "But I want to talk to my kids."

"There isn't a day goes by that Mel doesn't say he wishes she'd get married again. Or else die," Terri said. "For one thing," Terri said, "she's bankrupting us. Mel says it's just to spite him that she won't get married again. She has a boyfriend who lives with her and the kids, so Mel is supporting the boyfriend too."

"She's allergic to bees," Mel said. "If I'm not praying she'll get married again. I'm praying she'll get herself stung to death by a swarm of fucking bees."

"Shame on you," Laura said.

"Bzzzzzzz," Mel said, turning his fingers into bees and buzzin them at Terri's throat. Then he let his hands drop all the way to his sides.

"She's vicious," Mel said. "Sometimes I think I'll go up there dressed like a bee-keeper. You know, that hat that's like a helmet with the plate that comes down over your face, the big gloves, and the padded coat? I'll knock on the door and let loose a hive of bees in the house. But first I'd make sure the kids were out, of course."

He crossed one leg over the other. It seemed to take him a lot of time to do it. Then he put both feet on the floor and leaned forward, elbows on the table, his chin cupped in his hands.

"Maybe I won't call the kids, after all. Maybe it isn't such a hot idea. Maybe we'll just go eat. How does that sound?"

"Sounds fine to me," I said. "Eat or not eat. Or keep drinking. I could head right on out into the sunset."

"What does that mean, honey?" Laura said.

"It just means what I said," I said. "It means I could just keep going. That's all it means."

"I could eat something myself," Laura said. "I don't think I've ever been so hungry in my life. Is there something to nibble on?"

"I'll put out some cheese and crackers," Terri said.

But Terri just sat there. She did not get up to get anything.

Mel turned his glass over. He spilled it out on the table.

"Gin's gone," Mel said.

Terri said, "Now what?"

I could hear my heart beating. I could hear everyone's heart. I could hear the human noise we sat there making, not one of us moving, not even when the room went dark.

1981

Lawson Fusao Inada b. 1938

Lawson Inada is third-generation Japanese American, born and raised in Fresno, California. These autobiographical details are highlighted in Inada's volume of poetry *Legends from Camp:* Section II is titled "Fresno" and consists of poems that pay tribute to this agricultural region of California; Section I is titled "Camp," referring to the author's boyhood experience of internment during World War II along with other Japanese Americans. In his autobio-graphical recountings, Inada mentions going to the University of Iowa to study writing, then moving to Oregon. He has taught at Southern Oregon State College since 1966.

For both historical and aesthetic reasons, Lawson Inada is a significant figure in Asian American poetry and literature. He was one of the co-editors of the landmark anthology, *Aiiieeeee! An Anthology of Asian-American Writers,* and has participated in efforts to recover writing by earlier Japanese American authors such as Toshio Mori and John Okada. Legend has it that at a time of emerging Asian American consciousness but few visible Asian American writers, Frank Chin and his friends happened upon the book cover of *Down at the Santa Fe Depot* (1970), an anthology of Fresno-based poets. Struck by seeing an Asian face in the group photo of the poets, they discovered and contacted fellow Asian American writer Lawson Inada. Inada's collection *Before the War: Poems as They Happened* (1971) was one of the first Asian American single-author volumes of poetry from a major New York publishing house.

Inada's poetry stands out in its consistent engagement with jazz. *Before the War* begins with a whimsical portrait of a Japanese American figure playing "air bass"; includes tributes to jazz musicians and singers such as Charlie Parker, Lester Young, and Billie Holiday; and ends with poems written for Miles Davis and Charles Mingus. Riffing on the term "bluesman," Inada calls himself a "campsman," suggesting that his blues derive from Japanese American internment. He describes his project as "blowing shakuhachi versaphone" and cites jazz as the strongest influence on his writing. Leslie Marmon Silko calls Inada "a poet-musician in the tradition of Walt Whitman and James A. Wright."

Inada won the American Book Award in 1994 for *Legends from Camp* and was named Oregon State Poet of the Year in 1991. He has received a number of poetry fellowships from the National Endowment for the Arts and has performed his poetry in concert with numerous musicians. His poetics of performance posits his art not as an object that transcends time but as a process that shapes time. Calling live performance his favorite form of "publishing," Inada appropriates the value that is ascribed to a finalized, written text for a mode that is oral and dynamic.

Inada's poetics suggest that there is more than one way to tell a story, that many stories are embedded within a given story or within what we know as history. This multiple sense of time implicitly critiques the notion of a standard time or history that is equivalent for all subjects. Poems such as "Instructions to All Persons" and "Two Variations on a Theme by Thelonious Monk" shape time and history as variable and layered. "On Being Asian American" refers to an echo generated by the actualization of the racial subject. We can see a poetics of the echo in the repetition enacted in this poem as well as in the poems "Instructions" and "Two Variations." This repetition is what Henry Louis Gates, Jr., calls "repetition with a difference": a non-linear, non-teleological aesthetics of change.

Juliana Chang
Santa Clara University

PRIMARY WORKS

Before the War: Poems as They Happened, 1971; *The Buddha Bandits Down Highway 99,* with Garrett Kaoru Hongo and Alan Chong Lau, 1978; *Legends from Camp,* 1992; *Drawing the Line,* 1997.

Presidio of San Francisco, California
May 3, 1942

INSTRUCTIONS
TO ALL PERSONS OF
JAPANESE
ANCESTRY
Living in the Following Area:

All of that portion of the City of Los Angeles, State of California, within that boundary beginning at the point at which North Figueroa Street meets a line following the middle of the Los Angeles River; thence southerly and following the said line to East First Street; thence westerly on East First Street to Alameda Street; thence southerly on Alameda Street to East Third Street; thence northwesterly on East Third Street to Main Street; thence northerly on Main Street to First Street; thence northwesterly on First Street to Figueroa Street; thence northeasterly on Figueroa Street to the point of beginning.

Pursuant to the provisions of Civilian Exclusion Order No. 33, this Headquarters, dated May 3, 1942, all persons of Japanese ancestry, both alien and non-alien, will be evacuated from the above area by 12 o'clock noon, P. W. T., Saturday, May 9, 1942.

No Japanese person living in the above area will be permitted to change residence after 12 o'clock noon, P. W. T., Sunday, May 3, 1942, without obtaining special permission from the representative of the Commanding General, Southern California Sector, at the Civil Control Station located at:

> Japanese Union Church,
> 120 North San Pedro Street,
> Los Angeles, California.

Such permits will only be granted for the purpose of uniting members of a family, or in cases of grave emergency.

The Civil Control Station is equipped to assist the Japanese population affected by this evacuation in the following ways:

1. Give advice and instructions on the evacuation.
2. Provide services with respect to the management, leasing, sale, storage or other disposition of most kinds of property, such as real estate, business and professional equipment, household goods, boats, automobiles and livestock.
3. Provide temporary residence elsewhere for all Japanese in family groups.
4. Transport persons and a limited amount of clothing and equipment to their new residence.

The Following Instructions Must Be Observed:

1. A responsible member of each family, preferably the head of the family, or the person in whose name most of the property is held, and each individual living alone, will report to the Civil Control Station to receive further instructions. This must be done between 8:00 A. M. and 5:00 P. M. on Monday, May 4, 1942, or between 8:00 A. M. and 5:00 P. M. on Tuesday, May 5, 1942.
2. Evacuees must carry with them on departure for the Assembly Center, the following property:
   (a) Bedding and linens (no mattress) for each member of the family;
   (b) Toilet articles for each member of the family;
   (c) Extra clothing for each member of the family;
   (d) Sufficient knives, forks, spoons, plates, bowls and cups for each member of the family;
   (e) Essential personal effects for each member of the family.

All items carried will be securely packaged, tied and plainly marked with the name of the owner and numbered in accordance with instructions obtained at the Civil Control Station. The size and number of packages is limited to that which can be carried by the individual or family group.

3. No pets of any kind will be permitted.
4. No personal items and no household goods will be shipped to the Assembly Center.
5. The United States Government through its agencies will provide for the storage, at the sole risk of the owner, of the more substantial household items, such as iceboxes, washing machines, pianos and other heavy furniture. Cooking utensils and other small items will be accepted for storage if crated, packed and plainly marked with the name and address of the owner. Only one name and address will be used by a given family.
6. Each family, and individual living alone, will be furnished transportation to the Assembly Center or will be authorized to travel by private automobile in a supervised group. All instructions pertaining to the movement will be obtained at the Civil Control Station.

> Go to the Civil Control Station between the hours of 8:00 A.M. and 5:00 P.M.,
> Monday, May 4, 1942, or between the hours of 8:00 A.M. and 5:00 P.M.,
> Tuesday, May 5, 1942, to receive further instructions.

> J. L. DeWITT
> Lieutenant General, U. S. Army
> Commanding

SEE CIVILIAN EXCLUSION ORDER NO. 33.

Instructions to All Persons

Let us take
what we can
for the occasion:

    Ancestry. (*Ancestry*)
5   All of that portion. (*Portion*)
    With the boundary. (*Boundary*)
    Beginning. (*Beginning*)
    At the point. (*Point*)
    Meets a line. (*Line*)
10   Following the middle. (*Middle*)
    Thence southerly. (*Southerly*)
    Following the said line. (*Following*) (*Said*)
    Thence westerly. (*Westerly*)
    Thence northerly. (*Northerly*)
15   To the point. (*Point*)
    Of beginning. (*Beginning*) (*Ancestry*)

Let us bring
what we need
for the meeting:

20   Provisions. (*Provisions*)
    Permission. (*Permission*)
    Commanding. (*Commanding*)
    Uniting. (*Uniting*)
    Family (*Family*)

25 Let us have
what we have
for the gathering:

    Civil. (*Civil*)
    Ways. (*Ways*)
30   Services. (*Services*)

    Respect. (*Respect*)
    Management. (*Management*)
    Kinds. (*Kinds*)
    Goods. (*Goods*)
35   For all. (*All*)

Let us take
what we can
for the occasion:

> *Responsible.*
> 50 *Individual.*
> *Sufficient.*
> *Personal.*
> *Securely.*
> *Civil.*
> 45 *Substantial.*
> *Accepted.*
> *Given.*
> *Authorized.*
>
> Let there be
> 50 Order.
>
> Let us be
> Wise.
> 1992

Two Variations on a Theme by Thelonious Monk as Inspired by Mal Waldron

Introduction: Monk's Prosody

> "I can't do that right. I have to practice that."
> —Thelonious Monk, composer, to his pianist
> (himself) during a solo run-through of
> "Round Midnight," April 5, 1957

April 5, 1957: Maybe I'm sitting on a fire escape in Berkeley, trying to write some poetry. I know one thing: I was listening to Monk by then—particularly his solo on "Bags' Groove," on the Miles Davis 10-inch lp. You might say I was studying Monk's prosody—how each time he'd come out of the speakers in a different, distinctive way, and always swinging.

Years pass. Decades. Prosody.

January 15, 1987: I work a duo concert with Mal Waldron. Mal, even while checking out the tuning, makes reference, says hello, to Monk. The next time we blow, I want to do "Blue Monk."

June, 1987: Whenever the next time is, I'll be ready. I work out a linear, horn-like statement; it fits, like an overlay. Then I jump right into the tune and the piano, and blow something from the inside out—percussive—particularly building around and repeating "ricochet."

April, 1988: One of those long Oregon dusks. Larry Smith, editor of Caliban, calls up to ask if I'd be interested in doing something with Monk's prosody. Prosody— yeah. I have to practice that.

I. Blue Monk (linear)

Solid, as the man himself would say.
Solid, as the man at his instrument.
Solid, as the solid composition.

However, at the same time,
5 this elegant melody,
"Blue Monk,"

while certainly being solid enough—
as evidenced by
the ease of our ability
10 to hum and whistle it,
even in sleep—

is actually solid, fluid,
and a real gas combined;

you know what I mean:
15 like feelings, like atmosphere,
like right, like here,

you feel like you've been hearing
"Blue Monk" forever,
since the planet started dancing,
20 like its been around since sound,

since the blue wind got up
one blue summer morning,
looked across the cool, blue canyon
at that sweet, blue mountain,
25 and melodiously started to sing
"Blue Monk";
you know that lovely feeling,
"Blue Monk";
you know what

30 "Blue Monk" can do for you,
the melodious message it sends,
the melodious message that always comes

echoing back across the canyons as a result;
"Blue Monk,"

35 as a result of recognition,
as a consequence of confirmation,
as an accomplishment of affirmation—
"Blue Monk,"
"Blue Monk"
40 in the sun and rain, in all conditions;

and the song, therefore,
just by being what it is—
these huge, blue feelings
spaced and placed just so,
45 ascending,
these huge, blue feelings
descending, just so,
and including some delightful
dimensions for refreshment
50 on a huge, blue plateau.

"Blue Monk," then, by its very nature,
built into its basic structure,
encompasses and contains
all the properties of nature:

55 take a hold of it,
hold it up to the light;
see what I mean?—
"Blue Monk" has you dancing;

by now you're feeling confident about the song,
60 feeling like you've got it down,
feeling like you're part of its beauty,
feeling like it's part of you—
which is certainly true;

feeling fine with the freedom of it;
65 feeling like going for it
with expansiveness, abandon;

feeling exhilarated in your bones
like you want to do something about
exercising your own right
70 to rhythm and expression,

yes, you feel like you own the song—
which you certainly do—

since you went right down there on West 52nd Street
and got it directly from the man himself,
75 Blue Monk, who turns out to be,
not the imposing artist you had heard and read about,
but just the husband, the father, the neighbor
making his way out of the corner grocery
with some snow peas and stalks of celery
80 sticking out of a paper sack,
he just needs something back,
gladly giving you the tune
in exchange for a proven recipe of your own;

meanwhile, Blue Monk is smiling
85 that solid Blue Monk smile
while offering you directions for usage:

"Look, 'Blue Monk' is a solid song;
you can bend it; you can break it;
you can always remake it;
90 *it's hot and it's cool,*
it's suitable for digging
in whatever occasion you choose—
ceremonious, thelonious and such . . ."

Ah, the sheer joy of such ownership!
95 You take "Blue Monk" home and set it
glowing in your living room
like a luxurious lamp.
You stick it in the phone,
sending it out via satellite:

100 *"Hello, Mom? Dig this song!"*
"Hello, is this the White House?
Listen, I've got a solid
new anthem for the shaky republic!"

You take "Blue Monk" outside to the fire escape,
105 seeing how far you can throw it,
looping it smoothly over the moonlit harbor
as it becomes a bridge
of flowing blue lights:
"Blue Monk."
110 You're dancing, humming,
strolling slowly across,
tossing blue notes
floating over the wide, blue water
like you're a luminous, musical spider;
115 tossing cool, blue clusters high overhead,

creating a blue, musical constellation:
"Blue Monk";

by now, many others,
including birds, animals, insects,
120 have joined you on your excursion,
having just got wise
to mythology and fireworks combined,
staring awestruck up into the huge, blue night
to find the Blue Monk profile outlined,
125 pointing out and humming
each huge, blue star in the melody—
and, oh, those sweet, blue spaces in between . . .

Yes, indeed, this is some kind
of luxurious structure,
130 in architectural legacy

ascending, descending, with pliable plateaus
for ease of breathing, handling,
relaxing, building, dancing, laughing,
praying, creating, embracing, enhancing;

135 a structure as solid, fluid, strong,
translucent, luminous, freeing,
and bracing
as the man himself—

Mr. Blue Monk,
140 bringing everything we do,
we see, we know,
into melodious focus

through the blue keys
of his blue piano;

145 therefore, in this blue region,
with this blue vision, in this blue
body of being
we all know as home,
everything throbs and pulses and glows
150 with the true, blue beauty of his song:

"Blue Monk"!

II. *"Blue Monk" (percussive)*

Ricochet:

Radius:
Radiating:

Reciting: Realizing: Referring: Recapturing: Repercussion:
5   Revolving: Reflecting: Returning: Reconstituting: Republic:
Reshaping: Restructuring: Reversing: Reclaiming: Religion:
Respecting: Removing: Reforming: Receiving: Reality:
Refining: Reducing: Refreshing: Regenerating: Resource:
Regarding: Relating: Relaxing: Revering: Remembering:
10   Renewing: Revising: Repairing: Replacing: Residing:
Reviewing: Respecting: Resolving: Reviving: Responsible:
Retaining: Resuming: Revealing: Rehearsing: Resulting:
Restoring: Retrieving: Regaining: Recovering: Relying:
Redeeming: Replying: Reminding: Rewarding: Resounding:
15

Reverberating:

Remarkably:

Releasing:

Remaining:

Repeating:

1992

Kicking the Habit

Late last night, I decided to
stop using English.
I had been using it all day—

5   talking all day,
listening all day,
thinking all day,
reading all day,
remembering all day,
feeling all day,

10   and even driving all day,
in English—

when, finally I decided to
stop.

So I pulled off the main highway
15 onto a dark country road
and kept on going and going
until I emerged in another nation and . . .
stopped.

There, the insects
20 inspected my passport, the frogs
investigated my baggage, and the trees
pointed out lights in the sky,
saying,
  "Shhhhlllyyymmm"—
25 and I, of course, replied.
After all, I was a foreigner,
and had to comply . . .

Now don't get me wrong:
There's nothing "wrong"
30 with English,

and I'm not complaining
about the language
which is my native tongue.
I make my living with the lingo;
35 I was even in England once.
So you might say I'm actually
addicted to it;
yes, I'm an Angloholic,
  and I can't get along without the stuff:
40 It controls my life.

Until last night, that is.
Yes, I had had it
with the habit.

I was exhausted,
45 burned out,
by the habit.
And I decided to
kick the habit,
cold turkey,
50 right then and there
on the spot!

And, in so doing, I kicked
open the door of a cage
and stepped out from confinement
55 into the greater world.

Tentatively, I uttered,

"Chemawa? Chinook?"

and the pines said

"Clackamas, Siskiyou."

60 And before long, everything else
chimed in with their two cents' worth
and we had a fluid and fluent
conversation going,

communicating, expressing,
65 echoing whatever we needed to
know, know, know . . .

What was it like?
Well, just listen:

Ah, the exquisite seasonings
70 of syllables, the consummate consonants, the vigorous
vowels of varied vocabularies

clicking, ticking, humming,
growling, throbbing, strumming—

coming from all parts of orifices, surfaces,
15 in creative combinations, orchestrations,
resonating in rhythm with the atmosphere!

I could have remained there
forever—as I did, and will.
And when I resumed my way,
80 my stay could no longer be

"ordinary"—

as they say,
as *we* say, in English.

For on the road of life,
85 in the code of life,

there's much more to red than

"stop,"

there's much more to green than

"go,"

90 and there's much, much more to yellow than

"caution,"

for as the yellow
sun clearly enunciated to me this morning:

"Fusao. Inada."

1997

On Being Asian American

for our children

Of course, not everyone
can be an Asian American.
Distinctions are earned,
and deserve dedication.

5 Thus, from time of birth,
the journey awaits you—
ventures through time,
the turns of the earth.

When you seem to arrive,
10 the journey continues;
when you seem to arrive,
the journey continues.

Take me as I am, you cry,
I, I, am an individual.
15 *Which certainly is true.*
Which generates an echo.

Who are all your people
assembled in celebration,
with wisdom and strength,
20 *to which you are entitled.*

For you are at the head
of succeeding generations,
as the rest of the world
comes forward to greet you.

25 *As the rest of the world*
comes forward to greet you.

1992

Michael S. Harper b. 1938

The poetry of Michael S. Harper resists easy categorization. Alternately metaphysical and reflective, historical and biographical, musical and autobiographical, Harper's poetry demonstrates a "both/and" sensibility. He views poetry as a place where "the microcosm and the cosmos are united." Harper's poetic project occurs, then, in a conceptual space where he maintains the sacred nature of speech as a form of human connection, evidenced by his assertion that "the tongue is the customer of the ear." Harper is a poet whose work is oriented toward performance; his poems are heavily indebted to African American musical traditions such as jazz and the blues, for he is interested, above all, in the ways we improvise on the themes that compose human experience.

Born in Brooklyn, Harper spent the first thirteen years of his life in New York before his family relocated to Los Angeles. His father worked as a post office supervisor, his mother as a medical stenographer. Growing up in the 1940s and 1950s, Harper experienced the great cultural and artistic vitality manifested at that time in the African American community: Jackie Robinson's entry into pro baseball, the music of Billie Holiday (she played piano in the Harper home), the birth and growth of bebop, and the boxing prowess of Sugar Ray Robinson. Harper's poetry often celebrates African American examples of artistic and athletic excellence.

After graduating from high school, Harper continued his education at Los Angeles State College and, later, the University of Iowa, where he received an M.A. in English and did work at the Iowa Writer's Workshop. But he claims that his education also took place at the facing table in the post office, where he worked full-time to put himself through college. It was there that he encountered black men and women who were trained doctors, lawyers, and teachers whose race made the post office the only place they could find employment.

Harper is the author of many collections of poems, two of which, *Dear John, Dear Coltrane* (1970) and *Images of Kin* (1977), have been nominated for the National Book Award. He is co-editor of a critically acclaimed anthology, *Chant of Saints* (1979), and is responsible for bringing poet Sterling A. Brown's *Collected Poems* into print. Harper's books offer the reader a pantheon of heroes and heroines and a variety of geographical settings (often portraying aspects of Harper's travels through Mexico, West and South Africa, as well as New England and the South) that demonstrate his affinity for different personas and idioms, each of which allows him to create modes of address that call for a more cohesive sensibility.

Harper's poems also explore his connections to other artists—jazz saxophonists John Coltrane and Charlie Parker, writers Ralph Ellison, Sterling Brown, Robert Hayden, and James Wright—and what they teach him about the inherent responsibility of survival (a subject he has confronted in poems that concern the deaths of two of his children at birth and, more recently, of his brother). They provide models for his own poetic expressions. Jazz provides the "architectonic impulse" that informs the structures of his poems. The writers offer models of enduring craft and seriousness. All of these heroes exemplify the concept of modality that runs through the Harper oeuvre. It represents, in part, the act of resisting the Western impulse to compartmentalize knowledge and experience and thus culture as well.

Herman Beavers
University of Pennsylvania

PRIMARY WORKS

Dear John, Dear Coltrane, 1970; *History Is Your Own Heartbeat,* 1971; *Photographs: Negatives; History as Apple Tree,* 1972; *Song: I Want a Witness,* 1972; *Debridement,* 1973; *Nightmare Begins Responsibility,* 1975; *Images of Kin,* 1977; *Healing Song for the Inner Ear,* 1985; *Honorable Amendments,* 1995; *Songlines in Michaeltree,* 2000.

Song: I Want a Witness

Blacks in frame houses
call to the helicopters,
their antlered arms
spinning; jeeps pad
5 these glass-studded streets;
on this hill are tanks painted gold.
Our children sing
spirituals of *Motown,*
idioms these streets suckled
10 on a southern road.
This scene is about power,
terror, producing
love and pain and pathology;
in an army of white dust,
15 blacks here to *testify*
and *testify,* and *testify,*
and *redeem,* and *redeem,*
in black smoke coming,
as they wave their arms,
20 as they wave their tongues.

1972

Nightmare Begins Responsibility

I place these numbed wrists to the pane
watching white uniforms whisk over
him in the tube-kept
prison
5 fear what they will do in experiment
watch my gloved stickshifting gasolined hands
breathe *boxcar-information-please* infirmary tubes

distrusting white-pink mending paperthin
silkened end hairs, distrusting tubes
10 shrunk in his *trunk-skincapped*
shaven head, in thighs
distrusting-white-hands-picking-baboon-light
on this son who will not make his second night
of this wardstrewn intensive airpocket
15 where his father's asthmatic
hymns of *night-train,* train done gone
his mother can only know that he has flown
up into essential calm unseen corridor
going boxscarred home, *mamaborn, sweetsonchild*
20 *gonedowntown* into *researchtestingwarehousebatteryacid*
mama-son-done-gone/me telling her 'nother
train tonight, no music, no breathstroked
heartbeat in my infinite distrust of them:

and of my distrusting self
25 *white-doctor-who-breathed-for-him-all-night*
say it for two sons gone,
say nightmare, say it loud
panebreaking heartmadness:
nightmare begins responsibility.

1975

Here Where Coltrane Is

Soul and race
are private dominions,
memories and modal
songs, a tenor blossoming,
5 which would paint suffering
a clear color but is not in
this Victorian house
without oil in zero degree
weather and a forty-mile-an-hour wind;
10 it is all a well-knit family:
a love supreme.
Oak leaves pile up on walkway
and steps, catholic as apples
in a special mist of clear white
15 children who love my children.
I play "Alabama"

on a warped record player
skipping the scratches
on your faces over the fibrous
20   conical hairs of plastic
under the wooden floors.

Dreaming on a train from New York
to Philly, you hand out six
notes which become an anthem
25   to our memories of you:
oak, birch, maple,
apple, cocoa, rubber.
For this reason Martin is dead;
for this reason Malcolm is dead;
30   for this reason Coltrane is dead;
in the eyes of my first son are the browns
of these men and their music.

1977

A Narrative of the Life and Times of John Coltrane: Played by Himself

Hamlet, North Carolina

I don't remember train whistles,
or corroding trestles of ice
seeping from the hangband,
vaulting northward in shining triplets,
5   but the feel of the reed on my tongue
haunts me even now, my incisors
pulled so the pain wouldn't lurk
on "Cousin Mary";

in High Point I stared
10   at the bus which took us to band
practice on Memorial Day;
I could hardly make out, in the mud,
placemarks, separations of skin
sketched in plates above the rear bumper.

15   Mama asked, "what's the difference
'tween North and South Carolina,"
a capella notes of our church choir
doping me into arpeggios,

into *sheets of sound* labeling me
20 into dissonance.

I never liked the photo taken with
Bird, Miles without sunglasses,
me in profile almost out of exposure:
these were my images of movement;
25 when I hear the sacred songs,
auras of my mother at the stove,
I play the blues:

what good does it do to complain:
one night I was playing with Bostic,
30 blacking out, coming alive only to melodies
where I could play my parts:
And then, on a train to Philly,
I sang "Naima" locking the door
without exit no matter what song
35 I sang; with remonstrations on the ceiling
of that same room I practiced in
on my back when too tired to stand,
I broke loose from crystalline habits
I thought would bring me that sound.

1985

Camp Story

I look over the old photos
for the US Hotel fire,
1900 Saratoga Springs,
where your grandfather
5 was chef on loan
from Catskill
where you were born.

The grapes from his arbor
sing in my mouth:
10 the smoke from the trestle
of his backyard,
the engine so close
to the bedroom
I can almost touch it,
15 make bricks from the yards
of perfection,

the clear puddles from the Hudson River,
where you would make change
at the dayline,
20 keep the change from the five
Jackleg Diamonds would leave
on the counter top or the stool.

Where is the CCC camp
you labored in
25 to send the money home to the family,
giving up your scholarship
so you could save the family
homestead from the banks of the river.

All across America the refugees
30 find homes in these camps
and are made to eat
at a table of liberty
you could have had
if you could not spell
35 or count, or keep time.

I see you, silent, wordfully
talking to my brother, Jonathan,
as he labors on the chromatic
respirator; you kiss his brown
40 temple where his helmet left
a slight depression
near a neat line of stitches
at the back of his skull.

As he twitches to chemicals
45 the Asian nurses catheter
into the cavities and caves
of his throat and lungs:
the doctor repeats the story
of his chances.

1985

Joyce Carol Oates b. 1938

Critic, teacher, short story writer, poet, playwright, novelist, editor, and publisher, Joyce Carol Oates is an artist of amazing versatility, productivity, and range. She has written more than twenty novels and hundreds of shorter works; several of her plays have been produced off-Broadway; at least two of her stories have been made into films. Writing about men and women struggling for existence in "Eden Valley," a region strikingly like her own birthplace in upstate New York, Oates has been variously classified as a realist, a naturalist, a "gothic" artist, and "the dark lady of American Letters." She has won many prizes, including the National Book Award, a Guggenheim Fellowship, an O. Henry award for Special Achievement, and an award from the Lotos Club. Oates has been elected to the National Institute of Arts and Letters. While she calls herself a feminist, she prefers to be considered "a woman who writes." She has a wide readership: her work is as likely to be found on an academic syllabus as on the bestseller list.

Oates has often been considered a realist in the tradition of Dreiser; she is indeed a social critic, focusing on contemporary events and issues in fiction and essays. But she is also testing classical myths and established literary conventions beyond the limits of any one genre. Curiously, as if to expand her own boundaries, Oates has published fiction—a series of harrowing psychological mysteries—under a pseudonym, Rosamond Smith.

Perhaps Oates is best understood as an artist in residence—in the largest sense of that term. She studied at Syracuse and then in graduate school at the University of Wisconsin, and has taught literature and writing at Detroit and Windsor. As a scholar, she has written several collections of literary criticism, including *New Heaven, New Earth, (Woman) Writer,* and *The Profane Art.* She is on the Advisory Board of *The Kenyon Review;* she is a frequent reviewer of contemporary literature. Currently she is Roger S. Berlind Distinguished Professor of English at Princeton, where she lives and writes and works at the press she founded with her husband, Professor Raymond Smith.

Oates draws upon this complex and varied background in her fiction. In one way or another, all of Oates's characters struggle to find a place in a changing and often threatening world. In her early novels *With Shuddering Fall* and *A Garden of Earthly Delights,* she writes about rural America with its migrants, ragged prophets, and automobile junkyards; in contrast, *Expensive People* mocks the suburbanite, and her novel *them* dramatizes the violent lives of the urban poor. *Wonderland* is a novel of lost generations; the hero barely escapes from the gunfire of his crazed father; as a father himself, he is in danger of losing his daughter in the turbulence of the sixties. *Childwold* is a lyrical and experimental portrait of an artist as a young woman. Oates satirizes doctors, lawyers, preachers; she casts an especially critical eye at professors and resident artists in *Unholy Loves, Solstice, American Appetites,* and *Marya: A Life.*

Fascinated by the literary past and the work of other writers, she has also tried her hand at "imitations"—reimagining stories of Joyce, Thoreau, James, Chekhov, and Kafka. Oates produced a group of novels which represent her own imaginative view of nineteenth-century conventions, with particular emphasis on the constraints placed upon women both as writers and as hapless heroines.

But she is also inscribing the history of the present, memorializing the paranoia of the fifties in *You Must Remember This,* dramatizing explosive American race relations in *Because It is Bitter, and Because It Is My*

Heart, and publishing essays on boxing which have won her infrequent spots as a ringside commentator.

Joyce Carol Oates may be best known for her short stories, frequently included in the annual O. Henry Prize Selection and widely anthologized. Like her novels, many of her stories are experiments in form and character. Most focus on the personality at risk: on seemingly ordinary people whose lives are vulnerable to powerful threats from external society and the inner self.

"Where Are You Going, Where Have You Been?" is one of these. A frightening view of "coming of age" written in 1967, the story has appeared in several collections, including *The Wheel of Love;* it has also been adapted for the screen (*Smooth Talk,* 1986). Its central character, Connie, is a young woman fatally at ease in the world of adolescent ritual: high school flir-

tations, hamburger hangouts and drive-ins, movies and fan magazines; her dreams are shaped by popular song lyrics. She seems destined for a conventional future very much like her mother's, evident in their half-affectionate bickering. Yet as Oates deftly and gradually reveals, this sense of security is at best illusory; even the familiar language of popular song becomes the agency of seduction, making Connie the helpless victim of a grotesque and demonic caller she mistakes for a "friend." Asking the question posed by the sixties balladeer and youth culture cult figure, Bob Dylan (to whom this story is dedicated), "Where Are You Going, Where Have You Been?" powerfully represents the complex, open-ended literary project of author Joyce Carol Oates.

Eileen T. Bender
Indiana University

PRIMARY WORKS

By the North Gate, 1963; *With Shuddering Fall,* 1964; *A Garden of Earthly Delights,* 1967; *Expensive People,* 1968; *them,* 1969; *The Wheel of Love,* 1970; *Love and Its Derangements,* 1970; *Wonderland,* 1971; *Marriages and Infidelities,* 1972; *Angel Fire,* 1973; *Do with Me What You Will,* 1973; *New Heaven, New Earth,* 1974; *The Goddess and Other Women,* 1974; *The Hungry Ghosts,* 1974; *The Fabulous Beasts,* 1975; *The Seduction and Other Stories,* 1975; *The Assassins,* 1975; *Childwold,* 1976; *Crossing the Border,* 1976; *Triumph of the Spider Monkey,* 1976; *Night Side,* 1977; *Son of the Morning,* 1978; *All the Good People I've Left Behind,* 1978; *Cybele,* 1979; *Unholy Loves,* 1979; *Bellefleur,* 1980; *A Sentimental Education,* 1980; *Celestial Timepiece,* 1980; *Three Plays,* 1980; *Contraries,* 1981; *Angel of Light,* 1981; *A Bloodsmoor Romance,* 1982; *Invisible Woman,* 1982; *The Profane Art,* 1983; *Last Days,* 1984; *Mysteries of Winterhurn,* 1984; *Solstice,* 1985; *Raven's Wing,* 1986; *Marya: A Life,* 1986; *(Woman) Writer,* 1986; *You Must Remember This,* 1987; *On Boxing,* 1988; *The Assignation,* 1988; *American Appetites,* 1989; *The Time Traveler,* 1989; *I Lock My Door Upon Myself,* 1990; *Expensive People,* 1990; *Because It Is Bitter, and Because It Is My Heart,* 1991; *In Darkest America,* 1991; *Twelve Plays,* 1991; *The Rise of Life on Earth,* 1991; *Where Is Here?,* 1992; *Heat and Other Stories,* 1992; *Black Water,* 1992; *Where Are You Going, Where Have You Been?: Selected Early Stories,* 1993; *Foxfire,* 1993; *Haunted,* 1994; *What I Lived For,* 1994; *Zombie,* 1995; *The Perfectionist and Other Plays,* 1995; *First Love: A Gothic Tale,* 1996; *Will You Always Love Me?,* 1996; *Tenderness,* 1996; *We Were the Mulvaneys,* 1996; *Mancrazy,* 1997; *My Heart Laid Bare,* 1998; *The Collector of Hearts,* 1998; *New Plays,* 1998; *Broke Heart Blues,* 1999; *Where I've Been, and Where I'm Going,* 1999; *Blonde,* 2000; *Faithless,* 2001; *Middle Age,* 2001; *Beasts,* 2002; *I'll Take You There,* 2002; *The Tattooed Girl,* 2003; *Rope: A Love Story,* 2003; *The Falls,* 2004; *The Corn Maiden,* 2005; *Missing Mom,* 2005; *Black Girl/White Girl,* 2006; *The Gravedigger's Daughter,* 2007; *My Sister, My Love,* 2008.

Where Are You Going, Where Have You Been?

For Bob Dylan

Her name was Connie. She was fifteen and she had a quick, nervous giggling habit of craning her neck to glance into mirrors or checking other people's faces to make sure her own was all right. Her mother, who noticed everything and knew everything and who hadn't much reason any longer to look at her own face, always scolded Connie about it. "Stop gawking at yourself. Who are you? You think you're so pretty?" she would say. Connie would raise her eyebrows at these familiar old complaints and look right through her mother, into a shadowy vision of herself as she was right at that moment: she knew she was pretty and that was everything. Her mother had been pretty once too, if you could believe those old snapshots in the album, but now her looks were gone and that was why she was always after Connie.

"Why don't you keep your room clean like your sister? How've you got your hair fixed—what the hell stinks? Hair spray? You don't see your sister using that junk."

Her sister June was twenty-four and still lived at home. She was a secretary in the high school Connie attended, and if that wasn't bad enough—with her in the same building—she was so plain and chunky and steady that Connie had to hear her praised all the time by her mother and her mother's sisters. June did this, June did that, she saved money and helped clean the house and cooked and Connie couldn't do a thing, her mind was all filled with trashy daydreams. Their father was away at work most of the time and when he came home he wanted supper and he read the newspaper at supper and after supper he went to bed. He didn't bother talking much to them, but around his bent head Connie's mother kept picking at her until Connie wished her mother was dead and she herself was dead and it was all over. "She makes me want to throw up sometimes," she complained to her friends. She had a high, breathless, amused voice that made everything she said sound a little forced, whether it was sincere or not.

There was one good thing: June went places with girl friends of hers, girls who were just as plain and steady as she, and so when Connie wanted to do that her mother had no objections. The father of Connie's best girl friend drove the girls the three miles to town and left them at a shopping plaza so they could walk through the stores or go to a movie, and when he came to pick them up again at eleven he never bothered to ask what they had done.

They must have been familiar sights, walking around the shopping plaza in their shorts and flat ballerina slippers that always scuffed the sidewalk, with charm bracelets jingling on their thin wrists; they would lean together to whisper and laugh secretly if someone passed who amused or interested them. Connie had long dark blond hair that drew anyone's eye to it, and she wore part of it pulled up on her head and puffed out and the rest of it she let fall down her back. She wore a pull-over jersey blouse that looked one way when she was at home and another way when she was away from home. Everything about her had two sides to it, one for home and one for anywhere that was not home: her walk, which could be childlike and bobbing, or languid enough to make anyone think she was hearing music in her head; her mouth, which was pale and smirking most of the time, but bright and pink on these evenings out; her laugh, which was cynical and drawling at home—"Ha, ha, very funny,"—but high-pitched and nervous anywhere else, like the jingling of the charms on her bracelet.

Sometimes they did go shopping or to a movie, but sometimes they went across the highway, ducking fast across the busy road, to a drive-in restaurant where older kids hung out. The restaurant was shaped like a big bottle, though squatter than a real bottle, and on its cap was a revolving figure of a grinning boy holding a hamburger aloft. One night in midsummer they ran across, breathless with daring, and right away someone leaned out a car window and invited them over, but it was just a boy from high school they didn't like. It made them feel good to be able to ignore him. They went up through the maze of parked and cruising cars to the bright-lit, fly-infested restaurant, their faces pleased and expectant as if they were entering a sacred building that loomed up out of the night to give them what haven and blessing they yearned for. They sat at the counter and crossed their legs at the ankles, their thin shoulders rigid with excitement, and listened to the music that made everything so good: the music was always in the background, like music at a church service; it was something to depend upon.

A boy named Eddie came in to talk with them. He sat backwards on his stool, turning himself jerkily around in semicircles and then stopping and turning back again, and after a while he asked Connie if she would like something to eat. She said she would and so she tapped her friend's arm on her way out—her friend pulled her face up into a brave, droll look—and Connie said she would meet her at eleven, across the way. "I just hate to leave her like that," Connie said earnestly, but the boy said that she wouldn't be alone for long. So they went out to his car, and on the way Connie couldn't help but let her eyes wander over the windshields and faces all around her, her face gleaming with a joy that had nothing to do with Eddie or even this place; it might have been the music. She drew her shoulders up and sucked in her breath with the pure pleasure of being alive, and just at that moment she happened to glance at a face just a few feet from hers. It was a boy with shaggy black hair, in a convertible jalopy painted gold. He stared at her and then his lips widened into a grin. Connie slit her eyes at him and turned away, but she couldn't help glancing back and there he was, still watching her. He wagged a finger and laughed and said, "Gonna get you, baby," and Connie turned away again without Eddie noticing anything.

She spent three hours with him, at the restaurant where they ate hamburgers and drank Cokes in wax cups that were always sweating, and then down an alley a mile or so away, and when he left her off at five to eleven only the movie house was still open at the plaza. Her girl friend was there, talking with a boy. When Connie came up, the two girls smiled at each other and Connie said, "How was the movie?" and the girl said, "*You* should know." They rode off with the girl's father, sleepy and pleased, and Connie couldn't help but look back at the darkened shopping plaza with its big empty parking lot and its signs that were faded and ghostly now, and over at the drive-in restaurant where cars were still circling tirelessly. She couldn't hear the music at this distance.

Next morning June asked her how the movie was and Connie said, "So-so."

She and that girl and occasionally another girl went out several times a week, and the rest of the time Connie spent around the house—it was summer vacation—getting in her mother's way and thinking, dreaming about the boys she met. But all the boys fell back and dissolved into a single face that was not even a face but an idea, a feeling, mixed up with the urgent insistent pounding of the music and the humid night air of July. Connie's mother kept dragging her back to the daylight by finding things for her to do or saying suddenly, "What's this about the Pettinger girl?"

And Connie would say nervously, "Oh, her. That dope." She always drew thick clear lines between herself and such girls, and her mother was simple and kind enough to believe it. Her mother was so simple, Connie thought, that it was maybe cruel to fool her so much. Her mother went scuffling around the house in old bedroom slippers and complained over the telephone to one sister about the other, then the other called up and the two of them complained about the third one. If June's name was mentioned her mother's tone was approving, and if Connie's name was mentioned it was disapproving. This did not really mean she disliked Connie, and actually Connie thought that her mother preferred her to June just because she was prettier, but the two of them kept up a pretense of exasperation, a sense that they were tugging and struggling over something of little value to either of them. Sometimes, over coffee, they were almost friends, but something would come up—some vexation that was like a fly buzzing suddenly around their heads—and their faces went hard with contempt.

One Sunday Connie got up at eleven—none of them bothered with church—and washed her hair so that it could dry all day long in the sun. Her parents and sister were going to a barbecue at an aunt's house and Connie said no, she wasn't interested, rolling her eyes to let her mother know just what she thought of it. "Stay home alone then," her mother said sharply. Connie sat out back in a lawn chair and watched them drive away, her father quiet and bald, hunched around so that he could back the car out, her mother with a look that was still angry and not at all softened through the windshield, and in the back seat poor old June, all dressed up as if she didn't know what a barbecue was, with all the running yelling kids and the flies. Connie sat with her eyes closed in the sun, dreaming and dazed with the warmth about her as if this were a kind of love, the caresses of love, and her mind slipped over onto thoughts of the boy she had been with the night before and how nice he had been, how sweet it always was, not the way someone like June would suppose but sweet, gentle, the way it was in movies and promised in songs; and when she opened her eyes she hardly knew where she was, the back yard ran off into weeds and a fence-like line of trees and behind it the sky was perfectly blue and still. The asbestos "ranch house" that was now three years old startled her—it looked small. She shook her head as if to get awake.

It was too hot. She went inside the house and turned on the radio to drown out the quiet. She sat on the edge of her bed, barefoot, and listened for an hour and a half to a program called XYZ Sunday Jamboree, record after record of hard, fast, shrieking songs she sang along with, interspersed by exclamations from "Bobby King": "An' look here, you girls at Napoleon's—Son and Charley want you to pay real close attention to this song coming up!"

And Connie paid close attention herself, bathed in a glow of slow-pulsed joy that seemed to rise mysteriously out of the music itself and lay languidly about the airless little room, breathed in and breathed out with each gentle rise and fall of her chest.

After a while she heard a car coming up the drive. She sat up at once, startled, because it couldn't be her father so soon. The gravel kept crunching all the way in from the road—the driveway was long—and Connie ran to the window. It was a car she didn't know. It was an open jalopy, painted a bright gold that caught the sunlight opaquely. Her heart began to pound and her fingers snatched at her hair, checking it, and she whispered, "Christ. Christ," wondering how bad she looked. The car came to a stop at the side door and the horn sounded four short taps, as if this were a signal Connie knew.

She went into the kitchen and approached the door slowly, then hung out the screen door, her bare toes curling down off the step. There were two boys in the car and now she recognized the driver: he had shaggy, shabby black hair that looked crazy as a wig and he was grinning at her.

"I ain't late, am I?" he said.

"Who the hell do you think you are?" Connie said.

"Toldja I'd be out, didn't I?"

"I don't even know who you are."

She spoke sullenly, careful to show no interest or pleasure, and he spoke in a fast, bright monotone. Connie looked past him to the other boy, taking her time. He had fair brown hair, with a lock that fell onto his forehead. His sideburns gave him a fierce, embarrassed look, but so far he hadn't even bothered to glance at her. Both boys wore sunglasses. The driver's glasses were metallic and mirrored everything in miniature.

"You wanta come for a ride?" he said.

Connie smirked and let her hair fall loose over one shoulder.

"Don'tcha like my car? New paint job," he said. "Hey."

"What?"

"You're cute."

She pretended to fidget, chasing flies away from the door.

"Don'tcha believe me, or what?" he said.

"Look, I don't even know who you are," Connie said in disgust.

"Hey, Ellie's got a radio, see. Mine broke down." He lifted his friend's arm and showed her the little transistor radio the boy was holding, and now Connie began to hear the music. It was the same program that was playing inside the house.

"Bobby King?" she said.

"I listen to him all the time. I think he's great."

"He's kind of great," Connie said reluctantly.

"Listen, that guy's *great*. He knows where the action is."

Connie blushed a little, because the glasses made it impossible for her to see just what this boy was looking at. She couldn't decide if she liked him or if he was just a jerk, and so she dawdled in the doorway and wouldn't come down or go back inside. She said, "What's all that stuff painted on your car?"

"Can'tcha read it?" He opened the door very carefully, as if he were afraid it might fall off. He slid out just as carefully, planting his feet firmly on the ground, the tiny metallic world in his glasses slowing down like gelatine hardening, and in the midst of it Connie's bright green blouse. "This here is my name, to begin with," he said. ARNOLD FRIEND was written in tarlike black letters on the side, with a drawing of a round, grinning face that reminded Connie of a pumpkin, except it wore sunglasses. "I wanta introduce myself, I'm Arnold Friend and that's my real name and I'm gonna be your friend, honey, and inside the car's Ellie Oscar, he's kinda shy." Ellie brought his transistor radio up to his shoulder and balanced it there. "Now, these numbers are a secret code, honey," Arnold Friend explained. He read off the numbers 33, 19, 17 and raised his eyebrows at her to see what she thought of that, but she didn't think much of it. The left rear fender had been smashed and around it was written, on the gleaming gold background: DONE BY CRAZY WOMAN DRIVER. Connie had to laugh at that. Arnold Friend was pleased at her laughter and looked up at her. "Around the other side's a lot more—you wanta come and see them?"

"No."

"Why not?"

"Why should I?"

"Don'tcha wanta see what's on the car? Don'tcha wanta go for a ride?"

"I don't know."

"Why not?"

"I got things to do."

"Like what?"

"Things."

He laughed as if she had said something funny. He slapped his thighs. He was standing in a strange way, leaning back against the car as if he were balancing himself. He wasn't tall, only an inch or so taller than she would be if she came down to him. Connie liked the way he was dressed, which was the way all of them dressed: tight faded jeans stuffed into black, scuffed boots, a belt that pulled his waist in and showed how lean he was, and a white pull-over shirt that was a little soiled and showed the hard small muscles of his arms and shoulders. He looked as if he probably did hard work, lifting and carrying things. Even his neck looked muscular. And his face was a familiar face, somehow: the jaw and chin and cheeks slightly darkened because he hadn't shaved for a day or two, and the nose long and hawk-like, sniffing as if she were a treat he was going to gobble up and it was all a joke.

"Connie, you ain't telling the truth. This is your day set aside for a ride with me and you know it," he said, still laughing. The way he straightened and recovered from his fit of laughing showed that it had been all fake.

"How do you know what my name is?" she said suspiciously.

"It's Connie."

"Maybe and maybe not."

"I know my Connie," he said, wagging his finger. Now she remembered him even better, back at the restaurant, and her cheeks warmed at the thought of how she had sucked in her breath just at the moment she passed him—how she must have looked to him. And he had remembered her. "Ellie and I come out here especially for you," he said. "Ellie can sit in back. How about it?"

"Where?"

"Where what?"

"Where're we going?"

He looked at her. He took off the sunglasses and she saw how pale the skin around his eyes was, like holes that were not in shadow but instead in light. His eyes were like chips of broken glass that catch the light in an amiable way. He smiled. It was as if the idea of going for a ride somewhere, to someplace, was a new idea to him.

"Just for a ride, Connie sweetheart."

"I never said my name was Connie," she said.

"But I know what it is. I know your name and all about you, lots of things," Arnold Friend said. He had not moved yet but stood still leaning back against the side of his jalopy. "I took a special interest in you, such a pretty girl, and found out all about you—like I know your parents and sister are gone somewheres and I know where and how long they're going to be gone, and I know who you were with last night, and your best girl friend's name is Betty. Right?"

He spoke in a simple lilting voice, exactly as if he were reciting the words to a song. His smile assured her that everything was fine. In the car Ellie turned up the volume on his radio and did not bother to look around at them.

"Ellie can sit in the back seat," Arnold Friend said. He indicated his friend with a casual jerk of his chin, as if Ellie did not count and she should not bother with him.

"How'd you find out all that stuff?" Connie said.

"Listen: Betty Schultz and Tony Fitch and Jimmy Pettinger and Nancy Pettinger," he said in a chant. "Raymond Stanley and Bob Hutter—"

"Do you know all those kids?"

"I know everybody."

"Look, you're kidding. You're not from around here."

"Sure."

"But—how come we never saw you before?"

"Sure you saw me before," he said. He looked down at his boots, as if he were a little offended. "You just don't remember."

"I guess I'd remember you," Connie said.

"Yeah?" He looked up at this, beaming. He was pleased. He began to mark time with the music from Ellie's radio, tapping his fists lightly together. Connie looked away from his smile to the car, which was painted so bright it almost hurt her eyes to look at it. She looked at that name, ARNOLD FRIEND. And up at the front fender was an expression that was familiar—MAN THE FLYING SAUCERS. It was an expression kids had used the year before but didn't use this year. She looked at it for a while as if the words meant something to her that she did not yet know.

"What're you thinking about? Huh?" Arnold Friend demanded. "Not worried about your hair blowing around in the car, are you?"

"No."

"Think I maybe can't drive good?"

"How do I know?"

"You're a hard girl to handle. How come?" he said. "Don't you know I'm your friend? Didn't you see me put my sign in the air when you walked by?"

"What sign?"

"My sign." And he drew an X in the air, leaning out toward her. They were maybe ten feet apart. After his hand fell back to his side the X was still in the air, almost visible. Connie let the screen door close and stood perfectly still inside it, listening to the music from her radio and the boy's blend together. She stared at Arnold

Friend. He stood there so stiffly relaxed, pretending to be relaxed, with one hand idly on the door handle as if he were keeping himself up that way and had no intention of ever moving again. She recognized most things about him, the tight jeans that showed his thighs and buttocks and the greasy leather boots and the tight shirt, and even that slippery friendly smile of his, that sleepy dreamy smile that all the boys used to get across ideas they didn't want to put into words. She recognized all this and also the singsong way he talked, slightly mocking, kidding, but serious and a little melancholy, and she recognized the way he tapped one fist against the other in homage to the perpetual music behind him. But all these things did not come together.

She said suddenly, "Hey, how old are you?"

His smile faded. She could see then that he wasn't a kid, he was much older—thirty, maybe more. At this knowledge her heart began to pound faster.

"That's a crazy thing to ask. Can'tcha see I'm your own age?"

"Like hell you are."

"Or maybe a coupla years older. I'm eighteen."

"Eighteen?" she said doubtfully.

He grinned to reassure her and lines appeared at the corners of his mouth. His teeth were big and white. He grinned so broadly his eyes became slits and she saw how thick the lashes were, thick and black as if painted with a black tarlike material. Then, abruptly, he seemed to become embarrassed and looked over his shoulder at Ellie. "*Him,* he's crazy," he said. "Ain't he a riot? He's a nut, a real character." Ellie was still listening to the music. His sunglasses told nothing about what he was thinking. He wore a bright orange shirt unbuttoned halfway to show his chest, which was a pale, bluish chest and not muscular like Arnold Friend's. His shirt collar was turned up all around and the very tips of the collar pointed out past his chin as if they were protecting him. He was pressing the transistor radio up against his ear and sat there in a kind of a daze, right in the sun.

"He's kinda strange," Connie said.

"Hey, she says you're kinda strange! Kinda strange!" Arnold Friend cried. He pounded on the car to get Ellie's attention. Ellie turned for the first time and Connie saw with shock that he wasn't a kid either—he had a fair, hairless face, cheeks reddened slightly as if the veins grew too close to the surface of his skin, the face of a forty-year-old baby. Connie felt a wave of dizziness rise in her at this sight and she stared at him as if waiting for something to change the shock of the moment, make it all right again. Ellie's lips kept shaping words, mumbling along with the words blasting in his ear.

"Maybe you two better go away," Connie said faintly.

"What? How come?" Arnold Friend cried. "We come out here to take you for a ride. It's Sunday." He had the voice of the man on the radio now. It was the same voice, Connie thought. "Don'tcha know it's Sunday all day? And honey, no matter who you were with last night, today you're with Arnold Friend and don't you forget it! Maybe you better step out here," he said, and this last was in a different voice. It was a little flatter, as if the heat was finally getting to him.

"Hey."

"You two better leave."

"We ain't leaving until you come with us."

"Like hell I am—"

"Connie, don't fool around with me. I mean—I mean, don't fool *around*," he said shaking his head. He laughed incredulously. He placed his sunglasses on top of his head, carefully, as if he were indeed wearing a wig, and brought the stems down behind his ears. Connie stared at him, another wave of dizziness and fear rising in her so that for a moment he wasn't even in focus but was just a blur standing there against his gold car, and she had the idea that he had driven up the driveway all right but had come from nowhere before that and belonged nowhere and that everything about him and even about the music that was so familiar to her was only half real.

"If my father comes and sees you—"

"He ain't coming. He's at a barbecue."

"How do you know that?"

"Aunt Tillie's. Right now they're—uh—they're drinking. Sitting around," he said vaguely, squinting as if he were staring all the way to town and over to Aunt Tillie's back yard. Then the vision seemed to get clear and he nodded energetically. "Yeah. Sitting around. There's your sister in a blue dress, huh? And high heels, the poor sad bitch—nothing like you, sweetheart! And your mother's helping some fat woman with the corn, they're cleaning the corn—husking the corn—"

"What fat woman?" Connie cried.

"How do I know what fat woman, I don't know every goddamn fat woman in the world!" Arnold Friend laughed.

"Oh, that's Mrs. Hornsby. . . . Who invited her?" Connie said. She felt a little lightheaded. Her breath was coming quickly.

"She's too fat. I don't like them fat. I like them the way you are, honey," he said, smiling sleepily at her. They stared at each other for a while through the screen door. He said softly, "Now, what you're going to do is this: you're going to come out that door. You're going to sit up front with me and Ellie's going to sit in the back, the hell with Ellie, right? This isn't Ellie's date. You're my date. I'm your lover, honey."

"What? You're crazy—"

"Yes, I'm your lover. You don't know what that is but you will," he said. "I know that too. I know all about you. But look: it's real nice and you couldn't ask for nobody better than me, or more polite. I always keep my word. I'll tell you how it is, I'm always nice at first, the first time. I'll hold you so tight you won't think you have to try to get away or pretend anything because you'll know you can't. And I'll come inside you where it's all secret and you'll give in to me and you'll love me—"

"Shut up! You're crazy!" Connie said. She backed away from the door. She put her hands up against her ears as if she'd heard something terrible, something not meant for her. "People don't talk like that, you're crazy," she muttered. Her heart was almost too big now for her chest and its pumping made sweat break out all over her. She looked out to see Arnold Friend pause and then take a step toward the porch, lurching. He almost fell. But, like a clever drunken man, he managed to catch his balance. He wobbled in his high boots and grabbed hold of one of the porch posts.

"Honey?" he said. "You still listening?"

"Get the hell out of here!"

"Be nice, honey. Listen."

"I'm going to call the police—"

He wobbled again and out of the side of his mouth came a fast spat curse, an aside not meant for her to hear. But even this "Christ!" sounded forced. Then he began to smile again. She watched this smile come, awkward as if he were smiling from inside a mask. His whole face was a mask, she thought wildly, tanned down to his throat but then running out as if he had plastered make-up on his face but had forgotten about his throat.

"Honey—? Listen, here's how it is. I always tell the truth and I promise you this: I ain't coming in that house after you."

"You better not! I'm going to call the police if you—if you don't—"

"Honey," he said, talking right through her voice, "honey, I'm not coming in there but you are coming out here. You know why?"

She was panting. The kitchen looked like a place she had never seen before, some room she had run inside but that wasn't good enough, wasn't going to help her. The kitchen window had never had a curtain, after three years, and there were dishes in the sink for her to do—probably—and if you ran your hand across the table you'd probably feel something sticky there.

"You listening, honey? Hey?"

"—going to call the police—"

"Soon as you touch the phone I don't need to keep my promise and can come inside. You won't want that."

She rushed forward and tried to lock the door. Her fingers were shaking. "But why lock it," Arnold Friend said gently, talking right into her face. "It's just a screen door. It's just nothing." One of his boots was at a strange angle, as if his foot wasn't in it. It pointed out to the left, bent at the ankle. "I mean, anybody can break through a screen door and glass and wood and iron or anything else if he needs to, anybody at all, and specially Arnold Friend. If the place got lit up with a fire, honey, you'd come runnin' out into my arms, right into my arms an' safe at home—like you knew I was your lover and'd stopped fooling around. I don't mind a nice shy girl but I don't like no fooling around." Part of those words were spoken with a slight rhythmic lilt, and Connie somehow recognized them—the echo of a song from last year, about a girl rushing into her boy friend's arms and coming home again—

Connie stood barefoot on the linoleum floor, staring at him. "What do you want?" she whispered.

"I want you," he said.

"What?"

"Seen you that night and thought, that's the one, yes sir. I never needed to look anymore."

"But my father's coming back. He's coming to get me. I had to wash my hair first—" She spoke in a dry, rapid voice, hardly raising it for him to hear.

"No, your daddy is not coming and yes, you had to wash your hair and you washed it for me. It's nice and shining and all for me. I thank you, sweetheart," he said with a mock bow, but again he almost lost his balance. He had to bend and adjust his boots. Evidently his feet did not go all the way down; the boots must have been stuffed with something so that he would seem taller. Connie stared out at him and behind him at Ellie in the car, who seemed to be looking off toward

Connie's right, into nothing. This Ellie said, pulling the words out of the air one after another as if he were just discovering them, "You want me to pull out the phone?"

"Shut your mouth and keep it shut," Arnold Friend said, his face red from bending over or maybe from embarrassment because Connie had seen his boots. "This ain't none of your business."

"What—what are you doing? What do you want?" Connie said. "If I call the police they'll get you, they'll arrest you—"

"Promise was not to come in unless you touch that phone, and I'll keep that promise," he said. He resumed his erect position and tried to force his shoulders back. He sounded like a hero in a movie, declaring something important. But he spoke too loudly and it was as if he were speaking to someone behind Connie. "I ain't made plans for coming in that house where I don't belong but just for you to come out to me, the way you should. Don't you know who I am?"

"You're crazy," she whispered. She backed away from the door but did not want to go into another part of the house, as if this would give him permission to come through the door. "What do you . . . you're crazy, you. . . ."

"Huh? What're you saying, honey?"

Her eyes darted everywhere in the kitchen. She could not remember what it was, this room.

"This is how it is, honey: you come out and we'll drive away, have a nice ride. But if you don't come out we're gonna wait till your people come home and then they're all going to get it."

"You want that telephone pulled out?" Ellie said. He held the radio away from his ear and grimaced, as if without the radio the air was too much for him.

"I toldja shut up, Ellie," Arnold Friend said, "you're deaf, get a hearing aid, right? Fix yourself up. This little girl's no trouble and's gonna be nice to me, so Ellie keep to yourself, this ain't your date—right? Don't hem in on me, don't hog, don't crush, don't bird dog, don't trail me," he said in a rapid, meaningless voice, as if he were running through all the expressions he'd learned but was no longer sure which of them was in style, then rushing on to new ones, making them up with his eyes closed. "Don't crawl under my fence, don't squeeze in my chipmunk hole, don't sniff my glue, suck my popsicle, keep your own greasy fingers on yourself!" He shaded his eyes and peered in at Connie, who was backed against the kitchen table. "Don't mind him, honey, he's just a creep. He's a dope. Right? I'm the boy for you and like I said, you come out here nice like a lady and give me your hand, and nobody else gets hurt, I mean, your nice old bald-headed daddy and your mummy and your sister in her high heels. Because listen: why bring them in this?"

"Leave me alone," Connie whispered.

"Hey, you know that old woman down the road, the one with the chickens and stuff—you know her?"

"She's dead!"

"Dead? What? You know her?" Arnold Friend said.

"She's dead—"

"Don't you like her?"

"She's dead—she's—she isn't here any more—"

"But don't you like her, I mean, you got something against her? Some grudge or something?" Then his voice dipped as if he were conscious of a rudeness. He touched the sunglasses perched up on top of his head as if to make sure they were still there. "Now, you be a good girl."

"What are you going to do?"

"Just two things, or maybe three," Arnold Friend said. "But I promise it won't last long and you'll like me the way you get to like people you're close to. You will. It's all over for you here, so come on out. You don't want your people in any trouble, do you?"

She turned and bumped against a chair or something, hurting her leg, but she ran into the back room and picked up the telephone. Something roared in her ear, a tiny roaring, and she was so sick with fear that she could do nothing but listen to it— the telephone was clammy and very heavy and her fingers groped down to the dial but were too weak to touch it. She began to scream into the phone, into the roaring. She cried out, she cried for her mother, she felt her breath start jerking back and forth in her lungs as if it were something Arnold Friend was stabbing her with again and again with no tenderness. A noisy sorrowful wailing rose all about her and she was locked inside it the way she was locked inside this house.

After a while she could hear again. She was sitting on the floor with her wet back against the wall.

Arnold Friend was saying from the door, "That's a good girl. Put the phone back."

She kicked the phone away from her.

"No, honey. Pick it up. Put it back right."

She picked it up and put it back. The dial tone stopped.

"That's a good girl. Now, you come outside."

She was hollow with what had been fear but what was now just an emptiness. All that screaming had blasted it out of her. She sat, one leg cramped under her, and deep inside her brain was something like a pinpoint of light that kept going and would not let her relax. She thought, I'm not going to see my mother again. She thought, I'm not going to sleep in my bed again. Her bright green blouse was all wet.

Arnold Friend said, in a gentle-loud voice that was like a stage voice, "The place where you came from ain't there any more, and where you had in mind to go is cancelled out. This place you are now—inside your daddy's house—is nothing but a cardboard box I can knock down any time. You know that and always did know it. You hear me?"

She thought, I have got to think. I have got to know what to do.

"We'll go out to a nice field, out in the country here where it smells so nice and it's sunny," Arnold Friend said. "I'll have my arms tight around you so you won't need to try to get away and I'll show you what love is like, what it does. The hell with this house! It looks solid all right," he said. He ran a fingernail down the screen and the noise did not make Connie shiver, as it would have the day before. "Now, put your hand on your heart, honey. Feel that? That feels solid too but we know better. Be nice to me, be sweet like you can because what else is there for a girl like you but to be sweet and pretty and give in?—and get away before her people come back?"

She felt her pounding heart. Her hand seemed to enclose it. She thought for the first time in her life that it was nothing that was hers, that belonged to her, but just a pounding, living thing inside this body that wasn't really hers either.

"You don't want them to get hurt," Arnold Friend went on. "Now, get up, honey. Get up all by yourself."

She stood.

"Now, turn this way. That's right. Come over here to me.—Ellie, put that away, didn't I tell you? You dope. You miserable creepy dope," Arnold Friend said. His words were not angry but only part of an incantation. The incantation was kindly. "Now, come out through the kitchen to me, honey, and let's see a smile, try it, you're a brave, sweet little girl and now they're eating corn and hot dogs cooked to bursting over an outdoor fire, and they don't know one thing about you and never did and honey, you're better than them because not a one of them would have done this for you."

Connie felt the linoleum under her feet; it was cool. She brushed her hair back out of her eyes. Arnold Friend let go of the post tentatively and opened his arms for her, his elbows pointing in toward each other and his wrists limp, to show that this was an embarrassed embrace and a little mocking, he didn't want to make her self-conscious.

She put out her hand against the screen. She watched herself push the door slowly open as if she were back safe somewhere in the other doorway, watching this body and this head of long hair moving out into the sunlight where Arnold Friend waited.

"My sweet little blue-eyed girl," he said in a half-sung sigh that had nothing to do with her brown eyes but was taken up just the same by the vast sunlit reaches of the land behind him and on all sides of him—so much land that Connie had never seen before and did not recognize except to know that she was going to it.

1970

Ishmael Reed b. 1938

Ishmael Reed is a poet, novelist, actor, journalist, dramatist, and editor; his works reflect his artistic, ethnic, political, religious, and social interests. He spotlights black issues, but his themes are universal. His satiric barbs intentionally provoke his audiences in their wonderfully ironic and humorous way. Experimental forms, innovative style, and radical ideas place him in the forefront of contemporary writers. From black history to black humor, from Black Power to black magic, Reed integrates diverse themes and nontraditional styles.

Born on February 22, 1938, in Chattanooga, Tennessee, to Ben and Thelma (Coleman) Reed, Reed was raised in a blue-collar environment in Buffalo, New York, where the family moved when he was a child. From 1956 to 1960, he attended the University of New York at Buffalo. After moving to New York City, he founded the *East Village Other,* an independent newspaper, and published his first novel in 1967. This was followed by numerous books of poetry and fiction in addition to articles, plays, songs and very active editing after arriving in Oakland,

California, in 1968. Ishmael Reed has won a National Endowment fellowship and a Guggenheim Award, and he has been nominated twice for the National Book Award, once in poetry for *Conjure* and once in fiction for *Mumbo Jumbo*.

Although Reed is indebted to all the humorous, satiric, and bawdy writers from Ovid to Chaucer to Swift to Blake to Joyce, he emphasizes his debt to minority artists, especially black writers. He relies on African mythology, black sports heroes, and even rhythm and blues for his symbols and metaphors. Reed also weaves motifs of literary and contemporary allusions throughout his work: Amos and Andy, Eygptian gods, and famous figures (past and present) all appear in his mirror of society.

Controversial about race, sex, politics, freedom, religion, and everything else, Reed satirizes most institutions: "My main job I felt was to humble Judeo-Christian culture." In Reed's Neo-Hoo Doo Church, all poets are priests and historians. One of his favorite issues is that minority contributions to Western civilization seldom receive due credit. He stirs the fires of discord by satirizing the distorted versions of popular history. One function of the artist is to re-rewrite history to reveal the "truth," so Reed gleefully points out that cowboys were predominantly minorities, that Alexandre Dumas, the nineteenth-century French novelist who wrote *The Three Musketeers,* had African ancestry; and even that *Uncle Tom's Cabin* was stolen by Harriet Beecher Stowe from *The Life of Josiah Henson, Formerly a Slave*. But Reed is not a single-issue writer; he is a universal writer. His books are not solely about race issues, although race issues frequently serve as focal points. (He attacks the black establishment as harshly as he does the white.)

Reed's comic tone and joyous outlook in his parodies make us laugh at our foibles. Many of his works are comedies in the classical sense: Evil is punished and Good rewarded. Viewing life as a struggle between Dionysian and Apollonian forces, Reed chooses the laughter, dance, music, and joy: "I see life as mysterious, holy, profound, exciting, serious, and fun." So is his writing.

Michael Boccia
University of Southern Maine

PRIMARY WORKS

The Free Lance Pallbearers, 1967; *The Rise and Fall of . . . ? Adam Clayton Powell* (as Emmett Coleman), 1967; *Yellow Back Radio Broke-Down,* 1969; *19 Necromancers from Now,* 1970; *Catechism of D Neoamerican Hoo Doo Church,* 1970; *Mumbo Jumbo,* 1972; *Conjure,* 1972; *Chattanooga,* 1973; *The Last Days of Louisiana Red,* 1974; *A Secretary to the Spirits,* 1975; *Flight to Canada,* 1976; *Shrovetide in Old New Orleans,* 1978; *The Ace Booms,* 1980; *Mother Hubbard* (previously *Hell Hath No Fury),* 1982; *The Terrible Twos,* 1982; *God Made Alaska for the Indians,* 1982; *Savage Walls,* 1985. *Reckless Eyeballing,* 1986; *Points of View,* 1988; *Writin' Is Fightin',* 1988; *New and Collected Poems,* 1989; *The Terrible Threes,* 1989; *The Freelance Pallbearers,* 1990; *Japanese by Spring,* 1993; *Airing Dirty Laundry,* 1993; *The Reed Reader,* 2000; *Another Day at the Front,* 2003; *New and Collected Poems 1964–2007,* 2007; *Mixing It Up,* 2008.

I Am a Cowboy in the Boat of Ra

"The devil must be forced to reveal any such physical evil (potions, charms, fetishes, etc.) still outside the body and these must be burned." (Rituale Romanum, *published 1947, endorsed by the coat-of-arms and introductory letter from Francis cardinal Spellman*)[1]

I am a cowboy in the boat of Ra,[2]
sidewinders in the saloons of fools
bit my forehead   like   O
the untrustworthiness of Egyptologists
5   who do not know their trips. Who was that
dog-faced man?[3] they asked, the day I rode
from town.

School marms with halitosis cannot see
the Nefertiti[4] fake chipped on the run by slick
10 germans, the hawk behind Sonny Rollins'[5] head or
the ritual beard of his axe; a longhorn winding
its bells thru the Field of Reeds.

I am a cowboy in the boat of Ra. I bedded
down with Isis,[6] Lady of the Boogaloo, dove
15 down deep in her horny, stuck up her Wells-Far-ago[7]
in daring midday getaway. "Start grabbing the
blue," I said from top of my double crown.[8]

---

[1]Authentic citation. Francis Joseph Spellman was an American Roman Catholic who was archbishop of New York (1939) and cardinal (1946).

[2]Ancient Egyptian sun god and chief deity. He is represented as a hawk and the full sun. Father of Osiris, Isis, and Set.

[3]Anubis, the ancient Egyptian deity of the dead was depicted as a man with a jackal head. Like Hermes of Greek myth, his role was to bring the dead before the judge of the infernal regions.

[4]Translates literally as "the beautiful one has come"; wife of Egyptian Pharaoh Akenaten (1375–1358 B.C.) and influential in the spread of the arts in ancient Egypt. A bust of her head that the Germans looted from Egypt in the early part of the twentieth century and damaged now is in the State Museum of Berlin.

[5]African American tenor saxophonist among the leaders in of the "hardbop" or "soul" jazz movement of the 1950s.

[6]Egyptian nature goddess; a prototype for many Mediterranean Mother Earth goddesses; most popular goddess in the Roman Empire. Sister and wife of Osiris, mother of Horus; restores Osiris, king of the dead, to life after he has been murdered and dismembered by his brother Set.

[7]Wells Fargo was an overland stage company in the nineteenth-century American West.

[8]When the ancient Egyptian cults of Ra and Ammon were combined into the cult of Ammon Ra, their two ritual crowns were combined into a double crown signifying a unified Egypt.

I am a cowboy in the boat of Ra. Ezzard Charles[9]
of the Chisholm Trail.[10] Took up the bass but they
20 blew off my thumb. Alchemist in ringmanship but a
sucker for the right cross.

I am a cowboy in the boat of Ra. Vamoosed from
the temple i bide my time. The price on the wanted
poster was a-going down, outlaw alias copped my stance
25 and moody greenhorns were making me dance;
    while my mouth's
shooting iron got its chambers jammed.

I am a cowboy in the boat of Ra. Boning-up in
the ol West i bide my time. You should see
30 me pick off these tin cans whippersnappers. I
write the motown long plays for the comeback of
Osiris.[11] Make them up when stars stare at sleeping
steer out here near the campfire. Women arrive
on the backs of goats and throw themselves on
35 my Bowie.[12]

I am a cowboy in the boat of Ra. Lord of the lash,
the Loup Garou[13] Kid. Half breed son of Pisces and
Aquarius.[14] I hold the souls of men in my pot. I do
the dirty boogie with scorpions. I make the bulls
40 keep still and was the first swinger to grape the taste.

I am a cowboy in his boat. Pope Joan[15] of the
Ptah Ra.[16] C/mere a minute willya doll?
Be a good girl and
bring me my Buffalo horn of black powder
45 bring me my headdress of black feathers
bring me my bones of Ju-Ju[17] snake

[9]Black heavyweight boxing champion of the world from 1949 to 1951.

[10]Nineteenth-century wagon-train trail from Missouri to California.

[11]Translates literally as "many-eyed"; Egyptian judge of the dead. Osiris is the setting sun, Ra the midday sun, and Horus the morning sun. Osiris is reborn through the actions of Isis.

[12]A popular, large, and bulging bladed knife designed by Jim Bowie, the nineteenth-century frontiersman, who died at the Alamo.

[13]Werewolf.

[14]Two Zodiac signs from astrology. Being born on the cusp of Aquarius and Pisces is an omen of mystical powers.

[15]Tradition has it that Joan had a violent passion for the monk Folda and secretly followed him into the brotherhood. She was so popular among the clergymen that she was elected pope and succeeded Leo IV.

[16]Ptah, god of craftsmanship and chief god of Memphis, was combined with Ra, chief god of Heliopolis, when the two Egyptian city-states combined into a single nation.

[17]The mystical or magical powers associated with ancestors and places or an amulet or fetish of West African origin representing those magical attributes, usually consisting of red snake bones and feathers connected by snake skin.

go get my eyelids of red paint.
Hand me my shadow

I'm going into town after Set[18]

50 I am a cowboy in the boat of Ra

look out Set   here i come Set
to get Set   to sunset Set
to unseat Set   to Set down Set

usurper of the Royal couch
55   imposter RAdio of Moses' bush[19]
party pooper O hater of dance
vampire outlaw of the milky way

1972

Flight to Canada[1]

Dear Massa Swille:
What it was?
I have done my Liza Leap[2]
& am safe in the arms
5 of Canada, so
Ain't no use your Slave
Catchers waitin on me
At Trailways
I won't be there

10 I flew in non-stop
Jumbo jet this A.M. Had
Champagne
Compliments of the Cap'n

---

[18]Egyptian god of the setting sun, and hence night, he is the brother of Osiris, whom he murders and dismembers in order to steal the royal throne of the gods.
[19]Exodus 3:2: Yaweh appeared to Moses as a burning bush.
[1]Reed writes in the novel of the same name that this poem "kind of imitates" the style of William Wells Brown, the black satirist who wrote *Clotel* in 1853, the first known African American novel.
[2]In *Uncle Tom's Cabin,* by Harriet Beecher Stowe, a black female slave, Eliza, attains freedom by leaping from ice floe to ice floe across the Ohio River into the North and fleeing to Canada.

Who announced that a
15 Runaway Negro was on the
Plane. Passengers came up
And shook my hand
& within 10 min. I had
Signed up for 3 anti-slavery
20 Lectures. Remind me to get an
Agent

   Traveling in style
   Beats craning your neck after
   The North Star[3] and hiding in
25 Bushes anytime, Massa
   Besides, your Negro dogs
   Of Hays & Allen[4] stock can't
   Fly

   By now I s'pose that
30 Yellow Judas Cato[5] done tole
   You that I have snuck back to
   The plantation 3 maybe 4 times
   Since I left the first time

   Last visit I slept in
35 Your bed and sampled your
   Cellar. Had your prime
   Quadroon[6] give me
   She-Bear, Yes, yes

   You was away at a
40 Slave auction at Ryan's Mart[7]
   In Charleston & so I knowed
   You wouldn't mind
   Did you have a nice trip, Massa?

   I borrowed your cotton money
45 to pay for my ticket & to get
   Me started in this place called
   Saskatchewan[8] Brrrrrr!

---

[3]Polaris, the brightest star in the Little Dipper, was used by escaped slaves as the beacon for the Underground Railroad that would lead north to free states or Canada.

[4]Hays & Allen bred and trained dogs especially to track runaway slaves.

[5]High yellow, colloquial American black slang, refers to a light complectioned Negro. Judas Is-cariot was the apostle who betrayed Jesus at the Last Supper, and Cato (both the Elder and Younger) were Roman censors who led simple lives of self-denial.

[6]A person who is of one-quarter Negro ancestry.

[7]A slave market.

[8]A Canadian province.

It's cold up here but least
Nobody is collaring hobbling gagging
50 Handcuffing yoking chaining & thumbscrewing
You like you is they hobby horse

The Mistress Ms. Lady
Gived me the combination
To your safe, don't blame
55 The feeble old soul, Cap'n
I told her you needed some
More money to shop with &
You sent me from Charleston
To get it. Don't worry
60 Your employees won't miss
It & I accept it as a
Down payment on my back
Wages

I must close now
65 Massa, by the time you gets
This letter old Sam will have
Probably took you to the
Deep Six
That was rat poison I left
70 In your Old Crow[9]

Your boy
Quickskill

1976

Toni Cade Bambara 1939–1995

In a revealing essay called "Black English" (1972), Toni Cade Bambara summarized those attitudes that by 1970 had become the dramatic center of the fifteen stories included in her first short story collection, *Gorilla My Love* (1972). One of those attitudes, that "language is [as often] used to mis-inform, to mis-direct, to smoke out, to screen out, to block out, to intimidate as it is to inform," is one theme of the title story

of that collection; another, that "language certainly determines how we perceive the world" (limiting or expanding it), is the thematic core of "Playing with Punjab," "Maggie of the Green Bottles," and, especially, "My Man Bovanne." As superb a linguist as she was satirist, as splendid a storyteller as she was cultural ecologist, and as crucial a thinker as she was intrepid force for social transformation, Toni Cade,

---

[9]A famous southern whiskey.

adopting the name Bambara, which she discovered as a signature on a sketchbook in her great-grandmother's trunk, grew up like most of the narrators of her fiction, in an urban neighborhood whose rituals shaped her critical imagination.

In the New York City neighborhoods of Harlem, Bedford-Stuyvesant, and Queens, she and her brother Walter (now a painter) cut through the pernicious urban miasma which her fiction rigorously, often humorously, assails. Here in the "games, chants, jingles" of her peers, in the eloquence of the Seventh Avenue street speakers, in the elegance of the church-inspired club-inspired music of her neighborhood, in the talk and humor at home, and in the "space" allowed her by her parents, Walter and Helen (Henderson) Cade, who understood the necessity of encouraging a child's interior life, Toni Cade Bambara began to forge the language characteristic of the folk-based music, poetry, and prose of African American blues-jazz expressive modes. She completed a bachelor's degree in theater and literature from Queens College in 1959 and a master's in modern American literature from the City College of New York in 1963, studying, subsequently, at the Commedia del' Arte in Milan. She also studied filmmaking in England.

It is not surprising that during a period of tremendous political activism in which she matured—the struggle for civil rights in America, the struggle for the economic, political, and cultural empowerment of black Americans, an international resistance of colonialism, a demand for political and cultural self-determination in the Caribbean and on the continents of Africa and Asia, and a vigorous protest against war and nuclear weaponry—many young African American intellectuals, like Toni Cade Bambara, found a common cause. Still, her personal voice continues to find its deepest resonance in the cadences of the womanly themes of re-creation and renewal found in "My Man Bovanne," the story which opens *Gorilla My Love.* The pervasive melody harmonizing her work and embracing the specific emphasis of recent African American women writers is the theme of "a certain way of being in the world," nowhere more fully orchestrated than in her novel, *The Salt Eaters* (1980), and in her second book of short stories, *The Sea Birds Are Still Alive* (1977).

Eleanor W. Traylor
Howard University

PRIMARY WORKS

The Black Woman: An Anthology, 1970; *Tales and Stories for Black Folks,* 1971; *Gorilla My Love,* 1972; *The Sea Birds Are Still Alive: Collected Stories,* 1977; *The Salt Eaters,* 1980; *Raymond's Run,* 1990; *These Bones Are Not My Child,* 1999; *Deep Sightings and Rescue Missions,* 1999.

The Lesson

Back in the days when everyone was old and stupid or young and foolish and me and Sugar were the only ones just right, this lady moved on our block with nappy hair and proper speech and no makeup. And quite naturally we laughed at her, laughed the way we did at the junk man who went about his business like he was some bigtime president and his sorry-ass horse his secretary. And we kinda hated her too, hated the way we did the winos who cluttered up our parks and pissed on our handball walls and stank up our hallways and stairs so you couldn't halfway play hide-and-seek without a goddamn gas mask. Miss Moore was her name. The only woman on the block with no first name. And she was black as hell, cept for her feet, which were fish-white and spooky. And she was always planning these boring-ass things for us to do, us being my cousin, mostly, who lived on the block cause we all moved North the same time and to the same apartment then spread out gradual to breathe. And our parents would yank our heads into some kinda shape and crisp up our clothes so we'd be presentable for travel with Miss Moore, who always looked like she was going to church, though she never did. Which is just one of the things the grownups talked about when they talked behind her back like a dog. But when she came calling with some sachet she'd sewed up or some gingerbread she'd made or some book, why then they'd all be too embarrassed to turn her down and we'd get handed over all spruced up. She'd been to college and said it was only right that she should take responsibility for the young ones' education, and she not even related by marriage or blood. So they'd go for it. Specially Aunt Gretchen. She was the main gofer in the family. You got some ole dumb shit foolishness you want somebody to go for, you send for Aunt Gretchen. She been screwed into the go-along for so long, it's a blood-deep natural thing with her. Which is how she got saddled with me and Sugar and Junior in the first place while our mothers were in a la-de-da apartment up the block having a good ole time.

So this one day Miss Moore rounds us all up at the mailbox and it's purdee hot and she's knockin herself out about arithmetic. And school suppose to let up in summer I heard, but she don't never let up. And the starch in my pinafore scratching the shit outta me and I'm really hating this nappy-head bitch and her goddamn college degree. I'd much rather go to the pool or to the show where it's cool. So me and Sugar leaning on the mailbox being surly, which is a Miss Moore word. And Flyboy checking out what everybody brought for lunch. And Fat Butt already wasting his peanut-butter-and-jelly sandwich like the pig he is. And Junebug punchin on Q.T.'s arm for potato chips. And Rosie Giraffe shifting from one hip to the other waiting for somebody to step on her foot or ask her if she from Georgia so she can kick ass, preferably Mercedes'. And Miss Moore asking us do we know what money is, like we a bunch of retards. I mean real money, she say, like it's only poker chips or monopoly papers we lay on the grocer. So right away I'm tired of this and say so. And would much rather snatch Sugar and go to the Sunset and terrorize the West Indian kids and take their hair ribbons and their money too. And Miss Moore files that remark away for next week's lesson on brotherhood, I can tell. And finally I say we oughta get to the subway cause it's cooler and besides we might meet some cute boys. Sugar done swiped her mama's lipstick, so we ready.

So we heading down the street and she's boring us silly about what things cost and what our parents make and how much goes for rent and how money ain't divided up right in this country. And then gets to the part about we all poor and live in the slums, which I don't feature. And I'm ready to speak on that, but she steps out in the street and hails two cabs just like that. Then she hustles half the crew in with her and hands me a five-dollar bill and tells me to calculate 10 percent tip for the driver. And we're off. Me and Sugar and Junebug and Flyboy hangin out the window and hollering to everybody, putting lipstick on each other cause Flyboy a faggot anyway, and making farts with our sweaty armpits. But I'm mostly trying to figure how to spend this money. But they all fascinated with the meter ticking and Junebug starts laying bets as to how much it'll be when we get there. So I'm stuck. Don't nobody want to go for my plan, which is to jump out at the next light and run off to the first bar-b-que we can find. Then the driver tells us to get the hell out cause we there already. And the meter reads eight-five cents. And I'm stalling to figure out the tip and Sugar say give him a dime. And I decide he don't need it bad as I do, so later for him. But then he tries to take off with Junebug foot still in the door so we talk about his mama something ferocious. Then we check out that we on Fifth Avenue and everybody dressed up in stockings. One lady in a fur coat, hot as it is. White folks crazy.

"This is the place," Miss Moore say, presenting it to us in the voice she uses at the museum. "Let's look in the window before we go in."

"Can we steal?" Sugar asks very serious like she's getting the ground rules squared away before she plays. "I beg pardon," say Miss Moore, and we fall out. So she leads us around the windows of the toy store and me and Sugar screamin, "This is mine, that's mine, I gotta have that, that was made for me, I was born for that," till Big Butt drowns us out.

"Hey, I'm goin to buy that there."

"That there? You don't even know what it is, stupid."

"I do so," he say punchin on Rosie Giraffe. "It's a microscope."

"Whatcha gonna do with a microscope, fool?"

"Look at things."

"Like what, Ronald?" ask Miss Moore. And Big Butt ain't got the first notion. So here go Miss Moore gabbing about the thousands of bacteria in a drop of water and the somethinorother in a speck of blood and the million and one living things in the air around us is invisible to the naked eye. And what she say that for? Junebug to town on that "naked" and we rolling. Then Miss Moore ask what it cost. So we all jam into the window smudgin it up and the price tag say $300. So then she ask how long'd take for Big Butt and Junebug to save up their allowances. "Too long," I said. "Yeh," adds Sugar, "outgrown it by that time." And Miss Moore say no, you never outgrow learning instruments. "Why, even medical students and interns and," blah, blah, blah. And we ready to choke Big Butt for bringing it up in the first damn place.

"This here costs four hundred eighty dollars," say Rosie Giraffe. So we pile up all over her to see what she pointin out. My eyes tell me it's a chunk of glass cracked with something heavy and different-color inks dipped into the splits, then the whole thing put into a oven and something. But for $480 it don't make sense.

"That's a paperweight made of semi-precious stones fused together under tremendous pressure," she explains slowly, with her hands doing the mining and all the factory work.

"So what's a paperweight?" asks Rosie Giraffe.

"To weigh paper with, dumbbell," say Flyboy, the wise man from the East.

"Not exactly," say Miss Moore, which is what she say when you warm or way off too. "It's to weigh paper down so it won't scatter and make your desk untidy." So right away me and Sugar curtsy to each other and then to Mercedes who is more the tidy type.

"We don't keep paper on top of the desk in my class," say Junebug, figuring Miss Moore crazy of lyin one.

"At home, then," she say. "Don't you have a calendar and a pencil case and a blotter and a letter-opener on your desk at home where you do your homework?" And she know damn well what our homes look like cause she nosys around in them every chance she gets.

"I don't even have a desk," say Junebug. "Do we?"

"No. And I don't get no homework neither," say Big Butt.

"And I don't even have a home," say Flyboy like he do at school to keep the white folks off his back and sorry for him. Send this poor kid to camp posters, is his specialty.

"I do," say Mercedes. "I have a box of stationery on my desk and a picture of my cat. My godmother bought the stationery and the desk. There's a big rose on each sheet and the envelopes smell like roses."

"Who wants to know about your smelly-ass stationery," say Rosie Giraffe fore I can get my two cents in.

"It's important to have a work area all your own so that . . ."

"Will you look at this sailboat, please," say Flyboy, cuttin her off and pointin to the thing like it was his. So once again we tumble all over each other to gaze at this magnificent thing in the toy store which is just big enough to maybe sail two kittens across the pond if you strap them to the posts tight. We all start reciting the price tag like we in assembly. "Handcrafted sailboat of fiberglass at one thousand one hundred ninety-five dollars."

"Unbelievable," I hear myself say and am really stunned. I read it again for myself just in case the group recitation put me in a trance. Same thing. For some reason this pisses me off. We look at Miss Moore and she lookin at us, waiting for I dunno what.

"Who'd pay all that when you can buy a sailboat set for a quarter at Pop's, a tube of glue for a dime, and ball of string for eight cents? It must have a motor and a whole lot else besides," I say. "My sailboat cost me about fifty cents."

"But will it take water?" say Mercedes with her smart ass.

"Took mine to Alley Pond Park once," say Flyboy. "String broke. Lost it. Pity."

"Sailed mine in Central Park and it keeled over and sank. Had to ask my father for another dollar."

"And you got the strap," laugh Big Butt. "The jerk didn't even have a string on it. My old man wailed on his behind."

Little Q.T. was staring hard at the sailboat and you could see he wanted it bad. But he too little and somebody'd take it from him. So what the hell. "This boat for kids, Miss Moore?"

"Parents silly to buy something like that just to get all broke up," say Rosie Giraffe.

"That much money it should last forever," I figure.

"My father'd buy it for me if I wanted it."

"Your father, my ass," say Rosie Giraffe getting a chance to finally push Mercedes.

"Must be rich people shop here," say Q.T.

"You are a very bright boy," say Flyboy. "What was your first clue?" And he rap him on the head with the back of his knuckles, since Q.T. the only one he could get away with. Though Q.T. liable to come up behind you years later and get his licks in when you half expect it.

"What I want to know is," I say to Miss Moore though I never talk to her, I wouldn't give the bitch that satisfaction, "is how much a real boat costs? I figure a thousand'd get you a yacht any day."

"Why don't you check that out," she say, "and report back to the group?" Which really pains my ass. If you gonna mess up a perfectly good swim day least you could do is have some answers. "Let's go in," she say like she got something up her sleeve. Only she don't lead the way. So me and Sugar turn the corner to where the entrance is, but when we get there I kinda hang back. Not that I'm scared, what's there to be afraid of, just a toy store. But I feel funny, shame. But what I got to be shamed about? Got as much right to go in as anybody. But somehow I can't seem to get hold of the door, so I step away for Sugar to lead. But she hangs back too. And I look at her and she looks at me and this is ridiculous. I mean, damn, I have never ever been shy about doing nothing or going nowhere. But then Mercedes steps up and then Rosie Giraffe and Big Butt crowd in behind and shove, and next thing we all stuffed into the doorway with only Mercedes squeezing past us, smoothing out her jumper and walking right down the aisle. Then the rest of us tumble in like a glued-together jigsaw done all wrong. And people lookin at us. And it's like the time me and Sugar crashed into the Catholic church on a dare. But once we got in there and everything so hushed and holy and the candles and the bowin and the handkerchiefs on all the drooping heads, I just couldn't go through with the plan. Which was for me to run up to the altar and do a tap dance while Sugar played the nose flute and messed around in the holy water. And Sugar kept givin me the elbow. Then later teased me so bad I tied her up in the shower and turned it on and locked her in. And she'd be there till this day if Aunt Gretchen hadn't finally figured I was lyin about the boarder takin a shower.

Same thing in the store. We all walkin on tiptoe and hardly touchin the games and puzzles and things. And I watched Miss Moore who is steady watchin us like she waitin for a sign. Like Mama Drewery watches the sky and sniffs the air and takes note of just how much slant is in the bird formation. Then me and Sugar bump smack into each other, so busy gazing at the toys, 'specially the sailboat. But we don't laugh and go into our fat-lady bump-stomach routine. We just stare at the price tag. The Sugar run a finger over the whole boat. And I'm jealous and want to hit her. Maybe not her, but I sure want to punch somebody in the mouth.

"Watcha bring us here for, Miss Moore?"

"You sound angry, Slyvia. Are you mad about something?" Givin me one of them grins like she tellin a grown-up joke that never turns out to be funny. And she's lookin very closely at me like maybe she plannin to do my portrait from memory. I'm mad, but I won't give her the satisfaction. So I slouch around the store being very bored and say, "Let's go."

Me and Sugar at the back of the train watchin the tracks whizzin by large then small then gettin gobbled up in the dark. I'm thinkin about this tricky toy I saw in the store. A clown that somersaults on a bar then does chin-ups just cause you yank lightly at his leg. Cost $35. I could see me askin my mother for a $35 birthday clown. "You wanna who that costs what?" she'd say, cocking her head to the side to get a better view of the hole in my head. Thirty-five dollars could buy new bunk beds for Junior and Gretchen's boy. Thirty-five dollars and the whole household could go visit Granddaddy Nelson in the country. Thirty-five dollars would pay for the rent and the piano bill too. Who are these people that spend that much for performing clowns and $1,000 for toy sailboats? What kinda work they do and how they live and how come we ain't in on it? Where we are is who we are, Miss Moore always pointin out. But it don't necessarily have to be that way, she always adds then waits for somebody to say that poor people have to wake up and demand their share of the pie and don't none of us know what kind of pie she talkin about in the first damn place. But she ain't so smart cause I still got her four dollars from the taxi and she sure ain't gettin it. Messin up my day with this shit. Sugar nudges me in my pocket and winks.

Miss Moore lines us up in front of the mailbox where we started from, seem like years ago, and I got a headache for thinkin so hard. And we lean all over each other so we can hold up under the draggy-ass lecture she always finished us off with at the end before we thank her for borin us to tears. But she just looks at us like she readin tea leaves. Finally she say, "Well, what did you think of F.A.O. Schwarz?"

Rosie Giraffe mumbles, "White folks crazy."

"I'd like to go there again when I get my birthday money," says Mercedes, and we shove her out the pack so she has to lean on the mailbox by herself.

"I'd like a shower. Tiring day," said Flyboy.

Then Sugar surprises me by sayin, "You know, Miss Moore, I don't think all of us here put together eat in a year what the sailboat costs." And Miss Moore lights up like somebody goosed her. "And?" she say, urging Sugar on. Only I'm standin on her foot so she don't continue.

"Imagine for a minute what kind of society it is in which some people can spend on a toy what it would cost to feed a family of six or seven. What do you think?"

"I think," say Sugar pushing me off her feet like she never done before, cause I whip her ass in a minute, "that this is not much of a democracy if you ask me. Equal chance to pursue happiness means an equal crack at the dough, don't it?" Miss Moore is beside herself and I am disgusted with Sugar's treachery. So I stand on her foot one more time to see if she'll shove me. She shuts up, and Miss Moore looks at me, sorrowfully I'm thinkin. And somethin weird is goin on, I can feel it in my chest.

"Anybody else learn anything today?" lookin dead at me. I walk away and Sugar has to run to catch up and don't even seem to notice when I shrug her arm off my shoulder.

"Well, we got four dollars anyway," she said.

"Uh hunh."

"We could go to Hascombs and get a half a chocolate layer and then go to the Sunset and still have plenty money for potato chips and ice-cream sodas."

"Un hunh."

"Race you to Hascombs," she say.

We start down the block and she gets ahead which is O.K. by me cause I'm goin to the West End and then over to the Drive to think this day through. She can run if she want to and even run faster. But ain't nobody gonna beat me at nuthin.

1972

Frank Chin b. 1940

Frank Chin was born on February 25, 1940, in Berkeley, California. His father was an immigrant and his mother a fourth-generation resident of Oakland China-town, where Chin spent much of his child-hood. He attended the University of California at Berkeley and at Santa Barbara and participated in the Program in Creative Writing at the University of Iowa. Chin is a tireless and influential promoter of Asian American literature, though his vision of it has often been criticized for its exclusionary tendencies. He has written novels, short stories, plays, comic books, and numerous essays; produced documentaries; worked as a script consultant in Hollywood; taught college courses in Asian American literature; and helped form the Asian American Theatre Workshop in San Francisco.

He co-edited (with Jeffery Paul Chan, Lawson Fusao Inada, and Shawn Wong) a foundational anthology of Asian American writings entitled *Aiiieeeee!* (1974). A second volume, *The Big Aiiieeeee!*, was published in 1991. Much of Chin's notoriety stems from the positions he and his colleagues take in the introductory essays in those collections. One of their central concerns is the emasculating effect of anti-Asian racism as epitomized by stereotypical figures like Charlie Chan and Fu Manchu. Another controversial aspect of Chin's nonfictional writing has been his relentless criticism of writers such as David Henry Hwang, Maxine Hong Kingston, and Amy Tan; in his view, these writers falsify Asian and Asian American culture. Critics point out the misogyny and homophobia that propel Chin's polemics, but they also acknowledge the significance of his pioneering work as a literary historian. Indeed many of the writers that Chin and his colleagues champion—such as Louis Chu, John Okada, and Hisaye Yamamoto—

have been accorded a privileged place in Asia American literary studies.

The controversy generated by Chin's polemics has tended to overshadow his fictional and dramatic works. First staged in 1972, *The Chickencoop Chinaman* was one of the first plays written by an Asian American to be produced in New York. A second play, *The Year of the Dragon,* premiered two years later. Many of Chin's early writings contain an autobiographical element. They often revolve around a male protagonist—usually a would-be writer—alienated from his family or from his Chinatown community. This is the predicament shared by Johnny in Chin's first published short story, "Food for All His Dead" (1962), and by Fred in *The Year of the Dragon.* Much of Chin's early fiction was published in *The Chinaman Pacific & Frisco R.R. Co.* (1988), which won the National Book Award and from which "Railroad Standard Time" has been excerpted. The writings from this period tend to revel in masochistic self-loathing. The male heroes find only momentary relief when they are able to articulate their agony in elaborate monologues and when they gain tenuous access to a Chinese American history of mythical dimensions—a history usually associated with the railroad.

A shift can be detected in Chin's writings around the mid-eighties: he begins to forge a new vision of literary and racial authenticity based on a selective reading of classic Chinese texts, including *Romance of the Three Kingdoms, Water Margin,* and Sun Tzu's *The Art of War.* At the heart of the Chinese "real," Chin asserts, is an essentially martial view of the world: Life is War. His recent works feature protagonists who embrace these values; furthermore, they frequently allude to the figure of Kwan Kung, a warrior deified in Chinese folklore. The novel *Donald Duk* (1991) recounts the coming-of-age of its eponymous twelve-year-old protagonist: unlike the anti-heroes of Chin's earlier fiction, Donald is able to move beyond racial self-loathing by discovering the history of the Chinese American laborers who built the railroad and the world of Chinese mythology. The novel *Gunga Din Highway* (1994) features characters who are more exuberant and virile versions of the tortured protagonists of Chin's early writings, for the male heroes of this later work have access to the heroic tradition Chin identifies with

Kwan Kung. In *Bulletproof Buddhists and Other Essays* (1998) Chin finds evidence for the persistence of "real" Chinese values in a wide range of cultural locations: in the rituals of Southeast Asian youth gangs in southern California, in the Chinese American communities along the California-Mexico border, and in the works of dissident writers in Singapore.

Daniel Y. Kim
Brown University

PRIMARY WORKS

The Chickencoop Chinaman and The Year of the Dragon: Two Plays by Frank Chin, 1981; *The Chinaman Pacific & Frisco R.R. Co.*, 1988; *Donald Duk*, 1991; *Gunga Din Highway*, 1994; *Bulletproof Buddhists and Other Essays*, 1998; *Born in the USA: A Story of Japanese America*, 2002.

Railroad Standard Time

"This was your grandfather's," Ma said. I was twelve, maybe fourteen years old when Grandma died. Ma put it on the table. The big railroad watch, Elgin. Nineteen-jewel movement. American made. Lever set. Stem wound. Class facecover. Railroad standard all the way. It ticked on the table between stacks of dirty dishes and cold food. She brought me in here to the kitchen, always to the kitchen to loose her thrills and secrets, as if the sound of running water and breathing the warm soggy ghosts of stale food, floating grease, old spices, ever comforted her, as if the kitchen was a paradise for conspiracy, sanctuary for us *juk sing* Chinamen from the royalty of pure-talking China-born Chinese, old, mourning, and belching in the other rooms of my dead grandmother's last house. Here, private, to say in Chinese, "This was your grandfather's," as if now that her mother had died and she'd been up all night long, not weeping, tough and lank, making coffee and tea and little foods for the broken-hearted family in her mother's kitchen, Chinese would be easier for me to understand. As if my mother would say all the important things of the soul and blood to her son, me, only in Chinese from now on. Very few people spoke the language at me the way she did. She chanted a spell up over me that conjured the meaning of what she was saying in the shape of old memories come to call. Words I'd never heard before set me at play in familiar scenes new to me, and ancient.

She lay the watch on the table, eased it slowly off her fingertips down to the tabletop without a sound. She didn't touch me, but put it down and held her hands in front of her like a bridesmaid holding an invisible bouquet and stared at the watch. As if it were talking to her, she looked hard at it, made faces at it, and did not move or answer the voices of the old, calling her from other rooms, until I picked it up.

A two-driver, high stepping locomotive ahead of a coal tender and baggage car, on double track between two semaphores showing a stop signal was engraved on the back.

"Your grandfather collected railroad watches," Ma said. "This one is the best." I held it in one hand and then the other, hefted it, felt out the meaning of "the best," words that rang of meat and vegetables, oils, things we touched, smelled, squeezed, washed, and ate, and I turned the big cased thing over several times. "Grandma gives it to you now," she said. It was big in my hand. Gold. A little greasy. Warm.

I asked her what her father's name had been, and the manic heat of her all-night burnout seemed to go cold and congeal. "Oh," she finally said, "it's one of those Chinese names I . . ." in English, faintly from another world, woozy and her throat and nostrils full of bubbly sniffles, the solemnity of the moment gone, the watch in my hand turned to cheap with the mumbling of a few awful English words. She giggled herself down to nothing but breath and moving lips. She shuffled backward, one step at a time, fox-trotting dreamily backwards, one hand dragging on the edge of the table, wobbling the table, rattling the dishes, spilling cold soup. Back down one side of the table, she dropped her butt a little with each step then muscled it back up. There were no chairs in the kitchen tonight. She knew, but still she looked. So this dance and groggy mumbling about the watch being no good, in strange English, like an Indian medicine man in a movie.

I wouldn't give it back or trade it for another out of the collection. This one was mine. No other. It had belonged to my grandfather. I wore it braking on the Southern Pacific, though it was two jewels short of new railroad standard and an outlaw watch that could get me fired. I kept it on me, arrived at my day-off courthouse wedding to its time, wore it as a railroad relic/family heirloom/grin-bringing affectation when I was writing background news in Seattle, reporting from the shadows of race riots, grabbing snaps for the 11:00 P.M., timing today's happenings with a nineteenth-century escapement. (Ride with me, Grandmother.) I was wearing it on my twenty-seventh birthday, the Saturday I came home to see my son asleep in the back of a strange station wagon, and Sarah inside, waving, shouting through an open window, "Goodbye Daddy," over and over.

I stood it. Still and expressionless as some good Chink, I watched Barbara drive off, leave me, like some blonde white goddess going home from the jungle with her leather patches and briar pipe sweetheart writer and my kids. I'll learn to be a sore loser. I'll learn to hit people in the face. I'll learn to cry when I'm hurt and go for the throat instead of being polite and worrying about being obnoxious to people walking out of my house with my things, taking my kids away. I'll be more than quiet, embarrassed. I won't be likable anymore.

I hate my novel about a Chinatown mother like mine dying, now that Ma's dead. But I'll keep it. I hated after reading *Father and Glorious Descendant, Fifth Chinese Daughter, The House That Tai Ming Built.* Books scribbled up by a sad legion of snobby autobiographical Chinatown saps all on their own. Christians who never heard of each other, hardworking people who sweat out the exact same Chinatown book, the same cunning "Confucius says" joke, just like me. I kept it then and I'll still keep it. Part cookbook, memories of Mother in the kitchen slicing meat paper-thin with a cleaver. Mumbo jumbo about spices and steaming. The secret of Chinatown rice. The hands come down toward the food. The food crawls with culture. The thousand-year-old living Chinese meat makes dinner a safari into the unknown, a blood ritual. Food pornography. Black magic. Between the lines, I read a madman's detailed description of the preparation of shrunken heads. I never wrote to mean anything more than word fun with the food Grandma cooked at home. Chinese food. I read a list of what I remembered eating at my grandmother's table and knew I'd always be known by what I ate, that we come from a hungry tradition. Slop eaters following the wars on all fours. Weed cuisine and mud gravy in the shadow of corpses. We plundered the dust for fungus. Buried things. Seeds plucked out of the wind to feed a race of lace-boned skinnys, in high-school English, become transcendental Oriental art to make the dyke-ish spinster teacher cry. We always come to fake art and write the Chinatown book like bugs come to fly in the light. I hate my book now that ma's dead, but I'll keep it. I know she's not the woman I wrote up like my mother, and dead, in a book that was like everybody else's Chinatown book. Part word map of Chinatown San Francisco, shop to shop down Grant Avenue. Food again. The wind sucks the shops out and you breathe warm roast ducks dripping fat, hooks into the neck, through the head, out an eye. Stacks of iced fish, blue and fluorescent pink in the neon. The air is thin soup, sharp up the nostrils.

All mention escape from Chinatown into the movies. But we all forgot to mention how stepping off the streets into a faceful of Charlie Chaplin or a Western on a ripped and stained screen that became caught in the grip of winos breathing in unison in their sleep and billowed in and out, that shuddered when cars went by . . . we all of us Chinamans watched our own MOVIE ABOUT ME! I learned how to box watching movies shot by James Wong Howe. Cartoons were our nursery rhymes. Summers inside those neon-and-stucco downtown hole-in-the-wall Market Street Frisco movie houses blowing three solid hours of full-color seven-minute cartoons was school, was rows and rows of Chinamans learning English in a hurry from Daffy Duck.

When we ate in the dark and recited the dialogue of cartoon mice and cats out loud in various tones of voice with our mouths full, we looked like people singing hymns in church. We learned to talk like everybody in America. Learned to need to be afraid to stay alive, keep moving. We learned to run, to be cheerful losers, to take a sudden pie in the face, talk American with a lot of giggles. To us a cartoon is a desperate situation. Of the movies, cartoons were the high art of our claustrophobia. They understood us living too close to each other. How, when you're living too close to too many people, you can't wait for one thing more without losing your mind. Cartoons were a fine way out of waiting in Chinatown around the rooms. Those of our Chinamans who every now and then break a reverie with, "Thank you, Mighty Mouse," mean it. Other folks thank Porky Pig, Snuffy Smith, Woody Woodpecker.

The day my mother told me I was to stay home from Chinese school one day a week starting today, to read to my father and teach him English while he was captured in total paralysis from a vertebra in the neck on down, I stayed away from cartoons. I went to a matinee in a white neighborhood looking for the MOVIE ABOUT ME and was the only Chinaman in the house. I liked the way Peter Lorre ran along nonstop routine hysterical. I came back home with Peter Lorre. I turned out the lights in Pa's room. I put a candle on the dresser and wheeled Pa around in his chair to see me in front of the dresser mirror, reading Edgar Allan Poe out loud to him in the voice of Peter Lorre by candlelight.

The old men in the Chinatown books are all Muses for Chinese ceremonies. All the same. Loyal filial children kowtow to the old and whiff food laid out for the dead. The dead eat the same as the living but without the sauces. White food. Steamed chicken. Rice we all remember as children scrambling down to the ground, to all fours and bonking our heads on the floor, kowtowing to a dead chicken.

My mother and aunts said nothing about the men of the family except they were weak. I like to think my grandfather was a good man. Even the kiss-ass steward service, I like to think he was tough, had a few laughs and ran off with his pockets full of engraved watches. Because I never knew him, not his name, nor anything about him, except a photograph of him as a young man with something of my mother's face in his face, and a watch chain across his vest. I kept his watch in good repair and told everyone it would pass to my son someday, until the day the boy was gone. Then I kept it like something of his he'd loved and had left behind, saving it for him maybe, to give to him when he was a man. But I haven't felt that in a long time.

The watch ticked against my heart and pounded my chest as I went too fast over bumps in the night and the radio on, on an all-night run downcoast, down country, down old Highway 99, Interstate 5, I ran my grandfather's time down past road signs that caught a gleam in my headlights and came at me out of the night with the names of forgotten high school girlfriends, BELLEVUE KIRKLAND, ROBERTA GERBER, AURORA CANBY, and sang with the radio to Jonah and Sarah in Berkeley, my Chinatown in Oakland and Frisco, to raise the dead. Ride with me, Grandfather, this is your grandson the ragmouth, called Tampax, the burned scarred boy, called Barbecue, going to San Francisco to bury my mother, your daughter, and spend Chinese New Year's at home. When we were sitting down and into our dinner after Grandma's funeral, and ate in front of the table set with white food for the dead, Ma said she wanted no white food and money burning after her funeral. Her sisters were there. Her sisters took charge of her funeral and the dinner afterwards. The dinner would most likely be in a Chinese restaurant in Frisco. Nobody had these dinners at home anymore. I wouldn't mind people having dinner at my place after my funeral, but no white food.

The whiz goes out of the tires as their roll bites into the steel grating of the Carquinez Bridge. The noise of the engine groans and echoes like a bomber in flight through the steel roadway. Light from the water far below shines through the grate, and I'm driving high, above a glow. The voice of the tires hums a shrill rubber screechy mosquito hum that vibrates through the chassis and frame of the car into my meatless butt, into my tender asshole, my pelvic bones, the roots of my teeth. Over the Carquinez Bridge to CROCKETT MARTINEZ closer to home, roll the tires of Ma's Chevy, my car now, carrying me up over the water southwest toward rolls of fog. The fat man's coming home on a sneaky breeze. Dusk comes a drooly mess of sunlight, a slobber of cheap pawnshop gold, a slow building heat across the water, all through the milky air through the glass of the window into the closed atmosphere of a driven car, into one side of my bomber's face. A bomber, flying my mother's car into the unknown charted by the stars and the radio, feels the coming of some old night song climbing hand over hand, bass notes plunking as steady and shady as reminiscence to get on my nerves one stupid beat after the other crossing the high rhythm six-step of the engine. I drive through the shadows of the bridge's steel structure all over the road. Fine day. I've been on the road for sixteen hours straight down the music of Seattle, Spokane, Salt Lake, Sacramento, Los Angeles, and Wolfman Jack lurking in odd hours of darkness, at peculiar altitudes of darkness, favoring the depths of certain Oregon valleys and heat and moonlight of my miles. And I'm still alive. Country 'n' western music for the night road. It's pure white music. Like "The Star-Spangled Banner," it was the first official American music out of school into my jingling earbones sung by sighing white big tits in front of the climbing promise of FACE and Every Good Boy Does Fine chalked on the blackboard.

She stood up singing, one hand cupped in the other as if to catch drool slipping off her lower lip. Our eyes scouted through her blouse to elastic straps, lacy stuff, circular stitching, buckles, and in the distance, finally some skin. The color of her skin spread through the stuff of her blouse like melted butter through bread nicely to our tongues and was warm there. She sat flopping them on the keyboard as she breathed, singing "Home on the Range" over her shoulder, and pounded the tune out with her palms. The lonesome prairie was nothing but her voice, some hearsay country she stood up to sing *a capella* out of her. Simple music you can count. You can hear the words clear. The music's run through Clorox and Simonized, beating so insistently right and regular that you feel to sing it will deodorize you, make you clean. The hardhat hit parade. I listen to it a lot on the road. It's that get-outta-town beat and tune that makes me go.

Mrs. Morales was her name. Aurora Morales. The music teacher us boys liked to con into singing for us. Come-on opera, we wanted from her, not them Shirley Temple tunes the girls wanted to learn, but big notes, high long ones up from the navel that drilled through plaster and steel and skin and meat for bone marrow and electric wires on one long titpopping breath.

This is how I come home, riding a mass of spasms and death throes, warm and screechy inside, itchy, full of ghostpiss, as I drive right past what's left of Oakland's dark wooden Chinatown and dark streets full of dead lettuce and trampled carrot tops parallel all the time in line with the tracks of the Western Pacific and Southern Pacific railroads.

1988

Sheaf of Prison Literature

This sheaf brings together a number of contemporary writers under the term "prison literature," a category that refers to authors who began their writing careers in prison and also to prominent writers who have imagined the prison experience, perhaps observing it from the outside. Many of these professional writers, such as James Baldwin in his novel *If Beale Street Could Talk,* John Cheever in his novel *Falconer,* John Edgar Wideman in his book *Brothers and Keepers,* or Norman Mailer in his work *The Executioner's Song,* derive their authority through observation and through knowing prisoners: visiting them, listening to them, and imagining their experience. These famous writers did not learn to write in prison, although Baldwin was driven to suicidal despair after being incarcerated for a few days in Paris.

Other prison writers—those represented here—derive their authority directly. All five became writers in prison, though two—Kathy Boudin and Leonard Peltier—are better known for the controversy generated by their cases than for their writing. For them, as for many less famous prison writers, literature becomes the only way to escape, communicate with the outside world, or create something in the barren concrete wastelands of what might be called America's prison-industrial complex.

Regardless of which side of the bars the writer is on, prison literature always deals with a common theme: the devastating effect of incarceration on body, mind, and soul. Prison seeks to inhibit or prevent fundamental human desires, one of which is communication. If the prison represents a world hidden from sight, many Americans are oblivious to a significant number of their compatriots. In the twenty-first century, nearly 3 percent of American adults (1 in 37) have served time in prison, and the percentage is projected to grow to 3.4 percent by 2010. This startling statistic reflects a trend that began in the last three decades of the twentieth century: the United States tends to deal with most of its social problems through its prison system. This trend exists to make the general populace feel safe and secure. Yet even those who most accept the necessity for widespread incarceration must acknowledge that justice is not always served: that people are wrongfully imprisoned and even executed for crimes that they did not commit, that the system does not operate the same way for wealthy and poor inmates, and that alternatives to stiff prison sentences might result in a more humane society. Stories of petty shoplifters who serve twenty-five years in prison under California's controversial "three strikes and you're out" rule should give Americans pause. The infamous images of American guards torturing Iraqi inmates in Iraq's Abu Ghraib prison during the U.S. occupation in 2003–2004 should trigger some widespread soul searching about the cost to humanity in the name of safety and security.

Literature is a way to address some of these concerns. Prison literature is one way of allowing the voices of the imprisoned to be heard in the safe, secure living rooms of mainstream America. Yet prison literature is not unique to our time. Looking back to the classic American literature of the nineteenth century with this in mind, one might be surprised to discover how prominent a theme it is. Nathaniel Hawthorne's *The Scarlet Letter* begins in prison, Melville's "Bartleby the Scrivener" ends in prison, and Rebecca Harding Davis's "Life in the Iron Mills" and Henry David Thoreau's "Resistance to Civil Government" center on the prison experience. The literature of the civil rights era in the twentieth century also touches heavily on incarceration: Malcolm X discusses his prison experience extensively in *The Autobiography of Malcolm X* and Martin Luther King's "Letter from Birmingham Jail" is a superb example of how incarceration highlights injustice. It could be argued that prison writing is an essential component of American literature.

Contemporary prison literature is, for better or worse, an expanding field. In his introduction to *Prison Writing in Twentieth-Century America,* H. Bruce Franklin describes it as "far more bleak and desperate than the prison literature of any earlier period." Regardless of how one might feel about its message or about the individuals who write it, prison literature should not be ignored. Its very existence testifies to a basic American freedom that even prison cannot take away: the freedom to write.

D. Quentin Miller
Suffolk University

Etheridge Knight 1931–1991

Etheridge Knight was a black prison-born artist. Born in Corinth, Mississippi, in a large and relatively poor family of seven children, he was able to complete only a ninth grade education. Therefore, he discovered early in his life that his social and economic opportunities were limited. In Corinth, Knight found only menial jobs such as shining shoes available to him and, thus, spent much of his time hanging out in pool halls and barrooms. As a teenager, he turned to narcotics for what he felt would relieve him from his emotional anguish. Then, at sixteen, in his attempt to find a purpose in life, he enlisted in the army and later fought in the Korean War. During the war, Knight's addiction increased when he was treated with narcotics for a shrapnel wound. After his discharge from the service, he drifted aimlessly for several years throughout the country until he eventually settled in Indianapolis, Indiana. During these years, he learned through his experiences in bars and pool halls the art of telling toasts—long narrative poems from the black oral tradition that are acted out in a theatrical manner. Unfortunately, however, his drug addiction, not toast-telling, dominated Knight's life. In Indianapolis,

he snatched an old white woman's purse in order to support his addiction and was sentenced in 1960 to serve a ten- to twenty-five-year term in Indiana State Prison.

Embittered by his lengthy prison sentence, which he felt was unjust and racist in nature, Knight became rebellious, hostile, and belligerent during his first year of incarceration. However, *The Autobiography of Malcolm X* and other prison works influenced him to turn to writing in order to liberate his soul. As Knight once stated: "I died in Korea from a shrapnel wound and narcotics resurrected me. I died in 1960 from a prison sentence and poetry brought me back to life."

By drawing from his early experiences as a teller of toasts, Knight developed his verse into a transcribed-oral poetry of considerable power. His earlier poems, "The Idea of Ancestry," "The Violent Space," "Hard Rock Returns to Prison from the Hospital for the Criminal Insane," and "He Sees Through Stone," were so effective that Broadside publisher-poet Dudley Randall published Knight's first volume of verse, *Poems From Prison,* and hailed him as one of the major poets of the New Black Aesthetic. In addition, other poets such as Don L. Lee,

Gwendolyn Brooks, and Sonia Sanchez aided Knight in obtaining his parole in 1968.

Upon his release from prison, Knight married Sonia Sanchez. However, because of his drug addiction, the marriage was short-lived. He then married Mary McNally and they adopted two children and settled in Minneapolis, Minnesota, until 1977. Three years later, Knight published his volume of poems *Belly Songs and Other Poems*. Separated from Mary in the late 1970s, Knight resided in Memphis, Tennessee, where he received methadone treatments. In 1980 he published *Born of A Woman: New and Selected Poems* and in 1986, *The Essential Etheridge Knight*. He died of lung cancer in March of 1991.

Knight's poetry, much of it written in prison, ranges from expressions of loneliness and frustration to a sense of triumph over the soul's struggle. In his earlier prison poetry, Knight brings us mercilessly and straight on face to face with the infinite varieties of pain and sorrow of the prison world until, finally, the total prison soul stands before us anatomized. We meet the lobotomized inmate "Hard Rock," the raped convict Freckled-Faced Gerald, and the old black soothsayer lifer who "sees through stone" and waits patiently for the dawning of freedom. Above all, in "The Idea of Ancestry" and "The Violent Space," the two most powerful of his prison poems, we witness the poet himself deep in despair, alone in the freedomless void of his prison cell. However, Knight's best poems are his later ones, those that search for heritage, continuity, and meaning. In two of his post-prison poems, "The Bones of My Father," which shows his growing concern for image rather than the statement, and his masterful blues poem, "A Poem for Myself (Or Blues for A Mississippi Black Boy)," Knight's search takes him to the South, the ancestral home for blacks. Finally, in "Ilu, The Talking Drum," one of the finest poems in contemporary American poetry, Knight brings the black American life experience back full circle from Africa to the black South and then back to an Africa of the spirit.

Patricia Liggins-Hill
University of San Francisco

PRIMARY WORKS

Poems From Prison, 1968; *Black Voices from Prison*, 1972; *Belly Song and Other Poems,* 1973; *Born of A Woman: New and Selected Poems,* 1980; *The Essential Etheridge Knight,* 1986.

The Idea of Ancestry

1

Taped to the wall of my cell are 47 pictures: 47 black
faces: my father, mother, grandmothers (1 dead), grand
fathers (both dead), brothers, sisters, uncles, aunts,
cousins (1st & 2nd), nieces, and nephews. They stare
5 across the space at me sprawling on my bunk. I know
their dark eyes, they know mine. I know their style,
they know mine. I am all of them, they are all of me;
they are farmers, I am a thief, I am me, they are thee.

I have at one time or another been in love with my mother,
10 1 grandmother, 2 sisters, 2 aunts (1 went to the asylum),
and 5 cousins. I am now in love with a 7 yr old niece
(she sends me letters written in large block print, and
her picture is the only one that smiles at me).

I have the same name as 1 grandfather, 3 cousins, 3 nephews,
15 and 1 uncle. The uncle disappeared when he was 15, just took
off and caught a freight (they say). He's discussed each year
when the family has a reunion, he causes uneasiness in
the clan, he is an empty space. My father's mother, who is 93
and who keeps the Family Bible with everybody's birth dates
20 (and death dates) in it, always mentions him. There is no
place in her Bible for "whereabouts unknown."

2

Each Fall the graves of my grandfathers call me, the brown
hills and red gullies of mississippi send out their electric
messages, galvanizing my genes. Last yr/like a salmon quitting
25 the cold ocean—leaping and bucking up his birthstream/I
hitchhiked my way from L.A. with 16 caps in my pocket and a
monkey on my back. and I almost kicked it with the kinfolks.
I walked barefooted in my grandmother's backyard/I smelled the old
land and the woods/I sipped cornwhiskey from fruit jars with the men/
30 I flirted with the women/I had a ball till the caps ran out
and my habit came down. That night I looked at my grandmother
and split/my guts were screaming for junk/but I was almost
contented/I had almost caught up with me.
(The next day in Memphis I cracked a croaker's crib[1] for a fix.)

35 This yr there is a gray stone wall damming my stream, and when
the falling leaves stir my genes, I pace my cell or flop on my bunk
and stare at 47 black faces across the space. I am all of them,
they are all of me, I am me, they are thee, and I have no sons
to float in the space between.

1968

---

[1] A doctor's house.

The Violent Space
(Or When Your Sister Sleeps Around for Money)

Exchange in greed the ungraceful signs. Thrust
The thick notes between green apple breasts.
Then the shadow of the devil descends,
The violent space cries and angel eyes,
5   Large and dark, retreat in innocence and in ice.
(Run sister run—the Bugga man comes!)

The violent space cries silently,
Like you cried wide years ago
In another space, speckled by the sun
10   And the leaves of a green plum tree,
And you were stung
By a red wasp and we flew home.
(Run sister run—the Bugga man comes!)

Well, hell, lil sis, wasps still sting.
15   You are all of seventeen and as alone now
In your pain as you were with the sting
On your brow.
Well, shit, lil sis, here we are:
You and I and this poem.
20   And what should I do? should I squat
In the dust and make strange markings on the ground?
Shall I chant a spell to drive the demon away?
(Run sister run—the Bugga man comes!)

In the beginning you were the Virgin Mary,
25   And you are the Virgin Mary now.
But somewhere between Nazareth and Bethlehem
You lost your name in the nameless void.
O Mary don't you weep don't you moan
O Mary shake your butt to the violent juke,
30   Absorb the demon puke and watch the white eyes pop.
(Run sister run—the Bugga man comes!)

And what do I do. I boil my tears in a twisted spoon
And dance like an angel on the point of a needle.
I sit counting syllables like Midas gold.
35   I am not bold. I can not yet take hold of the demon
And lift his weight from your black belly,
So I grap the air and sing my song.
(But the air can not stand my singing long.)

1968

Ilu, the Talking Drum

The deadness was threatening us—15 Nigerians and 1 Mississippi
    nigger.
It hung heavily, like stones around our necks, pulling us down
to the ground, black arms and legs outflung
5 on the wide green lawn of the big white house
near the wide brown beach by the wide blue sea.
The deadness was threatening us, the day
was dying with the sun, the stillness—
unlike the sweet silence after love/making or
10 the pulsating quietness of a summer night—
the stillness was skinny and brittle and wrinkled
by the precise people sitting on the wide white porch
of the big white house. . . .
The darkness was threatening us, menacing . . .
15 we twisted, turned, shifted positions, picked our noses,
stared at our bare toes, hissed air thru our teeth. . . .
Then Tunji, green robes flowing as he rose,
strapped on *Ilu,* the talking drum,
and began:

20 kah doom/kah doom-doom/kah doom/kah doom-doom-doom
kah doom/kah doom-doom/kah doom/kah doom-doom-doom
kah doom/kah doom-doom/kah doom/kah doom-doom-doom
kah doom/kah doom-doom/kah doom/kah doom-doom-doom

the heart, the heart beats, the heart, the heart beats slow
25 the heart beats slowly, the heart beats
the blood flows slowly, the blood flows
the blood, the blood flows, the blood, the blood flows slow
kah doom/kah doom-doom/kah doom/kah doom-doom-doom
and the day opened to the sound
30 kah doom/kah doom-doom/kah doom/kah doom-doom-doom
and our feet moved to the sound of life
kah doom/kah doom-doom/kah doom/kah doom-doom-doom
and we rode the rhythms as one
from Nigeria to Mississippi
35 and back
kah doom/kah doom-doom/kah doom/kah doom-doom-doom

1980

A Poem for Myself
(Or Blues for a Mississippi Black Boy)

I was born in Mississippi;
I walked barefooted thru the mud.
Born black in Mississippi,
Walked barefooted thru the mud.
5   But, when I reached the age of twelve
I left that place for good.
My daddy he chopped cotton
And he drank his liquor straight.
Said my daddy chopped cotton
10   And he drank his liquor straight.
When I left that Sunday morning
He was leaning on the barnyard gate.
I left my momma standing
With the sun shining in her eyes.
15   Left her standing in the yard
With the sun shining in her eyes.
And I headed North
As straight as the Wild Goose Flies,
I been to Detroit & Chicago—
20   Been to New York city too.
I been to Detroit and Chicago
Been to New York city too.
Said I done strolled all those funky avenues
I'm still the same old black boy with the same old blues.
25   Going back to Mississippi
This time to stay for good
Going back to Mississippi
This time to stay for good—
Gonna be free in Mississippi
30   Or dead in the Mississippi mud.

1980

Jimmy Santiago Baca b. 1952

"Ignore all those myths about me," Jimmy Santiago Baca once said. "Just say I'm a writer who has earned my living for more than twenty years by writing." But Baca's story of redemption in prison has mythic dimensions. Voiceless and stripped to nothing, he was forced to discover inner resources he never knew he had. Now he is a major voice for Chicanos, prisoners, and the dispossessed.

Born in Santa Fe of Chicano and "detribalized Apache" parents, Baca was abandoned by his parents when he was two. He lived with his grandparents until he was placed in an orphanage. By the time he was twenty-one, life on the streets had landed him in prison for five years, convicted on charges of drug possession. The pivotal experience of his evolution was learning to read in prison, which Baca renders extravagantly in "Coming into Language" (*Working in the Dark*). A prisoner of twenty-one, made virtually insensate by bad luck and hard knocks, impulsively steals a book from a desk clerk. Despite his fear and contempt of books, he opens it at random and sounds out the letters. Ravished by the music of a Wordsworth poem, he suddenly recovers the whole spectrum of feeling. A few days later he picks up pencil and paper: "Until then, I had felt as if I had been born into a raging ocean where I swam relentlessly. . . . Never solid ground beneath me, never a resting place. I had lived with only the desperate hope to stay afloat. . . . But when at last I wrote my first words on the page, I felt an island rising beneath my feet like the back of a whale. As more and more words emerged, I could finally rest: I had a place to stand for the first time in my life." Having "a place to stand" freed Baca to recover his buried self, the child who had "waited so many years to speak again." With a place to stand, Baca could look around him and populate the page with his own unrecognized people. His memoir, *A Place to Stand: The Making of a Poet,* is a wrenching pilgrim's progress from loss, degradation, and crime to literacy and spiritual self-discovery that shares much with *The Autobiography of Malcolm X.* In prison Baca learns that neither religious grace nor the convict code can serve him, and he turns to the liberating and truth-disclosing power of poetry. Writing, he claims, enabled him "to rise from a victim of a barbarous colonization to a man in control of his life." And, "All of us who went to prison were lied to, and poetry is the only thing that didn't lie. Everything that is not a lie is po-

etry. In order to bring order to our world, we were forced to write. Writing was the only thing that could relieve the pain of betrayal, the only thing that filled the void of abandonment."

In 1976 "Letters Come to Prison," one of Baca's first poems, won an honorable mention in poetry from the PEN prison writing contest. Soon afterward, the poet Denise Levertov published some of his work in *Mother Jones;* she helped Baca find a publisher for his first major collection, *Immigrants in Our Own Land,* in 1978, the year he was released. Levertov discerned Baca's "intense lyricism" and "transformative vision which perceives the mythic and archetypal significance of life-events." In 1988 his spiritual quest novel in verse, *Martín: and Meditations on the South Valley,* received the Before Columbus American Book Award for poetry, bringing Baca international acclaim. He has also won a Wallace Stevens Yale Poetry Fellowship, a Pushcart Prize, the National Hispanic Heritage Award, the International Award (granted by the Frankfurt Book Fair), and he has been Champion of the International Poetry Slam. In addition to poetry, Baca has published short stories and essays; his screenplay, *Blood in, Blood out* (also known as *Bound by Honor*), about gang culture in Los Angeles, was released by Hollywood Pictures in 1993. Baca played a major role and was a key adviser in the making of the film, partly shot in San Quentin. In *Working in the Dark,* Baca recounts the traumatic experience of re-entering prison for the film. A combination of toughness, searing honesty, and tender vulnerability marks his best work.

Assimilation is an illusion, Baca says. He honors the *mestizaje,* the "braided cord," of Chicanismo. Earthbound and peaceful, most Chicanos reap "spiritual sustenance from their relationships with Mother Earth and *indio* Grandfather." Though famous, Baca mistrusts money because it dilutes "our poetry and our souls," he said in an interview, and it hurts his effort "of going into the projects and working with people in humble sort of way." As vital to him as writing is the act of sharing his conviction that language "is a very real living being." In a recent interview he said, "I began to provoke language to decreate me and then to give birth to me again." Baca teaches writing in countless schools and universities, reservations, barrio community centers, white ghettos, housing projects, and prisons nationwide. Of his students, he says, "If they were taught to be racist or violent, language has this amazing ability to unteach all that, and make them question it. It gives them back their power toward regaining their humanity." Literacy is linked to the growth of compassion for oneself and others. In the poem "El Gato" he enjoins men to cry: "our fists are tired from being clenched / and our faces just might break off! / And we need to cry all those good-byes out/ And get up in the middle of the night and cry / And we need to cry for no good reason, but to cry / For all those we never cried for / Cry to get our wings fluttering again!" Rob Allbee, a poet and ex-con in Sacramento, was overcome when he heard Baca read this on the air; Allbee began to read it in his healing circles with men in prison. When Baca was performing his work in Sacramento, he heard about Allbee and called him out of the audience to read the piece; Allbee became the "ghost reading in Sacramento" here. The power of Baca's

teaching and the example of his poetry have inspired countless prisoners.

With his love of his distinctive landscape and his compassion for struggling Chicanos and Native Americans, Baca owes much to Pablo Neruda. Emily Dickinson, he says, is also very important to him. He admires Levertov, Grace Paley, Adrienne Rich, and Marge Piercy for their courage, honesty, insight, and iconoclastic approach to poetry, and Raul Salinas and Ricardo Sanchez for breaking new ground for Chicano writers.

Baca has three sons and says he helps support "about ten adopted children." For many years, he has run his own school of writers; his students stay in New Mexico for a year or more and study writing with Baca while working in the community, painting, landscaping, or teaching literacy.

The poems selected here are from *Set This Book on Fire!* Writing remains for Baca a place endlessly to unfold more ways of being human. In his latest collection, "Winter Poems Along the Rio Grande," he continues to invite the world:

. . . *unexpectedly I see a bend in the river,
it stuns me
that one day I may be as sincere with myself,
through the changes of being a human being,
turn to see myself
flowingly, gracefully as the river.*

Bell Gale Chevigny
Purchase College, SUNY (emerita)

PRIMARY WORKS

Immigrants in Our Own Land, 1978; *Martín; and Meditations on the South Valley,* 1987; *Black Mesa Poems,* 1989; *Working in the Dark: Reflections of a Poet of the Barrio,* 1992; Screenplay: *Bound by Honor,* 1993; *Set This Book on Fire!,* 1999; *Healing Earthquakes,* 2001; *A Place to Stand: The Making of a Poet,* 2002; *C-Train and Thirteen Mexicans,* 2002; *Winter Poems Along the Rio Grande,* 2004; *The Importance of a Piece of Paper,* 2004.

I've Taken Risks

starting as a kid
when I stole choir uniforms
from an Episcopalian church
so I'd have something to keep me warm that winter.
5   I looked like a Biblical prophet
striding in six layers of robes through dark streets.

When you turned up the ace,
you kissed the card. And when the joker scoffed at you,
you were led away by authorities.
10 Second chances were for punks,
two-bit, jive-timing, nickel-diming
chumps.

It was beautiful in a way,
to see us kids at seven and eight
15 years old
standing before purple-faced authorities
screaming at us to ask forgiveness, muttering
how irresponsible we were, how impudent and defiant.

That same night
20 in the dark all alone, we wept in our blankets
for someone to love, to take care of us,
but we never asked for second chances.

1999

I Put on My Jacket

Wrapped up, I went out in winter light
climbing in volcanic rock on the west mesa
feeling softer and meaner than I've felt in years.
Amid arid scrub-brush, and bone-
5   biting cold, I thought of Half-Moon Bay,
how the ocean unscrolls on shore
with indecipherable messages.

Only those hiding out
from tormentors and tyrants, those in jail,
10 gypsies and outlaws, could understand.

the ocean talks to me
as one prisoner taps a spoon to another
through four feet of concrete
isolation-cell wall.

                              1999

Commitment

A county jail guard knocked out a tooth
smacking me across the face with his club once.
I took that tooth and sharpened it on my cell floor
to an arrowhead I tied to my toothbrush with floss
5 to stab him with it. I never did,
but with the same commitment, I once took my brogan
and a cot-leg of angle iron
hammering it against the bars to escape, which I did.
Hammering that metal leg for months,
10 I finally cut that bar they said was impossible
to cut through
with a boot and cot-leg.
It's a lesson that if I can do that,
when it comes to the business of living,
15 I can do anything.

                              1999

Ghost Reading in Sacramento

For days I feel a ghost
trailing me, memories aching and joyous,
from kitchen to basketball courts
to walking paths to driving around town,
5 a presence hovers about me
like the incipient, tight-furled rosebud
on the verge of breaking free, and I realize
miracles come in colors, soft bruises—
the mean scowl of a drunk
10 in a corner booth in a bar,

the elation a kid feels freed
of morning chores, leaping and running
out to the playground. I feel startled,
surrounded by memories,
15 like one of those sailors who finally comes ashore
to kneel before a humble altar, surrendering to feelings
that the world is too large for him to see it all, a man
whose heart once radiated stamina, strength, and firmness
yet now like a sail is folded to the mast:
20 from Charlie whirling in old songs
mimicking oldies but goodies
to Gilbert's miner's grubbing for gold
in his coal-shaft past
to your solitary dance
25 in a room filled with dreams
to David's hunting through jungles of cells
tracking a cure for AIDS
to that guy in Sacramento
who made us all realize something more beyond ourselves,
30 who drew our thinking out of our eyes
in tears, his voice a sudden catching,
kindling and flame,
reminding us of our own flickering journey.

1999

Kathy Boudin b. 1943

Kathy Boudin's name brings to mind the generation of student antiwar protesters of the 1960s and 1970s; however, her achievements in prison remain virtually unknown. Boudin was raised in New York City by social activist parents—Jean, a poet and a pacifist, and Leonard, a constitutional lawyer. Boudin spent some of the summer of 1963 in the South and committed herself to the civil rights struggle. After graduating from Bryn Mawr in 1965, she lived in Cleveland, Ohio, and with women on welfare wrote a welfare-rights manual that helped develop community leadership.

As opposition to the war in Vietnam intensified, Boudin co-authored *The Bust Book: What to Do Until the Lawyer Comes,* a legal self-defense guide for antiwar demonstrators. After three of her friends in the violent Weather Underground were killed while making bombs in a New York City townhouse in March 1970, Boudin went underground. She surfaced in 1981 when she was arrested for participating in a Black Liberation Army armored car robbery in which two police officers and a mall security guard were killed. Boudin was an unarmed passenger in the getaway vehicle driven by her lover, David Gilbert.

She pleaded guilty to felony murder and robbery and was sentenced to twenty years to life. At Bedford Hills Correctional Facility in New York, Boudin worked collaboratively with other inmates to develop programs and to write about them to help other incarcerated women do the same.

Parenting from Inside/out: Voices of Mothers in Prison, a book she coauthored with another prisoner, reflects her work with Bedford's Children's Center. Boudin also coauthored the *Foster Care Handbook for Incarcerated Parents,* which has been widely used in social service agencies and social work schools. Boudin applied Paolo Freire's *Pedagogy of the Oppressed* teaching basic literacy through learning by analysis and action and with others designed and created a prize-winning, peer-driven AIDS counseling and education project. With others, Boudin researched the importance of education to prisoners and their children and published the results; the Bedford Hills college program is now a model for other colleges and correctional institutions.

Boudin's interest in poetry sprang from her mother's work. She was influenced by the women's movement, the black movement, and writers in prison, and her poems treat family relations and prison experiences. In 1998, her "Trilogy of Journeys" won first prize in poetry in the PEN prison writing contest. Imagining her first day of freedom, Boudin wrote, "If only there were a place where the living and the dead could meet, to tell their tales, to weep. I would reach for you, not so that you could forgive me, but so that you could know that I have no pride for what I have done, only the wisdom and regret that came too late."

In 2003, Boudin was granted parole and was released. She works in the field of HIV/AIDS and continues to write poetry.

Bell Gale Chevigny
Purchase College, SUNY (emerita)

PRIMARY WORKS

With P. Bedell and J. Ashkin, *The Foster Care Handbook for Incarcerated Parents: A Manual of Your Legal Rights and Responsibilities,* 1994; with R. Greco, eds., *Parenting from Inside/out: Voices of Mothers in Prison: A Self-help Book for Incarcerated Parents, Social Workers and Community Service Centers,* 1998; *Breaking the Walls of Silence: AIDS and the Women in a New York State Maximum Security Prison,* 1998; with M. Fine et al., *Changing Minds: The Impact of College in a Maximum Security Prison,* 2001.

The Call

You might not be at the other end
of eight cells,
one garlic-coated cooking area
vibrating with the clatter of popcorn on
5   aluminum pot covers
two guards peering through blurry plexiglas,
the TV room echoing with
Jeopardy sing-song music and competing yells for
answers—
10   all lying between
my solitude and the telephone.

Or
you might answer

with a flat "hello,"
15 and I will hear your fingers
poking at plastic computer buttons,
your concentration focused on
the green and blue invaders and defenders.
My words only background
20 to your triumphs and defeats.

But I long for your voice.
Even the sound of your clicking fingers.
I journey past
eight cells submerged
25 in rap, salsa, heavy metal and soul
careening along the green metal corridor,
the guards perched on their raised platform,
dominoes clacking on plastic tabletops.
Past the line of roaches weaving
30 to the scent of overflowing garbage pails
voices shouting down the corridors,
legs halted by the line
that cannot be crossed.
Finally I sit on the floor
35 of the chairless smoky butt-filled room
to call you
who answers with an ever-deepening voice,
who barely sounds like my son.

"Hi, what are you doing?"
40 "I'm lying down, burning incense, listening to music.
    Do you want to hear it?"
With such relief
I barely utter "Yes," pushing my ear into the telephone,
my nose into the air.
45 Your flutes and organs become a soft carpet I walk along
in the musty sweetness and fruit smells
of orange peels and raspberries.
You begin to describe your new room
One wall   the dream catcher   a set of hatchets
50   and white feathers wrapped with beads
        of turquoise sky and sunset.
Your bed opposite a full length mirror
Perfect, you say, to view yourself,
a new body, six and half inches in one year.

55 Then you invite me
into your special boxes,
gifts from your father

made behind bars.
"I keep all my treasures."

60 I nod breathlessly
My son has taken my voice.
His words fill me in
A naming ceremony.
Slowly his hand lifts
65   a coffee brown belt
name carved across,
a menu of favorite food
   shared on the overnight visit.
Father-love.

70 The QEII ticket stub from
   the final ocean trip with Grandma.
"Eat your breakfast, pack your clothes, then you can watch TV,"
his grandfather's voice echoes
   from a note left by his bed.
75 He moves to the Christmas calendar
   of shared favorite books
Tales of Peter Rabbit to *Huck Finn*
   the story of fourteen years.
A birthday card
80   A photo
My son and I stand back to back.
His head inches past mine.

Then you dangle one sandstone earring
   the other in a box in my cell,
85 "We'll put them together when you get out."
   Your words hang like a glider.
Mother-love.

Then guitar notes rise and fall,
and I say, as always "I love you,"
90 and you say, as always, "I love you,"
and the phone clicks off.

1997

Our Skirt

You were forty-five and I was fourteen
when you gave me the skirt.
"It's from Paris!" you said
as if that would impress me
5   who at best had mixed feelings
about skirts.

But I was drawn by that summer cotton
with splashes of black and white—like paint
dabbed by an eager artist.
10 I borrowed your skirt
and it moved like waves
as I danced at a ninth-grade party.
Wearing it date after date
including my first dinner with a college man.
15 I never was much for buying new clothes,
once I liked something it stayed with me for years.

I remember the day I tried
ironing your skirt,
so wide it seemed to go on and on
20 like a western sky.
Then I smelled the burning
and, crushed, saw that I had left a red-brown scorch
on that painting.

But you, Mother, you understood
25 because ironing was not your thing either.
And over the years your skirt became my skirt
until I left it and other parts of home with you.

Now you are eighty and I almost fifty.
We sit across from each other
30 in the prison visiting room
Your soft gray-thin hair twirls into style.
I follow the lines on your face, paths lit by your eyes
until my gaze comes to rest
on the black and white,
35 on the years
that our skirt has endured.

1997

A Trilogy of Journeys

for my son on turning 18

I.

The day approaches
    when I begin
my yearly pilgrimage
    back in time,
5 the present no longer important,
only the exact hour and minutes on a clock.
They will bring me to that moment
    when you began
    the longest journey
10 man ever makes,
out of the sea that
rocked you and bathed you,
out of the darkness and warmth,
    that caressed you,
15 out of the space
that you stretched like the skin of a drum
    until it could no longer hold you
        and you journeyed through my tunnel
          with its twists and turns,
20 propelling yourself
on and on until
    your two feet danced into brightness
and you taught me
    the meaning
25   of miracles.

II.

Somewhere in the middle of the country
    you are driving a car,
sitting straight, seat belt tight across your well-exercised chest,
looking into the horizon,
30 the hum of the engine dwarfed by the
    laughter of your companions.
You are driving toward 18.
Two sets of parents
    on each side of the continent
35 await your arrival,
    anxiously,
And you leave them astounded

        by that drive,
     always a part of you,
40 to grow up as soon as possible
    You move toward the point
       that as parents we both celebrate and dread,
    foreshadowed by leavings that take place
      over and over again.
45 That leaving for kindergarten,
     that leaving for camp,
        that leaving parents home on a Saturday night.
    Until that time when you really leave,
      which is the point of it all,
50 And the sweet sadness.

III

My atlas sits
    on a makeshift desk,
a drawing board
    between two lock-boxes.
55 It was a hard-fought-for item,
     always suspect in the prison environment
as if I could slide into its multicolored shapes
    and take a journey.
In front of me is the United States
60   spread across two pages.
I search for Route 80,
    a thin red line
and imagine you,
    a dot moving along it.
65 You, an explorer now.
    Davenport, Iowa; Cheyenne, Wyoming; then Utah; Nevada;
     until you reach
     the Sierras, looking down on the golden land.
Roads once traveled by your father and me.
70 As I struggle within myself to let you go,
     and it is only within,
for you *will* go,
I am lifted out of the limits
    of this jail cell,
75 and on the road
    with you, my son,
who more than any map or dream
    extends my world.
    My freedom may be limited,
80 but I am your passenger.

1999

Leonard Peltier b. 1944

In prison since 1976, Leonard Peltier has spent nearly half of his life in an iron cage. "I am guilty only of being an Indian," he argues in his memoir. "Truth is, they actually need us. Who else would they fill up their jails and prisons with in places like the Dakotas and New Mexico if they didn't have Indians?"

Prison Writings: My Life Is My Sundance is Leonard Peltier's sole book-length publication, a tonally and stylistically fragmented text reflective of the burdens and pressures of writing from a maximum-security prison, perhaps reflective of years of experience with displacement. In poetry and prose, Peltier refers with irony to "Aboriginal Sin," pointing to the many ways that indigenous peoples are guilty at birth—"guilty of being ourselves." Citing government policies of enforced assimilation, perhaps none more damaging than removing children from their homes and placing them in boarding schools (such as the Bureau of Indian Affairs schools that forbade him to use his native language and cultural practices), Peltier asks us to reconceive his struggle for freedom as predating his conviction and incarceration for a crime that many argue he did not commit. Indeed, many have seen Leonard Peltier's life as emblematic of the colonization of indigenous people throughout the world. For thirty years, various individuals and groups, such as the Dalai Lama, Amnesty International, Nelson Mandela, and the European Parliament, have called for Peltier's release from prison, where he is serving two consecutive life sentences. Few individual cases, in fact, have garnered as much sustained attention as the Free Peltier movement.

Born on September 12, 1944, Leonard Peltier was raised on Sioux and Ojibway (Chippewa) reservations in North Dakota. The "rank racism and brutal poverty" that he experienced during these years set the foundation for his political activism, while the federal policies of "termination" and "relocation" initiated a crisis that had profound effects on his family and larger community. At the age of fifteen, he left the Turtle Mountain Reservation and made his way to the "red ghettoes" of the Pacific West. In 1965, he opened an auto-body shop that failed, he tells us, because of "that old Indian weakness: *sharing* with others." During this time, his political awareness grew even as his capitalist ventures failed, and during the 1960s and 1970s, he helped establish a halfway house for men prisoners, devoted time to native land rights, counseled others on alcohol abuse, and joined the American Indian Movement (AIM). This latter organization led him to the Pine Ridge Indian Reservation in South Dakota in 1972. In the early 1970s, AIM members (who were called Traditionalists) engaged in conflicts with other Native Americans (who were called Nontraditionalists). As part of an AIM security force, Peltier was at the scene of a shoot-out that resulted in the death of two FBI agents. He was extradited from Canada, convicted of two counts of first-degree murder, and sentenced to two consecutive life sentences.

Peltier's story, however, does not begin and end with this central event in his life. His commitment to transforming society, aiding the poor and the disenfranchised, and raising awareness for Native American rights continues even as his many supporters work for his release. Peltier is an artist, activist, and writer, and his life is, as his memoir conveys, his sundance: "Sundance is our religion, our strength. We take great pride in that strength, which enables us to resist pain, torture, any trial rather than betray the People."

Juda Bennett
The College of New Jersey

PRIMARY WORK

Prison Writings: My Life Is My Sundance, 1999.

from Prison Writings

10:00 P.M. Time for the nightly lockdown and head count. The heavy metal door to my cell lets out an ominous grinding sound, then slides abruptly shut with a loud clang. I hear other doors clanging almost simultaneously down the cellblock. The walls reverberate, as do my nerves. Even though I know it's about to happen, at the sudden noise my skin jumps. I'm always on edge in here, always nervous, always apprehensive. I'd be a fool not to be. You never let your guard down when you live in hell. Every sudden sound has its own terror. Every silence, too. One of those sounds—or one of those silences—could well be my last, I know. But which one? My body twitches slightly at each unexpected footfall, each slamming metal door. Will my death announce itself with a scream or do its work in silence? Will it come slowly or quickly? Does it matter? Wouldn't quick be better than slow, anyway?

A guard's shadow passes by the little rectangular window on the cell door. I hear his keys jangle, and the mindless squawking of his two-way radio. He's peering in, observing, observing. He sees me sitting here cross-legged in the half-light hunched over on my bed, writing on this pad. I don't look up at him. I can feel his gaze passing over me, pausing, then moving on, pausing again at the sleeping form of my cellmate snoring softly in the bunk above. Now he goes by. The back of my neck creeps.

Another day ends. That's good. But now another night is beginning. And that's bad. The nights are worse. The days just happen to you. The night's you've got to imagine, to conjure up, all by yourself. They're the stuff of your own nightmares. The lights go down but they never quite go out in here. Shadows lurk everywhere. Shadows within shadows. I'm one of those shadows myself. I, Leonard Peltier. Also known in my native country of Great Turtle Island as Gwarth-ee-lass—"He Leads the People." Also known among my Sioux brothers as Tate Wikuwa—"Wind Chases the Sun." Also known as U.S. Prisoner #89637-132.

I fold my pillow against the cinderblock wall behind me and lean back, half sitting, knees drawn up, here on my prison cot. I've put on my gray prison sweatpants and long-sleeved sweatshirt. They'll do for PJs. It's cool in here this late winter night. There's a shiver in the air. The metal and cinderblock walls and tile floors radiate a perpetual chill this time of year.

Old-timers will tell you how they used to get thrown, buck naked in winter, into the steel-walled, steel-floored Hole without even so much as a cot or a blanket to keep them warm; they had to crouch on their knees and elbows to minimize contact with the warmth-draining steel floor. Today you generally get clothes and a cot and blanket—though not much else. The Hole—with which I've become well acquainted at several federal institutions these past twenty-three years, having become something of an old-timer myself—remains, in my experience, one of the most inhuman of tortures. A psychological hell. Thankfully, I'm out of there right now.

I'm also out of the heat that used to afflict us until they finally installed air-conditioning in the cellblock about ten years back. Before that Leavenworth was infamous as the Hot House, because there was no air-conditioning here, just big wall-mounted fans that, during the mind-numbing heat of a Kansas hundred-degree summer day, blew the heavy, sluggish, unbreathable air at you like a welding torch, at times literally drying the sweat on your forehead before it could form, particularly on the stifling upper tiers of the five-tier cellblock.

But we still have the noise, always the noise. I suppose the outside world is noisy most of the time, too, but in here every sound is magnified in your mind. The ventilation system roars and rumbles and hisses. Nameless clanks and creakings, flushings and gurglings sound within the walls. Buzzers and bells grate at your nerves. Disembodied, often unintelligible voices drone and squawk on loudspeakers. Steel doors are forever grinding and slamming, then grinding and slamming again. There's an ever-present background chorus of shouts and yells and calls, demented babblings, crazed screams, ghostlike laughter. Maybe one day you realize one of those voices is your own, and then you really begin to worry.

From time to time they move you around from one cell to another, and that's always a big deal in your life. Your cell is just about all you've got, your only refuge. Like an animal's cage, it's your home—a home that would make anyone envy the homeless. Different cellblocks in this ancient penitentiary have different kinds of cells, some barred, some—like the one I'm currently in—a five-and-a-half-by-nine-foot cinderblock closet with a steel door. There's a toilet and sink, a double bunk bed, a couple of low wall-mounted steel cabinets that provide a makeshift and always cluttered desktop.

Right now they've put another inmate in here with me after I'd gotten used to being blissfully alone for some time. He's got the upper bunk and his inert, snoring form sags down nearly to my head as I try to half sit in here with this legal pad on my lap. At least I get the lower bunk because of the bad knee I've had for years. I presume that they put my new cellmate in here with me as a form of punishment—a punishment for both of us, I suppose—though for what, neither he nor I have the slightest idea.

The first thing you have to understand in here is that you never understand anything in here. For sure, they don't want you ever to get comfortable. Nor do they ever want you to have a sense of security. And, for sure, you don't. Security's the one thing you never get in a maximum-security prison.

Now, on this chilly night, I toss the rough green army blanket over my knees, and drape a hand towel over the back of my neck to keep the chill off. I keep my socks on under the sheets, at least until I finally go to sleep. On this yellow legal pad purchased at the prison commissary I scrawl as best I can with a pencil stub that somebody's been chewing on. I can barely make out my own handwriting in the semi-darkness, but no matter.

I don't know if anyone will ever read this. Maybe someone will. If so, that someone can only be you. I try to imagine who you might be and where you might be reading this. Are you comfortable? Do you feel secure? Let me write these words to you, then, personally. I greet you, my friend. Thanks for your time and attention, even your curiosity. Welcome to my world. Welcome to my iron lodge. Welcome to Leavenworth.

1999

Judee Norton b. 1949

Drawing on her prison experiences, Judee Norton writes short fiction that carries the history of women's prison literature to a new phase. Incarcerated women who write constitute a minority of the population of a women's prison, and their chosen genres have traditionally been forms of life writing, such as letters and prison memoirs. Norton, whose work has been honored by the PEN prison writing awards, writes autobiographical short fiction, a blend of fiction and women prisoners' traditional life writing. Contemporary women prisoners have moved away from earlier writers' need for the self-justification that is often the agenda of personal narrative. Instead, they choose poetry and fiction with assertive, even radical themes that both affirm the human rights of all prisoners and condemn the inhumanity of prison conditions.

Born in Arizona farming country, Judee Norton grew up in a poor family with five children. In her contribution to *Doing Time* (1999), she describes her background as one of "addiction, poverty, low self-esteem, and a general sense of bewilderment about the business of living." She received a five-year sentence on a drug charge and was incarcerated from 1988 to 1992 in the Arizona State Prison Complexes in Phoenix and Perryville. She became a writer in prison and has said that her writing helped her survive her incarceration.

Norton's characters are confined within a state women's prison, where events occur against the background of kitchen detail, exercise periods in the yard, or conversations in the dining hall or laundry room. This setting is deceptive in its relative lack of physical restrictions or deprivation of basic needs. In this topsy-turvy universe, the imprisoned protagonist stands for rationality and integrity against the threats of corrupt and irrational forces, represented by the prison administrators. For Norton, the absurd world of prison becomes, by default, her universe, and she must summon her personal will to withstand what she experiences as its objective—to destroy her by eroding her pride and identity. Attacks on a prisoner's spirit may be physical or deeply emotional, as in "Norton #59900."

Norton lives and works today in a small farm community at the foot of Arizona's Catalina Mountains near Tucson. She gives readings of her work at universities and has discussed her writing and prison life on various radio shows. She continues to write about her prison experience in *Slick,* a project of autobiographical fiction. She describes her work as "an account of my experiences in prison, along with some often stark revelations about why and how I came to be there." Most of the work offers accounts of Norton's incarceration, commenting on the corruption, injustice, and inhumanity of the prison system from the point of view of the female prisoner. By challenging prison administrators on environmental and human rights issues, Norton's protagonist creates an ironic space in which power is redefined as the preservation of self-respect through even the smallest acts of resistance.

Judith Scheffler
West Chester University

PRIMARY WORKS

"Arrival" (received a 1990 PEN prison writing award); "Gerta's Story" and "Slick and the Beanstalk," in *Wall Tappings: An International Anthology of Women's Prison Writings,* 2002.

Norton #59900

"Attention on the yard, attention in the units! Norton, five-nine-nine-zero-zero, obtain a pass and report to the captain's office immediately!" the public address speakers boom. The sound bounces around the yard, boomerangs between the buildings and my ears again and again. I am standing outside the schoolroom, smoking and sweating in the 112-degree summer afternoon, squinting at the sun and wondering idly whether this kind of weather would be more enjoyable if I were lying on a Mexican beach wearing only a string bikini and a smile, holding a frosty margarita in one hand and a fine, slender stick of Indika in the other. I have just decided that it most definitely would be when the summons comes.

At once I am approached from every direction by fellow inmates asking, "Did you hear them call you to the captain's office, Jude?" and, "What's going on? Why does the captain want you?" I feign indifference as I take a long final drag of my cigarette, then flip the butt with practiced skill into one of the pink-painted coffee cans nearby.

"Who the fuck knows," I respond with just the right degree of flippancy. My voice is sure and steady, and that pleases me. I can feel my face rearranging itself into a mask of haughty insolence, a half-sneer claims my mouth, one eyebrow hitches itself a quarter-inch upward on my forehead to indicate arrogant disregard. It is my intention to appear poised, untroubled, faintly amused, and slightly bored. I am quite sure I achieve such a look.

My guts belie my measured outward calm. They twist and grumble and roil, threatening to send my lunch to the sidewalk. My heart is beating much too fast. My mouth is dry, my tongue feels like a landed trout thrashing about in that arid, alien place. My hands are trembling, my knees belong to a stranger, I am grateful for the first time ever that it is so goddamn hot in Phoenix. Everyone glistens with a fine film of perspiration; perhaps no one will notice that I smell of fear.

I affect a hip-slung swagger for the amusement of the gathered crowd, and head for south unit control to ask for a pass. It strikes me that I am asking permission to go to a place I haven't the faintest glimmer of desire to go to, and I giggle. The officer issuing my pass looks up at me and says, "Hope you still think it's funny when you get back, Norton." I shrug. The walk across the yard is a long one, made longer by my determination to stroll casually under the scrutiny of a hundred watching eyes. I can feel them on me, can almost hear the thoughts behind them:

"Poor Jude!"

". . . 'bout time that goody-goody bitch got hers."

"Damn, hope it ain't bad news . . ."

"Gir'fren', please, look who be in trouble now!"

"Sheee-it . . ."

I knock purposefully at the polished wooden door with the brass plate that announces this as the Mount Olympus of DOC. CAPTAIN, it says in big carved block letters. Fuck you, I mouth silently.

After just enough time has elapsed to make me feel insignificant and small, the door is opened by a fat, oily sergeant. She is damp and rumpled in spite of the cool, air-conditioned comfort of the room. She turns wordlessly from me and installs her sloppy bulk at a desk littered with forms—applications, requests, petitions—paper prayers from the miserable and needy. She selects one and peers importantly at it over the tops of her smeary glasses, then picks up a red pen and makes a large unmistakable X in a box labeled DENIED. I imagine a look of malignant glee on her greasy flat features as she does it.

Having not been invited to sit, I am still standing near the door, feeling awkward and displaced, when the phone rings. She picks up the receiver, says, "Yeah?" into it, and after a moment looks at me, nods, and replaces it. She jerks her head in the direction of the door through which I have just come and says, "Go back outside for a minute, if you don't mind." Fleetingly, I wonder what she would say if I responded, "Oh, but I *do* mind, I mind very much, in fact; it's hotter than the devil's dick out there, you see, and I *so* much prefer it inside." What I actually say, though, is, "Oh, sure, no problem," and am mortified to find myself blushing.

Once outside, it occurs to me that if this was sly, psychological weaponry, designed to unseat and disadvantage me, it is quite effective. I feel humiliated and disgraced in a way I cannot identify. I light a cigarette and arrange my limbs carefully into a posture of indolent apathy. I hook my thumbs in my belt loops and squint with what I hope is an air of monumental unconcern through the smoke that curls up into my face.

At last the door opens again, and I am ushered into the cool depths of the anteroom, and this time I get a nod from the sergeant to proceed into the next room, the sacred chamber where sits the captain, enthroned behind a gleaming expanse of mahogany desk. He is leaning back in a maroon leather swivel chair, rolling a gold Cross pen between his startlingly white palms. He is a black giant, all teeth and long-fingered hands and military creases. His hair is cut very short on the sides and back, and the top flares out and up several inches. It is decidedly and perfectly flat on top, as though his barber used a T-square. I am reminded of the enchanting topiary at Disneyland's Small World; he appears a well-tended shrub. Then he smiles at me and I think to myself viciously that he looks like the offspring of Arsenio Hall and Jaws. He motions me to a small chair, carefully chosen and placed so that I am directly in front of him and several inches lower. I feel like a beggar, prostate at the foot of the king. I am determined that he should not know this. I meet his gaze with a cool look of studied dignity.

"You're Norton?" he asks.

No, you moron, I'm Smith, Jones, Appleby, Wellington, Mother Teresa, Doc Holliday, Jackie Onassis, anyone in the world besides Norton, at least I'd like to be right now, dontcha know, I think wildly. Aloud, I say, "Yes, sir. I'm Norton."

The chair creaks as he leans forward and picks up a piece of paper, pretends to study it. Without looking at me, he says, "Norton, I called you in to talk to you about your son's at-ti-tude," pronouncing all three syllables distinctly as though to a slow child.

"My son's attitude?" I repeat, feeling exquisitely stupid.

He gives a derisive little snort, as though to indicate that of course we both know what he's talking about and it's damned silly of me to pretend ignorance. Bewildered, I ask, "What attitude, sir?"

The captain closes his eyes and leans back again, rolling the gold pen in his hands. It clicks annoyingly against his rings.

"Your son, Adam," he begins with an air of great forbearance, "seems to cause a problem every time he comes to visit you. My officers tell me that he is rude and disrespectful, a troublemaker." He opens his eyes and looks at me expectantly.

I am dismayed to notice that my mouth is agape, that I have been caught so unawares as to be, for one of the very few times in my entire life, speechless. "A troublemaker, sir?" I say, realizing with no small degree of consternation that thus far I have only managed to echo what has been said to me.

"Ap-par-ent-ly," he replies, again dividing the word carefully into all its syllables, "he demanded a full explanation of the visitor's dress code a couple of weeks ago. And last Sunday, according to the report, he questioned the policy that forbids inmates or their visitors to sit on the grass."

I have a quick vision of an official report, complete with the Seal of the Great State of Arizona, titled TROUBLEMAKERS, and can see my son's name emblazoned at the top of a long list. His sins are red-lettered: DEMANDING EXPLANATIONS and QUESTIONING POLICY. Suddenly and against all reason and prudence, I have a powerful urge to laugh, to say, "You're kidding, right dude?" But I fight it and win, and say instead, "Sir?" as though it were a question in its own right, and the captain obliges me by treating it as such.

"Your son, Adam," he says with exaggerated patience, "insists upon knowing the reason for every rule and regulation DOC imposes, which we are in no way obligated to provide to him. He disrupts my officers in the performance of their duties."

I am beginning to hate the way he says my son's name, and I feel the first stirrings of anger. The visitation officers' "duties" consist of sitting in a cool, dark room with a bank of closed-circuit TV screens, looking out onto the baked parking lot where a line of parched visitors wait for the regal nod of approval that will allow them entry into the institution. Their "duties" include watching us chat with our loved ones, making sure that there is no "prolonged kissing," no hanky-panky under the tables, no exchanging of other than words. The most arduous task they will perform all day in the fulfillment of their "duties" is bending over to inspect my vagina after I squat and cough and "spread those cheeks *wide*" for a strip search at visit's end. I fail to comprehend how my son's questions interfere with these odious "duties," and I say so.

The captain's response is brusque, and it is obvious that he, too, is becoming annoyed. "It is not your place, Norton, to determine whether or not the officers' duties are being interfered with. It *is* your place to ensure that your visitors comply with procedure."

"What 'procedure,' sir, says that my boy can't ask questions?" I challenge, against my better judgment, which has long since flown. A little voice inside my head says, *Oh boy, now you've done it, you smartass,* and the voice is surely smarter than I am, for the captain stands up so fast he nearly topples his chair. His breath is coming fast and his eyes blaze.

As quickly as he is losing his calm, I am gaining mine, and from some place deep inside I thought was forever closed to me, I feel a surge of fearlessness. I stand also, and face him squarely and unblinkingly, an intrepid lioness defending her cub. It is a sensation that will not last.

"Sit," he commands.

I sit.

A moment later, he sits, crossing one elegantly trousered leg over the other and picking up the ubiquitous gold pen again. "Tell me," he says congenially, "what happened in the blue jeans incident two weeks ago."

"What happened, sir," I begin reasonably, "is that my son came to visit me wearing a pair of gray Dockers, you know, men's casual pants, and he was told that he could not see me because he was not in compliance with the dress code that specifies 'no blue jeans.' He was understandably upset, and asked that a higher authority be consulted."

"And were they?"

"Yes, sir, someone called the OIC,[1] who didn't want to take the responsibility for a decision; she in turn called the lieutenant, who ultimately allowed him in."

"So he *was* admitted," the captain says, in a tone which implies that, after all, the whole point is moot, and why ever in the world am I so agitated about it?

Warming to my subject, and not liking one bit the look of smug self-satisfaction on his face, I throw caution to the winds, full speed ahead and damn the torpedoes, devil take the hindmost. All pretense of civility leaves me, my instinct for self-preservation is gone.

"Oh, he was admitted all right," I say, making no attempt to disguise my disgust. I note with detachment that my hands and arms have bravely joined the recitation and are describing sharply eloquent shapes and forms in the air, punctuating my mounting fury, underlining my passion. The pitch and timbre of my voice have changed and the words rush from me, unstoppable. "He was admitted, sir, twenty whole minutes before the end of visitation, after taking a filthy stinking city bus all the way from Tempe and being allowed to stand in the blazing sun for three and a half hours without a square inch of shade or so much as an offer of a drink of water. He was admitted after he begged, pleaded, cajoled, and tried to reason with every know-nothing brownshirt in this whole sorry place. He was admitted after repeatedly pointing out to every available cretin with a badge that his gray, pleated, slash-pocketed, cuffed, pleated and creased, one-hundred-percent cotton *slacks* were, in fact, neither 'blue' nor 'jeans' and therefore did not violate the 'no blue jeans' rule. He was admitted after being chastised like a naughty schoolboy by that loser of a sergeant, after being called immature, impatient, juvenile, and demanding, after being threatened with dismissal from the premises, after being subjected to an outrageously erroneous judgment call on his goddamn *pants,* sir. Disrespectful? Oh, I hope so. With all due respect to you, sir, I hope to Christ he was disrespectful to them."

By this time, I am shaking with rage. I am remembering my fair-skinned boy's sunburned face. I am remembering the awful look in his sky-colored eyes, that bright liquidity that tells of a boy perched on the brink of manhood, trying not to cry. I am remembering my own inability to explain, to soothe, to mend as mothers do, as they must, for if not they, who?

It is an omission of some seriousness that I did not notice earlier the twin spots of color that had crept to the captain's cheekbones. On his ebony skin they are the

[1]Officer in charge [Norton's note].

color of dried blood, and his eyes snap and sparkle at me. There is a vein pulsing at his left temple. I have an abrupt vision of myself cutting out my tongue with his letter-opener and simply leaving it flopping about on his desk in expiation. Too late.

"Norton," he says slowly, "it is clear to me where your son got his attitude." I notice that he does not divide his words into all their separate parts for me now. He taps his chin thoughtfully with the pen. "It is my feeling that for the continued se-cure operation of this institution, it will be necessary to discontinue your son's visits until further notice. Perhaps he only needs time away from you to learn to deal with the fact of your incarceration in a mature and sensible manner. An attitude adjust-ment period." He smiles.

My heart lurches and I feel the color staining my own cheeks even as it leaves his. "Sir," I say, hating the quavering, desperate sound of my voice, "surely you're not saying he can't come to see me anymore." I can hear the humble, supplicating tone I use, and I despise myself for it. "Please," I say, strangling the word.

Having regained his equilibrium, the captain sits up straight in the chair and al-lows a wider smile. "That is pre-cise-ly what I am saying, Norton." In control, once more, he has gone back to hacking his words apart. I hate him for that.

I am consumed by impotent rage, I wrestle with a crushing and mighty urge to rise and beat that superior face of his into a bleeding pulp of unrecognizable jutting bones and torn flesh. The desire is so intense as to be palpable. I can hear the dull wet crunch of gristle and cartilage, can feel his warm slippery brains between my fin-gers, can smell the dark coppery odor of his blood, can see it splashing up, up, onto the walls, the carpet, the desk, my face, my hair, crimson and joyous.

I am dazed and shaken by this vision. I sit for a moment gripping the chair bot-tom with white-knuckled horror. Then I push the chair back gently, like a woman preparing to excuse herself from the dinner table and say softly, "May I leave, sir?"

"Certainly," replies the captain, ever the gracious host. He smiles at me. I do not return the smile.

With the grace and ironclad composure that have saved me from humiliation since early childhood, I hold my head high as I walk through the outer office past the inquisitive stare of the duty sergeant. I close the big door quietly, and slip unnoticed around the corner of the building.

I lean against the sun-baked wall and struggle with a host of emotions I cannot put name to. I feel the wall burning my shoulders through my blue workshirt. My knees become suddenly and utterly incapable of supporting me. They fold up and I slide bonelessly down the wall, heedless of the way its pebbled surface scrapes at my back. My teeth are clenched, but my lips part and turn downward. From them comes an awful keening sound I do not recognize. My eyes sting with the threat of unwel-come tears, I beg them silently not to betray me. But they do, traitorous things, and a great wash of tears pours unchecked down my cheeks, off my chin, into my lap, a flood of them, pent up all those years when to cry was a sign of weakness and to be weak was to be a victim. I lay my forehead on my knees and drop my hands loosely to the blistering cement beside me, like useless weapons that would not fire when so much was at stake. I am dimly aware that I am crying in the brokenhearted way of a small child, a sort of hitching and breathless uh-uh-uh-uh-uh, complete with snot running down into my mouth. I feel naked and wounded, unmanned by grief and hopelessness.

Finally I can no longer hear the sounds of my own weeping. I turn my head to one side and feel the sun begin to evaporate the tears, leaving my face tight and dry. I spit on the fingertips of my hands and scrub away the trails they left, wipe my nose on my sleeve, and pull a small black comb from my back pocket. I take my sunglasses from the top of my head and run the comb briskly through the matted and dampened strands and stand up. Straight. Tall. Shoulders back. Chin up. I put the dark glasses on my face and the mantle of hard-ass prisoner on my soul.

I saunter nonchalantly around the corner, past the door marked CAPTAIN, onto the yard. An acquaintance approaches me and asks in an excited whisper, "So, what happened in there? What's up?"

She is immediately joined by a second and a third and a fourth, all eager, questioning. I am comfortable now. This is my milieu, this is where I know exactly what is expected of me, precisely how to behave, what to do and say. I shove both hands jauntily into the hip pockets of my Levi's and allow a disdainful grin to own my face.

"Fuck him," I say with contempt. "He can't touch this."

We all laugh.

1991

James Welch (Blackfeet–Gros Ventre) 1940–2003

Welch was born in Browning, Montana, and attended the University of Montana. Half Blackfeet and half Gros Ventre, Welch drew on his Native American background but he refused to think of himself as "only" an Indian writer. The power of his fiction and poetry convinces the reader of his place in the mainstream of American literature, but that power derives as much from his subject matter as from his taut narrative style, laced with a laconic humor that adds a bitter complexity to his harsh tales.

In *Winter in the Blood* and *The Death of Jim Loney,* Welch drew with superb understatement the unlived lives of the contemporary Native American men, shut off from college educations because of family poverty and ignorance, warded away from financial respectability because of that education cut short. In each book, the protagonist had been a star high school athlete. Now, a decade or more after that athletic career ended, the men have no direction and no promise. They lead aimless lives of drinking, sex (and the promise that a healthy sexual relationship might hold is undercut by their own nihilistic attitudes), and apathy. Confused relationships with parents, especially with the father, whose life as an outsider to the white culture has set the model for the son, dominates what plot exists. But more than plot, these novels are marked by mood and tone, atmosphere as precisely drawn as anything by Hemingway or Richard Wright. Alienation and loss are what remain from reading these stunning texts.

Fools Crow, a truly Native American narrative in that its base plot is actual history from the nineteenth century, shares the somber tone of the earlier two novels at moments, but its texture has changed radically. This is a full panoply of native life—household customs, religious rites, love and family situations, war-making. Comedy, strength, ribaldry in the realization of the Native American lives of the past—in the height of power and cultural achievement—are set against the contemporary malaise, for an even more sadly ironic effect. *Indian Lawyer* places the Native American in the midst of that malaise and shows the inherent corruptibility of all people. Taking the four novels as a tetrology provokes a better sense of Welch's meaning: the pride of heritage makes more understandable the deep apathy and sense of loss of the present-day Montana Indians. That sense of loss is applicable to any culture, of course, but it need not be: it is enough for us to recognize the immense loss the Indian culture has experienced, for it is so much worse than anything mainstream inhabitants can visualize. Welch's work allows readers that visualization, and that convincing understanding.

In Welch's poems the strain that some critics have called comic surrealism is more evident—but for some readers *Winter in the Blood* also shares in that tone. Characteristic of Blackfeet responses to life, Welch's understated and oblique humor is a part of his world vision, and deserves to be recognized.

Linda Wagner-Martin
University of North Carolina at Chapel Hill

PRIMARY WORKS

Riding the Earthboy 40: Poems, 1971; *Winter in the Blood,* 1974; *The Death of Jim Loney,* 1979; *Fools Crow,* 1986; *Indian Lawyer,* 1990; *Killing Custer: The Battle of the Little Bighorn and the Fate of the Plains Indians,* 1994; *The Heartsong of Charging Elk,* 2000.

from Winter in the Blood

Part Four

38

"Hello," he said. "You are welcome."

"There are clouds in the east," I said. I could not look at him.

"I feel it, rain tonight maybe, tomorrow for sure, cats and dogs."

The breeze had picked up so that the willows on the irrigation ditch were gesturing in our direction.

"I see you wear shoes now. What's the meaning of this?" I pointed to a pair of rubber boots. His pants tucked inside them.

"Rattlesnakes. For protection. This time of year they don't always warn you."

"They don't hear you," I said. "You're so quiet you take them by surprise."

"I found a skin beside my door this morning. I'm not taking any chances."

"I thought animals were your friends."

"Rattlesnakes are best left alone."

"Like you," I said.

"Could be."

I pumped some water into the enamel basin for Bird, then I loosened his cinch.

"I brought some wine." I held out the bottle.

"You are kind—you didn't have to."

"It's French," I said. "Made out of roses."

"My thirst is not so great as it once was. There was a time . . ." A gust of wind ruffled his fine white hair. "Let's have it."

I pressed the bottle into his hand. He held his head high, resting one hand on his chest, and drank greedily, his Adam's apple sliding up and down his throat as though it were attached to a piece of rubber. "And now, you," he said.

Yellow Calf squatted on the white skin of earth. I sat down on the platform on which the pump stood. Behind me, Bird sucked in the cool water.

"My grandmother died," I said. "We're going to bury her tomorrow."

He ran his paper fingers over the smooth rubber boots. He glanced in my direction, perhaps because he heard Bird's guts rumble. A small white cloud passed through the sun but he said nothing.

"She just stopped working. It was easy."

His knees cracked as he shifted his weight.

"We're going to bury her tomorrow. Maybe the priest from Harlem. He's a friend . . ."

He wasn't listening. Instead, his eyes were wandering beyond the irrigation ditch to the hills and the muscled clouds above them.

Something about those eyes had prevented me from looking at him. It had seemed a violation of something personal and deep, as one feels when he comes upon a cow licking her newborn calf. But now, something else, his distance, made it all right to study his face, to see for the first time the black dots on his temples and the bridge of his nose, the ear lobes which sagged on either side of his head, and the bristles which grew on the edges of his jaw. Beneath his humped nose and above his chin, creases as well defined as cutbanks between prairie hills emptied into his mouth. Between his half-parted lips hung one snag, yellow and brown and worndown, like that of an old horse. But it was his eyes, narrow beneath the loose skin of his lids, deep behind his cheekbones, that made one realize the old man's distance was permanent. It was behind those misty white eyes that gave off no light that he lived, a world as clean as the rustling willows, the bark of a fox or the odor of musk during mating season.

I wondered why First Raise had come so often to see him. Had he found a way to narrow that distance? I tried to remember that one snowy day he had brought me with him. I remembered Teresa and the old lady commenting on my father's judgment for taking me out on such a day; then riding behind him on the horse, laughing at the wet, falling snow. But I couldn't remember Yellow Calf or what the two men talked about.

"Did you know her at all?" I said.

Without turning his head, he said, "She was a young woman; I was just a youth."

"Then you did know her then."

"She was the youngest wife of Standing Bear."

I was reaching for the wine bottle. My hand stopped.

"He was a chief, a wise man—not like these conniving devils who run the agency today."

"How could you know Standing Bear? He was Blackfeet."

"We came from the mountains," he said.

"You're Blackfeet?"

"My people starved that winter; we all starved but they died. It was the cruelest winter. My folks died, one by one." He seemed to recollect this without emotion.

"But I thought you were Gros Ventre. I thought you were from around here."

"Many people starved that winter. We had to travel light—we were running from the soldiers—so we had few provisions. I remember, the day we entered this valley it began to snow and blizzard. We tried to hunt but the game refused to move. All winter long we looked for deer sign. I think we killed one deer. It was rare that we even jumped a porcupine. We snared a few rabbits but not enough . . ."

"You survived," I said.

"Yes, I was strong in those days." His voice was calm and monotonous.

"How about my grandmother? How did she survive?"

He pressed down on the toe of his rubber boot. It sprang back into shape.

"She said Standing Bear got killed that winter," I said.

"He led a party against the Gros Ventres. They had meat. I was too young. I remember the men when they returned to camp—it was dark but you could see the white air from their horses' nostrils. We all stood waiting, for we were sure they would bring meat. But they brought Standing Bear's body instead. It was a bad time."

I tapped Yellow Calf's knee with the bottle. He drank, then wiped his lips on his shirt sleeve.

"It was then that we knew our medicine had gone bad. We had wintered some hard times before, winters were always hard, but seeing Standing Bear's body made us realize that we were being punished for having left our home. The people resolved that as soon as spring came we would go home, soldiers or not."

"But you stayed," I said. "Why?"

He drew an arc with his hand, palm down, taking in the bend of the river behind his house. It was filled with tall cottonwoods, most of them dead, with tangles of brush and wild rose around their trunks. The land sloped down from where we were sitting so that the bend was not much higher than the river itself.

"This was where we camped. It was not grown over then, only the cottonwoods were standing. But the willows were thick then, all around to provide a shelter. We camped very close together to take advantage of this situation. Sometimes in winter, when the wind has packed the snow and blown the clouds away, I can still hear the muttering of the people in their tepees. It was a very bad time."

"And your family starved . . ."

"My father died of something else, a sickness, pneumonia maybe. I had four sisters. They were among the first to go. My mother hung on for a little while but soon she went. Many starved."

"But if the people went back in the spring, why did you stay?"

"My people were here."

"And the old—my grandmother stayed too," I said.

"Yes. Being a widow is not easy work, especially when your husband had other wives. She was the youngest. She was considered quite beautiful in those days."

"But why did she stay?"

He did not answer right away. He busied himself scraping a star in the tough skin of earth. He drew a circle around it and made marks around it as a child draws the sun. Then he scraped it away with the end of his stick and raised his face into the thickening wind. "You must understand how people think in desperate times. When their bellies are full, they can afford to be happy and generous with each other—the meat is shared, the women work and gossip, men gamble—it's a good time and you do not see things clearly. There is no need. But when the pot is empty and your guts are tight in your belly, you begin to look around. The hunger sharpens your eye."

"But why her?"

"She had not been with us more than a month or two, maybe three. You must understand the thinking. In that time the soldiers came, the people had to leave their home up near the mountains, then the starvation and the death of their leader. She had brought them bad medicine."

"But you—you don't think that."

"It was apparent," he said.

"It was bad luck; the people grew angry because their luck was bad," I said.

"It was medicine."

I looked at his eyes. "She said it was because of her beauty."

"I believe it was that too. When Standing Bear was alive, they had to accept her. In fact, they were proud to have such beauty—you know how it is, even if it isn't yours." His lips trembled into what could have been a smile.

"But when he died, her beauty worked against her," I said.

"That's true, but it was more than that. When you are starving, you look for signs. Each event becomes big in your mind. His death was the final proof that they were cursed. The medicine man, Fish, interpreted the signs. They looked at your grandmother and realized that she had brought despair and death. And her beauty—it was as if her beauty made a mockery of their situation."

"They can't have believed this . . ."

"It wasn't a question of belief, it was the way things were," he said. "The day Standing Bear was laid to rest, the women walked away. Even his other wives gave her the silent treatment. It took the men longer—men are not sensitive. They considered her the widow of a chief and treated her with respect. But soon, as it must be, they began to notice the hatred in their women's eyes, the coolness with which they were treated if they brought your grandmother a rabbit leg or a piece of fire in the morning. And they became ashamed of themselves for associating with the young widow and left her to herself."

I was staring at the bottle on the ground before me. I tried to understand the medicine, the power that directed the people to single out a young woman, to leave her to fend for herself in the middle of a cruel winter. I tried to understand the thinking, the hatred of the women, the shame of the men. Starvation. I didn't know it. I couldn't understand the medicine, her beauty.

"What happened to her?"

"She lived the rest of the winter by herself."

"How could she survive alone?"

He shifted his weight and dug his stick into the earth. He seemed uncomfortable. Perhaps he was recalling things he didn't want to or he felt that he had gone too far. He seemed to have lost his distance, but he went on: "She didn't really leave. It was the dead of winter. To leave the camp would have meant a sure death, but there were tepees on the edge, empty—many were empty then."

"What did she do for food?"

"What did any of us do? We waited for spring. Spring came, we hunted—the deer were weak and easy to kill."

"But she couldn't hunt, could she?" It seemed important for me to know what she did for food. No woman, no man could live a winter like that alone without something.

As I watched Yellow Calf dig at the earth I remembered how the old lady had ended her story of the journey of Standing Bear's band.

There had been great confusion that spring. Should the people stay in this land of the Gros Ventres, should they go directly south to the nearest buffalo herd, or should they go back to the country west of here, their home up near the mountains? The few old people left were in favor of this last direction because they wanted to die in familiar surroundings, but the younger ones were divided as to whether they should stay put until they got stronger or head for the buffalo ranges to the south. They rejected the idea of going home because the soldiers were there. Many of them had encountered the Long Knives before, and they knew that in their condition they wouldn't have a chance. There was much confusion, many decisions and indecisions, hostility.

Finally it was the soldiers from Fort Assiniboine who took the choice away from the people. They rode down one late-spring day, gathered up the survivors and drove them west to the newly created Blackfeet Reservation. Because they didn't care to take her with them, the people apparently didn't mention her to the soldiers, and because she had left the band when the weather warmed and lived a distance away, the soldiers didn't question her. They assumed she was a Gros Ventre.

A gust of wind rattled the willows. The clouds towered white against the sky, but I could see their black underbellies as they floated toward us.

The old lady had ended her story with the image of the people being driven "like cows" to their reservation. It was a strange triumph and I understood it. But why hadn't she spoken of Yellow Calf? Why hadn't she mentioned that he was a member of that band of Blackfeet and had, like herself, stayed behind?

A swirl of dust skittered across the earth's skin.

"You say you were just a youth that winter—how old?" I said.

He stopped digging. "That first winter, my folks all died then."

But I was not to be put off. "How old?"

"It slips my mind," he said. "When one is blind and old he loses track of the years."

"You must have some idea."

"When one is blind . . ."

"Ten? Twelve? Fifteen?"

". . . and old, he no longer follows the cycles of the years. He knows each season in its place because he can feel it, but time becomes a procession. Time feeds upon itself and grows fat." A mosquito took shelter in the hollow of his cheek, but he didn't notice. He had attained that distance. "To an old dog like myself, the only cycle begins with birth and ends in death. This is the only cycle I know."

I thought of the calendar I had seen in his shack on my previous visit. It was dated 1936. He must have been able to see then. He had been blind for over thirty years, but if he was as old as I thought, he had lived out a lifetime before. He had lived a life without being blind. He had followed the calendar, the years, time—

I thought for a moment.

Bird farted.

And it came to me, as though it were riding one moment of the gusting wind, as though Bird had had it in him all the time and had passed it to me in that one instant of corruption.

"Listen, old man," I said. "It was you—you were old enough to hunt!"

But his white eyes were kneading the clouds.

I began to laugh, at first quietly, with neither bitterness nor humor. It was the laughter of one who understands a moment in his life, of one who has been let in on the secret through luck and circumstance. "You . . . you're the one." I laughed, as the secret unfolded itself. "The only one . . . you, her hunter . . ." And the wave behind my eyes broke.

Yellow Calf still looked off toward the east as though the wind could wash the wrinkles from his face. But the corners of his eyes wrinkled even more as his mouth fell open. Through my tears I could see his Adam's apple jerk.

"The only one," I whispered, and the old man's head dropped between his knees. His back shook, the bony shoulders squared and hunched like the folded wings of a hawk.

"And the half-breed, Doagie!" But the laughter again racked my throat. *He wasn't Teresa's father; it was you, Yellow Calf, the hunter!*

He turned to the sound of my laughter. His face was distorted so that the single snag seemed the only recognizable feature of the man I had come to visit. His eyes hid themselves behind the high cheekbones. His mouth had become the rubbery sneer of a jack-o'-lantern.

And so we shared this secret in the presence of ghosts, in wind that called forth the muttering tepees, the blowing snow, the white air of the horses' nostrils. The cottonwoods behind us, their dead white branches angling to the threatening clouds, sheltered these ghosts as they had sheltered the camp that winter. But there were others, so many others.

Yellow Calf stood, his hands in his pockets, suddenly withdrawn and polite. I pressed what remained of the bottle of wine into his hand. "Thank you," he said.

"You must come visit me sometime," I said.

"You are kind."

I tightened the cinch around Bird's belly. "I'll think about you," I said.

"You'd better hurry," he said. "It's coming."

I picked up the reins and led Bird to the rotting plank bridge across the irrigation ditch.

He lifted his hand.

39

Bird held his head high as he trotted down the fence line. He was anxious to get home. He was in a hurry to have a good pee and a good roll in the manure. Since growing old, he had lost his grace. With each step, I felt the leather of the saddle rub against my thighs.

It was a good time for odor. Alfalfa, sweet and dusty, came with the wind, above it the smell of rain. The old man would be lifting his nose to this odor, thinking of other things, of those days he stood by the widow when everyone else had failed her. So much distance between them, and yet they lived only three miles apart. But what created this distance? And what made me think that he was Teresa's father? After all, twenty-five years had passed between the time he had become my grandmother's hunter and Teresa's birth. They could have parted at any time. But he was the one. I knew that. The answer had come to me as if by instinct, sitting on the pump platform, watching his silent laughter, as though it was his blood in my veins that had told me.

I tried to imagine what it must have been like, the two of them, hunter and widow. If I was right about Yellow Calf's age, there couldn't have been more than four or five years separating them. If she was not yet twenty, he must have been fifteen or sixteen. Old enough to hunt, but what about the other? Could he have been more than hunter then, or did that come later? It seemed likely that they had never lived together (except perhaps that first winter out of need). There had never been any talk, none that I heard. The woman who had told me about Doagie had implied that he hadn't been Teresa's father. She hadn't mentioned Yellow Calf.

So for years the three miles must have been as close as an early morning walk down this path I was now riding. The fence hadn't been here in the beginning, nor the odor of alfalfa. But the other things, the cottonwoods and willows, the open spaces of the valley, the hills to the south, the Little Rockies, had all been here then; none had changed. Bird lifted his head and whinnied. He had settled into a gait that would have been a dance in his younger days. It was only the thudding of his hooves and the saddle rubbing against my thighs that gave him away. So for years the old man had made this trip; but could it have been twenty-five? Twenty-five years without living together, twenty-five years of an affair so solemn and secretive it had not even been rumored?

Again I thought of the time First Raise had taken me to see the old man. Again I felt the cold canvas of his coat as I clung to him, the steady clopping of the horse's hooves on the frozen path growing quieter as the wet snow began to pile up. I remembered the flour sack filled with frozen deer meat hanging from the saddle horn, and First Raise getting down to open the gate, then peeing what he said was my name in the snow. But I couldn't remember being at the shack. I couldn't remember Yellow Calf.

Yet I had felt it then, that feeling of event. Perhaps it was the distance, those three new miles, that I felt, or perhaps I had felt something of that other distance; but the event of distance was as vivid to me as the cold canvas of First Raise's coat against my cheek. He must have known then what I had just discovered. Although he told me nothing of it up to the day he died, he had taken me that snowy day to see my grandfather.

40

A glint of sunlight caught my eyes. A car was pulling off the highway onto our road. It was too far away to recognize. It looked like a dark beetle lumbering slowly over the bumps and ruts of the dusty tracks. I had reached the gate but I didn't get down. Bird pawed the ground and looked off toward the ranch. From this angle only the slough and corral were visible. Bird studied them. The buildings were hidden behind a rise in the road.

The clouds were now directly overhead, but the sun to the west was still glaring hot. The wind had died down to a steady breeze. The rain was very close.

It was Ferdinand Horn and his wife. As the dark green Hudson hit the stretch of raised road between the alfalfa fields, he honked the horn as if I had planned to disappear. He leaned out his window and waved. "Hello there, partner," he called. He turned off the motor and the car coasted to a stop. He looked up at me. "We just stopped to offer our condolences."

"What?"

Ferdinand Horn's wife leaned forward on the seat and looked up through the windshield. She had a pained look.

"Oh, the old lady!" It was strange, but I had forgotten that she was dead.

"She was a fine woman," Ferdinand Horn said. He gazed at the alfalfa field out his window.

"Teresa and Lame Bull went to Harlem to get her. They probably won't get back before dark."

"We saw them. We just came from there," he said. He seemed to be measuring the field. "A lovely woman."

Ferdinand Horn's wife stared at me through her turquoise-frame glasses. She had cocked her head to get a better look. It must have been uncomfortable.

"We're going to bury her tomorrow," I said.

"The hell you say."

"We're not doing anything fancy. You could probably come if you want to." I didn't know exactly how Teresa would act at the funeral.

"That's an idea." He turned to his wife. She nodded, still looking up through the windshield. "Oh hell, where's my manners." He fumbled in a paper sack between them. He punched two holes in the bottom of a can of beer. It had a pop-top on top. He handed it to me.

I took a sip, then a swallow, and another. The wine had left my mouth dry, and the beer was good and colder than I expected. "Jesus," I gasped. "That really hits the spot."

"I don't know what's wrong with me. What the hell are you doing on that damn plug?"

"I was just riding around. I visited Yellow Calf for a minute."

"No kidding? I thought he was dead." He looked at the field again. "How is he anyway?"

"He seems to be okay, living to the best of his ability," I said.

"You know, my cousin Louie used to bring him commodities when he worked for Reclamation. He used to regulate that head gate back by Yellow Calf's, and he'd bring him groceries. But hell, that was ten years ago—hell, twenty!"

I hadn't thought of that aspect. How did he eat now? "Maybe the new man brings him food," I said.

"He's kind of goofy, you know."

"The new man?"

"Yellow Calf."

Ferdinand Horn's wife pushed her glasses up, then wrinkled her nose to keep them there. She was holding a can of grape pop in her lap. She had wrapped a light blue hankie around it to keep her hand from getting cold or sticky.

"You have a low spot in that corner over there."

I followed his finger to an area of the field filled with slough grass and foxtail.

"Did you find her?" The muffled voice brought me back to the car.

"We're going to bury her tomorrow," I said.

"No, no," she shrieked, and hit Ferdinand Horn on the chest. "Your wife!" She hadn't taken her eyes off me. "Your wife!"

It was a stab in the heart. "I saw her . . . in Havre," I said.

"Well?"

"In Gable's . . ."

She leaned forward and toward Ferdinand Horn. Her upper lip lifted over her small brown teeth. "Was that white man with her?"

"No, she was all alone this time."

"I'll bet—"

"How many bales you get off this piece?"

"I'll bet she was all alone. As if a girl like that could ever be alone." She looked up like a muskrat through the thin ice of the windshield.

"We just came by to offer our condolences."

"Don't try to change the subject," she said, slapping Ferdinand Horn on the arm. "Did you bring her back?"

"Yes," I said. "She's in at the house now. Do you want to see her?"

"You mean you brought her back?" She sounded disappointed.

"You want to see her?"

"Did you get your gun back?" Ferdinand Horn was now looking at me.

"Yes. Do you want to see her?"

"Okay, sure, for a minute," he said.

His wife fell back against the seat. She was wearing the same wrinkled print dress she had worn the time before. Her thighs were spread beneath the bright butterflies. I couldn't see her face.

"We're late enough," she said.

"Well, just for a minute," Ferdinand Horn said.

"We just came by to offer our condolences."

Ferdinand Horn seemed puzzled. He turned toward her. Her thighs tightened. He looked up at me. Then he started the car. "How many bales you get off this piece?" he said.

41

As Bird and I rounded the bend of the slough, I could hear the calf bawling. It was almost feeding time. We passed the graveyard with its fresh dirt now turning tan beneath the rolling clouds. Bird loped straight for the corral, his ears forward and his legs stiffened. I could feel the tension in his body. I thought it was because of the storm which threatened to break at any time, but as we neared the corral, Bird pulled up short and glanced in the direction of the slough. It was the calf's mother. She was lying on her side, up to her chest in the mud. Her good eye was rimmed white and her tongue lolled from the side of her mouth. When she saw us, she made an effort to free herself, as though we had come to encourage her. Her back humped forward as her shoulders strained against the sucking mud. She switched her tail and a thin stream of crap ran down her backside.

Bird whinnied, then dropped his head, waiting for me to get down and open the gate. He had lost interest.

I wanted to ignore her. I wanted to go away, to let her drown in her own stupidity, attended only by clouds and the coming rain. If I turned away now, I thought, if I turned away—my hands trembled but did nothing. She had earned this fate by being stupid, and now no one could help her. Who would want to? As she stared at me, I saw beyond the immediate panic that hatred, that crazy hatred that made me aware of a quick hatred in my own heart. Her horns seemed tipped with blood, the dark blood of catastrophe. The muck slid down around her ears as she lowered her head, the air from her nostrils blowing puddles in the mud. I had seen her before, the image of catastrophe, the same hateful eye, the long curving horns, the wild-eyed spinster leading the cows down the hill into the valley. Stupid, stupid cow, hateful in her stupidity. She let out a long, bubbling call. I continued to glance at her, but now, as though energy, or even life, had gone out of her, she rolled her head to one side, half submerged in the mud, her one eye staring wildly at the clouds.

Stupid, stupid—

I slid down, threw open the corral gate and ran to the horse shed. The soft flaky manure cushioned the jolt of my bad leg. A rope hung from a nail driven into a two-by-four. I snatched it down and ran back to the gate. Bird was just sauntering through. I half led, half dragged him down to the edge of the slough. He seemed offended that I should ask this task of him. He tried to look around toward the pasture behind the corral. The red horse was watching us over the top pole, but there was no time to exchange horses. Already the cow lay motionless on her side.

I tied one end of the rope to the saddle horn to keep Bird from walking away, then threw open the loop to fit over the cow's head. But she would not lift it. I yelled and threw mud toward her, but she made no effort. My scalp began to sweat. A chilly breeze blew through my hair as I twirled the loop above my head. I tried for her horn but it was pointing forward toward me and the loop slid off. Again and again I threw for the horn, but the loop had nothing to tighten against. Each time I expected her to raise her head in response to the loop landing roughly against her neck and head, but she lay still. She must be dead, I thought, but the tiny bubbles around her nostrils continued to fizz. Then I was in the mud, up to my knees, wading out to the cow. With each step, the mud closed around my leg, then the heavy suck as I pulled the other free. My eyes fixed themselves on the bubbles and I prayed for them to stop so I could turn back, but the frothy mass continued to expand and move as though it were life itself. I was in up to my crotch, no longer able to lift my legs, able only to slide them through the greasy mire. The two or three inches of stagnant water sent the smell of dead things through my body. It was too late, it was taking too long—by leaning forward I could almost reach the cow's horn. One more step, the bubbles weren't moving, and I did clutch the horn, pulling myself toward her. She tried to lift her head, but the mud sucked it back down. Her open mouth, filling with slime, looked as pink as a baby mouse against the green and black. The wild eye, now trying to focus on me, was streaked with the red threads of panic.

By lifting on her horn, I managed to raise her head enough to slide the loop underneath, the mud now working to my advantage. I tightened up and yelled to Bird, at the same time pulling the rope against the saddle horn. The old horse shook his shoulders and backed up. He reared a few inches off the ground, as though the pressure of the rope had reminded him of those years spent as a cow horse. But the weight of the cow and mud began to pull the saddle forward, the back end lifting away from his body. It wouldn't hold. I gripped the taut rope and pulled myself up and out of the mud. I began to move hand over hand back toward the bank. Something had gone wrong with my knee; it wouldn't bend. I tried to arch my toes to keep my shoe from being pulled off, but there was no response. My whole leg was dead. The muscles in my arms knotted, but I continued to pull myself along the rope until I reached the edge of the bank. I lay there a moment, exhausted, then tried to get up but my arms wouldn't move. It was a dream. I couldn't move my arms. They lay at my sides, palms up, limp, as though they belonged to another body. I bent my good knee up under me, using my shoulders and chin as leverage.

Once again I yelled at Bird, but he would not come, would not slack up on the rope. I swore at him, coaxed him, reasoned with him, but I must have looked foolish to him, my ass in the air and the sweat running from my scalp.

Goddamn you, Bird, goddamn you. Goddamn Ferdinand Horn, why didn't you come in, together we could have gotten this damn cow out, why hadn't I ignored her? Goddamn your wife with her stupid turquoise glasses, stupid grape pop, your stupid car. Lame Bull! It was his cow, he had married this cow, why wasn't he here? Off riding around, playing the role, goddamn big-time operator, can't trust him, can't trust any of these damn idiots, damn Indians. Slack up, you asshole! Slack up! You want to strangle her? That's okay with me; she means nothing to me. What did I do to deserve this? Goddamn that Ferdinand Horn! Ah, Teresa, you made a terrible mistake. Your husband, your friends, your son, all worthless, none of them worth a shit. Slack up, you sonofabitch! Your mother dead, your father—you don't even know, what do you think of that? A joke, can't you see? Lame Bull! The biggest joke—can't you see that he's a joke, a joker playing a joke on you? Were you taken for a ride! Just like the rest of us, this country, all of us taken for a ride. Slack up, slack up! This greedy stupid country—

My arms began to tingle as they tried to wake up. I moved my fingers. They moved. My neck ached but the strength was returning. I crouched and spent the next few minutes planning my new life. Finally I was able to push myself from the ground and stand on my good leg. I put my weight on the other. The bones seemed to be wedged together, but it didn't hurt. I hobbled over to Bird. He raised his head and nodded wildly. As I touched his shoulder, he shied back even further.

"Here, you old sonofabitch," I said. "Do you want to defeat our purpose?"

He nodded his agreement. I hit the rope with the edge of my hand. I hit it again. He let off, dancing forward, the muscles in his shoulders working beneath the soft white hair. I looked back at the cow. She was standing up in the mud, her head, half of it black, straight up like a swimming water snake. I snapped the rope out toward her, but she didn't move. Her eyes were wild, a glaze beginning to form in them. The noose was still tight around her neck.

As I climbed aboard the horse, I noticed for the first time that it was raining. What I thought was sweat running through my scalp had been rain all along. I snapped the rope again, arcing a curve away from me toward the cow. This time the noose did loosen up. She seemed surprised. A loud gasp, as harsh as a dog's bark, came from her throat. As though that were her signal for a final death struggle, she went into action, humping her back, bawling, straining against the sucking mud. Bird tightened up on the rope and began to back away. The saddle came forward; I turned him so that he was headed away from the slough.

The rain was coming hard now, the big drops stinging the back of my neck and splattering into the dusty earth. A magpie, light and silent, flew overhead, then lit on a fence post beside the loading chute. He ruffled his sleek feathers, then squatted to watch.

The rope began to hum in the gathering wind, but the cow was coming, flailing her front legs out of the mud. Bird slipped once and almost went down, doing a strange dance, rolling quickly from side to side, but he regained his balance and continued to pull and the cow continued to come. I took another dally around the saddle horn and clung to the end of the rope. I slapped him on the shoulder. Somewhere in my mind I could hear the deep rumble of thunder, or maybe it was the rumble of energy, the rumble of guts—it didn't matter. There was only me, a white horse and a cow. The pressure of the rope against my thigh felt right. I sat to one side in the saddle, standing in the right stirrup, studying the rough strands of hemp against the pant leg. The cow had quit struggling and was now sliding slowly through the greasy mud.

Her head pointed up into the rain, but her eyes had lost that wild glare. She seemed to understand this necessary inconvenience.

It was all so smooth and natural I didn't notice that Bird had begun to slip in the rain-slick dirt. He turned sideways in an attempt to get more traction. He lowered his rump and raised his head. He lowered his head again so that he was stretched low to the ground. I leaned forward until I could smell the sweet warmth of his wet mane. Then I felt the furious digging of hooves, and I realized that he was about to go down. Before I could react, he whirled around, his front legs striking out at the air. His hind legs went out from under him. It was only the weight of the cow on the end of the rope that kept him from falling over backwards on top of me. His large white butt thumped the ground in front of me, he tottered for an instant, then he fell forward and it was quiet.

42

A flash of lightning to the south of me. I couldn't or wouldn't turn my head. I felt my back begin to stiffen. I didn't know if it was because of the fall or the damp, but I wasn't uncomfortable. The stiffness provided a reason for not moving. I saw the flash in the corner of my eye, as though it were mirrored countless times in the countless raindrops that fell on my face.

I wondered if Mose and First Raise were comfortable. They were the only ones I really loved, I thought, the only ones who were good to be with. At least the rain wouldn't bother them. But they would probably like it; they were that way, good to be with, even on a rainy day.

I heard Bird grunt twice as he tried to heave himself upright, but I couldn't find the energy to look at him. The magpie must have flown closer, for his metallic *awk! awk!* was almost conversational. The cow down in the slough had stopped gurgling. Her calf called once, a soft drone which ended on a quizzical high note. Then it was silent again.

Some people, I thought, will never know how pleasant it is to be distant in a clean rain, the driving rain of a summer storm. It's not like you'd expect, nothing like you'd expect.

1974

Bharati Mukherjee b. 1940

Bharati Mukherjee is one of the best-known South Asian American woman writers. She has stated that she wants to be viewed not as a hyphenated South Asian–American writer but as an American writer. In an interview with Bill Moyers, she commented, "I feel very American . . . I knew the moment I landed as a student in 1961 . . . that this is where I belonged. It was an instant kind of love."

One wonders, however, if one can really discard a part of one's personal/political history even in the process of transformation, especially since the past displays a tenacious, trickster-like ability to appear at the oddest times and in the most astonishing disguises. The insistence on being known as an American, without acknowledging one's Asian heritage, may grate on those who see the term "American" as denoting the *Euro*-American socio-politically dominant group only. For those of us who feel that it is absolutely necessary to continue emphasizing our essentially non-European, American identities until we are truly acknowledged as Americans with our own distinctive American presence, Mukherjee's stance may seem simplistic. Yet, as many of her stories show she is neither ignorant of nor insensitive to racism and oppression in the United States. In the interview with Moyers, she also said that "Multiculturalism, in a sense, is well intentioned, but it ends up marginalizing the person."

Mukherjee's ease with discovering her identity as a mainstream American, her skill with the dialogues and incidents familiar to the dominant society, her refusal to be marginalized, and her absolute mastery of English are not surprising when one looks at her biography. She was born in 1940 to an upper-middle-class Brahmin family in Calcutta. Her education in India was at a convent school run by Irish nuns. She was also educated in England and Switzerland. She came to the United States in 1961 to attend the Writer's Workshop at the University of Iowa, where she received an M.F.A. in creative writing and a Ph.D. in English and comparative literature. She and her husband, the Canadian writer Clark Blaise, lived in Canada from 1966 to 1980. They emigrated to the United States in 1980. Mukherjee teaches in the English Department at the University of California, Berkeley.

Mukherjee's first novel, *The Tiger's Daughter,* portrays Tara Banerjee Cartwright, a Western-educated, well-to-do Bengali woman married to an American. Her second novel, *Wife,* begins in Bengal, with the following opening sentence, which would do credit to Jane Austen: "Dimple Dasgupta had set her heart on marrying a neuro-surgeon, but her father was looking for engineers in the matrimonial ads." Her novels *Holder of the World, Jasmine,* and *Leave It to Me,* and her brilliantly written collections of short stories, *Darkness* and *Middleman and Other Stories,* extend Mukherjee's discussion into the more violent and grotesque yet very real aspects of collisions between cultures at different times in the histories of India and the United States.

"A Wife's Story" is a carefully crafted narrative, with an interesting twist: the wife comes to America to study, and the husband comes to visit her. The story begins with Panna watching a play that insults Indian men and women. It ends with Panna waiting for her husband, who is leaving for India the next morning without her, to make love to her: "The water is running in the bathroom. In the ten days he has been here he has learned American rites: deodorants, fragrances." Panna ends her narrative with "I am free, afloat, watching somebody else." One hears echoes of Mukherjee's statement about America being a place where one can choose "to discard . . . history . . . and invent a whole new history for myself." As Panna glories in her beautiful body and her freedom, one is haunted by the question of the price and texture of her freedom. "A Wife's Story," like many of the other stories by Mukherjee, leaves the narrative unresolved and open for discussion. It also raises important questions about the forging of cultural, national, and sexual alliances in a United States that glorifies individual freedom and urges the loss of a racial and ethnic memory that is not Eurocentric.

Roshni Rustomji-Kerns
Sonoma State University

PRIMARY WORKS

The Tiger's Daughter, 1971; *Wife*, 1975; *Days and Nights in Calcutta* (coauthored with Clark Blaise), 1977; *Darkness*, 1985; *The Sorrow and the Terror: The Haunting Legacy of the Air India Tragedy*, 1987; *The Middleman and Other Stories*, 1988; *Jasmine*, 1989; *Holder of the World*, 1993; *Leave It to Me*, 1997; *Desirable Daughters*, 2002; *The Tree Bride*, 2004.

A Wife's Story

Imre says forget it, but I'm going to write David Mamet.[1] So Patels are hard to sell real estate to. You buy them a beer, whisper Glengarry Glen Ross, and they smell swamp instead of sun and surf. They work hard, eat cheap, live ten to a room, stash their savings under futons in Queens, and before you know it they own half of Hoboken. You say, where's the sweet gullibility that made this nation great?

Polish jokes, Patel jokes: that's not why I want to write Mamet.

Seen their women?

Everybody laughs. Imre laughs. The dozing fat man with the Barnes & Noble sack between his legs, the woman next to him, the usher, everybody. The theater isn't so dark that they can't see me. In my red silk sari I'm conspicuous. Plump, gold paisleys sparkle on my chest.

The actor is just warming up. *Seen their women?* He plays a salesman, he's had a bad day and now he's in a Chinese restaurant trying to loosen up. His face is pink. His wool-blend slacks are creased at the crotch. We bought our tickets at half-price, we're sitting in the front row, but at the edge, and we see things we shouldn't be seeing. At least I do, or think I do. Spittle, actors goosing each other, little winks, streaks of makeup.

Maybe they're improvising dialogue too. Maybe Mamet's provided them with insult kits, Thursdays for Chinese, Wednesdays for Hispanics, today for Indians. Maybe they get together before curtain time, see an Indian woman settling in the front row off to the side, and say to each other: "Hey, forget Friday. Let's get *her* today. See if she cries. See if she walks out." Maybe, like the salesmen they play, they have a little bet on.

---

[1] David Mamet (b. 1947) is an American playwright, essayist, and film director. The narrator is referring to his 1984 play *Glengarry Glen Ross*, which is about the ethics of real estate salesmen. "Patel" is an Indian title (also a surname) that refers generally to a landowning caste.

Maybe I shouldn't feel betrayed.

Their women, he goes again. *They look like they've just been fucked by a dead cat.* The fat man hoots so hard he nudges my elbow off our shared armrest.

"Imre. I'm going home." But Imre's hunched so far forward he doesn't hear. English isn't his best language. A refugee from Budapest, he has to listen hard. "I didn't pay eighteen dollars to be insulted."

I don't hate Mamet. It's the tyranny of the American dream that scares me. First, you don't exist. Then you're invisible. Then you're funny. Then you're disgusting. Insult, my American friends will tell me, is a kind of acceptance. No instant dignity here. A play like this, back home, would cause riots. Communal, racist, and antisocial. The actors wouldn't make it off stage. This play, and all these awful feelings, would be safely locked up.

I long, at times, for clear-cut answers. Offer me instant dignity, today, and I'll take it.

"What?" Imre moves toward me without taking his eyes off the actor. "Come again?"

Tears come. I want to stand, scream, make an awful scene. I long for ugly, nasty rage.

The actor is ranting, flinging spittle. *Give me a chance. I'm not finished, I can get back on the board. I tell that asshole, give me a real lead. And what does that asshole give me? Patels. Nothing but Patels.*

This time Imre works an arm around my shoulders. "Panna, what is Patel? Why are you taking it all so personally?"

I shrink from his touch, but I don't walk out. Expensive girls' schools in Lausanne and Bombay have trained me to behave well. My manners are exquisite, my feelings are delicate, my gestures refined, my moods undetectable. They have seen me through riots, uprootings, separation, my son's death.

"I'm not taking it personally."

The fat man looks at us. The woman looks too, and shushes.

I stare back at the two of them. Then I stare, mean and cool, at the man's elbow. Under the bright blue polyester Hawaiian shirt sleeve, the elbow looks soft and runny. "Excuse me," I say. My voice has the effortless meanness of well-bred displaced Third World women, though my rhetoric has been learned elsewhere. "You're exploiting my space."

Startled, the man snatches his arm away from me. He cradles it against his breast. By the time he's ready with comebacks, I've turned my back on him. I've probably ruined the first act for him. I know I've ruined it for Imre.

It's not my fault; it's the *situation.* Old colonies wear down. Patels—the new pioneers—have to be suspicious. Idi Amin's lesson is permanent. AT&T wires move good advice from continent to continent. Keep all assets liquid. Get into 7-11s, get out of condos and motels. I know how both sides feel, that's the trouble. The Patel sniffing out scams, the sad salesmen on the stage: postcolonialism has made me their referee. It's hate I long for; simple, brutish, partisan hate.

After the show Imre and I make our way toward Broadway. Sometimes he holds my hand; it doesn't mean anything more than that crazies and drunks are crouched in doorways. Imre's been here over two years, but he's stayed very old-world, very courtly, openly protective of women. I met him in a seminar on special ed. last semester. His wife is a nurse somewhere in the Hungarian countryside. There are two sons, and miles of petitions for their emigration. My husband manages a mill two hundred miles north of Bombay. There are no children.

"You make things tough on yourself," Imre says. He assumed Patel was a Jewish name or maybe Hispanic; everything makes equal sense to him. He found the play tasteless, he worried about the effect of vulgar language on my sensitive ears. "You have to let go a bit." And as though to show me how to let go, he breaks away from me, bounds ahead with his head ducked tight, then dances on amazingly jerky legs. He's a Magyar, he often tells me, and deep down, he's an Asian too. I catch glimpses of it, knife-blade Attila cheekbones, despite the blondish hair. In his faded jeans and leather jacket, he's a rock video star. I watch MTV for hours in the apartment when Charity's working the evening shift at Macy's. I listen to WPLJ on Charity's earphones. Why should I be ashamed? Television in India is so uplifting.

Imre stops as suddenly as he'd started. People walk around us. The summer sidewalk is full of theatergoers in seersucker suits; Imre's year-round jacket is out of place. European. Cops in twos and threes huddle, lightly tap their thighs with night sticks and smile at me with benevolence. I want to wink at them, get us all in trouble, tell them the crazy dancing man is from the Warsaw Pact. I'm too shy to break into dance on Broadway. So I hug Imre instead.

The hug takes him by surprise. He wants me to let go, but he doesn't really expect me to let go. He staggers, though I weigh no more than 104 pounds, and with him, I pitch forward slightly. Then he catches me, and we walk arm in arm to the bus stop. My husband would never dance or hug a woman on Broadway. Nor would my brothers. They aren't stuffy people, but they went to Anglican boarding schools and they have a well-developed sense of what's silly.

"Imre." I squeeze his big, rough hand. "I'm sorry I ruined the evening for you."

"You did nothing of the kind." He sounds tired. "Let's not wait for the bus. Let's splurge and take a cab instead."

Imre always has unexpected funds. The Network, he calls it, Class of '56.

In the back of the cab, without even trying, I feel light, almost free. Memories of Indian destitutes mix with the hordes of New York street people, and they float free, like astronauts, inside my head. I've made it. I'm making something of my life. I've left home, my husband, to get a Ph.D. in special ed. I have a multiple-entry visa and a small scholarship for two years. After that, we'll see. My mother was beaten by her mother-in-law, my grandmother, when she'd registered for French lessons at the Alliance Française. My grandmother, the eldest daughter of a rich zamindar, was illiterate.

Imre and the cabdriver talk away in Russian. I keep my eyes closed. That way I can feel the floaters better. I'll write Mamet tonight. I feel strong, reckless. Maybe I'll write Steven Spielberg too; tell him that Indians don't eat monkey brains.

We've made it. Patels must have made it. Mamet, Spielberg: they're not condescending to us. Maybe they're a little bit afraid.

Charity Chin, my roommate, is sitting on the floor drinking Chablis out of a plastic wineglass. She is five foot six, three inches taller than me, but weighs a kilo and a half less than I do. She is a "hands" model. Orientals are supposed to have a monopoly in the hands-modelling business, she says. She had her eyes fixed eight or nine months ago and out of gratitude sleeps with her plastic surgeon every third Wednesday.

"Oh, good," Charity says. "I'm glad you're back early. I need to talk."

She's been writing checks. MCI, Con Ed, Bonwit Teller. Envelopes, already stamped and sealed, form a pyramid between her shapely, knee-socked legs. The checkbook's cover is brown plastic, grained to look like cowhide. Each time Charity flips back the cover, white geese fly over sky-colored checks. She makes good money, but she's extravagant. The difference adds up to this shared, rent-controlled Chelsea one-bedroom.

"All right. Talk."

When I first moved in, she was seeing an analyst. Now she sees a nutritionist.

"Eric called. From Oregon."

"What did he want?"

"He wants me to pay half the rent on his loft for last spring. He asked me to move back, remember? He *begged* me."

Eric is Charity's estranged husband.

"What does your nutritionist say?" Eric now wears a red jumpsuit and tills the soil in Rajneeshpuram.

"You think Phil's a creep too, don't you? What else can he be when creeps are all I attract?"

Phil is a flutist with thinning hair. He's very touchy on the subject of *flautists* versus *flutists*. He's touchy on every subject, from music to books to foods to clothes. He teaches at a small college upstate, and Charity bought a used blue Datsun ("Nissan," Phil insists) last month so she could spend weekends with him. She returns every Sunday night, exhausted and exasperated. Phil and I don't have much to say to each other—he's the only musician I know; the men in my family are lawyers, engineers, or in business—but I like him. Around me, he loosens up. When he visits, he bakes us loaves of pumpernickel bread. He waxes our kitchen floor. Like many men in this country, he seems to me a displaced child, or even a woman, looking for something that passed him by, or for something that he can never have. If he thinks I'm not looking, he sneaks his hands under Charity's sweater, but there isn't too much there. Here, she's a model with high ambitions. In India, she'd be a flat-chested old maid.

I'm shy in front of the lovers. A darkness comes over me when I see them horsing around.

"It isn't the money," Charity says. Oh? I think. "He says he still loves me. Then he turns around and asks me for five hundred."

What's so strange about that, I want to ask. She still loves Eric, and Eric, red jump suit and all, is smart enough to know it. Love is a commodity, hoarded like any other. Mamet knows. But I say, "I'm not the person to ask about love." Charity knows that mine was a traditional Hindu marriage. My parents, with the help of a marriage broker, who was my mother's cousin, picked out a groom. All I had to do was get to know his taste in food.

It'll be a long evening, I'm afraid. Charity likes to confess. I unpleat my silk sari—it no longer looks too showy—wrap it in muslin cloth and put it away in a dresser drawer. Saris are hard to have laundered in Manhattan, though there's a good man in Jackson Heights. My next step will be to brew us a pot of chrysanthemum tea. It's a very special tea from the mainland. Charity's uncle gave it to us. I like him. He's a humpbacked, awkward, terrified man. He runs a gift store on Mott Street, and though he doesn't speak much English, he seems to have done well. Once upon a time he worked for the railways in Chengdu, Szechwan Province, and during the Wuchang Uprising, he was shot at. When I'm down, when I'm lonely for my husband, when I think of our son, or when I need to be held, I think of Charity's uncle. If I hadn't left home, I'd never have heard of the Wuchang Uprising. I've broadened my horizons.

Very late that night my husband calls me from Ahmadabad, a town of textile mills north of Bombay. My husband is a vice president at Lakshmi Cotton Mills. Lakshmi is the goddess of wealth, but LCM (Priv.), Ltd., is doing poorly. Lockouts, strikes, rock-throwings. My husband lives on digitalis, which he calls the food for our *yuga* of discontent.

"We had a bad mishap at the mill today." Then he says nothing for seconds.

The operator comes on. "Do you have the right party, sir? We're trying to reach Mrs. Butt."

"Bhatt," I insist. "*B* for Bombay, *H* for Haryana, *A* for Ahmadabad, double *T* for Tamil Nadu." It's a litany. "This is she."

"One of our lorries was firebombed today. Resulting in three deaths. The driver, old Karamchand, and his two children."

I know how my husband's eyes look this minute, how the eye rims sag and the yellow corneas shine and bulge with pain. He is not an emotional man—the Ahmadabad Institute of Management has trained him to cut losses, to look on the bright side of economic catastrophes—but tonight he's feeling low. I try to remember a driver named Karamchand, but can't. That part of my life is over, the way *trucks* have replaced *lorries* in my vocabulary, the way Charity Chin and her lurid love life have replaced inherited notions of marital duty. Tomorrow he'll come out of it. Soon he'll be eating again. He'll sleep like a baby. He's been trained to believe in turnovers. Every morning he rubs his scalp with cantharidine oil so his hair will grow back again.

"It could be your car next." Affection, love. Who can tell the difference in a traditional marriage in which a wife still doesn't call her husband by his first name?

"No. They know I'm a flunky, just like them. Well paid, maybe. No need for undue anxiety, please."

Then his voice breaks. He says he needs me, he misses me, he wants me to come to him damp from my evening shower, smelling of sandalwood soap, my braid decorated with jasmines.

"I need you too."

"Not to worry, please," he says. "I am coming in a fortnight's time. I have already made arrangements."

Outside my window, fire trucks whine, up Eighth Avenue. I wonder if he can hear them, what he thinks of a life like mine, led amid disorder.

"I am thinking it'll be like a honeymoon. More or less."

When I was in college, waiting to be married, I imagined honeymoons were only for the more fashionable girls, the girls who came from slightly racy families, smoked Sobranies in the dorm lavatories and put up posters of Kabir Bedi, who was supposed to have made it as a big star in the West. My husband wants us to go to Niagara. I'm not to worry about foreign exchange. He's arranged for extra dollars through the Gujarati Network, with a cousin in San Jose. And he's bought four hundred more on the black market. "Tell me you need me. Panna, please tell me again."

* * *

I change out of the cotton pants and shirt I've been wearing all day and put on a sari to meet my husband at JFK. I don't forget the jewelry; the marriage necklace of mangalsutra, gold drop earrings, heavy gold bangles. I don't wear them every day. In this borough of vice and greed, who knows when, or whom, desire will overwhelm.

My husband spots me in the crowd and waves. He has lost weight, and changed his glasses. The arm, uplifted in a cheery wave, is bony, frail, almost opalescent.

In the Carey Coach, we hold hands. He strokes my fingers one by one. "How come you aren't wearing my mother's ring?"

"Because muggers know about Indian women," I say. They know with us it's 24-karat. His mother's ring is showy, in ghastly taste anywhere but India: a blood-red Burma ruby set in a gold frame of floral sprays. My mother-in-law got her guru to bless the ring before I left for the States.

He looks disconcerted. He's used to a different role. He's the knowing, suspicious one in the family. He seems to be sulking, and finally he comes out with it. "You've said nothing about my new glasses." I compliment him on the glasses, how chic and Western-executive they make him look. But I can't help the other things, necessities until he learns the ropes. I handle the money, buy the tickets. I don't know if this makes me unhappy.

Charity drives her Nissan upstate, so for two weeks we are to have the apartment to ourselves. This is more privacy than we ever had in India. No parents, no servants, to keep us modest. We play at housekeeping. Imre has lent us a hibachi, and I grill saffron chicken breasts. My husband marvels at the size of the Perdue hens. "They're big like peacocks, no? These Americans, they're really something!" He tries out pizzas, burgers, McNuggets. He chews. He explores. He judges. He loves it all, fears nothing, feels at home in the summer odors, the clutter of Manhattan streets. Since he thinks that the American palate is bland, he carries a bottle of red peppers in his pocket. I wheel a shopping cart down the aisles of the neighborhood Grand Union, and he follows, swiftly, greedily. He picks up hair rinses and high-protein diet powders. There's so much I already take for granted.

One night, Imre stops by. He wants us to go with him to a movie. In his work shirt and red leather tie, he looks arty or strung out. It's only been a week, but I feel as though I am really seeing him for the first time. The yellow hair worn very short at the sides, the wide, narrow lips. He's a good-looking man, but self-conscious, almost arrogant. He's picked the movie we should see. He always tells me what to see, what to read. He buys the *Voice*. He's a natural avant-gardist. For tonight he's chosen *Numéro Deux*.

"Is it a musical?" my husband asks. The Radio City Music Hall is on his list of sights to see. He's read up on the history of the Rockettes. He doesn't catch Imre's sympathetic wink.

Guilt, shame, loyalty. I long to be ungracious, not ingratiate myself with both men.

That night my husband calculates in rupees the money we've wasted on Godard. "That refugee fellow, Nagy, must have a screw loose in his head. I paid very steep price for dollars on the black market."

Some afternoons we go shopping. Back home we hated shopping, but now it is a lovers' project. My husband's shopping list startles me. I feel I am just getting to know him. Maybe, like Imre, freed from the dignities of old-world culture, he too could get drunk and squirt Cheez Whiz on a guest. I watch him dart into stores in his gleaming leather shoes. Jockey shorts on sale in outdoor bins on Broadway entrance him. White tube socks with different bands of color delight him. He looks for microcassettes, for anything small and electronic and smuggleable. He needs a garment bag. He calls it a "wardrobe," and I have to translate.

"All of New York is having sales, no?"

My heart speeds watching him this happy. It's the third week in August, almost the end of summer, and the city smells ripe, it cannot bear more heat, more money, more energy.

"This is so smashing! The prices are so excellent!" Recklessly, my prudent husband signs away traveller's checks. How he intends to smuggle it all back I don't dare ask. With a microwave, he calculates, we could get rid of our cook.

This has to be love, I think. Charity, Eric, Phil: they may be experts on sex. My husband doesn't chase me around the sofa, but he pushes me down on Charity's battered cushions, and the man who has never entered the kitchen of our Ahmadabad house now comes toward me with a dish tub of steamy water to massage away the pavement heat.

Ten days into his vacation my husband checks out brochures for sightseeing tours. Shortline, Grayline, Crossroads: his new vinyl briefcase is full of schedules and pamphlets. While I make pancakes out of a mix, he comparison-shops. Tour number one costs $10.95 and will give us the World Trade Center, Chinatown, and the United Nations. Tour number three would take us both uptown *and* downtown for $14.95, but my husband is absolutely sure he doesn't want to see Harlem. We settle for tour number four: Downtown and the Dame. It's offered by a new tour company with a small, dirty office at Eighth and Forty-eighth.

The sidewalk outside the office is colorful with tourists. My husband sends me in to buy the tickets because he has come to feel Americans don't understand his accent.

The dark man, Lebanese probably, behind the counter comes on too friendly. "Come on, doll, make my day!" He won't say which tour is his. "Number four? Honey, no! Look, you've wrecked me! Say you'll change your mind." He takes two twenties and gives back change. He holds the tickets, forcing me to pull. He leans closer. "I'm off after lunch."

My husband must have been watching me from the sidewalk. "What was the chap saying?" he demands. "I told you not to wear pants. He thinks you are Puerto Rican. He thinks he can treat you with disrespect."

The bus is crowded and we have to sit across the aisle from each other. The tour guide begins his patter on Forty-sixth. He looks like an actor, his hair bleached and blow-dried. Up close he must look middle-aged, but from where I sit his skin is smooth and his cheeks faintly red.

"Welcome to the Big Apple, folks." The guide uses a microphone. "Big Apple. That's what we native Manhattan degenerates call our city. Today we have guests from fifteen foreign countries and six states from this U.S. of A. That makes the Tourist Bureau real happy. And let me assure you that while we may be the richest city in the richest country in the world, it's okay to tip your charming and talented attendant." He laughs. Then he swings his hip out into the aisle and sings a song.

"And it's mighty fancy on old Delancey Street, you know. . . ."

My husband looks irritable. The guide is, as expected, a good singer. "The bloody man should be giving us histories of buildings we are passing, no?" I pat his hand, the mood passes. He cranes his neck. Our window seats have both gone to Japanese. It's the tour of his life. Next to this, the quick business trips to Manchester and Glasgow pale.

"And tell me what street compares to Mott Street, in July. . . ."

The guide wants applause. He manages a derisive laugh from the Americans up front. He's working the aisles now. "I coulda been somebody, right? I coulda been a star!" Two or three of us smile, those of us who recognize the parody. He catches my smile. The sun is on his harsh, bleached hair. "Right, your highness? Look, we gotta maharani with us! Couldn't I have been a star?"

"Right!" I say, my voice coming out a squeal. I've been trained to adapt; what else can I say?

We drive through traffic past landmark office buildings and churches. The guide flips his hands. "Art deco," he keeps saying. I hear him confide to one of the Americans: "Beats me. I went to a cheap guide's school." My husband wants to know more about this Art Deco, but the guide sings another song.

"We made a foolish choice," my husband grumbles. "We are sitting in the bus only. We're not going into famous buildings." He scrutinizes the pamphlets in his jacket pocket. I think, at least it's air-conditioned in here. I could sit here in the cool shadows of the city forever.

Only five of us appear to have opted for the "Downtown and the Dame" tour. The others will ride back uptown past the United Nations after we've been dropped off at the pier for the ferry to the Statue of Liberty.

An elderly European pulls a camera out of his wife's designer tote bag. He takes pictures of the boats in the harbor, the Japanese in kimonos eating popcorn, scavenging pigeons, me. Then, pushing his wife ahead of him, he climbs back on the bus and waves to us. For a second I feel terribly lost. I wish we were on the bus going back to the apartment. I know I'll not be able to describe any of this to Charity, or to Imre. I'm too proud to admit I went on a guided tour.

The view of the city from the Circle Line ferry is seductive, unreal. The skyline wavers out of reach, but never quite vanishes. The summer sun pushes through fluffy clouds and dapples the glass of office towers. My husband looks thrilled, even more than he had on the shopping trips down Broadway. Tourists and dreamers, we have spent our life's savings to see this skyline, this statue.

"Quick, take a picture of me!" my husband yells as he moves toward a gap of railings. A Japanese matron has given up her position in order to change film. "Before the Twin Towers disappear!"

I focus, I wait for a large Oriental family to walk out of my range. My husband holds his pose tight against the railing. He wants to look relaxed, an international businessman at home in all the financial markets.

A bearded man slides across the bench toward me. "Like this," he says and helps me get my husband in focus. "You want me to take the photo for you?" His name, he says, is Goran. He is Goran from Yugoslavia, as though that were enough for tracking him down. Imre from Hungary. Panna from India. He pulls the old Leica out of my hand, signaling the Orientals to beat it, and clicks away. "I'm a photographer," he says. He could have been a camera thief. That's what my husband would have assumed. Somehow, I trusted. "Get you a beer?" he asks.

"I don't. Drink, I mean. Thank you very much." I say those last words very loud, for everyone's benefit. The odd bottles of Soave with Imre don't count.

"Too bad." Goran gives back the camera.

"Take one more!" my husband shouts from the railing. "Just to be sure!"

The island itself disappoints. The Lady has brutal scaffolding holding her in. The museum is closed. The snack bar is dirty and expensive. My husband reads out the prices to me. He orders two french fries and two Cokes. We sit at picnic tables and wait for the ferry to take us back.

"What was that hippie chap saying?"

As if I could say. A day-care center has brought its kids, at least forty of them, to the island for the day. The kids, all wearing name tags, run around us. I can't help noticing how many are Indian. Even a Patel, probably a Bhatt if I looked hard enough. They toss hamburger bits at pigeons. They kick styrofoam cups. The pigeons are slow, greedy, persistent. I have to shoo one off the table top. I don't think my husband thinks about our son.

"What hippie?"

"The one on the boat. With the beard and the hair."

My husband doesn't look at me. He shakes out his paper napkin and tries to protect his french fries from pigeon feathers.

"Oh, him. He said he was from Dubrovnik." It isn't true, but I don't want trouble.

"What did he say about Dubrovnik?"

I know enough about Dubrovnik to get by. Imre's told me about it. And about Mostar and Zagreb. In Mostar white Muslims sing the call to prayer. I would like to see that before I die: white Muslims. Whole peoples have moved before me; they've adapted. The night Imre told me about Mostar was also the night I saw my first snow in Manhattan. We'd walked down to Chelsea from Columbia. We'd walked and talked and I hadn't felt tired at all.

"You're too innocent," my husband says. He reaches for my hand. "Panna," he cries with pain in his voice, and I am brought back from perfect, floating memories of snow, "I've come to take you back. I have seen how men watch you."

"What?"

"Come back, now. I have tickets. We have all the things we will ever need. I can't live without you."

A little girl with wiry braids kicks a bottle cap at his shoes. The pigeons wheel and scuttle around us. My husband covers his fries with spread-out fingers. "No kicking," he tells the girl. Her name, Beulah, is printed in green ink on a heart-shaped name tag. He forces a smile, and Beulah smiles back. Then she starts to flap her arms. She flaps, she hops. The pigeons go crazy for fries and scraps.

"Special ed. course is two years," I remind him. "I can't go back."

My husband picks up our trays and throws them into the garbage before I can stop him. He's carried disposability a little too far. "We've been taken," he says, moving toward the dock, though the ferry will not arrive for another twenty minutes. "The ferry costs only two dollars round-trip per person. We should have chosen tour number one for $10.95 instead of tour number four for $14.95."

With my Lebanese friend, I think. "But this way we don't have to worry about cabs. The bus will pick us up at the pier and take us back to midtown. Then we can walk home."

"New York is full of cheats and whatnot. Just like Bombay." He is not accusing me of infidelity. I feel dread all the same.

That night, after we've gone to bed, the phone rings. My husband listens, then hands the phone to me. "What is this woman saying?" He turns on the pink Macy's lamp by the bed. "I am not understanding these Negro people's accents."

The operator repeats the message. It's a cable from one of the directors of Lakshmi Cotton Mills. "Massive violent labor confrontation anticipated. Stop. Return posthaste. Stop. Cable flight details. Signed Kantilal Shah."

"It's not your factory," I say. "You're supposed to be on vacation."

"So, you are worrying about me? Yes? You reject my heartfelt wishes but you worry about me?" He pulls me close, slips the straps of my nightdress off my shoulder. "Wait a minute."

I wait, unclothed, for my husband to come back to me. The water is running in the bathroom. In the ten days he has been here he has learned American rites: deodorants, fragrances. Tomorrow morning he'll call Air India; tomorrow evening he'll be on his way back to Bombay. Tonight I should make up to him for my years away, the gutted trucks, the degree I'll never use in India. I want to pretend with him that nothing has changed.

In the mirror that hangs on the bathroom door, I watch my naked body turn, the breasts, the thighs glow. The body's beauty amazes. I stand here shameless, in ways he has never seen me. I am free, afloat, watching somebody else.

1988

Maxine Hong Kingston b. 1940

Born in Stockton, California, in 1940, Maxine Ting Ting Hong is the eldest of six surviving children of Tom Hong (scholar, laundry man, and manager of a gambling house) and Ying Lan Chew (midwife, laundress, field hand). She earned a B.A. from the University of California at Berkeley in 1962 and a teaching certificate in 1965. She has lived and worked both in California and in Honolulu, Hawaii.

Author of three award-winning books, The Woman Warrior (1976), China Men (1980), and Tripmaster Monkey (1989), Maxine Hong Kingston is undoubtedly the most-recognized Asian American writer today. Her work attracts attention from many arenas: Chinese Americans, feminist scholars, literary critics, and the media. In 1977 Kingston won the Mademoiselle Magazine Award, in 1978 the Anisfield-Wolf Book Award. In 1980 she was proclaimed Living Treasure of Hawaii. The Woman Warrior received the National Book Critics' Circle Award for the best book of nonfiction in 1976, and Time magazine proclaimed it one of the top ten nonfiction works of the decade. It is, however, a collage of fiction and fact, memory and imagination—a hybrid genre of Kingston's own devising. Through the Chinese legends and family stories that marked her childhood and the mysterious old-world customs that her mother enforced but did not explain, through Kingston's own experiences and her imaginative and poetic flights, *The Woman Warrior* details the complexities and difficulties in Kingston's development as a woman and as a Chinese American. It focuses on a difficult and finally reconciled mother/daughter relationship.

Kingston's second book, *China Men,* focuses on men and is shaped by a rather uncommunicative father/daughter relationship. It depends heavily on family history, American laws, and imaginative projections based loosely on historical fact. Its purpose, Kingston has stated, is to "claim America" for Chinese Americans by showing how indebted America is to the labor of Chinese men, her great-grandfathers and grandfathers, who cleared jungle for the sugar plantations in Hawaii, who split rock and hammered steel to build railroads in the United States, who created fertile farmland out of swamp and desert, yet faced fierce discrimination and persecution. In this text, too, Kingston blends myth and fact, autobiography and fiction, blurring the usual dividing lines.

In *Tripmaster Monkey,* her first novel, Kingston again blends Chinese myth with American reality. She combines allusions to a Chinese classic, *Monkey* or *Journey to the West,* the story of a magical, mischievous monkey who accompanies a monk to India for the sacred books of Buddhism, with the life of a 1960s Berkeley beatnik playwright.

Amy Ling
University of Wisconsin at Madison

King-Kok Cheung
University of California, Los Angeles

PRIMARY WORKS

The Woman Warrior: Memoirs of a Girlhood among Ghosts, 1975; *China Men,* 1980; *Hawai'i One Summer,* 1987; *Tripmaster Monkey: His Fake Book,* 1989; *To Be the Poet,* 2002; *The Fifth Book of Peace,* 2003.

No Name Woman

"You must not tell anyone," my mother said, "what I am about to tell you. In China your father had a sister who killed herself. She jumped into the family well. We say that your father has all brothers because it is as if she had never been born.

"In 1924 just a few days after our village celebrated seventeen hurry-up weddings—to make sure that every young man who went 'out on the road' would responsibly come home—your father and his brothers and your grandfather and his brothers and your aunt's new husband sailed for America, the Gold Mountain. It was your grandfather's last trip. Those lucky enough to get contracts waved good-bye from the decks. They fed and guarded the stowaways and helped them off in Cuba, New York, Bali, Hawaii. 'We'll meet in California next year,' they said. All of them sent money home.

"I remember looking at your aunt one day when she and I were dressing; I had not noticed before that she had such a protruding melon of a stomach. But I did not think, 'She's pregnant,' until she began to look like other pregnant women, her shirt pulling and the white tops of her black pants showing. She could not have been pregnant, you see, because her husband had been gone for years. No one said any-thing. We did not discuss it. In early summer she was ready to have the child, long after the time when it could have been possible.

"The village had also been counting. On the night the baby was to be born the villagers raided our house. Some were crying. Like a great saw, teeth strung with lights, files of people walked zigzag across our land, tearing the rice. Their lanterns doubled in the disturbed black water, which drained away through the broken bunds. As the villagers closed in, we could see that some of them, probably men and women we knew well, wore white masks. The people with long hair hung it over their faces. Women with short hair made it stand up on end. Some had tied white bands around their foreheads, arms, and legs.

"At first they threw mud and rocks at the house. Then they threw eggs and be-gan slaughtering our stock. We could hear the animals scream their deaths—the roosters, the pigs, a last great roar from the ox. Familiar wild heads flared in our night windows; the villagers encircled us. Some of the faces stopped to peer at us, their eyes rushing like searchlights. The hands flattened against the panes, framed heads, and left red prints.

"The villagers broke in the front and the back doors at the same time, even though we had not locked the doors against them. Their knives dripped with the blood of our animals. They smeared the blood on the doors and walls. One woman swung a chicken, whose throat she had slit, splattering blood in red arcs about her. We stood together in the middle of our house, in the family hall with the pictures and tables of the ancestors around us, and looked straight ahead.

"At that time the house had only two wings. When the men came back, we would build two more to enclose our courtyard and a third one to begin a second courtyard. The villagers pushed through both wings, even your grandparents' rooms, to find your aunt's, which was also mine until the men returned. From this room a new wing for one of the younger families would grow. They ripped up her clothes and shoes and broke her combs, grinding them underfoot. They tore her work from the loom. They scattered the cooking fire and rolled the new weaving in it. We could hear them in the kitchen breaking our bowls and banging the pots. They overturned the great waist-high earthenware jugs; duck eggs, pickled fruits, vegetables burst out and mixed in acrid torrents. The old woman from the next field swept a broom through the air and loosed the spirits-of-the-broom over our heads. 'Pig.' 'Ghost.' 'Pig,' they sobbed and scolded while they ruined our house.

"When they left, they took sugar and oranges to bless themselves. They cut pieces from the dead animals. Some of them took bowls that were not broken and clothes that were not torn. Afterward we swept up the rice and sewed it back up into sacks. But the smells from the spilled preserves lasted. Your aunt gave birth in the pigsty that night. The next morning when I went for the water, I found her and the baby plugging up the family well.

"Don't let your father know that I told you. He denies her. Now that you have started to menstruate, what happened to her could happen to you. Don't humiliate us. You wouldn't like to be forgotten as if you had never been born. The villagers are watchful."

Whenever she had to warn us about life, my mother told stories that ran like this one, a story to grow up on. She tested our strength to establish realities. Those in the emigrant generations who could not reassert brute survival died young and far from home. Those of us in the first American generations have had to figure out how the invisible world the emigrants built around our childhoods fits in solid America.

The emigrants confused the gods by diverting their curses, misleading them with crooked streets and false names. They must try to confuse their offspring as well, who, I suppose, threaten them in similar ways—always trying to get things straight, always trying to name the unspeakable. The Chinese I know hide their names; sojourners take new names when their lives change and guard their real names with silence.

Chinese-Americans, when you try to understand what things in you are Chinese, how do you separate what is peculiar to childhood, to poverty, insanities, one family, your mother who marked your growing up with stories, from what is Chinese? What is Chinese tradition and what is the movies?

If I want to learn what clothes my aunt wore, whether flashy or ordinary, I would have to begin, "Remember Father's drowned-in-the-well sister?" I cannot ask that. My mother has told me once and for all the useful parts. She will add nothing unless powered by Necessity, a riverbank that guides her life. She plants vegetable gardens rather than lawns; she carries the odd-shaped tomatoes home from the fields and eats food left for the gods.

Whenever we did frivolous things, we used up energy; we flew high kites. We children came up off the ground over the melting cones our parents brought home from work and the American movie on New Year's Day—*Oh, You Beautiful Doll* with Betty Grable one year, and *She Wore a Yellow Ribbon* with John Wayne another year. After the one carnival ride each, we paid in guilt; our tired father counted his change on the dark walk home.

Adultery is extravagance. Could people who hatch their own chicks and eat the embryos and the heads for delicacies and boil the feet in vinegar for party food, leaving only the gravel, eating even the gizzard lining—could such people engender a prodigal aunt? To be a woman, to have a daughter in starvation time was a waste enough. My aunt could not have been the lone romantic who gave up everything for sex. Women in the old China did not choose. Some man had commanded her to lie with him and be his secret evil. I wonder whether he masked himself when he joined the raid on her family.

Perhaps she had encountered him in the fields or on the mountain where the daughters-in-law collected fuel. Or perhaps he first noticed her in the marketplace. He was not a stranger because the village housed no strangers. She had to have dealings with him other than sex. Perhaps he worked an adjoining field, or he sold her the cloth for the dress she sewed and wore. His demand must have surprised, then terrified her. She obeyed him; she always did as she was told.

When the family found a young man in the next village to be her husband, she had stood tractably beside the best rooster, his proxy, and promised before they met that she would be his forever. She was lucky that he was her age and she would be the first wife, an advantage secure now. The night she first saw him, he had sex with her. Then he left for America. She had almost forgotten what he looked like. When she tried to envision him, she only saw the black and white face in the group photograph the men had had taken before leaving.

The other man was not, after all, much different from her husband. They both gave orders: she followed. "If you tell your family, I'll beat you. I'll kill you. Be here again next week." No one talked sex, ever. And she might have separated the rapes from the rest of living if only she did not have to buy her oil from him or gather wood in the same forest. I want her fear to have lasted just as long as rape lasted so that the fear could have been contained. No drawn-out fear. But women at sex hazarded birth and hence lifetimes. The fear did not stop but permeated everywhere. She told the man, "I think I'm pregnant." He organized the raid against her.

On nights when my mother and father talked about their life back home, sometimes they mentioned an "outcast table" whose business they still seemed to be settling, their voices tight. In a commensal tradition, where food is precious, the powerful older people made wrongdoers eat alone. Instead of letting them start separate new lives like the Japanese, who could become samurais and geishas, the Chinese family, faces averted but eyes glowering sideways, hung on to the offenders and fed them leftovers. My aunt must have lived in the same house as my parents and eaten at an outcast table. My mother spoke about the raid as if she had seen it, when she and my aunt, a daughter-in-law to a different household, should not have been living together at all. Daughters-in-law lived with their husbands' parents, not their own; a synonym for marriage in Chinese is "taking a daughter-in-law." Her husband's parents could have sold her, mortgaged her, stoned her. But they had sent her back to her own mother and father, a mysterious act hinting at disgraces not told me. Perhaps they had thrown her out to deflect the avengers.

She was the only daughter; her four brothers went with her father, husband, and uncles "out on the road" and for some years became western men. When the goods were divided among the family, three of the brothers took land, and the youngest, my father, chose an education. After my grandparents gave their daughter away to her husband's family, they had dispensed all the adventure and all the property. They expected her alone to keep the traditional ways, which her brothers, now among the barbarians, could fumble without detection. The heavy, deep-rooted women were to maintain the past against the flood, safe for returning. But the rare urge west had fixed upon our family, and so my aunt crossed boundaries not delineated in space.

The work of preservation demands that the feelings playing about in one's guts not be turned into action. Just watch their passing like cherry blossoms. But perhaps my aunt, my forerunner, caught in a slow life, let dreams grow and fade and after some months or years went toward what persisted. Fear at the enormities of the forbidden kept her desires delicate, wire and bone. She looked at a man because she liked the way the hair was tucked behind his ears, or she liked the question-mark line of a long torso curving at the shoulder and a straight at the hip. For warm eyes or a soft voice or a slow walk—that's all—a few hairs, a line, a brightness, a sound, a pace, she gave up family. She offered us up for a charm that vanished with tiredness, a pigtail that didn't toss when the wind died. Why, the wrong lighting could erase the dearest thing about him.

It could very well have been, however, that my aunt did not take subtle enjoyment of her friend, but, a wild woman, kept rollicking company. Imagining her free with sex doesn't fit, though. I don't know any women like that, or men either. Unless I see her life branching into mine, she gives me no ancestral help.

To sustain her being in love, she often worked at herself in the mirror, guessing at the colors and shapes that would interest him, changing them frequently in order to hit on the right combination. She wanted him to look back.

On a farm near the sea, a woman who tended her appearance reaped a reputation for eccentricity. All the married women blunt-cut their hair in flaps about their ears or pulled it back in tight buns. No nonsense. Neither style blew easily into heart-catching tangles. And at their weddings they displayed themselves in their long hair for the last time. "It brushed the backs of my knees," my mother tells me. "It was braided, and even so, it brushed the backs of my knees."

At the mirror my aunt combed individuality into her bob. A bun could have been contrived to escape into black streamers blowing in the wind or in quiet wisps about her face, but only the older women in our picture album wear buns. She brushed her hair back from her forehead, tucking the flaps behind her ears. She looped a piece of thread, knotted into a circle between her index fingers and thumbs, and ran the double strand across her forehead. When she closed her fingers as if she were making a pair of shadow geese bite, the string twisted together catching the little hairs. Then she pulled the thread away from her skin, ripping the hairs out neatly, her eyes watering from the needles of pain. Opening her fingers, she cleaned the thread, then rolled it along her hairline and the tops of her eyebrows. My mother did the same to me and my sisters and herself. I used to believe that the expression "caught by the short hairs" meant a captive held with a depilatory string. It especially hurt at the temples, but my mother said we were lucky we didn't have to have our feet bound when we were seven. Sisters used to sit on their beds and cry together, she said, as their mothers or their slaves removed the bandages for a few minutes each night and let the blood gush back into their veins. I hope that the man my aunt loved appreciated a smooth brow, that he wasn't just a tits-and-ass man.

Once my aunt found a freckle on her chin, at a spot that the almanac said predestined her for unhappiness. She dug it out with a hot needle and washed the wound with peroxide.

More attention to her looks than these pullings of hairs and pickings at spots would have caused gossip among the villagers. They owned work clothes and good clothes, and they wore good clothes for feasting the new seasons. But since a woman combing her hair hexes beginnings, my aunt rarely found an occasion to look her best. Women looked like great sea snails—the corded wood, babies, and laundry they carried were the whorls on their backs. The Chinese did not admire a bent back; goddesses and warriors stood straight. Still there must have been a marvelous freeing of beauty when a worker laid down her burden and stretched and arched.

Such commonplace loveliness, however, was not enough for my aunt. She dreamed of a lover for the fifteen days of New Year's, the time for families to exchange visits, money, and food. She plied her secret comb. And sure enough she cursed the year, the family, the village, and herself.

Even as her hair lured her imminent lover, many other men looked at her. Uncles, cousins, nephews, brothers would have looked, too, had they been home between journeys. Perhaps they had already been restraining their curiosity, and they left, fearful that their glances, like a field of nesting birds, might be startled and caught. Poverty hurt, and that was their first reason for leaving. But another, final reason for leaving the crowded house was the never-said.

She may have been unusually beloved, the precious daughter, spoiled and mirror gazing because of the affection the family lavished on her. When her husband left, they welcomed the chance to take her back from the in-laws; she could live like the little daughter for just a while longer. There are stories that my grandfather was different from other people, "crazy ever since the little Jap bayoneted him in the head." He used to put his naked penis on the dinner table, laughing. And one day he brought home a baby girl, wrapped up inside his brown western-style greatcoat. He had traded one of his sons, probably my father, the youngest, for her. My grandmother made him trade back. When he finally got a daughter of his own, he doted on her. They must have all loved her, except perhaps my father, the only brother who never went back to China, having once been traded for a girl.

Brothers and sisters, newly men and women, had to efface their sexual color and present plain miens. Disturbing hair and eyes, a smile like no other, threatened the ideal of five generations living under one roof. To focus blurs, people shouted face to face and yelled from room to room. The immigrants I know have loud voices, unmodulated to American tones even after years away from the village where they called their friendships out across the fields. I have not been able to stop my mother's screams in public libraries or over telephones. Walking erect (knees straight, toes pointed forward, no pigeon-toed, which is Chinese-feminine) and speaking in an inaudible voice, I have tried to turn myself American-feminine. Chinese communication was loud, public. Only sick people had to whisper. But at the dinner table, where the family members came nearest one another, no one could talk, not the outcasts nor any eaters. Every word that falls from the mouth is a coin lost. Silently they gave and accepted food with both hands. A preoccupied child who took his bowl with one hand got a sideways glare. A complete moment of total attention is due everyone alike. Children and lovers have no singularity here, but my aunt used a secret voice, a separate attentiveness.

She kept the man's name to herself throughout her labor and dying; she did not accuse him that he be punished with her. To save her inseminator's name she gave silent birth.

He may have been somebody in her own household, but intercourse with a man outside the family would have been no less abhorrent. All the village were kinsmen, and the titles shouted in loud country voices never let kinship be forgotten. Any man within visiting distance would have been neutralized as a lover—"brother," "younger brother," "older brother"—one hundred and fifteen relationship titles. Parents researched birth charts probably not so much to assure good fortune as to circumvent incest in a population that has but one hundred surnames. Everybody has eight million relatives. How useless then sexual mannerisms, how dangerous.

As if it came from an atavism deeper than fear, I used to add "brother" silently to boys' names. It hexed the boys, who would or would not ask me to dance, and made them less scary and as familiar and deserving of benevolence as girls.

But, of course, I hexed myself also—no dates. I should have stood up, both arms waving, and shouted out across the libraries, "Hey you! Love me back." I had no idea, though, how to make attraction selective, how to control its direction and magnitude. If I made myself American-pretty so that the five or six Chinese boys in the class fell in love with me, everyone else—the Caucasian, Negro, and Japanese boys—would too. Sisterliness, dignified and honorable, made much more sense.

Attraction eludes control so stubbornly that whole societies designed to organize relationships among people cannot keep order, not even when they bind people to one another from childhood and raise them together. Among the very poor and the wealthy, brothers married their adopted sisters, like doves. Our family allowed some romance, paying adult brides' prices and providing dowries so that their sons and daughters could marry strangers. Marriages promises to turn strangers into friendly relatives—a nation of siblings.

In the village structure, spirits shimmered among the live creatures, balanced and held in equilibrium by time and land. But one human being flaring up into violence could open up a black hole, a maelstrom that pulled in the sky. They frightened villagers, who depended on one another to maintain the real, went to my aunt to show her a personal, physical representation of the break she had made in the "roundness." Misallying couples snapped off the future, which was to be embodied in true offspring. The villagers punished her for acting as if she could have a private life, secret and apart from them.

If my aunt had betrayed the family at a time of large grain yields and peace, when many boys were born, and wings were being built on many houses, perhaps she might have escaped such severe punishment. But the men—hungry, greedy, tired of planting in dry soil—had been forced to leave the village in order to send food-money home. There were ghost plagues, bandit plagues, wars with the Japanese, floods. My Chinese brother and sister had died of an unknown sickness. Adultery, perhaps only a mistake during good times, became a crime when the village needed food.

The round moon cakes and round doorways, the round tables of graduated sizes that fit one roundness inside another, round windows and rice bowls—these talismans had lost their power to warn this family of the law: a family must be whole, faithfully keeping the descent line by having sons to feed the old and the dead, who in turn look after the family. The villagers came to show my aunt and her lover-in-hiding a broken house. The villagers were speeding up the circling of events because she was too shortsighted to see that her infidelity had already harmed the village, that waves of consequences would return unpredictably, sometimes in disguise, as now, to hurt her. This roundness had to be made coin-sized so that she would see its circumference: punish her at the birth of her baby. Awaken her to the inexorable. People who refused fatalism because they could invent small resources insisted on culpability. Deny accidents and wrest fault from the stars.

After the villagers left, their lanterns now scattering in various directions toward home, the family broke their silence and cursed her. "Aiaa, we're going to die. Death is coming. Death is coming. Look what you've done. You've killed us. Ghost! Dead ghost! Ghost! You've never been born." She ran out into the fields, far enough from the house so that she could no longer hear their voices, and pressed herself against the earth, her own land no more. When she felt the birth coming, she thought that she had been hurt. Her body seized together. "They've hurt me too much," she thought. "This is gall, and it will kill me." With forehead and knees against the earth, her body convulsed and then relaxed. She turned on her back, lay on the ground. The black well of sky and stars went out and out and out forever; her body and her complexity seemed to disappear. She was one of the stars, a bright dot in blackness, without home, without a companion, in eternal cold and silence. An agoraphobia rose in her, speeding higher and higher, bigger and bigger; she would not be able to contain it; there would no end to fear.

Flayed, unprotected against space, she felt pain return, focusing her body. This pain chilled her—a cold, steady kind of surface pain. Inside, spasmodically, the other pain, the pain of the child, heated her. For hours she lay on the ground, alternately body and space. Sometimes a vision of normal comfort obliterated reality: she saw the family in the evening gambling at the dinner table, the young people massaging their elders' backs. She saw them congratulating one another, high joy on the morning the rice shoots came up. When these pictures burst, the stars drew yet further apart. Black space opened.

She got to her feet to fight better and remembered that old-fashioned women gave birth in their pigsties to fool the jealous, pain-dealing gods, who do not snatch piglets. Before the next spasm could stop her, she ran to the pigsty, each step a rushing out into emptiness. She climbed over the fence and knelt in the dirt. It was good to have a fence enclosing her, a tribal person alone.

Laboring, this woman who had carried her child as a foreign growth that sickened her every day, expelled it at last. She reached down to touch the hot, wet, moving mass, surely smaller than anything human, and could feel that it was human after all—fingers, toes, nails, nose. She pulled it up on to her belly, and it lay curled there, butt in the air, feet precisely tucked on under the other. She opened her loose shirt and buttoned the child inside. After resting, it squirmed and thrashed and she pushed it up to her breast. It turned its head this way and that until it found her nipple. There, it made little snuffling noises. She clenched her teeth at its preciousness, lovely as a young calf, a piglet, a little dog.

She may have gone to the pigsty as a last act of responsibility: she would protect this child as she had protected its father. It would look after her soul, leaving supplies on her grave. But how would this tiny child without family find her grave when there would be no marker for her anywhere, neither in the earth nor the family hall? No one would give her a family hall name. She had taken the child with her into the wastes. At its birth the two of them had felt the same raw pain of separation, a wound that only the family pressing tight could close. A child with no descent line would not soften her life but only trail after her ghostlike, begging her to give it purpose. At dawn the vilagers on their way to the fields would stand around the fence and look.

Full of milk, the little ghost slept. When it awoke, she hardened her breasts against the milk that crying loosens. Toward morning she picked up the baby and walked toward the well.

Carrying the baby to the well shows loving. Otherwise abandon it. Turn its face into the mud. Mothers who love their children take them along. It was probably a girl; there is some hope of forgiveness for boys.

"Don't tell anyone you had an aunt. Your father does not want to hear her name. She has never been born." I have believed that sex was unspeakable and words so strong and fathers so frail that "aunt" would do my father mysterious harm. I have thought my family, having settled among immigrants who had also been their neighbors in the ancestral land, needed to clean their name, and a wrong word would incite the kinspeople even here. But there is more to this silence: they want me to participate in her punishment. And I have.

In the twenty years since I heard this story I have not asked for details nor said my aunt's name. I do not know it. People who can comfort the dead can also chase after them to hurt them further—a reverse ancestor worship. The real punishment was not the raid swiftly inflicted by the villagers, but the family's deliberate forgetting her. Her betrayal so maddened them, they saw to it that she would suffer forever, even after death. Always hungry, always needing, she would have to beg food from other ghosts, snatch and steal it from those whose living descendants give them gifts. She would have to fight the ghosts massed at the crossroads for the buns a few thoughtful citizens leave to decoy her away from the village and home so that the ancestral spirits could feast unharassed. At peace, they could act like gods, not ghosts, their descent lines providing them with paper suits and dresses, spirit money, paper houses, paper automobiles, chicken, meat, and rice into eternity—essences delivered up in smoke and flames, steam and incense rising from each rice bowl. In an attempt to make the Chinese care for people outside the family, Chairman Mao encourages us now to give our paper replicas to the spirits of outstanding soldiers and workers, no matter whose ancestors they may be. My aunt remains forever hungry. Goods are not distributed evenly among the dead.

My aunt haunts me—her ghost drawn to me because now, after fifty years of neglect, I alone devote pages of paper to her, though not origamied into houses and clothes. I do not think she always means me well. I am telling on her, and she was a spite suicide, drowning herself in the drinking water. The Chinese are always very frightened of the drowned one, whose weeping ghost, wet hair hanging and skin bloated, waits silently by the water to pull down a substitute.

1975–1976

Bobbie Ann Mason b. 1940

Bobbie Ann Mason's parents chose her masculine-sounding first name because they were certain that she would be a boy. Questions surrounding gender identity are prominent throughout her work, but they serve to highlight a broader theme illustrated by this anecdote: the difficulty of accepting change or difference. Although young women tend to be the protagonists of her fiction, Mason's consistent subjects are rural, working-class Americans who are facing or evading the rapidly changing late twentieth century.

Bobbie Ann Mason was born in Mayfield, Kentucky, on May 1, 1940. She grew up on a farm that had been in her father's family for generations. In the aftermath of the Great Depression, farming was a difficult way to earn a living, yet her father's stint in the army during World War II was for him a mystifying departure from the world that he had always known rather than a glimpse of the possibilities available in the wider world. Like many young people destined to become writers, Bobbie Ann escaped from her rural surroundings through books. She graduated from the University of Kentucky and went immediately to New York, the best place to begin a writing career. After writing fan magazine features about teen stars, she longed to return to more substantial literature and earned a Ph.D. at the University of Connecticut, where her childhood passion for detective stories developed into a fascination with Nabokov, the subject of her dissertation and her first book. After a half-dozen years of teaching at Mansfield State College in Pennsylvania, Mason began her career as a fiction writer.

Mason has published four collections of short stories, *Shiloh and Other Stories* (1982), *Love Life* (1989), *Zigzagging Down a Wild Trail* (2001), and *Nancy Culpepper* (2006). These stories, many originally published in the *New Yorker*, earned Mason the title of "regional writer," yet her regionalism is tempered to a large degree by her tendency to saturate her stories with references to contemporary popular culture, especially allusions to television and rock music. Virtually all her fiction takes place in her native Kentucky, and her main characters tend to be people who both desire and are mystified by change. The potent forces of accelerated change war against the conservative values of rural America in her fiction, and the battleground is often the flickering television screen in living rooms. Mason refuses to judge or romanticize the lives of her characters; she is more interested in allowing them to enact their dramas, occasionally experiencing moments of realization but unaware of what to do with them.

Of her three novels, the one that has gained the most attention is *In Country*

(1985), the story of a teenager's quest to learn the truth about her father, who died in the Vietnam War. The following story, "Airwaves," contains many of the same elements as *In Country*: confusion about appropriate gender roles, a female main character who longs to empower herself, and an almost spiritual turning to radio and television for insight into the mysteries of the contemporary world.

D. *Quentin Miller*
Suffolk University

PRIMARY WORKS

Shiloh and Other Stories, 1982; *In Country*, 1985; *Spence + Lila*, 1988; *Love Life*, 1989; *Feather Crowns*, 1993; *Midnight Magic*, 1998; *Clear Springs*, 1999; *Zigzagging Down a Wild Trail*, 2001; *An Atomic Romance: A Novel*, 2005; *Nancy Culpepper: Stories*, 2006.

Airwaves

When Jane lived with Coy Wilson, he couldn't listen to rock music before noon or after supper. In the morning, it was too jarring; at night, the vibrations lingered in his head and interfered with his sleep. But now that they are apart, Jane listens to Rock-95 all the time. Rock-95 is a college station—"your station for kick-ass rock and roll." She sets the radio alarm every night for 8 A.M., and when it goes off she dozes and dreams while the music blasts in her ears for an hour or more. Women rock singers snarl and scream their independence. The sounds are numbing. Jane figures if she can listen to hard rock in her sleep, she won't care that Coy has gone.

Jane stands in the window in pink shortie pajamas, watching her landlady, Mrs. Bush, hang out her wash. Today is white things: sheets, socks, underwear, towels. Jane's mother used to say, "Always separate your colored things from your white things!" as though there were something morally significant about the way you do laundry. Jane never follows the rules. All her sheets have flowers on them, and her underwear is bright colors. Anything white is outnumbered. The men's shorts on Mrs. Bush's wash line flap in the breeze like flags of surrender.

The coffee is bitter. She bought the store brand, because Mrs. Bush gave her a fifty-cent coupon and the store paid double coupons. Mrs. Bush, who is a waitress at the Villa Romano, keeps asking Jane when she is going to get a job. When Coy lived there, Mrs. Bush was always asking him when he was going to marry Jane. Six weeks ago, not long after she split up with Coy, Jane was laid off from the Holiday Clothing Company. First she was a folder, then a presser. Folding was more satisfying than pressing—the heat from the presser took the curl out of her hair—but when she was switched to the pressing room, she got a fifty-cents-an-hour raise. She was hoping to go to the Villa Romano that night with Coy and have a spaghetti supper to celebrate, but he chose that day to move back home with his mother. His unemployment had run out two weeks before, and he had been at loose ends. He thought he was getting an ulcer. When Jane got home, he had lined up their joint possessions on the floor—the toaster, the blender, the records, the TV tables, a whatnot, even the kitchen utensils.

"The TV's mine," he said apologetically. "I had it when we started out."

"I told you I'd pay the rent," she said, as he punched his jeans into a duffle bag. When he wouldn't answer, she set the coffeepot in the cabinet and shut the door. "I got the coffeepot with Green Stamps," she said.

"I'm going to cut out coffee anyway."

"Good. It makes you irritable."

Coy set the toaster in a grocery box with some shaving cream and socks—all his mateless socks from what Jane called his Lonely Sock Drawer. Jane tried to keep from crying as she pleaded with him to stay.

"I can't let you go on supporting me," he said. "I wasn't raised that way."

"What's the difference? Your mother will support you. You could even watch her TV."

He divided the record albums as though he were dealing out cards. "One for you and one for me." He left his favorite Willie Nelson record on her pile.

When he left, she said, "You just let me know when you get yourself straightened out, and we'll take it from there."

"That's my whole point," said Coy. "I have to work things out."

Jane knew she should have been more understanding. He was appreciative of delicate, fine things most men wouldn't notice, such as flowers and pretty dishes. Coy was tender in his lovemaking, with more sensitivity than men were usually given credit for. On Phil Donahue's show, when the topic was sex, the women in the audience always said they wanted men who were gentle and considerate and involved in a lot of touching during the day instead of "wham-bam-thank-you-ma'am" at the end of the day. Coy was the answer to those women's prayers, but he went too far. He was so fragile, with his nervous stomach. He couldn't watch meat being cut up. Jane still finds broken rolls of Tums stashed around the apartment.

Unemployed, Jane is adrift. She watches a lot of TV. She managed to buy a TV on sale before she lost her job. She has had to stop smoking (not a serious problem) and eating out so that she can keep up her car and TV payments. She canceled her subscription to a cosmetics club. She has accumulated a lot of bizarre eye shadows and creams that she doesn't use. When she goes out to a job interview, she paints her face and feels silly. Job-hunting is like going to church—a pointless ritual of dressing up. At the factory, she had to wear a blue smock over a dark skirt. Pants weren't allowed. "I wish I could get on at the Villa Romano," she tells Mrs. Bush. "The uniform is nice, and I could wear pants."

Coy used to go to Kentucky Lake alone sometimes, for the whole weekend, to meditate and restore himself. She once thought his desire to be alone was peculiar, but now she appreciates it. Being alone is incredibly easy. Her mind sails off into unexpected trances. Sometimes she pretends she is an invalid recovering from a coma, and she rediscovers everything around her—simple things, like the noise the rotary antenna makes, a sound she never heard when the TV volume was loud. Or she pretends she is in a wheelchair, viewing the world from one certain level. She likes to see things suddenly, from new angles. Once when Coy lived there, she stepped up on a crate to dust the top of a shelf, and Coy suddenly appeared and caught her in an embrace. On the crate, she was exactly his height. The dusty shelf was at eye level. For a day or two, she went around noticing the spaces that would be in his line of vision—the top of the refrigerator, the top of an old cardboard wardrobe her father had given her, curtain rods, moldings.

Today, when Jane leaves the apartment to pick up her unemployment check, Mrs. Bush is outside, watering her petunias. She pulls a letter from her pocket and waves it at Jane.

"My boy's in California," she says. "They're going to let him have a furlough, but he likes it so much out there he won't come home."

"I don't blame him," says Jane. "It's too far, and California must be a lot more fun than here."

"They start him out on heavy-duty equipment, but that didn't suit him and they've switched him to electronics. They take a hundred dollars out of his pay every month, and then when he gets out they'll double it and give him a bonus so he can go to school."

Mrs. Bush fires water at a border of hollyhocks. Jane steps over the coiled hose and casually thinks of evil serpents. She says, "My brother couldn't get in the Army because he had high arches, so he became a Holy Roller preacher instead. He used to cuss like the devil, but now he's preaching up a storm." Jane looks Mrs. Bush straight in the eyes. She's not old but looks old. If she died, maybe Jane could get her job.

"My cousin was a Holy Roller," says Mrs. Bush. "He got sanctified and then got hit by a truck the next day."

Nervously, Mrs. Bush tears off the edging of paper where she has ripped open the letter from her son. She balls the bit of paper and drops it into a pot of hen and chickens.

Jane's mother died when she was fifteen, and her father, Vernon Motherall, has never learned to cook for himself. "What's in this?" he asks suspiciously that weekend, when she takes him a tuna casserole.

"Macaroni. Tuna fish. Mushroom soup."

"I don't like mushrooms. Mushrooms is poison."

"This isn't poison. It's Campbell's." Jane has brought him this same kind of casserole dozens of times, and he always argues against mushrooms. He's convinced that someday a mushroom is going to get him.

Vernon rents the bottom of a dilapidated clapboard house. He has two dump trucks in the backyard. He hauls rock and sand and asphalt—"whatever needs hauling," his ad in the yellow pages says. His dingy office is filled with greasy papers on spikes and piles of *Field and Stream* magazines. In a ray of sunlight, the dust whirls and sparkles. Jane sweeps her hand through it.

"I wish I had some money," she says. "I'd buy one of those things that takes the negative ions out of the air."

"What good's that do?" Vernon is swigging a Pabst, though it's still morning.

"It knocks the dust out of the air."

"What for?" The way Jane's father speaks is more like an extended grunt than conversation. He sits in a large stuffed chair that seems to be part of his own big lumpy body.

"I don't know. I think the dust just falls down instead of circulating. If you had one of those, your sinuses wouldn't be so bad."

"They ain't been bothering me none lately."

"Those ionizers make you feel good, too. They do something to your mood."

"I've got all I need for my mood," he says, lifting his bottle of beer.

"You drink too much."

"Don't look at my beer belly."

"I will if I want to," Jane says, playfully thumping his belt buckle. "You get loaded and go out and have wrecks. You're going to get yourself killed."

Vernon grins at her mockingly. They always have this conversation, and he never takes her seriously.

"Here, eat this," Jane says, plopping a scoop of casserole on a melamine plate that has discoloration on it.

Vernon plucks another beer from the refrigerator and sits down at the card table in his dirty kitchen. He eats without comment, then mops his plate with a bread heel. When he finishes, he says, "I went to hear Joe preach at his new church the other Sunday. How did I turn out a boy like that? He's bound and determined to make a fool out of himself. His wife runs out on him, and he turns around and starts preaching Holy Roller. Did you know he talks in tongues now? What will he think of next?"

"Well, Joe goes at anything like killing snakes," says Jane. "It's all or nothing."

Vernon laughs. "His text for the day was the Twenty-third Psalm, and he comes to the part where the Lord maketh me lie down in green pastures and restoreth my soul? And he reads it 'he *storeth* my soul,' and starts preaching on the Lord's store-houses." Vernon doubles over laughing. "He thinks the Lord stores souls—like corn in a grain elevator!"

"I wonder what ever happened to all those grain-elevator explosions we used to hear about," Jane says, giggling.

"If the Lord stores some of those pitiful souls Joe's dragged in, his storehouse is liable to explode!" Vernon laughs, and beer sprays out of his mouth.

"Have some more tuna casserole," Jane says affectionately. When it comes to her brother, who was always in trouble, she and her father are in cahoots.

"You should have a good man to cook for. Not Coy Wilson. He's too prissy, and he took advantage of you, living with you with no intention of marrying."

"You're still feeling guilty 'cause you ran out on me and Joe and Mother that time," says Jane, shifting the subject.

"The trouble is, too many women are working and the men can't get jobs," her father says. "Women should stay home."

"Don't start in," Jane says in a warning voice. "I've got enough trouble."

"You could move back home with me," Vernon says plaintively. "Parents always used to take care of their kids till they married."

"I guess that's why Coy ran home to his mama."

"You can come home to your old daddy anytime," Vernon says, moving back to his easy chair. The vinyl upholstery makes obscene noises when he lands.

"It would never work," Jane says. "We don't like the same TV shows anymore."

Waiting in the unemployment line the next afternoon is tedious, and all the faces have deadpan expressions, but Jane is feeling elated, almost euphoric, though for no substantial reason. In the car, driving past a local radio transmitter, she suddenly realized that she had no idea how sound got from the transmitter to the radio. She felt so ignorant. The idea of sound waves seemed farfetched. She went to the library and asked for a book about radio. The librarian showed her a pamphlet about Nathan Stubblefield.

"He invented radio," the woman said. "They say it was Marconi, but Stubblefield was really the first, and he was from right around here. He lived about five miles from my house."

"I always heard radio was invented in Kentucky," Jane said.

"He just never got credit for it." The woman reminded Jane of a bouncy game-show contestant. "Kentucky never gets enough credit, if you ask me. We've go so much here to be proud of. Kentucky even has a Golden Pond, like in the movie."

Reading the pamphlet in the unemployment line, Jane feels strangely connected to something historically important. It is a miracle that sound can travel long distances through the air and then appear instantaneously, like a genie from a bottle, and that a man from Kentucky was the first to make it happen. Who can she tell? Who would care? This is the sort of thing that wouldn't register on her father, and Coy would think she was crazy. Her brother, though, would recognize the feeling. It occurs to Jane that he probably hears voices from heaven every day, just as though he were tuned in to heaven's airways. She wonders if he can really talk in tongues. Her brother is a radio! Jane feels like dancing. In her mind, the unemployment line suddenly turns into a chorus line, a movie scene. For a moment, she's afraid she's going nuts. The line inches forward.

After collecting her check, she cashes it at the bank's drive-in window, talking to the teller through a speaker, then goes to Jerry's Drive-In and orders a Coke through another speaker. A voice confirms her order, and in the background behind the voice, Jane hears a radio playing—Rock-95, the same station she is hearing on her car radio.

Coy calls up during a "Mary Tyler Moore" rerun that week, one Jane hasn't seen before. Jane is eating canned ravioli. The clarity of his voice startles her. He could be in the same room.

"I got a job! Floorwalking at Wal-Mart."

"Oh, I'm glad." Jane spears a pillow of ravioli and listens while Coy describes his hours and his duties and the amount of take-home pay he gets—less than he made at the plant before his layoff, but with more security. The job sounds incredibly boring.

"When I get on my feet, maybe we can reconsider some things," he says.

"If you're floorwalking, you're already on your feet," she says. "That's a joke," she says, when he doesn't respond. "I don't want to get back together if money's the issue."

"I thought we went through all that."

"I've been thinking, and I can't let you support me."

"Well, I've got a job now, and you don't."

"You wouldn't let *me* support *you*," Jane says. Why should I let you support me?"

"If we got back together, you could go to school part-time."

"I have to find a job first. I'd go to school now if I could go and still draw unemployment, but they won't let you draw and go to school too. Let's change the subject. How's your stomach?"

Coy tells Jane that on the news he saw pictures of starving children in Africa, and managed to watch without getting queasy. Jane always told him he was too sensitive to misfortunes that had nothing to do with him.

An awkward silence follows. Finally, Jane says, "My brother's got a Holy Roller church. He's preaching."

"That sounds about like him," Coy says, without surprise.

"I think I'll go Sunday. I need some religion. Do you want to go?"

"Hell, no. I don't want to invite a migraine."

"I thought your nerves were getting better."

"They are, but they're not that good yet."

After Coy hangs up, Jane feels lonely, wishing Coy were there touching her lightly with promising caresses, like the women on "Donahue" always wanted. Once, Rita Jenrette, whose husband was involved in a political scandal, was on Donahue's show, and during the program her husband called up. Coy's job sounds so depressing. Jane wishes he were the host of a radio call-in show. She could call him up and talk to him, pretending there was nothing personal between them. She would ask him about love. She'd ask whether he thought the magic of love worked anything at all like radio waves. Her ravioli grows cold.

Joe's church is called the Foremost Evangelical Assembly. The church is a converted house trailer, with a perpendicular extension. There is a Coke machine in the corridor. People sit around drinking Cokes and 7-Ups. No one is dressed up.

"Can you believe it!" cries Joe, clasping both of Jane's hands and jerking her forward as though about to swing her around in a game children play.

"Can you pray for me to find a job?" Jane says, grinning. "Daddy says you could talk in tongues, and I thought that might help."

"Was Daddy drinking when you saw him last?" Joe asks anxiously.

"Of course. Is the Pope Catholic?"

"I told him I could stop him from that if he'd just get his tail down here every Sunday." Joe has on a pin-striped double-knit suit with an artificial daisy in the lapel. He looks the part.

"Are you going to talk in tongues today?" Jane asks. "I want to see how you do it."

"Watch close," he says with a wink. "But I'm not allowed to give away the secret."

"Is it like being a magician?"

Her brother only grins mysteriously.

Jane sits cross-legged on the floor behind the folding chairs. People turn around and stare at her, probably wondering if she is Joe's girlfriend. The congregation loves Joe. He is a large man, and his size makes him seem powerful and authoritative, like an Army general. He has always been a goof-off, calling attention to himself, staging some kind of show. If Alexander Haig became a stand-up comedian, he would be just like Joe. He stands behind a card table with two overturned plastic milk crates stacked on it. On his right, a TV set stares at the congregation.

The service is long and peculiar and filled with individual testimonials that seem to come randomly, interrupting Joe's talk. It's not really a sermon. It's just Joe telling stories about how bad he used to be before he found Christ. He always had the gift of the gab, Vernon used to say. Joe tells a long anecdote about how his wife's infidelity made him turn to the Lord. He exaggerates parts of the story that Jane recognizes. (He *never* gave his wife a beautiful house with a custom-built kitchen and a two-car garage. It was a dumpy old house that they rented.) She almost giggles aloud when he opens the Bible and reads from "the Philippines," and she makes a mental note to tell her father. A woman takes a crying baby into the corridor and tries to make it drink some Coke. Jane wishes she had a cigarette. In this crazy setting, if Joe talked in tongues, nobody would notice it as anything odd.

When a young couple brings forth a walleyed child to be healed, Joe cries out in astonishment, "Who, me? I can't heal nobody!" He paces around in front of the TV set. "But I can guarantee that if you just let the spirit in, miracles have been known to happen." He rambles along on this point, and the little girl's head droops indifferently. "Just open up your heart and let him in!" Joe shouts. "Let the spirit in, and the Lord will shake up the alignment of them eyes." A song from *Hair,* "Let the Sunshine In," starts going through Jane's head. The child's eye shoots out across the room. While Joe is ranting, Jane gets a Coke and stands in the doorway.

"Icky-bick-eye-bo!" Joe cries suddenly. He looks embarrassed and bows his head. "Freema-di-kibbi-frida," he says softly.

Jane has been thinking of talking in tongues as an involuntary expression—a kind of gibberish that pours forth when people are possessed by the spirit of God. But now, in amazement, she watches her brother, his hands folded and eyes closed, as though bowing his head for a moment of prayer, chanting strange words slowly and carefully, as methodically as Mrs. Bush hangs out her wash. He is speaking a singsong language made of hard, disturbing sounds. "Shecky-beck-be-floyt-I-shecky-tibby-libby. Dat-cree-la-croo-la-crow." He seems to be trying hard not to say "abracadabra" or any other familiar words. Jane, disappointed, doubts that these words are messages from heaven. Joe seems afraid that some repressed obscenity might rush out. He used to cuss freely. Now he probably really believes he is tuned in to heaven.

"Where's Coy?" he asks her after the service. He has failed to correct the child's eyes but won't admit it.

"We don't get along so good. After he lost his job, he couldn't handle it."

"Well, get him on down here! We'll help him."

He tries to talk Jane into bringing Coy for Wednesday-night prayer meeting. "There's two kinds of men," Joe says. "Them that goes to church and them that don't. You should never get mixed up with some boy who won't take you to church."

"I know."

Joe says goodbye, with his arms around her like a lover's. Jane can smell the Tic Tacs on his breath.

"Do you want one hamburger patty or two?" Jane asks her father.

"One. No, two." Vernon looks confused. "No, make it one."

They ate at the lake, in a trailer belonging to Jane's former boss, who had promised to let her use it some weekend. Jane, wanting a change of scene for her father, brought a cooler of supplies, and Vernon brought his dog, Buford. He grumbled because Jane wouldn't let him bring any beer, but he sneaked along a quart of Heaven Hill, and he is already drunk. Jane is furious.

"How can you watch 'Hogan's Heroes' on that cruddy TV?" she asks. "The reception's awful."

"I've seen this one so many times I know what's going on. See that machine gun? Watch that guy in the tower. He's going to shoot."

"That's a tower? I thought it was a giraffe."

When they sit down to eat at the picnic table outside, Buford tries to get in Jane's lap. He has the broad shoulders of a bulldog and the fine facial features of a chihuahua. He goes around in a little cloud of gnats.

"I can't eat with a dog in my lap," Jane says, pushing the dog away. "Coy wants to come back to me," she tells her father. "He's got his pride again."

"Don't let him."

"He's more of a man than you think." Jane laughs. "Joe says he can help us work things out. He wants us to come to Wednesday-night prayer meetings."

"How did I go wrong?" Vernon asks helplessly, addressing a tree. "One kid starts preaching just to stay out of jail, and the other one wants to live in sin and ruin her reputation." Vernon turns to the dog and says, "It's all my fault. Children always hurt you."

"And what about you?" Jane shouts at him. "You worry us half to death with your drinking and then expect us to be little angels."

She takes her plate indoors and turns on "M*A*S*H." The reception is so poor without a cable that the figures undulate on the screen. Hawkeye and B.J. turn into wavy lines, staggering drunks.

That night, Vernon's drunken sleep on the couch is loud and unrestrained. Jane thinks of his sleep as slumber. She always thought of Coy's sleep as catnapping. She misses Coy, but wonders if she can ever get along with any man. In all her relationships with people, she has to deal with one or another intolerable habit. Jane is not sure the hard-rock music has hardened her to pain and distraction. Her father is hopeless. He used to get drunk and throw her mother's good dishes against the wall. He lined them up on the table and broke them one by one until her mother relented and gave him the keys to the car. He had accidents. He was always apologetic afterward, and he made it up to them in lavish ways, bringing home absurd presents, such as a bushel of peaches or a pint of oysters in a little white fold-together cardboard container like the ones goldfish come in. Once, he brought goldfish, but Jane's mother had expected oysters. Her disappointment hurt him, and he went back and bought oysters. One year, he ran away to Detroit. When he came back months later, Jane's mother forgave him. By then, she was dying of cancer, and Jane suspects that he never really forgave himself for being there too late to make it up to her.

Buford paces around the trailer fretfully. Jane can't sleep. The bed is musty and lumpy. She recalls a story her mother once told her about a woman who was trapped in a lion cage by a lion who tried to mate with her. From outside the cage, the lion's trainer yelled instructions to her—how she had to stroke the lion until he was satisfied. Pinned under the lion, the woman saved her life by obeying the man's instructions. That was more or less how her mother always told her she had to be with a husband, or a rapist. She thinks of her mother as the woman in the cage, listening to the lion tamer shouting instructions—do anything to keep from being murdered. As Jane recalls her mother telling it, the lion's eyes went all dreamy, and he rolled over on his back and went to sleep.

Jane suspects that what she really wants is a man something like the lion. She loves Coy's gentleness, but she wants him to be aggressive at times. The women on "Donahue" said they wanted that, too. Someone in the audience said women can't have it both ways.

During the weekend, Jane tries to get Vernon to go fishing, but he hasn't renewed his fishing license since the price went up. He complains about the snack cakes she brought, and he sits around drinking. Jane listens to the radio and reads a book called *Working,* about people's jobs. "It takes all kinds," she tells her father when he asks about the book. She has given up trying to entertain him, but by Sunday evening he seems mellow and talkative.

At the picnic table, Jane watches the sun setting behind the oak trees. "Look how pretty it is. The light on the water looks like a melted orange Popsicle."

Vernon grunts, acknowledging the sunset.

"I want you to enjoy yourself," Jane says calmly.

"I'm an old fool," he says, sloshing his drink. "I never amounted to anything. This country is taking away every chance the little man ever had. If it weren't for the Republicans and the Democrats, we'd be better off."

"Don't we have to have one or the other?"

"Throw 'em all out. They cancel each other out anyway." Vernon snatches at a mosquito. "The minorities rule this country. They've meddled with the Constitution till it's all out of shape."

The sun disappears, and the mosquitoes come out. Jane slaps her arms. Her toes are under the dog, warming like buns in a toaster oven. She nudges him away, and he pads across the porch, taking his gnat cloud with him.

"Tell me something," Jane asks later, as they are eating. "What did you do in Detroit that time when you ran off and left Mom with Joe and me?"

Vernon shrugs and drinks from a fresh drink. "Worked a Chrysler."

"Why did you leave us?"

"Your mother couldn't put up with me."

Jane can't see her father's face in the growing dark, so she feels bolder. Taking a deep breath, she says, "I guess for a long time I felt guilty after you left—not because you left but because I wanted you to leave. Mom and Joe and me got along just fine without you. I liked moving into that restaurant, living upstairs with Mom, and her going downstairs to cook hamburgers for people. I think I liked it so much not just because I could have all the hamburgers and milk shakes I wanted but because *she* loved it. She loved waiting on people and cooking food for the public. But we were glad when you came back and we moved back home."

Vernon nods and nods, about to say something. Jane gets up and turns on the bug light on the porch. She says, "That's how I've been feeling, living by myself. If I found something I liked as much as Mom liked cooking for the public, I'd be happy."

Vernon pours some more bourbon into his Yosemite Sam jelly glass and nods thoughtfully. He sips his drink and looks out on the darkening lake for so long that Jane thinks he must be working up to a spectacular confession or apology. Finally, he says "The Constitution is damaged all to hell." He sets his plate on the ground for the dog to lick.

The next morning is work-pants day. On Mrs. Bush's line is a row of dark-green work pants and matching shirts. The pants are heavy and wrinkled. The sun comes out, and by afternoon, when Jane returns from shopping, the wrinkles are gone and the pants look fluffy. Jane reaches into the back seat of her car for her sack of groceries—soup, milk, cereal, and a Sara Lee cheesecake, marked down.

"Faired up nice, didn't it?" cries Mrs. Bush, appearing with her laundry basket. "They say another front's coming through and we'll have a storm."

"I hope so," says Jane, wishing it would be a tornado.

"I've got some news for you," Mrs. Bush says, as she drops clothespins into a plastic bucket. "A girl I work with is pregnant, and she's quitting work next week."

"I thought I wanted to work at the Villa Romano more than anything, but now I'm not sure," Jane says. What would it be like, waiting on tables with Mrs. Bush?

"It's a good job, and they feed you all you can eat. They've got the *best* ambrosia!"

She drops a clothespin and Jane picks it up. Jane says, "I think I'll join the Army."

Mrs. Bush laughs. "Jimmy's still in California. They would have flown him here and back, but he wouldn't come home. Is that any way for a boy to do his mama?" She tests a pant leg for dampness, and frowns. "I've got to go. Could you bring in these britches for me later?" she asks. "If I'm late to work, my boss will shoot me."

When Jane puts her groceries away, the cereal tumbles to the floor. The milk carton is leaking. She turns on Rock-95 full blast, then rips the cover off the cheesecake and starts eating from the middle. Jane feels strange, quivery. One simple idea could suddenly change everything, the same way a tornado could. Everything in her life is converging, narrowing, like a multitude of tiny lines trying to get through one pinhole. She imagines straightening out a rainbow and rolling it up in a tube. The sound waves travel on rainbows. She can't explain these notions to Coy. They don't even make sense to her. Today, he looked worried about her when she stopped in at Wal-Mart. It has been a crazy day, a stupid weekend. After picking up her unemployment check, she applied for a job at Betty's Boutique, but the opening had been filled five minutes earlier. At Wal-Mart, Coy was patrolling the pet department. In his brown plaid pants, blue shirt, and yellow tie, he looked stylish and comfortable, as though he had finally found a place where he belonged. He seemed like a man whose ambition was to get a service award so he could have his picture in the paper, shaking hands with his boss.

"I hope you're warming a place in bed for me," he whispered to her, within earshot of customers. He touched her elbow, and his thumb poked surreptitiously at her waist. "I have to work tonight," he went on. "We're doing inventory. But we've got to talk."

"O.K.," she said, her eyes fixing on a fish tank in which some remarkably blue fish were darting around like darning-needle flies.

On her way out of the store, without thinking, she stopped and bought a travel kit for her cosmetics, with plastic cases inside for her toothbrush, lotion, and soap. She wasn't sure where she was going. Driving out of the parking lot, she thought how proudly Coy had said, "We're taking inventory," as though he were in thick with Wal-Mart executives. It didn't seem like him. She had deluded herself, expecting more of him just because he was such a sweet lover. She had thought he was an ideal man, like the new contemporary man described in the woman's magazines, but he was just a floorwalker. There was not future in that. Women had been walking the floors for years. She remembered her mother walking the floor with worry, when her father was out late, drinking.

At the Army recruiting station, Jane stuffed the literature into her purse. She took one of everything. On a bulletin board, she read down a list of career-management fields, strange-sounding phrases like Air Defense Artillery, Missile Maintenance, Ballistic Maintenance, Cryptologic Operations, Topographic Engineering. The words stirred her, filled her with awe.

"Here's what I want," she said to the recruiter. "Communications and Electronics Operations."

"That's our top field," said the man, who was wearing a beautiful uniform trimmed with bright ribbons. "You join that and you'll get somewhere."

Later, in her kitchen, her mouth full of cheesecake, Jane reads the electronics brochure, pausing over the phrases "field radio," "teletype," and "radio relay equipment." Special security clearance is required for some electronics operations. She pictures herself someplace remote, in a control booth, sending signals for war, like an engineer in charge of a sports special on TV. She doesn't want to go to war, but if there is one, women should go. She imagines herself in a war, crouching in the jungle, sweating, on the lookout for something to happen. The sounds of warfare would be like the sounds of rock and roll, hard-driving and satisfying.

She sleeps so soundly that when Coy calls the next morning, the telephone rings several times. Rock-95 is already blasting away, and she wonders groggily if it is loud enough over the telephone to upset his equilibrium.

"I'm trying to remember what you used to say about waking up," she says sleepily.

"You know I could never talk till I had my coffee."

"I thought you were giving up coffee. Does your mama make you coffee?"

"Yeah."

"I knew she would." Jane sits up and turns down the radio. "Oh, now I remember what you said. You said it was like being born."

Coy had said that the relaxation of sleep left him defenseless and shattered, so that the daytime was spent restructuring himself, rebuilding defenses. Sleep was a forgetting, and in the daylight he had to gather his strength, remember who he was. For him, the music was an intrusion on a fragile life, and now it makes Jane sad that she hasn't been fair to him.

"Can I come for breakfast?" he asks.

"You took the toaster, and I can't make toast the way you like it."

"Let's go to the Dairy Barn and have some country ham and biscuits."

Jane's sheets are dirty. She was going to wash them at the laundromat and bring them home to dry—to save money and to score a point with her landlady. She says, "I'll meet you as soon as I drop off my laundry at the Washeteria. I've got something to tell you."

"I hope it's good."

"It's not what you think." On the radio, Rod Stewart is bouncing blithely away on "Young Turks." Jane feels older, too old for her and Coy to be young hearts together, free tonight, as the song directs. Jane says, "Red-eye gravy. That's what I want. Do you think they'll have red-eye gravy?"

"Of course they'll have red-eye gravy. Who ever heard of country ham without red-eye gravy?"

After hanging up, Jane lays the sheets on the living-room rug, and in the center she tosses her underwear and blouses and slacks. The colors clash. A tornado in a flower garden. After throwing in her jeans, she ties the corners of the sheets and sets the bundle by the door. As she puts on her makeup, she rehearses what she has to tell Coy. She has imagined his stunned silence. She imagines gathering everyone she knows in the same room, so she can make her announcement as if she were holding a press conference. It would be so much more official.

With her bundle of laundry, she goes bumping down the stairs. A stalk of light from a window on the landing shoots down the stairway. Jane floats through the light, with the dust motes shining all around her, penetrating silently, and then she remembers a dirty T-shirt in the bathroom. Letting the bundle slide to the bottom of the stairs, she turns back to her apartment. She has left the radio on, and for a moment on the landing she thinks that someone must be home.

1987

Simon Ortiz (Acoma Pueblo) b. 1941

Simon Ortiz was born in Albuquerque, New Mexico. After an elementary education in Indian schools, high school, and a stint in the army, he enrolled at the University of New Mexico, where he became aware of N. Scott Momaday, James Welch, and others among the first voices in Native American literature in the late '60s. Although he was always interested in writing, under the pressures of contemporary experience Ortiz found his motive for writing changed from self-expression to the desire to "express a Native American nationalistic (some may call it a tribalistic) literary voice."

Ortiz is a member of the Acoma Pueblo tribe, and his experiences in that community endowed him with several passionate concerns. From his father he learned to reverence the power and integrity of language. By choice, his poetry is fundamentally oral and frequently narrative, because he believes that one experiences life through poetry or, in the oral tradition, song, "Song as language," he has written, "is a way of touching." A second recurrent theme of Ortiz is that we establish our identity, individually and communally, in relation to a sense of place. For the most part, he argues, Anglo-Americans have been alienated from the land, a dislocation they try to valorize with an expansionist Frontier ideology. It is no wonder, then, that Ortiz is also deeply concerned with the political consequences of his writing. He grew up in the uranium mining area of northwest New Mexico, where laborers daily compromised their health and lives in the ruthless exploitation of the natural environment. Ortiz himself worked in such mines, and his identification with workers and the dehumanizing conditions under which they struggle, highlighted in his short story "To Change in a Good Way," permeates his work. Arguments that literature ought to be above politics, be concerned only with beauty and universal significance, do not sway him. Such a position, he argues, is taken by those who want to obscure the political consequences of their own work, "who do not want to hear the truth spoken by those who defend the earth."

Ortiz's interest in the transformative power of compelling language, a historical sense of place, and the political dimensions of poetry are especially evident in his most recent work, a cycle of poems entitled *from Sand Creek*. Based on his experiences as a veteran recovering at a VA hospital, the poems offer a series of discrete, but tonally unified moments of reflection, which contemplate the present condition of the speaker and his nation in view of each's past. Though the book is full of anger, grief, and pain, its dominant theme is compassion. "Love," he writes, "should be answerable for." Only by claiming responsibility for ourselves and our nation, present and past, can we create the possibility of hope.

Andrew O. Wiget
New Mexico State University

PRIMARY WORKS

Going for the Rain, 1976; *A Good Journey*, 1977; *Howbah Indians*, 1978; *Fight Back: For the Sake of the People, For the Sake of the Land*, 1980; *from Sand Creek*, 1981; *Fightin': New and Selected Short Stories*, 1983; *Woven Stone*, 1992; *After and Before the Lightning*, 1994; *Men on the Moon*, 1999; *Out There Somewhere*, 2002; *The Good Rainbow Road*, 2004.

from Sand Creek

November 29, 1864: On that cold dawn, about 600 Southern Cheyenne and Arapaho People, two-thirds of them women and children, were camped on a bend of Sand Creek in southeastern Colorado. The People were at peace. This was expressed two months before by Black Kettle, one of the principal elders of the Cheyennes, in Denver to Governor John Evans and Colonel John W. Chivington, head of the Colorado Volunteers. "I want you to give all these chiefs of the soldiers here to understand that we are for peace, and that we have made peace, that we may not be mistaken for enemies." The reverend Colonel Chivington and his Volunteers and Fort Lyon troops, numbering more than 700 heavily armed men, slaughtered 105 women and children and 28 men.

A U.S. flag presented by President Lincoln in 1863 to Black Kettle in Washington, D.C. flew from a pole above the elder's lodge on that gray dawn. The People had been assured they would be protected by the flag. By mid-1865, the Cheyenne and Arapaho People had been driven out of Colorado Territory.

* * *

This America
has been a burden
of steel and mad
death,
5   but, look now,
there are flowers
and new grass
and a spring wind
rising
10 from Sand Creek.

It was a national quest, dictated by economic motives. Europe was hungry for raw material, and America was abundant forest, rivers, land.

Many of them
built their sod houses
without windows.
Without madness.

5 But fierce, o
with a just determination.

Consulting axioms
and the dream called America.

Cotton Mather[1] was no fool.

10 A few remembered
Andrew Jackson,
knew who he was,
ruminating, savoring
fresh Indian blood.

15 Style is a matter
of preference,
performance,
judgement yearning
to be settled quickly.

20 The axiom
would be the glory of America

---

[1]Cotton Mather (1663–1728) was a Puritan minister and author whose writings were influential during the Salem witch trials of 1692–1693.

at last,
                    no wastelands,
            no forgiveness.

25 The child would be sublime.

                    *   *   *

There are ghost towns all over the West; some are profitable tourist attractions of the "frontier," others are merely sad and unknown.

            What should have been
            important and fruitful
            became bitter.
                    Wasted.
5   Spots appeared on their lungs.
                    Marrow dried
                            in their bones.
                    They ranted.
            Pointless utterances.
10 Truth did not speak for them.

            It is a wonder
            they even made it to California.

            But, of course,
            they did,
15 and they named it success.
            Conquest.
            Destiny.

            Frontiers ended for them
            and a dread settled upon them
20 and became remorseless
                    nameless
                    namelessness.

                    *   *   *

Colonel Chivington was a moral man, believed he was made in the image of God, and he carried out the orders of his nation's law; Kit Carson didn't mind stealing and killing either.

            At the Salvation Army
            a clerk
            caught me
            wandering
5 among old spoons

and knives,
sweaters and shoes.

I couldn't have stolen anything;
my life was stolen already.

10 In protest though,
I should have stolen.
My life. My life.

She caught me;
Carson caught Indians,
15 secured them with his lies.
Bound them with his belief.

After winter,
our own lives fled.

I reassured her
20 what she believed.
Bought a sweater.

And fled.

I should have stolen.
My life. My life.

*   *   *

There is a revolution going on; it is very spiritual and its manifestation is economic,
political, and social. Look to the horizon and listen.

The mind is stunned stark.

At night,
Africa is the horizon.

The cots of the hospital
5 are not part of the dream.

Lie awake, afraid.
Thinned breath.

Was it a scream again.
                                    Far
10 below, far below,
the basement speaks
for Africa, Saigon, Sand Creek.

Souls gather
around campfires.
15 Hills protect them.

Mercenaries gamble
for odds.
            They'll never know.
Indians stalk beyond the dike,
20 carefully measure the distance,
count their bullets.

Stark, I said,
stunned night in the VAH.

*   *   *

The blood poured unto the plains, steaming like breath on winter mornings; the breath
rose into the clouds and became the rain and replenishment.

They were amazed
at so much blood.
                    Spurting,
                    sparkling,
5 splashing, bubbling, steady
hot arcing streams.
                Red
and bright and vivid
unto the grassed plains.
10   Steaming.
So brightly and amazing.
They were awed.

It almost seemed magical
that they had so much blood.
15 It just kept pouring,
like rivers,
like endless floods from the sky,
thunder that had become liquid,
and the thunder surged forever
20 into their minds.
                Indeed,
they must have felt
they should get on their knees
and drink the red rare blood,
25 drink to replenish
their own vivid loss.

Their helpless hands
were like sieves.

*   *   *

*The land and Black Kettle took them in like lost children, and by 1876 land allotment
and reservations and private property were established.*

They must have known.

Surely,
they must have.
Black Kettle
5 met them at the open door
of the plains.

He swept his hand
all about them.
The vista of the mountains
10 was at his shoulder.
The rivers
run from the sky.
Stone soothes
every ache.
15   Dirt feeds us.
Spirit is nutrition.
Like a soul, the land
was open to them, like a child's heart.
There was no paradise,
20 but it would have gently and willingly
and longingly given them food and air
and substance for every comfort.
If they had only acknowledged
even their smallest conceit.

*   *   *

That dream
shall have a name
after all,
and it will not be vengeful
5 but wealthy with love
and compassion
and knowledge.
And it will rise
in this heart
10 which is our America.

1981

John Edgar Wideman b. 1941

John Edgar Wideman was born in Washington, D.C., and grew up in the black Homewood section of Pittsburgh, Pennsylvania. Wideman's parents struggled financially, but managed a decent standard of living for their family. During Wideman's high school years, circumstances allowed the family to move out of Homewood to Shadyside, a more economically prosperous neighborhood; Wideman attended the integrated Peabody High School in Shadyside, starred on the basketball team, became senior class president, and earned the honor of valedictorian.

It was at Peabody High School that Wideman's remarkable intellectual and creative career started to emerge clearly. In these early years, Wideman began to immerse himself in white, Western intellectual influences and traditions, which caused some estrangement from black cultural traditions and psychological separation from black people. After high school, he went on to the University of Pennsylvania to major in English, study the traditional curriculum, and develop his creative writing skills. He also became an All-Ivy-League basketball player. These very impressive credentials earned Wideman a Rhodes Scholarship at his graduation in 1963. Wideman went to Oxford and was one of the first two black Rhodes Scholars to complete the term in over fifty years. After Oxford, Wideman returned to the University of Pennsylvania to become that school's first black tenured professor.

In order to raise their children in a different environment, Wideman and his wife, Judy, moved to Laramie, Wyoming, and the University of Wyoming after he taught at the University of Pennsylvania. Wideman's distance from Homewood ironically drew him back to the African American experience. Listening to family stories while visiting Homewood for his grandmother's funeral in 1973, Wideman began to incorporate influences from the black cultural tradition into his writing (his first novel had been published in 1967, when he was twenty-six), and to move psychologically closer to his family and to black people in his personal life. Wideman spent the years between 1973 and 1981, during which he published none of what he wrote, studying African American cultural influences. He read a wide range of books about the black experience and also studied the culture firsthand, making his family in Homewood his main source. Wideman and his family left Laramie in the late 1980s; he now teaches at the University of Massachusetts at Amherst.

Wideman's first three novels, the third of which appeared in 1973, show strong influences from the mainstream modernist tradition that he studied and knew so thoroughly. These works have black settings and mostly black characters, but Wideman makes the bleak, pessimistic modernist voice dominant over a black cultural voice. These novels often show Wideman as a virtuoso craftsman and writer of great power; however, he did not feel satisfied with what he had done. His writing after 1981, when he refocused his fiction and himself toward blackness, displays very strong postmodernist influences, but postmodernism serves the needs of articulating African American racial concerns and African American cultural tradition, whose voice is dominant. Wideman has published fourteen books since 1981. The quality and volume of his work place him in the first rank of contemporary American writers.

James W. Coleman
University of North Carolina–Chapel Hill

PRIMARY WORKS

A Glance Away, 1967; *Hurry Home,* 1970; *The Lynchers,* 1973; *Hiding Place,* 1981; *Damballah,* 1981; *Sent for You Yesterday,* 1983; *Brothers and Keepers,* 1984; *The Homeward Trilogy,* 1985; *Reuben,* 1987; *Fever,* 1989; *Philadelphia Fire,* 1990; *All Stories Are True,* 1993; *Fatheralong: A Meditation on Fathers and Sons, Race and Society,* 1994; *The Cattle Killing,* 1996; *Two Cities,* 1998; *Hoop Roots,* 2001; *The Island: Martinique,* 2003; *God's Gym,* 2005; *Fanon,* 2008.

Valaida[1]

Whither shall I go from thy spirit?
Or whither shall I flee from thy presence?

Bobby tell the man what he wants to hear. Bobby lights a cigarette. Blows smoke and it rises and rises to where I sit on my cloud overhearing everything. Singing to no one. Golden trumpet from the Queen of Denmark across my knees. In my solitude. Dead thirty years now and meeting people still. Primping loose ends of my hair. Worried how I look. How I sound. Silly. Because things don't change. Bobby with your lashes a woman would kill for, all cheekbones, bushy brows and bushy upper lip, ivory when you smile. As you pretend to contemplate his jive questions behind your screen of smoke and summon me by rolling your big, brown-eyed-handsome-man eyeballs to the ceiling where smoke pauses not one instant, but scoots through and warms me where I am, tell him, Bobby, about "fabled Valaida Snow who traveled in an orchid-colored Mercedes-Benz, dressed in an orchid suit, her pet monkey rigged out in an orchid jacket and cap, with the chauffeur in orchid as well." If you need to, lie like a rug, Bobby. But don't waste the truth, either. They can't take that away from me. Just be cool. As always. Recite those countries and cities we played. Continents we conquered. Roll those faraway places with strange-sounding names around in your sweet mouth. Tell him they loved me at home too, a down-home girl from Chattanooga, Tennessee, who turned out the Apollo, not a mumbling word from wino heaven till they were on their feet hollering and clapping for more with the rest of the audience. Reveries of days gone by, yes, yes, they haunt me, baby, I can taste it. Yesteryears, yesterhours. Bobby, do you also remember what you're not telling him? Blues lick in the middle of a blind flamenco singer's moan. Mother Africa stretching her crusty, dusky hands forth, calling back her far-flung children. Later that same night both of us bad on bad red wine wheeling round and round a dark gypsy cave. Olé. Olé.

Don't try too hard to get it right, he'll never understand. He's watching your cuff links twinkle. Wondering if they're real gold and the studs real diamonds. You called me Minnie Mouse. But you never saw me melted down to sixty-eight pounds soaking wet. They beat me, and fucked me in every hole I had. I was their whore. Their maid.

---

[1]Valaida Snow (c. 1900–1956) was a jazz trumpeter, singer, and dancer of considerable talent whose life inspired this story.

A stool they stood on when they wanted to reach a little higher. But I never sang in their cage, Bobby. Not one note. Cost me a tooth once, but not a note. Tell him that one day I decided I'd had enough and walked away from their hell. Walked across Europe, the Atlantic Ocean, the whole U.S. of A. till I found a quiet spot to put peace back in my soul, and then I began performing again. My tunes. In my solitude. And yes. There was a pitiful little stomped-down white boy in the camp I tried to keep the guards from killing, but if he lived or died I never knew. Then or now. Monkey and chauffeur and limo and champagne and cigars and outrageous dresses with rhinestones, fringe and peekaboo slits. That's the foolishness the reporter's after. Stuff him with your MC b.s., and if he's still curious when you're finished, if he seems a halfway decent sort in spite of himself, you might suggest listening to the trumpet solo in My Heart Belongs to Daddy, *hip him to* Hot Snow, *the next to last cut, my voice and Lady Day's figure and ground, ground and figure* Dear Lord above, send back my love.

He heard her in the bathroom, faucets on and off, on and off, spurting into the sink bowl, the tub. Quick burst of shower spray, rain sound spattering plastic curtain. Now in the quiet she'll be polishing. Every fixture will gleam. *Shine's what people see. See something shiny, don't look no further, most people don't.* If she's rushed she'll wipe and polish faucets, mirrors, metal collars around drains. Learned that trick when she first came to the city and worked with gangs of girls in big downtown hotels. *Told me, said, Don't be fussing around behind in there or dusting under them things, child. Give that mirror a lick. Rub them faucets. Twenty more rooms like this one here still to do before noon.* He lowers the newspaper just enough so he'll see her when she passes through the living room, so she won't see him looking unless she stops and stares, something she never does. She knows he watches. Let him know just how much was enough once upon a time when she first started coming to clean the apartment. Back when he was still leaving for work some mornings. Before they understood each other, when suspicions were mutual and thick as the dust first time she bolted through his doorway, into his rooms, out of breath and wary eyed like someone was chasing her and it might be him.

She'd burst in his door and he'd felt crowded. Retreated, let her stake out the space she required. She didn't bully him but demanded in the language of her brisk, efficient movements that he accustom himself to certain accommodations. They developed an etiquette that spelled out precisely how close, how distant the two of them could be once a week while she cleaned his apartment.

Odd that it took him years to realize how small she was. Shorter than him and no one in his family ever stood higher than five foot plus an inch or so of that thick, straight, black hair. America a land of giants and early on he'd learned to ignore height. You couldn't spend your days like a country lout gawking at the skyscraper heads of your new countrymen. No one had asked him so he'd never needed to describe his cleaning woman. Took no notice of her height. Her name was Clara Jackson and when she arrived he was overwhelmed by the busyness of her presence. How much she seemed to be doing all at once. Noises she'd manufacture with the cleaning paraphernalia, her humming and singing, the gum she popped, heavy thump of her heels even though she changed into tennis sneakers as soon as she crossed the threshold of his apartment, her troubled breathing, asthmatic wheezes and snorts of wrecked sinuses getting worse and worse over the years, her creaking knees, layers of dresses, dusters, slips whispering, the sighs and moans and wincing ejaculations, addresses to invisible presences she smuggled with her into his domain. *Yes, Lord. Save me, Jesus. Thank you, Father.* He backed away from the onslaught, the clamorous weight of it, avoided her systematically. Seldom were they both in the same room at the same time more than a few minutes because clearly none was large enough to contain them and the distance they needed.

She was bent over, replacing a scrubbed rack in the oven when he'd discovered the creases in her skull. She wore a net over her hair like serving girls in Horn and Hardart's. Under the webbing were clumps of hair, defined by furrows exposing her bare scalp. A ribbed yarmulke of hair pressed down on top of her head. Hair he'd never imagined. Like balled yarn in his grandmother's lap. Like a nursery rhyme. *Black sheep. Black sheep, have you any wool?* So different from what grew on his head, the heads of his brothers and sisters and mother and father and cousins and everyone in the doomed village where he was born, so different that he could not truly consider it hair, but some ersatz substitute used the evening of creation when hair ran out. Easier to think of her as bald. Bald and wearing a funny cap fashioned from the fur of some swarthy beast. Springy wires of it jutted from the netting. One dark strand left behind, shocking him when he discovered it marooned in the tub's gleaming, white belly, curled like a question mark at the end of the sentence he was always asking himself. He'd pinched it up in a wad of toilet paper, flushed it away.

Her bag of fleece had grayed and emptied over the years. Less of it now. He'd been tempted countless times to touch it. Poke his finger through the netting into one of the mounds. He'd wondered if she freed it from the veil when she went to bed. If it relaxed and spread against her pillow or if she slept all night like a soldier in a helmet.

When he stood beside her or behind her he could spy on the design of creases, observe how the darkness was cultivated into symmetrical plots and that meant he was taller than Clara Jackson, that he was looking down at her. But those facts did not calm the storm of motion and noise, did not undermine her power any more than the accident of growth, the half inch he'd attained over his next tallest brother, the inch eclipsing the height of his father, would have diminished his father's authority over the family, if there had been a family, the summer after he'd shot up past everyone, at thirteen the tallest, the height he remained today.

Mrs. Clara. Did you know a colored woman once saved my life?

Why is she staring at him as if he's said, Did you know I slept with a colored woman once? He didn't say that. Her silence fusses at him as if he did, as if he'd blurted out something unseemly, ungentlemanly, some insult forcing her to tighten her jaw and push her tongue into her cheek, and taste the bitterness of the hard lump inside her mouth. Why is she ready to cry, or call him a liar, throw something at him or demand an apology or look right through him, past him, the way his mother stared at him on endless October afternoons, gray slants of rain falling so everybody's trapped indoors and she's cleaning, cooking, tending a skeletal fire in the hearth and he's misbehaving, teasing his little sister till he gets his mother's attention and then he shrivels in the weariness of those sad eyes catching him in the act, piercing him, ignoring him, the hurt, iron and distance in them accusing him. Telling him for this moment, and perhaps forever, for this cruel, selfish trespass, you do not exist.

No, Mistah Cohen. That's one thing I definitely did not know.

His fingers fumble with a button, unfastening the cuff of his white shirt. He's rolling up one sleeve. Preparing himself for the work of storytelling. She has laundered the shirt how many times. It's held together by cleanliness and starch. A shirt that ought to be thrown away but she scrubs and sprays and irons it; he knows the routine, the noises. She saves it how many times, patching, mending, snipping errant threads, the frayed edges of cuff and collar hardened again so he is decent, safe within them, the blazing white breast he puffs out like a penguin when it's spring and he descends from the twelfth floor and conquers the park again, shoes shined, the remnants of that glorious head of hair slicked back, freshly shaved cheeks raw as a baby's in the brisk sunshine of those first days welcoming life back and yes he's out there in it again, his splay-foot penguin walk and gentleman's attire, shirt like a pledge, a promise, a declaration framing muted stripes of his dark tie. Numbers stamped inside the collar. Mark of the dry cleaners from a decade ago, before Clara Jackson began coming to clean. Traces still visible inside the neck of some of his shirts she's maintained impossibly long past their prime, a row of faded numerals like those he's pushing up his sleeve to show her on his skin.

The humped hairs on the back of his forearm are pressed down like grass in the woods where a hunted animal has slept. Gray hairs the color of his flesh, except inside his forearm, just above his wrist, the skin is whiter, blue veined. All of it, what's gray, what's pale, what's mottled with dark spots is meat that turns to lard and stinks a sweet sick stink to high heaven if you cook it.

Would you wish to stop now? Sit down a few minutes, please. I will make a coffee for you and my tea. I tell you a story. It is Christmas soon, no?

She is stopped in her tracks. A tiny woman, no doubt about it. Lumpy now. Perhaps she steals and hides things under her dress. Lumpy, not fat. Her shoulders round and padded. Like the derelict women who live in the streets and wear their whole wardrobes winter spring summer fall. She has put on flesh for protection. To soften blows. To ease around corners. Something cushioned to lean against. Something to muffle the sound of bones breaking when she falls. A pillow for all the heads gone and gone to dust who still find ways at night to come to her and seek a resting place. He could find uses for it. Extra flesh on her bones was not excess, was a gift. The female abundance, her thickness, her bulk reassuring as his hams shrink, his fingers become claws, the chicken neck frets away inside those razor-edged collars she scrubs and irons.

Oh you scarecrow. Death's-head stuck on a stick. Another stick lashed crossways for arms. First time you see yourself dead you giggle. You are a survivor, a lucky one. You grin, stick out your tongue at the image in the shard of smoky glass because the others must be laughing, can't help themselves, the ring of them behind your back, peeking over your scrawny shoulders, watching as you discover in the mirror what they've been seeing since they stormed the gates and kicked open the sealed barracks door and rescued you from the piles of live kindling that were to be your funeral pyre. Your fellow men. Allies. Victors. Survivors. Who stare at you when they think you're not looking, whose eyes are full of shame, as if they've been on duty here, in this pit, this stewpot cooking the meat from your bones. They cannot help themselves. You laugh to help them forget what they see. What you see. When they herded your keepers past you, their grand uniforms shorn of buttons, braid, ribbons, medals, the twin bolts of frozen lightning, golden skulls, eagles' wings, their jackboots gone, feet bare or in peasant clogs, heads bowed and hatless, iron faces unshaven, the butchers still outweighed you a hundred pounds a man. You could not conjure up the spit to mark them. You dropped your eyes in embarrassment, pretended to nod off because your body was too weak to manufacture a string of spittle, and if you could have, you'd have saved it, hoarded and tasted it a hundred times before you swallowed the precious bile.

A parade of shambling, ox-eyed animals. They are marched past you, marched past open trenches that are sewers brimming with naked, rotting flesh, past barbed-wire compounds where the living sift slow and insubstantial as fog among the heaps of dead. No one believes any of it. Ovens and gas chambers. Gallows and whipping posts. Shoes, shoes, shoes, a mountain of shoes in a warehouse. Shit. Teeth. Bones. Sacks of hair. The undead who huddle into themselves like bats and settle down on a patch of filthy earth mourning their own passing. No one believes the enemy. He is not these harmless farmers filing past in pillaged uniforms to do the work of cleaning up this mess someone's made. No one has ever seen a ghost trying to double itself in a mirror so they laugh behind its back, as if, as if the laughter is a game and the dead one could muster up the energy to join in and be made whole again. I giggle. I say, Who in God's name would steal a boy's face and leave this thing?

Nearly a half century of rich meals with seldom one missed but you cannot fill the emptiness, cannot quiet the clamor of those lost souls starving, the child you were, weeping from hunger, those selves, those stomachs you watched swelling, bloating, unburied for days and you dreamed of opening them, of taking a spoon to whatever was growing inside because you were so empty inside and nothing could be worse than that gnawing emptiness. Why should the dead be ashamed to eat the dead? Who are their brothers, sisters, themselves? You hear the boy talking to himself, hallucinating milk, bread, honey. Sick when the spoiled meat is finally carted away.

Mistah Cohen, I'm feeling kinda poorly today. If you don mind I'ma work straight through and gwan home early. Got all my Christmas still to do and I'm tired.

She wags her head. Mumbles more he can't decipher. As if he'd offered many times before, as if there is nothing strange or special this morning at 10:47, him standing at the china cupboard prepared to open it and bring down sugar bowl, a silver cream pitcher, cups and saucers for the two of them, ready to fetch instant coffee, a tea bag, boil water and sit down across the table from her. As if it happens each day she comes, as if this once is not the first time, the only time he's invited this woman to sit with him and she can wag her old head, stare at him moon eyed as an owl and refuse what's never been offered before.

The tattoo is faint. From where she's standing, fussing with the vacuum cleaner, she won't see a thing. Her eyes, in spite of thick spectacles, watery and weak as his. They have grown old together, avoiding each other in these musty rooms where soon, soon, no way round it, he will wake up dead one morning and no one will know till she knocks Thursday, and knocks again, then rings, pounds, hollers, but no one answers and she thumps away to rouse the super with his burly ring of keys.

He requires less sleep as he ages. Time weighs more on him as time slips away, less and less time as each second passes but also more of it, the past accumulating in vast drifts like snow in the darkness outside his window. In the wolf hours before dawn this strange city sleeps as uneasily as he does, turning, twisting, groaning. He finds himself listening intently for a sign that the night knows he's listening, but what he hears is his absence. The night busy with itself, denying him. And if he is not out there, if he can hear plainly his absence in the night pulse of the city, where is he now, where was he before his eyes opened, where will he be when the flutter of breath and heart stop?

They killed everyone in the camps. The whole world was dying there. Not only Jews. People forget. All kinds locked in the camps. Yes. Even Germans who were not Jews. Even a black woman. Not gypsy. Not African. American like you, Mrs. Clara.

They said she was a dancer and could play any instrument. Said she could line up shoes from many countries and hop from one pair to the next, performing the dances of the world. They said the Queen of Denmark had honored her with a gold trumpet. But she was there, in hell with the rest of us.

A woman like you. Many years ago. A lifetime ago. Young then as you would have been. And beautiful. As I believe you must have been, Mrs. Clara. Yes. Before America entered the war. Already camps had begun devouring people. All kinds of people. Yet she was rare. Only woman like her I ever saw until I came here, to this country, this city. And she saved my life.

Poor thing.

I was just a boy. Thirteen years old. The guards were beating me. I did not know why. Why? They didn't need a why. They just beat. And sometimes the beating ended in death because there was no reason to stop, just as there was no reason to begin. A boy. But I'd seen it many times. In the camp long enough to forget why I was alive, why anyone would want to live for long. They were hurting me, beating the life out of me but I was not surprised, expected no explanation. I remember curling up as I had seen a dog once cowering from the blows of a rolled newspaper. In the old country lifetimes ago. A boy in my village staring at a dog curled and rolling on its back in the dust outside the baker's shop and our baker in his white apron and tall white hat striking this mutt again and again. I didn't know what mischief the dog had done. I didn't understand why the fat man with flour on his apron was whipping it unmercifully. I simply saw it and hated the man, felt sorry for the animal, but already the child in me understood it could be no other way so I rolled and curled myself against the blows as I'd remembered that spotted dog in the dusty village street because that's the way it had to be.

Then a woman's voice in a language I did not comprehend reached me. A woman angry, screeching. I heard her before I saw her. She must have been screaming at them to stop. She must have decided it was better to risk dying than watch the guards pound a boy to death. First I heard her voice, then she rushed in, fell on me, wrapped herself around me. The guards shouted at her. One tried to snatch her away. She wouldn't let go of me and they began to beat her too. I heard the thud of clubs on her back, felt her shudder each time a blow was struck.

She fought to her feet, dragging me with her. Shielding me as we stumbled and slammed into a wall.

My head was buried in her smock. In the smell of her, the smell of dust, of blood. I was surprised how tiny she was, barely my size, but strong, very strong. Her fingers dug into my shoulders, squeezing, gripping hard enough to hurt me if I hadn't been past the point of feeling pain. Her hands were strong, her legs alive and warm, churning, churning as she pressed me against herself, into her. Somehow she'd pulled me up and back to the barracks wall, propping herself, supporting me, sheltering me. Then she screamed at them in this language I use now but did not know one word of then, cursing them, I'm sure, in her mother tongue, a stream of spit and sputtering sounds as if she could build a wall of words they could not cross.

The kapos hesitated, astounded by what she'd dared. Was this black one a madwoman, a witch? Then they tore me from her grasp, pushed me down and I crumpled there in the stinking mud of the compound. One more kick, a numbing, blinding smash that took my breath away. Blood flooded my eyes. I lost consciousness. Last I saw of her she was still fighting, slim, beautiful legs kicking at them as they dragged and punched her across the yard.

You say she was colored?

Yes. Yes. A dark angel who fell from the sky and saved me.

Always thought it was just you people over there doing those terrible things to each other.

He closes the china cupboard. Her back is turned. She mutters something at the metal vacuum tubes she's unclamping. He realizes he's finished his story anyway. Doesn't know how to say the rest. She's humming, folding rags, stacking them on the bottom pantry shelf. Lost in the cloud of her own noise. Much more to his story, but she's not waiting around to hear it. This is her last day before the holidays. He'd sealed her bonus in an envelope, placed the envelope where he always does on the kitchen counter. The kitchen cabinet doors have magnetic fasteners for a tight fit. After a volley of doors clicking, she'll be gone. When he's alone preparing his evening meal, he depends on those clicks for company. He pushes so they strike not too loud, not too soft. They punctuate the silence, reassure him like the solid slamming of doors in big sedans he used to ferry from customer to customer. How long since he'd been behind the wheel of a car? Years, and now another year almost gone. In every corner of the city they'd be welcoming their Christ, their New Year with extravagant displays of joy. He thinks of Clara Jackson in the midst of her family. She's little but the others are brown and large, with lips like spoons for serving the sugary babble of their speech. He tries to picture them, eating and drinking, huge people crammed in a tiny, shabby room. Unimaginable, really. The faces of her relatives become his. Everyone's hair is thick and straight and black.

1989

Gloria Anzaldúa 1942–2004

When Gloria Anzaldúa described the United States and Mexico border as "una herida abierta" (an open wound), she spoke from her lived experience as a native border dweller. Born in the ranch settlement of Jesus Maria in south Texas, Anzaldúa grew up in the small town of Hargill, Texas, and later wrote and taught in northern California. In her poetry, fiction, essays, and autobiography, she wrote eloquently of the indignities a Chicana lesbian feminist overcomes as she escapes the strictures of patriarchal Chicano traditions and confronts the injustices of dominant culture.

Her highly acclaimed text, *Borderlands/La Frontera: The New Mestiza*, interweaves autobiography, history of the Chicana/o Southwest, essay, autobiography, and poetry in a manner that defies traditional categorization. Chicana *mestizaje* in the late twentieth century can be seen as a new genre that describes the cultural and linguistic global connections between Chicana writers and writers of the Americas. The bilingual title of her book illustrates the transcultural experience of border dwellers and border consciousness. English and Spanish co-exist for Mexican-descent people of the borderlands. In Anzaldúa's text, the pre-conquest language, Nahuatl, mixes with English and Spanish. Likewise, the Chicana language that Anzaldúa deploys in this text can be said to be a new Chicana language, one that legitimizes the intermingling of English and Spanish with indigenous Nahuatl.

In *Borderlands* Anzaldúa presents multiple issues that inform a radical political awareness. These issues culminate in what she called a new consciousness for the women who examine and question the restrictions placed on them in the borderlands of the United States. In Anzaldúa's political manifesto, a "new mestiza" emerges only after her oppositional consciousness develops.

The chapter "Entering into the Serpent" presents some *cuentos* (stories) that border families tell their children. For Prieta, the narrator of this section, the story of the snake that slithers into a woman's uterus and impregnates her provides the link to Anzaldúa's "serpentine" feminist theory. The new mestiza's task is to "winnow out the lies" as a Chicana feminist historian. She also provides alternative metaphors to the ones promoted by androcentric psychologists and priests. Anzaldúa's new mestiza invokes Olmec myth when she asserts that "Earth is a coiled Serpent" and rewrites the origin of the Catholic Guadalupe, empowering her as a pre-Columbian "*Coatlalopeuh, She Who Has Dominion over Serpents.*"

Like the constantly shifting identities of the Chicana in the contemporary world, the deities that Anzaldúa unearths and names become a pantheon of possible feminist icons. Through these icons mestizas can unlearn the masculinist versions of history, religion, and myth. She methodically shows how both the "male-dominated Azteca-Mexica culture" and the post-conquest church established the binary of the *virgen/puta* (Virgin/whore) when they split Coatlalopeuh/Coatlicue/Tonantsi/Tlazolteotl/Cihuacoatl into good and evil, light and dark, sexual and asexual beings. Guadalupe, then, is Coatlalopeuh with "the serpent/sexuality out of her."

Anzaldúa revises androcentric myths of the Chicano homeland, Aztlán, and of *La Llorona* (the Weeping Woman). She intertwines the familiar stories with new feminist threads so that her insistence on the recuperation of the feminist—the serpent—produces a tapestry at once familiar and radically different. While "la facultad" can be interpreted as a spiritual extrasensory perception, what Anzaldúa has in fact developed is the ability to rupture dominating belief systems that have been presented as ancient truths and accurate histories.

The second excerpt, "*La conciencia de la mestiza:* Towards a New Consciousness," is the final chapter of the prose section of the book. In this essay, Anzaldúa summarizes her mestiza methodology. Mestiza methodology offers strategies for unearthing a razed indigenous history as a process of coming to consciousness as political agents of change. Mestizas can turn to pre-conquest history and historical sites such as the Aztec temples to recover women's place in a past that has been satanized. With the new knowledge they learn of the central importance of female deities rendered passive with Western androcentric ideology. The mestiza/mestizo Aztec legacy focuses only on the blood sacrifices of this military power and further obscures the other indigenous tribal traditions that Aztec hegemony absorbed. Anzaldúa's reclamation of Aztec deities and traditions begins a reformulation of Aztlán from a male nation-state to a feminist site of resistance.

For Anzaldúa, Chicana feminism and lesbian politics emerged as forces that gave voice to her political agenda as a new mestiza, an identity that claims much more than the simple definition of *mestizo* (mixed blood) allows. In this section, Anzaldúa clearly presents her political ideology, which is historically grounded in the colonial legacy of the American Southwest in its relation to larger hemispheric events. In *Borderlands,* American and Mexican history, American and Mexican culture are contested fields.

Sonia Saldívar-Hull
University of California at Los Angeles

PRIMARY WORKS

This Bridge Called My Back: Writing by Radical Women of Color, ed. with Cherríe Moraga, 1981; *Borderlands/La Frontera: The New Mestiza,* 1987; *Interviews/Entrevistas,* 2000; *This Bridge We Call Home,* 2002.

from Borderlands/La Frontera

3

Entering into the Serpent

> Sueño con serpientes, con serpientes del mar,
> Con cierto mar, ay de serpientes sueño yo.
> Largas, transparentes, en sus barrigas llevan
> Lo que pueden arebatarle al amor.
> Oh, oh, oh, la mató y aparese una mayor.
> Oh, con mucho más infierno en digestión.
>
> I dream of serpents, serpents of the sea,
> A certain sea, oh, of serpents I dream.
> Long, transparent, in their bellies they carry
> All that they can snatch away from love.
> Oh, oh, oh, I kill one and a larger one appears.
> Oh, with more hellfire burning inside!
> —Silvio Rodríguez, *"Sueño Con Serpientes"*[1]

In the predawn orange haze, the sleepy crowing of roosters atop the trees. *No vayas al escusado en lo oscuro.* Don't go to the outhouse at night, Prieta, my mother would say. *No se te vaya a meter algo por allá.* A snake will crawl into your *nalgas,*[2] make you pregnant. They seek warmth in the cold. *Dicen que las culebras* like to suck *chiches,*[3] can draw milk out of you.

---

[1]From the song *"Sueño Con Serpientes"* by Silvio Rodríguez, from the album *Días y flores.* Translated by Barbara Dane with the collaboration of Rina Benmauor and Juan Flores. [All notes are Anzaldúa's—Ed.]

[2]Vagina, buttocks.
[3]They say snakes like to suck women's teats.

En el escusado in the half-light spiders hang like gliders. Under my bare buttocks and the rough planks the deep yawning tugs at me. I can see my legs fly up to my face as my body falls through the round hole into the sheen of swarming maggots below. Avoiding the snakes under the porch I walk back into the kitchen, step on a big black one slithering across the floor.

Ella tiene su tono[4]

Once we were chopping cotton in the fields of Jesus Maria Ranch. All around us the woods. *Quelite*[5] towered above me, choking the stubby cotton that had outlived the deer's teeth.

I swung *el azadón*[6] hard. *El quelite* barely shook, showered nettles on my arms and face. When I heard the rattle the world froze.

I barely felt its fangs. Boot got all the *veneno*.[7] My mother came shrieking, swinging her hoe high, cutting the earth, the writhing body.

I stood still, the sun beat down. Afterwards I smelled where fear had been: back of neck, under arms, between my legs; I felt its heat slide down my body. I swallowed the rock it had hardened into.

When Mama had gone down the row and was out of sight, I took out my pocketknife. I made an X over each prick. My body followed the blood, fell onto the soft ground. I put my mouth over the red and sucked and spit between the rows of cotton.

I picked up the pieces, placed them end on end. *Culebra de cascabel*.[8] I counted the rattlers: twelve. It would shed no more. I buried the pieces between the rows of cotton.

That night I watched the window sill, watched the moon dry the blood on the tail, dreamed rattler fangs filled my mouth, scales covered my body. In the morning I saw through snake eyes, felt snake blood course through my body. The serpent, *mi tono*, my animal counterpart. I immune to its venom. Forever immune.

Snakes, *víboras*: since that day I've sought and shunned them. Always when they cross my path, fear and elation flood my body. I know things older than Freud, older than gender. She—that's how I think of *la Víbora*, Snake Woman. Like the ancient Olmecs, I know Earth is a coiled Serpent. Forty years it's taken me to enter into the Serpent, to acknowledge that I have a body, that I am a body and to assimilate the animal body, the animal soul.

Coatlalopeuh, She Who Has Dominion over Serpents

Mi mamagrande Ramona toda su vida mantuvo un altar pequeño en la esquina del comedor. Siempre tenía las velas prendidas. Allí hacía promesas a la Virgen de Guadalupe. My family, like most Chicanos, did not practice Roman Catholicism but

---

[4]She has supernatural power from her animal soul, the *tono*.
[5]Weed.
[6]The hoe.
[7]Venom, poison.
[8]Rattlesnake.

a folk Catholicism with many pagan elements. *La Virgen de Guadalupe*'s Indian name is *Coatlalopeuh.* She is the central deity connecting us to our Indian ancestry.

Coatlalopeuh is descended from, or is an aspect of, earlier Mesoamerican fertility and Earth goddesses. The earliest is *Coatlicue,* or "Serpent Skirt." She had a human skull or serpent for a head, a necklace of human hearts, a skirt of twisted serpents and taloned feet. As creator goddess, she was mother of the celestial deities, and of *Huitzilopochtli* and his sister, *Coyolxauhqui,* She With Golden Bells, Goddess of the Moon, who was decapitated by her brother. Another aspect of *Coatlicue* is *Tonantsi.*[9] The Totonacs, tired of the Aztec human sacrifices to the male god, *Huitzilopochtli,* renewed their reverence for *Tonantsi* who preferred the sacrifice of birds and small animals.[10]

The male-dominated Azteca-Mexica culture drove the powerful female deities underground by giving them monstrous attributes and by substituting male deities in their place, thus splitting the female Self and the female deities. They divided her who had been complete, who possessed both upper (light) and underworld (dark) aspects. *Coatlicue,* the Serpent goddess, and her more sinister aspects, *Tlazolteotl* and *Cihuacoatl,* were "darkened" and disempowered much in the same manner as the Indian *Kali.*

Tonantsi—split from her dark guises, *Coatlicue, Tlazolteotl,* and *Cihuacoatl,*— became the good mother. The Nahuas, through ritual and prayer, sought to oblige *Tonantsi* to ensure their health and the growth of their crops. It was she who gave *México* the cactus plant to provide her people with milk and pulque. It was she who defended her children against the wrath of the Christian God by challenging God, her son, to produce mother's milk (as she had done) to prove that his benevolence equalled his disciplinary harshness.[11]

After the Conquest, the Spaniards and their Church continued to split *Tonantsi/Guadalupe.* They desexed *Guadalupe,* taking *Coatlalopeuh,* the serpent/sexuality, out of her. They completed the split begun by the Nahuas by making *la Virgen de Guadalupe/Virgen María* into chaste virgins and *Tlazolteotl/Coatlicue/la Chingada* into *putas;* into the Beauties and the Beasts. They went even further; they made all Indian deities and religious practices the work of the devil.

Thus *Tonantsi* became *Guadalupe,* the chaste protective mother, the defender of the Mexican people.

El nueve de diciembre del año 1531
a las cuatro de la madrugada
un pobre indio que se llamaba Juan Diego

---

[9]In some Nahuatl dialects *Tonantsi* is called *Tonatzin,* literally "Our Holy Mother." "*Tonan* was a name given in Nahuatl to several mountains, these being the congelations of the Earth Mother at spots convenient for her worship." The Mexica considered the mountain mass southwest of Chapultepec to be their mother. Burr Cartwright Brundage, *The Fifth Sun: Aztec Gods, Aztec World* (Austin, TX: University of Texas Press, 1979), 154, 242.

[10]Ena Campbell, "The Virgin of Guadalupe and the Female Self-Image: A Mexican Case History," *Mother Worship: Themes and Variations,* James J. Preston, ed. (Chapel Hill, NC: University of North Carolina Press, 1982), 22.

[11]Alan R. Sandstrom, "The Tonantsi Cult of the Eastern Nahuas," *Mother Worship: Themes and Variations,* James J. Preston, ed.

iba cruzando el cerro de Tepeyác
cuando oyó un cantó de pájaro.
Alzó al cabeza vío que en la cima del cerro
estaba cubierta con una brillante nube blanca.
Parada en frente del sol
sobre una luna creciente
sostenida por un ángel
estaba una azteca
vestida en ropa de india.
Nuestra Señora María de Coatlalopeuh
se le apareció.
"Juan Diegito, El-que-habla-como-un-águila,"
la Virgen le dijo en el lenguaje azteca.
"Para hacer mi altar este cerro eligo.
Dile a tu gente que yo soy la madre de Dios,
a los indios yo les ayudaré."
Estó se lo contó a Juan Zumarraga
pero el obispo no le creyo.
Juan Diego volvió, lleño su tilma[12]
con rosas de castilla
creciendo milagrosamente en la nieve.
Se las llevó al obispo,
y cuando abrió su tilma
el retrato de la Virgen
ahí estaba pintado.

Guadalupe appeared on December 9, 1531, on the spot where the Aztec goddess, *Tonantsi* ("Our Lady Mother"), had been worshipped by the Nahuas and where a temple to her had stood. Speaking Nahua, she told Juan Diego, a poor Indian crossing Tepeyac Hill, whose Indian name was *Cuautlaohuac* and who belonged to the *mazehual* class, the humblest within the Chichimeca tribe, that her name was *María Coatlalopeuh. Coatl* is the Nahuatl word for serpent. *Lopeuh* means "the one who has dominion over serpents." I interpret this as "the one who is at one with the beasts." Some spell her name *Coatlaxopeuh* (pronounced *"Cuatlashupe"* in Nahuatl) and say that *"xopeuh"* means "crushed or stepped on with disdain." Some say it means "she who crushed the serpent," with the serpent as the symbol of the indigenous religion, meaning that her religion was to take the place of the Aztec religion.[13] Because *Coatlalopeuh* was homophonous to the Spanish *Guadalupe,* the Spanish identified her with the dark Virgin, *Guadalupe,* patroness of West Central Spain.[14]

From that meeting, Juan Diego walked away with the image of *la Virgen* painted on his cloak. Soon after, Mexico ceased to belong to Spain, and *la Virgen de*

---

[12]An oblong cloth that hangs over the back and ties together across the shoulders.

[13]Andres Gonzales Guerrero, Jr., *The Significance of* Nuestra Señora de Gualdalupe *and* La Raza Cósmica *in the Development of a Chicano Theology of Liberation* (Ann Arbor, MI: University Microfilms International, 1984), 122.

[14]*Algunos dicen que Guadalupe es una palabra derivada del lenguaje árabe que significa "Río Oculto."* Tomie de Paola, *The Lady of Guadalupe* (New York: Holiday House, 1980), 44.

Guadalupe began to eclipse all the other male and female religious figures in Mexico, Central America and parts of the U.S. Southwest. *"Desde entonces para el mexicano ser Guadalupano es algo esencial/*Since then for the Mexican, to be a *Guadalupano* is something essential."[15]

Mi Virgen Morena	My brown virgin
Mi Virgen Ranchera	my country virgin
Eres nuestra Reina	you are our queen
México es tu tierra	Mexico is your land
Y tú su bandera.	and you its flag.

—*"La Virgen Ranchera"*[16]

In 1660 the Roman Catholic Church named her Mother of God, considering her synonymous with *la Virgen María;* she became *la Santa Patrona de los mexicanos.* The role of defender (or patron) has traditionally been assigned to male gods. During the Mexican Revolution, Emiliano Zapata and Miguel Hidalgo used her image to move *el pueblo mexicano* toward freedom. During the 1965 grape strike in Delano, California, and in subsequent Chicano farmworkers' marches in Texas and other parts of the Southwest, her image on banners heralded and united the farmworkers. *Pachucos* (zoot suiters) tattoo her image on their bodies. Today, in Texas and Mexico she is more venerated than Jesus or God the Father. In the Lower Rio Grande Valley of south Texas it is *la Virgen de San Juan de los Lagos* (an aspect of *Guadalupe*) that is worshipped by thousands every day at her shrine in San Juan. In Texas she is considered the patron saint of Chicanos. *Cuando Carito, mi hermanito,* was missing in action and, later, wounded in Viet Nam, *mi mamá* got on her knees *y le prometío a Ella que si su hijito volvía vivo* she would crawl on her knees and light novenas in her honor.

Today, *la Virgen de Guadalupe* is the single most potent religious, political and cultural image of the Chicano/*mexicano.* She, like my race, is a synthesis of the old world and the new, of the religion and culture of the two races in our psyche, the conquerors and the conquered. She is the symbol of the *mestizo* true to his or her Indian values. *La cultura chicana* identifies with the mother (Indian) rather than with the father (Spanish). Our faith is rooted in indigenous attributes, images, symbols, magic and myth. Because *Guadalupe* took upon herself the psychological and physical devastation of the conquered and oppressed *indio,* she is our spiritual, political and psychological symbol. As a symbol of hope and faith, she sustains and insures our survival. The Indian, despite extreme despair, suffering and near genocide, has survived. To Mexicans on both sides of the border, *Guadalupe* is the symbol of our rebellion against the rich, upper and middleclass; against their subjugation of the poor and the *indio.*

Guadalupe unites people of different races, religions, languages: Chicano protestants, American Indians and whites. *"Nuestra abogada siempre serás/*Our *mediatrix* you will always be." She mediates between the Spanish and the Indian cultures (or

[15] *"Desde el cielo una hermosa mañana,"* from *Propios de la misa de Nuestra Señora de Guadalupe,* Guerrero, 124.

[16] From *"La Virgen Ranchera,"* Guerrero, 127.

three cultures as in the case of *mexicanos* of African or other ancestry) and between Chicanos and the white world. She mediates between humans and the divine, between this reality and the reality of spirit entities. *La Virgen de Guadalupe* is the symbol of ethnic identity and of the tolerance for ambiguity that Chicanos-*mexicanos,* people of mixed race, people who have Indian blood, people who cross cultures, by necessity possess.

La gente Chicana tiene tres madres. All three are mediators: *Guadalupe,* the virgin mother who has not abandoned us, *la Chingada (Malinche),* the raped mother whom we have abandoned, and *la Llorona,* the mother who seeks her lost children and is a combination of the other two.

Ambiguity surrounds the symbols of these three "Our Mothers." *Guadalupe* has been used by the Church to mete out institutionalized oppression: to placate the Indians and *mexicanos* and Chicanos. In part, the true identity of all three has been subverted—*Guadalupe* to make us docile and enduring, *la Chingada* to make us ashamed of our Indian side, and *la Llorona* to make us long-suffering people. This obscuring has encouraged the *virgen/puta* (whore) dichotomy.

Yet we have not all embraced this dichotomy. In the U.S. Southwest, Mexico, Central and South America the *indio* and the *mestizo* continue to worship the old spirit entities (including *Guadalupe*) and their supernatural power, under the guise of Christian saints.[17]

Las invoco diosas mías, ustedes las indias
sumergidas en mi carne que son mis sombras.
Ustedes que persisten mudas en sus cuevas.
Ustedes Señoras que ahora, como yo,
     están en desgracia.

For Waging War Is My Cosmic Duty: The Loss of the Balanced Oppositions and the Change to Male Dominance

Therefore I decided to leave
The country (Aztlán),
Therefore I have come as one charged with a
     special duty,
Because I have been given arrows and shields,
For waging war is my duty,
And on my expeditions I
Shall see all the lands,
I shall wait for the people and meet them
In all four quarters and I shall give them
Food to eat and drinks to quench their thirst,
For here I shall unite all the different peoples!
—*Huitzilopochtli* speaking to the Azteca-Mexica[18]

[17]*La Virgen María* is often equated with the Aztec *Teleoinam,* the Maya *Ixchel,* the Inca *Mamacocha* and the Yuroba *Yemayá.*

[18]Geoffrey Parrinder, ed., *World Religions: From Ancient History to the Present* (New York, NY: Facts on File Publications, 1971), 72.

Before the Aztecs became a militaristic, bureaucratic state where male predatory warfare and conquest were based on patrilineal nobility, the principle of balanced opposition between the sexes existed.[19] The people worshipped the Lord and Lady of Duality, *Ometecuhtli* and *Omecihuatl.* Before the change to male dominance, *Coatlicue,* Lady of the Serpent Skirt, contained and balanced the dualities of male and female, light and dark, life and death.

The changes that led to the loss of the balanced oppositions began when the Azteca, one of the twenty Toltec tribes, made the last pilgrimage from a place called Aztlán. The migration south began about the year A.D. 820. Three hundred years later the advance guard arrived near Tula, the capital of the declining Toltec empire. By the 11th century, they had joined with the Chichimec tribe of Mexitin (afterwards called Mexica) into one religious and administrative organization within Aztlán, the Aztec territory. The Mexitin, with their tribal god *Tetzauhteotl Huitzilopochtli* (Magnificent Humming Bird on the Left), gained control of the religious system.[20] (In some stories *Huitzilopochtli* killed his sister, the moon goddess *Malinalxoch,* who used her supernatural power over animals to control the tribe rather than wage war.)

Huitzilopochtli assigned the Azteca-Mexica the task of keeping the human race (the present cosmic age called the Fifth Sun, *El Quinto Sol*) alive. They were to guarantee the harmonious preservation of the human race by unifying all the people on earth into one social, religious and administrative organ. The Aztec people considered themselves in charge of regulating all earthly matters.[21] Their instrument: controlled or regulated war to gain and exercise power.

After 100 years in the central plateau, the Azteca-Mexica went to Chapultepec, where they settled in 1248 (the present site of the park on the outskirts of Mexico City). There, in 1345, the Aztec-Mexica chose the site of their capital, Tenochtitlan.[22] By 1428, they dominated the Central Mexican lake area.

The Aztec ruler, *Itzcoatl,* destroyed all the painted documents (books called codices) and rewrote a mythology that validated the wars of conquest and thus continued the shift from a tribe based on clans to one based on classes. From 1429 to 1440, the Aztecs emerged as a militaristic state that preyed on neighboring tribes for tribute and captives.[23] The "wars of flowers" were encounters between local armies with a fixed number of warriors, operating within the Aztec World, and, according to set rules, fighting ritual battles at fixed times and on predetermined battlefields. The religious purpose of these wars was to procure prisoners of war who could be sacrificed to the deities of the capturing party. For if one "fed" the gods, the human race would be saved from total extinction. The social purpose was to enable males of noble families and warriors of low descent to win honor, fame and administrative offices, and to prevent social and cultural decadence of the elite. The Aztec people were free to have their own religious faith, provided it did not conflict too much with

---

[19]Levi-Stauss's paradigm which opposes nature to culture and female to male has no such validity in the early history of our Indian forebears. June Nash, "The Aztecs and the Ideology of Male Dominance," *Signs* (Winter, 1978), 349.

[20]Parrinder, 72.
[21]Parrinder, 77.
[22]Nash, 352.
[23]Nash, 350, 355.

the three fundamental principles of state ideology: to fulfill the special duty set forth by *Huitzilopochtli* of unifying all peoples, to participate in the wars of flowers, and to bring ritual offerings and do penance for the purpose of preventing decadence.[24]

Matrilineal descent characterized the Toltecs and perhaps early Aztec society. Women possessed property, and were curers as well as priestesses. According to the codices, women in former times had the supreme power in Tula, and in the beginning of the Aztec dynasty, the royal blood ran through the female line. A council of elders of the Calpul headed by a supreme leader, or *tlactlo,* called the father and mother of the people, governed the tribe. The supreme leader's vice-emperor occupied the position of "Snake Woman" or *Cihuacoatl,* a goddess.[25] Although the high posts were occupied by men, the terms referred to females, evidence of the exalted role of women before the Aztec nation became centralized. The final break with the democratic Calpul came when the four Aztec lords of royal lineage picked the king's successor from his siblings or male descendants.[26]

La Llorona's wailing in the night for her lost children has an echoing note in the wailing or mourning rites performed by women as they bid their sons, brothers and husbands good-bye before they left to go to the "flowery wars." Wailing is the Indian, Mexican and Chicana woman's feeble protest when she has no other recourse. These collective wailing rites may have been a sign of resistance in a society which glorified the warrior and war and for whom the women of the conquered tribes were booty.[27]

In defiance of the Aztec rulers, the *macehuales* (the common people) continued to worship fertility, nourishment and agricultural female deities, those of crops and rain. They venerated *Chalchiuhtlicue* (goddess of sweet or inland water), *Chicome-coatl* (goddess of food) and *Huixtocihuatl* (goddess of salt).

Nevertheless, it took less than three centuries for Aztec society to change from the balanced duality of their earlier times and from the egalitarian traditions of a wandering tribe to those of a predatory state. The nobility kept the tribute, the commoner got nothing, resulting in a class split. The conquered tribes hated the Aztecs because of the rape of their women and the heavy taxes levied on them. The *Tlaxcalans* were the Aztec's bitter enemies and it was they who helped the Spanish defeat the Aztec rulers, who were by this time so unpopular with their own common people that they could not even mobilize the populace to defend the city. Thus the Aztec nation fell not because *Malinali* (*la Chingada*) interpreted for and slept with Cortés, but because the ruling elite had subverted the solidarity between men and women and between noble and commoner.[28]

Sueño con serpientes

Coatl. In pre-Columbian America the most notable symbol was the serpent. The Olmecs associated womanhood with the Serpent's mouth which was guarded by rows of dangerous teeth, a sort of *vagina dentate.* They considered it the most sacred

---

[24]Parrinder, 355.

[25]Jacques Soustelle, *The Daily Life of the Aztecs on the Eve of the Spanish Conquest* (New York, NY: Macmillan Publishing Company, 1962). Soustelle and most other historians got their information from the Franciscan father Bernardino de Sahagún, chief chronicler of Indian religious life.

[26]Nash, 252–253.

[27]Nash, 358.

[28]Nash, 361–362.

place on earth, a place of refuge, the creative womb from which all things were born and to which all things returned. Snake people had holes, entrances to the body of the Earth Serpent; they followed the Serpent's way, identified with the Serpent deity, with the mouth, both the eater and the eaten. The destiny of humankind is to be devoured by the Serpent.[29]

> Dead,
> the doctor by the operating table said.
> I passed between the two fangs,
> the flickering tongue.
> Having come through the mouth of the serpent,
> swallowed,
> I found myself suddenly in the dark,
> sliding down a smooth wet surface
> down down into an even darker darkness.
> Having crossed the portal, the raised hinged mouth,
> having entered the serpent's belly,
> now there was no looking back, no going back.
>
> Why do I cast no shadow?
> Are there lights from all sides shining on me?
> Ahead, ahead.
> curled up inside the serpent's coils,
> the damp breath of death on my face.
> I knew at that instant: something must change
> or I'd die.
> *Algo tenía que cambiar.*

After each of my four bouts with death I'd catch glimpses of an otherworld Serpent. Once, in my bedroom, I saw a cobra the size of the room, her hood expanding over me. When I blinked she was gone. I realized she was, in my psyche, the mental picture and symbol of the instinctual in its collective impersonal, prehuman. She, the symbol of the dark sexual drive, the chthonic (underworld), the feminine, the serpentine movement of sexuality, of creativity, the basis of all energy and life.

The Presences

> She appeared in white, garbed in white,
> standing white, pure white.
> —Bernardino de Sahagún[30]

On the gulf where I was raised, *en el Valle del Río Grande* in South Texas—that triangular piece of land wedged between the river *y el golfo* which serves as the Texas-U.S./Mexican border—is a Mexican *pueblito* called Hargill (at one time in the

[29]Karl W. Luckert, *Olmec Religion: A Key to Middle America and Beyond* (Norman, OK: University of Oklahoma Press, 1976), 68, 69, 87, 109.

[30]Bernardino de Sahagún, *General History of* the *Things of New Spain* (Florentine Codex), Vol. I Revised, trans. Arthur Anderson and Charles Dibble (Sante Fe, NM: School of American Research, 1950), 11.

history of this one-grocery-store, two-service-stations town there were thirteen churches and thirteen *cantinas*). Down the road, a little ways from our house, was a deserted church. It was known among the *mexicanos* that if you walked down the road late at night you would see a woman dressed in white floating about, peering out the church window. She would follow those who had done something bad or who were afraid. *Los mexicanos* called her *la Jila*. Some thought she was *la Llorona*. She was, I think, *Cihuacoatl*, Serpent Woman, ancient Aztec goddess of the earth, of war and birth, patron of midwives, and antecedent of *la Llorona*. Covered with chalk, *Cihuacoatl* wears a white dress with a decoration half red and half black. Her hair forms two little horns (which the Aztecs depicted as knives) crossed on her forehead. The lower part of her face is a bare jawbone, signifying death. On her back she carries a cradle, the knife of sacrifice swaddled as if it were her papoose, her child.[31] Like *la Llorona*, *Cihuacoatl* howls and weeps in the night, screams as if demented. She brings mental depression and sorrow. Long before it takes place, she is the first to predict something is to happen.

Back then, I, an unbeliever, scoffed at these Mexican superstitions as I was taught in Anglo school. Now, I wonder if this story and similar ones were the culture's attempts to "protect" members of the family, especially girls, from "wandering." Stories of the devil luring young girls away and having his way with them discouraged us from going out. There's an ancient Indian tradition of burning the umbilical cord of an infant girl under the house so she will never stray from it and her domestic role.

> *A mis ancas caen los cueros de culebra,*
> *cuatro veces por año los arrastro,*
> *me tropiezo y me caigo*
> *y cada vez que miro una culebra le pregunto*
> *¿Qué traes conmigo?*

Four years ago a red snake crossed my path as I walked through the woods. The direction of its movement, its pace, its colors, the "mood" of the trees and the wind and the snake—they all "spoke" to me, told me things. I look for omens everywhere, everywhere catch glimpses of the patterns and cycles of my life. Stones "speak" to Luisah Teish, a Santera; trees whisper their secrets to Chrystos, a Native American. I remember listening to the voices of the wind as a child and understanding its messages. *Los espíritus* that ride the back of the south wind. I remember their exhalation blowing in through the slits in the door during those hot Texas afternoons. A gust of wind raising the linoleum under my feet, buffeting the house. Everything trembling.

We're not supposed to remember such otherworldly events. We're supposed to ignore, forget, kill those fleeting images of the soul's presence and of the spirit's presence. We've been taught that the spirit is outside our bodies or above our heads

---

[31]The Aztecs muted Snake Woman's patronage of childbirth and vegetation by placing a sacrificial knife in the empty cradle she carried on her back (signifying a child who died in childbirth), thereby making her a devourer of sacrificial victims. Snake Woman had the ability to change herself into a serpent or into a lovely young woman to entice young men who withered away and died after intercourse with her. She was known as a witch and a shape-shifter. Brundage, 168–171.

somewhere up in the sky with God. We're supposed to forget that every cell in our bodies, every bone and bird and worm has spirit in it.

Like many Indians and Mexicans, I did not deem my psychic experiences real. I denied their occurrences and let my inner senses atrophy. I allowed white rationality to tell me that the existence of the "other world" was mere pagan superstition. I accepted their reality, the "official" reality of the rational, reasoning mode which is connected with external reality, the upper world, and is considered the most developed consciousness—the consciousness of duality.

The other mode of consciousness facilitates images from the soul and the unconscious through dreams and the imagination. Its work is labeled "fiction," make-believe, wish-fulfillment. White anthropologists claim that Indians have "primitive" and therefore deficient minds, that we cannot think in the higher mode of consciousness—rationality. They are fascinated by what they call the "magical" mind, the "savage" mind, the *participation mystique* of the mind that says the world of the imagination—the world of the soul—and of the spirit is just as real as physical reality.[32] In trying to become "objective," Western culture made "objects" of things and people when it distanced itself from them, thereby losing "touch" with them. This dichotomy is the root of all violence.

Not only was the brain split into two functions but so was reality. Thus people who inhabit both realities are forced to live in the interface between the two, forced to become adept at switching modes. Such is the case with the *india* and the *mestiza*.

Institutionalized religion fears trafficking with the spirit world and stigmatizes it as witchcraft. It has strict taboos against this kind of inner knowledge. It fears what Jung calls the Shadow, the unsavory aspects of ourselves. But even more it fears the supra-human, the god in ourselves.

"The purpose of any established religion . . . is to glorify, sanction and bless with a superpersonal meaning all personal and interpersonal activities. This occurs through the 'sacraments,' and indeed through most religious rites."[33] But it sanctions only its own sacraments and rites. Voodoo, Santeria, Shamanism and other native religions are called cults and their beliefs are called mythologies. In my own life, the Catholic Church fails to give meaning to my daily acts, to my continuing encounters with the "other world." It and other institutionalized religions impoverish all life, beauty, pleasure.

The Catholic and Protestant religions encourage fear and distrust of life and of the body; they encourage a split between the body and the spirit and totally ignore the soul; they encourage us to kill off parts of ourselves. We are taught that the body is an ignorant animal; intelligence dwells only in the head. But the body is smart. It

---

[32]Anthropologist Lucien Levy-Bruhl coined the word *participation mystique*. According to Jung, "It denotes a peculiar kind of psychological connection . . . (in which) the subject cannot clearly distinguish himself from the object but is bound to it by a direct relationship which amounts to partial identity." Carl Jung, "Def-initions," in *Psychological Types, The Collected Works of C. G. Jung*, Vol. 6 (Princeton, NJ: Princeton University Press, 1953), par. 781.

[33]I have lost the source of this quote. If anyone knows what it is, please let the publisher know.

does not discern between external stimuli and stimuli from the imagination. It reacts equally viscerally to events from the imagination as it does to "real" events.

So I grew up in the interface trying not to give countenance to *el mal aigre,*[34] evil non-human, non-corporeal entities riding the wind, that could come in through the window, through my nose with my breath. I was not supposed to believe in *susto,* a sudden shock or fall that frightens the soul out of the body. And growing up between such opposing spiritualities how could I reconcile the two, the pagan and the Christian?

No matter to what use my people put the supranatural world, it is evident to me now that the spirit world, whose existence the whites are so adamant in denying, does in fact exist. This very minute I sense the presence of the spirits of my ancestors in my room. And I think *la Jila* is *Cihuacoatl,* Snake Woman; she is *la Llorona,* Daughter of Night, traveling the dark terrains of the unknown searching for the lost parts of herself. I remember *la Jila* following me once, remember her eerie lament. I'd like to think that she was crying for her lost children, *los* Chicanos/*mexicanos.*

La facultad

La facultad is the capacity to see in surface phenomena the meaning of deeper realities, to see the deep structure below the surface. It is an instant "sensing," a quick perception arrived at without conscious reasoning. It is an acute awareness mediated by the part of the psyche that does not speak, that communicates in images and symbols which are the faces of feelings, that is, behind which feelings reside/hide. The one possessing this sensitivity is excruciatingly alive to the world.

Those who are pushed out of the tribe for being different are likely to become more sensitized (when not brutalized into insensitivity). Those who do not feel psychologically or physically safe in the world are more apt to develop this sense. Those who are pounced on the most have it the strongest—the females, the homosexuals of all races, the darkskinned, the outcast, the persecuted, the marginalized, the foreign.

When we're up against the wall, when we have all sorts of oppressions coming at us, we are forced to develop this faculty so that we'll know when the next person is going to slap us or lock us away. We'll sense the rapist when he's five blocks down the street. Pain makes us acutely anxious to avoid more of it, so we hone that radar. It's a kind of survival tactic that people, caught between the worlds, unknowingly cultivate. It is latent in all of us.

I walk into a house and I know whether it is empty or occupied. I feel the lingering charge in the air of a recent fight or lovemaking or depression. I sense the emotions someone near is emitting—whether friendly or threatening. Hate and fear—the more intense the emotion, the greater my reception of it. I feel a tingling on my skin when someone is staring at me or thinking about me. I can tell how oth-

---

[34]Some *mexicanos* and Chicanos distinguish between *aire,* air, and *mala aigre,* the evil spirits which reside in the air.

ers feel by the way they smell, where others are by the air pressure on my skin. I can spot the love or greed or generosity lodged in the tissues of another. Often I sense the direction of and my distance from people or objects—in the dark, or with my eyes closed, without looking. It must be a vestige of a proximity sense, a sixth sense that's lain dormant from long-ago times.

Fear develops the proximity sense aspect of *la facultad*. But there is a deeper sensing that is another aspect of this faculty. It is anything that breaks into one's everyday mode of perception, that causes a break in one's defenses and resistance, anything that takes one from one's habitual grounding, causes the depths to open up, causes a shift in perception. This shift in perception deepens the way we see concrete objects and people; the senses become so acute and piercing that we can see through things, view events in depth, a piercing that reaches the underworld (the realm of the soul). As we plunge vertically, the break, with its accompanying new seeing, makes us pay attention to the soul, and we are thus carried into awareness—an experiencing of soul (Self).

We lose something in this mode of initiation, something is taken from us: our innocence, our unknowing ways, our safe and easy ignorance. There is a prejudice and a fear of the dark, chthonic (underworld), material such as depression, illness, death and the violations that can bring on this break. Confronting anything that tears the fabric of our everyday mode of consciousness and that thrusts us into a less literal and more psychic sense of reality increases awareness and *la facultad*.

7

La conciencia de la mestiza/Towards a New Consciousness

Por la mujer de mi raza
hablará el espíritu.[35]

Jose Vasconcelos, Mexican philosopher, envisaged *una raza mestiza, una mezcla de razas afines, una raca de color—la primera raza síntesis del globo.* He called it a cosmic race, *la raza cósmica,* a fifth race embracing the four major races of the world.[36] Opposite to the theory of the pure Aryan, and to the policy of racial purity that white America practices, his theory is one of inclusivity. At the confluence of two or more genetic streams, with chromosomes constantly "crossing over," this mixture of races, rather than resulting in an inferior being, provides hybrid progeny, a mutable, more malleable species with a rich gene pool. From this racial, ideological, cultural and biological cross-pollinization, an "alien" consciousness is presently in the making—a new *mestiza* consciousness, *una conciencia de mujer.* It is a consciousness of the Borderlands.

[35]This is my own "take off" on Jose Vasconcelos's idea. Jose Vasconcelos, *La Raza Cósmica: Misión de la Raza Ibero-Americana* (México: Aguilar S.A. de Ediciones, 1961).

[36]Vasconcelos.

Una lucha de fronteras/A Struggle of Borders

Because I, a *mestiza,*
continually walk out of one culture
and into another,
because I am in all cultures at the same time,
alma entre dos mundos, tres, cuatro,
me zumba la cabeza con lo contradictorio.
Estoy norteada por todas las voces que me hablan
simultáneamente.

The ambivalence from the clash of voices results in mental and emotional states of perplexity. Internal strife results in insecurity and indecisiveness. The mestiza's dual or multiple personality is plagued by psychic restlessness.

In a constant state of mental nepantilism, an Aztec word meaning torn between ways, *la mestiza* is a product of the transfer of the cultural and spiritual values of one group to another. Being tricultural, monolingual, bilingual, or multilingual, speaking a patois, and in a state of perpetual transition, the *mestiza* faces the dilemma of the mixed breed: which collectivity does the daughter of a darkskinned mother listen to?

El choque de un alma atrapado entre el mundo del espíritu y el mundo de la técnica a veces la deja entullada. Cradled in one culture, sandwiched between two cultures, straddling all three cultures and their value systems, *la mestiza* undergoes a struggle of flesh, a struggle of borders, an inner war. Like all people, we perceive the version of reality that our culture communicates. Like others having or living in more than one culture, we get multiple, often opposing messages. The coming together of two self-consistent but habitually incompatible frames of reference[37] causes *un choque,* a cultural collision.

Within us and within *la cultura chicana,* commonly held beliefs of the white culture attack commonly held beliefs of the Mexican culture, and both attack commonly held beliefs of the indigenous culture. Subconsciously, we see an attack on ourselves and our beliefs as a threat and we attempt to block with a counterstance.

But it is not enough to stand on the opposite river bank, shouting questions, challenging patriarchal, white conventions. A counterstance locks one into a duel of oppressor and oppressed; locked in mortal combat, like the cop and the criminal, both are reduced to a common denominator of violence. The counterstance refutes the dominant culture's views and beliefs, and, for this, it is proudly defiant. All reaction is limited by, and dependent on, what it is reacting against. Because the counterstance stems from a problem with authority—outer as well as inner—it's a step towards liberation from cultural domination. But it is not a way of life. At some point, on our way to a new consciousness, we will have to leave the opposite bank, the split between the two mortal combatants somehow healed so that we are on both shores at once and, at once, see through serpent and eagle eyes. Or perhaps we will decide to disengage from the dominant culture, write it off altogether as a lost cause, and cross the border into a wholly new and separate territory. Or we might go another route. The possibilities are numerous once we decide to act and not react.

---

[37] Arthur Koestler termed this "bisociation." Albert Rothenberg, *The Creative Process in Art, Science, and Other Fields* (Chicago, IL: University of Chicago Press, 1979), 12.

A Tolerance for Ambiguity

These numerous possibilities leave *la mestiza* floundering in uncharted seas. In perceiving conflicting information and points of view, she is subjected to a swamping of her psychological borders. She has discovered that she can't hold concepts or ideas in rigid boundaries. The borders and walls that are supposed to keep the undesirable ideas out are entrenched habits and patterns of behavior; these habits and patterns are the enemy within. Rigidity means death. Only by remaining flexible is she able to stretch the psyche horizontally and vertically. *La mestiza* constantly has to shift out of habitual formations; from convergent thinking, analytical reasoning that tends to use rationality to move toward a single goal (a Western mode), to divergent thinking,[38] characterized by movement away from set patterns and goals and toward a more whole perspective, one that includes rather than excludes.

The new *mestiza* copes by developing a tolerance for contradictions, a tolerance for ambiguity. She learns to be an Indian in Mexican culture, to be Mexican from an Anglo point of view. She learns to juggle cultures. She has a plural personality, she operates in a pluralistic mode—nothing is thrust out, the good the bad and the ugly, nothing rejected, nothing abandoned. Not only does she sustain contradictions, she turns the ambivalence into something else.

She can be jarred out of ambivalence by an intense, and often painful, emotional event which inverts or resolves the ambivalence. I'm not sure exactly how. The work takes place underground—subconsciously. It is work that the soul performs. That focal point or fulcrum, that juncture where the mestiza stands, is where phenomena tend to collide. It is where the possibility of uniting all that is separate occurs. This assembly is not one where severed or separated pieces merely come together. Nor is it a balancing of opposing powers. In attempting to work out a synthesis, the self has added a third element which is greater than the sum of its severed parts. That third element is a new consciousness—a mestiza consciousness—and though it is a source of intense pain, its energy comes from continual creative motion that keeps breaking down the unitary aspect of each new paradigm.

En unas pocas centurias, the future will belong to the mestiza. Because the future depends on the breaking down of paradigms, it depends on the straddling of two or more cultures. By creating a new mythos—that is, a change in the way we perceive reality, the way we see ourselves, and the ways we behave—*la mestiza* creates a new consciousness.

The work of *mestiza* consciousness is to break down the subject-object duality that keeps her a prisoner and to show in the flesh and through the images in her work how duality is transcended. The answer to the problem between the white race and the colored, between males and females, lies in healing the split that originates in the very foundation of our lives, our culture, our languages, our thoughts. A massive uprooting of dualistic thinking in the individual and collective consciousness is the beginning of a long struggle, but one that could, in our best hopes, bring us to the end of rape, of violence, of war.

[38]In part, I derive my definitions for "convergent" and "divergent" thinking from Rothenberg, 12–13.

La encrucijada/The Crossroads

A chicken is being sacrificed
    at a crossroads, a simple mound of earth
a mud shrine for *Eshu,*
    Yoruba god of indeterminacy,
who blesses her choice of path.
    She begins her journey.

Su cuerpo es una bocacalle. La mestiza has gone from being the sacrificial goat to becoming the officiating priestess at the crossroads.

As a *mestiza* I have no country, my homeland cast me out; yet all countries are mine because I am every woman's sister or potential lover. (As a lesbian I have no race, my own people disclaim me; but I am all races because there is the queer of me in all races.) I am cultureless because, as a feminist, I challenge the collective cultural/religious male-derived beliefs of Indo-Hispanics and Anglos; yet I am cultured because I am participating in the creation of yet another culture, a new story to explain the world and our participation in it, a new value system with images and symbols that connect us to each other and to the planet. *Soy un amasamiento,* I am an act of kneading, of uniting and joining that not only has produced both a creature of darkness and a creature of light, but also a creature that questions the definitions of light and dark and gives them new meanings.

We are the people who leap in the dark, we are the people on the knees of the gods. In our very flesh, (r)evolution works out the clash of cultures. It makes us crazy constantly, but if the center holds, we've made some kind of evolutionary step forward. *Nuestra alma el trabajo,* the opus, the great alchemical work; spiritual *mestizaje,* a "morphogenesis,"[39] an inevitable unfolding. We have become the quickening serpent movement.

Indigenous like corn, like corn, the *mestiza* is a product of crossbreeding, designed for preservation under a variety of conditions. Like an ear of corn—a female seed-bearing organ—the *mestiza* is tenacious, tightly wrapped in the husks of her culture. Like kernels she clings to the cob; with thick stalks and strong race roots, she holds tight to the earth—she will survive the crossroads.

Lavando y remojando el maíz en agua de cal, despojando el pellejo. Moliendo, mixteando, amasando, haciendo tortillas de masa.[40] She steeps the corn in lime, it swells,

---

[39]To borrow chemist Ilya Prigogine's theory of "dissipative structures." Prigogine discovered that substances interact not in predictable ways as it was taught in science, but in different and fluctuating ways to produce new and more complex structures, a kind of birth he called "morphogenesis," which created unpredictable innovations. Harold Gilliam, "Searching for a New World View," *This World* (January, 1981), 23.

[40]Corn tortillas are of two types, the smooth uniform ones made in a tortilla press and usually bought at a tortilla factory or supermarket, and *gorditas,* made by mixing *masa* with lard or shortening or butter (my mother sometimes puts in bits of bacon or *chicharrones*).

softens. With stone roller on *metate,* she grinds the corn, then grinds again. She kneads and moulds the dough, pats the round balls into *tortillas.*

> We are the porous rock in the stone *metate*
> squatting on the ground.
> We are the rolling pin, *el maíz y agua,*
> *la masa harina. Somos e amasijo.*
> *Somos lo molido en el metate.*
> We are the *comal* sizzling hot,
> the hot *tortilla,* the hungry mouth.
> We are the coarse rock.
> We are the grinding motion,
> the mixed potion, *somos el molcajete.*
> We are the pestle, the *comino, ajo, pimienta,*
> We are the *chile colorado,*
> the green shoot that cracks the rock.
> We will abide.

El camino de la mestiza/The Mestiza Way

Caught between the sudden contraction, the breath sucked in and the endless space, the brown woman stands still, looks at the sky. She decides to go down, digging her way along the roots of trees. Sifting through the bones, she shakes them to see if there is any marrow in them. Then, touching the dirt to her forehead, to her tongue, she takes a few bones, leaves the rest in their burial place.

She goes through her backpack, keeps her journal and address book, throws away the muni-bart metromaps. The coins are heavy and they go next, then the greenbacks flutter through the air. She keeps her knife, can opener and eyebrow pencil. She puts bones, pieces of bark, hierbas, eagle feather, snakeskin, tape recorder, the rattle and drum in her pack and she sets out to become the complete tolteca.[41]

Her first step is to take inventory. *Despojando, desgranando, quitando paja.* Just what did she inherit from her ancestors? This weight on her back—which is the baggage from the Indian mother, which the baggage from the Spanish father, which the baggage from the Anglo?

Pero es difícil differentiating between *lo heredado, lo adquirido, lo impuesto.* She puts history through a sieve, winnows out the lies, looks at the forces that we as a race, as women, have been a part of. *Luego bota lo que no vale, los desmientos, los desencuentos, el embrutecimiento. Aguarda el juicio, hondo y enraízado, de la gente antigua.* This step is a conscious rupture with all oppressive traditions of all cultures and religions. She communicates that rupture, documents the struggle. She reinterprets history and, using new symbols, she shapes new myths. She adopts new perspectives toward the darkskinned, women and queers. She strengthens her tolerance (and intolerance) for ambiguity. She is willing to share, to make herself vulnerable to

---

[41]Gina Valdés, *Puentes y Fronteras: Coplas Chicanas* (Los Angeles: Castle Lithograph, 1982), 2.

foreign ways of seeing and thinking. She surrenders all notions of safety, of the familiar. Deconstruct, construct. She becomes a *nahual,* able to transform herself into a tree, a coyote, into another person. She learns to transform the small "I" into the total Self. *Se hace moldeadora de su alma. Según la concepción que tiene de sí misma, así será.*

Que no se nos olvide los hombres

"Tú no sirves pa' nada—
you're good for nothing.
Eres pura vieja."

"You're nothing but a woman" means you are defective. Its opposite is to be *un macho.* The modern meaning of the word "machismo," as well as the concept, is actually an Anglo invention. For men like my father, being "macho" meant being strong enough to protect and support my mother and us, yet being able to show love. Today's macho has doubts about his ability to feed and protect his family. His "machismo" is an adaptation to oppression and poverty and low self-esteem. It is the result of hierarchical male dominance. The Anglo, feeling inadequate and inferior and powerless, displaces or transfers these feelings to the Chicano by shaming him. In the Gringo world, the Chicano suffers from excessive humility and self-effacement, shame of self and self-deprecation. Around Latinos he suffers from a sense of language inadequacy and its accompanying discomfort; with Native Americans he suffers from a racial amnesia which ignores our common blood, and from guilt because the Spanish part of him took their land and oppressed them. He has an excessive compensatory hubris when around Mexicans from the other side. It overlays a deep sense of racial shame.

The loss of a sense of dignity and respect in the macho breeds a false machismo which leads him to put down women and even to brutalize them. Coexisting with his sexist behavior is a love for the mother which takes precedence over that of all others. Devoted son, macho pig. To wash down the shame of his fears, of his very being, and to handle the brute in the mirror, he takes to the bottle, the snort, the needle, and the fist.

Though we "understand" the root causes of male hatred and fear, and the subsequent wounding of women, we do not excuse, we do not condone, and we will no longer put up with it. From the men of our race, we demand the admission/acknowledgment/disclosure/testimony that they wound us, violate us, are afraid of us and of our power. We need them to say they will begin to eliminate their hurtful put-down ways. But more than the words, we demand acts. We say to them: We will develop equal power with you and those who have shamed us.

It is imperative that mestizas support each other in changing the sexist elements in the Mexican-Indian culture. As long as woman is put down, the Indian and the Black in all of us is put down. The struggle of the mestiza is above all a feminist one. As long as *los hombres* think they have to *chingar mujeres* and each other to be men, as long as men are taught that they are superior and therefore culturally favored over *la mujer,* as long as to be a *vieja* is a thing of derision, there can be no real healing of our psyches. We're halfway there—we have such love of the Mother, the good mother. The first step is to unlearn the *puta/virgen* dichotomy and to see *Coatlapopeuh-Coatlicue* in the Mother, *Guadalupe.*

Tenderness, a sign of vulnerability, is so feared that it is showered on women with verbal abuse and blows. Men, even more than women, are fettered to gender roles. Women at least have had the guts to break out of bondage. Only gay men have had the courage to expose themselves to the woman inside them and to challenge the current masculinity. I've encountered a few scattered and isolated gentle straight men, the beginnings of a new breed, but they are confused, and entangled with sexist behaviors that they have not been able to eradicate. We need a new masculinity and the new man needs a movement.

Lumping the males who deviate from the general norm with man, the oppressor, is a gross injustice. *Asombra pensar que nos hemos quedado en ese pozo oscuro donde el mundo encierra a las lesbianas. Asombra pensar que hemos, como femenistas y lesbianas, cerrado nuestros corazónes a los hombres, a nuestros hermanos los jotos, desheredados y marginales como nosotros.* Being the supreme crossers of cultures, homosexuals have strong bonds with the queer white, Black, Asian, Native American, Latino, and with the queer in Italy, Australia and the rest of the planet. We come from all colors, all classes, all races, all time periods. Our role is to link people with each other—the Blacks with Jews with Indians with Asians with whites with extraterrestrials. It is to transfer ideas and information from one culture to another. Colored homosexuals have more knowledge of other cultures; have always been at the forefront (although sometimes the closet) of all liberation struggles in this country; have suffered more injustices and have survived them despite all odds. Chicanos need to acknowledge the political and artistic contributions of their queer. People, listen to what your *jotería* is saying.

The mestizo and the queer exist at this time and point on the evolutionary continuum for a purpose. We are a blending that proves that all blood is intricately woven together, and that we are spawned out of similar souls.

Somos una gente

Hay tantísimas fronteras
que dividen a la gente,
pero por cada frontera
existe también un puente
—Gina Valdés[42]

Divided Loyalties. Many women and men of color do not want to have any dealings with white people. It takes too much time and energy to explain to the downwardly mobile, white middle-class women that it's okay for us to want to own "possessions," never having had any nice furniture on our dirt floors or "luxuries" like washing

[42]Richard Wilhelm, *The I Ching or Book of Changes,* trans. Cary F. Baynes (Princeton, NJ: Princeton University Press, 1950), 98.

machines. Many feel that whites should help their own people rid themselves of race hatred and fear first. I, for one, choose to use some of my energy to serve as mediator. I think we need to allow whites to be our allies. Through our literature, art, *corridos,* and folktales we must share our history with them so when they set up committees to help Big Mountain Navajos or the Chicano farmworkers or *los Nicaragüenses* they won't turn people away because of their racial fears and ignorances. They will come to see that they are not helping us but following our lead.

Individually, but also as a racial entity, we need to voice our needs. We need to say to white society: We need you to accept the fact that Chicanos are different, to acknowledge your rejection and negation of us. We need you to own the fact that you looked upon us as less than human, that you stole our lands, our personhood, our self-respect. We need you to make public restitution: to say that, to compensate for your own sense of defectiveness, you strive for power over us, you erase our history and our experience because it makes you feel guilty—you'd rather forget your brutish acts. To say you've split yourself from minority groups, that you disown us, that your dual consciousness splits off parts of yourself, transferring the "negative" parts onto us. (Where there is persecution of minorities, there is shadow projection. Where there is violence and war, there is repression of shadow.) To say that you are afraid of us, that to put distance between us, you wear the mask of contempt. Admit that Mexico is your double, that she exists in the shadow of this country, that we are irrevocably tied to her. Gringo, accept the doppelganger in your psyche. By taking back your collective shadow the intracultural split will heal. And finally, tell us what you need from us.

By Your True Faces We Will Know You

I am visible—see this Indian face—yet I am invisible. I both blind them with my beak nose and am their blind spot. But I exist, we exist. They'd like to think I have melted in the pot. But I haven't, we haven't.

The dominant white culture is killing us slowly with its ignorance. By taking away our self-determination, it has made us weak and empty. As a people we have resisted and we have taken expedient positions, but we have never been allowed to develop unencumbered—we have never been allowed to be fully ourselves. The whites in power want us people of color to barricade ourselves behind our separate tribal walls so they can pick us off one at a time with their hidden weapons; so they can white-wash and distort history. Ignorance splits people, creates prejudices. A misinformed people is a subjugated people.

Before the Chicano and the undocumented worker and the Mexican from the other side can come together, before the Chicano can have unity with Native Americans and other groups, we need to know the history of their struggle and they need to know ours. Our mothers, our sisters and brothers, the guys who hang out on street corners, the children in the playgrounds, each of us must know our Indian lineage, our afro-*mestizaje,* our history of resistance.

To the immigrant *mexicano* and the recent arrivals we must teach our history. The 80 million *mexicanos* and the Latinos from Central and South America must know of our struggles. Each one of us must know basic facts about Nicaragua, Chile and the rest of Latin America. The Latinoist movement (Chicanos, Puerto Ricans, Cubans and other Spanish-speaking people working together to combat racial discrimination in the market place) is good but it is not enough. Other than a common culture we will have nothing to hold us together. We need to meet on a broader communal ground.

The struggle is inner: Chicano, *indio,* American Indian, *mojado, mexicano,* immigrant Latino, Anglo in power, working class Anglo, Black, Asian—our psyches resemble the bordertowns and are populated by the same people. The struggle has always been inner, and is played out in the outer terrains. Awareness of our situation must come before inner changes, which in turn come before changes in society. Nothing happens in the "real" world unless it first happens in the images in our heads.

El día de la Chicana

> I will not be shamed again
> Nor will I shame myself.

I am possessed by a vision: that we Chicanas and Chicanos have taken back or uncovered our true faces, our dignity and self-respect. It's a validation vision.

Seeing the Chicana anew in light of her history. I seek an exoneration, a seeing through the fictions of white supremacy, a seeing of ourselves in our true guises and not as the false racial personality that has been given to us and that we have given to ourselves. I seek our woman's face, our true features, the positive and the negative seen clearly, free of the tainted biases of male dominance. I seek new images of identity, new beliefs about ourselves, our humanity and worth no longer in question.

Estamos viviendo en la noche de la Raza, un tiempo cuando el trabajo se hace a lo quieto, en el oscuro. El día cuando aceptamos tal y como somos y para en donde vamos y porque—ese día será el día de la Raza. Yo tengo el compromiso de expresar mi visión, mi sensibilidad, mi percepción de la revalidación de la gente mexicana, su mérito, estimación, honra, aprecio, y validez.

On December 2nd when my sun goes into my first house, I celebrate *el día de la Chicana y el Chicano.* On that day I clean my altars, light my *Coatlalopeuh* candle, burn sage and copal, take *el baño para espantar basura,* sweep my house. On that day I bare my soul, make myself vulnerable to friends and family by expressing my feelings. On that day I affirm who we are.

On that day I look inside our conflicts and our basic introverted racial temperament. I identify our needs, voice them. I acknowledge that the self and the race have been wounded. I recognize the need to take care of our personhood, of our racial self. On that day I gather the splintered and disowned parts of *la gente mexicana* and hold them in my arms. *Todas las partes de nosotros valen.*

On that day I say, "Yes, all you people wound us when you reject us. Rejection strips us of self-worth; our vulnerability exposes us to shame. It is our innate identity you find wanting. We are ashamed that we need your good opinion, that we need your acceptance. We can no longer camouflage our needs, can no longer let defenses and fences sprout around us. We can no longer withdraw. To rage and look upon you with contempt is to rage and be contemptuous of ourselves. We can no longer blame you, nor disown the white parts, the male parts, the pathological parts, the queer parts, the vulnerable parts. Here we are weaponless with open arms, with only our magic. Let's try it our way, the mestiza way, the Chicana way, the woman way."

On that day, I search for our essential dignity as a people, a people with a sense of purpose—to belong and contribute to something greater than our *pueblo*. On that day I seek to recover and reshape my spiritual identity. *¡Anímate! Raza, a celebrar el día de la Chicana.*

El retorno

All movements are accomplished in six stages,
and the seventh brings return.
—I Ching

Tanto tiempo sin verte casa mía,
mi cuna, mi hondo nido de la huerta.
—"Soledad"[43]

I stand at the river, watch the curving, twisting serpent, a serpent nailed to the fence where the mouth of the Rio Grande empties into the Gulf.

I have come back. *Tanto dolor me costó el alejamiento.* I shade my eyes and look up. The bone beak of a hawk slowly circling over me, checking me out as potential carrion. In its wake a little bird flickering its wings, swimming sporadically like a fish. In the distance the expressway and the slough of traffic like an irritated sow. The sudden pull in my gut, *la tierra, los aguacerros.* My land, *el viento soplando la arena, el lagartijo debajo de un nopalito. Me acuerdo como era antes. Una región desértica de vasta llanuras, costeras de baja altura, de escasa lluvia, de chaparrales formados por mesquites y huizaches.* If I look real hard I can almost see the Spanish fathers who were called "the cavalry of Christ" enter this valley riding their burros, see the clash of cultures commence.

Tierra natal. This is home, the small towns in the Valley, *los pueblitos* with chicken pens and goats picketed to mesquite shrubs. *En las colonias* on the other side of the tracks, junk cars line the front yards of hot pink and lavender-trimmed houses— Chicano architecture we call it, self-consciously. I have missed the TV shows where hosts speak in half and half, and where awards are given in the category of Tex-Mex music. I have missed the Mexican cemeteries blooming with artificial flowers, the fields of aloe vera and red pepper, rows of sugar cane, of corn hanging on the stalks, the cloud of *polvareda* in the dirt roads behind a speeding pickup truck, *el sabor de tamales de rez y venado.* I have missed *la yegua colorada* gnawing the wooden gate of her stall, the smell of horse flesh from Carito's corrals. *He hecho menos las noches calientes sin aire, noches de linternas y lechuzas* making holes in the night.

I still feel the old despair when I look at the unpainted, dilapidated, scrap lumber houses consisting mostly of corrugated aluminum. Some of the poorest people in the

---

[43] "Soledad" is sung by the group, Haciendo Punto en Otro Son.

U.S. live in the Lower Rio Grande Valley, an arid and semi-arid land of irrigated farming, intense sunlight and heat, citrus groves next to chaparral and cactus. I walk through the elementary school I attended so long ago, that remained segregated until recently. I remember how the white teachers used to punish us for being Mexican.

How I love this tragic valley of South Texas, as Ricardo Sánchez calls it; this borderland between the Nueces and the Rio Grande. This land has survived possession and ill-use by five countries: Spain, Mexico, the Republic of Texas, the U.S., the Confederacy, and the U.S. again. It has survived Anglo-Mexican blood feuds, lynchings, burnings, rapes, pillage.

Today I see the Valley still struggling to survive. Whether it does or not, it will never be as I remember it. The borderlands depression that was set off by the 1982 peso devaluation in Mexico resulted in the closure of hundreds of Valley businesses. Many people lost their homes, cars, land. Prior to 1982, U.S. store owners thrived on retail sales to Mexicans who came across the border for groceries and clothes and appliances. While goods on the U.S. side have become 10, 100, 1000 times more expensive for Mexican buyers, goods on the Mexican side have become 10, 100, 1000 times cheaper for Americans. Because the Valley is heavily dependent on agriculture and Mexican retail trade, it has the highest unemployment rates along the entire border region; it is the Valley that has been hardest hit.[44]

"It's been a bad year for corn," my brother, Nune, says. As he talks, I remember my father scanning the sky for a rain that would end the drought, looking up into the sky, day after day, while the corn withered on its stalk. My father has been dead for 29 years, having worked himself to death. The life span of a Mexican farm laborer is 56—he lived to be 38. It shocks me that I am older than he. I, too, search the sky for rain. Like the ancients, I worship the rain god and the maize goddess, but unlike my father I have recovered their names. Now for rain (irrigation) one offers not a sacrifice of blood, but of money.

"Farming is in a bad way," my brother says. "Two to three thousand small and big farmers went bankrupt in this country last year. Six years ago the price of corn was $8.00 per hundred pounds," he goes on. "This year it is $3.90 per hundred pounds." And, I think to myself, after taking inflation into account, not planting anything puts you ahead.

I walk out to the back yard, stare at *los rosales de mamá*. She wants me to help her prune the rose bushes, dig out the carpet grass that is choking them. *Mamagrande Ramona también tenía rosales.* Here every Mexican grows flowers. If they don't have a piece of dirt, they use car tires, jars, cans, shoe boxes. Roses are the Mexican's favorite flower. I think, how symbolic—thorns and all.

---

[44]Out of the twenty-two border counties in the four border states, Hidalgo County (named for Father Hidalgo who was shot in 1810 after instigating Mexico's revolt against Spanish rule under the banner of *la Virgen de Guadalupe*) is the most poverty-stricken county in the nation as well as the largest home base (along with Imperial in California) for migrant farmworkers. It was here that I was born and raised. I am amazed that both it and I have survived.

Yes, the Chicano and Chicana have always taken care of growing things and the land. Again I see the four of us kids getting off the school bus, changing into our work clothes, walking into the field with Papí and Mamí, all six of us bending to the ground. Below our feet, under the earth lie the watermelon seeds. We cover them with paper plates, putting *terremotes* on top of the plates to keep them from being blown away by the wind. The paper plates keep the freeze away. Next day or the next, we remove the plates, bare the tiny green shoots to the elements. They survive and grow, give fruit hundreds of times the size of the seed. We water them and hoe them. We harvest them. The vines dry, rot, are plowed under. Growth, death, decay, birth. The soil prepared again and again, impregnated, worked on. A constant changing of forms, *renacimientos de la tierra madre.*

> This land was Mexican once
> was Indian always
> and is.
> And will be again.

1987

Janice Mirikitani b. 1942

Janice Mirikitani, sansei, a third-generation Japanese American, was born in Stockton, California, just before World War II, during which she and her family were interned in concentration camps, along with 110,000 other Japanese Americans. Mirikitani is the editor of several anthologies, including *Third World Women, Time to Greez! Incantations from the Third World,* and *AYUMI, A Japanese American Anthology,* a 320-page bilingual anthology featuring four generations of Japanese American writers, poets, and graphic artists. She has published in many anthologies, textbooks and periodicals, including *Asian American Heritage, The Third Woman: Minority Women Writers of the United States, Amerasia,* and *Bridge.*

Mirikitani is a poet, dancer, and teacher, as well as a social and political activist; she has been program director of Glide Church/Urban Center since 1967 and director of the Glide Theater Group. Her commitment to Third World positions against racism and oppression is reflected in the protest content in her major collections, *Awake in the River* (1978) and *Shedding Silence* (1987). George Leong says of her: "From the eye of racist relocation fever which came about and plagued America during World War II, Janice Mirikitani grew/bloomed/fought as a desert flower behind barbed wire. She grew with that pain, of what it all represented; from the multinational corporations to war from Korea to Vietnam to Latin America to Africa to Hunter's Point and Chinatown" ("Afterword," *Awake in the River*).

Much of her work seeks defiantly to break the stereotypes of Asian Americans prevalent in mainstream American culture. Her voice is often angry, aggressive, blunt, and direct. But it can also be elegiac. Because she is finding new ground, Mirikitani takes the time to explore her family history, and she anchors her identity securely in the details of Asian American experience. In this manner she manages to escape easy nostalgia and cultural sentimentality. Mirikitani does not separate her writing from a social and political platform and sees the necessity to write out of a political agenda. Identifying her community as Third World, she says, "I don't think that Third World writers can really afford to separate themselves from the ongoing struggles of their people. Nor can we ever not embrace our history."

Shirley Geok-lin Lim
University of California, Santa Barbara

PRIMARY WORKS

Awake in the River, 1978; *Shedding Silence,* 1987; *We the Dangerous,* 1995; *Love Works,* 2000.

For My Father

He came over the ocean
carrying Mt. Fuji
on his back/Tule Lake on his chest
hacked through the brush
5   of deserts
and made them grow
strawberries

we stole berries
from the stem
10   we could not afford them
for breakfast

his eyes held
nothing
as he whipped us
15   for stealing.

the desert had dried
his soul.

wordless
he sold
20   the rich,
full berries
to hakujines
whose children
pointed at our eyes

25   they ate fresh
strawberries
with cream.

Father,
I wanted to scream
30 at your silence.
Your strength
was a stranger
I could never touch.
iron
35 in your eyes
to shield
the pain
to shield desert-like wind
from patches
40 of strawberries
grown
from
tears.

                    1978

Desert Flowers

Flowers
faded
in the desert wind.
No flowers grow
5 where dust winds blow
and rain is like
a dry heave moan.

                Mama, did you dream about that
                beau who would take you
10   away from it all,
                who would show you
                in his '41 ford
                and tell you how soft
                your hands
15   like the silk kimono
                you folded for the wedding?
                Make you forget
                about That place,
                the back bending
20   wind that fell like a wall,
                drowned all your geraniums
                and flooded the shed
                where you tried to sleep
                away hyenas?

25 And mama,
bending in the candlelight,
after lights out in barracks,
an ageless shadow
grows victory flowers
30 made from crepe paper,
shaping those petals
like the tears
your eyes bled.

Your fingers
35 knotted at knuckles
wounded, winding around wire stems
the tiny, sloganed banner:

"america for americans".

Did you dream
40 of the shiny ford
(only always a dream)
ride your youth
like the wind
in the headless night?
45 Flowers
2 ¢ a dozen,
flowers for American Legions
worn like a badge
on america's lapel
50 made in post-concentration camps
by candlelight.
Flowers
watered
by the spit
55 of "no japs wanted here",
planted in poverty
of postwar relocations,
plucked by
victory's veterans.

60 Mama, do you dream
of the wall of wind
that falls
on your limbless desert,
on stems
65 brimming with petals/crushed
crepepaper
growing
from the crippled
mouth of your hand?

70   Your tears, mama,
      have nourished us.
      Your children
      like pollen
      scatter in the wind.

          1978

Breaking Tradition

for my Daughter

My daughter denies she is like me,
her secretive eyes avoid mine.
      She reveals the hatreds of womanhood
      already veiled behind music and smoke and telephones.
5   I want to tell her about the empty room
      of myself.
      This room we lock ourselves in
      where whispers live like fungus,
      giggles about small breasts and cellulite,
10   where we confine ourselves to jealousies,
      bedridden by menstruation.
      This waiting room where we feel our hands
      are useless, dead speechless clamps
      that need hospitals and forceps and kitchens
15   and plugs and ironing boards to make them useful.
  I deny I am like my mother. I remember why:
      She kept her room neat with silence,
      defiance smothered in requirements to be otonashii,
      passion and loudness wrapped in an obi,
20   her steps confined to ceremony,
      the weight of her sacrifice she carried like
      a foetus. Guilt passed on in our bones.
  I want to break tradition—unlock this room
      where women dress in the dark
25   Discover the lies my mother told me.
      The lies that we are small and powerless
      that our possibilities must be compressed
      to the size of pearls, displayed only as
      passive chokers, charms around our neck.
30   Break Tradition.
      I want to tell my daughter of this room
      of myself
      filled with tears of shakuhachi,

the light in my hands,
35 poems about madness,
the music of yellow guitars—
sounds shaken from barbed wire and
goodbyes and miracles of survival.
This room of open window where daring ones escape.

40 My daughter denies she is like me
her secretive eyes are walls of smoke
and music and telephones,
her pouting ruby lips, her skirts
swaying to salsa, Madonna and the Stones,
45 her thighs displayed in carnavals of color.
I do not know the contents of her room.
She mirrors my aging.

She is breaking tradition.

1978

Recipe

Round Eyes

Ingredients: scissors, Scotch magic transparent tape,
eyeliner—water based, black.
Optional: false eyelashes.

5 Cleanse face thoroughly.

For best results, powder entire face, including eyelids.
(lighter shades suited to total effect desired)

With scissors, cut magic tape 1/16" wide, 3/4"–1/2" long—
depending on length of eyelid.

10 Stick firmly onto mid-upper eyelid area
(looking down into handmirror facilitates finding
adequate surface)

If using false eyelashes, affix first on lid, folding any
excess lid over the base of eyelash with glue.

15 Paint black eyeliner on tape and entire lid.

Do not cry.

1987

Pat Mora b. 1942

A Chicana from El Paso, Texas, Pat Mora has written three books of poetry, a children's book, and a collection of essays. She earned both a B.A. and an M.A. in English from the University of Texas at El Paso while she raised three children, all of whom attended universities. She lives and writes in Cincinnati, Ohio.

The poem "University Avenue" presents Chicanas, working-class women, who only recently gained front-door entry to universities, particularly in traditionally racist institutions in Texas that historically relegated Mexican women to roles as faceless workers pushing the broomcarts, mopping the corridors of academia, and cleaning the departments' bathrooms. Mora's poem recognizes that the "first of our people" to attend universities as students, administrators, and faculty, however, need not sacrifice Mexican indigenous traditions that inform Chicana/ Chicano identity. Implicit in her use of Spanish words is the succor that bilingualism offers, the richness that biculturalism should evoke. The lessons whispered in Spanish are also the stories, the rich oral traditions that we carry with us to seminars, meetings, and lectures.

In "Unnatural Speech" Mora explores the dual voices of this bilingual, bicultural student. She speaks to the pain that the Chicana confronts as she makes the transition from Spanish speaker to English dominant speaker. Must the Spanish oral tradition of childhood nursery rhymes remain in the past, hidden in the memory of carefree childhood? Is there danger in learning and internalizing the "new rules" of the dominant language too well? The dilemma remains: will accommodating the dominant culture in the United States erase the songs of the other, the indigenous Mexican culture?

"Border Town: 1938" presents the other side of the bicultural dilemma. While we can now assert the importance of keeping both the Mexican and the American languages and traditions, Mora's poetry urges us to remember the specificities of Chicana history in the United States; that history has been one of separate and unequal educational systems. Evoking that memory of segregated "Mexican Schools" in Texas of the recent past, Mora does not allow the reader to romanticize that history. The problem she presents in these poems from her collection, *Borders,* is one where Mexican Americans on the border too often are forced to choose one side or the other, one language or the other, one culture or the other. Struggling to gain a foothold in the land of their ancestors, Chicanas must learn to gain power from a constantly shifting, ambiguous, multiple identity: as Mora asserts in a poem from *Chants,* "Legal Alien": "an American to Mexicans/a Mexican to Americans/a handy token/sliding back and forth/between the fringes of both worlds/by smiling/by masking the discomfort/of being pre-judged/Bi-laterally."

Sonia Saldívar-Hull
University of California, Los Angeles

PRIMARY WORKS

Chants, 1984; Borders, 1986; Communion, 1991; Nepantla: Essays from the Land in the Middle, 1993; Agua Santa/Holy Water, 1995; House of Houses, 1997; Aunt Carmen's Book of Practical Saints, 1997; Adobe Odes, 2006.

Border Town: 1938

She counts cement cracks
little Esperanza with the long brown braids,
counts so as not to hear
the girls in the playground singing,
5   "the farmer's in the dell
          the farmer's in the dell"
laughing and running round-round
while little Esperanza walks head down
eyes full of tears.
10   "The nurse takes the child"
but Esperanza walks alone across the loud
street, through the graveyard gates
down the dirt path, walks faster,
faster . . . away
15 from ghosts with long arms,
no "hi-ho the dairy-o" here,
runs to that other school
for Mexicans
every day wanting to stay close to home,
20 every day wanting to be the farmer in the dell,
little Esperanza in the long brown braids
counts cement cracks

ocho, nueve, diez.

1986

Unnatural Speech

The game has changed
girl/child, no humming
or singing in these halls,
long, dark, ending at the desk
5 you want, where you'd sit
adding numbers one by one,
a C.P.A., daisies on your desk.
                    I study hard
you say, your smile true,
10 like dawn is, fresh, vulnerable,
but my English language scares

you, makes your palms sweat
when you speak before a class
                    I say my speeches
15   to my dolls
you say. Dolls? The game
has changed, girl/child.
I hear you once singing
to those unblinking eyes
20 lined up on your bed
                    Víbora, víbora de la mar,
your words light in your mouth.

Now at twenty
you stand before
25 those dolls tense,
feet together,
tongue thick, dry,
pushing heavy English
words out.
30   In class I hide
                    my hands behind
                    my back. They shake.
                    My voice too.
I know the new rules,
35 girl/child, one by one,
víboras I've lived with
all my life, learned to hold
firmly behind the head.
If I teach you, will your songs
40 evaporate, like dawn?

                                        1986

University Avenue

We are the first
of our people to walk this path.
We move cautiously
unfamiliar with the sounds,
5   guides for those who follow.
Our people prepared us
with gifts from the land
            fire
                    herbs and song

10   *hierbabuena* soothes us into morning
rhythms hum in our blood
abrazos linger round our bodies
cuentos whisper lessons *en español.*
We do not travel alone.
15   Our people burn deep within us.

1986

Lee Smith b. 1944

Lee Smith has been making up stories—or letting stories tell themselves—since she was a child; she said once that she did it to keep herself from lying. Her first novel, written while she was an undergraduate at Hollins College, appeared in 1968 and won an award. The novels and stories, and the awards, have kept on coming. When Lee Smith gives a reading, her audiences are enthralled; at a book signing, people—women, mostly—line up and loop around, waiting for a chance to meet and speak to the writer. Smith's subjects, like her stories and her voices, are many; but one continuing theme is the way it feels to be a southern woman today. She casts her many voices through as many places and times, yet she writes with special tenderness for her gender and her generation.

In the story Smith has called the closest to her own life, "Tongues of Fire," a gap or gulf between classes separates and attracts the protagonist (a girl whom Dorothy Smith describes as "strangled by a mother rigidly dedicated to keeping up appearances") and her schoolmate, who lives in a very different world among the contemporary rural poor. Her schoolmate's mother speaks in tongues: "Tongues of fire just come down on my head," she tells her daughter's city friend. "I envy this," Smith herself has said, "and aspire to it more than I can tell you."

To many readers, it is Smith herself who speaks in tongues. She has an uncanny ear for voices and an uncommon range.

In *Oral History,* Smith's "breakthrough" novel, for example, we hear first the voice of a college student filled with the new pomposities of academic talk. She is convinced that she can "capture" her own past through oral history. But when her tape recorder records the ghostly historical voices of Granny Younger, Red Emmy, Richard Burlage, Dory Cantrell, those voices become for the reader more real and alive that the utterances of present-day characters. Smith brings the lyricism of mountain ballads to life in their talk. In her many other narratives, the voices come from southern cities, mountains, and coasts; they come from the deep past and the "Phil Donahue Show"; they come from men and women, the young and the aged, rich and poor.

The voices of Smith's characters emerge in patterns that suggest thematic preoccupations as well as sheer lyricism. Richard Burlage (*Oral History*), the educated Richmonder who comes to the mountains in search of "the very roots of consciousness and belief," betrays those very roots by abandoning his mountain love, Dory, and by returning to his "real" life in Richmond. At the same time, his language, which had moved close to incoherence in his passion for Dory, regresses to the highly literate—and controlling—diction of his origins, and even the phrase above, "the very roots," is exposed as a cliché. Yet the mountains do not emerge as the dichotomous victor in a thematic battle with civilization: Smith exposes Richard's mountain fantasies as primitivist projections by showing, for example, Dory's own longings for something other and different from what she has known. "Artists" deals with gaps between classes, arts, and artists. Jennifer's ultimate choice of the art of Molly Crews should not be read as a simple victory for one side either, however. Smith consistently explores the sentimentality implied in privileging difference, particularly when the person doing the privileging comes from an already privileged position.

Smith's first novel, *The Last Day the Dogbushes Bloomed* (1968), tackles the question of difference and its relation to art head on. The narrator is a child whose summer sees the collapse of her fantasies about her family and about her own safety (a visiting boy forces Susan into sex through the rhetorical power of his imaginary friend). The power of the imagination to construct and to destroy is a major force as well in *Something in the Wind,* the story of a college student. In *Black Mountain Breakdown,* overwhelmed by an early rape and by her (not irrelevant) willingness to please, hence her inability to assert herself, Crystal Spangler ends up self-paralyzed.

Crystal Spangler marked the "bottom" in a sense for Lee Smith's women; since then, their capacity for resilience,

strength, pain, and sheer joy has grown steadily. Smith's tour de force character, surely, is Ivy Rowe of *Fair and Tender Ladies,* an epistolary novel that takes Ivy from her first words to her death. Ivy inspired a one-woman play by Barbara Smith and Mark Hunter that ran off-Broadway in 1990. Smith's 1992 novel, *Devil's Dream,* renders country music into narrative by telling the stories of country musicians. It too has inspired another creative enterprise, a traveling show and audiotape starring Smith reading and the writer Clyde Edgerton singing, along with other expert country musicians.

Lee Smith has an irrepressible love of play that pervades her fiction. There is tummy-crunching humor in her lighter novels (*Fancy Strut, Family Linen*) and in many of her stories (collected in *Cakewalk* and *Me and My Baby View the Eclipse*), as well as in fugitive pieces like her parody of romance novels (and of her own most tragic character) in "Desire on Silhouette Lagoon: A Harleque'en Romanza by Crystal Spangler." Beyond the humor, her sense of play means that Smith's writing is constantly in process: she does not stop inventing new characters, new stories, and new literary strategies, showing—and giving—through it all a great and lasting pleasure.

Anne Goodwyn Jones
Allegheny College

PRIMARY WORKS

The Last Day the Dogbushes Bloomed, 1968; *Something in the Wind,* 1971; *Fancy Strut,* 1973; *Black Mountain Breakdown,* 1980; *Cakewalk,* 1981; *Oral History,* 1983; *Family Linen,* 1985; *Fair and Tender Ladies,* 1988; *Me and My Baby View the Eclipse,* 1990; *Devil's Dream,* 1992; *Saving Grace,* 1994; *Christmas Letters,* 1996; *News of the Spirit,* 1990; *The Last Girls,* 2002; *On Agate Hill,* 2006.

The Bubba Stories

Even now when I think of my brother Bubba, he appears instantly just as he was then, rising up before me in the very flesh, grinning that one-sided grin, pushing his cowlick out of his tawny eyes, thumbs hooked in the loops of his wheat jeans, Bass Weejuns held together with electrical tape, leaning against his green MGB. Lawrence Leland Christian III—Bubba—in the days of his glory, Dartmouth College, ca. 1965. Brilliant, Phi Beta Kappa his junior year. The essence of cool. The essence not only of cool but of *bad,* for Bubba was a legendary wild man in those days; and while certain facts in his legend varied, this constant remained: Bubba would do anything. *Anything.*

I was a little bit in love with him myself.

I made Bubba up in the spring of 1963 in order to increase my popularity with my girlfriends at a small women's college in Virginia. I was a little bit in love with them, too. But at first I was ill at ease among them: a thistle in the rose garden, a mule at the racetrack, Cinderella at the fancy dress ball. Take your pick—I was into images then. More than anything else in the world, I wanted to be a writer. I didn't want to *learn to write,* of course. I just wanted to *be a writer,* and I often pictured myself poised at the foggy edge of a cliff someplace in the south of France, wearing a cape, drawing furiously on a long cigarette, hollow-cheeked and haunted, trying to make up my mind between two men. Both of them wanted me desperately.

But in fact I was Charlene Christian, a chunky size twelve, plucked up from a peanut farm near South Hill, Virginia, and set down in those exquisite halls through the intervention of my senior English teacher, Mrs. Bella Hood, the judge's wife, who had graduated from the school herself. I had a full scholarship. I would be the first person in my whole family ever to graduate from college, unless you counted my aunt Dee, who got her certificate from beauty college in Richmond. I was not going to count Aunt Dee. I was not even going to *mention* her in later years, or anybody else in my family. I intended to grow beyond them. I intended to become a famous hollow-cheeked author, with mysterious origins.

But this is the truth. I grew up in McKenney, Virginia, which consisted of nothing more than a crossroads with my father's store in the middle of it. I used to climb onto the tin roof of our house and turn slowly all around, scanning the horizon, looking for . . . what? I found nothing of any interest, just flat brown peanut fields that stretched in every direction as far as I could see, with a farmhouse here and there. I knew who lived in every house. I knew everything about them and about their families, what kind of car they drove and where they went to church, and they knew everything about us.

Not that there was much to know. My father, Hassell Christian, would give you the shirt off his back, and everybody knew it. At the store, he'd extend credit indefinitely to people down on their luck, and he let some families live in his tenant houses for free. Our own house adjoined the store.

My mother's younger brother Sam, who lived with us, was what they then called a Mongoloid. Some of the kids at school referred to him as a "Mongolian idiot." Now the preferred term is "Down's syndrome." My uncle Sam was sweet, small, and no trouble at all. I played cards with him endlessly, every summer of my childhood—Go Fish, rummy, Old Maid, hearts, blackjack. Sam loved cards and sunshine and his cat, Blackie. He liked to sit on a quilt in the sun, playing cards with me. He liked to sit on the front porch with Blackie and watch the cars go by. He loved it when I told him stories.

My mother, who was high-strung, was always fussing around after Sam, making him pick up paper napkins and turn off the TV and put his shoes in a line. My mother had three separate nervous breakdowns before I went away to college. My father always said we had to "treat her with kid gloves." When I think about it now, I am surprised that my mother was able to hold herself together long enough to conceive a child at all, or come to term. After me, there were two miscarriages, and then, I was told, they "quit trying." I was never sure what this meant, exactly. But certainly I could never imagine my parents having a sexual relationship in the first place—he was too fat and gruff, she was too fluttery and crazy. The whole idea was gross.

Whenever my mother had a nervous breakdown, my grandmother, Memaw, would come over from next door to stay with Sam full-time, and I would be sent to South Hill to stay with my aunt Dee and my cousins. I loved my Aunt Dee, who was as different from Mama as day from night. Aunt Dee wore her yellow hair in a beehive and smoked Pall Mall cigarettes. After work she'd come in the door, kick off her shoes, put a record on the record player, and dance all over the living room to "Ooh-Poo-Pa-Doo." She said it "got the kinks out." She taught us all to do the shag, even little Melinda.

I was always sorry when my dad appeared in his truck, ready to take me back home.

When I think of home now, the image that comes most clearly to mind is my whole family lined up in the flickering darkness of our living room, watching TV. We never missed *The Ed Sullivan Show, Bonanza, The Andy Griffith Show,* or *Candid Camera*—Sam's favorite. Sam used to laugh and laugh when they'd say, "Smile! You're on *Candid Camera!*" It was the only time my family ever did anything together. I can just see us now in the light from that black-and-white Zenith: me, Sam, and Memaw on the couch, Daddy and Mama in the recliner and the antique wing chair, respectively, facing the television. We always turned off the lights and sat quietly, and didn't eat anything.

No wonder I got a boyfriend with a car as soon as possible, to get out of there. Don Fetterman had a soft brown crew cut and wide brown eyes, and reminded me, in the nicest possible way, of the cows that he and his family raised. Don was president of the 4-H Club and the Glee Club. I was vice-president of the Glee Club (how we met). We were both picked "Most Likely to Succeed."

We rubbed our bodies together at innumerable dances in the high school gym while they played our song—"The Twelfth of Never"—but we never, never went all the way. Don wouldn't. He believed we should save ourselves for marriage. I, on the other hand, having read by this time a great many novels, was just dying to lose my virginity so that I would mysteriously begin to "live," so that my life would finally *start*. I knew for sure that I would never become a great writer until I could rid myself of this awful burden. But Don Fetterman stuck to his guns, refusing to cooperate. Instead, for graduation, he gave me a pearl "pre-engagement" ring, which I knew for a fact had cost $139 at Snow's Jewelers in South Hill, where I worked after school and on weekends. This was a lot of money for Don Fetterman to spend.

Although I didn't love him, by then he thought I did; and after I got the ring, I didn't have the nerve to tell him the truth. So I kept it, and kissed Don good-bye for hours and hours the night before he went off to join the Marines. My tears were real at this point, but after he left I relegated him firmly to the past. Ditto my whole family. Once I got to college, I was determined to become a new person.

Luckily my freshman roommate turned out to be a kind of prototype, the very epitome of a popular girl. The surprise was that she was nice, too. Dixie Claiborne came from Memphis, where she was to make her debut that Christmas at the Swan Ball. She had long, perfect blond hair, innumerable cashmere sweater sets, and real pearls. She had lots of friends already, other girls who had gone to St. Cecilia's with her. (It seemed to me a good two-thirds of the girls at school had gone to St. Something-or-other.) They had a happy ease in the world and a strangely uniform appearance, which I immediately began to copy—spending my whole first semester's money, saved up from my job at the jeweler's, on several A-line skirts, McMullen blouses, and a pair of red Pappagallo shoes. Dixie had about a thousand cable-knit sweaters, which she was happy to lend me.

In addition to the right clothes, she came equipped with the right boyfriend, already a sophomore at Washington and Lee University, the boys' school just over the mountain. His name was Trey (William Hill Dunn III). Trey would be so glad, Dixie said, smiling, to get all of us dates for the Phi Gam mixer. "All of us" meant our entire suite—Dixie and me in the front room overlooking the old quadrangle with its massive willow oaks, Melissa and Donnie across the hall, and Lily in the single just beyond our study room.

Trey fixed us up with several Phi Gams apiece, but nothing really clicked; and in November, Melissa, Donnie, Lily, and I signed up to go to a freshman mixer at UVA. As our bus approached the university's famous serpentine wall, we went into a flurry of teasing our hair and checking our makeup. Looking into my compact, I stuck out my lips in a way I'd been practicing. I had a pimple near my nose, but I'd turned it into a beauty spot with eyebrow pencil. I hoped to look like Sandra Dee.

Freshman year, everybody went to mixers, where freshman boys, as uncomfortable as we were, stood nervously about in the social rooms of their fraternity houses, wearing navy-blue blazers, ties, and chinos. Nobody really knew how to date in this rigid system so unlike high school—and certainly so unlike prep school, where many of these boys had been locked away for the past four years. If they could have gotten their own dates, they would have. But they couldn't. They didn't know anybody, either. They pulled at their ties and looked at the floor. They seemed to me generally gorgeous, completely unlike Don Fetterman with his feathery crew cut and his 4-H jacket, now at Camp LeJeune. But I still wrote to Don, informative, stilted notes about my classes and the weather. His letters in return were lively and real, full of military life ("the food sucks") and vague sweet plans for our future—a future that did not exist, as far as I was concerned, and yet these letters gave me a secret thrill. My role as Don Fetterman's girl was the most exciting I'd had yet, and I couldn't quite bring myself to give it up, even as I attempted to transform myself into another person altogether.

"Okay," the upperclassman-in-charge announced casually, and the St. Anthony's Hall pledges wandered over in our direction.

"Hey," the cutest one said to a girl.

"Hey," she said back.

The routine never varied. In a matter of minutes, the four most aggressive guys would walk off with the four prettiest girls, and the rest of us would panic. On this occasion the social room at St. Anthony's Hall was cleared in a matter of minutes, and I was left with a tall, gangly, bucktoothed boy whose face was as pocked as the moon. Still, he had a shabby elegance I already recognized. He was from Mississippi.

"What do you want to do?" he asked me.

I had not expected to be consulted. I glanced around the social room, which looked like a war zone. I didn't know where my friends were.

"What do *you* want to do?" I asked.

His name (his *first* name) was Rutherford. He grinned at me. "Let's get drunk," he said, and my heart leaped up as I realized that my burden might be lifted in this way. We walked across the beautiful old campus to an open court where three or four fraternities had a combo going, wild-eyed electrified Negroes going through all kinds of gyrations on the bandstand. It was Doug Clark and the Hot Nuts. The music was so loud, the beat so strong, that you couldn't listen to it and stand still. The Hot Nuts were singing an interminable song; everybody seemed to know the chorus, which went, "Nuts, hot nuts, get 'em from the peanut man. Nuts, hot nuts, get 'em any way you can." We started dancing. I always worried about this—all I'd ever done before college, in the way of dancing, was the shag with my aunt Dee and a long, formless *clutch* with Don Fetterman, but with Rutherford it didn't matter.

People made a circle around us and started clapping. Nobody looked at me. All eyes were on Rutherford, whose dancing reminded me of the way chickens back home flopped around after Daddy cut their heads off. At first I was embarrassed. But then I caught on—Rutherford was a real *character*. I kept up with him the best I could, and then I got tickled and started laughing so hard I could barely dance. *This is fun,* I realized suddenly. This is what I'm *supposed* to be doing. This is college.

About an hour later we heard the news, which was delivered to us by a tweed-jacketed professor who walked on-stage, bringing the music to a ragged, grinding halt. He grabbed the microphone. "Ladies and gentlemen," he said thickly—and I remember thinking how odd this form of address seemed—"ladies and gentlemen, the President has been shot."

The whole scene started to churn, as if we were in a kaleidoscope—the blue day, the green grass, the stately columned buildings. People were running and sobbing. Rutherford's hand under my elbow steered me back to his fraternity house, where everyone was clustered around several TVs, talking too loud. All the weekend festivities were canceled. We were to return to school immediately. Rutherford seemed relieved by this prospect, having fallen silent—perhaps because he'd quit drinking, or because conversation alone wasn't worth the effort it took if nothing else (sex) might be forthcoming. He gave me a perfunctory kiss on the cheek and turned to go.

I was about to board the bus when somebody grabbed me, hard, from behind. I whirled around. It was Lily, red-cheeked and glassy-eyed, her blond hair springing out wildly above her blue sweater. Her hot-pink lipstick was smeared; her pretty, pointed face looked vivid and alive. A dark-haired boy stood close behind her, his arm around her waist.

"Listen," Lily hissed at me. "Sign me in, will you?"

"What?" I had heard her, but I couldn't believe it.

"Sign me in." Lily squeezed my shoulder. I could smell her perfume. Then she was gone.

I sat in a rear seat by myself and cried all the way back to school.

I caught on fast that as far as college boys were concerned, girls fell into either the Whore or the Saint category. Girls knew that if they gave in and *did it,* then boys wouldn't respect them, and word would get around, and they would never get a husband. The whole point of college was to get a husband.

I had not known anything about this system before I arrived there. It put a serious obstacle in my path toward becoming a great writer.

Lily, who clearly had given up her burden long since, fell into the Whore category. But the odd thing about it was that she didn't seem to mind, and she swore she didn't want a husband, anyway. "Honey, a husband is the *last* thing on my list!" she'd say, giggling. Lily was the smartest one of us, even though she went to great lengths to hide this fact.

Later, in 1966, she and the head of the philosophy department, Dr. Wiener, would stage the only demonstration ever held on our campus, walking slowly around the blooming quadrangle carrying signs that read "Get out of Vietnam," while the rest of us, well oiled and sunning on the rooftops, clutched our bikini tops and peered down curiously at the two of them.

If Lily was the smartest, Melissa was the dumbest, the nicest, and the least interested in school. Melissa came from Charleston, South Carolina, and spoke so slowly that I was always tempted to leap in and finish her sentences for her. All she wanted to do was marry her boyfriend, now at the University of South Carolina, and have babies. Donnie, Melissa's roommate, was a big, freckled, friendly girl from Texas. We didn't have any idea how rich she was until her mother flew up and bought a cabin at nearby Goshen Lake so "Donnie and her friends" would have a place to "relax."

By spring, Dixie was the only one of us who was actually pinned. It seemed to me that she was not only pinned but almost married, in a funny way, with tons and tons of children—Trey, her boyfriend; and me; and the other girls in our suite; and the other Phi Gams, Trey's fraternity brothers at Washington and Lee. Dixie had a notebook in which she made a list of things to do each day, and throughout the day she checked them off, one by one. She always got everything done. At the end of first semester, she had a 4.0 average; Trey had a 0.4. Dixie didn't mind. Totally, inexplicably, she loved him.

By then, most of the freshman girls who weren't going with somebody had several horror stories to tell about blind dates at UVA or W&L fraternities—about boys who "dropped trou," or threw up in their dates' purses. I had only one horror story, but I never told it, since the most horrible element in it was me.

This is what happened. It was Spring Fling at the Phi Gam house, and Trey had gotten me a date with a red-headed boy named Eddy Turner. I was getting desperate.

I'd made a C in my first semester of creative writing, while Lily had made an A. Plus, I'd gained eight pounds. Both love and literature seemed to be slipping out of my sights. And I was drinking too much—we'd been drinking Yucca Flats, a horrible green punch made with grain alcohol in a washtub, all afternoon before I ended up in bed with Eddy Turner.

The bed was his, on the second floor of the Phi Gam house—not the most private setting for romance. I could scarcely see Eddy by the light from the street lamp coming in through the single high window. Faintly, below, I could hear music, and the house shook slightly with the dancing. I thought of Hemingway's famous description of sex from *For Whom the Bell Tolls,* which I'd typed out neatly on an index card: "The earth moved under the sleeping bag." The whole Phi Gam house was moving under me. After wrestling with my panty girdle for what seemed like hours, Eddy tossed it in the corner and got on top of me. Drunk as I was, I wanted him to. I wanted him to *do it.* But I didn't think it would hurt so much, and suddenly I wished he would kiss me or say something. He didn't. He was done and lying on his back beside me when the door to the room burst open and the light came on. I sat up, grasping for the sheet that I couldn't find. My breasts are large, and they had always embarrassed me. Until that night, Don Fetterman was the only boy who had seen them. It was a whole group of Phi Gams, roaming from room to room. Luckily I was blinded by the light, so I couldn't tell exactly who they were.

"Smile!" they yelled. "You're on *Candid Camera!*" They laughed hysterically, slammed the door, and were gone, leaving us in darkness once again. I sobbed into Eddy's pillow, because what they said reminded me of Sam, whose face would not leave my mind then for hours while I cried and cried and cried and sobered up. I didn't tell Eddy what I was crying about, nor did he ask. He sat in a chair and smoked cigarettes while he waited for me to stop crying. Finally I did. Eddy and I didn't date after that, but we were buddies in the way I was buddies with the whole Phi Gam house due to my status as Dixie's roommate. I was like a sister, giving advice to the lovelorn, administering Cokes and aspirin on Sunday mornings, typing papers.

It was not the role I'd had in mind, but it was better than nothing, affording me at least a certain status among the girls at school; and the Phi Gams saw to it that I attended all the big parties, usually with somebody whose girlfriend couldn't make it. Often, when the weekend was winding down, I could be found in the Phi Gam basement alone, playing "Tragedy," my favorite song, over and over on the jukebox.

> Blown by the wind,
> Kissed by the snow,
> All that's left
> Is the dark below.
> Gone from me,
> Oh, oh,
> Trag-e-dy.

It always brought me to the edge of tears, because I had never known any tragedy myself, or love, or drama. *Wouldn't anything ever happen to me?*

Meanwhile, my friends' lives were like soap operas—Lily's period was two weeks late, which scared us all, and then Dixie went on the pill. Melissa and her boyfriend split up (she lost seven pounds, he slammed his hand into a wall) and then made up again.

Melissa was telling us about it, in her maddeningly slow way, one day when we were out at Donnie's lake cabin, sunning. "It's not the same, though," she said. "He just gets *too mad.* I don't know what it is—he scares me."

"Dump him," Lily said, applying baby oil with iodine in it, our suntan lotion of choice.

"But I *love* him," Melissa wailed. Lily snorted.

"Well . . ." Dixie began diplomatically, but suddenly I sat up.

"Maybe he's got a wild streak," I said. "Maybe he just can't control himself. That's always been Bubba's problem." The little lake before us took on a deeper, more intense hue. I noticed the rotting pier, the old fisherman up at the point, Lily's painted toenails. I noticed *everything.*

"Who's Bubba?" Donnie asked.

Dixie eyed me expectantly, thinking I meant one of the Phi Gams, since several of them had that nickname.

"My brother," I said. I took a deep breath.

"*What?* You never said you had a *brother!*" Dixie's pretty face looked really puzzled now.

Everybody sat up and stared at me.

"Well, I do," I said. "He's two years older than me, and he stayed with my father when my parents split up. So I've never lived with him. In fact, I don't know him real well at all. This is very painful for me to talk about. We were inseparable when we were little," I added, hearing my song in the back of my mind. *Oh, oh . . . trag-e-dy!*

"Oh Charlene, I'm so sorry! I had no idea!" Dixie was hugging me, slick hot skin and all.

I started crying. "He was a real problem child," I said, "and now he's just so wild. I don't know what's going to become of him."

"How long has it been since you've seen him?" Melissa asked.

"About two years," I said. "Our parents won't have anything at all to do with each other. They *hate* each other, especially since Mama remarried. They won't let us get together, not even for a day. It's just awful."

"So how did you see him two years ago?" Lily asked. They had all drawn closer, clustering around me.

"He ran away from school," I said, and "came to my high school, and got me right out of class. I remember it was biology lab," I said. "I was dissecting a frog."

"Then what?"

"We spent the day together," I said. "We got some food and went out to this quarry and ate, and just drove around. We talked and talked," I said. "And you know what? I felt just as close to him then as I did when we were babies. Just like all those years had never passed at all. It was great," I said.

"Then he went back to school? Or what?"

"No." I choked back a sob. "It was almost dark, and he was taking me back to my house, and then he was planning to head on down to Florida, he said, when all of a sudden these blue lights came up behind us, and it was the police."

"The *police?*" Dixie was getting very nervous. She was such a good girl.

"Well, it was a stolen car, of course," I explained. "They nailed him. If he hadn't stopped in to see me, he might have gotten away with it," I said, "if he'd just headed straight to Florida. But he came to see me. Mama and Daddy wouldn't even bail him out. They let him go straight to prison."

"Oh, Charlene, *no wonder* you never talk about your family!" Dixie was in tears now.

"But he was a model prisoner," I went on. I felt exhilarated. "They gave all the prisoners this test, and he scored the highest that anybody in the whole history of the prison had *ever* scored, so they let him take these special classes, and he did so well that he got out a whole year early, and now he's in college."

"Where?"

I thought fast. "Dartmouth," I said wildly. I knew it had to be a northern school, since Dixie and Melissa seemed to know everybody in the South. But neither of them, as far as I could recall, had ever mentioned Dartmouth.

"He's got a full scholarship," I added. "But he's so bad, I don't know if he'll be able to keep it or not." Donnie got up and went in and came back with cold Cokes for us all, and we stayed out at Goshen Lake until the sun set, and I told them about Bubba.

He was a KA, the wildest KA of them all. Last winter, I said, he got drunk and passed out in the snow on the way back to his fraternity house; by the time a janitor found him the following morning, his cheek was frozen solid to the road. It took two guys from maintenance, with torches, to melt the snow around Bubba's face and get him loose. And now the whole fraternity was on probation because of this really gross thing he'd made the pledges do. "What really gross thing?" they asked. "Oh, you don't want to know," I said. "You really don't."

"I *really do.*" Lily pushed her sunburned face into mine. "Come on. After Trey, nothing could be that bad." Even Dixie grinned.

"Okay," I said, launching into a hazing episode that required the KA pledges to run up three flights of stairs, holding alum in their mouths. On each landing, they had to dodge past these two big football players. If they swallowed the alum during the struggle, well, alum makes you vomit immediately, so you can imagine. . . . They could imagine. But the worst part was that when one pledge wouldn't go past the second landing, the football players threw him down the stairs, and he broke his back.

"That's just disgusting," Donnie drawled. "Nobody would ever do that in Texas."

But on the other hand, I said quickly, Bubba was the most talented poet in the school, having won the Iris Nutley Leach Award for Poetry two years in a row. I pulled the name Iris Nutley Leach right out of the darkening air. I astonished myself. And girls were just crazy about Bubba, I added. In fact, this girl from Washington tried to kill herself after they broke up, and then she had to be institutionalized at Sheppard Pratt in Baltimore. I knew all about Sheppard Pratt because my mother had gone there.

"But he doesn't have a girlfriend right now," I said. Everybody sighed, and a warm breeze came up over the pines and ruffled our little lake. By then, Bubba was as real to me as the Peanuts towel I sat on, as real as the warm gritty dirt between my toes.

During the next year or so, Bubba would knock up a girl and then nobly help her get an abortion (Donnie offered to contribute); he would make Phi Beta Kappa;

he would be arrested for assault; he would wreck his MGB; he would start writing folk songs. My creativity knew no bounds when it came to Bubba, but I was a dismal failure in my first writing class, where my teacher, Mr. Lefcowicz, kept giving me B's and C's and telling me, "Write what you know."

I didn't want to write what I knew. I had no intention of writing a word about my own family, or those peanut fields. Who would want to read about *that?* I had wanted to write in order to *get away* from my own life. I couldn't give up that tormented woman on the cliff in the south of France. I intended to write about glamorous heroines with exciting lives. One of my first—and worst—stories involved a stewardess in Hawaii. I had never been to Hawaii, of course. At that time, I had never even been on a plane. The plot, which was very complicated, had something to do with international espionage. I remember how kindly my young teacher smiled at me when he handed my story back. He asked me to stay for a minute after class. "Charlene," he said, "I want you to write something true next time."

Instead, I decided to give up on plot and concentrate on theme, intending to pull some heartstrings. It was nearly Christmas, and this time we had to read our stories aloud to the whole group. But right before that class, Mr. Lefcowicz, who had already read our stories, pulled me aside and told me that I didn't have to read mine out loud if I didn't want to.

"Of course I want to," I said.

We took our seats.

My story took place in a large, unnamed city on Christmas Eve. In this story, a whole happy family was trimming the Christmas tree, singing carols, and drinking hot chocolate while it snowed outside. I think I had "softly falling flakes." Each person in the family was allowed to open one present—selected from the huge pile of gifts beneath the glittering tree—before bed. Then everyone went to sleep, and a "pregnant silence" descended. At three o'clock a fire broke out, and the whole house burned to the ground, and they all burned up, dying horrible deaths, which I described individually—conscious, as I read aloud, of some movement and sound among my listeners. But I didn't dare look up as I approached the story's ironic end: "When the fire trucks arrived, the only sign of life to be found was a blackened music box in the smoking ashes, softly playing 'Silent Night.'"

By the end of my story, one girl had put her head down on her desk; another was having a coughing fit. Mr. Lefcowicz was staring intently out the window at the wintry day, his back to us. Then he made a great show of looking at his watch. "Whoops! Class dismissed!" he cried, grabbing his bookbag. He rushed from the room like the White Rabbit, already late.

But I was not that stupid.

As I walked across the cold, wet quadrangle toward my dormitory, I understood perfectly well that my story was terrible, laughable. I wanted to die. The gray sky, the dripping, leafless trees, fit my mood perfectly, and I remembered Mr. Lefcowicz saying, in an earlier class, that we must never manipulate nature to express our characters' emotions. "Ha!" I muttered scornfully to the heavy sky.

The very next day, I joined the staff of the campus newspaper. I became its editor in the middle of my sophomore year—a job nobody else wanted, a job I really enjoyed. I had found a niche, a role, and although it was not what I had envisioned for myself, it was okay. Thus I became the following things: editor of the newspaper; member of Athena, the secret honor society; roommate of Dixie, the May Queen; friend of Phi Gams; and—especially—sister of Bubba, whose legend loomed ever larger. But I avoided both dates and creative writing classes for the next two years, finding Mr. Lefcowicz's stale advice, "Write what you know," more impossible with each visit home.

The summer between my sophomore and junior years was the hardest. The first night I was home, I realized that something was wrong with Mama when I woke up to hear water splashing in the downstairs bathroom. I went to investigate. There she was, wearing a lacy pink peignoir and her old gardening shoes, scrubbing the green tub.

"Oh, hi, Charlene!" she said brightly, and went on scrubbing, humming tune-lessly to herself. A mop and bucket stood in the corner. I said good night and went back to my bedroom, where I looked at the clock; it was three-thirty a.m.

The next day, Mama burst into tears when Sam spilled a glass of iced tea, and the day after that, Daddy took her over to Petersburg and put her in the hospital. Memaw came in to stay with Sam during the day while I worked at Snow's in South Hill, my old job.

I'd come home at suppertime each day to find Sam in his chair on the front porch, holding Blackie, waiting for me. He seemed to have gotten smaller some-how—and for the first time I realized that Sam, so much a part of my childhood, was not growing up along with me. In fact, he would *never* grow up, and I thought about that a lot on those summer evenings as I swung gently in the porch swing, back and forth through the sultry air, suspended.

In August, I went to Memphis for a week to visit Dixie, whose house turned out to be like Tara in *Gone With the Wind,* only bigger, and whose mother turned out to drink sherry all day long. I came back to find Mama out of the hospital already, much improved by shock treatments, and another surprise—a baby-blue Chevrolet con-vertible, used but great-looking, in the driveway. My father handed me the keys.

"Here, honey," he said, and then he hugged me tight, smelling of sweat and to-bacco. "We're so proud of you." He had traded a man a combine or something for the car.

So I drove back to school in style, and my junior year went smoothly until Don-nie announced that her sister Susannah, now at Pine Mountain Junior College, was going to Dartmouth for Winter Carnival, to visit a boy she'd met that summer. Su-sannah just *couldn't wait* to look up Bubba.

Unfortunately this was not possible, as I got a phone call that very night saying that Bubba had been kicked out of school for leading a demonstration against the war. Lily, who had become much more political herself by that time, jumped up from her desk and grabbed my hand.

"Oh, no!" she shrieked. "He'll be drafted!" The alarm that filled our study room was palpable—as real as the mounting body count on TV—as we stared white-faced at each other.

"Whatever will he do now?" Donnie was wringing her hands.

"I don't know," I said desperately. "I just don't know." I went to my room—a single, this term—and thought about it. It was clear that he would have to do some-thing, something to take him far, far away.

But Bubba's problem was soon to be superseded by Melissa's. She was pregnant, really pregnant, and in spite of all the arguments we could come up with, she wanted to get married and have the baby. She wanted to have lots of babies, and one day live in the big house on the Battery that her boyfriend would inherit, and this is exactly what she's done. Her life has been predictable and productive. So violent in his college days, Melissa's husband turned out to be a model of stability in later life. And their first child, Anna, kept him out of the draft.

As she got into her mother's car to leave, Melissa squeezed my hand and said, "Keep me posted about Bubba, and don't worry so much. I'm sure everything will work out all right."

It didn't.

Bubba burned his draft card not a month later and headed for Canada, where he lived in a commune. I didn't hear from him for a long time after that, tangled up as I was by then in my affair with Dr. Pierce.

Dr. Pierce was a fierce, bleak, melancholy man who looked like a bird of prey. Not surprisingly, he was a Beckett scholar. He taught the seminar in contemporary literature that I took in the spring of my junior year. We read Joseph Heller, Kurt Vonnegut, Flannery O'Connor, John Barth, and Thomas Pynchon, among others. Flannery O'Connor would become my favorite, and I would do my senior thesis on her work, feeling a secret and strong kinship, by then, with her dire view. But this was later, after my affair with Dr. Pierce was over.

At first I didn't know what to make of him. I hated his northern accent, his lugubrious, glistening dark eyes, his all-encompassing pessimism. He told us that contemporary literature was absurd because the world was absurd. He told us that the language in the books we were reading was weird and fractured because true communication is impossible in the world today. Dr. Pierce told us this in a sad, cynical tone full of infinite world-weariness, which I found both repellent and attractive.

I decided to go in and talk to him. I am still not sure why I did this—I was making good grades in his course, I understood everything. But one blustery, unsettling March afternoon I found myself sitting outside his office. He was a popular teacher, rumored to be always ready to listen to his students' problems. I don't know what I meant to talk to him about. The hour grew late. The hall grew dark. I smoked four or five cigarettes while other students, ahead of me, went in and out. Then Dr. Pierce came and stood in the doorway. He took off his glasses and rubbed his eyes. He looked tired, but not nearly as old as he did in class, where he always wore a tie. Now he wore jeans and a blue work shirt, and I could see the dark hair at his neck.

"Ah," he said in that way of his that rendered all his remarks oddly significant. "Ah! Miss Christian, is it not?"

He knew it was. I felt uncomfortable, like he was mocking me. He made a gesture; I preceded him into his office and sat down.

"Now," he said, staring at me. I looked out the window at the skittish, blowing day, at the girls who passed by on the sidewalk, giggling and trying to hold their skirts down. *"Miss Christian,"* Dr. Pierce said. Maybe he'd said it before. I looked at him.

"I presume you had some reason for this visit," he said sardonically.

To my horror, I started crying. Not little ladylike sniffles, either, but huge groaning sobs. Dr. Pierce thrust a box of Kleenex in my direction, then sat drumming his fingers on his desk. I kept on crying. Finally I realized what he was drumming: the *William Tell* overture. I got tickled. Soon I was crying and laughing at the same time. I was still astonished at myself.

"Blow your nose," Dr. Pierce said.

I did.

"That's better," he said. It was. He got up and closed his office door, although there was no need to do so, since the hall outside was empty now. Dr. Pierce sat back down and leaned across his desk toward me. "What is it?" he asked.

But I still didn't know what it was. I said so, and apologized. "One thing, though," I said. "I'd like to complain about the choice of books on our reading list."

"Aha!" Dr. Pierce said. He leaned back in his chair and made his fingers into a tent. "You liked Eudora Welty," he said. This was true; I nodded. "You liked *Lie Down in Darkness,*" he said. I nodded again.

"But I just *hate* this other stuff!" I burst out. "I just hated *The End of the Road,* I hated it! It's so depressing."

He nodded rapidly. "You think literature should make you feel good?" he asked.

"It used to," I said. Then I was crying again. I stood up. "I'm so sorry," I said.

Dr. Pierce stood up, too, and walked around his desk and came to stand close to me. The light in his office was soft, gray, furry. Dr. Pierce took both my hands in his. "Oh, Miss Christian," he said. "My very dear, very young Miss Christian, I know what you mean." And I could tell, by the pain and weariness in his voice, that this was true. I could see Dr. Pierce suddenly as a much younger man, as a boy, with a light in his eyes and a different feeling about the world. I reached up and put my hands in his curly hair and pulled his face down to mine and kissed him fiercely, in a way I had never kissed anybody. I couldn't imagine myself doing this, yet I did it naturally. Dr. Pierce kissed me back. We kissed for a long time, while it grew completely dark outside, and then he locked the door and turned back to me. He sighed deeply, almost a groan—a sound, I felt, of regret—then unbuttoned my shirt. We made love on the rug on his office floor. Immediately we were caught up in a kind of fever that lasted for several months—times like these in his office after hours, or in the backseat of my car parked by Goshen Lake, or in cheap motels when I'd signed out to go home.

Nobody suspected a thing. I was as good at keeping secrets as I was at making up lies. Plus, I was a campus leader, and Dr. Pierce was a married man.

He tried to end it that June. I was headed home, and he was headed to New York, where he had a fellowship to do research at the Morgan Library.

"Charlene—" Dr. Pierce said. We were in public, out on the quadrangle right after graduation. His wife walked down the hill at some distance behind us, with other faculty wives. Dr. Pierce's voice was hoarse, the way it got when he was in torment (which he so often was, which was one of the most attractive things about him. Years later, I'd realize this). "Let us make a clean break," he sort of mumbled. "Right now. It cannot go on, and we both know it."

We had reached the parking lot in front of the chapel; the sunlight reflected off the cars was dazzling.

Dr. Pierce stuck out his hand in an oddly formal gesture. "Have a good summer, Charlene," he said, "and good-bye."

Dr. Pierce had chosen his moment well. He knew I wouldn't make a scene in front of all these people. But I refused to take his hand. I rushed off madly through the parked cars to my own and gunned it out of there and out to the lake, where I parked on the bluff above Donnie's cabin, in the exact spot where Dr. Pierce and I had been together so many times. I sat at the wheel and looked out at the lake, now full of children on a school outing. Their shrill screams and laughter drifted to me thinly, like the sounds of birds in the trees around my car. I leaned back on the seat and stared straight up at the sun through the trees—just at the top of the tent of green, where light filtered through in bursts like stars.

But I couldn't give him up, not yet, not ever.

I resolved to surprise Dr. Pierce in New York, and that's exactly what I did, telling my parents I'd gone on a trip to Virginia Beach with friends. I got his summer address from the registrar's office. I drove up through Richmond and Washington, a seven-hour drive. It was crazy and even a dangerous thing to do, since I had never been to New York. But at last I ended up in front of the brownstone in the Village where Dr. Pierce and his wife were subletting an apartment. It was midafternoon and hot; I had not imagined New York to be so hot, hotter even than McKenney, Virginia. I was still in a fever, I think. I rang the doorbell, without even considering what I would do if his wife answered. But nobody answered. Nobody was home. Somehow, this possibility had not occurred to me. I felt exhausted. I leaned against the wall and then slid down it, until I was sitting on the floor in the vestibule. I pulled off my panty hose and stuffed them into my purse. They were too hot. I was too hot. I wore a kelly-green linen dress; I'd thought I needed to be all dressed up to go to New York.

I don't even remember falling asleep, but I was awakened by Dr. Pierce shaking my shoulder and saying my name.

Whatever can be said of Dr. Pierce, he was not a jerk. He told me firmly that our relationship was over, and just as firmly that I should not be going around New York City at night by myself, not in the shape I was in.

By the time his wife came home with groceries, I was lying on the studio bed, feeling a little better. He told her I was having a breakdown, which seemed suddenly true. Dr. Pierce and I looked at the news on TV while she made spaghetti. After dinner she lit a joint and handed it to me. It was the first time anybody had offered me marijuana. I shook my head. I thought I was crazy enough already. Dr. Pierce's wife was nice, though. She was pale, with long, long blond hair, which she had worn in a braid on campus, or twisted on top of her head. Now it fell over her shoulders like water. She was not much—certainly not ten years—older than I was, and I wondered if she, too, had been his student. But I was exhausted. I fell asleep on the studio bed in front of a fan that drowned out the sound of their voices as they cleaned up from dinner.

I woke up very early the next morning. I wrote the Pierces a thank-you note on an index card I found in Dr. Pierce's briefcase, and left it propped conspicuously against the toaster. The door to their bedroom was open, but I did not look in.

On the street, I was horrified to find that I had gotten a parking ticket and that my convertible top had been slashed—gratuitously, since there was nothing in the car to steal. This upset me more than anything else about my trip to New York, more than Dr. Pierce's rejection, or his renunciation, as I preferred to consider it—which is how I did consider it, often, during that summer at home while I had the rest of my nervous breakdown.

My parents were very kind. They thought it all had to do with Don Fetterman, who was missing in action in Vietnam, and maybe it did, sort of. I was "nervous," and cried a lot. Finally my aunt Dee got tired of me mooning around, as she called it. She frosted my hair and took me to Myrtle Beach, where it proved impossible to continue the nervous breakdown. The last night of the trip, Aunt Dee and I double-dated with some realtors she'd met by the pool.

Aunt Dee and I got back to McKenney just in time for me to pack and drive to school, where I was one of the seniors in charge of freshman orientation. Daddy had gotten the top fixed on my car; I was a blonde; and I'd lost twenty-five pounds.

The campus seemed smaller to me as I drove through the imposing gates. My foot-steps echoed as I carried my bags up to the third floor of Old North, where Dixie and I would have the coveted "turret room." I was the first one back in the dorm, but as I hauled things in from my car, other seniors began arriving. We hugged and squealed, following a script as old as the college. At least three girls stopped in mid-hug to push me back, scrutinize me carefully, and exclaim that they wouldn't have recognized me. I didn't know what they meant.

Sweaty and exhausted after carrying everything up to the room, I decided to shower before dinner. I was standing naked in our room, toweling my hair dry, when the dinner bell rang. Its somber tone sounded elegiac to me in that moment. On im-pulse, I started rummaging around in one of my boxes, until I found the mirror I was looking for. I went to stand at the window while the last of the lingering chimes died on the August air.

I held the mirror out at arm's length and looked at myself. I had cheekbones. I had hipbones. I could see my ribs. My eyes were darker, larger in my face. My wild damp hair was as blond as Lily's.

Clearly, *something had finally happened to me.*

That weekend, Dixie, Donnie, Lily, and I went out to Donnie's cabin to drink beer and catch up on the summer. We telephoned Melissa, now eight months preg-nant, who claimed to be blissfully happy and said she was making curtains.

Lily snorted. She got up and put Simon and Garfunkel on the stereo, and got us each another beer. Donnie lit candles and switched off the overhead lamp. Dixie waved her hand, making her big diamond sparkle in the candlelight. Trey, now in law school at Vanderbilt, had given it to her in July. She was already planning her wed-ding. We would all be bridesmaids, of course. (That marriage would last for only a few years, and Dixie would divorce once more before she went to law school herself.) Donnie told us about her mother's new boyfriend. We gossiped on as the hour grew late and bugs slammed suicidally into the porch light. The moon came up big and bright. I kept playing "The Sounds of Silence" over and over; it matched my mood, my new conception of myself. I also liked "I Am a Rock, I Am an Island."

Then Lily announced that she was in love, *really in love* this time, with a young poet she'd met that summer on Cape Cod, where she'd been waitressing. We waited while she lit a cigarette. "We lived together for two months," Lily said, "in his room at the inn, where we could look out and see the water." We stared at her. None of us had ever lived with anybody, or known anyone who had. Lily looked around at us.

"It was wonderful," she said. "It was heaven. But it was not what you might think," she added enigmatically, "living with a man."

I started crying.

There was a long silence, and the needle on the record started scratching. Donnie got up and cut it off. They were all looking at me.

"And what about you, Charlene?" Lily said softly. "What happened to you this summer, anyway?"

It was a moment I had rehearsed again and again in my mind. I would tell them about my affair with Dr. Pierce and how I had gone to New York to find him, and how he had renounced me because his wife was pregnant. I had just added this part. But I was crying too hard to speak. "It was awful," I said finally, and Dixie came over and hugged me. "What was awful?" she said, but I couldn't even speak, my mind filled suddenly, surprisingly, with Don Fetterman as he'd looked in high school, presiding over the Glee Club.

"Come on," Dixie said, "tell us."

The candles were guttering, the moon made a path across the lake. I took a deep breath.

"Bubba is dead," I said.

"Oh, God! Oh, no!" A sort of pandemonium ensued, which I don't remember much about, although I remember the details of my brother's death vividly. Bubba drowned in a lake in Canada, attempting to save a friend's child who had fallen overboard. The child died, too. Bubba was buried there, on the wild shore of that northern lake, and his only funeral was what his friends said as they spoke around the grave one by one. His best friend had written to me, describing the whole thing.

"Charlene, Charlene, why didn't you tell us sooner?" Donnie asked.

I just shook my head. "I couldn't," I said.

Later that fall, I finally wrote a good story—about my family, back in McKenney—and then another, and then another. I won a scholarship to graduate school at Columbia University in New York, where I still live, with my husband, on the West Side, free-lancing for several magazines and writing fiction.

It was here, only a few weeks ago, that I last saw Lily, now a prominent feminist scholar. She was in town for the MLA convention. We went to a bistro near my apartment for lunch, lingering over wine far into the late-December afternoon while my husband baby-sat. Lily was in the middle of a divorce. "You know," she said at one point, twirling her tulip wineglass, "I have often thought that the one great tragedy of my life was never getting to meet your brother. Somehow I always felt that he and I were just meant for each other." We sat in the restaurant for a long time, at the window where we could see the passersby hurrying along the sidewalk in the dismal sleet outside, each one so preoccupied, so caught up in his own story. We sat there all afternoon.

1997

Pedro Pietri 1944–2004

Born in Ponce, Puerto Rico, Pedro Pietri lived most of his life in New York City. He wrote poetry and plays, some of which have been presented in off-Broadway theaters. *Illusions of a Revolving Door,* a collection of his plays in English, was published in Puerto Rico in 1992, the first time a Nuyorican writer published his work in English on the island.

His texts illustrate the literature of protest and denunciation that characterizes the work of Nuyorican writers, who address their literature to Puerto Rican readers in order to raise consciousness of social and political oppression within American society. Nuyorican poets began to read at the Nuyorican Poet's Cafe, at 505 East Sixth Street in New York City, where they met with other writers, artists, and community people. Their "poetic" language is anti-lyrical and harsh; it is the street language of blacks and Puerto Ricans in El Barrio. Such a stylistic choice implies a resistance to Americanization and an expression of dignity and pride in the *puertorriqueño's* heritage.

In *Puerto Rican Obituary,* a key text for Nuyorican poets, Pietri creates a mock epic of the Puerto Rican community in the United States. Through humor, sarcasm, and an irreverent irony, the poet presents the American Dream—which motivated many Puerto Ricans to emigrate to this country—not as a dream but as a nightmare and, ultimately, as death. The *puertorriqueños* find themselves shut out of America's economic opportunities and lifestyle and realize that they are unemployed, living on welfare, bitter, degraded. Pietri's image of a collective death is symbolic, denouncing the death of the Puerto Ricans' dignity as a people and individually. Yet Pietri is not altogether pessimistic, for the poem proposes a utopian symbolic space of Puerto Rican identity.

In *Traffic Violations,* Pietri moves away from the specificity of the social conditions of Puerto Ricans in New York, and expresses a broader poetic vision of life as absurd. As his title indicates, his poetry reaffirms the need to break away from norms, the healthy rupturing of expectations, logic, and civilization. By inverting many American idiomatic expressions and clichés, he surprises and moves the reader. This book presents the figure of the poet as a self-willed outcast, who drinks and uses drugs in order to avoid falling into any mechanization of the self. It is a surrealist work.

As representative of the literature of protest in Nuyorican culture, Pedro Pietri's work is a strong denunciation of the American system and of Western capitalism. To struggle against these forces, Pietri's poetry invites the *puertorriqueños* to acquire a sense of dignity and pride in their heritage and to avoid complete cultural assimilation.

Frances R. Aparicio
University of Illinois at Chicago

PRIMARY WORKS

Puerto Rican Obituary, 1973; *Lost in the Museum of Natural History/Perdido en el Museo de Historia Natural,* 1981; *Traffic Violations,* 1983; *The Masses Are Asses,* 1984; *Illusions of a Revolving Door: Plays, Teatro,* 1992.

Puerto Rican Obituary

They worked
They were always on time
They were never late
They never spoke back
5   when they were insulted
They worked
They never took days off
that were not on the calendar
They never went on strike
10   without permission
They worked
ten days a week
and were only paid for five
They worked
15   They worked
They worked
and they died
They died broke
They died owing
20   They died never knowing
what the front entrance
of the first national city bank looks like
Juan
Miguel
25   Milagros
Olga
Manuel
All died yesterday today
and will die again tomorrow
30   passing their bill collectors
on to the next of kin
All died
waiting for the garden of eden
to open up again
35   under a new management
All died
dreaming about america
waking them up in the middle of the night
screaming: *Mira Mira*[1]
40   your name is on the winning lottery ticket
for one hundred thousand dollars

[1]Spanish: Look, Look.

All died
hating the grocery stores
that sold them makebelieve steak
45 and bulletproof rice and beans
All died waiting dreaming and hating

Dead Puerto Ricans
Who never knew they were Puerto Ricans
Who never took a coffee break
50 from the ten commandments
to KILL KILL KILL
the landlords of their cracked skulls
and communicate with their latino souls
Juan
55 Miguel
Milagros
Olga
Manuel
From the nervous breakdown streets
60 where the mice live like millionaires
and the people do not live at all
are dead and were never alive

Juan
died waiting for his number to hit
65 Miguel
died waiting for the welfare check
to come and go and come again
Milagros
died waiting for her ten children
70 to grow up and work
so she could quit working
Olga
died waiting for a five dollar raise
Manuel
75 died waiting for his supervisor to drop dead
so he could get a promotion

It's a long ride
from Spanish Harlem
to long island cemetery
80 where they were buried
First the train
and then the bus
and the cold cuts for lunch
and the flowers
85 that will be stolen

when visiting hours are over
It's very expensive
It's very expensive
But they understand
90 Their parents understood
It's a long nonprofit ride
from Spanish Harlem
to long island cemetery

Juan
95 Miguel
Milagros
Olga
Manuel
All died yesterday today
100 and will die again tomorrow
Dreaming
Dreaming about queens
Cleancut lilywhite neighborhood
Puerto Ricanless scene
105 Thirty thousand dollar home
The first spics on the block
Proud to belong to a community
of gringos who want them lynched
Proud to be a long distance away
110 from the sacred phrase: *Qué Pasa*[2]
These dreams
These empty dreams
from the makebelieve bedrooms
their parents left them
115 are the aftereffects
of television programs
about the ideal
white american family
with black maids
120 and latino janitors
who are well trained
to make everyone
and their bill collectors
laugh at them
125 and the people they represent

Juan
died dreaming about a new car

---

[2]Spanish: What's happening?

Miguel
died dreaming about new antipoverty programs

130 Milagros
died dreaming about a trip to Puerto Rico
Olga
died dreaming about real jewelry
Manuel
135 died dreaming about the irish sweepstakes

They all died
like a hero sandwich dies
in the garment district
at twelve o'clock in the afternoon
140 social security number to ashes
union dues to dust

They knew
they were born to weep
and keep the morticians employed
145 as long as they pledge allegiance
to the flag that wants them destroyed
They saw their names listed
in the telephone directory of destruction
They were trained to turn
150 the other cheek by newspapers
that mispelled mispronounced
and misunderstood their names
and celebrated when death came
and stole their final laundry ticket
155 They were born dead
and they died dead

It's time
to visit sister lópez again
the number one healer
160 and fortune card dealer
in Spanish Harlem
She can communicate
with your late relatives
for a reasonable fee

165 Good news is guaranteed

Rise Table Rise Table
death is not dumb and disabled
Those who love you want to know

the correct number to play
170 Let them know this right away
Rise Table Rise Table
death is not dumb and disabled
Now that your problems are over
and the world is off your shoulders
175 help those who you left behind
find financial peace of mind
Rise Table Rise Table
death is not dumb and disabled
If the right number we hit
180 all our problems will split
and we will visit your grave
on every legal holiday
Those who love you want to know
the correct number to play
185 Let them know this right away
We know your spirit is able
Death is not dumb and disabled
RISE TABLE RISE TABLE

Juan
190 Miguel
Milagros
Olga
Manuel
All died yesterday today
195 and will die again tomorrow
Hating fighting and stealing
broken windows from each other
Practicing a religion without a roof
The old testament
200 The new testament
according to the gospel
of the internal revenue
the judge and jury and executioner
protector and eternal bill collector

205 Secondhand shit for sale
Learn how to say *Cómo Está Usted*[3]
and you will make a fortune
They are dead
They are dead
210 and will not return from the dead

[3]Spanish: How are you?

        until they stop neglecting
        the art of their dialogue
        for broken english lessons
        to impress the mister goldsteins
215   who keep them employed
        as *lavaplatos*[4] porters messenger boys
        factory workers maids stock clerks
        shipping clerks assistant mailroom
        assistant, assistant assistant
220   to the assistant's assistant
        assistant lavaplatos and automatic
        artificial smiling doormen
        for the lowest wages of the ages
        and rages when you demand a raise
225   because it's against the company policy
        to promote SPICS SPICS SPICS

        Juan
        died hating Miguel because Miguel's
        used car was in better running condition
230   than his used car
        Miguel
        died hating Milagros because Milagros
        had a color television set
        and he could not afford one yet
235   Milagros
        died hating Olga because Olga
        made five dollars more on the same job
        Olga
        died hating Manuel because Manuel
240   had hit the numbers more times
        than she had hit the numbers
        Manuel
        died hating all of them
        Juan
245   Manuel
        Milagros
        and Olga
        because they all spoke broken english
        more fluently than he did

250   And now they are together
        in the main lobby of the void
        Addicted to silence

[4]Spanish: Dishwashers.

Off limits to the wind
Confined to worm supremacy
255 in long island cemetery
This is the groovy hereafter
the protestant collection box
was talking so loud and proud about

Here lies Juan
260 Here lies Miguel
Here lies Milagros
Here lies Olga
Here lies Manuel
who died yesterday today
265 and will die again tomorrow
Always broke
Always owing
Never knowing
that they are beautiful people
270 Never knowing
the geography of their complexion

PUERTO RICO IS A BEAUTIFUL PLACE
PUERTORRIQUEÑOS ARE A BEAUTIFUL RACE

If only they
275 had turned off the television
and tuned into their own imaginations
If only they
had used the white supremacy bibles
for toilet paper purpose
280 and made their latino souls
the only religion of their race
If only they
had returned to the definition of the sun
after the first mental snowstorm
285 on the summer of their senses
If only they
had kept their eyes open
at the funeral of their fellow employees
who came to this country to make a fortune
290 and were buried without underwear

Juan
Miguel
Milagros
Olga
295 Manuel
will right now be doing their own thing

where beautiful people sing
and dance and work together
where the wind is a stranger
300 to miserable weather conditions
where you do not need a dictionary
to communicate with your people
Aquí[5] *Se habla Español*[6] all the time
Aquí you salute your flag first
305 Aquí there are no dial soap commercials
Aquí everybody smells good
Aquí tv dinners do not have a future
Aquí the men and women admire desire
and never get tired of each other
310 Aquí Qué Pasa Power is what's happening
Aquí to be called *negrito*[7]
means to be called LOVE

1973

Traffic Violations

you go into chicken delight
and order dinosaurs
because you are hungry
and want something different
5 now that you no longer
eat meat or fish or vegetables
you are told politely
is against company policies
to be that different
10 so you remove a button off
your absentminded overcoat
the scenery changes
you are waiting in line
to take a mean leak
15 at one of those public toilets
in the times square area
the line is 3 weeks long
many waited with their lunch
inside brown paper bags

[5]Spanish: Here.
[6]Spanish: We speak Spanish.
[7]Spanish: Black (diminutive form).

20 singing the battle hymn
of the republic to keep warm

you remove another button off
your absentminded overcoat
all you can see now are
25 high heels and low quarter shoes
coming at your eyeballs
disappearing when they come
close enough to make contact

you try to get up off the floor
30 but you forgot how to move
umbrellas open up inside your head
you start screaming backwards
your legs behave like flat tires
your mind melts in slow motion

35 you remove another button off
your absentminded overcoat
is late in the evening
according to everybody
who keeps track of time
40 you are about to jump off the roof
emergency sirens are heard

A crowd of skilled & unskilled
Laborers on their mental lunch break
congregate on the street below
45 the roof you are about to jump from
they are laughing hysterically
nobody tries to talk you out of it
everybody wants you to jump
so they can get some sleep tonight—
50 should you change your mind about jumping
All the spectators will get uptight

red white and blue representatives
from the suicide prevention bureau
order you to jump immediately
55 you refuse to obey their orders
they sendout a helicopter to push you
off the roof into the morning headlines
the laughter from the crowd
on the street breaks the sound barrier

60 you try removing another button off
your absentminded overcoat

but that button is reported missing
the helicopter pushes you off the roof
everybody is feeling much better
65 you are losing your memory real fast
the clouds put on black arm bands
it starts raining needles and thread

a few seconds before having breakfast
at a cafeteria in the hereafter
70 you remove your absentminded overcoat

you are on the front and back seat
of a bi-lingo spaceship
smoking grass with your friends
from the past present and future
75 nothing unusual is happening
you are all speeding
without moving an inch
making sure nobody does the driving

1983

Richard Rodriguez b. 1944

Richard Rodriguez is probably the best-known Mexican American writer today, his fame propelling him to regular appearances on radio and television talk shows and even to the pages of *People* magazine. His essays have appeared in prestigious journals and newspapers such as the *American Scholar* and the *Los Angeles Times.* Rodriguez is also perhaps the most controversial of contemporary Latino authors, having been applauded by the political right, especially in his early career, for stands against affirmative action and bilingual education, and vilified by the left for precisely the same positions. In any event, Rodriguez commands attention for the thoughtfulness and craftsmanship of his prose and his willingness to take on provocative issues. Over the years, Rodriguez has become less susceptible to easy political categorization as his arguments have become more nuanced.

Rodriguez was born in San Francisco,
the child of Mexican immigrants ambitious for their four children and eager for admission into the American middle class. The Rodriguezes soon moved to Sacramento and brought a "gaudy yellow" house among white bungalows "many blocks from the Mexican south side of town." Sensitive and introspective, Richard began Catholic school armed with only a few words of English. As Rodriguez recalls in his autobiographical narrative, *The Hunger of Memory,* his movement through the American educational system to affluence and a certain celebrity was wrenching both to himself and to his parents. Quickly noticing Richard's academic gifts, the nuns insisted that he speak English at home to accelerate his intellectual development, thereby opening a cultural chasm between boy and parents that only widens. Rodriguez observes that he had to choose between the "public identity" of the American mainstream and the "private identity"

of his parents' Mexican home, finally concluding that assimilation is a "necessity." In *Hunger of Memory,* Rodriguez seems willfully ignorant that large immigration movements—like the one that brought his parents to the United States—typically create bi-directional acculturation, immigrants and native-born residents transforming and revitalizing one another. Furthermore, Rodriguez ignores the well-established fact that many—perhaps most—of us have rich and varied identities that allow us to function in a number of cultural settings.

In *Days of Obligation,* Rodriguez blends autobiographical explorations with musings on such topics as Mexican history and character, the California missions, and the AIDS epidemic. Sprawling and sometimes opaque, *Days of Obligation* nonetheless reveals a more mature Rodriguez, uncomfortable with some of the facile conclusions of *Hunger of Memory.* Here,

very much aware of his mortality, Rodriguez wishes to understand his parents' cultural heritage, which earlier he had been all-too-willing to jettison. *Hunger of Memory* ends with a family Christmas dinner at which Rodriguez and his father have almost nothing to say to each other; in *Days of Obligation,* we see Rodriguez throughout beseeching his parents for more information about Mexico and their lives there.

The selection reproduced here comes from the chapter "Complexion" in *Hunger of Memory.* Rodriguez treats the complex of attitudes he encountered because of his dark skin: from his family, from Anglo outsiders, from himself. One of Rodriguez's virtues as a writer of autobiography is to reveal honestly his insecurities, even in connection with such difficult issues as his adolescent sexuality.

Raymund A. Paredes
University of California–Los Angeles

PRIMARY WORKS

Hunger of Memory: The Education of Richard Rodriguez, 1982; *Days of Obligation: An Argument with My Mexican Father,* 1992; *Brown: The Last Discovery of America,* 1999.

from Hunger of Memory

Visiting the East Coast or the gray capitals of Europe during the long months of winter, I often meet people at deluxe hotels who comment on my complexion. (In such hotels it appears nowadays a mark of leisure and wealth to have a complexion like mine.) Have I been skiing? In the Swiss Alps? Have I just returned from a Caribbean vacation? No. I say no softly but in a firm voice that intends to explain: My complexion is dark. (My skin is brown. More exactly, terra-cotta in sunlight, tawny in shade. I do not redden in sunlight. Instead, my skin becomes progressively dark; the sun singes the flesh.)

When I was a boy the white summer sun of Sacramento would darken me so, my T-shirt would seem bleached against my slender dark arms. My mother would see me come up the front steps. She'd wait for the screen door to slam at my back. "You look like a *negrito,*" she'd say, angry, sorry to be angry, frustrated almost to laughing, scorn. "You know how important looks are in this country. With *los gringos* looks are all that they judge on. But you! Look at you! You're so careless!" Then she'd start in all over again. "You won't be satisfied till you end up looking like *los pobres* who work in the fields, *los braceros.*"

(*Los braceros:* Those men who work with their *brazos,* their arms; Mexican nationals who were licensed to work for American farmers in the 1950s. They worked very hard for very little money, my father would tell me. And what money they earned they sent back to Mexico to support their families, my mother would add. *Los pobres*— the poor, the pitiful, the powerless ones. But paradoxically also powerful men. They were the men with brown-muscled arms I stared at in awe on Saturday mornings when they showed up downtown like gypsies to shop at Woolworth's or Penney's. On Monday nights they would gather hours early on the steps of the Memorial Auditorium for the wrestling matches. Passing by on my bicycle in summer, I would spy them there, clustered in small groups, talking—frightening and fascinating men—some wearing Texas *sombreros* and T-shirts which shone fluorescent in the twilight. I would sit forward in the back seat of our family's '48 Chevy to see them, working alongside Valley highways: dark men on an even horizon, loading a truck amid rows of straight green. Powerful, powerless men. Their fascinating darkness—like mine—to be feared.)

"You'll end up looking just like them." . . .

2

Complexion. My first conscious experience of sexual excitement concerns my complexion. One summer weekend, when I was around seven years old, I was at a public swimming pool with the whole family. I remember sitting on the damp pavement next to the pool and seeing my mother, in the spectators' bleachers, holding my younger sister on her lap. My mother, I noticed, was watching my father as he stood on a diving board, waving to her. I watched her wave back. Then saw her radiant, bashful, astonishing smile. In that second I sensed that my mother and father had a relationship I knew nothing about. A nervous excitement encircled my stomach as I saw my mother's eyes follow my father's figure curving into the water. A second or two later, he emerged. I heard him call out. Smiling, his voice sounded, buoyant, calling me to swim to him. But turning to see him, I caught my mother's eyes. I heard her shout over to me. In Spanish she called through the crowd: "Put a towel on over your shoulders." In public, she didn't want to say why. I knew.

That incident anticipates the shame and sexual inferiority I was to feel in later years because of my dark complexion. I was to grow up an ugly child. Or one who thought himself ugly. (*Feo.*) One night when I was eleven or twelve years old, I locked myself in the bathroom and carefully regarded my reflection in the mirror over the sink. Without any pleasure I studied my skin. I turned on the faucet. (In my mind I heard the swirling voices of aunts, and even my mother's voice, whispering, whispering incessantly about lemon juice solutions and dark, *feo* children.) With a bar of soap, I fashioned a thick ball of lather. I began soaping my arms. I took my father's straight razor out of the medicine cabinet. Slowly, with steady deliberateness, I put the blade against my flesh, pressed it as close as I could without cutting, and moved it up and down across my skin to see if I could get out, somehow lessen, the dark. All I succeeded in doing, however, was in shaving my arms bare of their hair. For as I noted with disappointment, the dark would not come out. It remained. Trapped. Deep in the cells of my skin.

Throughout adolescence, I felt myself mysteriously marked. Nothing else about my appearance would concern me so much as the fact that my complexion was dark.

My mother would say how sorry she was that there was not money enough to get braces to straighten my teeth. But I never bothered about my teeth. In three-way mirrors at department stores, I'd see my profile dramatically defined by a long nose, but it was really only the color of my skin that caught my attention.

I wasn't afraid that I would become a menial laborer because of my skin. Nor did my complexion make me feel especially vulnerable to racial abuse. (I didn't really consider my dark skin to be a racial characteristic. I would have been only too happy to look as Mexican as my light-skinned older brother.) Simply, I judged myself ugly. And, since the women in my family had been the ones who discussed it in such worried tones, I felt my dark skin made me unattractive to women.

Thirteen years old. Fourteen. In a grammar school art class, when the assignment was to draw a self-portrait, I tried and I tried but could not bring myself to shade in the face on the paper to anything like my actual tone. With disgust then I would come face to face with myself in mirrors. With disappointment I located myself in class photographs—my dark face undefined by the camera which had clearly described the white faces of classmates. Or I'd see my dark wrist against my long-sleeved white shirt.

I grew divorced from my body. Insecure, overweight, listless. On hot summer days when my rubber-soled shoes soaked up the heat from the sidewalk, I kept my head down. Or walked in the shade. My mother didn't need anymore to tell me to watch out for the sun. I denied myself a sensational life. The normal, extraordinary, animal excitement of feeling my body alive—riding shirtless on a bicycle in the warm wind created by furious self-propelled motion—the sensations that first had excited in me a sense of my maleness, I denied. I was too ashamed of my body. I wanted to forget that I had a body because I had a brown body. I was grateful that none of my classmates ever mentioned the fact.

I continued to see the *braceros,* those men I resembled in one way and, in another way, didn't resemble at all. On the watery horizon of a Valley afternoon, I'd see them. And though I feared looking like them, it was with silent envy that I regarded them still. I envied them their physical lives, their freedom to violate the taboo of the sun. Closer to home I would notice the shirtless construction workers, the roofers, the sweating men tarring the street in front of the house. And I'd see the Mexican gardeners. I was unwilling to admit the attraction of their lives. I tried to deny it by looking away. But what was denied became strongly desired.

In high school physical education classes, I withdrew, in the regular company of five or six classmates, to a distant corner of a football field where we smoked and talked. Our company was composed of bodies too short or too tall, all graceless and all—except mine—pale. Our conversation was usually witty. (In fact we were intelligent.) If we referred to the athletic contests around us, it was with sarcasm. With savage scorn I'd refer to the "animals" playing football or baseball. It would have been important for me to have joined them. Or for me to have taken off my shirt, to have let the sun burn dark on my skin, and to have run barefoot on the warm wet grass. It would have been very important. Too important. It would have been too telling a gesture—to admit the desire for sensation, the body, my body.

Fifteen, sixteen. I was a teenager shy in the presence of girls. Never dated. Barely could talk to a girl without stammering. In high school I went to several dances, but I never managed to ask a girl to dance. So I stopped going. I cannot remember high school years now with the parade of typical images: bright drive-ins or gliding blue shadows of a Junior Prom. At home most weekend nights, I would pass evenings reading. Like those hidden, precocious adolescents who have no real-life sexual experiences, I read a great deal of romantic fiction. "You won't find it in your books," my brother would playfully taunt me as he prepared to go to a party by freezing the crest of the wave in his hair with sticky pomade. Through my reading, however, I developed a fabulous and sophisticated sexual imagination. At seventeen, I may not have known how to engage a girl in small talk, but I had read *Lady Chatterley's Lover.*

It annoyed me to hear my father's teasing: that I would never know what "real work" is; that my hands were so soft. I think I knew it was his way of admitting pleasure and pride in my academic success. But I didn't smile. My mother said she was glad her children were getting their educations and would not be pushed around like *los pobres.* I heard the remark ironically as a reminder of my separation from *los braceros.* At such times I suspected that education was making me effeminate. The odd thing, however, was that I did not judge my classmates so harshly. Nor did I consider my male teachers in high school effeminate. It was only myself I judged against some shadowy, mythical Mexican laborer—dark like me, yet very different.

Language was crucial. I knew that I had violated the ideal of the *macho* by becoming such a dedicated student of language and literature. *Machismo* was a word never exactly defined by the persons who used it. (It was best described in the "proper" behavior of men.) Women at home, nevertheless, would repeat the old Mexican dictum that a man should be *feo, fuerte, y formal.* "The three F's," my mother called them, smiling slyly. *Feo* I took to mean not literally ugly so much as ruggedly handsome. (When my mother and her sisters spent a loud, laughing afternoon determining ideal male good looks, they finally settled on the actor Gilbert Roland, who was neither too pretty nor ugly but had looks "like a man.") *Fuerte,* "strong," seemed to mean not physical strength as much as inner strength, character. A dependable man is *fuerte. Fuerte* for that reason was a characteristic subsumed by the last of the three qualities, and the one I most often considered—*formal.* To be *formal* is to be steady. A man of responsibility, a good provider. Someone *formal* is also constant. A person to be relied upon in adversity. A sober man, a man of high seriousness.

I learned a great deal about being *formal* just by listening to the way my father and other male relatives of his generation spoke. A man was not silent necessarily. Nor was he limited in the tones he could sound. For example, he could tell a long, involved, humorous story and laugh at his own humor with high-pitched giggling. But a man was not talkative the way a woman could be. It was permitted a woman to be gossipy and chatty. (When one heard many voices in a room, it was usually women who were talking.) Men spoke much less rapidly and often men spoke in monologues. (When one voice sounded in a crowded room, it was most often a man's voice one heard.) More important than any of this was the fact that a man never verbally revealed his emotions. Men did not speak about their unease in moments of crisis or danger. It was the woman who worried aloud when her husband got laid off from work. At times of illness or death in the family, a man was usually quiet, even silent. Women spoke up to voice prayers. In distress, women always sounded quick ejaculations to God or the Virgin; women prayed in clearly audible voices at a wake held in a funeral parlor. And on the subject of love, a woman was verbally expansive. She spoke of her yearning and delight. A married man, if he spoke publicly about love, usually did so with playful, mischievous irony. Younger, unmarried men more often were quiet. (The *macho* is a silent suitor. *Formal.*)

At home I was quiet, so perhaps I seemed *formal* to my relations and other Spanish-speaking visitors to the house. But outside the house—my God!—I talked. Particularly in class or alone with my teachers, I chattered. (Talking seemed to make teachers think I was bright.) I often was proud of my way with words. Though, on other occasions, for example, when I would hear my mother busily speaking to women, it would occur to me that my attachment to words made me like her. Her son. Not *formal* like my father. At such times I even suspected that my nostalgia for sounds—the noisy, intimate Spanish sounds of my past—was nothing more than effeminate yearning.

High school English teachers encouraged me to describe very personal feelings in words. Poems and short stories I wrote, expressing sorrow and loneliness, were awarded high grades. In my bedroom were books by poets and novelists—books that I loved—in which male writers published feelings the men in my family never revealed or acknowledged in words. And it seemed to me that there was something unmanly about my attachment to literature. Even today, when so much about the myth of the *macho* no longer concerns me, I cannot altogether evade such notions. Writing these pages, admitting my embarrassment or my guilt, admitting my sexual anxieties and my physical insecurity, I have not been able to forget that I am not being *formal.*

So be it.

1982

Alice Walker b. 1944

Alice Walker was born in Eatonton, Georgia, the youngest of eight children of Minnie and Willie Lee Walker, black sharecroppers. Her early life in the South was marked by the pressures of segregation and economic hardship on one hand, and the nurturing refuge of family, church, and black community on the other. Summer visits with her older brothers who had settled in the North gave Walker her first glimpses of the world beyond the rural South. Her poetry, often quite personal, and at times starkly intimate, in its themes of family connections, romantic passion, and political integrity, draws frequently on remembrances of childhood.

In 1961 Walker entered Spelman College, a black women's school in Atlanta,

Georgia. Finding Spelman too traditional, Walker transferred in 1963 to Sarah Lawrence College, a school noted for its avant-garde curriculum in the arts. There, under the tutelage of poet Muriel Rukeyser and others, she began her writing career.

After college, Walker worked briefly for the New York City Welfare Department and in 1967 married Mel Leventhal, a civil rights attorney. The couple moved to Mississippi, where he prosecuted school-desegregation cases and she taught at Jackson State College and also conducted adult education courses in black history. Their life in Mississippi as an interracial, activist couple was harrowing; they lived with constant threats of lethal violence against themselves and their infant daughter. During that time Walker published *The Third Life of Grange Copeland,* a novel of personal and political confrontation and transformation in the lives of three generations of a southern black family. A later novel, *Meridian,* explores the complex psychological burden borne throughout the rest of their lives by those young men and women, black and white, who came of age living and working at the center of the civil rights movement of the nineteen sixties.

In 1971, Walker accepted a fellowship from the Radcliffe Institute in Cambridge, Massachusetts, where she worked on poetry and short fiction, as well as on her landmark essay *In Search of Our Mothers' Gardens.* In 1982, Walker published *The Color Purple,* an epistolary novel about the lives of two sisters, Celie and Nettie, raised in a rural, southern, black community and separated through years of tragedy, pain, struggle, and ultimate triumph. The novel was awarded both the American Book Award and the Pulitzer Prize in 1983.

Alice Walker has been from the start of her career a prolific and diversified writer, adept at poetry, novels, short stories, and essays. Throughout her work, a central theme is the courage, resourcefulness, and creativity of black women of various ages, circumstances, and conditions. Whether in rescuing from oblivion the writing and reputation of novelist, folklorist, and anthropologist Zora Neale Hurston, or in producing her own portraits unique in American letters of black women whose rich and complex lives have been little known and frequently devalued, Alice Walker continues to be a central figure in reshaping and expanding the canon of American literature.

Marilyn Richardson
Independent Scholar

PRIMARY WORKS

Once, 1968; *The Third Life of Grange Copeland* , 1970; *Revolutionary Petunias,* 1973; *In Love & Trouble,* 1973; *Meridian,* 1976; *Goodnight, Willie Lee, I'll See You in the Morning,* 1979; *You Can't Keep a Good Woman Down,* 1981; *The Color Purple,* 1982; *In Search of Our Mothers' Gardens,* 1983; *Horses Make a Landscape Look More Beautiful,* 1984; *The Temple of My Familiar,* 1989; *Possessing the Secret of Joy,* 1992; *Warrior Marks: Her Blue Body Everything We Knew: Earthling Poems, 1965–1990,* 1991; *Female Genital Mutilation and the Sexual Blinding of Women,* 1993; *The Same River Twice: Honoring the Difficult,* 1996; *Anything We Love Can Be Saved: A Writer's Activism,* 1997; *By the Light of My Father's Smile: A Novel,* 1998; *The Way Forward Is with a Broken Heart,* 2000; *Sent by Earth: A Message from the Grandmother Spirit after the Bombing of the World Trade Center and Pentagon,* 2002; *Absolute Trust in the Goodness of the Earth: New Poems,* 2003; *Collected Poems,* 2005; *Now Is the Time to Open Your Heart,* 2005.

Laurel

It was during that summer in the mid-sixties that I met Laurel.

There was a new radical Southern newspaper starting up . . . it was only six months old at the time, and was called *First Rebel.* The title referred, of course, to the black slave who was rebelling all over the South long before the white rebels fought the Civil War. Laurel was in Atlanta to confer with the young people on its staff, and, since he wished to work on a radical, racially mixed newspaper himself, to see if perhaps *First Rebel* might be it.

I was never interested in working on a newspaper, however radical. I agree with Leonard Woolf that to write against a weekly deadline deforms the brain. Still, I attended several of the editorial meetings of *First Rebel* because while wandering out of the first one, fleeing it, in fact, I bumped into Laurel, who, squinting at me through cheap, fingerprint-smudged blue-and-gray-framed bifocals, asked if I knew where the meeting was.

He seemed a parody of the country hick; he was tall, slightly stooped, with black-ish hair cut exactly as if someone had put a bowl over his head. Even his ears stuck out, and were large and pink.

Really, I thought.

Though he was no more than twenty-two, two years older than me, he seemed older. No doubt his bifocals added to this impression, as did his nonchalant gait and slouchy posture. His eyes were clear and brown and filled with an appropriate country slyness. It was his voice that held me. It had a charming lilt to it.

"Would you say that again?" I asked.

"Sure," he said, making it two syllables, the last syllable a higher pitch than the first. "I'm looking for where *First Rebel,* the newspaper, is meeting. What are *you* doing?"

The country slyness was clumsily replaced by a look of country seduction.

Have mercy! I thought. And burst into laughter.

Laurel grinned, his ears reddening.

And so we became involved in planning a newspaper that was committed to combating racism and other violence in the South . . . (until it ran out of funds and folded three years and many pieces of invaluable investigative journalism later).

Laurel's was not a variation of a Southern accent, as I'd first thought. His ancestors had immigrated to the United States in the early 1800s. They had settled in California because there they found the two things they liked best: wine grapes and apples.

I'd never heard anything like Laurel's speech. He could ask a question like "How d'you happen t' be here?" and it sounded as if two happy but languid children were slowly jumping rope under apple trees in the sun. And on Laurel himself, while he spoke, I seemed to smell apples and the faint woodruffy bouquet of May wine.

He was also effortlessly complimentary. He would say, as we went through the cafeteria line, "You're beaut-ti-ful, reel-i," and it was like hearing it and caring about hearing it for the first time. Laurel, who loved working among the grapes, and had done so up to the moment of leaving the orchards for Atlanta, had dirt, lots of it, under his nails.

That's it, I thought. I can safely play here. No one brings such dirty nails home to dinner. That was Monday. By Tuesday I thought that dirty nails were just the right nonbourgeois attribute and indicated a lack of personal concern for appearances that included the smudged bifocals and the frazzled but beautifully fitting jeans; in a back pocket of which was invariably a half-rolled, impressively battered paperback book. It occurred to me that I could not look at Laurel without wanting to make love with him.

He was the same.

For a while, I blamed it on Atlanta in the spring . . . the cherry trees that blossomed around the campus buildings, the wonderful honeysuckle smells of our

South, the excitement of being far away from New York City and its never-to-be-gotten-used-to dirt. But it was more: if we both walked into a room from separate doors, even if we didn't see each other, a current dragged us together. At breakfast neither of us could eat, except chokingly, so intense was our longing to be together. Minus people, table, food.

A veritable movie.

Throughout the rest of the week we racked our brains trying to think of a place to make love. But the hotels were still segregated, and once, after a Movement party at somebody's house, we were severely reprimanded for walking out into the Southern night, blissfully hand in hand.

"Don't you know this is outrageous?" a young black man asked us, pulling us into his car, where I sat on Laurel's lap in a kind of sensual stupor—hearing his words, agreeing with them, knowing the bloody History behind them . . . but not caring in the least.

In short, there was no place for us to make love, as that term is popularly understood. We were housed in dormitories. Men in one. Women in another. Interracial couples were under surveillance wherever the poor things raised their heads anywhere in the city. We were reduced to a kind of sexual acrobatics on a bench close beside one of the dormitories. And, as lovers know, acrobatics of a sexual sort puts a strain on one's power of physical ingenuity while making one's lust all the more a resident of the brain, where it quickly becomes all-pervading, insatiable, and profound.

The state of lust itself is not a happy one if there is no relief in sight. Though I am happy enough to enter that state whenever it occurs, I have learned to acknowledge its many and often devastating limitations. For example, the most monumental issues fade from one's consciousness as if erased by a swift wind. Movements of great social and political significance seem but backdrops to one's daily exchanges—be they ever so muted and circumscribed—with the Object of One's Desire. (I at least was not yet able to articulate how the personal is the political, as was certainly true in Laurel's and my case. Viz., nobody wanted us to go to bed with each other, except us, and they had made laws to that effect. And of course whether we slept together or not was nobody's business, except ours.)

The more it became impossible to be with Laurel, to make love fully and naturally, the more I wanted nothing but that. If the South had risen again during one of our stolen kisses—his hands on my breasts, my hands on his (his breasts were sensitive, we discovered quite by acrobatic invention and accident)—we would have been hard pressed to notice. This is "criminal" to write, of course, given the myths that supposedly make multiracial living so much easier to bear, but it is quite true. And yet, after our week together—passionate, beautiful, haunting, and never, never to be approximated between us again, our desire to make love never to be fulfilled (though we did not know this then), we went our separate ways. Because in fact, while we kissed and said Everything Else Be Damned! the South *was* rising again. *Was* murdering people. Was imprisoning our colleagues and friends. Was keeping us from strolling off to a clean, cheap hotel.

It was during our last night together that he told me about his wife. We were dancing in a local Movement-oriented nightclub. What would today be called a disco. He had an endearing way of dancing, even to slow tunes (during which we clung together shamelessly); he did a sort of hop, fast or slow depending on the music, from one foot to the other, almost in time with the music—and that was dance to him. It didn't bother me at all. Our bodies easily found their own rhythms anyway, and touching alone was our reason for being on the floor. *There* we could make a sort of love, in a dark enough corner, that was not exactly grace but was not, was definitely not, acrobatics.

He peered at me through the gray-and-blue-framed glasses.

"I've got a wife back home."

What I've most resented as "the other woman" is being made responsible for the continued contentment and happiness of the wife. On our last night together, our lust undiminished and apparently not to be extinguished, given our surroundings, what was I supposed to do with this information?

All I could think was: She's not *my* wife.

She was, from what he said, someone admirable. She was away from home for the summer, studying for an advanced degree. He seemed perplexed by this need of hers to continue her education instead of settling down to have his children, but lonely rather than bitter.

So it was *just sex* between us, after all, I thought.

(To be fair, I was engaged to a young man in the Peace Corps. I didn't mind if it *was* just sex, since by that time our mutual lust had reached a state, almost, of mysticism.)

Laurel, however, was tormented.

(I never told him about my engagement. As far as I was concerned, it remained to be seen whether my engagement was relevant to my relationship with others. I thought not, but realized I was still quite young.)

That night, Laurel wrung his hands, pulled his strangely cut hair and cried, as we brazenly walked out along Atlanta's dangerous, cracker-infested streets.

I cried because he did, and because in some odd way it relieved my lust. Besides, I enjoyed watching myself pretend to suffer . . . Such moments of emotional dishonesty are always paid for, however, and that I did not know this at the time attests to my willingness to believe our relationship would not live past the moment itself.

And yet.

There was one letter from him to me after I'd settled in a small Georgia town (a) to picket the jailhouse where a local schoolteacher was under arrest for picketing the jailhouse where a local parent was under arrest for picketing the jailhouse where a local child was under arrest for picketing . . . and (b) to register voters.

He wrote that he missed me.

I missed him. He was the principal other actor in all my fantasies. I wrote him that I was off to Africa, but would continue to write. I gave him the address of my school, to which he could send letters.

Once in Africa, my fiancé (who was conveniently in the next country from mine and free to visit) and I completed a breakup that had been coming for our entire two-year period of engagement. He told me, among other things, that it was not uncommon for Peace Corps men to sleep with ten-year-old African girls. *At that age, you see, they were still attractive.* I wrote about that aspect of the Peace Corps' activities to Laurel, as if I'd heard about it from a stranger.

Laurel, I felt, would never take advantage of a ten-year-old child. And I loved him for it.

Loving him, I was not prepared for the absence of letters from him, back at my school. Three months after my return I still had heard nothing. Out of depression over this and the distraction schoolwork provided, I was a practicing celibate. Only rarely did I feel lustful, and then of course I always thought of Laurel, as of a great opportunity, much missed. I thought of his musical speech and his scent of apples and May wine with varying degrees of regret and tenderness. However, our week of passion—magical, memorable, but far too brief—gradually assumed a less than central place even in my most sanguine recollections.

In late November, six months after Laurel and I met, I received a letter from his wife.

My first thought, when I saw the envelope, was: She has the same last name as his. It was the first time their marriage was real for me. I was also frightened that she wrote to accuse me of disturbing her peace. Why else would a wife write?

She wrote that on July fourth of the previous summer (six weeks after Laurel and I met) Laurel had had an automobile accident. He was driving his van, delivering copies of *First Rebel.* He had either fallen asleep at the wheel or been run off the road by local rebels of the other kind. He had sustained a broken leg, a fractured back, and a severely damaged brain. He had been in a coma for the past four months. Nothing could rouse him. She had found my letter in his pocket. Perhaps I would come to see him.

(I was never to meet Laurel's wife, but I admired this gesture then, and I admire it now.)

It was a small Catholic hospital in Laurel's hometown. In the entryway a bloody, gruesome, ugly Christ the color of a rutabaga, stood larger than life. Nuns dressed in black and white habits reminded one of giant flies. Floating moonlike above their "wings," their pink, cherubic faces were kind and comical.

Laurel's father looked very much like Laurel. The same bifocals, the same plain clothing, the same open-seeming face—but on closer look, wide rather than open. The same lilt to his voice. Laurel's sister was also there. She, unaccountably, embraced me.

"We're so glad you came," she said.

She was like Laurel too. Smaller, pretty, with short blond hair and apple cheeks. She reached down and took Laurel's hand.

Laurel alone did not look like Laurel. He who had been healthy, firm-fleshed, virile, lay now on his hospital bed a skeleton with eyes. Tubes entered his body everywhere. His head was shaved, a bandage covering the hole that had been drilled in the top. His breathing was hardly a whistle through a hole punched in his throat.

I took the hands that had given such pleasure to my breasts, and they were bones, unmoving, cold, in mine. I touched the face I'd dreamed about for months as I would the face of someone already in a coffin.

His sister said, "Annie is here," her voice carrying the lilt.

Laurel's eyes were open, jerking, twitching, in his head. His mouth was open. But he was not there. Only his husk, his shell. His father looked at me—as he would look at any other treatment. Speculatively. Will it work? Will it revive my son?

I did not work. I did not revive his son. Laurel lay, wheezing through the hole in his throat, helpless, insensate. I was eager to leave.

Two years later, the letters began to arrive. Exactly as if he thought I still waited for them at school.

"My darling," he wrote, "I am loving you. Missing you and out of coma after a year and everybody given up on me. My brain damaged. Can you come to me? I am still bedridden."

But I was not in school. I was married, living in the South.

"Tell him you're married now," my husband advised. "He should know not to hurt himself with dreaming."

I wrote that I was not only married but "happily."

My marital status meant nothing to Laurel.

"Please come," he wrote. "There are few black people here. You would be lonesome but I will be here loving you."

I wrote again. This time I reported I was married, pregnant, and had a dog for protection.

"I dream of your body so luscious and fertile. I want so much to make love to you as we never could do. I hope you know how I lost part of my brain working for your people in the South. I miss you. Come soon."

I wrote: "Dear Laurel, I am so glad you are better. I'm sorry you were hurt. So sorry. I cannot come to you because I am married. I love my husband. I cannot bear to come. I am pregnant—nauseous all the time and anxious because of the life I/We lead." Etc., etc.

To which he replied: "You married a jew. [I had published a novel and apparently reviewers had focused on my marriage instead of my work as they often did.] There are no jews here either. I guess you have a taste for the exotic though I was not exotic. I am a cripple now with part of my brain in somebody's wastepaper basket. We could have children if you will take responsibility for bringing them up. I cannot be counted on. Ha Ha."

I asked my husband to intercept the letters that came to our house. I asked the president of my college to collect and destroy those sent to me there. I dreaded seeing them.

"I dream of your body, so warm and brown, whereas mine is white and cold to me now. I could take you as my wife here the people are prejudiced against blacks they were happy martin luther king was killed. I want you here. We can be happy and black and beautiful and crippled and missing part of my brain together. I want you but I guess you are tied up with that jew husband of yours. I mean no disrespect to him but we belong together and you know that."

"Dear Laurel, I am a mother. [I hoped this would save me. It didn't.] I have a baby daughter. I hope you are well. My husband sends his regards."

Most of Laurel's letters I was not shown. Assuming that my husband confiscated his letters without my consent, Laurel telegraphed: ANNIE, I AM COMING BY GREYHOUND BUS DON'T LET YOUR DOG BITE ME, LAUREL.

My husband said: "Fine, let him come. Let him see that you are not the woman he remembers. His memory is frozen on your passion for each other. Let him see how happy you and I are."

I waited, trembling.

It was a cold, clear evening. Laurel hobbled out of the taxi on crutches, one leg shorter than the other. He had regained his weight and, though pale, was almost handsome. He glanced at my completely handsome husband once and dismissed him. He kept his eyes on me. He smiled on me happily, pleased with me.

I knew only one dish then, chicken tarragon; I served it.

I was frightened. Not of Laurel, exactly, but of feeling all the things I felt.

(My husband's conviction notwithstanding, I suspected marriage could not keep me from being, in some ways, exactly the woman Laurel remembered.)

I woke up my infant daughter and held her, disgruntled, flushed and ludicrously alert, in front of me.

While we ate, Laurel urged me to recall our acrobatic nights on the dormitory bench, our intimate dancing. Before my courteous husband, my cheeks flamed. Those nights that seemed so far away to me seemed all he clearly remembered; he recalled less well how his accident occurred. Everything before and after that week had been swept away. The moment was real to him. I was real to him. Our week together long ago was very real to him. But that was all. His speech was as beautifully lilting as ever, with a zaniness that came from a lack of connective knowledge. But he was hard to listen to: he was both overconfident of his success with me—based on what he recalled of our mutual passion—and so intense that his gaze had me on the verge of tears.

Now that he was here and almost well, I must drop everything, including the baby on my lap—whom he barely seemed to see—and come away with him. Had I not flown off to Africa, though it meant leaving the very country in which he lived?

Finally, after the riddles within riddles that his words became (and not so much riddles as poems, and disturbing ones), my husband drove Laurel back to the bus station. He had come over a thousand miles for a two-hour visit.

My husband's face was drawn when he returned. He loved me, I was sure of that. He was glad to help me out. Still, he wondered.

"It lasted a week!" I said. "Long before I met you."

"I know," he said. "Sha, sha, baby," he comforted me. I had crept into his arms, trembling from head to foot. "It's all right. We're safe."

But *were we?*

And Laurel? Zooming through the night back to his home? The letters continued. Sometimes I asked to read one that came to the house.

"I am on welfare now. I hate being alive. Why didn't my father let me die? The people are prejudiced here. If you came they would be cruel to us but maybe it would help them see something. You are more beautiful than ever. You are so sexy you make me ache—it is not only because you are black that would be racism but because when you are in the same room with me the room is full of color and scents and I am all alive."

He offered to adopt my daughter, shortly after he received a divorce from his wife.

After my husband and I were divorced (some seven years after Laurel's visit and thirteen years after Laurel and I met), we sat one evening discussing Laurel. He recalled him perfectly, with characteristic empathy and concern.

"If I hadn't been married to you, I would have gone off with him," I said, "Maybe."

"Really?" He seemed surprised.

Out of habit I touched his arm. "I loved him, in a way."

"I know," he said, and smiled.

"A lot of love was lust. That threw me off for years until I realized lust can be a kind of love."

He nodded.

"I felt guilty about Laurel. When he wrote me, I became anxious. When he came to visit us, I was afraid."

"He was not the man you knew."

"I don't think I knew him well enough to tell. Even so, I was afraid the love and lust would come flying back, along with the pity. And that even if they didn't come back, I would run off with him anyway, because of the pity—*and for the adventure.*"

It was the word "adventure" and the different meaning it had for each of us that finally separated us. We had come to understand that, and to accept it without bitterness.

"I wanted to ask you to let me go away with him, for just a couple of months," I said. *"To let me go . . ."*

"He grew steadily worse, you know. His last letters were brutal. He blamed you for everything, even the accident, accusing you of awful, nasty things. He became a bitter, vindictive man."

He knew me well enough to know I heard this and I did not hear it.

He sighed. "It would have been tough for me," he said. "Tough for our daughter. Tough for you. Toughest of all for Laurel."

(*"Tell me it's all right that I didn't go!"* I wanted to plead, but didn't.)

"Right," I said instead, shrugging, and turning our talk to something else.

1971

Cluster: Nature and Spirituality—Ecocriticism

Although many of us affiliate with particular spiritual traditions, we don't always think about how our fundamental relationship with the planet—with specific places, vast natural forces, and other living species—is relevant to our deepest beliefs about what it means to be human, what it means to be a living being, and what it means to reside in particular communities. The search for such meanings usually occurs during private moments of spiritual reflection—and sometimes through the act of literary expression. The five selections included in this section offer a diverse range of meditations on spirituality and nature.

African American sociologist bell hooks, originally from Kentucky but now a resident of New York City, takes a psychological and historical perspective in "Touching the Earth," arguing that the Great Migration in the early and mid-twentieth century, when many people moved from the rural South to the urban, industrial North, "wounded the psyches of black folk." hooks suggests that in the past, "living close to nature, black folks were able to cultivate a spirit of wonder and reverence for life." But rather than calling for a reversal of history and a nostalgic return to rural ways of life, she urges her readers—readers of all cultural backgrounds—to appreciate the importance of "touching the earth," no matter where they live.

In her essay, hooks cites Kentucky author Wendell Berry's writing on the value of agricultural work as a means of fostering "human spiritual well-being." In this cluster, we have included Berry's essay "Word and Flesh," which focuses on the importance of appreciating our specific interactions and relationships, on the *meaning* we derive through such contact. Many people these days find themselves worried about the overwhelming planetary changes that are occurring—vast processes such as climate change and extinction. How can we even begin to understand what these processes mean? How to care about them? Berry asserts that we must determine what nature means to us by figuring out what we *love*—and, he writes, "love is never abstract."

For journalist Bill McKibben, a writer-in-residence at Middlebury College in Vermont, it is valuable to understand our relationship to nature in terms of scale. In an excerpt from his book *The Comforting Whirlwind: God, Job, and the Scale of Creation,* McKibben examines the human ability to cause widespread changes in nature through modern technology and draws readers' attention to the ancient biblical story of Job, suggesting that we might do well to shrink our impact on the planet, not only as a means of protecting earth's ecological health but also as a way of restoring the vivid meaning of nature in our lives.

In her essay "All My Relations," Linda Hogan, a Colorado writer of Chickasaw descent, emphasizes the power of particular ceremonies in reminding us of our strong connections to the planet. The telling of stories is in itself a form of ceremony, a strategy for remembering.

Minnesota activist and author Winona LaDuke, an enrolled member of the Mississippi Band of Anishinaabeg, uses the phrase "all our relations" as the title of her book about "native struggles for land and life," the first two pages of which are included in this cluster. Here, LaDuke describes the extraordinary sense of connectedness—indeed, the sense of *kinship*—between humans and other living organisms that native people on this continent felt, like native people elsewhere in the world, before what she calls "the toxic invasion" by colonial cultures.

Scott Slovic
University of Nevada, Reno

Bill McKibben b. 1960

from The Comforting Whirlwind

Overcoming the orthodoxy that places us at the center is, I think, necessary not only for our individual souls, but also for the collective future of the churches. As I have tried to show, our faith, like our planet, is incompatible over the long run with any culture that puts people forever at its core and makes their material satisfaction its only goal. Standing up to that culture will not be in any sense easy—we are all participants in it, by the very time and place of our birth. For me, however, that imprinting has lessened slightly over the years as I have spent more time outdoors and more time in church. The church, because of its professed values, is the only institution left in society that has even, shall we say, a prayer of mounting a challenge to this dominant culture. And if it did I am convinced that it would be healthy not only for the environment but for the church. Because our message need not—should not—be only negative. It should be positive—replacing the ersatz joy of the consumer society with the real joy of God and creation. This, in a sense, is our ace in the hole. The consumer society has one great weakness, one flank left unprotected. And that is that for all its superficial sugary jazzy sexy appeal, it has not done a particularly good job of making people *happy*. It has left unsatisfied some basic human needs, or has tried to satisfy them inappropriately. There was a commercial for one brand of cosmetic airing the day I was watching television, and its punchline was, "Love you have to wait for. Pantene, you can just go get." All things being equal, people would prefer love, I think. That we can offer. In the end, we need deeper answers to the deepest questions. Why are we here? At least in part, or so God implies in his answer to Job, to be a part of the great play of life, but only a part. We are not bigger than everything else—we are *like* everything else, meant to be exuberant and wild and *limited.* The very fact of the variety of life implies that—simple observation of the profusion around us should undermine our insistence on eternal primacy. Julian Barnes, in his magnificently irreverent novel *A History of the World in Ten and One Half Chapters,* describes the voyage of Noah's Ark from the viewpoint of a stowaway termite. The trip taught the animals a lot of things, he says, but "the main thing was this: that man is a very unevolved species compared to the animals. We don't deny, of course, your cleverness, your considerable potential. But you are, as yet an early stage of your development. We, for instance, are always ourselves. That is what it means to be evolved. We are what we are, and we know what that is. You don't expect a cat suddenly to start barking, do you, or a pig to start lowing? But this is what, in a manner of speaking, [we] learned to expect from your species. One moment you bark, one moment you mew; one moment you wish to be wild, one moment you wish to be tame. We knew where we were with Noah only in this one respect: we never knew where we were with him."

But *what* part should we play? Even if we accept that our role is somehow to be limited, we know that our peculiar brains set us apart from the rest of creation. We have powers unique to ourselves; to refuse them would be like a bird refusing flight. Luckily, of course, there are whole huge categories of activity for which reason is utterly suited and which do not also spell destruction for the rest of the ecosystem. *Witnessing* the glory around us—that is a role no other creature can play. When God tells us we are created in his image, the only thing we know about God is that he finds creation beautiful—"Good. Very good." Perhaps that is a clue as to how we should see ourselves. Humans—the animal that appreciates. Appreciates each other, loves each other, protects each other from harm. Appreciates the rest of creation, loves the rest of creation, protects the rest of creation. These activities are deeply linked, of course—I have tried to show that any solution of our environmental problems is in large measure dependent on solving great numbers of social and political problems. Caring for the rain forest means caring for the Chinese means caring to ride bicycles appreciating migratory songbirds means living mindful of the fourth generation down the road. All these are deeply human impulses, reflective of what is unique to our species. Most of our other accomplishments—huge dams, huge populations, huge abundance—are magnifications of the traits of all animals. They are uses of reason to do *better* than other creatures but not to do *different*. They reflect only a small percentage of the gifts we have been given as *humans,* and often they interfere with those gifts. Excessive materialism of the type deemed normal in Western societies clearly constitutes such an obstacle; so, even more, does the poverty of the Third World. You cannot fully exercise your unique human gifts—appreciation, witness, caring—when you are bowed down by hunger. The argument that we should free people to act as humans necessarily means, therefore, that we must address the deep economic chasm on this planet. The argument that the current approach of the industrialized countries is nearly as soul-deadening as the poverty of the South means that we must pull the sides of that chasm closer together, instead of trying to provide a bridge so that they can cross to our doubtful nirvana.

As Wendell Berry once asked in the title of an essay, "What are people for?" What feels most right to us? Find that and we will find the answers to what our place is, what our limits should be. And the answers, as I have said before, are paradoxical. We really want not utter individualism but a strong sense of community, not endless luxury but a large taste of the joy of service, not a totally packaged world but a reintroduction to the gorgeousness of the physical planet. The secret weapon of environmental change and of social justice must be this—living with simple elegance is more *pleasurable* than living caught in the middle of our consumer culture. What do I mean by simple elegance? There are a hundred examples, some of which I've already given: riding a bike or walking, so that you can hear your body again and feel the terrain; eating a simple diet, low enough on the food chain that you cause neither the environmental damage nor the arteriosclerosis promoted by our current menus; working less because you need less money which means someone else can share your job and you can reduce the stress and increase the satisfaction of your life; when nightfall comes, instead of turning on half the lights in the house and separating to the various television sets, lighting a candle or two and watching the sunset and talking or reading aloud. (It takes one power plant the size of Chernobyl simply to provide the continuous current that allows all our TV sets to turn on instantly when we flip the switch instead of taking a few seconds to warm up. But that is not the only drain from television—television is the constant stimulus of our desire for more stuff, and the constant wedge that prevents fellowship.) Many of us have spent time at retreat houses or monasteries, and sensed the peace that those experiences provide. But of course we're allowed to recreate that at home, to whatever extent we can. Many of us have experienced the pleasure that comes when there's a huge snowstorm in the winter and the power goes out for a day or two. Sure it's a nuisance, but it's also quiet—you can't drive and have to walk or ski. You gather with the neighbors, working and eating together. That experience too can be repeated, voluntarily, even in the middle of the summer. Instead of shopping at the supermarket for everything, we can grow more of our own food, and extra for our neighbors. Church communities provide natural places to organize some of these practices; if their members can be persuaded to try them, and if all we have been promised by God is true, then the satisfaction and joy of the experiment will begin to spread. We will find ourselves a little strengthened in the face of the vapid, empty culture we have created. The great laugh will start to spread, till with a chuckle and a shake of our heads we begin to turn our backs on the way we were and create new ways of being. We were born for community; we were born for service; we were born for joy; we were born to feel at home in this beautiful world; we were born to share certain unique gifts.

And of those gifts, the most unique and the most paradoxical is the ability to restrain ourselves. Conscious self-restraint belongs to no other creature, and for us it is the hardest of all tasks, both as individuals and as societies. Can we learn to genetically engineer plants and animals? Of course we can. Can we stop ourselves from genetically engineering plants and animals? Can we set strict limits so that such work is okay for dealing with childhood diseases but taboo for anything else? Can we wean ourselves from cheap fossil fuel? Can we ignore the easy path? Can we muster the discipline to learn what we *really* want, and to follow that desire unwaveringly? When I said that this generation witnesses a confluence of thinking from atmospheric chemists and mystics, that is what I meant.

The easy answer, of course, is to say no. One of our current orthodoxies is to say that we are "destined" to behave in certain ways. Isn't human momentum forever forward, towards more control and power? Isn't it "human nature" to keep growing our economies forever, to reject a humbler approach to living our lives? I don't know the answer to that—no one does, because we've never made a concerted and society-wide effort. But I do think there is one at least mildly hopeful analogue, something that gives me some comfort. Fifty years ago, with World War II at its height, one could have made a convincing argument that people were destined to keep fighting ever larger and bloodier wars—certainly history would have supported such an argument. But then, at the end of the war, the atom bomb was exploded. In a way, this invention gave us all the Godlike power I have been describing today. It gave us the right to talk back to the God of Job, to say we had ultimate and total strength. J. Robert Oppenheimer, on witnessing the first explosion at Alamagordo, quoted from the Bhagavad Gita—"We are become Gods, destroyers of the worlds." But something interesting happened. So far, having that power, we have chosen not to exercise it. Indeed, and with ever increasing strength, we have built a taboo around this power. We still have wars, of course—too many wars, bloody wars, devastating and highly technological wars. But nuclear war, which many people expected in the early days of the Cold War, has become steadily more unthinkable.

One prays that this taboo will hold as nuclear weapons spread to new countries. And it is not a perfect analogy. We have built this taboo because each of us can imagine what a nuclear explosion would be like and that imagining spurs us to act. The greenhouse effect, by contrast, results from a billion explosions of a billion pistons every second of every day around the world. Its impact is nearly invisible, much harder to build a myth around. Still the analogy gives me hope. With the atomic bomb a new physical fact came into the world, a fact so far-reaching that it is slowly changing the ways we conduct ourselves, leading us to greater restraint. And it was a new theological and philosophical fact as well—atomic war raised questions that conventional war never did. Even those comfortable with killing were queasy at the thought of such utter destruction—it seemed like more power than human beings could possibly justify, and so we have been slowly backing away from it. The greenhouse effect, and the other global environmental problems that we face, are new facts of the same magnitude. Already there are signs that people and nations around the world are ready to take on these facts. Not enough people, not the most powerful people—but there are enough of us that we've begun to constitute a force. Perhaps, just perhaps, in the mighty words of James Russell Lowell, new occasions will once more teach new duties, and time make ancient good uncouth.

And if we can teach ourselves those new duties, then the immense recuperative power of God's creation may be enough to erase at least the most horrible of our damage. I live, as I said, in the Adirondack mountains of upstate New York. The Adirondacks are among the oldest mountains on earth and eons ago they were the tallest. Time has slowly worn them away, but they are still impressive and remote. Twenty years after Lewis and Clark returned from the West, the tallest mountain in New York State, Mt. Marcy, still had not been climbed by a European. Once settlers came, however, they came with a vengeance. The streams were dammed for power; the hemlocks were stripped so that their bark could be used for tanning; most of all the loggers attacked the woods with amazing vigor. A hundred years ago, they were largely logged off—these remote mountains, the headwaters of the Hudson River, stripped bare of their pine and hemlock. But then some very visionary New Yorkers decided to preserve them. They carved out a six million-acre park, half public and half private, and amended the state constitution so that on the public land no tree could be cut again. It is a curious place, a rare hybrid of park and settlement—a true experiment in people living near nature. A century has not been enough to restore the primeval forest but it has been long enough to create again a true wilderness, the largest by far in the eastern United States. It is wild country—bear and coyote and mink and lynx. Out my back door you can wander through several hundred thousand acres of contiguous wilderness, land without road or cabin. It has revived, this land—it's a tremendously inspiring place, a symbol of what we might be able to do if we set our minds to it. And of what nature will do on its own, given half a chance. In the last five years, moose have begun to wander in again from the north and the east—an animal absent for a century is now taking up root again in these mountains. The first eagle chicks in nearly thirty years fledged in the park last spring. There is a re-creation going on—the world of the first chapter of Genesis is slowly reasserting itself, and many people are in fact doing their best to exercise responsible dominion over the land, to act as stewards. The state government has enacted some of the world's toughest land-use laws for the people who live in the Adirondacks. Forty-acre zoning is the rule for much of the park. You need special permits, granted only after environmental review, to make even small alterations to your home. Big projects, like golf courses, are routinely turned down. Not everyone likes it, but the voters of New York by and large continue to support the regulations—continue to say that at least in this special place the desire of human beings will not be the ultimate arbiter. It should be a model for much of the rest of the country and the world. I see each day that we do not face a hopeless task.

Merely a daunting one. It is always easier to cling to orthodoxy. Though the other world looks appealing, it is a trapeze swing away, and we fear. Often, I must be goaded to think, to realize, to try to grasp what is truly human. I was hiking in the hills behind my house last summer when I stepped on a hornet's nest. I was stung at least seventy times, and it hurt like nothing I have ever felt. And, alone, half an hour's hike from home, I was scared—I knew I was having some sort of reaction because hives were swelling across my chest. I have a good imagination, so it was not much of a stretch to believe that I might not make it back home. And yet the strongest feeling, as I ran back down the ridge, was a feeling of prayer—the simplest sort of prayer. Thank you God for those birds. Thank you God for these trees. Even, I think, thank you God for the hornets. Thank you that I am somehow linked to all of this. Never before had I felt quite so profoundly the rightness of the world around me—perhaps because it was my first experience as a potential link in the food chain. It was the least separated I had ever been, the closest to a creature. A trip to the hospital eventually erased my myriad bumps, but not the feeling of desperate at-homeness that I felt that afternoon. These reflections are largely an outgrowth of that stumble into the hornet's nest. If they draw from the book of Job any one lesson for our time, it is this: We need to stop thinking so much in terms of our "environment." An environment is a human creation: the home environment, the office environment. It counts—we need clean air and clean water, of course. But our environment is only a small part of something much larger. A planet, filled with the vast order of creation. It is a buzzing, weird, stoic, abundant, reckless, haunting, painful, perfect planet. All of it matters, all of it is glorious. And all of it can speak to us in the deepest and most satisfying ways, if only we will let it.

2005

bell hooks b. 1952

Touching the Earth

*I wish to live because life has within it that which is good, that which
is beautiful, and that which is love. Therefore, since I have known all
these things, I have found them to be reason enough and—I wish to live.
Moreover, because this is so, I wish others to live for generations and
generations and generations and generations.*
—Lorraine Hansberry, *To Be Young, Gifted, and Black*

When we love the earth, we are able to love ourselves more fully. I believe this. The
ancestors taught me it was so. As a child I loved playing in dirt, in that rich Kentucky
soil, that was a source of life. Before I understood anything about the pain and exploitation of the southern system of sharecropping, I understood that grown-up black
folks loved the land. I could stand with my grandfather Daddy Jerry and look out at
fields of growing vegetables, tomatoes, corn, collards, and know that this was his
handiwork. I could see the look of pride on his face as I expressed wonder and awe
at the magic of growing things. I knew that my grandmother Baba's backyard garden
would yield beans, sweet potatoes, cabbage, and yellow squash, that she too would
walk with pride among the rows and rows of growing vegetables showing us what the
earth will give when tended lovingly.

From the moment of their first meeting, Native American and African people
shared with one another a respect for the life-giving forces of nature, of the earth.
African settlers in Florida taught the Creek Nation runaways, the "Seminoles," methods for rice cultivation. Native peoples taught recently arrived black folks all about
the many uses of corn. (The hotwater cornbread we grew up eating came to our black
southern diet from the world of the Indians.) Sharing the reverence for the earth,
black and red people helped one another remember that, despite the white man's
ways, the land belonged to everyone. Listen to these words attributed to Chief Seattle in 1854:

> How can you buy or sell the sky, the warmth of the land? The idea is strange to us.
> If we do not own the freshness of the air and the sparkle of the water, how can you buy
> them? Every part of this earth is sacred to my people. Every shining pine needle,
> every sandy shore, every mist in the dark woods, every clearing and humming insect
> is holy in the memory and experience of my people. . . . We are part of the earth and
> it is part of us. The perfumed flowers are our sisters; the deer, the horse, the great
> eagle, these are our brothers. The rocky crests, the juices in the meadows, the body
> heat of the pony, and man—all belong to the same family.

The sense of union and harmony with nature expressed here is echoed in testimony by black people who found that even though life in the new world was "harsh,

harsh," in relationship to the earth one could be at peace. In the oral autobiography of granny midwife Onnie Lee Logan, who lived all her life in Alabama, she talks about the richness of farm life—growing vegetables, raising chickens, and smoking meat. She reports:

> We lived a happy, comfortable life to be right outa slavery times. I didn't know nothin else but the farm so it was happy and we was happy. . . . We couldn't do anything else but be happy. We accept the days as they come and as they were. Day by day until you couldn't say there was any great hard time. We overlooked it. We didn't think nothin about it. We just went along. We had what it takes to make a good livin and go about it.

Living in modern society, without a sense of history, it has been easy for folks to forget that black people were first and foremost a people of the land, farmers. It is easy for folks to forget that at the first part of the 20th century, the vast majority of black folks in the United States lived in the agrarian south.

Living close to nature, black folks were able to cultivate a spirit of wonder and reverence for life. Growing food to sustain life and flowers to please the soul, they were able to make a connection with the earth that was ongoing and life-affirming. They were witnesses to beauty. In Wendell Berry's important discussion of the relationship between agriculture and human spiritual well-being, *The Unsettling of America,* he reminds us that working the land provides a location where folks can experience a sense of personal power and well-being:

> We are working well when we use ourselves as the fellow creature of the plants, animals, material, and other people we are working with. Such work is unifying, healing. It brings us home from pride and despair, and places us responsibly within the human estate. It defines us as we are: not too good to work without our bodies, but too good to work poorly or joylessly or selfishly or alone.

There has been little or no work done on the psychological impact of the "great migration" of black people from the agrarian south to the industrialized north. Toni Morrison's novel *The Bluest Eye* attempts to fictively document the way moving from the agrarian south to the industrialized north wounded the psyches of black folk. Estranged from a natural world, where there was time for silence and contemplation, one of the "displaced" black folks in Morrison's novel, Miss Pauline, loses her capacity to experience the sensual world around her when she leaves southern soil to live in a northern city. The south is associated in her mind with a world of sensual beauty most deeply expressed in the world of nature. Indeed, when she falls in love for the first time she can name that experience only by evoking images from nature, from an agrarian world and near wilderness of natural splendor:

> When I first seed Cholly, I want you to know it was like all the bits of color from that time down home when all us chil'ren went berry picking after a funeral and I put some in the pocket of my Sunday dress, and they mashed up and stained my hips. My whole dress was messed with purple, and it never did wash out. Not the dress nor me. I could feel that purple deep inside me. And that lemonade Mama used to make when Pap came in out of the fields. It be cool and yellowish, with seeds floating near the bottom. And the streak of green them june bugs made on the trees that night we left from down home. All of them colors was in me. Just sitting there.

Certainly, it must have been a profound blow to the collective psyche of black people to find themselves struggling to make a living in the industrial north away from the land. Industrial capitalism was not simply changing the nature of black work life, it altered the communal practices that were so central to survival in the agrarian south. And it fundamentally altered black people's relationship to the body. It is the loss of any capacity to appreciate her body, despite its flaws, Miss Pauline suffers when she moves north.

The motivation for black folks to leave the south and move north was both material and psychological. Black folks wanted to be free of the overt racial harassment that was a constant in southern life and they wanted access to material goods— to a level of material well-being that was not available in the agrarian south where white folks limited access to the spheres of economic power. Of course, they found that life in the north had its own perverse hardships, that racism was just as virulent there, that it was much harder for black people to become landowners. Without the space to grow food, to commune with nature, or to mediate the starkness of poverty with the splendor of nature, black people experienced profound depression. Working in conditions where the body was regarded solely as a tool (as in slavery), a profound estrangement occurred between mind and body. The way the body was represented became more important than the body itself. It did not matter if the body was well, only that it appeared well.

Estrangement from nature and engagement in mind/body splits made it all the more possible for black people to internalize white-supremacist assumptions about black identity. Learning contempt for blackness, southerners transplanted in the north suffered both culture shock and soul loss. Contrasting the harshness of city life with an agrarian world, the poet Waring Cuney wrote this popular poem in the 1920s, testifying to lost connection:

> She does not know her beauty
> She thinks her brown body
> has no glory,
> If she could dance naked,
> Under palm trees
> And see her image in the river
> She would know.
> But there are no palm trees on the street,
> And dishwater gives back no images.

For many years, and even now, generations of black folks who migrated north to escape life in the south, returned down home in search of a spiritual nourishment, a healing, that was fundamentally connected to reaffirming one's connection to nature, to a contemplative life where one could take time, sit on the porch, walk, fish, and catch lightning bugs. If we think of urban life as a location where black folks learned to accept a mind/body split that made it possible to abuse the body, we can better understand the growth of nihilism and despair in the black psyche. And we can know that when we talk about healing that psyche we must also speak about restoring our connection to the natural world.

Wherever black folks live we can restore our relationship to the natural world by taking the time to commune with nature, to appreciate the other creatures who share this planet with humans. Even in my small New York City apartment I can pause to listen to birds sing, find a tree and watch it. We can grow plants—herbs, flowers, vegetables. Those novels by African-American writers (women and men) that talk about black migration from the agrarian south to the industrialized north describe in detail the way folks created space to grow flowers and vegetables. Although I come from country people with serious green thumbs, I have always felt that I could not garden. In the past few years, I have found that I can do it—that many gardens will grow, that I feel connected to my ancestors when I can put a meal on the table of food I grew. I especially love to plant collard greens. They are hardy, and easy to grow.

In modern society, there is also a tendency to see no correlation between the struggle for collective black self-recovery and ecological movements that seek to restore balance to the planet by changing our relationship to nature and to natural resources. Unmindful of our history of living harmoniously on the land, many contemporary black folks see no value in supporting ecological movements, or see ecology and the struggle to end racism as competing concerns. Recalling the legacy of our ancestors who knew that the way we regard land and nature will determine the level of our self-regard, black people must reclaim a spiritual legacy where we connect our well-being to the well-being of the earth. This is a necessary dimension of healing. As Berry reminds us:

> Only by restoring the broken connections can we be healed. Connection is health. And what our society does its best to disguise from us is how ordinary, how commonly attainable, health is. We lose our health—and create profitable diseases and dependencies—by failing to see the direct connections between living and eating, eating and working, working and loving. In gardening, for instance, one works with the body to feed the body. The work, if it is knowledgeable, makes for excellent food. And it makes one hungry. The work thus makes eating both nourishing and joyful, not consumptive, and keeps the eater from getting fat and weak. This health, wholeness, is a source of delight.

Collective black self-recovery takes place when we begin to renew our relationship to the earth, when we remember the way of our ancestors. When the earth is sacred to us, our bodies can also be sacred to us.

1993

Wendell Berry b. 1934

from Word and Flesh

We have failed to produce new examples of good home and community economies, and we have nearly completed the destruction of the examples we once had. Without examples, we are left with theory and the bureaucracy and meddling that come with theory. We change our principles, our thoughts, and our words, but these are changes made in the air. Our lives go on unchanged.

For the most part, the subcultures, the countercultures, the dissenters, and the opponents continue mindlessly—or perhaps just helplessly—to follow the pattern of the dominant society in its extravagance, its wastefulness, it dependencies, and its addictions. The old problem remains: How do you get intelligence *out* of an institution or an organization?

My small community in Kentucky has lived and dwindled for at least a century under the influence of four kinds of organizations: governments, corporations, schools, and churches—all of which are distant (either actually or in interest), centralized, and consequently abstract in their concerns.

Governments and corporations (except for employees) have no presence in our community at all, which is perhaps fortunate for us, but we nevertheless feel the indifference or the contempt of governments and corporations for communities such as ours.

We have had no school of our own for nearly thirty years. The school system takes our young people, prepares them for "the world of tomorrow"—which it does not expect to take place in any rural area—and gives back "expert" (that is, extremely generalized) ideas.

The church is present in the town. We have two churches. But both have been used by their denominations, for almost a century, to provide training and income for student ministers, who do not stay long enough even to become disillusioned.

For a long time, then, the minds that have most influenced our town have not been *of* the town and so have not tried even to perceive, much less to honor, the good possibilities that are there. They have not wondered on what terms a good and conserving life might be lived there. In this my community is not unique but is like almost every other neighborhood in our country and in the "developed" world.

The question that *must* be addressed, therefore, is not how to care for the planet, but how to care for each of the planet's millions of human and natural neighborhoods, each of its millions of small pieces and parcels of land, each one of which is in some precious way different from all the others. Our understandable wish to preserve the planet must somehow be reduced to the scale of our competence—that is, to the wish to preserve all of its humble households and neighborhoods.

What can accomplish this reduction? I will say again, without overweening hope but with certainty nonetheless, that only love can do it. Only love can bring intelligence out of the institutions and organizations, where it aggrandizes itself, into the presence of the work that must be done.

Love is never abstract. It does not adhere to the universe or the planet or the nation or the institution or the profession, but to the singular sparrows of the street, the lilies of the field, "the least of these my brethren." Love is not, by its own desire, heroic. It is heroic only when compelled to be. It exists by its willingness to be anonymous, humble, and unrewarded.

The older love becomes, the more clearly it understands its involvement in partiality, imperfection, suffering, and mortality. Even so, it longs for incarnation. It can live no longer by thinking.

And yet to put on flesh and do the flesh's work, it must think.

In his essay on Kipling, George Orwell wrote: "All left-wing parties in the highly industrialized countries are at bottom a sham, because they make it their business to fight against something which they do not really wish to destroy. They have internationalist aims, and at the same time they struggle to keep up a standard of life with which those aims are incompatible. We all live by robbing Asiatic coolies, and those of us who are 'enlightened' all maintain that those coolies ought to be set free; but our standard of living, and hence our 'enlightenment,' demands that the robbery shall continue."

This statement of Orwell's is clearly applicable to our situation now; all we need to do is change a few nouns. The religion and the environmentalism of the highly industrialized countries are at bottom a sham, because they make it their business to fight against something that they do not really wish to destroy. We all live by robbing nature, but our standard of living demands that the robbery shall continue.

We must achieve the character and acquire the skills to live much poorer than we do. We must waste less. We must do more for ourselves and each other. It is either that or continue merely to think and talk about changes that we are inviting catastrophe to make.

The great obstacle is simply this: the conviction that we cannot change because we are dependent on what is wrong. But that is the addict's excuse, and we know it will not do.

How dependent, in fact, are we? How dependent are our neighborhoods and communities? How might our dependencies be reduced? To answer these questions will require better thoughts and better deeds than we have been capable of so far.

We must have the sense and the courage, for example, to see that the ability to transport food for hundreds or thousands of miles does not necessarily mean that we are well off. It means that the food supply is more vulnerable and more costly than a local food supply would be. It means that consumers do not control or influence the healthfulness of their food supply and that they are at the mercy of the people who have the control and influence. It means that, in eating, people are using large quantities of petroleum that other people in another time are almost certain to need.

Our most serious problem, perhaps, is that we have become a nation of fantasists. We believe, apparently, in the infinite availability of finite resources. We persist in land-use methods that reduce the potentially infinite power of soil fertility to a finite quantity, which we then proceed to waste as if it were an infinite quantity. We have an economy that depends not on the quality and quantity of necessary goods and services but on the moods of a few stockbrokers. We believe that democratic freedom can be preserved by people ignorant of the history of democracy and indifferent to the responsibilities of freedom.

Our leaders have been for many years as oblivious to the realities and dangers of their time as were George III and Lord North. They believe that the difference between war and peace is still the overriding political difference—when, in fact, the difference has diminished to the point of insignificance. How would you describe the difference between modern war and modern industry—between, say, bombing and strip mining, or between chemical warfare and chemical manufacturing? The difference seems to be only that in war the victimization of humans is directly intentional and in industry it is "accepted" as a "trade-off."

Were the catastrophes of Love Canal, Bhopal, Chernobyl, and the *Exxon Valdez* episodes of war or of peace? They were, in fact, peacetime acts of aggression, intentional to the extent that the risks were known and ignored.

We are involved unremittingly in a war not against "foreign enemies," but against the world, against our freedom, and indeed against our existence. Our so-called industrial accidents should be looked upon as revenges of Nature. We forget that Nature is necessarily party to all our enterprises and that she imposes conditions of her own.

Now she is plainly saying to us: "If you put the fates of whole communities or cities or regions or ecosystems at risk in single ships or factories or power plants, then I will furnish the drunk or the fool or the imbecile who will make the necessary small mistake."

1989

Winona LaDuke b. 1959

from All Our Relations

The last 150 years have seen a great holocaust. There have been more species lost in the past 150 years than since the Ice Age. During the same time, Indigenous peoples have been disappearing from the face of the earth. Over 2,000 nations of Indigenous peoples have gone extinct in the western hemisphere, and one nation disappears from the Amazon rainforest every year.

There is a direct relationship between the loss of cultural diversity and the loss of biodiversity. Wherever Indigenous peoples still remain, there is also a corresponding enclave of biodiversity. Trickles of rivers still running in the Northwest are home to the salmon still being sung back by Native people. The last few Florida panthers remain in the presence of traditional Seminoles, hidden away in the great cypress swamps of the Everglades. Some of the largest patches of remaining prairie grasses sway on reservation lands. One half of all reservation lands in the United States is still forested, much of it old-growth. Remnant pristine forest ecosystems, from the northern boreal forests to the Everglades, largely overlap with Native territories.

In the Northwest, virtually every river is home to a people, each as distinct as a species of salmon. The Tillamook, Siletz, Yaquina, Alsea, Siuslaw, Umpqua, Hanis, Miluk, Colville, Tututni, Shasta, Costa, and Chetco are all people living at the mouths of salmon rivers. One hundred and seven stocks of salmon have already become extinct in the Pacific Northwest, and 89 are endangered. "Salmon were put here by the Creator, and it is our responsibility to harvest and protect the salmon so that the cycle of life continues," explains Pierson Mitchell of the Columbia River Intertribal Fishing Commission. "Whenever we have a funeral, we mourn our loved one, yes, but we are also reminded of the loss of our salmon and other traditional foods," laments Bill Yallup Sr., the Yakama tribal chairman.

The stories of the fish and the people are not so different. Environmental destruction threatens the existence of both. The Tygh band of the Lower Deschutes River in Oregon includes a scant five families, struggling to maintain their traditional way of life and relationship to the salmon. "I wanted to dance the salmon, know the salmon, say goodbye to the salmon," says Susana Santos, a Tygh artist, fisherwoman, and community organizer. "Now I am looking at the completion of destruction, from the Exxon Valdez to . . . those dams . . . seventeen fish came down the river last year. None this year. The people are the salmon, and the salmon are the people. How do you quantify that?"

Native American teachings describe the relations all around—animals, fish, trees, and rocks—as our brothers, sisters, uncles, and grandpas. Our relations to each other, our prayers whispered across generations to our relatives, are what bind our cultures together. The protection, teachings, and gifts of our relatives have for generations preserved our families. These relations are honored in ceremony, song, story, and life that keep relations close—to buffalo, sturgeon, salmon, turtles, bears, wolves, and panthers. These are our older relatives—the ones who came before and taught us how to live. Their obliteration by dams, guns, and bounties is an immense loss to Native families and cultures. Their absence may mean that a people sing to a barren river, a caged bear, a buffalo far away. It is the struggle to preserve that which remains and the struggle to recover that characterizes much of Native environmentalism. It is these relationships that industrialism seeks to disrupt. Native communities will resist with great determination.

> *Salmon was presented to me and my family through our religion as our brother. The same with the deer. And our sisters are the roots and berries. And you would treat them as such. Their life to you is just as valuable as another person's would be.*
>
> —*Margaret Saluskin, Yakama*

1999

Linda Hogan b. 1947

from Dwellings

All My Relations

It is a sunny, clear day outside, almost hot, and a slight breeze comes through the room from the front door. We sit at the table and talk. As is usual in an Indian household, food preparation began as soon as we arrived, and now there is the snap of potatoes frying in the black skillet, the sweet smell of white bread overwhelming even the grease, and the welcome black coffee. A ringer washer stands against the wall of the kitchen, and the counter space is taken up with dishes, pans, and boxes of food.

I am asked if I still read books and I admit that I do. Reading is not "traditional" and education has long been suspect in communities that were broken, in part, by that system, but we laugh at my confession because a television set plays in the next room.

In the living room there are two single beds. People from reservations, travelers needing help, are frequent guests here. The man who will put together the ceremony I have come to request sits on one, dozing. A girl takes him a plate of food. He eats. He is a man I have respected for many years, for his commitment to the people, for his intelligence, for his spiritual and political involvement in concerns vital to Indian people and nations. Next to him sits a girl eating potato chips, and from this room we hear the sounds of the freeway.

After eating and sitting, it is time for me to talk to him, to tell him why we have come here. I have brought him tobacco and he nods and listens as I tell him about the help we need.

I know this telling is the first part of the ceremony, my part in it. It is story, really, that finds its way into language, and story is at the very crux of healing, at the heart of every ceremony and ritual in the older America.

The ceremony itself includes not just our own prayers and stories of what brought us to it, but also includes the unspoken records of history, the mythic past, and all the other lives connected to ours, our families, nations, and all other creatures.

I am sent home to prepare. I tie fifty tobacco ties, green. This I do with Bull Durham tobacco, squares of cotton that are tied with twine and left strung together. These are called prayer ties. I spend the time preparing alone and in silence. Each tie has a prayer in it. I will also need wood for the fire, meat and bread for food.

On the day of the ceremony, we meet in the next town and leave my car in public parking. My daughters and I climb into the backseat. The man who will help us is drumming and singing in front of us. His wife drives and chats. He doesn't speak. He is moving between the worlds, beginning already to step over the boundaries of what we think, in daily and ordinary terms, is real and present. He is already feeling, hearing, knowing what else is there, that which is around us daily but too often unacknowledged, a larger life than our own. We pass billboards and little towns and gas stations. An eagle flies overhead. It is "a good sign," we all agree. We stop to watch it.

We stop again, later, at a convenience store to fill the gas tank and to buy soda. The leader still drums and is silent. He is going into the drum, going into the center, even as we drive west on the highway, even with our conversation about other people, family, work.

It is a hot balmy day, and by the time we reach the site where the ceremony is to take place, we are slow and sleepy with the brightness and warmth of the sun. Others are already there. The children are cooling off in the creek. A woman stirs the fire that lives inside a circle of black rocks, pots beside her, a jar of oil, a kettle, a can of coffee. The leaves of the trees are thick and green.

In the background, the sweat lodge structure stands. Birds are on it. It is still skeletal. A woman and man are beginning to place old rugs and blankets over the bent cottonwood frame. A great fire is already burning, and the lava stones that will be the source of heat for the sweat are being fired in it.

A few people sit outside on lawn chairs and cast-off couches that have the stuffing coming out. We sip coffee and talk about the food, about recent events. A man tells us that a friend gave him money for a new car. The creek sounds restful. Another man falls asleep. My young daughter splashes in the water. Heat waves rise up behind us from the fire that is preparing the stones. My tobacco ties are placed inside, on the framework of the lodge.

By late afternoon we are ready, one at a time, to enter the enclosure. The hot lava stones are placed inside. They remind us of earth's red and fiery core, and of the spark inside all life. After the flap, which serves as a door, is closed, water is poured over the stones and the hot steam rises around us. In a sweat lodge ceremony, the entire world is brought inside the enclosure. The soft odor of smoking cedar accompanies this arrival. It is all called in. The animals come from the warm and sunny distances. Water from dark lakes is there. Wind. Young, lithe willow branches bent overhead remember their lives rooted in ground, the sun their leaves took in. They remember that minerals and water rose up their trunks, and birds nested in their leaves, and that planets turned above their brief, slender lives. The thunderclouds travel in from far regions of earth. Wind arrives from the four directions. It has moved through caves and breathed through our bodies. It is the same air elk have inhaled, air that passed through the lungs of a grizzly bear. The sky is there, with all the stars whose lights we see long after the stars themselves have gone back to nothing. It is a place grown intense and holy. It is a place of immense community and of humbled solitude; we sit together in our aloneness and speak, one at a time, our deepest language of need, hope, loss, and survival. We remember that all things are connected.

Remembering this is the purpose of the ceremony. It is part of a healing and restoration. It is the mending of a broken connection between us and the rest. The participants in a ceremony say the words "All my relations" before and after we pray; those words create a relationship with other people, with animals, with the land. To have health it is necessary to keep all these relations in mind. The intention of a ceremony is to put a person back together by restructuring the human mind. This reorganization is accomplished by a kind of inner map, a geography of the human spirit and the rest of the world. We make whole our broken-off pieces of self and world. Within ourselves, we bring together the fragments of our lives in a sacred act of renewal, and we reestablish our connections with others. The ceremony is a point of return. It takes us toward the place of balance, our place in the community of all things. It is an event that sets us back upright. But it is not a finished thing. The real ceremony begins where the formal one ends, when we take up a new way, our minds and hearts filled with the vision of earth that holds us within it, in compassionate relationship to and with our world.

We speak. We sing. We swallow water and breathe smoke. By the end of the ceremony, it is as if skin contains land and birds. The places within us have become filled. As inside the enclosure of the lodge, the animals and ancestors move into the human body, into skin and blood. The land merges with us. The stones come to dwell inside the person. Gold rolling hills take up residence, their tall grasses blowing. The red light of canyons is there. The black skies of night that wheel above our heads come to live inside the skull. We who easily grow apart from the world are returned to the great store of life all around us, and there is the deepest sense of being at home here in this intimate kinship. There is no real aloneness. There is solitude and the nurturing silence that is relationship with ourselves, but even then we are part of something larger.

After a sweat lodge ceremony, the enclosure is abandoned. Quieter now, we prepare to drive home. We pack up the kettles, the coffeepot. The prayer ties are placed in nearby trees. Some of the other people prepare to go to work, go home, or cook a dinner. We drive. Everything returns to ordinary use. A spider weaves a web from one of the cottonwood poles to another. Crows sit inside the framework. It's evening. The crickets are singing. All my relations.

1995

Art Spiegelman b. 1948

Art Spiegelman, arguably the world's most influential living progenitor of the idea that comic books can be literature, is a material and cultural blacksmith, as he puts it, and he is important to any study of today's narrative forms. As a conceptual thinker and as an author, Spiegelman enlivens any inquiry into comics, and the publication of his book *Maus: A Survivor's Tale* in 1986 marked a transformative moment in the field of contemporary literature.

Spiegelman was born in Sweden in 1948 to Anja and Vladek Spiegelman, Polish Jews who had survived Auschwitz. His older brother, Richieu, was a child when he died during the war. Spiegelman grew up in Rego Park, Queens, where his love for comics began at an early age. After dropping out of Harpur College (now the State University of New York at Binghamton), Spiegelman moved to San Francisco, where in the early 1970s he produced work in the underground comix community that led directly to the serious, textured, rigorous work that today is known as the graphic novel.

Spiegelman's influential underground pieces (collected in his large-format book *Breakdowns* in 1977) include experimental work like "Ace Hole: Midget Detective" and "Don't Get around Much Anymore"— but also two autobiographical strips, "Prisoner on the Hell Planet: A Case Study," and "Maus," the prototype for the book-length version. "Don't Get around Much Anymore," a dense, compact one-page strip from 1973 that looks both cubist and art deco–inspired, is a vigorous exploration of how comics present time and space. Here Spiegelman unmoors the two from each other. While nothing much happens in the strip, its modernist exploration of the medium's formal capacities pointed the way to the rich formal capacities of comics and has had an enduring influence.

Spiegelman has said that he had to subsume his more formal interests to produce *Maus,* but *Maus* (which was published in two volumes; the second appeared in 1991) shows the same kinds of aesthetic concerns as his underground work, expanded and enriched by a postmodern emphasis on narrative. The seemingly disparate strands of Spiegelman's underground-era comic strips finally coalesce in *Maus,* his novel-length, career-defining work that is engaged with form and the power of narrative.

Maus changed the way that the public at large—as well as academic audiences—think about comics. Thirteen years in the making, *Maus* is a black-and-white text that is driven by Vladek Spiegelman's Holocaust testimony. It represents Jews as mice and Nazis as cats, inhabiting and reversing stereotypes created by Nazi propaganda. It is also self-reflexive, meditating on and rupturing its own established frameworks, including its animal metaphor and its past-and-present narrative structure. It has won numerous awards, including a special Pulitzer Prize in 1992 that celebrated its achievement and marked its challenge to traditional classification (a comic book about the Holocaust was at that time an utterly foreign phenomenon). Translated into more than twenty languages, *Maus* is probably the most famous graphic narrative ever produced in the United States.

Spiegelman was a contributor to the *New Yorker* for more than ten years. His book on 9/11, *In the Shadow of No Towers,* came out in 2004. A reprint of his now-classic *Breakdowns,* with a new comics introduction titled "Portrait of the Artist as a Young %@?*!" was published by Pantheon in 2008. He is preparing a book titled *Meta Maus,* about the making of *Maus.*

Hillary Chute
Harvard University

Don't Get Around Much Anymore

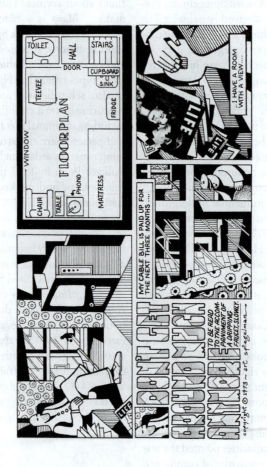

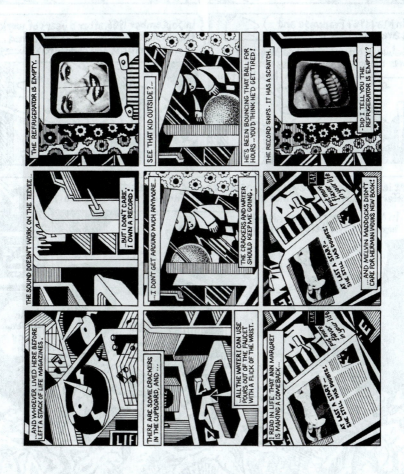

from Maus II

WITH THE OTHER BOYS THERE, I GOT ALONG FINE.

DON'T WORRY... YOU JUST HAVE TO KNOW HOW TO HANDLE YIDL ...

BRING HIM A FEW EGGS, SOME BUTTER OR CHEESE ... YOU'LL SEE. HE'LL SING A DIFFERENT TUNE.

HA! AND WHERE DO I GET ALL THIS FOOD?

JUST KEEP YOUR EYES OPEN. YOU CAN *ORGANIZE* THINGS WITH THE POLES HERE.

POLES FROM NEARBY THEY HIRED TO WORK ALSO HERE— NOT PRISONERS, BUT SPECIALIST BUILDING WORKERS ...

(PSST—I CAN GET YOU A FINE GOLD WATCH FOR A POUND OF SAUSAGE AND SIX EGGS.)

(AGREED.)

THEY HAD **NOTHING**, ONLY FOOD FROM THEIR FARMS. THEY WERE HAPPY TO MAKE EXCHANGES.

THE HEAD GUY FROM THE AUSCHWITZ LAUNDRY WAS A FINE FELLOW WHAT KNEW WELL MY FAMILY BEFORE THE WAR ...

FROM HIM I GOT CIVILIAN **CLOTHINGS** TO SMUGGLE OUT BELOW MY UNIFORM. I WAS SO THIN THE GUARDS DIDN'T SEE IF I WORE EXTRA.

HERE YIDL. I'VE GOT A BIG PIECE OF CHEESE FOR YOU.

A GIFT? VERY NICE, SPIEGELMAN.

AND WHAT ELSE DO YOU HAVE THERE? A LOAF OF BREAD? YOU'RE A RICH MAN!

WAIT! I NEED THAT TO PAY OFF THE GUY WHO HELPED ME ORGANIZE THE CHEESE!

HMPH.

HE WAS SO GREEDY, YIDL, HE WANTED I RISK ONLY FOR HIM EVERYTHING. I TOO HAD TO EAT.

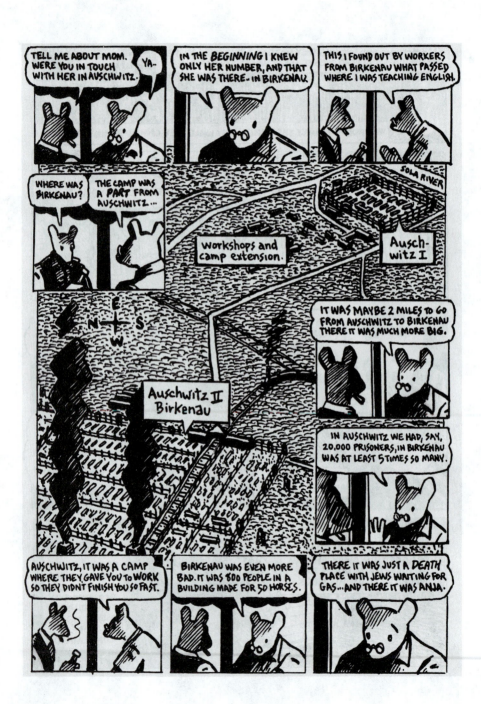

Leslie Marmon Silko (Laguna) b. 1948

Leslie Marmon Silko grew up on the Laguna Pueblo Reservation in the house where her father, Lee H. Marmon, was born. Her mother, Virginia, worked outside the home, and Silko spent most of her preschool years with her great-grandmother, who lived next door.

She attended Bureau of Indian Affairs schools at Laguna until high school in Albuquerque. Then she attended the University of New Mexico, graduating *magna cum laude* in 1969. She then attended three semesters of law school before deciding to devote herself to writing and to enter graduate school in English.

Silko has taught at Navajo Community College, Many Farms, Arizona, at the University of New Mexico, and at the University of Arizona. She was formerly married to attorney John Silko. She has two sons, Robert, born in 1966, and Cazimir, born in 1972. The family lived in Alaska during the mid-seventies when Silko was writing *Ceremony*. Although Alaska is the setting for the title story of her book *Storyteller*, most of her early fiction and poetry is set in the Laguna area.

Many cultures have influenced the history of Laguna. Hopi, Jemez, and Zuni people had married into the pueblo by the time it was established at its present site in the early 1500s. Later Navajos, Spanish settlers, and others of European ancestry intermarried with the Lagunas. The incorporation of rituals and stories from other tribes and cultures into their oral tradition occurred early in Laguna society and became an ongoing practice. Silko's own ancestry is mixed. Her father's people were Laguna and white. Her mother, born in Montana, was from a Plains tribe. Silko also has Mexican ancestry.

Her first book, *Laguna Woman* (1974), a collection of her poetry, shows an awareness of the interrelationships between the people and the river, mesas, hills, and mountains surrounding Laguna. But this awareness of place is not narrowly regional. For example, "Prayer to the Pacific" affirms the dependence of the Lagunas on the rain which west winds blow from as far as China.

The nearly 500-year existence of present-day Laguna makes it possible for Silko to write out of a culture intricately knowledgeable about the natural environment. This landscape and culture suffered severe trauma during the past half-century. During World War II, the atomic bomb was developed at nearby Los Alamos; and the first atomic explosion, at the Trinity site, occurred only 150 miles from Laguna. In the early 1950s the Anaconda company opened a large open-pit uranium mine on Laguna land, and uranium mining became a major source of income for Laguna and neighboring Pueblo and Navajo peoples. Nuclear destruction is a central concern in *Ceremony* (1977), Silko's first novel. An important theme in all of Silko's work is the recurrence of everything that happens. As "old Grandma" in *Ceremony* simply states, "'It seems like I already heard these stories before . . . only thing is, the names sound different.'"

Silko's second novel, *Almanac of the Dead* (1991), sounds an alarm in the face of escalating interpersonal violence and greed threatening to destroy humanity at the end of the twentieth century. A wide-ranging analysis and critique of contemporary American culture, the novel ends with the prophetic vision of a revolution in which the buffalo, the indigenous people, and the poor regain their land. Silko's third novel, *Gardens in the Dunes* (1999), juxtaposes the world of the indigenous peoples of the desert Southwest with that of the European and American upper class during the period between the Ghost Dance era at the end of the nineteenth century and World War I.

The most useful guide to understanding the cultural and social contexts of *Ceremony* and *Almanac of the Dead* is Silko's *Yellow Woman and a Beauty of the Spirit: Essays on Native American Life Today.* (1996). Silko models her fiction on the Laguna storytelling tradition, which she describes as patterned like the web of a spider.

Norma C. Wilson
University of South Dakota

PRIMARY WORKS

Laguna Woman, 1974; *Ceremony*, 1977; *Storyteller*, 1981; *Almanac of the Dead*, 1991; *Yellow Woman and a Beauty of the Spirit. Essays on Native American Life Today*, 1996; *Gardens in the Dunes*, 1999.

Lullaby

The sun had gone down but the snow in the wind gave off its own light. It came in thick tufts like new wool—washed before the weaver spins it. Ayah reached out for it like her own babies had, and she smiled when she remembered how she had laughed at them. She was an old woman now, and her life had become memories. She sat down with her back against the wide cottonwood tree, feeling the rough bark on her back bones; she faced east and listened to the wind and snow sing a high-pitched Yeibechei[1] song. Out of the wind she felt warmer, and she could watch the wide fluffy snow fill in her tracks, steadily, until the direction she had come from was gone. By the light of the snow she could see the dark outline of the big arroyo a few feet away. She was sitting on the edge of Cebolleta Creek, where in the springtime the thin cows would graze on grass already chewed flat to the ground. In the wide deep creek bed where only a trickle of water flowed in the summer, the skinny cows would wander, looking for new grass along winding paths splashed with manure.

Ayah pulled the old Army blanket over her head like a shawl. Jimmie's blanket— the one he had sent to her. That was a long time ago and the green wool was faded, and it was unraveling on the edges. She did not want to think about Jimmie. So she thought about the weaving and the way her mother had done it. On the tall wooden loom set into the sand under a tamarack tree for shade. She could see it clearly. She had been only a little girl when her grandma gave her the wooden combs to pull the twigs and burrs from the raw, freshly washed wool. And while she combed the wool, her grandma sat beside her, spinning a silvery strand of yarn around the smooth cedar spindle. Her mother worked at the loom with yarns dyed bright yellow and red and gold. She watched them dye the yarn in boiling black pots full of beeweed petals, juniper berries, and sage. The blankets her mother made were soft and woven so tight that rain rolled off them like birds' feathers. Ayah remembered sleeping warm on cold windy nights, wrapped in her mother's blankets on the hogan's[2] sandy floor.

---

[1] Navajo Night Chant—a song of healing.
[2] Traditional six-sided Navajo dwelling, the door of which faces east.

The snow drifted now, with the northwest wind hurling it in gusts. It drifted up around her black overshoes—old ones with little metal buckles. She smiled at the snow which was trying to cover her little by little. She could remember when they had no black rubber overshoes; only the high buckskin leggings that they wrapped over their elkhide moccasins. If the snow was dry or frozen, a person could walk all day and not get wet; and in the evenings the beams of the ceiling would hang with lengths of pale buckskin leggings, drying out slowly.

She felt peaceful remembering. She didn't feel cold any more. Jimmie's blanket seemed warmer than it had ever been. And she could remember the morning he was born. She could remember whispering to her mother, who was sleeping on the other side of the hogan, to tell her it was time now. She did not want to wake the others. The second time she called to her, her mother stood up and pulled on her shoes; she knew. They walked to the old stone hogan together, Ayah walking a step behind her mother. She waited alone, learning the rhythms of the pains while her mother went to call the old woman to help them. The morning was already warm even before dawn and Ayah smelled the bee flowers blooming and the young willow growing at the springs. She could remember that so clearly, but his birth merged into the births of the other children and to her it became all the same birth. They named him for the summer morning and in English they called him Jimmie.

It wasn't like Jimmie died. He just never came back, and one day a dark blue sedan with white writing on its doors pulled up in front of the boxcar shack where the rancher let the Indians live. A man in a khaki uniform trimmed in gold gave them a yellow piece of paper and told them that Jimmie was dead. He said the Army would try to get the body back and then it would be shipped to them; but it wasn't likely because the helicopter had burned after it crashed. All of this was told to Chato because he could understand English. She stood inside the doorway holding the baby while Chato listened. Chato spoke English like a white man and he spoke Spanish too. He was taller than the white man and he stood straighter too. Chato didn't explain why; he just told the military man they could keep the body if they found it. The white man looked bewildered; he nodded his head and he left. Then Chato looked at her and shook his head, and then he told her, "Jimmie isn't coming home anymore," and when he spoke, he used the words to speak of the dead. She didn't cry then, but she hurt inside with anger. And she mourned him as the years passed, when a horse fell with Chato and broke his leg, and the white rancher told them he wouldn't pay Chato until he could work again. She mourned Jimmie because he would have worked for his father then; he would have saddled the big bay horse and ridden the fence lines each day, with wire cutters and heavy gloves, fixing the breaks in the barbed wire and putting the stray cattle back inside again.

She mourned him after the white doctors came to take Danny and Ella away. She was at the shack alone that day they came. It was back in the days before they hired Navajo women to go with them as interpreters. She recognized one of the doctors. She had seen him at the children's clinic at Cañoncito about a month ago. They were wearing khaki uniforms and they waved papers at her and a black ball-point pen, trying to make her understand their English words. She was frightened by the way they looked at the children, like the lizard watches the fly. Danny was swinging on the tire swing on the elm tree behind the rancher's house, and Ella was toddling around the front door, dragging the broomstick horse Chato made for her. Ayah could see they wanted her to sign the papers, and Chato had taught her to sign her name. It was something she was proud of. She only wanted them to go, and to take their eyes away from her children.

She took the pen from the man without looking at his face and she signed the papers in three different places he pointed to. She stared at the ground by their feet and waited for them to leave. But they stood there and began to point and gesture at the children. Danny stopped swinging. Ayah could see his fear. She moved suddenly and grabbed Ella into her arms; the child squirmed, trying to get back to her toys. Ayah ran with the baby toward Danny; she screamed for him to run and then she grabbed him around his chest and carried him too. She ran south into the foothills of juniper trees and black lava rock. Behind her she heard the doctors running, but they had been taken by surprise, and as the hills became steeper and the cholla cactus were thicker, they stopped. When she reached the top of the hill, she stopped to listen in case they were circling around her. But in a few minutes she heard a car engine start and they drove away. The children had been too surprised to cry while she ran with them. Danny was shaking and Ella's little fingers were gripping Ayah's blouse.

She stayed up in the hills for the rest of the day, sitting on a black lava boulder in the sunshine where she could see for miles all around her. The sky was light blue and cloudless, and it was warm for late April. The sun warmth relaxed her and took the fear and anger away. She lay back on the rock and watched the sky. It seemed to her that she could walk into the sky, stepping through clouds endlessly. Danny played with little pebbles and stones, pretending they were birds eggs and then little rabbits. Ella sat at her feet and dropped fistfuls of dirt into the breeze, watching the dust and particles of sand intently. Ayah watched a hawk soar high above them, dark wings gliding; hunting or only watching, she did not know. The hawk was patient and he circled all afternoon before he disappeared around the high volcanic peak the Mexicans called Guadalupe.

Late in the afternoon, Ayah looked down at the gray boxcar shack with the paint all peeled from the wood; the stove pipe on the roof was rusted and crooked. The fire she had built that morning in the oil drum stove had burned out. Ella was asleep in her lap now and Danny sat close to her, complaining that he was hungry; he asked when they would go to the house. "We will stay up here until your father comes," she told him, "because those white men were chasing us." The boy remembered then and he nodded at her silently.

If Jimmie had been there he could have read those papers and explained to her what they said. Ayah would have known then, never to sign them. The doctors came back the next day and they brought a BIA[3] policeman with them. They told Chato they had her signature and that was all they needed. Except for the kids. She listened to Chato sullenly; she hated him when he told her it was the old woman who died in the winter, spitting blood; it was her old grandma who had given the children this disease. "They don't spit blood," she said coldly. "The whites lie." She held Ella and Danny close to her, ready to run to the hills again. "I want a medicine man first," she said to Chato, not looking at him. He shook his head. "It's too late now. The policeman is with them. You signed the paper." His voice was gentle.

[3]U.S. Bureau of Indian Affairs.

It was worse than if they had died: to lose the children and to know that somewhere, in a place called Colorado, in a place full of sick and dying strangers, her children were without her. There had been babies that died soon after they were born, and one that died before he could walk. She had carried them herself, up to the boulders and great pieces of the cliff that long ago crashed down from Long Mesa; she laid them in the crevices of sandstone and buried them in fine brown sand with round quartz pebbles that washed down the hills in the rain. She had endured it because they had been with her. But she could not bear this pain. She did not sleep for a long time after they took her children. She stayed on the hill where they had fled the first time, and she slept rolled up in the blanket Jimmie had sent her. She carried the pain in her belly and it was fed by everything she saw: the blue sky of their last day together and the dust and pebbles they played with; the swing in the elm tree and broomstick horse choked life from her. The pain filled her stomach and there was no room for food or for her lungs to fill with air. The air and the food would have been theirs.

She hated Chato, not because he let the policeman and doctors put the screaming children in the government car, but because he had taught her to sign her name. Because it was like the old ones always told her about learning their language or any of their ways: it endangered you. She slept alone on the hill until the middle of November when the first snows came. Then she made a bed for herself where the children had slept. She did not lie down beside Chato again until many years later, when he was sick and shivering and only her body could keep him warm. The illness came after the white rancher told Chato he was too old to work for him anymore, and Chato and his old woman should be out of the shack by the next afternoon because the rancher had hired new people to work there. That had satisfied her. To see how the white man repaid Chato's years of loyalty and work. All of Chato's fine-sounding English talk didn't change things.

It snowed steadily and the luminous light from the snow gradually diminished into the darkness. Somewhere in Cebolleta a dog barked and other village dogs joined with it. Ayah looked in the direction she had come, from the bar where Chato was buying the wine. Sometimes he told her to go on ahead and wait; and then he never came. And when she finally went back looking for him, she would find him passed out at the bottom of the wooden steps to Azzie's Bar. All the wine would be gone and most of the money too, from the pale blue check that came to them once a month in a government envelope. It was then that she would look at his face and his hands, scarred by ropes and the barbed wire of all those years, and she would think, this man is a stranger; for forty years she had smiled at him and cooked his food, but he remained a stranger. She stood up again, with the snow almost to her knees, and she walked back to find Chato.

It was hard to walk in the deep snow and she felt the air burn in her lungs. She stopped a short distance from the bar to rest and readjust the blanket. But this time he wasn't waiting for her on the bottom step with his old Stetson hat pulled down and his shoulders hunched up in his long wool overcoat.

She was careful not to slip on the wooden steps. When she pushed the door open, warm air and cigarette smoke hit her face. She looked around slowly and deliberately, in every corner, in every dark place that the old man might find to sleep.

The bar owner didn't like Indians in there, especially Navajos, but he let Chato come in because he could talk Spanish like he was one of them. The men at the bar stared at her, and the bartender saw that she left the door open wide. Snowflakes were flying inside like moths and melting into a puddle on the oiled wood floor. He motioned to her to close the door, but she did not see him. She held herself straight and walked across the room slowly, searching the room with every step. The snow in her hair melted and she could feel it on her forehead. At the far corner of the room, she saw red flames at the mica window of the old stove door; she looked behind the stove just to make sure. The bar got quiet except for the Spanish polka music playing on the jukebox. She stood by the stove and shook the snow from her blanket and held it near the stove to dry. The wet wool smell reminded her of new-born goats in early March, brought inside to warm near the fire. She felt calm.

In past years they would have told her to get out. But her hair was white now and her face was wrinkled. They looked at her like she was a spider crawling slowly across the room. They were afraid; she could feel the fear. She looked at their faces steadily. They reminded her of the first time the white people brought her children back to her that winter. Danny had been shy and hid behind the thin white woman who brought them. And the baby had not known her until Ayah took her into her arms, and then Ella had nuzzled close to her as she had when she was nursing. The blonde woman was nervous and kept looking at a dainty gold watch on her wrist. She sat on the bench near the small window and watched the dark snow clouds gather around the mountains; she was worrying about the unpaved road. She was frightened by what she saw inside too: the strips of venison drying on a rope across the ceiling and the children jabbering excitedly in a language she did not know. So they stayed for only a few hours. Ayah watched the government car disappear down the road and she knew they were already being weaned from these lava hills and from this sky. The last time they came was in early June, and Ella stared at her the way the men in the bar were now staring. Ayah did not try to pick her up; she smiled at her instead and spoke cheerfully to Danny. When he tried to answer her, he could not seem to remember and he spoke English words with the Navajo. But he gave her a scrap of paper that he had found somewhere and carried in his pocket; it was folded in half, and he shyly looked up at her and said it was a bird. She asked Chato if they were home for good this time. He spoke to the white woman and she shook her head. "How much longer?" he asked, and she said she didn't know; but Chato saw how she stared at the boxcar shack. Ayah turned away then. She did not say good-bye.

She felt satisfied that the men in the bar feared her. Maybe it was her face and the way she held her mouth with teeth clenched tight, like there was nothing anyone could do to her now. She walked north down the road, searching for the old man. She did this because she had the blanket, and there would be no place for him except with her and the blanket in the old adobe barn near the arroyo. They always slept there when they came to Cebolleta. If the money and the wine were gone, she would be relieved because then they could go home again; back to the old hogan with a dirt roof and rock walls where she herself had been born. And the next day the old man could go back to the few sheep they still had, to follow along behind them, guiding them, into dry sandy arroyos where sparse grass grew. She knew he did not like walking behind old ewes when for so many years he rode big quarter horses and worked with cattle. But she wasn't sorry for him; he should have known all along what would happen.

There had not been enough rain for their garden in five years; and that was when Chato finally hitched a ride into the town and brought back brown boxes of rice and sugar and big tin cans of welfare peaches. After that, at the first of the month they went to Cebolleta to ask the postmaster for the check; and then Chato would go to the bar and cash it. They did this as they planted the garden every May, not because anything would survive the summer dust, but because it was time to do this. The journey passed the days that smelled silent and dry like the caves above the canyon with yellow painted buffaloes on their walls.

He was walking along the pavement when she found him. He did not stop or turn around when he heard her behind him. She walked beside him and she noticed how slowly he moved now. He smelled strong of woodsmoke and urine. Lately he had been forgetting. Sometimes he called her by his sister's name and she had been gone for a long time. Once she had found him wandering on the road to the white man's ranch, and she asked him why he was going that way; he laughed at her and said, "You know they can't run that ranch without me," and he walked on determined, limping on the leg that had been crushed many years before. Now he looked at her curiously, as if for the first time, but he kept shuffling along, moving slowly along the side of the highway. His gray hair had grown long and spread out on the shoulders of the long overcoat. He wore the old felt hat pulled down over his ears. His boots were worn out at the toes and he had stuffed pieces of an old red shirt in the holes. The rags made his feet look like little animals up to their ears in snow. She laughed at his feet; the snow muffled the sound of her laugh. He stopped and looked at her again. The wind had quit blowing and the snow was falling straight down; the southeast sky was beginning to clear and Ayah could see a star.

"Let's rest awhile," she said to him. They walked away from the road and up the slope to the giant boulders that had tumbled down from the red sandrock mesa throughout the centuries of rainstorms and earth tremors. In a place where the boulders shut out the wind, they sat down with their backs against the rock. She offered half of the blanket to him and they sat wrapped together.

The storm passed swiftly. The clouds moved east. They were massive and full, crowding together across the sky. She watched them with the feeling of horses—steely blue-gray horses startled across the sky. The powerful haunches pushed into the distances and the tail hairs streamed white mist behind them. The sky cleared. Ayah saw that there was nothing between her and the stars. The light was crystalline. There was no shimmer, no distortion through earth haze. She breathed the clarity of the night sky; she smelled the purity of the half moon and the stars. He was lying on his side with his knees pulled up near his belly for warmth. His eyes were closed now, and in the light from the stars and the moon, he looked young again.

She could see it descend out of the night sky: an icy stillness from the edge of the thin moon. She recognized the freezing. It came gradually, sinking snowflake by snowflake until the crust was heavy and deep. It had the strength of the stars in

Orion, and its journey was endless. Ayah knew that with the wine he would sleep. He would not feel it. She tucked the blanket around him, remembering how it was when Ella had been with her; and she felt the rush so big inside her heart for the babies. And she sang the only song she knew to sing for babies. She could not remember if she had ever sung it to her children, but she knew that her grandmother had sung it and her mother had sung it:

> *The earth is your mother,*
> *she holds you.*
> *The sky is your father,*
> *he protects you.*
> *Sleep,*
> *sleep.*
> *Rainbow is your sister,*
> *she loves you.*
> *The winds are your brothers,*
> *they sing to you.*
> *Sleep,*
> *sleep.*
> *We are together always*
> *We are together always*
> *There never was a time*
> *when this*
> *was not so.*

1981

Wendy Rose (Hopi) b. 1948

Wendy Rose was born in Oakland, California, and is of Hopi, Miwok, English, Scottish, Irish, and German extraction. She spent her childhood in the Bay Area just as that region experienced its postwar boom and urban sprawl. She grew up coming to terms with her ethnicity, her gender, and with an Indian's place (or lack of it) in an urban setting. In 1976 she married Arthur Murata while she was an anthropology student at the University of California, Berkeley, which she had entered as an undergraduate in 1974. She received her master's degree there in cultural anthropology in 1978. She taught from 1979 to 1983 at the same school in both ethnic studies and Native American studies before going to teach (1983–1984) at Fresno State University and then in 1984 to her current position as the coordinator of the American Indian Studies Program at Fresno City College, California. She serves on the Modern Language Association Commission on Languages and Literatures of America. In response to her ethnic role, she is active in a wide array of American Indian community affairs. At the same time, Wendy Rose works on more poems as well as on a bilingual Hopi-English manuscript. She still collects entries for a massive compilation of an annotated bibliography of published books by Native American authors in the United States and Canada.

She is best known as an American Indian poet. She is one of the premier American Indian women poets of today. Her work is widely anthologized in American literary titles. Her poems show a persistent evolution and understanding of her own voice as an Indian, as a woman, and as a poet. Her poetry serves as a bridge between ancient storytellers and singers and the modern analyst of literature and culture. She sees American culture critically from the inside as well as from the outside. Her poems project the defiance of indigenous peoples in this century, the poignancy of a precarious survival in an occupied land, and a challenge to the Eurocentric poetic tradition while at the same time using its medium to convey her images. Her verse combines pieces from her own background, glimpses of modern American life, and bits from Indian tradition to weave a tapestry of contemporary indigenous poetry that is unsurpassed in its realism and

beauty. Wendy Rose's poetry also carries the rage of a mixed-blood American Indian and that of a woman in a male-dominated academic environment, as seen in her 1977 *Academic Squaw.* Her poems present the tragedy of the loss of millions of native lives under the onslaught of Europeans coming to the New World, yet also preserve the strength for survival of the remaining Indian women of the hemisphere. This sense of poignancy is captured in her poem "To the Hopi in Richmond." Rose's poetry offers a slice of contemporary American Indian existence in the United States, bringing back to the late twentieth century the sacredness and balance of the ancients among the American Indians.

C. B. Clark
Oklahoma City University

PRIMARY WORKS

Hopi Roadrunner Dancing, 1973; *Long Division: A Tribal History,* 1977; *Academic Squaw: Reports to the World from the Ivory Tower,* 1977; *Poetry of the American Indian* Series, 1978; *Builder Kachina: A Home-Going Cycle,* 1979; *Lost Copper,* 1980; *What Happened When the Hopi Hit New York,* 1982; *Halfbreed Chronicles,* 1985; *Great Pretenders: Further Reflections on Whiteshamanism,* 1992; *Going to War with All My Relations,* 1993; *Now Proof She Is Gone,* 1994; *Bone Dance: New and Selected Poems, 1965–1993,* 1994; *Itch Like Crazy,* 2002.

Throat Song: The Rotating Earth

"Eskimo throat singers imitate the sounds the women hear . . .
listening to the sound of wind going through the cracks of an igloo
. . . the sound of the sea shore, a river of geese, the sound of the
northern lights while the lights are coming closer . . . in the old days
the people used to think the world was flat, but when they learned
the world was turning, they made a throat-singing song about it."
—INUKTITUT MAGAZINE, DECEMBER 1980

I always knew you were singing!

As my fingers have pulled your clay,
as your mountains have pulled the clay of me;
as my knees have deeply printed your mud,
5   as your winds have drawn me down and dried the mud of me;

around me always the drone and scrape of stone,
small movements atom by atom I heard like tiny drums;
I heard flutes and reeds that whine in the wind,
the bongo scratch of beetles in redwood bark,

10 the constant rattle that made of this land
a great gourd!

Oh I always knew you were singing!

1982

Loo-wit[1]

The way they do
this old woman
no longer cares
what others think
5 but spits her black tobacco
any which way
stretching full length
from her bumpy bed.
Finally up
10 she sprinkles ash on the snow,
cold and rocky buttes
that promise nothing
but winter is going at last.
Centuries of cedar
15 have bound her to earth,
huckleberry ropes
lay prickly about her neck.
Her children play games
(no sense of tomorrow);
20 her eyes are covered
with bark and she wakes
at night, fears
she is blind.
Nothing but tricks
25 left in this world,
nothing to keep

---

[1]Loo-wit: "Lady of Fire," Mt. St. Helens.

an old woman home.
Around her
machinery growls,
30   snarls and ploughs
great patches of her skin.
She crouches
in the north,
the source
35   of her trembling—
dawn appearing
with the shudder
of her slopes.
Blackberries unravel,
40   stones dislodge;
it's not as if
they weren't warned.

She was sleeping
but she heard the boot scrape;
45   the creaking floor;
felt the pull of the blanket
from her thin shoulder.
With one free heand
she finds her weapons
50   and raises them high;
clearing the twigs from her throat
she sings, she sings,
shaking the sky like a blanket about her
Loo-wit sings and sings and sings!

1983

To the Hopi in Richmond[1] (Santa Fe Indian Village)

My people in boxcars
my people   my pain
united by the window steam
of lamb stew cooking

[1] A small colony of Hopi were brought to the San Francisco Bay area to build railroads and they remained.

5 and the metal
of your walls,
your floors with cracks and crickets,
your tin roofs
full of holes;

10 that rain you prayed for
thousands of years
comes now
when you live
in a world
15 of water.

So remember
the sun
remember it was not easy
the gentle sun
20 of August mornings
remember it

as you pray today
for the rain
below the mesas;
25 the moisture
in your fields.

1985

If I Am Too Brown or Too White for You

remember I am a garnet woman
whirling into precision
as a crystal arithmetic
or a cluster and so

5 why the dream
in my mouth,
the flutter of blackbirds
at my wrists?

In the morning
10 there you are
at the edge of the river
on one knee

and you are selecting me
from among polished stones
15 more definitely red or white
between which tiny serpents swim

and you see that my body
is blood frozen
into giving birth
20 over and over in a single motion

and you touch the matrix
shattered in winter
and begin to piece together
the shape of me

25 wanting the fit in your palm
to be perfect
and the image less
clouded, less mixed

but you always see
30 just in time
working me around
in the evening sun

there is a small light
in the smoke, a tiny sun
35 in the blood, so deep
it is there and not there,

so pure
it is singing.

1985

Story Keeper

The stories would be braided in my hair
between the plastic combs and blue wing tips
but as the rattles would spit,
the drums begin,
5 along would come someone
to stifle and stop the sound

and the story keeper I would have been
must melt into the cave
of artifacts discarded

10 and this is a wound
to be healed
in the spin of winter,
the spiral
of beginning.
15 This is the task:
to find the stories now
and to heave at the rocks,
dig at the moss
with my fingernails,
20 let moisture seep along my skin
and fall within
soft and dark
to the blood

and I promise
25 I will find them
even after so long: where underground
they are albino
and they listen, they shine,
and they wait
30 with tongues shriveled like leaves
and fearful of their names
that would crystallize them,
make them fossils
with the feathers on their backs
35 frozen hard
like beetle wings.

ΔΔΔΔ   ΔΔΔΔ

But spring is floating
to the canyon rim;
needles burst yellow
40 from the pine branch
and the stories have built a new house.
Oh they make us dance
the old animal dances
that go a winding way
45 back and back
to the red clouds
of our first
Hopi morning.

Where I saw them last
50 they are still: antelope and bear
dancing in the dust,
prairie dog and lizard
whirling just whirling,
pinyon and willow
55 bending, twisting,
we women
rooting into the earth
our feet becoming water
and our hair pushing up
60 like tumbleweed

and the spirits should have noticed
how our thoughts wandered those first days,
how we closed our eyes against them
and forgot the signs;
65 the spirits were never smart about this
but trusted us to remember it right
and we were distracted,
we were new.
We mapped the trails
70 the spirits had walked
as if the footprints had more meaning
than the feet.
color after color,
designs that spin and sprout
75 were painted on the sky
but we were only confused
and turned our backs
and now we are trapped
inside our songlessness.

80 We are that kind of thing
that pushes away
the very song
keeping us alive
so the stories have been strong
85 and tell themselves
to this very day,
with or without us
it no longer matters.
The flower merges with the mud,
90 songs are hammered onto spirits
and spirits onto people;
every song is danced out loud
for we are the spirits,

we are the people,
95 descended from the ones
who circled the underworld
and return to circle again.

I feel the stories
rattle under my hand
100 like sun-dried greasy
gambling bones.

1985

Julia

[Julia Pastrana was a mid-nineteenth century singer and dancer in the circus who was billed as "The Ugliest Woman in the World," or sometimes, "The Lion Lady." She was a Mexican Indian who had been born with facial deformities and with long hair growing from all over her body, including her face. In an effort to maintain control over her professional life, her manager persuaded her to marry him and she expressed her belief that he was actually in love with her. She bore him a son who lived for only six hours and had inherited his mother's physical appearance. She died three days later. Her husband, unwilling to forfeit his financial investment, had Julia and her infant boy stuffed, mounted and put on display in a case made of wood and glass. As recently as 1975, Julia Pastrana and her little baby were exhibited in Europe and in the United States.]

Tell me it was just a dream,
my husband, a clever trick
made by some tin-faced village god
or ghost coyote, to frighten me
5 with his claim that our marriage is made
of malice and money.
Oh tell me again
how you admire my hands,
how my jasmine tea is rich and strong,
10 my singing sweet, my eyes so dark
you would lose yourself swimming
man into fish
as you mapped the pond
you would own.
15 That was not all.
The room grew cold
as if to joke
with these warm days;
the curtains blew out

20 and fell back
    against the moon-painted sill.

    I rose from my bed like a spirit
    and, not a spirit at all, floated slowly
    to my great glass oval
25 to see myself reflected
    as the burnished bronze woman
    skin smooth and tender
    I know myself to be
    in the dark
30 above the confusion
    of French perfumes
    and I was there in the mirror
    and I was not.

    I had become hard
35 as the temple stones
    of O'tomi,[1] hair grown over my ancient face
    like black moss, gray as jungle fog
    soaking green the tallest tree tops.
    I was frail
40 as the breaking dry branches
    of my winter sand canyons,
    standing so still as if
    to stand forever.

    Oh such a small room!
45 No bigger than my elbows outstretched
    and just as tall as my head.
    A small room from which to sing
    open the doors
    with my cold graceful mouth,
50 my rigid lips, my silences
    dead as yesterday,
    cruel as the children
    and cold as the coins
    that glitter
55 in your pink fist.

    And another magic
    in the cold
    of that small room:
    in my arms
60 or standing near me

[1] An Indian tribe in east central Mexico.

on a tall table
by my right side:
a tiny doll
that looked
65   like me.

Oh my husband
tell me again
this is only a dream
I wake from warm
70   and today is still today,
summer sun and quick rain;
tell me, husband, how you love me
for my self one more time.
It scares me so
75   to be with child,
lioness
with cub.

1985

Jamaica Kincaid b. 1949

Jamaica Kincaid began life on May 25, 1949, as Elaine Potter Richardson, the oldest daughter of a determined Dominican woman who was descended from Carib Indians and who had fled a tyrannical father for the tiny island of Antigua. The largest and most developed of the Leeward Islands in the West Indies, this "small place" (about the size of Staten Island) had an indigenous population of Arawak Indians who were nearly exterminated by contact with Europeans. In the seventeenth century, Antigua was occupied by English colonists who started tobacco cultivation and, later, sugar production and who imported slave labor from Africa to plant and tend the sugarcane. Antigua remained a British colony, becoming an associated, self-governing state of the United Kingdom in 1967 and gaining its full independence in 1981.

After an Anglophilic upbringing in colonial schools, Kincaid left her powerful mother and her island home in 1965 for New York City. In the heady atmosphere of the women's movement and sexual revolution, she worked as an au pair, studied photography, and in 1973 reinvented herself with a name that alludes to her island origins. At this time, she was writing for magazines like *Ingenue* and *Rolling Stone.* She did not return to Antiqua until 1985, when her brother was dying of AIDS.

Her break came when she met William Shawn, the exacting editor of the *New Yorker* who became her mentor. She worked at the magazine as a staff writer until 1995. Most of the stories and essays that form her books were published and continue to appear in its pages. They focus almost obsessively on her West Indian background.

In 1979, Kincaid married Shawn's son Allen Shawn, a composer and professor of music at Bennington College, and moved to Vermont, where she had two children, converted to Judaism, divorced, and still lives, gardens, and writes.

Kincaid's books have been both popular successes as coming-of-age tales and critically acclaimed chronicles of the immigrant experience. Stylistically, she uses powerful rhythms, repetition, mimicry, satire, and deceptively simple sentences to push beyond the "rationality" of canonical and masculinist prose. Her works interrogate gender relations, sexuality, family, colonial history, and diasporic identities. Her first collection of stories, *At the Bottom of the River* (1983), uses an incantatory style to evoke West Indian speech and surreal poetic imagery to express the harrowing power struggles and fierce attachment between mothers and daughters.

This theme also defined her next book, *Annie John* (1985), the story of an Antiguan girl whose growing maturity forces a separation from her mother and father. Readers found this book charming and universal because its critique of postcolonial privilege was largely inferential. Kincaid dropped this indirection in her next book, *A Small Place* (1988), from which the excerpt included here is taken; it is a bitter indictment of the legacy of British colonialism in Antigua.

Since this breakthrough, Kincaid's work has looked unsparingly at the effects of colonization on individuals and families in a series of novels and memoirs—*Lucy* (1990), about a young Antiguan au pair in freewheeling New York; *The Autobiogra-*

phy of My Mother (1995), a despairing portrait of lives enmeshed in the colonial past; *My Brother* (1997), a poignant account of her younger brother's death from AIDS; *Mr. Potter: A Novel* (2002), episodes in the life of an ordinary Antiguan man.

In 1999, Kincaid published *My Garden [Book:],* essays that connect the pleasures of gardening to Europe's botanical theft of the Americas and to Kincaid's familiar themes of power, conquest, and betrayal. More recently, *Among Flowers: A Walk in the Himalayas* (2005) describes a trek through the Himalayas to gather the seeds of rare plants when Kincaid seems to enact the role of thief.

In an interview, Kincaid said about *A Small Place,* "I realized in writing that book that the first step to claiming yourself is anger." In acidic prose, Kincaid indicts the legacy of British colonialism and the tourism industry as the sources of the corruption of the Antiguan government and the suffering of the Antiguan people. This quasi-memoir was so incendiary that the *New Yorker* refused to publish it. Parts of it form the narrative for the 2001 documentary film *Life and Debt,* about the economic decline of Jamaica and other small nations despoiled by globalism.

Ivy Schweitzer
Dartmouth College

PRIMARY WORKS

At the Bottom of the River (1983); *Annie John* (1985); *A Small Place* (1988); *Annie, Gwen, Lilly, Pam, and Tulip* (1989); *Lucy* (1990); *Biography of a Dress* (1990); *The Autobiography of My Mother* (1995); *My Brother* (1997); *My Favorite Plant: Writers and Gardeners on the Plants They Love* (1998, editor); *My Garden [Book:]* (1999); *Talk Stories* (2000); *Life and Debt* (2001, narrator, film); *Mr. Potter: A Novel* (2002); *Among Flowers: A Walk in the Himalayas* (2005).

from A Small Place

The Antigua that I knew, the Antigua in which I grew up, is not the Antigua you, a tourist, would see now. That Antigua no longer exists. That Antigua no longer exists partly for the usual reason, the passing of time, and partly because the bad-minded people who used to rule over it, the English, no longer do so. (But the English have become such a pitiful lot these days, with hardly any idea what to do with themselves now that they no longer have one quarter of the earth's human population bowing and scraping before them. They don't seem to know that this empire business was all wrong and they should, at least, be wearing sackcloth and ashes in token penance of the wrongs committed, the irrevocableness of their bad deeds, for no natural disaster imaginable could equal the harm they did. Actual death might have been better. And so all this fuss over empire—what went wrong here, what went wrong there—always makes me quite crazy, for I can say to them what went wrong: they should never have left their home, their precious England, a place they loved so much, a place they had to leave but could never forget. And so everywhere they went they turned it into England; and everybody they met turned English. But no place could ever really be England, and nobody who did not look exactly like them would ever be English, so you can imagine the destruction of people and land that came from that. The English hate each other and they hate England, and the reason they are so miserable now is that they have no place else to go and nobody else to feel better than.) But let me show you the Antigua that I used to know.

In the Antigua that I knew, we lived on a street named after an English maritime criminal, Horatio Nelson, and all the other streets around us were named after some other English maritime criminals. There was Rodney Street, there was Hood Street, there was Hawkins Street, and there was Drake Street. There were flamboyant trees and mahogany trees lining East Street. Government House, the place where the Governor, the person standing in for the Queen, lived, was on East Street. Government House was surrounded by a high white wall—and to show how cowed we must have been, no one ever wrote bad things on it; it remained clean and white and high. (I once stood in hot sun for hours so that I could see a putty-faced Princess from England disappear behind these walls. I was seven years old at the time, and I thought, She has a putty face.) There was the library on lower High Street, above the Department of the Treasury, and it was in the part of High Street that all colonial government business took place. In that part of High Street, you could cash a cheque at the Treasury, read a book in the library, post a letter at the post office, appear before a magistrate in court. (Since we were ruled by the English, we also had their laws. There was a law against using abusive language. Can you imagine such a law among people for whom making a spectacle of yourself through speech is everything? When West Indians went to England, the police there had to get a glossary of bad West Indian words so they could understand whether they were hearing abusive language or not.) It was in the same part of High Street that you could get a passport in another government office. In the middle of High Street was the Barclays Bank. The Barclay brothers, who started Barclays Bank, were slave-traders. That is how they made their money. When the English outlawed the slave trade, the Barclay brothers went into banking. It made them even richer. It's possible that when they saw how rich banking made them, they gave themselves a good beating for opposing an end to slave trading (for surely they would have opposed that), but then again, they may have been visionaries and agitated for an end to slavery, for look at how rich they became with their banks borrowing from (through their savings) the descendants of the slaves and then lending back to them. But people just a little older than I am can recite the name of and the day the first black person was hired as a cashier at this very same Barclays Bank in Antigua. Do you ever wonder why some people blow things up? I can imagine that if my life had taken a certain turn, there would be the Barclays Bank, and there I would be, both of us in ashes. Do you ever try to understand why people like me cannot get over the past, cannot forgive and cannot forget? There is the Barclays Bank. The Barclay brothers are dead. The human beings they traded, the human beings who to them were only commodities, are dead. It should not have been that they came to the same end, and heaven is not enough of a reward for one or hell enough of a punishment for the other. People who think about these things believe that every bad deed, even every bad thought, carries with it its own retribution. So do you see the queer thing about people like me? Sometimes we hold your retribution. . . .

And what were these people from North America, these people from England, these people from Europe, with their bad behaviour, doing on this little island? For they so enjoyed behaving badly, as if there was pleasure immeasurable to be had from not acting like a human being. Let me tell you about a man; trained as a dentist, he took it on himself to say he was a doctor, specialising in treating children's illnesses. No one objected—certainly not us. He came to Antigua as a refugee (running away from Hitler) from Czechoslovakia. This man hated us so much that he would send his wife to inspect us before we were admitted into his presence, and she would make sure that we didn't smell, that we didn't have dirt under our fingernails, and that nothing else about us—apart from the colour of our skin—would offend the doctor. (I can remember once, when I had whooping cough and I took a turn for the worse, that my mother, before bundling me up and taking me off to see this man, examined me carefully to see that I had no bad smells or dirt in the crease of my neck, behind my ears, or anywhere else. Every horrible thing that a housefly could do was known by heart to my mother, and in her innocence she thought that she and the doctor shared the same crazy obsession—germs.) Then there was a headmistress of a girls' school, hired through the colonial office in England and sent to Antigua to run this school which only in my lifetime began to accept girls who were born outside a marriage; in Antigua it had never dawned on anyone that this was a way of keeping black children out of this school. This woman was twenty-six years old, not too long out of university, from Northern Ireland, and she told these girls over and over again to stop behaving as if they were monkeys just out of trees. No one ever dreamed that the word for any of this was racism. We thought these people were so ill-mannered and we were so surprised by this, for they were far away from their home, and we believed that the farther away you were from your home the better you should behave. (This is because if your bad behaviour gets you in trouble you have your family not too far off to help defend you.) We thought they were un-Christian-like; we thought they were small-minded; we thought they were like animals, a bit below human standards as we understood those standards to be. We felt superior to all these people; we thought that perhaps the English among them who behaved this way weren't English at all, for the English were supposed to be civilised, and this behaviour was so much like that of an animal, the thing we were before the English rescued us, that maybe they weren't from the real England at all but from another England, one we were not familiar with, not at all from the England we were told about, not at all from the England we could never be from, the England that was so far away, the England that not even a boat could take us to, the England that, no matter what we did, we could never be of. We felt superior, for we were so much better behaved and we were full of grace, and these people were so badly behaved and they were so completely empty of grace. (Of course, I now see that good behaviour is the proper posture of the weak, of children.) We were taught the names of the Kings of England. In Antigua, the twenty-fourth of May was a holiday—Queen Victoria's official birthday. We didn't say to ourselves, Hasn't this extremely unappealing person been dead for years and years? Instead, we were glad for a holiday. Once, at dinner (this happened in my present life), I was sitting across from an Englishman, one of those smart people who know how to run things that England still turns out but who now, since the demise of the empire, have nothing to do; they look so sad, sitting on the rubbish heap of history. I was reciting my usual litany of things I hold against England and the English, and to round things off I said, "And do you know that we had to celebrate Queen Victoria's birthday?" So he said that every year, at the school he attended in England, they marked the day she died. I said, "Well, apart from the fact that she belonged to you and so anything you did about her was proper, at least you know she died." So that was England to us—Queen Victoria and the glorious day of her coming into the world, a beautiful place, a blessed place, a living and blessed thing, not the ugly, piggish individuals we met. I cannot tell you how angry it makes me to hear people from North America tell me how much they love England, how beautiful England is, with its traditions. All they see is some frumpy, wrinkled-up person passing by in a carriage waving at a crowd. But what I see is the millions of people, of whom I am just one, made orphans: no motherland, no fatherland, no gods, no mounds of earth for holy ground, no excess of love which might lead to the things that an excess of love sometimes brings, and worst and most painful of all, no tongue. (For isn't it odd that the only language I have in which to speak of this crime is the language of the criminal who committed the crime? And what can that really mean? For the language of the criminal can contain only the goodness of the criminal's deed. The language of the criminal can explain and express the deed only from the criminal's point of view. It cannot contain the horror of the deed, the injustice of the deed, the agony, the humiliation inflicted on me. When I say to the criminal, "This is wrong, this is wrong, this is wrong," or, "This deed is bad, and this other deed is bad, and this one is also very, very bad," the criminal understands the word "wrong" in this way: It is wrong when "he" doesn't get his fair share of profits from the crime just committed; he understand the word "bad" in this way: a fellow criminal betrayed a trust. That must be why, when I say, "I am filled with rage," the criminal says, "But why?" And when I blow things up and make life generally unlivable for the criminal (is my life not unlivable, too?) the criminal is shocked, surprised. But nothing can erase my rage—not an apology, not a large sum of money, not the death of the criminal—for this wrong can never be made right, and only the impossible can make me still: can a way be found to make what happened not have happened? And so look at this prolonged visit to the bile duct that I am making, look at how bitter, how dyspeptic just to sit and think about these things makes me. . . . Have I given you the impression that the Antigua I grew up in revolved almost completely around England? Well, that was so. I met the world through England, and if the world wanted to meet me it would have to do so through England.

Are you saying to yourself, "Can't she get beyond all that, everything happened so long ago, and how does she know that if things had been the other way around her ancestors wouldn't have behaved just as badly, because, after all, doesn't everybody behave badly given the opportunity?"

Our perception of this Antigua—the perception we had of this place ruled by these bad-minded people—was not a political perception. The English were ill-mannered, not racists; the school headmistress was especially ill-mannered, not a racist; the doctor was crazy—he didn't even speak English properly, and he came from a strangely named place, he also was not a racist; the people at the Mill Reef Club were puzzling (why go and live in a place populated mostly by people you cannot stand), not racists.

Have you ever wondered to yourself why it is that all people like me seem to have learned from you is how to imprison and murder each other, how to govern badly, and how to take the wealth of our country and place it in Swiss bank accounts? Have you ever wondered why it is that all we seem to have learned from you is how to corrupt our societies and how to be tyrants? You will have to accept that this is mostly your fault. Let me just show you how you looked to us. You came. You took things that were not yours, and you did not even, for appearances' sake, ask first. You could have said, "May I have this, please?" and even though it would have been clear to everybody that a yes or no from us would have been of no consequence you might have looked so much better. Believe me, it would have gone a long way. I would have had to admit that at least you were polite. You murdered people. You imprisoned people. You robbed people. You opened your own banks and you put our money in them. The accounts were in your name. The banks were in your name. There must have been some good people among you, but they stayed home. And that is the point. That is why they are good. They stayed home. But still, when you think about it, you must be a little sad. The people like me, finally, after years and years of agitation, made deeply moving and eloquent speeches against the wrongness of your domination over us, and then finally, after the mutilated bodies of you, your wife, and your children were found in your beautiful and spacious bungalow at the edge of your rubber plantation—found by one of your many house servants (none of it was ever yours; it was never, ever yours)—you say to me, "Well, I wash my hands of all of you, I am leaving now," and you leave, and from afar you watch as we do to ourselves the very things you used to do to us. And you might feel that there was more to you than that, you might feel that you had understood the meaning of the Age of Enlightenment (though, as far as I can see, it had done you very little good); you loved knowledge, and wherever you went you made sure to build a school, a library (yes, and in both of these places you distorted or erased my history and glorified your own). But then again, perhaps as you observe the debacle in which I now exist, the utter ruin that I say is my life, perhaps you are remembering that you had always felt people like me cannot run things, people like me will never grasp the idea of Gross National Product, people like me will never be able to take command of the thing the most simple-minded among you can master, people like me will never understand the notion of rule by law, people like me cannot really think in abstractions, people like me cannot be objective, we make everything so personal. You will forget your part in the whole setup, that bureaucracy is one of your inventions, that Gross National Product is one of your inventions, and all the laws that you know mysteriously favour you. Do you know why people like me are shy about being capitalists? Well, it's because we, for as long as we have known you, *were* capital, like bales of cotton and sacks of sugar, and you were the commanding, cruel capitalists, and the memory of this is so strong, the experience so recent, that we can't quite bring ourselves to embrace this idea that you think so much of. As for what we were like before we met you, I no longer care. No periods of time over which my ancestors held sway, no documentation of complex civilisations, is any comfort to me. Even if I really came from people who were living like monkeys in trees, it was better to be that than what happened to me, what I became after I met you.

1988

Sandra María Esteves b. 1948 and Luz María Umpierre b. 1947

While Sandra María Esteves and Luz María Umpierre have rather different backgrounds and life experiences, their strong commitment to issues of women's liberation and social justice and their involvement in the struggles of Puerto Rican communities and those of people of color have brought them close together. Both women began their poetic careers in the 1970s, have published widely, and are especially famous for the four-poem poetic dialogue that they have sustained since 1980.

The daughter of a Puerto Rican father and a Dominican mother, Esteves was born and raised in the Bronx. She describes herself as "Puerto Rican-Dominican-Borinqueña-Quisqueyana-Taino-African-American," stressing her black, Caribbean, and indigenous ancestry. Traumatic childhood anti-Spanish educational experiences led her away from language and toward the visual arts. She began writing poetry as a college student after attending a transformative community reading in Harlem, and after Toshio Idata, a Japanese

sculptor-teacher at the Pratt Institute in Brooklyn led her to create art through words. In the early seventies, Esteves became part of the group of poets identified as the Nuyorican poets movement and was mentored by Louis Reyes Rivera and Jesús Papoleto Meléndez; for many years she was one of the very few women associated with this group, which also included Pedro Pietri and Tato Laviera. Important themes in Esteves's work include motherhood and the celebration of Afro-Diasporic culture, particularly music, dance, and popular religious traditions such as Santería. Her poetry is predominantly in English, with some exceptions; she also code-switches between English and Spanish. Esteves was not schooled in Spanish and as such has always felt that English is her dominant language of poetic expression.

Umpierre was born and raised in Puerto Rico in a working-class neighborhood in San Juan, received scholarships to elite schools, and came to the United States in 1974 to pursue graduate studies in Spanish at Bryn Mawr College. She has publicly stated in interviews that one of the main motivations for her migration was the harassment and persecution that she experienced in Puerto Rico for being a lesbian, as well as her need to distance herself from her domineering father. Umpierre most explicitly addresses the theme of lesbianism in *The Margarita Poems* (1987) although other poems hinted at this in . . . *Y Otras Desgracias/And Other Misfortunes* (1985).

Umpierre grew up hearing migration histories because her mother had lived for an extended period in New York. As a result, when Umpierre first arrived in the United States, she already had a profound affinity and knowledge of diasporic experience. In general, Umpierre's poetry has been marked by its progressive move away from Spanish toward English. Cultural and political tensions are manifested in the poems of both poets through this linguistic interchange, and the poems require that realms be bilingual in order to fully appreciate and understand the poets' craft.

The "Maria Cristina" poetic exchange between Esteves and Umpierre is one of the most interesting in contemporary U.S. Latina literature. This "controversy" is notable for several reasons: it extends a centuries-old rural Puerto Rican tradition of poetic "battles" in Spanish called *controversias* in which one (usually male) poet challenges another to improvise on a specific topic; the improvisation is conducted in *décimas,* that is, ten-verse rhymed stanzas with a refrain, and is expected to be witty in order to outsmart one's opponent. Of course, Esteves and Umpierre's *controversia* differs radically in many respects: it is between women; it was not staged as a spontaneous public performance (except at least once); it is conducted in English; and it articulates the precise tensions and differences between diasporic Puerto Rican women who struggle with tradition and modernity in the light of cultural oppression.

The first two poems in this exchange are marked by their strong oral and mili-

tant tone. It is useful to think of them in a *performative* context, as texts that should be recited out loud, in which the words serve as a crucial part of a communicative gesture that is focusing on a political struggle through poetry. These poems are ideological manifestos that represent two very different notions of the position of Puerto Rican women in the United States in the 1970s and 1980s, of the tensions inherent in two social movements (civil rights and feminism) that often saw each other as polar opposites.

Esteves widely performed her first poem in the exchange and disseminated it in the context of Puerto Rican community spaces and the political struggles supported by the Nuyorican poets. Umpierre's poem comes out of her experiences in Philadelphia and New Jersey, from the contrast between disenfranchised Puerto Rican communities and elite educational environments such as those at Bryn Mawr College and Rutgers University; it also stems from her direct involvement with Third World feminists of color in the United States, whose positions are most clearly articulated in Gloria Anzaldúa and Cherríe Moraga's landmark 1981 anthology, *This Bridge Called My Back: Writings by Radical Women of Color,* a volume that also includes contributions by Aurora Levins Morales and Audre Lorde. In fact, it is notable that several of Umpierre's books from the 1980s were published by Third Woman Press, which was started by the Chicana scholar Norma Alarcón precisely to give voice to such writers.

The third and fourth poems in this exchange are more nuanced texts, in which the poets try to reconcile each other's viewpoint. They are expressions of solidarity and gestures toward the establishment of female poetic genealogies, most explicitly stated in the allusions to "titi," or auntie, Julia, a clear reference to Julia de Burgos (1971–1953), a Puerto Rican feminist poet who died destitute and anonymous on the streets of New York. De Burgos wrote most of her poetry in Spanish but toward the end of her life wrote several important poems in English, such as "Farewell in Welfare Island" (1953). Mentions of other women writers such as Marge Piercy, Ana Castillo, and Julia Alvarez abound in Umpierre's work, as do intertextual allusions to the work of poets such as Sylvia Plath and Virginia Woolf.

Lawrence La Fountain-Stokes
University of Michigan, Ann Arbor

PRIMARY WORKS

Sandra María Esteves: *Yerba Buena: Dibujos y Poemas*, 1980; *Tropical Rains: A Bilingual Downpour*, 1984; *Bluestown Mockingbird Mambo*, 1990; *Undelivered Love Poems*, 1997; *Contrapunto in the Open Field*, 1998; *Finding Your Way; Poems for Young Folks*, 1999.

Luz María Umpierre: *Una Puertorriqueña en Penna*, 1979; *En el país de las maravillas (Kempis puertorriqueño)*, 1982; *. . . Y Otras Desgracias/And Other Misfortunes . . .*, 1985; *The Margarita Poems*, 1987; *For Christine: Poems and One Letter*, 1995.

A Poetry Exchange

A la Mujer Borrinqueña

My name is Maria Christina
I am a Puerto Rican woman born in el barrio

Our men . . . they call me negra because they love me
and in turn I teach them to be strong

5 I respect their ways
inherited from our proud ancestors
I do not tease them with eye catching clothes
I do not sleep with their brothers and cousins
although I've been told that this is a liberal society
10 I do not poison their bellies with instant chemical foods
our table holds food from earth and sun

My name is Maria Christina
I speak two languages broken into each other
but my heart speaks the language of people
15 born in oppression

I do not complain about cooking for my family
because abuela taught me that woman is the master of fire
I do not complain about nursing my children
because I determine the direction of their values

20 I am the mother of a new age of warriors
I am the child of a race of slaves
I teach my children how to respect their bodies
so they will not o.d. under the stairway's shadow of shame
I teach my children to read and develop their minds
25 so they will understand the reality of oppression
I teach them with discipline . . . and love
so they will become strong and full of life

My eyes reflect the pain
of that which has shamelessly raped me
30   but my soul reflects the strength of my culture
My name is Maria Christina
I am a Puerto Rican woman born in el barrio
Our men . . . they call me negra because they love me
and in turn I teach them to be strong.

                                                                         1980

In Response

My name is not María Cristina.
I am a Puerto Rican woman born in another barrio.
Our men . . . they call me pushie
for I speak without a forked tongue
5 and I do fix the leaks in all faucets.

I don't accept their ways,
shed down from macho-men ancestors.
I sleep around whenever it is possible;
no permission needed from dearest *marido*
10 or kissing-loving papa.
I need not poison anyone's belly but my own;
no cooking mama here;
I cook but in a different form.

My name is not María Cristina.
15 I speak, I think,
I express myself in any voice,
in any tone, in any language that conveys
my house within.
The only way to fight oppression is through
20   resistance:
I do complain
I will complain
I do revise,
I don't conceal,

25 I will reveal,
    I will revise.

    I am not the mother of rapist warriors,
    I am the child that was molested.
    I teach my students to question all authority,
30 to have no fears, no nail biting in class,
    no falling in love with the teacher.

    My eyes reflect myself,
    the strengths that I am trying to attain,
    the passions of a woman who at 35 is 70.
35 My soul reflects my past,
    my soul deflects the future.

    My name is not María Cristina.
    I am a Puerto Rican woman born in another barrio.
    Our men . . . they call me bitchie
40 for I speak without a twisted tongue
    and I do fix all leaks in my faucets.

                                              1985

So Your Name Isn't María Cristina

for Luz María Umpierre

    All right. I'll accept that.
    She was just a young woman. Another Puertorriqueña among many.
    Desperate to define self within worlds of contradictions.
    Caught somewhere inbetween the casera traditions of Titi Julia
5   and the progressive principles of a Young Lords cousin.

    I'll admit she was barely a child, with no definitions of her own.
    No recognition of her vast cultural inheritance.

    She didn't used to know herself.
    Having to pick and choose from surrounding reflections.
10 Needing alternatives to focus by.
    So she found them here and there,
    tried them on for size and feeling,
    taking pieces from different places,
    coordinated like a wardrobe,
15 sometimes elegant, most times plain.

    María Cristina was naive when she wrote her first poem,
    just beginning her metamorphosis,
    struggling for explanations in the complications of being,

searching her unique place in the world, purpose for existence.
20 Discovering new meanings for old words
listed in the encyclopedia of colonialism.
Each day becoming reference volumes,
forming bridges of correspondence from old to new worlds.

She's not young anymore, not like before.
25 Anyone can change.
In fact, she's become someone else since those old times,
even though her name is still the same.

So your name isn't María Cristina,
but it really doesn't matter in which barrio you were born.
30 We all get the same kick in the ass
by faces that are similar.
You're still her older sister, teacher of many metaphors.
When she was ignorant you pulled her closer,
explaining the fruits of your experiences.
35 She watched how you fixed your own faucets,
defending yourself against heartless violations.
How you marked out your path with defiant resistance
against all forms of enslavement.
How you fought, yelled back,
40 at those who wanted you to fail, expected it, crossing you.
She watched it all, and learned from the watching
that weeding the garden is constant to its cultivation.

It's a good thing you were around.

Now she can build her own house
45 as well as sew, cook, wash, have babies,
even if her name hasn't changed.

So your name isn't María Cristina,
but you forgot to tell me if you understood
she was just one person,
50 one Borinqueña within our universal identity.
In some ways a lot like Titi Julia
who took care of her when Mami went to work.
You remember her, don't you?

The point is she grew,
55 and watched, and studied, and learned,
awakening into womanhood.

But María Cristina isn't a little girl anymore.
Everything came the hard way,
like breathing and walking the first time.

60 Self perception took time to evolve into new values,
   to patiently believe in her possibilities.

Now she can build her own house,
even though her name hasn't changed.

Thank God,
65 it was a good thing you were around.

1990

Music d'Orsay

[To Sandra María Esteves]

My pain, Sandra, is mine.
I stitch my wounds
and mend my entrails
torn, teared, ripped
5 by hands that have
no caring for me—or you.

I take on others' pain;
    so I took on yours and
    rocked it against,
10   within my heart
    in such a strong devotion
    in silence
    in absence not seen—like air—
that no one saw my bleeding.

15 Dissonant   ears   heard words
         that were not mine;
         they never heard my moans
         in seeing lesser minds
         exalted and bestowed
20   and yours, ignored.

And if I dared defy you
in a poem it was just sure enough
because I cared; I cared too much;
I loved intensely
25 the You that chose
another road—parallel to mine.

And no one wished for
        intersections,

between
30   Your Self
and
I.

Envy, Sandra, is putrefaction.
And envy rose in masculine minds
35 because I built my side of a bridge of
words
between
our
lives
40   with
just
one
single
poem;
45   one
repetitive
stanza
which
i
50   just
read
and
read
hoping
55   for you
to hear
and join
your words
to mine, complete
60   this structure
that now connects us—firmly—
because you have responded back,
the link is made.

I sit in pain
65 looking at Claude Monet's, Musée d'Orsay—exact
location—
purple flowers like my wounded flesh,
his bluish garden like a healing wound
and the green that builds his background; his
70   backdrop.

This last, I wish for you :
green palms to sooth you,
green morivíví to survive,

green waters of a sea normally blue
75 green, green everywhere
because,
Sandy,
it was in green
in
80 Puerto Rican
hope
of foliage
intertwined
on country roads
85 to give us shade,
that I defied your poem
with

my

answer.

1995

Jessica Hagedorn b. 1949

Born in the Santa Mesa section of Manila in 1949, Jessica Hagedorn traces her early inspiration to a mother devoted to painting and a maternal grandfather who was an accomplished writer and political cartoonist. Situated within a colonial heritage of Catholic schooling and U.S. cultural hegemony, Hagedorn found herself drawn to Hollywood movies and Western literary classics—but equally to melodramas and radio serials in Tagalog. This predilection for crossing boundaries defines Hagedorn's cultural productions, which include poetry and fiction, theater pieces and performance art, and music and screenplays.

Moving to San Francisco at the age of fourteen proved pivotal in shaping Hagedorn's consciousness. Although eventually attending the American Conservatory Theater, Hagedorn attributes a substantial part of her artistic development to her early exposure to San Francisco's social and literary scene. The family's frequent moves through diverse neighborhoods con-

tributed, along with her unimpeded appetite for browsing bookstores, to her sense of multiculturalism. She cites Bienvenido Santos, Amiri Baraka, Ishmael Reed, Jayne Cortez, and Víctor Hernández Cruz, as well as Gabriel García Márquez, Manuel Puig, and Stéphane Mallarmé, as among her literary influences. No less vital was her participation in San Francisco's Kearny Street Writers' Workshop, which introduced her to Asian American history and literature and helped infuse her with the spirit, passion, and social commitment of the late 1960s.

Hagedorn's urban American experience also stimulated an abiding interest in music, particularly rock, jazz, and rhythm and blues. Her poetry propels itself along rhythms inflected by music and urban vernacular. In 1973 her poetry appeared in *Four Young Women: Poems,* an anthology edited by Kenneth Rexroth. She continued experimenting in *Dangerous Music,* a 1975 collection whose poetry occasionally resembles a literal "dance" of words and whose offbeat prose fiction opens a space for rewriting of immigration narratives.

Also in 1975, along with Thulani Davis and Ntozake Shange, Hagedorn formed a band called the West Coast Gangster Choir, rechristened in 1978 in New York City as the Gangster Choir. Upon moving to the East Coast, she participated in New York's Basement Workshop. Earlier experiments using dramatic sketches during the pauses between songs contributed to the development of her performance art. Following the production of several theatrical works and teleplays, in 1981 her *Pet Food & Tropical Apparitions* appeared, which featured sexually charged poems and in the title story took a hard but sympathetic look at the capacity of inner-city culture to evince simultaneously an incomparable vitality and a lurid self-destructiveness. Between 1988 and 1992, she participated in the performance/theater trio Thought Music.

In 1990 Hagedorn produced her first novel, *Dogeaters,* a mordant exploration of class and ethnic divisions, rampant commercialism, plutocratic machinations, revolutionary insurgency, and the varieties of corruption in a country caught in the grasp of a Marcos-like regime and laboring beneath the shadow of Western colonialism. Nominated for the National Book Award and recipient of the American Book Award, *Dogeaters* is also noteworthy for its stylistic daring. Playfully splicing together book and letter excerpts, poetry, a gossip column, dramatic dialogue, and news items into a conventional storytelling frame, the novel explores the possibilities of combining postmodern narrative practices with a postcolonial political agenda.

In 1993 Hagedorn edited *Charlie Chan Is Dead: An Anthology of Contemporary Asian American Fiction.* Significantly, although the book included many well-known Asian American writers, such as Carlos Bulosan, Hisaye Yamamoto, Maxine Hong Kingston, Amy Tan, and Bharati Mukherjee, nearly half of the forty-eight writers enjoyed publication in a major collection for the first time.

Hagedorn's second novel, *The Gangster of Love,* appeared in 1996. It experiments with shifting points of view and engages dream as a supplementary narrative strategy but otherwise tells a conventional story of a young woman from the Philippines struggling to establish her musical and artistic career in America and later grappling with the encroachments of age.

Hagedorn remains ideologically aligned with the radical 1960s politics that helped shape her sensibility, but ultimately she is interested not in social realism but in reinvention and the varieties of liberation. Just as her work resists easy categorization into "high" or "pop" culture, it seeks to cross conventional boundaries of self and country and of writing and art.

George Uba
California State University, Northridge

PRIMARY WORKS

Dangerous Music, 1975; *Pet Food & Tropical Apparitions,* 1981; *Teenytown* (performance piece), 1988; *Dogeaters,* 1990; *Danger and Beauty,* 1993; *Airport Music* (performance piece), 1994; *The Gangster of Love,* 1996; *Burning Heart: A Portrait of the Philippines,* 1999; *Dream Jungle,* 2003.

The Blossoming of Bongbong

Antonio Gargazulio-Duarte, also fondly known as Bongbong to family and friends, had been in America for less than two years and was going mad. He didn't know it, of course, having left the country of his birth, the Philippines, for the very reason that his sanity was at stake. As he often told his friend, the painter Frisquito, "I can no longer tolerate contradiction. This country is full of contradiction. I have to leave before I go crazy."

His friend Frisquito would only laugh. His laugh was eerie because it was soundless. When he laughed, his body would shake—and his face, which was already grotesque, would distort—but no sound would emit from him.

People were afraid of Frisquito. They bought his paintings, but they stayed away from him. Especially when he was high. Frisquito loved to get high. He had taken acid more than fifty times, and he was only twenty-six years old. He had once lived in New York, where people were used to his grotesque face, and ignored him. Frisquito had a face that resembled a retarded child: eyes slanted, huge forehead, droopy mouth, and pale, luminous skin. Bongbong once said to him, "You have skin like the surface of the moon." Frisquito's skull was also unusually large, which put people off, especially women. Frisquito soon learned to do without women or men. "My paintings are masturbatory," he once said to the wife of the president of the Philippines. She never blinked an eye, later commissioning three obscene murals. She was often referred to as a "trendsetter."

Frisquito told Bongbong, "There's nothing wrong with being crazy. The thing to do is to get comfortable with it."

Not only had Frisquito taken acid more than fifty times, he had also taken peyote and cocaine and heroin at a rate that doctors often said would normally kill a man. "But I'm like a bull," he would say. "Nothing can really hurt me, except the creator of the universe."

At which point he would smile.

Bongbong finally left Manila on a plane for San Francisco. He was deathly afraid. He wore an olive-green velvet jacket, and dark velvet pants, with a long scarf thrown casually around his scrawny neck. Frisquito saw him off to the airport. "You look like a faggot," he said to Bongbong, who was once named best-dressed young VIP in Manila. Bongbong felt ridiculously out of place and took two downers so he could sleep during the long ride to America. He arrived, constipated and haggard, and was met by his sister and brother-in-law, Carmen and Pochoy Guevara. "You look terrible," his sister said. She was embarrassed to be seen with him. Secretly she feared he was homosexual, especially since he was such good friends with Frisquito.

Bongbong had moved in with his sister and brother-in-law, who lived in a plush apartment on Twin Peaks. His brother-in-law Pochoy, who had graduated as a computer programmer from Heald's Business College, worked for the Bank of America. His sister Carmen, who was rather beautiful in a bland, colorless kind of way, had enrolled in an Elizabeth Arden beauty course, and had hopes of being a fashion model.

"Or maybe I could go into merchandising," she would say, in the afternoons when she wouldn't go to class. She would sit in her stainless-steel, carpeted electric kitchen. She drank cup after cup of instant Yuban coffee, and changed her nail polish every three days.

"You should wear navy blue on your nails," Bongbong said to her one of those afternoons, when she was removing her polish with Cutex lemon-scented polish remover. "It would look wonderful with your sallow complexion." "Sallow" was a word Bongbong had learned from Frisquito.

"Sallow? What does that mean?" Carmen never knew if her brother was insulting or complimenting her.

"It means pale and unhealthy," Bongbong said. "Anyway, it's in style now. I've seen lots of girls wearing it."

He wrote Frisquito a letter:

Dear Frisquito,

Everyone is a liar. My sister is the biggest one of them all. I am a liar. I lie to myself every second of the day. I look in the mirror and I don't know what's there. My sister hates me. I hate her. She is inhuman. But then, she doesn't know how to be human. She thinks I'm inhuman. I am surrounded by androids. Do you know what that is? I'm glad I never took acid.

I wish I was a movie star.

Love,
Bongbong

The apartment had two bedrooms. Pochoy had bought a leather couch and a Magnavox record player on credit. He owned the largest and most complete collection of Johnny Mathis records. At night Bongbong would lie awake and listen to their silent fucking in the next room, and wonder if Carmen was enjoying herself. Sometimes they would fuck to "Misty."

Carmen didn't cook too often, and Pochoy had a gluttonous appetite. Since he didn't believe in men cooking, they would often order Chinese food or pizzas to be delivered. Once in a while Bongbong would try to fix a meal, but he was never talented in that direction. Frisquito had taught him how to cook two dishes: fried chicken & spaghetti.

Dear Frisquito,

I can't seem to find a job. I have no skills, and no college degree. Carmen thinks I should apply at Heald's Business College and go into computer programming. The idea makes me sick. I am twenty-six years old and no good at anything. Yesterday I considered getting a job as a busboy in a restaurant, but Carmen was horrified. She was certain everyone in Manila would hear about it (which they will), and she swears she'll kill herself out of shame. Not a bad idea, but I am not a murderer. If I went back to Manila I could be a movie star.

Love,
Bongbong

Bongbong stood in the middle of a Market Street intersection, slowly going mad. He imagined streetcars melting and running him over, grinding his flesh and bones into one hideous, bloody mess. He saw the scurrying Chinese women, no more than four feet tall, run amok and beat him to death with their shopping bags, which were filled to the brim with slippery, silver-scaled fish.

He watched a lot of television. His eyes became bloodshot. He began to read—anything from best-sellers to plays to political science to poetry. A lot of it he didn't quite understand, but the names and events fascinated him. He would often visit bookshops just to get out of the apartment. He chose books at random, sometimes for their titles or the color of their book jackets. His favorite before he went crazy was *Vibration Cooking* by Verta Mae Grosvenor. He even tried out some of Verta Mae's recipes, when he was in better moods on the days when Carmen and Pochoy were away. He had found Verta Mae's book for seventy-five cents in a used-book store he frequented.

"What is this?" Carmen asked, staring at the book cover, which featured Verta Mae in her colorful African motif outfit.

"That, my dear, is a cookbook," Bongbong answered, snatching the book out of her hands, now decorated in Max Factor's "Regency Red."

On the bus going home there was a young girl sitting behind Bongbong wearing a Catholic school uniform and carrying several books in her pale, luminous arms, which reminded him of the surface of the moon. When the bus came to a stop, she walked quietly to the front and before getting off she turned, very slowly and deliberately, and stared deeply into Bongbong's eyes. "You will get what you deserve," she said.

One time when Bongbong was feeling particularly lonely, he went to a bar on Union Street where young men and women stand around and drink weak Irish coffees. The bar was sometimes jokingly known as a "meat factory." The young men were usually executives, or trying to look like executives. They wore their hair slightly long, with rather tacky muttonchop whiskers, and they all smoked dope. The women were usually chic or terribly hip. Either way they eyed each other coolly and all wore platform shoes.

A drink was sent to Bongbong from the other end of the bar by a twenty-eight-year-old sometime actress and boutique salesgirl named Charmaine. She was from Nicaragua, and quite stunning, with frizzy brown hair and the biggest ass Bongbong had ever seen.

"What're you having?" she asked, grinning. Her lips were moist and glossy, and the Fertile Crescent was tattooed in miniature on her left cheek.

Bongbong, needless to say, was silent for a moment. Ladies like Charmaine were uncommon in Manila. "Gimlet," he murmured, embarrassed because he disliked the idea of being hustled.

Charmaine had a habit of tossing her head back, so that her frizzy curls bounced, as if she were always secretly dancing. "Awright," she said, turning to the bartender, "bring the gentleman a gimlet." She giggled, turning to look fully at Bongbong. "I'm Charmaine. Wha's your name?"

Bongbong blushed. "Antonio," he said, "But I go by my nickname." He dreaded her next question, but braced himself for it, feeling the familiar nausea rising within him. Once Frisquito had told him that witches and other types of human beings only had power over you if they knew your name. Since that time Bongbong always hesitated when anyone asked him for his name, especially women. "Women are more prone to occult powers than men," Frisquito warned. "It comes natural to them."

Charmaine was smiling now. "Oh yeah? Whatisit?"

"Bongbong."

The bartender handed him the gimlet, and Charmaine shrugged. "Tha's a funky name, man. You Chicano?"

Bongbong was offended. He wanted to say No, I'm Ethiopian, or Moroccan, or Nepalese, what the fuck do you care . . . Silently he drank his gimlet. Then he decided, the nausea subsiding, that Charmaine wasn't malicious, and left the bar with her shortly after.

Charmaine showed him the boutique where she worked, which was next door to the bar. Bongbong stared at the platform shoes in the display window as if he were seeing them for the first time. Their glittering colors and whimsical designs intrigued him. Charmaine watched his face curiously as he stood with his face pressed against the glass like a small child; then she took his arm and led him to her VW.

She lived in a large flat in the Fillmore district with another sometime actress and boutique salesgirl named Colelia. They had six cats, and the place smelled like a combination of cat piss and incense.

Colelia thought she was from Honey Patch, South Carolina, but she wasn't sure. "I'm all mixed up," she said. Sometimes she thought she was a geechee. She was the only person Bongbong knew who had ever read *Vibration Cooking*. She had even met Verta Mae at a party in New York.

Bongbong spent the night in Charmaine's bed, but he couldn't bring himself to even touch her. She was amused, and asked him if he was gay. At first he didn't understand the term. English sometimes escaped him, and certain colloquialisms, like "gay," never made sense. He finally shook his head and mumbled no. Charmaine told him she didn't really mind. Then she asked him to go down on her.

Dear Frisquito:

I enrolled at Heald's College today so that Carmen would shut up. I plan on leaving the house every morning and pretending I'm going to school. That way no one will bother me.

I think I may come back to Manila soon, but somehow I feel I'm being trapped into staying here. I don't understand anything. Everyone is an artist, but I don't see them doing anything. Which is what I don't understand . . . but one good thing is I am becoming a good cook.

Enclosed is a copy of *Vibration Cooking* by Verta Mae.

Love,
B.

Sometimes Bongbong would open the refrigerator door and oranges would fly out at him. He was fascinated by eggs, and would often say to his sister, "We're eating the sunset," or "We're eating embryos." Or he would frown and say, "I never did like chickens."

He began riding streetcars and buses from one end of the city to the other, often going into trances and reliving the nightmare of the streetcar melting and running him over. Always the Chinese women would appear, beating him to death with silver-scaled fish, or eggs.

Bongbong saw Charmaine almost every day for a month. His parents sent him an allowance, thinking he was in school. This allowance he spent lavishly on her. He bought her all the dazzling platform shoes her heart desired. He took her to fancy nightclubs so she could dance and wiggle her magnificent ass to his delight. She loved Sly Stone and Willie Colon, so he bought her all their records. They ate curry and spice cake every night of the week (sometimes alternating with yogurt pie and gumbo) and Charmaine put on ten pounds.

He never fucked her. Sometimes he went down on her, which she liked even better. She had replaced books and television in his life. He thought he was saved.

One afternoon while he was waiting for Charmaine in the bar where they had met, Bongbong had a vision. A young woman entered the bar, wearing a turban on her head made of torn rags. Her hair was braided and stood out from her scalp like branches on a young tree. Her skin was so black she was almost blue.

Around her extremely firm breasts she wore an old yellow crocheted doily, tied loosely. Her long black skirt was slit up the front all the way to her crotch, and underneath she wore torn black lace tights, and shocking-pink suede boots, laced all the way up to her knees. She carried a small basket as a handbag, and she was smoking Eve cigarettes elegantly, as if she were a dowager empress.

She sat next to Bongbong and gazed at him coolly and deliberately. People in the bar turned their heads and stared at her, some of them laughing. She asked Bongbong for a match. He lit her cigarette. His hands were trembling. She smiled, and he saw that some of her teeth were missing. After she smoked her cigarette, she left the bar.

Another day while Bongbong was walking in the Tenderloin, he had another vision. A young woman offered to fuck him for a mere twenty-five dollars. He hesitated, looking at her. She had shoulder-length, greasy blond hair. She had several teeth missing too, and what other teeth she had left were rotten. Her eyes, which were a dull brown, were heavily painted with midnight-blue mascara. She wore a short red skirt, a tight little sweater, and her black sheer tights had runs and snags all over them. Bongbong noticed that she had on expensive silver platform shoes that were sold in Charmaine's boutique.

He asked her name.

Her voice was as dull as her eyes. "Sandra," she replied.

He suddenly felt bold in her presence. "How old are you?"

"Nineteen. How old are you, honey?" She leered at him, then saw the blank look on his face, and all the contempt washed out of her. He took her to a restaurant where they served watery hamburgers and watery coffee. He asked her if she had a pimp.

"Yup. And I been busted ten times. I been a hooker since I was thirteen, and my parents are more dead than alive. Anything else you wanna know?"

Her full name was Sandra Broussard. He told her she was beautiful. She laughed. She said her pimp would kill her if she ever left the business. She showed him her scars. "He cut my face once, with a razor," she said.

He felt useless. He went back to the apartment and Carmen was waiting for him. "We've decided you should move out of this place as soon as possible," she said. "I'm pregnant, and I want to redecorate your room for the baby. I'm going to paint your room pink."

He went into the bathroom and stared at the bottles of perfume near the sink, the underarm deodorant, the foot deodorant, the cinnamon-flavored mouthwash, and the vaginal spray. They used Colgate brand toothpaste. Dove soap. Zee toilet paper. A Snoopy poster hung behind the toilet. It filled him with despair.

Bongbong moved into Charmaine's flat shortly after. He brought his velvet suit and his books. Colelia reacted strangely at first. She had been Charmaine's lover for some time, and felt Bongbong would be an intrusion. But all he did was read his books and watch television. He slept on a mattress in the living room. He hardly even spoke to Charmaine anymore. Sometimes they would come home from work in the evenings and find Bongbong in the kitchen, preparing Verta Mae's Kalalou Noisy Le Sec or her Codfish with Green Sauce for all of them. Colelia realized he wasn't a threat to her love life at all. Life became peaceful for her and Charmaine.

During the long afternoons when Colelia and Charmaine were gone and the cats were gone and the smell of piss from the catbox lingered in the chilly air, Bongbong would put on his velvet suit and take long walks in the Tenderloin, trying to find Sandra Broussard. He thought he saw her once, inside a bar, but when he went in, he found it was a mistake. The woman turned out to be much older, and when she turned to smile at him, he noticed she wore the hand of Fatima on a silver chain around her neck.

When he really thought about it, in his more lucid moments, he realized he didn't even remember what Sandra looked like anymore. Dullness was all he could conjure of her presence. Her fatigue and resignation.

Charmaine, on the other hand, was bright, beautiful, and selfish. She was queen of the house, and most activity revolved around her. Colelia always came home from work with a gift for Charmaine, which they both referred to as "prizes." Sometimes they were valuable, like jade rings or amethyst stones for Charmaine's pierced nose, or silly—like an old Walt Disney cup with Donald Duck painted on it.

Bongbong found the two women charming and often said so when he was in a talkative mood. "You are full of charm and your lives will be full of success," he would say to them, as they sat in their antique Chinese robes, painting each other's faces.

"You sound like a fortune cookie," Charmaine would say, glaring at him.

He would be silent at her outbursts, which naturally made her more furious. "I wish you'd tell me how much you want me," she would demand, ignoring her female lover's presence in the room.

Sometimes Charmaine would watch Bongbong as he read his books, and she would get evil with him out of boredom. She was easily distracted and therefore easily bored, especially when she wasn't the center of attention. This was often the case when Colelia was at work and it was Charmaine's day off.

Bongbong said to her, "Once you were a witch, but you misused your powers. Now you resent me because I remind you of those past days."

Charmaine circled Bongbong as he sat in the living room immersed in *Green Mansions* by W. H. Hudson. He had found the hardback novel for one dollar in another secondhand-book shop, called Memory Lane.

"I'm going to take my clothes off, Bongbong," Charmaine would tease. "What're you going to do about it?" Bongbong would look up at her, puzzled. Then she would put her hands on her enormous hips. "Men like me most of all because of my ass, Bongbong . . . but they can't really get next to me. Most of them have no style . . . but you have a sort of style—" By this time she often removed her skirt. "I don't wear panties," she said, "so whenever I want, Colelia can feel me up." Bongbong tried to ignore her. He was getting skilled in self-hypnosis, and whenever external disturbances would occur, he would stare off into the distance and block them slowly from his mind.

The more skilled he became in his powers, the more furious Charmaine would get with him. One time she actually wrenched the book from his hands and threw it out the window. Then she lay on the couch in front of him and spread her legs. "You know what I've got, Bongbong? Uterina Furor . . . That's what my mother used to say . . . Nuns get it all the time. Like a fire in the womb."

To make her smile, Bongbong would kiss her between the legs, and then Colelia would come home and pay more attention to Charmaine and Bongbong would cook more of Verta Mae's recipes, such as Stuffed Heart Honky Style (one of Charmaine's favorites), and everything would be all right.

Charmaine's destructive moods focused on Bongbong twice a month, and got worse when the moon was full. "You're in a time of perennial menstruation," Bongbong told her solemnly after one of her fits.

One morning while they were having breakfast together, Colelia accused Charmaine of being in love with Bongbong. "Why, I don't know—" Colelia said. "He's so funny-looking and weird. You're just into such an ego trip you want what you can't have."

Charmaine giggled. "Forever analyzing me! Don't I love you enough?"

"It's not that."

"Well, then—why bring him up? You never understood him from the very beginning," Charmaine said. "Or why I even brought him here in the first place. I must confess—I don't quite know why I brought him home myself. Somehow, I knew he wasn't going to fuck me . . . I really didn't want a fuck though. It was more like I wanted him around to teach me something about myself . . . Something like that, anyway."

Colelia looked away. "That's vague enough."

"Are you really jealous of him?" Charmaine asked.

Colelia finally shook her head. "Not in that way . . . but maybe because I don't understand him, or the two of you together—I am jealous. I guess because I feel left out of his mystique."

Charmaine embraced her, and the two of them wept.

Bongbong's visions and revelations were becoming more frequent. A Chinese woman with a blond wig and a map of the world on her legs. A black man with three breasts. A cat turning doorknobs. A tortoise crawling out of a sewer on the sidewalk, and junkies making soup out of him. Frisquito assassinating the president of the Philippines who happens to be his wife in drag who happens to be a concert pianist's mother . . . The visions were endless, circular, and always moving.

Dear Frisquito:

Yesterday a friend of Charmaine's named Ra brought a record over by a man named John Coltrane. Ra tells me that Mr. Coltrane died not too long ago, I believe when we were just out of high school. Ra decided that I could keep the record, which is called "Meditations." I believe it is the title of one of your paintings.

Every morning I plan on waking up to this man's music. It keeps my face from disintegrating. You once said your whole being had disintegrated long ago, and that you had the power to pick up the pieces from time to time, when it was necessary—such as the time you gave an exhibit of your works, for the benefit of the First Lady. I think there may be some hope left for me.

Yesterday I cooked Verta Mae's Uptight Ragout in your honor.

Love,
B.

Bongbong now referred to himself as "B." He could not stand to speak in long sentences, and tried to live and speak as minimally as possible. Charmaine worried about him, especially when he would go on one of his rampages and cook delicious gumbo dinners for herself and Colelia, and not eat with them.

"But B," she protested, "I never see you eat anymore."

One time he said, "Maybe I eat a saxophone."

He loved the word "saxophone."

His parents stopped sending money, since Carmen wrote them that he had never attended one day of school at Heald's Business College. His father wrote him and warned him never to set foot in the Philippines again, or he would have him executed for the crime of deception and subversion to one's parents, a new law put into practice in the current dictator's regime.

Bongbong decided to visit Carmen. She was almost six months pregnant, and very ugly. Her face had broken out in rashes and pimples, and her whole body was swollen. Her once shimmering black hair was now dry and brittle, and she had cut it short. He stared at her for a long time as they sat in the kitchen in silence. She finally suggested that he see the baby's room.

She had decorated the room with more Snoopy posters, and mobiles with wooden angels hung from the ceiling. A pink baby bed stood in the center of the room, which was heavily scented with floral spray.

"It's awful," Bongbong said.

"Oh, you're always insulting everything!" his sister screamed, shoving him out the door. She shut the door behind her, as if guarding a sacred temple, and looked at him, shaking with rage. "You make everything evil. Are you on drugs? I think you're insane," she said. "Leave this house before I call the police." She hated him because he made her feel ashamed in his presence, but she couldn't understand why.

Frisquito, who never answered any of his letters, sent him a check for a considerable amount of money. A postcard later arrived with "Don't Worry" scratched across it, and Frisquito's signature below the message. Bongbong, who now wore his velvet suit every day, went to a pawnshop and bought a soprano saxophone.

In the mornings he would study with Ra, who taught him circular breathing. He never did understand chords and scales, but he could hear what Ra was trying to teach him and he surprised everyone in the house with the eerie sounds he was making out of his new instrument. Charmaine told Colelia that she thought Bongbong was going to be all right, because Bongbong had at last found his "thing."

Which was wrong, because Bongbong's music only increased his natural visionary powers. He confessed to Ra that he could actually see the notes in the air, much as he could see the wind. Ra would smile, not saying anything.

Bongbong watched Charmaine at the kitchen table eating breakfast, and when she looked up at him, she would suddenly turn into his mother, with Minnie Mouse ears and long, exaggerated Minnie Mouse eyelashes, which glittered and threw off sparks when she blinked. This frightened him sometimes because he would forget who Charmaine was. As long as he could remember who everyone was, he felt a surge of relief. But these moments were becoming more and more confusing, and it was getting harder and harder for him to remember everyone's name, including his own.

Colelia decided that Bongbong was a "paranoid schizophrenic" and that she and Charmaine should move out, for their own safety. "One of these days we'll come home from work and find all our kitty cats with their throats slit," she said. She refused to eat any more of Bongbong's cooking, for fear he would poison her. "He doesn't like women basically. That's the root of his problem" she told Charmaine. "I mean, the guy doesn't even jack off! How unnatural can he be? Remember Emil Kemper!"

"Remember Emil Kemper" became the motto of the household. Emil Kemper was a young madman in Santa Cruz, California, who murdered his grandmother when he was something like thirteen years old, murdered his mother later on after he was released from the looney bin—cut her head off—and murdered about a million other female hitchhikers.

Charmaine sympathized with Bongbong, but she wasn't sure about him either. Only Ra vouched for his sanity. "Sure the cat is crazy," he said, "but he'll never hurt any of you."

Bongbong practiced the saxophone every day, and seemed to survive on a diet of water and air. Charmaine came home from the boutique one night and brought him two pairs of jeans and two T-shirts. One T-shirt had glittery blue and silver thread woven into it, and Bongbong saw the shirt become a cloud floating above his narrow bed. "Well," Charmaine said, trying to sound casual as she watched Bongbong drift off dreamily, "aren't you going to try it on? Do you like it? I seriously think you should have your velvet suit dry-cleaned, before it falls apart."

Bongbong touched the cloud. "Oh, how beautiful," he said.

He never wore the shirt. He hung it above his bed like a canopy, where he could study it at night. His ceiling became a galaxy. To appease Charmaine (he was very sensitive to her feelings, and loved her in his own way), he wore the other shirt and sent his velvet suit to the cleaners.

Frisquito sent him more money the next month, and Bongbong bought a telescope.

Dear Frisquito,

Do you know I am only five feet and two inches tall? Without my platform shoes, of course. Why do people like to look like cripples? Yesterday I saw a fat young woman wearing platform shoes that made her feet look like boats. Her dress was too short on her fat body and you could see her cellulite wobbling in her forest-green pantyhose. Cellulite is the new fad in America. Some French-woman discovered it and is urging everyone to feel for it in their skin. It's sort of like crepe-paper tissue that happens when you put on too much weight. I told the fat young woman she was beautiful, and she told me to fuck off. She was very angry, and I realized there are a lot of angry people around me. Except in the house I live in, which is why I've stayed so long.

The Coltrane record is warped from having been left in the sun. I am writing a song about it in my head.

> With my telescope I can see
> everyone, and they don't have to
> see me.

                                        Love,
                                          B.

Bongbong often brought the telescope up to the roof of their building and watched the people on the streets below. Then at night he would watch the stars in the sky and try to figure out different constellations. Charmaine took him to the planetarium for his birthday, and they watched a show on Chinese astronomy called "The Emperor of the Heavens," narrated by a man called Alvin. Bongbong was moved to tears. "I love you," he told Charmaine, as they lay back in their seats and watched the heavens.

But he had forgotten that she was Charmaine Lopez, and that she lived with him. He thought she was Sandra Broussard, or the blue lady with the rag turban on her head. When the show was over, he asked her to marry him.

He didn't say another word until they reached the flat. He cooked Verta Mae's Jamaican Curried Goat for birthday dinner and Colelia baked him a cake decorated with a sugar-coated model airplane. Bongbong removed the airplane and hung it next to the canopy above his bed.

After dinner he asked Charmaine if she would sleep with him. She didn't have the heart to refuse, and kissing Colelia on her forehead, followed Bongbong into his room. The next morning Charmaine told Colelia they should both move out.

"Was he a freak? I mean, did he hurt you?" Colelia asked.

Charmaine shook her head. "No. But I don't want to live around him anymore. It may be best if we left today."

They packed their clothes and rounded up their cats and drove away in Charmaine's VW, leaving Bongbong with a note on the kitchen table: "We will send for the rest of our things. Forgive us. C & C."

Bongbong awoke from a beautiful dream, in which he had learned how to fly. Everything in the dream had an airy quality. He floated and glided through the atmosphere, and went swimming in the clouds, which turned out to be his glittery blue sweater. Charmaine Lopez and her dancing girls did the rhumba in the heavens, which were guarded by smiling Chinese deities. Alvin from the planetarium sang "Stardust" for him as he flew by. He was happy. He could play his saxophone forever. Then he saw Frisquito flying far away, waving to him. He tried and tried, but he couldn't get any closer to him. Frisquito became smaller and smaller, then vanished, and when Bongbong opened his eyes, he found Charmaine gone.

He decided to stay in the flat, and left the other rooms just as they were. Even Ra stopped coming to visit, so Bongbong had to teach himself about the saxophone. There were brief moments when he found that the powers of levitation were within him, so while he practiced the saxophone he would also practice levitating.

Frisquito,

Just two things. The power of flight has been in me all along. All I needed was to want it bad enough.

Another is something someone once said to me. Never is forever, she said.

Love

He didn't sign his name or his initial, because he had finally forgotten who he was.

1975

The Death of Anna May Wong

My mother is very beautiful
And not yet old.
A Twin,
Color of two continents:
5 I stroll through Irish tenderloin
Nightmare doors—drunks spill out
Saloon alleys falling asleep
At my feet . . .

My mother wears a beaded
10 Mandarin coat:
In the dryness
Of San Diego's mediterrannean parody
I see your ghost, Belen
As you clean up
15 After your sweet señora's

mierda

Jazz,
Don't do me like that.
Mambo,
20 Don't do me like that.
Samba, calypso, funk and
Boogie
Don't cut me up like that

Move my gut so high up
25 Inside my throat
I can only strangle you
To keep from crying . . .

My mother serves crêpes suzettes
With a smile
30 And a puma
Slithers down
            19th street and Valencia
Gabriel o.d.'s on reds
As we dance together

35 Dorothy Lamour undrapes
Her sarong
And Bing Crosby ignores
The mierda.

My mother's lavender lips
40 Stretch in a slow smile.
And beneath
The night's cartoon sky
Cold with rain
           Alice Coltrane
45 Kills the pain
And I know
I can't go home again.

          1971

Filipino Boogie

Under a ceiling-high Christmas tree
I pose
      in my Japanese kimono
My mother hands me
5   a Dale Evans cowgirl skirt
and
     baby cowgirl boots

Mommy and daddy split
No one else is home

10 I take some rusty scissors
               and cut the skirt up
     in
        little pieces

(don't give me no bullshit fringe,
15 Mama)

Mommy and daddy split
No one else is home

     I take my baby cowgirl boots
              and flush them
20   down
                the
                    toilet

(don't hand me no bullshit fringe,
(Papa)

25 I seen the Indian Fighter
Too many times
             dug on Sitting Bull
                 before Donald Duck

In my infant dream
30 These warriors weaved a magic spell
        more blessed than Tinker Bell

(Kirk Douglas rubs his chin
and slays Minnehaha by the campfire)

Mommy and daddy split
35 There ain't no one else home

         I climb a mango tree
            and wait for Mohawk drums

(Mama—World War II
is over . . . why you cryin'?)

40 Is this San Francisco?
Is this San Francisco?
Is this Amerika?

buy me Nestle's Crunch
        buy me Pepsi in a can

45 *Ladies' Home Journal*
        and *Bonanza*

I seen Little Joe in Tokyo
I seen Little Joe in Manila
I seen Laramie in Hong Kong
50 I seen Yul Brynner in San Diego
and the bloated ghost
                of Desi Arnaz

dancing
        in Tijuana

55 Rip-off synthetic ivory
                to send
                the natives
        back home

and

60   North Beach boredom
        escapes
        the barber shops
    on Kearny street
            where
65   they spit out
                    red tobacco

                    patiently
        waiting
            in 1930s suits

70 and in another dream
            I climb a mango tree
    and Saturday
        afternoon
            Jack Palance
75   bazookas

                the krauts

and

the YELLOW PERIL
bombs
80   Pearl Harbor
1971

Homesick

Blame it on the mambo and the cha-cha, voodoo amulets worn on the same chain with tiny crucifixes and scapulars blessed by the Pope. Chains of love, medals engraved with the all-seeing Eye, ascending Blessed Virgins floating toward heaven surrounded by erotic cherubs and archangels, the magnificent torso of a tormented, half-naked Saint Sebastian pierced by arrows dripping blood. A crown of barbed-wire thorns adorns the holy subversive's head, while we drown in the legacy of brutal tropical generals stuffed in khaki uniforms, their eyes shielded by impenetrable black sunglasses, Douglas MacArthur style.

And Douglas MacArthur and Tom Cruise are painted on billboards lining Manila's highways, modeling *Ray-Ban* shades and Jockey underwear. You choose between the cinema version starring Gregory Peck smoking a corncob pipe, or the real thing. "I shall return," promised the North American general, still revered by many as the savior of the Filipino people, who eagerly awaited his return. As the old saying goes, this is how we got screwed, screwed real good. According to Nick Joaquin, "The Philippines spent three hundred years trapped in a convent, and fifty years in Hollywood . . ." Or was it four hundred years? No matter—there we were, seduced and abandoned in a confusion of identities, then granted our independence. Hollywood pretended to leave us alone. An African American saying also goes: "Nobody's *given* freedom." Being granted our independence meant we were owned all along by someone other than ourselves.

I step off the crowded plane onto the tarmac of the newly named Ninoy Aquino Airport. It is an interesting appropriation of the assassinated senator's name, don't you think? So I think, homesick for this birthplace, my country of supreme ironies and fatalistic humor, mountains of foul garbage and breathtaking women, men with the fierce faces of wolves and steamy streets teeming with abandoned children.

The widow of the assassinated senator is Corazon Aquino, now president of the Republic of the Philippines in a deft stroke of irony that left the world stunned by a sudden turn of events in February 1986. She is a beloved figure, a twentieth-century icon who has inherited a bundle of cultural contradictions and an economic nightmare in a lush paradise of corrupt, warring factions. In a Manila department store, one of the first souvenirs I buy my daughter is a rather homely Cory Aquino doll made out of brown cloth; the doll wears crooked wire eyeglasses, a straw shoulder bag, plastic high-heeled shoes, and Cory's signature yellow dress, with "I Love Cory" embroidered on the front. My daughter seems delighted with her doll, and the notion of a woman president.

Soldiers in disguise, patrol the countryside . . . Jungle not far away. So goes a song I once wrote, pungent as the remembered taste of mangoes overripe as my imagination, the memory of Manila the central character of the novel I am writing, the novel that brings me back to this torrid zone, my landscape haunted by ghosts and movie-lovers.

Nietzsche once said, "A joke is an epitaph for an emotion." Our laughter is pained, self-mocking. Blame it on *Rambo, Platoon,* and *Gidget Goes Hawaiian.* Cory Aquino has inherited a holy war, a class war, an amazing nation of people who've endured incredible poverty and spiritual loss with inherent humor and grace. Member of the ruling class, our pious president has also inherited an army of divided, greedy men. Yet probably no one will bother assassinating her, as icons are always useful.

My novel sits in its black folder, an obsession with me for over ten years. Home is now New York, but home in my heart will also always be Manila, and the rage of a marvelous culture stilled, confused, and diverted. Manila is my river of dreams choked with refuse, the refuse of refusal and denial, a denial more profound than the forbidding Catholic Church in all its ominous presence.

Blame it on the mambo and the cha-cha, a cardinal named Sin, and an adviser named Joker. Blame it on a former beauty queen with a puffy face bailed out of a jam by Doris Duke. Blame it on *Imeldification.* Blame it on children named Lourdes, Maria, Jesus, Carlos, Peachy, Baby, and Elvis. Blame it on the rich, who hang on in spite of everything. Blame it on the same people who are still in power, before Marcos, after Marcos. You name it, we'll blame it. The NPA, the vigilantes, rebel colonels nicknamed "Gringo," and a restless army plotting coups. Blame it on signs in nightclubs that warn: NO GUNS OR DRUGS.

Cards have been reshuffled, roles exchanged. The major players are the same, even those who suffered long years in prison under one regime, even those who died by the bullet. Aquino, Lopez, Cojuangco, Zobel, Laurel, Enrile, etc. etc. Blood against blood, controlling the destinies of so many disparate tribes in these seven thousand islands.

I remember my grandmother, Lola Tecla, going for drives with me as a child down the boulevard along Manila Bay. The boulevard led to Luneta Park, where Rizal was executed by the Spanish colonizers; it was then known as Dewey Boulevard, after an American admiral. From history books forced on me as a child at a convent school run by strict nuns, I learned a lopsided history of myself, one full of lies and blank spaces, a history of omission—a colonial version of history which scorned the "savage" ways of precolonial Filipinos. In those days even our language was kept at a distance; Tagalog was studied in a course called "National Language" (*sic*), but it was English that was spoken, English that was preferred. Tagalog was a language used to address servants. I scorned myself, and it was only later, after I had left the Philippines to settle in the country of my oppressor, that I learned to confront my demons and reinvent my own history.

I am writing a novel set in contemporary Philippines. It is a journey back I am always taking. I leave one place for the other, welcomed and embraced by the family I have left—fathers and brothers and cousins and uncles and aunts. Childhood sweethearts, now with their own children. I am unable to stay. I make excuses, adhere to tight schedules. I return, only to depart, weeks or months later, depending on finances and the weather, obligations to my daughter, my art, my addiction to life in the belly of one particular beast. I am the other, the exile within, afflicted with permanent nostalgia for the mud. I return, only to depart: Manila, New York, San Francisco, Manila, Honolulu, Detroit, Manila, Guam, Hong Kong, Zamboanga, Manila, New York, San Francisco, Tokyo, Manila again, Manila again, Manila again.

1992

Vulva Operetta

In my dream, sweaters are referred to as "vulvas." They are mohair or angora wool, of a soft, warm texture—gray, bleeding into a deep, rich red—similar to Japanese raku pottery.

We wear these sweaters.

5 *People say things like: "It's hot. I think I'll take my vulva off."*
Or: "It's cold. I think I'll put my vulva on."

Foppish men and women ask each other questions like: "Where did you get that BEE-YOO-TEE-FUL vulva?"
Followed by remarks like:
10 *"I think I'm gonna put my vulva in the closet. I think I'm gonna put my vulva in the closet. I think I'm gonna put my vulva. I'm gonna. My vulva. I."*

1992

Dorothy Allison b. 1949

Born in Greenville, South Carolina, to a fourteen-year-old mother, Dorothy Allison was raised near her large extended family. After her mother married, her aunts provided occasional refuge from an abusive stepfather. The violence and chaos of her upbringing, stemming largely from her family's poverty, fuel Allison's writing, as does the strength she saw in her relatives' survival despite such hopeless conditions. Her chance to escape came when a National Merit Scholarship paid for her to at-tend Florida Presbyterian College. She later earned a master's degree in anthro-pology from the New School for Social Re-search in New York.

Allison became active in the women's movement in the early seventies, working for several feminist publications and help-ing establish Herstore, a feminist book-store in Tallahassee, Florida. She credits feminism for enabling her to become a writer. Although she had begun writing as a child, she viewed writing the truth as such a dangerous activity that she burned everything she wrote. But in 1973 friends in the lesbian-feminist collective where she was living convinced her to stop destroying her work.

Her first book, *The Women Who Hate Me,* was a collection of poems, most written in reaction to the protest surrounding the 1982 Barnard College "Towards a Politics of Sexuality" conference. The intent of that feminist conference was to discuss sexuality in all its complexity, but anti-pornography protesters effectively shut down the event by appealing to university administrators and personally attacking conference participants. Allison's poems, which are frequently angry, focus on women's relationships and lesbian sexuality. An expanded version of the book was published in 1991 with the subtitle *Poetry 1980–1990.*

In 1988 Allison published *Trash,* a collection of emotionally intense, frequently violent, and often comic short stories. Class difference is a predominant theme, as many of her characters confront others' stereotypical expectations of rural southerners. The misunderstandings created by often romantic stereotypes are particularly poignant in stories depicting lesbian relationships. Given Allison's subject matter, it is not surprising that among the writers she credits as influences are Flannery O'Connor, James Baldwin, Eudora Welty, Tennessee Williams, Carson McCullers, Muriel Rukeyser, and Toni Morrison.

Allison's earliest published work established her audience and reputation primarily in the lesbian community. Her first novel, *Bastard out of Carolina* (1992), gained her national attention. It won the Lambda Award and was a finalist for the National Book Award. Loosely autobiographical, the compelling first-person narrative follows Bone Boatwright's survival of her stepfather's sexual abuse. In 1996 the novel became a film directed by Anjelica Huston.

Two or Three Things I Know for Sure, composed after Allison completed the novel, debuted as a performance piece at The Lab in San Francisco in August 1991. Revised for publication in 1995, the work, which traces Allison's family history by describing family photographs, explores the paradoxical power of stories to both support and delude. While Allison writes of her need to tell stories as part of her own survival, she also describes the "meanest" ones as those "the women [she] loved told themselves in secret—the stories that sustained and broke them." A short documentary based on the work, *Two or Three Things and Nothing for Sure,* by Tina DiFeliciantonio and Jane Wagner, won prizes at both the Aspen and the Toronto film festivals and aired on PBS in 1998.

In 1994 Allison published a collection of critical and political essays under the descriptive title *Skin: Talking About Sex, Class, and Literature.* Her second novel appeared in 1998. *Cavedweller,* a *New York Times* bestseller, portrays the relationships between a woman and her three daughters, two of whom she abandoned when she fled from their father. Reviews praised the language, characterization, and emotional power of the story but noted that the novel's structure weakens in the latter half. Allison is currently working on a project inspired by Janis Joplin. She lives in northern California with her partner Alix and her son Wolf.

Kelly Lynch Reames
Oklahoma State University

PRIMARY WORKS

The Women Who Hate Me, 1983; *Trash,* 1988; *The Women Who Hate Me: Poetry 1980–1990,* 1991; *Bastard out of Carolina,* 1992; *Skin: Talking About Sex, Class, and Literature,* 1994; *Two or Three Things I Know for Sure,* 1995; *Cavedweller,* 1998.

Don't Tell Me You Don't Know

I came out of the bathroom with my hair down wet on my shoulders. My Aunt Alma, my mama's oldest sister, was standing in the middle of Casey's dusty hooked rug looking like she had just flown in on it, her grey hair straggling out of its misshapen bun. For a moment I was so startled I couldn't move. Aunt Alma just stood there looking around at the big bare room with its two church pews bracketing the only other furniture—a massive pool table. I froze while the water ran down from my hair to dampen the collar of the oversized tuxedo shirt I used for a bathrobe.

"Aunt Alma," I stammered, "well . . . welcome. . . ."

"You really live here?" she breathed, as if, even for me, such a situation was quite past her ability to believe. "Like this?"

I looked around as if I were seeing it for the first time myself, shrugged and tried to grin. "It's big," I offered, "lots of space, four porches, all these windows. We get along well here, might not in a smaller place." I looked back through the kitchen to Terry's room with its thick dark curtains covering a wall of windows. Empty. So was Casey's room on the other side of the kitchen. It was quiet and still, with no one even walking through the rooms overhead.

"Thank God," I whispered to myself. Nobody else was home.

Aunt Alma turned around slowly and stepped over to the mantel with the old fly-spotted mirror over it. She pushed a few of her loose hairs back and then laid her big rattan purse up by a stack of fliers Terry had left there, brushing some of the dust away first.

"My God," she echoed, "dirtier than we ever lived. Didn't think you'd turn out like this."

I shrugged again, embarrassed and angry and trying not to show it. Well hell, what could I do? I hadn't seen her in so long. She hadn't even been around that last year I'd lived with Mama, and I wasn't sure I particularly wanted to see her now. But why was she here anyway? How had she found me?

I closed the last two buttons on my shirt and tried to shake some of the water out of my hair. Aunt Alma watched me through the dark spots of the mirror, her mouth set in an old familiar line. "Well," I said, "I didn't expect to see you." I reached up to push hair back out of my eyes. "You want to sit down?"

Aunt Alma turned around and bumped her hip against the pool table. "Where?" One disdainful glance rendered the pews for what they were—exquisitely uncomfortable even for my hips. Her expression reminded me of my Uncle Jack's jokes about her, about how she refused to go back to church till they put in rocking chairs.

"No rocking chairs here," I laughed, hoping she'd laugh with me. Aunt Alma just leaned forward and rocked one of the balls on the table against another. Her mouth kept its flat, impartial expression. I tried gesturing across the pool table to my room and the big waterbed outlined in sunlight and tree shade from the three windows overlooking it.

"It's cleaner in there," I offered, "it's my room. This is our collective space." I gestured around.

"Collective," my aunt echoed me again, but the way she said the word expressed clearly her opinion of such arrangements. She looked toward my room with its narrow cluttered desk and stacks of books, then turned back to the pool table as by far the more interesting view. She rocked the balls again so that the hollow noise of the thump resounded against the high, dim ceiling.

"Pitiful," she sighed, and gave me a sharp look, her washed-out blue eyes almost angry. Two balls broke loose from the others and rolled idly across the matted green surface of the table. The sunlight reflecting through the oak leaves outside made Aunt Alma's face seem younger than I remembered it, some of the hard edge eased off the square jaw.

"Your mama is worried about you."

"I don't know why." I turned my jaw to her, knowing it would remind her of how much alike we had always been, the people who had said I was more her child than my mama's. "I'm fine. Mama should know that. I spoke to her not too long ago."

"How long ago?"

I frowned, mopped at my head some more. Two months, three, last month? "I'm not sure . . . Reese's birthday. I think it was Reese's birthday."

"Three months." My aunt rocked one ball back and forth across her palm, a yellow nine ball. The light filtering into the room went a shade darker. The -9- gleamed pale through her fingers. I looked more closely at her. She looked just as she had when I was thirteen, her hair grey in that loose bun, her hands large and swollen, her body straining the seams of the faded print dress. She'd worn her hair short for a while, but it was grown long again now, and the print dress under her coat could have been any dress she'd worn in the last twenty years. She'd gotten old, suddenly, after the birth of her eighth child, but since then she seemed not to change at all. She looked now as if she would go on forever—a worn stubborn woman who didn't care what you saw when you looked at her.

I drew breath in slowly, carefully. I knew from old experience to use caution in dealing with any of my aunts, and this was the oldest and most formidable. I'd seen grown men break down and cry when she'd kept that look on them too long; little children repent and swear to change their ways. But I'd also seen my other aunts stare her right back, and like them I was a grown woman minding my own business. I had a right to look her in the eye, I told myself. I was no wayward child, no half-drunk, silly man. I was her namesake, my mama's daughter. I had to be able to look her in the eye. If I couldn't, I was in trouble, and I didn't want that kind of trouble here, 500 miles and half a lifetime away from my aunts and the power of their eyes.

Slow, slow, the balls rocked one against the other. Aunt Alma looked over at me levelly. I let the water run down between my breasts, looked back at her. My mama's sister. I could feel the tears pushing behind my eyes. It had been so long since I'd seen her or any of them! The last time I'd been to Old Henderson Road had been years back. Aunt Alma had stood on that sagging porch and looked at me, memorizing me, both of us knowing we might not see each other again. She'd moved her mouth and I'd seen the pain there, the shadow of the nephew behind her—yet another one she was raising since her youngest son, another cousin of mine, had run off and left the girl who'd birthed that boy. The pain in her eyes was achingly clear to me, the certain awful knowledge that measured all her children and wrenched her heart.

Something wrong with that boy, my uncles had laughed.

Yeah, something. Dropped on his head one too many times, you think?

I think.

My aunt, like my mama, understood everything, expected nothing, and watched her own life like a terrible fable from a Sunday morning sermon. It was the perspective that all those women shared, the view that I could not, for my life, accept. I believed, I believed with all my soul that death was behind it, that death was the seed and the fruit of that numbed and numbing attitude. More than anything else, it was my anger that had driven me away from them, driven them away from me—my unpredictable, automatic anger. Their anger, their hatred, always seemed shielded, banked and secret, and because of that—shameful. My uncles were sudden, violent, and daunting. My aunts wore you down without ever seeming to fight at all. It was my anger that my aunts thought queer, my wild raging temper they respected in a boy and discouraged in a girl. That I slept with girls was curious, but not dangerous. That I slept with a knife under my pillow and refused to step aside for my uncles was more than queer. It was crazy.

Aunt Alma's left eye twitched, and I swallowed my tears, straightened my head, and looked her full in the face. I could barely hold myself still, barely return her look. Again those twin emotions, the love and the outrage that I'd always felt for my aunt, warred in me. I wanted to put out my hand and close my fingers on her hunched, stubborn shoulder. I wanted to lay my head there and pull tight to her, but I also wanted to hit her, to scream and kick and make her ashamed of herself. Nothing was clean between us, especially not our love.

Between my mama and Aunt Alma there were five other sisters. The most terrible and loved was Bess, the one they swore had always been so smart. From the time I was eight Aunt Bess had a dent in the left side of her head—a shadowed dent that emphasized the twitch of that eye, just like the twitch Aunt Alma has, just like the twitch I sometimes get, the one they tell me is nerves. But Aunt Bess wasn't born with that twitch as we were, just as she wasn't born with that dent. My uncle, her husband, had come up from the deep dust on the road, his boots damp from the river, picking up clumps of dust and making mud, knocking it off on her steps, her screen door, her rug, the back rung of a kitchen chair. She'd shouted at him, "Not on my clean floor!" and he'd swung the bucket, river-stained and heavy with crawfish. He'd hit her in the side of the head—dented her into a lifetime of stupidity and half-blindness. Son of a bitch never even said he was sorry, and all my childhood he'd laughed at her, the way she'd sometimes stop in the middle of a sentence and grope painfully for a word.

None of *them* had told me that story. I had been grown and out of the house before one of the Greenwood cousins had told it so I understood, and as much as I'd hated him then, I'd raged at them more.

"You let him live?" I'd screamed at them. "He did that to her and you did nothing! You did nothing to him, nothing for her."

"What'd you want us to do?"

My Aunt Grace had laughed at me. "You want us to cut him up and feed him to the river? What good would that have done her or her children?"

She'd shaken her head, and they had all stared at me as if I were still a child and didn't understand the way the world was. The cold had gone through me then, as if the river were running up from my bowels. I'd felt my hands curl up and reach, but there was nothing to reach for. I'd taken hold of myself, my insides, and tried desperately to voice the terror that was tearing at me.

"But to leave her with him after he did that, to just let it stand, to let him get away with it." I'd reached and reached, trying to get to them, to make them feel the wave moving up and through me. "It's like all of it, all you let them get away with."

"Them?" My mama had watched my face as if afraid of what she might find there. "Who do you mean? And what do you think we could do?"

I couldn't say it. I'd stared into mama's face, and looked from her to all of them, to those wide, sturdy cheekbones, those high, proud eyebrows, those set and terrible mouths. I had always thought of them as mountains, mountains that everything conspired to grind but never actually broke. The women of my family were all I had ever believed in. What was I if they were not what I had shaped them in my own mind? All I had known was that I had to get away from them—all of them—the men who could do those terrible things and the women who would let it happen to you. I'd never forgiven any of them.

It might have been more than three months since I had talked to Mama on the telephone. It had been far longer than that since I had been able to really talk to any of them. The deepest part of me didn't believe that I would ever be able to do so. I dropped my eyes and pulled myself away from Aunt Alma's steady gaze. I wanted to reach for her, touch her, maybe cry with her, if she'd let me.

"People will hurt you more with pity than with hate," she'd always told me. "I can hate back, or laugh at them, but goddamn the son of a bitch that hands me pity."

No pity. Not allowed. I reached to rock a ball myself.

"Want to play?" I tried looking up into her eyes again. It was too close. Both of us looked away.

"I'll play myself." She set about racking up the balls. Her mouth was still set in that tight line. I dragged a kitchen stool in and sat in the doorway out of her way, telling myself I had to play this casually, play this as family, and wait and see what the point was.

"Where's Uncle Bill?" I was rubbing my head again and trying to make conversation.

"What do you care? I don't think Bill said ten words to you in your whole life." She rolled the rack forward and back, positioning it perfectly for the break. "'Course he didn't say many more to anybody else either." She grinned, not looking at me, talking as if she were pouring tea at her own kitchen table. "Nobody can say I married that man for his conversation."

She leaned into her opening shot, and I leaned forward in appreciation. She had a great stance, her weight centered over her massive thighs. My family runs to heavy women, gravy-fed working women, the kind usually seen in pictures taken at mining disasters. Big women, all of my aunts move under their own power and stalk around telling everybody else what to do. But Aunt Alma was the prototype, the one I had loved most, starting back when she had given us free meals in the roadhouse she'd run for a while. It had been one of those bad times when my stepfather had been out of work and he and Mama were always fighting. Mama would load us all in the Pontiac and crank it up on seventy-five cents worth of gas, just enough to get to Aunt Alma's place on the Eustis Highway. Once there, we'd be fed on chicken gravy and biscuits, and Mama would be fed from the well of her sister's love and outrage.

You tell that bastard to get his ass out on the street. Whining don't make money. Cursing don't get a job . . .

Bitching don't make the beds and screaming don't get the tomatoes planted. They had laughed together then, speaking a language of old stories and older jokes.

You tell him.

I said.

Now girl, you listen to me.

The power in them, the strength and the heat! How could anybody not love my mama, my aunts? How could my daddy, my uncles, ever stand up to them, dare to raise hand or voice to them? They were a power on the earth.

I breathed deep, watching my aunt rock on her stance, settling her eye on the balls, while I smelled chicken gravy and hot grease, the close thick scent of love and understanding. I used to love to eat at Aunt Alma's house, all those home-cooked dinners at the roadhouse; pinto beans with peppers for fifteen, nine of them hers. Chow-chow on a clean white plate passed around the table while the biscuits passed the other way. My aunt always made biscuits. What else stretched so well? Now those starch meals shadowed her loose shoulders and dimpled her fat white elbows.

She gave me one quick glance and loosed her stroke. The white ball punched the center of the table. The balls flew to the edges. My sixty-year-old aunt gave a grin that would have scared piss out of my Uncle Bill, a grin of pure, fierce enjoyment. She rolled the stick in fingers loose as butter on a biscuit, laughed again, and slid her palms down the sides of polished wood, while the anger in her face melted into skill and concentration.

I rocked back on my stool and covered my smile with my wet hair. Goddamn! Aunt Alma pushed back on one ankle, swung the stick to follow one ball, another, dropping them as easily as peas on potatoes. Goddamn! She went after those balls like kids on a dirt yard, catching each lightly and dropping them lovingly. Into the holes, move it! Turning and bracing on ankles thickened with too many years of flour and babies, Aunt Alma blitzed that table like a twenty-year-old hustler, not sparing me another glance.

Not till the eighth stroke did she pause and stop to catch her breath.

"You living like this—not for a man, huh?" she asked, one eyebrow arched and curious.

"No," I shrugged, feeling more friendly and relaxed. Moving like that, aunt of mine I wanted to say, don't tell me you don't understand.

"Your mama said you were working in some photo shop, doing shit work for shit money. Not much to show for that college degree, is that?"

"Work is work. It pays the rent."

"Which ought not to be much here."

"No," I agreed, "not much. I know," I waved my hands lightly, "it's a wreck of a place, but it's home. I'm happy here. Terry, Casey and everybody—they're family."

"Family." Her mouth hardened again. "You have a family, don't you remember? These girls might be close, might be important to you, but they're not family. You know that." Her eyes said more, much more. Her eyes threw the word *family* at me like a spear. All her longing, all her resentment of my abandonment was in that word, and not only hers, but Mama's and my sisters' and all the cousins' I had carefully not given my new address.

"How about a beer?" I asked. I wanted one myself. "I've got a can of Pabst in the icebox."

"A glass of water," she said. She leaned over the table to line up her closing shots.

I brought her a glass of water. "You're good," I told her, wanting her to talk to me about how she had learned to play pool, anything but family and all this stuff I so much did not want to think about.

"Children," she stared at me again. "What about children?" There was something in her face then that waited, as if no question were more important, as if she knew the only answer I could give.

Enough, I told myself, and got up without a word to get myself that can of Pabst. I did not look in her eyes. I walked into the kitchen on feet that felt suddenly unsteady and tender. Behind me, I heard her slide the cue stick along the rim of the table and then draw it back to set up another shot.

Play it out, I cursed to myself, just play it out and leave me alone. Everything is so simple for you, so settled. Make babies. Grow a garden. Handle some man like he's just another child. Let everything come that comes, die that dies; let everything go where it goes. I drank straight from the can and watched her through the doorway. All my uncles were drunks, and I was more like them than I had ever been like my aunts.

Aunt Alma started talking again, walking around the table, measuring shots and not even looking in my direction. "You remember when ya'll lived out on Greenlake Road? Out on that dirt road where that man kept that old egg-busting dog? Your mama couldn't keep a hen to save her life till she emptied a shell and filled it again with chicken shit and baby piss. Took that dog right out of himself when he ate it. Took him right out of the taste for hens and eggs." She stopped to take a deep breath, sweat glittering on her lip. With one hand she wiped it away, the other going white on the pool cue.

"I still had Annie then. Lord, I never think about her anymore."

I remembered then the last child she had borne, a tiny girl with a heart that fluttered with every breath, a baby for whom the doctors said nothing could be done, a baby they swore wouldn't see six months. Aunt Alma had kept her in an okra basket and carried her everywhere, talking to her one minute like a kitten or a doll and the next minute like a grown woman. Annie had lived to be four, never outgrowing the vegetable basket, never talking back, just lying there and smiling like a wise old woman, dying between a smile and a laugh while Aunt Alma never interrupted the story that had almost made Annie laugh.

I sipped my beer and watched my aunt's unchanging face. Very slowly she swung the pool cue up and down, not quite touching the table. After a moment she stepped in again and leaned half her weight on the table. The 5-ball became a bird murdered in flight, dropping suddenly into the far right pocket.

Aunt Alma laughed out loud, delighted. "Never lost it," she crowed. "Four years in the roadhouse with that table set up in the back. Every one of them sons of mine thought he was going to make money on it. Lord those boys! Never made a cent." She swallowed the rest of her glass of water.

"But me," she wiped the sweat away again. "I never would have done it for money. I just loved it. Never went home without playing myself three or four games. Sometimes I'd set Annie up on the side and we'd pretend we was playing. I'd tell her when I was taking her shots. And she'd shout when I'd sink 'em. I let her win most every time."

She stopped, put both hands on the table, closed her eyes.

"'Course, just after we lost her, we lost the roadhouse." She shook her head, eyes still closed. "Never did have anything fine that I didn't lose."

The room was still, dust glinted in the sunlight past her ears. She opened her eyes and looked directly at me.

"I don't care," she began slowly, softly. "I don't care if you're queer or not. I don't care if you take puppydogs to bed, for that matter, but your mother was all my heart for twenty years when nobody else cared what happened to me. She stood by me. I've stood by her and I always thought to do the same for you and yours. But she's sitting there, did you know that? She's sitting there like nothing's left of her life, like . . . like she hates her life and won't say shit to nobody about it. She wouldn't tell me. She won't tell me what it is, what has happened."

I sat the can down on the stool, closed my own eyes, dropped my head. I didn't want to see her. I didn't want her to be there. I wanted her to go away, disappear out of my life the way I'd run out of hers. Go away, old woman. Leave me alone. Don't talk to me. Don't tell me your stories. I an't a baby in a basket, and I can't lie still for it.

"You know. You know what it is. The way she is about you. I know it has to be you—something about you. I want to know what it is, and you're going to tell me. Then you're going to come home with me and straighten this out. There's a lot I an't never been able to fix, but this time, this thing, I'm going to see it out. I'm going to see it fixed."

I opened my eyes and she was still standing there, the cue stick shiny in her hand, her face all flushed and tight.

"Go," I said and heard my voice, a scratchy, strangling cry in the big room. "Get out of here."

"What did you tell her? What did you say to your mama?"

"Ask her. Don't ask me. I don't have nothing to say to you."

The pool cue rose slowly, slowly till it touched the right cheek, the fine lines of broken blood vessels, freckles, and patchy skin. She shook her head slowly. My throat pulled tighter and tighter until it drew my mouth down and open. Like a shot the cue swung. The table vibrated with the blow. Her cheeks pulled tight, the teeth all a grimace. The cue split and broke. White dust rose in a cloud. The echo hurt my ears while her hands rose up as fists, the broken cue in her right hand as jagged as the pain in her face.

"Don't you say that to me. Don't you treat me like that. Don't you know who I am, what I am to you? I didn't have to come up here after you. I could have let it run itself out, let it rest on your head the rest of your life, just let you carry it—your mama's life. YOUR MAMA'S LIFE, GIRL. Don't you understand me? I'm talking about your mama's life."

She threw the stick down, turned away from me, her shoulders heaving and shaking, her hands clutching nothing. "I an't talking about your stepfather. I an't talking about no man at all. I'm talking about your mama sitting at her kitchen table, won't talk to nobody, won't eat, won't listen to nothing. What'd she ever ask from you? Nothing. Just gave you your life and everything she had. Worked herself ugly for you and your sister. Only thing she ever hoped for was to do the same for your children, someday to sit herself back and hold her grandchildren on her lap. . . ."

It was too much. I couldn't stand it.

"GODDAMN YOU!" I was shaking all over. "CHILDREN! All you ever talk about—you and her and all of you. Like that was the end-all and be-all of everything. Never mind what happens to them once they're made. That don't matter. It's only the getting of them. Like some goddamned crazy religion. Get your mother a grandchild and solve all her problems. Get yourself a baby and forget everything else. It's what you were born for, the one thing you can do with no thinking about it at all. Only I can't. To get her a grandchild, I'd have to steal one!"

I was wringing my own hands, twisting them together and pulling them apart. Now I swung them open and slapped down at my belly, making my own hollow noise in the room.

"No babies in there, aunt of mine, and never going to be. I'm sterile as a clean tin can. That's what I told Mama, and not to hurt her. I told her because she wouldn't leave me alone about it. Like you, like all of you, always talking about children, never able to leave it alone." I was walking back and forth now, unable to stop myself from talking. "Never able to hear me when I warned her to leave it be. Going on and on till I thought I'd lose my mind."

I looked her in the eye, loving her and hating her, and not wanting to speak, but hearing the words come out anyway. "Some people never do have babies, you know. Some people get raped at eleven by a stepfather their mama half-hates but can't afford to leave. Some people then have to lie and hide it 'cause it would make so much trouble. So nobody will know, not the law and not the rest of the family. Nobody but the women supposed to be the ones who take care of everything, who know what to do and how to do it, the women who make children who believe in them and trust in them, and sometimes die for it. Some people never go to a doctor and don't find out for ten years that the son of a bitch gave them some goddamned disease."

I looked away, unable to stand how grey her face had gone.

"You know what it does to you when the people you love most in the world, the people you believe in—cannot survive without believing in—when those people do nothing, don't even know something needs to be done? When you cannot hate them but cannot help yourself? The hatred grows. It just takes over everything, eats you up and makes you somebody full of hate."

I stopped. The roar that had been all around me stopped, too. The cold was all through me now. I felt like it would never leave me. I heard her move. I heard her hip bump the pool table and make the balls rock. I heard her turn and gather up her purse. I opened my eyes to see her moving toward the front door. That cold cut me then like a knife in fresh slaughter. I knew certainly that she'd go back and take care of Mama, that she'd never say a word, probably never tell anybody she'd been here. 'Cause then she'd have to talk about the other thing, and I knew as well as she that however much she tried to forget it, she'd really always known. She'd done nothing then. She'd do nothing now. There was no justice. There was no justice in the world.

When I started to cry it wasn't because of that. It wasn't because of babies or no babies, or pain that was so far past I'd made it a source of strength. It wasn't even that I'd hurt her so bad, hurt Mama when I didn't want to. I cried because of the things I hadn't said, didn't know how to say, cried most of all because behind everything else there was no justice for my aunts or my mama. Because each of them to save their lives had tried to be strong, had become, in fact, as strong and determined as life would let them. I and all their children had believed in that strength, had believed in them and their ability to do anything, fix anything, survive anything. None of us had ever been able to forgive ourselves that we and they were not strong enough, that strength itself was not enough.

Who can say where that strength ended, where the world took over and rolled us all around like balls on a pool table? None of us ever would. I brought my hands up to my neck and pulled my hair around until I clenched it in my fists, remembering how my aunt used to pick up Annie to rub that baby's belly beneath her chin—Annie bouncing against her in perfect trust. Annie had never had to forgive her mama anything.

"Aunt Alma, wait. Wait!"

She stopped in the doorway, her back trembling, her hands gripping the doorposts. I could see the veins raised over her knuckles, the cords that stood out in her neck, the flesh as translucent as butter beans cooked until the skins come loose. Talking to my mama over the phone, I had not been able to see her face, her skin, her stunned and haunted eyes. If I had been able to see her, would I have ever said those things to her?

"I'm sorry."

She did not look back. I let my head fall back, rolled my shoulders to ease the painful clutch of my own muscles. My teeth hurt. My ears stung. My breasts felt hot and swollen. I watched the light as it moved on her hair.

"I'm sorry. I would . . . I would . . . anything. If I could change things, if I could help. . . ."

I stopped. Tears were running down my face. My aunt turned to me, her wide pale face as wet as mine. "Just come home with me. Come home for a little while. Be with your mama a little while. You don't have to forgive her. You don't have to forgive anybody. You just come to love her the way she loves you. Like I love you. Oh girl, don't you know how we love you!"

I put my hands out, let them fall apart on the pool table. My aunt was suddenly across from me, reaching across the table, taking my hands, sobbing into the cold dirty stillness—an ugly sound, not softened by the least self-consciousness. When I leaned forward, she leaned to me and our heads met, her grey hair against my temple brightened by the sunlight pouring in the windows.

"Oh, girl! Girl, you are our precious girl."

I cried against her cheek, and it was like being five years old again in the roadhouse, with Annie's basket against my hip, the warmth in the room purely a product of the love that breathed out from my aunt and my mama. If they were not mine, if I was not theirs, who was I? I opened my mouth, put my tongue out, and tasted my aunt's cheek and my own. Butter and salt, dust and beer, sweat and stink, flesh of my flesh.

"Precious," I breathed back to her.

"Precious."

1988

Víctor Hernández Cruz b. 1949

Born in Aguas Buenas, a small mountain town in Puerto Rico, Víctor Hernández Cruz moved with his family to the States when he was five. He attended Benjamin Franklin High School in New York City and was associated with The Gut Theater on East 104th Street. He published *Snaps,* his first collection of poetry, when he was twenty. From the early 1970s, Hernández Cruz lived in San Francisco; in 1990 he returned to Aguas Buenas, where he continues to write in both English and Spanish.

His poetry has been described as "the most conscious of literary forms, and the most influenced by present tendencies in American literature" among Puerto Rican writers in the United States. It is, indeed, highly introspective and abstract, preoccupied with form, rhythm, and language. His poems lack the referential context to popular culture and life in El Barrio which characterizes the work of Tato Laviera and Miguel Algarín, for example. Rather, his intellectualizing voice exhibits influences of various literary movements, such as minimalism and concrete poetry, among others. Nonetheless, his poems and prose pieces capture Hispanic images and symbols in the urban milieu.

One distinguishing feature of Hernández Cruz's poetry is its conscious language choices. The poet plays with both English and Spanish words, with spelling and phonetics, suggesting at times simultaneous American and Puerto Rican readings. The title of his book *By Lingual Wholes* illustrates his playful and witty use of language. *By Lingual* echoes the word "bilingual," and the concept *wholes,* which implies both totality and absence—(w)holes—unifies the poems in this collection. The book

itself is a collage in which spatial and visual signs are part of the poem's meaning, as they are in the work of the Brazilian concrete poets. Poetry and prose are intertwined with one-word poems, haikus, short stories, prose poems, and an empty appendix. The epigraph to the book signals this playful yet serious hybridization: "Speech changing within space."

Hernández Cruz's vision of the transformation of literary English because of its contact with Spanish is his unique contribution to American literature. Just as Spanish in the States has been transforming itself into the distinct dialects of the various Hispanic groups who live here, English also has been affected by Hispanic writers. Hernández Cruz believes that the English syntax is being changed through the Spanish influence. His work is substantially enriched by the mixture and interplay of the two languages, and by the meaningful intersections between English and Spanish. However, in *Panoramas,* he proposes that English and Spanish not be mixed.

His poetry has evolved from the fragmented and often violent images of urban life, experiences with drugs, and existential beliefs during his youth—as in *Snaps*—to a dynamic and sometimes profound expression of biculturalism and bilingualism. Cosmopolitan and urban, his poetry stands without sacrificing images of Hispanic origin, culture, and tradition. His is the language of the urban, intellectual Latino who nevertheless cannot survive without transforming the past into the present.

Frances R. Aparicio
University of Illinois at Chicago

PRIMARY WORKS

Snaps, 1969; *Mainland,* 1973; *Tropicalization,* 1976; *By Lingual Wholes,* 1982; *Rhythm, Content and Flavor,* 1989; *Red Beans,* 1991; *Panoramas,* 1997; *Maraca,* 2001; *The Mountain in the Sea,* 2006.

urban dream

1

there was fire & the people were yelling.   running crazing.
screaming & falling.   moving up side down.   there was fire.
fires.   & more fires.   & walls caving to the ground.   & mercy
mercy.   death.   bodies falling down.   under bottles flying in the
5 air. garbage cans going up against windows.   a car singing
brightly a blue flame.   a snatch. a snag.   sounds of bombs.   &
other things blowing up.
times square
electrified.   burned.   smashed. stomped
10 hey over here
hey you.   where you going.
no walking.   no running.   no standing.
STOP
you crazy.   running.   stick
15 this stick up your eyes.   pull your heart out.
hey.

2

after noise.   comes silence.   after brightness (or great big flames)
comes darkness.   goes with whispering.   (even soft music can be heard)
even lips smacking.   foots stepping all over bones & ashes, all over
20 blood & broken lips that left their head somewhere else, all over
livers, & bright white skulls with hair on them. standing over a river
watching hamburgers floating by.   steak with teeth in them.
flags.   & chairs.   & beds.   & golf sets.   & mickeymouse broken
in
25 half.
governors & mayors step out the show.   they split.

3

dancing arrives.

1969

Mountain Building

The mountains have changed to buildings
Is this hallway the inside of a stem
That has a rattling flower for a head,
Immense tree bark with roots made out of
5　Mailboxes?
In the vertical village moons fly out of
Apartment windows and though what you
See is a modern city
The mountain's guitars pluck inside
10　It's agriculture taking an elevator
Through urban caves which lead to
Paths underground They say Camuy
To Hutuado[1]
Taino subground like the IRT in
15　constant motion

The streets take walks in your dark eyes
Seashell necklaces make music in the
Origin of silence
What are we stepping on? Pineapple
20　Fields frozen with snow
Concrete dirt later the rocks of the
Atlantic
The sculpture of the inner earth
Down there where you thought only worms
25　and unnamed crocodiles parade
Lefty stands on a corner
Analyzing every seed
Squeezing the walls as he passes
Through at the bottom of the basement
30　Where the boiler makes heat

The flesh arrives out of a hole
In the mountain that goes up like a
Green wall
Bodies come in making *maraca*[2] sounds
35　An invisible map out of the flora
Bees arrive in the vicinity and sing
Chorus while woody woodpeckers make
Women out of trees and place flowers
On their heads

[1]Refers to the underground caves at Camuy,　　[2]Rattle—musical instrument of Taíno origin.
Puerto Rico.

40 Waterfalls like Hurakan's faucets
    Caress the back of Yuquiyu[3]
    Arawak's echoes

    Hallway of graffiti like the master
    Cave drawings made by owls when they
45 Had hands
    You see the fish with pyramids inside
    Their stomachs
    Hanging near the doorways where
    San Lazaro[4] turns the keys
50 Villa Manhattan
    Breeze of saint juice made from
    Coconuts
    Slide down the stairs to your
    Belly and like a hypnotized *guanábana*[5]
55 You float down the street
    And win all your hands at dominoes

    The Moros live on the top floor eating
    Roots and have a rooster on the roof
    Africans import okra from the bodega
60 The Indians make a base of *guava*
    On the first floor
    The building is spinning itself into
    a spiral of *salsa*
    Heaven must be calling or the
65 Residents know the direction
    Because there is an upward pull
    If you rise too quickly from your seat
    You might have to comb a spirit's
    Hair
70 They float over the chimneys
    Arrive through the smog
    Appear through the plaster of Paris
    It is the same people in the windowed
    Mountains.

                                1982

---

[3]Hurakan and Yuquiyu: Indian deities (Taíno).   [5]Soursop.
[4]Saint Lazarus.

Table of Contents

Your tablet is your inner workings, your grasp on the board, which is shifting, trying to knock the items balanced on the table kitchen or desk, motion *contestivis* of accumulated objects. Objectivity too is matter of this piece of wood. A *tabla* is in the dictionary, transporting itself like: *tabla* (1) *(de madera)* of wood: if you lose this you lose grip as implied in conversation somewhere like Rio Piedras, Puerto Rico; (2) *(de metal)* sheets: moments among buildings, big structures, boats, autos, irons ironing your skull base for greater irony; (3) *(de piedra)* slab: also chunk of reality, let's say a piece of voice not knowing its pretty qualities are being used beyond its own life; (4) *(de tierra)* strip: episode which should be recalled right in the strip; this feels like going through distance back to a time that was slowly being eaten by this moment when it is still trying to hold onto the table; (5) *(cuadro pintado en una tabla):* situation which has been thoroughly explained into your metabolism or a framework, something that works within a frame of four sides painted clearly so you can distinguish shapes, and *contenido* reversed means *nest contained.* This is a list of tables. Broken legs will lose the tablet, and you will place your fingers on the wrong weather. Whether you at the time thought perfect your box of index, this tablature will accurately give you all the stops on a road for which you have an unsecured map with inscriptions and designs.

   Let us not lose our table as we praise the importance of its acquisition. So the flow goes that it is also a catalogue *catalogo—cadaloco* means each crazy one of all the material involved. Such a list is the one you have to have faith in to maintain your tables analogous to your mind health. This wealth leads to a Spanish *(table de lavar)* wash table where the surgeons reconstruct dilapidated jungles inside of your vision from which they (this) move you (to a *tabla de planchar*) and stretch you out (to *tabla de salvación*), at which point you might have capreached and you would *(tener tablas)* to present your presence on a stage to the world and bad light would not harm you. Tablear cuts you into pieces, separates you into patches / streams / numbers / notes till you level to approachable grade for tabletear signifies to rattle, ultimately, realizations that a table has four legs and within it contains space, unless it is the table of multiplication, whereupon you will see everything in doubles or substance folded. Tabloid stretched out has many stories that are placed one by the other into pictures and features done so you can continue to follow your interests and arrange them in your pocket neatly like a well-versed drum alphabetizing names of peoples and whereabouts of mountains visible and under earth. Figures pop into your *tabula rasa,* empty where there is no grease or *grasa,* a simple search for *gracia* gracing this directory which has given deep tales and details of detours so we may come to a *principio* or principles. Let us now table this tablederia of context tabled.

1982

Carolyn Forché b. 1950

Carolyn Forché's spirited paternal grand-mother, Anna, a Slovak immigrant, spoke "a funny English," in the poet's words, partly to display her resistance to American culture. Forché's life and poetry have responded to the challenge in Anna's declaration: "in your country / you have nothing" ("Endurance"). Anna nicknamed Carolyn *Piskata*, "Chatterbox," and passed on to her granddaughter an old homily: "Eat Bread and Salt and Speak the Truth" ("Burning the Tomato Worms"). Forché was born in Detroit; her father, Michael Sidlosky, labored as a tool and die maker ten and twelve hours a day, six and sometimes seven days a week. Her mother, Louise, bore seven children before attending college.

Forché was educated in Catholic schools and then graduated from Michigan State University. She has an M.F.A. from Bowling Green State University (1975) and an honorary doctorate from Russell Sage College (1985).

Her first book of poems, *Gathering the Tribes,* received the Yale Series of Younger Poets Award in 1975. These poems derived partly from Forché's alternately living among Pueblo Indians near Taos, New Mexico, and backpacking in the desert regions of Utah, on the Pacific Crest Trail, and in the Okanogan region of British Columbia. As its title suggests, this volume is characterized not by the self-absorption of much twentieth-century American verse but by a desire for community—incorporating, among other voices, those of the "silenced" Pueblo Indians and her own Slovak ancestors.

From January 1978 to March 1980, Forché made a number of trips to El Salvador; during this period she documented human rights violations for Amnesty International, verifying information and evaluating the organization's reports on El Salvador. While living in El Salvador, she also wrote seven of the 22 poems included in *The Country Between Us,* her second collection and the Academy of American Poets' 1981 Lamont Poetry Selection. In 1980 Forché worked closely with Monsignor Oscar Romero, the beloved Archbishop of San Salvador who was assassinated that year by a right-wing death squad; after several attempts had been made on Forché's life, Monsignor Romero asked that she return to the United States to "tell the American people what is happening." She has said that her El Salvador experience transformed her life and work: it "prevent[s] me from ever viewing myself or my country again through precisely the same fog of unwitting connivance" ("El Salvador: An Aide Memoire").

Forché continues to travel and to act on her beliefs. In 1983 she accompanied a congressional fact-finding delegation to Israel; in 1984 she contributed to the program *All Things Considered* on National Public Radio from Beirut, Lebanon; from December 1985 to March 1986 she lived in South Africa. She has held numerous teaching positions at American universities.

Denise Levertov's praise for *The Country Between Us* suggests what Forché accomplishes: a seamless merging of the "personal and political, lyrical and engaged." Her important anthology, *Against Forgetting: Twentieth Century Poetry of Witness,* and her 1994 collection of poems, *The Angel of History,* a consummate book of fragmented images and characters who voice the largely untold narratives of modern wars, brought her the Swedish Edita and Ira Morris Award for Peace and Culture in 1998.

Constance Coiner
State University of New York at Binghamton

Linda Wagner-Martin
University of North Carolina–Chapel Hill

PRIMARY WORKS

Gathering the Tribes, 1976; *The Country Between Us,* 1982; *Flowers from the Volcano,* translations of the poetry of Claribel Alegría, 1982; *El Salvador: Work of Thirty Photographers,* 1983; *The Angel of History,* 1994; *Sorrow,* 1999; *Blue Hour,* 2003.

from The Country between Us

The Colonel

WHAT YOU HAVE HEARD IS TRUE. I was in his house. His wife carried a tray of coffee and sugar. His daughter filed her nails, his son went out for the night. There were daily papers, pet dogs, a pistol on the cushion beside him. The moon swung bare on its black cord over the house. On the television was a cop show. It was in English. Broken bottles were embedded in the walls around the house to scoop the kneecaps from a man's legs or cut his hands to lace. On the windows there were gratings like those in liquor stores. We had dinner, rack of lamb, good wine, a gold bell was on the table for calling the maid. The maid brought green mangoes, salt, a type of bread. I was asked how I enjoyed the country. There was a brief commercial in Spanish. His wife took everything away. There was some talk then of how difficult it had become to govern. The parrot said hello on the terrace. The colonel told it to shut up, and pushed himself from the table. My friend said to me with his eyes: say nothing. The colonel returned with a sack used to bring groceries home. He spilled many human ears on the table. They were like dried peach halves. There is no other way to say this. He took one of them in his hands, shook it in our faces, dropped it into a water glass. It came alive there. I am tired of fooling around he said. As for the rights of anyone, tell your people they can go fuck themselves. He swept the ears to the floor with his arm and held the last of his wine in the air. Something for your poetry, no? he said. Some of the ears on the floor caught this scrap of his voice. Some of the ears on the floor were pressed to the ground.

May 1978

1982

Because One Is Always Forgotten

In Memoriam, José Rudolfo Viera[1] 1939–1981: El Salvador

When Viera was buried we knew it had come to an end,
his coffin rocking into the ground like a boat or a cradle.

I could take my heart, he said, and give it to a *campesino*[2]
and he would cut it up and give it back:

5 you can't eat heart in those four dark
chambers where a man can be kept years.

A boy soldier in the bone-hot sun works his knife
to peel the face from a dead man

and hang it from the branch of a tree
10 flowering with such faces.

The heart is the toughest part of the body.
Tenderness is in the hands.

1982

As Children Together

Under the sloped snow
pinned all winter with Christmas
lights, we waited for your father
to whittle his soap cakes
5 away, finish the whisky,
your mother to carry her coffee
from room to room closing lights

---

[1]Labor activist and director of El Salvador's Institute of Agrarian Reform from October 1979 until his death in January 1981. Along with two U.S. agrarian reform specialists, Michael Hammer and Mark Pearlman, Viera was gunned down in the Sheraton Hotel coffee shop in San Salvador. As Forché reports in *El Salvador: Work of Thirty Photographers,* "Shortly before his murder, Viera appeared on television demanding an investigation of a $40 million fraud by the former military administrators of [El Salvador's] Institute of Agrarian Transformation." U.S. newspapers reported Hammer and Pearlman's deaths but failed to report Viera's.

[2]Peasant, farmer, one who works the land.

cubed in the snow at our feet.
Holding each other's
10 coat sleeves we slid down
the roads in our tight
black dresses, past
crystal swamps and the death
face of each dark house,
15 over the golden ice
of tobacco spit, the blue
quiet of ponds, with town
glowing behind the blind
white hills and a scant
20 snow ticking in the stars.
You hummed *blanche comme
la neige*[1] and spoke of Montreal
where a *quebeçoise*[2] could sing,
take any man's face
25 to her unfastened blouse
and wake to wine
on the bedside table.
I always believed this,
Victoria, that there might
30 be a way to get out.

You were ashamed of that house,
its round tins of surplus flour,
chipped beef and white beans,
relief checks and winter trips
35 that always ended in deer
tied stiff to the car rack,
the accordion breath of your uncles
down from the north, and what
you called the stupidity
40 of the Michigan French.

Your mirror grew ringed
with photos of servicemen
who had taken your breasts
in their hands, the buttons
45 of your blouses in their teeth,
who had given you the silk
tassles of their graduation,
jackets embroidered with dragons
from the Far East. You kept

---

[1]French for "white as the snow," this is the title
of a traditional song of Quebec.   [2]A female native of Quebec.

50 the corks that had fired
from bottles over their beds,
their letters with each city
blackened, envelopes of hair
from their shaved heads.
55 I am going to have it, you said.
Flowers wrapped in paper from carts
in Montreal, a plane lifting out
of Detroit, a satin bed, a table
cluttered with bottles of scent.

60 So standing in a platter of ice
outside a Catholic dance hall
you took their collars
in your fine chilled hands
and lied your age to adulthood.

65 I did not then have breasts of my own,
nor any letters from bootcamp
and when one of the men who had
gathered around you took my mouth
to his own there was nothing
70 other than the dance hall music
rising to the arms of iced trees.

I don't know where you are now, Victoria.
They say you have children, a trailer
in the snow near our town,
75 and the husband you found as a girl
returned from the Far East broken
cursing holy blood at the table
where nightly a pile of white shavings
is paid from the edge of his knife.

80 If you read this poem, write to me.
I have been to Paris since we parted.

1982

from The Recording Angel

I

Memory insists she stood there, able to go neither forward nor back, and in that
Unanimous night, time slowed, in light pulsing through ash, light of which the coat was made
5 Light of their brick houses
In matter's choreography of light, time slowed, then reversed until memory
Held her, able to go neither forward nor back
They were alone where once hundreds of thousands lived

10 Doves, or rather their wings, heard above the roof and the linens floating
Above a comic wedding in which corpses exchange vows. A grand funeral celebration
Everyone has died at once
15 Walking home always, always on this same blue road, cold through the black-and-white trees
Unless the film were reversed, she wouldn't reach the house
As she doesn't in her memory, or in her dream
Often she hears him calling out, half her name, his own, behind her in
20 a room until she turns
Standing forever, where often she hears him calling out

He is there, hidden in the blue winter fields and the burnt acreage of summer
As if, in reflecting the ruins, the river were filming what their city had
25 been
And *had it not been for this* lines up behind *if it weren't for that*
Until the past is something of a regiment
Yet looking back down the row of marching faces one sees one face
Before the shelling, these balconies were for geraniums and children
30 The slate roofs for morning

Market flowers in a jar, a string of tied garlic, and a voice moving off as if fearing itself
Under the leprous trees a white siren of light searches
Under the leprous trees a white siren of sun

II

35 A row of cabanas with white towels near restorative waters where once it was possible to be cured

A town of vacant summer houses
Mists burning the slightest lapse of sea
The child has gone to the window filled with desire, a glass light
40   passing through its hand
There are tide tables by which the sea had been predictable, as were
    the heavens
As sickness chose from among us we grew fewer
There were jetty lights where there was no jetty
45 What the rain forests had been became our difficult breath

At the moment when the snow geese lifted, thousands at once after
    days of crying in the wetlands
At once they lifted in a single ascent, acres of wind in their wingbones
Wetlands of morning light in their lift moving as one over the
50   continent
As a white front, one in their radiance, in their crying, a cloud of one
    desire

The child plays with its dead telephone. The father blows a kiss. The
    child laughs
55 The fire of his few years is carried toward the child on a cake
The child can't help itself. Would each day be like this?

And the geese, rising and falling in the rain on a surf of black hands
Sheets of rain and geese invisible or gone

Someone was supposed to have come
60 Waves turning black with the beach weed called dead men's hands
The sea strikes a bottle against a rock

III

The photographs were found at first by mistake in the drawer. After
    that I went to them often
She was standing on her toes in a silk *yukata,* her arms raised
65 Wearing a girl's white socks and near her feet a vase of calla lilies:
Otherwise she wore nothing
And in this one, her long hair is gathered into a white towel
Or tied back not to interfere
She had been wounded by so many men, abused by them
70 From behind in a silk *yukata,* then like this
One morning they were gone and I searched his belongings for them
    like a madwoman
In every direction, melted railyards, felled telegraph poles
For two months to find some trace of her
75 Footsteps on the floor above. More birds

It might have been less painful had it not been for the photographs
And beyond the paper walls, the red maple
Shirt in the wind of what the past meant
The fresh claw of a swastika on Rue Boulard
80 A man walking until he can no longer be seen
Don't say I was there. Always say I was never there.

1994

Elegy

The page opens to snow on a field: boot-holed month, black hour
the bottle in your coat half vodka half winter light.
To what and to whom does one say *yes*?
If God were the uncertain, would you cling to him?

5 Beneath a tattoo of stars the gate opens, so silent so like a tomb.
This is the city you most loved, an empty stairwell
where the next rain lifts invisibly from the Seine.

With solitude, your coat open, you walk
steadily as if the railings were there and your hands weren't passing
10   through them.

"When things were ready, they poured on fuel and touched off the
      fire.
They waited for a high wind. It was very fine, that powdered bone.
It was put into sacks, and when there were enough we went to a
15   bridge on the Narew River."

And even less explicit phrases survived:
"To make charcoal.
For laundry irons."
And so we revolt against silence with a bit of speaking.
20 The page is a charred field where the dead would have written
We went on. And it was like living through something again one could
      not live through again.

The soul behind you no longer inhabits your life: the unlit house
25 with its breathless windows and a chimney of ruined wings
where wind becomes an aria, your name, voices from a field,
And you, smoke, dissonance, a psalm, a stairwell.

1994

Paula Vogel b. 1951

Paula Vogel's writing has always been outside the box, with a provocative string of uncompromising plays aimed at exploring gender inequities, nontraditional families, and the darker side of human nature through AIDS, pornography, prostitution, sexual abuse, and gay and lesbian relationships. An outspoken lesbian since the age of seventeen, she continually pushes the boundaries of censorship with her language and choice of subject. As the scholar, David Savran explains, she likes to "stage the impossible" and "defy traditional theater logic." That she does so with such eloquent compassion and innovation is testament to her skilled writing, which offers a balanced view of sensitive topics against an often scathing commentary, nuanced by the disconcerting humor that she frequently employs.

Vogel was born into a divisive household. Her Jewish father walked out when she was eleven, and her Catholic mother, once divorced, was constantly on the move in a series of low-paying jobs. Vogel got involved in stage management during her sophomore year in high school. She obtained an undergraduate degree from the Catholic University of America and spent three years doing graduate work at Cornell University. Since then she has been involved in the theater as both writer and consultant, won a series of grants and awards, and taught play writing at Brown University as well as the Maximum Security Center for women at the Adult Corrections Institute in Rhode Island.

Her first full-length play, *Meg* (1977), a study of the relationship between Margaret Roper and her father, Sir Thomas More, was produced at the Kennedy Center and won the American College Theatre Festival Award for best new play. The two-act *Desdemona: A Play about a Handkerchief* (1980) drew attention in its blatant disregard of both theatrical and social conventions. Its retelling of Shakespeare's *Othello* from the viewpoint of Desdemona, whom she portrays as a conniving prostitute rather than innocent victim, offers a comedic but astute feminist spin on the original play.

During the 1980s Vogel established a solid reputation as an Off-Broadway and Off-Off-Broadway dramatist, with plays like the one-act *The Oldest Profession* (1981), a satire on sexuality and old age about five elderly prostitutes, and *And Baby Makes Seven* (1984), a play partly inspired by Edward Albee's *Who's Afraid of Virginia Woolf* (1962), that looks at so-called family values in its tale of two lesbians, a gay man, and their fantasy children, whom they kill to make room for the new arrival.

The Obie-winning *Baltimore Waltz* (1992), partly a reaction to the death of her brother from AIDS, was Vogel's first widely acclaimed play. It uses its heroine's fictional ATD (acquired toilet disease) to force audiences to re-examine their views about AIDS and women's sexuality. *The Mineola Twins* (1996), a political satire and exposure of the complacency of suburbia, relates the parallel lives of two distinctly different sisters, and helped cement Vogel's reputation, but it was the memory play, *How I Learned to Drive* (1997), that put Vogel firmly on the critical radar. Despite its uncomfortable subject matter, incest and sexual predation, this dark comedy–drama won the New York Drama Critics' Circle Award, the Pulitzer Prize, and an Obie Award for Playwriting.

Vogel often uses someone else's work as a springboard, and *How I Learned to Drive* is both an homage and response to Vladimir Nabokov's *Lolita,* in its tale of a young girl's sexual awakening through the attentions of an older man. In *How I Learned to Drive,* Vogel uses the metaphor of driving lessons to relate a complex tale of the relationship between the abused and the abuser, although the play is finally more about growth and maturation than the destructive force of abuse. Boldly theatrical, it uses scant sets, nonlinear narrative, and a three-person Greek chorus to play the supporting roles of family and passers-by. Vogel resists portraying the central protagonist, Li'l Bit, as victim, and by depicting her uncle Peck as an attractive and kindly person, she emphasizes the ambiguities of the situation. She has stated that this is not a play about pedophilia but about survival and "coming of age" in our difficult contemporary culture.

Vogel continues to write and test her audiences, with plays like *Hot 'n' Throbbing* (1994; rev. 2000), which explores pornography and its relation to domestic abuse and violence, and *The Long Christmas Ride Home* (2003), which ingeniously features puppets alongside the actors. She is also working on a screenplay for *How I Learned to Drive*.

Susan Abbotson
Rhode Island College

PRIMARY WORKS

Meg, 1977; *The Oldest Profession,* 1981; *And Baby Makes Seven,* 1984; *Desdemona: A Play about a Handkerchief,* 1994; *Hot 'n' Throbbing,* 1994 (rev. 2000); *The Baltimore Waltz and Other Plays,* 1996; *The Mineola Twins,* 1996; *How I Learned to Drive,* 1997; *The Mammary Plays,* 1998; *The Long Christmas Ride Home,* 2003; *A Civil War Christmas,* 2008.

How I Learned to Drive

CHARACTERS

LI'L BIT A woman who ages forty-something to eleven years old. (See Notes on the New York Production.)

PECK Attractive man in his forties. Despite a few problems, he should be played by an actor one might cast in the role of Atticus in *To Kill a Mockingbird.*

THE GREEK CHORUS If possible, these three members should be able to sing three-part harmony.

MALE GREEK CHORUS Plays Grandfather, Waiter, High School Boys. Thirties–forties. (See Notes on the New York Production.)

FEMALE GREEK CHORUS Plays Mother, Aunt Mary, High School Girls. Thirty–fifty. (See Notes on the New York Production.)

TEENAGE GREEK CHORUS Plays Grandmother, high school girls and the voice of eleven-year-old Li'l Bit. Note on the casting of this actor: I would strongly recommend casting a young woman who is "of legal age," that is, twenty-one to twenty-five years old who can look as close to eleven as possible. The contrast with the other cast members will help. If the actor is too young, the audience may feel uncomfortable. (See Notes on the New York Production.)

PRODUCTION NOTES

I urge directors to use the GREEK CHORUS *in staging as environment and, well, part of the family—with the exception of the* TEENAGE GREEK CHORUS *member who, after the last time she appears onstage, should perhaps disappear.*

As For Music: Please have fun. I wrote sections of the play listening to music like Roy Orbison's "Dream Baby" and The Mamas and the Papa's "Dedicated to the One I Love." The vaudeville sections go well to the Tijuana Brass or any music that sounds like a *Laugh-In* soundtrack. Other sixties music is rife with pedophilish (?) reference: the "You're Sixteen" genre hits; The Beach Boys' "Little Surfer Girl"; Gary Puckett and the Union Gap's "This Girl Is a Woman Now"; "Come Back When You Grow Up," etc.

And whenever possible, please feel free to punctuate the action with traffic signs: "No Passing," "Slow Children," "Dangerous Curves," "One Way," and the visual signs for children, deer crossings, hills, school buses, etc. (See Notes on the New York Production.)

This script uses the notion of slides and projections, which were not used in the New York production of the play.

On Titles: Throughout the script there are bold-faced titles. In production these should be spoken in a neutral voice (the type of voice that driver education films employ). In the New York production these titles were assigned to various members of the Greek Chorus and were done live.

NOTES ON THE NEW YORK PRODUCTION

The role of LI'L BIT *was originally written as a character who is forty-something. When we cast Mary-Louise Parker in the role of* LI'L BIT, *we cast the* GREEK CHORUS *members with younger actors as the* FEMALE GREEK *and the* MALE GREEK, *and cast the* TEENAGE GREEK *with an older (that is, mid-twenties) actor as well. There is a great deal of flexibility in age. Directors should change the age in the last monologue for* LI'L BIT *("And before you know it, I'll be thirty-five. . . .") to reflect the actor's age who is playing* LI'L BIT.

As the house lights dim, a Voice announces:

SAFETY FIRST—YOU AND DRIVER EDUCATION.

Then the sound of a key turning the ignition of a car. LI'L BIT *steps into a spotlight on the stage; "well-endowed," she is a softer-looking woman in the present time than she was at seventeen.*

LI'L BIT Sometimes to tell a secret, you first have to teach a lesson. We're going to start our lesson tonight on an early, warm summer evening.

In a parking lot overlooking the Beltsville Agricultural Farms in suburban Maryland.

Less than a mile away, the crumbling concrete of U.S. One wends its way past one-room revival churches, the porno drive-in, and boarded up motels with For Sale signs tumbling down.

Like I said, it's a warm summer evening.

Here on the land the Department of Agriculture owns, the smell of sleeping farm animal is thick on the air. The smells of clover and hay mix in with the smells of the leather dashboard. You can still imagine how Maryland used to be, before the malls took over. This countryside was once dotted with farmhouses—from their porches you could have witnessed the Civil War raging in the front fields.

Oh yes. There's a moon over Maryland tonight, that spills into the car where I sit beside a man old enough to be—did I mention how still the night is? Damp soil and tranquil air. It's the kind of night that makes a middle-aged man with a mortgage feel like a country boy again.

It's 1969. And I am very old, very cynical of the world, and I know it all. In short, I am seventeen years old, parking off a dark lane with a married man on an early summer night.

(Lights up on two chairs facing front—or a Buick Riviera, if you will. Waiting patiently, with a smile on his face, PECK *sits sniffing the night air.* LI'L BIT *climbs in beside him, seventeen years old and tense. Throughout the following, the two sit facing directly front. They do not touch. Their bodies remain passive. Only their facial expressions emote.)*

PECK Ummm. I love the smell of your hair.

LI'L BIT Uh-huh.

PECK Oh, Lord. Ummmm. *(Beat)* A man could die happy like this.

LI'L BIT Well, *don't.*

PECK What shampoo is this?

LI'L BIT Herbal Essence.

PECK Herbal Essence. I'm gonna buy me some. Herbal Essence. And when I'm alone in the house, I'm going to get into the bathtub and uncap the bottle and—

LI'L BIT —Be good.

PECK What?

LI'L BIT Stop being . . . bad.

PECK What did you think I was going to say? What do you think I'm going to do with the shampoo?

LI'L BIT I don't want to know. I don't want to hear it.

PECK I'm going to wash my hair. That's all.

LI'L BIT Oh.

PECK What did you think I was going to do?

LI'L BIT Nothing. . . . I don't know. Something . . . nasty.

PECK With shampoo? Lord, gal—your mind!

LI'L BIT And whose fault is it?

PECK Not mine. I've got the mind of a boy scout.

LI'L BIT Right. A horny boy scout.

PECK Boy scouts are always horny. What do you think the first Merit Badge is for?

LI'L BIT There. You're going to be nasty again.

PECK Oh, no. I'm good. Very good.

LI'L BIT It's getting late.

PECK Don't change the subject. I was talking about how good I am. (Beat) Are you ever gonna let me show you how good I am?

LI'L BIT Don't go over the line now.

PECK I won't. I'm not gonna do anything you don't want me to do.

LI'L BIT That's right.

PECK And I've been good all week.

LI'L BIT You have?

PECK Yes. All week. Not a single drink.

LI'L BIT Good boy.

PECK Do I get a reward? For not drinking?

LI'L BIT A small one. It's getting late.

PECK Just let me undo you. I'll do you back up.

LI'L BIT All right. But be quick about it. (PECK *pantomimes undoing* LI'L BIT's *brassiere with one hand*) You know, that's amazing. The way you can undo the hooks through my blouse with one hand.

PECK Years of practice.

LI'L BIT You would make an incredible brain surgeon with that dexterity.

PECK I'll bet Clyde—what's the name of the boy taking you to the prom?

LI'L BIT Claude Souders.

PECK Claude Souders. I'll bet it takes him two hands, lights on, and you helping him on to get to first base.

LI'L BIT Maybe.

(Beat.)

PECK Can I . . . kiss them? Please?

LI'L BIT I don't know.

PECK Don't make a grown man beg.

LI'L BIT Just one kiss.

PECK I'm going to lift your blouse.

LI'L BIT It's a little cold.

(PECK *laughs gently.*)

PECK That's not why you're shivering. (*They sit, perfectly still, for a long moment of silence.* PECK *makes gentle, concentric circles with his thumbs in the air in front of him*) How does that feel?

(LI'L BIT *closes her eyes, carefully keeps her voice calm:*)

LI'L BIT It's . . . okay.

(*Sacred music, organ music or a boy's choir swells beneath the following.*)

PECK I tell you, you can keep all the cathedrals of Europe. Just give me a second with these—these celestial orbs—

(PECK *bows his head as if praying. But he is kissing her nipple.* LI'L BIT, *eyes still closed, rears back her head on the leather Buick car seat.*)

LI'L BIT Uncle Peck—we've got to go. I've got graduation rehearsal at school tomorrow morning. And you should get on home to Aunt Mary—

PECK —All right, Li'l Bit.

LI'L BIT —*Don't* call me that no more. (*Calmer*) Any more. I'm a big girl now, Uncle Peck. As you know.

(LI'L BIT *pantomimes refastening her bra behind her back.*)

PECK That you are. Going on eighteen. Kittens will turn into cats.
(*Sighs*) I live all week long for these few minutes with you—you know that?

LI'L BIT I'll drive.

(*A Voice cuts in with:*)

IDLING IN THE NEUTRAL GEAR.

(*Sound of car revving cuts off the sacred music;* LI'L BIT, *now an adult, rises out of the car and comes to us.*)

LI'L BIT In most families, relatives get names like "Junior," or "Brother," or "Bubba." In my family, if we call someone "Big Papa," it's not because he's tall. In my family, folks tend to get nicknamed for their genitalia. Uncle Peck, for example. My mama's adage was "the titless wonder," and my cousin Bobby got branded for life as "B.B."
  (*In unison with* GREEK CHORUS:)

LI'L BIT For blue balls.   GREEK CHORUS For blue balls.

FEMALE GREEK CHORUS (*As* MOTHER) And of course, we were so excited to have a baby girl that when the nurse brought you in and said, "It's a girl! It's a baby girl!" I just had to see for myself. So we whipped your diapers down and parted your chubby little legs—and right between your legs there was—

(PECK *has come over during the above and chimes along:*)

PECK Just a little bit.   GREEK CHORUS Just a little bit.

FEMALE GREEK CHORUS (*As* MOTHER) And when you were born, you were so tiny that you fit in Uncle Peck's outstretched hand.

(PECK *stretches his hand out.*)

PECK Now that's a fact. I held you, one day old, right in this hand.

(*A traffic signal is projected of a bicycle in a circle with a diagonal red slash.*)

LI'L BIT Even with my family background, I was sixteen or so before I realized that pedophilia did not mean people who loved to bicycle. . . .

(*A Voice intrudes:*)

DRIVING IN FIRST GEAR.

LI'L BIT 1969. A typical family dinner.

FEMALE GREEK CHORUS (As MOTHER) Look, Grandma. Li'l Bit's getting to be as big in the bust as you are.

LI'L BIT Mother! Could we please change the subject?

TEENAGE GREEK CHORUS (As GRANDMOTHER) Well, I hope you are buying her some decent bras. I never had a decent bra, growing up in the Depression, and now my shoulders are just crippled—crippled from the weight hanging on my shoulders—the dents from my bra straps are big enough to put your finger in.—Here, let me show you—

(As GRANDMOTHER starts to open her blouse:)

LI'L BIT Grandma! Please don't undress at the dinner table.

PECK I thought the entertainment came after the dinner.

LI'L BIT (To the audience) This is how it always starts. My grandfather, Big Papa, will chime in next with—

MALE GREEK CHORUS (As GRANDFATHER) Yup. If Li'l Bit gets any bigger, we're gonna haveta buy her a wheelbarrow to carry in front of her—

LI'L BIT—Damn it—

PECK—How about those Redskins on Sunday, Big Papa?

LI'L BIT (To the audience) The only sport Big Papa followed was chasing Grandma around the house—

MALE GREEK CHORUS (As GRANDFATHER)—Or we could write to Kate Smith. Ask her for somma her used brassieres she don't want anymore—she could maybe give to Li'l Bit here—

LI'L BIT—I can't stand it. I can't.

PECK Now, honey, that's just their way—

FEMALE GREEK CHORUS (As MOTHER) I tell you, Grandma, Li'l Bit's at that age. She's so sensitive, you can't say boo—

LI'L BIT I'd like some privacy, that's all. Okay? Some goddamn privacy—

PECK—Well, at least she didn't use the savior's name—

LI'L BIT (To the audience) And Big Papa wouldn't let a dead dog lie. No sirree.

MALE GREEK CHORUS (As GRANDFATHER) Well, she'd better stop being so sensitive. 'Cause five minutes before Li'l Bit turns the corner, her tits turn first—

LI'L BIT (Starting to rise from the table) —That's it. That's it.

PECK Li'l Bit, you can't let him get to you. Then he wins.

LI'L BIT I hate him. Hate him.

PECK That's fine. But hate him and eat a good dinner at the same time.

(Li'l Bit calms down and sits with perfect dignity.)

LI'L BIT The gumbo is really good, Grandma.

MALE GREEK CHORUS (As GRANDFATHER) A'course, Li'l Bit's got a big surprise coming for her when she goes to that fancy college this fall—

PECK Big Papa—let it go.

MALE GREEK CHORUS (As GRANDFATHER) What does she need a college degree for? She's got all the credentials she'll need on her chest.

LI'L BIT—Maybe I want to learn things. Read. Rise above my cracker background—
PECK—Whoa, now, Li'l Bit—
MALE GREEK CHORUS (*As* GRANDFATHER) What kind of things do you want to read?
LI'L BIT There's a whole semester course, for example, on Shakespeare—

(GREEK CHORUS, *as* GRANDFATHER, *laughs until he weeps.*)

MALE GREEK CHORUS (*As* GRANDFATHER) Shakespeare. That's a good one. Shakespeare is really going to help you in life.
PECK I think it's wonderful. And on scholarship!
MALE GREEK CHORUS (*As* GRANDFATHER) How is Shakespeare going to help her lie on her back in the dark?

(*Li'l Bit is on her feet.*)

LI'L BIT You're getting old, Big Papa. You are going to die—very very soon. Maybe even tonight. And when you get to heaven, God's going to be a beautiful black woman in a long white robe. She's gonna look at your chart and say: Uh-oh. Fornication. Dog-ugly mean with blood relatives. Oh. Uh-oh. Voted for George Wallace. Well, one last chance: If you can name the play, all will be forgiven. And then she'll quote: "The quality of mercy is not strained." Your answer? Oh, too bad—*Merchant of Venice:* Act IV, Scene iii. And then she'll send your ass to fry in hell with all the other crackers. Excuse me, please.
   (*To the audience*) And as I left the house, I would always hear Big Papa say:
MALE GREEK CHORUS (*As* GRANDFATHER) Lucy, your daughter's got a mouth on her. Well, no sense in wasting good gumbo. Pass me her plate, Mama.
LI'L BIT And Aunt Mary would come up to Uncle Peck:
FEMALE GREEK CHORUS (*As* AUNT MARY) Peck, go after her, will you? You're the only one she'll listen to when she gets like this.
PECK She just needs to cool off.
FEMALE GREEK CHORUS (*As* AUNT MARY) Please, honey—Grandma's been on her feet cooking all day.
PECK All right.
LI'L BIT And as he left the room, Aunt Mary would say:
FEMALE GREEK CHORUS (*As* AUNT MARY) Peck's so good with them when they get to be this age.

(LI'L BIT *has stormed to another part of the stage, her back turned, weeping with a teenage fury.* PECK, *cautiously, as if stalking a deer, comes to her. She turns away even more. He waits a bit.*)

PECK I don't suppose you're talking to family. (*No response*) Does it help that I'm in-law?
LI'L BIT Don't you dare make fun of this.
PECK I'm not. There's nothing funny about this. (*Beat*) Although I'll bet when Big Papa is about to meet his maker, he'll remember *The Merchant of Venice.*
LI'L BIT I've got to get away from here.
PECK You're going away. Soon. Here, take this.

(PECK *hands her his folded handkerchief.* LI'L BIT *uses it, noisily. Hands it back. Without her seeing, he reverently puts it back.*)

LI'L BIT I hate this family.

PECK Your grandfather's ignorant. And you're right—he's going to die soon. But he's family. Family is . . . family.

LI'L BIT Grown-ups are always saying that. Family.

PECK Well, when you get a little older, you'll see what we're saying.

LI'L BIT Uh-huh. So family is another acquired taste, like French kissing?

PECK Come again?

LI'L BIT You know, at first it really grosses you out, but in time you grow to like it?

PECK Girl, you are . . . a handful.

LI'L BIT Uncle Peck—you have the keys to your car?

PECK Where do you want to go?

LI'L BIT Just up the road.

PECK I'll come with you.

LI'L BIT No—please? I just need to . . . to drive for a little bit. Alone.

(PECK *tosses her the keys.*)

PECK When can I see you alone again?

LI'L BIT Tonight.

(LI'L BIT *crosses to center stage where the lights dim around her. A Voice directs:*)

SHIFTING FORWARD FROM FIRST TO SECOND GEAR.

LI'L BIT There were a lot of rumors about why I got kicked out of that fancy school in 1970. Some say I got caught with a man in my room. Some say as a kid on scholarship I fooled around with a rich man's daughter.

(LI'L BIT *smiles innocently at the audience*) I'm not talking.

But the real truth was I had a constant companion in my dorm room—who was less than discrete. Canadian V.O. A fifth a day.

1970. A Nixon recession. I slept on the floors of friends who were out of work themselves. Took factory work when I could find it. A string of dead-end jobs that didn't last very long.

What I did, most nights, was cruise the Beltway and the back roads of Maryland, where there was still country, past the battlefields and farm houses. Racing in a 1965 Mustang—and as long as I had gasoline for my car and whiskey for me, the nights would pass. Fully tanked, I would speed past the churches and the trees and the bend, thinking just one notch of the steering wheel would be all it would take, and yet some . . . reflex took over. My hands on the wheel in the nine and three o'-clock position—I never so much as got a ticket. He taught me well.

(*A Voice announces:*)

YOU AND THE REVERSE GEAR.

LI'L BIT Back up. 1968. On the Eastern Shore. A celebration dinner.

(LI'L BIT *joins* PECK *at a table in a restaurant.*)

PECK Feeling better, missy?

LI'L BIT The bathroom's really amazing here, Uncle Peck! They have these little soaps—instead of borax or something—and they're in the shape of shells.

PECK I'll have to take a trip to the gentlemen's room just to see.

LI'L BIT How did you know about this place?

PECK This inn is famous on the Eastern shore—it's been open since the seventeenth century. And I know how you like history . . .

(LI'L BIT *is shy and pleased.*)

LI'L BIT It's great.

PECK And you've just done your first, legal, long-distance drive. You must be hungry.

LI'L BIT I'm starved.

PECK I would suggest a dozen oysters to start, and the crab imperial . . . (LI'L BIT *is genuinely agog*) You might be interested to know the town history. When the British sailed up this very river in the dead of night—see outside where I'm pointing?—they were going to bombard the heck out of this town. But the town fathers were ready for them. They crept up all the trees with lanterns so that the British would think they saw the town lights and they aimed their cannons too high. And that's why the inn is still here for business today.

LI'L BIT That's a great story.

PECK (*Casually*) Would you like to start with a cocktail?

LI'L BIT You're not . . . you're not going to start drinking, are you, Uncle Peck?

PECK Not me. I told you, as long as you're with me, I'll never drink. I asked you if you'd like a cocktail before dinner. It's nice to have a little something with the oysters.

LI'L BIT But . . . I'm not . . . legal. We could get arrested. Uncle Peck, they'll never believe I'm twenty-one!

PECK So? Today we celebrate your driver's license—on the first try. This establishment reminds me a lot of places back home.

LI'L BIT What does that mean?

PECK In South Carolina, like here on the Eastern Shore, they're . . . (*Searches for the right euphemism*) . . . "European." No so puritanical. And very understanding if gentlemen wish to escort very attractive young ladies who might want a before-dinner cocktail. If you want one, I'll order one.

LI'L BIT Well—sure. Just . . . one.

(*The* FEMALE GREEK CHORUS *appears in a spot.*)

FEMALE GREEK CHORUS (*As* MOTHER) A Mother's Guide to Social Drinking:
    A lady never gets sloppy—she may, however, get tipsy and a little gay.

Never drink on an empty stomach. Avail yourself of the bread basket and generous portions of butter. Slather the butter on your bread.

Sip your drink, slowly, let the beverage linger in your mouth—interspersed with interesting, fascinating conversation. Sip, never . . . slurp or gulp. Your glass should always be three-quarters full when his glass is empty.

Stay away from ladies' drinks: drinks like pink ladies, slow gin fizzes, daiquiris, gold cadillacs, Long Island iced teas, margaritas, piña coladas, mai tais, planters punch, white Russians, black Russians, red Russians, melon balls, blue balls, hummingbirds, hemorrhages and hurricanes. In short, avoid anything with sugar, or anything with an umbrella. Get your vitamin C from fruit. Don't order anything with Voodoo or Vixen in the title or sexual positions in the name like Dead Man Screw or the Missionary. (*She sort of titters*)

Believe me, they are lethal. . . . I think you were conceived after one of those.

Drink, instead, like a man: straight up or on the rocks, with plenty of water in between.

Oh, yes. And never mix your drinks. Stay with one all night long, like the man you came in with: bourbon, gin, or tequila till dawn, damn the torpedoes, full speed ahead!

(*As the* FEMALE GREEK CHORUS *retreats, the* MALE GREEK CHORUS *approaches the table as a* WAITER.)

MALE GREEK CHORUS (*As* WAITER) I hope you all are having a pleasant evening. Is there something I can bring you, sir, before you order?

(LI'L BIT *waits in anxious fear. Carefully,* UNCLE PECK *says with command:*)

PECK I'll have a plain iced tea. The lady would like a drink, I believe.

(*The* MALE GREEK CHORUS *does a double take; there is a moment when* UNCLE PECK *and he are in silent communication.*)

MALE GREEK CHORUS (*As* WAITER) Very good. What would the . . . lady like?
LI'L BIT (*A bit flushed*) Is there . . . is there any sugar in a martini?
PECK None that I know of.
LI'L BIT That's what I'd like then—a dry martini. And could we maybe have some bread?
PECK A drink fit for a woman of the world.—Please bring the lady a dry martini, be generous with the olives, straight up.

(*The* MALE GREEK CHORUS *anticipates a large tip.*)

MALE GREEK CHORUS (*As* WAITER) Right away. Very good sir.

(*The* MALE GREEK CHORUS *returns with an empty martini glass which he puts in front of* LI'L BIT.)

PECK Your glass is empty. Another martini, madam?
LI'L BIT Yes, thank you. (PECK *signals the* MALE GREEK CHORUS, *who nods*) So why did you leave South Carolina, Uncle Peck?
PECK I was stationed in D.C. after the war, and decided to stay. Go North, Young Man, someone might have said.

LI'L BIT What did you do in the service anyway?

PECK *(Suddenly taciturn)* I . . . I did just this and that. Nothing heroic or spectacular.

LI'L BIT But did you see fighting? Or go to Europe?

PECK I served in the Pacific Theater. It's really nothing interesting to talk about.

LI'L BIT It is to me. *(The* WAITER *has brought another empty glass)* Oh, goody. I love the color of the swizzle sticks. What were we talking about?

PECK Swizzle sticks.

LI'L BIT Do you ever think of going back?

PECK To the Marines?

LI'L BIT No—to South Carolina.

PECK Well, we do go back. To visit.

LI'L BIT No, I mean to live.

PECK Not very likely. I think it's better if my mother doesn't have a daily reminder of her disappointment.

LI'L BIT Are these floorboards slanted?

PECK Yes, the floor is very slanted. I think this is the original floor.

LI'L BIT Oh, good.

(The FEMALE GREEK CHORUS *as* MOTHER *enters swaying a little, a little past tipsy.)*

FEMALE GREEK CHORUS *(As* MOTHER*)* Don't leave your drink unattended when you visit the ladies' room. There is such a thing as white slavery; the modus operandi is to spike an unsuspecting young girl's drink with a "mickey" when she's left the room to powder her nose.

But if you feel you have had more than your sufficiency in liquor, do go to the ladies' room—often. Pop your head out of doors for a refreshing breath of the night air. If you must, wet your face and head with tap water. Don't be afraid to dunk your head if necessary. A wet woman is still less conspicuous than a drunk woman.

(The FEMALE GREEK CHORUS *stumbles a little; conspiratorially)* When in the course of human events it becomes necessary, go to a corner stall and insert the index and middle finger down the throat almost to the epiglottis. Divulge your stomach before rejoining your beau waiting for you at your table.

Oh, no. Don't be shy or embarrassed. In the very best of establishments, there's always one or two debutantes crouched in the corner stalls, their beaded purses tossed willy-nilly, sounding like cats in heat, heaving up the contents of their stomachs.

(The FEMALE GREEK CHORUS *begins to wander off)* I wonder what it is they do in the men's rooms . . .

LI'L BIT So why is your mother disappointed in you, Uncle Peck?

PECK Every mother in Horry County has Great Expectations.

LI'L BIT—Could I have another mar-ti-ni, please?

PECK I think this is your last one.

*(*PECK *signals the* WAITER. *The* WAITER *looks at* LI'L BIT *and shakes his head no.* PECK *raises an eyebrow, raises his finger to indicate one more, and then rubs his fingers together. It looks like a secret code. The* WAITER *sighs, shakes his head sadly, and brings over another empty martini glass. He glares at* PECK.*)*

LI'L BIT The name of the county where you grew up is "Horry?" (LI'L BIT, *plastered, begins to laugh. Then she stops*) I think your mother should be proud of you.

(PECK *signals for the check.*)

PECK Well, missy, she wanted me to do—to *be* everything my father was not. She wanted me to amount to something.
LI'L BIT But you have! You've amounted a lot. . . .
PECK I'm just a very ordinary man.

(*The* WAITER *has brought the check and waits.* PECK *draws out a large bill and hands it to the* WAITER. LI'L BIT *is in the soppy stage.*)

LI'L BIT I'll bet your mother loves you, Uncle Peck.

(PECK *freezes a bit. To* MALE GREEK CHORUS *as* WAITER:)

PECK Thank you. The service was exceptional. Please keep the change.
MALE GREEK CHORUS (*As* WAITER, *in a tone that could freeze*) Thank you, sir. Will you be needing any help?
PECK I think we can manage, thank you.

(*Just then, the* FEMALE GREEK CHORUS *as* MOTHER *lurches on stage; the* MALE GREEK CHORUS *as* WAITER *escorts her off as she delivers:*)

FEMALE GREEK CHORUS (*As* MOTHER) Thanks to judicious planning and several trips to the ladies' loo, your mother once out-drank an entire regiment of British officers on a good-will visit to Washington! Every last man of them! Milquetoasts! How'd they ever kick Hitler's cahones, huh? No match for an American lady—I could drink every man in here under the table.
  (*She delivers one last crucial hint before she is gently "bounced"*) As a last resort, when going out for an evening on the town, be sure to wear a skin-tight girdle— so tight that only a surgical knife or acetylene torch can get it off you—so that if you do pass out in the arms of your escort, he'll end up with rubber burns on his fingers before he can steal your virtue—

(*A Voice punctures the interlude with:*)

VEHICLE FAILURE.

Even with careful maintenance and preventive operation of your automobile, it is all too common for us to experience an unexpected breakdown. If you are driving at any speed when a breakdown occurs, you must slow down and guide the automobile to the side of the road.

(PECK *is slowly propping up* LI'L BIT *as they work their way to his car in the parking lot of the inn.*)

PECK How are you doing, missy?

LI'L BIT It's so far to the car, Uncle Peck. Like the lanterns in the trees the British fired on . . .

(LI'L BIT *stumbles.* PECK *swoops her up in his arms.*)

PECK Okay. I think we're going to take a more direct route.
(LI'L BIT *closes her eyes*) Dizzy? (*She nods her head*) Don't look at the ground. Almost there—do you feel sick to your stomach? (LI'L BIT *nods. They reach the "car."* PECK *gently deposits her on the front seat*) Just settle here a little while until things stop spinning. (LI'L BIT *opens her eyes*)

LI'L BIT What are we doing?

PECK We're just going to sit here until your tummy settles down.

LI'L BIT It's such nice upholst'ry—

PECK Think you can go for a ride, now?

LI'L BIT Where are you taking me?

PECK Home.

LI'L BIT You're not taking me—upstairs? There's no room at the inn? (LI'L BIT *giggles*)

PECK Do you want to go upstairs? (LI'L BIT *doesn't answer*) Or home?

LI'L BIT—This isn't right, Uncle Peck.

PECK What isn't right?

LI'L BIT What we're doing. It's wrong. It's very wrong.

PECK What are we doing? (LI'L BIT *does not answer*) We're just going out to dinner.

LI'L BIT You know. It's not nice to Aunt Mary.

PECK You let me be the judge of what's nice and not nice to my wife.

(*Beat.*)

LI'L BIT Now you're mad.

PECK I'm not mad. It's just that I thought you . . . understood me, Li'l Bit. I think you're the only one who does.

LI'L BIT Someone will get hurt.

PECK Have I forced you to do anything?

(*There is a long pause as* LI'L BIT *tries to get sober enough to think this through.*)

LI'L BIT . . . I guess not.

PECK We are just enjoying each other's company. I've told you, nothing is going to happen between us until you want it to. Do you know that?

LI'L BIT Yes.

PECK Nothing is going to happen until you want it to. (*A second more, with* PECK *staring ahead at the river while seated at the wheel of his car. Then, softly:*) Do you want something to happen?

(PECK *reaches over and strokes her face, very gently.* LI'L BIT *softens, reaches for him, and buries her head in his neck. Then she kisses him. Then she moves away, dizzy again.*)

LI'L BIT . . . I don't know.

(PECK *smiles; this has been good news for him—it hasn't been a "no."*)

PECK Then I'll wait. I'm a very patient man. I've been waiting for a long time. I don't mind waiting.

LI'L BIT Someone is going to get hurt.

PECK No one is going to get hurt. *(LI'L BIT closes her eyes)* Are you feeling sick?

LI'L BIT Sleepy.

(Carefully, PECK *props* LI'L BIT *up on the seat.)*

PECK Stay here a second.

LI'L BIT Where're you going?

PECK I'm getting something from the back seat.

LI'L BIT *(Scared: too loud)* What? What are you going to do?

*(*PECK *reappears in the front seat with a lap rug.)*

PECK Shhh. *(*PECK *covers* LI'L BIT. *She calms down)* There. Think you can sleep?

*(*LI'L BIT *nods. She slides over to rest on his shoulder. With a look of happiness,* PECK *turns the ignition key. Beat.* PECK *leaves* LI'L BIT *sleeping in the car and strolls down to the audience. Wagner's* Flying Dutchman *comes up faintly.*

A Voice interjects:)

IDLING IN THE NEUTRAL GEAR.

TEENAGE GREEK CHORUS Uncle Peck Teaches Cousin Bobby How to Fish.

PECK I get back once or twice a year—supposedly to visit Mama and the family, but the real truth is to fish. I miss this the most of all. There's a smell in the Low country—where the swamp and fresh inlet join the saltwater—a scent of sand and cypress, that I haven't found anywhere yet.

I don't say this very often up North because it will just play into the stereotype everyone has, but I will tell you: I didn't wear shoes in the summertime until I was sixteen. It's unnatural down here to pen up your feet in leather. Go ahead—take 'em off. Let yourself breathe—it really will make you feel better.

We're going to aim for some pompano today—and I have to tell you, they're a very shy, mercurial fish. Takes patience, and psychology. You have to believe it doesn't matter if you catch one or not.

Sky's pretty spectacular—there's some beer in the cooler next to the crab salad I packed, so help yourself if you get hungry. Are you hungry? Thirsty? Holler if you are.

Okay. You don't want to lean over the bridge like that—pompano feed in shallow water, and you don't want to get too close—they're frisky and shy little things—wait, check your line. Yep, something's been munching while we were talking.

Okay, look: We take the sand flea and you take the hook like this—right through his little sand flea rump. Sand fleas should always keep their backs to the wall. Okay. Cast it in, like I showed you. That's great! I can taste that pompano now, sautéed with some pecans and butter, and a little bourbon—now—let it lie on the bottom—now, reel, jerk, reel, jerk—

Look—look at your line. There's something calling, all right. Okay, tip the rod up—not too sharp—hook it—all right, now easy, reel and then rest—let it play. And reel—play it out, that's right—really good! I can't believe it! It's a pompano.—Good work! Way to go! You are an official fisherman now. Pompano are hard to catch. We are going to have a delicious little—

What? Well, I don't know how much pain a fish feels—you can't think of that. Oh, no, don't cry, come on now, its just a fish—the other guys are going to see you.—No, no, you're just real sensitive, and I think that's wonderful at your age— look, do you want me to cut it free? You do?

Okay, hand me those pliers—look—I'm cutting the hook—okay? And we're just going to drop it in—no I'm not mad. It's just for fun, okay? There—it's going to swim back to its lady friend and tell her what a terrible day it had and she's going to stroke him with her fins until he feels better, and then they'll do something alone together that will make them both feel good and sleepy. . . .

(PECK *bends down, very earnest*) I don't want you to feel ashamed about crying. I'm not going to tell anyone, okay? I can keep secrets. You know, men cry all the time. They just don't tell anybody, and they don't let anybody catch them. There's nothing you could do that would make me feel ashamed of you. Do you know that? Okay. (PECK *straightens up, smiles*)

Do you want to pack up and call it a day? I tell you what—I think I can still remember—there's a really neat tree house where I used to stay for days. I think it's still here—it was the last time I looked. But it's a secret place—you can't tell anybody we've gone there—least of all your mom or your sisters.—This is something special just between you and me. Sound good? We'll climb up there and have a beer and some crab salad—okay, B.B.? Bobby? Robert . . .

(LI'L BIT *sits at a kitchen table with the two* FEMALE GREEK CHORUS *members.*)

LI'L BIT (*To the audience*) Three women, three generations, sit at the kitchen table. On Men, Sex, and Women: Part I:

FEMALE GREEK CHORUS (*As* MOTHER) Men only want one thing.

LI'L BIT (*Wide-eyed*) But what? What is it they want?

FEMALE GREEK CHORUS (*As* MOTHER) And once they have it, they lose all interest. So Don't Give It to Them.

TEENAGE GREEK CHORUS (*As* GRANDMOTHER) I never had the luxury of the rhythm method. Your grandfather is just a big bull. A big bull. Every morning, every evening.

FEMALE GREEK CHORUS (*As* MOTHER, *whispers to* LI'L BIT) And he used to come home for lunch every day.

LI'L BIT My god, Grandma!

TEENAGE GREEK CHORUS (*As* GRANDMOTHER)Your grandfather only cares that I do two things: have the table set and the bed turned down.

FEMALE GREEK CHORUS (*As* MOTHER) And in all that time, Mother, you never have experienced—?

LI'L BIT (*To the audience*)—No my grandmother believed in all the sacraments of the church, to the day she died. She believed in Santa Claus and the Easter Bunny until she was fifteen. But she didn't believe in—

TEENAGE GREEK CHORUS (*As* GRANDMOTHER)—Orgasm! That's just something you and Mary have made up! I don't believe you.

FEMALE GREEK CHORUS (*As* MOTHER) Mother, it happens to women all the time—

TEENAGE GREEK CHORUS (*As* GRANDMOTHER)—Oh, now you're going to tell me about the G force!

LI'L BIT No, Grandma, I think that's astronauts—

FEMALE GREEK CHORUS (*As* MOTHER) Well, Mama, after all, you were a child bride when Big Papa came and got you—you were a married woman and you still believed in Santa Claus.

TEENAGE GREEK CHORUS (*As* GRANDMOTHER) It was legal, what Daddy and I did! I was fourteen and in those days, fourteen was a grown-up woman—

(BIG PAPA *shuffles in the kitchen for a cookie.*)

MALE GREEK CHORUS (*As* GRANDFATHER)—Oh, now we're off on Grandma and the Rape of the Sa-bean Women!

TEENAGE GREEK CHORUS (*As* GRANDMOTHER) Well, you were the one in such a big hurry—

MALE GREEK CHORUS (*As* GRANDFATHER *to* LI'L BIT)—I picked your grandmother out of that herd of sisters just like a lion chooses the gazelle—the plump, slow, flaky gazelle dawdling at the edge of the herd—your sisters were too smart and too fast and too scrawny—

LI'L BIT (*To the audience*)—The family story is that when Big Papa came for Grandma, my Aunt Lily was waiting for him with a broom—and she beat him over the head all the way down the stairs as he was carrying out Grandma's hope chest—

MALE GREEK CHORUS (*As* GRANDFATHER)—and they were mean. 'Specially Lily.

FEMALE GREEK CHORUS (*As* MOTHER) Well, you were robbing the baby of the family!

TEENAGE GREEK CHORUS (*As* GRANDMOTHER) I still keep a broom handy in the kitchen! And I know how to use it! So get your hand out of the cookie jar and don't you spoil your appetite for dinner—out of the kitchen!

(MALE GREEK CHORUS *as* GRANDFATHER *leaves chuckling with a cookie.*)

FEMALE GREEK CHORUS (*As* MOTHER) Just one think a married woman needs to know how to use—the rolling pin or the broom. I prefer a heavy, cast-iron fry pan—they're great on a man's head, no matter how thick the skull is.

TEENAGE GREEK CHORUS (*As* GRANDMOTHER) Yes, sir, your father is ruled by only two bosses! Mr. Gut and Mr. Peter! And sometimes, first thing in the morning, Mr. Sphincter Muscle!

FEMALE GREEK CHORUS (*As* MOTHER) It's true. Men are like children. Just like little boys.

TEENAGE GREEK CHORUS (*As* GRANDMOTHER) Men are bulls! Big bulls!

(THE GREEK CHORUS *is getting aroused.*)

FEMALE GREEK CHORUS (*As* MOTHER) They'd still be crouched on their haunches over a fire in a cave if we hadn't cleaned them up!

TEENAGE GREEK CHORUS (*As* GRANDMOTHER, *flushed*) Coming in smelling of sweat—

FEMALE GREEK CHORUS (*As* MOTHER)—Looking at those naughty pictures like boys in a dime store with a dollar in their pockets!

TEENAGE GREEK CHORUS (*As* GRANDMOTHER; *raucous*) No matter to them what they smell like! They've got to have it, right then, on the spot, right there! Nasty!—

FEMALE GREEK CHORUS (*As* MOTHER)—Vulgar!

TEENAGE GREEK CHORUS (*As* GRANDMOTHER) Primitive!—

FEMALE GREEK CHORUS (*As* MOTHER)—Hot!—

LI'L BIT And just about then, Big Papa would shuffle in with—

MALE GREEK CHORUS (*As* GRANDFATHER)—What are you all cackling about in here?

TEENAGE GREEK CHORUS (*As* GRANDMOTHER) Stay out of the kitchen! This is just for girls!

(*As* GRANDFATHER *leaves:*)

MALE GREEK CHORUS (*As* GRANDFATHER) Lucy, you'd better not be filling Mama's head with sex! Every time you and Mary come over and start in about sex, when I ask a simple question like, "What time is dinner going to be ready?" Mama snaps my head off!

TEENAGE GREEK CHORUS (*As* GRANDMOTHER) Dinner will be ready when I'm good and ready! Stay out of this kitchen!

(LI'L BIT *steps out.*
   A Voice directs:)

WHEN MAKING A LEFT TURN, YOU MUST DOWNSHIFT WHILE GOING FORWARD.

LI'L BIT 1979. A long bus trip to Upstate New York. I settled in to read, when a young man sat beside me.

MALE GREEK CHORUS (*As* YOUNG MAN; *voice cracking*) "What are you reading?"

LI'L BIT He asked. His voice broke into that miserable equivalent of vocal acne, not quite falsetto and not tenor, either. I glanced a side view. He was appealing in an odd way, huge ears at a defiant angle springing forward at ninety degrees. He must have been shaving, because his face, with a peach sheen, was speckled with nicks and styptic. "I have a class tomorrow," I told him.

MALE GREEK CHORUS (*As* YOUNG MAN) "You're taking a class?"

LI'L BIT "I'm teaching a class." He concentrated on lowering his voice.

MALE GREEK CHORUS (*As* YOUNG MAN) "I'm a senior. Walt Whitman High."

LI'L BIT The light was fading outside, so perhaps he was—with a very high voice.

I felt his "interest" quicken. Five steps ahead of the hopes in his head, I slowed down, waited, pretended surprise, acted at listening, all the while knowing we would get off the bus, he would just then seem to think to ask me to dinner, he would chivalrously insist on walking me home, he would continue to converse in the street until I would casually invite him up to my room—and—I was only into the second moment of conversation and I could see the whole evening before me.

And dramaturgically speaking, after the faltering and slightly comical "first act," there was the very briefest of intermissions, and an extremely capable and forceful and sustained second act. And after the second act climax and a gentle denouement—before the post-play discussion—I lay on my back in the dark and I thought about you, Uncle Peck. Oh. Oh—this is the allure. Being older. Being the first. Being the translator, the teacher, the epicure, the already jaded. This is how the giver gets taken.

(LI'L BIT *changes her tone*) On Men, Sex, and Women: Part II:

(LI'L BIT *steps back into the scenes as a fifteen-year-old, gawky and quiet, as the gazelle at the edge of the herd.*)

TEENAGE GREEK CHORUS (As GRANDMOTHER; *to* LI'L BIT) You're being mighty quiet, missy. Cat Got Your Tongue?

LI'L BIT I'm just listening. Just thinking.

TEENAGE GREEK CHORUS (As GRANDMOTHER) Oh, yes, Little Miss Radar Ears? Soaking it all in? Little Miss Sponge? Penny for your thoughts?

(LI'L BIT *hesitates to ask but she really wants to know.*)

LI'L BIT Does it—when you do it—you know, theoretically when I do it and I haven't done it before—I mean—does it hurt?

FEMALE GREEK CHORUS (As MOTHER) Does what hurt, honey?

LI'L BIT When a . . . when a girl does it for the first time—with a man—does it hurt?

TEENAGE GREEK CHORUS (As GRANDMOTHER; *horrified*) That's what you're thinking about?

FEMALE GREEK CHORUS (As MOTHER; *calm*) Well, just a little bit. Like a pinch. And there's a little blood.

TEENAGE GREEK CHORUS (As GRANDMOTHER) Don't tell her that! She's too young to be thinking those things!

FEMALE GREEK CHORUS (As MOTHER) Well, if she doesn't find out from me, where is she going to find out? In the street?

TEENAGE GREEK CHORUS (As GRANDMOTHER) Tell her it hurts! It's agony! You think you're going to die! Especially if you do it before marriage!

FEMALE GREEK CHORUS (As MOTHER) Mama! I'm going to tell her the truth! Unlike you, you left me and Mary completely in the dark with fairy tales and told us to go to the priest! What does an eighty-year-old priest know about love-making with girls!

LI'L BIT (*Getting upset*) It's not fair!

FEMALE GREEK CHORUS (As MOTHER) Now, see, she's getting upset—you're scaring her.

TEENAGE GREEK CHORUS (As GRANDMOTHER) Good! Let her be good and scared! It hurts! You bleed like a stuck pig! And you lay there and say, "Why, O Lord, have you forsaken me?!"

LI'L BIT It's not fair! Why does everything have to hurt for girls? Why is there always blood?

FEMALE GREEK CHORUS (As MOTHER) It's not a lot of blood—and it feels wonderful after the pain subsides . . .

TEENAGE GREEK CHORUS (*As* GRANDMOTHER) You're encouraging her to just go out and find out with the first drugstore joe who buys her a milk shake!

FEMALE GREEK CHORUS (*As* MOTHER) Don't be scared. It won't hurt you—if the man you go to bed with really loves you. It's important that he loves you.

TEENAGE GREEK CHORUS (*As* GRANDMOTHER)—Why don't you just go out and rent a motel room for her, Lucy?

FEMALE GREEK CHORUS (*As* MOTHER) I believe in telling my daughter the truth! We have a very close relationship! I want her to be able to ask me anything—I'm not scaring her with stories about Eve's sin and snakes crawling on their bellies for eternity and women bearing children in mortal pain—

TEENAGE GREEK CHORUS (*As* GRANDMOTHER)—If she stops and thinks before she takes her knickers off, maybe someone in this family will finish high school!

(LI'L BIT *knows what is about to happen and starts to retreat from the scene at this point.*)

FEMALE GREEK CHORUS (*As* MOTHER) Mother! If you and Daddy had helped me—I wouldn't have had to marry that—that no-good-son-of-a—

TEENAGE GREEK CHORUS (*As* GRANDMOTHER)—He was good enough for you on a full moon! I hold you responsible!

FEMALE GREEK CHORUS (*As* MOTHER)—You could have helped me! You could have told me something about the facts of life!

TEENAGE GREEK CHORUS (*As* GRANDMOTHER)—I told you what my mother told me! A girl with her skirt up can outrun a man with his pants down!

(*The* MALE GREEK CHORUS *enters the fray;* LI'L BIT *edges further downstage.*)

FEMALE GREEK CHORUS (*As* MOTHER) And when I turned to you for a little help, all I got afterwards was—

MALE GREEK CHORUS (*As* GRANDFATHER) You Made Your Bed; Now Lie On It!

(*The* GREEK CHORUS *freezes, mouths open, argumentatively.*)

LI'L BIT (*To the audience*) Oh, please! I still can't bear to listen to it, after all these years—

(*The* MALE GREEK CHORUS *"unfreezes," but out of his open mouth as if to his surprise, comes a base refrain from a Motown song.*)

MALE GREEK CHORUS "Do-Bee-Do-Wha!"

(*The* FEMALE GREEK CHORUS *member is also surprised; but she, too, unfreezes.*)

FEMALE GREEK CHORUS "Shoo-doo-be-doo-be-doo; shoo-doo-be-doo-be-doo."

(*The Male and* FEMALE GREEK CHORUS *members continue with their harmony, until the* TEENAGER *member of the* CHORUS *starts in with Motown lyrics such as "Dedicated to the One I Love," or "In the Still of the Night," or "Hold Me"—any Sam Cooke will do. The three modulate down into three-part harmony, softly, until they are submerged by the actual recording playing over the radio in the car in which* UNCLE PECK *sits in the driver's seat, waiting.* LI'L BIT *sits in the passenger's seat.*)

LI'L BIT Ahh. That's better.

(Uncle PECK *reaches over and turns the volume down; to* LI'L BIT:)

PECK How can you hear yourself think?

*(*LI'L BIT *does not answer.*
A Voice insinuates itself in the pause:)

BEFORE YOU DRIVE.

Always check under your car for obstructions—broken bottles, fallen tree branches, and the bodies of small children. Each year hundreds of children are crushed beneath the wheels of unwary drivers in their own driveways. Children depend on you to watch them.

(Pause.
The Voice continues:)

YOU AND THE REVERSE GEAR.

(In the following section, it would be nice to have slides of erotic photographs of women and cars: women posed over the hood; women draped along the sideboards; women with water hoses spraying the car; and the actress playing LI'L BIT *with a Bel Air or any 1950s car one can find for the finale.)*

LI'L BIT 1967. In a parking lot of the Beltsville Agriculture Farms. The Initiation into a Boy's First Love.

PECK *(With a soft look on his face)* Of course, my favorite care will always be the '56 Bel Air Sports Coupe. Chevy sold more '55s, but the '56!—a V-8 with Corvette option, 225 horsepower; went from zero to sixty miles per hour in 8.9 seconds.

LI'L BIT *(To the audience)* Long after a mother's tits, but before a woman's breasts:

PECK Super-Turbo-Fire! What a Power Pack—mechanical lifters, twin four-barrel carbs, lightweight valves, dual exhausts—

LI'L BIT *(To the audience)* After the milk but before the beer:

PECK A specific intake manifold, higher-lift camshaft, and the tightest squeeze Chevy had ever made—

LI'L BIT *(To the audience)* Long after he's squeezed down the birth canal but before he's pushed his way back in: The boy falls in love with the thing that bears his weight with speed.

PECK I want you to know your automobile inside and out. —Are you there? Li'l Bit?

(Slides end here.)

LI'L BIT—What?
PECK You're drifting. I need you to concentrate.
LI'L BIT Sorry.

PECK Okay. Get into the driver's seat. (LI'L BIT *does*) Okay. Now. Show me what you're going to do before you start the car.

(LI'L BIT *sits, with her hands in her lap. She starts to giggle.*)

PECK Now, come on. What's the first thing you're going to adjust?

LI'L BIT My bra strap?—

PECK—Li'l Bit. What's the most important thing to have control of on the inside of the car?

LI'L BIT That's easy. The radio. I tune the radio from Mama's old fart tunes to—

(LI'L BIT *turns the radio up so we can hear a 1960s tune. With surprising firmness,* PECK *commands:*)

PECK—Radio off. Right now. (LI'L BIT *turns the radio off*) When you are driving your car, with your license, you can fiddle with the stations all you want. But when you are driving with a learner's permit in my car, I want all your attention to be on the road.

LI'L BIT Yes, sir.

PECK Okay. Now the seat—forward and up. (LI'L BIT *pushes it forward*) Do you want a cushion?

LI'L BIT No—I'm good.

PECK You should be able to reach all the switches and controls. Your feet should be able to push the accelerator, brake and clutch all the way down. Can you do that?

LI'L BIT Yes.

PECK Okay, the side mirrors. You want to be able to see just a bit of the right side of the car in the right mirror—can you?

LI'L BIT Turn it out more.

PECK Okay. How's that?

LI'L BIT A little more. . . . Okay, that's good.

PECK Now the left—again, you want to be able to see behind you—but the left lane—adjust it until you feel comfortable. (LI'L BIT *does so*) Next. I want you to check the rearview mirror. Angle it so you have a clear vision of the back. (LI'L BIT *does so*) Okay. Lock your door. Make sure all the doors are locked.

LI'L BIT (*Making a joke of it*) But then I'm locked in with you.

PECK Don't fool.

LI'L BIT All right. We're locked in.

PECK We'll deal with the air vents and defroster later. I'm teaching you on a manual—once you learn manual, you can drive anything. I want you to be able to drive any car, any machine. Manual gives you control. In ice, if your brakes fail, if you need more power—okay? It's a little harder at first, but them it becomes like breathing. Now. Put your hands on the wheel. I never want to see you driving with one hand. Always two hands. (LI'L BIT *hesitates*) What? What is it now?

LI'L BIT If I put my hands on the wheel—how do I defend myself?

PECK (*Softly*) Now listen. Listen up close. We're not going to fool around with this. This is serious business. I will never touch you when you are driving a car. Understand?

LI'L BIT Okay.

PECK Hands on the nine o'clock and three o'clock position gives you maximum control and turn.

(PECK *goes silent for a while.* LI'L BIT *waits for more instruction*)

Okay. Just relax and listen to me, Li'l Bit, okay? I want you to lift your hands for a second and look at them. (LI'L BIT *feels a bit silly, but does it*)

Those are your two hands. When you are driving, you life is in your own two hands. Understand? (LI'L BIT *nods*)

I don't have any sons. You're the nearest to a son I'll ever have—and I want to give you something. Something that really matters to me.

There's something about driving—when you're in control of the car, just you and the machine and the road—that nobody can take from you. A power. I feel more myself in my car than anywhere else. And that's what I want to give to you.

There's a lot of assholes out there. Crazy men, arrogant idiots, drunks, angry kids, geezers who are blind—and you have to be ready for them. I want to teach you to drive like a man.

LI'L BIT What does that mean?

PECK Men are taught to drive with confidence—when aggression. The road belongs to them. They drive defensively—always looking out for the other guy. Women tend to be polite—to hesitate. And that can be fatal.

You're going to learn to think what the other guy is going to do before he does it. If there's an accident, and ten cars pile up, and people get killed, you're the one who's gonna steer through it, put your foot on the gas if you have to, and be the only one to walk away. I don't know how long you or I are going to live, but we're for damned sure not going to die in a car.

So if you're going to drive with me, I want you to take this very seriously.

LI'L BIT I will, Uncle Peck. I want you to teach me to drive.

PECK Good. You're going to pass your test on the first try. Perfect score. Before the next four weeks are over, you're going to know this baby inside and out. Treat her with respect.

LI'L BIT Why is it a "she"?

PECK Good question. It doesn't have to be a "she"—but when you close your eyes and think of someone who responds to your touch—someone who performs just for you and gives you what you ask for—I guess I always see a "she." You can call her what you like.

LI'L BIT (*To the audience*) I closed my eyes—and decided not to change the gender.

(*A Voice:*)

Defensive driving involves defending yourself from hazardous and sudden changes in your automotive environment. By thinking ahead, the defensive driver can adjust to weather, road conditions and road kill. Good defensive driving involves mental and physical preparation. Are you prepared?

(*Another Voice chimes in:*)

YOU AND THE REVERSE GEAR.

LI'L BIT 1966. The Anthropology of the Female Body in Ninth Grade—Or A Walk Down Mammary Lane.

(Throughout the following, there is occasional rhythmic beeping, like a transmitter signaling. LI'L BIT *is aware of it, but can't figure out where it is coming from. No one else seems to hear it.)*

MALE GREEK CHORUS In the hallway of Francis Scott Key Middle School.

(A bell rings; the GREEK CHORUS *is changing classes and meets in the hall, conspiratorially.)*

TEENAGE GREEK CHORUS She's coming!

*(*LI'L BIT *enters the scene; the* MALE GREEK CHORUS *member has a sudden, violent sneezing and lethal allergy attack.)*

FEMALE GREEK CHORUS Jerome? Jerome? Are you all right?
MALE GREEK CHORUS I—don't—know. I can't breathe—get Li'l Bit—
TEENAGE GREEK CHORUS—He needs oxygen!—
FEMALE GREEK CHORUS—Can you help us here?
LI'L BIT What's wrong? Do you want me to get the school nurse—

(The MALE GREEK CHORUS *member wheezes, grabs his throat and sniffs at* LI'L BIT'S *chest, which is beeping away.)*

MALE GREEK CHORUS No—it's okay—I only get this way when I'm around an allergy trigger—
LI'L BIT Golly. What are you allergic to?
MALE GREEK CHORUS *(With a sudden grab of her breast)* Foam rubber.

(The GREEK CHORUS *members break up with hilarity;* JEROME *leaps away from* LI'L BIT'S *kicking rage with agility; as he retreats:)*

LI'L BIT Jerome! Creep! Cretin! Cro-Magnon!
TEENAGE GREEK CHORUS Rage is not attractive in a girl.
FEMALE GREEK CHORUS Really. Get a Sense of Humor.

(A voice echoes:)

GOOD DEFENSIVE DRIVING INVOLVES MENTAL AND PHYSICAL PREPARATION. WERE YOU PREPARED?

FEMALE GREEK CHORUS Gym Class: In the showers.

(The sudden sound of water; the FEMALE GREEK CHORUS *members and* LI'L BIT, *while fully clothed, drape towels across their fronts, miming nudity. They stand, hesitate, at an imaginary shower's edge.)*

LI'L BIT Water looks hot.

FEMALE GREEK CHORUS Yesss. . . .

(FEMALE GREEK CHORUS *members are not going to make the first move. One dips a ten-tative toe under the water, clutching the towel around her.*)

LI'L BIT Well, I guess we'd better shower and get out of here.

FEMALE GREEK CHORUS Yep. You go ahead. I'm still cooling off.

LI'L BIT Okay. —Sally? Are you gonna shower?

TEENAGE GREEK CHORUS After you—

(LI'L BIT *takes a deep breath for courage, drops the towel and plunges in: The two* FEMALE GREEK CHORUS *members look at* LI'L BIT *in the all together, laugh, gasp and high-five each other.*)

TEENAGE GREEK CHORUS Oh my god! Can you believe—

FEMALE GREEK CHORUS Told you it's not foam rubber! I win! Jerome owes me fifty cents.

(*A Voice editorializes:*)

WERE YOU PREPARED?

(LI'L BIT *tries to cover up; she is exposed, as suddenly 1960s Motown fills the room and we segue into:*)

FEMALE GREEK CHORUS The Sock Hop.

(LI'L BIT *stands against the wall with her female classmates.* TEENAGE GREEK CHORUS *is mesmerized by the music and just sways alone, lip-synching the lyrics.*)

LI'L BIT I don't know. Maybe it's just me—but—do you ever feel like you're just a walking Mary Jane joke?

FEMALE GREEK CHORUS I don't know what you mean.

LI'L BIT You haven't heard the Mary Jane jokes? (FEMALE GREEK CHORUS *member shakes her head no*) Okay. "Little Mary Jane is walking through the woods, when all of a sudden this man who was hiding behind a tree jumps out, rips open Mary Jane's blouse, and plunges his hands on her breasts. And Little Mary Jane just laughed and laughed because she knew her money was in her shoes."

(LI'L BIT *laughs; the* FEMALE GREEK CHORUS *does not.*)

FEMALE GREEK CHORUS You're weird.

(*In another space, in a strange light,* UNCLE PECK *stands and stares at* LI'L BIT's *body. He is setting up a tripod, but he just stands, appreciative, watching her.*)

LI'L BIT Well, don't you ever feel . . . self-conscious? Like you're being looked at all the time?

FEMALE GREEK CHORUS That's not a problem for me. —Oh—look—Greg's coming over to ask you to dance.

(TEENAGE GREEK CHORUS *becomes attentive, flustered.* MALE GREEK CHORUS *member, as Greg, bends slightly as a very short young man, whose head is at* LI'L BIT'S *chest level. Ardent, sincere and socially inept,* GREG *will become a successful gynecologist.*)

TEENAGE GREEK CHORUS *(Softly)* Hi, Greg.

(GREG *does not hear. He is intent on only one thing.*)

MALE GREEK CHORUS *(As* GREG, *to* LI'L BIT) Good Evening. Would you care to dance?

LI'L BIT *(Gently)* Thank you very much, Greg—but I'm going to sit this one out.

MALE GREEK CHORUS *(As* GREG) Oh. Okay. I'll try my luck later.

(*He disappears.*)

TEENAGE GREEK CHORUS Oohhh.

(LI'L BIT *relaxes. Then she tenses, aware of* PECK'S *gaze.*)

FEMALE GREEK CHORUS Take pity on him. Someone should.

LI'L BIT But he's too short.

TEENAGE GREEK CHORUS He can't help it.

LI'L BIT But his head comes up to (LI'L BIT *gestures*) here. And I think he asks me on the fast dances so he can watch me—you know—jiggle.

FEMALE GREEK CHORUS I wish I had your problems.

(*The tune changes;* GREG *is across the room in a flash.*)

MALE GREEK CHORUS *(As* GREG) Evening again. May I ask you for the honor of a spin on the floor?

LI'L BIT I'm . . . very complimented, Greg. But I . . . I just don't do fast dances.

MALE GREEK CHORUS *(As* GREG) Oh. No problem. That's okay.

(*He disappears.* TEENAGE GREEK CHORUS *watches him go.*)

TEENAGE GREEK CHORUS That is just so—sad.

(LI'L BIT *becomes aware of* PECK *waiting.*)

FEMALE GREEK CHORUS You know, you should take it as a compliment that the guys want to watch you jiggle. They're guys. That's what they're supposed to do.

LI'L BIT I guess you're right. But sometimes I feel like these alien life forces, these two mounds of flesh have grafted themselves onto my chest, and they're using me until they can "propagate" and take over the world and they'll just keep growing, with a mind of their own until I collapse under their weight and they suck all the nourishment out of my body and I finally just waste away while they get bigger and bigger and— (LI'L BIT'S *classmates are just staring at her in disbelief*)

FEMALE GREEK CHORUS—You are the strangest girl I have ever met.

(LI'L BIT'S *trying to joke but feels on the verge of tears.*)

LI'L BIT Or maybe someone's implanted radio transmitters in my chest at a frequency I can't hear, that girls can't detect, but they're sending out these signals to men who get mesmerized, like sirens, calling them to dash themselves on these "rocks"—

(Just then, the music segues into a slow dance, perhaps a Beach Boys tune like "Little Surfer," but over the music there's a rhythmic, hypnotic beeping transmitted, which both GREG *and* PECK *hear.* LI'L BIT *hears it too, and in horror she stares at her chest. She, too, is almost hypnotized. In a trance,* GREG *responds to the signals and is called to her side—actually, her front. Like a zombie, he stands in front of her, his eyes planted on her two orbs.)*

MALE GREEK CHORUS *(As* GREG) This one's a slow dance. I hope your dance card isn't . . . filled?

*(*LI'L BIT *is aware of* PECK; *but the signals are calling her to him. The signals are no longer transmitters, but an electromagnetic force, pulling* LI'L BIT *to his side, where he again waits for her to join him. She must get away from the dance floor.)*

LI'L BIT Greg—you really are a nice boy. But I don't like to dance.
MALE GREEK CHORUS *(As* GREG) That's okay. We don't have to move or anything. I could just hold you and we could just sway a little—
LI'L BIT—No! I'm sorry—but I think I have to leave; I hear someone calling me—
   *(*LI'L BIT *starts across the dance floor, leaving* GREG *behind. The beeping stops. The lights change, although the music does not. As* LI'L BIT *talks to the audience, she continues to change and prepare for the coming session. She should be wearing a tight tank top or a sheer blouse and very tight pants. To the audience:)*
   In every man's home some small room, some zone in his house, is set aside. It might be the attic, or the study, or a den. And there's an invisible sign as if from the old treehouse: Girls Keep Out.
   Here, away from female eyes, lace doilies and crochet, he keeps his manly toys: the Vargas pinups, the tackle. A scent of tobacco and WD-40. *(She inhales deeply)* A dash of his Bay Rum. Ahh . . . *(*LI'L BIT *savors it for just a moment more)*
   Here he keeps his secrets: a violin or saxophone, drum set or darkroom, and the stacks of *Playboy*. *(In a whisper)* Here, in my aunt's home, it was the basement. Uncle Peck's turf.

(A Voice commands:)

YOU AND THE REVERSE GEAR.

LI'L BIT 1965. The Photo Shoot.

*(*LI'L BIT *steps into the scene as a nervous but curious thirteen-year-old. Music, from the previous scene, continues to play, changing into something like Roy Orbison later— something seductive with a beat.* PECK *fiddles, all business, with his camera. As in the driving lesson, he is all competency and concentration.* LI'L BIT *stands awkwardly. He looks through the Leica camera on the tripod, adjusts the back lighting, etc.)*

PECK Are you cold? The lights should heat up some in a few minutes—
LI'L BIT—Aunt Mary is?
PECK At the National Theatre matinee. With your mother. We have time.
LI'L BIT But—what if—
PECK—And so what if they return? I told them you and I were going to be working

with my camera. They won't come down. (LI'L BIT *is quiet, apprehensive*)—Look, are you sure you want to do this?

LI'L BIT I said I'd do it. But—

PECK—I know. You've drawn the line.

LI'L BIT (*Reassured*) That's right. No frontal nudity.

PECK Good heavens, girl, where did you pick that up?

LI'L BIT (*Defensive*) I read.

(PECK *tries not to laugh.*)

PECK And I read *Playboy* for the interviews. Okay. Let's try some different music.

(PECK *goes to an expensive reel-to-reel and forwards. Something like "Sweet Dreams" begins to play.*)

LI'L BIT I didn't know you listened to this.

PECK I'm not dead, you know. I try to keep up. Do you like this song? (LI'L BIT *nods with pleasure*) Good. Now listen—at professional photo shoots, they always play music for the models. Okay? I want you to just enjoy the music. Listen to it with your body, and just—respond.

LI'L BIT Respond to the music with my . . . body?

PECK Right. Almost like dancing. Here—let's get you on the stool, first. (PECK *comes over and helps her up*)

LI'L BIT But nothing showing—

(PECK *firmly, with his large capable hands, brushes back her hair, angles her face.* LI'L BIT *turns to him like a plant to the sun.*)

PECK Nothing showing. Just a peek.
(*He holds her by the shoulders, looking at her critically. Then he unbuttons her blouse to the midpoint, and runs his hands over the flesh of her exposed sternum, arranging the fabric, just touching her. Deliberately, calmly. Asexually.* LI'L BIT *quiets, sits perfectly still, and closes her eyes*)
Okay?

LI'L BIT Yes.

(PECK *goes back to his camera.*)

PECK I'm going to keep talking to you. Listen without responding to what I'm saying; you want to *listen* to the music. Sway, move just your torso or your head—I've got to check the light meter.

LI'L BIT But—you'll be watching.

PECK No—I'm not here—just my voice. Pretend you're in your room all alone on a Friday night with your mirror—and the music feels good—just move for me, Li'l Bit—
(LI'L BIT *closes her eyes. At first self-conscious; then she gets more into the music and begins to sway. We hear the camera start to whir. Throughout the shoot, there can be a slide montage of actual shots of the actor playing* LI'L BIT—*interspersed with other models à la Playboy, Calvin Klein and Victoriana/Lewis Carroll's Alice Liddell*)
That's it. That looks great. Okay. Just keep doing that. Lift your head up a bit

more, good, good, just keep moving, that a girl—you're a beautiful young woman. Do you know that? (LI'L BIT *looks up, blushes.* PECK *shoots the camera. The audience should see this shot on the screen*)

LI'L BIT No. I don't know that.

PECK Listen to the music. (LI'L BIT *closes her eyes again*) Well you are. For a thirteen-year-old, you have a body a twenty-year-old woman would die for.

LI'L BIT The boys in school don't think so.

PECK The boys in school are little Neanderthals in short pants. You're ten years ahead of them in maturity; it's gonna take a while for them to catch up.

(PECK *clicks another shot; we see a faint smile on* LI'L BIT *on the screen*)

Girls turn into women long before boys turn into men.

LI'L BIT Why is that?

PECK I don't know, Li'l Bit. But it's a blessing for men.

(LI'L BIT *turns silent*) Keep moving. Try arching your back on the stool, hands behind you, and throw your head back. (*The slide shows a* Playboy *model in this pose*) Oohh, great. That one was great. Turn head away, same position. (*Whir*) Beautiful.

(LI'L BIT *looks at him a bit defiantly.*)

LI'L BIT I think Aunt Mary is beautiful.

(PECK *stands still.*)

PECK My wife is a very beautiful woman. Her beauty doesn't cancel yours out. (*More casually; he returns to the camera*) All the women in your family are beautiful. In fact, I think all women are. You're not listening to the music. (PECK *shoots some more film in silence*) All right, turn your head to the left. Good. Now take the back of your right hand and put it on your right cheek—your elbow angled up—now slowly, slowly, stroke your cheek, draw back your hair with the back of your hand. (*Another classic* Playboy *or* Vargas) Good. One hand above and behind your head; stretch your body; smile. (*Another pose*)

Li'l Bit. I want you to think of something that makes you laugh—

LI'L BIT I can't think of anything.

PECK Okay. Think of Big Papa chasing Grandma around the living room. (LI'L BIT *lifts her head and laughs. Click. We should see this shot*) Good. Both hands behind your head. Great! Hold that. (*From behind his camera*) You're doing great work. If we keep this up, in five years we'll have a really professional portfolio.

(LI'L BIT *stops.*)

LI'L BIT What do you mean in five years?

PECK You can't submit work to *Playboy* until you're eighteen.—

(PECK *continues to shoot; he knows he's made a mistake.*)

LI'L BIT—Wait a minute. You're joking aren't you, Uncle Peck?

PECK Heck, no. You can't get into *Playboy* unless you're the very best. And you are the very best.

LI'L BIT I would never do that!

(PECK *stops shooting. He turns off the music.*)

PECK Why? There's nothing wrong with *Playboy*—it's a very classy maga—

LI'L BIT *(More upset)* But I thought you said I should go to college!

PECK Wait—Li'l Bit—it's nothing like that. Very respectable women model for *Playboy*—actresses with major careers—women in college—there's an Ivy League issue every—

LI'L BIT—I'm never doing anything like that! You'd show other people these—other *men*—these—what I'm doing.—Why would you do that?! Any *boy* around here could just pick up, just go to The Stop & Go and *buy*— Why would you ever want to—to share—

PECK—Whoa, whoa. Just stop a second and listen to me. Li'l Bit. Listen. There's nothing wrong in what we're doing. I'm very proud of you. I think you have a wonderful body and an even more wonderful mind. And of course I want other people to *appreciate* it. It's not anything shameful.

LI'L BIT *(Hurt)* But this is something—that I'm only doing for you. This is something—that you said was just between us.

PECK It is. And if that's how you feel, five years from now, it will remain that way. Okay? I know you're not going to do anything you don't feel like doing.
   (He walks back to the camera) Do you want me to stop now? I've got just a few more shots on this roll—

LI'L BIT I don't want anyone seeing this.

PECK I swear to you. No one will. I'll treasure this—that you're doing this only for me.
   (LI'L BIT *still shaken, sits on the stool. She closes her eyes*) Li'l Bit? Open your eyes and look at me. (LI'L BIT *shakes her head no*) Come on. Just open your eyes, honey.

LI'L BIT If I look at you—if I look at the camera: You're gonna know what I'm thinking. You'll see right through me—

PECK—No, I won't. I want you to look at me. All right, then. I just want you to listen. Li'l Bit. *(She waits)* I love you. (LI'L BIT *opens her eyes; she is startled.* PECK *captures the shot. On the screen we see right through her.* PECK *says softly)* Do you know that? (LI'L BIT *nods her head yes*) I have loved you every day since the day you were born.

LI'L BIT Yes.

(LI'L BIT *and* PECK *just look at each other. Beat. Beneath the shot of herself on the screen,* LI'L BIT, *still looking at her uncle, begins to unbutton her blouse.*
   A neutral Voice cuts off the above scene with:)

IMPLIED CONSENT

As an individual operating a motor vehicle in the state of Maryland, you must abide by "Implied Consent." If you do not consent to take the blood alcohol content test,

there may be severe penalties: a suspension of license, a fine, community service and a possible jail sentence.

(The Voice shifts tone:)

IDLING IN NEUTRAL GEAR.

MALE GREEK CHORUS *(Announcing)* Aunt Mary on behalf of her husband.

(FEMALE GREEK CHORUS checks her appearance, and with dignity comes to the front of the stage and sits down to talk to the audience.)

FEMALE GREEK CHORUS *(As AUNT MARY)* My husband was such a good man—is. Is such a good man. Every night, he does the dishes. The second he comes home, he's taking out the garbage, or doing the yard work, lifting the heavy things I can't. Everyone in the neighborhood borrows Peck—it's true—women with husbands of their own, men who just don't have Peck's abilities—there's always a knock on our door for a jump start on cold mornings, when anyone else needs a ride, or help shoveling the sidewalk—I look out, and there Peck is, without a coat, pitching in.

I know I'm lucky. The man works from dawn to dusk. And the overtime he does every year—my poor sister. She sits every Christmas when I come to dinner with a new stole, or diamonds, or with the tickets to Bermuda.

I know he has troubles. And we don't talk about them. I wonder, sometimes, what happened to him during the war. The men who fought World War II didn't have "rap sessions" to talk about their feelings. Men in his generation were expected to be quiet about it and get on with their lives. And sometimes I can feel him just fighting the trouble—whatever has burrowed deeper than the scar tissue—and we don't talk about it. I know he's having a bad spell because he comes looking for me in the house, and just hangs around me until it passes. And I keep my banter light—I discuss a new recipe, or sales, or gossip—because I think domesticity can be a balm for men when they're lost. We sit in the house and listen to the peace of the clock ticking in his well-ordered living room, until it passes.

(Sharply) I'm not a fool. I know what's going on. I wish you could feel how hard Peck fights against it—he's swimming against the tide, and what he needs is to see me on the shore, believing in him, knowing he won't go under, he won't give up—

And I want to say this about my niece. She's a sly one, that one is. She knows exactly what she's doing; she's twisted Peck around her little finger and thinks it's all a big secret. Yet another one who's borrowing my husband until it doesn't suit her anymore.

Well. I'm counting the days until she goes away to school. And she manipulates someone else. And then he'll come back again, and sit in the kitchen while I bake, or beside me on the sofa when I sew in the evenings. I'm a very patient woman. But I'd like my husband back.

I am counting the days.

(A Voice repeats:)

YOU AND THE REVERSE GEAR.

MALE GREEK CHORUS Li'l Bit's Thirteenth Christmas. Uncle Peck Does the Dishes. Christmas 1964.

(PECK stands in a dress shirt and tie, nice pants, with an apron. He is washing dishes. He's in a mood we haven't seen. Quiet, brooding. LI'L BIT *watches him a moment before seeking him out.)*

LI'L BIT Uncle Peck? *(He does not answer. He continues to work on the pots)* I didn't know where you'd gone to *(He nods. She takes this as a sign to come in)* Don't you want to sit with us for a while?
PECK No. I'd rather do the dishes.

(Pause. LI'L BIT *watches him.)*

LI'L BIT You're the only man I know who does dishes. *(PECK says nothing)* I think it's really nice.
PECK My wife has been on her feet all day. So's your grandmother and your mother.
LI'L BIT I know. *(Beat)* Do you want some help?
PECK No. *(He softens a bit towards her)* You can help by just talking to me.
LI'L BIT Big Papa never does the dishes. I think it's nice.
PECK I think men should be nice to women. Women are always working for us. There's nothing particularly manly in wolfing down food and then sitting around in a stupor while the women clean up.
LI'L BIT That looks like a really neat camera that Aunt Mary got you.
PECK It is. It's a very nice one.

(Pause, as PECK *works on the dishes and some demon that* LI'L BIT *intuits.)*

LI'L BIT Did Big Papa hurt your feelings?
PECK *(Tired)* What? Oh, no—it doesn't hurt me. Family is family. I'd rather have him picking on me than—I don't pay him any mind, Li'l Bit.
LI'L BIT Are you angry with us?
PECK No, Li'l Bit. I'm not angry.

(Another pause.)

LI'L BIT We missed you at Thanksgiving. . . . I did. I missed you.
PECK Well, there were . . . "things" going on. I didn't want to spoil anyone's Thanksgiving.
LI'L BIT Uncle Peck? *(Very carefully)* Please don't drink anymore tonight.
PECK I'm not . . . overdoing it.
LI'L BIT I know. *(Beat)* Why do you drink so much?

(PECK stops and thinks, carefully.)

PECK Well, Li'l Bit—let me explain it this way. There are some people who have a . . . a "fire" in the belly. I think they go to work on Wall Street or they run for office. And then there are people who have a "fire" inside their heads—and they become writers or scientists or historians. *(He smiles a little at her)* You. You've got a "fire" in the head. And then there are people like me.

LI'L BIT Where do you have . . . a fire?

PECK I have a fire in my heart. And sometimes the drinking helps.

LI'L BIT There's got to be other things that can help.

PECK I suppose there are.

LI'L BIT Does it help—to talk to me?

PECK Yes. I does. *(Quietly)* I don't get to see you very much.

LI'L BIT I know. (LI'L BIT *thinks*) You could talk to me more.

PECK Oh?

LI'L BIT I could make a deal with you, Uncle Peck.

PECK I'm listening.

LI'L BIT We could meet and talk—once a week. You could just store up whatever's bothering you during the week—and then we could talk.

PECK Would you like that?

LI'L BIT As long as you don't drink. I'd meet you somewhere for lunch or for a walk— on the weekends—as long as you stop drinking. And we could talk about whatever you want.

PECK You would do that for me?

LI'L BIT I don't think I'd want Mom to know. Or Aunt Mary. I wouldn't want them to think—

PECK—No. It would just be us talking.

LI'L BIT I'll tell Mom I'm going to a girlfriend's. To study. Mom doesn't get home until six, so you can call me after school and tell me where to meet you.

PECK You get home at four?

LI'L BIT We can meet once a week. But only in public. You've got to let me—draw the line. And once it's drawn, you mustn't cross it.

PECK Understood.

LI'L BIT Would that help?

(PECK *is very moved*.)

PECK Yes. Very much.

LI'L BIT I'm going to join the others in the living room now. (LI'L BIT *turns to go*)

PECK Merry Christmas, Li'l Bit.

(LI'L BIT *bestows a very warm smile on him*.)

LI'L BIT Merry Christmas, Uncle Peck.

(A Voice dictates:)

SHIFTING FORWARD FROM SECOND TO THIRD GEAR.

(The Male and FEMALE GREEK CHORUS *members come forward*.)

MALE GREEK CHORUS 1969. Days and Gifts: A Countdown:

FEMALE GREEK CHORUS A note. "September 3, 1969. Li'l Bit: You've only been away two days and it feels like months. Hope your dorm room is cozy. I'm sending you this tape cassette—it's a new model—so you'll have some music in your room. Also that music you're reading about for class—*Carmina Burana.* Hope you enjoy. Only ninety days to go!—Peck."

MALE GREEK CHORUS September 22. A bouquet of roses. A note: "Miss you like crazy. Sixty-nine days . . ."

TEENAGE GREEK CHORUS September 25. A box of chocolates. A card: "Don't worry about the weight gain. You still look great. Got a post office box—write to me there. Sixty-six days.—Love, your candy man."

MALE GREEK CHORUS October 16. A note: "Am trying to get through the Jane Austin you're reading—*Emma*—here's a book in return: *Liaisons Dangereuses.* Hope you're saving time for me." Scrawled in the margin the number: "47."

FEMALE GREEK CHORUS November 16. "Sixteen days to go!—Hope you like the perfume.—Having a hard time reaching you on the dorm phone. You must be in the library a lot. Won't you think about me getting you your own phone so we can talk?"

TEENAGE GREEK CHORUS November 18. "Li'l Bit—got a package and returned it to the P.O. Box. Have you changed dorms? Call me at work or write to the P.O. Am still on the wagon. Waiting to see you. Only two weeks more!"

MALE GREEK CHORUS November 23. A letter: "Li'l Bit. So disappointed you couldn't come home for the turkey. Sending you some money for a nice dinner out—nine days and counting!"

GREEK CHORUS *(In unison)* November 25th. A letter:

LI'L BIT "Dear Uncle Peck: I am sending this to you at work. Don't come up next weekend for my birthday. I will not be here—"

(A Voice directs:)

SHIFTING FORWARD FROM THIRD TO FOURTH GEAR.

MALE GREEK CHORUS December 10, 1969. A hotel room. Philadelphia. There is no moon tonight.

(PECK sits on the side of the bed while LI'L BIT paces. He can't believe she's in his room, but there's a desperate edge to his happiness. LI'L BIT is furious, edgy. There is a bottle of champagne in an ice bucket in a very nice hotel room.)

PECK Why don't you sit?

LI'L BIT I don't want to.—What's the champagne for?

PECK I thought we might toast your birthday—

LI'L BIT—I am so pissed off at you, Uncle Peck.

PECK Why?

LI'L BIT I mean, are you crazy?

PECK What did I do?

LI'L BIT You scared the holy crap out of me—sending me that stuff in the mail—

PECK—They were gifts! I just wanted to give you some little perks your first
semester—

LI'L BIT—Well, what the hell were those numbers all about! Forty-four days to go—
only two more weeks.—And then just numbers—69—68—67—like some serial
killer!

PECK Li'l Bit! Whoa! This is me you're talking to—I was just trying to pick up your
spirits, trying to celebrate your birthday.

LI'L BIT My *eighteenth* birthday. I'm not a child, Uncle Peck. You were counting
down to my eighteenth birthday.

PECK So?

LI'L BIT So? So statutory rape is not in effect when a young woman turns eighteen.
And you and I both know it.

(PECK *is walking on ice.*)

PECK I think you misunderstand.

LI'L BIT I think I understand all too well. I know what you want to do five steps ahead
of you doing it: Defensive Driving 101.

PECK Then why did you suggest we meet here instead of the restaurant?

LI'L BIT I don't want to have this conversation in public.

PECK Fine. Fine. We have a lot to talk about.

LI'L BIT Yeah. We do.
    (LI'L BIT *doesn't want to do what she has to do*) Could I . . . have some of that
champagne?

PECK Of course, madam! (PECK *makes a big show of it*) Let me do the honors. I
wasn't sure which you might prefer—Tattingers or Veuve Clicquot—so I thought
we'd start out with an old standard—Pierrier Jouet. (*The bottle is popped*)
    Quick—Li'l Bit—your glass! (UNCLE PECK *fills* LI'L BIT's *glass. He puts the bottle
back in the ice and goes for a can of ginger ale*) Let me get some of this ginger ale—
my bubbly—and toast you.

(*He turns and sees that* LI'L BIT *has not waited for him.*)

LI'L BIT Oh—sorry, Uncle Peck. Let me have another. (PECK *fills her glass and reaches
for his ginger ale; she stops him*) Uncle Peck—maybe you should join me in the
champagne.

PECK You want me to—drink?

LI'L BIT It's not polite to let a lady drink alone.

PECK Well, missy, if you insist. . . . (PECK *hesitates*)—Just one. It's been a while. (PECK
fills another flute for himself) There. I'd like to propose a toast to you and your
birthday! (PECK *sips it tentatively*) I'm not used to this anymore.

LI'L BIT You don't have anywhere to go tonight, do you?

(PECK *hopes this is a good sign.*)

PECK I'm all yours.—God, it's good to see you! I've gotten so used to . . . to . . . talking to you in my head. I'm used to seeing you every week—there's so much—I
don't quite know where to begin. How's school, Li'l Bit?

LI'L BIT I—it's hard. Uncle Peck. Harder than I thought it would be. I'm in the middle of exams and papers and—I don't know.

PECK You'll pull through. You always do.

LI'L BIT Maybe. I . . . might be flunking out.

PECK You always think the worse, Li'l Bit, but when the going gets tough— (LI'L BIT *shrugs and pours herself another glass*) —Hey, honey, go easy on that stuff, okay?

LI'L BIT Is it very expensive?

PECK Only the best for you. But the cost doesn't matter—champagne should be "sipped." (LI'L BIT *is quiet*) Look—if you're in trouble in school—you can always come back home for a while.

LI'L BIT No— (LI'L BIT *tries not to be so harsh*) —Thanks, Uncle Peck, but I'll figure some way out of this.

PECK You're supposed to get in scrapes, your first year away from home.

LI'L BIT Right. How's Aunt Mary?

PECK She's fine. *(Pause)* Well—how about the new car?

LI'L BIT It's real nice. What is it, again?

PECK It's a Cadillac El Dorado.

LI'L BIT Oh. Well, I'm real happy for you, Uncle Peck.

PECK I got it for you.

LI'L BIT What?

PECK I always wanted to get a Cadillac—but I thought, Peck, wait until Li'l Bit's old enough—and thought maybe you'd like to drive it, too.

LI'L BIT *(Confused)* Why would I want to drive your car?

PECK Just because it's the best—I want you to have the best.

(They are running out of "gas"; small talk.)

LI'L BIT Listen, Uncle Peck, I don't know how to begin this, but—	PECK I have been thinking of how to say this in my head, over and over—

PECK Sorry.

LI'L BIT You first.

PECK Well, your going away—has just made me realize how much I miss you. Talking to you and being alone with you. I've really come to depend on you, Li'l Bit. And it's been so hard to get in touch with you lately—the distance and—and you're never in when I call—I guess you've been living in the library—

LI'L BIT—No—the problem is, I haven't been in the library—

PECK—Well, it doesn't matter—I hope you've been missing me as much.

LI'L BIT Uncle Peck—I've been thinking a lot about this—and I came here tonight to tell you that—I'm not doing very well. I'm getting very confused—I can't concentrate on my work—and now that I'm away—I've been going over and over it in my mind—and I don't want us to "see" each other anymore. Other than with the rest of the family.

PECK *(Quiet)* Are you seeing other men?

LI'L BIT *(Getting agitated)* I—no, that's not the reason—I—well, yes, I am seeing other—listen, it's not really anybody's business!

PECK Are you in love with anyone else?

LI'L BIT That's not what this is about.

PECK Li'l Bit—you're scared. Your mother and your grandparents have filled your head with all kinds of nonsense about men—I hear them working on you all the time—and you're scared. It won't hurt you—if the man you go to bed with really loves you. (LI'L BIT *is scared. She starts to tremble*) And I have loved you since the day I held you in my hand. And I think everyone's just gotten you frightened to death about something that is just like breathing—

LI'L BIT Oh, my god—(*She takes a breath*) I can't see you anymore, Uncle Peck.

(PECK *downs the rest of his champagne.*)

PECK Li'l Bit. Listen. Listen. Open your eyes and look at me. Come on. Just open your eyes, honey. (LI'L BIT, *eyes squeezed shut, refuses*) All right then. I just want you to listen. Li'l Bit—I'm going to ask you this just once. Of your own free will. Just lie down on the bed with me—our clothes on—just lie down with me, a man and a woman . . . and let's . . . hold one another. Nothing else. Before you say anything else. I want the chance to . . . hold you. Because sometimes the body knows things that the mind isn't listening to . . . and after I've held you, then I want you to tell me what you feel.

LI'L BIT You'll just . . . hold me?

PECK Yes. And then you can tell me what you're feeling.

(LI'L BIT—*half wanting to run, half wanting to get it over with, half wanting to be held by him:*)

LI'L BIT Yes. All right. Just hold. Nothing else.

(PECK *lies down on the bed and holds his arms out to her.* LI'L BIT *lies beside him, putting her head on his chest. He looks as if he's trying to soak her into his pores by osmosis. He strokes her hair, and she lies very still. The* MALE GREEK CHORUS *member and the* FEMALE GREEK CHORUS *member as* AUNT MARY *come into the room.*)

MALE GREEK CHORUS Recipe for a Southern Boy:
FEMALE GREEK CHORUS (*As* AUNT MARY) A drawl of molasses in the way he speaks.
MALE GREEK CHORUS A gumbo of red and brown mixed in the cream of his skin.

(*While* PECK *lies, his eyes closed,* LI'L BIT *rises in the bed and responds to her aunt.*)

LI'L BIT Warm brown eyes—
FEMALE GREEK CHORUS (*As* AUNT MARY) Bedroom eyes—
MALE GREEK CHORUS A dash of Southern Baptist Fire and Brimstone—
LI'L BIT A curl of Elvis on his forehead—
FEMALE GREEK CHORUS (*As* AUNT MARY) A splash of Bay Rum—
MALE GREEK CHORUS A closely shaven beard that he razors just for you—
FEMALE GREEK CHORUS (*As* AUNT MARY) Large hands—rough hands—
LI'L BIT Warm hands—
MALE GREEK CHORUS The steel of the military in his walk—
LI'L BIT The slouch of the fishing skiff in his walk—
MALE GREEK CHORUS Neatly pressed khakis—
FEMALE GREEK CHORUS (*As* AUNT MARY) And under the wide leather of his belt—
LI'L BIT Sweat of cypress and sand—
MALE GREEK CHORUS Neatly pressed khakis—

LI'L BIT His heart beating Dixie—

FEMALE GREEK CHORUS (*As* AUNT MARY) The whisper of the zipper—you could reach out with your hand and—

LI'L BIT His mouth—

FEMALE GREEK CHORUS (*As* AUNT MARY) You could just reach out and—

LI'L BIT Hold him in your hand—

FEMALE GREEK CHORUS (*As* AUNT MARY) And his mouth—

(LI'L BIT *rises above her uncle and looks at his mouth; she starts to lower herself to kiss him—and wrenches herself free. She gets up from the bed.*)

LI'L BIT—I've got to get back.

PECK Wait—Li'l Bit. Did you . . . feel nothing?

LI'L BIT (*Lying*) No. Nothing.

PECK Do you—do you think of me?

(*The* GREEK CHORUS *whispers:*)

FEMALE GREEK CHORUS Khakis—

MALE GREEK CHORUS Bay Rum—

FEMALE GREEK CHORUS The whisper of the—

LI'L BIT—No.

(PECK, *in a rush, trembling, gets something out of his pocket.*)

PECK I'm forty-five. That's not old for a man. And I haven't been able to do anything else but think of you. I can't concentrate on my work—Li'l Bit. You've got to—I want you to think about what I am about to ask you.

LI'L BIT I'm listening.

(PECK *opens a small ring box.*)

PECK I want you to be my wife.

LI'L BIT This isn't happening.

PECK I'll tell Mary I want a divorce. We're not blood-related. It would be legal—

LI'L BIT—What have you been thinking! You are married to my aunt, Uncle Peck. She's my family. You have—you have gone way over the line. Family is family.

(*Quickly,* LI'L BIT *flies through the room, gets her coat*) I'm leaving. Now. I am not seeing you. Again.

(PECK *lies down on the bed for a moment, trying to absorb the terrible news. For a moment, he almost curls into a fetal position*)

I'm not coming home for Christmas. You should go home to Aunt Mary. Go home now, Uncle Peck.

(PECK *gets control, and sits, rigid*)

Uncle Peck?—I'm sorry but I have to go.

(*Pause*)

Are you all right?

(*With a discipline that comes from being told that boys don't cry,* PECK *stands upright.*)

PECK I'm fine. I just think—I need a real drink.

(The MALE GREEK CHORUS *has become a bartender. At a small counter, he is lining up shots for* PECK. *As* LI'L BIT *narrates, we see* PECK *sitting, carefully and calmly downing shot glasses.)*

LI'L BIT *(To the audience)* I never saw him again. I stayed away from Christmas and Thanksgiving for years after.

It took my uncle seven years to drink himself to death. First he lost his job, then his wife, and finally his driver's license. He retreated to his house, and had his bottles delivered.

(PECK stands, and puts his hands in front of him—almost like Superman flying)

One night he tried to go downstairs to the basement—and he flew down the steep basement stairs. My aunt came by weekly to put food on the porch, and she noticed the mail and the papers stacked up, uncollected.

They found him at the bottom of the stairs. Just steps away from his dark room.

Now that I'm old enough, there are some questions I would have liked to have asked him. Who did it to you, Uncle Peck? How old were you? Were you eleven?

(PECK moves to the driver's seat of his car and waits)

Sometimes I think of my uncle as a kind of Flying Dutchman. In the opera, the Dutchman is doomed to wander the sea; but every seven years he can come ashore, and if he finds a maiden who will love him of her own free will—he will be released.

And I see Uncle Peck in my mind, in his Chevy '56, a spirit driving up and down the back roads of Carolina—looking for a young girl who, of her own free will, will love him. Release him.

(A Voice states:)

YOU AND THE REVERSE GEAR.

LI'L BIT The summer of 1962. On Men, Sex, and Women: Part III:

*(*LI'L BIT *steps, as an eleven year old, into:)*

FEMALE GREEK CHORUS *(As* MOTHER*)* It is out of the question. End of Discussion.
LI'L BIT But why?
FEMALE GREEK CHORUS *(As* MOTHER*)* Li'l Bit—we are not discussing this. I said no.
LI'L BIT But I could spend an extra week at the beach! You're not telling me why!
FEMALE GREEK CHORUS *(As* MOTHER*)* Your uncle pays entirely too much attention to you.
LI'L BIT He listens to me when I talk. And—and he talks to me. He teaches me about things. Mama—he knows an awful lot.
FEMALE GREEK CHORUS *(As* MOTHER*)* He's a small town hick who's learned how to mix drinks from Hugh Hefner.
LI'L BIT Who's Hugh Hefner?

(Beat.)

FEMALE GREEK CHORUS *(As* MOTHER*)* I am not letting an eleven-year-old girl spend seven hours alone in the car with a man. . . . I don't like the way your uncle looks at you.

LI'L BIT For god's sake, mother! Just because you've gone through a bad time with my father—you think every man is evil!

FEMALE GREEK CHORUS *(As* MOTHER*)* Oh no, Li'l Bit—not all men. . . . We . . . we just haven't been very lucky with the men in our family.

LI'L BIT Just because you lost your husband—I still deserve a chance at having a father! Someone! A man who will look out for me! Don't I get a chance?

FEMALE GREEK CHORUS *(As* MOTHER*)* I will feel terrible if something happens.

LI'L BIT Mother! It's in your head! Nothing will happen! I can take care of myself. And I can certainly handle Uncle Peck.

FEMALE GREEK CHORUS *(As* MOTHER*)* All right. But I'm warning you—if anything happens, I hold you responsible.

(LI'L BIT *moves out of this scene and toward the car.*)

LI'L BIT 1962 On the Back Roads of Carolina: The First Driving Lesson.

(The TEENAGE GREEK CHORUS *member stands apart on stage. She will speak all of* LI'L BIT*'s lines.* LI'L BIT *sits beside* PECK *in the front seat. She looks at him closely, remembering.)*

PECK Li'l Bit? Are you getting tired?

TEENAGE GREEK CHORUS A little.

PECK It's a long drive. But we're making really good time. We can take the back road from here and see . . . a little scenery. Say—I've got an idea—(PECK *checks his rearview mirror)*

TEENAGE GREEK CHORUS Are we stopping, Uncle Peck.

PECK There's no traffic here. Do you want to drive?

TEENAGE GREEK CHORUS I can't drive.

PECK It's easy. I'll show you how. I started driving when I was your age. Don't you want to?—

TEENAGE GREEK CHORUS—But it's against the law at my age!

PECK And that's why you can't tell anyone I'm letting you do this—

TEENAGE GREEK CHORUS—But—I can't reach the pedals.

PECK You can sit in my lap and steer. I'll push the pedals for you. Did your father ever let you drive his car?

TEENAGE GREEK CHORUS No way.

PECK Want to try?

TEENAGE GREEK CHORUS Okay. (LI'L BIT *moves into* PECK*'s lap. She leans against him, closing her eyes)*

PECK You're just a little thing, aren't you? Okay—now think of the wheel as a big clock—I want you to put your right hand on the clock where three o'clock would be; and your left hand on the nine—

(LI'L BIT *puts one hand to* PECK*'s face, to stroke him. Then, she takes the wheel.)*

TEENAGE GREEK CHORUS Am I doing this right?

PECK That's right. Now, whatever you do, don't let go of the wheel. You tell me whether to go faster or slower—

TEENAGE GREEK CHORUS Not so fast, Uncle Peck!

PECK Li'l Bit—I need you to watch the road—

(PECK puts his hands on LI'L BIT's breasts. She relaxes against him, silent, accepting his touch.)

TEENAGE GREEK CHORUS Uncle Peck—what are you doing?

PECK Keep driving. *(He slips his hand under her blouse)*

TEENAGE GREEK CHORUS Uncle Peck—please don't do this—

PECK—Just a moment longer . . . *(PECK tenses against LI'L BIT)*

TEENAGE GREEK CHORUS *(Trying not to cry)* This isn't happening.

(PECK tenses more, sharply. He buries his face in LI'L BIT's neck, and moans softly. The
TEENAGE GREEK CHORUS *exits, and* LI'L BIT *steps out of the car.* PECK, *too, disappears.*
   A Voice reflects:)

DRIVING IN TODAY'S WORLD.

LI'L BIT That day was the last day I lived in my body. I retreated above the neck, and I've lived inside the "fire" in my head ever since.

And now that seems like a long, long time ago. When we were both very young.

And before you know it, I'll be thirty-five. That's getting up there for a woman. And I find myself believing in things that a younger self vowed never to believe in. Things like family and forgiveness.

I know I'm lucky. Although I still have never known what it feels like to jog or dance. Any thing like that . . . "jiggles." I do like to watch people on the dance floor, or out on the running paths, just jiggling away. And I say—good for them. *(LI'L BIT moves to the car with pleasure)*

The nearest sensation I feel—of flight in the body—I guess I feel when I'm driving. On a day like today. It's five A.M. The radio says it's going to be clear and crisp. I've got five hundred miles of highway ahead of me —and some back roads too. I filled the tank last night, and had the oil checked. Checked the tires, too. You've got to treat her . . . with respect.

First thing I do is: Check under the car. To see if any two-year-olds or household cats have crawled beneath, and strategically placed their skulls behind my back tires. *(LI'L BIT crouches)*

Nope. Then I get in the car. *(LI'L BIT does so)*

I lock the doors. And turn the key. Then I adjust the most important control on the dashboard—the radio—*(LI'L BIT turns the radio on: We hear all of the GREEK CHORUS overlapping, and static:)*

FEMALE GREEK CHORUS *(Overlapping)* —"You were so tiny you fit in his hand—"

MALE GREEK CHORUS *(Overlapping)* —"How is Shakespeare gonna help her lie on her back in the—"

TEENAGE GREEK CHORUS *(Overlapping)* —"Am I doing it right?"

(LI'L BIT *fine-tunes the radio station. A song like "Dedicated to the One I Love" or Orbison's "Sweet Dreams" comes on, and cuts off the* GREEK CHORUS.)

LI'L BIT Ahh . . . *(Beat)* I adjust my seat. Fasten my seat belt. Then I check the right side mirror—check the left side. *(She does)* Finally I adjust the rearview mirror. *(As* LI'L BIT *adjust the rearview mirror, a faint light strikes the spirit of* UNCLE PECK, *who is sitting in the back seat of the car. She sees him in the mirror. She smiles at him, and he nods at her. They are happy to be going for a long drive together.* LI'L BIT *slips the car into first gear; to the audience:)* And then—I floor it. *(Sound of a car taking off. Blackout)*

END OF PLAY

Karen Tei Yamashita b. 1951

Karen Tei Yamashita's writing, like her life, has been specially attuned to the histories, stories, and meanings of movement and migration. Born in Oakland, California, Yamashita moved to Los Angeles when she was one. Her writing career properly began in 1975 when she traveled to Brazil to study the experiences of Japanese immigrant women there. What was to have been a one-year research project turned into a nine-year stay that gave her the material for her first two books, *Through the Arc of the Rain Forest* and *Brazil-Maru,* both published after her return to Los Angeles in the mid-1980s.

Those novels bear traces of Yamashita's experiences in Brazil, a country that she describes as having a "generous and gracious acceptance . . . of strangers," in a peculiar mix of developed and developing worlds. They also attest to her range as a writer, which moves from the complexly woven, multiply narrated voices that make a three-generation tapestry of Japanese immigrants in *Brazil-Maru* to, in *Through the Arc,* the fantastic world of miraculous pilgrimages, which draws equal parts from Latin American magical realism and Brazilian soap operas.

Long before the term *globalization* was being bandied about by politicians and cultural critics, Yamashita was chronicling the sometimes tragic and sometimes beautiful effects of a world folding in on itself. This view of the shrinking world finds expression in the frequent lists that populate her fiction, such as the one from *Through the Arc,* which describes a junkyard of "F-86 Sabres, F-4 Phantoms, Huey Cobras, Lear Jets and Piper Cubs, Cadillacs, Volkswagens, Dodges and an assorted mixture of gas guzzlers," swallowed up by the vegetation to create a "rainforest parking lot." But while Yamashita, with her eye for the irreconcilably polyglot—that which simultaneously demands and denies easy categorization—describes the collision of worlds in Brazil, her sensibility has also been nourished by the equally fascinating racial, geographical, architectural, and migratory stew that is Los Angeles. In her third novel, *Tropic of Orange* (from which the following selection is taken), she turns her attention to this city. Not only does her characterization of Los Angeles stand in stark contrast to Hollywood's schizophrenic treatment, which shuttles between Pacific paradise and disaster-prone dystopia, but she accurately describes the extent to which the city of angels is being shaped and re-shaped by those who have traveled to make their homes there. A character like Bobby Ngu, "Chinese from Singapore with a Vietnam name speaking like a Mexican living in Koreatown," speaks of a place where disparate worlds collide and commingle.

The consistent line that links Yamashita's novels is her deep engagement with the social world and her continual questioning of "standards" of justice and equity through characters who struggle to make such abstract concepts real in the collective project of community. Whether through the destruction of rain forest in the name of corporate expansion, through the corrupting influence of "business" and

war on a commune of Japanese idealists, or through the unsettling contradictions that the global marketplace has thrown up between the United States and Mexico, Yamashita's narratives and characters speak to the necessity of making community in spite of and because of a humanity that struggles against its own flawed nature to realize that which it has imagined to be possible.

A world traveler herself, Yamashita currently makes her home in Santa Cruz, California. She teaches creative writing at the University of California, Santa Cruz.

Michael Murashige
Independent scholar

PRIMARY WORKS

Through the Arc of the Rain Forest, 1990; *Brazil-Maru,* 1992; *Tropic of Orange,* 1997; *Circle K Cycles,* 2001.

from Tropic of Orange

2. Benefits—Koreatown

Check it out, ése. You know this story? Yeah, over at Sanitary Supply they always tell it. This dude drives up, drives up to Sanitary. Makes a pickup like always. You know. Paper towels. Rags. Mop handles. Gallon of Windex. Stuff like that. Drives up in a Toyota pickup. Black shiny deal, all new, big pinche wheels. Very nice. Yeah. Asian dude. Kinda skinny. Short, yeah. But so what? Dark glasses. Cigarette in the mouth. He's getting out the truck, see. In the parking lot. Big tall dude comes by with a gun. Yeah, a gun. Puts it to his head and says, GIMME THE KEYS! It's a jacker. Asian dude don't lose no time, man. No time. Not a doubt. Rams the door closed. WHAM! Just like that. Slams the door on the jacker's hand. On the jacker's gun! Smashes the gun! Smashes the hand. Gun ain't worth shit. Hand's worth even less. Jacker loses it bad. He's crying. Screaming. It's not over. Asian dude swings the door open. Attacks the jacker. Pushes him up to the wall of Sanitary and beats the shit out. Dude don't come up to the jacker's nose. But it don't matter. Got every trick in the books. Bruce Lee moves. Kick. VAP! WHOP! Damn. Don't mess with this man. By now Sanitary's called the police. Crowd's seen it all. Jacker's a mess. Blood everywhere. Never seen so much blood. But not a drop on the Asian. Not a drop. Never took off his shades. Never even stopped smoking. Turns over the jacker's remains to the police. Don't say nothing. That's it. Goes into Sanitary. Picks up the mop handles, Windex, rags. Gets in the pickup. He's gone. That's it. That's it.

That's Bobby. If you know your Asians, you look at Bobby. You say, that's Vietnamese. That's what you say. Color's pallid. Kinda blue just beneath the skin. Little underweight. Korean's got rounder face. Chinese's taller. Japanese's dressed better. If you know your Asians. Turns out you'll be wrong. And you gonna be confused. Dude speaks Spanish. Comprende? So you figure it's one of those Japanese from Peru. Or maybe Korean from Brazil. Or Chinamex. Turns out Bobby's from Singapore. You say, okay, Indonesian. Malaysian. Wrong again. You say, look at his name. That's gotta be Vietnam. Ngu. Bobby Ngu. They all got Ngu names. Hey, it's not his real name. Real name's Li Kwan Yu. But don't tell nobody. Go figure. Bobby's Chinese. Chinese from Singapore with a Vietnam name speaking like a Mexican living in Koreatown. That's it.

Bobby's story. It's a long story. Gotta be after hours for Bobby to tell it. And then, he might not. He was twelve. His brother eight. Dad had a bicycle business in Singapore. Mother dies. Business went bad. Can't sell no more bicycles. Dad says, you wanna future? Better go to America. Better start out something new. For the family. You better go. Don't worry about us. You start a future all new.

Bobby's only twelve. How you get from Singapore to America? It's 1975. People getting on boats, rafts, dinghies, anything, swimming south out of Vietnam. Get to Singapore, but Singapore don't want them. They tell the Americans, its your problem. Put them in camps. Keep them there. Count them. Sort them out. Ask questions. Americans lost the war. Gotta take care of the casualties. Call them boat people. Call them refugees. Call for humanitarian aid. Call for political asylum. Meanwhile, they're in camps. Singapore don't want them. What's America gonna do? Count them again. Sort them out. Ask more questions. Pretty soon refugees get put on planes. Little by little. Distributed to America.

Every day, Bobby gets up early. He and his little brother. Walk over to the camp. Gates open in the morning. Walk in. Stand around with the refugees. Eat with the refugees. Guards don't notice. Who's gonna notice? But he's there every day. Maybe he belongs there. So maybe they notice. Bobby and his brother. Looking like orphans. Sad situation. Orphans everywhere. The war did this. Got to help the children. It's the children who suffer. Bobby and his little brother don't understand nothing. Don't understand Vietnamese. Just get some language here and there. That's all. Looks like they can't talk. Why not? War does that. You can't talk. Gets to be nighttime. Bobby and his brother go home. Slip out. Walk back into Singapore town. Go home and eat. Sleep. Get up early. Go back every morning. Spend the day sitting and eating with refugees. It's like that every day. Every day for months. That's it.

Then, pretty soon Bobby and the brother get counted. They get sorted. Get questions. Bobby's gotta have a name. He says Ngu. Everybody's Ngu. He's Ngu too. He's on the list. He's counted. Brother's counted, too. Get their pictures taken. Get some papers. American passports. Bobby's dad gives him money. U.S. money. Saved from the black market. Hides it in his pants. Sews it there. It's everything his dad can give. Money's there. Ready. Just in case. Every morning, Bobby gets his brother up early. Every morning, they slip into the refugee camp. Every night they slip out. One night they do not come home. One night Bobby's dad and the two sisters eat dinner. They leave two bowls out like always. They stare at the bowls. Silent. Staring at the two bowls.

Bobby'll tell you this story. But only after hours. After some beers and lots of smokes. He don't have time to tell stories. Too busy. Never stops. Got only a little time to sleep even. Always working. Hustling. Moving. That's why he beat that guy up and never stopped. Just kept on going. Never stops smoking either. Gonna die from smoking. He can't stop. Daytime, works the mailroom at a big-time newspaper. Sorts mail nonstop. Tons of it. Never stops. Nighttime got his own business. Him and his wife. Cleaning buildings. Clean those buildings that still got defense contracts. Bobby's got clearance. Got it for his wife too. Go around everywhere. Dump the stuff that's shredded. Wipe up the conference tables. Dust everything. Wipe down the computer monitors. Vacuum staples and hole punches and donuts out of carpets. Scrub the urinals. Mop down the floors. Bobby only stops for a smoke with the nighttime guard.

Bobby's wife likes to study. She's got a Walkman in her ears. Running the vacuum and the Walkman. It's not music. She's studying English. She's Mexican. Bobby don't teach her English. Speaks to her in Spanish. She's got to learn by herself. She's smart. Really smart. Got her degree at LACC. She told Bobby, janitors like them got to make better money. Got to get benefits. Some don't even get the minimum. Can we live on $4.25 an hour? No way. She joined Justice for Janitors. Bobby got mad. This is his business. He's independent. All the money is his. What's she talking about? It's solidarity she said. Some work for the companies. They need to organize. For protection. Bobby don't understand this. He says he works the morning job and gets benefits. Why is she complaining?

Maybe this was the reason. Maybe not. Bobby got in an argument with his wife. So she split. She took the boy with her. Drives him crazy. He can't see straight. Never been so happy as when he got married to that woman. Can't explain. Happier he is, harder he works. Can't stop. Gotta make money. Provide for his family. Gotta buy his wife nice clothes. Gotta buy his kid the best. Bobby's kid's gonna know the good life. That's how Bobby sees it.

It's not just the kid and the wife. Bobby's gotta send money to his dad. Back in Singapore. Keep the old man alive. Wanted the old man to come to L.A., but he wouldn't do it. Says he's too old. Says Bobby's got the future. All new future. And Bobby's baby brother. He's in college. Smart kid. Gets all As. Bobby put him in college. Pays for everything. Books, dorm, tuition, extras. Got him a car, too. Bobby don't forget his baby bro. His carnalito. Don't forget the kid cried every day when they arrived. Every day for two weeks. Cried for his mom who was already dead. Cried for his dad. For his sisters. Cried. Carnalito don't cry no more. Bobby don't forget.

Used to be, back in Singapore, Bobby had it easy. Dad had a factory. Putting out bicycles. Had a good life. Good money. Only had to go to school. One day, American bicycle company put up a factory. Workers all went over there. New machines. Paid fifty cents more. Pretty soon, American company's selling all over. Exporting. Bicycles go to Hong Kong. Go to Thailand. To India. To Japan. To Taiwan. Bobby's dad losing business. Can't compete. That's it.

But that's the past. Everything had to change. Change like the seasons. Rainy season. Dry season. Rainy season'll come again. Bobby's working on it. Gonna flood with the rainy season. Gonna fly back to Singapore and see his dad. Gonna see his sisters. See his nephews and nieces. Gonna bring the kid bro and the family along, too. But he's gotta get that woman back. Gotta bring the boy home. Can't be happy without his family. Can't work. Can't keep running. Can't keep fighting. After hours, Bobby keeps thinking. What's he gonna do? Rafaela said he's gotta stop smoking. That's it.

After hours, Bobby goes home. House's in Koreatown, edge of Pico-Union. Maybe it's Koreatown, but he owns it. Stucco job with two palm trees in front. Nobody home. Just him. Woman said to stop smoking. That's it. That's the last cigarette. Boil some water. Get out the ginseng. Get a good piece of the root. Grind it up good. Hot water. Ginseng. Steam goes up just like the root. That's the smell. Clean up the system. Clear the head. It's an old root. Takes a long time to grow. Don't waste it.

1997

Garrett Kaoru Hongo b. 1951

Garrett Kaoru Hongo is a prolific and accomplished Asian American poet. His poetry is characterized by striking images and unexpected, luminous lines. He has a special talent for close observation, an eye for the telling detail, and an ability to make the mundane beautiful, as in the vivid food images of "Who Among You Knows the Essence of Garlic?" In dramatic monologues, such as "The Unreal Dwelling: My Years in Volcano," he gives voice to figures from his familial past or from a communal past. Of his writing, Hongo has written, "My project as a poet has been motivated by a search for origins of various kinds— quests for ethnic and familial roots, cultural identities, and poetic inspiration. . . . I find the landscapes, folkways, and societies of Japan, Hawaii, and even Southern California to continually charm and compel me to write about them and inform myself of their specificities."

Born in Volcano, Hawaii, Hongo moved as a child to Laie, to Kahuku, and then to California—the San Fernando Valley—where he and his brother were the only Japanese in the public school. His family finally settled in Gardena, a Japanese American community in South Los Angeles adjoining the black community of Watts and the white community of Torrance. Hongo graduated from Pomona College, then traveled in Japan on a Thomas J. Watson Fellowship. He returned for graduate work at the University of Michigan, where he won the Hopwood poetry prize and studied with poet-professors Bert Meyers, Donald Hall, and Philip Levine. Later, he earned an M.F.A. from the University of California at Irvine. He taught at various universities, including the University of Missouri, where he was poetry editor of the *Missouri Review*. He is presently professor of English and creative writing at the University of Oregon.

Hongo has produced three volumes of poetry. The first, a joint publication with fellow poets Lawson Fusao Inada and Alan Chong Lau called *The Buddha Bandits down Highway 99* (1978), is a tripartite work of youthful exuberance. Hongo's contribution to that first volume, "Cruising 99," is included in his second book, *Yellow Light* (1982), from which most of the poems in this selection were taken. *Yellow Light* won the Wesleyan Poetry Prize. *The River of Heaven* (1988), his third book of poetry, was awarded the Lamont Poetry Selection for 1987 by the Academy of American Poets and two years later was a finalist for the Pulitzer Prize in Poetry. "The Unreal Dwelling: My Years in Volcano" comes from this collection. In 1995, Hongo published *Volcano*, a poetic memoir exploring in greater depth some of the themes he had introduced in his poetry: his continuing search for family history and his rediscovery of the land of his childhood.

Hongo has also contributed to the Asian American literary/historical/critical opus by compiling and editing three significant anthologies. *The Open Boat* (1993) showcases the poetry of thirty-one Asian American poets; *Songs My Mother Taught Me* (1994) collects stories, plays, and memoirs of Wakako Yamauchi; *Under Western Eyes* (1995) assembles personal narratives by Asian American writers. Hongo's de-

scription of the Asian American poets he has gathered together in *The Open Boat* applies equally to his own poetry: "We come to consciousness aware of the history of immigration and the Asian diaspora, singing from the fissures and fragmentations of culture in order to bring about their momentary unity in the kind of evanescent beauty that the figure of a poem makes."

Amy Ling
University of Wisconsin at Madison

King-Kok Cheung
University of California, Los Angeles

PRIMARY WORKS

The Buddha Bandits down Highway 99, with Alan Chong Lau and Lawson Fusao Inada, 1978; *Yellow Light,* 1982; *The River of Heaven,* 1988; *Volcano: A Memoir of Hawaii,* 1995.

Yellow Light

One arm hooked around the frayed strap
of a tar-black patent-leather purse,
the other cradling something for dinner:
fresh bunches of spinach from a J-Town *yaoya,*
5 sides of split Spanish mackerel from Alviso's,
maybe a loaf of Langendorf; she steps
off the hissing bus at Olympic and Fig,
begins the three-block climb up the hill,
passing gangs of schoolboys playing war,
10 Japs against Japs, Chicanas chalking sidewalks
with the holy double-yoked crosses of hopscotch,
and the Korean grocer's wife out for a stroll
around this neighborhood of Hawaiian apartments
just starting to steam with cooking
15 and the anger of young couples coming home
from work, yelling at kids, flicking on
TV sets for the Wednesday Night Fights.

If it were May, hydrangeas and jacaranda
flowers in the streetside trees would be
20 blooming through the smog of late spring.
Wisteria in Masuda's front yard would be
shaking out the long tresses of its purple hair.

Maybe mosquitoes, moths, a few orange butterflies
settling on the lattice of monkey flowers
25 tangled in chain-link fences by the trash.

But this is October, and Los Angeles
seethes like a billboard under twilight.
From used-car lots and the movie houses uptown,
long silver sticks of light probe the sky.
30 From the Miracle Mile, whole freeways away,
a brilliant fluorescence breaks out
and makes war with the dim squares
of yellow kitchen light winking on
in all the side streets of the Barrio.

35 She climbs up the two flights of flagstone
stairs to 201-B, the spikes of her high heels
clicking like kitchen knives on a cutting board,
props the groceries against the door,
fishes through memo pads, a compact,
40 empty packs of chewing gum, and finds her keys.

The moon then, cruising from behind
a screen of eucalyptus across the street,
covers everything, everything in sight,
in a heavy light like yellow onions.

1982

Off from Swing Shift

Late, just past midnight,
freeway noise from the Harbor
and San Diego leaking in
from the vent over the stove,
5 and he's off from swing shift at Lear's.
Eight hours of twisting circuitry,
charting ohms and maximum gains
while transformers hum
and helicopters swirl
10 on the roofs above the small factory.
He hails me with a head-fake,
then the bob and weave
of a weekend middleweight

learned at the Y on Kapiolani
15 ten years before I was born.

The shoes and gold London Fogger
come off first, then the easy grin
saying he's lucky as they come.
He gets into the slippers
20 my brother gives him every Christmas,
carries his Thermos over to the sink,
and slides into the one chair at the table
that's made of wood and not yellow plastic.
He pushes aside stacks
25 of *Sporting News* and *Outdoor Life,*
big round tins of Holland butter cookies,
and clears a space for his elbows, his pens,
and the *Racing Form's* Late Evening Final.

His left hand reaches out,
30 flicks on the Sony transistor
we bought for his birthday
when I was fifteen.
The right ferries in the earphone,
a small, flesh-colored star,
35 like a tiny miracle of hearing,
and fits it into place.
I see him plot black constellations
of figures and calculations
on the magazine's margins,
40 alternately squint and frown
as he fingers the knob of the tuner
searching for the one band
that will call out today's results.

There are whole cosmologies
45 in a single handicap,
a lifetime of two-dollar losing
in one pick of the Daily Double.

Maybe tonight is his night
for winning, his night
50 for beating the odds
of going deaf from a shell
at Anzio still echoing
in the cave of his inner ear,
his night for cashing in
55 the blue chips of shrapnel still grinding
at the thickening joints of his legs.

But no one calls
the horse's name, no one
says Shackles, Rebate, or Pouring Rain.
60 No one speaks a word.

1982

Who among You Knows the Essence of Garlic?

Can your foreigner's nose smell mullets
roasting in a glaze of brown bean paste
and sprinkled with novas of sea salt?

Can you hear my grandmother
5 chant the mushroom's sutra?

Can you hear the papayas crying
as they bleed in porcelain plates?

I'm telling you that the bamboo
slips the long pliant shoots
10 of its myriad soft tongues
into your mouth that is full of oranges.

I'm saying that the silver waterfalls
of bean threads will burst in hot oil
and stain your lips like zinc.

15 The marbled skin of the blue mackerel
works good for men. The purple oils
from its flesh perfume the tongues of women.

If you swallow them whole, the rice cakes
soaking in a broth of coconut milk and brown sugar
20 will never leave the bottom of your stomach.

Flukes of giant black mushrooms
leap from their murky tubs
and strangle the toes of young carrots.

Broiling chickens ooze grease,
25 yellow tears of fat collect
and spatter in the smoking pot.

Soft ripe pears, blushing
on the kitchen window sill,
kneel like plump women
30 taking a long luxurious shampoo,
and invite you to bite their hips.

Why not grab basketfuls of steaming noodles,
lush and slick as the hair of a fine lady,
and squeeze?

35 The shrimps, big as Portuguese thumbs,
stew among cut guavas, red onions,
ginger root, and rosemary in lemon juice,
the palm oil bubbling to the top,
breaking through layers and layers
40 of shredded coconut and sliced cashews.

Who among you knows the essence
of garlic and black lotus root,
of red and green peppers sizzling
among squads of oysters in the skillet,
45 of crushed ginger, fresh green onions,
and pale-blue rice wine simmering
in the stomach of a big red fish?

                                            1982

And Your Soul Shall Dance

for Wakako Yamauchi

Walking to school beside fields
of tomatoes and summer squash,
alone and humming a Japanese love song,
you've concealed a copy of *Photoplay*
5 between your algebra and English texts.
Your knee socks, saddle shoes, plaid dress,
and blouse, long-sleeved and white
with ruffles down the front,
come from a Sears catalogue
10 and neatly complement your new Toni curls.
All of this sets you apart from the landscape:
flat valley grooved with irrigation ditches,
a tractor grinding through alkaline earth,

the short stands of windbreak eucalyptus
15 shuttering the desert wind
from a small cluster of wooden shacks
where your mother hangs the wash.
You want to go somewhere.
Somewhere far away from all the dust
20 and sorting machines and acres of lettuce.
Someplace where you might be kissed
by someone with smooth, artistic hands.
When you turn into the schoolyard,
the flagpole gleams like a knife blade in the sun,
25 and classmates scatter like chickens,
shooed by the storm brooding on your horizon.

1982

The Unreal Dwelling: My Years in Volcano

What I did, I won't excuse,
except to say it was a way to change,
the way new flows add to the land,
making things new, clearing the garden.
5 I left two sons, a wife behind—
and does it matter? The sons grew,
became their own kinds of men,
lost in the swirl of robes, cries
behind a screen of mist and fire
10 I drew between us, gambles I lost
and walked away from like any bad job.
I drove a cab and didn't care,
let the wife run off too, her combs
loose in some shopkeeper's bed.
15 When hope blazed up in my heart for the fresh start,
I took my daughters with me to keep house,
order my living as I was taught and came to expect.
They swept up, cooked, arranged flowers,
practiced tea and *buyō,* the classical dance.
20 I knew how because I could read and ordered books,
let all movements be disciplined and objects arranged
by an idea of order, the precise sequence of images
which conjure up the abstract I might call
yūgen, or Mystery, *chikara,* . . . Power.
25 The principles were in the swordsmanship
I practiced, in the package of loans

and small thefts I'd managed since coming here.
I could count, keep books, speak English
as well as any white, and I had false papers
30 recommending me, celebrating the fiction
of my long tenure with Hata Shōten of Honolulu.
And my luck was they bothered to check
only those I'd bribed or made love to.
Charm was my collateral, a willingness to move
35 and live on the frontier my strongest selling point.
So they staked me, a small-time hustler
good with cars, odds, and women,
and I tossed some boards together,
dug ponds and a cesspool,
40 figured water needed tanks, pipes,
and guttering on the eaves
to catch the light-falling rain,
and I had it—a store and a house out-back
carved out of rainforests and lava land
45 beside this mountain road seven leagues from Hilo.
I never worried they'd come this far—
the banks, courts, and police—
mists and sulphur clouds from the crater
drenching the land, washing clean my tracks,
50 bleaching my spotted skin the pallor of long-time residents.
I regularized my life and raised my girls,
put in gas pumps out front, stocked varieties of goods
and took in local fruit, flowers on consignment.
And I had liquor—plum wine and *saké*
55 from Japan, whiskey from Tennessee—
which meant I kept a pistol as well.
My girls learned to shoot, and would have
only no one bothered to test us.
It was known I'd shot cats and wild pigs
60 from across the road rummaging through garbage.
I never thought of my boys,
or of women too much
until my oldest bloomed,
suddenly, vanda-like, from spike
65 to scented flower almost overnight.
Young men in Model A's came up from town.
One even bussed, and a Marine from Georgia
stole a Jeep to try taking her
to the coast, or, more simply,
70 down a mountain road for the night.
The Shore Patrol found him.
And I got married again, to a country girl
from Kona who answered my ad.

I approved of her because,
75 though she was rough-spoken and squat-legged,
    and, I discovered, her hair
    slightly red in the groin,
    she could carry 50-lbs. sacks of California Rose
    without strain or grunting.
80 As postmaster and Territorial official,
    I married us myself, sent announcements
    and champagne in medicine vials
    to the villagers and my "guarantors" in town.
    The toasts tasted of vitamin-B and cough syrup.
85 My oldest moved away, herself married
    to a dapper Okinawan who sold Oldsmobiles
    and had the leisure to play golf on weekends.
    I heard from my boy then, my oldest son,
    back from the war and writing to us,
90 curious, formal, and not a little proud
    he'd done his part. What impressed me
    was his script—florid but under control,
    penmanship like pipers at the tideline
    lifting and settling on the sand-colored paper.
95 He wrote first from Europe, then New York,
    finally from Honolulu. He'd fought,
    mustered out near the Madison Square Garden
    in time to see LaMotta smash the pretty one,
    and then came home to a girl he'd met in night school.
100 He said he won out over a cop because he danced better,
    knew from the service how to show up in a tie,
    bring flowers and silk in nice wrappings.
    I flew the Island Clipper to the wedding,
    the first time I'd seen the boy in twenty years,
105 gave him a hundred cash and a wink
    since the girl was pretty,
    told him to buy, not rent his suits,
    and came home the next day, hungover,
    a raw ache in my throat.
110 I sobered up, but the ache
    stayed and doctors tell me
    it's this sickness they can't get rid of,
    pain all through my blood and nerve cells.
    I cough too much, can't smoke or drink
115 or tend to things. Mornings, I roll
    myself off the damp bed, wrap
    a blanket on, slip into the wooden clogs,
    and take a walk around my pond and gardens.
    On this half-acre, calla lilies in bloom,
120 cream-white cups swollen with milk,

heavy on their stems, and rocking in the slight wind,
cranes coming to rest on the wet, coppery soil.
The lotuses ride, tiny flamingoes, sapphired
pavilions buoyed on their green keels on the pond.
125 My fish follow me, snorting to be fed,
gold flashes and streaks of color
like blood satin and brocade in the algaed waters.
And when the sky empties of its many lights,
I see the quarter moon, horned junk,
130 sailing over the Ka'u and the crater rim.
This is the River of Heaven. . . .
Before I cross, I know I must bow down,
call to my oldest son, say what I must
to bring him, and all the past, back to me.

1985

Joy Harjo (Creek) b. 1951

Joy Harjo is a Creek Indian, born in the heart of the Creek Nation in Tulsa, Oklahoma. After graduation from the Institute of American Indian Arts in Santa Fe, New Mexico, she subsequently taught there from 1978 to 1979 and again from 1983 to 1984. In 1978 she earned an M.F.A. after studying at the University of Iowa Writers' Workshop. She is a professor at the University of New Mexico. Along with her continuing poetry, she is presently involved in writing screenplays and has just completed in collaboration with an astronomer her fourth book.

Joy Harjo's poetry is widely praised and recognized. She has seen her work published in many literary reviews in the United States, as well as in magazines and anthologies. A cadence marks her work that is reminiscent of the repetitions of the Indian ceremonial drum, exemplified in the energy and motion of her "She Had Some Horses." Her poetic voice and imagery have steadily developed as she resurrects the carnage of the early conflict between native and European, "the fantastic and terrible story of our survival" ("An-chorage" poem), and the rejoicing experienced by those who carry on Indian traditions and culture. Her work provides a unique perspective and a piquant examination of American culture from a native point of view. Her verse cries out for the lost, the dispossessed, and the forgotten of reservation, rural, and urban America. Her rigorous words pronounce an awakening for those left voiceless in the past. She relentlessly pursues in print tensions surrounding gender and ethnicity. She explores the pain of existence and the dream fusion of the individual with the landscape, especially the mesa-strewn Southwest. Like so many other Native Americans, Joy Harjo has traveled across the nation and her poetry reflects the exuberance for sight and sound of the Indian powwow circuit, moving through the culture of pan-Indian America, and participation in Indian-related conferences. Her lyricism mirrors the lushness of feel for the countryside and rich images of the people she encounters. Her work mingles realism and the philosophy of American Indian spirituality. She recalls the wounds of the past, the agony of the Indian present, and dream visions of a better future for indigenous peoples. Her work continues to deal with themes which call forth rage and elation at the same time. The multiplicity of emotions she touches is encompassed in her 1983 *She Had Some Horses* in the title poem:

She had some horses she loved.
She had some horses she hated.
These were the same horses.

C. B. Clark
Oklahoma City University

PRIMARY WORKS

The Last Song, 1975; *What Moon Drove Me to This,* 1979; *She Had Some Horses,* 1983; *Secrets from the Center of the World,* with Steven Strom, 1989; *In Mad Love and War,* 1990; *The Woman Who Fell from the Sky,* 1994; "Letter from the End of the Twentieth Century" (compact disk album), 1996; *The Spiral of Memory: Interviews,* 1996; *A Map to the Next World: Poetry and Tales,* 2000; *How We Became Human,* 2002.

The Woman Hanging from the Thirteenth Floor Window

She is the woman hanging from the 13th floor
window. Her hands are pressed white against the
concrete moulding of the tenement building. She
hangs from the 13th floor window in east Chicago,
5 with a swirl of birds over her head. They could
be a halo, or a storm of glass waiting to crush her.

She thinks she will be set free.

The woman hanging from the 13th floor window
on the east side of Chicago is not alone.
10 She is a woman of children, of the baby, Carlos,
and of Margaret, and of Jimmy who is the oldest.
She is her mother's daughter and her father's son.
She is several pieces between the two husbands
she has had. She is all the women of the apartment
15 building who stand watching her, watching themselves.

When she was young she ate wild rice on scraped down
plates in warm wood rooms. It was in the farther
north and she was the baby then. They rocked her.

She sees Lake Michigan lapping at the shores of
20 herself. It is a dizzy hole of water and the rich
live in tall glass houses at the edge of it. In some
places Lake Michigan speaks softly, here, it just sputters

and butts itself against the asphalt. She sees
other buildings just like hers. She sees other
25 women hanging from many-floored windows
counting their lives in the palms of their hands
and in the palms of their children's hands.

She is the woman hanging from the 13th floor window
on the Indian side of town. Her belly is soft from
30 her children's births, her worn levis swing down below
her waist, and then her feet, and then her heart.
She is dangling.

The woman hanging from the 13th floor hears voices.
They come to her in the night when the lights have gone
35 dim. Sometimes they are little cats mewing and scratching
at the door, sometimes they are her grandmother's voice,
and sometimes they are gigantic men of light whispering
to her to get up, to get up, to get up. That's when she wants
to have another child to hold onto in the night, to be able
40 to fall back into dreams.

And the woman hanging from the 13th floor window
hears other voices. Some of them scream out from below
for her to jump, they would push her over. Others cry softly
from the sidewalks, pull their children up like flowers and gather
45 them into their arms. They would help her, like themselves.

But she is the woman hanging from the 13th floor window,
and she knows she is hanging by her own fingers, her
own skin, her own thread of indecision.

She thinks of Carlos, of Margaret, of Jimmy.
50 She thinks of her father, and of her mother.
She thinks of all the women she has been, of all
the men. She thinks of the color of her skin, and
of Chicago streets, and of waterfalls and pines.
She thinks of moonlight nights, and of cool spring storms.
55 Her mind chatters like neon and northside bars.
She thinks of the 4 a.m. lonelinesses that have folded
her up like death, discordant, without logical and
beautiful conclusion. Her teeth break off at the edges.
She would speak.

60 The woman hangs from the 13th floor window crying for
the lost beauty of her own life. She sees the
sun falling west over the grey plane of Chicago.
She thinks she remembers listening to her own life
break loose, as she falls from the 13th floor

65 window on the east side of Chicago, or as she
climbs back up to claim herself again.

1983

New Orleans

This is the south. I look for evidence
of other Creeks, for remnants of voices,
or for tobacco brown bones to come wandering
down Conti Street, Royale, or Decatur.
5 Near the French Market I see a blue horse
caught frozen in stone in the middle of
a square. Brought in by the Spanish on
an endless ocean voyage he became mad
and crazy. They caught him in blue
10 rock, said

          don't talk.

I know it wasn't just a horse

                  that went crazy.

Nearby is a shop with ivory and knives.
15 There are red rocks. The man behind the
counter has no idea that he is inside
magic stones. He should find out before
they destroy him. These things
have memory,

20   you know.
I have a memory.

                  It swims deep in blood,
a delta in the skin. It swims out of Oklahoma,
deep the Mississippi River. It carries my
25 feet to these places: the French Quarter,
stale rooms, the sun behind thick and moist
clouds, and I hear boats hauling themselves up
and down the river.

My spirit comes here to drink.
30 My spirit comes here to drink.
Blood is the undercurrent.

There are voices buried in the Mississippi
mud. There are ancestors and future children

buried beneath the currents stirred up by
35 pleasure boats going up and down.
There are stories here made of memory.

I remember DeSoto. He is buried somewhere in
this river, his bones sunk like the golden
treasure he traveled half the earth to find,
40 came looking for gold cities, for shining streets
of beaten gold to dance on with silk ladies.

He should have stayed home.

               (Creeks knew of him for miles
                  before he came into town.
45   Dreamed of silver blades
                       and crosses.)
And knew he was one of the ones who yearned
for something his heart wasn't big enough
to handle.
50   (And DeSoto thought it was gold.)

The Creeks lived in earth towns,
                  not gold,
       spun children, not gold.
That's not what DeSoto thought he wanted to see
55 The Creeks knew it, and drowned him in
          the Mississippi River
              so he wouldn't have to drown himself.

Maybe his body is what I am looking for
as evidence. To know in another way
60 that my memory is alive.
But he must have got away, somehow,
because I have seen New Orleans,
the lace and silk buildings,
trolley cars on beaten silver paths,
65 graves that rise up out of soft earth in the rain,
shops that sell black mammy dolls
holding white babies.

And I know I have seen DeSoto,
             having a drink on Bourbon Street,
70   mad and crazy
                dancing with a woman as gold
                as the river bottom.

                             1983

Remember

Remember the sky that you were born under,
know each of the star's stories.
Remember the moon, know who she is.
Remember the sun's birth at dawn, that is the
5 strongest point of time. Remember sundown
and the giving away to night.
Remember your birth, how your mother struggled
to give you form and breath. You are evidence of
her life, and her mother's, and hers.
10 Remember your father. He is your life, also.
Remember the earth whose skin you are:
red earth, black earth, yellow earth, white earth
brown earth, we are earth.
Remember the plants, trees, animal life who all have their
15 tribes, their families, their histories, too. Talk to them,
listen to them. They are alive poems.
Remember the wind. Remember her voice. She knows the
origin of this universe.
Remember you are all people and all people are you.
20 Remember you are this universe and this
universe is you.
Remember all is in motion, is growing, is you.
Remember language comes from this.
Remember the dance language is, that life is.
25 Remember.

1983

Vision

The rainbow touched down
"somewhere in the Rio Grande,"
we said. And saw the light of it
from your mother's house in Isleta.[1]
5 How it curved down between earth
and the deepest sky to give us horses
of color
      horses that were within us all of this time
but we didn't see them because
10 we wait for the easiest vision
        to save us.

---

[1]An Indian pueblo in New Mexico.

In Isleta the rainbow was a crack
in the universe. We saw the barest
of all life that is possible.
15 Bright horses rolled over
and over the dusking sky.
I heard the thunder of their beating
hearts. Their lungs hit air
and sang. All the colors of horses
20 formed the rainbow,
                and formed us
watching them.

                              1983

Anchorage

for Audre Lorde

This city is made of stone, of blood, and fish.
There are Chugatch Mountains[1] to the east
and whale and seal to the west.
It hasn't always been this way, because glaciers
5 who are ice ghosts create oceans, carve earth
and shape this city here, by the sound.
They swim backwards in time.

Once a storm of boiling earth cracked open
the streets, threw open the town.
10 It's quiet now, but underneath the concrete
is the cooking earth,
                and above that, air
which is another ocean, where spirits we can't see
are dancing   joking   getting full
15 on roasted caribou, and the praying
goes on, extends out.

Nora and I go walking down 4th Avenue
and know it is all happening.

[1] A range extending about 280 miles along the
coast of south Alaska just above the panhandle.
Chugach Eskimo (Ahtnas) reside there.

On a park bench we see someone's Athabascan[2]
20 grandmother, folded up, smelling like 200 years
of blood and piss, her eyes closed against some
unimagined darkness, where she is buried in an ache
in which nothing makes
            sense.

25 We keep on breathing, walking, but softer now,
the clouds whirling in the air above us.
What can we say that would make us understand
better than we do already?
Except to speak of her home and claim her
30 as our own history, and know that our dreams
don't end here, two blocks away from the ocean
where our hearts still batter away at the muddy shore.

And I think of the 6th Avenue jail, of mostly Native
and Black men, where Henry told about being shot at
35 eight times outside a liquor store in L.A., but when
the car sped away he was surprised he was alive,

no bullet holes, man, and eight cartridges strewn
on the sidewalk
            all around him.

40 Everyone laughed at the impossibility of it,
but also the truth. Because who would believe
the fantastic and terrible story of all of our survival
those who were never meant
            to survive?

                     1983

Deer Dancer

Nearly everyone had left that bar in the middle of winter except the
hardcore. It was the coldest night of the year, every place shut down,
but not us. Of course we noticed when she came in. We were Indian
ruins. She was the end of beauty. No one knew her, the stranger

---

[2]Athabascan is a complicated but wide-spread Indian language, part of the Na-Dene Indian language superstock of North America. Indians speak Athabascan in the sub-Arctic interior of Alaska, along the Pacific Northwest Coast (Tlingit of Alaska panhandle, Tolowa of Oregon, and Hupa of California), and in the American Southwest (Apache and Navajo).

5   whose tribe we recognized, her family related to deer, if that's who she
     was, a people accustomed to hearing songs in pine trees, and making
     them hearts.

     The woman inside the woman who was to dance naked in the bar of
     misfits blew deer magic. Henry Jack, who could not survive a sober
10   day, thought she was Buffalo Calf Woman[1] come back, passed out, his
     head by the toilet. All night he dreamed a dream he could not say.
     The next day he borrowed money, went home, and sent back the
     money I lent. Now that's a miracle. Some people see vision in a
     burned tortilla, some in the face of a woman.

15   This is the bar of broken survivors, the club of shotgun, knife wound,
     of poison by culture. We who were taught not to stare drank our beer.
     The players gossiped down their cues. Someone put a quarter in the
     jukebox to relive despair. Richard's wife dove to kill her. We had to
     hold her back, empty her pockets of knives and diaper pins, buy her
20   two beers to keep her still, while Richard secretly bought the beauty a
     drink.

     How do I say it? In this language there are no words for how the real
     world collapses. I could say it in my own and the sacred mounds
     would come into focus, but I couldn't take it in this dingy envelope.
25   So I look at the stars in this strange city, frozen to the back of the sky,
     the only promises that ever make sense.

     My brother-in-law hung out with white people, went to law school
     with a perfect record, quit. Says you can keep your laws, your words.
     And practiced law on the street with his hands. He jimmied to the
30   proverbial dream girl, the face of the moon, while the players racked a
     new game. He bragged to us, he told her magic words and that's
     when she broke, became human. But we all heard his bar voice crack:

     What's a girl like you doing in a place like this?

     That's what I'd like to know, what are we all doing in a place like this?

35   You would know she could hear only what she wanted to; don't we
     all? Left the drink of betrayal Richard bought her, at the bar. What
     was she on? We all wanted some. Put a quarter in the juke. We all
     take risks stepping into thin air. Our ceremonies didn't predict this.
     Or we expected more.

---

[1]The culture heroine of the Lakota, who brought them the sacred pipe and the seven central rites of the Sioux. In myth she is re-markably beautiful and stirs the desire of the men who first meet her. See "Wohpe and the Gift of the Pipe" in Volume A.

40 I had to tell you this, for the baby inside the girl sealed up with a lick
of hope and swimming into praise of nations. This is not a rooming
house, but a dream of winter falls and the deer who portrayed the
relatives of strangers. The way back is deer breath on icy windows.

The next dance none of us predicted. She borrowed a chair for the
45 stairway to heaven and stood on a table of names. And danced in the
room of children without shoes.

You picked a fine time to leave me, Lucille.
With four hungry children and a crop in the field.

And then she took off her clothes. She shook loose memory, waltzed
50 with the empty lover we'd all become.

She was the myth slipped down through dreamtime. The promise of
feast we all knew was coming. The deer who crossed through knots of
a curse to find us. She was no slouch, and neither were we, watching.

The music ended. And so does the story. I wasn't there. But I
55 imagined her like this, not a stained red dress with tape on her heels
but the deer who entered our dream in white dawn, breathed mist into
pine trees, her fawn a blessing of meat, the ancestors who never left.

1990

We Must Call a Meeting

I am fragile, a piece of pottery smoked from fire
                                        made of dung,
the design drawn from nightmares. I am an arrow, painted
                                        with lightning
5 to seek the way to the name of the enemy,
                                        but the arrow has now created
its own language.
                    It is a language of lizards and storms, and we have
begun to hold conversations
10   long into the night.
                                        I forget to eat.
I don't work. My children are hungry and the animals who live
in the backyard are starving.
                                I begin to draw maps of stars.
15 The spirits of old and new ancestors perch on my shoulders.
I make prayers of clear stone
                            of feathers from birds
                                        who live closest to the gods.

The voice of the stone is born
20   of a meeting of yellow birds
who circle the ashes of a smoldering volcano.
                                    The feathers sweep the prayers up
and away.
                I, too, try to fly but get caught in the cross fire of signals
25   and my spirit drops back down to earth.
I am lost; I am looking for you
            who can help me walk this thin line between the breathing
                                  and the dead.
You are the curled serpent in the pottery of nightmares.
30 You are the dreaming animal who paces back and forth in my head.
We must call a meeting.
                   Give me back my language and build a house
Inside it.
         A house of madness.
35   A house for the dead who are not dead.
And the spiral of the sky above it.
And the sun
           and the moon.
                 And the stars to guide us called promise.

1990

Tato Laviera b. 1951

Tato Laviera was born in Puerto Rico and has lived in New York City since 1960. A second-generation Puerto Rican writer, a poet and playwright, he is deeply committed to the social and cultural development of Puerto Ricans in New York. In addition, he has taught Creative Writing at Rutgers and other universities on the East Coast.

His poetry and plays are linguistic and artistic celebrations of Puerto Rican culture, African Caribbean traditions, the fast rhythms of life in New York City, and of life in general. Laviera writes in English, Spanish, and Spanglish, a mixture of the two. His superior command of both languages and the playful yet serious value he imparts to Spanglish, distinguishes his writing from others of his generation. For example, the titles of two of his books, *Enclave* and *AmeRícan*, suggest double readings in Spanish and

English. Laviera's poetry is highly relevant to the study of bilingual and bicultural issues, for in it he documents, examines, and questions what it means to be a Puerto Rican in the United States. His texts have reflected the changes and transitions that his community has undergone since the major migrations of the 1940s and, moreover, offer a paradigm of what pluralistic America should really be all about.

In *La Carreta Made a U-Turn* one finds forceful poems denouncing the hardships, injustices, and social problems that the poor Puerto Rican confronts in New York City: cold, hunger, high rents, eviction, drug addiction, linguistic alienation, unemployment. The second part of this collection, entitled "Loisaida (Lower East Side) Streets: Latinas Sing," examines the issues and problems affecting today's Latina women.

This is, perhaps, one of the few instances in which a Hispanic male writer conscientiously and sympathetically addresses the conflicts of bicultural Hispanic women. Laviera concludes this book with a series of poems which celebrate African Caribbean music, both in its traditional functions as well as in its resurgence within the contemporary urban context of New York City.

Laviera has been called a "chronicler of life in El Barrio" and rightly so. His poetic language is not influenced by the written, academic tradition of poetry, but instead it is informed by popular culture, by the oral tradition of Puerto Rico and the Caribbean, and by the particular voices spoken and heard in El Barrio. Gossip, refrains, street language, idiomatic expressions, interjections, poetic declamation, and African Caribbean music such as *salsa,* rhumbas, *mambos, sones* and *música jíbara* (mountain music), are but some of the raw material with which Laviera constructs his poems. Though published in a written format. Laviera's poetry is meant to be sung and recited.

A central tenet to Laviera's work is his identification with the African American community in this country. On the one hand, he reinforces the unity and common roots of blacks and Puerto Ricans: "it is called Africa in all of us." This tendency also reflects the new multi-ethnic constitution of America, which has supplanted the old myth of the melting pot. In this context Laviera's poems are reaffirmations of his Puetroricanness and of his community's as a new national identity that diverges from the insular Puerto Rican. He proposes a new ethnic identity that includes other minority groups in the country. New York City becomes the space where this convergence and cultural *mestizaje* (mixing) takes place. While maintaining a denunciative stance through the use of irony and tongue-in-cheek humor, Laviera's work flourishes with a contagious optimism, and his poems are true songs to the joy of living which Puerto Ricans profoundly feel despite the harsh circumstances in which they live.

Frances R. Aparicio
University of Illinois–Chicago

PRIMARY WORKS

La Carreta Made a U-Turn, 1976; *Olú Clemente* (theatre), 1979; *Enclave,* 1981; *AmeRícan,* 1985; *Mainstream Ethics,* 1988; *Mixturao and Other Poems,* 2008.

frío[1]

```
      35 mph winds
      & the 10 degree
      weather
      penetrated the pores
    5 of our windows
      mr. steam rested for
      the night
      the night we most
      needed him
```

[1]Spanish: the cold.

10 everybody arropándose[2]
    on their skin blankets
    curled-up like the embryo
    in my mother's womb
    a second death birth
15 called nothingness

    & the frío made more
    asustos[3] in our empty
    stomachs

                     the toilet has not
                     been flushed for
20   three days

                             1976

AmeRícan

    we gave birth to a new generation,
    AmeRícan, broader than lost gold
    never touched, hidden inside the
    puerto rican mountains.

5 we gave birth to a new generation,
    AmeRícan, it includes everything
    imaginable you-name-it-we-got-it
    society.

    we gave birth to a new generation,
10 AmeRícan salutes all folklores,
    european, indian, black, spanish,
    and anything else compatible:

    AmeRícan,   singing to composer pedro flores'[1] palm
                     trees high up in the universal sky!

15 AmeRícan,   sweet soft spanish danzas gypsies
                     moving lyrics la española[2] cascabelling
                     presence always singing at our side!

---

[2]Spanish: covering themselves.
[3]Spanish: frightening.
[1]Pedro Flores, Puerto Rican composer of popular romantic songs.

[2]"Spanish" (feminine).

AmeRícan,   beating jíbaro[3] modern troubadours
                  crying guitars romantic continental
20   bolero love songs!

AmeRícan,   across forth and across back
                  back across and forth back
                  forth across and back and forth
                  our trips are walking bridges!

25   it all dissolved into itself, the attempt
                  was truly made, the attempt was truly
                  absorbed, digested, we spit out
                  the poison, we spit out the malice,
                  we stand, affirmative in action,
30   to reproduce a broader answer to the
                  marginality that gobbled us up abruptly!

AmeRícan,   walking plena-[4] rhythms in new york,
                  strutting beautifully alert, alive,
                  many turning eyes wondering,
35   admiring!

AmeRícan,   defining myself my own way any way many
                  ways Am e Rícan, with the big R and the
                  accent on the í!

AmeRícan,   like the soul gliding talk of gospel
40   boogie music!

AmeRícan,   speaking new words in spanglish tenements,
                  fast tongue moving street corner *"que
                  corta"*[5] talk being invented at the insistence
                  of a smile!

45 AmeRícan,   abounding inside so many ethnic english
                  people, and out of humanity, we blend
                  and mix all that is good!

AmeRícan,   integrating in new york and defining our
                  own *destino,*[6] our own way of life,

---

[3]Term referring to the Puerto Rican farmer who lives in the mountains. The jíbaros have a particular musical style.

[4]African Puerto Rican folklore music and dance.

[5]Spanish: that cuts.

[6]Spanish: destiny.

50 AmeRícan,   defining the new america, humane america,
                admired america, loved america, harmonious
                america, the world in peace, our energies
                collectively invested to find other civili-
                zations, to touch God, further and further,
55   to dwell in the spirit of divinity!

    AmeRícan,   yes, for now, for i love this, my second
                land, and i dream to take the accent from
                the altercation, and be proud to call
                myself american, in the u.s. sense of the
60   word, AmeRícan, America!

                                                    1985

Latero[1] Story

i am a twentieth-century welfare recipient
moonlighting in the sun as a latero
a job invented by national state laws
designed to re-cycle aluminum cans
5 returned to consumer's acid laden
gastric inflammation pituitary glands
coca diet rites low cal godsons
of artificially flavored malignant
indigestions somewhere down the line
10 of a cancerous cell

i collect garbage cans in outdoor facilities
congested with putrid residues
my hands shelving themselves
opening plastic bags never knowing
15 what they'll encounter

several times a day i touch evil rituals
cut throats of chickens
tongues of poisoned rats
salivating my index finger
20 smells of month old rotten foods
next to pamper's diarrhea
        dry blood infectious diseases
hypodermic needles tissued with

---

[1]From Spanish *lata:* can. A man who picks up
cans from garbage containers and the streets.

heroin water drops pilfered in
25 slimy greases hazardous waste materials
but i cannot use rubber gloves
they undermine my daily profits

i am a twentieth-century welfare recipient
moonlighting in the day as a latero
30 that is the only opportunity i have
to make it big in america
some day i might become experienced enough
to offer technical assistance
to other lateros
35 i am thinking of publishing
my own guide to latero's collection
and founding a latero's union offering
medical dental benefits

i am a twentieth-century welfare recipient
40 moonlighting in the night as a latero
i am considered some kind of expert
at collecting cans during fifth avenue parades
i can now hire workers at twenty
five cents an hour guaranteed salary
45 and fifty per cent of two and one half cents
profit on each can collected

i am a twentieth-century welfare recipient
moonlighting in midnight as a latero
i am becoming an entrepreneur
50 an american success story
i have hired bag ladies to keep peddlers
from my territories
i have read in some guide to success
that in order to get rich
55 to make it big
i have to sacrifice myself
moonlighting until dawn by digging
deeper into the extra can
margin of profit
60 i am on my way up the opportunistic
ladder of success
in ten years i will quit welfare
to become a legitimate businessman
i'll soon become a latero executive
65 with corporate conglomerate intents
god bless america

1988

Judith Ortiz Cofer b. 1952

The daughter of a teenage mother and a career Navy father, Judith Ortiz Cofer spent her childhood traveling back and forth between the U.S. mainland and Puerto Rico, her birthplace, experiencing schools and neighborhoods in both Spanish and English and adjusting and readjusting to different cultural environments. After retirement, her father settled the family in Georgia, which stabilized Judith's education. During college she married and, with husband and daughter, moved to Florida where she finished an M.A. in English. A fellowship allowed her to pursue graduate work at Oxford, after which she returned to Florida and simultaneously began teaching English and writing poetry. In 1981 and 82, she received scholarships to the Bread Loaf Writers' Conference, and continued on the program's staff until 1985. *Peregrina* won first place in the Riverstone International Poetry Chapbook Competition in 1985. *Reaching for the Mainland* and *Terms of Survival* appeared in 1987. Since then, she has concentrated on prose, publishing *The Line of the Sun* (1989), a novel; *Silent Dancing* (1990), autobiographical essays; and *The Latin Deli* (1993) and *An Island Like You* (1995), short stories.

As a child, living amid the violence and racial tensions of the Paterson, New Jersey slums, the library became her refuge, and books her English teachers; on the island, the written word gave way to the oral tradition of her Spanish speaking grandmother. Though strongly determined by the English language and literary tradition of her academic training, her writing still reflects the tension of that dynamic intercultural background. Spanish lingers, filtering through in emotion-packed words or phrases that remind us we are reading something other than a monolingual text. Her poems offer continual overlays and blends of cultures and languages that refuse to settle completely into either side, hence defining their ever-shifting, never-ending synthesis as authentic Puerto Rican life. She calls it the "habit of movement," a state of instability that informs and stimulates her creativity.

One pattern her exploration takes is that of gathering, like an anthropologist, sayings, expressions, or words from Puerto Rican Spanish and recasting them into English poems in which the essence is conveyed across linguistic borders. In the process, she charts the experience of intercultural life, exposing readers to alternative perspectives on everyday matters that can seem so common and simple when safely encapsulated in the familiar words of one's own language. That is, Ortiz Cofer achieves what many claim to be the function of poetry: she rarifies language and experience to an intensity that enables it to stir the reader's otherwise callous sensibilities. At a more pedestrian level, this experience is and has been fundamental to the development of the U.S. idiom and culture, themselves a product of the continual intercultural synthesis that makes them so rich and dynamic. Thus, beyond displaying the particularities of Puerto Rican experience, Ortiz Cofer reminds us of our common national character.

While much of her poetry and prose displays the texture of her interwoven cultures, the underlying preoccupation is more sexual than cultural. More than languages and geographic locations, the figures gripped in an unstable embrace are men and women, with the former more an ever-absent presence, and the latter a long-suffering presence longing for that absence. Perhaps her works document the disintegration of the traditional family resulting from the pressures of migratory life, but even in the pieces that recall prior lives in more settled times, stable relationships are illusions. Ortiz Cofer's concern is not simply ethnic, but profoundly sexual—the key to any stable culture is the viability of the male-female relationship. Her basic question is the essential one of desire and its fulfillment. Everything else—ethnic strife, social injustice, gender conflict, religion, tradition, language itself—becomes mere incarnation of frustrated desire. *Silent Dancing* plays with memory and the power of media to document events, despite its inability to convey the emotive value of images. A powerful commentary on lost moments, it is equally forceful as a recovery of the ephemeral quality of experience.

Juan Bruce-Novoa
University of California at Irvine

PRIMARY WORKS

Latin Women Pray, 1980; *The Native Dancer,* 1981; *Among the Ancestors,* 1981; *Peregrina,* 1986; *Reaching for the Mainland,* 1987; *Terms of Survival,* 1988; *The Line of the Sun,* 1989; *Silent Dancing,* 1990; *The Latin Deli,* 1993; *An Island Like You,* 1995; *Reaching for the Mainland,* 1995; *The Year of Our Revolution,* 1998; *Sleeping with One Eye Open,* 1999; *Woman in Front of the Sun,* 2000; *The Meaning of Consuelo,* 2003; *Call Me Maria,* 2004.

Claims

Last time I saw her, Grandmother
had grown seamed as a Bedouin tent.
She had claimed the right
to sleep alone, to own
5   her nights, to never bear
the weight of sex again nor to accept
its gift of comfort, for the luxury
of stretching her bones.
She'd carried eight children,
10 three had sunk in her belly, *náufragos*[1]
she called them, shipwrecked babies
drowned in her black waters.
Children are made in the night and
steal your days
15 *for the rest of your life, amen.* She said this
to each of her daughters in turn. Once she had made a pact
with man and nature and kept it. Now like the sea,
she is claiming back her territory.

1987

---

[1]Spanish: victims of shipwrecks.

The Woman Who Was Left at the Altar

She calls her shadow Juan,
looking back often as she walks.
She has grown fat, her breasts huge
as reservoirs. She once opened her blouse
5   in church to show the silent town
what a plentiful mother she could be.
Since her old mother died, buried in black,
she lives alone.
Out of the lace she made curtains for her room,
10   doilies out of the veil. They are now
yellow as malaria.
She hangs live chickens from her waist to sell,
walks to the town swinging her skirts of flesh.
She doesn't speak to anyone. Dogs follow
15   the scent of blood to be shed. In their hungry,
yellow eyes she sees his face. She takes him
to the knife time after time.

1987

My Father in the Navy:
A Childhood Memory

Stiff and immaculate
in the white cloth of his uniform
and a round cap on his head like a halo,
he was an apparition on leave from a shadow-world
5   and only flesh and blood when he rose from below
the waterline where he kept watch over the engines
and dials making sure the ship parted the waters
on a straight course.
Mother, brother and I kept vigil
10   on the nights and dawns of his arrivals,
watching the corner beyond the neon sign of a quasar
for the flash of white our father like an angel
heralding a new day.
His homecomings were the verses
15   we composed over the years making up
the siren's song that kept him coming back
from the bellies of iron whales
and into our nights
like the evening prayer.

1987

En Mis Ojos No Hay Días[1]

from Borges'[2] poem "The Keeper of the Books"

Back before the fire burned in his eyes,
in the blast furnace which finally consumed him,
Father told us about the reign of little terrors
of his childhood beginning
5   at birth with a father who cursed him
for being the twelfth and the fairest
too blond and pretty to be from his loins,
so he named him the priest's pauper son.
He said the old man kept:
10   a mule for labor
a horse for sport
wine in his cellar
a mistress in town
and a wife to bear him daughters,
15   to send to church
to pray for his soul.
And sons,
to send to the fields
to cut the cane
20   and raise the money
to buy his rum.
He was only ten when he saw his father
split a man in two with his machete
and walk away proud to have rescued his honor
25   like a true "hombre."

Father always wrapped these tales
in the tissue paper of his humor
and we'd listen at his knees rapt,
warm and safe,
30   by the blanket of his caring,
but he himself could not be saved,
"What on earth drove him mad?"
his friends still ask,
remembering Prince Hamlet, I reply,
35   "Nothing on earth,"
but no one listens to ghost stories anymore.

1987

[1]Spanish: In My Eyes There Are No Days.
[2]Jorge Luis Borges (1899–1986), Argentine
writer.

Latin Women Pray

Latin women pray
In incense sweet churches
They pray in Spanish to an Anglo God
With a Jewish heritage.
5 And this Great White Father
Imperturbable in his marble pedestal
Looks down upon his brown daughters
Votive candles shining like lust
In his all seeing eyes
10 Unmoved by their persistent prayers.

Yet year after year
Before his image they kneel
Margarita Josefina Maria and Isabel
All fervently hoping
15 That if not omnipotent
At least he be bilingual

1987

Rita Dove b. 1952

Former U.S. poet laureate Rita Dove has an international poetic vision. The settings of her enigmatic lyrics move from Ohio to Germany to Israel; the time frames shift from the present to a past both historical and personal. In a single volume, slaves, biblical characters, mythological figures, and members of Dove's own family stand side by side. Although she has been rightly celebrated as an eloquent African American female voice, her frequently shifting viewpoint suggests that she sees her work transcending race and gender as well as time and place.

Born in 1952 in Akron, Ohio, Dove was the second of four children in a middle-class family. Both her paternal grandfather and her father worked for the Goodyear Tire and Rubber Company in Akron. Her father, Ray Dove, earned a master's degree and became the company's first black chemist, though at the time of his oldest daughter's birth he was still restricted to running the company elevator.

Rita Dove attended the public schools in Akron and then enrolled at Miami University in Ohio, where she graduated *summa cum laude* in 1973. She then attended the University of Tübingen on a Fulbright Scholarship and earned an MFA from the University of Iowa in 1977.

Dove's poetry is grounded in reality yet capable of sky-high buoyancy. Her oblique, sometimes otherworldly metaphors indicate a literary kinship with contemporary Scandinavian poets such as Tomas Tranströmer. In her poems ("Ö," for instance), language itself often appears to be a form of salvation. As Dove put it in a 1991 interview, "I think one reason I became primarily a poet rather than a fiction writer is that though I am interested in stories, I am profoundly fascinated by the ways in which language can change your perceptions."

In 1987 Dove won the Pulitzer Prize for *Thomas and Beulah,* a sequence of poems about her grandparents' courtship, marriage, and subsequent life in Akron. More recently, she has published a sonnet sequence based on the Persephone myth, *Mother Love* (1995); a verse drama, *The Darker Face of the Earth* (1994, rev. ed. 1996), an Oedipal tale set in antebellum South Carolina; and a collection of lyrics,

On the Bus with Rosa Parks (1999). In addition to verse, she has published short stories, essays, and a novel.

A resident of Charlottesville, Virginia, Dove is Commonwealth Professor of English at the University of Virginia.

Hilary Holladay
University of Massachusetts, Lowell

PRIMARY WORKS

The Yellow House on the Corner, 1980; *Museum,* 1983; *Fifth Sunday,* 1985; *Thomas and Beulah,* 1986; *Grace Notes,* 1989; *Through the Ivory Gate,* 1992; *Selected Poems,* 1993; *The Darker Face of the Earth: A Verse Play in Fourteen Scenes,* 1994; *Mother Love: Poems,* 1995; *The Poet's World,* 1995; *The Darker Face of the Earth* (rev. 2nd ed.), 1996; *On the Bus with Rosa Parks,* 1999; *American Smooth,* 2004.

Kentucky, 1833

It is Sunday, day of roughhousing. We are let out in the woods. The
young boys wrestle and butt their heads together like sheep—a circle
forms; claps and shouts fill the air. The women, brown and glossy,
gather round the banjo player, or simply lie in the sun, legs and
5 aprons folded. The weather's an odd monkey—any other day he's on
our backs, his cotton eye everywhere; today the light sifts down like
the finest cornmeal, coating our hands and arms with a dust. God's
dust, old woman Acker says. She's the only one who could read to us
from the Bible, before Massa forbade it. On Sundays, something
10 hangs in the air, a hallelujah, a skitter of brass, but we can't call it by
name and it disappears.

Then Massa and his gentlemen friends come to bet on the boys. They
guffaw and shout, taking sides, red-faced on the edge of the boxing
ring. There is more kicking, butting, and scuffling—the winner gets a
15 dram of whiskey if he can drink it all in one swig without choking.

Jason is bucking and prancing about—Massa said his name reminded
him of some sailor, a hero who crossed an ocean, looking for a golden
cotton field. Jason thinks he's been born to great things—a suit with
gold threads, vest and all. Now the winner is sprawled out under a
20 tree and the sun, that weary tambourine, hesitates at the rim of the
sky's green light. It's a crazy feeling that carries through the night; as if
the sky were an omen we could not understand, the book that, if we
could read, would change our lives.

1980

Ö

Shape the lips to an *o,* say *a.*
That's *island.*

One word of Swedish has changed the whole neighborhood.
When I look up, the yellow house on the corner
5 is a galleon stranded in flowers. Around it

the wind. Even the high roar of a leaf-mulcher
could be the horn-blast from a ship
as it skirts the misted shoals.

We don't need much more to keep things going.
10 Families complete themselves
and refuse to budge from the present,
the present extends its glass forehead to sea
(backyard breezes, scattered cardinals)

and if, one evening, the house on the corner
15 took off over the marshland,
neither I nor my neighbor
would be amazed. Sometimes

a word is found so right it trembles
at the slightest explanation.
20 You start out with one thing, end
up with another, and nothing's
like it used to be, not even the future.

1980

Daystar

She wanted a little room for thinking:
but she saw diapers steaming on the line,
a doll slumped behind the door.

So she lugged a chair behind the garage
5 to sit out the children's naps.

Sometimes there were things to watch—
the pinched armor of a vanished cricket,

a floating maple leaf. Other days
she stared until she was assured
10   when she closed her eyes
she'd see only her own vivid blood.

She had an hour, at best, before Liza appeared
pouting from the top of the stairs.
And just *what* was mother doing
15   out back with the field mice? Why,
building a palace. Later
that night when Thomas rolled over and
lurched into her, she would open her eyes
and think of the place that was hers
20   for an hour—where
she was nothing,
pure nothing, in the middle of the day.

1986

The Oriental Ballerina

twirls on the tips of a carnation
while the radio scratches out a morning hymn.
Daylight has not ventured as far

as the windows—the walls are still dark,
5   shadowed with the ghosts
of oversized gardenias. The ballerina

pirouettes to the wheeze of the old
rugged cross, she lifts
her shoulders past the edge

10   of the jewelbox lid. Two pink slippers
touch the ragged petals, no one
should have feet that small! In China

they do everything upside down:
this ballerina has not risen but drilled
15   a tunnel straight to America

where the bedrooms of the poor
are papered in vulgar flowers
on a background the color of grease, of

teabags, of cracked imitation walnut veneer.
20 On the other side of the world
they are shedding robes sprigged with

roses, roses drifting with a hiss
to the floor by the bed
as, here, the sun finally strikes the windows

25 suddenly opaque,
noncommital as shields. In this room
is a bed where the sun has gone

walking. Where a straw nods over
the lip of its glass and a hand
30 reaches for a tissue, crumpling it to a flower.

The ballerina had been drilling all night!
She flaunts her skirts like sails,
whirling in a disk so bright,

so rapidly she is standing still.
35 The sun walks the bed to the pillow
and pauses for breath (in the Orient,

breath floats like mist
in the fields), hesitating
at a knotted handkerchief that has slid

40 on its string and has lodged beneath
the right ear which discerns
the most fragile music

where there is none. The ballerina dances
at the end of a tunnel of light,
45 she spins on her impossible toes—

the rest is shadow.
The head on the pillow sees nothing
else, though it feels the sun warming

its cheeks. *There is no China;*
50 no cross, just the papery kiss
of a kleenex above the stink of camphor,

the walls exploding with shabby tutus. . . .

1986

Naomi Shihab Nye b. 1952

At the age of six, as Naomi Shihab Nye learned how to write, she began creating poems. She published her first poem one year later in a children's magazine, *Wee Wisdom.* She was encouraged by her mother, who read poetry to her, and later by a teacher, who asked students to memorize lines of William Blake and Langston Hughes.

Naomi and her brother grew up in a bicultural home, born to a German American mother and a Palestinian American father. Although her mother was raised Lutheran and her father Muslim, they sent her to Unity Sunday School as well as the Vedanta Society of St. Louis to study Hinduism, where the swami modeled the value of peace in his teachings.

In 1966, her family sold its business and moved to the Middle East, to a town eight miles north of Jerusalem, then located inside the borders of Jordan. There her father edited the *Jerusalem Times,* for which his fourteen-year-old daughter wrote a weekly column and often composed letters to the editor. Until this move, the Shihab home heard only fragments of Arabic. Yet the language and the oral narratives shared by her father and her grandmother, Sitta Khadara, left an indelible imprint on some of Nye's most important writing. Stories that punctuated the headlines also left a lasting impression on her poetry and prose, as did the history behind her father's emigration to the United States.

The way that historical events affect people's daily lives is an important theme in Nye's writing, shaped largely by a familial legacy of dispossession. Sitti Khadara became a refugee in 1948, when she lost her home in Jerusalem to Israeli settlers. And just a year after the Shihabs moved to the Middle East, Naomi and her family had to flee Jerusalem on the eve of the Six Day War. Upon returning to the United States the Shihabs moved to Texas, where Naomi found herself homesick for Palestine—for the muezzin, the olive groves,

and her grandmother's stories. She continued to weave those narratives into images at Trinity University in San Antonio, where she received her bachelor's degree in 1974.

The borderland culture of Texas provides Nye with striking thematic parallels of invisible and dispossessed peoples. In "Where the Soft Air Lives," her images of events and people in the Southwest often double as allusions to the circumstances that Palestinians in the diaspora face: "There is no border in the sky," a Mexican woman observes. A product of Texas, where Nye has spent the bulk of her life with her husband and son, she has been profoundly influenced by Latino/a and Native American art and literature.

Nye's poems blend lyricism and realism as a way of poetically documenting stories that would otherwise be rendered invisible. Her work has a reportorial tone but manages to portray what newspapers cannot. Images of healing accent her poem, "Blood," in which the speaker's father reveals her Arab ethnicity and her relationship to the world around her as it appears in "the headlines [which] clot in my blood." With these images, Nye bears witness to the suffering of the people in her poems. She intervenes in the headlines by using poetry to ease tensions in the world by recognizing one another's humanity, as, for example, in "Ducks," which represents daily life in Iraq before and after the war.

Her grandmother and father often are the vehicles through which Nye humanizes Arab people in her writing. In "My Father and the Figtree," she reminisces about the folktales that feature Johan, a trickster figure, and figs, which symbolize the Palestinian land that her father left behind. When her grandmother figures as a character in the poem "The Words Under the Words," Nye details the pain of displacement and diaspora, and the power of words and storytelling, to travel across those distances among relatives.

Humanizing people who are often de-humanized in the media and history is a standard feature of Nye's poetry and prose. Many of the works that she has translated and written are for children, a way to encourage her younger audience to see similarities across the visible differences. *Sitti's Secret* is a picture book that features a young girl who lives in the United States and who misses her grandmother in Palestine. For young adult readers, Nye wrote a novel, *Habibi*, that draws on her experience as fourteen-year-old in Jerusalem. In San Antonio, Nye continues to write for children and adults and conducts writing workshops for the Writers in the Schools program and for the Texas Commission on the Arts to increase literacy and writing for children and teenagers. Her work with children has also generated a rich body of translation work about Mexico and the Middle East. In collaboration with translators, poets, and artists from these regions, Nye has published two volumes of poetry and art aimed to help children enjoy poetry while dispelling stereotypes.

Marcy Jane Knopf-Newman
Boise State University

PRIMARY WORKS

Different Ways to Pray: Poems, 1980; *Hugging the Jukebox,* 1982; *Yellow Glove,* 1986; *Fuel: Poems,* 1988; *Red Suitcase: Poems,* 1994; *Travel Alarm,* 1993; *Sitti's Secrets,* 1994; *Words Under the Words: Selected Poems,* 1995; *Never in a Hurry: Essays on People and Places,* 1996; *Habibi,* 1997; *What Holds Us Up: Poems,* 2000; *Mint Snowball,* 2001; *19 Varieties of Gazelle,* 2002; *You and Yours,* 2005.

Ducks

We thought of ourselves as people of culture.
How long will it be till others see us that way again?
Iraqi friend

In her first home each book had a light around it.
The voices of distant countries
floated in through open windows,
entering her soup and her mirror.
5   They slept with her in the same thick bed.

Someday she would go there.
Her voice, among all those voices.
In Iraq a book never had one owner—it had ten.
Lucky books, to be held often
10   and gently, by so many hands.

Later in American libraries she felt sad
for books no one ever checked out.

She lived in a country house beside a pond
and kept ducks, two male, one female.

15 She worried over the difficult relations
of triangles. One of the ducks
often seemed depressed.
But not the same one.

During the war between her two countries
20 she watched the ducks more than usual.
She stayed quiet with the ducks.
Some days they huddled among reeds
or floated together.

She could not call her family in Basra
25 which had grown farther away than ever
nor could they call her. For nearly a year
she would not know who was alive,
who was dead.

The ducks were building a nest.

1994

Different Ways to Pray

There was the method of kneeling,
a fine method, if you lived in a country
where stones were smooth.
The women dreamed wistfully of bleached courtyards,
5 hidden corners where knee fit rock.
Their prayers were weathered rib bones,
small calcium words uttered in sequence,
as if this shedding of syllables could somehow
fuse them to the sky.

10 There were the men who had been shepherds so long
they walked like sheep.
Under the olive trees, they raised their arms—
Hear us! We have pain on earth!
We have so much pain there is no place to store it!
15 But the olives bobbed peacefully
in fragrant buckets of vinegar and thyme.
At night the men ate heartily, flat bread and white cheese,
and were happy in spite of the pain,
because there was also happiness.

20 Some prized the pilgrimage,
wrapping themselves in new white linen
to ride buses across miles of vacant sand.
When they arrived at Mecca
they would circle the holy places,
25 on foot, many times,
they would bend to kiss the earth
and return, their lean faces housing mystery.

While for certain cousins and grandmothers
the pilgrimage occurred daily,
30 lugging water from the spring
or balancing the baskets of grapes.
These were the ones present at births,
humming quietly to perspiring mothers.
The ones stitching intricate needlework into children's dresses,
35 forgetting how easily children soil clothes.

There were those who didn't care about praying.
The young ones. The ones who had been to America.
They told the old ones, you are wasting your time.
        Time?—The old ones prayed for the young ones.
40 They prayed for Allah to mend their brains,
for the twig, the round moon,
to speak suddenly in a commanding tone.

And occasionally there would be one
who did none of this,
45 the old man Fowzi, for example, Fowzi the fool,
who beat everyone at dominoes,
insisted he spoke with God as he spoke with goats,
and was famous for his laugh.

                                                        1994

My Father and the Figtree

For other fruits my father was indifferent.
He'd point at the cherry trees and say,
"See those? I wish they were figs."
In the evening he sat by my bed
5 weaving folktales like livid little scarves.
They always involved a figtree.
Even when it didn't fit, he'd stick it in.
Once Joha was walking down the road and he saw a figtree.

Or, he tied his camel to a figtree and went to sleep.
10 Or, later when they caught and arrested him,
   his pockets were full of figs.

At age six I ate a dried fig and shrugged.
"That's not what I'm talking about!" he said,
"I'm talking about a fig straight from the earth—
15 gift of Allah!—on a branch so heavy it touches the ground.
I'm talking about picking the largest fattest sweetest fig
in the world and putting it in my mouth."
(Here he'd stop and close his eyes.)

Years passed, we lived in many houses, none had figtrees.
20 We had lima beans, zucchini, parsley, beets.
"Plant one!" my mother said, but my father never did.
He tended garden half-heartedly, forgot to water,
let the okra get too big.
"What a dreamer he is. Look how many things he starts
25 and doesn't finish."

The last time he moved, I got a phone call.
My father, in Arabic, chanting a song I'd never heard.
"What's that?"
"Wait till you see!"
30 He took me out to the new yard.
There, in the middle of Dallas, Texas,
a tree with the largest, fattest, sweetest figs in the world.
"It's a figtree song!" he said,
plucking his fruits like ripe tokens,
35 emblems, assurance
of a world that was always his own.

1997

Blood

"A true Arab knows how to catch a fly in his hands,"
my father would say. And he'd prove it,
cupping the buzzer instantly
while the host with the swatter stared.

5 In the spring our palms peeled like snakes.
True Arabs believed watermelon could heal fifty ways.
I changed these to fit the occasion.

Years before, a girl knocked,
wanted to see the Arab.

10 I said we didn't have one.
    After that, my father told me who he was,
    "Shihab"—"shooting star"—
    a good name, borrowed from the sky.
    Once I said, "When we die, we give it back?"
15 He said that's what a true Arab would say.

    Today the headlines clot in my blood.
    A little Palestinian dangles a truck on the front page.
    Homeless fig, this tragedy with a terrible root
    is too big for us. What flag can we wave?
20 I wave the flag of stone and seed,
    table mat stitched in blue.

    I call my father, we talk around the news.
    It is too much for him,
    neither of his two languages can reach it.
25 I drive into the country to find sheep, cows,
    to plead with the air:
    Who calls anyone *civilized*?
    Where can the crying heart graze?
    What does a true Arab do now?

                                        1997

Where the Soft Air Lives

"Meanwhile Dean and I went out to dig the streets of Mexican San
Antonio. It was fragrant and soft—the softest air I'd ever known—
and dark, and mysterious, and buzzing. Sudden figures of girls in
white bandannas appeared in the humming dark."
                    Jack Kerouac, *On the Road*

1.
She placed her babies in the sink
stroking off the heat with an old damp rag.
Coo-coo little birdies, she sang,
then she tied the hair up in ponytails
5 pointing to the moon. It made them look
like little fruits with a pointed end.
She said, You don't think about poverty
till someone comes over.

2.
The man on Guadalupe Street is
10 guarding the cars. On his porch

the lights of Virgin Mary flash
endlessly, prayer-time, vigilante,
he rocks with his wife every night
rocking, while the bakery seals its cases
15 of pumpkin tart and the boys
with T-shirts slashed off below the nipples
strut big as buses past his gate.
He is keeping an eye on them.
And on fenders, hubcaps,
20 a grocery cart let loose
and lodged against a fence.
Cars roar past, but they will have
to got home again. He is happy
in this life, blinking Mother of God,
25 his wife placing one curl of mint in the tea,
saying always the same line,
Is it sweet enough? and the porch
painted three shades of green.

3.
I mended my ways, he said.
30 I took a needle and big thread and mended them.
You would not know me to see me now.
Sometimes I see myself sweeping the yard,
watering the dog, and I think
who is that guy? He looks like an old guy.
35 He looks like a guy who tells you
fifteen dead stories and mixes them up.
So that explains it:
why I don't tell you nuthin.

4.
She feeds her roses coffee
40 to make them huge. When her son was in Vietnam
the bougainvillea turned black once overnight.
But he didn't die. She prescribes lemongrass,
manzanilla: in her album the grandchildren
smile like seed packets.
She raises the American flag on her pole
45 because she is her own Mexican flag
and the wind fluttering the hem of her dress
says there is no border in the sky.

5.
Lisa's husband left, so she dyed her hair
a different color every day. Once pale silk,
50 next morning, a flame. She shaped her nails,
wore a nightgown cut down so low

the great canyon between her bosoms
woke up the mailman dragging his bag.
She pulled the bed into the dining room,
55 placed it dead center, never went out.
TV, eyelash glue, pools of perfume.
She was waiting for the plumber,
the man who sprays the bugs. Waiting
to pay a newspaper bill, to open her arms,
60 unroll all her front pages
and the sad unread sections too,
the ads for bacon and cleanser,
the way they try to get you to come to the store
by doubling your coupons,
65 the way they line the ads in red.

6.
Air filled with hearts,
we pin them to our tongues,
follow the soft air back to its cave
between tires, river of air
70 pouring warm speech, two-colored speech
into the streets. *Make a house*
and live in it.

At the Mission Espada
the priest keeps a little goat
75 tied to a stump.
His people come slowly out
of the stone-white room,
come lifting their feet suddenly heavy,
trying to remember far back before
80 anything had happened twice.
Someone lit a candle, and it caught.
A girl in a white dress,
singing in a window.
And you were getting married,
85 getting born, seeing the slice of blue
that meant *shore*;
the goat rises,
his bitten patch of land around him.
The priest bends to touch his head.
90 And goes off somewhere.
But the air behind him
still holding that hand, and the little goat
still standing.

1997

Gary Soto b. 1952

Gary Soto was born in Fresno, California, in the heart of the San Joaquin Valley, one of the world's richest agricultural regions. Raised in a working-class family, Soto attended parochial and public schools before enrolling in Fresno State College, intending to study geography and urban planning. His interests soon shifted to literature, however, especially after studying with the prominent poet Philip Levine. Soto published his first poem in 1973 in the *Iowa Review* as a college senior. After graduation, he entered the creative writing program at the University of California, Irvine and earned a master of fine arts degree in 1976. Soto then resided briefly in Mexico. His first book of poetry, *The Elements of San Joaquin,* appeared in 1977 to much critical acclaim. That same year, Soto began teaching at the University of California, Berkeley where he remains. After four volumes of poetry, Soto has more recently published three collections of autobiographical sketches and essays. He is the winner of various prestigious prizes including a Guggenheim fellowship and the Academy of American Poets Award.

Like much contemporary American verse, Soto's poetry is largely autobiographical, recalling childhood and adolescent incidents, and delineating family experience. Soto possesses the skill of converting ordinary, even banal, events into poetic occasions; much of his power and appeal as a poet derives precisely from the accessibility and familiarity of his subjects: a grandmother's courage, a youthful failure as an athlete, a father's relationship with his curious, energetic daughter. Soto's preference for clear, uncomplicated language and concrete images also enhances his work's accessibility. In terms of technique, the most striking feature of Soto's poetry is enjambment, the device of carrying meaning, without pause, from one line to the next.

Soto's ethnic consciousness—his sense of himself as a Mexican American—animates much of his work without delimiting it. Soto moves easily between the United States and Mexico to find his settings, his themes, and his protagonists. He often focuses on peculiarly Mexican American issues and he frequently delineates, especially in poems recalling his childhood, the Mexican Americans' sense of community. But Soto presents Mexican American experience and culture as they fit within a broader context of human events and values. It is fair to say that Soto's largest concern as a poet is the plight of that segment of humanity that is exploited, ignored, unheard. Soto lifts his voice in their behalf; as he once wrote: "I believe in the culture of the poor."

Raymund Paredes
University of California–Los Angeles

PRIMARY WORKS

The Elements of San Joaquin, 1977; *The Tale of Sunlight,* 1978; *Where Sparrows Work Hard,* 1981; *Black Hair,* 1985; *Living Up the Street,* 1985; *Small Faces,* 1986; *Lesser Evils: Ten Quartets,* 1988; *Who Will Know Us?: New Poems,* 1990; *A SummerLife,* 1990; *A Fire in My Hands: A Book of Poems,* 1990; *Baseball in April and Other Stories,* 1990; *Home Course in Religion: New Poems,* 1991; *Pacific Crossing,* 1992; *Neighborhood Odes,* 1992; *Local News,* 1993; *Crazy Weekend,* 1994; *Jesse,* 1994; *New and Selected Poems,* 1995; *Petty Crimes,* 1998; *Nerdlandia: A Play,* 1999; *A Natural Man,* 1999; *Buried Onions,* 1999; *Nickel and Dime,* 2000; *The Effects of Knut Hamsun on a Fresno Boy: Recollections and Short Essays,* 2000; *Poetry Lover,* 2001; *Baseball in April and Other Stories,* 2000; *A Simple Plan,* 2006; *Accidental Love,* 2007.

Braly Street

   Every summer
   The asphalt softens
   Giving under the edge
   Of boot heels and the trucks
5 That caught radiators
   Of butterflies.
   Bottle caps and glass
   Of the '40s and '50s
   Hold their breath
10 Under the black earth
   Of asphalt and are silent
   Like the dead whose mouths
   Have eaten dirt and bermuda.
   Every summer I come
15 To this street
   Where I discovered ants bit,
   Matches flare,
   And pinto beans unraveled
   Into plants; discovered
20 Aspirin will not cure a dog
   Whose fur twiches.
   It's 16 years
   Since our house
   Was bulldozed and my father
25 Stunned into a coma . . .
   Where it was,
   An oasis of chickweed
   And foxtails.
   Where the almond tree stood
30 There are wine bottles
   Whose history
   Is a liver. The long caravan
   Of my uncle's footprints
   Has been paved
35 With dirt. Where my father
   Cemented a pond
   There is a cavern of red ants
   Living on the seeds
   The wind brings
40 And cats that come here
   To die among
   The browning sage.

   It's 16 years
   Since bottle collectors

45 Shoveled around
    The foundation
    And the almond tree
    Opened its last fruit
    To the summer.
50 The houses are gone,
    The Molinas, Morenos,
    The Japanese families
    Are gone, the Okies gone
    Who moved out at night
55 Under a canopy of
    Moving stars.

    In '57 I sat
    On the porch, salting
    Slugs that came out
60 After the rain,
    While inside my uncle
    Weakened with cancer
    And the blurred vision
    Of his hands
65 Darkening to earth.
    In '58 I knelt
    Before my father
    Whose spine was pulled loose.
    Before his face still
70 Growing a chin of hair,
    Before the procession
    Of stitches behind
    His neck, I knelt
    And did not understand.

75 Braly Street is now
    Tin ventilators
    On the warehouses, turning
    Our sweat
    Towards the yellowing sky;
80 Acetylene welders
    Beading manifolds,
    Stinging the half-globes
    Of retinas. When I come
    To where our house was,
85 I come to weeds
    And a sewer line tied off
    Like an umbilical cord;
    To the chinaberry
    Not pulled down

90 And to its rings
My father and uncle
Would equal, if alive.

                    1977

The Cellar

I entered the cellar's cold,
Tapping my way deeper
Than light reaches,
And stood in a place
5 Where the good lumber
Ticked from its breathing
And slept in a weather
Of fine dust.
Looking for what we
10 Discarded some time back,
I struck a small fire
And stepped back
From its ladder of smoke,
Watching the light
15 Pull a chair
And a portion of the wall
From where they crouched
In the dark.
I saw small things—
20 Hat rack and suitcase,
Tire iron and umbrella
That closed on a great wind—
Step slowly, as if shy,
From their kingdom of mold
25 Into a new light.

Above, in the rented rooms,
In the lives
I would never know again,
Footsteps circled
30 A bed, the radio said
What was already forgotten.
I imagined the sun
And how a worker
Home from the fields

35 Might glimpse at it
    Through the window's true lens
    And ask it not to come back.
    And because I stood
    In this place for hours,
40 I imagined I could climb
    From this promise of old air
    And enter a street
    Stunned gray with evening
    Where, if someone
45 Moved, I could turn,
    And seeing through the years,
    Call him brother, call him Molina.

                 1978

Mexicans Begin Jogging

    At the factory I worked
    In the fleck of rubber, under the press
    Of an oven yellow with flame,
    Until the border patrol opened
5 Their vans and my boss waved for us to run.
    "Over the fence, Soto," he shouted,
    And I shouted that I was American.
    "No time for lies," he said, and pressed
    A dollar in my palm, hurrying me
10 Through the back door.

    Since I was on his time, I ran
    And became the wag to a short tail of Mexicans—
    Ran past the amazed crowds that lined
    The street and blurred like photographs, in rain.
15 I ran from that industrial road to the soft
    Houses where people paled at the turn of an autumn sky.
    What could I do but yell *vivas*
    To baseball, milkshakes, and those sociologists
    Who would clock me
20 As I jog into the next century
    On the power of a great, silly grin.

                 1981

Black Hair

At eight I was brilliant with my body.
In July, that ring of heat
We all jumped through, I sat in the bleachers
Of Romain Playground, in the lengthening
5   Shade that rose from our dirty feet.
The game before us was more than baseball.
It was a figure—Hector Moreno
Quick and hard with turned muscles,
His crouch the one I assumed before an altar
10   Of worn baseball cards, in my room.

I came here because I was Mexican, a stick
Of brown light in love with those
Who could do it—the triple and hard slide,
The gloves eating balls into double plays.
15   What could I do with 50 pounds, my shyness,
My black torch of hair, about to go out?
Father was dead, his face no longer
Hanging over the table or our sleep,
And mother was the terror of mouths
20   Twisting hurt by butter knives.
In the bleachers I was brilliant with my body,
Waving players in and stomping my feet,
Growing sweaty in the presence of white shirts.
I chewed sunflower seeds. I drank water
25   And bit my arm through the late innings.
When Hector lined balls into deep
Center, in my mind I rounded the bases
With him, my face flared, my hair lifting
Beautifully, because we were coming home
30   To the arms of brown people.

                                                    1985

Kearney Park

True Mexicans or not, let's open our shirts
And dance, a spark of heels
Chipping at the dusty cement. The people
Are shiny like the sea, turning

5   To the clockwork of rancheras,
     The accordion wheezing, the drum-tap
     Of work rising and falling.
     Let's dance with our hats in hand.
     The sun is behind the trees,
10 Behind my stutter of awkward steps
     With a woman who is a brilliant arc of smiles,
     An armful of falling water. Her skirt
     Opens and closes. My arms
     Know no better but to flop
15 On their own, and we spin, dip
     And laugh into each other's faces—
     Faces that could be famous
     On the coffee table of my abuelita.
     But grandma is here, at the park, with a beer
20 At her feet, clapping
     And shouting, "Dance, hijo, dance!"
     Laughing, I bend, slide, and throw up
     A great cloud of dust,
     Until the girl and I are no more.

1985

Rane Arroyo b. 1954

Born in Chicago to parents from Puerto Rico, Rane Ramón Arroyo is a prize-winning poet and playwright who has also lived in Ohio and Pennsylvania; he received a Ph.D. in American literature and cultural studies from the University of Pittsburgh. A self-professed gay writer, he is also a literary critic and performance artist and directs the University of Toledo's creative writing program. Arroyo's work is marked by his references to Caribbean and Latino life in the Midwest (particularly in Chicago), his consistent engagement with canonical literary figures of American and English modernism as well as with Latin American and Spanish poets, and his exploration of his personal experiences, including his long-standing relationship with the poet Glenn Sheldon, affection for his cat Diva, and awareness of his own process of aging.

Arroyo's self-reflexive poetry often focuses on the inner conscience of a poetic persona, a gay Puerto Rican bard who feels out of place in the world and who is constantly grappling with what it means to be a poet marked by racial, sexual, and linguistic difference. In this universe, poetry is construed as the space where memory comes together, the space for appreciating that which surrounds the individual, a way to come to terms with the world and to reflect about politics, news, racial relations, and the migrant experience, and, quite markedly, what it means to be an American.

At the core of Arroyo's universe are his family and the Puerto Rican traditions (dance, music, food, the Spanish language) and social experiences (factory work, poverty, migration) that characterize his relatives. A recurrent set of characters appears throughout Arroyo's four books: these include Mami, Papi, Aunt Sylvia, Uncle "Rachel" (the transvestite uncle), as well as many cousins. The poems often express intimate (and evolving) relationships with these individuals, highlighting issues of masculinity and gender in relation to the father and uncle, of tradition and assimilation in relation to the mother, and of youth and coming of age with the cousins.

One of the most striking features of Arroyo's poetry is his play with traditional forms (what appear to be rigid stanza sequences, often couplets and tercets, and set-length verses), which he uses to give shape to strongly prosaic content; the verses constantly make use of enjambment. Arroyo's poetry is marked by the variety of topics that it covers in a most colloquial way, wandering from considerations of Latino popular and mass culture (Andy García, Antonio Banderas, Desi Arnaz, Rita Moreno and *West Side Story,* Speedy González, Taco Bell) to revisionist historic dialogues with Christopher Columbus and conquistadors such as Juan Ponce de León to profound analysis about the specific environs of a particular neighborhood or serious critiques of racism or of the effects of drug trafficking and drug addiction His poetry tries to reconcile geographic specificity (his own love of Chicago, his parents' Puerto Rico) with cosmopolitanism (a learned engagement with the Western tradition and extensive travels throughout the world). He makes a clear attempt to address dominant conceptions of Latinos in the United States, engaging with damaging stereotypes as well as with issues specific to Mexican-Americans/Chicanos, Cuban-Americans, and Puerto Ricans.

The strong literary bent of Arroyo's work is established by constant mentions of and dialogues with poets such as William Carlos Williams (whose mother was Puerto Rican), Wallace Stevens, Hart Crane, Diane Williams, Seamus Heaney, as well as such Hispanic greats as Sor Juana Inés de la Cruz, Federico García Lorca, Octavio Paz, and Pablo Neruda. In fact, the poet's careful attention to form and literary language as *writerly* phenomena bring him closer to Víctor Hernández Cruz than to other Puerto Rican poets.

Lawrence La Fountain-Stokes
University of Michigan—Ann Arbor

PRIMARY WORKS

Columbus's Orphan, 1993; *The Singing Shark,* 1996; *Pale Ramón,* 1998; *Home Movies of Narcissus,* 2002; *Same-Sex Séances,* 2008; *The Roswell Poems,* 2008.

My Transvestite Uncle Is Missing

1. *Questions*
I remember you so Elvis Presley-thin
and ever about to join the army (now I know

the whys of that), and I remember remembering you:
before breasts, before European wigs, when

5   the etc. of your sexuality was a secret,
and you babysat me, and we danced to Aretha,

and you taught me to scream for the joy of
a song on the radio ("Romeo requests this from

his grave!"), and I can't call you, what's
10 your new legal name? Is it in the phone book?

Are you that official? I've heard you're
dead, call me collect please, I'm on my own,

and Uncle Rachel if you were here tonight I'd . . .
I'd sing to you: "Pretty woman walking down

15 the street of dreams," and you could tell me
that story again where gold is spun out of straw

2. Answers
News of your old death, first I danced in the shower with
clothes on, cracked my green head against a corner gave you a
bloody birth in my mind, gave myself a satisfying scar,
20 watched an Annie Lennox video where she has a red towel on
her head, I mirrored her, white towel to stop the bleeding
inside my own nest of a skull, then I screamed and screamed,
but the police never came, snow fell from the constellations,
everything was on fire, fast forward, tumbling and I stupidly
25 read the Song of Solomon for comfort, my eye filled up with
blood, I strapped a big bandage around my head, I'm a poor
man's Wilfred Owen, I'm my own damnation, you're dead,
I won't sing at the funeral that took place without me, the
sun will hear my confessions, my naked body on a rooftop
30 cruel cock crowing as if another ordinary morning, and it is,
I did survive, I, someone shows up to make sure I'm not in a
coma, I'm not, not with all these memories, I touch myself as
if I'm still loved, Uncle Rachel, does Death look sexy without
a fig leaf?

1996

Caribbean Braille

My blind father doesn't
want a volunteer
reader to describe
someone else's depluming.
5 He'd rather spend his rosary
time remembering, but
what does he long for in his

short attention span?
He has been reflecting
10 upon the color *wine-red,*
the idea of it in the world,
wine-red as wine and red.
The last thing Father saw
before his eyes burned into
15 industrial nothingness
was a nova in the shape
of a rose with hot thorns:
my eyes burst into flames
without warning. In his
20 youth's Old San Juan,
the norteamericano hotels
had roses and wine on tables
which he'd spy on from
cobblestone streets. *Who needs*
25 *fiction?* he asks, sure that
I have no answer, but
the son reads his father
to sleep. We wake up in
the morning, compare
30 mosquito bites. We laugh:
how silly to think someone
might send us love letters via
Caribbean mosquitoes. We
read this Braille by rubbing
35 our hands over and over
the bright bites. Our bodies are
the books we cannot read.

                                      1998

Write What You Know

But what do I know? I know Papi
worked in factories reigned by melodrama
(a sick day = the righteous anger of

waltzing bosses in K-Mart suits). I know
5 the word "knowledge" has the words
"now" and "ledge." I know that

my parents dared to color the suburbs
with their shy children. I'm no longer shy.
"Chew garlic," Mami said just yesterday after

10 I was diagnosed with pneumonia (I can't yet
breathe in the America I so love). I must write
about the time a museum guard yelled

at Papi: "The service entrance is over there."
Forgive me, Papi, for wanting to see dinosaurs.
15 (He's an aging man who abandoned me as an adult.)

Papi was silly, but he stopped dreaming
after citizen classes (but Puerto Ricans are
Americans I must still tell my frowning

scholarship geniuses). I know that Uncle
20 Manolo, who died in the green disgrace
of gangrene, did want to teach me the 12-string

guitar, but we visited less and less until
we were merely scars to each other, sad
genealogies. I know una tía became religious

25 decades after offering me a *Playboy* and
an egg timer. I know another tía talks
to spirits between epilepsy carnivals.

She is sweet and tough, what the grave
yearns for when thinking of honey.
30 I know that in poetry workshops I've lied:

"I'm not autobiographical." *They* don't need
to know Mami ripped a real blouse while
screaming at Heaven as if an eavesdropper

with a big diary. Papi's pornography was
35 disappointing because it wasn't imaginative.
I know I was judgmental, one way

to survive. I know that I miss feeding the camels
of the Three Wise Men. (Forget the presents—
camels in Chicago!) I know my teacher in

40 elementary school told me she was glad that
someday I'd be raped in prison. I know that
I've masturbated towards fake passports.

I've always loved details as if they are
sharable coins. I know that some colleagues
45 treating me to one dinner were naive in thinking

I knew the Mexican waiters who cursed them
every time they smiled under the parachutes of
fragile mustaches. We were and weren't strangers.

Will I get an award for knowing Miami hid her silver
50 Jack Kennedy dollars in the bathroom? I know God
has plans for me, but I'd rather do it myself, gracias.

I write without permission and no one knows how
often I'm rejected, and when I do publish, *they* smirk,
"Affirmative Action." My future is as an antique.

55 In know a man's morning beard can rub me raw
so that it feels that even sandpaper has a soul.
I know that I want to be known in my earned bed,

that it's worth it to be kept out of anthologies
because machos clone themselves without end.
60 My crotch has a mind of its own; I'm a double exile.

Sí, I know that none of this matters and yet
it hurts, it hurts. I know that once upon a time,
I used to be a brave little brown boy. The man I am

has memory losses that medicine can't help.
65 I know there are evil men trying to trade
new poems for old poems: newer, swifter,

correct models. I know that the writing
workshop is a minefield. I know that I cannot
stop writing, that the involuntary muscles

70 are in it for the long run. I know I must
write to scare myself. I know that my beloved
Hardy Boys may never recognize me

from other migrant workers while solving
The Mystery of the Lost Muchacho.
75 I'm waving to them: here I am, here I am.

Hombres, how many more clues do you need?

2002

That Flag

The Motel 6 clerk thinks I'm
Italian and complains to me
about Puerto Ricans, and I
nod because she has the key
5 to the last cheap room in town.
I unpack and go for a ride
down Joe Peréz Road and watch
two white, shirtless men do drug deals.
One looks at me, laughs. What does
10 he see? This sexy thug has
a Confederate flag in his truck
window. He rubs himself again
and again and I watch the way
one is possessed by a wreck.
15 The deal done, the two men then
slap each other on the ass,
and ride dust storms back to town.
I sit there thinking the fuckers
are right, that they are big
20 handsome, that they are our
America's perfect heirs and
that I'm not—aging Puerto Rican
homosexual poet exiled
to a borrowed bed. I walk
25 past the clerk and sing "Buenas
noches," but it isn't one, for I dream
of that flag, of a terrible army
of soldiers in uniforms of skin
sent to steal from me the head
30 of Joe Peréz. But I've hidden it
inside my own skull. It is safe.

2002

Louise Erdrich (Chippewa) b. 1954

Karen Louise Erdrich was born in Little Falls, Minnesota. She is an enrolled member of the Turtle Mountain Chippewa tribe of North Dakota. The daughter of Bureau of Indian Affairs educators, she received degrees from Dartmouth College and Johns Hopkins, and later served for a time as editor of the *Circle,* a newspaper published by the Boston Indian Council, before earning residential fellowships to the distinguished writers' colonies. Her initial reputation was founded on a series of successful short stories, for which she received the Nelson Algren Award in 1982 and a Pushcart Prize in 1983.

In 1984 Erdrich published her first book of poetry, *Jacklight*, which focuses upon both her own personal experiences and her observations of small town, upper-midwestern life. The classic themes of this poetry—the fragility and power of a life in the flesh, the desperation of longing, the need for transcendence—return in her second book of poetry, *Baptism of Desire* (1989), rendered almost surrealistically by combining an urgent and vivid organicism with a crackling, electrical imagery. Indeed, the virtuosity of Erdrich's acclaimed prose style is founded in the disciplined craft of her poetry, most of it written before her more widely known fiction.

Erdrich's first novel, *Love Medicine* (1984), was generously praised in the United States, where it won the National Book Critics' Circle Award for the Best Work of Fiction for 1984. The novel is structured as a series of separate narratives—several of which were first published as short stories—spanning a period of fifty years, from 1934 to 1984. Set on a North Dakota reservation, the stories focus on relations between three Chippewa families: the Kashpaws and their relations, the Lamartine/Nanapush, and the Morrisey families. The novel opens in 1981 with a young college student's return to the reservation on the occasion of the death of June Kashpaw. Coming home she sees clearly the pain and personal devastation the years have wrought on her family, and she struggles in her first-person narrative to comprehend what force or attraction in that situation would compel her Aunt June to set out for her home across an empty, snow-covered field on the night she froze

to death. The stories that follow probe the relations between these families and in so doing focus on three major characters: Marie Lazarre, a strong-willed woman of great spirit and beauty whose sense of principle is founded on feelings of inadequacy that have bedeviled her all her life; Lulu Lamartine, a woman of passionate intensity, who learned early in her life of the frailty of the flesh and its enormous capacity to heal life's pain and redeem its guilt; and Nector Kashpaw, a man of good looks and popular appeal, who is irresistibly drawn to Lulu but marries Marie (June is their daughter). The selection which follows is the second chapter of the book, the first in which we meet Marie Lazarre and come to understand her need for a "love medicine," a medicine which would create love, a love that would be a medicine.

Erdrich's second novel, *Beet Queen*, returns to the upper midwest in the same time frame as *Love Medicine*, but focuses on the Euro-American townspeople near the reservation. The action of the third novel in the trilogy, *Tracks*, precedes that of the other two, removing the story to the turn of the century and setting the stage for the other novels by exploring the different fates of young Fleur Pillager and Pauline Puyat and the traditional presence of the elder, Nanapush. In *Tracks* we learn that before she went into the convent and became Sister Leopolda, Pauline gave birth to a daughter, Marie (later Lazarre), whom she gave up to Bernadette Morrissey. Erdrich's work is marked by a generous, compassionate spirit, a marvelous sense of comic invention, a sometimes acute irony, and a finely honed sense of imagery and style.

Andrew O. Wiget
New Mexico State University

PRIMARY WORKS

Jacklight, 1984; *Love Medicine,* 1984; *Beet Queen,* 1986; *Tracks,* 1988; *Baptism of Fire,* 1989; *The Crown of Columbus,* 1991 (with Michael Dorris); *The Bingo Palace,* 1994; *The Blue Jay's Dance: A Birth Year,* 1995; *Grandmother's Pigeon,* 1996; *Tales of Burning Love,* 1996; *The Antelope Wife,* 1998; *The Birchbark House,* 1999; *The Last Report on the Miracles at Little No Horse,* 2001; *The Master Butcher's Singing Club,* 2003; *The Painted Drum,* 2005; *The Plague of Doves,* 2008.

from Love Medicine

Saint Marie (1934)

Marie Lazarre

So when I went there, I knew the dark fish must rise. Plumes of radiance had soldered on me. No reservation girl had ever prayed so hard. There was no use in trying to ignore me any longer. I was going up there on the hill with the black robe women. They were not any lighter than me. I was going up there to pray as good as they could. Because I don't have that much Indian blood. And they never thought they'd have a girl from this reservation as a saint they'd have to kneel to. But they'd have me. And I'd be carved in pure gold. With ruby lips. And my toenails would be little pink ocean shells, which they would have to stoop down off their high horse to kiss.

I was ignorant. I was near age fourteen. The length of sky is just about the size of my ignorance. Pure and wide. And it was just that—the pure and wideness of my ignorance—that got me up the hill to Sacred Heart Convent and brought me back down alive. For maybe Jesus did not take my bait, but them Sisters tried to cram me right down whole.

You ever see a walleye strike so bad the lure is practically out its back end before you reel it in? That is what they done with me. I don't like to make that low comparison, but I have seen a walleye do that once. And it's the same attempt as Sister Leopolda made to get me in her clutch.

I had the mail-order Catholic soul you get in a girl raised out in the bush, whose only thought is getting into town. For Sunday Mass is the only time my father brought his children in except for school, when we were harnessed. Our soul went cheap. We were so anxious to get there we would have walked in on our hands and knees. We just craved going to the store, slinging bottle caps in the dust, making fool eyes at each other. And of course we went to church.

Where they have the convent is on top of the highest hill, so that from its windows the Sisters can be looking into the marrow of the town. Recently a windbreak was planted before the bar "for the purposes of tornado insurance." Don't tell me that. That poplar stand was put up to hide the drinkers as they get the transformation. As they are served into the beast of their burden. While they're drinking, that body comes upon them, and then they stagger or crawl out the bar door, pulling a weight that can't move past the poplars. They don't want no holy witness to their fall.

Anyway, I climbed. That was a long-ago day. There was a road then for wagons that wound in ruts to the top of the hill where they had their buildings of painted brick. Gleaming white. So white the sun glanced off in dazzling display to set forms whirling behind your eyelids. The face of God you could hardly look at. But that day it drizzled, so I could look all I wanted. I saw the homelier side. The cracked whitewash and swallows nesting in the busted ends of eaves. I saw the boards sawed the size of broken windowpanes and the fruit trees, stripped. Only the tough wild rhubarb flourished. Goldenrod rubbed up their walls. It was a poor convent. I didn't see that then but I know that now. Compared to others it was humble, ragtag, out in the middle of no place. It was the end of the world to some. Where the maps stopped. Where God had only half a hand in the creation. Where the Dark One had put in thick bush, liquor, wild dogs, and Indians.

I heard later that the Sacred Heart Convent was a catchall place for nuns that don't get along elsewhere. Nuns that complain too much or lose their mind. I'll always wonder now, after hearing that, where they picked up Sister Leopolda. Perhaps she had scarred someone else, the way she left a mark on me. Perhaps she was just sent around to test her Sisters' faith, here and there, like the spot-checker in a factory. For she was the definite most-hard trial of anyone's endurance, even when they started out with veils of wretched love upon their eyes.

I was that girl who thought the black hem of her garment would help me rise. Veils of love which was only hate petrified by longing—that was me. I was like those bush Indians who stole the holy black hat of a Jesuit and swallowed little scraps of it to cure their fevers. But the hat itself carried smallpox and was killing them with belief. Veils of faith! I had this confidence in Leopolda. She was different. The other Sisters had long ago gone blank and given up on Satan. He slept for them. They never noticed his comings and goings. But Leopolda kept track of him and knew his habits, minds he burrowed in, deep spaces where he hid. She knew as much about him as my grandma, who called him by other names and was not afraid.

In her class, Sister Leopolda carried a long oak pole for opening high windows. It had a hook made of iron on one end that could jerk a patch of your hair out or throttle you by the collar—all from a distance. She used this deadly hook-pole for catching Satan by surprise. He could have entered without your knowing it— through your lips or your nose or any one of your seven openings—and gained your mind. But she would see him. That pole would brain you from behind. And he would gasp, dazzled, and take the first thing she offered, which was pain.

She had a stringer of children who could only breathe if she said the word. I was the worst of them. She always said the Dark One wanted me most of all, and I believed this. I stood out. Evil was a common thing I trusted. Before sleep sometimes he came and whispered conversation in the old language of the bush. I listened. He told me things he never told anyone but Indians. I was privy to both worlds of his knowledge. I listened to him, but I had confidence in Leopolda. She was the only one of the bunch he even noticed.

There came a day, though, when Leopolda turned the tide with her hook-pole.

It was a quiet day with everyone working at their desks, when I heard him. He had sneaked into the closets in the back of the room. He was scratching around, tasting crumbs in our pockets, stealing buttons, squirting his dark juice in the linings and the boots. I was the only one who heard him, and I got bold. I smiled. I glanced back and smiled and looked up at her sly to see if she had noticed. My heart jumped. For she was looking straight at me. And she sniffed. She had a big stark bony nose stuck to the front of her face for smelling out brimstone and evil thoughts. She had smelled him on me. She stood up. Tall, pale, a blackness leading into the deeper blackness of the slate wall behind her. Her oak pole had flown into her grip. She had seen me glance at the closet. Oh, she knew. She knew just where he was. I watched her watch him in her mind's eye. The whole class was watching now. She was staring, sizing, following his scuffle. And all of a sudden she tensed down, posed on her bent kneesprings, cocked her arm back. She threw the oak pole singing over my head, through my braincloud. It cracked through the thin wood door of the back closet, and the heavy pointed hook drove through his heart. I turned. She'd speared her own black rubber overboot where he'd taken refuge in the tip of her darkest toe.

Something howled in my mind. Loss and darkness. I understood. I was to suffer for my smile.

He rose up hard in my heart. I didn't blink when the pole cracked. My skull was tough. I didn't flinch when she shrieked in my ear. I only shrugged at the flowers of hell. He wanted me. More than anything he craved me. But then she did the worst. She did what broke my mind to her. She grabbed me by the collar and dragged me, feet flying, through the room and threw me in the closet with her dead black overboot. And I was there. The only light was a crack beneath the door. I asked the Dark One to enter into me and boost my mind. I asked him to restrain my tears, for they was pushing behind my eyes. But he was afraid to come back there. He was afraid of her sharp pole. And I was afraid of Leopolda's pole for the first time, too. I felt the cold hook in my heart. How it could crack through the door at any minute and drag me out, like a dead fish on a gaff, drop me on the floor like a gutshot squirrel.

I was nothing. I edged back to the wall as far as I could. I breathed the chalk dust. The hem of her full black cloak cut against my cheek. He had left me. Her spear could find me any time. Her keen ears would aim the hook into the beat of my heart.

What was that sound?

It filled the closet, filled it up until it spilled over, but I did not recognize the crying wailing voice as mine until the door cracked open, brightness, and she hoisted me to her camphor-smelling lips.

"He *wants* you," she said. "That's the difference. I give you love."

Love. The black hook. The spear singing through the mind. I saw that she had tracked the Dark One to my heart and flushed him out into the open. So now my heart was an empty nest where she could lurk.

Well, I was weak. I was weak when I let her in, but she got a foothold there. Hard to dislodge as the year passed. Sometimes I felt him—the brush of dim wings—but only rarely did his voice compel. It was between Marie and Leopolda now, and the struggle changed. I began to realize I had been on the wrong track with the fruits of hell. The real way to overcome Leopolda was this: I'd get to heaven first. And then, when I saw her coming, I'd shut the gate. She'd be out! That is why, besides the bowing and the scraping I'd be dealt, I wanted to sit on the altar as a saint.

To this end, I went up on the hill. Sister Leopolda was the consecrated nun who had sponsored me to come there.

"You're not vain," she said. "You're too honest, looking into the mirror, for that. You're not smart. You don't have the ambition to get clear. You have two choices. One, you can marry a no-good Indian, bear his brats, die like a dog. Or two, you can give yourself to God."

"I'll come up there," I said, "but not because of what you think."

I could have had any damn man on the reservation at the time. And I could have made him treat me like his own life. I looked good. And I looked white. But I wanted Sister Leopolda's heart. And here was the thing: sometimes I wanted her heart in love and admiration. Sometimes. And sometimes I wanted her heart to roast on a black stick.

She answered the back door where they had instructed me to call. I stood there with my bundle. She looked me up and down.

"All right," she said finally. "Come in."

She took my hand. Her fingers were like a bundle of broom straws, so thin and dry, but the strength of them was unnatural. I couldn't have tugged loose if she was leading me into rooms of white-hot coal. Her strength was a kind of perverse miracle, for she got it from fasting herself thin. Because of this hunger practice her lips were a wounded brown and her skin deadly pale. Her eye sockets were two deep lashless hollows in a taut skull. I told you about the nose already. It stuck out far and made the place her eyes moved even deeper, as if she stared out the wrong end of a gun barrel. She took the bundle from my hands and threw it in the corner.

"You'll be sleeping behind the stove, child."

It was immense, like a great furnace. There was a small cot close behind it.

"Looks like it could get warm there," I said.

"Hot. It does."

"Do I get a habit?"

I wanted something like the thing she wore. Flowing black cotton. Her face was strapped in white bandages, and a sharp crest of starched white cardboard hung over her forehead like a glaring beak. If possible, I wanted a bigger, longer, whiter beak than hers.

"No," she said, grinning her great skull grin. "You don't get one yet. Who knows, you might not like us. Or we might not like you."

But she had loved me, or offered me love. And she had tried to hunt the Dark One down. So I had this confidence.

"I'll inherit your keys from you," I said.

She looked at me sharply, and her grin turned strange. She hissed, taking in her breath. Then she turned to the door and took a key from her belt. It was a giant key, and it unlocked the larder where the food was stored.

Inside there was all kinds of good stuff. Things I'd tasted only once or twice in my life. I saw sticks of dried fruit, jars of orange peel, spice like cinnamon. I saw tins of crackers with ships painted on the side. I saw pickles. Jars of herring and the rind of pigs. There was cheese, a big brown block of it from the thick milk of goats. And besides that there was the everyday stuff, in great quantities, the flour and the coffee.

It was the cheese that got to me. When I saw it my stomach hollowed. My tongue dripped. I loved that goat-milk cheese better than anything I'd ever ate. I stared at it. The rich curve in the buttery cloth.

"When you inherit my keys," she said sourly, slamming the door in my face, "you can eat all you want of the priest's cheese."

Then she seemed to consider what she'd done. She looked at me. She took the key from her belt and went back, sliced a hunk off, and put it in my hand.

"If you're good you'll taste this cheese again. When I'm dead and gone," she said.

Then she dragged out the big sack of flour. When I finished that heaven stuff she told me to roll my sleeves up and begin doing God's labor. For a while we worked in silence, mixing up the dough and pounding it out on stone slabs.

"God's work," I said after a while. "If this is God's work, then I've done it all my life."

"Well, you've done it with the Devil in your heart then," she said. "Not God."

"How do you know?" I asked. But I knew she did. And I wished I had not brought up the subject.

"I see right into you like a clear glass," she said. "I always did."

"You don't know it," she continued after a while, "but he's come around here sulking. He's come around here brooding. You brought him in. He knows the smell of me, and he's going to make a last ditch try to get you back. Don't let him." She glared over at me. Her eyes were cold and lighted. "Don't let him touch you. We'll be a long time getting rid of him."

So I was careful. I was careful not to give him an inch. I said a rosary, two rosaries, three, underneath my breath. I said the Creed. I said every scrap of Latin I knew while we punched the dough with our fists. And still, I dropped the cup. It rolled under that monstrous iron stove, which was getting fired up for baking.

And she was on me. She saw he'd entered my distraction.

"Our good cup," she said. "Get it out of there, Marie."

I reached for the poker to snag it out from beneath the stove. But I had a sinking feel in my stomach as I did this. Sure enough, her long arm darted past me like a whip. The poker lighted in her hand.

"Reach," she said. "Reach with your arm for that cup. And when your flesh is hot, remember that the flames you feel are only one fraction of the heat you will feel in his hellish embrace."

She always did things this way, to teach you lessons. So I wasn't surprised. It was playacting, anyway, because a stove isn't very hot underneath right along the floor. They aren't made that way. Otherwise a wood floor would burn. So I said yes and got down on my stomach and reached under. I meant to grab it quick and jump up again, before she could think up another lesson, but here it happened. Although I groped for the cup, my hand closed on nothing. That cup was nowhere to be found. I heard her step toward me, a slow step. I heard the creak of thick shoe leather, the little *plat* as the folds of her heavy skirts met, a trickle of fine sand sifting, somewhere, perhaps in the bowels of her, and I was afraid. I tried to scramble up, but her foot came down lightly behind my ear, and I was lowered. The foot came down more firmly at the base of my neck, and I was held.

"You're like I was," she said. "He wants you very much."

"He doesn't want me no more," I said. "He had his fill. I got the cup!"

I heard the valve opening, the hissed intake of breath, and knew that I should not have spoke.

"You lie," she said. "You're cold. There is a wicked ice forming in your blood. You don't have a shred of devotion for God. Only wild cold dark lust. I know it. I know how you feel. I see the beast . . . the beast watches me out of your eyes sometimes. Cold."

The urgent scrape of metal. It took a moment to know from where. Top of the stove. Kettle. Lessons. She was steadying herself with the iron poker. I could feel it like pure certainty, driving into the wood floor. I would not remind her of pokers. I heard the water as it came, tipped from the spout, cooling as it fell but still scalding as it struck. I must have twitched beneath her foot, because she steadied me, and then the poker nudged up beside my arm as if to guide. "To warm your cold ash heart," she said. I felt how patient she would be. The water came. My mind went dead blank. Again. I could only think the kettle would be cooling slowly in her hand. I could not stand it. I bit my lip so as not to satisfy her with a sound. She gave me more reason to keep still.

"I will boil him from your mind if you make a peep," she said, "by filling up your ear."

Any sensible fool would have run back down the hill the minute Leopolda let them up from under her heel. But I was snared in her black intelligence by then. I could not think straight. I had prayed so hard I think I broke a cog in my mind. I prayed while her foot squeezed my throat. While my skin burst. I prayed even when I heard the wind come through, shrieking in the busted bird nests. I didn't stop when pure light fell, turning slowly behind my eyelids. God's face. Even that did not disrupt my continued praise. Words came. Words came from nowhere and flooded my mind.

Now I could pray much better than any one of them. Than all of them full force. This was proved. I turned to her in a daze when she let me up. My thoughts were gone, and yet I remember how surprised I was. Tears glittered in her eyes, deep down, like the sinking reflection in a well.

"It was so hard, Marie," she gasped. Her hands were shaking. The kettle clattered against the stove. "But I have used all the water up now. I think he is gone."

"I prayed," I said foolishly. "I prayed very hard."

"Yes," she said. "My dear one, I know."

We sat together quietly because we had no more words. We let the dough rise and punched it down once. She gave me a bowl of mush, unlocked the sausage from a special cupboard, and took that in to the Sisters. They sat down the hall, chewing their sausage, and I could hear them. I could hear their teeth bite through their bread and meat. I couldn't move. My shirt was dry but the cloth stuck to my back, and I couldn't think straight. I was losing the sense to understand how her mind worked. She'd gotten past me with her poker and I would never be a saint. I despaired. I felt I had no inside voice, nothing to direct me, no darkness, no Marie. I was about to throw that cornmeal mush out to the birds and make a run for it, when the vision rose up blazing in my mind.

I was rippling gold. My breasts were bare and my nipples flashed and winked. Diamonds tipped them. I could walk through panes of glass. I could walk through windows. She was at my feet, swallowing the glass after each step I took. I broke through another and another. The glass she swallowed ground and cut until her starved insides were only a subtle dust. She coughed. She coughed a cloud of dust. And then she was only a black rag that flapped off, snagged in bob wire, hung there for an age, and finally rotted into the breeze.

I saw this, mouth hanging open, gazing off into the flagged boughs of trees.

"Get up!" she cried. "Stop dreaming. It is time to bake."

Two other Sisters had come in with her, wide women with hands like paddles. They were evening and smoothing out the firebox beneath the great jaws of the oven.

"Who is this one?" they asked Leopolda. "Is she yours?"

"She is mine," said Leopolda. "A very good girl."

"What is your name?" one asked me.

"Marie."

"Marie. Star of the Sea."

"She will shine," said Leopolda, "when we have burned off the dark corrosion."

The others laughed, but uncertainly. They were mild and sturdy French, who did not understand Leopolda's twisted jokes, although they muttered respectfully at things she said. I knew they wouldn't believe what she had done with the kettle. There was no question. So I kept quiet.

"*Elle est docile,*"[1] they said approvingly as they left to starch the linens.

"Does it pain?" Leopolda asked me as soon as they were out the door.

I did not answer. I felt sick with the hurt.

"Come along," she said.

The building was wholly quiet now. I followed her up the narrow staircase into a hall of little rooms, many doors. Her cell was the quietest, at the very end. Inside, the air smelled stale, as if the door had not been opened for years. There was a crude straw mattress, a tiny bookcase with a picture of Saint Francis hanging over it, a ragged palm, a stool for sitting on, a crucifix. She told me to remove my blouse and sit on the stool. I did so. She took a pot of salve from the bookcase and began to smooth it upon my burns. Her hands made slow, wide circles, stopping the pain. I closed my eyes. I expected to see blackness. Peace. But instead the vision reared up again. My chest was still tipped with diamonds. I was walking through windows. She was chewing up the broken litter I left behind.

"I am going," I said. "Let me go."

But she held me down.

"Don't go," she said quickly. "Don't. We have just begun."

I was weakening. My thoughts were whirling pitifully. The pain had kept me strong, and as it left me I began to forget it; I couldn't hold on. I began to wonder if she'd really scalded me with the kettle. I could not remember. To remember this seemed the most important thing in the world. But I was losing the memory. The scalding. The pouring. It began to vanish. I felt like my mind was coming off its hinge, flapping in the breeze, hanging by the hair of my own pain. I wrenched out of her grip.

"He was always in you," I said. "Even more than in me. He wanted you even more. And now he's got you. Get thee behind me!"

I shouted that, grabbed my shirt, and ran through the door throwing it on my body. I got down the stairs and into the kitchen, even, but no matter what I told myself, I couldn't get out the door. It wasn't finished. And she knew I would not leave. Her quiet step was immediately behind me.

"We must take the bread from the oven now," she said.

She was pretending nothing happened. But for the first time I had gotten through some chink she'd left in her darkness. Touched some doubt. Her voice was so low and brittle it cracked off at the end of her sentence.

"Help me, Marie," she said slowly.

But I was not going to help her, even though she had calmly buttoned the back of my shirt up and put the big cloth mittens in my hands for taking out the loaves. I could have bolted for it then. But I didn't. I knew that something was nearing completion. Something was about to happen. My back was a wall of singing flame. I was turning. I watched her take the long fork in one hand, to tap the loaves. In the other hand she gripped the black poker to hook the pans.

"Help me," she said again, and I thought, Yes, this is part of it. I put the mittens on my hands and swung the door open on its hinges. The oven gaped. She stood back a moment, letting the first blast of heat rush by. I moved behind her. I could feel the

[1]French: She is docile.

heat at my front and at my back. Before, behind. My skin was turning to beaten gold. It was coming quicker than I thought. The oven was like the gate of a personal hell. Just big enough and hot enough for one person, and that was her. One kick and Leopolda would fly in headfirst. And that would be one-millionth of the heat she would feel when she finally collapsed in his hellish embrace.

Saints know these numbers.

She bent forward with her fork held out. I kicked her with all my might. She flew in. But the outstretched poker hit the back wall first, so she rebounded. The oven was not so deep as I had thought.

There was a moment when I felt a sort of thin, hot disappointment, as when a fish slips off the line. Only I was the one going to be lost. She was fearfully silent. She whirled. Her veil had cutting edges. She had the poker in one hand. In the other she held that long sharp fork she used to tap the delicate crusts of loaves. Her face turned upside down on her shoulders. Her face turned blue. But saints are used to miracles. I felt no trace of fear.

If I was going to be lost, let the diamonds cut! Let her eat ground glass!

"Bitch of Jesus Christ!" I shouted. "Kneel and beg! Lick the floor!"

That was when she stabbed me through the hand with the fork, then took the poker up alongside my head, and knocked me out.

It must have been a half an hour later when I came around. Things were so strange. So strange I can hardly tell it for delight at the remembrance. For when I came around this was actually taking place. I was being worshiped. I had somehow gained the altar of a saint.

I was laying back on the stiff couch in the Mother Superior's office. I looked around me. It was as though my deepest dream had come to life. The Sisters of the convent were kneeling to me. Sister Bonaventure. Sister Dympna. Sister Cecilia Saint-Claire. The two French with hands like paddles. They were down on their knees. Black capes were slung over some of their heads. My name was buzzing up and down the room, like a fat autumn fly lighting on the tips of their tongues between Latin, humming up the heavy blood-dark curtains, circling their little cosseted heads. Marie! Marie! A girl thrown in a closet. Who was afraid of a rubber overboot. Who was half overcome. A girl who came in the back door where they threw their garbage. Marie! Who never found the cup. Who had to eat their cold mush. Marie! Leopolda had her face buried in her knuckles. Saint Marie of the Holy Slops! Saint Marie of the Bread Fork! Saint Marie of the Burnt Back and Scalded Butt!

I broke out and laughed.

They looked up. All holy hell burst loose when they saw I'd woke. I still did not understand what was happening. They were watching, talking, but not to me.

"The marks . . ."

"She has her hand closed."

"Je ne peux pas voir."[2]

I was not stupid enough to ask what they were talking about. I couldn't tell why I was laying in white sheets. I couldn't tell why they were praying to me. But I'll tell you this: it seemed entirely natural. It was me. I lifted up my hand as in my dream. It was completely limp with sacredness.

---

[2]French: I cannot see.

"Peace be with you."

My arm was dried blood from the wrist down to the elbow. And it hurt. Their faces turned like flat flowers of adoration to follow that hand's movements. I let it swing through the air, imparting a saint's blessing. I had practiced. I knew exactly how to act.

They murmured. I heaved a sigh, and a golden beam of light suddenly broke through the clouded window and flooded down directly on my face. A stroke of perfect luck! They had to be convinced.

Leopolda still knelt in the back of the room. Her knuckles were crammed halfway down her throat. Let me tell you, a saint has senses honed keen as a wolf. I knew that she was over my barrel now. How it happened did not matter. The last thing I remembered was how she flew from the oven and stabbed me. That one thing was most certainly true.

"Come forward, Sister Leopolda." I gestured with my heavenly wound. Oh, it hurt. It bled when I reopened the slight heal. "Kneel beside me," I said.

She kneeled, but her voice box evidently did not work, for her mouth opened, shut, opened, but no sound came out. My throat clenched in noble delight I had read of as befitting a saint. She could not speak. But she was beaten. It was in her eyes. She stared at me now with all the deep hate of the wheel of devilish dust that rolled wild within her emptiness.

"What is it you want to tell me?" I asked. And at last she spoke.

"I have told my Sisters of your passion," she managed to choke out. "How the stigmata . . . the marks of the nails . . . appeared in your palm and you swooned at the holy vision. . . ."

"Yes," I said curiously.

And then, after a moment, I understood.

Leopolda had saved herself with her quick brain. She had witnessed a miracle. She had hid the fork and told this to the others. And of course they believed her, because they never knew how Satan came and went or where he took refuge.

"I saw it from the first," said the large one who put the bread in the oven. "Humility of the spirit. So rare in these girls."

"I saw it too," said the other one with great satisfaction. She sighed quietly. "If only it was me."

Leopolda was kneeling bolt upright, face blazing and twitching, a barely held fountain of blasting poison.

"Christ has marked me," I agreed.

I smiled the saint's smirk into her face. And then I looked at her. That was my mistake.

For I saw her kneeling there. Leopolda with her soul like a rubber overboot. With her face of a starved rat. With the desperate eyes drowning in the deep wells of her wrongness. There would be no one else after me. And I would leave. I saw Leopolda kneeling within the shambles of her love.

My heart had been about to surge from my chest with the blackness of my joyous heat. Now it dropped. I pitied her. I pitied her. Pity twisted in my stomach like that hook-pole was driven through me. I was caught. It was a feeling more terrible than any amount of boiling water and worse than being forked. Still, still, I could not help what I did. I had already smiled in a saint's mealy forgiveness. I heard myself speaking gently.

"Receive the dispensation of my sacred blood," I whispered.

But there was no heart in it. No joy when she bent to touch the floor. No dark leaping. I fell back into the white pillows. Blank dust was whirling through the light shafts. My skin was dust. Dust my lips. Dust the dirty spoons on the ends of my feet.

Rise up! I thought. Rise up and walk! There is no limit to this dust!

1984

Lorna Dee Cervantes b. 1954

This northern California native typifies the young Chicano writers who began appearing in the mid-1970s, ten years after the Chicano Movement began. Younger authors, having access to Chicano literature in school and in the community, could recast and adjust images and concepts Chicano Movement writers offered as self-defining, and the forms they utilized. The new writers, without rejecting the importance of cultural identity, emphasized questions of style and form, bringing polish and control to the ideologically overloaded earlier poetry. Age, however, was not the only difference. Women, excluded from the first decade of Chicano publishing, found outlets for their work. A new female, often feminist, voice forced the Chicano image into a more balanced perspective, with a mixture of cultural concern and gender-based criticism. And although Cervantes resisted academics for a number of years during which she attempted to survive strictly as a writer and publisher—she founded her own press and poetry magazine, *Mango*—like many of her generation, she now combines university life with writing. She presently teaches in the Creative Writing Program of the University of Colorado, Boulder.

Cervantes' work exemplifies these characteristics. Influenced by Carlos Castaneda, Cervantes sees life as a struggle with the enemy/guide, incarnations of the spiritual forces in Nature that can destroy if not brought into harmony and control, but once mastered, help one reach fulfillment.

At the personal level, men are the enemy; at the ethnic level, machismo and male dominance threaten familial unity; at the social level, it is Anglo-American society and racial prejudice; and at the artistic level, English and words themselves must be mastered. Cervantes defines her terms through poems about male/female struggle within the context of class and cultural struggle. Men are trained to exploit their environment, which leads them to abuse women, a situation that forces women to become self-reliant. Cervantes' feminism seems to culminate in "Beneath the Shadow of the Freeway," the image of the multi-generation, all-women family, surviving in the midst of social alienation and menaced by the male adversary.

Yet, ethnic unity, necessary to combat anti-Chicano prejudice, demands sexual harmony, so the author synthesizes from the older generations the wisdom of female oral tradition: a balance of strength and tenderness, of openness and caution, of sincerity and reserve. Castaneda's lesson—struggle with the enemy to turn it into your assistant—is applied to men and Nature. She learns to live with them, although never completely at ease. Survival depends on constant vigilance against betrayal, because despite the façade of peace, society and Nature are essentially a battle. Her manner of self-defense is to develop a harmonious identity through personal symbols in Nature—birds—related to a chosen cultural emphasis—the Native American element in her Mexican American past.

Then she blends them into the image of her art in the metaphor of the pen through an interlingual play on words—*pluma* in Spanish means pen and feather, so to be *emplumada* is to be feathered like a bird or an Indian, or to be armed with a pen like a writer. That she too can rework the rhetoric of warrior-like struggle is clear in "Poem for the Young White Man," reminiscent of the stringent Movement poetry. However, she is most successful when she eschews the easy clichés of political rhetoric to pursue her vision of the spirit of nature hidden under the surface of everyday existence, one which struggles to express itself through the tenuous harmony of lovers and writers. The last half of *Emplumada* and the entire second book, *From the Cables of Genocide,* explore and construct female-male relationships to feed a society starved for love. "Bananas" is a favorite of Cervantes and her audiences. Through the image of fruit, Cervantes creates a vast web of international sociopolitical forces at play and war. Yet she always keeps close contact with concrete reality in individual terms.

Juan Bruce-Novoa
University of California–Irvine

PRIMARY WORKS

Emplumada, 1981; *From the Cables of Genocide: Poems of Love and Hunger,* 1991; *Drive: The First Quartet,* 2006.

Beneath the Shadow of the Freeway

1

Across the street—the freeway,
blind worm, wrapping the valley up
from Los Altos[1] to Sal Si Puedes.[2]
I watched it from my porch
5 unwinding. Every day at dusk
as Grandma watered geraniums
the shadow of the freeway lengthened.

2

We were a woman family:
Grandma, our innocent Queen;
10 Mama, the Swift Knight, Fearless Warrior.
Mama wanted to be Princess instead.
I know that. Even now she dreams of taffeta
and foot-high tiaras.

Myself: I could never decide.
15 So I turned to books, those staunch, upright men.
I became Scribe: Translator of Foreign Mail,

[1]Spanish: The Heights.   [2]Spanish: Escape If You Can.

interpreting letters from the government, notices
of dissolved marriages and Welfare stipulations.
I paid the bills, did light man-work, fixed faucets,
20 insured everything
against all leaks.

3

Before rain I notice seagulls.
They walk in flocks,
cautious across lawns: splayed toes,
25 indecisive beaks. Grandma says
seagulls mean storm.
In California in the summer,
mockingbirds sing all night.
Grandma says they are singing for their nesting wives.
30 "They don't leave their families
borrachando."[3]

She likes the ways of birds,
respects how they show themselves
for toast and a whistle.

35 She believes in myths and birds.
She trusts only what she builds
with her own hands.

4

She built her house,
cocky, disheveled carpentry,
40 after living twenty-five years
with a man who tried to kill her.

Grandma, from the hills of Santa Barbara,
I would open my eyes to see her stir mush
in the morning, her hair in loose braids,
45 tucked close around her head
with a yellow scarf.

Mama said, "It's her own fault,
getting screwed by a man for that long.
Sure as shit wasn't hard."
50 soft she was soft

---

[3]Spanish: getting drunk.

5

in the night I would hear it
glass bottles shattering the street
words cracked into shrill screams
inside my throat   a cold fear
55 as it entered the house in hard
unsteady steps   stopping at my door
my name   bathrobe   slippers
outside a 3 A.M. mist heavy
as a breath full of whiskey
60 stop it   go home   come inside
mama if he comes here again
I'll call the police

inside
a gray kitten   a touchstone
65 purring beneath the quilts
grandma stitched
from his suits
the patchwork singing
of mockingbirds

6

70 "You're too soft . . . always were.
You'll get nothing but shit.
Baby, don't count on nobody."

—a mother's wisdom.
Soft. I haven't changed,
75 maybe grown more silent, cynical
on the outside.

"O Mama, with what's inside of me
I could wash that all away. I could."

"But Mama, if you're good to them
80 they'll be good to you back."

Back. The freeway is across the street.
It's summer now. Every night I sleep with a gentle man
to the hymn of mockingbirds,

and in time, I plant geraniums.
85 I tie up my hair into loose braids,
and trust only what I have built
with my own hands.

1981

Poem for the Young White Man Who Asked Me How I, an Intelligent, Well-Read Person, Could Believe in the War between Races

In my land there are no distinctions.
The barbed wire politics of oppression
have been torn down long ago. The only reminder
of past battles, lost or won, is a slight
5 rutting in the fertile fields.

In my land
people write poems about love,
full of nothing but contented childlike syllables.
Everyone reads Russian short stories and weeps.
10 There are no boundaries.
There is no hunger, no
complicated famine or greed.

I am not a revolutionary.
I don't even like political poems.
15 Do you think I can believe in a war between races?

I can deny it. I can forget about it
when I'm safe,
living on my own continent of harmony
and home, but I am not
20 there.

I believe in revolution
because everywhere the crosses are burning,
sharp-shooting goose-steppers round every corner,
there are snipers in the schools . . .
25 (I know you don't believe this.
You think this is nothing
but faddish exaggeration. But they
are not shooting at you.)

I'm marked by the color of my skin.
30 The bullets are discrete and designed to kill slowly.
They are aiming at my children.
These are facts.
Let me show you my wounds: my stumbling mind, my
"excuse me" tongue, and this
35 nagging preoccupation
with the feeling of not being good enough.

These bullets bury deeper than logic.
Racism is not intellectual.
I can not reason these scars away.

40 Outside my door
there is a real enemy
who hates me.

I am a poet
who yearns to dance on rooftops,
45 to whisper delicate lines about joy
and the blessings of human understanding.
I try. I go to my land, my tower of words and
bolt the door, but the typewriter doesn't fade out
the sounds of blasting and muffled outrage.
50 My own days bring me slaps on the face.
Every day I am deluged with reminders
that this is not
my land

and this is my land.

55 I do not believe in the war between races
but in this country
there is war.

1981

Macho

Slender, you are, secret as rail
under a stairwell of snow, slim
as my lips in the shallow hips.

I had a man of gristle and flint,
5 fingered the fine lineament of flexed
talons under his artifice of grit.

Every perfect body houses force
or deception. Every calculated figure
fears the summing up of age.

10 You're a beautiful mess of thread and silk,
a famous web of work and waiting, an

angular stylus with the patience of lead.

Your potent lure links hunger to flesh
as a frail eagle alights on my chest,
15 remember: the word for *machismo* is *real*.

1991

Bananas

for Indrek

I

In Estonia, Indrek is taking his children
to the Dollar Market to look at bananas.
He wants them to know about the presence of fruit,
about globes of light tart to the tongue, about the
5 twang of tangelos, the cloth of persimmons,
the dull little mons of kiwi. There is not a chance
for a taste. Where rubles are scarce, dollars are harder.
Even beef is doled out welfare-thin on Saturday's platter.
They light the few candles not reserved for the dead,
10 and try not to think of small bites in the coming winter,
of irradiated fields or the diminished catch in the fisherman's
net. They tell of bananas yellow as daffodils. And mango—
which tastes as if the whole world came out from her womb.

II

Colómbia, 1928, bananas rot in the fields.
15 A strip of lost villages between railyard
and cemetery. The United Fruit Company train,
a yellow painted slug, eats up the swamps and jungle.
Campesinos replace Indians who are a dream
and a rubble of bloody stones hacked into coffins:
20 malaria, tuberculosis, cholera, machetes of the jefes.
They become like the empty carts that shatter
the landscape. Their hands, no longer pulling the teats
from the trees, now twist into death, into silence
and obedience. They wait in Aracataca, poised as

25 statues between hemispheres. They would rather be
tilling the plots for black beans. They would rather grow
wings and rise as *pericos*—parrots, poets, clowns—a word
which means all this and whose task is messenger from
Mítla, the underworld where the ancestors of the slain
30 arise with the vengeance of Tiáloc. A stench permeates
the wind as bananas, black on the stumps, char
into odor. The murdered Mestizos have long been cleared
and begin their new duties as fertilizer for the plantations.
Feathers fall over the newly spaded soil: turquoise,
35 scarlet, azure, quetzál, and yellow litters
the graves like gold claws of bananas.

III

Dear I,

The 3′ × 6′ boxes in front of the hippy
market in Boulder are radiant with marigolds, some
40 with heads big as my Indian face. They signify
death to me, as it is Labor Day and already
I am making up the guest list for my *Dia de los Muertos*
altár. I'll need *maravillas* so this year I plant *caléndulas*
for blooming through snow that will fall before November.
45 I am shopping for "no-spray" bananas. I forego
the Dole and *Chiquita,* that name that always made me
blush for being christened with that title. But now
I am only a little small, though still brown enough
for the—*Where are you from?* Perhaps my ancestors
50 planted a placenta here as well as on my Califas coast
where alien shellfish replaced native mussels,
clams and oysters in 1886. *I'm from the 21st Century,*
I tell them, and feel rude for it—when all I desire
is bananas without pesticides. They're smaller
55 than plantains which are green outside and firm
and golden when sliced. Fried in butter
they turn yellow as over-ripe fruit. And sweet.
I ask the produce manager how to crate and
pack bananas to Estonia. She glares at me
60 suspiciously: *You can't do that. I know.*
There must be some law. You might spread
diseases. They would arrive as mush, anyway.
I am thinking of children in Estonia with
no fried *plátanos* to eat with their fish as
65 the Blond turns away, still without shedding
a smile at me—me, Hija del Sól, Earth's Daughter, lover

of bananas. I buy up Baltic wheat. I buy up organic
bananas, butter y canéla. I ship banana bread.

IV

At Big Mountain uranium
70 sings through the dreams of the people.
Women dress in glowing symmetries, sheep
clouds gather below the bluffs, sundown
sandstone blooms in four corners. Smell of sage
penetrates as state tractors with chains trawl the resistant
75 plants, gouging anew the tribal borders, uprooting
all in their path like Amazonian ants, breaking
the hearts of the widows. Elders and children
cut the fence again and again as wind whips
the waist of ancient rock. Sheep nip across
80 centuries in the people's blood, and are carried
off by the Federal choppers waiting in the canyon
with orders and slings. A long winter, little wool
to spin, medicine lost in the desecration of the desert.
Old women weep as the camera rolls on the dark
85 side of conquest. Encounter rerun. Uranium. 1992.

V

I worry about winter in a place
I've never been, about exiles in their
homeland gathered around a fire,
about the slavery of substance and
90 gruel: *Will there be enough to eat?*
Will there be enough to feed? And
they dream of beaches and pies, hemispheres
of soft fruit found only in the heat of the planet.
Sugar canes, like Geiger counters, seek out tropics;
95 and dictate a Resolution to stun the tongues of those
who can afford to pay: imported plums, bullets,
black caviar large as peas, smoked meats
the color of Southern lynchings, what we don't
discuss in letters.
100   You are out of work.
Not many jobs today for high physicists
in Estonia, you say. *Poetry, though, is food*
for the soul. And bread? What is cake before
corn and the potato? Before the encounter
105 of animals, women and wheat? Stocks high

these days in survival products; 500 years later tomato
size tumors bloom in the necks of the pickers.
On my coast, Diablo dominates the golden hills,
the faultlines. On ancestral land Vandenberg shoots nuclear
110 payloads to Kwajalein, a Pacific atoll, where 68% of all
infants are born amphibian or anemones. But poetry
is for the soul. I speak of spirit, the yellow seed
in air as life is the seed in water, and the poetry
of Improbability, the magic in the Movement
115 of quarks and sunlight, the subtle basketry
of hadrons and neutrinos of color, how what you do
is what you get—bananas or worry.
What do you say? Your friend,
                                        a Chicana poet.

                                                        1991

Helena María Viramontes b. 1954

Chronicler of the West Coast urban barrios, Helena María Viramontes was born, raised, and educated in East Los Angeles, California. Daughter of working-class parents, she and her nine brothers and sisters grew up surrounded by the family friends and relatives who found temporary sanctuary in the Viramontes household as they made the crossing from Mexico to the United States. Her writings reveal the political and aesthetic significance of the contemporary Chicana feminist's entrance into the publishing world. Viramontes's aesthetics are a practice of political intervention carried out in literary form. Her tales of the urban barrios, of the border cities, of the Third World metropolis that cities such as Los Angeles have become, record the previously silenced experiences of life on the border for Chicanas and Latinas. Viramontes remains an exemplar of the organic intellectual; she organizes the community to protest the closing of local public libraries in areas populated with Chicanos and Latinos; she gives readings and literary presentations to a population that is represented by the media as gang-infested and whose young men are more represented in the prison system than in the education system.

Viramontes's first short story collection, *The Moths and Other Stories* (1985), is a feminist statement on the status of the family in the Chicana/o community. In many of the stories, she transforms the concept of "*familia*" as the community itself changes with the last decade's infusion of refugees from war-torn countries in Central America; what were once predominantly Mexican American areas are now international Latina/o communities within the borders of the United States. The new immigrants bring with them specific histories which produce new stories that further emphasize the resemblances between Chicanas/os and "*los otros Americanos*": people Cherríe Moraga calls "refugees of a world on fire."

Viramontes's project in her short stories also gives historical context and voice to the women who many Chicano writers silenced through their appropriation of female historicity. As she challenges an uncritical view of the traditional Chicano family, she presents an altered version of *familia* that makes more sense in a world where governments continue to exert power over women's bodies by hiding behind the rhetoric of the sacred family as they simultaneously exploit and destroy members of families who do not conform to a specific political agenda or whose class positions or race automatically disqualifies them from inclusion.

In "The Cariboo Cafe," Viramontes makes explicit the connection between Chicanas and refugees from Central America. Written in early 1984 after Viramontes learned of the atrocities that the U.S. policies in countries such as El Salvador had enabled, this story embodies a Chicana feminist's critique of the political and economic policies of the United States government and its collaborators south of its border. Viramontes presents the oppression and exploitation of the reserve army of laborers that such policies create and then designate as "other," the "illegal" immigrants. Combining feminism with race and class consciousness, Viramontes commits herself, in this Chicana political discourse, to a transnational solidarity with the working-class political refugee seeking asylum from right-wing death squads in countries such as El Salvador.

In addition, the narrative structure of "The Cariboo Cafe" connects Chicana aesthetics to the literary traditions of such Latin American political writers as Gabriel García Márquez and Isabel Allende. The fractured narrative employed in this story hurls the reader into a complicated relationship with the text. The reader enters the text as an alien to this refugee culture; Viramontes crafts a fractured narrative to reflect the disorientation that the immigrant workers feel when they are subjected to life in a country that controls their labor but does not value their existence as human beings.

Further, the narrative structure shoots the reader into a world where she or he is as disoriented as the story's characters: two lost Mexican children; a refugee woman (possibly from El Salvador), whose mental state reflects the trauma of losing her five-year-old son to the labyrinth of the disappeared in Latin American countries ruled by armies and dictators the United States trains and supports; and a working-class man, an ironic representative of dominant Anglo-American culture, who runs the "double zero" cafe. The reader, particularly one unfamiliar with life in the border regions of that other America, must work to decipher the signs much in the same way the characters do. Through the artistry of her narrative, Helena María Viramontes shows how a Chicana oppositional art form also becomes an arena that reflects politics.

Sonia Saldívar-Hull
University of California–Los Angeles

PRIMARY WORKS

The Moths and Other Stories, 1985; *Paris Rats in E. L. A.*, 1993; *Under the Feet of Jesus*, 1995; *Their Dogs Came with Them*, 2007.

The Cariboo Cafe

I

They arrived in the secrecy of night, as displaced people often do, stopping over for a week, a month, eventually staying a lifetime. The plan was simple. Mother would work too until they saved enough to move into a finer future where the toilet was one's own and the children needn't be frightened. In the meantime, they played in the back allies, among the broken glass, wise to the ways of the streets. Rule one: never talk to strangers, not even the neighbor who paced up and down the hallways talking to himself. Rule two: the police, or "polie" as Sonya's popi pronounced the word, was La Migra in disguise and thus should always be avoided. Rule three: keep your key with you at all times—the four walls of the apartment were the only protection against the streets until Popi returned home.

Sonya considered her key a guardian saint and she wore it around her neck as such until this afternoon. Gone was the string with the big knot. Gone was the key. She hadn't noticed its disappearance until she picked up Macky from Mrs. Avila's house and walked home. She remembered playing with it as Amá walked her to school. But lunch break came, and Lalo wrestled her down so that he could see her underwear, and it probably fell somewhere between the iron rings and sandbox. Sitting on the front steps of the apartment building, she considered how to explain the missing key without having to reveal what Lalo had seen, for she wasn't quite sure which offense carried the worse penalty.

She watched people piling in and spilling out of the buses, watched an old man asleep on the bus bench across the street. He resembled a crumbled ball of paper, huddled up in the security of a tattered coat. She became aware of their mutual loneliness and she rested her head against her knees blackened by the soot of the playground asphalt.

The old man eventually awoke, yawned like a lion's roar, unfolded his limbs and staggered to the alley where he urinated between two trash bins. (She wanted to peek, but it was Macky who turned to look.) He zipped up, drank from a paper bag and she watched him until he disappeared around the corner. As time passed, buses came less frequently, and every other person seemed to resemble Popi. Macky became bored. He picked through the trash barrel; later, and to Sonya's fright, he ran into the street after a pigeon. She understood his restlessness for waiting was as relentless as long lines to the bathroom. When a small boy walked by, licking away at a scoop of vanilla ice cream, Macky ran after him. In his haste to outrun Sonya's grasp, he fell and tore the knee of his denim jeans. He began to cry, wiping snot against his sweater sleeve.

"See?" She asked, dragging him back to the porch steps by his wrist. "See? God punished you!" It was a thing she always said because it seemed to work. Terrified by the scrawny tortured man on the cross, Macky wanted to avoid his wrath as much as possible. She sat him on the steps in one gruff jerk. Seeing his torn jeans, and her own scraped knees, she wanted to join in his sorrow, and cry. Instead she snuggled so close to him, she could hear his stomach growling.

"Coke," he asked. Mrs. Avila gave him an afternoon snack which usually held him over until dinner. But sometimes Macky got lost in the midst of her own six children and . . .

Mrs. Avila! It took Sonya a few moments to realize the depth of her idea. They could wait there, at Mrs. Avila's. And she'd probably have a stack of flour tortillas, fresh off the comal, ready to eat with butter and salt. She grabbed his hand. "Mrs. Avila has Coke."

"Coke!" He jumped up to follow his sister. "Coke," he cooed.

At the major intersection, Sonya quietly calculated their next move while the scores of adults hurried to their own destinations. She scratched one knee as she tried retracing her journey home in the labyrinth of her memory. Things never looked the same when backwards and she searched for familiar scenes. She looked for the newspaperman who sat in a little house with a little T.V. on and selling magazines with naked girls holding beach balls. But he was gone. What remained was a little closet-like shed with chains and locks, and she wondered what happened to him, for she thought he lived there with the naked ladies.

They finally crossed the street at a cautious pace, the colors of the street lights brighter as darkness descended, a stereo store blaring music from two huge, blasting speakers. She thought it was the disco store she passed, but she didn't remember if the sign was green or red. And she didn't remember it flashing like it was now. Studying the neon light, she bumped into a tall, lanky dark man. Maybe it was Raoul's Popi. Raoul was a dark boy in her class that she felt sorry for because everyone called him sponge head. Maybe she could ask Raoul's Popi where Mrs. Avila lived, but before she could think it all out, red sirens flashed in their faces and she shielded her eyes to see the polie.

The polie is men in black who get kids and send them to Tijuana, says Popi. Whenever you see them, run, because they hate you, says Popi. She grabs Macky by his sleeve and they crawl under a table of bargain cassettes. Macky's nose is running, and when he sniffles, she puts her finger to her lips. She peeks from behind the poster of Vincente Fernandez to see Raoul's father putting keys and stuff from his pockets onto the hood of the polie car. And it's true, they're putting him in the car and taking him to Tijuana. Popi, she murmured to herself. Mamá.

"Coke." Macky whispered, as if she had failed to remember.

"Ssssh. Mi'jo, when I say run, you run, okay?" She waited for the tires to turn out, and as the black and white drove off, she whispered "Now," and they scurried out from under the table and ran across the street, oblivious to the horns.

They entered a maze of allies and dead ends, the long, abandoned warehouses shadowing any light. Macky stumbled and she continued to drag him until his crying, his untied sneakers, and his raspy breathing finally forced her to stop. She scanned the boarded up boxcars, the rows of rusted rails to make sure the polie wasn't following them. Tired, her heart bursting, she leaned him against a tall, chain-link fence. Except for the rambling of some railcars, silence prevailed, and she could hear Macky sniffling in the darkness. Her mouth was parched and she swallowed to rid herself of the metallic taste of fear. The shadows stalked them, hovering like nightmares. Across the tracks, in the distance, was a room with a yellow glow, like a beacon light at the end of a dark sea. She pinched Macky's nose with the corner of her dress, took hold of his sleeve. At least the shadows will be gone, she concluded, at the zero zero place.

II

Don't look at me. I didn't give it the name. It was passed on. Didn't even know what it meant until I looked it up in some library dictionary. But I kinda liked the name. It's, well, romantic, almost like the name of a song, you know, so I kept it. That was before JoJo turned fourteen even. But now if you take a look at the sign, the paint's peeled off 'cept for the two O's. The double zero cafe. Story of my life. But who cares, right? As long as everyone 'round the factories know I run an honest business.

The place is clean. That's more than I can say for some people who walk through that door. And I offer the best prices on double burger deluxes this side of Main Street. Okay, so its not pure beef. Big deal, most meat markets do the same. But I make no bones 'bout it. I tell them up front, 'yeah, it ain't dogmeat, but it ain't sirloin either.' Cause that's the sort of guy I am. Honest.

That's the trouble. It never pays to be honest. I tried scrubbing the stains off the floor, so that my customers won't be reminded of what happened. But they keep walking as if my cafe ain't fit for lepers. And that's the thanks I get for being a fair guy.

Not once did I hang up all those stupid signs. You know, like 'We reserve the right to refuse service to anyone,' or 'No shirt, no shoes, no service.' To tell you the truth—which is what I always do though it don't pay—I wouldn't have nobody walking through that door. The streets are full of scum, but scum gotta eat too is the way I see it. Now, listen. I ain't talkin 'bout out-of-luckers, weirdos, whores, you know. I'm talking 'bout five-to-lifers out of some tech. I'm talking Paulie.

I swear Paulie is thirty-five, or six. JoJo's age if he were still alive, but he don't look a day over ninety. Maybe why I let him hang out 'cause he's JoJo's age. Shit, he's okay as long as he don't bring his wigged out friends whose voices sound like a record at low speed. Paulie's got too many stories and they all get jammed up in his mouth so I can't make out what he's saying. He scares the other customers too, acting like he is shadow boxing, or like a monkey hopping on a frying pan. You know, nervous, jumpy, his jaw all falling and his eyes bulgy and dirt yellow. I give him the last booth, coffee and yesterday's donut holes to keep him quiet. After a few minutes, out he goes, before lunch. I'm too old, you know, too busy making ends meet to be nursing the kid. And so is Delia.

That Delia's got these unique titties. One is bigger than another. Like an orange and grapefruit. I kid you not. They're like that on account of when she was real young she had some babies, and they all sucked only one favorite tittie. So one is bigger than the other, and when she used to walk in with Paulie, huggy huggy and wearing those tight leotard blouses that show the nipple dots, you could see the difference. You could tell right off that Paulie was proud of them, the way he'd hang his arm over her shoulder and squeeze the grapefruit. They kill me, her knockers. She'd come in real queen-like, smacking gum and chewing the fat with the illegals who work in that garment warehouse. They come in real queen-like too, sitting in the best booth near the window, and order cokes. That's all. Cokes. Hey, but I'm a nice guy, so what if they mess up my table, bring their own lunches and only order small cokes, leaving a dime as tip? So sometimes the place ain't crawling with people, you comprende buddy? A dime's a dime as long as its in my pocket.

Like I gotta pay my bills too, I gotta eat. So like I serve anybody whose got the greens, including that crazy lady and the two kids that started all the trouble. If only

I had closed early. But I had to wash the dinner dishes on account of I can't afford a dishwasher. I was scraping off some birdshit glue stuck to this plate, see, when I hear the bells jingle against the door. I hate those fucking bells. That was Nell's idea. Nell's my wife; my ex-wife. So people won't sneak up on you, says my ex. Anyway, I'm standing behind the counter staring at this short woman. Already I know that she's bad news because she looks street to me. Round face, burnt toast color, black hair that hangs like straight ropes. Weirdo, I've had enough to last me a lifetime. She's wearing a shawl and a dirty slip is hanging out. Shit if I have to dish out a free meal. Funny thing, but I didn't see the two kids 'til I got to the booth. All of a sudden I see these big eyes looking over the table's edge at me. It shook me up, the way they kinda appeared. Aw, maybe they were there all the time.

The boy's a sweetheart. Short Order don't look nothing like his mom. He's got dried snot all over his dirty cheeks and his hair ain't seen a comb for years. She can't take care of herself, much less him or the doggie of a sister. But he's a tough one, and I pinch his nose 'cause he's a real sweetheart like JoJo. You know, my boy.

It's his sister I don't like. She's got these poking eyes that follow you 'round 'cause she don't trust no one. Like when I reach for Short Order, she flinches like I'm 'bout to tear his nose off, gives me a nasty, squinty look. She's maybe five, maybe six, I don't know, and she acts like she owns him. Even when I bring the burgers, she doesn't let go of his hand. Finally, the fellow bites it and I wink at him. A real sweetheart.

In the next booth, I'm twisting the black crud off the top of the ketchup bottle when I hear the lady saying something in Spanish. Right off I know she's illegal, which explains why she looks like a weirdo. Anyway, she says something nice to them 'cause it's in the same tone that Nell used when I'd rest my head on her lap. I'm surprised the illegal's got a fiver to pay, but she and her tail leave no tip. I see Short Order's small bites on the bun.

You know, a cafe's the kinda business that moves. You get some regulars but most of them are on the move, so I don't pay much attention to them. But this lady's face sticks like egg yolk on a plate. It ain't 'til I open a beer and sit in front of the B & W to check out the wrestling matches that I see this news bulletin 'bout two missing kids. I recognize the mugs right away. Short Order and his doggie sister. And all of a sudden her face is out of my mind. Aw fuck, I say, and put my beer down so hard that the foam spills onto last months Hustler. Aw fuck.

See, if Nell was here, she'd know what to do: call the cops. But I don't know. Cops ain't exactly my friends, and all I need is for bacon to be crawling all over my place. And seeing how her face is vague now, I decide to wait 'til the late news. Short Order don't look right neither. I'll have another beer and wait for the late news.

The alarm rings at four and I have this headache, see, from the sixpak, and I gotta get up. I was supposed to do something, but I got all suck-faced and forgot. Turn off the T.V., take a shower, but that don't help my memory any.

Hear sirens near the railroad tracks. Cops. I'm supposed to call the cops. I'll do it after I make the coffee, put away the eggs, get the donuts out. But Paulie strolls in looking partied out. We actually talk 'bout last night's wrestling match between BoBo Brazil and the Crusher. I slept through it, you see. Paulie orders an O.J. on account of he's catching a cold. I open up my big mouth and ask about De. Drinks the rest of his O.J., says real calm like, that he caught her eaglespread with the Vegetable fatso down the block. Then, very polite like, Paulie excuses himself. That's one thing

I gotta say about Paulie. He may be one big Fuck-up, but he's got manners. Juice gave him shit cramps, he says.

Well, leave it to Paulie. Good ole Mr. Fuck-Up himself to help me with the cops. The prick O.D.'s in my crapper; vomits and shits are all over—I mean all over the fuckin' walls. That's the thanks I get for being Mr. Nice Guy. I had the cops looking up my ass for the stash; says one, the one wearing a mortician's suit, We'll be back, we'll be back when you ain't looking. If I was pushing, would I be burning my god-damn balls off with spitting grease? So fuck 'em, I think. I ain't gonna tell you noth-ing 'bout the lady. Fuck you, I say to them as they drive away. Fuck your mother.

That's why Nell was good to have 'round. She could be a pain in the ass, you know, like making me hang those stupid bells, but mostly she knew what to do. See, I go bananas. Like my mind fries with the potatoes and by the end of the day, I'm deader than dogshit. Let me tell you what I mean. A few hours later, after I swore I wouldn't give the fuckin' pigs the time of day, the green vans roll up across the street. While I'm stirring the chili con carne I see all these illegals running out of the factory to hide, like roaches when the lightswitch goes on. I taste the chile, but I really can't taste nothing on account of I've lost my appetite after cleaning out the crapper, when three of them run into the Cariboo. They look at me as if I'm gonna stop them, but when I go on stirring the chile, they run to the bathroom. Now look, I'm a nice guy, but I don't like to be used, you know? Just 'cause they're regulars don't mean jackshit. I run an honest business. And that's what I told them Agents. See, by that time, my stomach being all dizzy, and the cops all over the place, and the three ille-gals running in here, I was all confused, you know. That's how it was, and well, I haven't seen Nell for years, and I guess that's why I pointed to the bathroom.

I don't know. I didn't expect handcuffs and them agents putting their hands up and down their thighs. When they walked passed me, they didn't look at me. That is the two young ones. The older one, the one that looked silly in the handcuffs on ac-count of she's old enough to be my grandma's grandma, looks straight at my face with the same eyes Short Order's sister gave me yesterday. What a day. Then, to top off the potatoes with the gravy, the bells jingle against the door and in enters the lady again with the two kids.

III

He's got lice. Probably from living in the detainers. Those are the rooms where they round up the children and make them work for their food. I saw them from the win-dow. Their eyes are cut glass, and no one looks for sympathy. They take turns, sort-ing out the arms from the legs, heads from the torsos. Is that one your mother? one guard asks, holding a mummified head with eyes shut tighter than coffins. But the children no longer cry. They just continue sorting as if they were salvaging cans from a heap of trash. They do this until time is up and they drift into a tunnel, back to the womb of sleep, while a new group comes in. It is all very organized. I bite my fist to keep from retching. Please God, please don't let Geraldo be there.

For you see, they took Geraldo. By mistake, of course. It was my fault. I shouldn't have sent him out to fetch me a mango. But it was just to the corner. I did-n't even bother to put his sweater on. I hear his sandals flapping against the gravel. I follow him with my eyes, see him scratching his buttocks when the wind picks up swiftly, as it often does at such unstable times, and I have to close the door.

The darkness becomes a serpent's tongue, swallowing us whole. It is the night of La Llorona. The women come up from the depths of sorrow to search for their children. I join them, frantic, desperate, and our eyes become scrutinizers, our bodies opiated with the scent of their smiles. Descending from door to door, the wind whips our faces. I hear the wailing of the women and know it to be my own. Geraldo is nowhere to be found.

Dawn is not welcomed. It is a drunkard wavering between consciousness and sleep. My life is fleeing, moving south towards the sea. My tears are now hushed and faint.

The boy, barely a few years older than Geraldo, lights a cigarette, rests it on the edge of his desk, next to all the other cigarette burns. The blinds are down to keep the room cool. Above him hangs a single bulb that shades and shadows his face in such a way as to mask his expressions. He is not to be trusted. He fills in the information, for I cannot write. Statements delivered, we discuss motives.

"Spies," says he, flicking a long burning ash from the cigarette onto the floor, then wolfing the smoke in as if his lungs had an unquenchable thirst for nicotine. "We arrest spies. Criminals." He says this with cigarette smoke spurting out from his nostrils like a nose bleed.

"Spies? Criminal?" My shawl falls to the ground. "He is only five and a half years old." I plead for logic with my hands. "What kind of crimes could a five year old commit?"

"Anyone who so willfully supports the contras in any form must be arrested and punished without delay." He knows the line by heart.

I think about moths and their stupidity. Always attracted by light, they fly into fires, or singe their wings with the heat of the single bulb and fall on his desk, writhing in pain. I don't understand why nature has been so cruel as to prevent them from feeling warmth. He dismisses them with a sweep of a hand. "This," he continues, "is what we plan to do with the contras, and those who aid them." He inhales again.

"But, Señor, he's just a baby."

"Contras are tricksters. They exploit the ignorance of people like you. Perhaps they convinced your son to circulate pamphlets. You should be talking to them, not us." The cigarette is down to his yellow finger tips, to where he can no longer continue to hold it without burning himself. He throws the stub on the floor, crushes it under his boot. "This," he says, screwing his boot into the ground, "is what the contras do to people like you."

"Señor. I am a washer woman. You yourself see I cannot read or write. There is my X. Do you think my son can read?" How can I explain to this man that we are poor, that we live as best we can? "If such a thing has happened, perhaps he wanted to make a few centavos for his mamá. He's just a baby."

"So you are admitting his guilt?"

"So you are admitting he is here?" I promise, once I see him, hold him in my arms again, I will never, never scold him for wanting more than I can give. "You see, he needs his sweater . . ." The sweater lies limp on my lap.

"Your assumption is incorrect."

"May I check the detainers for myself?"

"In time."

"And what about my Geraldo?"

"In time." He dismisses me, placing the forms in a big envelope crinkled by the day's humidity.

"When?" I am wringing the sweater with my hands.

"Don't be foolish, woman. Now off with your nonsense. We will try to locate your Pedro."

"Geraldo."

Maria came by today with a bowl of hot soup. She reports in her usual excited way, that the soldiers are now eating the brains of their victims. It is unlike her to be so scandalous. So insane. Geraldo must be cold without his sweater.

"Why?" I ask as the soup gets cold. I will write Tavo tonight.

At the plaza a group of people are whispering. They are quiet when I pass, turn to one another and put their finger to their lips to cage their voices. They continue as I reach the church steps. To be associated with me is condemnation.

Today I felt like killing myself, Lord. But I am too much of a coward. I am a washer woman, Lord. My mother was one, and hers too. We have lived as best we can, washing other people's laundry, rinsing off other people's dirt until our hands crust and chap. When my son wanted to hold my hand, I held soap instead. When he wanted to play, my feet were in pools of water. It takes such little courage, being a washer woman. Give me strength, Lord.

What have I done to deserve this, Lord? Raising a child is like building a kite. You must bend the twigs enough, but not too much, for you might break them. You must find paper that is delicate and light enough to wave on the breath of the wind, yet must withstand the ravages of a storm. You must tie the strings gently but firmly so that it may not fall apart. You must let the string go, eventually, so that the kite will stretch its ambition. It is such delicate work, Lord, being a mother. This I understand, Lord, because I am, but you have snapped the cord, Lord. It was only a matter of minutes and my life is lost somewhere in the clouds. I don't know, I don't know what games you play, Lord.

These four walls are no longer my house, the earth beneath it, no longer my home. Weeds have replaced all good crops. The irrigation ditches are clodded with bodies. No matter where we turn, there are rumors facing us and we try to live as best we can, under the rule of men who rape women, then rip their fetuses from their bellies. Is this our home? Is this our country? I ask Maria. Don't these men have mothers, lovers, babies, sisters? Don't they see what they are doing? Later, Maria says, these men are babes farted out from the Devil's ass. We check to make sure no one has heard her say this.

Without Geraldo, this is not my home, the earth beneath it, not my country. This is why I have to leave. Maria begins to cry. Not because I am going, but because she is staying.

Tavo. Sweet Tavo. He has sold his car to send me the money. He has just married and he sold his car for me. Thank you, Tavo. Not just for the money. But also for making me believe in the goodness of people again . . . The money is enough to buy off the border soldiers. The rest will come from the can. I have saved for Geraldo's schooling and it is enough for a bus ticket to Juarez. I am to wait for Tavo there.

I spit. I do not turn back.

Perhaps I am wrong in coming. I worry that Geraldo will not have a home to return to, no mother to cradle his nightmares away, soothe the scars, stop the hemorrhaging of his heart. Tavo is happy I am here, but it is crowded, the three of us, and I hear them arguing behind their closed door. There is only so much a nephew can provide. I must find work. I have two hands willing to work. But the heart. The heart wills only to watch the children playing in the street.

The machines, their speed and dust, make me ill. But I can clean. I clean toilets, dump trash cans, sweep. Disinfect the sinks. I will gladly do whatever is necessary to repay Tavo. The baby is due any time and money is tight. I volunteer for odd hours, weekends, since I really have very little to do. When the baby comes I know Tavo's wife will not let me hold it, for she thinks I am a bad omen. I know it.

Why would God play such a cruel joke, if he isn't my son? I jumped the curb, dashed out into the street, but the street is becoming wider and wider. I've lost him once and can't lose him again and to hell with the screeching tires and the horns and the headlights barely touching my hips. I can't take my eyes off him because, you see, they are swift and cunning and can take your life with a snap of a finger. But God is a just man and His mistakes can be undone.

My heart pounds in my head like a sledge hammer against the asphalt. What if it isn't Geraldo? What if he is still in the detainer waiting for me? A million questions, one answer: Yes. Geraldo, yes. I want to touch his hand first, have it disappear in my own because it is so small. His eyes look at me in total bewilderment. I grab him because the earth is crumbling beneath us and I must save him. We both fall to the ground.

A hot meal is in store. A festival. The cook, a man with shrunken cheeks and the hands of a car mechanic, takes a liking to Geraldo. Its like birthing you again, mi'jo. My baby.

I bathe him. He flutters in excitement, the water grey around him. I scrub his head with lye to kill off the lice, comb his hair out with a fine tooth comb. I wash his rubbery penis, wrap him in a towel and he stands in front of the window, shriveling and sucking milk from a carton, his hair shiny from the dampness.

He finally sleeps. So easily, she thinks. On her bed next to the open window he coos in the night. Below the sounds of the city become as monotonous as the ocean waves. She rubs his back with warm oil, each stroke making up for the days of his absence. She hums to him softly so that her breath brushes against his face, tunes that are rusted and crack in her throat. The hotel neon shines on his back and she covers him.

All the while the young girl watches her brother sleeping. She removes her sneakers, climbs into the bed, snuggles up to her brother, and soon her breathing is raspy, her arms under her stomach.

The couch is her bed tonight. Before switching the light off, she checks once more to make sure this is not a joke. Tomorrow she will make arrangements to go home. Maria will be the same, the mango stand on the corner next to the church plaza will be the same. It will all be the way it was before. But enough excitement. For the first time in years, her mind is quiet of all noise and she has the desire to sleep.

The bells jingle when the screen door slaps shut behind them. The cook wrings his hands in his apron, looking at them. Geraldo is in the middle, and they sit in the booth farthest away from the window, near the hall where the toilets are, and right away the small boy, his hair now neatly combed and split to the side like an adult, wrinkles his nose at the peculiar smell. The cook wipes perspiration off his forehead with the corner of his apron, finally comes over to the table.

She looks so different, so young. Her hair is combed slick back into one thick braid and her earrings hang like baskets of golden pears on her finely sculptured ears. He can't believe how different she looks. Almost beautiful. She points to what she wants on the menu with a white, clean fingernail. Although confused, the cook is sure of one thing—it's Short Order all right, pointing to him with a commanding finger, saying his only English word: coke.

His hands tremble as he slaps the meat on the grill; the patties hiss instantly. He feels like vomiting. The chile overboils and singes the fires, deep red trail of chile crawling to the floor and puddling there. He grabs the handles, burns himself, drops the pot on the wooden racks of the floor. He sucks his fingers, the patties blackening and sputtering grease. He flips them, and the burgers hiss anew. In some strange way he hopes they have disappeared, and he takes a quick look only to see Short Order's sister, still in the same dress, still holding her brother's hand. She is craning her neck to peek at what is going on in the kitchen.

Aw, fuck, he says, in a fog of smoke his eyes burning tears. He can't believe it, but he's crying. For the first time since JoJo's death, he's crying. He becomes angry at the lady for returning. At JoJo. At Nell for leaving him. He wishes Nell here, but doesn't know where she's at or what part of Vietnam JoJo is all crumbled up in. Children gotta be with their parents, family gotta be together, he thinks. It's only right. The emergency line is ringing.

Two black and whites roll up and skid the front tires against the curb. The flashing lights carousel inside the cafe. She sees them opening the screen door, their guns taut and cold like steel erections. Something is wrong, and she looks to the cowering cook. She has been betrayed, and her heart is pounding like footsteps running, faster, louder, faster and she can't hear what they are saying to her. She jumps up from the table, grabs Geraldo by the wrist, his sister dragged along because, like her, she refuses to release his hand. Their lips are mouthing words she can't hear, can't comprehend. Run, Run is all she can think of to do, Run through the hallway, out to the alley, Run because they will never take him away again.

But her legs are heavy and she crushes Geraldo against her, so tight, as if she wants to conceal him in her body again, return him to her belly so that they will not castrate him and hang his small, blue penis on her door, not crush his face so that he is unrecognizable, not bury him among the heaps of bones, and ears, and teeth, and jaws, because no one, but she, cared to know that he cried. For years he cried and she could hear him day and night. Screaming, howling, sobbing, shriveling and crying because he is only five years old, and all she wanted was a mango.

But the crying begins all over again. In the distance, she hears crying.

She refuses to let go. For they will have to cut her arms off to take him, rip her mouth off to keep her from screaming for help. Without thinking, she reaches over to where two pots of coffee are brewing and throws the streaming coffee into their faces. Outside, people begin to gather, pressing their faces against the window glass to get a good view. The cook huddles behind the counter, frightened, trembling. Their faces become distorted and she doesn't see the huge hand that takes hold of

Geraldo and she begins screaming all over again, screaming so that the walls shake, screaming enough for all the women of murdered children, screaming, pleading for help from the people outside, and she pushes an open hand against an officer's nose, because no one will stop them and he pushes the gun barrel to her face.

And I laugh at his ignorance. How stupid of him to think that I will let them take my Geraldo away, just because he waves that gun like a flag. Well, to hell with you, you pieces of shit, do you hear me? Stupid, cruel pigs. To hell with you all, because you can no longer frighten me. I will fight you for my son until I have no hands left to hold a knife. I will fight you all because you're all farted out of the Devil's ass, and you'll not take us with you. I am laughing, howling at their stupidity. Because they should know by now that I will never let my son go and then I hear something crunching like broken glass against my forehead and I am blinded by the liquid darkness. But I hold onto his hand. That I can feel, you see, I'll never let go. Because we are going home. My son and I.

1984

Aurora Levins Morales b. 1954

Aurora Levins Morales was born in Indiera, Puerto Rico, on February 24, 1954, to a Puerto Rican mother and a Jewish father. She came to the United States with her family in 1967 and lived in Chicago and New Hampshire. She presently works in the San Francisco Bay Area, where she has resided since 1976. Her short stories have appeared in *This Bridge Called My Back, Cuentos: Stories by Latinas,* and in *Revista Chicano-Riqueña.* In 1986 she published *Getting Home Alive,* a collection of short stories, essays, prose poems, and poetry in English authored in collaboration with her mother, Rosario Morales.

Levins Morales does not belong to the group of writers who were brought up in New York City and whose works deal with life in El Barrio. Her experiences have taken her, instead, from the urban world of Chicago, to the rural quiet of New Hampshire, and to the pluralistic and politically radical culture of the San Francisco Bay Area. Her writing has been profoundly influenced by two major literary streams: first, by North American feminists like Adrienne Rich, Susan Griffin, and in particular by Alice Walker. She has also read extensively the works of major Latin American writers such as Pablo Neruda and Eduardo Galeano. Her Puerto Rican–Jewish heritage has also been an important source of creativity. Her search for a language that will express a Latina woman's experience and struggle identifies her with the body of literature produced by U.S. women of color, and closely connects her with the work of contemporary Chicana writers.

She tries to define her *mestiza* and female identity through an analysis and critique of her two cultures. While considering herself "a child of the Americas," and not just Puerto Rican, Aurora employs in her writings the cultural symbols of her country, and her childhood memories of the Puerto Rican countryside. A unique element of *Getting Home Alive* is the generational dialogue and "cross-fertilization," as she describes it, between her mother's voice and her own. Along with Víctor Hernández Cruz, Levins Morales illustrates the gradual diversification that is taking place in Puerto Rican literature.

Following a first moment of protest which denounced the social and economic conditions of the *puertorriqueños* in the Bronx and El Barrio, younger Puerto Rican writers are exploring other issues, such as language, multiple subjectivities, international politics, class, feminism, and transnational identities. Their denunciations are not expressed directly but are embedded in a more lyrical and individual poetic language. Writers like Cruz and Morales exemplify a synthesis between the North American literary tradition and a broad Latin American culture. As Puerto Ricans have moved away from New York City and settled in other urban centers throughout the United States, their life experiences have varied, and the emerging writings are thus characterized by a greater diversity of voices.

Frances R. Aparicio
University of Illinois–Chicago

PRIMARY WORKS

Getting Home Alive, coauthored with Rosario Morales, 1986; *Medicine Stories: History, Culture, and the Politics of Integrity,* 1998; *Remedios: Stories of Earth and Iron from the History of Puertorriquenas,* 1998; *Telling to Live,* 2001.

Child of the Americas

I am a child of the Americas,
a light-skinned mestiza of the Caribbean,
a child of many diaspora, born into this continent at a crossroads.

I am a U.S. Puerto Rican Jew,
5   a product of the ghettos of New York I have never known.
An immigrant and the daughter and granddaughter of immigrants.
I speak English with passion: it's the tongue of my consciousness,
a flashing knife blade of crystal, my tool, my craft.

I am Caribeña,[1] island grown. Spanish is in my flesh,
10   ripples from my tongue, lodges in my hips:
the language of garlic and mangoes,
the singing in my poetry, the flying gestures of my hands.
I am of Latinoamerica, rooted in the history of my continent:
I speak from that body.

15   I am not african. Africa is in me, but I cannot return.
I am not taína.[2] Taíno is in me, but there is no way back.
I am not european. Europe lives in me, but I have no home there.

---

[1]Caribbean woman.
[2]Taínos were the Indian tribe indigenous to Puerto Rico.

I am new. History made me. My first language was spanglish.[3]
I was born at the crossroads
20 and I am whole.

1986

Puertoricanness

It was Puerto Rico waking up inside her. Puerto Rico waking her up at 6:00 a.m., remembering the rooster that used to crow over on 59th Street and the neighbors all cursed "that damn rooster," but she loved him, waited to hear his harsh voice carving up the Oakland sky and eating it like chopped corn, so obliviously sure of himself, crowing all alone with miles of houses around him. She was like that rooster.

Often she could hear them in her dreams. Not the lone rooster of 59th Street (or some street nearby . . . she had never found the exact yard though she had tried), but the wild careening hysterical roosters of 3:00 a.m. in Bartolo, screaming at the night and screaming again at the day.

It was Puerto Rico waking up inside her, uncurling and shoving open the door she had kept neatly shut for years and years. Maybe since the first time she was an immigrant, when she refused to speak Spanish in nursery school. Certainly since the last time, when at thirteen she found herself between languages, between countries, with no land feeling at all solid under her feet. The mulberry trees of Chicago, that first summer, had looked so utterly pitiful beside her memory of flamboyan and banana and. . . . No, not even the individual trees and bushes but the mass of them, the overwhelming profusion of green life that was the home of her comfort and nest of her dreams.

The door was opening. She could no longer keep her accent under lock and key. It seeped out, masquerading as dyslexia, stuttering, halting, unable to speak the word which will surely come out in the wrong language, wearing the wrong clothes. Doesn't that girl know how to dress? Doesn't she know how to date, what to say to a professor, how to behave at a dinner table laid with silver and crystal and too many forks?

Yesterday she answered her husband's request that she listen to the whole of his thoughts before commenting by screaming. "This is how we talk. I will not wait sedately for you to finish. Interrupt me back!" She drank pineapple juice three or four

---

[3] Refers to the mixture of Spanish and English,
  mostly in speech.

times a day. Not Lotus, just Co-op brand, but it was *piña,*[1] and it was sweet and yellow. And she was letting the clock slip away from her into a world of morning and afternoon and night, instead of "five-forty-one-and-twenty seconds—beep."

There were things she noticed about herself, the Puertoricanness of which she had kept hidden all these years, but which had persisted as habits, as idiosyncracies of her nature. The way she left a pot of food on the stove all day, eating out of it whenever hunger struck her, liking to have something ready. The way she had lacked food to offer Elena in the old days and had stamped on the desire to do so because it *was* Puerto Rican: Come, mija . . . ¿quieres café?[2] The way she was embarrassed and irritated by Ana's unannounced visits, just dropping by, keeping the country habits after a generation of city life. So unlike the cluttered datebooks of all her friends, making appointments to speak to each other on the phone days in advance. Now she yearned for that clocklessness, for the perpetual food pots of her childhood. Even in the poorest houses a plate of white rice and brown beans with calabaza[3] or green bananas and oil.

She had told Sally that Puerto Ricans lived as if they were all in a small town still, a small town of six million spread out over tens of thousands of square miles, and that the small town that was her country needed to include Manila Avenue in Oakland now, because she was moving back into it. She would not fight the waking early anymore, or the eating all day, or the desire to let time slip between her fingers and allow her work to shape it. Work, eating, sleep, lovemaking, play—to let them shape the day instead of letting the day shape them. Since she could not right now, in the endless bartering of a woman with two countries, bring herself to trade in one-half of her heart for the other, exchange this loneliness for another perhaps harsher one, she would live as a Puerto Rican lives en la isla,[4] right here in north Oakland, plant the bananales[5] and cafetales[6] of her heart around her bedroom door, sleep under the shadow of their bloom and the carving hoarseness of the roosters, wake to blue-rimmed white enamel cups of jugo de piña[7] and plates of guineo verde,[8] and heat pots of rice with bits of meat in them on the stove all day.

There was a woman in her who had never had the chance to move through this house the way she wanted to, a woman raised to be like those women of her childhood, hardworking and humorous and clear. That woman was yawning up out of sleep and into this cluttered daily routine of a Northern California writer living at the edges of Berkeley. She was taking over, putting doilies on the word processor, not bothering to make appointments, talking to the neighbors, riding miles on the bus to buy bacalao,[9] making her presence felt . . . and she was all Puerto Rican, every bit of her.

1986

[1]Pineapple.
[2]"Eat, darling, you want some coffee?"
[3]Pumpkin.
[4]On the island.
[5]Banana plants.
[6]Coffee trees.
[7]Pineapple juice.
[8]Green bananas or plantains.
[9]Codfish.

Heart of My Heart, Bone of My Bone

You were my first grief. From the death of you, so intimate, so much an unexplained event of the universe, I made my first decision to live.

You have no name. That was before names. There were comets plunging into the sun and cells dividing in a frenzy of life too intense, too bright for anything like thinking, but I remember. There was a great space of floating motes and dim light and growing. There were three hearts beating. One, a deep repetition of thunder that was the weather of the universe, a slow rumbling music. And two hearts pitter-pattering, interweaving, fingerlacing, first me then you then me then you, *patta-pun* patta-pun *patta-pun.*

I reconstruct this story from the outside, from knowing what things were, from having names. On the inside, I grew stronger and you grew weaker. I grew and you grew still. I felt your sadness and fear and loneliness without having to interpret signs, read your expressions. The fluids of our bodies mingled in one chemical response: I knew *exactly* how you felt, and never, since then, have I been so completely known.

It was there from the beginning, the thing that was wrong with you. Something I knew but at first was hardly aware of. That grew to trouble me, until slowly I knew that I would lose you. Would be as naked without you as the pulsing electric cord of your spine was naked, unprotected. It was a failure of some part of your body to develop, a loss in the genetic gamble, a part that was necessary and was not there, did not work. *A part that was necessary and is gone.*

On the outside, I read about fetal development, look at pictures, watch *The Miracle of Life* on TV. I am shivering as I watch: ten days, two weeks, four weeks, seven weeks, twelve weeks, fourteen . . . then nothing. The picture of the sixteen week fetus comes up on the screen, and I feel I have never seen this shape before, pinpointing your death in the shadowy places of my body's memory, a kind of emotional sonogram.

Cell of my cell, bone of my bone, when your heart fluttered and whispered and was still, when you floated passive in the salty water and slowly came undone, frilling and fraying at the edges, becoming strands of protein, disappearing into the walls, the glowing cord my flesh—the stillness that followed was terrible, patta-pun *and nothing,* patta-pun *and nothing.*

You were heart of my heart and my own single heart murmurs and mutters now, an extra beat in each movement, patta-pa-pun, patta-pa-bun, beating "Are you still here? Are you still here?" Trying to find you in the stillness of the house, too big now without you, my own small heart and the thunder above me.

This is all I know: You were the closest being in the world and then you were gone. I have looked for you everywhere, though for years I had no name for the longing, crying in my child's bunk bed at night for someone I missed, not knowing who. Turning over all the stones to find you: If I get sick, too, will you come back? If I promise to die young, will you come back? If I promise never to have another baby close to my heart, will you come back? Patta-pun and no answer. Patta-pun and nothing.

I am a woman rich in brothers. Ricardo, who came when I was two. At my wedding he said, "You were my first coconspirator and soulmate." Partner in all the games of my childhood. Sibling to the wild guava bushes, friend of dogs in every alley of Chicago, companion of my homesickness, with whom I learned the meaning of solidarity.

Alejandro, who was born when I was nearly twelve. The golden treasure we took with us to Chicago, the child of my adolescence, the one I sang to, took mountain climbing, hitchhiked with. The almost-my-son one. The one who reminds me I survived.

I am rich in brothers, rich in love, and still, tiny as my little finger, curled up inside me, is the first seed of myself, wailing to the edges of the empty universe, for my brother, my self, my first lost love.

1986

Sandra Cisneros b. 1954

Born in Chicago, Sandra Cisneros spent much of her early life moving between various homes in the United States and her father's family home in Mexico City. As a student at the Writers' Workshop at the University of Iowa in the late 1970s, Cisneros drew upon her bicultural experience to write "the stories that haven't been written to fill a literary void." Since then, she has made the border state of Texas her home and the bicultural site in which much of her work is located.

The National Endowment for the Arts, the University of Texas, the University of California, and the MacArthur Foundation have acknowledged Cisneros's border aesthetic by awarding her fellowships, grants, and visiting appointments. Yet it is this same successful career trajectory that has generated some controversy

among her literary peers. Her first book, a collection of poetry entitled *Bad Boys,* appeared in 1980 as part of a series of Chicano chapbooks. Like most Chicana/Chicano literature, Cisneros's early work was distributed by small presses specializing in Latina/Latino literature. But the interest generated by her first collection of fiction, *The House on Mango Street* (1984) enabled Cisneros to break into the world of major New York publishers. Her crossover appeal during the late 1980s and early 1990s facilitated a larger movement of Chicana writers, whose commercial and critical success has generated greater mainstream appreciation of Chicana/Chicano literature as well as some anxiety about their uneven reception. No one can understand recent history of Chicana/Chicano literature without making Cisneros a central figure in that reading.

In *Mango Street* Cisneros adapted the experimental form used by a number of other Chicana/o writers: the collection of related stories and sketches. *Mango Street* recalls Tomás Rivera's *. . . y no se lo tragó la tierra/And the Earth Did Not Devour Him* (selections from Rivera's novel appear elsewhere in this anthology) inasmuch as it uses a central protagonist to give short prose pieces coherence. About a young girl living in a segregated neighborhood in Chicago during the 1970s, *Mango Street* concludes with the Chicana artist's withdrawal from her community and, in a Joycean gesture, commitment to return. "I have gone away to come back," read *Mango Street*'s closing lines. "For the ones I left behind. For the ones who cannot get out."

Cisneros's second collection of poetry, *My Wicked, Wicked Ways* (1987), also invokes a developmental narrative; only here the narrative is ironic. The "bad girl" of the opening section develops into the "evil woman" of the next two sections, an artist whose escapades include adultery and a sexual romp through Europe. Cisneros's female speakers are complex, as they represent both defiance and fulfillment of cultural expectations. Her terse poetry evokes and ironically venerates the archetypal Chicana/Mexicana evil woman: La Malinche, the Indian mistress of Hernán Cortés, the "whore" who is said to have sold out her people to the conqueror. Like other Chicana feminists, Cisneros attempts to recover and revise La Malinche's tarnished reputation. Her project of mythic reclamation revises Chicana/Chicano cultural archaeology and bears the urgency of remembering everyday women whose lives would otherwise be anathematized or even forgotten.

Cisneros's feminism is even more evident in *Woman Hollering Creek* (1991). The first section contains a series of sketches told through the juvenile perspective familiar to readers of *Mango Street*. The rest of the book explores in greater detail the "wicked" woman of Cisneros's verse: the sultry seductress, perceived in her own culture as a sellout not just because of her sexuality but also because of her relative assimilation into Anglo-American culture. If *Mango Street* tries to solve the problem of the ethnic intellectual's estrangement from her community through a promise of return, *Woman Hollering Creek* demonstrates that making good on that promise creates another set of problems, negotiations, and anxieties.

In 1994, Cisneros published a book for children, using excerpts from *Mango Street*. *Hairs/Pelitos* illustrates the cultural diversity that takes place even within families by describing the different types of hair among members of Cisneros's own family; the book conveys a portrait of a family living in "heterogeneous harmony." With illustrations by Terry Ybanez, *Hair/Pelitos* is written, appropriately, in both Spanish and English. Also in 1994, Cisneros published her third book of poetry, *Loose Woman*, in which the much-maligned "wicked woman" brashly expresses a vision of history, sexuality, and community that celebrates poems that "fart in the bath" as much as it lambasts "politically-correct-Marxist-tourists/voyeurs." The poems are to date the best at capturing Cisneros's sense of outrageousness always made funnier, stronger, and deeper when shared with another as in her poem, "Las Girlfriends": "Been to hell and back again/Girl, me too."

Lora Romero
Stanford University

James Kyung-Jin Lee
University of Texas–Austin

PRIMARY WORKS

Bad Boys, 1980; *The House on Mango Street,* 1984, 1991; *My Wicked, Wicked Ways,* 1987, 1992; *Woman Hollering Creek and Other Stories,* 1991; *Hairs/Pelitos,* 1994; *Loose Woman,* 1994; *Caramelo,* 2002.

Eleven

What they don't understand about birthdays and what they never tell you is that when you're eleven, you're also ten, and nine, and eight, and seven, and six, and five, and four, and three, and two, and one. And when you wake up on your eleventh birthday you expect to feel eleven, but you don't. You open your eyes and everything's just like yesterday, only it's today. And you don't feel eleven at all. You feel like you're still ten. And you are—underneath the year that makes you eleven.

Like some days you might say something stupid, and that's the part of you that's still ten. Or maybe some days you might need to sit on your mama's lap because you're scared, and that's the part of you that's five. And maybe one day when you're all grown up maybe you will need to cry like if you're three, and that's okay. That's what I tell Mama when she's sad and needs to cry. Maybe she's feeling three.

Because the way you grow old is kind of like an onion or like the rings inside a tree trunk or like my little wooden dolls that fit one inside the other, each year inside the next one. That's how being eleven years old is.

You don't feel eleven. Not right away. It takes a few days, weeks even, sometimes even months before you say Eleven when they ask you. And you don't feel smart eleven, not until you're almost twelve. That's the way it is.

Only today I wish I didn't have only eleven years rattling inside me like pennies in a tin Band-Aid box. Today I wish I was one hundred and two instead of eleven because if I was one hundred and two I'd have known what to say when Mrs. Price put the red sweater on my desk. I would've known how to tell her it wasn't mine instead of just sitting there with that look on my face and nothing coming out of my mouth.

"Whose is this?" Mrs. Price says, and she holds the red sweater up in the air for all the class to see. "Whose? It's been sitting in the coatroom for a month."

"Not mine," says everybody. "Not me."

"It has to belong to somebody," Mrs. Price keeps saying, but nobody can remember. It's an ugly sweater with red plastic buttons and a collar and sleeves all stretched out like you could use it for a jump rope. It's maybe a thousand years old and even if it belonged to me I wouldn't say so.

Maybe because I'm skinny, maybe because she doesn't like me, that stupid Sylvia Saldívar says, "I think it belongs to Rachel." An ugly sweater like that, all raggedy and old, but Mrs. Price believes her. Mrs. Price takes the sweater and puts it right on my desk, but when I open my mouth nothing comes out.

"That's not, I don't, you're not . . . Not mine," I finally say in a little voice that was maybe me when I was four.

"Of course it's yours," Mrs. Price says. "I remember you wearing it once." Because she's older and the teacher, she's right and I'm not.

Not mine, not mine, not mine, but Mrs. Price is already turning to page thirty-two, and math problem number four. I don't know why but all of a sudden I'm feeling sick inside, like the part of me that's three wants to come out of my eyes, only I squeeze them shut tight and bite down on my teeth real hard and try to remember today I am eleven, eleven. Mama is making a cake for me for tonight, and when Papa comes home everybody will sing Happy birthday, happy birthday to you.

But when the sick feeling goes away and I open my eyes, the red sweater's still sitting there like a big red mountain. I move the red sweater to the corner of my desk with my ruler. I move my pencil and books and eraser as far from it as possible. I even move my chair a little to the right. Not mine, not mine, not mine.

In my head I'm thinking how long till lunchtime, how long till I can take the red sweater and throw it over the schoolyard fence, or leave it hanging on a parking meter, or bunch it up into a little ball and toss it in the alley. Except when math period ends Mrs. Price says loud and in front of everybody, "Now, Rachel, that's enough," because she sees I've shoved the red sweater to the tippy-tip corner of my desk and it's hanging all over the edge like a waterfall, but I don't care.

"Rachel," Mrs. Price says. She says it like she's getting mad. "You put that sweater on right now and no more nonsense."

"But it's not—"

"Now!" Mrs. Price says.

This is when I wish I wasn't eleven, because all the years inside of me—ten, nine, eight, seven, six, five, four, three, two, and one—are pushing at the back of my eyes when I put one arm through one sleeve of the sweater that smells like cottage cheese, and then the other arm through the other and stand there with my arms apart like if the sweater hurts me and it does, all itchy and full of germs that aren't even mine.

That's when everything I've been holding in since this morning, since when Mrs. Price put the sweater on my desk, finally lets go, and all of a sudden I'm crying in front of everybody. I wish I was invisible but I'm not. I'm eleven and it's my birthday today and I'm crying like I'm three in front of everybody. I put my head down on the desk and bury my face in my stupid clown-sweater arms. My face all hot and spit coming out of my mouth because I can't stop the little animal noises from coming out of me, until there aren't any more tears left in my eyes, and it's just my body shaking like when you have the hiccups, and my whole head hurts like when you drink milk too fast.

But the worst part is right before the bell rings for lunch. That stupid Phyllis Lopez, who is even dumber than Sylvia Saldívar, says she remembers the red sweater is hers! I take it off right away and give it to her, only Mrs. Price pretends like everything's okay.

Today I'm eleven. There's a cake Mama's making for tonight, and when Papa comes home from work we'll eat it. There'll be candles and presents and everybody will sing Happy birthday, happy birthday to you, Rachel, only it's too late.

I'm eleven today. I'm eleven, ten, nine, eight, seven, six, five, four, three, two, and one, but I wish I was one hundred and two. I wish I was anything but eleven, because I want today to be far away already, far away like a runaway balloon, like a tiny *o* in the sky, so tiny-tiny you have to close your eyes to see it.

1991

Gish Jen b. 1955

Born in Long Island, New York, Gish Jen comes from a family of five children with parents who were educated in Shanghai, China (her mother in educational psychology and her father in engineering), and who separately emigrated to the United States around World War II. As a pre-med and English major at Harvard University, Jen earned a B.A. in 1977. She then attended Stanford Business School for a year and, from 1981 to 1983, completed an M.F.A. at the University of Iowa. She lives in Cambridge, Massachusetts, with her husband, son, and daughter.

Although Jen's works have appeared in various journals and anthologies, including *The Atlantic* and *The Best American Short Stories 1988,* the 1991 novel *Typical American* marks her arrival as a much-acclaimed fiction writer. Callie and Mona, two sisters who appear in several of Jen's short stories, play minor roles in this work. The novel focuses on the girls' father, Ralph Chang, who, in line with the 1950s atmosphere of upward mobility and conformity in America, becomes absorbed with pursuing the American Dream. Jen's next novel, *Mona in the Promised Land,* focuses on Mona Chang, the daughter who converts to Judaism after the family moves to the upscale Jewish neighborhood of "Scarshill" (Jen grew up in Scarsdale, New York). Her collection of eight short stories, *Who's Irish?,* includes new and previously published works such as "The Water Faucet Vision" and "In the American Society."

In an interview, Jen said that the scene in "In the American Society" where Ralph throws the polo shirt into the swimming pool convinced her to use Ralph as the protagonist for her first novel. This dramatic act, she stated, indicated that Ralph was the kind of make-things-happen character she needed. The first part of "In the American Society" depicts a Chinese immigrant's vain attempt to impose the feudal practices and attitudes of an old-world Chinese village lord on his American restaurant employees. Placed in a different setting, the second part of the story suggests that this same background enables Ralph to resist being ridiculed. The parallel structures of the two scenes and the resolution of the story offer an insightful analysis of cross-cultural and racial issues in American society.

In this short story and in her other works, Jen displays a seamless, engaging, and comic narrative voice. Her ironic wit is apparent in disarmingly straightforward language. Jen's style contrasts markedly with the styles of Amy Tan and Maxine Hong Kingston, two other contemporary Chinese American writers with whom she is inevitably compared. However, although all three are Chinese American, each is a highly effective artist in her own right and should be read and enjoyed for her individual style. Like Kingston and Tan, Jen comes out of a specific Asian American historical-cultural experience. She takes her rightful place in an American literary tradition that is being redefined to include writers from the various cultures that compose American society.

Bonnie TuSmith
Northeastern University

PRIMARY WORKS

Typical American, 1991; *Mona in the Promised Land,* 1996; *Who's Irish?,* 1999; *The Love Wife,* 2004.

In the American Society

I. His Own Society

When my father took over the pancake house, it was to send my little sister Mona and me to college. We were only in junior high at the time, but my father believed in getting a jump on things. "Those Americans always saying it," he told us. "Smart guys thinking in advance." My mother elaborated, explaining that businesses took bringing up, like children. They could take years to get going, she said, years.

In this case, though, we got rich right away. At two months we were breaking even, and at four, those same hotcakes that could barely withstand the weight of butter and syrup were supporting our family with ease. My mother bought a station wagon with air conditioning, my father an oversized, red vinyl recliner for the back room; and as time went on and the business continued to thrive, my father started to talk about his grandfather and the village he had reigned over in China—things my father had never talked about when he worked for other people. He told us about the bags of rice his family would give out to the poor at New Year's, and about the people who came to beg, on their hands and knees, for his grandfather to intercede for the more wayward of their relatives. "Like that Godfather in the movie," he would tell us as, his feet up, he distributed paychecks. Sometimes an employee would get two green envelopes instead of one, which meant that Jimmy needed a tooth pulled, say, or that Tiffany's husband was in the clinker again.

"It's nothing, nothing," he would insist, sinking back into his chair. "Who else is going to take care of you people?"

My mother would mostly just sigh about it. "Your father thinks this is China," she would say, and then she would go back to her mending. Once in a while, though, when my father had given away a particularly large sum, she would exclaim, outraged, "But this here is the U—S—of—A!"—this apparently having been what she used to tell immigrant stock boys when they came in late.

She didn't work at the supermarket anymore; but she had made it to the rank of manager before she left, and this had given her not only new words and phrases, but new ideas about herself, and about America, and about what was what in general. She had opinions, now, on how downtown should be zoned; she could pump her own gas and check her own oil; and for all she used to chide Mona and me for being "copycats," she herself was now interested in espadrilles, and wallpaper, and most recently, the town country club.

"So join already," said Mona, flicking a fly off her knee.

My mother enumerated the problems as she sliced up a quarter round of watermelon: There was the cost. There was the waiting list. There was the fact that no one in our family played either tennis or golf.

"So what?" said Mona.

"It would be waste," said my mother.

"Me and Callie can swim in the pool."

"Plus you need that recommendation letter from a member."

"Come *on*," said Mona. "Annie's mom'd write you a letter in *sec*."

My mother's knife glinted in the early summer sun. I spread some more news-paper on the picnic table.

"*Plus* you have to eat there twice a month. You know what that means." My mother cut another, enormous slice of fruit.

"No, I *don't* know what that means," said Mona.

"It means Dad would have to wear a jacket, dummy," I said.

"Oh! Oh! Oh!" said Mona, clasping her hand to her breast. "Oh! Oh! Oh! Oh! Oh!"

We all laughed: my father had no use for nice clothes, and would wear only ten-year-old shirts, with grease-spotted pants, to show how little he cared what anyone thought.

"Your father doesn't believe in joining the American society," said my mother. "He wants to have his own society."

"So go to dinner without him." Mona shot her seeds out in long arcs over the lawn. "Who cares what he thinks?"

But of course we all did care, and knew my mother could not simply up and do as she pleased. For in my father's mind, a family owed its head a degree of loyalty that left no room for dissent. To embrace what he embraced was to love; and to embrace something else was to betray him.

He demanded a similar sort of loyalty of his workers, whom he treated more like servants than employees. Not in the beginning, of course. In the beginning all he wanted was for them to keep on doing what they used to do, and to that end he con-centrated mostly on leaving them alone. As the months passed, though, he expected more and more of them, with the result that for all his largesse, he began to have trou-ble keeping help. The cooks and busboys complained that he asked them to fix ra-diators and trim hedges, not only at the restaurant, but at our house; the waitresses that he sent them on errands and made them chauffeur him around. Our head wait-ress, Gertrude, claimed that he once even asked her to scratch his back.

"It's not just the blacks don't believe in slavery," she said when she quit.

My father never quite registered her complaint, though, nor those of the others who left. Even after Eleanor quit, then Tiffany, then Gerald, and Jimmy, and even his best cook, Eureka Andy, for whom he had bought new glasses, he remained mostly convinced that the fault lay with them.

"All they understand is that assembly line," he lamented. "Robots, they are. They want to be robots."

There *were* occasions when the clear running truth seemed to eddy, when he would pinch the vinyl of his chair up into little peaks and wonder if he was doing things right. But with time he would always smooth the peaks back down; and when business started to slide in the spring, he kept on like a horse in his ways.

By the summer our dishboy was overwhelmed with scraping. It was no longer just the hashbrowns that people were leaving for trash, and the service was as bad as the food. The waitresses served up French pancakes instead of German, apple juice instead of orange, spilt things on laps, on coats. On the Fourth of July some green-horn sent an entire side of fries slaloming down a lady's *massif centrale*. Meanwhile in the back room, my father labored through articles on the economy.

"What is housing starts?" he puzzled. "What is GNP?"

Mona and I did what we could, filling in as busgirls and bookkeepers and, one af-ternoon, stuffing the comments box that hung by the cashier's desk. That was Mona's idea. We rustled up a variety of pens and pencils, checked boxes for an hour, smeared the cards up with coffee and grease, and waited. It took a few days for my father to notice that the box was full, and he didn't say anything about it for a few days more. Finally, though, he started to complain of fatigue; and then he began to complain that the staff was not what it could be. We encouraged him in this—pointing out, for instance, how many dishes got chipped—but in the end all that happened was that, for the first time since we took over the restaurant, my father got it into his head to fire someone. Skip, a skinny busboy who was saving up for a sportscar, said nothing as my father mumbled on about the price of dishes. My father's hands shook as he wrote out the severance check; and he spent the rest of the day napping in his chair once it was over.

As it was going on midsummer, Skip wasn't easy to replace. We hung a sign in the window and advertised in the paper, but no one called the first week, and the person who called the second didn't show up for his interview. The third week, my father phoned Skip to see if he would come back, but a friend of his had already sold him a Corvette for cheap.

Finally a Chinese guy named Booker turned up. He couldn't have been more than thirty, and was wearing a lighthearted seersucker suit, but he looked as though life had him pinned: his eyes were bloodshot and his chest sunken, and the muscles of his neck seemed to strain with the effort of holding his head up. In a single dry breath he told us that he had never bussed tables but was willing to learn, and that he was on the lam from the deportation authorities.

"I do not want to lie to you," he kept saying. He had come to the United States on a student visa, had run out of money, and was now in a bind. He was loath to go back to Taiwan, as it happened—he looked up at this point, to be sure my father wasn't pro-KMT—but all he had was a phony social security card and a willingness to absorb all blame, should anything untoward come to pass.

"I do not think, anyway, that it is against law to hire me, only to be me," he said, smiling faintly.

Anyone else would have examined him on this, but my father conceived of laws as speed bumps rather than curbs. He wiped the counter with his sleeve, and told Booker to report the next morning.

"I will be good worker," said Booker.

"Good," said my father.

"Anything you want me to do, I will do."

My father nodded.

Booker seemed to sink into himself for a moment. "Thank you," he said finally. "I am appreciate your help. I am very, very appreciate for everything." He reached out to shake my father's hand.

My father looked at him. "Did you eat today?" he asked in Mandarin.

Booker pulled at the hem of his jacket.

"Sit down," said my father. "Please, have a seat."

My father didn't tell my mother about Booker, and my mother didn't tell my father about the country club. She would never have applied, except that Mona, while over at Annie's, had let it drop that our mother wanted to join. Mrs. Lardner came by the very next day.

"Why, I'd be honored and delighted to write you people a letter," she said. Her skirt billowed around her.

"Thank you so much," said my mother. "But it's too much trouble for you, and also my husband is . . ."

"Oh, it's no trouble at all, no trouble at all. I tell you." She leaned forward so that her chest freckles showed. "I know just how it is. It's a secret of course, but you know, my natural father was Jewish. Can you see it? Just look at my skin."

"My husband," said my mother.

"I'd be honored and delighted," said Mrs. Lardner with a little wave of her hands. "Just honored and delighted."

Mona was triumphant. "See, Mom," she said, waltzing around the kitchen when Mrs. Lardner left. "What did I tell you? 'I'm just honored and delighted, just honored and delighted.'" She waved her hands in the air.

"You know, the Chinese have a saying," said my mother. "To do nothing is better than to overdo. You mean well, but you tell me now what will happen."

"I'll talk Dad into it," said Mona, still waltzing. "Or I bet Callie can. He'll do anything Callie says."

"I can try, anyway," I said.

"Did you hear what I said?" said my mother. Mona bumped into the broom closet door. "You're not going to talk anything; you've already made enough trouble." She started on the dishes with a clatter.

Mona poked diffidently at a mop.

I sponged off the counter. "Anyway," I ventured. "I bet our name'll never even come up."

"That's if we're lucky," said my mother.

"There's all these people waiting," I said.

"Good," she said. She started on a pot.

I looked over at Mona, who was still cowering in the broom closet. "In fact, there's some black family's been waiting so long, they're going to sue," I said.

My mother turned off the water. "Where'd you hear that?"

"Patty told me."

She turned the water back on, started to wash a dish, then put it back down and shut the faucet.

"I'm sorry," said Mona.

"Forget it," said my mother. "Just forget it."

Booker turned out to be a model worker, whose boundless gratitude translated into a willingness to do anything. As he also learned quickly, he soon knew not only how to bus, but how to cook, and how to wait table, and how to keep the books. He fixed the walk-in door so that it stayed shut, reupholstered the torn seats in the dining room, and devised a system for tracking inventory. The only stone in the rice was that he tended to be sickly; but, reliable even in illness, he would always send a friend to take his place. In this way we got to know Ronald, Lynn, Dirk, and Cedric, all of whom, like Booker, had problems with their legal status and were anxious to please. They weren't all as capable as Booker, though, with the exception of Cedric, whom my father often hired even when Booker was well. A round wag of a man who called Mona and me *shou hou*—skinny monkeys—he was a professed non-smoker who was nevertheless always begging drags off of other people's cigarettes. This last habit drove our head cook, Fernando, crazy, especially since, when refused a hit, Cedric would occasionally snitch one. Winking impishly at Mona and me, he would steal up to an ashtray, take a quick puff, and then break out laughing so that the smoke came rolling out of his mouth in a great incriminatory cloud. Fernando accused him of stealing fresh cigarettes too, even whole packs.

"Why else do you think he's weaseling around in the back of the store all the time," he said. His face was blotchy with anger. "The man is a frigging thief."

Other members of the staff supported him in this contention and joined in on an "Operation Identification," which involved numbering and initialing their cigarettes—even though what they seemed to fear for wasn't so much their cigarettes as their jobs. Then one of the cooks quit; and rather than promote someone, my father hired Cedric for the position. Rumors flew that he was taking only half the normal salary, that Alex had been pressured to resign, and that my father was looking for a position with which to placate Booker, who had been bypassed because of his health.

The result was that Fernando categorically refused to work with Cedric.

"The only way I'll cook with that piece of slime," he said, shaking his huge tattooed fist, "is if it's his ass frying on the grill."

My father cajoled and cajoled, to no avail, and in the end was simply forced to put them on different schedules.

The next week Fernando got caught stealing a carton of minute steaks. My father would not tell even Mona and me how he knew to be standing by the back door when Fernando was on his way out, but everyone suspected Booker. Everyone but Fernando, that is, who was sure Cedric had been the tip-off. My father held a staff meeting in which he tried to reassure everyone that Alex had left on his own, and that he had no intention of firing anyone. But though he was careful not to mention Fernando, everyone was so amazed that he was being allowed to stay that Fernando was incensed nonetheless.

"Don't you all be putting your bug eyes on me," he said. "*He's* the frigging crook." He grabbed Cedric by the collar.

Cedric raised an eyebrow. "Cook, you mean," he said.

At this Fernando punched Cedric in the mouth; and the words he had just uttered notwithstanding, my father fired him on the spot.

With everything that was happening, Mona and I were ready to be getting out of the restaurant. It was almost time: the days were still stuffy with summer, but our window shade had started flapping in the evening as if gearing up to go out. That year the breezes were full of salt, as they sometimes were when they came in from the East, and they blew anchors and docks through my mind like so many tumbleweeds, filling my dreams with wherries and lobsters and grainy-faced men who squinted, day in and day out, at the sky.

It was time for a change, you could feel it; and yet the pancake house was the same as ever. The day before school started my father came home with bad news.

"Fernando called police," he said, wiping his hand on his pant leg.

My mother naturally wanted to know what police; and so with much coughing and hawing, the long story began, the latest installment of which had the police calling immigration, and immigration sending an investigator. My mother sat stiff as whalebone as my father described how the man summarily refused lunch on the house and how my father had admitted, under pressure, that he knew there were "things" about his workers.

"So now what happens?"

My father didn't know. "Booker and Cedric went with him to the jail," he said. "But me, here I am." He laughed uncomfortably.

The next day my father posted bail for "his boys" and waited apprehensively for something to happen. The day after that he waited again, and the day after that he called our neighbor's law student son, who suggested my father call the immigration department under an alias. My father took his advice; and it was thus that he discovered that Booker was right: it was illegal for aliens to work, but it wasn't to hire them.

In the happy interval that ensued, my father apologized to my mother, who in turn confessed about the country club, for which my father had no choice but to forgive her. Then he turned his attention back to "his boys."

My mother didn't see that there was anything to do.

"I like to talking to the judge," said my father.

"This is not China," said my mother.

"I'm only talking to him. I'm not give him money unless he wants it."

"You're going to land up in jail."

"So what else I should do?" My father threw up his hands. "Those are my boys."

"Your boys!" exploded my mother. "What about your family? What about your wife?"

My father took a long sip of tea. "You know," he said finally. "In the war my father sent our cook to the soldiers to use. He always said it—the province comes before the town, the town comes before the family."

"A restaurant is not a town," said my mother.

My father sipped at his tea again. "You know, when I first come to the United States, I also had to hide-and-seek with those deportation guys. If people did not helping me, I'm not here today."

My mother scrutinized her hem.

After a minute I volunteered that before seeing a judge, he might try a lawyer.

He turned. "Since when did you become so afraid like your mother?"

I started to say that it wasn't a matter of fear, but he cut me off.

"What I need today," he said, "is a son."

My father and I spent the better part of the next day standing in lines at the immigration office. He did not get to speak to a judge, but with much persistence he managed to speak to a judge's clerk, who tried to persuade him that it was not her place to extend him advice. My father, though, shamelessly plied her with compliments and offers of free pancakes until she finally conceded that she personally doubted anything would happen to either Cedric or Booker.

"Especially if they're 'needed workers,'" she said, rubbing at the red marks her glasses left on her nose. She yawned. "Have you thought about sponsoring them to become permanent residents?"

Could he do that? My father was overjoyed. And what if he saw to it right away? Would she perhaps put in a good word with the judge?

She yawned again, her nostrils flaring. "Don't worry," she said. "They'll get a fair hearing."

My father returned jubilant. Booker and Cedric hailed him as their savior, their Buddha incarnate. He was like a father to them, they said; and laughing and clapping, they made him tell the story over and over, sorting over the details like jewels. And how old was the assistant judge? And what did she say?

That evening my father tipped the paperboy a dollar and bought a pot of mums for my mother, who suffered them to be placed on the dining room table. The next night he took us all out to dinner. Then on Saturday, Mona found a letter on my father's chair at the restaurant.

> Dear Mr. Chang,
>
> You are the grat boss. But, we do not like to trial, so will runing away now. Plese to excus us. People saying the law in America is fears like dragon. Here is only $140. We hope some day we can pay back the rest bale. You will getting intrest, as you diserving, so grat a boss you are. Thank you for every thing. In next life you will be burn in rich family, with no more pancaks.
>
> Yours truley,
> Booker + Cedric

In the weeks that followed my father went to the pancake house for crises, but otherwise hung around our house, fiddling idly with the sump pump and boiler in an effort, he said, to get ready for winter. It was as though he had gone into retirement, except that instead of moving south, he had moved to the basement. He even took to showering my mother with little attentions, and to calling her "old girl," and when we finally heard that the club had entertained all the applications it could for the year, he was so sympathetic that he seemed more disappointed than my mother.

II.   In the American Society

Mrs. Lardner tempered the bad news with an invitation to a bon voyage "bash" she was throwing for a friend of hers who was going to Greece for six months.

"Do come," she urged. "You'll meet everyone, and then, you know, if things open up in the spring . . ." She waved her hands.

My mother wondered if it would be appropriate to show up at a party for someone they didn't know, but "the honest truth" was that this was an annual affair. "If it's not Greece, it's Antibes," sighed Mrs. Lardner. "We really just do it because his wife left him and his daughter doesn't speak to him, and poor Jeremy just feels so *unloved*."

She also invited Mona and me to the goings on, as "*demi*-guests" to keep Annie out of the champagne. I wasn't too keen on the idea, but before I could say anything, she had already thanked us for so generously agreeing to honor her with our presence.

"A pair of little princesses, you are!" she told us. "A pair of princesses!"

The party was that Sunday. On Saturday, my mother took my father out shopping for a suit. As it was the end of September, she insisted that he buy a worsted rather than a seersucker, even though it was only ten, rather than fifty percent off. My father protested that it was as hot out as ever, which was true—a thick Indian summer had cozied murderously up to us—but to no avail. Summer clothes, said my mother, were not properly worn after Labor Day.

The suit was unfortunately as extravagant in length as it was in price, which posed an additional quandary, since the tailor wouldn't be in until Monday. The salesgirl, though, found a way of tacking it up temporarily.

"Maybe this suit not fit me," fretted my father.

"Just don't take your jacket off," said the salesgirl.

He gave her a tip before they left, but when he got home refused to remove the price tag.

"I like to asking the tailor about the size," he insisted.

"You mean you're going to *wear* it and then *return* it?" Mona rolled her eyes.

"I didn't say I'm return it," said my father stiffly. "I like to asking the tailor, that's all."

The party started off swimmingly, except that most people were wearing bermudas or wrap skirts. Still, my parents carried on, sharing with great feeling the complaints about the heat. Of course my father tried to eat a cracker full of shallots and burnt himself in an attempt to help Mr. Lardner turn the coals of the barbeque; but on the whole he seemed to be doing all right. Not nearly so well as my mother, though, who had accepted an entire cupful of Mrs. Lardner's magic punch, and seemed indeed to be under some spell. As Mona and Annie skirmished over whether some boy in their class inhaled when he smoked, I watched my mother take off her shoes, laughing and laughing as a man with a beard regaled her with navy stories by the pool. Apparently he had been stationed in the Orient and remembered a few words of Chinese, which made my mother laugh still more. My father excused himself to go to the men's room then drifted back and weighed anchor at the hors d'oeuvres table, while my mother sailed on to a group of women, who tinkled at length over the clarity of her complexion. I dug out a book I had brought.

Just when I'd cracked the spine, though, Mrs. Lardner came by to bewail her shortage of servers. Her caterers were criminals, I agreed; and the next thing I knew I was handing out bits of marine life, making the rounds as amiably as I could.

"Here you go, Dad," I said when I got to the hors d'oeuvres table.

"Everything is fine," he said.

I hesitated to leave him alone; but then the man with the beard zeroed in on him, and though he talked of nothing but my mother, I thought it would be okay to get back to work. Just that moment, though, Jeremy Brothers lurched our way, an empty, albeit corked, wine bottle in hand. He was a slim, well-proportioned man, with a Roman nose and small eyes and a nice manly jaw that he allowed to hang agape.

"Hello," he said drunkenly. "Pleased to meet you."

"Pleased to meeting you," said my father.

"Right," said Jeremy. "Right. Listen. I have this bottle here, this most recalcitrant bottle. You see that it refuses to do my bidding. I bid it open sesame, please, and it does nothing." He pulled the cork out with his teeth, then turned the bottle upside down.

My father nodded.

"Would you have a word with it please?" said Jeremy. The man with the beard excused himself. "Would you please have a goddamned word with it?"

My father laughed uncomfortably.

"Ah!" Jeremy bowed a little. "Excuse me, excuse me, excuse me. You are not my man, not my man at all." He bowed again and started to leave, but then circled back. "Viticulture is not your forte, yes I can see that, see that plainly. But may I trouble you on another matter? Forget the damned bottle." He threw it into the pool, and winked at the people he splashed. "I have another matter. Do you speak Chinese?"

My father said he did not, but Jeremy pulled out a handkerchief with some characters on it anyway, saying that his daughter had sent it from Hong Kong and that he thought the characters might be some secret message.

"Long life," said my father.

"But you haven't looked at it yet."

"I know what it says without looking." My father winked at me.

"You do?"

"Yes, I do."

"You're making fun of me, aren't you?"

"No, no, no," said my father, winking again.

"Who are you anyway?" said Jeremy.

His smile fading, my father shrugged.

"*Who are you?*"

My father shrugged again.

Jeremy began to roar. "This is my party, *my party,* and I've never seen you before in my life." My father backed up as Jeremy came toward him. "*Who are you? WHO ARE YOU?*"

Just as my father was going to step back into the pool, Mrs. Lardner came running up. Jeremy informed her that there was a man crashing his party.

"Nonsense," said Mrs. Lardner. "This is Ralph Chang, who I invited extra especially so he could meet you." She straightened the collar of Jeremy's peach-colored polo shirt for him.

"Yes, well, we've had a chance to chat," said Jeremy.

She whispered in his ear; he mumbled something; she whispered something more.

"I do apologize," he said finally.

My father didn't say anything.

"I do." Jeremy seemed genuinely contrite. "Doubtless you've seen drunks before, haven't you? You must have them in China."

"Okay," said my father.

As Mrs. Lardner glided off, Jeremy clapped his arm over my father's shoulders. "You know, I really am quite sorry, quite sorry."

My father nodded.

"What can I do, how can I make it up to you?"

"No thank you."

"No, tell me, tell me," wheedled Jeremy. "Tickets to casino night?" My father shook his head. "You don't gamble. Dinner at Bartholomew's?" My father shook his head again. "You don't eat." Jeremy scratched his chin. "You know, my wife was like you. Old Annabelle could never let me make things up—never, never, never, never, never."

My father wriggled out from under his arm.

"How about sport clothes? You are rather overdressed, you know, excuse me for saying so. But here." He took off his polo shirt and folded it up. "You can have this with my most profound apologies." He ruffled his chest hairs with his free hand.

"No thank you," said my father.

"No, take it, take it. Accept my apologies." He thrust the shirt into my father's arms. "I'm so very sorry, so very sorry. Please, try it on."

Helplessly holding the shirt, my father searched the crowd for my mother.

"Here, I'll help you off with your coat."

My father froze.

Jeremy reached over and took his jacket off. "Milton's, one hundred twenty-five dollars reduced to one hundred twelve-fifty," he read. "What a bargain, what a bargain!"

"Please give it back," pleaded my father. "Please."

"Now for your shirt," ordered Jeremy.

Heads began to turn.

"Take off your shirt."

"I do not take orders like a servant," announced my father.

"Take off your shirt, or I'm going to throw this jacket right into the pool, just right into this little pool here." Jeremy held it over the water.

"Go ahead."

"One hundred twelve-fifty," taunted Jeremy. "One hundred twelve . . ."

My father flung the polo shirt into the water with such force that part of it bounced back up into the air like a fluorescent fountain. Then it settled into a soft heap on top of the water. My mother hurried up.

"You're a sport!" said Jeremy, suddenly breaking into a smile and slapping my father on the back. "You're a sport! I like that. A man with spirit, that's what you are. A man with panache. Allow me to return to you your jacket." He handed it back to my father. "Good value you got on that, good value."

My father hurled the coat into the pool too. "We're leaving," he said grimly. "Leaving!"

"Now, Ralphie," said Mrs. Lardner, bustling up; but my father was already stomping off.

"Get your sister," he told me. To my mother: "Get your shoes."

"That was *great*, Dad," said Mona as we walked down to the car. "You were *stupendous*."

"Way to show 'em," I said.

"What?" said my father offhandedly.

Although it was only just dusk, we were in a gulch, which made it hard to see anything except the gleam of his white shirt moving up the hill ahead of us.

"It was all my fault," began my mother.

"Forget it," said my father grandly. Then he said, "The only trouble is I left those keys in my jacket pocket."

"Oh *no*," said Mona.

"Oh no is right," said my mother.

"So we'll walk home," I said.

"But how're we going to get into the *house*," said Mona.

The noise of the party churned through the silence.

"Someone has to going back," said my father.

"Let's go to the pancake house first," suggested my mother. "We can wait there until the party is finished, and then call Mrs. Lardner."

Having all agreed that that was a good plan, we started walking again.

"God, just think," said Mona. "We're going to have to *dive* for them."

My father stopped a moment. We waited.

"You girls are good swimmers," he said finally. "Not like me."

Then his shirt started moving again, and we trooped up the hill after it, into the dark.

1991

Kimiko Hahn b. 1955

Kimiko Hahn's poetics are strongly intertextual, often explicitly so. She responds to phrases in other texts that she finds evocative. One text that she frequently returns to for such "cannibalization" (her term) is *Genji monogatari (The Tale of Genji)*, by Lady Murasaki Shikibu (978?–1026), generally considered not only the first Japanese novel but the first psychological novel. Hahn also refers in her writing to the influence and inspiration of other women writers from Japan's Heian period (794–1185).

Hahn's literary debt to Japanese women writers, however, should not be thought of as due to some essentialist connection between Asian American and Asian writers. In her poem "Cruising Barthes," Hahn explores the profoundly ambivalent nature of her exploration of Japanese language and literature: "The way I fear speaking Japanese and adore/speaking it. . . ./What is Japanese? blood,/geography, translation by white, Occupation-trained/academic men?" Her relationship to Japanese literature and culture were shaped, she says, not only by her Japanese American mother but also by her German American father's aesthetic interests in Japanese culture and her own formal study of East Asian cultures in college and graduate school. Language for her is not only a writing tool but also subject matter. Fluency in more than one language highlights language itself as a construction that can be interrogated and played with.

Kimiko Hahn was born in 1955 in Mt. Kisco, New York, to two artists, her mother from Hawaii and her father from Wisconsin. Hahn majored in English and East Asian Studies as an undergraduate at the University of Iowa; she received an M.A. in Japanese literature at Columbia University. Her poetry was first collected in book form in *We Stand Our Ground* (1988), a collaboration with two other women poets. Hahn is the author of five collections of poetry: *Air Pocket* (1989); *Earshot* (1992), which was awarded the Theodore Roethke Memorial Poetry Prize and an Association of Asian America Studies Literature Award; *The Unbearable Heart* (1995), which received an American Book Award; *Volatile* (1999); and *Mosquito and Ant* (1999). A recipient of fellowships from the National Endowment for the Arts and the New York Foundation for the Arts, she has also been awarded a Lila Wallace–Reader's Digest Writer's Award. Hahn was an editor of the magazine *Bridge: Asian-American Perspectives.* She cites her experience with the American Writers Congress as having a major impact, and she identifies Marxism as a strong intellectual and political influence.

Thematically, Hahn's poems explore the relationship between gender, language, body, desire, and subjectivity. Formally, her poetics of fragmentation, quotation, and multivocality propose new models of gendered and racialized subjectivity. The notion of the autonomous individual is questioned and replaced by a sense of the subject as inhabited and haunted by "other" voices. Her poetics of female intersubjectivity are manifested in the arcs of *The Unbearable Heart,* a collection of poems that mourn her mother, and *Mosquito and Ant,* arranged as a series of correspondences between the speaker and an older-sister figure.

Desire is the strongest thread running throughout Hahn's poems. The passion she uses to write love poetry is similar to the passion she uses to write political poetry. The libidinal charge of Hahn's poetry confounds distinctions between private and public, the intimate and the global. Her poems are sensual, lyrical, heartbreaking, intellectual, and political. They are challenging in the most pleasurable sense.

Meditative yet urgent, full of integrity and sensuality, suffused with a multilingual sensibility and "sense memory" (the title of a poem), Hahn's poetry is extremely compelling in its inscriptions of Asian American female desire and subjectivity.

Juliana Chang
University of Illinois, Urbana-Champaign

PRIMARY WORKS

We Stand Our Ground, with Gale Jackson and Susan Sherman, 1988; *Air Pocket,* 1989; *Earshot,* 1992; *The Unbearable Heart,* 1995; *Volatile,* 1999; *Mosquito and Ant,* 1999; *The Artist's Daughter,* 2002; *The Narrow Road to the Interior,* 2006.

Strands

The key warmed in your hand
and you knew the password
was *sea*
instead of *ocean.* Once in
5 he had blown the weekend
talking about documentaries.
Your head rested on his neck
then conked out
in bas relief.
10 The sound and smell
of the steam
across the room warmed you.
Later you figure
it was an extra blanket
15 tossed over your waist.
Your patience at that point
was unassuming. It was here
you turned into a piece
of wood
20 he spotted as sculptural.
You couldn't scream
till he pulled out
his tongue.

The key word was sea
25 not ocean.
Trudging through sixteen inches

your mind goes to drifts
there at the shore;
first last fall
30 with your husband and dog
slugging coffee from a thermos
and bracing against the wind.
You had gone for the dog
to taste sea salt
35 and expanse. The apricot cake
reminded you of earwax.
Now snow and crusts of ice
over sand
plays in your mind.
40 You wouldn't know
and call him again
by names. Seaweed. Oats. Bran.
Apricot jam. Jam.
And the word transforms from would
45 to wood as the key warms
in your hand.

Your hair is short
as spruce
and when you shake
50 short hairs
fall on the newspaper.
He had blown the afternoon
talking about El Salvador
without seeing the connection
55 to, say, Puerto Ricans
in Springfield, Mass.
The banks
of snow incite riot
or strand. The imagination
60 conks out
like the hemisphere.
Looking for an employer
you figure is looking
for what kills
65 the love between us
but not your vision
and never grandma's sea.

Your hair is short
as spruce or pine
70 and you think of his face
brushed by it.
Cellophaning, she suggested,

stains strands of hair
blue, green—whatever.
75 But you shied away
because of him.
Why? Would he walk out?
When you flirted he backed off
yet when you spoke
80 about newspaper clippings
or goldfish he glowed.
And now this. Something
you can't handle as he touches
your hair yet makes
85 for his coat. He doesn't understand
how paint fits into
this narration. So you take the hand
and dip it in.

                                    1992

Resistance: A Poem on Ikat Cloth[1]

By the time the forsythia blossomed
in waves along the parkway
the more delicate cherry and apple
had blown away, if you remember
5 correctly. Those were days
when you'd forget socks and books
after peeing in the privacy
of its branches and soft earth.
What a house you had
10 fit for turtles or sparrows.
One sparrow[2]
wrapped in a silk kimono
wept for her tongue
clipped off by the old woman.
15 You'll never forget that
or its vengeance as striking
as the yellow around your small shoulders.
        shitakirisuzume mother called her.

---

[1]Ikat: "the technique of resist-dying yarn before
it is woven" (*African Textiles,* John Picton and
John Mack, London, 1979).
[2]Sparrow references from the Japanese folk tale,

"Shitakirisuzume" (literally, "the tongue-cut-
sparrow"). The sparrow received the punishment after eating the old woman's rice starch.
The sparrow got even.

<pre>
            You didn't need to understand
20   exactly.
        a process of resistance
        in Soemba, Sumatra, Java, Bali,
        Timor,³
            Soon came mounds of flesh
25   and hair here and there.
            Centuries earlier
            you'd have been courted
        or sold.
            "Inu has let out my sparrow—the little one
30   that I kept in the clothes-basket she said,
            looking very unhappy."
        For a Eurasian, sold.
            Murasaki⁴
        mother
35   She soaked the cloth
            in incense
            then spread it on the floor
            standing there in bleached cotton,
            red silk and bare feet.
40   And you fell in love with her
        deeply as only a little girl could.
        Pulling at your nipples
        you dreamt of her body
        that would become yours.
45   "Since the day we first boarded the ship
            I have been unable to wear
            my dark red robe.
            That must not be done
            out of danger of attracting
50   the god of the sea."
        red as a Judy Chicago plate
        feast your eyes on this
        jack
            "when I was bathing along the shore
55   scarcely screened by reeds
            I lifted my robe revealing my leg
            and more."⁵
        roll up that skirt
        and show those calves
60   cause if that bitch thinks
        she can steal your guy
</pre>

---

³Locations in Indonesia known for ikat.
⁴*Murasaki* also means "purple."
⁵*Tosanikki* (*The Tosa Diary* by Ki no Tsurayuki

translated by Earl Miner), written in the female persona.

she's crazy

    The cut burned

    so she flapped her wings

65   and cried out

    but choked

    on blood.

The thread wound around your hand

so tight your fingers

70 turn indigo

    Murasaki

The Shining Prince[6] realized

he could form her

into the one forbidden him. For that

75 he would persist

into old age.

      rice starch

envelope bone, bride

    you can't resist

80 The box of the sparrow's vengeance

contained evils comparable to agent orange

or the minamata disease. The old man

lived happily

without the old woman. But why her?

85 except that she was archetypal.

    She depended on her child

    to the point that when her daughter died

    and she left Tosa

    she could only lie down

90   on the boat's floor

    and sob loudly

    while the waves

    crashed against her side

    almost pleasantly.

95 This depth lent the writer

the soft black silt

on the ocean floor

where all life, some men say, began.

    warp

100 "Mr. Ramsay, stumbling along a passage

one dark morning, stretched his arms out,

but Mrs. Ramsay, having died rather suddenly

the night before, his arms though stretched out,

remained empty."[7]

---

[6]"The Shining Prince" refers to Genji. *Genji-monogatari* (*The Tale of Genji* by Murasaki Shikibu, translated by Arthur Waley). This is the first time Genji hears the child Murasaki whom he later adopts, then marries.
[7]*To the Lighthouse,* Virginia Woolf.

105   when the men wove and women dyed
  mother—
   mutha
  Orchids you explained
  represent female genitalia
110 in Chinese verse.
  Hence the orchid boat.
  Patricia liked that
  and would use it in her collection
  Sex and Weather.
115 the supremes soothed like an older sister
  rubbing your back
  kissing your neck and pulling you into
  motor city, usa
  whether you like it
120 or not that
  was the summer
  of watts and though you
  were in a coma
  as far as that
125 the ramifications
  the ramifications
  bled through transistors
   a *class* act
  blues from indigo, reds
130 from mendoekoe root, yellows, boiling
  tegaran wood
  and sometimes by mudbath
   when you saw her bathing in the dark
   you wanted to dip your hand in
135 *mamagoto suruno?*[8]
   The bride transforms
   into water
   while the groom moves
   like the carp
140   there just under the bridge—
   like the boy with you
   under the forsythia
   scratching and rolling around.
   No, actually you just lay there
145   still and moist.
   still and moist.
   Wondering what next.
  pine

---

[8]*Mamagoto suruno,* Japanese, "playing house."

You're not even certain
which you see—
150   The carp or the reflection of your hand.
the forsythia curled
like cupped hands covering
        bound and unbound
As if blood
155   "The thought of the white linen
        spread out on the deep snow
        the cloth and the snow
        glowing scarlet was enough
        to make him feel that"[9]
160 The sight of him squeezing melons
sniffing one
then splitting it open in the park
was enough to make you feel that
        Naha, Ryukyu Island, Taketome, Shiga,
165   Karayoshi, Tottori, Izo,
resistance does not mean
not drawn it means
        sasou mizu araba
        inamu to zo omou[10]
170 bind the thread
with hemp or banana leaves
before soaking it in the indigo
black as squid as seaweed as his hair
        as his hair
175   as I lick his genitals
        first taking one side
        deep in my mouth then the other
        till he cries softly
        please
180 for days
        Though practical
        you hate annotations
        to the *kokinshu*;[11]
        each note vivisects
185   a *waka*
        like so many petals
        off a stem
        until your lap
        is full of blossoms.

[9]*Yukiguni* (*Snow Country*, Kawabata Yasunari, translated by Edward Seidensticker).

[10]*Sasou* etc. is a quote from a waka (classical Japanese poem) by Ono no Komachi. Donald Keene translated these lines, "were there wa-ter to entice me/ I would follow it, I think." (*Anthology of Japanese Literature*, p. 79).

[11]*Kokinshu* is the Imperial Anthology of poetry completed in 905.

190   How many you destroyed!
        You can't imagine
        Komachi's world
        as real. Hair
        so heavy it adds
195   another layer of brocade
        (black on wisteria,
        plum—)
        forsythia too raw
            and the smell
200   of fresh *tatami*.[12]
            But can you do without
            kono yumei no naka ni[13]
        Can you pull apart the line
        "my heart chars"
205   *kokoro yakeori*
        corridors of thread
            "creating the pattern from memory
            conforming to a certain style
            typical of each island"[14]
210   "K.8. Fragment of ramie kasuri, medium
        blue, with repeating double ikat, and mantled
        turtles and maple leaves of weft ikat.
        Omi Province, Shiga Prefecture,
        Honshu.
215   L. 16.5 cm. W. 19.5 cm."
            "the turtle with strands of seaweed
            growing from its back forming a mantle,
            reputed to live for centuries,"
        Komachi also moved
220   like those shadows in the shallows
        you cannot reach
        though they touch you.
        Wading and feeling
        something light as a curtain
225   around your calves you turn
        to see very small scallops
        rise to the surface
        for a moment of oxygen
        then close up and descend.
230   Caught, you look
        at what he calls their eyes
        (ridges of blue)

---

[12]*Tatami,* straw matting for the floor in Japanese homes.
[13]*Kono* etc., Japanese, for "in this dream."

[14]From another Ono no Komachi poem translated by Earl Miner (*Introduction to Japanese Court Poetry,* p. 82).

and are afraid to touch
that part.
235   from memory or history
sasou mizu
          Grandmother's *ofuro*[15]
          contained giant squid
killer whales
240   hot
omou
          You were afraid he would
          turn to the sea
          to say something
245   that would separate you
          forever
          so kept talking.
          Of course he grew irritable
          and didn't really want
250   a basket of shells
          for the bathroom.
"his arms though stretched out"
          The line shocked you
          like so much of Kawabata
255   who you blame
          for years of humiliation,
          katakana, hiragana, kanji,[16]
at each stroke
          You first hear the squall
260   coming across the lake
          like a sheet of glass.
          You start to cry and daddy
          rows toward the shore and mother.
in the Malayan Archipelago
265   Georgia O'Keeffe's orchid shocked you
          so even now you can picture the fragrance
"Should a stranger witness the performance
he is compelled to dip his finger
into the dye and taste it. Those employed
270 must never mention the names of dead people
or animals. Pregnant or sick women
are not allowed to look on;
should this happen they are punished
as strangers."
275   in the Malayan Archipelago

---

[15] *Ofuro,* Japanese bathtub.
[16] *Katakana,* etc., are the Japanese syllabaries
  and the Chinese characters, respectively.

where boys give their sweethearts
shuttles they will carve, burn,
name,
"language does not differ
280 from instruments of production,
from machines, let us say,"[17]
knocked down
knocked *up girl*
"the superstructure"
285 he wouldn't stop talking
about *deep structure*
and mention in prayer
but you need more than the female persona.
A swatch of cloth.
290 A pressed flower. The taste of powder
brushed against your lips.
pine
matsu[18]
The wedding day chosen
295 he brought you animal crackers
cloths
Pushing aside the branches
you crawl in
on your hands and knees,
300 lie back,
and light up.
tabako chodai[19]
because the forsythia
symbolizes so much
305 of sneakers,
cloth ABC books, charms,
sankyu[20]
the "charred heart"
would be reconstructed thus:
310 "Before the golden Buddha, I will lay
Poems as my flowers,
Entering in the Way,
Entering in the Way."[21]
fuck that shit
315 Link the sections
with fragrance: *matsu*

---

[17]Joseph Stalin, *Marxism and the Problems of Linguistics.*

[18]*Matsu,* Japanese, "pine tree" and "wait."

[19]*Tabako chodai,* Japanese, "give me a cigarette [tobacco]."

[20]*Sankyu,* Japanese pronunciation of "thank you."

[21]Noh play by Kan'ami Kiyotsugu, "Sotoba Komachi," supposedly about Ono no Komachi's repentance. (Keene, p. 270.)

shards of ice
The bride spread out her dress
for the dry cleaners
320 then picked kernels of rice
off the quilt and from her hair.
bits of china
the lining unfolds
out of the body
325 through hormonal revolutions
gravity and chance
lick that plate clean
can I get a cigarette
got a match
330 click clack, click
clack
chodai
in this dream
She wrapped the ikat
335 around her waist and set out
for Hausa, Yoruba, Ewe of Ghana,
Baule, Madagascar, and Northern Edo
I pull off my dress
and take a deep breath.
340 The cupped hands open then
onto the loom.
click clack click
clack
and in the rhythmic chore
345 I imagine a daughter in my lap
who I will never give away
but see off
with a bundle of cloths
dyed with resistance

1989

Cuttings

a zuihitsu for father

My younger sister and I, cleaning father's house before he returns from a week in intensive care, rush to dispose of mother's cosmetics, store her jewelry for a later date, and phone a woman's shelter to pick up bags of dresses, size 4, and shoes, 4½, even stopping to laugh at the platforms

5 from "the mod era" she swore would come back. We collapse into
each other's arms and cry *mommy mommy* as if she could hear us if we
wept loud enough.

I look out the taxi window at everyone else's life. Certainly all the
people in all the little apartments have gone about their business
10 making money off other people's mortgages or addictions, without the
knowledge my mother died last week, someone who found pleasure in
baking oddly shaped biscuits with her granddaughters.

I keep my father talking about his boyhood—his passion for deep-sea
diving though he grew up on Lake Michigan, his going AWOL for art
15 courses, the four books at the Naval Library on "Oriental Art." Here
we turn, always return, to Maude who *wasn't supposed to go first.* He
said he had her convinced.

I ask Marie how to tell the girls, Miya now six and Rei, four. She advises
we speak to them separately, to allow each their own reactions.

20 The funeral director says, "She doesn't look 68, but then oriental
women never look their age." He then reminisces about "The War."

I want to throw out as much as possible—a half-jar of expensive cream,
a suede jacket—belongings my sister wishes to hold on to. I go to the
Funeral Home. I find comfort in The 10 O'clock News; she resents the
25 superficial, even stupid resemblance of normality.

Two weeks now since mother died. Tuesday nights, I stay with father
now a man who can barely contain what, in a second, became memory.
He lurches from each small room testing himself against souvenirs:
animal puppets from Rome, 1956; a Noh mask, Kyoto, '64; silver
30 rabbit, Phnom Penh, '65; hotel towel, Chicago, '70. Even after
discarding her dresses and middle-class perfumes she inhabits every
corner of every project—collage, painting, carving. He recalls telling
her when they first met at the Art Institute that art would always come
before any thing and any one.

35 We toast Maude at a neighbor's, drinking what we like since she
couldn't tolerate liquor. Janet remembers the day she knew they'd be
friends: "We were looking at the peonies by the stone wall and your
mother said, *Know what these remind me of? Penises.*" Our laughter
resembles sobbing.

40 She reread stories as often as I demanded.

Convinced and convincing me through my early twenties I could not
sew or cook despite home ec. classes and odd advice, she cooked and

froze stews, checked if I ever baked potatoes and the last day we
saw her, sent us home with turkey leftovers. It's true I've never roasted
45 one.

The first thing I saw when I returned to clean their house were my three
skirts, pinned and draped across the ironing board.

How suddenly grievances against father evaporate, steam rising from
an icy river. He even corrects himself, calling mother, *a woman.*

50 Why is pain deeper than pleasure, though it is a pleasure to cry so loud
the arthritic dog hobbles off the sunny carpet, so loud I do not hear the
phone ring, so loud I feel a passion for mother I thought I reserved for
lovers. I insert a CD and sing about a love abandoned, because there
are no other lyrics for this.

55 Pulling off a crewneck sweater I bend my glasses and for the next few
days wear the frames off-center not realizing the dizzy view is in fact
physical.

Theresa, David, Liz, Mark, Sharon, Denise, Carmen, Sonia, Susan, Lee,
Cheryl, Susan, Jo, John, Jerry, Doug, Earlene, Marie, Robbin, Jessica,
60 Kiana, Patricia, Bob, Donna, Orinne, Shigemi—

Suddenly the tasks we put off need to get done: defrost the freezer, pay
the preschool bill, order more checks.

For 49 days after her own mother's death she did not eat meat. I didn't
know, mother. I'm sorry, I didn't know.

65 The sudden scent of her spills from her handbag—leather, lotion,
mints, coins. I cannot stand.

She had marked April 28 to see Okinawan dancers.

He has not yet slept in their bed, because the couch in front of the
television *feels firmer* to his seven broken ribs.

70 At dinner we play a story game; the younger one asks, "about
grandma?" then corrects herself quickly "about bunny rabbit" as she
momentarily trips on her own preoccupation.

Father tells me there is a Japanese story about a mask maker who has a
daughter renowned for her stunning beauty. Upon her untimely death,
75 how he does not recall, the father sits by her side to sketch the exquisite
features. Poetic license. Though mother did look beautiful I had never
seen a face devoid of any expression, an aspect even a painting would
somehow contain.

The children notice he has taken off his wedding ring.

80 At a favorite cafe I hear a newborn in the next booth wailing for, probably,
the mother's breast, as if his life will end this second. It is my cry.

Shrimp. An image of my parents at a card table shelling shrimp the
night before my sister's wedding, the peels translucent pink as my
mother's fingernails. Primitive and reassuring.

85 At the house in Paia where grandma washed other people's laundry
and raised her chickens, and grandpa sat in his wheelchair, we had a
toilet inside but also the old outhouse, a rickety two-seater. I would go
in, close the gray-painted door, latch the hook and sit on the edge
holding my breath against the frothy stench of shit. You could hear
your waste
90 hit bottom. The dim light lent privacy against peeping cousins.

She taught me to pluck or cut flowers near the roots for the long stems.
Recut under water. She taught me to rub my finger and thumb together
over the silver dollar sheath, to rub off the brown membrane and
scatter the seeds on my skirt. Gently so as not to tear the silver inside. I
95 see them and think of her name, not Maude, but Mother.

Father and I bring the ashes into the City and plan to drop them off at
the temple. Mrs. K has Buddhist robes over her blue jeans and suggests
she recite a sutra. We light incense in the half-light. I forget tissues. My
face and sleeves are covered with tears and mucus. My shoulders shake
100 silently as listening.

Three months have past. I count the days from March 10th to the 100th
day for another memorial service.

lotus suture

As if a metaphor for mother's death the Rodney King verdict and
105 rebellion in Los Angeles breaks open urban areas across the country. It
is a complex set of issues where some Korean shops and whites are
attacked as the emblems of the establishment. But what is the
establishment? Why not the actual property relations? Who actually
owns the buildings, makes the laws—I feel helpless. Embittered.

110 Cuttings she had placed in tumblers in the kitchen and bathroom offer
their fragile roots.

Rei discusses mother's death with me. A babysitter told her not to talk
about it. Another told her it is *like sleep.* I tell her to talk. I tell her it is
not sleep although the person looks asleep but he or she will not wake.
115 She wants to talk to grandma and asks if she can. I tell her if she wants

to she can; then I ask her what she wants to say. She wants to tell her to wake up.

People who have died but were revived speak of a dark tunnel with a fierce light at the end. Is it a passage or is it the memory of birth?

120 Miya speaks of dying—to see grandma again. I am shocked and try to say something.

I can see her body, not *her,* her body lying in a pine box, hands folded, black and white hair combed back, the funeral home odor saturating the drapes and carpets of the respectfully lit parlors. I said goodbye but 125 it was really *to myself.*

I wish I had snipped off a bit of hair. I recall the braid she kept for a while in her drawer.

I purchase an expensive "anti-wrinkle defense cream" at the discount pharmacy. The third morning my skin really feels smoother though the 130 burgeoning lines have not faded. I think something I've only thought the night before the plane trip: will I live to see the bottom of this jar.

Miya has shelved her grief and when admonished she declares: everything was fine until grandma died.

For the first time father harvests a half-dozen bamboo shoots from a 135 small grove on the side of the house. Mother had spoken of gathering them as a child in Hawaii, soaking then boiling then sizzling them. He finds a recipe and experiments. He sends some home with me. They taste like artichoke hearts. We all think of mother. And I think of a poem from the *Manyōshu* about a trowel.

140 He plays her lottery numbers.

The lawyer of the kid who broadsided their car sends a letter threatening to sue father if he does not respond in five days with information. We feel naive, in a state of disbelief at the vulgar tone of the letter.

145 I wear the silk pants she altered for me: a forgotten pin, sewn into the hem, sticks into my ankle.

At any moment of the day I can hear her admonishment: *oh, Kimi.* She especially disliked spills.

I do not want to write about her death. But I do not want to lose these 150 strong feelings.

Rei does not stop chattering about her: We have no one to make slush. She always had gum in her handbag. She read to us in Japanese and knew "cat's cradle" backward.

155 The 100th Day Anniversary. The weather is already warm. Her brother from Honolulu tells about her letters to him during World War II when he was in the 442nd.

We vacation on Fire Island. A few deer walk by the porch so close we can see how fuzzy their antlers are.

160 I keep recalling the diagram of the accident scene. Mother's body lying on the highway where medics attempted CPR. I imagine the wet black road, the traffic signals changing despite the halt.

Christmas ornaments last packed away by her: the balls she and father decorated with cherubs and glitter, old wooden angels and soldiers from my childhood, tinsel carefully rewrapped.

165 Some days I have a thought to write down but let it go.

During a week-long visit to the snowy fields of Vermont, I hear of a car bomb explosion at the World Trade Center, killing and injuring many people. The world continues outside this quiet. And the death of those who happen to step in its ordinary traffic.

170 I stop writing altogether. And when I must—postcards, single lines after a commute—the writing ends with mother.

Afraid father is "seeing someone" and hopeful. I extend mother's jealousy into the afterlife. It becomes my own hell.

I begin to feel impatient with father over little things like whether my
175 hair is trimmed evenly. I wonder if my annoyance indicates we are moving on.

Father finds an envelope of marigold seeds mother saved and lets the children scatter them. The composted earth smells fertile like the pail she kept with egg shells and melon rinds.

1995

Lynda Barry b. 1956

In the volume *The Best American Comics 2006,* the cartoonist, novelist, and writing teacher Lynda Barry's biography notes that she was born in Wisconsin "to a woman who came from the Philippines on a military transport plane and a navy man who drank and bowled." Barry spent much of her childhood in working-class Seattle, and many of her stories take place in racially mixed neighborhoods not unlike the one in which she grew up. She lives in Wisconsin today.

The author of fourteen books, Barry is one of the best-known active literary cartoonists and a chronicler of American adolescence. Her weekly syndicated comic strip, *Ernie Pook's Comeek,* has been running for thirty years. In reviewing Barry's 2002 comics work *One Hundred Demons* in the *New York Times,* the author Nick Hornby wrote, "Barry seems to me to almost single-handedly justify the form; she's one of America's very best contemporary writers." *One Hundred Demons,* like Barry's other major work, is finely tuned to capturing the cadences of childhood.

Barry attended Evergreen State College and shortly thereafter began producing comic strips for an alternative newspaper, the *Chicago Reader.* Her first book collections, *Girls and Boys* (1981) and *Big Ideas* (1983), focus on the often absurd and painful ins and outs of adult romantic relationships. Texts such as the so-called coloring book with fiction, *Naked Ladies! Naked Ladies! Naked Ladies!* (1984), and *Everything in the World* (1986) explore more fully the voices and consciousness of children. An examination of the creative texture of children's everyday lives has marked and defined Barry's work in the intervening years, when she published eight comics collections; two illustrated prose novels, *The Good Times Are Killing Me* (1988) and *Cruddy* (1999); and one ambiguous foray into comics nonfiction, *Demons,* which she called an "autobifictionalography."

In works such as *The Fun House* (1987), *Down the Street* (1989), and *My Perfect Life* (1992), Barry demonstrates the powerful economy of comics prose and expressive drawing to provide humor, insight, and pathos. According to Hornby, Barry's stories "contain little grenades of meaning that tend to explode just after you've read the last line." Many of her pieces—most of which are told in short, four-panel segments—show how the comics form doesn't simply illustrate words with pictures but offers two separate narrative tracks to dramatic effect. In "Help You," for example, the voice of a teenager speculating about her father's whereabouts during a school typing class is stamped over images of a man in a bar far away.

Although Barry is often funny, her oeuvre is unflinching and dark. In *It's So Magic* (1994), for instance, she looks at the horror of sexual abuse and acknowledges that the brutality of childhood is as much a part of the terrain as is playing and its unexpected elations. Writing the Unthinkable, the title of her popular writing course centered on memory, reflects this breadth. The unthinkable in the course's title isn't trauma but the positive ability to see any detail—good or bad, big or small—as relevant to the construction of experience.

Hillary Chute
Harvard University

Messed Up and Confused

Help You

Family Pictures

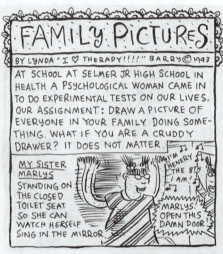

It's Cool

IT'S COOL

BY LYNDA "BACHELOR PARTY" BARRY © 1991

"THERE'S JUST SOME THINGS THAT MEN HAVE TO KEEP TO THEMSELVES." IS WHAT THE BOY EDDIE DAVIS SAID WHEN I GOT TO THE SNEAK OUT PLACE WHERE I WAS SUPPOSED TO MEET CINDY LUDERMYER. IT WAS 1 AM AND SHE WASN'T THERE. ONLY EDDIE AND ANOTHER GUY VINCENT.

"SO SHE WAS ALREADY HERE THEN?" I ASK. EDDIE SAYS "MAYBE YES AND MAYBE NO." I GO, "QUIT BEING A SPAZ. WHERE IS SHE?" ON A ROCK I SEE HER SWEATER. THAT'S WHEN HE SAYS THE MEN THING AND WHEN VINCENT PUTS HIS ARM AROUND ME. "IT'S COOL." HE SAYS. "IT'S COOL. DON'T FREAK OUT." I GO "I'M NOT FREAKING OUT."

BUT I WAS FREAKING OUT. SLIGHTLY FREAKING OUT. FREAKING OUT FOR ME AND FREAKING OUT FOR CINDY WHO LOVES BOONES FARM APPLE WINE AND THERE'S THE BOTTLE EMPTY ON ITS SIDE BY THE ROCK. CINDY WHO I SAID I WOULD GUARD. "COME ON YOU GUYS TELL ME WHERE SHE'S AT." THEN A WALKING NOISE IN THE BUSHES. "CINDY?" I SAY. "CINDY?"

NO. IT'S DAN. THE ORIGINAL GUY OF THE CATHOLIC BOYS WHO CINDY LIKED. HE'S BRUSHING HIS PANTS OFF AND WIPING HIS MOUTH. "EDDIE." HE SAYS. "EDDIE." THEN HE POINTS INTO THE WOODS. "SHE'S ASKIN' FOR YOU." EDDIE GOES AND I TRY TO FOLLOW. "HEY." DAN SAYS. HE PUSHES HIS HANDS AGAINST MY SHOULDERS. "DON'T FREAK OUT, MAN. IT'S COOL. IT'S COOL."

She Wanted It, She Wanted It

If You Want to Know Teenagers by Mar Lys

Li-Young Lee b. 1957

Li-Young Lee has been praised for his passionate poetry and its deceptively simple style. His poems are unique in their emotional intensity and metaphysical abstraction, particularly at a time when many contemporary American poets are breaking away from the "lyric I" in order to articulate an unstable and plural "I." Lee's three prize-winning books, *Rose* (1986), *The City in Which I Love You* (1990), and *The Winged Seed: A Remembrance* (1995), share recurrent themes of love, exile, and mortality. Haunted by memories, Lee's poems are exploratory, showing a relentless search for understanding and for the right language to give form to what is invisible and evanescent. He once said, "When I write, I'm trying to make that which is *visible*—this face, this body, this person—*invisible,* and at the same time, make what is *invisible*—that which exists at the level of pure *being*—completely visible." Critics who celebrate the disappearance of the "lyric I" from postmodern poetry as the only possible way of opening the poetic to the historical and political might take issue with Lee's poetics. Yet for minority American poets like Lee to explore the interior and the abstract may not be as escapist or politically inconsequential as some critics might think.

Lee was born in 1957 in Indonesia of Chinese parents. His mother, a granddaughter of Yuan Shi-kai, China's first president (1912–1916), married the son of a gangster and an entrepreneur. His parents' marriage in Communist China was much frowned upon, and they eventually fled to Indonesia, where Lee's father taught medicine and philosophy at Gamliel University in Jakarta and served as President Sukarno's medical adviser. In 1959, when Sukarno launched a violent ethnic purge of the Chinese, Lee's father was incarcerated for his interest in Western culture and ideas; he loved Shakespeare, opera, and Kierkegaard, and he taught the King James version of the Bible. After nineteen months of imprisonment, he escaped; with his family, he traveled to Macao, Japan, and Singapore before settling in Hong Kong, where he became a revered evangelist minister. In 1964, the family emigrated to the United States. Lee's father studied at the Pittsburgh Theological Seminary and later became a Presbyterian minister. Lee went to the University of Pittsburgh, where he took Gerald Stern's poetry writing class and earned his B.A. in 1979; he continued to study creative writing at the University of Arizona and the State University of New York at Brockport. He lives in Chicago with his wife and their two sons.

Lee's father and his family's experience of exile have had a significant impact on Lee's poetry. As a child, he learned to recite Chinese poems from the Tang dynasty (618–907) and was often enchanted by his father's poetic preaching and reading of the Psalms. Many of his poems recall his father, who is portrayed as strict and tender, powerful and vulnerable, godlike and human.

Breaking away from linear, rhetorical structure, Lee's poems unfold and expand from a central image, which holds together the discontinuous narratives and fragmentary scenes. Similar to the functions of imagery in classical Chinese poetry, his composition method gives him greater freedom in making leaps from narrative to lyricism and from the concrete to the abstract. Lee's poems bring together Eastern and Western ideas and traditions. Among the literary influences that Lee has acknowledged are the biblical Song of Songs, Gerald Stern's *Lucky Life,* Kierkegaard's *Fear and Trembling,* Meister Eckhart's sermons, and Rainer Maria Rilke's "Duino Elegies." The spiritual and emotional experience of the poems is accompanied by a down-to-earth sensualness that Lee says "comes from my obsession with the body, man-body, earth-body, woman-body, father-body, mother-body, mind-body (for I experience the mind as another body) and the poem body." This vision may suggest the influence of Whitman, but it is also rooted in Daoism. Lee is familiar with Daoist texts and admires Lao Zi, Lie Zi, and Zhuang Zi, whose sense of wonder and mystery and whose paradoxical and skeptical characteristics are evident in Lee's poems and prose-poem memoir.

Xiaojing Zhou

State University of New York–Buffalo

PRIMARY WORKS

Rose, 1986; *The City in Which I Love You,* 1990; *The Winged Seed,* 1995; *Book of My Nights,* 2001; *Behind My Eyes,* 2008.

I Ask My Mother to Sing

She begins, and my grandmother joins her.
Mother and daughter sing like young girls.
If my father were alive, he would play
his accordion and sway like a boat.

5   I've never been in Peking, or the Summer Palace,
nor stood on the great Stone Boat to watch
the rain begin on Kuen Ming Lake, the picnickers
running away in the grass.

But I love to hear it sung;
10 how the waterlilies fill with rain until
they overturn, spilling water into water,
then rock back, and fill with more.

Both women have begun to cry.
But neither stops her song.

                                        1986

My Father, in Heaven, Is Reading Out Loud

My father, in heaven, is reading out loud
to himself Psalms or news. Now he ponders what
he's read. No. He is listening for the sound
of children in the yard. Was that laughing
5   or crying? So much depends upon the
answer, for either he will go on reading,

or he'll run to save a child's day from grief.
As it is in heaven, so it was on earth.

Because my father walked the earth with a grave,
10 determined rhythm, my shoulders ached
from his gaze. Because my father's shoulders
ached from the pulling of oars, my life now moves
with a powerful back-and-forth rhythm:
nostalgia, speculation. Because he
15 made me recite a book a month, I forget
everything as soon as I read it. And knowledge
never comes but while I'm mid-stride a flight
of stairs, or lost a moment on some avenue.

A remarkable disappointment to him,
20 I am like anyone who arrives late
in the millennium and is unable
to stay to the end of days. The world's
beginnings are obscure to me, its outcomes
inaccessible. I don't understand
25 the source of starlight, or starlight's destinations.
And already another year slides out
of balance. But I don't disparage scholars;
my father was one and I loved him,
who packed his books once, and all of our belongings,
30 then sat down to await instruction
from his god, yes, but also from a radio.
At the doorway, I watched, and I suddenly
knew he was one like me, who got my learning
under a lintel; he was one of the powerless,
35 to whom knowledge came while he sat among
suitcases, boxes, old newspapers, string.

He did not decide peace or war, home or exile,
escape by land or escape by sea.
He waited merely, as always someone
40 waits, far, near, here, hereafter, to find out:
is it praise or lament hidden in the next moment?

1990

With Ruins

Choose a quiet
place, a ruins, a house no more
a house,

under whose stone archway I stood
5 one day to duck the rain.

The roofless floor, vertical
studs, eight wood columns
supporting nothing,
two staircases careening to nowhere, all
10 make it seem

a sketch, notes to a house, a three-
dimensional grid negotiating
absences,
an idea
15 receding into indefinite rain,

or else that idea
emerging, skeletal
against the hammered sky, a
human thing, scoured, seen clean
20 through from here to an iron heaven.

A place where things
were said and done,
there you can remember
what you need to
25 remember. Melancholy is useful. Bring yours.

                   1990

This Room and Everything in It

Lie still now
while I prepare for my future,
certain hard days ahead,
when I'll need what I know so clearly this moment.

5 I am making use
of the one thing I learned
of all the things my father tried to teach me:
the art of memory.

I am letting this room
10 and everything in it
stand for my ideas about love
and its difficulties.

I'll let your love-cries,
those spacious notes

15 of a moment ago,
     stand for distance.

     Your scent,
     that scent
     of spice and a wound,
20 I'll let stand for mystery.

     Your sunken belly
     is the daily cup
     of milk I drank
     as a boy before morning prayer.

25 The sun on the face
     of the wall
     is God, the face
     I can't see, my soul,

     and so on, each thing
30 standing for a separate idea,
     and those ideas forming the constellation
     of my greater idea.
     And one day, when I need
     to tell myself something intelligent
35 about love,

     I'll close my eyes
     and recall this room and everything in it:
     My body is estrangement.
     This desire, perfection.
40 Your closed eyes my extinction.
     Now I've forgotten my
     idea. The book
     on the windowsill, riffled by wind . . .
     the even-numbered pages are
45 the past, the odd-
     numbered pages, the future.
     The sun is
     God, your body is milk . . .

     useless, useless . . .
50 your cries are song, my body's not me . . .
     no good . . . my idea
     has evaporated . . . your hair is time, your thighs are song . . .
     it had something to do
     with death . . . it had something
55 to do with love.

                                                              1990

Alison Bechdel b. 1960

Alison Bechdel's comic strip, *Dykes to Watch Out For,* chronicles the contemporary lives and loves of various characters—mostly, although not entirely, lesbian ones. It first appeared in 1983 and continues to be read widely in national newspaper syndication and on the Internet (at www .dykestowatchoutfor.com).

Bechdel, who was born and raised in rural Pennsylvania, describes her formative influences as "Chas. Addams, *Mad Magazine,* Norman Rockwell, and Edward Gorey." Shortly after she graduated from Oberlin College, she became aware of the magazine *Gay Comix.* As she explains in an interview in *Modern Fiction Studies,* seeing this title—which was part of the comix scene of independently published, often radical and experimental, work— she felt, "'Oh, man! You can do cartoons about your own real life as a gay person.'" Bechdel explains, "And that was quite momentous for me. . . . It was right around then that I started doing my own comics."

Although Bechdel's experiences as a gay woman have informed *DTWOF,* she did not delve into her own life as a subject until she started work on *Fun Home: A Family Tragicomic* in 2000. *Fun Home* explores Bechdel's relationship with her father—an English teacher, part-time undertaker, obsessive restorer of the family's Victorian gothic house, and closeted gay man.

It is a breakthrough book in several different ways. First, it catapulted Bechdel, who lives in Vermont, from a popular alternative cartoonist to a mainstream literary figure. Widely acclaimed for its intricacy, density, and intelligence, *Fun Home* made the *New York Times* best-seller list, a rarity for literary graphic narratives since *Maus. Fun Home* was also nominated for a 2006 National Book Critics Circle Award in memoir/autobiography. Second, *Fun Home* became a crossover hit as a book

about gayness and as a book in the form of comics. In 2006, *Fun Home* made *People* magazine's list of the top ten books of the year, was named *Entertainment Weekly's* best nonfiction book of the year, and was named *Time* magazine's all-around, number one book of the year in any category.

Fun Home's success is an indicator of the acceptance that serious work in the form of comics is finally gaining in the United States and is also a testament to Bechdel's skill as a researcher and archivist of her own life and as an author who can create complex and moving narratives out of life experience. The book is thick with archival materials (including maps, arrest records, letters, diaries, sketchbooks, and photographs) that Bechdel meticulously reproduces as she weaves past and present events and ruminations together.

A highly crafted work, *Fun Home* is engaged with modernist fiction as a kind of lens through which it unfurls its story. In a related way—through references to Joyce's *Ulysses*—it also draws on Greek mythology to figure the relationship between Bruce Bechdel, a petty tyrant who often treated his children coldly and eventually committed suicide, and Alison, whose exploration of her father's early death is driven by both intense identification and disidentification. *Fun Home,* like the best works of literature, suggests that there are no easy answers. As Bechdel puts it in "In the Shadow of Young Girls in Flower," a chapter whose title is taken from Proust, "Perhaps this undifferentiation, this nonduality, is the point." *Fun Home* explores the knotty filial connection brilliantly, its words and images dependent on each other for meaning.

Hillary Chute
Harvard University

from Fun Home: A Family Tragicomic

I DEVELOPED A CONTEMPT FOR USE-LESS ORNAMENT. WHAT FUNCTION WAS SERVED BY THE SCROLLS, TASSELS, AND BRIC-A-BRAC THAT INFESTED OUR HOUSE?

IF ANYTHING, THEY OBSCURED FUNCTION. THEY WERE EMBELLISHMENTS IN THE WORST SENSE.

INCIPIENT YELLOW LUNG DISEASE

THEY WERE LIES.

MY FATHER BEGAN TO SEEM MORALLY SUSPECT TO ME LONG BEFORE I KNEW THAT HE ACTUALLY HAD A DARK SECRET.

MOM SAYS HURRY UP.

"BRONZING STICK"

HE USED HIS SKILLFUL ARTIFICE NOT TO MAKE THINGS, BUT TO MAKE THINGS APPEAR TO BE WHAT THEY WERE NOT.

MASS WILL BE OVER BEFORE WE GET THERE.

THAT IS TO SAY, IMPECCABLE.

STILL, SOMETHING VITAL WAS MISSING.

WELL?

ME, AGE 4

MY BROTHER CHRISTIAN, AGE 3

AN ELASTICITY, A MARGIN FOR ERROR.

HOW DID THIS VASE GET SO CLOSE TO THE EDGE OF THE TABLE?

BUT I DIDN'T DO ANYTHING!

MOST PEOPLE, I IMAGINE, LEARN TO ACCEPT THAT THEY'RE NOT PERFECT.

BUT AN IDLE REMARK ABOUT MY FATHER'S TIE OVER BREAKFAST COULD SEND HIM INTO A TAILSPIN.

PEACE, MAN.

IF WE COULDN'T CRITICIZE MY FATHER, SHOWING AFFECTION FOR HIM WAS AN EVEN DICIER VENTURE.

THIS EMBARRASSMENT ON MY PART WAS A TINY SCALE MODEL OF MY FATHER'S MORE FULLY DEVELOPED SELF-LOATHING.

HIS SHAME INHABITED OUR HOUSE AS PERVASIVELY AND INVISIBLY AS THE AROMATIC MUSK OF AGING MAHOGANY.

IN FACT, THE METICULOUS, PERIOD INTERIORS WERE EXPRESSLY DESIGNED TO CONCEAL IT.

MIRRORS, DISTRACTING BRONZES, MULTIPLE DOORWAYS. VISITORS OFTEN GOT LOST UPSTAIRS.

GRACIOUS, I ALMOST WALKED RIGHT INTO THIS!

MY MOTHER, MY BROTHERS, AND I KNEW OUR WAY AROUND WELL ENOUGH, BUT IT WAS IMPOSSIBLE TO TELL IF THE MINOTAUR LAY BEYOND THE NEXT CORNER.

AND THE CONSTANT TENSION WAS HEIGHTENED BY THE FACT THAT SOME ENCOUNTERS COULD BE QUITE PLEASANT.

HIS BURSTS OF KINDNESS WERE AS INCANDESCENT AS HIS TANTRUMS WERE DARK.

ALTHOUGH I'M GOOD AT ENUMERATING MY FATHER'S FLAWS, IT'S HARD FOR ME TO SUSTAIN MUCH ANGER AT HIM.

I EXPECT THIS IS PARTLY BECAUSE HE'S DEAD, AND PARTLY BECAUSE THE BAR IS LOWER FOR FATHERS THAN FOR MOTHERS.

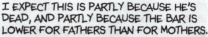

MY MOTHER MUST HAVE BATHED ME HUNDREDS OF TIMES. BUT IT'S MY FATHER RINSING ME OFF WITH THE PURPLE METAL CUP THAT I REMEMBER MOST CLEARLY.

...THE SUDDEN, UNBEARABLE COLD OF ITS ABSENCE.

WAS HE A GOOD FATHER? I WANT TO SAY, "AT LEAST HE STUCK AROUND." BUT OF COURSE, HE DIDN'T.

IT'S TRUE THAT HE DIDN'T KILL HIMSELF UNTIL I WAS NEARLY TWENTY.

BUT HIS ABSENCE RESONATED RETRO-ACTIVELY, ECHOING BACK THROUGH ALL THE TIME I KNEW HIM.

MAYBE IT WAS THE CONVERSE OF THE WAY AMPUTEES FEEL PAIN IN A MISSING LIMB.

HE REALLY WAS THERE ALL THOSE YEARS, A FLESH–AND–BLOOD PRESENCE STEAMING OFF THE WALLPAPER, DIGGING UP THE DOGWOODS, POLISHING THE FINIALS...

...SMELLING OF SAWDUST AND SWEAT AND DESIGNER COLOGNE.

BUT I ACHED AS IF HE WERE ALREADY GONE.

David Foster Wallace 1962–2008

One of the defining publishing events of the 1900s was surely the 1996 release of *Infinite Jest,* an anaconda text (more than a thousand pages, with more than nine hundred explanatory notes) that was only the second novel of a soft-spoken creative writing professor from Illinois State University, whose scruffy demeanor and trademark bandanna quickly became elements of his new celebrity. Critical estimations and fan websites quickly dubbed this reluctant celebrity, at thirty-four, the Literary Voice of Generation X, the Heir Apparent to Thomas Pynchon, the Grunge Wunderkind, a hip cross between Charles Dickens and Robin Williams, James Joyce and Hunter Thompson. Born in Ithaca, New York, the son of two respected academics, Wallace enjoyed a remarkably unremarkable childhood in Illinois (save for a time as a nationally ranked player on the junior tennis circuit), a bookworm given to the indiscriminate absorption of television. Although he evidenced promise in mathematical philosophy at Amherst, Wallace felt more compelled by fiction (he cites reading the metafictionist Donald Barthelme in particular). He completed his B.A. *summa cum laude* in 1985 and went on for his M.F.A. from the University of Arizona in 1987. By then he had already published his first novel, *The Broom of the System* (1986), his senior thesis at Amherst, a rollicking speculation on Ludwig Wittgenstein's language theories that centers on a mass exodus from a Cleveland nursing home.

After ten years and a growing reputation from his short stories and essays, Wallace released *Infinite Jest.* Because of its massive intricacy; its savvy indulgence of pop culture referents; its scores of eccentric characters; its labyrinthine plot (centering on a halfway house for recovering addicts and a nearby tennis academy); its multiple genres and shifting perspectives; its encyclopedic command of the metaphors of recreational pharmaceuticals, information theory, and mathematical sciences; its exuberant wordplay, its deliberate excess, and its often sophomoric humor, *Infinite Jest* was immediately linked to the dense avant-garde experimental texts of postmodernism that had audaciously—and self-consciously—extended fiction's form, including Pynchon's *Gravity's Rainbow* and William Gaddis's *The Recognitions.* Wallace's ambitious novel, clearly informed by these narrative audacities, was both hailed as innovative and energetic, seductive and playful, and derided as imitative and self-indulgent, inaccessible and unreadable.

Wallace himself qualified the assessment. Moved by the minimalist fiction of the late 1970s, especially Raymond Carver's restrained and unpretentious examinations of the strangled lives of ordinary people, Wallace argued that formal experimentation overintellectualized narrative and inevitably prized authorial ingenuity and self-justifying novelty, thus alienating a contemporary readership already diminished by seductive entertainment technologies, most prominently television. As he told the *Review of Contemporary Fiction* in 1993, "If a piece of fiction can allow us imaginatively to identify with a character's pain, we might then more easily conceive of others identifying with our own. This is nourishing, redemptive." That dynamic agenda moved Wallace to the forefront of a group of fin-de-millennium postpostmodern writers—among them, Richard Powers, Rick Moody, William Vollmann, and Jonathan Franzen—who balance postmodernism's radical experimentation with traditional explorations of character and theme, most often the inviolable loneliness at the heart of the Information Age. "The Devil Is a Busy Man," published after the hoopla of *Infinite Jest,* is just such a fiction: a subversive experiment in form—an uninterrupted monologue, a concise verbal construct, a voice without context (nameless, genderless)—in which a character struggles with the tangled motivation behind a simple act of charity and comes to reveal a paralyzing self-consciousness, a character trapped by decency and stranded in a moral universe where good and evil are ultimately indistinguishable and motivation is unreadable.

Wallace's work has been accorded several prestigious awards and has compelled the significant academic attention that sig-nals that he is more than a trendy celebrity. His post-*Infinite Jest* publications—innovative short fictions, insightful essays on popular culture, and a provocative study on the mathematical principle of infinity—herald a defining voice for the new century, tragically silenced by his premature death by suicide in 2008.

Joseph Dewey
University of Pittsburgh at Johnstown

PRIMARY WORKS

The Broom of the System (a novel), 1986; *Girl with Curious Hair* (short stories), 1989; *Signifying Rappers: Rap and Race in the Urban Present* (co-written with Mark Costello), 1990; *Infinite Jest* (a novel), 1996; *A Supposedly Fun Thing I'll Never Do Again: Essays and Argument*, 1997; *Brief Interviews with Hideous Men: Stories*, 1999; *Everything and More: A Compact History of Infinity*, 2003; *Oblivion: Stories*, 2004.

The Devil Is a Busy Man

Three weeks ago, I did a nice thing for someone. I can not say more than this, or it will empty what I did of any of its true, ultimate value. I can only say: a nice thing. In a general context, it involved money. It was not a matter of out and out "giving money" to someone. But it was close. It was more classifiable as "diverting" money to someone in "need." For me, this is as specific as I can be.

It was two weeks, six days, ago that the nice thing I did occurred. I can also mention that I was out of town—meaning, in other words, I was not where I live. Explaining why I was out of town, or where I was, or what the overall situation that was going on was, however, unfortunately, would endanger the value of what I did further. Thus, I was explicit with the lady that the person who would receive the money was to in no way know who had diverted it to them. Steps were explicitly taken so that my namelessness was structured into the arrangement which led to the diversion of the money. (Although the money was, technically, not mine, the secretive arrangement by which I diverted it was properly legal. This may lead one to wonder in what way the money was not "mine," but, unfortunately, I am unable to explain in detail. It is, however, true.) This is the reason. A lack of namelessness on my part would destroy the ultimate value of the nice act. Meaning, it would infect the "motivation" for my nice gesture—meaning, in other words, that part of my motivation for it would be, not generosity, but desiring gratitude, affection, and approval towards me to result. Despairingly, this selfish motive would empty the nice gesture of any ultimate value, and cause me to once again fail in my efforts to be classifiable as a nice or "good" person.

Thus, I was very intransigent about the secrecy of my own name in the arrangement, and the lady, who was the only other person with any knowing part in the arrangement (she, because of her job, could be classified as "the instrument" of the diversion of the money) whatsoever, acquiesced, to the best of my knowledge, in full to this.

Two weeks, five days, later, one of the people I had done the nice thing for (the generous diversion of funds was to two people—more specifically, a common law married couple—but only one of them called) called, and said, "hello," and that did I, by any possible chance, know anything about who was responsible for _____, because he just wanted to tell that person, "thank you!," and what a God-send this ____ dollars that came, seemingly, out of nowhere from the _____ was, etc.

Instantly, having cautiously rehearsed for such a possibility at great lengths, already, I said, coolly, and without emotion, "no," and that they were barking completely up the wrong tree for any knowledge on my part. Internally, however, I was almost dying with temptation. As everyone is well aware, it is so difficult to do something nice for someone and not want them, desperately, to know that the identity of the individual who did it for them was you, and to feel grateful and approving towards you, and to tell myriads of other people what you "did" for them, so that you can be widely acknowledged as a "good" person. Like the forces of darkness, evil, and hopelessness in the world at large itself, the temptation of this frequently can overwhelm resistance.

Therefore, impulsively, during the grateful, but inquisitive, call, unprescient of any danger, I said, after saying, very coolly, "no," and "the wrong tree," that, although I had no knowledge, I could well imagine that whoever, in fact, was, mysteriously responsible for _____ would be enthusiastic to know how the needed money, which they had received, was going to be utilized—meaning, for example, would they now plan to finally acquire health insurance for their new-born baby, or service the consumer debt in which they were deeply mired, or etc.?

My uttering this, however, was, in a fatal instant, interpreted by the person as an indirect hint from me that I was, despite my prior denials, indeed, the individual responsible for the generous, nice act, and he, throughout the remainder of the call, became lavish in his details on how the money would be applied to their specific needs, underlining what a God-send it was, with the tone of his voice's emotion transmitting both gratitude, approval, and something else (more specifically, something almost hostile, or embarrassed, or both, yet I can not describe the specific tone which brought this emotion to my attention adequately). This flood of emotion, on his part, caused me, sickeningly, too late, to realize, that what I had just done, during the call, was to not only let him know that I was the individual who was responsible for the generous gesture, but to make me do so in a subtle, sly manner that appeared to be, insinuationally, euphemistic, meaning, employing the euphemism: "whoever was responsible for _____," which, combined together with the interest I revealed in the money's "uses" by them, could fool no one about its implying of me as ultimately responsible, and had the effect, insidiously, of insinuating that, not only was I the one who had done such a generous, nice thing, but also, that I was so "nice"— meaning, in other words, "modest," "unselfish," or "untempted by a desire for their gratitude"—a person, that I did not even want them to know that I was who was responsible. And I had, despairingly, in addition, given off these insinuations so "slyly," that not even I, until afterward—meaning, after the call was over—, knew what I had done. Thus, I showed an unconscious and, seemingly, natural, automatic ability to both deceive myself and other people, which, on the "motivational level," not only completely emptied the generous thing I tried to do of any true value, and caused me to fail, again, in my attempts to sincerely be what someone would classify as truly a "nice" or "good" person, but, despairingly, cast me in a light to myself which could only be classified as "dark," "evil," or "beyond hope of ever sincerely becoming good."

1999

Chang-rae Lee b. 1965

Chang-rae Lee is not only the best-known Korean American writer but also one of the most acclaimed contemporary American novelists today. Although he is still at the beginning of his literary career, he has received numerous honors for his work, including the Hemingway Foundation/PEN Award, the American Book Award, and the Anisfield-Wolf Book Award. In addition, Lee has been hailed as one of the most accomplished young writers by two venerable literary magazines. The *New Yorker* identified him as one of twenty most important American writers younger than forty, and *Granta* selected him as a finalist for its list of best young American writers. He has written three novels—*Native Speaker* (1995), *A Gesture Life* (1999), and *Aloft* (2004).

Born in Seoul, South Korea, in 1965, Lee came to the United States with his family in 1968. He attended Yale University, where he majored in English and graduated with a B.A. degree in 1987. After college, Lee worked on Wall Street but left his job to concentrate on his writing. He enrolled in the M.F.A. program at the University of Oregon and submitted a draft of *Native Speaker,* his first novel, as his thesis. He now teaches creative writing at Princeton University and lives in New Jersey with his wife and two daughters.

Lee's work explores the themes of identity and alienation. His two earlier novels, *Native Speaker* and *A Gesture Life,* focus on the plight of being an outsider in a community, particularly the marginalized existence of Asian immigrant families in the United States. Although the emphasis of Lee's third novel, *Aloft,* which is about the life of an Italian American suburbanite, represents a departure from the subject matter of the previous works, the theme of emotional detachment remains.

Lee is celebrated for his elegant, elliptical prose and his delicately understated rendering of powerful emotional experiences, traits that are evident in his memoir, "Coming Home Again." In this carefully crafted piece, Lee writes poignantly about his mother and her untimely death from stomach cancer. While much of the essay is devoted to the writer's memories of the Korean dishes that his mother prepared during her lifetime, food signifies more broadly as a symbol of participation within the family and larger social groups. The preparation and consumption of food, in this piece, signal the shifts in the son's relationship with his mother.

Lee's memoir details the complex and often painful negotiations that inevitably occur in the parent-child relationship when the children begin to make their way to adulthood and when the parents cope with illness and death. Cutting back and forth in time, the essay juxtaposes the son's grief at his mother's death with the mother's sorrow at the son's departure for boarding school, an event that marks the growing distance between her and her child. Lee's deftly nuanced depiction of alienation is his noteworthy contribution to American literature.

Grace H. Park
University of California at Los Angeles

PRIMARY WORKS

Native Speaker, 1995; *A Gesture Life*, 1999; *Aloft*, 2004.

Coming Home Again

When my mother began using the electronic pump that fed her liquids and medication, we moved her to the family room. The bedroom she shared with my father was upstairs, and it was impossible to carry the machine up and down all day and night. The pump itself was attached to a metal stand on casters, and she pulled it along wherever she went. From anywhere in the house, you could hear the sound of the wheels clicking out a steady time over the grout lines of the slate-tiled foyer, her main thoroughfare to the bathroom and the kitchen. Sometimes you would hear her halt after only a few steps, to catch her breath or steady her balance, and whatever you were doing was instantly suspended by a pall of silence.

I was usually in the kitchen, preparing lunch or dinner, poised over the butcher block with her favorite chef's knife in my hand and her old yellow apron slung around my neck. I'd be breathless in the sudden quiet, and, having ceased my mincing and chopping would stare blankly at the brushed sheen of the blade. Eventually, she would clear her throat or call out to say she was fine, then begin to move again, starting her rhythmic *ka-jug;* and only then could I go on with my cooking, the world of our house turning once more, wheeling through the black.

I wasn't cooking for my mother but for the rest of us. When she first moved downstairs she was still eating, though scantily, more just to taste what we were having than from any genuine desire for food. The point was simply to sit together at the kitchen table and array ourselves like a family again. My mother would gently set herself down in her customary chair near the stove. I sat across from her, my father and sister to my left and right, and crammed in the center was all the food I had made—a spicy codfish stew, say, or a casserole of gingery beef, dishes that in my youth she had prepared for us a hundred times.

It had been ten years since we'd all lived together in the house, which at fifteen I had left to attend boarding school in New Hampshire. My mother would sometimes point this out, by speaking of our present time as being "just like before Exeter," which surprised me, given how proud she always was that I was a graduate of the school.

My going to such a place was part of my mother's not so secret plan to change my character, which she worried was becoming to much like hers. I was clever and able enough, but without outside pressure I was readily given to sloth and vanity. The famous school—which none of us knew the first thing about—would prove my mettle. She was right, of course, and while I was there I would falter more than a few times, academically and otherwise. But I never thought that my leaving home then would ever be a problem for her, a private quarrel she would have even as her life waned.

Now her house was full again. My sister had just resigned from her job in New York City, and my father, who typically saw his psychiatric patients until eight or nine in the evening, was appearing in the driveway at four-thirty. I had been living at home for nearly a year and was in the final push of work on what would prove a dismal failure of a novel. When I wasn't struggling over my prose, I kept occupied with the things she usually did—the daily errands, the grocery shopping, the vacuuming and the cleaning, and, of course, all the cooking.

When I was six or seven years old, I used to watch my mother as she prepared our favorite meals. It was one of my daily pleasures. She shooed me away in the beginning, telling me that the kitchen wasn't my place, and adding, in her half-proud, half-deprecating way, that her kind of work would only serve to weaken me. "Go out and play with your friends," she'd snap in Korean, "or better yet, do your reading and homework." She knew that I had already done both and that as the evening approached there was no place to go save her small and tidy kitchen, from which the clatter of her mixing bowls and pans would ring through the house.

I would enter the kitchen quietly and stand beside her, my chin lodging upon the point of her hip. Peering through the crook of her arm, I beheld the movements of her hands. For *kalbi,* she would take up a butchered short rib in her narrow hand, the flinty bone shaped like a section of an airplane wing and deeply embedded in gristle and flesh, and with the point of her knife cut so that the bone fell away, though not completely, leaving it connected to the meat by the barest opaque layer of tendon. The she methodically butterflied the flesh, cutting and unfolding, repeating the action until the meat lay out on her board, glistening and ready for seasoning. She scored it diagonally, then sifted sugar into the crevices with her pinched fingers, gently rubbing in the crystals. The sugar would tenderize as well as sweeten the meat. She did this with each rib, and then set them all aside in a large shallow bowl. She minced a half-dozen cloves of garlic, a stub of gingerroot, sliced up a few scallions, and spread it all over the meat. She wiped her hands and took out a bottle of sesame oil, and, after pausing for a moment, streamed the dark oil in two swift circles around the bowl. After adding a few splashes of soy sauce, she thrust her hands in and kneaded the flesh, careful not to dislodge the bones. I asked her why it mattered that they remain connected. "The meat needs the bone nearby," she said, "to borrow its richness." She wiped her hands clean of the marinade, except for her little finger, which she would flick with her tongue from time to time, because she knew that the flavor of a good dish developed not at once but in stages.

Whenever I cook, I find myself working just as she would, readying the ingredients—a mash of garlic, a julienne of red peppers, fantails of shrimp—and piling them in little mounds about the cutting surface. My mother never left me any recipes, but this is how I learned to make her food, each dish coming not from a list or a card but from the aromatic spread of a board.

I've always thought it was particularly cruel that the cancer was in her stomach, and that for a long time at the end she couldn't eat. The last meal I made for her was on New Year's Eve, 1990. My sister suggested that instead of a rib roast or a bird, or the usual overflow of Korean food, we make all sorts of finger dishes that our mother might fancy and pick at.

We set the meal out on the glass coffee table in the family room. I prepared a tray of smoked-salmon canapés, fried some Korean bean cakes, and made a few other dishes I thought she might enjoy. My sister supervised me, arranging the platters, and then with some pomp carried each dish in to our parents. Finally, I brought out a bottle of champagne in a bucket of ice. My mother had moved to the sofa and was sitting up, surveying the low table. "It looks pretty nice," she said. "I think I'm feeling hungry."

This made us all feel good, especially me, for I couldn't remember the last time she had felt any hunger or had eaten something I cooked. We began to eat. My mother picked up a piece of salmon toast and took a tiny corner in her mouth. She rolled it around for a moment and then pushed it out with the tip of her tongue, letting it fall back onto her plate. She swallowed hard, as if to quell a gag, then glanced up to see if we had noticed. Of course we all had. She attempted a bean cake, some cheese, and then a slice of fruit, but nothing was any use.

She nodded at me anyway, and said, "Oh, it's very good." But I was already feeling lost and I put down my plate abruptly, nearly shattering it on the thick glass. There was an ugly pause before my father asked me in a weary, gentle voice if anything was wrong, and I answered that it was nothing, it was the last night of a long year, and we were together, and I was simply relieved. At midnight, I poured out glasses of champagne, even one for my mother, who took a deep sip. Her manner grew playful and light, and I helped her shuffle to her mattress, and she lay down in the place where in a brief week she was dead.

My mother could whip up anything, but during our first years of living in this country we ate only Korean foods. At my harangue-like behest, my mother set herself to learning how to cook exotic American dishes. Luckily, a kind neighbor, Mrs. Churchill, a tall florid young woman with flaxen hair, taught my mother her most trusted recipes. Mrs. Churchill's two young sons, palish, weepy boys with identical crew cuts, always accompanied her, and though I liked them well enough, I would slip away from them after a few minutes, for I knew that the real action would be in the kitchen, where their mother was playing guide. Mrs. Churchill hailed from the state of Maine, where the finest Swedish meatballs and tuna casserole and angel food cake in America are made. She readily demonstrated certain techniques—how to layer wet sheets of pasta for a lasagna or whisk up a simple roux, for example. She often brought gift shoeboxes containing curious ingredients like dried oregano, instant yeast, and cream of mushroom soup. The two women, though at ease and jolly with each other, had difficulty communicating, and this was made worse by the often confusing terminology of Western cuisine ("corned beef," "deviled eggs"). Although I was just learning the language myself, I'd gladly play the interlocutor, jumping back and forth between their places at the counter, dipping my fingers into whatever sauce lay about.

I was an insistent child, and, being my mother's firstborn, much too prized. My mother could say no to me, and did often enough, but anyone who knew us— particularly my father and sister—could tell how much the denying pained her. And if I was overconscious of her indulgence even then, and suffered the rushing pangs of guilt that she could inflict upon me with the slightest wounded turn of her lip, I was too happily obtuse and venal to let her cease. She reminded me daily that I was her sole son, her reason for living, and that if she were to lose me, in either body or spirit, she wished God would mercifully smite her, strike her down like a weak branch.

In the traditional fashion, she was the house accountant, the maid, the launderer, the disciplinarian, the driver, the secretary, and, of course, the cook. She was also my first basketball coach. In South Korea, where girls' high school basketball is a popular spectator sport, she had been a star, the point guard for the national high school team that once won the all-Asia championship. I learned this one Saturday during the summer, when I asked my father if he would go down to the schoolyard and shoot some baskets with me. I had just finished the fifth grade, and wanted desperately to make the middle school team the coming fall. He called for my mother and sister to come along. When we arrived, my sister immediately ran off to the swings, and I recall being annoyed that my mother wasn't following her. I dribbled clumsily around the key, on the verge of losing control of the ball, and flung a flat shot that caromed wildly off the rim. The ball bounced to my father, who took a few not so graceful dribbles and made an easy layup. He dribbled out and then drove to the hoop for a layup on the other side. He rebounded his shot and passed the ball to my mother, who had been watching us from the foul line. She turned from the basket and began heading the other way.

"*Um-mah,*" I cried at her, my exasperation already bubbling over, "the basket's over *here!*"

After a few steps she turned around, and from where the professional three-point line must be now, she effortlessly flipped the ball up in a two-handed set shot, its flight truer and higher than I'd witnessed from any boy or man. The ball arced cleanly into the hoop, stiffly popping the chain-link net. All afternoon, she rained in shot after shot, as my father and I scrambled after her.

When we got home from the playground, my mother showed me the photograph album off her team's championship run. For years I kept it in my room, on the same shelf that housed the scrapbooks I made of basketball stars, with magazine clippings of slick players like Bubbles Hawkins and Pistol Pete and George (the Iceman) Gervin.

It puzzled me how much she considered her own history to be immaterial, and if she never patently diminished herself, she was able to finesse a kind of self-removal by speaking of my father whenever she could. She zealously recounted his excellence as a student in medical school and reminded me, each night before I started my homework, of how hard he drove himself in his work to make a life for us. She said that because of his Asian face and imperfect English, he was "working two times the American doctors." I knew that she was building him up, buttressing him with both genuine admiration and her own brand of anxious braggadocio, and that her overarching concern was that I might fail to see him as she wished me to—in the most dawning light, his pose steadfast and solitary.

In the year before I left for Exeter, I became weary of her oft-repeated accounts of my father's success. I was a teenager, and so ever inclined to be dismissive and bitter toward anything that had to do with family and home. Often enough, my mother was the object of my derision. Suddenly, her life seemed so small to me. She was there, and sometimes, I thought, *always* there, as if she were confined to the four walls of our house. I would even complain about her cooking. Mostly, though I was getting more and more impatient with the difficulty she encountered in doing everyday things. I was afraid for her. One day, we got into a terrible argument when she asked me to call the bank, to question a discrepancy she had discovered in the monthly statement. I asked her why she couldn't call herself. I was stupid and brutal, and I knew exactly how to wound her.

"Whom do I talk to?" she said. She would mostly speak to me in Korean, and I would answer in English.

"The bank manager, who else?"

"What do I say?"

"Whatever you want to say."

"Don't speak to me like that!" she cried.

"It's just that you should be able to do it yourself," I said.

"You know how I feel about this!"

"Well, maybe then you should consider it *practice,*" I answered lightly, using the Korean word to make sure she understood.

Her face blanched, and her neck suddenly became rigid, as if were throttling her. She nearly struck me right then, but instead she bit her lip and ran upstairs. I followed her, pleading for forgiveness at her door. But it was the one time in our life that I couldn't convince her, melt her resolve with the blandishments of a spoiled son.

When my mother was feeling strong enough, or was in particularly good spirits, she would roll her machine into the kitchen and sit at the table and watch me work. She wore pajamas day and night, mostly old pairs of mine.

She said, "I can't tell, what are you making?"

"*Mahn-doo* filling."

"You didn't salt the cabbage and squash."

"Was I supposed to?"

"Of course. Look, it's too wet. Now the skins will get soggy before you can fry them."

"What should I do?"

"It's too late. Maybe it'll be OK if you work quickly. Why didn't you ask me?"

"You were finally sleeping."

"You should have woken me."

"No way."

She sighed, as deeply as her weary lungs would allow.

"I don't know how you were going to make it without me."

"I don't know, either. I'll remember the salt next time."

"You better. And not too much."

We often talked like this, our tone decidedly matter-of-fact, chin up, just this side of being able to bear it. Once, while inspecting a potato fritter batter I was making, she asked me if she had ever done anything that I wished she hadn't done. I thought for a moment, and told her no. In the next breath, she wondered aloud if it was right of her to have let me go to Exeter, to live away from the house while I was so young. She tested the batter's thickness with her finger and called for more flour. Then she asked if, given a choice, I would go to Exeter again.

I wasn't sure what she was getting at, and I told her that I couldn't be certain, but probably yes, I would. She snorted at this and said it was my leaving home that had once so troubled our relationship. "Remember how I had so much difficulty talking to you? Remember?"

She believed back then that I had found her more and more ignorant each time I came home. She said she never blamed me, for this was the way she knew it would be with my wonderful new education. Nothing I could say seemed to quell the notion. But I knew that the problem wasn't simply the *education;* the first time I saw her again after starting school, barely six weeks later, when she and my father visited me on Parents Day, she had already grown nervous and distant. After the usual campus events, we had gone to the motel where they were staying in a nearby town and sat on the beds in our room. She seemed to sneak looks at me, as though I might discover a horrible new truth if our eyes should meet.

My own secret feeling was that I had missed my parents greatly, my mother especially, and much more than I had anticipated. I couldn't tell them that these first weeks were a mere blur to me, that I felt completely overwhelmed by all the studies and my much brighter friends and the thousand irritating details of living alone, and that I had really learned nothing, save perhaps how to put on a necktie while sprinting to class. I felt as if I had plunged too deep into the world, which, to my great horror, was much larger than I had ever imagined.

I welcomed the lull of the motel room. My father and I had nearly dozed off when my mother jumped up excitedly, murmured how stupid she was, and hurried to the closet by the door. She pulled out our old metal cooler and dragged it between the beds. She lifted the top and began unpacking plastic containers, and I thought she would never stop. One after the other they came out, each with a dish that traveled well—a salted stewed meat, rolls of Korean-style sushi. I opened a container of radish kimchi and suddenly the room bloomed with its odor, and I reveled in the very peculiar sensation (which perhaps only true kimchi lovers know) of simultaneously drooling and gagging as I breathed it all in. For the next few minutes, they watched me eat. I'm not certain that I was even hungry. But after weeks of pork parmigiana and chicken patties and wax beans, I suddenly realized that I had lost all the savor in my life. And it seemed I couldn't get enough of it back. I ate and I ate, so much and so fast that I actually went to the bathroom and vomited. I came out dizzy and sated with the phantom warmth of my binge.

And beneath the face of her worry, I thought my mother was smiling.

From that day, my mother prepared a certain meal to welcome me home. It was always the same. Even as I rode the school's shuttle bus from Exeter to Logan airport, I could already see the exact arrangement of my mother's table.

I knew that we would eat in the kitchen, the table brimming with plates. There was the *kalbi,* of course, broiled or grilled depending on the season. Leaf lettuce, to wrap the meat with. Bowls of garlicky clam broth with miso and tofu and fresh spinach. Shavings of cod dusted in flour and then dipped in egg wash and fried. Glass noodles with onions and shiitake. Scallion-and-hot-pepper pancakes. Chilled steamed shrimp. Seasoned salads of bean sprouts, spinach, and white radish. Crispy squares of seaweed. Steamed rice with barley and red beans. Homemade kimchi. It was all there—the old flavors I knew, the beautiful salt, the sweet, the excellent taste.

After the meal, my father and I talked about school, but I could never say enough for it to make any sense. My father would often recall his high school principal, who had gone to England to study the methods and traditions of the public schools, and regaled students with stories of the great Eton man. My mother sat with us, paring fruit, not saying a word but taking everything in. When it was time to go to bed, my father said good night first. I usually watched television until the early morning. My mother would sit with me for an hour or two, perhaps until she was accustomed to me again, and only then would she kiss me and head upstairs to sleep.

During the following days, it was always the cooking that started our conversations. She'd hold an inquest over the cold leftovers we ate at lunch, discussing each dish in terms of its balance of flavors or what might have been prepared differently. But mostly I begged her to leave the dishes alone. I wish I had paid more attention. After her death, when my father and I were the only ones left in the house, drifting through the rooms like ghosts, I sometimes tried to make that meal for him. Though it was too much for two, I made each dish anyway, taking as much care as I could. But nothing turned out quite right—not the color, not the smell. At the table, neither of us said much of anything. And we had to eat the food for days.

I remember washing rice in the kitchen one day and my mother's saying in English, from her usual seat, "I made a big mistake."

"About Exeter?"

"Yes. I made a big mistake. You should be with us for that time. I should never have let you go there."

"So why did you? I said.

"Because I didn't know I was going to die."

I let her words pass. For the first time in her life, she was letting herself speak her full mind, so what else could I do?

"But you know what?" she spoke up. "It was better for you. If you stayed home, you would not like me so much now."

I suggested that maybe I would like her even more.

She shook her head. "Impossible."

Sometimes I still think about what she said, about having made a mistake. I would have left home for college, that was never in doubt, but those years I was away at boarding school grew more precious to her as her illness progressed. After many months of exhaustion and pain and the haze of the drugs, I thought that her mind was beginning to fade, for more and more it seemed that she was seeing me again as her fifteen-year-old boy, the one she had dropped off in New Hampshire on a cloudy September afternoon.

I remember the first person I met, another new student, named Zack, who walked to the welcome picnic with me. I had planned to eat with my parents—my mother had brought a coolerful of food even that first day—but I learned of the cookout and told her that I should probably go. I wanted to go, of course. I was excited, and no doubt fearful and nervous, and I must have thought I was only thinking ahead. She agreed wholeheartedly, saying I certainly should. I walked them to the car, and perhaps I hugged them, before saying goodbye. One day, after she died, my father told me what happened on the long drive home to Syracuse.

He was driving the car, looking straight ahead. Traffic was light on the Massachusetts Turnpike, and the sky was nearly dark. They had driven for more than two hours and had not yet spoken a word. He then heard a strange sound from her, a kind of muffled chewing noise, as if something inside her were grinding its way out.

"So, what's the matter?" he said, trying to keep an edge to his voice.

She looked at him with her ashen face and she burst into tears. He began to cry himself, and pulled the car over onto the narrow shoulder of the turnpike, where they stayed for the next half hour or so, the blank-faced cars droning by them in the cold, on-rushing night.

Every once and a while, when I think of her, I'm driving alone somewhere on the highway. In the twilight, I see their car off to the side, a blue Olds coupe with a landau top, and as I pass them by I look back in the mirror and I see them again, the two figures huddled together in the front seat. Are they sleeping? Or kissing? Are they all right?

1996

Sherman Alexie (Spokane–Coeur d'Alene) b. 1966

Sherman Alexie was born in 1966 in Wellpinit, Washington, on the Spokane Indian Reservation. Born hydrocephalic, Alexie underwent brain surgery at the age of six months. Although the surgery was successful, he experienced seizures throughout his childhood. Alexie was a voracious reader, reading Steinbeck by the age of five and finishing all the books in the Wellpinit library by the age of twelve. He attended Reardon High School, an all-white school just outside the reservation, where, ironically, he played basketball for the Reardon "Indians." He attended Gonzaga University in Spokane and eventually graduated from Washington State University with a degree in American Studies. He battled alcoholism during this time and became sober at the age of twenty-three.

Alexie first encountered contemporary American Indian literature in college. Reading about his own experiences in poems and stories was a life-changing experience. After reading this line from a poem by Paiute poet Adrian Louis, "I'm in the reservation of my mind," Alexie felt that somebody understood him, and he knew that he would begin writing. That was in 1989. Three years later, Alexie's first book of poetry, *The Business of Fancydancing,* was published by Hanging Loose Press and received a

tremendous amount of critical attention from Native American as well as non-Indian critics. Joy Harjo, renowned Creek poet, called Alexie "one of the most vital writers to emerge in the late twentieth century." After the *New York Times Book Review* hailed Alexie as "one of the major lyric voices of our time" and the *New York Times Book Review* declared *Fancydancing* the 1992 Notable Book of the Year, Alexie's career skyrocketed. Since then, he has published nine books of poetry and four books of fiction and has won numerous awards, including the 1993 Lila Wallace–Reader's Digest Writers' Award, the 1993 PEN/Hemingway Best First Book of Fiction Citation for *The Lone Ranger and Tonto Fistfight in Heaven,* and the 1996 Before Columbus Foundation American Book Award. He was also named one of the Twenty Best American Novelists Under the Age of 40 by *Granta Magazine* in 1997 and one of Twenty Writers for the 21st Century by the *New Yorker* in 1999.

Alexie is perhaps best known for the movie *Smoke Signals,* the screenplay of which he adapted from his short story "This Is What It Means to Say Phoenix, Arizona," from 1993's *Lone Ranger and Tonto. Smoke Signals* was the first movie written, directed, and produced entirely by American Indians. The film premiered at the Sundance Film Festival in 1998 and won the Audience Award and the Filmmakers Trophy for Cheyenne-Arapaho director Chris Eyre.

Alexie is a significant writer and a controversial figure, known for his brutally honest depictions of contemporary reservation life and razor sharp wit. His goal is to challenge and poke fun at traditional stereotypes of American Indian people. In poems about basketball on the reservation and stories such as "Because My Father Always Said He Was the Only Indian Who Saw Jimi Hendrix Play 'The Star-Spangled Banner' at Woodstock" he drives home the point that American Indian people are not trapped in the nineteenth century but are members of living, vital cultures and, furthermore, participants in and part of American popular culture. Alexie takes his responsibilities as a Native American writer seriously, realizing that he is a political spokesperson for native peoples, like it or not; he participated in President Clinton's roundtable discussion on race. He frequently attacks non-natives who write about Native Americans or appropriate Native American themes. He receives much criticism for his viewpoints but remains outspoken and unapologetic.

Alexie currently lives in Seattle with his wife, Diane, a member of the Hidatsa Nation, and their son. He shows no signs of slowing his pace and is working on screenplays, in addition to his fiction and poetry.

Amanda J. Cobb
University of New Mexico, Albuquerque

PRIMARY WORKS

The Business of Fancydancing: Stories and Poems, 1992; *I Would Steal Horses,* 1993; *Old Shirts and New Skins,* 1993; *First Indian on the Moon,* 1993; *The Lone Ranger and Tonto Fistfight in Heaven,* 1993; *Seven Mourning Songs for the Cedar Flute I Have Yet to Learn to Play,* 1995; *Reservation Blues,* 1995; *Water Flowing Home,* 1996; *The Summer of Black Widows,* 1996; *Indian Killer,* 1996; *The Man Who Loves Salmon,* 1998; *Smoke Signals,* 1998; *One-Stick Song,* 1999; *The Toughest Indian in the World,* 2000; *Ten Little Indians,* 2003; *Dangerous Astronomy,* 2005; *Flight,* 2007.

Because My Father Always Said
He Was the Only Indian
Who Saw Jimi Hendrix Play
"The Star-Spangled Banner" at Woodstock

During the sixties, my father was the perfect hippie, since all the hippies were trying to be Indians. Because of that, how could anyone recognize that my father was trying to make a social statement?

But there is evidence, a photograph of my father demonstrating in Spokane, Washington, during the Vietnam war. The photograph made it onto the wire service and was reprinted in newspapers throughout the country. In fact, it was on the cover of *Time.*

In the photograph, my father is dressed in bell-bottoms and flowered shirt, his hair in braids, with red peace symbols splashed across his face like war paint. In his hands my father holds a rifle above his head, captured in that moment just before he proceeded to beat the shit out of the National Guard private lying prone on the ground. A fellow demonstrator holds a sign that is just barely visible over my father's left shoulder. It read MAKE LOVE NOT WAR.

The photographer won a Pulitzer Prize, and editors across the country had a lot of fun creating captions and headlines. I've read many of them collected in my father's scrapbook, and my favorite was run in the *Seattle Times*. The caption under the photograph read DEMONSTRATOR GOES TO WAR FOR PEACE. The editors capitalized on my father's Native American identity with other headlines like ONE WARRIOR AGAINST WAR and PEACEFUL GATHERING TURNS INTO NATIVE UPRISING.

Anyway, my father was arrested, charged with attempted murder, which was reduced to assault with a deadly weapon. It was a high-profile case so my father was used as an example. Convicted and sentenced quickly, he spent two years in Walla Walla State Penitentiary. Although his prison sentence effectively kept him out of the war, my father went through a different kind of war behind bars.

"There was Indian gangs and white gangs and black gangs and Mexican gangs," he told me once. "And there was somebody new killed every day. We'd hear about somebody getting it in the shower or wherever and the word would go down the line. Just one word. Just the color of his skin. Red, white, black, or brown. Then we'd chalk it up on the mental scoreboard and wait for the next broadcast."

My father made it through all that, never got into any serious trouble, somehow avoided rape, and got out of prison just in time to hitchhike to Woodstock to watch Jimi Hendrix play "The Star-Spangled Banner."

"After all the shit I'd been through," my father said, "I figured Jimi must have known I was there in the crowd to play something like that. It was exactly how I felt."

Twenty years later, my father played his Jimi Hendrix tape until it wore down. Over and over, the house filled with the rockets' red glare and the bombs bursting in air. He'd sit by the stereo with a cooler of beer beside him and cry, laugh, call me over and hold me tight in his arms, his bad breath and body odor covering me like a blanket.

Jimi Hendrix and my father became drinking buddies. Jimi Hendrix waited for my father to come home after a long night of drinking. Here's how the ceremony worked:

1. I would lie awake all night and listen for the sounds of my father's pickup.
2. When I heard my father's pickup, I would run upstairs and throw Jimi's tape into the stereo.
3. Jimi would bend his guitar into the first note of "The Star-Spangled Banner" just as my father walked inside.
4. My father would weep, attempt to hum along with Jimi, and then pass out with his head on the kitchen table.
5. I would fall asleep under the table with my head near my father's feet.
6. We'd dream together until the sun came up.

The days after, my father would feel so guilty that he would tell me stories as a means of apology.

"I met your mother at a party in Spokane," my father told me once. "We were the only two Indians at the party. Maybe the only two Indians in the whole town. I thought she was so beautiful. I figured she was the kind of woman who could make buffalo walk on up to her and give up their lives. She wouldn't have needed to hunt.

Every time we went walking, birds would follow us around. Hell, tumbleweeds would follow us around."

Somehow my father's memories of my mother grew more beautiful as their relationship became more hostile. By the time the divorce was final, my mother was quite possibly the most beautiful woman who ever lived.

"Your father was always half crazy," my mother told me more than once. "And the other half was on medication."

But she loved him, too, with a ferocity that eventually forced her to leave him. They fought each other with the kind of graceful anger that only love can create. Still, their love was passionate, unpredictable, and selfish. My mother and father would get drunk and leave parties abruptly to go home and make love.

"Don't tell your father I told you this," my mother said. "But there must have been a hundred times he passed out on top of me. We'd be right in the middle of it, he'd say *I love you,* his eyes would roll backwards, and then out went his lights. It sounds strange, I know, but those were good times."

I was conceived during one of those drunken nights, half of me formed by my father's whiskey sperm, the other half formed by my mother's vodka egg. I was born a goofy reservation mixed drink, and my father needed me just as much as he needed every other kind of drink.

One night my father and I were driving home in a near-blizzard after a basketball game, listening to the radio. We didn't talk much. One, because my father didn't talk much when he was sober, and two, because Indians don't need to talk to communicate.

"Hello out there, folks, this is Big Bill Baggins, with the late-night classics show on KROC, 97.2 on your FM dial. We have a request from Betty in Tekoa. She wants to hear Jimi Hendrix's version of 'The Star-Spangled Banner' recorded live at Woodstock."

My father smiled, turned the volume up, and we rode down the highway while Jimi led the way like a snowplow. Until that night, I'd always been neutral about Jimi Hendrix. But, in that near-blizzard with my father at the wheel, with the nervous silence caused by the dangerous roads and Jimi's guitar, there seemed to be more to all that music. The reverberation came to mean something, took form and function.

That song made me want to learn to play guitar, not because I wanted to be Jimi Hendrix and not because I thought I'd ever play for anyone. I just wanted to touch the strings, to hold the guitar tight against my body, invent a chord, and come closer to what Jimi knew, to what my father knew.

"You know," I said to my father after the song was over, "my generation of Indian boys ain't ever had no real war to fight. The first Indians had Custer to fight. My great-grandfather had World War I, my grandfather had World War II, you had Vietnam. All I have is video games."

My father laughed for a long time, nearly drove off the road into the snowy fields.

"Shit," he said. "I don't know why you're feeling sorry for yourself because you ain't had to fight a war. You're lucky. Shit, all you had was that damn Desert Storm. Should have called it Dessert Storm because it just made the fat cats get fatter. It was all sugar and whipped cream with a cherry on top. And besides that, you didn't even have to fight it. All you lost during that war was sleep because you stayed up all night watching CNN."

We kept driving through the snow, talked about war and peace.

"That's all there is," my father said. "War and peace with nothing in between. It's always one or the other."

"You sound like a book," I said.

"Yeah, well, that's how it is. Just because it's in a book doesn't make it not true. And besides, why the hell would you want to fight a war for this country? It's been trying to kill Indians since the very beginning. Indians are pretty much born soldiers anyway. Don't need a uniform to prove it."

Those were the kinds of conversations that Jimi Hendrix forced us to have. I guess every song has a special meaning for someone somewhere. Elvis Presley is still showing up in 7-11 stores across the country, even though he's been dead for years, so I figure music just might be the most important thing there is. Music turned my father into a reservation philosopher. Music had powerful medicine.

"I remember the first time your mother and I danced," my father told me once. "We were in this cowboy bar. We were the only real cowboys there despite the fact that we're Indians. We danced to a Hank Williams song. Danced to that real sad one, you know, 'I'm So Lonesome I Could Cry.' Except your mother and I weren't lonesome or crying. We just shuffled along and fell right goddamn down into love."

"Hank Williams and Jimi Hendrix don't have much in common," I said.

"Hell, yes, they do. They knew all about broken hearts," my father said.

"You sound like a bad movie."

"Yeah, well, that's how it is. You kids today don't know shit about romance. Don't know shit about music either. Especially you Indian kids. You all have been spoiled by those drums. Been hearing them beat so long, you think that's all you need. Hell, son, even an Indian needs a piano or guitar or saxophone now and again."

My father played in a band in high school. He was the drummer. I guess he'd burned out on those. Now, he was like the universal defender of the guitar.

"I remember when your father would haul that old guitar out and play me songs," my mother said. "He couldn't play all that well but he tried. You could see him thinking about what chord he was going to play next. His eyes got all squeezed up and his face turned all red. He kind of looked that way when he kissed me, too. But don't tell him I said that."

Some nights I lay awake and listened to my parents' lovemaking. I know white people keep it quiet, pretend they don't ever make love. My white friends tell me they can't even imagine their parents getting it on. I know exactly what it sounds like when my parents are touching each other. It makes up for knowing exactly what they sound like when they're fighting. Plus and minus. Add and subtract. It comes out just about even.

Some nights I would fall asleep to the sounds of my parents' lovemaking. I would dream Jimi Hendrix. I could see my father standing in the front row in the dark at Woodstock as Jimi Hendrix played "The Star-Spangled Banner." My mother was at home with me, both of us waiting for my father to find his way back home to the reservation. It's amazing to realize I was alive, breathing and wetting my bed, when Jimi was alive and breaking guitars.

I dreamed my father dancing with all these skinny hippie women, smoking a few joints, dropping acid, laughing when the rain fell. And it did rain there. I've seen actual news footage. I've seen the documentaries. It rained. People had to share food. People got sick. People got married. People cried all kinds of tears.

But as much as I dream about it, I don't have any clue about what it meant for my father to be the only Indian who saw Jimi Hendrix play at Woodstock. And maybe he wasn't the only Indian there. Most likely there were hundreds but my father thought he was the only one. He told me that a million times when he was drunk and a couple hundred times when he was sober.

"I was there," he said. "You got to remember this was near the end and there weren't as many people as before. Not nearly as many. But I waited it out. I waited for Jimi."

A few years back, my father packed up the family and the three of us drove to Seattle to visit Jimi Hendrix's grave. We had our photograph taken lying down next to the grave. There isn't a gravestone there. Just one of those flat markers.

Jimi was twenty-eight when he died. That's younger than Jesus Christ when he died. Younger than my father as we stood over the grave.

"Only the good die young," my father said.

"No," my mother said. "Only the crazy people choke to death on their own vomit."

"Why you talking about my hero that way?" my father asked.

"Shit," my mother said. "Old Jesse WildShoe choked to death on his own vomit and he ain't nobody's hero."

I stood back and watched my parents argue. I was used to these battles. When an Indian marriage starts to fall apart, it's even more destructive and painful than usual. A hundred years ago, an Indian marriage was broken easily. The woman or man just packed up all their possessions and left the tipi. There were no arguments, no discussions. Now, Indians fight their way to the end, holding onto the last good thing, because our whole lives have to do with survival.

After a while, after too much fighting and too many angry words had been exchanged, my father went out and bought a motorcycle. A big bike. He left the house often to ride that thing for hours, sometimes for days. He even strapped an old cassette player to the gas tank so he could listen to music. With that bike, he learned something new about running away. He stopped talking as much, stopped drinking as much. He didn't do much of anything except ride that bike and listen to music.

Then one night my father wrecked his bike on Devil's Gap Road and ended up in the hospital for two months. He broke both his legs, cracked his ribs, and punctured a lung. He also lacerated his kidney. The doctors said he could have died easily. In fact, they were surprised he made it through surgery, let alone survived those first few hours when he lay on the road, bleeding. But I wasn't surprised. That's how my father was.

And even though my mother didn't want to be married to him anymore and his wreck didn't change her mind about that, she still came to see him every day. She sang Indian tunes under her breath, in time with the hum of the machines hooked into my father. Although my father could barely move, he tapped his finger in rhythm.

When he had the strength to finally sit up and talk, hold conversations, and tell stories, he called for me.

"Victor," he said. "Stick with four wheels."

After he began to recover, my mother stopped visiting as often. She helped him through the worst, though. When he didn't need her anymore, she went back to the life she had created. She traveled to powwows, started to dance again. She was a champion traditional dancer when she was younger.

"I remember your mother when she was the best traditional dancer in the world," my father said. "Everyone wanted to call her sweetheart. But she only danced for me. That's how it was. She told me that every other step was just for me."

"But that's only half of the dance," I said.

"Yeah," my father said. "She was keeping the rest for herself. Nobody can give everything away. It ain't healthy."

"You know," I said, "sometimes you sound like you ain't even real."

"What's real? I ain't interested in what's real. I'm interested in how things should be."

My father's mind always worked that way. If you don't like the things you remember, then all you have to do is change the memories. Instead of remembering the bad things, remember what happened immediately before. That's what I learned from my father. For me, I remember how good the first drink of that Diet Pepsi tasted instead of how my mouth felt when I swallowed a wasp with the second drink.

Because of all that, my father always remembered the second before my mother left him for good and took me with her. No. I remembered the second before my father left my mother and me. No. My mother remembered the second before my father left her to finish raising me all by herself.

But however memory actually worked, it was my father who climbed on his motorcycle, waved to me as I stood in the window, and rode away. He lived in Seattle, San Francisco, Los Angeles, before he finally ended up in Phoenix. For a while, I got postcards nearly every week. Then it was once a month. Then it was on Christmas and my birthday.

On a reservation, Indian men who abandon their children are treated worse than white fathers who do the same thing. It's because white men have been doing that forever and Indian men have just learned how. That's how assimilation can work.

My mother did her best to explain it all to me, although I understood most of what happened.

"Was it because of Jimi Hendrix?" I asked her.

"Part of it, yeah," she said. "This might be the only marriage broken up by a dead guitar player."

"There's a first time for everything, enit?"

"I guess. Your father just likes being alone more than he likes being with other people. Even me and you."

Sometimes I caught my mother digging through old photo albums or staring at the wall or out the window. She'd get that look on her face that I knew meant she missed my father. Not enough to want him back. She missed him just enough for it to hurt.

On those nights I missed him most I listened to music. Not always Jimi Hendrix. Usually I listened to the blues. Robert Johnson mostly. The first time I heard Robert Johnson sing I knew he understood what it meant to be Indian on the edge of the twenty-first century, even if he was black at the beginning of the twentieth. That must have been how my father felt when he heard Jimi Hendrix. When he stood there in the rain at Woodstock.

Then on the night I missed my father most, when I lay in bed and cried, with that photograph of him beating that National Guard private in my hands, I imagined his motorcycle pulling up outside. I knew I was dreaming it all but I let it be real for a moment.

"Victor," my father yelled. "Let's go for a ride."

"I'll be right down. I need to get my coat on."

I rushed around the house, pulled my shoes and socks on, struggled into my coat, and ran outside to find an empty driveway. It was so quiet, a reservation kind of quiet, where you can hear somebody drinking whiskey on the rocks three miles away. I stood on the porch and waited until my mother came outside.

"Come on back inside," she said. "It's cold."

"No," I said. "I know he's coming back tonight."

My mother didn't say anything. She just wrapped me in her favorite quilt and went back to sleep. I stood on the porch all night long and imagined I heard motorcycles and guitars, until the sun rose so bright that I knew it was time to go back inside to my mother. She made breakfast for both of us and we ate until we were full.

1993

Chris Ware b. 1967

When Chris Ware's book *Jimmy Corrigan, the Smartest Kid on Earth*—which compiled episodes that had previously been printed as part of his ongoing cartoon pamphlet series *The Acme Novelty Library*—was published by Pantheon in 2000, it bewildered and amazed critics and readers. A story of family abandonment that tracks at least three generations of Corrigan men in meticulously rendered, experimental color pages, *Jimmy Corrigan* registers a deep level of aesthetic attention and narrative sophistication that has not always easily been understood as belonging to the realm of comics. *Jimmy Corrigan* won an American Book Award in 2000 and a Guardian First Book Award in 2001, the first graphic novel to win a major literary prize in the United Kingdom. The exploration of isolation within families and the intricate page layouts that made *Jimmy* famous are present in Ware's previous and subsequent work.

Ware was born in Omaha, Nebraska, and graduated from the University of Texas at Austin's School of Fine Art. He lives in Chicago with his wife and daughter, and he works as a historian and editor of comics. He edited the *McSweeney's Quarterly Concern* volume on comics and the most recent edition of *Best American Comics,* publishes a magazine called the *Ragtime Ephemeralist,* and creates installments of his continuing series *The Acme Novelty Library.* He also contributes covers and stories to the *New Yorker,* and his narrative "Building Stories" was serialized in the *New York Times Magazine* in 2005 and 2006. Ware's comics have been exhibited at the Whitney Museum of American Art, Cooper-Hewitt Museum, and Museum of Contemporary Art in Chicago (where he was the focus of a major exhibit).

Ware's work has an emotional rigor, and a formal, graphic rigor that often looks architectural. Indeed, Ware has been influenced by architecture and has made it a theme in his work. Ware has compared not only comics and architecture but also comics and music, calling attention to the timing and syncopation present in both forms.

Ware got his major start when the cartoonist Art Spiegelman noticed his work in the student newspaper of the University of Texas in the late 1980s and asked him to contribute to *RAW,* the high-profile magazine that billed itself as the cutting edge of comics and was published in New York by Spiegelman and his wife, Françoise Mouly. "Thrilling Adventure Stories (I Guess)" from 1991 marked Ware's second appearance in *RAW,* and it contains the hallmarks of Ware's work—its engagement with popular culture and comics history (here, through the trope of the superhero), investigation of family structure, visual precision, and experimental intricacy. In "Thrilling Adventure Stories (I Guess)," the first-person narration shifts from overarching text boxes to dialogue that is spoken by various characters throughout the story.

Ware disturbs naturalism—both by distributing the narration across characters and by destabilizing a visual reference for the narrator himself, a man who is recalling his childhood—but also anchors the piece in a realism through its direct and emotionally frank tone. Although many readers have noted its gloomy themes, Ware's work is not so much about loneliness as about a haunting sensibility that the visual texture of comics has the ability to evoke with its experiments in time and space on the page.

Hillary Chute
Harvard University

Thrilling Adventure Stories (I Guess)

Jhumpa Lahiri b. 1967

Jhumpa (née Nilanjana Sudeshna) Lahiri was born on July 11, 1967, in London to Bengali immigrants from Calcutta and moved to Rhode Island when she was one year old. Her father was a librarian at the University of Rhode Island and her mother a schoolteacher. Most of her fiction is located in and around Boston, in small New England towns, or in New York City, where she now lives with her husband and son. Since 2001 she has been married to Alberto Vourvoulias-Bush, an American-born Guatemalan Greek who is now the editor of *El Diario/La Prensa,* the biggest Spanish-language newspaper in New York; they were wed in a traditional Bengali Hindu ceremony in Calcutta.

Lahiri received a bachelor's degree from Barnard College and three master's degrees (in English, creative writing, and comparative studies in literature and the arts) and a Ph.D. in Renaissance literature from Boston University. She then received a two-year fellowship from Provincetown's Fine Arts Work Center, where she wrote much of *Interpreter of Maladies,* a collection of nine short stories. Three of these stories, "The Interpreter of Maladies," "A Real Durwan," and "The Treatment of Bibi Haldar," are set in Calcutta, where her parents visited their families every few years during her childhood.

Interpreter of Maladies won the 2000 Pulitzer Prize and the Pen/Hemingway Award, and the title story received the O'Henry Award. Lahiri received a Guggenheim fellowship in 2002, and her stories frequently appear in magazines and anthologies.

Her novel *The Namesake* (2003) portrays the life of a Bengali couple, Ashoke and Ashima Ganguly, who emigrate from Calcutta to Boston, and the coming of age of their son, Nikhil/Gogol, who struggles with the internal conflicts between his In-dian and American identities. The novel was made into a film by Mira Nair.

Lahiri's fiction deals with universal themes such as love, loss, death, birth, marriage, home, and homelessness. Her audience includes those studying minority or multicultural literature as well as those who are interested in the psychological and emotional impact of immigration as depicted in American literature. Lahiri has told an interviewer: "For immigrants, the challenges of exile, the loneliness, the constant sense of alienation, the knowledge of and longing for a lost world, are more explicit and distressing than for their children. On the other hand, the problem for the children of immigrants, those with strong ties to their country of origin, is that they feel neither one thing nor the other. The feeling that there was no single place to which I fully belonged bothered me growing up. It bothers me less now."

Although many Indian American writers are working today—including Bharati Mukherjee, Kiran Desai, Ved Mehta, and Vikram Seth—Lahiri is one of the few who represents the perspectives of first-generation immigrants who attempt to assimilate and yet are torn between two worlds. She is also unusual among ethnic writers in her depictions of interactions between the immigrant protagonists and well-rounded and sympathetic Euro-American characters, such as the 103-year-old Victorian landlady in "The Third and Final Continent"; the twenty-two-year-old midwesterner Miranda in "Sexy," who has an adulterous affair with the Boston investment banker Dev Mitra; the nine-year-old Bostonian Eliot, whom Mrs. Sen babysits in "Mrs. Sen's"; and Gogol's Euro-American girlfriends, Ruth and Maxine, in *The Namesake.*

In "When Mr. Pirzada Came to Dine," Lahiri seems to question whether identity is based on language, religion, nationality, knowledge of history, or cultural traits and practices. Perhaps Lahiri has hit on what is quintessentially American—an obsession with the places that one has either chosen or been forced to leave and those where one has moved.

Lavina D. Shankar
Bates College

PRIMARY WORKS

Interpreter of Maladies, 1999; *The Namesake,* 2003; *Unaccustomed Earth,* 2008.

When Mr. Pirzada Came to Dine

In the autumn of 1971 a man used to come to our house, bearing confections in his pocket and hopes of ascertaining the life or death of his family. His name was Mr. Pirzada, and he came from Dacca, now the capital of Bangladesh, but then a part of Pakistan. That year Pakistan was engaged in civil war. The eastern frontier, where Dacca was located, was fighting for autonomy from the ruling regime in the west. In March, Dacca had been invaded, torched, and shelled by the Pakistani army. Teachers were dragged onto streets and shot, women dragged into barracks and raped. By the end of the summer, three hundred thousand people were said to have died. In Dacca Mr. Pirzada had a three-story home, a lectureship in botany at the university, a wife of twenty years, and seven daughters between the ages of six and sixteen whose names all began with the letter A. "Their mother's idea," he explained one day, producing from his wallet a black-and-white picture of seven girls at a picnic, their braids tied with ribbons, sitting cross-legged in a row, eating chicken curry off of banana leaves. "How am I to distinguish? Ayesha, Amira, Amina, Aziza, you see the difficulty."

Each week Mr. Pirzada wrote letters to his wife, and sent comic books to each of his seven daughters, but the postal system, along with most everything else in Dacca, had collapsed, and he had not heard word of them in over six months. Mr. Pirzada, meanwhile, was in America for the year, for he had been awarded a grant from the government of Pakistan to study the foliage of New England. In spring and summer he had gathered data in Vermont and Maine, an in autumn he moved to a university north of Boston, where we lived, to write a short book about his discoveries. The grant was a great honor, but when converted into dollars it was not generous. As a result, Mr. Pirzada lived in a room in a graduate dormitory, and did not own a proper stove or a television set of his own. And so he came to our house to eat dinner and watch the evening news.

At first I knew nothing of the reason for his visits. I was ten years old, and was not surprised that my parents, who were from India, and had a number of Indian acquaintances at the university, should ask Mr. Pirzada to share our meals. It was a small campus, with narrow brick walkways and white pillared buildings, located on the fringes of what seemed to be an even smaller town. The supermarket did not carry mustard oil, doctors did not make house calls, neighbors never dropped by without an invitation, and of these things, every so often, my parents complained. In search of compatriots, they used to trail their fingers, at the start of each new semester, through the columns of the university directory, circling surnames familiar to their part of the world. It was in this manner that they discovered Mr. Pirzada, and phoned him, and invited him to our home.

I have no memory of his first visit, or of his second or his third, but by the end of September I had grown so accustomed to Mr. Pirzada's presence in our living room that one evening, as I was dropping ice cubes into the water pitcher, I asked my mother to hand me a fourth glass from a cupboard still out of my reach. She was busy at the stove, presiding over a skillet of fried spinach with radishes, and could not hear me because of the drone of the exhaust fan and the fierce scrapes of her spatula. I turned to my father, who was leaning against the refrigerator, eating spiced cashews from a cupped fist.

"What is it, Lilia?"

"A glass for the Indian man."

"Mr. Pirzada won't be coming today. More importantly, Mr. Pirzada is no longer considered Indian," my father announced, brushing salt from the cashews out of his trim black beard. "Not since Partition. Our country was divided. 1947."

When I said I thought that was the date of India's independence from Britain, my father said, "That too. One moment we were free and then we were sliced up," he explained, drawing an X with his finger on the countertop, "like a pie. Hindus here, Muslims there. Dacca no longer belongs to us." He told me that during Partition Hindus and Muslims had set fire to each other's homes. For many, the idea of eating in the other's company was still unthinkable.

It made no sense to me. Mr. Pirzada and my parents spoke the same language, laughed at the same jokes, looked more or less the same. They ate pickled mangoes with their meals, ate rice every night for supper with their hands. Like my parents, Mr. Pirzada took off his shoes before entering a room, chewed fennel seeds after meals as a digestive, drank no alcohol, for dessert dipped austere biscuits into successive cups of tea. Nevertheless my father insisted that I understand the difference, and he led me to a map of the world taped to the wall over his desk. He seemed concerned that Mr. Pirzada might take offense if I accidentally referred to him as an Indian, though I could not really imagine Mr. Pirzada being offended by much of anything. "Mr. Pirzada is Bengali, but he is a Muslim," my father informed me. "Therefore he lives in East Pakistan, not India." His finger trailed across the Atlantic, through Europe, the Mediterranean, the Middle East, and finally to the sprawling orange diamond that my mother once told me resembled a woman wearing a sari with her left arm extended. Various cities had been circled with lines drawn between them to indicate my parents' travels, and the place of their birth, Calcutta, was signified by a small silver star. I had been there only once and had no memory of the trip. "As you see, Lilia, it is a different country, a different color," my father said. Pakistan was yellow, not orange. I noticed that there were two distinct parts to it, one much larger than the other, separated by an expanse of Indian territory; it was as if California and Connecticut constituted a nation apart from the U.S.

My father rapped his knuckles on top of my head. "You are, of course, aware of the current situation? Aware of East Pakistan's fight for sovereignty?"

I nodded, unaware of the situation.

We returned to the kitchen, where my mother was draining a pot of boiled rice into a colander. My father opened up the can on the counter and eyed me sharply over the frames of his glasses as he ate some more cashews. "What exactly do they teach you at school? Do you study history? Geography?"

"Lilia has plenty to learn at school," my mother said. "We live here now, she was born here." She seemed genuinely proud of the fact, as if it were a reflection of my character. In her estimation, I knew, I was assured a safe life, an easy life, a fine education, every opportunity. I would never have to eat rationed food, or obey curfews, or watch riots from my rooftop, or hide neighbors in water tanks to prevent them from being shot, as she and my father had. "Imagine having to place her in a decent school. Imagine her having to read during power failures by the light of kerosene lamps. Imagine the pressures, the tutors, the constant exams." She ran a hand through her hair, bobbed to a suitable length for her part-time job as a bank teller. "How can you possibly expect her to know about Partition? Put those nuts away."

"But what does she learn about the world?" My father rattled the cashew can in his hand. "What is she learning?"

We learned American history, of course, and American geography. That year, and every year, it seemed, we began by studying the Revolutionary War. We were taken in school buses on field trips to visit Plymouth Rock, and to walk the Freedom Trail, and to climb to the top of the Bunker Hill Monument. We made dioramas out of colored construction paper depicting George Washington crossing the choppy waters of the Delaware River, and we made puppets of King George wearing white tights and a black bow in his hair. During tests we were given blank maps of the thirteen colonies, and asked to fill in names, dates, capitals. I could do it with my eyes closed.

The next evening Mr. Pirzada arrived, as usual, at six o'clock. Though they were no longer strangers, upon first greeting each other, he and my father maintained the habit of shaking hands.

"Come in, sir. Lilia, Mr. Pirzada's coat, please."

He stepped into the foyer, impeccably suited and scarved, with a silk tie knotted at his collar. Each evening he appeared in ensembles of plums, olives, and chocolate browns. He was a compact man, and though his feet were perpetually splayed, and his belly slightly wide, he nevertheless maintained an efficient posture, as if balancing in either hand two suitcases of equal weight. His ears were insulated by tufts of graying hair that seemed to block out the unpleasant traffic of life. He had thickly lashed eyes shaded with a trace of camphor, a generous mustache that turned up playfully at the ends, and a mole shaped like a flattened raisin in the very center of his left cheek. On his head he wore a black fez made from the wool of Persian lambs, secured by bobby pins, without which I was never to see him. Though my father always offered to fetch him in our car, Mr. Pirzada preferred to walk from his dormitory to our neighborhood, a distance of about twenty minutes on foot, studying trees and shrubs on his way, and when he entered our house his knuckles were pink with the effects of crisp autumn air.

"Another refugee, I am afraid, on Indian territory."

"They are estimating nine million at the last count," my father said.

Mr. Pirzada handed me his coat, for it was my job to hang it on the rack at the bottom of the stairs. It was made of finely checkered gray-and-blue wool, with a striped lining and horn buttons, and carried in its weave the faint smell of limes. There were no recognizable tags inside, only a hand-stitched label with the phrase "Z. Sayeed, Suitors" embroidered on it in cursive with glossy black thread. On certain days a birch or maple leaf was tucked into a pocket. He unlaced his shoes and lined them against the baseboard; a golden paste clung to the toes and heels, the result of walking through our damp, unraked lawn. Relieved of his trappings, he grazed my throat with his short, restless fingers, the way a person feels for solidity behind a wall before driving in a nail. Then he followed my father to the living room, where the television was tuned to the local news. As soon as they were seated my mother appeared from the kitchen with a plate of mincemeat kebabs with coriander chutney. Mr. Pirzada popped one into his mouth.

"One can only hope," he said, reaching for another, "that Dacca's refugees are as heartily fed. Which reminds me." He reached into his suit pocket and gave me a small plastic egg filled with cinnamon hearts. "For the lady of the house," he said with an almost imperceptible splay-footed bow.

"Really, Mr. Pirzada," my mother protested. "Night after night. You spoil her."

"I only spoil children who are incapable of spoiling."

It was an awkward moment for me, one which I awaited in part with dread, in part with delight. I was charmed by the presence of Mr. Pirzada's rotund elegance, and flattered by the faint theatricality of his attentions, yet unsettled by the superb ease of his gestures, which made me feel, for an instant, like a stranger in my own home. It had become our ritual, and for several weeks, before we grew more comfortable with one another, it was the only time he spoke to me directly. I had no response, offered no comment, betrayed no visible reaction to the steady stream of honey-filled lozenges, the raspberry truffles, the slender rolls of sour pastilles. I could not even thank him, for once, when I did, for an especially spectacular peppermint lollipop wrapped in a spray of purple cellophane, he had demanded, "What is this thank-you? The lady at the bank thanks me, the cashier at the shop thanks me, the librarian thanks me when I return an overdue book, the overseas operator thanks me as she tries to connect me to Dacca and fails. If I am buried in this country I will be thanked, no doubt, at my funeral."

It was inappropriate, in my opinion, to consume the candy Mr. Pirzada gave me in a casual manner. I coveted each evening's treasure as I would a jewel, or a coin from a buried kingdom, and I would place it in a small keepsake box made of carved sandalwood beside my bed, in which, long ago in India, my father's mother used to store the ground areca nuts she ate after her morning bath. It was my only memento of a grandmother I had never known, and until Mr. Pirzada came to our lives I could find nothing to put inside it. Every so often before brushing my teeth and laying out my clothes for school the next day, I opened the lid of the box and ate one of his treats.

That night, like every night, we did not eat at the dining table, because it did not provide an unobstructed view of the television set. Instead we huddled around the coffee table, without conversing, our plates perched on the edges of our knees. From the kitchen my mother brought forth the succession of dishes: lentils with fried onions, green beans with coconut, fish cooked with raisins in a yogurt sauce. I followed with the water glasses, and the plate of lemon wedges, and the chili peppers, purchased on monthly trips to Chinatown and stored by the pound in the freezer, which they liked to snap open and crush into their food.

Before eating Mr. Pirzada always did a curious thing. He took out a plain silver watch without a band, which he kept in his breast pocket, held it briefly to one of his tufted ears, and wound it with three swift flicks of his thumb and forefinger. Unlike the watch on his wrist, the pocket watch, he had explained to me, was set to the local time in Dacca, eleven hours ahead. For the duration of the meal the watch rested on his folded paper napkin on the coffee table. He never seemed to consult it.

Now that I had learned Mr. Pirzada was not an Indian, I began to study him with extra care, to try to figure out what made him different. I decided that the pocket watch was one of those things. When I saw it that night, as he wound it and arranged it on the coffee table, an uneasiness possessed me; life, I realized, was being lived in Dacca first. I imagined Mr. Pirzada's daughters rising from sleep, tying ribbons in their hair, anticipating breakfast, preparing for school. Our meals, our actions, were only a shadow of what had already happened there, a lagging ghost of where Mr. Pirzada really belonged.

At six-thirty, which was when the national news began, my father raised the volume and adjusted the antennas. Usually I occupied myself with a book, but that night my father insisted that I pay attention. On the screen I saw tanks rolling through dusty streets, and fallen buildings, and forests of unfamiliar trees into which East Pakistan refugees had fled, seeking safety over the Indian border. I saw boats with fan-shaped sails floating on wide coffee-colored rivers, a barricaded university, newspaper offices burnt to the ground. I turned to look at Mr. Pirzada; the images flashed in miniature across his eyes. As he watched he had an immovable expression on his face, composed but alert, as if someone were giving him directions to an unknown destination.

During the commercial my mother went to the kitchen to get more rice, and my father and Mr. Pirzada deplored the policies of a general named Yahyah Khan. They discussed intrigues I did not know, a catastrophe I could not comprehend. "See, children your age, what they do to survive," my father said as he served me another piece of fish. But I could no longer eat. I could only steal glances at Mr. Pirzada, sitting beside me in his olive green jacket, calmly creating a well in his rice to make room for a second helping of lentils. He was not my notion of a man burdened by such grave concerns. I wondered if the reason he was always so smartly dressed was in preparation to endure with dignity whatever news assailed him, perhaps even to attend a funeral at a moment's notice. I wondered, too, what would happen if suddenly his seven daughters were to appear on television, smiling and waving and blowing kisses to Mr. Pirzada from a balcony. I imagined how relieved he would be. But this never happened.

That night when I placed the plastic egg filled with cinnamon hearts in the box beside my bed, I did not feel the ceremonious satisfaction I normally did. I tried not to think about Mr. Pirzada, in his lime-scented overcoat, connected to the unruly, sweltering world we had viewed a few hours ago in our bright, carpeted living room. And yet for several moments that was all I could think about. My stomach tightened as I worried whether his wife and seven daughters were now members of the drifting, clamoring crowd that had flashed at intervals on the screen. In an effort to banish the image I looked around my room, at the yellow canopied bed with matching flounced curtains, at framed class pictures mounted on white and violet papered walls, at the penciled inscriptions by the closet door where my father recorded my height on each of my birthdays. But the more I tried to distract myself, the more I began to convince myself that Mr. Pirzada's family was in all likelihood dead. Eventually I took a square of white chocolate out of the box, and unwrapped it, and then I did something I had never done before. I put the chocolate in my mouth, letting it soften until the last possible moment, and then as I chewed it slowly, I prayed that Mr. Pirzada's family was safe and sound. I had never prayed for anything before, had never been taught or told to, but I decided, given the circumstances, that it was something I should do. That night when I went to the bathroom I only pretended to brush my teeth, for I feared that I would somehow rinse the prayer out as well. I wet the brush and rearranged the tube of paste to prevent my parents from asking any questions, and fell asleep with sugar on my tongue.

No one at school talked about the war followed so faithfully in my living room. We continued to study the American Revolution, and learned about the injustices of taxation without representation, and memorized passages from the Declaration of Independence. During recess the boys would divide in two groups, chasing each other wildly around the swings and seesaws, Redcoats against the colonies. In the class-room our teacher, Mrs. Kenyon, pointed frequently to a map that emerged like a movie screen from the top of the chalkboard, charting the route of the *Mayflower,* or showing us the location of the Liberty Bell. Each week two members of the class gave a report on a particular aspect of the Revolution, and so one day I was sent to the school library with my friend Dora to learn about the surrender at Yorktown. Mrs. Kenyon handed us a slip of paper with the names of three books to look up in the card catalogue. We found them right away, and sat down at a low round table to read and take notes. But I could not concentrate. I returned to the blond-wood shelves, to a section I had noticed labeled "Asia." I saw books about China, India, Indonesia, Korea. Eventually I found a book titled *Pakistan: A Land and Its People.* I sat on a footstool and opened the book. The laminated jacket crackled in my grip. I began turning the pages, filled with photos of rivers and rice fields and men in military uni-forms. There was a chapter about Dacca, and I began to read about its rainfall, and its jute production. I was studying a population chart when Dora appeared in the aisle.

"What are you doing back here? Mrs. Kenyon's in the library. She came to check up on us."

I slammed the book shut, too loudly. Mrs. Kenyon emerged, the aroma of her perfume filling up the tiny aisle, and lifted the book by the tip of its spine as if it were a hair clinging to my sweater. She glanced at the cover, then at me.

"Is this book a part of your report, Lilia?"

"No, Mrs. Kenyon."

"Then I see no reason to consult it," she said, replacing it in the slim gap on the shelf. "Do you?"

As weeks passed it grew more and more rare to see any footage from Dacca on the news. The report came after the first set of commercials, sometimes the second. The press had been censored, removed, restricted, rerouted. Some days, many days, only a death toll was announced, prefaced by a reiteration of the general situation. More poets were executed, more villages set ablaze. In spite of it all, night after night, my parents and Mr. Pirzada enjoyed long, leisurely meals. After the television was shut off, and the dishes washed and dried, they joked, and told stories, and dipped biscuits in their tea. When they tired of discussing political matters they discussed, instead, the progress of Mr. Pirzada's book about the deciduous trees of New England, and my father's nomination for tenure, and the peculiar eating habits of my mother's American coworkers at the bank. Eventually I was sent upstairs to do my homework, but through the carpet I heard them as they drank more tea, and listened to cassettes of Kishore Kumar, and played Scrabble on the coffee table, laughing and arguing long into the night about the spellings of English words. I wanted to join them, wanted, above all, to console Mr. Pirzada somehow. But apart from eating a piece of candy for the sake of his family and praying for their safety, there was nothing I could do. They played Scrabble until the eleven o'clock news, and then, sometime around midnight, Mr. Pirzada walked back to his dormitory. For this reason I never saw him leave, but each night as I drifted off to sleep I would hear them, anticipating the birth of a nation on the other side of the world.

One day in October Mr. Pirzada asked upon arrival, "What are these large orange vegetables on people's doorsteps? A type of squash?"

"Pumpkins," my mother replied. "Lilia, remind me to pick one up at the supermarket."

"And the purpose? It indicates what?"

"You make a jack-o'-lantern," I said, grinning ferociously. "Like this. To scare people away."

"I see," Mr. Pirzada said, grinning back. "Very useful."

The next day my mother bought a ten-pound pumpkin, fat and round, and placed it on the dining table. Before supper, while my father and Mr. Pirzada were watching the local news, she told me to decorate it with markers, but I wanted to carve it properly like others I had noticed in the neighborhood.

"Yes, let's carve it," Mr. Pirzada agreed, and rose from the sofa. "Hang the news tonight." Asking no questions, he walked into the kitchen, opened a drawer, and returned, bearing a long serrated knife. He glanced at me for approval. "Shall I?"

I nodded. For the first time we all gathered around the dining table, my mother, my father, Mr. Pirzada, and I. While the television aired unattended we covered the tabletop with newspapers. Mr. Pirzada draped his jacket over the chair behind him, removed a pair of opal cuff links, and rolled up the starched sleeves of his shirt.

"First go around the top, like this," I instructed, demonstrating with my index finger.

He made an initial incision and drew the knife around. When he had come full circle he lifted the cap by the stem; it loosened effortlessly, and Mr. Pirzada leaned over the pumpkin for a moment to inspect and inhale its contents. My mother gave him a long metal spoon with which he gutted the interior until the last bits of string and seeds were gone. My father, meanwhile, separated the seeds from the pulp and set them out to dry on a cookie sheet, so that we could roast them later on. I drew two triangles against the ridged surface for the eyes, which Mr. Pirzada dutifully carved, and crescents for eyebrows, and another triangle for the nose. The mouth was all that remained, and the teeth posed a challenge. I hesitated.

"Smile or frown?" I asked.

"You choose," Mr. Pirzada said.

As a compromise I drew a kind of grimace, straight across, neither mournful nor friendly. Mr. Pirzada began carving, without the least bit of intimidation, as if he had been carving jack-o'-lanterns his whole life. He had nearly finished when the national news began. The reporter mentioned Dacca, and we all turned to listen: An Indian official announced that unless the world helped to relieve the burden of East Pakistani refugees, India would have to go to war against Pakistan. The reporter's face dripped with sweat as he relayed the information. He did not wear a tie or a jacket, dressed instead as if he himself were about to take part in the battle. He shielded his scorched face as he hollered things to the cameraman. The knife slipped from Mr. Pirzada's hand and made a gash dripping toward the base of the pumpkin.

"Please forgive me." He raised a hand to one side of his face, as if someone had slapped him there. "I am—it is terrible. I will buy another. We will try again."

"Not at all, not at all," my father said. He took the knife from Mr. Pirzada, and carved around the gash, evening it out, dispensing altogether with the teeth I had drawn. What resulted was a disproportionately large hole the size of a lemon, so that our jack-o'-lantern wore an expression of placid astonishment, the eyebrows no longer fierce, floating in frozen surprise above a vacant, geometric gaze.

For Halloween I was a witch. Dora, my trick-or-treating partner, was a witch too. We wore black capes fashioned from dyed pillowcases and conical hats with wide cardboard brims. We shaded our faces green with a broken eye shadow that belonged to Dora's mother, and my mother gave us two burlap sacks that had once contained basmati rice, for collecting candy. That year our parents decided that we were old enough to roam the neighborhood unattended. Our plan was to walk from my house to Dora's, from where I was to call to say I had arrived safely, and then Dora's mother would drive me home. My father equipped us with flashlights, and I had to wear my watch and synchronize it with his. We were to return no later than nine o'clock.

When Mr. Pirzada arrived that evening he presented me with a box of chocolate-covered mints.

"In here," I told him, and opened up the burlap sack. "Trick or treat!"

"I understand that you don't really need my contribution this evening," he said, depositing the box. He gazed at my green face, and the hat secured by a string under my chin. Gingerly he lifted the hem of the cape, under which I was wearing a sweater and a zipped fleece jacket. "Will you be warm enough?"

I nodded, causing the hat to tip to one side.

He set it right. "Perhaps it is best to stand still."

The bottom of our staircase was lined with baskets of miniature candy, and when Mr. Pirzada removed his shoes he did not place them there as he normally did, but inside the closet instead. He began to unbutton his coat, and I waited to take it from him, but Dora called me from the bathroom to say that she needed my help drawing a mole on her chin. When we were finally ready my mother took a picture of us in front of the fireplace, and then I opened the front door to leave. Mr. Pirzada and my father, who had not gone into the living room yet, hovered in the foyer. Outside it was already dark. The air smelled of wet leaves, and our carved jack-o'-lantern flickered impressively against the shrubbery by the door. In the distance came the sounds of scampering feet, and the howls of the older boys who wore no costume at all other than a rubber mask, and the rustling apparel of the youngest children, some so young that they were carried from door to door in the arms of their parents.

"Don't go into any of the houses you don't know," my father warned.

Mr. Pirzada knit his brows together. "Is there any danger?"

"No, no," my mother assured him. "All the children will be out. It's a tradition."

"Perhaps I should accompany them?" Mr. Pirzada suggested. He looked suddenly tired and small, standing there in his splayed, stockinged feet, and his eyes contained a panic I had never seen before. In spite of the cold I began to sweat inside my pillowcase.

"Really, Mr. Pirzada," my mother said. "Lilia will be perfectly safe with her friend."

"But if it rains? If they lose their way?"

"Don't worry," I said. It was the first time I had uttered those words to Mr. Pirzada, two simple words I had tried but failed to tell him for weeks, had said only in my prayers. It shamed me now that I had said them for my own sake.

He placed one of his stocky fingers on my cheek, then pressed it to the back of his own hand, leaving a faint green smear. "If the lady insists," he conceded, and offered a small bow.

We left, stumbling slightly in our black pointy thrift-store shoes, and when we turned at the end of the driveway to wave good-bye, Mr. Pirzada was standing in the frame of the doorway, a short figure between my parents, waving back.

"Why did that man want to come with us?" Dora asked.

"His daughters are missing." As soon as I said it, I wished I had not. I felt that my saying it made it true, that Mr. Pirzada's daughters really were missing, and that he would never see them again.

"You mean they were kidnapped?" Dora continued. "From a park or something?"

"I didn't mean they were missing. I meant, he misses them. They live in a different country, and he hasn't seen them in a while, that's all."

We went from house to house, walking along pathways and pressing doorbells. Some people had switched off all their lights for effect, or strung rubber bats in their windows. At the McIntyres' a coffin was placed in front of the door, and Mr. McIntyre rose from it in silence, his face covered with chalk, and deposited a fistful of candy corns into our sacks. Several people told me that they had never seen an Indian witch before. Others performed the transaction without comment. As we paved our way with the parallel beams of our flashlights we saw eggs cracked in the middle of the road, and cars covered with shaving cream, and toilet paper garlanding branches of trees. By the time we reached Dora's house our hands were chapped from carrying our burlap bags, and our feet were sore and swollen. Her mother gave us bandages for our blisters and served us warm cider and caramel popcorn. She reminded me to call my parents to tell them that I had arrived safely, and when I did I could hear the television in the background. My mother did not seem particularly relieved to hear from me. When I replaced the phone on the receiver it occurred to me that the television wasn't on at Dora's house at all. Her father was lying on the couch, reading a magazine, with a glass of wine on the coffee table, and there was saxophone music playing on the stereo.

After Dora and I had sorted through our plunder, and counted and sampled and traded until we were satisfied, her mother drove me back to my house. I thanked her for the ride, and she waited in the driveway until I made it to the door. In the glare of her headlights I saw that our pumpkin had been shattered, its thick shell strewn in chunks across the grass. I felt the sting of tears in my eyes, and a sudden pain in my throat, as if it had been stuffed with the sharp tiny pebbles that crunched with each step under my aching feet. I opened the door, expecting the three of them to be standing in the foyer, waiting to receive me, and to grieve for our ruined pumpkin, but there was no one. In the living room Mr. Pirzada, my father, and mother were sitting side by side on the sofa. The television was turned off, and Mr. Pirzada had his head in his hands.

What they heard that evening, and for many evenings after that, was that India and Pakistan were drawing closer and closer to war. Troops from both sides lined the border, and Dacca was insisting on nothing short of independence. The war was to be waged on East Pakistani soil. The United States was siding with West Pakistan, the Soviet Union with India and what was soon to be Bangladesh. War was declared officially on December 4, and twelve days later, the Pakistani army, weakened by having to fight three thousand miles from their source of supplies, surrendered in Dacca. All of these facts I know only now, for they are available to me in any history book, in any library. But then it remained, for the most part, a remote mystery with haphazard clues. What I remember during those twelve days of the war was that my father no longer asked me to watch the news with them, and that Mr. Pirzada stopped bringing me candy, and that my mother refused to serve anything other than boiled eggs with rice for dinner. I remember some nights helping my mother spread a sheet and blankets on the couch so that Mr. Pirzada could sleep there, and high-pitched voices hollering in the middle of the night when my parents called our relatives in Calcutta to learn more details about the situation. Most of all I remember the three of them operating during that time as if they were a single person, sharing a single meal, a single body, a single silence, and a single fear.

In January, Mr. Pirzada flew back to his three-story home in Dacca, to discover what was left of it. We did not see much of him in those final weeks of the year; he was busy finishing his manuscript, and we went to Philadelphia to spend Christmas with friends of my parents. Just as I have no memory of his first visit, I have no memory of his last. My father drove him to the airport one afternoon while I was at school. For a long time we did not hear from him. Our evenings went on as usual, with dinners in front of the news. The only difference was that Mr. Pirzada and his extra watch were not there to accompany us. According to reports Dacca was repairing itself slowly, with a newly formed parliamentary government. The new leader, Sheikh Mujib Rahman, recently released from prison, asked countries for building materials to replace more than one million houses that had been destroyed in the war. Countless refugees returned from India, greeted, we learned, by unemployment and the threat of famine. Every now and then I studied the map above my father's desk and pictured Mr. Pirzada on that small patch of yellow, perspiring heavily, I imagined, in one of his suits, searching for his family. Of course, the map was outdated by then.

Finally, several months later, we received a card from Mr. Pirzada commemorating the Muslim New Year, along with a short letter. He was reunited, he wrote, with his wife and children. All were well, having survived the events of the past year at an estate belonging to his wife's grandparents in the mountains of Shillong. His seven daughters were a bit taller, he wrote, but otherwise they were the same, and he still could not keep their names in order. At the end of the letter he thanked us for our hospitality, adding that although he now understood the meaning of the words "thank you" they still were not adequate to express his gratitude. To celebrate the good news my mother prepared a special dinner that evening, and when we sat down to eat at the coffee table we toasted our water glasses, but I did not feel like celebrating. Though I had not seen him for months, it was only then that I felt Mr. Pirzada's absence. It was only then, raising my water glass in his name, that I knew what it meant to miss someone who was so many miles and hours away, just as he had missed his wife and daughters for so many months. He had no reason to return to us, and my parents predicted, correctly, that we would never see him again. Since January, each night before bed, I had continued to eat, for the sake of Mr. Pirzada's family, a piece of candy I had saved from Halloween. That night there was no need to. Eventually, I threw them away.

2000

Joe Sacco b. 1960

Joe Sacco, one of the pioneers of comics journalism, was born in Malta in 1960 and is now a permanent U.S. resident. Sacco was born to a Catholic family in the village of Kirkop, which has a population of eight hundred. His family moved to Australia when he was a child and then to Los Angeles before settling in Oregon, where Sacco lives now. Sacco's southern European parents survived terrifying German and Italian air raids on British-controlled Malta during World War II.

When Sacco was a child, the experiences of his parents drew him, like fellow cartoonist Art Spiegelman, into the physical and emotional consequences of war for targeted civilians: "The fact that I grew up always hearing about war and what the consequences were made it so that war is a fact of life," he told the *Journal News*. The twenty-one-page comic-strip story "More

Women, More Children, More Quickly: Malta 1935–43 as Recounted by Carmen M. Sacco" (1990), in which he interviews his mother about her experiences during raids that injured and killed her friends and family, is one of Sacco's first pieces of mature work. Here for the first time he displays the anchoring, structural aspect of his later, groundbreaking work—his visual re-creation of testimony by witnesses to historical trauma.

Before he decided to merge literary comics' strong autobiographical genre with the narrative aims and style of New Journalism, Sacco wrote a lengthy comics story about the Vietnam War (which failed to find a publisher), and he illustrated a book that collected case studies of human rights abuses. These two early projects represent his fascination with the horizon of history, but they are missing the feature that makes

"More Women" and his subsequent books successful—Sacco's firsthand eliciting of testimony.

As an author who has largely funded his own travels and works independently, Sacco is answerable only to his own fierce "journalistic ethic," as he puts it. As he explained this to me in an interview, "I want to show the truth of what I saw more than what I want people to see, or what I think is, the right way of seeing things. . . . Honesty means showing things that you think are going to hurt the cause you support."

In late 1991 and early 1992, Sacco spent two months in Palestine and Israel, where he interviewed hundreds of people on both sides of the conflict there. The American Book Award–winning *Palestine,* his first major work of comics journalism, takes place at the end of the first intifada (1987–1993). Its nine chapters present fifty episodes that range from one to thirty-two pages and that have titles such as "Hebron," "Ansar III," "'Moderate Pressure' Part 2," and "A Boy in the Rain."

The heart of the book takes place in the Jabalia refugee camp, where Sacco often stayed with a camp resident and translator named Sameh. Sacco interviews American Jews, Israeli Jews, survivors who fled Palestine in 1948, Palestinian hospital workers and patients, families testifying to violence, former Israeli prison inmates, torture victims, feminist activists, lawyers who defend stone throwing and honor killings, tomato farmers, teenagers and young men active in the intifada, disabled shooting victims, bereaved mothers and widows, and everyday destitute citizens.

His second major work, *Safe Area Gorazde,* takes place at the end of the Bosnian War. It focuses on the residents of the so-called U.N.-designated safe area of Gorazde, a largely Muslim enclave in Bosnian Serb territory that Sacco visited four times in late 1995 and early 1996.

His next Balkans-related project, *The Fixer,* is set in Sarajevo and jumps around in time, from 1995 to 2001, with frequent flashbacks to the early 1990s. Although Sacco interviews Serbian and Muslim Sarajevans and journalists, and government figures such as a Bosnian army colonel and intelligence chief, Sacco's chief subject and witness is Neven, an exploitative, morally ambiguous, and yet magnetic "fixer." Here, as elsewhere, Sacco's work incorporates the instability of journalism itself and investigates the nexus of trauma and memory.

Sacco, who has contributed his comics reporting to various publications, including *Time,* the *New York Times Magazine, Details,* and *Harper's,* is at work on a book about the Gaza Strip. In 2007, Fantagraphics published the special anniversary edition of *Palestine.*

Hillary Chute
Harvard University

A Boy in the Rain

Cluster: America in the World / The World in America— Globalization and Post-9/11 American Culture

When asked what has defined American culture in the early twenty-first century, many might point to the destruction of New York's World Trade Center towers, the U.S.-led war in Iraq, and Hurricane Katrina in the Gulf Coast states. As the authors in this cluster make clear, such events reveal a painful paradox. As U.S. economic and cultural domination has increased, the country has become a focus for the frustrations of violent religious zealots. And their attacks—both physical and ideological—have challenged U.S. domination itself.

As the readings in this cluster progress from the general to the local, from readings of culture to readings of literature, they wrestle with this and related paradoxes. Literary scholar Wai Chee Dimock asks whether American literature is autonomous or "dependent," and her answer begins with a discussion not of novels or poems but of what she calls the failed model of the nation-state. Dimock's observation that post-Katrina New Orleans resembled an underdeveloped country reflects a fundamental shift from a notion of the United States as a distinct and clearly defined "container" to one that emphasizes its porousness and instability.

A similar split between boundary and dispersal is central to the French philosopher and social theorist Jean Baudrillard's influential discussion of the 9/11 attacks. But while Dimock sees the unmaking of national boundaries as an effect of globalization, Baudrillard emphasizes the failure of globalization. For Baudrillard, the end of the cold war permitted U.S. power and influence to expand without hindrance.

The terrorist rhetoric of self-sacrifice disrupts this power and with it the postnational ideal of a unified or boundary-less world. Baudrillard distinguishes the methods and ideology of the terrorist attackers from those of industrialized powers, but he also undermines this us-versus-them rhetoric by claiming that Americans imagined and—more controversially—wanted the attacks. Baudrillard also argues that the attacks were from the outset inseparable from the symbolic ways that they were represented. Their reality was "everywhere infiltrated by images, virtuality and fiction" in ways that challenged the notion of reality itself.

Baudrillard's claim about the centrality of images and symbols in the attacks helps explain recent U.S. writers' preoccupation with describing these attacks, and the cluster's final three readings offer quite different responses. The celebrated American novelist Don DeLillo's 2001 essay, published at nearly the same time as Baudrillard's, also challenges the objective reality of the attacks. DeLillo, though, focuses on the ways that the attacks undermined our notion of and faith in the future and on the function of narrative itself. In response to the destructive plot perpetuated by attackers, DeLillo explores counternarratives, many of which complicate the notion of truth. DeLillo's essay is a case in point: he gives us no way to determine whether the account of Karen and Marc is true or fictional.

DeLillo's essay implies that the artificiality and uncertainty of narrative offer an alternative to the reductiveness and, by implication, the destructiveness of the attacks.

Literary scholars Michael Rothberg and David Simpson ask whether literature can offer an antidote to terrorism or at least to its treatment by the mass media. For Rothberg, literature allows the private realm of feeling to be assimilated to the public realm of seeing. Simpson takes a different approach to 9/11 literature, delineating the challenges facing two different modes of literary response to disaster. Literature filled with graphic details risks numbing its readers. Yet Simpson also sees a danger in the tendency of some post-9/11 novels to assimilate 9/11 into its characters' ordinary lives, a tendency that risks trivializing the disaster in ways that recall the glib and reductive narratives of what he calls the mainstream. Literature is thus for Simpson less powerful than for Rothberg; it often fails to challenge its readers' complacency.

As the differences among these excerpts suggest, stories—including the stories of globalization and 9/11—are seldom consistent. In this way, the discrepancies between these accounts point to the importance of storytelling itself and thus to literature. These essays do not resolve the recurrent questions they raise about truth, symbol, narrative, and the relation of the private to the public, but they create a space for literature itself, which, as several of them imply, is well suited to consider just these questions.

Ann Keniston
University of Nevada, Reno

Jean Baudrillard 1929–2007

from The Spirit of Terrorism

When it comes to world events, we had seen quite a few. From the death of Diana to the World Cup. And violent, real events, from wars right through to genocides. Yet, when it comes to symbolic events on a world scale—that is to say not just events that gain worldwide coverage, but events that represent a setback for globalization itself— we had had none. Throughout the stagnation of the 1990s, events were "on strike" (as the Argentinian writer Macedonio Fernandez put it). Well, the strike is over now. Events are not on strike any more. With the attacks on the World Trade Center in New York, we might even be said to have before us the absolute event, the "mother" of all events, the pure event uniting within itself all the events that have never taken place.

The whole play of history and power is disrupted by this event, but so, too, are the condition of analysis. You have to take your time. While events were stagnating, you had to anticipate and move more quickly than they did. But when they speed up this much, you have to move more slowly—though without allowing yourself to be buried beneath a welter of words, or the gathering clouds of war, and preserving intact the unforgettable incandescence of the images.

All that has been said and written is evidence of a gigantic aberation to the event itself, and the fascination it exerts. The moral condemnation and the holy alliance against terrorism are on the same scale as the prodigious jubilation at seeing this global superpower destroyed—better, at seeing it, in a sense, destroying itself, committing suicide in a blaze of glory. For it is that superpower which, by its unbearable power, has fomented all this violence which is endemic throughout the world, and hence that (unwittingly) terroristic imagination which dwells in all of us.

The fact that we have dreamt of this event, that everyone without exception has dreamt of it—because no one can avoid dreaming of the destruction of any power that has become hegemonic to this degree—is unacceptable to the Western moral conscience. Yet it is a fact, and one which can indeed be measured by the emotive violence of all that has been said and written in the effort to dispel it.

At a pinch, we can say that they *did it,* but we *wished for* it. If this is not taken into account, the event loses any symbolic dimension. It becomes a pure accident, a purely arbitrary act, the murderous phantasmagoria of a few fanatics, and all that would then remain would be to eliminate them. Now, we know very well that this is not how it is. Which explains all the counterphobic ravings about exorcizing evil: it is because it is there, everywhere, like an obscure object of desire. Without this deep-seated complicity, the event would not have had the resonance it has, and in their symbolic strategy the terrorists doubtless know that they can count on this unavowable complicity.

This goes far beyond hatred for the dominant world power among the disinherited and the exploited, among those who have ended up on the wrong side of the global order. Even those who share in the advantages of that order have this malicious desire in their hearts. Allergy to any definitive order, to any definitive power, is—happily—universal, and the two towers of the World Trade Center were perfect embodiments, in their very twinness, of that definitive order.

No need, then, for death drive or a destructive instinct, or even for perverse, unintended effects. Very logically—and inexorably—the increase in the power of power heightens the will to destroy it. And it was party to its own destruction. When the two towers collapsed, you had the impression that they were responding to the suicide of the suicide-planes with their own suicides. It has been said that "Even God cannot declare war on Himself." Well, He can. The West, in the position of God (divine omnipotence and absolute moral legitimacy), has become suicidal, and declared war on itself.

The countless disaster movies bear witness to this fantasy, which they clearly attempt to exorcise with images, drowning out the whole thing with special effects. But the universal attraction they exert, which is on a par with pornography, shows that acting-out is never very far away, the impulse to reject any system growing all the stronger as it approaches perfection or omnipotence.

It is probable that the terrorists had not foreseen the collapse of the Twin Towers (any more than had the experts!), a collapse which—much more than the attack on the Pentagon—had the greatest symbolic impact. The symbolic collapse of a whole system came about by an unpredictable complicity, as though the towers, by collapsing on their own, by committing suicide, had joined in to round off the event. In a sense, the entire system, by its internal fragility, lent the initial action a helping hand.

The more concentrated the system becomes globally, ultimately forming one single network, the more it becomes vulnerable at a single point (already a single little Filipino hacker had managed, from the dark recesses of his portable computer, to launch the "I love you" virus, which circled the globe devastating entire networks).

Here it was eighteen suicide attackers who, thanks to the absolute weapon of death, enhanced by technological efficiency, unleashed a global catastrophic process.

When global power monopolizes the situation to this extent, when there is such a formidable condensation of all functions in the technocratic machinery, and when no alternative form of thinking is allowed, what other way is there but a *terroristic situational transfer?* It was the system itself which created the objective conditions for this brutal retaliation. By seizing all the cards for itself, it forced the Other to change the rules. And the new rules are fierce ones, because the stakes are fierce. To a system whose very excess of power poses an insoluble challenge, the terrorists respond with a definitive act which is also not susceptible of exchange. Terrorism is the act that restores an irreducible singularity to the heart of a system of generalized exchange. All the singularities (species, individuals and cultures) that have paid with their deaths for the installation of a global circulation governed by a single power are taking their revenge today through this *terroristic situational transfer.*

This is terror against terror—there is no longer any ideology behind it. We are far beyond ideology and politics now. No ideology, no cause—not even the Islamic cause—can account for the energy which fuels terror. The aim is no longer even to transform the world, but (as the heresies did in their day) to radicalize the world by sacrifice. Whereas the system aims to realize it by force.

Terrorism, like viruses, is everywhere. There is a global perfusion of terrorism, which accompanies any system of domination as though it were its shadow, ready to activate itself anywhere, like a double agent. We can no longer draw a demarcation line around it. It is at the very heart of this culture which combats it, and the visible fracture (and the hatred) that pits the exploited and the underdeveloped globally against the Western world secretly connects with the fracture internal to the dominant system. That system can face down any visible antagonism. But against the other kind, which is viral in structure—as though every machinery of domination secreted its own counterapparatus, the agent of its own disappearance—against that form of almost automatic reversion of its own power, the system can do nothing. And terrorism is the shock wave of this silent reversion.

This is not, then, a clash of civilizations or religions, and it reaches far beyond Islam and America, on which efforts are being made to focus the conflict in order to create the delusion of a visible confrontation and a solution based on force. There is, indeed, a fundamental antagonism here, but one which points past the spectre of America (which is, perhaps, the epicentre, but in no sense the sole embodiment, of globalization) and the spectre of Islam (which is not the embodiment of terrorism either), to *triumphant globalization battling against itself.* In this sense, we can indeed speak of a world war—not the Third World War, but the Fourth and the only really global one, since what is at stake is globalization itself. The first two world wars corresponded to the classical image of war. The first ended the supremacy of Europe and the colonial era. The second put an end to Nazism. The third, which has indeed taken place, in the form of cold war and deterrence, put an end to Communism. With each succeeding war, we have moved further towards a single world order. Today that order, which has virtually reached its culmination, finds itself grappling with the antagonistic forces scattered throughout the very heartlands of the global, in all the current convulsions. A fractal war of all cells, all singularities, revolting in the form of antibodies. A confrontation so impossible to pin down that the idea of war has to be rescued from time to time by spectacular set-pieces, such as the Gulf War or the war in Afghanistan. But the Fourth World War is elsewhere. It is what haunts every world order, all hegemonic domination—if Islam dominated the world, terrorism would rise against Islam, *for it is the world, the globe itself, which resists globalization.* . . .

In all these vicissitudes, what stays with us, above all else, is the sight of the images. This impact of the images, and their fascination, are necessarily what we retain, since images are, whether we like it or not, our primal scene. And, at the same time as they have radicalized the world situation, the events in New York can also be said to have radicalized the relation of the image to reality. Whereas we were dealing before with an uninterrupted profusion of banal images and a seamless flow of sham events, the terrorist act in New York has resuscitated both images and events.

Among the other weapons of the system which they turned round against it, the terrorists exploited the "real time" of images, their instantaneous worldwide transmission, just as they exploited stock-market speculation, electronic information and air traffic. The role of images is highly ambiguous. For, at the same time as they exalt the event, they also take it hostage. They serve to multiply it to infinity and, at the same time, they are a diversion and a neutralization (this was already the case with the events of 1968). The image consumes the event, in the sense that it absorbs it and offers it for consumption. Admittedly, it gives it unprecedented impact, but impact as image-event.

How do things stand with the real event, then, if reality is everywhere infiltrated by images, virtuality and fiction? In the present case, we thought we had seen (perhaps with a certain relief) a resurgence of the real, and of the violence of the real, in an allegedly virtual universe. "There's an end to all your talk about the virtual— this is something real!" Similarly, it was possible to see this as a resurrection of history beyond its proclaimed end. But does reality actually outstrip fiction? If it seems to do so, this is because it has absorbed fiction's energy, and has itself become fiction. We might almost say that reality is jealous of fiction, that the real is jealous of the image. . . . It is a kind of duel between them, a contest to see which can be the most unimaginable.

The collapse of the World Trade Center towers is unimaginable, but that is not enough to make it a real event. An excess of violence is not enough to open on to reality. For reality is a principle, and it is this principle that is lost. Reality and fiction are inextricable, and the fascination with the attack is primarily a fascination with the image (both its exultatory and its catastrophic consequences are themselves largely imaginary).

In this case, then, the real is superadded to the image like a bonus of terror, like an additional *frisson:* not only is it terrifying, but, what is more, it is real. Rather than the violence of the real being there first, and the *frisson* of the image being added to it, the image is there first, and the *frisson* of the real is added. Something like an additional fiction, a fiction surpassing fiction. Ballard[1] (after Borges)[2] talked like this of reinventing the real as the ultimate and most redoubtable fiction.

---

[1] J. G. Ballard (b. 1930) is a British author whose subject matter is the dystopian future.

[2] Jorge Luis Borges (1899–1986) was an Argentine writer of postmodern fiction.

The terrorist violence here is not, then, a blowback of reality, any more than it is a blowback of history. It is not "real." In a sense, it is worse: it is symbolic. Violence in itself may be perfectly banal and inoffensive. Only symbolic violence is generative of singularity. And in this singular event, in this Manhattan disaster movie, the twentieth century's two elements of mass fascination are combined: the white magic of the cinema and the black magic of terrorism; the white light of the image and the black light of terrorism.

We try retrospectively to impose some kind of meaning on it, to find some kind of interpretation. But there is none. And it is the radicality of the spectacle, the brutality of the spectacle, which alone is original and irreducible. The spectacle of terrorism forces the terrorism of spectacle upon us. And, against this immoral fascination (even if it unleashes a universal moral reaction), the political order can do nothing. This is *our* theatre of cruelty, the only one we have left—extraordinary in that it unites the most extreme degree of the spectacular and the highest level of challenge. . . . It is at one and the same time the dazzling micromodel of a kernel of real violence with the maximum possible echo—hence the purest form of spectacle—and a sacrificial model mounting the purest symbolic form of defiance to the historical and political order. . . .

20xx

Wai Chee Dimock b. 1953

Planet and America, Set and Subset

What exactly is "American literature"? Is it a sovereign domain, self-sustained and self-governing, integral as a body of evidence? Or is it less autonomous than that, not altogether freestanding, but more like a municipality: a second-tier phenomenon, resting on a platform preceding it and encompassing it, and dependent on the latter for its infrastructure, its support network, its very existence as a subsidiary unit?

This jurisdictional language is meant to highlight American literature as a constituted domain and the variously imagined *ground* for its constitution. That ground, though methodologically crucial, is often left implicit. On what footing can the field call itself a field, and according to what integrating principle? What degree of self-determination can it lay claim to? And what does it have in common with the territorial jurisdiction whose name it bears, whose clear-cut borders contain an attribute we are tempted to call "American-ness"?

After the World Trade Center, and after Katrina, few of us are under the illusion that the United States is sovereign in any absolute sense. The nation seems to have come literally "unbundled" before our eyes, its fabric of life torn apart by extremist militant groups, and by physical forces of even greater scope, wrought by climate change and the intensified hurricane cycles. Territorial sovereignty, we suddenly realize, is no more than a legal fiction, a man-made fiction. This fiction is not honored by religious adherents who have a different vision of the world; nor is it honored by the spin of hurricanes accelerated by the thermodynamics of warming oceans. In each case, the nation is revealed to be what it is: an epiphenomenon, literally a superficial construct, a set of erasable lines on the face of the earth. It is no match for that grounded entity called the planet, which can wipe out those lines at a moment's notice, using weapons of mass destruction more powerful than any homeland defense.

"Globalization" is the familiar term used to describe this unraveling of national sovereignty. This process, seemingly inevitable, has been diagnosed in almost antithetical ways. On the one hand, theorists from Michael Walzer to Jürgen Habermas see an enormous potential in the decline of the nation-state; for them, this jurisdictional form, historically monopolizing violence, and now increasingly outmoded, must give way to other forms of human association: a "global civil society," a "postnational constellation." On the other hand, theorists such as Fredric Jameson caution against such optimism, pointing to the "McDonaldization" of the world, a regime of standardization and homogenization ushered in by the erosion of national borders, presided over by global capital and the "unchallenged primacy of the United States."

What Katrina dramatizes, however, is a form of "globalization" different from either scenario. Not benign, it is at the same time not predicated on the primacy of any nation. Long accustomed to seeing itself as the de facto center of the world—the military superpower, the largest economy, and the moral arbiter to boot—the United States suddenly finds itself downgraded to something considerably less. "It's like being in a Third World country," Mitch Handler, a manager in Louisiana's biggest public hospital, said to the Associated Press about the plight of hurricane victims. This Third-Worlding of a superpower came with a shock not only to Louisiana and Mississippi but to unbelieving eyes everywhere. Not the actor but the acted upon, the United States is simply the spot where catastrophe hits, the place on the map where large-scale forces, unleashed elsewhere, come home to roost. What does it mean for the United States to be on the receiving end of things? The experience is novel, mind-shattering in many ways, and a numbing patriotism is not incompatible with a numbing shame. To the rest of the world, however, this massive systemic failure confirms their view of the United States not only as a miscreant abroad—a "rogue nation" both in its rejection of the Kyoto Protocol and in its conduct of the Iraq War—but as one equally inept at home, falling far below an acceptable standard of care for its own citizens. Scale enlargement has stripped from this nation any dream of unchallenged primacy. If Europe has already been "provincialized"—has been revealed to be a smaller player in world history than previously imagined, as Dipesh Chakrabarty argues—the United States seems poised to follow suit.

In this context, it seems important to rethink the adequacy of a nation-based paradigm. Is "America" an adjective that can stand on its own, uninflected, unentangled, and unconstrained? Can an autonomous field be built on its chronology and geography, equal to the task of phenomenal description and causal explanation? Janice Radway, in her presidential address to the American Studies Association in 1998, answers with a resounding "no," and proposes a name change for the association for just that reason. A field calling itself "American" imagines that there is something exceptional about the United States, manifesting itself as "a distinctive set of properties and themes in all things American, whether individuals, institutions, or cultural products. This premise of exceptionalism translates into a methodology that privileges the nation above all else. The field can legitimize itself as a field only because the nation does the legitimizing. The disciplinary sovereignty of the former owes everything to the territorial sovereignty of the latter. Against this conflation of nation and field, Radway proposes a rigorous decoupling, a methodology predicated on the *noncoincidence* between the two. The nation has solid borders; the field, on the other hand, is fluid and amorphous, shaped and reshaped by emerging forces, by "intricate interdependencies" between "the near and far, the local and the distant." In short, as a domain of inquiry, the "Americanist" field needs to be kept emphatically distinct from the nation. Its vitality resides in a carefully maintained and carefully theorized zone, a penumbra intervening between it and the conceptual foreclosure dictated by its name. That penumbra makes the field a continuum rather than a container:

> It suggests that far from being conceived on the model of a container—that is, as a particular kind of hollowed out object with evident edges or skin enclosing certain organically uniform contents—territories and geographies need to be reconceived as spatially-situated and intricately intertwined networks of social relationships that tie specific locales to particular histories.

Radway's challenge to the "container" model turns the United States from a discrete entity into a porous network, with no tangible edges, its circumference being continually negotiated, its criss-crossing pathways continually modified by local input, local inflections. These dynamic exchanges suggest that the American field has never been unified, and will never be. Still, though not unified, the nation remains central for Radway: it is a first-order phenomenon, a primary field of inquiry. If it is no longer a "hollowed out object" filled with contents unique to it and homogenized within it, it remains a *disciplinary* object second to none, conceptually front and center, and naturalizing itself as the methodological baseline, a set of founding coordinates, reproducing its boundaries in the very boundaries of the field.

What sort of distortion comes with this nation-centered mapping? And how best to rectify it? . . . Rather than taking the nation as the default position, the totality we automatically reach for, we come up with alternate geographies that deny it this totalizing function. Forging such geographies might be one of the most critical tasks now facing the field. How best to fashion a domain of inquiry not replicating the terms of territorial sovereignty? What landscape would emerge then? And what would American literature look like when traced through these redrawn and realigned entities?

The language of set and subset is especially helpful here as a heuristic guide. While that language can sometimes conjure up a hierarchical ordering of part to whole, its interest for us lies in a different direction: not in stratification, but in modularization. What it highlights is the strategic breakup of a continuum, the carving of it into secondary units, and the premises and consequences attending that process. For units are not given but made. They are not an objective fact in the world, but an artifact, a postulate, aggregated as such for some particular purpose. Their lengths and widths, the size of their grouping, their criteria of selection, the platforms they rest on—all of these can be differently specified. Each specifying throws into relief a different kind of entity: mapped on a different scale, performing a different function, implementing a different set of membership criteria. And looming over all of these is the long-standing, still evolving, and always to be theorized relation between each unit and the larger continuum. A language of set and subset, in short, allows us to "modularize" the world into smaller entities: able to stand provisionally and do analytic work, but not self-contained, not fully sovereign, resting continually and non-trivially on a platform more robust and more extensive.

"American literature" is best understood as a subset in this sense. The field does stand to be classified apart, as a nameable and adducible unit. It is taxonomically useful as an entity. At the same time, that taxonomic usefulness should not lure us into thinking that this entity is natural, that its shape and size will hold all the way up and all the way down, staying intact regardless of circumstances, not varying with specifying frames. On the contrary, what we nominate as "American literature" is simply an effect of that nomination, which is to say, it is epiphenomenal, domain-specific, binding only at one register and extending no farther than that register. Once it is transposed, its membership will change also, going up and down with the ascending or descending scales of aggregation. And, across those scales, at every level of re-description, it can be folded back into a larger continuum from which it has only been momentarily set apart.

In *Gödel, Escher, Bach* (1979), Douglas Hofstadter discusses these ascending and descending scales and their intricate enfolding as "recursive structures and processes," to be found not only in mathematics, the visual arts, and music, but also in domains still more elementary: the grammar of languages, the geometry of the branches of trees, even particle physics. What all of these have in common is the phenomenon of "nesting": a generative process that modulates continually from the outside to the inside, from the background to the foreground, with several units, differently scaled, reciprocally cradling one another and overlapping with one another, creating an ever wider circumference as well as an ever greater recessional depth. Rather than proceeding as a straight line, recursive structures and processes give us a reversible landscape that can be either convex or concave, either bulging out or burrowing in, sometimes pivoted on the smallest embedded unit and sometimes radiating out to take in the largest embedding circumference. Hofstadter calls this reversible hierarchy a *heterarchy*. "The whole world is built out of recursion," he says. This entanglement between inner and outer limits allows entities to snowball, with each feedback loop generating an "increasing complexity of behavior," so much so that "suitably recursive systems might be strong enough to break out of any predetermined patterns," modifying the input to such an extent that the outcome becomes utterly unpredictable. Such unpredictability, Hofstadter adds, "probably lies at the heart of intelligence."

We explore the intelligence of American literature in just this light, as the unpredictable outcome stemming from the interplay between encapsulation and its undoing: between the modularity of the subset and an infinite number of larger aggregates that might count as its embedding "set." What are some of these aggregates? They are uncharted and uncataloged for the most part. One thing is clear, though. In order for American literature to be nested in them, these aggregates would have to rest on a platform broader and more robustly empirical than the relatively arbitrary and demonstrably ephemeral borders of the nation. They require alternate geographies, alternate histories. At their most capacious, they take their measure from the durations and extensions of the human species itself, folding in American literature as one fold among others, to be unfolded and refolded into our collective fabric.

Gayatri Chakravorty Spivak and Paul Gilroy have proposed the term "planet" as one aggregate that might do this work of enfolding. In *Death of a Discipline* (2003), Spivak argues that "planetarity" is a term worth exploring precisely because it is an unknown quantum, barely intimated, not yet adequate to the meaning we would like it to bear, and stirring for just that reason. It stands as a horizon impossible to define, and hospitable in that impossibility. Its very sketchiness makes it a "catachresis[1] for inscribing collective responsibility," for that sketchiness preserves a space for phenomena as yet emerging, not quite in sight. In *After Empire* (2004), Paul Gilroy also invokes the "planet" in this loose-fitting sense. The concept can be helpful only in the optative mood, as a generative principle fueled by its less than actualized status. For its heuristic value lies in its not having come into being: it is a habitat still waiting for its inhabitants, waiting for a humanity that has yet to be born, yet to be wrested from a seemingly boundless racism.

What are the consequences of invoking the planet, in its actualized and unactualized dimensions, as a research program? What practical difficulties might arise? What professional training is required? And what sort of creatures would literary scholars have to become to be practitioners of this new craft? It is helpful here to turn another presidential address, delivered by Philip Curtin to the American Historical Association in 1983, one that eerily speaks to the current situation. Entitled "Depth, Span, and Relevance," this presidential address zeroes in on the very question of professional training. "The discipline of history has broadened in the postwar decades, but historians have not," Curtin observes. "We teach the history of Africa and Asia, but specialists in American history know no more about the history of Africa than their predecessors did in the 1940s." Nor is Africa alone terra incognita in the minds of scholars. Europe, it seems, is also a dark continent: "Americanists know less European history than they did thirty years ago." Expertise so narrowly defined has serious consequences for the field as a whole. Americanists seem to have forgotten "that one of the prime values of a liberal education is breadth, not narrow specialization. Even before the explosion of new kinds of historical knowledge, historical competence required a balance between deep mastery of a particular field and a span of knowledge over other fields of history. Depth was necessary to discover and validate the evidence. Span was necessary to know what kind of evidence to look for—and to make some sense of it, once discovered." . . .

2007

---

[1]The improper use of words.

Don DeLillo b. 1936

In the Ruins of the Future

In the past decade the surge of capital markets has dominated discourse and shaped global consciousness. Multinational corporations have come to seem more vital and influential than governments. The dramatic climb of the Dow and the speed of the Internet summoned us all to live permanently in the future, in the utopian glow of cyber-capital, because there is no memory there and this is where markets are uncontrolled and investment potential has no limit.

All this changed on September 11. Today, again, the world narrative belongs to terrorists. But the primary target of the men who attacked the Pentagon and the World Trade Center was not the global economy. It is America that drew their fury. It is the high gloss of our modernity. It is the thrust of our technology. It is our perceived godlessness. It is the blunt force of our foreign policy. It is the power of American culture to penetrate every wall, home, life, and mind.

Terror's response is a narrative that has been developing over years, only now becoming inescapable. It is our lives and minds that are occupied now. This catastrophic event changes the way we think and act, moment to moment, week to week, for unknown weeks and months to come, and steely years. Our world, parts of our world, have crumbled into theirs, which means we are living in a place of danger and rage.

The protestors in Genoa, Prague, Seattle, and other cities want to decelerate the global momentum that seemed to be driving unmindfully toward a landscape of consumer-robots and social instability, with the chance of self-determination probably diminishing for most people in most countries. Whatever acts of violence marked the protests, most of the men and women involved tend to be a moderating influence, trying to slow things down, even things out, hold off the white-hot future.

The terrorists of September 11 want to bring back the past.

Our tradition of free expression and our justice system's provisions for the rights of the accused can only seem an offense to men bent on suicidal terror.

We are rich, privileged, and strong, but they are willing to die. This is the edge they have, the fire of aggrieved belief. We live in a wide world, routinely filled with exchange of every sort, an open circuit of work, talk, family, and expressible feeling. The terrorist, planted in a Florida town, pushing his supermarket cart, nodding to his neighbor, lives in a far narrower format. This is his edge, his strength. Plots reduce the world. He builds a plot around his anger and our indifference. He lives a certain kind of apartness, hard and tight. This is not the self-watcher, the soft white dangling boy who shoots someone to keep from disappearing into himself. The terrorist shares a secret and a self. At a certain point he and his brothers may begin to feel less motivated by politics and personal hatred than by brotherhood itself. They share the codes and protocols of their mission here and something deeper as well, a vision of judgment and devastation.

Does the sight of a woman pushing a stroller soften the man to her humanity and vulnerability, and her child's as well, and all the people he is here to kill?

This is his edge, that he does not see her. Years here, waiting, taking flying lessons, making the routine gestures of community and home, the credit card, the bank account, the post-office box. All tactical, linked, layered. He knows who we are and what we mean in the world—an idea, a righteous fever in the brain. But there is no defenseless human at the end of his gaze.

The sense of disarticulation we hear in the term "Us and Them" has never been so striking, at either end.

We can tell ourselves that whatever we've done to inspire bitterness, distrust, and rancor, it was not so damnable as to bring this day down on our heads. But there is no logic in apocalypse. They have gone beyond the bounds of passionate payback. This is heaven and hell, a sense of armed martyrdom as the surpassing drama of human experience.

He pledges his submission to God and meditates on the blood to come.

The Bush Administration was feeling a nostalgia for the Cold War. This is over now. Many things are over. The narrative ends in the rubble, and it is left to us to create the counter-narrative.

There are a hundred thousand stories crisscrossing New York, Washington, and the world. Where we were, whom we know, what we've seen or heard. There are the doctors' appointments that saved lives, the cell phones that were used to report the hijackings. Stories generating others and people running north out of the rumbling smoke and ash. Men running in suits and ties, women who'd lost their shoes, ops running from the skydive of all that towering steel.

People running for their lives are part of the story that is left to us.

There are stories of heroism and encounters with dread. There are stories that carry around their edges the luminous ring of coincidence, fate, or premonition. They take us beyond the hard numbers of dead and missing and give us a glimpse of elevated being. For a hundred who are arbitrarily dead, we need to find one person saved by a flash of forewarning. There are configurations that chill and awe us both. Two women on two planes, best of friends, who die together and apart, Tower 1 and Tower 2. What desolate epic tragedy might bear the weight of such juxtaposition? But we can also ask what symmetry, bleak and touching both, takes one friend, spares the other's grief?

The brother of one of the women worked in one of the towers. He managed to escape.

In Union Square Park, about two miles north of the attack site, the improvised memorials are another part of our response. The flags, flower beds, and votive candles, the lamppost hung with paper airplanes, the passages from the Koran and the Bible, the letters and poems, the cardboard John Wayne, the children's drawings of the Twin Towers, the hand-painted signs for Free Hugs, Free Back Rubs, the graffiti of love and peace on the tall equestrian statue.

There are many photographs of missing persons, some accompanied by hopeful lists of identifying features. (Man with panther tattoo, upper right arm.) There is the saxophonist, playing softly. There is the sculptured flag of rippling copper and aluminum, six feet long, with two young people still attending to the finer details of the piece.

Then there are the visitors to the park. The artifacts on display represent the confluence of a number of cultural tides, patriotic and multidevotional and retro hippie. The visitors move quietly in the floating aromas of candlewax, roses, and bus fumes. There are many people this evening, and in their voices, manner, clothing, and in the color of their skin they recapitulate the mix we see in the photocopied faces of the lost.

For the next fifty years, people who were not in the area when the attacks occurred will claim to have been there. In time, some of them will believe it. Others will claim to have lost friends or relatives, although they did not.

This is also the counter-narrative, a shadow history of false memories and imagined loss.

The Internet is a counter-narrative, shaped in part by rumor, fantasy, and mystical reverberation.

The cell phones, the lost shoes, the handkerchiefs mashed in the faces of running men and women. The box cutters and credit cards. The paper that came streaming out of the towers and drifted across the river to Brooklyn back yards: status reports, résumés, insurance forms. Sheets of paper driven into concrete, according to witnesses. Paper slicing into truck tires, fixed there.

These are among the smaller objects and more marginal stories in the sifted ruins of the day. We need them, even the common tools of the terrorists, to set against the massive spectacle that continues to seem unmanageable, too powerful a thing to set into our frame of practiced response.

Ash was spattering the windows. Karen was half dressed, grabbing the kids and trying to put on some clothes and talking with her husband and scooping things to take out to the corridor, and they looked at her, twin girls, as if she had fourteen heads.

They stayed in the corridor for a while, thinking there might be secondary explosions. They waited, and began to feel safer, and went back to the apartment.

At the next impact, Marc knew in the sheerest second before the shock wave broadsided their building that it was a second plane, impossible, striking the second tower. Their building was two blocks away, and he'd thought the first crash was an accident.

They went back to the hallway, where others began to gather, fifteen or twenty people.

Karen ran back for a cell phone, a cordless phone, a charger, water, sweaters, snacks for the kids, and then made a quick dash to the bedroom for her wedding ring.

From the window she saw people running in the street, others locked shoulder to shoulder, immobilized, with debris coming down on them. People were trampled, struck by falling objects, and there was ash and paper everywhere, paper whipping through the air, no sign of light or sky.

Cell phones were down. They talked on the cordless, receiving information measured out in eyedrops. They were convinced that the situation outside was far more grave than it was here.

Smoke began to enter the corridor.

Then the first tower fell. She thought it was a bomb. When she talked to someone on the phone and found out what had happened, she felt a surreal relief. Bombs and missiles were not falling everywhere in the city. It was not all-out war, at least not yet.

Marc was in the apartment getting chairs for the older people, for the woman who'd had hip surgery. When he heard the first low drumming rumble, he stood in a strange dead calm and said, "Something is happening." It sounded exactly like what it was, a tall tower collapsing.

The windows were surfaced with ash now, blacked out completely, and he wondered what was out there. What remained to be seen and did he want to see it?

They all moved into the stairwell, behind a fire door, but smoke kept coming in. It was gritty ash, and they were eating it.

He ran back inside, grabbing towels off the racks and washcloths out of drawers and drenching them in the sink, and filling his bicycle water bottles, and grabbing the kids' underwear.

He thought the crush of buildings was the thing to fear most. This is what would kill them.

Karen was on the phone, talking to a friend in the district attorney's office, about half a mile to the north. She was pleading for help. She begged, pleaded, and hung up. For the next hour a detective kept calling with advice and encouragement.

Marc came back out to the corridor. I think we might die, he told himself, hedging his sense of what would happen next.

The detective told Karen to stay where they were.

When the second tower fell, my heart fell with it. I called Marc, who is my nephew, on his cordless. I couldn't stop thinking of the size of the towers and the meager distance between those buildings and his. He answered, we talked. I have no memory of the conversation except for his final remark, slightly urgent, concerning someone on the other line, who might be sending help.

Smoke was seeping out of the elevator shaft now. Karen was saying goodbye to her father in Oregon. Not hello-goodbye. But goodbye-I-think-we-are-going-to-die. She thought smoke would be the thing that did it.

People sat on chairs along the walls. They chatted about practical matters. They sang songs with the kids. The kids in the group were cooperative because the adults were damn scared.

There was an improvised rescue in progress. Karen's friend and a colleague made their way down from Centre Street, turning up with two policemen they'd enlisted en route. They had dust masks and a destination, and they searched every floor for others who might be stranded in the building.

They came out into a world of ash and near night. There was no one else to be seen now on the street. Gray ash covered the cars and pavement, ash falling in large flakes, paper still drifting down, discarded shoes, strollers, briefcases. The members of the group were masked and toweled, children in adults' arms, moving east and then north on Nassau Street, trying not to look around, only what's immediate, one step and then another, all closely focused, a pregnant woman, a newborn, a dog.

They were covered in ash when they reached shelter at Pace University, where there was food and water, and kind and able staff members, and a gas-leak scare, and more running people.

Workers began pouring water on the group. Stay wet, stay wet. This was the theme of the first half hour.

Later a line began to form along the food counter.

Someone said, "I don't want cheese on that."

Someone said, "I like it better not so cooked."

Not so incongruous really, just people alive and hungry, beginning to be themselves again.

Technology is our fate, our truth. It is what we mean when we call ourselves the only superpower on the planet. The materials and methods we devise make it possible for us to claim our future. We don't have to depend on God or the prophets or other astonishments. We are the astonishment. The miracle is what we ourselves produce, the systems and networks that change the way we live and think.

But whatever great skeins of technology lie ahead, ever more complex, connective, precise, micro-fractional, the future has yielded, for now, to medieval expedience, to the old slow furies of cutthroat religion.

Kill the enemy and pluck out his heart.

If others in less scientifically advanced cultures were able to share, wanted to share, some of the blessings of our technology, without a threat to their faith or traditions, would they need to rely on a God in whose name they kill the innocent? Would they need to invent a God who rewards violence against the innocent with a promise of "infinite paradise," in the words of a handwritten letter found in the luggage of one of the hijackers?

For all those who may want what we've got, there are all those who do not. These are the men who have fashioned a morality of destruction. They want what they used to have before the waves of Western influence. They surely see themselves as the elect of God whether or not they follow the central precepts of Islam. It is the presumptive right of those who choose violence and death to speak directly to God. They will kill and then die. Or they will die first, in the cockpit, in clean shoes, according to instructions in the letter.

Six days after the attacks, the territory below Canal Street is hedged with barricades. There are few civilians in the street. Police at some checkpoints, troops in camouflage gear at others, wearing gas masks, and a pair of state troopers in conversation, and ten burly men striding east in hard hats, work pants, and NYPD jackets. A shop owner tries to talk a cop into letting him enter his place of business. He is a small elderly man with a Jewish accent, but there is no relief today. Garbage bags are everywhere in high broad stacks. The area is bedraggled and third-worldish, with an air of permanent emergency, everything surfaced in ash.

It is possible to pass through some checkpoints, detour around others. At Chambers Street I look south through the links of the National Rent-A-Fence barrier. There stands the smoky remnant of filigree that marks the last tall thing, the last sign in the mire of wreckage that there were towers here that dominated the skyline for over a quarter of a century.

Ten days later and a lot closer, I stand at another barrier with a group of people, looking directly into the strands of openwork façade. It is almost too close. It is almost Roman, I-beams for stonework, but not nearly so salvageable. Many here describe the scene to others on cell phones.

"Oh my god I'm standing here," says the man next to me.

The World Trade towers were not only an emblem of advanced technology but a justification, in a sense, for technology's irresistible will to realize in solid form whatever becomes theoretically allowable. Once defined, every limit must be reached. The tactful sheathing of the towers was intended to reduce the direct threat of such straight-edge enormity, a giantism that eased over the years into something a little more familiar and comfortable, even dependable in a way.

Now a small group of men have literally altered our skyline. We have fallen back in time and space. It is their technology that marks our moments, the small lethal devices, the remote-controlled detonators they fashion out of radios, or the larger technology they borrow from us, passenger jets that become manned missiles.

Maybe this is a grim subtext of their enterprise. They see something innately destructive in the nature of technology. It brings death to their customs and beliefs. Use it as what it is, a thing that kills.

Nearly eleven years ago, during the engagement in the Persian Gulf, people had trouble separating the war from coverage of the war. After the first euphoric days, coverage became limited. The rush of watching all that eerie green night-vision footage, shot from fighter jets in combat, had been so intense that it became hard to honor the fact that the war was still going on, untelevised. A layer of consciousness had been stripped away. People shuffled around, muttering. They were lonely for their war.

The events of September 11 were covered unstintingly. There was no confusion of roles on TV. The raw event was one thing, the coverage another. The event dominated the medium. It was bright and totalizing, and some of us said it was unreal. When we say a thing is unreal, we mean it is too real, a phenomenon so unaccountable and yet so bound to the power of objective fact that we can't tilt it to the slant of our perceptions. First the planes struck the towers. After a time it became possible for us to absorb this, barely. But when the towers fell. When the rolling smoke began moving downward floor to floor. This was so vast and terrible that it was outside imagining even as it happened. We could not catch up to it. But it was real, punishingly so, an expression of the physics of structural limits and a void in one's soul, and there was the huge antenna falling out of the sky, straight down, blunt end first, like an arrow moving backward in time.

The event itself has no purchase on the mercies of analogy or simile. We have to take the shock and horror as it is. But living language is not diminished. The writer wants to understand what this day has done to us. Is it too soon? We seem pressed for time, all of us. Time is scarcer now. There is a sense of compression, plans made hurriedly, time forced and distorted. But language is inseparable from the world that provokes it. The writer begins in the towers, trying to imagine the moment, desperately. Before politics, before history and religion, there is the primal terror. People falling from the towers hand in hand. This is part of the counter-narrative, hands and spirits joining, human beauty in the crush of meshed steel.

In its desertion of every basis for comparison, the event asserts its singularity. There is something empty in the sky. The writer tries to give memory, tenderness, and meaning to all that howling space.

We like to think America invented the future. We are comfortable with the future, intimate with it. But there are disturbances now, in large and small ways, a chain of reconsiderations. Where we live, how we travel, what we think about when we look at our children. For many people, the event has changed the grain of the most routine moment.

We may find that the ruin of the towers is implicit in other things. The new PalmPilot at fingertip's reach, the stretch limousine parked outside the hotel, the midtown skyscraper under construction, carrying the name of a major investment bank—all haunted in a way by what has happened, less assured in their authority, in the prerogatives they offer.

There is fear of other kinds of terrorism, the prospect that biological and chemical weapons will contaminate the air we breathe and the water we drink. There wasn't much concern about this after earlier terrorist acts. This time we are trying to name the future, not in our normally hopeful way but guided by dread.

What has already happened is sufficient to affect the air around us, psychologically. We are all breathing the fumes of lower Manhattan, where traces of the dead are everywhere, in the soft breeze off the river, on rooftops and windows, in our hair and on our clothes.

Think of a future in which the components of a microchip are the size of atoms. The devices that pace our lives will operate from the smart quantum spaces of pure information. Now think of people in countless thousands massing in anger and vowing revenge. Enlarged photos of martyrs and holy men dangle from balconies, and the largest images are those of a terrorist leader.

Two forces in the world, past and future. With the end of Communism, the ideas and principles of modern democracy were seen clearly to prevail, whatever the inequalities of the system itself. This is still the case. But now there is a global theocratic state, unboundaried and floating and so obsolete it must depend on suicidal fervor to gain its aim.

Ideas evolve and de-evolve, and history is turned on end.

On Friday of the first week a long series of vehicles moves slowly west on Canal Street. Dump trucks, flatbeds, sanitation sweepers. There are giant earthmovers making a tremendous revving sound. A scant number of pedestrians, some in dust masks, others just standing, watching, the indigenous people, clinging to walls and doorways, unaccustomed to traffic that doesn't bring buyers and sellers, goods and cash. The fire rescue car and state police cruiser, the staccato sirens of a line of police vans. Cops stand at the sawhorse barriers, trying to clear the way. Ambulances, cherry pickers, a fleet of Con Ed trucks, all this clamor moving south a few blocks ahead, into the cloud of sand and ash.

One month earlier I'd taken the same walk, early evening, among crowds of people, the panethnic swarm of shoppers, merchants, residents and passersby, with a few tourists as well, and the man at the curbstone doing acupoint massage, and the dreadlocked kid riding his bike on the sidewalk. This was the spirit of Canal Street, the old jostle and stir unchanged for many decades and bearing no sign of SoHo just above, with its restaurants and artists' lofts, or TriBeCa below, rich in architectural textures. Here were hardware bargains, car stereos, foam rubber and industrial plastics, the tattoo parlor and the pizza parlor.

Then I saw the woman on the prayer rug. I'd just turned the corner, heading south to meet some friends, and there she was, young and slender, in a silk headscarf. It was time for sunset prayer, and she was kneeling, upper body pitched toward the edge of the rug. She was partly concealed by a couple of vendors' carts, and no one seemed much to notice her. I think there was another woman seated on a folding chair near the curbstone. The figure on the rug faced east, which meant most immediately a storefront just a foot and a half from her tipped head but more distantly and pertinently toward Mecca, of course, the holiest city of Islam.

Some prayer rugs include a mihrab in their design, an arched element representing the prayer niche in a mosque that indicates the direction of Mecca. The only locational guide the young woman needed was the Manhattan grid.

I looked at her in prayer and it was clearer to me than ever, the daily sweeping taken-for-granted greatness of New York. The city will accommodate every language, ritual, belief, and opinion. In the rolls of the dead of September 11, all these vital differences were surrendered to the impact and flash. The bodies themselves are missing in large numbers. For the survivors, more grief. But the dead are their own nation and race, one identity, young or old, devout or unbelieving—a union of souls. During the hadj, the annual pilgrimage in Mecca, the faithful must eliminate every sign of status, income, and nationality, the men wearing identical strips of seamless white cloth, the women with covered heads, all recalling in prayer their fellowship with the dead.

Allahu akbar. God is great.

2002

Michael Rothberg b. 1966

Seeing Terror, Feeling Art: Public and Private in Post-9/11 Literature

More than five years after the attacks of September 11, 2001, it is not yet clear what "literature after 9/11" will be. The question of whether September 11 represents a cultural rupture remains open. Indeed, there is much continuity to be found. While post-9/11 literary works replay many familiar themes and techniques of post–World War II American literature, numerous pre-9/11 works foreshadow contemporary concerns, sometimes in quite uncanny ways. . . . [Here] I advance an argument about literature's potential social and political contribution in a post-9/11 age defined by a seemingly endless "war on terror."

My overarching claim is that literature and other forms of art are important sites of response to terrorism because . . . they illustrate the interconnectedness of the public and the private and allow us to reconnect our faculties of seeing and feeling, two forms of connection that both terrorism and mass society threaten. These characteristics of literature suggest that the aesthetic has a particular role to play in responding both to acts of extreme violence and to the political processes in which they unfold and to which they give rise. The aesthetic is neither an apolitical zone closed off from violence nor a realm that can simply be subsumed under the seemingly more urgent activity of politics, even in a moment of perpetual emergency. Rather, the aesthetic constitutes a bridging realm that connects subjective experience to larger collectivities. In Kant's canonical understanding in the *Critique of the Power of Judgment,* aesthetic judgment provides a "transition" across the "incalculable gulf between the domain of the concept of nature, as the sensible, and the domain of the concept of freedom, as the supersensible" (63). In [post-9/11 literature,] I find an attempt to bridge seeing, feeling, and understanding, on the one hand, and the subjective and the collective, on the other. This latter bridging is close to Kant's general definition of judgment as "the faculty for thinking of the particular as contained under the universal" (66). In the case of aesthetics, as Kant makes clear, the particular form of judgment is reflective, which is to say that the universal is not given in advance as it is in determinate judgment (67).[1] Aesthetic reflection consists of a groping after the universal from a particular, embodied position. Thus, although focused on the question of disinterested reception, Kantian aesthetic judgment does not presuppose a passive spectator but rather a spectator actively engaged with the world in both cognitive and affective registers. Within this context, the purely ideological concept of the "war on terror" reveals its moment of truth. By focusing on feeling ("terror") instead of a particular political tactic ("terrorism"), the phrase draws our attention to the affective level of politics and points us toward literature's potential counter-force—a reconstruction of relations between thinking and feeling that both acts of terrorism and the imperial war on terror attempt to sever. . . .

Literature and other forms of art are especially important after 9/11 because they allow us to imagine alternative responses to the violence of terrorism and the spectacles of mass-mediated culture. Literature and art can become sites for exploring the intersections between the public and the private and for understanding the feelings that terrorism draws on and produces. . . . Aesthetic acts (in other words, works of art) allow us to see and to feel simultaneously in a way that is different both from terrorism and from the mass media through which we inevitably experience terrorist acts.

2008

From Ann Keniston and Jeanne Follansbee Quinn, eds., *Literature after 9/11* (New York: Routledge, 2008).
[1] The Paul Guyer and Eric Matthews translation (Cambridge University Press, 2001) renders reflective and determinate judgment as "reflecting" and "determining," respectively.

David Simpson b. 1951

from Telling It Like It Isn't

Literature, we know and expect, takes time. Politicians and their accomplices in the mass media are in a hurry, anxious to get on with acts of retribution, with invading foreign countries, with whipping up the national imaginary to a point where all sorts of liberties can be taken and pushed aside, and above all with justifying their own short-term perspicacity and indispensability.[1] 9/11 gave rise to lots of rushed judgments and reflex responses, but literature was generally recalcitrant, in the spirit of Jacques Derrida's remark that the telegraphic condensation of the very phrase 9/11—which caught on so fast and so thoroughly—indicates that "we do not yet know how to qualify, that we do not know what we are talking about."[2] It takes time to write a novel or craft a poem, even for the most opportunistically facile writers. And a deliberate delay in the face of pressures to offer immediate findings is received as a mark of literary quality in a culture of mass communication and instant replay.

So our novelists and their publishers have waited a while. . . . But as time passes and the massive implications of such radically dishonest responses as the invasion of Iraq by a U.S.-led "coalition of the willing" become more and more apparent to more and more people, the expectations placed upon the slower literary response may tend to become greater and more and more intimidating, as if we who are elite, specialized readers are supposed to confirm our own patience and caution by discovering in the novel something we cannot find in politics or television, something we can think of as a truth. . . . It is indeed the language of the movie that slow reading and high literature both commonly conceive as that which they must work hardest to unseat. How true must that be of *this* movie, the endlessly replayed fifteen-second epic of impacting planes and falling towers that has produced a narrative sound-bite (or sight-bite) open to world-wide distribution and iconic adaptation without straining anyone's attention span and above all without (after the falling bodies were disappeared, as they soon were) asking anyone to come face to face with the deaths of people and the destruction of frail human bodies. The very currency of this movie (which is not a movie, though as everyone remarked it was as if they had seen it already) as it repeats itself over and over without further clarification or analysis has by

From Ann Keniston and Jeanne Follansbee Quinn, eds., *Literature after 9/11* (New York: Routledge, 2008).

[1][Jörg] Friedrich remarks rather wryly that after the assiduous clean-ups and compensations extended by the Nazi party to the victims of the bombings, "surveys showed that 58 percent were satisfied with the care they received" (*The Fire[: The Bombing of Germany, 1940–1945* (New York: Columbia University Press, 2006)], p. 390). The other end of the carrot was the high incidence of state executions carried out among those accused of looting (p. 396f).

[2]Giovanna Borradori, *Philosophy in a Time of Terror: Dialogues with Jürgen Habermas and Jacques Derrida* (Chicago and London: U of Chicago P, 2003), p. 86.

now become the motif of a deliberate opacity, a piece of history before the history has even been properly projected or deciphered. Now more than ever, one might say, is the time for taking time, the time of the novel.[3] . . .

What is a novelist, a practitioner of slow writing and a prophet of slow reading, to do? To seek to represent the material details of dismembering and dying bodies and minds is one way to go, but as Rousseau and Wordsworth among others well knew, there is no guarantee that literary representations of the sufferings of others will produce active sympathy in the world; they can equally well serve as inoculations against further responsiveness. The attempt might still be worth making, and Abu Ghraib gave evidence that it can work at least for a time.[4] The hegemonic assembly of corporate media and governing elites that produces the news and tries to limit how it will be received is certainly frightened of this, enough so to do what it can to keep the sordid realities of death as far away as possible, and to blame those alternative sources (like the now-infamous *Al Jazeera*) for doing things differently. The *New York Times* from time to time gives out images of dead Iraqis and Palestinians, but (with the honorable exceptional of some columnists) more for variety than out of any apparent commitment to what [W. G.] Sebald called reality. It is much too early to suggest that the contemporary novel is going in some clearly visible directions rather than others, but [several post 9-11 authors] share certain instincts about what can and should be said of our response to 9/11, a response that they (or their books) suggest is, after all, distinctly local and arguably even parochial, and by no means as far from the ideological mainstream as we or they might like.

2008

---

[3]The images of falling towers that were so ubiquitous in the days following 9/11 are, notably, not included in Paul Greengrass's impressive movie *United 93,* which also generally withholds and marginalizes scenes of graphic, proto-pornographic violence or subdues them by the use of montage. Oliver Stone's *World Trade Center* employs a much more conventional plot and cinematography but also avoids these images, representing the passage of the second plane only as a shadow and having most of the important information circulate by cellphone or on TV rather than as epic cinema.

[4]See David Simpson, "The Mourning Paper," *London Review of Books* 26:10 (20 May 2004), 3-5; and *9/11,* pp. 103–19.

Don DeLillo b. 1936

Don DeLillo has become one of the most respected and widely read American novelists associated with the term *postmodernism*. DeLillo shares with other postmodernist literary giants, such as Thomas Pynchon and John Barth, a tendency toward absurd humor that thinly covers a sense of dread, despair, or paranoia. Like these writers, he is concerned with the inability of the individual to gain any measure of control in a world gone mad with technological or governmental control.

DeLillo plunges his readers into a world where individuals have lost their bearings, where conspiracy theories become reality, and where the forces of history are stronger than free will. This world tends to sprawl in many directions, emphasizing (as postmodern novels tend to) surface rather than depth. In a 1997 essay, he relates the form and content of his work to the geography of his country: "The sweeping range of American landscape and experience can be a goad, a challenge, an affliction and an inspiration [to the novelist], pretty much in one package. The novel can be a foolhardy form, bristling with risk."

Since his first book, *Americana* (1971), DeLillo has published thirteen other novels, as well as a number of essays, plays, and short fiction, many of which have been incorporated into his novels.

DeLillo grew up in the Bronx, the son of Italian immigrant parents. He was raised Catholic, and he claims that his faith has had an effect on his aesthetic because of its emphasis on ritual and because it instructs its adherents to live according to a certain code so that death will not bring eternal damnation. Like his fictional rendition of Lee Harvey Oswald, JFK's assassin, in *Libra*, DeLillo was not fond of school and instead preferred to learn from alternative sources. He cites jazz (especially the innovative bop of Charles Mingus), film (especially the avant-garde French filmmaker Jean-Luc Godard), and abstract expressionist painting as the primary influences on his writing, though he also frequently mentions pick-up games of baseball and shooting pool as formative experiences. Although he attended Fordham University, he takes pains to diminish the influence of education on his work and says that his explorations of New York City are really what formed him. Even so, his most famous novel, *White Noise* (1985), takes place on a midwestern college campus and is narrated by a college professor.

One of the greatest influences on DeLillo's work is history itself, specifically the history that has occurred during his lifetime. Two of DeLillo's most enduring novels, *Libra* (1988) and *Underworld* (1997), are initiated by what he has referred to as forgotten newspaper headlines. *Libra* is an inventive rendition of the life and death of Lee Harvey Oswald, JFK's assassin, whose life is dictated by forces much greater than himself: not only history proper but the conspiracy theories that have dominated the popular imagination since the president's death. As one character puts it, history is "the sum total of all the things they aren't telling us." In this novel, information becomes overwhelming. A character named Nicholas Branch, who is trying to sort through all the evidence related to the case, grows despondent when the little room he is filling with information begins to overflow. Coincidence becomes stronger than cause and effect, and the randomness or chaos of the postmodern world triumphs over logic and order.

DeLillo's massive epic *Underworld* begins with two different events that coincided—the Soviets' exploding their first nuclear bomb and the Giants' winning the World Series with a home run that became known as "the shot heard 'round the world." The forces of what might be called official history (the events that are publicly shared and discussed) grind against the shadowy underworld (the hidden events that control the lives of individuals and that do not find their way into history books). In a memorable moment from *White Noise,* following a catastrophic "airborne toxic event," the narrator's wife solemnly reads absurd tabloid headlines to a rapt group of listeners. In all these cases, newspaper headlines actually eclipse the realities of history rather than illuminate them.

The story that follows focuses on a recent moment in history—the terror attacks of September 11, 2001. Initially published as part of a story called "Still Life," the piece became the first chapter of DeLillo's later novel *Falling Man* (2007).

D. Quentin Miller
Suffolk University

PRIMARY WORKS

Americana (1971), *End Zone* (1972), *Great Jones Street* (1973), *Ratner's Star* (1976), *Players* (1977), *Running Dog* (1978), *The Names* (1982), *White Noise* (1985), *Libra* (1988), *Mao II* (1991), *Underworld* (1997), *The Body Artist* (2001), *Cosmopolis* (2003), *Falling Man* (2007).

from Falling Man

It was not a street anymore but a world, a time and space of falling ash and near night. He was walking north through rubble and mud and there were people running past holding towels to their faces or jackets over their heads. They had handkerchiefs pressed to their mouths. They had shoes in their hands, a woman with a shoe in each hand, running past him. They ran and fell, some of them, confused and ungainly, with debris coming down around them, and there were people taking shelter under cars.

The roar was still in the air, the buckling rumble of the fall. This was the world now. Smoke and ash came rolling down streets and turning corners, busting around corners, seismic tides of smoke, with office paper flashing past, standard sheets with cutting edge, skimming, whipping past, otherworldly things in the morning pall.

He wore a suit and carried a briefcase. There was glass in his hair and face, marbled bolls of blood and light. He walked past a Breakfast Special sign and they went running by, city cops and security guards running, hands pressed down on gun butts to keep the weapons steady.

Things inside were distant and still, where he was supposed to be. It happened everywhere around him, a car half buried in debris, windows smashed and noises coming out, radio voices scratching at the wreckage. He saw people shedding water as they ran, clothes and bodies drenched from the sprinkler systems. There were shoes discarded in the street, handbags and laptops, a man seated on the sidewalk coughing up blood. Paper cups went bouncing oddly by.

The world was this as well, figures in windows a thousand feet up, dropping into free space, and the stink of fuel fire, and the steady rip of sirens in the air. The noise lay everywhere they ran, stratified sound collecting around them, and he walked away from it and into it at the same time.

There was something else then, outside all this, not belonging to this, aloft. He watched it coming down. A shirt came down out of the high smoke, a shirt lifted and drifting in the scant light and then falling again, down toward the river.

They ran and then they stopped, some of them, standing there swaying, trying to draw breath out of the burning air, and the fitful cries of disbelief, curses and lost shouts, and the paper massed in the air, contracts, resumés blowing by, intact snatches of business, quick in the wind.

He kept on walking. There were the runners who'd stopped and others veering into sidestreets. Some were walking backwards, looking into the core of it, all those writhing lives back there, and things kept falling, scorched objects trailing lines of fire.

He saw two women sobbing in their reverse march, looking past him, both in running shorts, faces in collapse.

He saw members of the tai chi group from the park nearby, standing with hands extended at roughly chest level, elbows bent, as if all of this, themselves included, might be placed in a state of abeyance.

Someone came out of a diner and tried to hand him a bottle of water. It was a woman wearing a dust mask and a baseball cap and she withdrew the bottle and twisted off the top and then thrust it toward him again. He put down the briefcase to take it, barely aware that he wasn't using his left arm, that he'd had to put down the briefcase before he could take the bottle. Three police vans came veering into the street and sped downtown, sirens sounding. He closed his eyes and drank, feeling the water pass into his body taking dust and soot down with it. She was looking at him. She said something he didn't hear and he handed back the bottle and picked up the briefcase. There was an aftertaste of blood in the long draft of water.

He started walking again. A supermarket cart stood upright and empty. There was a woman behind it, facing him, with police tape wrapped around her head and face, yellow caution tape that marks the limits of a crime scene. Her eyes were thin white ripples in the bright mask and she gripped the handle of the cart and stood there, looking into the smoke.

In time he heard the sound of the second fall. He crossed Canal Street and began to see things, somehow, differently. Things did not seem charged in the usual ways, the cobbled street, the cast-iron buildings. There was something critically missing from the things around him. They were unfinished, whatever that means. They were unseen, whatever that means, shop windows, loading platforms, paint-sprayed walls. Maybe this is what things look like when there is no one here to see them.

He heard the sound of the second fall, or felt it in the trembling air, the north tower coming down, a soft awe of voices in the distance. That was him coming down, the north tower.

The sky was lighter here and he could breathe more easily. There were others behind him, thousands, filling the middle distance, a mass in near formation, people walking out of the smoke. He kept going until he had to stop. It hit him quickly, the knowledge that he couldn't go any farther.

He tried to tell himself he was alive but the idea was too obscure to take hold. There was no taxis and little traffic of any kind and then an old panel truck appeared, Electrical Contractor, Long Island City, and it pulled alongside and the driver leaned toward the window on the passenger's side and examined what he saw, a man scaled in ash, in pulverized matter, and asked him where he wanted to go. It wasn't until he got in the truck and shut the door that he understood where he'd been going all along.

2007

Edwidge Danticat b. 1969

In the epilogue to her short story collection *Krik? Krak!* (1995), Edwidge Danticat explains, "When you write, it's like braiding your hair. Taking a handful of coarse unruly strands and attempting to bring them unity." In a variety of literary forms, Danticat deftly weaves tales of Haiti, her country of origin, with her experiences as a young emigrant to the United States, rendering the pain of cultural dislocation with compelling poetic restraint. Born in Port-au-Prince, Danticat was raised by an uncle, who was a Baptist minister, and an aunt because both of her parents had relocated to New York by the time Danticat was four years old. Although her home was in the Haitian capital, she spent summers with extended family in the countryside, an experience that would influence her literary representation of women's work, storytelling, and domestic relationships. In 1981, Danticat and two of her brothers left Haiti to join their parents, and as an adolescent in Brooklyn she found some difficulty bridging the cultural divide between American and Haitian experience. She describes the hostility toward Haitians from American youth who associated the country unfairly with refugees and the AIDS crisis: "It was very hard. 'Haitian' was like a curse." In high school, Danticat's anxiety about her accent prevented her from speaking in full voice, but she soon discovered the rewards of mediating between Creole and English: "You have to take some things from one culture and combine them with another to create a common language. That merging becomes creative."

After graduating from Barnard College in 1990 with a degree in French literature, Danticat enrolled in the masters of fine arts program at Brown University. Her thesis was an early draft on her first novel, *Breath, Eyes, Memory* (1994), the story of a young Haitian woman's emigration to New York to join her mother. The *New York Times Book Review* exclaimed that its "calm clarity of vision takes on the resonance of folk art" and praised the novel's "extraordinary ambitious" thematic complexity and "extraordinarily successful" execution. However, the Haitian American middle class took issue with the text's depiction of virginity-testing practices, and Danticat found herself defending what she calls the "singularity" of the protagonist's story. After Brown University, Danticat returned to the East Flatbush section of Brooklyn and worked for a time under the film director Jonathan Demme. The stories in her next publication, *Krik? Krak!* a National Book Award finalist, focus on personal and domestic relationships in Haiti and in the United States. The *New York Times Book Review* declared that "the best of these stories humanize, particularize, give poignancy to the lives of people we may have come to think of as faceless emblems of misery, poverty and brutality." With an impressive range of attention, the tales recount Haitian emigrant deaths at sea, the artistic and economic ambitions of the working class, and the intricate cultural expectations among Haitian American families. In "New York Day Women," the young narrator struggles to understand her mother and her family's Haitian roots as she tracks her mother on a walk through midtown Manhattan. At each turn the narrator reflects on her mother's history, folkways, and advice, recognizing finally the dignity of her mother's experience and acknowledging her mother's participation in a community of displaced immigrant women.

Danticat's second novel, *The Farming of Bones* (1998), an American Book Award winner, diverges from her previous work to explore a particular historical incident: the 1937 massacre of Haitians at the border with the Dominican Republic. This text connects with Danticat's other work in its emphasis on the protagonist's cultural liminality, since she lives in close contact with

Dominicans, and in its exploration of working-class Haitian subjectivity. Her novel for young adults, *Behind the Mountains* (2002), returns to the subject of Haitian emigration, as its protagonist adjusts to a new life in New York. *After the Dance* (2002) is a travel narrative, describing Carnival celebrations in Jacmel, Haiti. Danticat is also an active editor, most prominently of *The Butterfly's Way: Voices from the Haitian Dyaspora in the United States* (2001). She returned to the short story in *The Dew Breaker* (2004), a collection that focuses on a man who worked as a torturer under François Duvalier. The collection's nine stories all rotate around this "dew breaker," as Danticat explores the possibility of reinvention and liberation in America. The *Washington Post Book World* hailed *The Dew Breaker* as "a brilliant book, undoubtedly the best one yet by an enormously talented writer." Because of her powerful renderings of Haitian American politics and customs, Danticat has been acclaimed as the culture's spokesperson. She balks at that role, insisting, "I don't really see myself as the voice for the Haitian-American experience. There are many. I'm just one."

Katharine Capshaw Smith
University of Connecticut

PRIMARY WORKS

Breath, Eyes, Memory, 1994; *Krik? Krak!* 1995; *The Farming of Bones*, 1998; ed., *The Butterfly's Way: Voices from the Haitian Dyaspora in the United States*, 2001; *Behind the Mountains*, 2002; *After the Dance: A Walk through Carnival in Jacmel, Haiti*, 2002; *The Dew Breaker*, 2004; *Brother, I'm Dying*, 2007.

New York Day Women

Today, walking down the street, I see my mother. She is strolling with a happy gait, her body thrust toward the DON'T WALK sign and the yellow taxicabs that make forty-five-degree turns on the corner of Madison and Fifty-seventh Street.

I have never seen her in this kind of neighborhood, peering in Chanel and Tiffany's and gawking at the jewels glowing in the Bulgari windows. My mother never shops outside of Brooklyn. She has never seen the advertising office where I work. She is afraid to take the subway, where you may meet those young black militant street preachers who curse black women for straightening their hair.

Yet, here she is, my mother, who I left at home that morning in her bathrobe, with pieces of newspapers twisted like rollers in her hair. My mother, who accuses me of random offenses as I dash out of the house.

Would you get up and give an old lady like me your subway seat? In this state of mind, I bet you don't even give up your seat to a pregnant lady.

My mother, who is often right about that. Sometimes I get up and give my seat. Other times, I don't. It all depends on how pregnant the woman is and whether or not she is with her boyfriend or husband and whether or not *he* is sitting down.

As my mother stands in front of Carnegie Hall, one taxi driver yells to another, "What do you think this is, a dance floor?"

My mother waits patiently for this dispute to be settled before crossing the street.

In Haiti when you get hit by a car, the owner of the car gets out and kicks you for getting blood on his bumper.

My mother who laughs when she says this and shows the large gap in her mouth where she lost three more molars to the dentist last week. My mother, who at fifty-nine, says dentures are okay.

You can take them out when they bother you. I'll like them. I'll like them fine.

Will it feel empty when Papa kisses you?

Oh no, he doesn't kiss me that way anymore.

My mother, who watches the lottery drawing every night on channel 11 without ever having played the numbers.

A third of that money is all I would need. We would pay the mortgage, and your father could stop driving that taxicab all over Brooklyn.

I follow my mother, mesmerized by the many possibilities of her journey. Even in a flowered dress, she is lost in a sea of pinstripes and gray suits, high heels and elegant short skirts, Reebok sneakers, dashing from building to building.
My mother, who won't go out to dinner with anyone.

If they want to eat with me, let them come to my house, even if I boil water and give it to them.

My mother, who talks to herself when she peels the skin off poultry.

Fat, you know, and cholesterol. Fat and cholesterol killed your aunt Hermine.

My mother, who makes jam with grapefruit peel and then puts in cinnamon bark that I always think is cockroaches in the jam. My mother, whom I have always bought household appliances for, on her birthday. A nice rice cooker, a blender.
I trail the red orchids in her dress and the heavy faux leather bag on her shoulders. Realizing the ferocious pace of my pursuit, I stop against a wall to rest. My mother keeps on walking as though she owns the sidewalk under her feet.
As she heads toward the Plaza Hotel, a bicycle messenger swings so close to her that I want to dash forward and rescue her, but she stands dead in her tracks and lets him ride around her and then goes on.
My mother stops at a corner hot-dog stand and asks for something. The vendor hands her a can of soda that she slips into her bag. She stops by another vendor selling sundresses for seven dollars each. I can tell that she is looking at an African print dress, contemplating my size. I think to myself, Please Ma, don't buy it. It would be just another thing that I would bury in the garage or give to Goodwill.

Why should we give to Goodwill when there are so many people back home who need clothes? We save our clothes for the relatives in Haiti.

Twenty years we have been saving all kinds of things for the relatives in Haiti. I need the place in the garage for an exercise bike.

You are pretty enough to be a stewardess. Only dogs like bones.

This mother of mine, she stops at another hot-dog vendor's and buys a frankfurter that she eats on the street. I never knew that she ate frankfurters. With her blood pressure, she shouldn't eat anything with sodium. She has to be careful with her heart, this day woman.

I cannot just swallow salt. Salt is heavier than a hundred bags of shame.

She is slowing her pace, and now I am too close. If she turns around, she might see me. I let her walk into the park before I start to follow.

My mother walks toward the sandbox in the middle of the park. There a woman is waiting with a child. The woman is wearing a leotard with biker's shorts and has small weights in her hands. The woman kisses the child good-bye and surrenders him to my mother; then she bolts off, running on the cemented stretches in the park.

The child given to my mother has frizzy blond hair. His hand slips into hers easily, like he's known her for a long time. When he raises his face to look at my mother, it is as though he is looking at the sky.

My mother gives the child the soda that she bought from the vendor on the street corner. The child's face lights up as she puts in a straw in the can for him. This seems to be a conspiracy just between the two of them.

My mother and the child sit and watch the other children play in the sandbox. The child pulls out a comic book from a knapsack with Big Bird on the back. My mother peers into his comic book. My mother, who taught herself to read as a little girl in Haiti from the books that her brothers brought home from school.

My mother, who has now lost six of her seven sisters in Ville Rose and has never had the strength to return for their funerals.

Many graves to kiss when I go back. Many graves to kiss.

She throws away the empty soda can when the child is done with it. I wait and watch from a corner until the woman in the leotard and biker's shorts returns, sweaty and breathless, an hour later. My mother gives the woman her child back and strolls farther into the park.

I turn around and start to walk out of the park before my mother can see me. My lunch hour is long since gone. I have to hurry back to work. I walk through a cluster of joggers, then race to a *Sweden Tours* bus. I stand behind the bus and take a peek at my mother in the park. She is standing in a circle, chatting with a group of women who are taking other people's children on an afternoon outing. They look like a Third World Parent-Teacher Association meeting.

I quickly jump into a cab heading back to the office. Would Ma have said hello had she been the one to see me first?

As the cab races away from the park, it occurs to me that perhaps one day I would chase an old woman down a street by mistake and that old woman would be somebody else's mother, who I would have mistaken for mine.

Day women come out when nobody expects them.

Tonight on the subway, I will get up and give my seat to a pregnant woman or a lady about Ma's age.

My mother, who stuffs thimbles in her mouth and then blows up her cheeks like Dizzy Gillespie while sewing yet another Raggedy Ann doll that she names Suzette after me.

I will have all these little Suzettes in case you never have any babies, which looks more and more like it is going to happen.

My mother who had me when she was thirty-three—*l'âge du Christ*—at the age that Christ died on the cross.

That's a blessing, believe you me, even if American doctors say by that time you can make retarded babies.

My mother, who sews lace collars on my company softball T-shirts when she does my laundry.

Why, you can't you look like a lady playing softball?

My mother, who never went to any of my Parent-Teacher Association meetings when I was in school.

You're so good anyway. What are they going to tell me? I don't want to make you ashamed of this day woman. Shame is heavier than a hundred bags of salt.

1995

Minh Duc Nguyen b. 1972

Born in Nha Trang, Vietnam, in 1972, Minh Duc Nguyen came to the United States when he was eight. Minh's family was one of hundreds of thousands of "boat people" who fled Vietnam after the fall of Saigon in 1975. His parents had lost their business after the war, and they left Vietnam with their ten children for political and economic reasons. After staying in the refugee camps in Thailand, Minh was sponsored by his brothers, who were already living in the United States, and he was resettled in San Jose, California, in 1981.

Minh began writing fiction while earning a B.A. in molecular and cell biology at the University of California—Berkeley. Dissatisfied with his studies in science and eager to find an outlet outside the laboratory, Minh enrolled in a creative writing class taught by Bharati Mukherjee and quickly discovered that writing was his passion. After completing his undergraduate degree in 1994, Minh earned an M.F.A. in film and television at the University of Southern California in 1998. He wrote the early drafts of "Tale of Apricot" in Mukherjee's creative writing class at Berkeley. The final version of the story initially appeared in the journal UC Berkeley *Occident* and has subsequently been featured in *Watermark: Vietnamese American Poetry and Prose* and *Asian American Studies: A Reader*.

Cautious of the label "Asian American writer," Minh says that he takes the term "with a grain of salt." Minh characterizes his writings as containing an element of fantasy, because creative writing served as a form of escapism for him from his studies in science. Yet he found that this genre would itself become confined by the literary and political expectations of him as an "ethnic writer." His early experiences with publishers and literary critics revealed their bias for stories written in a "realistic" style, favoring only narratives concerning the plight of boat people and/or racial discrimination and hardship in the United States. Minh does not reject these themes in his writings but contends that Asian American literature needs to move beyond the state where stories are published only if they contain a political statement or biographical accounts of trauma. Furthermore, he maintains that even these conventional themes can be told in innovative ways.

"Tale of Apricot" is the story of a Vietnamese woman's memories of her past, from her youth as an orphan in the streets of Saigon, raised by a crippled, homeless man who teaches her the ways of begging and survival, to her adult life in Fresno, California, where she works in an apricot cannery with a multiethnic immigrant community. The short story was received with mixed reviews precisely because of its fantastic elements and departures from an "accurate" or plausible depiction of life in Vietnam. The duality of realism and fantasy is evident throughout the story, most notably, the narrator's ghostly existence and the material reality of poverty in Vietnam and factory labor in Fresno. Another important distinction is the significance of water in the story. In Vietnamese, the word for water (*nuoc*) is also the word for country or homeland. Thus, when the narrator seeks to join her body with the creek's water, the metaphor serves not just as a reference to her union with the spirit of Chu Que but also to Vietnam. Although "Tale of Apricot" addresses issues of exilic longing characterized by the sense of loss, wandering, and a desire to return to the homeland, the story does not completely fit the category of exilic writing because the narrator forever postpones the possibility of a return of reunion with water/homeland. Her quest to "become the creek" is not necessarily a unidirectional passage home but, rather, a desire to exist in fluid continuity, where "[a] body of water merges into other bodies of water, no matter how different they are in volume, in salt concentration, or in geography."

For Minh, the experience of leaving Vietnam by boat, successful after four attempts, undoubtedly is a poignant memory that surfaces briefly in "Tale of Apricot." Yet Minh's approach is closer to what Michele Janette has dubbed "tales of witness." Although Janette was writing about Vietnamese American literature in English that focuses on memoir, the dominant genre of the early postwar years, her observation, that tales of witness generate "a sense of movement and connection" to the homeland with a "multicultural rather than exilic perspective," also reflects the changing currents of newer Vietnamese American fiction.

The growing body of literature by Vietnamese Americans has had a significant influence on the scholarship and literary canons of both Asian American Studies, which in its early formations was mostly comprised of writers of Chinese and Japanese ancestry, and Vietnam War Studies, a field that predominantly featured the perspectives of U.S. veterans. Minh Duc Nguyen's works have also appeared in *The Viet Nam Forum, On a Bed of Rice—An Asian American Erotic Feast, Amerasia Journal, ZYZZYVA,* and *A Magazine.*

Christine Cao
University of California—Los Angeles

Tale of Apricot

I wake up this morning and feel no different than when I went to sleep. For hours, I lie here and observe the branches of the apricot tree that I slept under. I have recently made a promise not to sleep under any tree more than once. This third tree, so far, has the most complicated structure to remember.

I get up and wander around the apricot orchard. These days I have a lot of free time. And I don't have any friends left. They either died or disappeared some time ago. But I'm too old to need friends. The only face that I can remember anyway is that of Chu Que. At times, I look at my hands like they are the young faces of me and him, and I watch them speak to each other. At other times, I just laugh with the crickets and roll around on the wild grass, and I hug the yellow sand by the creek and sleep with the fallen apricots. And slowly, I feel more and more like, what if, I am a ghost.

I can't help but walk toward the apricot cannery. From where I am, the cannery appears as a gray umbrella, shielding the workers inside from the harsh sun of Fresno. Beneath that faded roof, each family, mainly of mothers and daughters, gathers around a long wooden table, slicing apricots in halves. They peel out the large brown seed inside the apricot and assemble the halves on a tray as large as the table. They stack one full tray on top of another. And at the end of each day, Mr. and Mrs. Best, the owners of this plantation, would give them two-fifty cash for each tray. Time is money, as people say, so they cut fast.

Inside the warehouse, I walk from one family to another. It is something that I have done for the past two days. I eavesdrop on their conversation but I keep my distance. I hear all kind of languages: Spanish, Chinese, Cambodian, Vietnamese, and more, but rarely English. The only time these workers would make an effort to speak English is when Mr. Best is around. But his tall frame is nowhere to be seen today. His wife, a small but attractive Chinese woman in her late thirties, is now chatting freely in her dialect among the Chinese families. Mrs. Best lets her dog, a black mutt with a stubby tail, skip around from one table to the next. The dumb dog jumps on everyone it sees and leaves prints of its dirty paws on their shirts.

"No, Vita! No!" Mrs. Best yells at her dog.

Briefly still, Vita stares back at its owner, confused. Then it runs away and resumes its bad manners.

I move toward the right wing of the cannery where all the Vietnamese families are concentrated, and I find the spot where I can be in the center of all of them. I hear that Mrs. Tan is giving Mrs. Anh tips on how to cook bun bo Hue without using MSG—just stew the beef back and tail bones in a large pot for three days to maximize the richness of the broth. Mrs. Nga is telling her daughter Linh not to go out with her boyfriend Minh any longer since he's not going to college. Mrs. Bich, probably the youngest mother there, is pregnant again. She wants a boy this time. Mrs. Thi, who stands in the corner, still hasn't said a word since I first saw her, but rumors tell me that her husband has left her for another woman. Mrs. Ha, a recent immigrant, complains that there aren't any good Vietnamese restaurants in Fresno, how the dishes that they make here are so plain, more like for the American healthy taste, and how the chicken meat here is too tender. She longs for egg noodles from Da Lat, fresh nuoc mam from Phu Quoc, longans from My Tho.

I stand here and listen to the Vietnamese that these families speak. Their words dance in my mind and it doesn't take many beats before I am back in Saigon.

I was three and was already wandering around the main streets day after day with Chu Que, my one-legged uncle, begging for spare change. Chu Que was not my blood relative but it didn't really matter because he was the only one who took care of me, and I didn't know how I came into existence anyway. He said he found me one night in a garbage can located in the back of a dog-meat restaurant. It was dark at the time he picked up my arm and thought that it was a dog bone with some skin left on it. I started to cry when he bit me, and Chu Que then thought that I was a dog with some horrible disease that the chef didn't want to cook and threw away half-killed. But when he saw my fingers grabbing tightly on his crutch, he knew right away that I was someone who had come into his life to fill in as his missing right leg. He lifted me out of the garbage can and into this world, and he bandaged my bleeding arm with a banana leaf. He found a rope and tightened one end around my neck and the other end on his crutch. And Chu Que called me Cho Con, his little dog, until he died.

I was lucky, Chu Que told me. My life could have been much worse. I could have been found by other beggars, perhaps a leper who would pass me his disease, and my hands and feet would have deteriorated when I reached ten, and I would have had to push my body around on a four-wheeled cart, or I could have been found by a desperate beggar who would have twisted my arms and legs and turned me into a freak—a showcase of pity to get more spare change. I asked Chu Que if that was what happened to him, that perhaps some beggars had kidnapped him from his family and broke off one of his legs. But Chu Que didn't say anything. To this day, I still don't know how he'd lost half of his right leg. Well anyway, at least with Chu Que, I still had all my body parts and grew up somewhat normally in the place I knew best. At least with him, I turned out somewhat a human being, or partly.

And standing here in the apricot cannery and in the middle of these families who speak my language, I am not asking for their pity. I am not asking for their spare change. I only seek their recognition that I have the same body parts as them, that I am a human being like them. I want them to see me, if not all of me, then parts of me.

Standing very close to me is little Trang. She has a dirty face even though the morning is still young. Her hands and slingshot are tucked deeply in her pant pockets. The rubber bands on the slingshot hang loose outside. She is standing around with nothing to do, so she decides to try her luck again.

"Ma," says Trang. "Can I help, please?"

Mrs. Ly and her oldest daughter Ngoc are busy with the apricots in their hands. The left hand holds the apricot with three fingers. The right hand holds the small knife with a short curve blade. The right thumb presses the sharp blade deep into the apricot. The three fingers on the left hand rotate the fruit, allowing the blade to slit along the groove that nature imprints on every apricot.

"I can do it, Ma. Let me show you." Little Trang sneaks her hand into Mrs. Ly's blouse pocket where she keeps the extra knife.

"Go away." Mrs. Ly pushes Trang's hand away. "You don't know how."

"Ma, I know how. It's like cutting apple."

"How many times have I told you that this is not an apple? This is an apricot, like a small peach. There's a large seed inside. You have to cut around it, and you have to cut right to get two equal halves. Otherwise, the lady boss will yell, understand? You don't know how. Now, go go, so I can work!"

Sister Ngoc feels pity for her much younger sister, so she says, "Trang, you can help me peel out the seed."

"I don't want to peel seed. I want to cut. Why don't you peel seed and I cut?"

Sister Ngoc smiles. "All right. Let me see if you can cut." And she is about to hand little Trang her knife, but Mrs. Ly stops her.

"No. I said she's too young to know how to cut. She'll cut her fingers instead. Girls with scars are ugly." Mrs. Ly rumbles on to explain that a girl's hands should be soft and white like steamed rice. The fingers should be long and somewhat fat where they meet the knuckles and pointed at the tips. But most importantly, the hands should be free of scars. If a hardworking girl has beautiful hands, it is a sign that she is kheo leo, clever, and she will know how to keep her house together when she has a family of her own. It's strange how Mrs. Ly's hands are nothing like what she described. Her frail hands appear used and dry around the fingertips. Red marks rest on her palms and long veins emerge through the brown skin. Perhaps they were once white and soft.

"Why don't you go play with the other kids?" Sister Ngoc tells little Trang, who is still staring at the knife. "Go go and come back later for lunch."

Finally, little Trang trots away toward the apricot orchard, kicking her feet high. She raises her hands and gazes at them. Her fingers clench into tight fists. I don't think she realizes how small her hands are.

I follow her. The poor girl must not think of herself as useless. I have a feeling she will do something of great importance for me.

I wish I could stop little Trang at this moment and talk to her and teach her the art of begging. All she had to do was to look deeply at her mother's hands with her light brown eyes and say, "Ma, you have beautiful hands." And I'm sure Mrs. Ly would soften and wrap her daughter's hands inside her own and they would cut together.

I knew all there was to know about begging. Chu Que taught me all the tricks, and I formulated some myself. The secret was to look like a beggar but talk like a poet.

"Cho Con, don't beg and they will give," said Chu Que. He often used breakfast as an example to show his point.

"It's early morning, and you are hungry and you want to eat breakfast. A man walks by. He's neither rich nor poor. Cho Con, what would you do?"

"Chu Que, I'd say, 'Chu a Chu, I'm hungry. Would you be kind and spare me some change?'"

"Well, that's not bad, Cho Con. You asked politely. And you look like a cute little girl, although very dirty. The man will pity and give you two dong. With that, you can buy one Chinese donut for breakfast. But suppose you want more. Suppose you want a bowl of porridge with stuffed pork intestines to go with your donut. How do you convince this man to give you five more dong?"

"Hmmm? . . . I'll say that you are my father . . . and you are very sick . . . and . . . that I need money to go buy you medicine."

"Oh, Cho Con, you lie. That's very good. You're learning every day. But there's no need to lie unless it's a matter of life and death. And besides, what if I'm not with you? Who would be your father?"

"Chu Que, what would you do?"

"Now, listen. You're a little girl. People like little girls. It's early morning, a man walks by, you're hungry and want to eat breakfast. If you wave your hand at him, look him straight in the eyes, and greet him with a smile, just this much I'll guarantee you that most of the time the man will already give two dong so you can buy a Chinese donut. But now you want a bowl of porridge, so it's a little trickier. You'll have to play a game with the man. Nothing is for free, understand? You play a game with him and he'll pay you for it."

"What game, Chu Que?"

"A game of words. Man likes to play games to test his wit. It's his stupid nature. So you ask him a silly question that makes him think but he cannot answer . . . like . . . 'Chu a Chu, do you know how big the moon is?' Hah, see? The man probably stops, thinks about it for a few seconds, and says, 'I really don't know. Why do you ask, little girl?' Now, this is when what you say counts the most! How much more the man will give you depends on how smart your answer is. You'd say something like this, 'Chu a Chu, last night I was so hungry that I couldn't sleep. So I laid here on the street awake all night and I watched the moon. The moon was so beautiful. It was bright, round and large, as large as your face! But I think the moon is probably much bigger than that. Chu a Chu, am I right?' What can he say now? Nothing! The man will nod his head in defeat. He'll pay you on the head and give you the extra five dong for your bowl of porridge, and he'll walk away smiling at his own kindness."

By the time I was seven, I had mastered this game of wit, which was played differently with a rich man or a poor man, young man or old man, a man or woman, tourists or local people. I rarely had to say "please" or even "spare change." But things became worse as I got older. I was no longer a cute little girl. I had to readjust and that was a new lesson. When I came to America, I encountered several beggars in San Francisco. They either sat in their corners and shook their paper cups with a few coins inside, or they just said, "Spare change?" And I laughed so hard at them.

Little Trang runs as fast as she can across the apricot orchard. She is anxious to meet the other children at the wild blackberry shrubs by the creek. But at halfway, her right foot steps into a squirrel's hole, and she falls down hard and scratches her left elbow on a sharp stone. Slowly, little Trang sits up. She holds her bleeding elbow close to her face and observes her wound carefully, with admiration. Then, with her fingertips, she rubs saliva off her tongue and cleans her wound. The touch of saliva on her injury must have created a burning pain, for her left cheek twitches continuously. But she remains still and quiet. The blood on the round scrape, which seems redder then a Tet good luck money envelope, soon clots in the dry summer heat. In a week, she'll have a new scar, and she'll have to hide it from her mother. The girl stands up on her feet. She kicks the dirt off her pants. As if she's forgotten about her fall, she races toward the creek, as fast as she can, like a wild mustang.

I run after her.

She stops to rest under an apricot tree with a few fruits left. She pulls down a drooping branch, shaking it vigorously until an apricot falls. She bends down and picks up the overripe fruit. With her long thumbnail, she stabs through the yellowish pink skin. Golden juice rushes out, racing down her thumb and wrist, cooling the pores of her skin along the way. She slides her sharp nail around the apricot and tears it apart into two messy halves. The large seed on one half stares at her.

"It's not that hard," she mumbles. "I can cut anything."

A large, black creature runs toward her and dives on her back. Little Trang falls, face down, but eases her crash with her hands. The apricot halves crush in her palms.

"Uneducated dog! I'll teach you a lesson!" she curses.

Dumb Vita licks her ear and then quickly runs away. Little Trang pushes herself up. She pulls out her slingshot from her pocket. She takes the wet apricot seed in her hand and shoots it at Vita. But she misses badly. Vita barks and disappears behind some bushes.

Trang swallows her anger and continues down until she reaches the narrow creek curving behind the apricot orchard. She finds the blackberry shrubs but sees no one. Usually the children gather here and play hide-and-seek, or they hunt for squirrels and birds with their slingshots or fish for crawdads in the muddy creek with the raw chicken parts that they brought from home. She walks farther down along the creek. Tall pines embed both sides of the creek now. Perhaps the children have hiked deep down the creek to find a perfect tree that extends its large branches from one side of the creek to the other, and the boys can climb up and tie a long rope on that branch so they can swing like monkeys from one side to the other.

After a long while, I become more and more reluctant to follow the little girl. I recognize this path, and I know what secret lies ahead. And suddenly, I feel weak, and I don't want to follow her any longer. But she's going down there no matter what, with or without me. Why can't a secret be a secret? But nothing can be a secret if it isn't discovered. Sometimes it is better to leave something unknown.

Chu Que always treated me like I was his pupil. But when I was old enough, I realized that he was only about fifteen years older than me, so I told him to cut that act out. And he did. I was a young woman now, and I could easily live on my own any day. In a way, Chu Que was relieved to be rid of the fatherly responsibility of all those years.

We became friends, friends in the way that we could swear at each other freely, and run away from each other for a few days, until we crawled back in the same corner and shared our cup again. Our difference in age didn't matter anymore. In a way, we were immortal.

"We're angels on the streets," Chu Que described us.

"But angels are the slaves of God," I contradicted him. "They are worse off than beggars."

Chu Que was very handsome. A brave soldier dressed in a new uniform couldn't be as handsome. He was neither tall nor did he carry himself well, especially with his limp. But he had the saddest face in Saigon. Every time I looked at him I felt very fortunate for my own life. His eyes, which were long and deep as the creek here, could see through any soul. Every day, we sat around and observed people on the streets. And randomly as he chose, Chu Que would point his finger at any person and tell me about him or her like he had known that person for years.

So I began to love. I don't know how or exactly when or what for, but I did, like I can't help but dream when I sleep. And everybody has to sleep, even if they live outside on the streets, and it's raining. And in Saigon, did it rain. It was late that August when the monsoon had come down hard for eight straight days and still wouldn't quit. Standing on the sidewalk, the flood had risen to our knees. That night I lost my sandals as we waded for many blocks to find a high step on some house or building. But with Chu Que's leg, we moved slowly, so all the dry spots were occupied by other beggars. We searched for miles with no luck.

"We're going to drown tonight," I said to him.

"Don't be silly. There must be a dry place somewhere in this damn city." He cried.

I could hardly hear him. The storm pounded hard against metal sheet rooftops, and water gushed down the sidewalks. The wind shoved violently, snapping tree branches and knocking over parked cyclos and scooters. Our streets became a river of floating trash. Wind and rain, earth and heaven, there must be a dry spot somewhere. We stared real hard, into the corners of brick walls, the pits of long alleys, under iron balconies and behind trash cans. And slowly, from these darkest places, round eyes, many of them, began to light up like stars, gazing out at us. We looked down with shame. We could not see our feet.

Then Chu Que said, "Follow me."

He held my hand and led me to a motel nearby. He pulled me inside the office room where the owner of the motel was leaning at the front counter. He was sipping hot tea. His wife and children were eating rice in the back.

"No," I said. "They would never—"

But Chu Que motioned me to say no more.

"How much for a room?" Chu Que asked the owner.

The owner didn't bother to answer. But his wife, she noticed how serious Chu Que seemed. So she replied, "Four hundred dong."

Chu Que slowly bent his back. He untied the knot on the short leg of his trouser. A tightly-wrapped plastic bag fell out, and Chu Que caught it. He took off the rubber band and unwrapped the plastic bag. Inside was a roll of money, a big roll of small bills. He counted the money in front of the owner and his wife.

"Here's the four hundred," Chu Que said. "And there are twenty-three left. I will throw that in if you make us a pot of hot tea like that and give us your left-over rice."

Astonished, the owner nodded. His wife took the money.

The owner showed us our room. A short while later, the wife served us hot tea and rice with salted fish and sour cabbage.

Chu Que and I both removed our soaked clothes, and we wrapped ourselves with the blankets that the room provided. We ate our rice and drank our tea. It was our best meal together.

After that, we crawled onto the bed and laid next to each other, like we always did on the street anyway. Only this time we were naked. I asked him about the money since I was as surprised as the motel owner. Chu Que shook his head in regret. He said he had been saving it to buy me a sweater. I inched closer to him. I told him that I already had him to keep me warm. Then his hand crawled slowly beneath the blankets and found its place on my small breast and covered my cold nipple. And just like that, we discovered ourselves all over again. And after an hour or so, we held tightly to each other and rolled down to the floor because we weren't used to lying on a soft mattress. I remember we giggled like little kids.

After that night, our lives changed completely. We still begged and dragged ourselves on the streets as usual. But I mean the invisible changes that you can't see. Whatever it was, it was comforting to know that someone would always be there for me, even though he was there since the beginning.

But nothing lasts. Money has to be spent, and food has to be eaten or it will spoil. Why discover something when one cannot hold on to it forever?

The night Chu Que died, we were sitting on Le Loi Boulevard, near Ben Thanh Market. Many things had changed. For one thing, Saigon was now Ho Chi Minh City, but we beggars couldn't care less. I was only worried about Chu Que's health. He was in constant pain. At night, he couldn't sleep in peace, always tossing and turning inside our blanket, ending up crouching like a fetus that tucks its hands in front of its stomach. I held him still as much as I could with one hand, and with the other hand, I massaged his head since it helped to ease his pain a little. I took him to the hospital, but it was no use. The doctor told us that he would require surgery, and there were other poor sick people with worse cases waiting.

"What are we supposed to do?" I asked the doctor. "Just wait to die on the street?"

The doctor said nothing.

"Let's go," Chu Que told me. "It's not his fault."

That night we sat in our corner. I was too tired to beg so I leaned back against the wall. The apartment's balcony above cast a shadow over my body. Chu Que, skinny and weak, crawled out to the sidewalk to be visible under the streetlights. It was nice to see him from a distance. He was indeed a poet in the degradation of time and mass. Sitting by myself, I watched him play his last game of words.

A man with black boots walked by.

"Chu a Chu, do you know what time it is?" asked Chu Que before he looked up and saw that the man's green hat glittered with a red metal star.

"It's ten after nine." The man's metal watchband and the large buttons on his khaki uniform shined at us. "Why do you ask? Does it matter to you what time it is?"

"No. I guess not. But a long time ago, I used to have a nice watch and I always knew what time it was . . . and . . . and I used to wear leather shoes that warmed my feet . . . and I used to live in a large house that had a tall ceiling to shield my head from the rain . . . like your beautiful hat there. No. I guess I don't need to know what time it is. It's just an old habit of this . . . poor . . . bum." And then Chu Que coughed abruptly.

The tall man stared at Chu Que for a while before, finally, he pulled out a hundred dong bill and dropped it in Chu Que's bowl.

"And did you used to have two legs, too?" asked the man.

"Huh? Two legs, one leg, what's the difference, dong chi?" Chu Que acknowledged him as Comrade.

"It's obvious."

"No, it's not. I'm almost blind, so why don't you tell me the difference between two legs and one leg."

The man shook his head and was about to leave.

"Tell me, or you don't know, dong chi!"

"All right, since you want to know so bad. I walk, you skip. I run, you crawl."

"You forget that you work and I beg, you give and I take!"

"You're right." The man laughed and dropped the second hundred dong bill. As the man turned to away, Chu Que suddenly coughed out in a fury.

"Let me tell you what's the difference between two legs and one leg. Listen up. There's no difference! You and I are stuck together like a kite with a tail and a head, understand? Without my tail, you can't fly straight with your big head. Without a beggar like me, you'd have no one to show off your wealth to. Without me, you're nothing!"

The man in black boots laughed even louder. He walked away in long strides.

Chu Que died that night, in defeat at his own game, leaving his Cho Con by herself in this world. Before he passed away, he gasped by my neck, "Leave this place."

I wrapped his body and crutch inside two blankets, his and mine, and tightened them with the same rope that he once used to put around my neck. I paid a cyclo to take us to the border of the Saigon River. There, I slid his body into the black water. I was hoping that his body would flow out to reach the South China Sea and then to the Pacific Ocean. But instead, Chu Que's body just sank and vanished, carrying all the weight of his pain with him.

I knew that I couldn't play the game of wit any longer. It wasn't a game anymore. It was begging now. Chu Que and I had lied to ourselves. In truth, we weren't poets. We were bums on the streets who begged for a living. We begged for meals. We begged for cigarettes. We begged for clothes. We begged for shelter. And after Chu Que died, I begged my way to America.

I took the bus from Ho Chi Minh City to Vung Tau, the peninsula where the Bay of Boats was located. In the daytime, I went to the restaurants, the villas, and the cafes that lined the resort's beach, and I begged. But at night, I walked to the Bay of Boats, and I sat and waited. I waited for weeks before one night I saw people creeping out like spiders from the darkest corners. I knew it was the moment, and I quickly changed into a clean outfit that I had saved. I crawled quietly from behind and slowly, I rose and joined them. No one noticed that I was an outsider. We waited, at least fifty of us, by the shore with our heads low, until these small boats that looked like coffins because visible in front of us. We waded out quietly and climbed on. The small boats rowed out in an hour between water and blackness. We reached a much larger fishing boat that had been waiting for us, and we crawled over quickly. The fishing boat sailed out for hours before daring to turn on its motor. The boat people crouched on deck, leaning on each other, seasick, like spiders entangled in their own web.

We reached Malaysia in seven days. No one knew I cheated. They were too happy to care. I spent seventeen months at a refugee camp before I was sponsored to America by a Catholic church in Fresno.

For many years, I worked as a custodian in an elementary school. I swept and mopped and days dried by. I sorted the papers, pencils and crayons that were dropped on the floor, and I tried to piece my life together. But most of the time, I picked up little pieces of trash and threw them in a large garbage can, and I dumped the loose fragments of my life in with them. Eventually, I had nothing left of myself to throw away.

And now I stare at the muddy water in this creek, and I wonder if this water carries any trace of Chu Que. It must. A body of water merges into other bodies of water, no matter how different they are in volume, in salt concentration, or in geography. Water from a river in one country flows out to join a sea, then meets an ocean, then travels a long distance to meet another sea, then joins a river in a new country, and ends up in a little creek. What do I know anyway? One leg or two legs, on boat or not, it still takes one to the same place. There's no difference.

I see no more need to follow little Trang. Obviously, she would never see me, and even if she could, she doesn't need my teaching. In this land, no one wants to beg, even if one is a beggar, and no one wants to play a game of wit, and definitely one would not pay for it. One just gives what one feels like, and one takes more than one can carry.

I jump into the creek and let the water carry me. It's something that I wanted to do three days ago but never had a chance. The water encloses my body, merges into me and stretches me. If I stay in this water long enough, gradually, I'll become the creek.

The water carries me, and I flow past little Trang who is still trotting anxiously further down the creek. The water takes me by many pines before it brings me back to the pathetic woman sitting by the creek with her bare feet in the water. Her back leans against a large trunk, but her head tilts toward the ground like she is about to fall down. She has one skinny hand clutching at her neck. Her eyes, pale yellow and barely open, gaze down at the water.

What are you staring at, you miserable woman? Why are you sitting there by yourself at a place like this? How did you end up her, Cho Con?

I grab her feet and pull myself out of the water. I sit next to her. I ask her many questions, but she does not respond. I wave my hand in front of her eyes, but she does not blink. I poke and tickle her feet but she does not move. At one point, I try to creep inside her.

Damn you, you're worthless, useless, nothing but a heavy bag of rice.

Soon little Trang walks by, and she sees the woman sitting by the creek with her bare feet in the water. She stops before the woman and asks, "Aunty, have you seen any boys and girls walking by here?"

Forget it little girl. She won't answer you. She can't. She's dead.

"I've been looking for them, but I can't find them anywhere. We were supposed to meet and play down there." She points to the direction where she came from.

Then she grins, showing off her little teeth. "Have you seen them, Aunty? They're small like me."

The woman has a black bag open on her lap. A strong breeze flies by and knocks the bag off her lap. Green bills of ones, fives, and tens roll out of the bag and hang loose at its mouth.

"Aunty, there's your money. You better put them back inside your bag, or they're going to fly into the water and get all wet."

Take the money, little girl. There are twenty-four dollars and some coins there. This woman does not need money any longer. She has begged all her life, and now she has a chance to give some back. Please take her money, little girl. Don't you want to help your mother? Take the money and give it to her. Take the spare change, little girl, and return this woman a favor.

A stronger wind rushes by. The bills flap loose, but little Trang quickly kneels down and grabs them. She puts the bills on the ground and rolls them into a tight bundle. Then she tucks the money back inside the bag. As she does this, she sees several apricots resting inside.

"My mother thinks I cannot cut apricots. I can, I know I can, if only she gives me a chance. What's so hard about cutting apricots?" asks little Trang. "There you go, Aunty. I put your money back inside your bag. Be careful now."

You old fool. You didn't think this would happen to you, right? You thought that on the anniversary of Chu Que's death, you would walk across the broad apricot orchard near where you live, pick a few apricots, and hike to the little creek here. You thought that at this creek, you could take off your shoes and cool your feet in the water. And you thought that you would have time to do all that before you'd drown yourself so you could join him in the creek. But what do you know? You died before you could do much. You died as you choked on an apricot's seed.

"What's in your hand? What are you hiding?" asks little Trang. "My sister plays a guessing game with me all the time. She hides a coin in one hand and makes me guess."

Little girl, would you do me a favor and push my body into the water. As long as it sits here, I cannot rest in peace. As long as it stays there, I'll never join him.

Little Trang bends down and holds up the tight left fist of the woman. She peels out one finger at a time. Resting inside the white palm is the other rotten half of the apricot, the half without the large brown seed.

Loud barking suddenly echoes through the pines. Little Trang turns around. Black Vita is charging toward her. She drops the woman's hand to pull out her slingshot. She picks up several pebbles from the ground. And quickly, she races toward Vita, head to head. She aims at its nose. The dog sees the slingshot and retreats. But little Trang chases after it.

"I'll get you this time, you dumb dog! I'll get you this time!"

Please don't go.

But little Trang has disappeared after Vita.

I lean back on the pine and stare at the profile of the dead woman. She's there and I'm not, like an apricot without the seed inside. I pity her, love her more. I think I will sleep under this tree tonight.

1997

Acknowledgments

Text

Edward Albee. "The Sandbox." Copyright © 1959, renewed 1987 by Edward Albee. Reprinted by permission of William Morris Agency, LLC on behalf of the author.

Sherman Alexie. "Because My Father Always Said He Was the Only Indian Who Saw Jimi Hendrix Play 'The Star-Spangled Banner' at Woodstock," from *The Lone Ranger and Tonto Fist-Fight in Heaven* by Sherman Alexie. Copyright © 1993 by Sherman Alexie. Used with permission of Grove/Atlantic, Inc.

Dorothy Allison. "Don't Tell Me You Don't Know," from *Trash* by Dorothy Allison (Ithaca, NY: Firebrand Books, 1988). Reprinted by permission of the author.

Rudolfo Anaya. Excerpt from *Bless Me, Ultima.* Copyright © Rudolfo Anaya 1974. Published in hardcover and mass market paperback by Warner Books Inc., 1994; originally published by TQS Publications. Reprinted by permission of Susan Bergholz Literary Services, New York, NY, and Lamy, NM. All rights reserved.

Gloria Anzaldúa. "Entering into the Serpent" and "La conciencia de la mestiza/Towards a New Consciousness," from *Borderlands/La Frontera: The New Mestiza.* Copyright © 1987, 1999 by Gloria Anzaldúa. Reprinted by permission of Aunt Lute Books.

Rane Arroyo. "Caribbean Braille" from *Pale Ramón* (Cambridge, MA: Zoland Books, 1998). Reprinted by permission of the author. "My Transvestite Uncle Is Missing," from *The Singing Shark* (Tempe, AZ: Arizona State University, Bilingual Press/Editorial Bilingüe, 1996). Reprinted by permission of the publisher. "That Flag" and "Write What You Know," from *Home Movies of Narcissus* by Rane Arroyo, © 2002 Rane Arroyo. Reprinted by permission of the University of Arizona Press.

John Ashbery. "As You Came from the Holy Land," from *Self-Portrait in a Convex Mirror* by John Ashbery, copyright © 1973 by John Ashbery, used by permission of Viking Penguin, a division of Penguin Group (USA) Inc. "Farm Implements and Rutabagas in a Landscape," from *The Double Dream of Spring* by John Ashbery, copyright © 1966, 1970 by John Ashbery, reprinted by permission of Georges Borchardt, Inc., on behalf of the author. "The Instruction Manual," from *Some Trees* by John Ashbery, copyright © 1956 by John Ashbery, reprinted by permission of Georges Borchardt, Inc., on behalf of the author.

Jimmy Santiago Baca. "Commitment," "Ghost Readings in Sacramento," "I Put on My Jacket," and "I've Taken Risks" from *Set This Book on Fire!* (Cedar Hill Publications, 2001). Grateful acknowledgement to Cedar Hills Books for permission to reprint Jimmy Santiago Baca's poems.

James Baldwin. "Sonny's Blues," © 1957 by James Baldwin was originally published in *Partisan Review.* Copyright renewed. Collected in *Going to Meet the Man,* published by Vintage Books. Reprinted by arrangement with the James Baldwin Estate.

Toni Cade Bambara. "The Lesson," copyright © 1972 by Toni Cade Bambara, from *Gorilla, My Love* by Toni Cade Bambara. Used by permission of Random House, Inc.

John Barth. "Lost in the Funhouse," copyright © 1967 by The Atlantic Monthly, from *Lost in the Funhouse* by John Barth. Used by permission of Doubleday, a division of Random House, Inc.

Donald Barthelme. "At the End of the Mechanical Age," from *Amateurs,* pp. 197–207. Copyright © 1976 by Donald Barthelme, reprinted with permission of The Wylie Agency, Inc.

Jean Baudrillard. Excerpt from *The Spirit of Terrorism and Other Essays,* Verso, 3–13, 26–30. Reprinted by permission of Verso Books.

Saul Bellow. "Looking for Mr. Green," copyright 1951, renewed © 1979 by Saul Bellow, from *Mosby's Memoirs and Other Stories* by Saul Bellow. Used by permission of Viking Penguin, a division of Penguin Group (USA) Inc.

Wendell Berry. Excerpt from "Word and Flesh," copyright © 2009 by Wendell Berry from *What Are People For? Essays.* Reprinted by permission of Counterpoint.

Elizabeth Bishop. "At the Fishhouses," "Filling Station," "The Fish," and "The Man-Moth" from *The Complete Poems: 1927–1979* by Elizabeth Bishop. Copyright © 1979, 1983 by Alice Helen Methfessel. Reprinted by permission of Farrar, Straus and Giroux, LLC.

Robert Bly. All lines from "Counting Small-Boned Bodies" from *The Light around the Body* by Robert Bly, copyright © 1967 by Robert Bly, copyright renewed 1995 by Robert Bly, reprinted by permission of HarperCollins Publishers. All lines from "The Teeth Mother Naked at Last" from *Sleepers Joining Hands* by Robert Bly, copyright © 1970 by Robert Bly, reprinted by permission of Harper-Collins Publishers.

Kathy Boudin. "The Call," from *Prison Writing in Twentieth-Century America* (New York: Penguin Books, 1998), reprinted by permission of the author. "Our Skirt" and "A Trilogy of Journeys," copyright © 1999 by PEN American Center, reprinted from *Doing Time: Twenty-Five Years of Prison Writing,* a PEN American Center Prize Anthology, edited by Bell Gale Chevigny, published by Arcade Publishing, New York, New York.

Gwendolyn Brooks. "A Bronzeville Mother Loiters in Mississippi. Meanwhile, a Mississippi Mother Burns Bacon," "The Last Quatrain of the Ballad of Emmett Till," "The Mother," The Sundays of Satin-Legs Smith," "Ulysses," and "We Real Cool." Reprinted by permission of the author.

Carlos Bulosan. Chapter XIII and Chapter XIV from *America Is in the Heart.* Reprinted by permission.

Raymond Carver. "What We Talk About When We Talk About Love," from *What We Talk About When We Talk About Love* by Raymond Carver, copyright © 1974, 1976, 1978, 1980, 1981 by Raymond Carver. Used by permission of Alfred A. Knopf, a division of Random House, Inc.

Lorna Dee Cervantes. "Bananas," from *Daughters of the Fifth Sun,* Riverhead Books, 1993, reprinted by permission of Lorna Dee Cervantes. "Beneath the Shadow of the Freeway," reprinted by permission of the publisher, *Latin American Literary Review,* volume 5, number 10, 1977, Pittsburgh, Pennsylvania. "Macho" is reprinted with permission from the publisher of *From the Cables of Genocide: Poems of Love and Hunger* (Houston: Arte Publico Press, University of Houston, 1991). "Poem for the Young White Man Who Asked Me How I, an Intelligent, Well-Read Person, Could Believe in the War between Races," from *Emplumada,* by Lorna Dee Cervantes, © 1982, reprinted by permission of the University of Pittsburgh Press.

Frank Chin. "Railroad Standard Time," from *The Chinaman Pacific & Frisco R.R. Co.* Reprinted with permission.

Sandra Cisneros. "Eleven," from *Woman Hollering Creek.* Copyright © 1991 by Sandra Cisneros. Published by Vintage Books, a division of Random House, Inc., and originally in hardcover by Random House, Inc. Reprinted by permission of Susan Bergholz Literary Services, New York, NY, and Lamy, NM. All rights reserved.

Lucille Clifton. "at the cemetery, walnut grove plantation, south carolina, 1989," "i am accused of tending to the past," and "reply" from *Quilting: Poems 1987–1990,* copyright © 1991 by Lucille Clifton, reprinted with the permission of BOA Editions, Ltd., www.boaeditions.org. "in white america," from *Next,* copyright © 1987 by Lucille Clifton, reprinted with the permission of BOA Editions, Ltd., www.boaeditions.org. "the thirty eighth year," from *Good Woman: Poems and a Memoir 1969–1980,* copyright © 1987 by Lucille Clifton, reprinted with the permission of BOA Editions, Ltd., www.boaeditions.org.

Judith Ortiz Cofer. "Claims," "En Mis Ojos No Hay Dias," "Latin Women Pray," "My Father in the Navy: A Childhood Memory," and "The Woman Who Was Left at the Altar," from *Triple Crown,* © 1987, Bilingual Press/Arizona State University, Tempe, AZ. Reprinted by permission.

Combahee River Collective. "A Black Feminist Statement," from *Capitalist Patriarchy and the Case for Socialist Feminism,* ed. Zillah R. Eisenstein (New York: Monthly Review, 1979). Copyright © 1979 by Monthly Review Press. Reprinted by permission of Monthly Review Foundation.

Robert Creeley. "America," "For Love," "Hart Crane," "I Know a Man," and "Words," from *For Love: Poems 1950–1960* by Robert Creeley. Reprinted by permission of the University of California Press.

Víctor Hernández Cruz. "Mountain Building" and "Table of Contents," from *Bilingual Wholes.* "Urban Dream," from *Snaps*, 1969. Reprinted by permission of the author.

Edwidge Danticate. "New York Day Women," from *Krik? Krak!*, © 1995, is published by permission of Soho Press, Inc. All rights reserved.

Don DeLillo. Chapter 1 from *Falling Man*, reprinted with the permission of Scribner, a Division of Simon & Schuster Adult Publishing Group, copyright © 2007 by Don DeLillo, all rights reserved. "In the Ruins of the Future: Reflections on Terror, Loss and Time in the Shadow of September," copyright © 2001 by Don DeLillo, first printed in *Harper's Magazine*, December 2001, used by permission of Wallace Literary Agency, Inc.

Vine Deloria, Jr. Excerpt from *Custer Died for Your Sins: An Indian Manifesto*, reprinted with the permission of Scribner, a Division of Simon & Schuster Adult Publishing Group. Copyright © 1969 by Vine Deloria, Jr. Copyright renewed © 1997 by Vine Deloria, Jr. All rights reserved.

Wai Chee Dimock, Wai Chee. "Planet America, Set and Subset," from *Shades of the Planet*, ed. Wai Chee Dimock. © 2007 by Princeton University Press. Reprinted by permission of Princeton University Press.

Rita Dove. "Daystar" and "The Oriental Ballerina" from *Thomas and Beulah*, Carnegie Mellon University Press, © 1986 by Rita Dove. "Kentucky, 1833" and "O" from *The Yellow House on the Corner*, Carnegie Mellon University Press, copyright © 1980 by Rita Dove. Reprinted by permission of the author.

Ralph Ellison. "Brave Words for a Startling Occasion," edited by John F. Callahan, copyright 1953 by Ralph Ellison, from *The Collected Essays of Ralph Ellison* by Ralph Ellison, used by permission of Modern Library, a division of Random House, Inc. "A Party Down at the Square" copyright © 1966 by Fanny Ellison and "Flying Home" copyright © 1996 by Fanny Ellison, from *Flying Home and Other Stories* by Ralph Ellison. Used by permission of Random House, Inc.

Louise Erdrich. "Saint Marie," from the book *Love Medicine* by Louise Erdrich. Copyright © 1984, 1993 by Louise Erdrich. Reprinted by permission of Henry Holt and Company, LLC.

Sandra María Esteves. "A la Mujer Borrinqueña," © 1980 Sandra María Esteves, reprinted from *Yerba Buena*, Greenfield Review, ISBN 0912678-47-X, by permission of the author. "So Your Name Isn't María Cristina" is reprinted with permission from the publisher of Bluestown Mockingbird Mambo (Houston: Arte Publico Press, University of Houston, 1990).

Lawrence Ferlinghetti. "Dove Sta Amore" and "I Am Waiting," from *A Coney Island of the Mind*, copyright © 1958 by Lawrence Ferlinghetti, reprinted by permission of New Directions Publishing Corp. "The Old Italians Dying" from *These Are My Rivers*, copyright © 1979 by Lawrence Ferlinghetti, reprinted by permission of New Directions Publishing Corp.

Carolyn Forché. All lines from "As Children Together" copyright © 1980 by Carolyn Forché, "Because One Is Always Forgotten" copyright © 1981 by Carolyn Forché, "The Colonel" copyright © 1981 (originally appeared in *Women's International Resource Exchange*), from *The Country between Us* by Carolyn Forché, reprinted by permission of HarperCollins Publishers. All lines from "Elegy" and "The Recording Angel" from *The Angel of History* by Carolyn Forché, copyright © 1994 by Carolyn Forché, reprinted by permission of HarperCollins Publishers.

Brenda (Bonnie) Frazer. Excerpt from *Troia: Mexican Memoirs* (New York: Croton Press, Ltd., 1969), pp. 9–15. Reprinted by permission of the author.

Ernest J. Gaines. "The Sky Is Gray," copyright © 1963 by Ernest J. Gaines, from *Bloodline* by Ernest J. Gaines. Used by permission of Doubleday, a division of Random House, Inc.

Allen Ginsberg. All lines from "America" copyright © 1956, 1959 by Allen Ginsberg, "Howl" copyright © 1955 by Allen Ginsberg, and "A Supermarket in California" copyright © 1955 by Allen Ginsberg from *Collected Poems 1947–1980* by Allen Ginsberg. Reprinted by permission of HarperCollins Publishers.

Jessica Hagedorn. "The Blossoming of Bongbong," "The Death of Anna May Wong," "Filipino

Boogie," "Homesick," and "Vulva Operetta" from *Danger and Beauty*, © 1993. Copyright © 2002 by Jessica Hagedorn. Reprinted by permission of City Lights Books.

Kimiko Hahn. "Cuttings," from *The Unbearable Heart*. Copyright © 1995 by Kimiko Hahn. Reprinted by permission of Kaya. "Resistance: A Poem on Ikat Cloth," from *Air Pocket* by Kimiko Hahn. Copyright © 1989 by Kimiko Hahn. Reprinted by permission of Hanging Loose Press. "Strands," from *Earshot* by Kimiko Hahn. Copyright © 1992 by Kimiko Hahn.

Joy Harjo. "Anchorage," "New Orleans," "Remember," "Vision," and "The Woman Hanging from the 13th Floor Window" from *She Had Some Horses*, copyright © 1983 by Joy Harjo, used by permission of the publisher, Thunder's Mouth Press. "Deer Dancer" and "We Must Call a Meeting," from *In Mad Love and War*, copyright © 1990 by Joy Harjo, reprinted by permission of University Press of New England.

Michael Harper. "Camp Story," "Here Where Coltrane Is," "History as Apple Tree," "Nightmare Begins Responsibility," "A Narrative of the Life and Times of John Coltrane: Played by Himself," and "Song: I Want a Witness" are reprinted by permission of the author.

Robert Hayden. "Summertime and the Living . . ." copyright © 1962, 1966 by Robert Hayden, "Mourning Poem for the Queen of Sunday" and "Those Winter Sundays" copyright © 1966 by Robert Hayden, "Tour 5" copyright © 1962, 1966 by Robert Hayden, from *Collected Poems of Robert Hayden* by Robert Hayden, edited by Frederick Glaysher. Used by permission of Liveright Publishing Corporation.

Le Ly Hayslip. "A Different View," from *When Heaven and Earth Changed Places* by Le Ly Hayslip, copyright © 1989 by Le Ly Hapslip and Charles Jay Wurts. Used by permission of Doubleday, a division of Random House, Inc.

Michael Herr. Excerpt from *Dispatches* by Michael Herr, copyright © 1977 by Michael Herr. Used by permission of Alfred A. Knopf, a division of Random House, Inc.

Linda Hogan. "All My Relations," from *Dwellings: A Spiritual History of the Living World* by Linda Hogan. Copyright © 1995 by Linda Hogan. Used by permission of W. W. Norton & Company, Inc.

Rolando Hinojosa-Smith. "Sometimes It Just Happens That Way, That's All," from *The Valley* (Bilingual Review Press, 1983). Reprinted by permission.

Garrett Kaoru Hongo. "And Your Soul Shall Dance," "Off from Swing Shift," "Who among You Knows the Essence of Garlic?," and "Yellow Light," from *Yellow Light*, copyright © 1982 by Garrett Kaoru Hongo, Wesleyan University Press, reprinted by permission of University Press of New England. "The Unreal Dwelling: My Years in Volcano," from *The River of Heaven* by Garrett Hongo, used by permission of University Press of New England.

bell hooks. "touching the earth," from *Sisters of the Yam*, South End Press, 1993, pp. 175–182. Reprinted by permission of South End Press.

Lawson Fusao Inada. "Kicking the Habit," "Instructions to All Persons," and "Two Variations on a Theme" are reprinted by permission of Coffee House Press. "On Being Asian American" is reprinted by permission.

Gish Jen. "In the American Society," from *Imagining America*. Copyright © 1986 by Gish Jen. First published in *The Southern Review*. Reprinted by permission of the author.

Joyce Johnson. Excerpts from *Minor Characters: A Beat Memoir* copyright © 1983, 1994 by Joyce Johnson. Used by permission of Penguin, a division of Penguin Group (USA) Inc. "July 26, 1957," from *Door Wide Open: A Beat Love Affair in Letters* by Joyce Johnson and Jack Kerouac, copyright © 2000 by Joyce Johnson, copyright © 2000 by the Estate of Stella Kerouac, John Sampras, Literary Representative. Used by permission of Viking Penguin, a division of Penguin Group (USA) Inc.

LeRoi Jones (Amiri Baraka). "An Agony. As Now," "Black People: This Is Our Destiny," "Ka 'Ba," "Numbers, Letters," and "A Poem Some People Will Have to Understand," reprinted by permission of SLL/Sterling Lord Literistic, Inc., copyright 1964 by Amiri Baraka LeRoi Jones (Amiri Baraka). "Dutchman and the Slave," reprinted by permission of SLL/Sterling Lord Literistic, Inc., copyright 1964 by Amiri Baraka.

June Jordan. "Moving toward Home," from *Living Room* by June Jordan, copyright © 1985 by June Jordan, reprinted by permission of Avalon/Thunder's Mouth, a member of Perseus Books Group.

"Poem about My Rights" and "To Free Nelson Mandela," from *Naming Our Destiny* by June Jordan, copyright © 1989 by June Jordan, reprinted by permission of Basic/Thunder's Mouth, a member of Perseus Books Group.

Jack Kerouac. "The Vanishing American Hobo," from *Lonesome Traveler* (1960). Reprinted by permission of SLL/Sterling Lord Literistic, Inc. Copyright © 1988 by Estate of Jan Kerouac. Excepts from Jack Kerouac, Albert Saijo, and Lew Welch, *Trip Trap: Haiku on the Road*, edited by Donald Allen, Grey Fox Press, 1998, pp. 42–43, 46–47. Reprinted by permission of Albert Saijo. "July 26, 1957," from *Door Wide Open: A Beat Love Affair in Letters* by Joyce Johnson and Jack Kerouac, copyright © 2000 by Joyce Johnson, copyright © 2000 by the Estate of Stella Kerouac, John Sampras, Literary Representative. Used by permission of Viking Penguin, a division of Penguin Group (USA) Inc.

Jamaica Kincaid. Excerpt from *A Small Place* by Jamaica Kincaid. Copyright © 1988 by Jamaica Kincaid. Reprinted by permission of Farrar, Straus and Giroux, LLC.

Martin Luther King Jr. "I Have a Dream" and "Letter from Birmingham Jail" are reprinted by arrangement with The Heirs to the Estate of Martin Luther King Jr., c/o Writers House as agent for the proprietor New York, NY. Copyright 1963 Dr. Martin Luther King Jr., copyright renewed 1991 Coretta Scott King.

Maxine Hong Kingston. "No Name Woman," from *The Woman Warrior* by Maxine Hong Kingston. Copyright © 1975, 1976 by Maxine Hong Kingston. Used by permission of Alfred A. Knopf, a division of Random House, Inc.

Etheridge Knight. "The Idea of Ancestry," "Ilu, the Talking Drum," "A Poem for Myself," and "The Violent Space," from *The Essential Etheridge Knight*, by Etheridge Knight, © 1986. Reprinted by permission of the University of Pittsburgh Press.

Yusef Komunyakaa. "Facing It," "Fog Galleon," "Prisoners," "Thanks," and "TuDo Street," from *Neon: New and Selected Poems*. Reprinted by permission of University Press of New England.

Winona LaDuke. Excerpt from *All Our Relations*, South End Press, 1999, pp. 1–2. Reprinted by permission of South End Press.

Jhumpra Lahiri. "When Mr. Pirzada Came to Dine," from *Interpreter of Maladies* by Jhumpa Lahiri. Copyright © 1999 by Jhumpa Lahiri. Reprinted by permission of Houghton Mifflin Harcourt Publishing Company. All rights reserved.

Tato Laveria. "AmeRican," from *AmeRican*, 1985; "frio," from *Lacarreta Made a U-Turn*, 1976; and "Latero Story (can pickers)," from *Mainstream Ethics*, are reprinted with permission of the publisher (Houston: Arte Publico Press, University of Houston).

Chang-Rae Lee. "Coming Home Again," published in *The New Yorker*, October 6, 1995), pp. 164–168. Reprinted by permission of International Creative Management, Inc. Copyright © 1995 by Chang-Rae Lee.

Li-Young Lee. "I Ask My Mother to Sing," from *Rose*, copyright © 1986 by Li-Young Lee, reprinted with the permission of BOA Editions, Ltd., www.boaeditions.org. "My Father, in Heaven, Is Reading Out Loud," "This Room and Everything in It," and "With Ruins," from *The City in Which I Love You*, copyright © 1990 by Li-Young Lee, reprinted with the permission of BOA Editions, Ltd., www.boaeditions.org.

Denise Levertov. "Fragrance of Life, Odor of Death," "In Thai Binh (Peace) Province," and "A Poem at Christmas, 1972 during the Terror-Bombing of North Vietnam," from *The Freeing of the Dust*, by Denise Levertov, copyright © 1975 by Denise Levertov, reprinted by permission of New Directions Publishing Corp. "Overheard over S.E. Asia," from *Poems 1968–1972*, by Denise Levertov, copyright © 1972 by Denise Levertov, reprinted by permission of New Directions Publishing Corp.

Philip Levine. "Coming Home, Detroit, 1968," "The Everlasting Sunday," and "The Rats," from *Not This Pig*, © 1968 by Philip Levine and reprinted by permission of Wesleyan University Press. "The Lesson," copyright © 2004 by Philip Levine, from *Breath: Poems* by Philip Levine, used by permission of Alfred A. Knopf, a division of Random House, Inc. "The Simple Truth," from *The Simple Truth* by Philip Levine, copyright © 1994 by Philip Levine, used by permission of Alfred A. Knopf, a division of Random House, Inc.

Audre Lorde. "The Art of Response" and "Stations," from *Our Dead behind Us* by Audre Lorde, copyright © 1986 by Audre Lorde, used by permission of W. W. Norton & Company, Inc. "The

Master's Tools Will Never Dismantle the Master's House," reprinted with permission from *Sister Outsider* by Audre Lorde, copyright © 1984, 2007 by Audre Lorde, Crossing Press, Berkeley, CA, www.tenspeed.com. "Never Take Fire from a Woman," "Power," and "Walking Our Boundaries," from *The Black Unicorn* by Audre Lorde, copyright © 1978 by Audre Lorde, used by permission of W. W. Norton & Company, Inc.

Robert Lowell. "For Theodore Roethke," "For the Union Dead," "Memories of West Street and Lepke," "Near the Ocean," and "Skunk Hour," from *Collected Poems* by Robert Lowell. Copyright © 2003 by Harriet Lowell and Sheridan Lowell. Reprinted by permission of Farrar, Straus and Giroux, LLC.

Wing Tek Lum. "Chinese New Year" and "Minority Poem," from *Time to Greez! Incantations from the Third World*, ed. Janice Mirikitani, Buriel Clay II, Janet Campbell Hall, et al. (San Francisco: Glide Publications / Third World Communications, 1975), p. 61. Reprinted by permission of Wing Tek Lum.

Norman Mailer. Excerpt from *The Armies of the Night* by Norman Mailer, copyright © 1968 by Norman Mailer. Used by permission of Dutton Signet, a division of Penguin Group (USA) Inc.

Bernard Malamud. "The Magic Barrel," from *The Magic Barrel* by Bernard Malamud. Copyright © 1950, 1958, renewed 1977, 1986 by Bernard Malamud. Reprinted by permission of Farrar, Straus and Giroux, LLC.

Paule Marshall. "To Da-duh: In Memoriam," from *Reena and Other Stories*. Copyright © 1983 by The Feminist Press. Reprinted with the permission of The Feminist Press at the City University of New York, www.feministpress.org.

Bobbie Ann Mason. "Airwaves," from *Love Life* (New York: Harper & Row, 1989). Reprinted by permission of International Creative Management, Inc. Copyright © 1989 by Bobbie Ann Mason.

Bill McKibben. Excerpt from *The Comforting Whirlwind* by Bill McKibben, © 1994 Wm. B. Eerdmans Publishing Company, Grand Rapids, Michigan. Reprinted by permission of the publisher; all rights reserved.

Arthur Miller. From *The Crucible* by Arthur Miller, copyright 1952, 1953, 1954, renewed © 1980, 1981, 1982 by Arthur Miller. Used by permission of Viking Penguin, a division of Penguin Group (USA) Inc.

Janice Mirikitani. "Breaking Tradition" and "Recipe," from *Shedding Silence: Poetry and Prose by Janice Mirikitani*, reprinted by permission of the author. "Desert Flowers" and "For My Father," from *Awake in the River: Poetry and Prose by Janice Mirikitani*, reprinted by permission of the author.

Nicholasa Mohr. "A Thanksgiving Celebration," from *Rituals of Survival*. Reprinted by permission of Arte Publico Press.

N. Scott Momaday. "Headwaters," "Prologue" (pp. 3–4), from "Introduction" (pp. 11–12), IV (pp. 22–23), XVI (pp. 54–55), XVII (pp. 56, 59), XXIV (pp. 82–83), "Epilogue" (pp. 85–86, 88), and "Rainy Mountain Cemetery," from *The Way to Rainy Mountain*. Used by permission.

Pat Mora. "Border Town: 1938," "University Avenue," and "Unnatural Speech," from *Borders*. Reprinted by permission of Arte Publico Press.

Aurora Levins Morales. "Child of the Americas," "Heart of My Heart, Bone of My Bone," and "Puertoricanness," reprinted with permission from *Getting Home Alive* by Aurora Levins Morales and Rosario Morales, published by Firebrand Books, Ann Arbor, MI. Copyright © 1986 by Aurora Levins Morales and Rosario Morales.

Toni Morrison. "Recitatif," from *Ancestral House*, pp. 422–436 (New York: Westview Press, 1995). Reprinted by permission of International Creative Management, Inc. Copyright © 1995 by Toni Morrison.

Bharati Mukherjee. "A Wife's Story," from *The Middleman and Other Stories* by Bharati Mukherjee. Copyright © 1988 by Bharati Mukherjee. Used with permission of Grove/Atlantic, Inc.

Name withheld. "White Male Qualities," from *Roots: An Asian American Reader*, UCLA Asian American Studies Center, Regents of the University of California, 1971, pp. 44–45. Reprinted by permission of UCLA Asian American Studies Center.

Larry Neal. "Some Reflections on the Black Aesthetic," from *The Black Aesthetic*, edited by Addison Gayle, Jr., Doubleday, 1971, 12–14. Reprinted by permission of Evelyn Neal.

Minh Duc Nguyen. "Tale of Apricot," from *Watermark: Vietnamese American Poetry and Prose* (New York: Asian American Writers' Workshop, 1998). Reprinted by permission of the author.

Judee Norton. "Norton #59900," from *Doing Time: Twenty-Five Years of Prison Writing*, a PEN American Center Prize Anthology, edited by Bell Gale Chevigny, published Arcade Publishing, New York, New York. Copyright © 1999 by PEN American Center.

Naomi Shihab Nye. "Blood" and "Where the Soft Air Lives," from *Yellow Glove* (Portland, OR: Breitenbush Publications, 1986), reprinted by permission of the author, Naomi Shihab Nye, 2004. "Different Ways to Pray" and "My Father the Figtree," from *Different Ways to Pray* (Portland, OR: Breitenbush Publications, 1980), reprinted by permission of the author, Naomi Shihab Nye, 2004. "Ducks," from *Fuel*, copyright © 1998 by Naomi Shihaab Nye, reprinted with the permission of BOA Editions, Ltd., www.boaeditions.org.

Joyce Carol Oates. "Where Are You Going, Where Have You Been?," 1965. Copyright © 1970 by Ontario Review. Reprinted by permission of John Hawkins & Associates, Inc.

Tim O'Brien. "In the Field," from *The Things They Carried* by Tim O'Brien. Copyright © 1990 by Tim O'Brien. Reprinted by permission of Houghton Mifflin Harcourt Publishing Company. All rights reserved.

Flannery O'Connor. "A Good Man Is Hard to Find," from *A Good Man Is Hard to Find and Other Stories*, copyright 1953 by Flannery O'Connor and renewed 1981 by Regina O'Connor, reprinted by permission of Houghton Mifflin Harcourt Publishing Company.

Frank O'Hara. "The Day Lady Died" and "Poem," from *Collected Poems*, reprinted by permission of City Lights Books. "My Heart" from *Collected Poems* by Frank O'Hara, copyright © 1970 by Maureen Granville-Smith, Administratrix of the Estate of Frank O'Hara, reprinted by permission of Alfred A. Knopf, Inc. "Why I Am Not a Painter" by Frank O'Hara, copyright © 1958 by Maureen Granville-Smith, Administratrix of the Estate of Frank O'Hara, reprinted by permission of Alfred A. Knopf, Inc.

John Okada. Chapter 6, from *No-No Boy*. Reprinted by permission of the University of Washington Press.

Tillie Olsen. "O Yes," from *Tell Me a Riddle* by Tillie Olsen, Dell Publishing, 1961, pp. 39-62. Reprinted by permission of The Frances Goldin Literary Agency.

Charles Olson. "For Sappho, Back," "I, Maximus of Gloucester, to You," "The Kingfishers," and "Maximus, to Himself," from *The Collected Poems of Charles Olson*, translated and edited by George Butterick. Copyright © 1987 Estate of Charles Olson (previously published poetry), © 1987 University of Connecticut (previously unpublished poetry). Reprinted by permission of the University of California Press.

Simon Ortiz. Excerpts from *From Sand Creek*. Reprinted by permission of the author.

Cynthia Ozick. "The Shawl," from *The Shawl* by Cynthia Ozick, copyright © 1980, 1983 by Cynthia Ozick. Used by permission of Alfred A. Knopf, a division of Random House, Inc.

Grace Paley. "The Expensive Moment," from *Later the Same Day* by Grace Paley. Copyright © 1985 by Grace Paley. Reprinted by permission of Farrar, Straus and Giroux, LLC.

Leonard Peltier. Excerpt from *Prison Writings* by Leonard Peltier. Copyright © 1999 by Leonard Peltier. Used with permission of St. Martin's Press, LLC. All rights reserved.

Thomas Pynchon. "Entropy," from *Slow Learner* by Thomas Pynchon. Copyright © 1984 by Thomas Pynchon. By permission of Little, Brown and Company.

Ann Petry. "The Witness," from *Miss Muriel and Other Stories*, 1989. Reprinted by the permission of Russell & Volkening as agents for the author. Copyright © 1971 by Ann Petry, renewed in 1999 by Elizabeth Petry. Story originally appeared in *Redbook*, 1971.

Pedro Pietri. "Puerto Rican Obituary," from *Puerto Rican Obituary* by Pedro Pietri. Reprinted by permission of Monthly Review Press. "Traffic Violations," from *Traffic Violations* (Waterfront Press, 1983). Reprinted by permission of the author.

Sylvia Plath. All lines from "Daddy," "Fever 103°," "Lady Lazarus," and "Stings," from *Ariel* by Sylvia Plath, copyright © 1963 by Ted Hughes, reprinted by permission of HarperCollins Publishers. All lines from "For a Fatherless Son," from *Winter Trees* by Sylvia Plath, copyright © 1971 by Ted Hughes, reprinted by permission of HarperCollins Publishers.

Ishmael Reed. "Flight to Canada" and "I Am a Cowboy in the Boat of Ra." Reprinted by permission of the author.

Adrienne Rich. "Coast to Coast" from *A Wild Patience Has Taken Me This Far: Poems 1978–1981* by Adrienne Rich, copyright © 1981 by Adrienne Rich, used by permission of W. W. Norton & Company, Inc.; "Diving into the Wreck" and "From a Survivor" copyright © 2002 by Adrienne Rich, copyright © 1973 by W. W. Norton & Company, Inc.; "Frame" copyright © 2002, 1981 by Adrienne Rich and "Power" copyright © 2002 by Adrienne Rich, copyright © 1978 by W. W. Norton & Company, Inc., from *The Fact of a Doorframe: Selected Poems 1950–2001* by Adrienne Rich, copyright © 1981, 1984 by Adrienne Rich, copyright © 1975, 1978 by W. W. Norton & Company, Inc.; "Not Somewhere Else, but Here" from *The Dream of a Common Language: Poems 1974–1977* by Adrienne Rich, copyright © 1978 by W. W. Norton & Company, Inc.

Tomás Rivera. ". . . y no se lo trago la tierra / And the Earth Did Not Part" (English only), pp. 2, 47–56, 107–115 (12 pages). Reprinted by permission of Arte Publico Press.

Richard Rodriguez. "Complexion," from *Hunger of Memory* by Richard Rodriguez. Reprinted by permission of David R. Godine, Publisher, Inc. Copyright © 1982 by Richard Rodriguez.

Theodore Roethke. "Big Wind" copyright 1947 by The United Chapters of Phi Beta Kappa, "Elegy for Jane" copyright 1950 by Theodore Roethke, "Frau Bauman, Frau Schmidt and Frau Schwartze" copyright 1952 by Theodore Roethke, "The Lost Son" copyright 1947 by Theodore Roethke, "Meditations of an Old Woman" copyright 1958 by Theodore Roethke, "My Papa's Waltz" copyright 1942 by Hearst Magazines, Inc., and "Root Cellar" copyright 1943 by Modern Poetry Association, Inc., from *Collected Poems of Theodore Roethke* by Theodore Roethke. Used by permission of Doubleday, a division of Random House, Inc.

Wendy Rose. "If I Am Too Brown or Too White for You," "Julia," "Loo-wit," "Story Keeper," "Throat Song: The Rotating Earth," and "To the Hopi in Richmond," reprinted by permission of the author.

Philip Roth. "You Can't Tell a Man by the Song He Sings," from *Goodbye, Columbus* by Philip Roth. Copyright © 1959, renewed 1987 by Philip Roth. Reprinted by permission of Houghton Mifflin Co. All rights reserved.

Michael Rothberg. "Seeing Terror, Feeling Art: Public and Private in Post 9/11 Literature," from *Literature after 9/11*, ed. Ann Keniston and Jeanne Quinn (New York: Routledge, 2008). Copyright 2008 by Taylor & Francis Group LLC – Books. Reproduced with permission of Taylor & Francis Group LLC – Books in the format Textbook via Copyright Clearance Center.

Muriel Rukeyser. "Absolom," "How We Did It," "Martin Luther Kind, Malcolm X," "The Minotaur," "The Poem as Mask," and "Rite," from *Collected Poems* by Muriel Rukeyser. Reprinted with permission of William Rukeyser.

Albert Saijo. "Bodhisattva Vows," from *New Spiritual Homes: Religion and Asian Americans* by David Yoo, University of Hawaii Press, 1999, 235, copyright © 1999 University of Hawaii Press, reprinted with permission. "Your Head," from *The Backpacker*, 101 Productions, 1977, 165–167, copyright © 1977 by Albert Saijo, reprinted by permission of the author.

Rita Sánchez. "Chicana Writer Breaking Out of Silence," from *Chicana Feminist Thought*, edited by Alma M. Garcia, Routledge, 1997, pp. 66–68. Reproduced with permission of Routledge in the format Textbook via Copyright Clearance Center.

Sonia Sanchez. "to blk/record/buyers," "Father and Daughter," "Just Don't Never Give Up on Love," and "Masks," "A Letter to Dr. Martin Luther King," and "Masks," from the book *homegirls and handgrenades* by Sonia Sanchez. Copyright © 1984 by Sonia Sanchez. Reprinted by permission of the publisher, Thunder's Mouth Press, a member of Perseus Books Group.

Bienvenido N. Santos. "Scent of Apples," from *Scent of Apples* by Bienvenido N. Santos. Copyright © 1955, 1967 by Bienvenido N. Santos. Reprinted by permission of the University of Washington Press.

Anne Sexton. "Housewife" and "Young," from *All My Pretty Ones* by Anne Sexton, copyright © 1962 by Anne Sexton, © renewed 1990 by Linda G. Sexton, reprinted by permission of Houghton Mifflin Harcourt Publishing Company, all rights reserved. "Her Kind," from *To Bedlam and Part Way Back* by Anne Sexton, copyright © 1960 by Anne Sexton, renewed 1988 by Linda G. Sexton, reprinted by permission of Houghton Mifflin Harcourt Publishing Company, all rights reserved. "Somewhere in Africa," from *Live or Die* by Anne Sexton, copyright © 1966 by Anne Sexton, reprinted by permission of Houghton Mifflin Harcourt Publishing Company, all rights reserved.

Leslie Marmon Silko. "Lullaby." Copyright © 1981 by Leslie Marmon Silko, reprinted with the permission of the The Wylie Agency, Inc.

David Simpson. Excerpt from "Telling It Like It Isn't," from *Literature after 9/11*, ed. Ann Keniston and Jeanne Quinn (New York: Routledge, 2008). Reprinted by permission of the author.

Lee Smith. "The Bubba Stories," from *News of the Spirit* by Lee Smith, copyright © 1997 by Lee Smith. Used by permission of G. P. Putnam's Sons, a division of Penguin Group (USA) Inc.

Gary Snyder. "It Was When" and "Wave," from *Regarding Wave*, copyright © 1970 by Gary Snyder, reprinted by permission of New Directions Publishing Corp. "Riprap," from *Riprap and Cold Mountain Poems*, copyright © 2003 by Gary Snyder, reprinted by permission of the publisher, Counterpoint, Berkeley, CA. "Vapor Trails," from *The Back Country*, copyright © 1968 by Gary Snyder, reprinted by permission of New Directions Publishing Corp.

Gary Soto. "Black Hair," "Braly Street," "Kearney Park," and "Mexicans Begin Jogging," from *New and Selected Poems* © 1995 by Gary Soto, used with permission of Chronicle Books LLC, San Francisco, visit ChronicleBooks.com. "The Cellar," from *The Tale of Sunlight*, copyright © 1978 by Gary Soto, reprinted by permission of the poet.

Ronald Tanaka. "I Hate My Wife for Her Flat Yellow Face . . . ," from *Gidra*, September 1969. Reprinted by permission of the Family of Ronald Tanaka.

Luz Maria Umpierre-Herrera. "In Response," from *. . . Y Otras Desgracias (And Other Misfortunes)* (Third Woman Press, 1985). Reprinted by permission of Dr. Luzma Umpierre. "Music d'Or-say," from *For Christine* (Professional Press, 1995). Reprinted by permission of Dr. Luzma Umpierre.

John Updike. From *Trust Me* by John Updike, copyright © 1987 by John Updike. Used by permission of Alfred A. Knopf, a division of Random House, Inc.

Helen Maria Viramontes. "The Cariboo Cafe," from *The Moth and Other Stories*. Reprinted with permission of the publisher (Houston: Arte Publico Press–University of Houston, 1985).

Paula Vogel. "How I Learned to Drive," from *The Mammary Plays* by Paula Vogel. Copyright © 1998 by Paula Vogel. Published by Theatre Communications Group.

Alice Walker. "Laurel," from *You Can't Keep a Good Woman Down*, copyright © 1978 by Alice Walker, reprinted by permission of Houghton Mifflin Harcourt Publishing Company.

David Foster Wallace. "The Devil Is a Busy Man," from *Brief Interviews with Hideous Men* by David Foster Wallace. Copyright © 1999 by David Foster Wallace. By permission of Little, Brown and Company, Inc.

James Welch. From *Winter in the Blood*, Harper & Row, 1974. Copyright © 1974 by James Welch. All rights reserved. Reprinted by permission of Elaine Markson Agency.

Eudora Welty. "The Wide Net," from *The Wide Net and Other Stories*, copyright 1942 and renewed 1970 by Eudora Welty, reprinted by permission of Houghton Mifflin Harcourt Publishing Company.

John Edgar Wideman. "Valaida," from the book *Fever* by John Edgar Wideman. Copyright © 1989 by John Edgar Wideman. Reprinted by permission of Henry Holt and Company, LLC.

Tennessee Williams. "Portrait of a Madonna," from *Twenty-Seven Wagons Full of Cotton*, copyright © 1945 by The University of the South. Reprinted by permission of New Directions Publishing Corp.

Malcolm X and Alex Haley. Excerpt from Chapter 19, "1965," from *The Autobiography of Malcolm X* by Malcolm X and Alex Haley, copyright © 1964 by Alex Haley and Malcolm X. Copyright © 1965 by Alex Haley and Betty Shabazz. Used by permission of Random House, Inc.

Hisaye Yamamoto. "Seventeen Syllables," from *Seventeen Syllables and Other Stories*. Reprinted by permission of the author.

Karen Tei Yamashita. "Benefits-Koreatown," reprinted from *Tropic of Orange*. Copyright © 1997 by Karen Tei Yamashita (Coffee House Press, Minneapolis). Reprinted by permission of the publisher.

Photos

Page 3024: Library of Congress.

Pages 3252–3253: Copyright © 1973 by Art Spiegelman.

Pages 3254–3264: Copyright © 1986, 1989, 1990, 1991 by Art Spiegelman.

Pages 3506–3511: © 1992 by Lynda Barry.

Pages 3518–3526: Copyright © 2006 by Alison Bechdel. All rights reserved.

Pages 3547–3552: © 1991 Chris Ware.

Pages 3566–3572: © 1993, 1994, 1995, 1996, 2001 Joe Sacco. All rights reserved.

Insert page 1: Hulton Archive / Getty Images.

Insert page 2: Top, © The Pollock-Krasner Foundation / Artists Rights Society (ARS), New York / The Museum of Modern Art / Licensed by SCALA / Art Resource, NY; bottom, Yale University Art Gallery / Art Resource, NY.

Insert page 3: Copyright © 1997–2007 Levittowners.com. All rights reserved.

Insert page 4: © Bettmann/Corbis.

Insert page 5: © The Museum of Modern Art / Licensed by SCALA / Art Resource, NY / Artists Rights Society (ARS), New York.

Insert page 6: Top: Burt Shavitz / Pix Inc. / Time Life Pictures / Getty Images; bottom, AP Photo.

Insert page 7: Top: AP Photo / Nick Ut; bottom, AP Photo / NASA.

Insert page 8: Don Murray / Getty Images.

Index of Authors, Titles, and First Lines of Poems